ARCHITECT REGISTRATION EXAM

ARE REVIEW MANUAL

SECOND EDITION

DAVID KENT BALLAST, FAIA
STEVEN E. O'HARA, PE

Professional Publications, Inc. • Belmont, California

Benefit by Registering This Book with PPI

- Get book updates and corrections.
- Hear the latest exam news.
- Obtain exclusive exam tips and strategies.
- Receive special discounts.

Register your book at **www.ppi2pass.com/register**.

Report Errors and View Corrections for This Book

PPI is grateful to every reader who notifies us of a possible error. Your feedback allows us to improve the quality and accuracy of our products. You can report errata and view corrections at **www.ppi2pass.com/errata**.

ARE REVIEW MANUAL
Second Edition

Current printing of this edition: 1

Printing History

edition number	printing number	update
1	3	Minor corrections.
1	4	Minor corrections. Copyright update.
2	1	Code update. New material. Copyright update.

Printed in the United States of America.

PPI
1250 Fifth Avenue, Belmont, CA 94002
(650) 593-9119
www.ppi2pass.com

ISBN: 978-1-59126-321-0

Library of Congress Control Number: 2010941647

TABLE OF CONTENTS

List of Figures . . . xi

List of Tables . . . xix

Preface and Acknowledgments . . . xxiii

Introduction
- About This Book . . . xxv
- The Architect Registration Examination . . . xxv
- Study Guidelines . . . xxvii
- Taking the Exam . . . xxix
- After the Exam . . . xxxii

How SI Units Are Used in This Book . . . xxxiii

Codes and Standards Used in This Book . . . xxxv

Section 1: Mathematics

Chapter 1: Mathematics
- Architects' and Engineers' Dimensioning Systems . . . 1-1
- Trigonometry . . . 1-2
- Logarithms . . . 1-2

Section 2: Programming, Planning & Practice

Chapter 2: Environmental Analysis and Project Planning
- Influences on Urban Development . . . 2-1
- Community Influences on Design . . . 2-8
- Land Analysis . . . 2-9
- Transportation and Utility Influences . . . 2-13
- Climatic Influences . . . 2-14
- Sustainable Design . . . 2-15
- Legal and Economic Influences . . . 2-17
- Evaluating Existing Structures . . . 2-23
- Evaluating Historic Structures . . . 2-25
- Architectural Practice and Services During Pre-Design . . . 2-28
- Definitions . . . 2-29

Chapter 3: Building Programming

Functional Requirements . . . 3-1
Design Considerations . . . 3-4
Psychological and Social Influences . . . 3-8
Budgeting and Scheduling . . . 3-9
Codes and Regulations . . . 3-16
The Programming Process . . . 3-16

Chapter 4: Solving the Site Zoning Vignette

Tips for Completing the Site Zoning Vignette . . . 4-1

Section 3: Site Planning & Design

Chapter 5: Site Analysis and Design

Topography . . . 5-1
Climate . . . 5-3
Drainage . . . 5-7
Utilities . . . 5-8
Circulation . . . 5-8
Parking . . . 5-10
Landscaping . . . 5-13
Property Descriptions . . . 5-13
Site Acoustics . . . 5-16
Site Security . . . 5-17
Other Design Considerations . . . 5-19

Chapter 6: Solving the Site Design Vignette

Tips for Completing the Site Design Vignette . . . 6-1

Chapter 7: Solving the Site Grading Vignette

Tips for Completing the Site Grading Vignette . . . 7-1

Section 4: Schematic Design

Chapter 8: Solving the Building Layout Vignette

Tips for Completing the Building Layout Vignette . . . 8-1

Chapter 9: Solving the Interior Layout Vignette

Tips for Completing the Interior Layout Vignette . . . 9-1

Section 5: Structural Systems

Chapter 10: Selection of Structural Systems

Standard Structural Systems . . . 10-1
Complex Structural Systems . . . 10-7
Structural System Selection Criteria . . . 10-11

Chapter 11: Loads on Buildings

Gravity Loads . . . 11-1
Lateral Loads . . . 11-6
Miscellaneous Loads . . . 11-7

Chapter 12: Structural Fundamentals

Statics and Forces . . . 12-1
Properties of Sections . . . 12-5
Structural Analysis . . . 12-7

Chapter 13: Beams and Columns
Beams . . . 13-1
Columns . . . 13-9

Chapter 14: Trusses
Basic Principles . . . 14-1
Truss Analysis . . . 14-3

Chapter 15: Soil and Foundations
Soil Properties . . . 15-1
Foundation Systems . . . 15-6
Retaining Walls . . . 15-11

Chapter 16: Connections
Wood Connections . . . 16-1
Steel Connections . . . 16-7
Concrete Connections . . . 16-17

Chapter 17: Building Code Requirements on Structural Design
Loading . . . 17-1
Allowable Stresses . . . 17-3
Construction Requirements . . . 17-4
Fireproofing . . . 17-5

Chapter 18: Wood Construction
Properties of Structural Lumber . . . 18-1
Wood Beams . . . 18-5
Miscellaneous Provisions . . . 18-9
Wood Columns . . . 18-10
Joists . . . 18-11
Glued-Laminated Construction . . . 18-11
Planking . . . 18-13

Chapter 19: Steel Construction
Properties of Structural Steel . . . 19-1
Steel Beams . . . 19-3
Steel Columns . . . 19-11
Built-Up Sections . . . 19-12
Open-Web Steel Joists . . . 19-15

Chapter 20: Concrete Construction
Concrete Materials and Placement . . . 20-2
Safety Factors . . . 20-5
Concrete Beams . . . 20-5
Concrete Slabs . . . 20-13
Concrete Columns . . . 20-13
Prestressed Concrete . . . 20-14

Chapter 21: Wall Construction
Masonry Walls . . . 21-1
Stud Walls . . . 21-5
Concrete Walls . . . 21-7
Building Envelope . . . 21-7

Chapter 22: Lateral Forces—Wind
Basic Principles . . . 22-1
Analysis of Wind Loading . . . 22-4
Design of Wind-Resisting Structures . . . 22-9

Chapter 23: Lateral Forces—Earthquakes

Basic Principles 23-2
Structural Systems to Resist Lateral Loads 23-6
Building Configuration 23-12
Analysis of Earthquake Loading 23-16
Additional Considerations 23-25

Chapter 24: Long Span Structures—One-Way Systems

Types of One-Way Systems 24-1
Design and Selection Considerations 24-6
Technical Considerations 24-8

Chapter 25: Long Span Structures—Two-Way Systems

Types of Two-Way Long Span Systems 25-2
Design and Selection Considerations 25-8
Technical Considerations 25-9

Chapter 26: Solving the Structural Layout Vignette

Tips for Completing the Structural Layout Vignette 26-1

Section 6: Building Systems

Chapter 27: Human Comfort and Mechanical System Fundamentals

Definitions 27-1
Human Comfort 27-2
Measurement Systems 27-4
External and Internal Loads 27-6
Climatic Types and Design Responses 27-9

Chapter 28: HVAC Systems

Energy Sources 28-1
Energy Conversion 28-2
HVAC Systems 28-4
System Sizing 28-10
Energy Conservation 28-10
Definitions 28-15

Chapter 29: Energy Efficiency and Alternative Energy Sources

Part 1: Energy Efficiency 29-1
Building Orientation 29-1
Building Shape 29-2
Landscaping 29-3
Building Shading 29-4
Earth Sheltering 29-4
Green Roofs 29-5
Air Locks 29-7
Insulation and Weather Sealing 29-7
Glazing 29-9
Double Envelope 29-10
Daylighting 29-10
Part 2: Alternative Energy Sources 29-13
Solar Design 29-13
Wind 29-18
Geothermal 29-18
Photovoltaics 29-18
Definitions 29-19

Chapter 30: Sustainable Design
Site Development . . . 30-1
Water Use . . . 30-1
Alternative Energy Sources and Energy Efficiency . . . 30-3
Materials . . . 30-3
Indoor Air Quality . . . 30-11
Recycling and Reuse . . . 30-16
Hazardous Material Mitigation . . . 30-16
Life-Cycle Cost Analysis . . . 30-18
Sustainable Building Programs, Rating Systems, and Standards . . . 30-18
Product Certification . . . 30-20
Regulations and Industry Standards Related to Sustainability . . . 30-22
Definitions . . . 30-23

Chapter 31: Plumbing Systems
Water Supply . . . 31-1
Water Supply Design . . . 31-4
Sanitary Drainage and Venting . . . 31-17
Waste Disposal and Treatment . . . 31-19
Storm Drainage . . . 31-19
Fire Protection and Life Safety . . . 31-20

Chapter 32: Electrical Systems
Electrical Fundamentals . . . 32-1
Power Supply . . . 32-4
Lighting Fundamentals . . . 32-9
Light Sources . . . 32-12
Lighting Design . . . 32-16
Signal and Safety Alarm Systems . . . 32-21

Chapter 33: Acoustics
Definitions . . . 33-1
Fundamentals of Sound and Human Hearing . . . 33-2
Sound Transmission . . . 33-4
Sound Absorption . . . 33-6
Sound Control . . . 33-8
Room Acoustics . . . 33-13

Chapter 34: Solving the Mechanical and Electrical Plan Vignette
Tips for Completing the Mechanical and Electrical Plan Vignette . . . 34-1

Section 7: Building Design & Construction Systems

Chapter 35: Site Work
Soil . . . 35-1
Earthwork . . . 35-5
Shoring and Bracing . . . 35-5
Site Drainage . . . 35-6
Site Improvements . . . 35-7

Chapter 36: Concrete
History of Concrete . . . 36-1
Formwork . . . 36-1
Moisture Migration and Vapor Barriers . . . 36-3
Reinforcement . . . 36-4

Concrete Materials 36-5
New Concrete Products 36-7
Curing and Testing 36-8
Placing and Finishing 36-10
Joints and Accessories 36-11
Precast Concrete 36-12
Precast, Prestressed Concrete 36-13

Chapter 37: Masonry
Mortar 37-1
Brick 37-2
Other Unit Masonry 37-8
Stone 37-12

Chapter 38: Metals
History of Metals 38-1
Basic Materials and Processes 38-2
Ferrous Metals 38-4
Nonferrous Metals 38-6
Structural Metals 38-8
Metal Fabrications 38-11
Ornamental Metals 38-11

Chapter 39: Structural and Rough Carpentry
Characteristics of Lumber 39-1
Framing 39-4
Engineered Wood Products 39-7
Heavy Timber Construction 39-9
Fasteners 39-10
Wood Treatment 39-11

Chapter 40: Finish Carpentry and Architectural Woodwork
Finish Carpentry 40-1
Architectural Woodwork 40-4
Finishes 40-14

Chapter 41: Moisture Protection and Thermal Insulation
Dampproofing 41-1
Waterproofing 41-1
Building Insulation 41-2
Types of Building Insulation 41-3
Shingles and Roofing Tile 41-8
Preformed Roofing and Siding 41-10
Membrane Roofing 41-11
Flashing 41-13
Roof Accessories 41-13
Caulking and Sealants 41-13
Exterior Insulation and Finish Systems 41-15

Chapter 42: Doors, Windows, and Glazing
Door Openings 42-1
Metal Doors and Frames 42-2
Wood Doors and Frames 42-4
Glass Doors 42-5
Special Doors 42-7
Hardware 42-7

Building Code Requirements 42-13
Windows 42-15
Glass and Glazing 42-16
Curtain Wall Systems 42-20

Chapter 43: Finish Materials
Lath and Plaster 43-1
Gypsum Wallboard 43-2
Tile 43-5
Terrazzo 43-7
Stone Finishes 43-8
Acoustical Treatment 43-8
Wood Flooring 43-11
Laminate Flooring 43-13
Resilient Flooring 43-13
Seamless Flooring 43-15
Carpet 43-15
Painting 43-16
Color 43-17

Chapter 44: Vertical Transportation
Hydraulic Elevators 44-1
Electric Elevators 44-1
Elevator Design 44-3
Freight Elevators 44-6
Escalators 44-6
Stairs and Ramps 44-7

Chapter 45: Solving the Accessibility/Ramp Vignette
Tips for Completing the Accessibility/Ramp Vignette 45-1

Chapter 46: Solving the Stair Design Vignette
Tips for Completing the Stair Design Vignette 46-1

Chapter 47: Solving the Roof Plan Vignette
Tips for Completing the Roof Plan Vignette 47-1

Section 8: Construction Documents & Services

Chapter 48: Construction Drawings and Details
Developing and Evaluating Construction Details 48-1
Organization and Layout of Construction Drawings 48-6
Coordination 48-9
Building Information Modeling 48-9

Chapter 49: The Project Manual and Specifications
The Project Manual 49-1
Specifications 49-2

Chapter 50: The Primary Contractual Documents
Approaches to Project Delivery 50-1
Owner-Architect Agreements—AIA Document B101 50-4
Owner-Contractor Agreements—AIA Document A101 50-9
General Conditions of the Contract—AIA Document A201 50-11
Supplementary Conditions of the Contract 50-17

Chapter 51: Bidding Procedures and Documents
Bidding Procedures 51-1
Bidding Documents 51-3
Cost Control 51-5

Chapter 52: Construction Administration Services
Submittals 52-1
Changes in the Work 52-2
Field Administration 52-3
Progress Payments 52-5
Project Closeout 52-6

Chapter 53: Project and Practice Management
Part 1: Practice Management 53-1
Business Organization 53-1
Office Organization 53-3
Legal Issues 53-3
Part 2: Project Management 53-6
Planning and Scheduling 53-6
Monitoring 53-8
Coordinating 53-9
Documentation 53-9

Chapter 54: Solving the Building Section Vignette
Tips for Completing the Building Section Vignette 54-1

Section 9: Building Regulations

Chapter 55: Building Codes and Regulations
History of Building Codes 55-1
Building Regulations 55-2
Building Codes 55-2
Testing and Material Standards 55-3
Fire-Resistance Standards 55-6
Administrative Requirements of Building Codes 55-10
Requirements Based on Occupancy 55-10
Classification Based on Construction Type 55-12
Means of Egress 55-16
Corridors 55-21
Doors 55-23
Stairways 55-24
Other Code Requirements 55-26
Definitions 55-30

Chapter 56: Barrier-Free Design
Accessible Routes 56-1
Doorways 56-3
Plumbing Fixtures and Toilet Rooms 56-3
Floor Surfaces 56-9
Ramps and Stairs 56-9
Protruding Objects 56-9
Detectable Warnings 56-9
Signage and Alarms 56-10
Telephones 56-11
Seating 56-11
Elevators 56-11

Index I-1

LIST OF FIGURES

1.1 Functions of a Right Triangle 1-2
1.2 The Law of Sines and the Law of Cosines 1-2

2.1 Medieval City Form 2-2
2.2 Star-Shaped City Form 2-2
2.3 Diagram of Ebenezer Howard's Garden City Concept 2-3
2.4 Patterns of Urban Development 2-5
2.5 Superblock Concept 2-6
2.6 Topographic Map 2-10
2.7 Representation of Land Slope with Contour Lines 2-11
2.8 Guides for Road Layout at Intersections 2-13
2.9 Examples of Floor Area Ratios 2-19

3.1 Methods of Recording Space Relationships 3-4
3.2 Organization Concepts 3-5
3.3 Circulation Patterns 3-7
3.4 Gantt Chart 3-15
3.5 CPM Schedule 3-15

5.1 Common Contour Conditions 5-2
5.2 New and Existing Contour Lines 5-3
5.3 South Wall Sun Control 5-3
5.4 Climatic Regions of the United States 5-5
5.5 Drainage Around Buildings 5-7
5.6 Sewer Layout Based on Slope Required 5-8
5.7 Design Guidelines for On-Site Roads 5-9
5.8 Design Guidelines for Road Grades 5-9
5.9 Design Guidelines for Exterior Walks 5-10
5.10 Access Requirements for the Physically Disabled 5-10
5.11 Design Guidelines for Exterior Stairs 5-11
5.12 Design Guidelines for Service Drives 5-11
5.13 Parking Layouts 5-11
5.14 Parking for the Physically Disabled 5-12
5.15 Drainage Patterns in Parking Lots 5-12
5.16 U.S. Survey System 5-14
5.17 Typical Boundary Survey Description 5-15
5.18 Outdoor Sound Barriers 5-16

6.1 Preferred Locations of Automobile and Pedestrian Entries to Streets 6-3

8.1	Site Constraints Notes	8-2
8.2	Space Groupings	8-2
8.3	Organizing Concepts	8-3
10.1	Wood Structural Systems	10-2
10.2	Common Steel Structural Systems	10-3
10.3	Concrete Structural Systems	10-4
10.4	Typical Precast Concrete Shapes	10-5
10.5	Types of Masonry Construction	10-6
10.6	Typical Composite Construction	10-7
10.7	Reactions of a Hinged Arch	10-8
10.8	Post-and-Beam and Rigid Frames	10-8
10.9	Gabled Rigid Frame	10-9
10.10	Typical Space Frame	10-9
10.11	Folded Plate Construction	10-10
10.12	Cable-Supported Structures	10-10
11.1	Forces on a Building Due to Wind	11-6
11.2	Load from Soil on Retaining Wall	11-8
12.1	Types of Forces	12-2
12.2	Addition of Collinear Forces	12-2
12.3	Hypothetical Stress-Strain Graph	12-3
12.4	Moments in Equilibrium	12-4
12.5	Centroid of a Symmetrical Area	12-5
12.6	Centroids for Some Common Shapes	12-5
12.7	Centroidal Axes of Steel Angle with Unequal Legs	12-6
12.8	Transfer of Moment of Inertia	12-7
12.9	Resultant of Collinear Forces	12-7
12.10	Finding the Resultant of Concurrent Coplanar Forces	12-8
12.11	Free-Body Diagrams	12-9
13.1	Behavior of Simply Supported Beam Under Load	13-1
13.2	Shear Forces in Beams	13-2
13.3	Types of Beams	13-3
13.4	Types of Loads	13-3
13.5	Shear Diagram of Uniformly Loaded Beam	13-5
13.6	Relationship of Shear and Moment Diagrams	13-6
13.7	Static Formulas for Some Common Loads	13-9
13.8	End Conditions for Columns	13-11
14.1	Types of Trusses	14-1
14.2	Typical Steel Truss Construction	14-2
14.3	Typical Wood Trussed Rafter Construction	14-2
14.4	Alignment of Lines of Force in a Truss	14-2
14.5	Determining Horizontal and Vertical Truss Components	14-3
15.1	Typical Boring Log	15-2
15.2	Unified Soil Classification System	15-4
15.3	Methods of Controlling Subsurface Water	15-5
15.4	Types of Spread Footings	15-6
15.5	Pile Types	15-7
15.6	Pile Caps	15-7
15.7	Load Action on Simple Spread Footings	15-8
15.8	Critical Sections for Wall Footings	15-8
15.9	Individual Column Footings	15-9

15.10 Types of Retaining Walls 15-11
15.11 Forces Acting on a Retaining Wall 15-12
15.12 Resisting Forces on Retaining Walls 15-13

16.1 Wood Connector Design Variables 16-3
16.2 Orientation of Wood Fasteners 16-3
16.3 Typical Bolted Connection Conditions 16-4
16.4 Timber Connectors 16-7
16.5 Special Connection Hardware 16-8
16.6 Location of Bolt Threads in Relation to Shear Plane 16-8
16.7 Tearing Failures at Bolted Connection 16-11
16.8 Typical Steel Framing Connections 16-12
16.9 Types of Welded Connections 16-15
16.10 Weld Dimensions 16-16
16.11 Welding Symbols 16-16
16.12 Concrete Joints Tied with Rebars 16-18
16.13 Keyed Concrete Connections 16-18
16.14 Precast Concrete Connections 16-18
16.15 Shear Connectors 16-19

17.1 Relation of Strength to Duration of Load for Wood Structural Members 17-3

18.1 Notching of Beams 18-9
18.2 K_e-Values for Wood Columns 18-11
18.3 Glued-Laminated Beam 18-13

19.1 Structural Steel Shapes 19-2
19.2 K-Values for Various End Conditions 19-12
19.3 Plate Girder 19-15
19.4 Open-Web Steel Joist 19-15

20.1 Reinforcing Bar Identification 20-4
20.2 Stress Distribution in Concrete Beams 20-6
20.3 Typical Shear Cracking Pattern near End of Beam 20-9
20.4 Methods of Providing Web Reinforcement 20-9
20.5 Continuity in Concrete Construction 20-12
20.6 T-Beams 20-13
20.7 Concrete Columns 20-14

21.1 Masonry Wall Types 21-3
21.2 Horizontal Joint Reinforcement 21-3
21.3 Arch Action in a Masonry Wall over an Opening 21-5
21.4 Masonry Lintels 21-5
21.5 Platform Construction 21-6
21.6 Typical Wood Stud Wall Framing 21-6
21.7 Precast Concrete Wall Panel Connections 21-8
21.8 Typical Attachment of Brick Facing at Intermediate Floor 21-8
21.9 Typical Attachment of Curtain Wall 21-9
21.10 Typical Horizontal Attachment of Masonry to Primary Structure 21-10

22.1 Forces on a Building Due to Wind 22-2
22.2 Basic Wind Speeds 22-3
22.3 Wind Velocity as a Function of Terrain 22-4
22.4 Methods of Calculating Pressures 22-7
22.5 Diaphragm Loading 22-9
22.6 Effect of Building Shape on Efficiency 22-10
22.7 Framing Systems to Resist Lateral Loads 22-11
22.8 Beam-to-Column Connections 22-15

23.1 Building Motion During an Earthquake 23-3
23.2(a) Maximum Considered Earthquake Ground Motion of 0.2 sec Spectral Response Acceleration 23-4
23.2(b) Maximum Considered Earthquake Ground Motion of 1.0 sec Spectral Response Acceleration 23-5
23.3 Shear Walls 23-6
23.4 Braced Frames 23-10
23.5 Moment-Resisting Frames 23-11
23.6 Diaphragm Load Distribution 23-12
23.7 Development of Torsion 23-14
23.8 Problem Plan Shapes 23-14
23.9 Solutions to Reentrant Corners 23-15
23.10 Variation in Perimeter Stiffness 23-15
23.11 Discontinuous Shear Walls 23-16
23.12 Soft First Stories 23-17
23.13 Distribution of Base Shear 23-23
23.14 Overturning Moment 23-25

24.1 Built-Up Steel Sections 24-2
24.2 Transfer Girder 24-2
24.3 Rigid Frame 24-3
24.4 Truss Configurations 24-3
24.5 Open-Web Steel Joist Configurations 24-4
24.6 Vierendeel Truss 24-4
24.7 Typical Prestressed Concrete Shapes 24-5
24.8 Types of Arches 24-6

25.1 One-Way and Two-Way Systems 25-1
25.2 Two-Way Truss Space Frame 25-2
25.3 Offset Grid Space Frame 25-3
25.4 Methods of Space Frame Support 25-3
25.5 Dome Structural Behavior 25-4
25.6 Schwedler Dome 25-4
25.7 Thin-Shell Barrel Vault 25-5
25.8 Types of Thin-Shell Surfaces 25-5
25.9 Shear Stresses in Domes 25-5
25.10 Four-Section Hyperbolic Paraboloid Roof 25-6
25.11 Membrane Structures 25-6
25.12 Folded Plate Structure 25-7
25.13 Cable Structures 25-8

27.1 Body Heat Generated and Lost at Rest 27-2
27.2 Comfort Chart for Temperate Zones 27-4
27.3 Psychrometric Chart 27-5

28.1 Compressive Refrigeration 28-3
28.2 Absorption Cooling 28-3
28.3 Variable Air Volume System 28-4
28.4 High-Velocity Dual-Duct System 28-5
28.5 Constant Volume with Reheat 28-5
28.6 Multizone System 28-6
28.7 Four-Pipe All-Water System 28-6
28.8 Air-Water Induction System 28-7
28.9 Fan Coil with Supplementary Air 28-7
28.10 Displacement Ventilation 28-12

28.11 Water-Loop Heat Pump System 28-12
28.12 Energy Transfer Wheel 28-13

29.1 Optimum Building Orientation 29-1
29.2 Building Shape Affects Energy Use 29-2
29.3 Building Shapes Based on Climate Type and Type of Load 29-3
29.4 Building Shading 29-4
29.5 Green Roof Construction 29-6
29.6 Daylighting Variables 29-11
29.7 Effect of Light Shelf 29-12
29.8 Seasonal Variation of Sun Angle 29-13
29.9 Sun Angles 29-14
29.10 Typical Sun Chart 29-14
29.11 Sun Path Projections 29-16
29.12 Passive Solar Heating Types 29-17

30.1 Life-Cycle Inventory Model 30-4

31.1(a) Upfeed System 31-6
31.1(b) Downfeed System 31-7
31.2 Plumbing Fittings 31-9
31.3 Valves 31-9
31.4 Flow Chart for Type L Copper Pipe 31-13
31.5 Expansion Devices for Hot Water Piping 31-14
31.6 Water Heater Types 31-16
31.7 Drainage and Vent System 31-18
31.8 Private Sewage Disposal 31-19
31.9 Smoke Control in High-Rise Buildings 31-22

32.1 Basic Electric Current 32-1
32.2 Sine Wave of Alternating Current 32-2
32.3 Basic Circuit Types 32-3
32.4 Electrical Service Types 32-5
32.5 Light Reflections 32-9
32.6 Human Eye 32-10
32.7 Relationship of Light Source and Illumination 32-10
32.8 Glare Zones 32-11
32.9 Incandescent Lamp Shapes 32-13
32.10 Candlepower Distribution Curve 32-16
32.11 Lighting Systems 32-17
32.12 Spectral Energy Distribution Curve 32-18
32.13 Illumination at an Angle to a Point Source 32-18

33.1 NC (Noise Criteria) Curves 33-5
33.2 Noise Reduction 33-8
33.3 Details for Low-Frequency Sound Absorption 33-9
33.4 Potential Sources of Sound Leaks Through Partitions 33-9
33.5 Principles of Acoustic Control for Doors 33-10
33.6 Glazing Assembly for Sound Control 33-10

35.1 Typical Boring Log 35-2
35.2 Unified Soil Classification System 35-4
35.3 Excavation Shoring 35-6
35.4 Unit Paving 35-7
35.5 Unit Paving Patterns 35-8

36.1 Concrete Formwork 36-2
36.2 Reinforcing Bar Identification 36-4

36.3 Concrete Joints 36-11
36.4 Typical Precast Concrete Shapes 36-12

37.1 Sizes and Faces of Brick 37-3
37.2 Brick Courses 37-3
37.3 Brick Bond Patterns 37-4
37.4 Brick Joints 37-5
37.5 Typical Attachment of Brick Facing at Intermediate Floor 37-5
37.6 Types of Brick Walls 37-6
37.7 Brick Wall Construction 37-7
37.8 Masonry Lintels 37-7
37.9 Arch Action in a Masonry Wall over an Opening 37-7
37.10 Typical Concrete Block Shapes 37-9
37.11 Reinforced, Grouted Concrete Masonry Wall 37-9
37.12 Reinforced Masonry Wall at Parapet 37-9
37.13 Structural Clay Tile 37-10
37.14 Glass Block Partition at Sill and Head 37-11
37.15 Stone Patterns 37-14
37.16 Veneer Stone Anchoring Details 37-15
37.17 Veneer Stone Corner Joints 37-15
37.18 Stone Veneer at Parapet 37-16

38.1 Structural Steel Shapes 38-8
38.2 Open-Web Steel Joist 38-9
38.3 Steel Decking 38-10
38.4 Light-Gage Metal Framing 38-11
38.5 Expansion Joint Cover Assemblies 38-12
38.6 Standard Brass and Bronze Shapes 38-12

39.1 Common Wood Defects 39-2
39.2 Yard Lumber Types 39-3
39.3 Wood Shrinkage 39-4
39.4 Light Frame Construction 39-5
39.5 Wood Framing into Masonry 39-6
39.6 Framing for Openings 39-6
39.7 Prefabricated Structural Wood 39-7
39.8 Types of Trusses 39-8
39.9 Glued-Laminated Beams 39-9
39.10 Special Connection Hardware 39-11
39.11 Timber Connectors 39-11

40.1 Methods of Sawing Boards 40-3
40.2 Wood Siding 40-3
40.3 Typical Stair Construction 40-4
40.4 Interior Trim 40-4
40.5 Veneer Cuts 40-5
40.6 Wood Joints 40-6
40.7 Typical Wood Cabinet 40-6
40.8 Typical Countertop Details 40-7
40.9 HPDL Edge Treatments 40-7
40.10 Types of Cabinet Door Framing 40-8
40.11 Typical Upper Cabinet 40-8
40.12 Veneer Matching 40-9
40.13 Panel Matching Veneers 40-9
40.14 Matching Panels Within a Room 40-10

40.15 Flush Panel Joints 40-11
40.16 Stile and Rail Panel Construction 40-11
40.17 Stile and Rail Components 40-12

41.1 Waterproofed Wall and Slab 41-2
41.2 Roof Types 41-9
41.3 Wood Shingle Installation 41-10
41.4 Clay Roofing Tile Profiles 41-10
41.5 Standing Seam Metal Roof 41-11
41.6 Three-Ply Built-Up Roof 41-11
41.7 Metal Flashing Details 41-14
41.8 Elastomeric Flashing Details 41-14
41.9 Expansion Joints 41-15
41.10 Typical Joint with Sealant 41-15

42.1 Parts of a Door 42-1
42.2 Door Handing 42-2
42.3 Types of Swinging Doors 42-2
42.4 Door Classification by Operation 42-2
42.5 Standard Steel Door Frames 42-4
42.6 Types of Wood Doors 42-5
42.7 Standard Wood Door Frame 42-6
42.8 Standard Glass Door Configurations 42-6
42.9 Glass Door Panic Hardware 42-7
42.10 Common Hinge Types 42-8
42.11 Special Hinges 42-8
42.12 Types of Locksets 42-10
42.13 Door Pivots 42-11
42.14 Miscellaneous Door Hardware 42-11
42.15 Parts of a Window 42-15
42.16 Types of Windows 42-15
42.17 Methods of Glazing 42-19
42.18 Selected Safety Glazing Locations 42-21

43.1 Expanded Metal Lath 43-1
43.2 Gypsum Wallboard Framing 43-4
43.3 Gypsum Wallboard Trim 43-4
43.4 Gypsum Wallboard Partitions 43-5
43.5 Ceramic Tile Shapes 43-6
43.6 Methods of Terrazzo Installation 43-7
43.7 Stone Flooring Installation Methods 43-8
43.9 Lay-In Suspended Acoustical Ceiling 43-9
43.10 Partition Bracing for Zones 3 and 4 43-10
43.11 Detail of Runners at Perimeter Partition 43-10
43.12 Ceiling Grid Bracing 43-11
43.13 Types of Wood Flooring 43-11
43.14 Wood Flooring Installation 43-13
43.15 Wood Flooring on Wood Framing 43-13
43.16 Brewster Color Wheel 43-17
43.17 Modifying Values of a Hue 43-18
43.18 Munsell Color System 43-18
43.19 Simultaneous Contrast 43-19

44.1 Traction Elevator 44-2
44.2 Elevator Lobby Space Requirements 44-5
44.3 Escalator Configuration 44-7

44.4 Basic Stair Configurations . . . 44-8
44.5 Stair Planning Guidelines . . . 44-8
44.6 Building Code Requirements for Nonstraight Stairs . . . 44-9
44.7 IBC Requirements for Enclosed Exit Stairs . . . 44-9

48.1 Construction Floor Plan . . . 48-10
48.2 Reflected Ceiling Plan . . . 48-11
48.3 Structural Plan . . . 48-12
48.4 Mechanical Plan . . . 48-13
48.5 Plumbing Plan . . . 48-14
48.6 Power Plan . . . 48-15
48.7 Telephone/Electrical Plan . . . 48-16
48.8 Lighting Plan . . . 48-17
48.9 Site Plan Symbols . . . 48-18
48.10 Architectural Symbols . . . 48-18
48.11 Electrical and Lighting Symbols . . . 48-19
48.12 Mechanical Symbols . . . 48-20
48.13 Material Indications in Section . . . 48-21

49.1 MasterFormat 2010 Divisions . . . 49-4
49.2 SectionFormat Outline . . . 49-8

53.1 Fee Projection Chart . . . 53-7
53.2 Project Monitoring Chart . . . 53-8

55.1 Options for Fire Partition Construction . . . 55-8
55.2 The Egress System . . . 55-17
55.3 Common Path of Egress Travel . . . 55-19
55.4 Arrangement of Exits . . . 55-20
55.5 Allowable Projections into Exit Corridors . . . 55-21
55.6 Exit Door Swing . . . 55-24
55.7 Acceptable Nosing Shapes for Safety and Accessibility . . . 55-25
55.8 Code Requirements for Stairways . . . 55-26
55.9 Handrail Configurations . . . 55-27
55.10 Fireplace Hearth and Trim Dimensions . . . 55-29

56.1 Maneuvering Clearances . . . 56-2
56.2 Wheelchair Clearances . . . 56-2
56.3 Turn in Corridors or Around Obstructions . . . 56-2
56.4 Doorway Clearances . . . 56-3
56.5 Maneuvering Clearances at Doors . . . 56-5
56.6 Double Door Clearances . . . 56-5
56.7 Toilet Stall Dimensions . . . 56-5
56.8 Ambulatory Toilet Stall Dimensions . . . 56-6
56.9 Clear Floor Space at Water Closets . . . 56-6
56.10 Clear Floor Space at Lavatories . . . 56-6
56.11 Water Fountain Access . . . 56-7
56.12 Clear Floor Space at Bathtubs . . . 56-7
56.13 Grab Bars at Bathtubs . . . 56-8
56.14 Accessible Shower Stalls . . . 56-8
56.15 Requirements for Protruding Objects . . . 56-10
56.16 Telephone Access . . . 56-12
56.17 International TDD and Hearing Loss Symbols . . . 56-13
56.18 Minimum Clearances for Seating and Tables . . . 56-13

LIST OF TABLES

2.1 Recommended Grade Slopes for Various Uses . . . 2-10

3.1 Some Common Space Planning Guidelines . . . 3-2
3.2 Some Common Efficiency Ratios . . . 3-3
3.3 Space Requirements for Estimating Non-assignable Areas . . . 3-3
3.4 Project Budget Line Items . . . 3-10
3.5 System Cost Budget of Office Buildings . . . 3-12

5.1 Solar Angles for Representative Latitudes and Cities . . . 5-3
5.2 Climate Zone Descriptions . . . 5-6

11.1 Weights of Some Common Building Materials . . . 11-2
11.2 Uniform and Concentrated Loads . . . 11-4
11.3 Live Load Element Factor, K_{LL} . . . 11-5
11.4 Soil Lateral Loads . . . 11-8

12.1 Coefficients of Linear Expansion . . . 12-3
12.2 Modulus of Elasticity of Some Common Building Materials . . . 12-4

15.1 IBC Allowable Foundation and Lateral Pressure . . . 15-5

16.1(a) Bolt Lateral Design Values (Z) for Single Shear (Two Member) Connections . . . 16-5
16.1(b) Bolt Lateral Design Values (Z) for Double Shear (Three Member) Connections . . 16-6
16.2 Available Shear Strength of Bolts . . . 16-9
16.3 Available Shear Strength of Bole Hole Based on Bolt Spacing . . . 16-10
16.4 All-Bolted Double-Angle Connections $^3/_4$ in Bolts . . . 16-13
16.5 All-Bolted Double-Angle Connections $^7/_8$ in Bolts . . . 16-14
16.6 Allowable Working Strengths of Fillet Welds . . . 16-16
16.7 Minimum Size of Fillet Welds . . . 16-17

18.1 Sectional Properties of Standard Dressed Lumber . . . 18-2
18.2(a) Design Values for Visually Graded Dimension Lumber . . . 18-3
18.2(b) Adjustment Factors . . . 18-4
18.3 Floor Joist Spans for Common Lumber Species . . . 18-12

19.1 Standard Designations for Structural Shapes . . . 19-3
19.2 Selected Allowable Strengths for 50 ksi Steel . . . 19-4
19.3 Properties of Wide Flange Shapes . . . 19-6
19.4 Section Modulus and Moment of Resistance of Selected Structural Shapes . . . 19-7
19.5 Maximum Total Uniform Load . . . 19-9
19.6 Available Critical Stress for Compression Members . . . 19-13
19.7 Available Strength in Axial Compression . . . 19-14

19.8 Open-Web Steel Joist Series 19-15
19.9 Standard Load Table for Open-Web Steel Joists, K-Series 19-17

20.1 Properties of Reinforcing Bars 20-3
20.2 Strength Reduction Factors 20-5
20.3 Maximum Computed Deflections 20-11
20.4 Minimum Thickness of Nonprestressed Beams or One-Way Slabs Unless Deflections Are Computed 20-11

21.1(a) Compressive Strength of Clay Masonry 21-2
21.1(b) Compressive Strength of Concrete Masonry 21-2

22.1 K_z Values 22-5
22.2 C_p Values 22-6
22.3 I Values 22-7
22.4 Allowable Shear for Wood Structural Diaphragms 22-13

23.1 Seismic Force Resisting Systems 23-7
23.2 Vertical Structural Irregularities 23-13
23.3 Horizontal Structural Irregularities 23-13
23.4(a) Occupancy Categories and Requirements 23-18
23.4(b) Importance Factor, I 23-19
23.4(c) Importance Factor, I (snow loads) 23-19
23.4(d) Importance Factor, I (wind loads) 23-19
23.5 Seismic Site Coefficient F_α 23-19
23.6 Seismic Site Coefficient F_v 23-19
23.7 Site Class Definitions 23-20
23.8 Seismic Design Categories for Short-Period Response 23-20
23.9 Seismic Design Categories for 1 sec Period Response 23-21
23.10 Upper Limit Period Coefficient, C_u 23-21
23.11 Approximate Period Parameters, C_t and x 23-21

24.1 One-Way Long Span Systems 24-1

25.1 Two-Way Long Span Systems 25-2

28.1 Approximate Efficiencies of Fuels 28-2
28.2 HVAC Systems for Building Types 28-9
28.3 Location of Exhaust Outlets 28-10

30.1 Embodied Energy in Common Building Materials 30-5
30.2 LEED for New Construction Point Categories 30-20

31.1 Plastic Pipe Types and Uses 31-8
31.2 Minimum Flow Pressure for Various Fixtures 31-10
31.3 Load Values Assigned to Fixtures 31-11
31.4 Table for Estimating Demand 31-12
31.5 Allowance in Equivalent Length of Pipe for Friction Loss in Valves and Threaded Fittings 31-14

32.1 Characteristics of Some Common Light Sources 32-12

33.1 Common Sound Intensity Levels 33-3
33.2 Subjective Change in Loudness Based on Decibel Level Change 33-4
33.3 Addition of Decibels 33-4
33.4 Some Representative Noise Criteria 33-6
33.5 Effect of Barrier STC on Hearing 33-6
33.6 Recommended Reverberation Times 33-8
33.7 Effect of SIL on Communication 33-12
33.8 Wavelengths Based on Frequency 33-13

36.1	Minimum Concrete Protection for Reinforcement	36-5
37.1	Types of Mortar	37-2
37.2	Selection of Mortar	37-2
37.3	Stones Used in Construction	37-12
37.4	Types of Stone Finishes	37-13
38.1	Coefficients of Thermal Expansion for Metals	38-4
38.2	Composition and Description of Copper Alloys	38-7
38.3	Standard Designations for Structural Shapes	38-9
38.4	Open-Web Steel Joists—Spans and Depths	38-10
39.1	Nominal and Actual Sizes of Lumber	39-4
40.1	Selected Grades for Appearance Grades of Western Lumber	40-2
41.1	*R*-Values for Insulation	41-4
41.2	Perm Rating Terminology	41-8
41.3	Recommended Slopes for Roofing	41-9
41.4	Comparative Properties of Sealants	41-16
42.1	Door Type Advantages and Disadvantages	42-3
42.2	How to Determine Hinge Heights	42-9
42.3	Hardware Finishes	42-13
42.4	Fire Door Classifications	42-13
42.5	Maximum Size of Wire Glass in Fire-Protection-Rated Doors	42-14
44.1	Recommended Elevator Capacities	44-4
44.2	Metric Equivalents of Elevator Capacity	44-4
44.3	Car Passenger Capacity	44-4
44.4	Recommended Elevator Speeds	44-5
44.5	Metric Equivalents of Elevator Speed	44-5
55.1	Flame-Spread Ratings	55-5
55.2	Fire-Resistance Rating Requirements for Building Elements	55-7
55.3	Interior Wall and Ceiling Finish Requirements by Occupancy	55-9
55.4	Occupancy Groups Summary	55-12
55.5	Incidental Accessory Occupancies	55-13
55.6	Fire-Resistance Requirements for Exterior Walls Based on Fire Separation Distance	55-14
55.7	Allowable Building Heights and Areas	55-15
55.8	Maximum Floor Area Allowances per Occupant	55-18
55.9	Maximum Occupant Load for Spaces with One Exit	55-19
55.10	Exit Access Travel Distances	55-20
55.11	Corridor Fire-Resistance Ratings	55-22
55.12	Required Ratings of Doors Based on Partition Type	55-24
56.1	Minimum Number of Wheelchair Spaces for Assembly Areas	56-14

PREFACE AND ACKNOWLEDGMENTS

This book is tailored to the needs of those studying for version 4.0 of the Architect Registration Examination (ARE 4.0). For the second edition, we have updated the content to reflect the most recent editions of a number of codes and standards, including

- 2005 *Americans with Disabilities Act and Architectural Barriers Act Accessibility Guidelines*
- 2005 AISC *Steel Construction Manual,* 13th edition
- 2007 AIA Contract Documents
- 2008 ACI 318, *Building Code Requirements for Structural Concrete*
- 2008 *National Electrical Code* (NFPA 70)
- 2008 SectionFormat
- 2009 *International Building Code*
- 2009 *Life Safety Code* (NFPA 101)
- 2009 LEED Rating Systems
- 2009 *International Plumbing Code*
- 2009 *International Mechanical Code*
- 2009 *International Energy Conservation Code*
- 2010 CSI MasterFormat

In addition, throughout the book we've updated old material and added new material to cover any developments in architecture and construction that emerged since the first edition of this book was published. For example, this edition includes new or greatly expanded sections on energy conservation, restoration of historic buildings, green roofs, sustainable building programs, site acoustics, site security, the use of color, emergency and standby power systems, building information modeling, integrated project delivery, dispute resolution, project financing, water treatment methods, waste stabilization ponds, lighting control, new kinds of lighting fixtures and lamps, supplementary cementitious materials, insulation, and air barriers, among many other topics.

In the ARE, there is considerable overlap in what you need to study for the various divisions. For this reason, this book, *ARE Review Manual*, covers topics from all seven divisions in a single volume. Sample problems and practice exams can be found in seven companion volumes, one for each division. We believe that this organization will help you study for individual divisions most effectively.

You will find that this book and the related volumes are valuable parts of your exam preparation. Although there is no substitute for a good formal education and the broad-based experience provided by your internship with a practicing architect, this review guide will help direct your study efforts to increase your chances of passing the ARE.

Many people have helped in the production of this book. For this new edition, we would like to thank all the fine people at PPI including Scott Marley (project editor), Cathy Schrott (typesetter), Amy Schwertman (cover designer and illustrator), and Thomas Bergstrom (illustrator). For the first edition, thanks also to technical reviewer Gary E. Demele, AIA, who kept us on the right track and provided valuable input, and to Heather Kinser (project editor) and Kate Hayes (typesetter), who prepared much of this material when it first appeared.

Although we had much help in preparing this new edition, the responsibility for any errors is our own. A current list of known errata for this book is maintained at **www.ppi2pass.com/errata**, and you can let us know of any errors you find at the same place. We greatly appreciate the time our readers take to help us keep this book accurate and up to date.

David Kent Ballast, FAIA

Steven E. O'Hara, PE

INTRODUCTION

ABOUT THIS BOOK

ARE Review Manual is written to give you a thorough review of the subjects most likely to appear on the Architect Registration Examination (ARE).

The book is organized into sections that follow the exam divisions, and the chapters are arranged by subject to help you organize your study efforts. The first section, Mathematics, and the last, Building Regulations, cover information that may appear in any division of the ARE. In between these are seven other sections, each section covering the subject areas of a different one of the seven divisions of the ARE.

- Programming, Planning & Practice
- Site Planning & Design
- Schematic Design
- Structural Systems
- Building Systems
- Building Design & Construction Systems
- Construction Documents & Services

Sample problems and practice exams for the ARE can be found in seven companion volumes published by PPI.

- *Programming, Planning & Practice: ARE Sample Problems and Practice Exam*
- *Site Planning & Design: ARE Sample Problems and Practice Exam*
- *Schematic Design: ARE Sample Problems and Practice Exam*
- *Structural Systems: ARE Sample Problems and Practice Exam*
- *Building Systems: ARE Sample Problems and Practice Exam*
- *Building Design & Construction Systems: ARE Sample Problems and Practice Exam*
- *Construction Documents & Services: ARE Sample Problems and Practice Exam*

THE ARCHITECT REGISTRATION EXAMINATION

Congratulations on completing (or nearing the end of) the Intern Development Program! You are two-thirds of the way to being able to call yourself an architect. NAAB degree? Check. IDP? Check. Now on to step three.

The final hurdle is the Architect Registration Examination. The ARE is a uniform test administered to candidates who wish to become licensed architects after they have served their required internships. It is given throughout the United States, the U.S. territories, and Canada.

The ARE has been developed to protect the health, safety, and welfare of the public by testing a candidate's entry-level competence to practice architecture. Its content relates as closely as possible to situations encountered in practice. It tests for the kinds of knowledge, skills, and abilities required of an entry-level architect, with particular emphasis on those services that affect public health, safety, and welfare. In order to accomplish these objectives, the exam tests for

- knowledge in specific subject areas
- the ability to make decisions
- the ability to consolidate and use information to solve a problem
- the ability to coordinate the activities of others on the building team

The ARE also includes some professional practice and project management problems, and problems that are based on particular editions of codes as specified in the *ARE 4.0 Guidelines*. (However, the editions specified by the *ARE Guidelines* are not necessarily the most current editions available.)

The ARE is developed jointly by the National Council of Architectural Registration Boards (NCARB) and the Committee of Canadian Architectural Councils (CCAC), with the assistance of the Chauncey Group International and

Prometric. The Chauncey Group serves as NCARB's test development and operations consultant, and Prometric operates and maintains the test centers where the ARE is administered.

Although the responsibility of professional licensing rests with each individual state, every state's board requires successful completion of the ARE to achieve registration or licensure. One of the primary reasons for a uniform test is to facilitate reciprocity—that is, to enable an architect to more easily gain a license to practice in states other than the one in which he or she was originally licensed.

The ARE is administered and graded entirely by computer. All divisions of the exam are offered six days a week at a network of test centers across North America. The results are scored by computer, and the results are forwarded to individual state boards of architecture, which process them and send them to candidates. If you fail a division, you must wait six months before you can retake that division.

First Steps

As you begin to prepare for the exam, you should first obtain a current copy of the *ARE Guidelines* from NCARB. This booklet will get you started with the exam process and will be a valuable reference throughout. It includes descriptions of the seven divisions, instructions on how to apply, pay for, and take the ARE, and other useful information. You can download a PDF version at www.ncarb.org, or you can request a printed copy through the contact information provided at that site.

The NCARB website also gives current information about the exam, education requirements, training, examination procedures, and NCARB reciprocity services. It includes sample scenarios of the computer-based examination process and examples of costs associated with taking the computer-based exam.

The PPI website is also a good source of exam info (at **www.ppi2pass.com/areinfo**) and answers to frequently asked questions (at **www.ppi2pass.com/arefaq**).

To register as an examinee, you should obtain the registration requirements from the board in the state, province, or territory where you want to be registered. The exact requirements vary from one jurisdiction to another, so contact your local board. Links to state boards can be found at **www.ppi2pass.com/areinfo**.

As soon as NCARB has verified your qualifications and you have received your "Authorization to Test" letter, you may begin scheduling examinations. The exams are offered on a first come, first served basis and must be scheduled at least 72 hours in advance. See the *ARE Guidelines* for instructions on finding a current list of testing centers. You may take the exams at any location, even outside the state in which you intend to become registered.

You may schedule any division of the ARE at any time and may take the divisions in any order. Divisions can be taken one at a time, to spread out preparation time and exam costs, or can be taken together in any combination.

However, you must pass all seven divisions of the ARE within a single five-year period. This period, or "rolling clock," begins on the date of the first division you passed. If you have not completed the ARE within five years, the divisions that you passed more than five years ago are no longer credited, and the content in them must be retaken. Your new five-year period begins on the date of the earliest division you passed within the last five years.

Examination Format

The ARE is organized into seven divisions that test various areas of architectural knowledge and problem-solving ability.

Programming, Planning & Practice

85 multiple-choice problems
1 graphic vignette: Site Zoning

Site Planning & Design

65 multiple-choice problems
2 graphic vignettes: Site Design, Site Grading

Schematic Design

2 graphic vignettes: Building Layout, Interior Layout

Structural Systems

125 multiple-choice problems
1 graphic vignette: Structural Layout

Building Systems

95 multiple-choice problems
1 graphic vignette: Mechanical & Electrical Plan

Building Design & Construction Systems

85 multiple-choice problems
3 graphic vignettes: Accessibility/Ramp, Roof Plan, Stair Design

Construction Documents & Services

100 multiple-choice problems
1 graphic vignette: Building Section

Experienced test-takers will tell you that there is quite a bit of overlap among these divisions. Problems that seem better suited to the Construction Documents & Services division may show up on the Building Design & Construction Systems division, for example, and problems on architectural history and building regulations might show up anywhere. That's why it's important to have a comprehensive strategy for studying and taking the exams.

The ARE is given entirely by computer. There are two kinds of problems on the exam. Multiple-choice problems are short questions presented on the computer screen; you answer them by clicking on the right answer or answers, or by filling in a blank. Graphic vignettes are longer problems in design; you solve a vignette by planning and drawing your solution on the computer. Six of the seven divisions contain both multiple-choice sections and graphic vignettes; the Schematic Design division contains only vignettes. Both kinds of problems are described later in this Introduction.

STUDY GUIDELINES

After the five to seven years (or even more) of higher education you've received to this point, you probably have a good idea of the study strategy that works best for you. The trick is figuring out how to apply that to the ARE. Unlike many college courses, there isn't a textbook or set of class notes from which all the exam problems will be derived. The exams are very broad and draw problems from multiple areas of knowledge.

The first challenge, then, is figuring out what to study. The ARE is never quite the same exam twice. The field of knowledge tested is always the same, but the specific problems asked are drawn randomly from a large pool, and will differ from one candidate to the next. One division may contain many code-related problems for one candidate and only a few for the next. This makes the ARE a challenge to study for.

The *ARE Guidelines* contain lists of resources recommended by NCARB. That list can seem overwhelming, though, and on top of that, many of the recommended books are expensive or no longer in print. In one volume, however, the *ARE Review Manual* gives you an overview of the concepts and information that will be most useful in passing the ARE. The seven companion volumes also contain lists of helpful resources for preparing for the individual divisions.

Your method of studying for the ARE should be based on both the content and form of the exam and on your school and work experience. Because the exam covers such a broad range of subject matter, it cannot possibly include every detail of practice. Rather, it tends to focus on what is considered entry-level knowledge and knowledge that is important for the protection of the public's health, safety, and welfare. Other types of problems are asked, too, but this knowledge should be the focus of your review schedule.

Your recent work experience should also help you determine what areas to study the most. If, for example, you have been working with construction documents for several years, you will probably need less review in that area than in others you have not had much recent experience with.

The *ARE Review Manual* and its companion volumes are structured to help you focus on the topics that are more likely to be included in the exam in one form or another. Some subjects may seem familiar or may be easy to recall from memory, and others may seem completely foreign; the latter are the ones to give particular attention to. It may be wise to study additional sources on these subjects, take review seminars, or get special help from someone who is knowledgeable in the topic.

A typical candidate might spend about forty hours preparing for and taking each exam. Some will need to study more, some less. Forty hours is about one week of studying eight hours a day, or two weeks of four hours a day, or a month of two hours a day, along with reasonable breaks and time to attend to other responsibilities. As you probably work full time and have other family and personal obligations, it is important to develop a realistic schedule and do your best to stick to it. The ARE is not the kind of exam you can cram for the night before.

Also, since the fees are high and retaking a test is expensive, you want to do your best and pass in as few tries as possible. Allowing enough time to study and going into each exam well prepared will help you relax and concentrate on the problems.

The following steps may provide a useful structure for an exam study program.

Step 1: Start early. You can't review for a test like this by starting two weeks before the date. This is especially true if you are taking all portions of the exam for the first time.

Step 2: Go through the *ARE Review Manual* quickly to get a feeling for the scope of the subject matter and how the major topics are organized. Whatever division you're studying for, plan to review the chapters on building regulations as well. Review the *ARE Guidelines*.

Step 3: Based on your review of the *ARE Review Manual* and *ARE Guidelines*, and on a realistic appraisal of your strong and weak areas, set priorities for study and determine which topics need more study time.

Step 4: Divide review subjects into manageable units and organize them into a sequence of study. It is generally best to start with the less familiar subjects. Based on the exam date and plans for beginning study, assign a time limit to each study unit. Again, your knowledge of a subject should determine the time devoted to it. You may want to devote an entire week to earthquake design if it is an unfamiliar subject, and only one day to timber design if it is a familiar one. In setting up a schedule, be realistic about other life commitments as well as your personal ability to concentrate on studying over a length of time.

Step 5: Begin studying, and stick with the schedule. Of course, this is the most difficult part of the process and the one that requires the most self-discipline. The job should be easier if you have started early and if you are following a realistic schedule that allows time for recreation and personal commitments.

Step 6: Stop studying a day or two before the exam. Relax. By this time, no amount of additional cramming will help.

At some point in your studying, you will want to spend some time becoming familiar with the program you will be using to solve the graphic vignettes, which does not resemble commercial CAD software. The software and sample vignettes can be downloaded from the NCARB website at www.ncarb.org.

There are many schools of thought on the best order for taking the divisions. One factor to consider is the six-month waiting period before you can retake a particular division. It's never fun to predict what you might fail, but if you know that a specific area might give you trouble, consider taking that exam near the beginning. You might be pleasantly surprised when you check the mailbox, but if not, as you work through the rest of the exams, the clock will be ticking and you can schedule the retest six months later.

Here are some additional tips.

- Learn concepts first, and then details later. For example, it is much better to understand the basic ideas and theories of waterproofing than it is to attempt to memorize dozens of waterproofing products and details. Once the concept is clear, the details are much easier to learn and to apply during the exam.
- Use the *ARE Review Manual's* index to focus on particular subjects in which you feel weak, especially subjects that can apply to more than one division.
- Don't tackle all your hardest subjects first. Make one of your early exams one that you feel fairly confident about. It's nice to get off on the right foot with a PASS.
- Programming, Planning & Practice and Building Design & Construction Systems both tend to be "catch-all" divisions that cover a lot of material from the Construction Documents & Services division as well as others. Consider taking Construction Documents & Services first among those three, and then the other two soon after.
- Many past candidates recommend taking the Programming, Planning & Practice division last or nearly last, so that you will be familiar with the body of knowledge for all the other divisions as well.
- Brush up on architectural history before taking any of the divisions with multiple-choice sections. Know major buildings and their architects, particularly structures that are representative of an architect's philosophy (for example, Le Corbusier and the Villa Savoye) or that represent "firsts" or "turning points."
- Try to schedule your exams so that you'll have enough time to get yourself ready, eat, and review a little. If you'll have a long drive to the testing center, try to avoid having to make it during rush hour.
- If you are planning to take more than one division at a time, do not overstudy any one portion of the exam. It is generally better to review the concepts than to try to become an overnight expert in one area. For example, you may need to know general facts about plate girders, but you will not need to know how to complete a detailed design of a plate girder.
- Even though you may have a good grasp of the information and knowledge in a particular subject area, be prepared to address problems on the material in a variety of forms and from different points of view. For example, you may have studied and know definitions, but you will also need to be able to apply that knowledge when a problem includes a definition-type word as part of a more complex situation-type of problem.
- Solve as many sample problems as possible, including those provided with NCARB's practice program, the books of sample problems and practice exams published by PPI, and any others that are available.
- Take advantage of the community of intern architects going through this experience with you. Some local AIA chapters offer ARE preparation courses or may be able to help you organize a study group with other interns in your area. PPI's Passing Zones are interactive online reviews to help you prepare for individual divisions of the ARE. Find out more at **www.ppi2pass.com/passingzone**.

  Visit website forums to discuss the exam with others who have taken it or are preparing to take it. The Architecture Exam Forum at **www.ppi2pass.com/areforum** is a great online resource for questions, study advice, and encouragement. Even though the special problems on the ARE change daily, it is a good idea to get a feeling for the ARE's format, its general emphasis, and the subject areas that previous candidates have found particularly troublesome.

- A day or two before the first test session, stop studying in order to relax as much as possible. Get plenty of sleep the night before the test.
- Try to relax as much as possible during study periods and during the exam itself. Worrying is counterproductive. Candidates who have worked diligently in school, have obtained a wide range of experience during internship, and have started exam review early will be in the best possible position to pass the ARE.

TAKING THE EXAM

What to Bring

Bring multiple forms of photo ID and your Authorization to Test letter to the test site.

It is neither necessary nor permitted to bring any reference materials or scratch paper into the test site. Pencils and scratch paper are provided by the proctor and must be returned when leaving the exam room. Earplugs will also be provided. Leave all your books and notes in the car. Most testing centers have lockers for your keys, small personal belongings, and cell phone.

Do not bring a calculator into the test site. A calculator built into the testing software will be available in all divisions.

Arriving at the Testing Center

Allow plenty of time to get to the exam site, to avoid transportation problems such as getting lost or stuck in traffic jams. If you can, arrive a little early, and take a little time in the parking lot to review one last time the formulas and other things you need to memorize. Then relax, take a few deep breaths, and go take the exam.

Once at the test site, you will check in with the attendant, who will verify your identification and your Authorization to Test. (Don't forget to take this home with you after each exam; you'll need it for the next one.) After you check in, you'll be shown to your testing station.

When the exam begins, you will have the opportunity to click through a tutorial that explains how the computer program works. You'll probably want to read through it the first time, but after that initial exam, you will know how the software works and you won't need the tutorial. Take a deep breath, organize your paper and pencils, and take advantage of the opportunity to dump all the facts floating around in your brain onto your scratch paper—write down as much as you can. This includes formulas, ratios ("if x increases, y decreases"), and so on—anything that you are trying desperately not to forget. If you can get all the things you've crammed at the last minute onto that paper, you'll be able to think a little more clearly about the problems posed on the screen.

Taking the Multiple-Choice Sections

The ARE multiple-choice sections include several types of problems.

One type of multiple-choice problem is based on written, graphic, or photographic information. You will need to examine the information and select the correct answer from four given options. Some problems may require calculations.

A second type of multiple-choice problem lists four or five items or statements, which are given Roman numerals from I to IV or I to V. For example, the problem may give five statements about a subject, and you must choose the statements that are true. The four answer choices are combinations of these numerals, such as "I and III" or "II, IV, and V."

A third type of multiple-choice problem describes a situation that could be encountered in actual practice. Drawings, diagrams, photographs, forms, tables, or other data may also be given. The problem requires you to select the best answer from four options.

Two kinds of problems that NCARB calls "alternate item types" also show up in the multiple-choice sections. In a "fill in the blank" problem, you must fill a blank with a number derived from a table or calculation. In a "check all that apply" problem, six options are given, and you must choose all the correct answers. The problem tells how many of the options are correct, from two to four. You must choose all the correct answers to receive credit; partial credit is not given.

Between 10% and 15% of the problems in a multiple-choice section will be these "alternate item type" problems. Every problem on the ARE, however, counts the same toward your total score.

Keep in mind that multiple-choice problems often require the examinee to do more than just select an answer based on memory. At times it will be necessary to combine several facts, analyze data, perform a calculation, or review a drawing. You will probably not need the entire time allotted for the multiple-choice sections. If you have time for more than one pass through the problems, you can make good use of it.

Here are some tips for the multiple-choice problems.

- Go through the entire section in one somewhat swift pass, answering the problems that you're sure about and marking the others so you can return to them later. If a problem requires calculations, skip it for now unless it's very simple. Then go back to the beginning and work your way through the exam again, taking a little more time to read each problem and think through the answer.

- Another benefit of going through the entire section at the beginning is that occasionally there is information in one problem that may help you answer another problem somewhere else.
- If you are very unsure of a problem, pick your best answer, mark it, and move on. You will probably have time at the end of the test to go back and recheck these answers. But remember, your first response is usually the best.
- Always answer all the problems. Unanswered problems are counted wrong, so even if you are just guessing, it's better to choose an answer and have a chance of it being correct than to skip it and be certain of getting it wrong. When faced with four options, the old SAT strategy of eliminating the two options that are definitely wrong and making your best guess between the two that remain is helpful on the ARE, too.
- Some problems may seem too simple. Although a few very easy and obvious problems are included on the ARE, more often the simplicity should serve as a red flag to warn you to reevaluate the problem for exceptions to a rule or special circumstances that make the obvious, easy response incorrect.
- Watch out for absolute words in a problem, such as "always," "never," and "completely." These are often a clue that some little exception exists, turning what reads like a true statement into a false one or vice versa.
- Be alert for words like "seldom," "usually," "best," and "most reasonable." These indicate that some judgment will be involved in answering the problem. Look for two or more options that appear to be very similar.
- Some divisions will provide an on-screen reference sheet with useful formulas and other information that will help you solve some problems. Skim through the reference sheet so you know what information is there, and then use it as a resource.
- Occasionally there may be a defective problem. This does not happen very often, but if it does, make the best choice possible under the circumstances. Flawed problems are usually discovered, and either they are not counted on the test or any one of the correct answers is credited.

Solving the Vignettes

Each of the eleven graphic vignettes is designed to test a particular area of knowledge and skill. Each one presents a base plan of some kind and gives programmatic and other requirements. You must create a plan that satisfies the requirements.

Site Design. This vignette requires you to prepare a schematic site plan in response to various programmatic, functional, orientation, and setback requirements. You must place buildings, accommodate both pedestrian and vehicular circulation, plan parking spaces, respond to climatic influences, and consider land use, views, and other requirements.

Size Zoning. On a site plan, you must draw the areas suitable for surface improvements and building construction, taking into account limitations imposed by zoning, setback, and other regulatory and programmatic requirements. On a corresponding grid, you must draw the profile of the contour lines indicated on the site plan, and draw a profile line showing the maximum buildable envelope.

Site Grading. This vignette tests your ability to manipulate site topography. The problem presents a site plan with contours, and a program. You must manipulate the contour lines on the site to satisfy certain requirements.

Interior Layout. This vignette tests your understanding of the principles of design and accessibility that govern basic interior space planning. A background floor plan is present, along with a program and code requirements. You must plan the required spaces, including furniture, and show access to these spaces.

Building Layout. This vignette presents a site plan, a program, and code requirements, and requires you to produce floor plans for a small, two-story building on the site. You must satisfy the requirements while considering relevant features and limitations of the site.

Building Section. You must develop a schematic section of a two-story building, given the partial floor plans where the section is cut. Information is given about building materials, structural systems, frost depth, mechanical systems, and heights and elevations of some elements. You must show how structural elements, mechanical systems, and space for lighting are integrated into the solution, and indicate appropriate footing and foundation depths and sizes, bearing walls, beams, and correct thicknesses for the given floor and roof assemblies. Parapets must be shown. Rated assemblies may be part of the problem.

Structural Layout. You are given the floor plan of a small building and must sketch a structural system that meets certain requirements. The structural system includes columns, bearing walls, and roof structure. Spacing of beams and joists must be reasonable for the spans and layout of the building.

All elements of structural continuity must be shown so that loads are carried from the roof to the foundation.

Accessibility/Ramp. This vignette tests your understanding of accessibility requirements as they relate to the design of ramp and stair systems. The problem presents a base plan, a program, and code requirements, and you must design a stair and ramp system connecting two floor elevations.

Mechanical & Electrical Plan. You are given a background drawing, a program, code requirements, and a lighting diagram, and must complete a reflected ceiling plan by placing the ceiling grid and arranging the mechanical and electrical system components within it. The problem can include considerations for structural element sizes, duct sizes and types, footcandle levels, fire dampers, rated vertical shafts, placement of diffusers, and mechanical system requirements.

Stair Design. This vignette tests your understanding of the three-dimensional nature of stair design and of the basic functional and code issues involved. The problem presents partial background floor plans of two levels, a building section, a program, and code requirements. You must complete the floor plan with a stair system.

Roof Plan. You must demonstrate understanding of the basic concepts related to roof design by completing the roof plan for a small building. You are given the outline of the roof, a background floor plan, and a program, and must complete the roof plan by indicating slopes, directions and elevations, and the locations of roof accessories and equipment.

The computer scores the vignettes by a complex grading method. Design criteria are given various point values, and responses are categorized as Acceptable, Unacceptable, or Indeterminate.

General Tips for the Vignettes

Here are some general tips for approaching the vignettes. More detailed solving tips can be found in the vignette solutions in this book.

- Remember that with the current format and computer grading, each vignette covers only a very specific area of knowledge and offers a limited number of possible solutions. In a few cases only one solution is really possible. Use this as an advantage.
- Read everything thoroughly, twice. Follow the requirements exactly, letting each problem solve itself as much as possible. Be careful not to read more into the instructions than is there. The test writers are very specific about what they want; there is no need to add to the vignette requirements. If a particular type of solution is strongly suggested, follow that lead.
- Consider only those code requirements given in the vignette, even if they deviate from familiar codes. Do not read anything more into the vignette. The code requirements may be slightly different from what you use in practice.
- Use the scratch paper provided to sketch possible solutions before starting the final solution.
- Make sure all programmed elements are included in the final design.
- When the functional requirements of the vignette have been solved, use the vignette directions as a checklist to make sure all criteria have been satisfied.

General Tips for Using the Vignette Software

It is important to practice with the vignette software that will be used in the exam. The program is unique to the ARE and unlike standard CAD software. If you are unfamiliar with the software interface you will waste valuable time learning to use it, and are likely to run out of time before completing the vignettes. Practice software can be downloaded at no charge from NCARB's website at www.ncarb.org. Usage time for the practice program can also be purchased at Prometric test centers. The practice software includes tutorials, directions, and one practice vignette for each of the eleven vignettes.

Here are some general tips for using the vignette software.

- When elements overlap on the screen, it may be difficult to select a particular element. If this happens, repeatedly click on the element without moving the mouse until the desired element is highlighted.
- Try to stay in "ortho" mode. This mode can be used to solve most vignettes, and it makes the solution process much easier and quicker. Unless obviously required by the vignette, creating additional angles only complicates things and eats up your limited time.
- If the vignette relates to contour modifications, it may help to draw schematic sections through the significant existing slopes. This provides a three-dimensional image of the situation.
- When drawing, if the program states that elements should connect, make sure they touch at their boundaries only and do not overlap. Use the *check* tool to determine if there are any overlaps. Walls that do not align correctly can cause a solution to be downgraded or even rejected. Remember, walls between spaces change color temporarily when properly aligned.

- Make liberal use of the *zoom* tool for sizing and aligning components accurately. Zoom in as closely as possible on the area being worked. When aligning objects, it is also helpful to use the full-screen cursor.
- Turn on the grid and verify spacing. This makes it easier to align objects and get a sense of the sizes of objects and the distances between them. Use the *measure* tool to check exact measurements if needed.
- Make liberal use of the sketch tools. These can be turned on and off and do not count during the grading, but they can be used to show relationships and for temporary guidelines and other notations.
- Use sketch circles to show required distances, setbacks, clearances, and similar measures.

AFTER THE EXAM

When you've clicked the button to end the test, the computer may prompt you to provide some demographic information about yourself and your education and experience. Then gather your belongings, turn in your scratch paper and materials—you must leave them with the proctor—and leave the test site. (For security reasons, you can't remove anything from the test site.) If the staff has retained your Authorization to Test and your identification, don't forget to retrieve both.

If you should encounter any problems during the exam or have any concerns, be sure to report them to the test site administrator and to NCARB as soon as possible. If you wait longer than ten days after you test, NCARB will not respond to your complaint. You must report your complaint immediately and directly to NCARB and copy your state registration board for any hope of assistance.

Then it's all over but the wait for the mail. How long it takes to get your scores will vary with the efficiency of your state registration board, which reviews the scores from NCARB before passing along the results. But four to six weeks is typical.

As you may have heard from classmates and colleagues, the ARE is a difficult exam—but it is certainly not impossible to pass. A solid architectural education and a well-rounded internship are the best preparation you can have. Watch carefully and listen to the vocabulary used by architects with more experience. Look for opportunities to participate in all phases of project delivery so that you have some "real world" experience to apply to the scenarios you will inevitably find on the exam.

One last piece of advice is not to put off taking the exams. Take them as soon as you become eligible. You will probably still remember a little bit from your college courses and you may even have your old textbooks and notes handy. As life gets more complicated—with spouses and children and work obligations—it is easy to make excuses and never find time to get around to it. Make the commitment, and do it now. After all, this is the last step to reaching your goal of calling yourself an architect.

HOW SI UNITS ARE USED IN THIS BOOK

This book includes equivalent measurements in the text and illustrations using the Système International (SI), or the *metric system* as it is commonly called. However, the use of SI units for construction and book publishing in the United States is problematic. This is because the building construction industry in the United States (with the exception of federal construction) has generally not adopted the metric system. As a result, equivalent measurements of customary U.S. units (also called English or inch-pound units) are usually given as a *soft* conversion, in which customary U.S. measurements are simply converted into SI units using standard conversion factors. This always results in a number with excessive significant digits. When construction is done using SI units, the building is designed and drawn according to *hard* conversions, where planning dimensions and building products are based on a metric module from the beginning. For example, studs are spaced 400 mm on center to accommodate panel products that are manufactured in standard 1200 mm widths.

During the present time of transition to the Système International in the United States, code-writing bodies, federal laws such as the ADA and the ABA, product manufacturers, trade associations, and other construction-related industries typically still use the customary U.S. system and make soft conversions to develop SI equivalents. Some manufacturers produce the same products in sizes for each measuring system. Although there are industry standards for developing SI equivalents, there is no perfect consistency for rounding off when conversions are made. For example, the *International Building Code* shows a 152 mm equivalent when a 6 in dimension is required, while the *Americans with Disabilities Act and Architectural Barriers Act Accessibility Guidelines (ADA/ABA Guidelines)* give a 150 mm equivalent for the same customary U.S. dimension.

To further complicate matters, each book publisher may employ a slightly different house style in handling SI equivalents when customary U.S. units are used as the primary measuring system. The confusion is likely to continue until the United States construction industry adopts the SI system completely, eliminating the need for dual dimensioning in publishing.

For the purposes of this book, the following conventions have been adopted.

Throughout the book, the customary U.S. measurements are given first with the SI equivalent shown in parentheses. When the measurement is millimeters, units are not shown. For example, a dimension may be indicated as 4 ft 8 in (1422). When the SI equivalent is some other unit, such as for volume or area, the units are indicated. For example, 250 ft^2 (23 m^2).

Following standard conventions, all SI distance measurements in illustrations are in millimeters unless specifically indicated as meters.

When a measurement is given as part of a problem scenario, the SI measurement is not necessarily meant to be roughly equal to the U.S. measurement. For example, a hypothetical force on a beam might be given as 12 kips (12 kN). 12 kips is actually equal to about 53.38 kN, but the intention in such cases is only to provide two problems, one in U.S. units and one in SI units, of about the same difficulty. Solve the entire problem in either U.S. or SI units; don't try to convert from one to the other in the middle of solving a problem.

When dimensions are for informational use, the SI equivalent rounded to the nearest millimeter is used.

When dimensions are given and they relate to planning or design guidelines, the SI equivalent is rounded to the nearest 5 mm for numbers over a few inches and to the nearest 10 mm for numbers over a few feet. When the dimension exceeds several feet, the number is rounded to the nearest 100 mm. For example, if you need a space about 10 ft wide for a given activity, the modular, rounded SI equivalent will be given as 3000 mm. More exact conversions are not required.

When an item is only manufactured to a customary U.S. measurement, the nearest SI equivalent rounded to the nearest millimeter is given, unless the dimension is very small (as for metal gages), in which case a more precise decimal equivalent will be given. Some materials, such as glass, are often manufactured to SI sizes. So, for example, a nominal $^1/_2$ in thick piece of glass will have an SI equivalent of 13 mm but can be ordered as 12 mm.

When there is a hard conversion in the industry and an SI equivalent item is manufactured, the hard conversion is given. For example, a 24 × 24 ceiling tile would have the hard conversion of 600 × 600 (instead of 610) because these are manufactured and available in the United States.

When an SI conversion is used by a code, such as the *International Building Code*, or published in another regulation, such as the *ADA/ABA Guidelines*, the SI equivalents used by the issuing agency are printed in this book. For example, the same 10 ft dimension given previously as 3000 mm for a planning guideline would have an SI equivalent of 3048 mm in the context of the IBC because this is what that code requires. The *ADA/ABA Guidelines* generally follow the rounding rule, to take SI dimensions to the nearest 10 mm. For example, a 10 ft requirement for accessibility will be shown as 3050 mm. The code requirements for readers outside the United States may be slightly different.

This book uses different abbreviations for pounds of force and pounds of mass in customary U.S. units. The abbreviation used for pounds of force (pounds-force) is lbf, and the abbreviation used for pounds of mass (pounds-mass) is lbm.

CODES AND STANDARDS USED IN THIS BOOK

ACI 318-08: *Building Code Requirements for Structural Concrete*, 2008. American Concrete Institute, Farmington Hills, MI.

ADA/ABA Guidelines: *Americans with Disabilities Act and Architectural Barriers Act Accessibility Guidelines*, 2005. U.S. Architectural and Transportation Barriers Compliance Board, Washington, DC.

AIA: Contract Documents, 2007. American Institute of Architects, Washington, DC.

AISC: *Steel Construction Manual*, 13th ed, 2005. American Institute of Steel Construction, Chicago, IL.

ANSI/ASHRAE 62.1-2007: *Ventilation for Acceptable Indoor Air Quality*, 2007. American Society of Heating, Refrigerating and Air-Conditioning Engineers, Atlanta, GA.

ANSI/ASHRAE 62.2-2007: *Ventilation and Acceptable Indoor Air Quality in Low-Rise Residential Buildings*, 2007. American Society of Heating, Refrigerating and Air-Conditioning Engineers, Atlanta, GA.

ANSI/ASHRAE/IESNA 90.1-2007: *Energy Standard for Buildings Except Low-Rise Residential Buildings*, 2007. American Society of Heating, Refrigerating and Air-Conditioning Engineers, Atlanta, GA.

ANSI/BOMA Z65.1-2010: *Office Buildings: Standard Methods of Measurement*, 2010. Building Owners and Managers Association, Washington, DC.

ASCE/SEI 7-05: *Minimum Design Loads for Buildings and Other Structures*, 2005. American Society of Civil Engineers, Reston, VA.

CSI: MasterFormat, 2010. Construction Specifications Institute, Alexandria, VA.

CSI: SectionFormat, 2008. Construction Specifications Institute, Alexandria, VA.

IBC: *International Building Code*, 2009. International Code Council, Washington, DC.

ICC/ANSI A117.1-2003: *Accessible and Usable Buildings and Facilities*, 2003. International Code Council. Washington, DC.

IECC: *International Energy Conservation Code*, 2009. International Code Council, Washington, DC.

IMC: *International Mechanical Code*, 2009. International Code Council, Washington, DC.

IPC: *International Plumbing Code*, 2009. International Code Council, Washington, DC.

LEED 2009: Leadership in Energy and Environmental Design (LEED) 2009 Green Building Rating System for New Construction. U.S. Green Building Council, Washington, DC.

NDS: *National Design Specification for Wood Construction, ASD/LRFD*, 2005. American Forest & Paper Association, Washington, DC.

NEC (NFPA 70): *National Electrical Code*, 2008. National Fire Protection Association, Quincy, MA.

NFPA 101: *Life Safety Code*, 2009. National Fire Protection Association, Quincy, MA.

The Secretary of the Interior's Standards for Rehabilitation, 2010. *Code of Federal Regulations*, Title 36, Part 67.

SECTION 1: MATHEMATICS

Chapter 1: Mathematics

1 MATHEMATICS

Completing the ARE successfully does not require any complex mathematics. Calculations are usually simple and straightforward, requiring the four basic math functions with a few additional bits of knowledge. The following sections should provide sufficient refresher information for the exam.

ARCHITECTS' AND ENGINEERS' DIMENSIONING SYSTEMS

Architects usually work with units of feet, inches, and fractions of an inch or in SI units (metric), whereas engineers and landscape architects work with decimals of a foot and with feet and inches. Engineering dimensions are typically found on site drawings, with both elevations and distances being shown in decimal format. Examinees should be able to convert from one to the other. (See also How SI Units Are Used in This Book in the front of this book.)

Calculators are available that allow the user to add, subtract, multiply, and divide in feet and inches. But even without this type of calculator, the conversion is fairly simple. Remember that the basic unit of measurement is the foot; only the fractions of a foot are different.

To convert from an architectural to an engineering dimension, first divide the common fraction of an inch (if any) as it appears to convert it to a decimal fraction. Then combine this with the number of inches. Finally, divide the inches, including the decimal fraction, by 12 to obtain the decimal part of a foot.

Example 1.1

Convert 4 ft $5^5/_8$ in to decimal format.

First, convert $^5/_8$ in.

$$\frac{5}{8}\ \text{in} = 0.625\ \text{in}$$

Combined with the number of inches, the fractional part of a foot ($5^5/_8$ in) is 5.625 in.

Dividing by 12,

$$\frac{5.625\ \text{in}}{12\ \frac{\text{in}}{\text{ft}}} = 0.469\ \text{ft}$$

The number of feet stays the same, so the equivalent decimal dimension is 4.469 ft.

Example 1.2

Convert 15.875 ft to feet and inches format.

First, multiply by 12 to convert the decimal fraction of a foot to inches.

$$(0.875\ \text{ft})(12\ \text{in}) = 10.50\ \text{in}$$

Then, convert the decimal fraction of an inch to a common fraction, by multiplying the decimal by the number that is wanted in the numerator; this product becomes the denominator. For instance, to convert to eighths of an inch, multiply by 8.

$$(0.50\ \text{in})(8) = 4$$

$$0.50\ \text{in} = 4/8\ \text{in (or } 1/2\ \text{in)}$$

The complete conversion is then the sum of the whole feet, the whole inches, and the fraction of an inch, or 15 ft $10^1/_2$ in.

TRIGONOMETRY

Trigonometric functions occur frequently in various types of architectural applications. Some of the most common functions, such as the sine, cosine, and tangent, relate to the right triangle. See Fig. 1.1. A useful mnemonic device is to remember the old Indian chief SOH-CAH-TOA. In other words, the sine of an angle, *S*, is equal to the side opposite the angle, *O*, divided by the hypotenuse, *H*. The cosine of an angle, *C*, is equal to the side adjacent to the angle, *A*, divided by the hypotenuse, *H*. Finally, the tangent of an angle, *T*, is equal to the side opposite the angle, *O*, divided by the side adjacent, *A*.

Knowing any two sides of a right triangle, the third side can be found with the Pythagorean theorem, which states that the sum of the squares of the two sides adjacent to the right angle equals the square of the hypotenuse.

$$A^2 + O^2 = H^2 \qquad 1.1$$

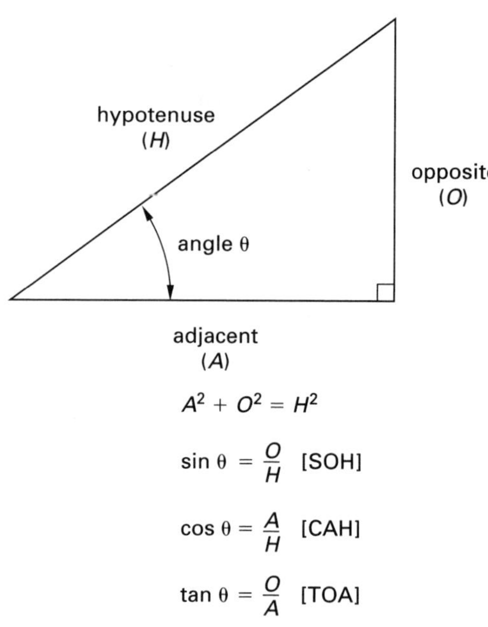

$$A^2 + O^2 = H^2$$

$$\sin\theta = \frac{O}{H} \quad \text{[SOH]}$$

$$\cos\theta = \frac{A}{H} \quad \text{[CAH]}$$

$$\tan\theta = \frac{O}{A} \quad \text{[TOA]}$$

Figure 1.1 Functions of a Right Triangle

The perimeter, *p*, and area, *A*, of a circle are related to its radius, *r*, by the formulas

$$p = 2\pi r$$

$$A = \pi r^2 = \frac{p^2}{4\pi}$$

The area of a triangle is

$$A = \tfrac{1}{2}bh$$

The base, *b*, can be any side of the triangle. The height, *h*, is the distance from the base to the apex (the corner opposite the base), measured perpendicularly to the base.

The *law of sines* says that for any triangle

$$\frac{a}{\sin A} = \frac{b}{\sin B} = \frac{c}{\sin C}$$

A, *B*, and *C* are the angles opposite sides *a*, *b*, and *c*, respectively, as shown in Fig. 1.2.

The *law of cosines* says that for any triangle

$$c^2 = a^2 + b^2 - 2ab\cos C$$

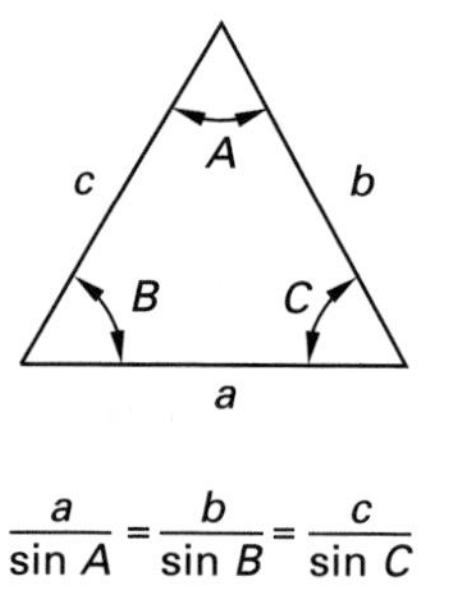

$$\frac{a}{\sin A} = \frac{b}{\sin B} = \frac{c}{\sin C}$$

$$c^2 = a^2 + b^2 - 2ab\cos C$$

Figure 1.2 The Law of Sines and the Law of Cosines

LOGARITHMS

In the past, logarithms were used to multiply and divide very large numbers. Multiplication could be accomplished simply by adding the logarithms of two numbers and converting the resulting logarithm back to a whole number. Logarithms are no longer used for this purpose, but they are used with acoustical calculations, so examinees should be familiar with the concept.

The logarithm of a number *x* is that number which, when used as the exponent of another number (known as the *base*), will yield the original number *x*. 10 is the commonly used base in architectural work. 10 raised to the power of 2 equals 100, so the logarithm of 100 is 2. This is written as

$$\log 100 = 2$$

Logarithms that use 10 as the base are called *common logarithms*, or *common logs* for short. Some common logs are

$$\log 1000 = 3$$
$$\log 100 = 2$$
$$\log 10 = 1$$
$$\log 1 = 0$$
$$\log 0.1 = -1$$
$$\log 0.01 = -2$$
$$\log 0.001 = -3$$

When a logarithmic measurement (e.g., sound power level) increases by one, the measured characteristic has actually increased by a factor of 10.

(Two other bases are often used for logarithms in other fields. *Natural logarithms* are based on the mathematical constant e, approximately 2.718, and *binary logarithms* use a base of 2.)

For numbers that fall between exact powers of 10, the log is given as a fraction in decimal form. For example,

$$\log 78 = 1.89209$$

The whole number part of the decimal (in this case, 1) is called the *characteristic*, and the fractional part (0.89209) is called the *mantissa*.

Because 78 is between 10 and 100, you can expect without calculating that the log will be between 1 and 2. Logarithms of numbers can be found in log tables, but any good calculator also has log functions available at the touch of a button.

In performing acoustical calculations, logarithms must be manipulated. The following formulas are useful to remember.

$$\log xy = \log x + \log y \qquad 1.2$$

$$\log \frac{x}{y} = \log x - \log y \qquad 1.3$$

$$\log x^n = n \log y \qquad 1.4$$

$$\log 1 = 0 \qquad 1.5$$

SECTION 2: PROGRAMMING, PLANNING & PRACTICE

Chapter 2: Environmental Analysis and Project Planning
Chapter 3: Building Programming
Chapter 4: Solving the Site Zoning Vignette

2 ENVIRONMENTAL ANALYSIS AND PROJECT PLANNING

Nomenclature

d	vertical distance between contours	ft (m)
G	slope of land	%
L	horizontal distance between points of a slope	ft (m)

Competent architectural design depends on thoroughly understanding the environmental factors that affect how a building site is selected and developed. These factors include the larger context of the surrounding community and urban setting as well as the smaller scale influences from the immediate site. This chapter reviews the effects of the larger environmental issues on the planning of a building project. Chapter 5 focuses on site analysis prior to starting design work.

Included here is a review of historical patterns of urban development, planning concepts, the effects of development patterns on social behavior, land analysis, transportation influences, climatic and ecological considerations, legal constraints, economic influences, and the ways in which all these affect the development of a building site.

INFLUENCES ON URBAN DEVELOPMENT

Contemporary city and community planning has antecedents in the historical development of the city and in the theories of many designers and planners who felt that rational development of the land and cities could improve living conditions. Many development concepts and city forms have been tried; some have failed, but portions of others have been successfully employed in urban planning.

An architect must know of the history and theory of city planning in order to understand the relationships between an individual building project and the larger context of the community and city in which it is located. The larger environment first affects how the site is developed and how the building is designed, and then the building in turn affects the community of which it is a part.

Historical Influences

The first human settlements began as collections of people engaged in agricultural pursuits rather than leading a nomadic life. As surplus food became available and ceremony, religion, and leadership began to develop, the embryonic form of the city was apparent. Living quarters surrounded the archetypes of the granary (the place where food was stored), the temple (where ceremonial rites and social interaction took place), and the palace (where the administration of the village was conducted). For security, villages were often walled in or otherwise situated for protection from other village populations or nomadic tribes seeking to take the food they could not produce.

All these basic components of the city were present in the Greek cities, but in a more highly developed form. The activities of the palace, which included trade and exchange of goods as well as religious ceremony, had developed to a point where separate places were required for these activities. The temple became the center for religious activity, while the agora became the marketplace. The agora was not just a location for the trading of goods but was also a place for meeting people, exchanging news, and conducting other business. The walled Greek cities also had special facilities, such as theaters and stadiums, for other activities.

The form of the medieval city was similar to that of earlier villages; it started at the crossroads of two main streets and was irregular in layout. Medieval cities were organized around the church and the market because these represented the two most important aspects of life. The structures were near the center of the city, and surrounding them was an informal ring of streets loosely connected, with intersecting streets running from the church to the gates of the city wall. See Fig. 2.1.

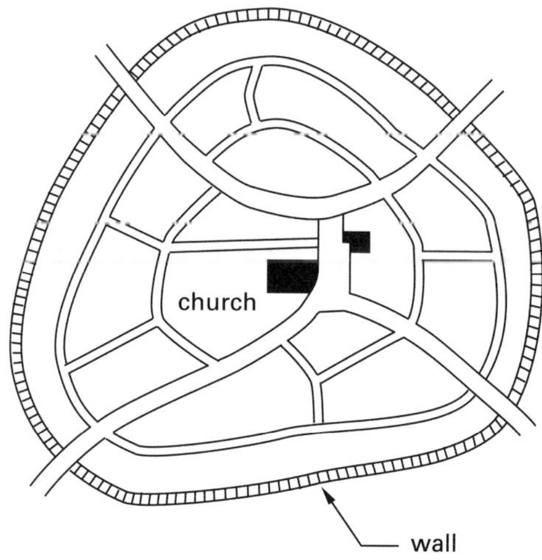

Figure 2.1 Medieval City Form

With the invention of gunpowder, the usual medieval fortification of the high wall was no longer sufficient to protect the city. The star-shaped city developed with regularly spaced bastions at points around the wall so that the entire enclosure and all approaches to the city could be defended before the enemy could get close enough for their cannons to be effective. Streets radiated out from the center, thus allowing the defense to be controlled from one point and making it possible to easily move troops and materials. See Fig. 2.2.

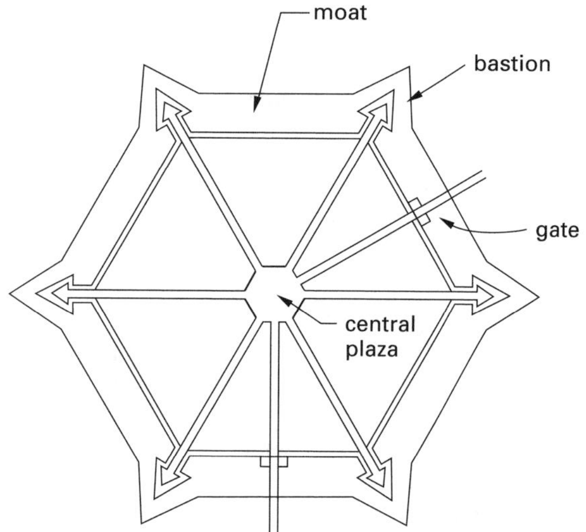

Figure 2.2 Star-Shaped City Form

During the Renaissance, city planning took on greater importance. Although military and defense considerations were still important, planners paid more attention to the aesthetics of urban design. City plans combined symmetrical order with radial layout of streets focused on points of interest. The primary organization of the radial boulevards was overlaid on a grid of secondary streets or over an existing road system.

Christopher Wren's plan for the rebuilding of London after the great fire of 1666 and Haussmann's plan for Paris reflect the Renaissance and Baroque approaches. In the unrealized London plan, Wren proposed main avenues linking major religious and commercial facilities. These were to be superimposed on a gridiron plan for other streets.

In Paris, Georges-Eugène Haussmann advocated straight, arterial boulevards connecting principal historic buildings, monuments, and open squares. These were designed to create vistas and work in conjunction with the major buildings that were part of the plan. During the period from 1853 to 1869, a large part of Paris was demolished to implement Haussmann's plan. Although the purpose of the plan was to minimize riots, facilitate defense of the city, and clear out slums, the plan also improved transportation and beautified the city.

In contrast to the use of straight boulevards promoted by Haussmann, the Austrian architect and town planner Camillo Sitte advocated just the opposite. In his book *City Planning According to Artistic Principles*, published in 1889, Sitte proposed that cities be laid out on the principles of medieval towns, with curving and irregular streets. He felt this street configuration would provide a variety of views and be much more interesting than the standard grid and radial city layouts of the time. From a practical standpoint, Sitte proposed using T-intersections to reduce the possible number of intersection traffic conflicts. He also suggested creating civic spaces around a pinwheel arrangement of streets, which became known as a *turbine square*.

The Industrial Revolution of the eighteenth and nineteenth centuries in England brought about a fundamental change in the design of cities. The factory system required that the work force be close to the factory, and therefore to the source of power, and to transportation. As production expanded, so did the population of the factory towns. The emphasis was on turning out the goods, and the cities soon became overcrowded, filthy, and devoid of open space and recreational activities. Although the Industrial Revolution began in England, it rapidly spread to northwestern Europe and the northeastern United States, carrying with it the resulting ills of its environment.

The response to the living conditions brought about by the Industrial Revolution spawned a reform movement. The first concerns of many reformers were to alleviate the unspeakable housing conditions that existed, to reduce crowding, and to improve the water supply and sewage systems. Later, reformers and planners realized that there was also a need for open space and recreation. All these concerns sparked interest in the planning of cities where factories, housing, and other features of urban life could coexist.

One of the best-known results of the reform movement is the *Garden City* concept published by Ebenezer Howard in 1898. Howard attempted to combine the best of city and country living in his town-country idea. He proposed that a 6000 ac (2428 ha) tract of land be privately owned by the residents. At the center of his idealized city, there would be civic buildings in a park. These would include a town hall, a concert hall, a theater, a library, and other municipal buildings. See Fig. 2.3. Surrounding this core would be housing and shops with industrial facilities in the outermost ring. The urban part of the town would support 30,000 people on 1000 ac (405 ha) of land. The remaining 5000 ac (2023 ha) would be reserved for a greenbelt and agricultural use and house 2000 people. (A hectare [ha] is 10 000 m^2. One acre [ac] contains 4046.87 m^2.)

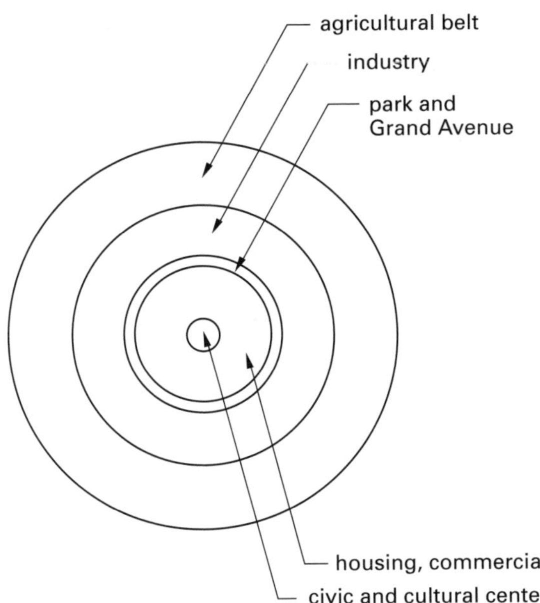

Figure 2.3 Diagram of Ebenezer Howard's Garden City Concept

Two cities were built in England using Howard's ideas: Letchworth in 1903 and Welwyn Garden City in 1920. Although they followed the garden city concept, they did not become independent cities but instead were satellite towns.

Another city plan developed as a reaction to the conditions of the Industrial Revolution was the *cité industrielle* by Tony Garnier in 1917. This planned city was to have been built in France and included separate zones for residential, public, industrial, and agricultural use, linked by separated circulation paths for vehicles and pedestrians. The buildings would be placed on long, narrow lots with ample open space between them. Garnier's plan was one of the first to emphasize the idea of zoning, an idea that would later become vital for city planning.

In the United States, early attempts at city planning reflected the diversity of ideas and styles brought from the Old World. Towns laid out in the colonies were a reaction to the Renaissance ideals and reflected the agrarian lifestyles of the settlers. They were planned around a central commons, which was the focus of community life. Houses were free-standing structures set back from the front street, and the lots included backyards as well. This was one of the influences that helped set a precedent for single-family detached housing, prevalent even today.

Philadelphia was typical of many of the early towns. Begun in 1682, it was based on a *gridiron street system* with regularly planned public open spaces and uniform spacing and setback of buildings. Its use of the grid system became the model for later planning in America and for the new towns established as the West was settled.

Savannah, Georgia, was similarly designed in 1733. It was based on a ward of 40 house lots bounded by major streets in a grid system and contained an interior square, two sides of which were reserved for public use.

The grid system was encouraged by the Ordinance of 1785, which established the rectangular survey system of the United States. This system divided the country into a grid of 24 mi squares, each subdivided into 16 townships, each 6 mi on a side. These were further subdivided into 36 1 mi^2 sections.

One early American city that broke with the grid system was Washington, DC. Its layout represented a significant step in city planning because of the scale of the project and because it was America's capital city. Pierre Charles L'Enfant was the designer. Unlike the simple grid systems of Philadelphia and Savannah, L'Enfant's design was based on the Renaissance and Baroque planning concepts of diagonal and radial streets superimposed on a rectangular grid.

The Washington plan centered on the Capitol, the Mall, and the executive mansion. These and other, smaller circles and squares were connected with broad avenues, creating a coherent transportation system based on vistas terminating in either a building or monument. Modifications were made to the original L'Enfant plan over the years, but the basic layout of the city remains true to L'Enfant's vision.

In landscape and park design, Frederick Law Olmsted was one of the preeminent leaders. He was one of the first landscape architects to preserve the natural features of an area while adding naturalistic elements. With architect Calvert Vaux, Olmsted designed New York's Central Park in the 1850s, which inspired similar designs for metropolitan parks across the country and in Canada. Later, Olmsted designed Prospect Park in Brooklyn, Riverside Park in New York, Audubon Park in New Orleans, the Metropolitan Parks System in Boston, and the grounds of the U.S. Capitol in Washington, DC.

One of the most profound changes in American urban design began with the *Columbian Exposition* in Chicago in 1893. Designed by architects Daniel Burnham and John Root and by landscape architect Frederick Law Olmsted, the Exposition grouped classical buildings symmetrically around formal courts of honor, reflecting pools, and large promenades. It started the *City Beautiful* movement in the United States and revived interest in urban planning. Some of the typical results of emulating the layout of the Columbian Exposition included civic centers organized around formal parks, a proliferation of classical public buildings, and broad, tree-lined parkways and streets.

In the 1920s and 1930s, architects such as Frank Lloyd Wright and Le Corbusier envisioned cities with vast open spaces. Wright proposed in his plan for Broadacre City that every home should be situated on at least an acre of land. Le Corbusier saw the city consisting of office and housing towers surrounded by large green spaces. Most city planners agree that both schemes would have resulted in very dull cities and a type of urban sprawl probably worse than what exists today.

A fairly recent notion of town planning is the *new town* concept. It is an extension of the idea that entirely new communities can be built away from the crowding and ugliness of existing cities. The idea started in Great Britain in the 1940s and soon spread to the United States and elsewhere. New towns were supposed to be autonomous centers including housing, shopping, and business, surrounded by a greenbelt. Originally, the population was to be limited to about 30,000, but this was later increased to 70,000 to 250,000 people.

Several new towns were built in England. However, they never became truly independent cities because they lacked significant employment centers; they still depended on nearby cities for jobs. In the United States, Columbia, Maryland, and Reston, Virginia, began as new towns but suffered from the same problems as their British counterparts. They never became truly separate cities; instead, they depended on the jobs of nearby Washington, DC, and other areas.

These new towns and previous visions of utopia have all suffered from the same problems: they are usually static in their conception, and they lack the vitality and interest of a city that has evolved over time.

New urbanism is a more recent planning philosophy that attempts to counter the many undesirable aspects of city development, including suburban sprawl, reliance on the automobile, environmental deterioration, housing segregation, loss of farmland, and single-use development. The movement was begun in the late 1980s with the construction of Seaside, Florida, by Andrès Duany and Elizabeth Plater-Zyberk. Other planners and architects who developed the principles of new urbanism include Peter Calthorpe and Peter Katz.

New urbanism planning concepts work at the building, neighborhood, district, and regional levels in new developments as well as urban and suburban infill projects. One of the primary urban design features is the development of neighborhoods intended for mixed use: housing within walking distance of shops, offices, and other services, and a variety of residential types, from apartments above shops to single-family houses. At the regional level, new urbanism promotes the connection of neighborhoods and towns to regional patterns of pedestrian, bicycle, and public transit systems while reducing dependence on the automobile and establishing connections to open space and natural systems. At the street and building level, new urbanism encourages individual buildings to be integrated with their surroundings, to support the street as a place for pedestrians, and to provide users with a clear sense of location and time. The preservation or reuse of historic structures is also supported.

There are many other precepts of the new urbanism movement, including regional planning, a mix of residential types (including affordable housing), safe streets, sustainable design principles, and the integration of civic, institutional, and educational facilities into neighborhoods. Some of the small-scale design features that may be found in new urbanism designs include village squares, backyard garages, front porches, and picket fences.

Development Patterns

The form of urban development can be viewed at two scales: the larger scale of the city or metropolitan region and the smaller scale of the community and neighborhood. In the twentieth century, the pattern of development at the city scale has generally been determined by geographic features and the layout of transportation, most notably the highway. In some cases where effective city and regional planning has been undertaken, land use plans have also determined, to a certain degree, the form of development.

Cities begun near a major geographic feature such as the junction of two rivers or a large body of water tended to develop along the water and ultimately away from it. When begun in less confining circumstances, cities have grown more or less equally in all directions, usually in a uniform grid pattern.

With the proliferation of the automobile, cities have expanded in a number of typical patterns. These are shown diagrammatically in Fig. 2.4. Each of these patterns affects the planning of the smaller-scale communities and neighborhoods and ultimately can have an effect on the design of individual building projects.

The simplest pattern is the *expanding grid*. In this pattern a city is formed at the junction of two roads and laid out in the prevalent pattern exemplified in the initial plan of Philadelphia. Growth simply follows the grid pattern until some natural feature, limiting population, or economics stops it. The strict grid pattern is usually characteristic of smaller cities. Larger United States metropolitan areas follow other patterns but are almost always infilled with some type of grid.

The *star pattern* revolves around the urban core, and development follows radiating spokes of main highways or mass transit routes. Higher density development tends to form around the spokes, with lower density development between.

The *field pattern* has no central focus or apparent overall organization scheme. Development takes place in an amorphous network of highways and natural features. Los Angeles is a typical example of this type of pattern.

With the *satellite pattern*, there is a central urban core with other major cores surrounding it. The central core is linked to the others with major highways, and often the outer cores are connected with a road system called a *beltway*. It is then possible to travel from center to center or around the

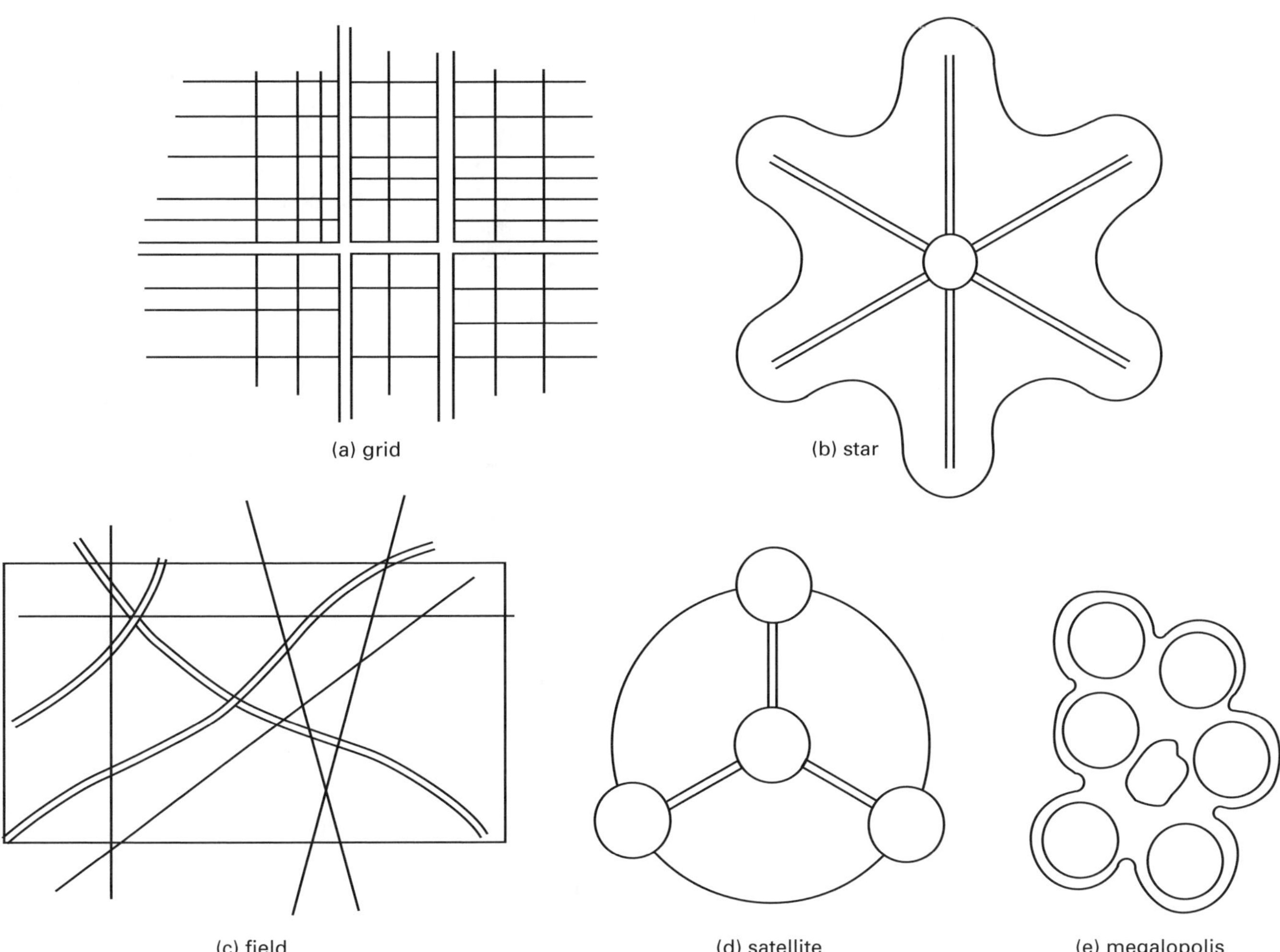

Figure 2.4 Patterns of Urban Development

city without having to go through the core. The outer cores often begin as major shopping areas, peripheral business centers, or transportation centers. Houston is an example of this type of pattern. Often, a satellite pattern starts out as a star pattern.

Finally, the ultimate in urban development is the *megalopolis*. Here, two or more major urban centers near each other grow together as the space between is developed. Many sections of the northeastern United States and Southern California can be considered megalopolises.

Although large-scale urban development can affect the way people view the city and how individual parcels of land are developed, it is within the smaller community and neighborhood scale that architects must plan sites and design buildings. One idea that is useful in linking the urban scale with the community scale is the concept of imageability proposed by Kevin Lynch.

Imageability is the quality of a physical environment that gives it a high probability of evoking a strong image in the mind of a given observer. For example, the hills of San Francisco are part of the image of that city in the minds of most people who visit it or live there. Everyone maintains a mental image of the environment; it is vital to orientation, way-finding, and general well-being.

In *The Image of the City*, Kevin Lynch identified five basic elements of the urban image: paths, edges, districts, nodes, and landmarks. These are created by buildings, natural features, roads, and other components of the city. Site planning and building design should respond to existing image elements and enhance them if possible.

A *path* is a way of circulation along which people customarily, occasionally, or potentially move. A path may be a street, pedestrian walkway, railroad, transit line, or river. Since circulation is an important part of any physical environment, paths are usually at the center of a person's image.

Edges are linear elements other than paths that form boundaries between two districts or that break continuity. An edge may be a shoreline, a line of buildings against a park, a wall, or a similar feature. Sometimes an element is a path if used for circulation and an edge if seen from afar. For example, a highway can be perceived as an edge of one neighborhood and a path when one is traveling on it. Edges may be either solid or penetrable.

Districts are two-dimensional areas that people perceive as having some common, identifying character and that they can enter. A district can be perceived from the inside if one is in it or can be identified as an element of the city if one is outside. Back Bay in Boston and Georgetown in Washington, DC, are examples of districts.

Nodes are strategic centers of interest that people can enter. They may be the intersections of paths, places where modes of transportation change, plazas, public squares, or centers of districts.

Landmarks are similar to nodes in that they are point references, but people cannot enter them—they are viewed from the exterior. A tower, monument, building, or natural feature can be a landmark.

Many of the large-scale elements of imageability are interwoven with the smaller community and neighborhood. However, there are additional patterns of development that are also intimately related to an individual site. One is the street pattern. Initially, community and neighborhood development followed the layout of the streets, usually a grid. Blocks between streets were subdivided into lots, and each lot was developed as a separate entity. Although this development method persists today, other approaches have emerged.

One of these approaches is the superblock, which is an outgrowth of the new town concept. This is shown diagrammatically in Fig. 2.5. One of the first trials of this development scheme was in the new town of Radburn, New Jersey, by Henry Wright. Here, the attempt was made to plan a large piece of land that limited the intrusion of the automobile. The superblock was surrounded by a continuous street, and vehicular access was provided with cul-de-sacs.

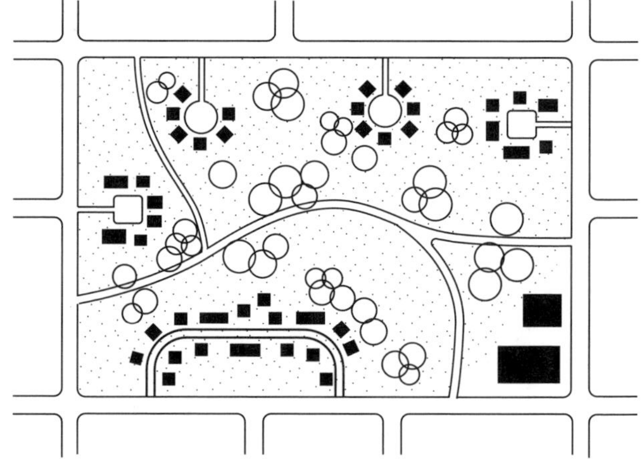

Figure 2.5 Superblock Concept

The superblock concept minimizes the impact of the car on housing and allows the development of pedestrian circulation and park space within the block. This concept was used in the planning of Chandigarh, India, by Le Corbusier, and of Brasilia by Lucio Costa and Oscar Niemeyer. In theory, the separation of the automobile on the side of the house that faces the street from the pedestrian and living area on the other side seems to be an admirable goal. However, because much of contemporary life revolves around the automobile, this separation can be counterproductive to neighborhood social interaction. As a result, the driveways and parking spaces of superblocks are often used more than the quiet park spaces.

A variation and extension of the superblock idea is the *planned unit development*, or PUD. With this approach, each large parcel of land can have a mix of uses: residential, commercial, recreational, and open space designed with variable lot sizes and densities. Industrial developments can also be planned as PUDs. PUDs must conform to certain standards as promulgated by the local planning agency and must be approved by the planning agency, but within the restrictions the planner has wide latitude in determining how the site is developed.

The standards for PUDs include such things as the uses permitted, total floor area ratio (ratio of developed floor space to land area), amount of open space required, parking spaces required, living space ratio (open space less parking space), maximum heights, and setbacks at the perimeter.

Planned unit developments offer many advantages. They make more efficient use of land by grouping compatible uses without the sometimes unnecessary requirements of setback regulations in zoning ordinances. This grouping allows the extra land to be given over to open space or common use areas. They also provide a variety of housing options, from single-family detached to row houses to high-rise apartments and condominiums. PUDs also recapture some of the diversity and variety of urban living that many people find desirable.

The Effects of Development Patterns on Social Behavior

The physical environment affects human behavior. This is true at any scale, from the plan of a city to the arrangement of furniture in a room. A great deal of research has been conducted in the field of environmental psychology; some of the results remain inconclusive, while other theories have been shown to provide a reliable basis for making design decisions. Be familiar with the following principles.

Density is one characteristic of human settlements that has received a great deal of attention. It refers to the number of people per unit of area. For example, a city might be referred to as having a density of 50 people per acre. Density refers only to a ratio, not to the total number of people or how they are distributed. The 50 people could be evenly distributed over the acre or they could all be housed in a few high-rise buildings in one part of the land parcel.

For a long time, high density was equated with undesirable living conditions. However, research has shown that there is much more involved when talking about density. The first consideration is that density should not be confused with crowding. Four people sharing a bedroom would be crowding, but if each of the same four people had adequate personal space while still occupying the same overall living space (the same density) they probably would not be crowded.

The perception of crowding also depends on cultural influences and circumstances. Some cultures find living in closer proximity to one another normal and desirable, whereas people from other cultures would find the same density crowded. In a similar way, being densely packed in a restaurant for a few hours would not seem crowded to most people, but trying to relax on a park bench at the same density would be uncomfortable. Regardless of the interpretation of density, however, there are limits to the density under which people can comfortably live, work, and play. Studies have shown that excessive density can cause poor physical and mental health and spawn a variety of antisocial behaviors.

Different cultures and socioeconomic groups respond to and use physical environments differently. The entire range of a particular group's pattern of living, working, playing, and socializing may flourish under one kind of environment and suffer under another. Taking cultural and social differences into account when designing housing and other facilities is critical to a successful project.

Regardless of the specific culture of a group, all people need and want social interaction with their family, friends, neighbors, and other groups to which they belong. A building, neighborhood, or city can promote or hinder such interaction. Providing spaces to gather, to watch other people, to cross paths, and to meet informally is a way the architect can encourage this vital part of human life. Spaces, buildings, rooms, and even furniture can be considered *sociopetal* if they tend to bring people together. A group of chairs facing each other, circular gathering spaces, and radial street plans are examples of sociopetal environments. *Sociofugal* refers to conditions that do just the opposite; they tend to discourage interaction or social contact.

In addition to interaction, people need a place they can call their own, whether it is their house, a seat at a conference table, or one end of a park bench. This is the concept of *territoriality* and is a fundamental part of animal behavior (humans included). When someone personalizes a desk at the office with family pictures, plants, individual coffee mugs, and the like, he or she is staking a claim to a personal territory, small and temporary as it may be. In a more permanent living environment, such as a house or apartment, territorial boundaries are provided by walls, fences, and property lines. Often, boundaries are more subtle. A street, a row of trees, or something very small such as a change in level may serve to define a person's or group's territory.

Closely related to territoriality is the concept of *personal spaces* that surround each individual. This idea, proposed by Edward T. Hall, states that there are four basic distances that can be used to study human behavior and serve as a guide for designing environments. The actual dimensions of the four distances vary with the circumstances and with cultural and social differences, but they always exist. The architect should be aware of personal distance needs and design accordingly, as forcing people closer together than the situation suggests can have a negative effect on them.

The closest is *intimate distance*. This ranges from physical contact to a distance of about 6 in to 18 in (150 to 460). People only allow other people to come within this distance under special conditions. If forced this close together, as on a crowded bus, people have defense mechanisms, such as avoiding eye contact, to minimize the effect of the physical contact.

The next distance is the *personal distance*, from about $1^1/_2$ ft to $2^1/_2$ ft (460 to 760) for some cultures, or more for others. If given the choice, people will maintain this distance between themselves and other people.

Social distance is the next invisible sphere, ranging from about 4 ft to 12 ft (1200 to 3660). This is the distance at which most impersonal business, work, and other interaction takes place between strangers or in more formal situations.

Public distance is the farthest, ranging from about 12 ft (3660) outward. The greatest amount of formality can be achieved at this distance. In addition, this distance allows people to escape if they sense physical danger from another person.

Another principle concerning the effects of development patterns on social behavior is *diversity*. The human animal needs a diverse and stimulating environment. In a monotonous urban setting, community, or building, people tend to become depressed, become irritated, or suffer some other type of negative influence. Over a long period of time, living in a dull, nonstimulating environment can even affect personality development.

Environment can also have an effect on criminal behavior. Oscar Newman developed concepts of what he called defensible space, and published them in the book *Defensible Space* and later in an expanded volume called *Creating Defensible Space*. The concepts of defensible space have spawned the newer term "crime prevention through environmental design" (CPTED).

Newman's original concept of *defensible space* described a range of design elements that used the basic concepts of surveillance, territoriality, and real and symbolic barriers to reduce crime. For example, instead of having the entry to an apartment building open directly to the public area of a street, a low wall could be built to indicate a separation of public and semipublic space. A large window could also be placed next to the front door so residents and passersby could observe activity both inside and outside the door.

Newman's research showed that relatively simple changes in design could reduce criminal behavior. CPTED takes the idea further and includes additional methods to reduce crime, such as electronic surveillance, alarms, and human resources. Refer to Ch. 5 for a discussion of site security.

COMMUNITY INFLUENCES ON DESIGN

Catchment Areas

Nearly all land development is dependent on or affected by some surrounding base of population within a geographical region. The term used to describe this is the *catchment area*. For example, the developer of a grocery store bases the decision to build on the number of people within a certain distance from the proposed store location. The population within this catchment area is the primary market for the services of the store. In a similar way, a school district is the catchment area for a particular school building.

The boundaries of catchment areas may be determined by physical features such as a highway or river, by artificial political boundaries such as a city line or school district limit, or by nebulous demarcations such as the division between two ethnic neighborhoods. Often, when site location studies are being made, a developer knows that a certain number of people must reside within a specified distance from the proposed site to make the project economically feasible. By using population information from census data or other types of surveys, a determination can be quickly made to see if the catchment area will support the land development.

The size and boundaries of a catchment area are dependent on several factors. A residential catchment area, for example, may increase in size with an increase in the population of the surroundings, either through a geographical expansion or with the construction of new housing. Conversely, the expansion of an employment center may create the demand for more workers and increase the employment catchment area. Boundaries are often determined by the availability of transportation. A convenience store that depends on neighborhood customers will have closer boundaries than will a shopping center accessible by major highways.

In many cases, the composition of a catchment area must be known in some detail in order to make development decisions. Simple gross population numbers are not enough. The developer of a high-end retail store needs to know how many people or families with an average income over a particular amount reside within a certain distance from the store site. A school district would have to know how many children of a particular age reside within an area. This kind of information is usually available from census data and local planning agencies.

Accessibility to Transportation

Transportation of all types is critical to the selection and development of a building site. This is true at all scales, from accessibility by major freeways to the individual road system and pedestrian paths around a small site. Something as simple as a one-way street that makes turning into a site from one direction difficult or impossible may be enough to render the property undesirable for some uses.

The following considerations should be examined when analyzing a site for development.

- Is there an adequate highway system to bring the catchment area population to the site?
- Are there adequate traffic counts for businesses that depend on drive-by trade?
- Would the development create additional traffic that would overload the existing road system or require new roads to be built or expanded?
- Is there adequate truck access for servicing the site?
- Does the surrounding transportation network create an undesirable environment for the development? For example, a small site bounded by two freeways may be too noisy for an apartment building.
- Is there safe and convenient pedestrian access to the site if required?
- Are there public transportation lines nearby? How can people get from the mass transit stops to the site?
- Are rail lines available for industrial projects?

Neighborhoods

Any development project is an intimate part of the area in which it is located. Architects must be sensitive to the existing fabric of a neighborhood that may influence how a project is designed as well as to the impact the project may have on the surroundings. A *neighborhood* can be defined as a relatively small area in which a number of people live who share similar needs and desires in housing, social activities, and other aspects of day-to-day living.

The original concept of the neighborhood as a part of city planning was developed by Clarence Perry in 1929. Although his ideas had physical design implications, they were primarily proposed as a way of bringing people together to discuss common problems and to become involved in the planning process. He felt that the ideal way to do this was to base the neighborhood on an area within walking distance of an elementary school, which would serve as the community center of neighborhood activity. Additionally, Perry proposed that the district be surrounded by major streets rather than intersected by them.

The neighborhood has become the basic planning unit for contemporary American urban design. This is in part due to the need for a manageable size on which to base city planning, as well as to the increased importance placed on citizen participation in the planning process, as suggested by Perry. The neighborhood is the scale most people can readily understand and identify with, the part of a city that people come in contact with on a daily basis and that influences their life the most.

Site development must be sensitive to the existing neighborhood. This can include such criteria as respecting pedestrian paths, maintaining the size and scale of the surrounding buildings, using similar or compatible materials, not creating uses that conflict with the surroundings, respecting views and access to important structures in the area, and trying to fit within the general context of the district.

Public Facilities

Public facilities include such places as schools, shops, fire stations, churches, post offices, and recreational centers. Their availability, location, and relative importance in a neighborhood can affect how a site is developed. For example, if a church is the center of social activity in a neighborhood, the designer should maintain easy access to it, surrounding development should be subordinate to or compatible with it, and the designer should give consideration to maintaining views or enhancing the church's prominence in the community. In another case, the path from a school to a recreation center may have special importance. The neighborhood may want the link maintained and improved by any new building along the way.

LAND ANALYSIS

Topography

A study of a site's topography is an important part of environmental analysis because existing land conditions affect how development can take place, what modifications need to be made, and what costs might be involved. Topography describes the surface features of land. Commonly used in land planning and architectural site development, a topographic map shows the slope and contour of the land as well as other natural and artificial features.

A topographic map is developed from a topographic survey by a land surveyor. In addition to information on the contours of a site, a survey will include such data as property boundaries, existing buildings, utility poles, roads and other manufactured features, and trees and other natural features like rock outcroppings and heavy vegetation. Figure 2.6 shows a simplified example of a topographic map.

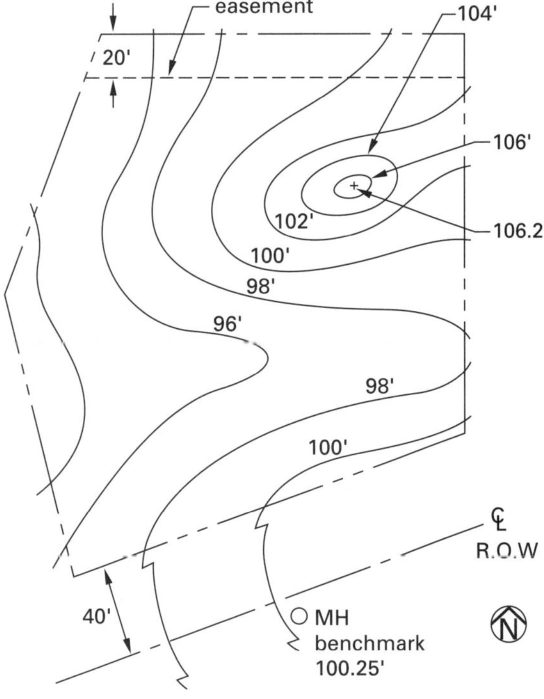

Figure 2.6 Topographic Map

The *contour lines* on a map are a graphic way to show the elevations of the land in a plan view and are used to make a slope analysis to determine the suitability of the land for various uses. Each contour line represents a continuous line of equal elevation above some reference benchmark. The *contour interval* is the vertical distance between adjacent contour lines. The contour interval on a map will vary depending on the steepness of the slope, the scale of the map, and the amount of detail required. Many large-scale maps of individual building sites use 1, 2, or 5 ft (0.5 m or 1 m) contour intervals, and small-scale maps of large regions may use 20 ft or 40 ft (5 m or 10 m) contours. The relationship between a contour map and a section through the contours is illustrated in Fig. 2.7.

Knowing the contour interval and the horizontal distance between any two contour lines, the slope of the land at that point can be determined. The slope is represented as a percentage, each 1% being 1 ft (1 m) of vertical rise for every 100 ft (100 m) of horizontal distance. Thus, a slope of $6^1/_2$% would rise (or drop) $6^1/_2$ ft ($6^1/_2$ m) within 100 ft (100 m).

The slope is found using the formula

$$G = \left(\frac{d}{L}\right) \times 100\% \qquad 2.1$$

Example 2.1

Find the slope between points A and B in Fig. 2.7 if the horizontal distance between them is 80 ft.

Because the contour interval is 5 ft, the vertical distance between the two points is 15 ft. The slope is

$$G = \left(\frac{15 \text{ ft}}{80 \text{ ft}}\right) \times 100\%$$
$$= 19\%$$

For slope analysis, the existing contours can be divided into general categories according to their potential for various types of uses. Slopes from 0% to 4% are usable for all types of intense activity and are easy to build on. Slopes from 4% to 10% are suitable for informal movement and outdoor activity and can also be built on without much difficulty. Slopes over 10% are difficult to climb or use for outdoor activity and are more difficult and expensive to build on. Depending on the condition of the soil, very steep slopes, over 25%, are subject to erosion and become more expensive to build on. Table 2.1 gives some recommended minimum and maximum slopes for various uses.

Table 2.1

Recommended Grade Slopes for Various Uses

	slopes (%)		
	min.	preferred	max.
ground areas for drainage	2.0	4.0	
grass areas for recreation	2.0		3.0
paved parking areas	1.5	2.5	5.0
roads	0.5		10.0
sanitary sewers			
(depends on size)	0.5–1.5		
approach walks to buildings	1.0		5.0
landscaped slopes	2.0		50.0
ramps	5.0		8.33

Respecting the natural contours and slope of the land is important not only from an ecological and aesthetic standpoint but also from an economic standpoint. Moving large quantities of earth costs money, and importing or exporting soil to or from a site is not desirable. Ideally, the amount of

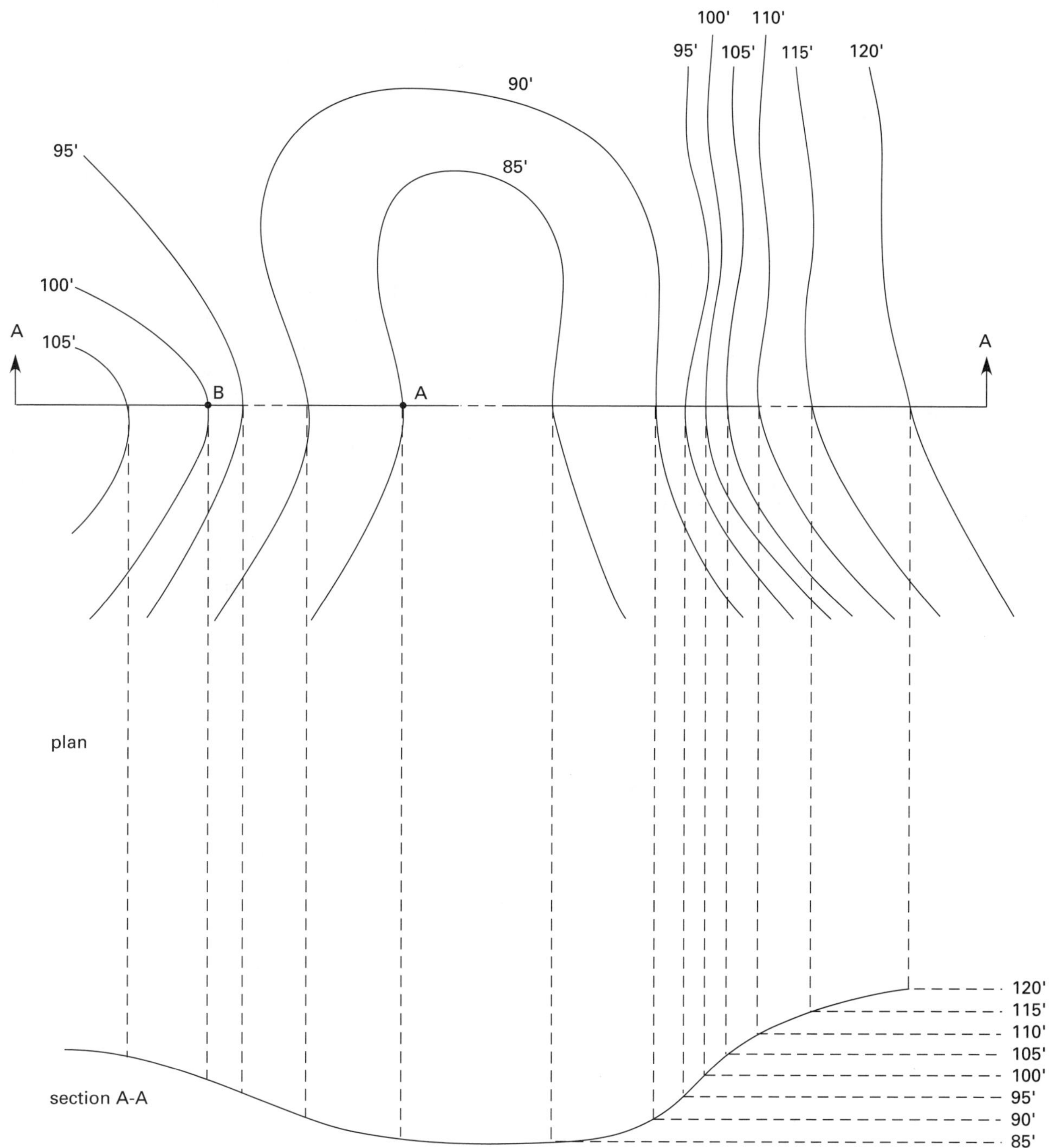

Figure 2.7 Representation of Land Slope with Contour Lines

earth cut away in grading operations should equal the amount required to fill in other portions of the site. Topography and the use of contours is described in more detail in Ch. 5.

Natural Features

Every site has natural features that may be either desirable or undesirable. A complete site analysis will include a study of these features.

A view analysis may be required to determine the most desirable ways to orient buildings, outdoor areas, and approaches to the buildings. Undesirable views can be minimized or blocked with landscaping or other manufactured features.

Significant natural features such as rock outcroppings, cliffs, caves, and bogs should be identified to determine whether they must be avoided or can be used as positive design features in the site design.

Subsurface conditions of groundwater and rock must be known also. Sites with high water tables (about 6 ft to 8 ft [1800 to 2400] below grade) can cause problems with excavations, foundations, utility placement, and landscaping. The water table is the level underground in which the soil is saturated with water. Generally, the water follows the slope of the grade above, but it may vary slightly. Boring logs will reveal whether groundwater is present and how deep it is.

Sites with a preponderance of rocks near the surface can be very expensive and difficult (sometimes impossible) to develop. Blasting is usually required, which can increase the site development costs significantly (and may not be allowed by city code restrictions).

Drainage

Every site has some type of natural drainage pattern that must be taken into account during design. In some cases the drainage may be relatively minor, consisting only of the runoff from the site itself and a small amount from adjacent sites. This type of drainage can easily be diverted around roads, parking lots, and buildings with curbs, culverts, and minor changes in the contours of the land. In other cases, major drainage paths such as gullies, dry gulches, or rivers may traverse the site. These will have a significant influence on potential site development because they must, in most cases, be maintained. Buildings need to be built away from them or must bridge them so that water flow is not restricted and potential damage is avoided. If modification to the contours is required, the changes must be done in such a way that the contours of the adjacent properties are not disturbed.

The development of a site may be so extensive that excessive runoff is created due to roof areas, roads, and parking lots. All of these increase the *runoff coefficient*, the fraction of total precipitation that is not absorbed into the ground. If the runoff is greater than the capacity of the natural or artificial drainage from the site, holding ponds must be constructed to temporarily collect site runoff and release it at a controlled rate.

During construction, runoff drainage must be controlled to prevent sediment from draining into waterways and stormwater drainage systems. Sediment-laden runoff has been shown to degrade stream habitats for fish and other aquatic species, make it more difficult to filter drinking water, and decrease the capacity of drinking water storage. Construction runoff is controlled by constructing a silt fence before any earth moving or other soil disturbance begins. A *silt fence* is a temporary fence designed to allow water to pass through while filtering out sediment. The silt fence is placed along the perimeter of a construction site at places where drainage would normally occur. Although the exact construction requirements vary by jurisdiction, most silt fences are a few feet high and are constructed of a geotextile or other filter fabric stretched between support stakes with the bottom edge of the fabric trenched into the soil. The fence is placed perpendicularly to the slope of the land (that is, along a horizontal contour level) so that the fence causes the stormwater to gather and seep through, rather than merely changing the direction of its flow.

Soil

Soil is the pulverized upper layer of the earth, formed by the erosion of rocks and plant remains and modified by living plants and organisms. Generally, the visible upper layer is topsoil, a mixture of mineral and organic material. The thickness of topsoil may range from just a few inches to a foot or more. Below this is a layer of mostly mineral material, which is above a layer of the fractured and weathered parent material of the soil above. Below all of these layers is solid *bedrock*.

Soil is classified according to grain size and as either organic or inorganic. The grain size classification is

Gravel: particles over 2 mm in diameter

Sands: particles from 0.05 mm to 2 mm in diameter; the finest grains just visible to the eye

Silt: particles from 0.002 mm to 0.05 mm in diameter; the grains are invisible but can be felt as smooth

Clay: particles under 0.002 mm in diameter; smooth and floury when dry, plastic and sticky when wet

All soils are a combination of the preceding types, and any site analysis must include a subsurface investigation to determine the types of soil present as well as the water content. Some soils are unsuitable for certain uses, and layers of different soil types may create planes of potential slippage or slides and make the land useless for development.

Gravels and sands are excellent for construction loads and drainage and for sewage drain fields, but they are unsuitable for landscaping.

Silt is stable when dry or damp but unstable when wet. It swells and heaves when frozen and compresses under load. Generally, building foundations and road bases must extend below it or must be elastic enough to avoid damage. Some nonplastic silts are usable for lighter loads.

Clay expands when wet and is subject to slippage. It is poor for foundations unless it can be kept dry. It is also poor for landscaping and unsuitable for sewage drain fields or other types of drainage.

Peat and other organic materials are excellent for landscaping but unsuitable for building foundations and road bases. Usually, these soils must be removed from the site and replaced with sands and gravels for foundations and roads. Refer to Ch. 35 for more information on soil.

TRANSPORTATION AND UTILITY INFLUENCES

This section reviews some general guidelines for analyzing the transportation and utilities servicing a site. Review Ch. 5 for more detailed design criteria.

Roads

Roads provide a primary means of access to a site. Their availability and capacity may be prime determinants in whether and how a parcel of land can be developed. There are four basic categories of roads: local, collector, arterial, and expressway.

Local streets have the lowest capacity and provide direct access to building sites. They may be in the form of continuous grid or curvilinear systems or may be cul-de-sacs or loops.

Collector streets connect local streets and arterial streets. They, of course, have a higher capacity than local streets but are usually not intended for through traffic. Intersections of collector and local roads may be controlled by stop signs, whereas intersections with arterial streets will be controlled with stop lights.

Arterial streets are intended as major, continuous circulation routes that carry large amounts of traffic on two or three lanes. They usually connect expressways. Parking on the street is typically not allowed, and direct access from arterial streets to building sites should be avoided.

Expressways are limited access roads designed to move large volumes of traffic between, through, and around population centers. Intersections are made by various types of ramp systems, and pedestrian access is not allowed. Expressways have a major influence on the land due to the space they require and their noise and visual impact.

Site analysis must take into account the existing configuration of the street system and fit into the hierarchy of roads. Entrances and exits from the site must be planned to minimize congestion and dangerous intersections. Figure 2.8 illustrates some general guidelines for road layout.

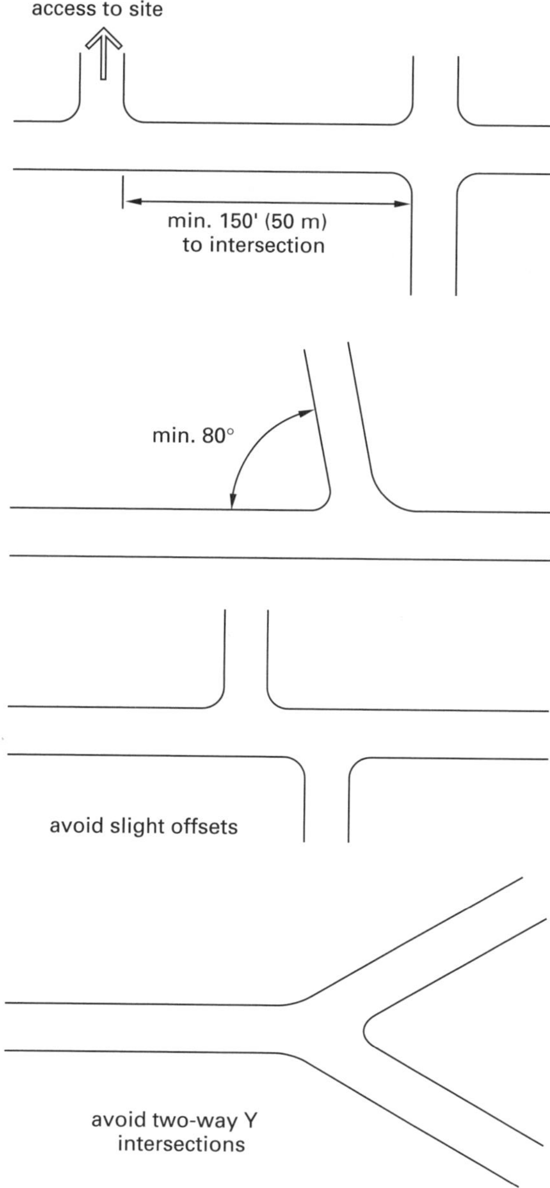

Figure 2.8 Guides for Road Layout at Intersections

Roads must be laid out both in the horizontal direction and the vertical direction, called *horizontal alignment* and *vertical alignment*, respectively. The straight sections of roads are called *tangents*, and the curved portions are arcs of a circle so that a vehicle can be steered easily and safely. Simple curves with a uniform radius between tangents are preferred. There should generally be a minimum of 100 ft (30 m) between curves in opposite directions and 200 ft (60 m) between curves in the same direction. Multiple-radius curves should be avoided.

Vertical alignment must be designed to provide a smooth transition between grade changes and to avoid overly steep grades. Depending on weather conditions and design speeds, streets should not have more than a 10% grade.

Public Transit

The availability and location of public transit lines can influence site design. A site analysis should include a determination of the types of public access available (whether bus, subway, rail line, or taxi stop) and the location relative to the site. Building entrances and major site features should be located conveniently to the public transit. In large cities, site development may have to include provisions for public access to subway and rail lines.

Service Access

Service to a site includes provisions for truck loading, moving vans, and daily delivery services. Ideally, service access should be separate from automobile and pedestrian access to a site and a building. Space for large-truck turning and loading dock berths needs to be provided. Local zoning ordinances usually specify the number and size of loading berths, but generally they should be 10 ft to 12 ft (3050 to 3660) wide, at least 40 ft (12 200) long, and have a 14 ft (4270) vertical clearance. A minimum turning radius of 60 ft (18 300) should be provided unless some other maneuvering method is possible.

Utility Availability

Site analysis must determine the availability, location, and capacity of existing utilities. The development potential of a site is dependent on the availability of the necessary utilities of water, sanitary sewers, storm sewers, telephone service, gas service, electric service, and other public utilities. Utility lines that have to be extended from a considerable distance add greatly to the cost of development.

Generally, utility lines follow the street layout and right-of-way. Sanitary sewers, storm sewers, and water mains are located under the road, whereas electric and communication lines are adjacent to the roads. Gas lines may either be under the road or next to it within the right-of-way. Utilities can also be located in easements, portions of privately owned land that public utility companies can use for the installation and maintenance of their lines.

When new services must be installed, sanitary and storm sewer location takes precedence because sewers must use the flow of gravity and therefore depend on the natural slope of the land. Collection systems drain to municipal disposal systems or to private, on-site treatment facilities.

Municipal Services

Depending on the location of the site, municipal services may include police protection, fire protection, trash removal, and street cleaning. The development site plan must provide access for these services, many of which require large land areas. For example, local fire protection officials may require an unobstructed strip of land around buildings to allow for fire fighting, in addition to suitable access roads from the street to the building. In some climates, adequate provisions must be made for snow removal or snow stacking.

CLIMATIC INFLUENCES

For any given site there are two aspects to climatic analysis: the macroclimate and the microclimate. The *macroclimate* refers to the overall climate of the region and is reflected in the weather data available from the National Weather Service. From this information a region can be classified as cool, temperate, hot-arid, or hot-humid. The *microclimate* refers to the site-specific modification of the macroclimate by such features as land slope, trees and other vegetation, bodies of water, and buildings.

The microclimate of a site can have a significant influence on its development; undesirable climatic effects can be minimized by careful planning, and desirable effects can be used to enhance the comfort of the inhabitants.

Wind Patterns

Both prevailing wind patterns and microclimate wind effects must be studied during site analysis. Buildings can then be located to take advantage of breezes or to avoid cold winds. Wind on the top of a hill, for example, can be about 20% higher than wind on flat ground. The *leeward* side of a hill (the side away from the wind direction) experiences less wind than the *windward* side. Near large bodies of water, warm air rises over the warmer land during the day and causes a breeze from the water. At night the pattern may be reversed; cold air flows down a hill and settles in low-lying regions, causing pockets that remain colder than higher elevations during the first part of the day. On a large scale, this results in an inversion where warmer air holds colder air below, trapping pollution.

Wind patterns can be modified by buildings and trees. For a line of trees 50 ft to 150 ft (15 m to 46 m) deep, wind velocity can be reduced from 30% to 60% to a distance 10 times the height of the tree line, depending on the density of the trees, and about half that to a distance of 20 times the tree height. For a single row of trees the effect is different. Refer to Ch. 29. Buildings can affect similar types of wind modification.

In general, in temperate climates the best microclimates for wind are on south- or southeast-facing slopes, in the middle of the slope or toward the top of a hill rather than at the very top or bottom of the slope.

Solar Orientation

The amount of solar radiation received on the ground surface depends on the angle of the sun's rays to the surface. At the macroclimate scale, this is the main reason that summer is warmer than winter: the sun is higher in the sky. (Also, there are longer days.) It also accounts for the fact that lower latitudes are warmer than higher latitudes. On a microclimate scale, in the Northern Hemisphere south-facing slopes tend to be warmer, especially in the winter, than other slope orientations or flat surfaces. Ski runs in northern latitudes, for example, are usually located on north-facing mountains to avoid the direct radiation of the sun.

The amount of radiation absorbed or reflected is affected by the surface material. The fraction of the radiant energy received on a surface that is reflected is called the albedo and is expressed as a number from zero to 1.0. A flat black surface that absorbs all the energy and reflects none has an albedo of zero, whereas an albedo of 1.0 corresponds to a mirror that reflects all the energy striking it. Natural materials such as grass and vegetation have low albedos; snow and pavement have high albedos.

Closely related to albedo is *conductivity*, which is the time rate of flow of heat through a material. Highly conductive materials let heat pass through them quickly, whereas materials of low conductivity retard the passage of heat. Natural materials generally have low conductivity, and metal, concrete, and masonry have relatively high conductivities.

Combined, albedo and conductivity affect the microclimate. Ground surfaces with low albedo and high conductivity tend to moderate and stabilize the microclimate because excess heat is quickly absorbed, stored, and released when the temperature drops. Surfaces with grass and other vegetation are cooler in hot weather for this reason. On the other hand, surfaces with high albedo and low conductivity, such as pavements or concentrations of buildings, are much hotter than what the macroclimate would normally produce.

SUSTAINABLE DESIGN

Sustainable building design, also known as *green building design*, is an increasingly important part of architectural design. Sustainable design addresses a wide range of concerns, including the environmental impact of a building, the wise use of materials, energy conservation, the use of alternative energy sources, adaptive reuse, indoor air quality, recycling, reuse, and other strategies to achieve a balance between the consumption of environmental resources and the renewal of those resources. Sustainable design considers the full life cycle of a building and of the materials that comprise the building. Accordingly, it considers the impact that raw material extraction will have through all the stages of fabrication, installation, operation, maintenance, and disposal.

This section discusses sustainable design as it affects site evaluation, site selection, and the development of project concepts. Subsequent chapters cover alternative energy systems, new material technologies, building systems, hazardous material mitigation, indoor air quality, energy conservation, and adaptive reuse.

General Ecological Considerations

Ecology is the study of living organisms in relation to their environment. Applied to site development, the word takes on a slightly broader meaning. The need to understand the impact of construction on the surrounding natural environment is a key factor in the ecology of site development. This concern has been codified with the requirement that federal agencies file environmental impact statements (EISs). This requirement was started as one of the provisions of the National Environmental Policy Act of 1969 and is enforced by the Environmental Protection Agency (EPA). It requires a formal process to predict how a development will affect the environment, including the air, water, land, and wildlife. Many states have similar laws that require EISs for state-sponsored development. Another factor in the ecology of site development is the need to be cognizant of the impact of smaller-scale building on the surroundings, whether the environment is rural or in the heart of a city.

One concern that should be investigated during site analysis for semirural or rural development is the impact on natural landforms, water runoff, wildlife, and existing vegetation. The development should disturb the natural contours of the land as little as possible. Existing drainage patterns must be left intact, and additional runoff caused by roofs and paving should not exceed the capacity of the existing drainage paths. The development should also avoid significantly disturbing existing ecological systems of plants and wildlife.

For urban sites, slightly different concerns should be studied. The relationship of the building and its users to the surrounding environment remains a factor, but the impact of this relationship is more on artificial systems than on natural ecosystems. The development should minimize the production of noise, pollution, or other detrimental emissions. Building placement should avoid undesirable wind conditions, either on the site itself or around nearby buildings. The effect of a building blocking sunlight from adjacent buildings and outdoor spaces should be studied and minimized when possible. Similarly, the development should avoid any possible annoying reflection or glare on neighboring buildings. Finally, the impact of development on the utility and transportation systems must be thoroughly understood. Specific guidelines for achieving these goals are given in the following sections and in Ch. 30.

Wetlands

A *wetland* is defined by the Environmental Protection Agency as an area whose soil is inundated or saturated by surface water or groundwater frequently enough that it can support plants that are adapted to living in saturated soil. Wetlands are sometimes also referred to as *jurisdictional wetlands*. In the United States, wetlands are protected by the federal government through the Clean Water Act of 1972 (CWA). States and local governmental jurisdictions may also have regulations related to wetlands.

Wetlands regulations are aimed at protecting wetlands, and areas interrelated with them, from damage due to nearby development, discharge of dredged or fill material, or outright destruction. Discharge into wetlands may be allowed but Section 404 of the CWA requires a permit from the U.S. Army Corps of Engineers, except for certain farming, forestry, and other activities that are exempt from this requirement.

Site Analysis

In addition to the previously discussed influences of community, land, transportation, and climate on site selection and building design, a number of sustainability issues should be considered when analyzing a site. These include the following.

- Determine what sites or portions of a site should *not* be built on. These include wetlands or sites within 100 ft (30 m) of wetlands, elevations lower than 5 ft (1.5 m) above a 100-year floodplain, habitats for endangered species, potential historic sites (i.e., burial grounds), and prime farmland.

- Determine the historical and cultural qualities of the surrounding area. An area with significant historical or cultural importance may suggest that new development should reflect the massing, architectural style, and landscape design of surrounding development to integrate with the community and preserve the area's cultural heritage.

- Analyze what types of development might surround the site in the future. Such development could affect the location of the building, connection with transportation or other infrastructure, solar access, local microclimate, view corridors, and shared facilities such as parking or service access.

- Analyze existing air quality. This should be done by a qualified laboratory or service and should include an assessment of the existing air quality as well as an estimation of the effects of the proposed development on air quality in the area.

- Have the soil and groundwater tested for contamination. Contaminated soil or water could make the proposed project infeasible or affect building location and mitigation methods.

- Determine the presence of endangered species. These may include plants, insects, and animals.

Site and Building Concepts Using Sustainability

The early stages of project planning and site analysis offer many ways to help create a sustainable project. The following sustainability guidelines may affect project concepts.

Building Location

- Give preference to urban sites or other sites with existing infrastructure, to minimize disruption of undeveloped land and maximize efficient use of transportation and utility services.

- Encourage mixed-use development of residential, commercial, retail, and entertainment facilities, to give people the option of living near the buildings where they work and do much of their shopping and relaxation.

- Locate buildings near public transportation.

- Locate buildings in such a way as to minimize tree and vegetation clearing, take advantage of solar access, and minimize the detrimental effects of wind.

- Minimize solar shadows on adjacent properties with setbacks or low building heights.

- Locate buildings in such a way as to maximize desirable airflow patterns.

- Locate buildings in such a way as to use gravity sewer systems.

Building Size, Shape, and Design

- Minimize the building footprint by using multiple floors, when possible.
- Design the building dimensions to optimize material use and reduce waste.
- Consider using garden roofs or highly reflective roof coverings to reduce the heat island effect.
- Plan buildings to include bicycle storage and shower/changing facilities.

Site Disturbance

- Plan buildings and parking on previously disturbed areas.
- Position buildings along landscape contours and shallow slopes, to minimize earthwork and site clearing.
- Plan utility corridors along new road or walk construction or along previously disturbed areas on the site.
- Limit site disturbance to 40 ft (12 m) beyond the building perimeter, 5 ft (1.5 m) beyond primary roadway curbs and walks, and 25 ft (7.6 m) beyond constructed areas with permeable surfaces.

Site Development

- Minimize the site development area by providing all or some parking under the building.
- Develop a site plan to minimize road length, parking, and service areas. Consolidate pedestrian, automobile, and service paths whenever possible. Double load parking lots to share access lanes and minimize paving.
- Do not develop more than the minimum parking required by the local zoning ordinance.
- Reduce heat islands by providing shade or using high-albedo materials with a minimum reflectance of 0.3.
- Use open-grid paving or other pervious paving to reduce storm water runoff.
- Plan pedestrian surfaces using permeable materials such as loose aggregate, permeable concrete, wooden decks, and spaced paving stones.
- Use mechanical or natural treatment systems for stormwater, such as constructed wetlands, vegetated filter strips, infiltration basins, and bioswales. A *bioswale* is a shallow grass-lined ditch or channel designed to detain storm runoff and remove sediments and other contaminants while allowing the water to seep into the ground through a process known as *phytoremediation*.
- Design vegetative buffer areas around parking lots to mitigate runoff of water containing pollutants such as oil and sediments.
- Minimize site lighting, and prevent light from spilling onto adjacent properties or into the sky.
- If allowed by local and state regulations, consider using collected rainwater for supplemental irrigation. However, the annual rainfall must be enough to make this feasible. Also, areas with poor air quality may yield water not suitable for its intended purpose. Roofing materials must be carefully selected, and the costs of collection, storage, and filtration must be evaluated. Refer to Ch. 30 for more information on rainwater collection.

  If rainwater cannot be collected, an infiltration basin may be used. An *infiltration basin* is a closed depression in the earth from which water can escape only into the soil. Do not confuse this with a *catch basin*, which is an area that temporarily contains excessive runoff until it can flow at a controlled rate into the storm sewer system.
- Use native plant materials, and minimize the use of high-maintenance lawns. Good landscaping practices can improve the aesthetics of a site, reduce water runoff, and minimize erosion while minimizing the need for irrigation and providing habitats for animal and insect species.

LEGAL AND ECONOMIC INFLUENCES

In the United States, legal regulations and economic conditions have a great influence on how land is developed. For example, most commercial, for-profit landowners attempt to maximize their return on investment while working within the legal constraints of zoning ordinances and other types of building regulations. This practice may dictate the best economic uses of the property, how much square footage must be built, and even the overall architectural form of the structure. An architect must have an understanding of these influences and how they affect site development and building design.

Zoning

The most common form of legal constraint on land development is zoning. Although human settlements have been informally separated into areas of different uses for centuries, it was not until the first part of the twentieth century that zoning took on legal status. It was originally an attempt to improve the problems of the rapidly expanding cities: crowding, factories being built too close to housing, and tall buildings blocking light and air.

The first zoning ordinance was passed in 1916 in New York City and was the first attempt by a municipal government to control the use and location of buildings throughout a city. Zoning began as a way of regulating land use, but today it has grown into one means of implementing planning policy.

Zoning is the division of a city or other governmental unit into districts, and the regulation of the use of land and the location and bulk of buildings on property within those districts. Its legal basis is largely founded on the right of the state to protect the health, safety, and welfare of the public. Municipalities receive the power to zone through the states with enabling legislation.

Zoning primarily regulates

- the uses allowed on a parcel of land depending on the zoning district
- the area of the land that may be covered with buildings
- the bulk of the structures
- the distances the buildings must be set back from the property lines
- parking and loading space requirements

Other requirements, such as regulation of signs and bonuses for providing plazas and open space, may also be included. Although zoning is primarily used in cities, special types of zoning are sometimes used. These types may include rural zoning to separate agricultural uses from forestry or recreational use, floodplain zoning, airport zoning, and historic area zoning.

Uses are established for the zoning districts and are based on residential, commercial, and industrial occupancies with subdivisions within each of these. Residential zones may include, for example, single-family, low-density multifamily, and high-density multifamily dwellings. For each zoning district, a list of permissible uses is specified, with single-family zones being the most restrictive. Each zone may be used for the purposes listed for that zone and for any use listed in a more restrictive zone. For instance, a single-family house could be constructed within a dense business zone, though it probably would not be for economic and aesthetic reasons.

The amount of land that can be covered is determined by the interrelationship of two zoning restrictions: floor area ratio and setbacks. *Floor area ratio* is the ratio of the gross floor area within a structure to the area of the lot on which the structure is situated. For example, if the floor area ratio is 1.0 and a lot is 75,000 ft^2 in area, the maximum permissible gross floor space is 75,000 ft^2. Within the constraints of setbacks and bulk planes, this 75,000 ft^2 of floor space may be configured in any number of ways.

Figure 2.9(a) shows a structure occupying only 50% of the ground area. If the floor area ratio (sometimes referred to as FAR) is 1.0, then a two-story building can be constructed.

Figures 2.9(b) and 2.9(c) illustrate two instances where the same floor area ratio can result in two different building forms. In Fig. 2.9(b), the building occupies only 25% ground area. If the FAR is 3.0, then a 12-story building can be erected. In Fig. 2.9(c), the building occupies 50% of the land, so only six stories can be built. In both cases, the building area is three times the land area.

Floor area ratios must always be developed with regard to setbacks. A *setback* is the minimum distance a building must be placed from a property line. Setback distances usually vary depending on which property line is involved. The distance from the property line facing the street or the primary front of the property is known as the *front setback*, usually the greatest setback distance. The distance from the back of the lot is the *rear setback*, and the distance from the side property line is known as the *side setback*. In the example of Fig. 2.9(a), for instance, setbacks might preclude covering 50% of the site, so to reach the maximum allowable floor area ratio, the building would have to be more than two stories. Setbacks also regulate the bulk of a building and how much space results between structures.

Another common zoning tool is the bulk plane restriction. This sets up an imaginary inclined plane beginning at the lot line or the center of the street and sloping at a prescribed angle toward and over the lot. The building cannot extend into this plane. The purpose of the restriction is to ensure adequate light and air to neighboring properties and to the open space and streets around the land.

Sometimes, zoning ordinances will also place maximum limits on the number of stories of a building or the height in feet above grade level.

There are many instances when zoning restrictions create an undue hardship on a property owner or a zoning ordinance does not completely cover unusual conditions. For these cases, the property owner can apply for a *variance*, which is a deviation from the zoning regulations. Municipalities have a procedure by which owners can describe their situation and apply for a variance. A public hearing is a part of the process to allow nearby property owners and anyone interested to object to the application if they wish.

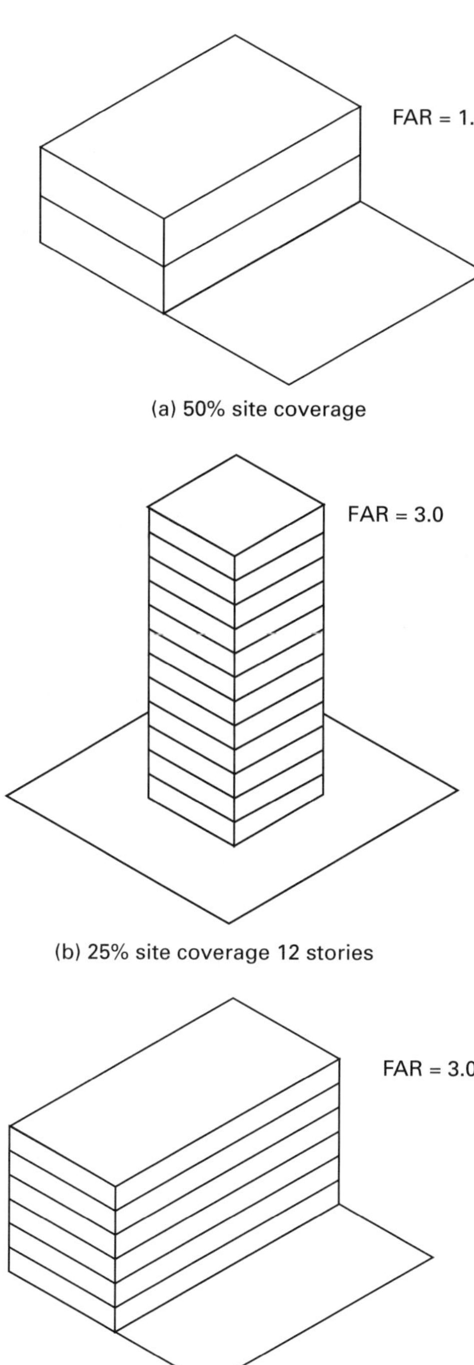

Figure 2.9 Examples of Floor Area Ratios

If a new zoning ordinance is being applied to existing development, there may be properties that contain nonconforming uses. These are allowed to remain unless the owner stops using the property in its original fashion or the property is demolished or destroyed by fire. Then, any new use must conform to the zoning requirements.

A zoning board (or planning commission) may also grant a *conditional use permit*, which allows a nonconforming use or other use in the zoning ordinance if the property owner meets certain restrictions. This is often done if the exception is in the public interest. For example, a zoning board may allow a temporary street fair in a location where it would normally be prohibited, or it might allow a church to violate a setback provision with the condition that other open space be provided for the community.

Refer to Ch. 5 for more information on zoning.

Easements and Rights-of-Way

An *easement* is the right of one party to use a portion of the land of another party in a particular way. It is a legal instrument and is normally recorded. There are many types of easements, one of the most common being a *utility easement*. This allows a utility company to install and maintain lines above or below the ground within the boundaries of the easement. Although the land belongs to the property owner, no permanent structures can be erected within the easement without permission from the party holding the easement.

Another type of easement is the *access easement*. If one parcel of land is not served by a public road and another parcel separates the first parcel from the street, an access easement may be granted, which allows the public and the owner of the inaccessible land the right to cross.

Other types of easements include *support easements* for the construction of common party walls between properties, *joint use easements* that allow two or more property owners to share a common feature such as a driveway, *scenic easements* that protect views and development in scenic areas, and *conservation easements* that limit land use in large areas. Scenic and conservation easements are often used by public agencies to control land use without the need to purchase large tracts of property.

A *right-of-way* is the legal right of one party or the public to traverse land belonging to another. In its most common form, a right-of-way refers to the public land used for streets and sidewalks. The boundary of a right-of-way usually corresponds to the property line of adjacent property owners. In most cases, the street occupies only a portion of the right-of-way; the remainder is used for sidewalks, landscaping, and utilities. An access easement, as previously described, creates a private or public right-of-way.

Deed Restrictions

Deeds to property can contain provisions that restrict the use of the property by the buyer. These are called *restrictive covenants* and are legal and enforceable if they are reasonable and in the public interest. It is quite common for the developer of a large tract of land that is being subdivided to include restrictive covenants in the deeds. They may include such limitations as setbacks, minimum square footage of houses, the types of materials that can and cannot be used on the exterior, and similar provisions.

Two other types of deed restrictions are affirmative covenants and conditional covenants. An *affirmative covenant* requires a buyer to perform a specific duty in the future. For example, the purchaser of property may be required to construct and maintain a fence as a condition of purchase. A *conditional covenant* permits the title to the property to revert to the original owner if the restrictions prescribed in the deed are not followed.

Because the covenants are in the deed, they are known to the potential buyer before purchase so the buyer can decide not to purchase if the covenants are not acceptable. Restrictive covenants are often used in residential subdivisions to maintain a desired uniformity of appearance, site development, and quality of construction. Most deed restrictions, however, are generally established for a certain period of years such as 10, 15, 20, or 30 years.

Land Values

As part of the overall economic analysis of a site for potential development (or adaptive reuse of an existing building), the cost of the property is vital in making a decision concerning site selection. In addition to land acquisition costs, there are costs of site improvements, building construction, appraisal, financing, professional fees, permits, and maintenance of the completed structure. If all of these cannot be paid off in a reasonable amount of time and yield a profit to the owner or developer, the site is probably a poor economic choice.

Land values are generally based on location, potential profit-making use, and local market conditions, which includes demand for the land. Location includes such things as a potential surrounding market area, population density in the region, special features of the site (such as being waterfront property), and proximity to transportation and utilities, which are especially important to residential and industrial development. Land values are based on the concept of "highest and best use," which means that the property is to be used and developed in such a way as to yield the highest return on investment. Property that is not used to this capacity is said to be underdeveloped.

There are three basic ways land is valued. A fairly common technique is the *market approach*. The surrounding neighborhood or region is investigated to find properties that have recently sold or are on the market that are similar to the property being valued. Except for adjustments to reflect the unique nature of the property, the property is assumed to have the same value as that of the similar properties. For example, if three nearby house lots in a subdivision recently sold for around \$40,000 and they were all about the same size, then a fourth lot of similar size would also be valued at about \$40,000. Quite often, the value is based on a unit quantity that can more easily be applied to another property that is not exactly the same. Land is commonly assigned a value per square foot or per acre, and buildings are often valued at a cost per square foot. The assumed value of another property can then be determined simply by multiplying the current market value per square foot times the area of the property being evaluated.

The second method is the *income approach*. Here, the basis is the potential the property has to yield a profit (income). The potential income is estimated (allowing for vacancies and credit losses), and then various expenses such as taxes, insurance, and maintenance are deducted. Because potential income is usually figured on a yearly basis, this amount must be capitalized to estimate the current, total value of the property.

The third method is the *cost approach*. With this method, the value of the land is estimated at its highest and best use. Then, the cost to replace the building or add improvements is calculated. The estimated accrued depreciation is figured and subtracted from the replacement cost or cost of the improvements. This adjusted amount is then added to the land value to give the total value of the property.

Tax Structure

The taxes to which a developer is subject can influence whether a project is undertaken and how the site is developed. Although the subject is very complicated, taxes become an ongoing operating cost of a development and can be estimated fairly easily if one knows the tax rate and what it is based on. Many tax rates are based on a mill levy on the assessed valuation of a piece of property. A mill is one-thousandth of a dollar, or one-tenth of a cent. The assessed valuation is a percentage of the actual value of the property, and the percentage is set by the taxing authority.

Example 2.2

The assessed valuation of developed property is based on 19% of actual value, and the mill levy is 0.04931. If a developed piece of property is estimated to have an actual valuation of \$150,000, what will the yearly tax be?

The assessed value is

$$(0.19)(\$150{,}000) = \$28{,}500$$

The yearly tax will be

$$(0.04931)(\$28{,}500) = \$1405$$

Taxing authorities may offer various types of tax incentives to developers as a way of implementing public policy. For instance, tax credits may be given for renovating historic structures as a way of encouraging historic preservation. New businesses may be encouraged to move to a city by reduction or elimination of taxes for a certain time period. In any case, tax incentives may turn an otherwise uneconomical project into a viable one.

Life-Cycle Cost Analysis

A *life-cycle cost analysis* (LCC) is used to evaluate the economic performance of a material or building system over the service life of the material or system. The LCC includes all the costs associated with purchasing, installing, maintaining, and disposing of an item from the time the item is installed in a building through the duration of the LCC study period. All costs during the study period are discounted to convert future costs to their equivalent present values and account for the time value of money.

Not to be confused with the LCC is the *life-cycle assessment analysis* (LCA). The LCA of a material evaluates the environmental impacts from initial raw material extraction to final recycling, reuse, or disposal. It includes raw material extraction, material processing, the manufacture of intermediate materials, fabrication, installation in the building, operation, maintenance, and final disposal or reuse.

Refer to Ch. 30 for a detailed discussion of both life-cycle cost analysis and life-cycle assessment.

Public Works Financing

There are several methods by which government agencies can finance public works projects. These include general sales and property taxes, special sales taxes, general obligation bonds, revenue bonds (or rate-supported bonds), public enterprise revenue bonds, tax-increment financing, development impact fees, subdivision exactions, and special district assessments. These methods have different requirements and are used for different purposes.

General Sales Taxes and Property Taxes

A *general tax* is any tax imposed for general governmental purposes. Property taxes are an *ad valorem tax*, a tax based on the value of property being taxed. The money collected by a municipality or other jurisdiction is placed in a general fund and used as required by that jurisdiction. Although general taxes may be used to fund public works, they are typically used to provide ongoing operation and maintenance of existing facilities and normal capital improvements, such as replacing curbs and gutters or remodeling schools. Major projects are typically funded with other methods as described in the following sections.

Depending on the local or state jurisdiction, general taxes or increases to general taxes may be limited or may require a vote of the general population. However, an increase in property taxes usually occurs when the value of property is increased by the local jurisdiction's tax assessment office, even if the rate of taxation is unchanged.

Special Sales Taxes

A *special tax* is any tax imposed for a specific purpose or by a single-purpose authority. Special sales taxes require a majority vote of the people in the district. An example this type of tax is one to fund a major transportation project.

General Obligation Bonds

General obligation bonds are issued by a city or state and backed by general tax revenue and the issuer's credit. They are used to finance the acquisition or construction of specific public capital facilities and to purchase real property. The jurisdiction issuing the bond is authorized to levy a property tax at the rate necessary to repay the principal and interest of the bonds, usually over a period of 10 to 30 years. Each general obligation bond measure requires approval of the voters. Examples of projects funded with general obligation bonds include schools, museums, and libraries. Because all taxpayers in the jurisdiction issuing the bonds must contribute a property tax to pay off the bonds, a voter majority is required.

Revenue Bonds or Rate-Supported Bonds

Revenue bonds (often called *rate-supported bonds*) are similar to general obligation bonds in that a local government issues them to pay for a facility or improvement. However, these bonds are backed by the revenue, or rates, from customers using the services that the bond funding paid for. In most cases rates increase to pay for retirement of the bonds. City water and sewer facilities often use this method of financing.

Public Enterprise Revenue Bonds

Public enterprise revenue bonds are issued by cities or counties to finance facilities for revenue-producing public enterprises. The bonds are paid off from revenues generated by the facility through the charges they impose. Airports, parking garages, and hospitals are examples of facilities that may use this method of financing.

Tax-Increment Financing

A city can use *tax-increment financing* to pay for improvements based on increased taxes due to the increased value of property. A city creates a special district and makes public improvements within that district that will generate private development. The assessed value of the property within the district is determined, and taxes based on that value are frozen for a defined period of time set forth in the development plan. Bonds are issued at the beginning of the redevelopment. Each taxing jurisdiction continues to receive its share of the taxes based on the original assessed valuation. At the end of the development period, the assessed valuation increases due to the new development, and the increased taxes (the tax increment) go into a special fund created to retire bonds issued to originate the development. Tax-increment financing is used for purchasing land, planning, and public works improvements to encourage private development. It does not require a vote by the people in the district.

Development Impact Fees

Development impact fees are costs charged to developers for off-site infrastructure improvements made necessary by new development. These fees are a way to make developers, rather than existing residents, responsible for the costs necessitated by the development. Impact fees may be made in addition to other exactions, such as hookup fees for utility service, and can be used for projects such as street improvements or construction of wastewater treatment plants. Because there is often the question of how the fee is calculated and who really benefits from the new public facilities, impact fees can be controversial.

Subdivision Exactions

Subdivision exactions are similar to development fees in that they put a burden on the developer, but in this case the exaction is not used to fund construction. Rather, subdivision exactions are requirements that developers either dedicate some land for public use or contribute cash for the purchase of land and facilities made necessary by local governments.

Special District Assessments

There are several variations of *special district assessments* (often called *business improvement districts*—BIDs—or *benefit assessments*). These fees are used to fund public space improvements, like parks and streetscapes, in order to enhance an area's appeal and, indirectly, its property values. A special district is established to include the properties that will benefit from the proposed improvements. If a majority of the property owners in the area agree to the arrangement, then all owners within the district's boundaries are required to contribute. Taxes are assessed on those property owners in the district who would benefit from the improvements. This type of funding is usually, but not always, used to improve or maintain existing facilities. It is not intended to encourage private development.

Project Financing

Building projects are financed in many ways. The following are some of the most common types of loans.

A *blanket loan* (sometimes called a *blanket mortgage*) is a type of loan often used to fund a large piece of real estate that the borrower intends to subdivide and resell as smaller parcels. With a traditional mortgage, every time a parcel was sold the borrower would have to repay the entire loan and secure a new mortgage on the unsold parcels. With a blanket mortgage, as each parcel is sold, a portion of the mortgage is paid back and retired, but the remainder of the mortgage is still in force.

A *bond* is a kind of debt security often issued by a government entity (such as the government of a city, state, or nation) to raise money to finance a construction project. The issuer of the bond receives money from the buyer, and in exchange promises to repay the principal with interest on a certain later date. Bonds are typically sold to individual investors or investment companies.

A *bridge loan* is a short-term loan used to purchase property or finance a project quickly, before long-term financing can be arranged.

A *construction loan* is used to finance the building of a project for the duration of construction. Once construction is complete, the loan must be converted into a long-term, permanent loan whereby the lender is repaid monthly.

A *hard money loan* is typically a relatively short-term loan used where there is a distressed financial situation, such as foreclosure, bankruptcy, or nonpayment of a previous loan. The loan is based on the quick-sale value (which is usually significantly less than the market value) of an asset such as a parcel of property or other real estate. High interest rates are usual.

A *mezzanine loan* is often used by a developer for a large project. The loan is secured by collateral in the stock of the development company, rather than in the developed property. In the event of default, the lender can seize the assets of the borrower more quickly than with a standard mortgage loan.

A *mortgage loan* provides cash to a borrower to purchase property in exchange for a lien on the property until the loan is repaid. This is the common method by which individuals purchase homes.

As part of project financing, a developer will develop a pro forma statement, which includes project financing. A *pro forma statement* is a statement or model of all the expected expenses (both initial and long term) of developing a project, compared against the expected income and increase in value of the project. (*Pro forma* is Latin for *as a matter of form*.) A pro forma statement is developed in order to determine whether the project is likely to be financially successful.

EVALUATING EXISTING STRUCTURES

In many cases, the architect is working on a project not to construct a new building on a piece of land, but to renovate or reuse an existing structure. In these situations, the architect must evaluate the existing structure to see if it is appropriate for the intended use. The evaluation process involves surveying the structure, documenting the survey, researching applicable regulations, and evaluating the information. This process usually involves existing buildings with no historic value, but may include historic structures, which require additional work on the part of the design professional.

The amount of work and detail included in the survey and documentation will vary depending on the basic information needed to test the project's feasibility. It may be that a quick, cursory survey of the structure's size and condition is enough to confirm that the project is not feasible within the budget and that no further survey work should be done. If the initial survey suggests that the project may work, a more extensive survey and evaluation may be undertaken. If the evaluation shows that the structure is workable for the proposed use, yet another more detailed survey may be scheduled, and documentation may be created to provide the basis for detailed design work and construction documents.

Surveying Existing Buildings

An existing building survey must include several components. In most cases, the survey requires laborious field measurements and site-survey techniques, unless accurate as-built drawings are available. An existing building survey should include the following.

- Site features, including parking, service access, pedestrian access, adjacent properties, microclimate, and amenities like views and water features.
- Size and configuration of the structure, including overall size and shape, height, location of columns and bearing walls, beams, and other major structural components. Also, the location of partitions, toilets, mechanical rooms, and other service areas.
- Structure, including the type, load capacity, and condition. The condition of the foundation and primary structural frame are most important because these support everything else, and correcting or reinforcing them is expensive. A structural engineering consultant is usually needed for this portion of the survey.
- Roof, including the type, condition, and expected remaining life. Are there any signs of water damage or leaking?
- Exterior envelope, including the type and condition. Are the windows in good condition? What type of existing insulation does it have and what *R*-value does it provide?
- Mechanical system, including the type of heating and cooling, the capacity of the central plant, and the condition of the distribution system. A mechanical engineering consultant is usually needed for this portion of the survey.
- Plumbing, including the capacity of service to the building, sewer capacity, condition of pipes and fixtures, and number of fixtures. A mechanical engineering consultant is usually needed for this portion of the survey.
- Electrical, including the capacity of service to the building, condition of primary and secondary service, condition of wiring and devices, and condition of lighting and other electrical components. An electrical engineering consultant is usually needed for this portion of the survey.
- Fire protection, including the condition of the system, pipe sizing, and spacing of heads. A mechanical engineering or fire protection consultant may be needed for this portion of the survey.
- Major equipment, if applicable. This component depends on the building type and may include such items as refrigeration equipment, commercial food service equipment, and laboratory equipment.
- Finishes, including the condition and expected life of major surface finishes.
- Condition of the structure for accessibility. Also, the condition of the egress system and fire-rated elements.

If the building is a designated historic structure or has historic value, additional issues need to be investigated. These are discussed in the next section of this chapter.

Although this is not part of the actual building survey, the architect must ask the client about cost and time constraints. This is a vital part of the evaluation process that will take place later. In some cases, the client may not have a budget and may want the architect to develop an estimate of the costs involved in adapting an existing building to a new use.

Documenting Building Surveys

The building survey is typically documented in several ways. These include manually drafted drawings, CAD drawings, notes, formal reports, photographs, and videos. If architectural drawings and specifications of the structure exist, the architect should obtain these and verify them against the actual structure. The architect should also obtain any existing site surveys, soils investigations, and other documentation.

Drawings, whether manually drafted or CAD generated, should include the building structure and exterior walls as well as the location of interior partitions, doors, equipment, woodwork, plumbing fixtures, and other pertinent items. The accuracy of the survey and the drawings depends on the structure's size and complexity, the time and equipment devoted to field measurements, and the requirements of the new use of the building. Normally, measurement accuracy to within $^1/_4$ in (6) is more than adequate, and even $^1/_2$ in (13) accuracy may be sufficient.

The documentation should also include elevations of floors and other major features. Drawings of some elevations may also be required. The locations of mechanical and electrical equipment to remain should also be noted as required. Elements that are to be removed should be highlighted.

Finally, the project should be documented with photographs, videos, or both.

Methods of Field Measuring and Recording

Traditionally, collecting information on the size and configuration of an existing building has required the architect to visit the site and make sketches and measurements using a tape measure and traditional surveying equipment. Drawings are then produced from the measurements taken on site. This method is labor intensive and susceptible to human error as well as errors introduced by measurement tools. However, hand measuring can be a useful, low-cost method to use when measuring buildings of moderate size and complexity. Hand measuring is also well suited for recording small details that cannot be seen by instruments using other techniques.

The use of simple tape measures has recently been augmented by more precise instruments. Low-cost, line-of-sight sonic devices can be used by one person and give reasonable accuracy for many uses. However, their range is limited and they cannot precisely differentiate between closely spaced elements.

A more accurate procedure is *electromagnetic distance measurement* (EDM). This process uses a laser-based instrument with an onboard computer to measure the distance, horizontal angle, and vertical angle of the instrument's laser beam to a reflective prism target. These instruments are accurate to $\pm^1/_{64}$ in at 1600 ft (±0.5 at 500 m). As with hand measuring, this method requires a knowledgeable operator to select the points to be measured. Two people are usually required to operate this instrument.

A similar technique is *reflectorless electromagnetic distance measurement* (REDM). The device used in this process does not require the use of a prism reflector, but instead relies on the return signal bounced from the object being measured. The accuracy is less precise: $\pm^1/_8$ in at 100 ft (±3 at 30 m). The accuracy of REDM is affected by the obliqueness of the laser beam on the targeted point, the distance from the instrument to the targeted point, and the reflective quality and texture of the targeted point.

Several image-based techniques, other than standard photography, are available to assist in the accurate surveying of existing structures. These include rectified photography, orthophotography, photogrammetry, and laser scanning.

Rectified Photography

Rectified photography uses large-format, film-based view cameras (the type typically used for high-quality architectural photography) to photograph facades. The camera's focal plane is set parallel to the facade and gives a flat image with no perspective distortion. Dimensions can be scaled off of the image, but to improve accuracy the building plane should be relatively flat. In addition to providing the ability to scale building elements not readily accessible to hand measuring, the photograph provides an accurate image of the building, as any photograph would.

Orthophotography

Orthophotography is similar to rectified photography except that it relies on digital photography and correction of optical distortion through computer software.

Photogrammetry

Photogrammetry is the surveying of objects or spaces through the use of photography and associated software. Common techniques for the application of this method are stereophotogrammetry and convergent photogrammetry.

Stereophotogrammetry uses two overlapping photographs in a computer program to produce a digital stereo image. The image can then be used to extract information to make a three-dimensional drawing. In addition to producing accurate three-dimensional drawings, this technique also produces a photographic record. It does require specialized equipment and computer software, as well as trained technicians to do the work.

Convergent photogrammetry uses multiple, oblique photographic images of an object taken at different angles. Measurements and three-dimensional models are derived by using software that traces the multiple overlapping photographs taken from the different angles. This field measuring technique requires that reference points be established by standard surveying techniques or by measuring distances between the reference points to establish a correctly scaled coordinate system that the software can use. Although relatively inexpensive, convergent photogrammetry is slower than laser scanning. It has an accuracy of about ±0.05%.

Laser Scanning

Laser scanning uses medium-range pulsing laser beams, which systematically sweep over an object or space to obtain three-dimensional coordinates of points on the surface of the object or space being scanned. The resulting image is a "point cloud" forming a three-dimensional image. From this image, plans, elevations, sections, and three-dimensional models are developed by computer software. The laser may scan from one or more points, depending on the exact system being used. For multiple room interiors, the images can be stitched together to give an overall image of an entire building. Unlike photogrammetry, no surveyed reference points are needed; all the information can be gathered from a single point rather than from multiple photographs. Laser scanning has an accuracy ranging from ±0.05% to ±0.01% or better.

Researching Applicable Regulations

Just as with new construction, the architect must obtain all the relevant regulations and codes that apply to the project. This includes zoning restrictions, easements, deed restrictions, covenants, historic preservation rules, energy conservation codes, and local agency regulations, as well as which building codes apply. The architect should determine from existing drawings or from the local building official the construction type of the building and its designated occupancy.

Evaluating Existing Structures

Evaluating the adequacy of an existing structure for a new use involves answering the following basic questions.

- Does the site work for the new use or can it be adapted for the new use within the constraints of time and budget?
- Is the size and configuration of the existing structure adaptable for the new use within the constraints of time and budget?
- Is the appearance and character of the structure consistent with the client's design goals and desired image?
- How much work and cost are needed to repair, renovate, modify, and add to the structure for the new use? Will seismic renovation be required? The analysis should first include the foundation and primary structural elements, as these are the most expensive to modify and are always required for any other work. Additions or modifications to the secondary structural elements are less costly and easier to accomplish.
- How much work and cost are needed to repair, renovate, modify, and add to the mechanical, plumbing, electrical, and life safety systems to make the building work for the new use? If the building is not fully sprinklered, is the cost of adding sprinklers justified based on code requirement trade-offs and possible lower insurance rates?
- Does the new occupancy work within the constraints of the existing building's construction type and area? If the maximum allowable area for the new occupancy is exceeded, the building may need to be separated into compartments with firewalls. This may prove to be economically unfeasible. Refer to Ch. 29 for a discussion of maximum allowable area and height based on occupancy and building type.
- What additional work is required to bring the structure in compliance with current applicable codes and regulations?
- How much of the existing structure must be modified to conform to code requirements? Can this be done within the constraints of time and budget?
- If a budget is not already established, how much will the minimum required amount of renovation cost? How much will the desired amount of work cost? How long might the project take to complete?

If extensive work and cost are needed, a detailed cost analysis should be performed to see if the project is economically feasible. Even an expensive and extensive remodeling may be less costly than new construction, or the cost may be justified if the return on investment meets the client's needs. In addition, during this cost analysis the client's true needs must be separated from their wish list of features.

EVALUATING HISTORIC STRUCTURES

Planning the reuse of a historic structure presents unique opportunities and challenges. Depending on its age, a historic building may use structural systems and construction materials that are difficult to evaluate based on modern needs and building codes. The Historic Preservation Service of the National Park Service has developed a wealth of information and regulations pertaining to national historic landmarks as well as historic preservation in general. Much of this information can be found on their website.

Defining the Scope of the Problem

The first determination the architect must make is whether the structure is a designated historic landmark or simply an old building that the client would like to reuse while maintaining its historic character. If the structure is a national historic landmark or has similar landmark status on the state or local level, specific requirements will influence the kind of rehabilitation work allowed. In addition, if the owner wants to receive federal tax credits, the rehabilitation must qualify as a certified rehabilitation. In this case, the Secretary of the Interior's Standards for Rehabilitation (described in the next section) must be met. Requirements for national historic properties can be found by contacting the National Park Service. If the property is designated as a state or local historic landmark, the state historic preservation officer should be contacted.

Regardless of whether the project falls under the scope of federal, state, or local regulations, the architect, with the client, should determine which of four treatment approaches will be undertaken. If the building is a designated landmark, the state preservation officer and National Park Service should also be consulted. The four treatments, listed in hierarchical order from most historically accurate to least, are preservation, rehabilitation, restoration, and reconstruction.

Preservation attempts to retain all historic fabric through conservation, maintenance, and repair. It reflects the building's continuum over time and the respectful changes and alterations that are made.

Rehabilitation emphasizes the retention and repair of historic materials, but gives more latitude to replacement because it assumes the property is more deteriorated prior to work. Both preservation and rehabilitation focus attention on the preservation of those materials, features, finishes, spaces, and spatial relationships that give a property its historic character.

Restoration focuses on the retention of materials from the most significant time in a property's history, while permitting the removal of materials from other periods.

Reconstruction is the least historically accurate and allows the opportunity to re-create a non-surviving site, landscape, building, structure, or object in new materials.

Specific standards and guidelines for each of these four treatments are given in detail and are available from the Historic Preservation Service office or at the National Park Service website.

Defining Regulatory Requirements

As codified in 36 CFR 67 for use in the Federal Historic Preservation Tax Incentives program, the Historic Preservation Service of the National Park Service has established ten general standards to guide historic preservation. These are often referred to as the Secretary of the Interior's Standards for Rehabilitation. They are to be applied to specific *rehabilitation* projects in a reasonable manner, taking into consideration economic and technical feasibility. When federal investment tax credits are involved, these standards take precedence over local requirements.

1. A property will be used for its historic purpose or be given a new use that requires minimal change to its distinctive materials, features, spaces, and spatial relationships.
2. The historic character of a property will be retained and preserved. The removal of distinctive materials or alteration of features, spaces, and spatial relationships that characterize a property will be avoided.
3. Each property will be recognized as a physical record of its time, place, and use. Changes that create a false sense of historical development, such as adding conjectural features or architectural elements from other historic properties, will not be undertaken.
4. Changes to a property that have acquired historic significance in their own right will be retained and preserved.
5. Distinctive features, finishes, and construction techniques or examples of craftsmanship that characterize a property will be preserved.
6. Deteriorated historic features will be repaired rather than replaced. Where the severity of deterioration requires replacement of a distinctive feature, the new feature will match the old in design, color, texture, and, where possible, materials. Replacement of missing features will be substantiated by documentary and physical evidence.
7. Chemical or physical treatments, if appropriate, will be undertaken using the gentlest means possible. Treatments that cause damage to historic materials will not be used.
8. Archeological resources will be protected and preserved in place. If such resources must be disturbed, mitigation measures will be undertaken.
9. New additions, exterior alterations, or related new construction will not destroy historic materials, features, and spatial relationships that characterize the property. The new work will be differentiated from the old and will be compatible with the historic materials, features, size, scale, proportion, and massing to protect the integrity of the property and its environment.

10. New additions and adjacent or related new construction will be undertaken in such a manner that, if removed in the future, the essential form and integrity of the historic property and its environment would be unimpaired.

The U.S. National Park Service has also established similar guidelines for preservation, for restoration, and for reconstruction. The ten general standards to guide the *restoration* of projects are as follows.

1. A property will be used as it was historically or be given a new use which reflects the property's restoration period.
2. Materials and features from the restoration period will be retained and preserved. The removal of materials or alteration of features, spaces, and spatial relationships that characterize the period will not be undertaken.
3. Each property will be recognized as a physical record of its time, place, and use. Work needed to stabilize, consolidate, and conserve materials and features from the restoration period will be physically and visually compatible, identifiable upon close inspection, and properly documented for future research.
4. Materials, features, spaces, and finishes that characterize other historical periods will be documented prior to their alteration or removal.
5. Distinctive materials, features, finishes, and construction techniques or examples of craftsmanship that characterize the restoration period will be preserved.
6. Deteriorated features from the restoration period will be repaired rather than replaced. Where the severity of deterioration requires replacement of a distinctive feature, the new feature will match the old in design, color, texture, and, where possible, materials.
7. Replacement of missing features from the restoration period will be substantiated by documentary and physical evidence. A false sense of history will not be created by adding conjectural features, features from other properties, or by combining features that never existed together historically.
8. Chemical or physical treatments, if appropriate, will be undertaken using the gentlest means possible. Treatments that cause damage to historic materials will not be used.
9. Archeological resources affected by a project will be protected and preserved in place. If such resources must be disturbed, mitigation measures will be undertaken.
10. Designs that were never executed historically will not be constructed.

These guidelines are widely used at the federal level as well as by states and local historic district and planning commissions. However, the architect must research any other specific regulations that may apply.

Surveying the Historic Structure

In addition to the survey components listed in the previous section, additional work is required. The structural survey must include an assessment of settlement, deflection of beams, and structural members damaged in previous renovations or for mechanical and electrical services. The physical survey should determine if original or historic elements have been removed or altered, and if so, what their original appearance was.

The architect should identify the aspects of the building that define its historic character and set them in a list of priorities. These characteristics include the overall form of the building, its materials, spaces, and workmanship, and other notable features that distinguish it from other buildings. A physical survey of the original appearance of the structure and its current condition may call for the services of a restoration specialist to perform tests and conduct other investigations.

Masonry in Historic Buildings

Many historic buildings were constructed of masonry, so the evaluation, repair, and restoration of this material is particularly important. The Historic Preservation Service of the National Park Service provides several recommendations for the treatment of historic masonry in several categories. The following are often covered in the ARE exam.

Identify, Retain, and Preserve

Unique masonry features from the restoration period should be identified and should not be altered or covered.

Protect and Maintain

To protect the masonry features from the restoration period, proper drainage should be provided so that water does not accumulate.

Masonry surfaces should be cleaned only when necessary to halt deterioration or remove heavy soiling. Tests should be conducted before cleaning in order to study which methods are best and what the long-term effects will be. The gentlest method possible should be used, such as cleaning with low-pressure water, detergents, and natural bristle brushes.

Sandblasting and chemical products that can damage masonry should not be used.

Paint should be removed only if it is damaged or deteriorated, and then only to the next sound layer using the gentlest method possible. Repainting should be done with colors that are documented to the restoration period of the building.

Repair

Masonry and mortar may be repaired or replaced if there are signs of deterioration, looseness, or other damage. Mortar should be repointed by hand-raking the joints and duplicating the mortar in strength, composition, color, texture, and joint profile. Electric saws and hammers should not be used to remove mortar from joints. Mortar with high portland cement content should not be used for repointing.

Damaged masonry units should be repaired by patching, piecing in, or otherwise reinforcing the masonry using recognized preservation methods. To a limited extent, extensively deteriorated or missing parts of masonry features may be replaced with similar pieces of the same material or a compatible substitute.

Replace

If a feature is too deteriorated to repair, it may be replaced with a reproduction. In reproducing the feature, existing physical evidence should be used as a model. If the same kind of material is not technically or economically feasible, then a compatible substitute material may be considered.

Remove Existing Features From Other Historic Periods

When the structure comprises both the original construction and construction from later historic periods, the items from other periods should be removed and, if possible, stored to facilitate future research.

Recreate Missing Features

If a masonry feature from the restoration period is entirely missing, a new feature may be recreated based on physical or documentary evidence. This should be considered only when none of the previous recommendations is feasible.

ARCHITECTURAL PRACTICE AND SERVICES DURING PRE-DESIGN

One of the first, and most important, decisions the architect must make during pre-design is whether or not to accept a project offered by a potential client. The factors that are involved in this decision include the current workload of the architect's office, the match between the project and the types of work the architect's office is qualified to do or prefers to do, the potential feasibility of the project, the owner's budget both for the project and for fees, and the reliability and reputation of the client.

In many cases, the amount of work the client requests exceeds the budget for either construction or professional fees, or both. In this case, the architect must either decline to accept the job, accept a lower profit margin, or negotiate with the owner to reduce the scope of the project or the scope of the architect's services. If the owner is unknown to the architect, the architect should investigate the client, including the client's ability to fund the project, past experience with building projects, and experience with working with design professionals.

If the architect decides to accept the job, the architect must first negotiate an agreement with the owner that determines the scope of the work, fees required, and other aspects of the contract. Refer to Ch. 50 for more information on owner-architect agreements. This agreement may also involve developing a preliminary design and construction schedule to help determine the project's feasibility, as well as the anticipated fees required by the architect.

If another architect or design professional is, or may be, involved with the project, the architect must determine if there is any formal or informal agreement between the owner and the other design professional. The architect cannot accept work from the owner unless the other architect or design professional has severed their relationship with the owner.

Coordination with Regulatory Agencies

If the building project requires approval from planning agencies or other governmental bodies before detailed design can begin, the architect is often the professional responsible for guiding the owner's project through the approval process. The work involved may include developing preliminary site plans and land-use proposals, sketching preliminary building designs, and meeting with governmental agencies and neighborhood groups. This work, of course, requires additional fees beyond the normal fee for building design, so the architect must estimate the time and costs required for the work.

If the building presents unusual design challenges and requires zoning variances or unusual building techniques or materials, the architect will have to work with building officials or zoning regulators early in the pre-design phase to obtain advice and approval of any deviation from zoning requirements, or to use alternate means and methods of construction as allowed by building codes.

Consultant Coordination

The architect should involve the consultants in the project as early as possible. Their advice and expertise is vital to determining the scope of the building project (especially if it involves the renovation of an existing building), developing broad conceptual approaches to designing the building, and understanding the concerns of the client and other design professionals working on the project.

One of the most important tasks for the architect during pre-design is the assembly and coordination of the various consultants on the project. These may include structural, mechanical, and electrical engineers at a minimum. Additional consultants may include soils engineers, civil engineers, fire protection engineers, historic preservation specialists, security consultants, interior designers, and audio-visual consultants. The expected services of each consultant must be determined with the advice of the consultant and the approval of the client. The involvement of the client is mandatory if the owner contracts directly with the consultant for services.

The contractual arrangement between the consultant and the architect or owner must also be determined. If the owner contracts directly with the consultant, the architect avoids any problems with contract provisions and payment, but may lose some ability to direct the consultant. If the architect writes an agreement directly with the consultant and is responsible for paying the consultant, the architect has more control but may encounter problems with paying the consultant's fees if there is delayed payment from the client.

Once the consultants are retained, the architect should inform the appropriate consultants about the applicable code requirements. The architect is also responsible for informing the consultants of any design decisions that may have code implications. Although the architect is responsible for ensuring that the drawings and specifications conform to the applicable codes, AIA Document C401, the Architect-Consultant Agreement, states that the consultant is responsible for code compliance regarding their area of work in the same way the architect is responsible to the owner under AIA B101, the Owner-Architect Agreement. By signing their drawings, the engineering consultants become responsible for compliance with applicable codes and regulations.

The AIA C401 document also states that each consultant is responsible for the accurate production of the consultant's own drawings and specifications. Further, the consultant is responsible for checking their own various documents for consistency. However, the architect is the prime consultant and is liable to the owner for the consultant's work.

Refer to Ch. 53 for more information on project and practice management, which is also tested in the Programming, Planning, and Practice division. Also refer to Chs. 55 and 56 for information on building regulations.

DEFINITIONS

Following are some of the many definitions that may appear in questions in the Programming, Planning, and Practice division.

Abatement: a reduction in the price of a property due to the discovery of some problem that tends to decrease the property's value

Accessory building: a building whose function is secondary to that of the main structure

Amenities: desirable features of a building or near a building that have the effect of increasing the property's value

Amortization: the payment of a loan over the life of the loan using equal payments at equal intervals. Each payment provides for a portion to be applied to the principal and the remainder to be applied to the interest.

Anchor tenant: a major tenant in shopping mall, such as a department store, that in theory serves to attract shoppers to the mall to the benefit of other, smaller stores. See also *Satellite tenant*.

Appraisal: an estimation of a property's value made by a qualified appraiser

Aquifer: a natural, underground reservoir from which wells draw water

Assessed value: the value given to a piece of property by a local jurisdiction, to be used to assess taxes on the property. The assessed value is a percentage of the actual value, that is, the value that the property would command on the open market.

Bedroom community: a region or small town that contains mainly housing and offers few employment opportunities

Blighted area: an area of a city that has been determined to contain buildings and infrastructure that are in a state of decay and in need of improvement

Boilerplate: a standard portion (generally a paragraph or more) of a written document, such as a contract or architectural specification, that appears in all similar documents

Buffer zone: a piece of land used to separate two incompatible uses

Capital expenditure: an amount of money used to make physical improvements to a property to enhance the property's value over an extended period of time

Cash flow: the amount of money that is net income from a property after expenses are paid

CC&Rs: abbreviation for "covenants, conditions, and restrictions," which are all the rules that apply to a property owner in a subdivision, condominium, or cooperative housing facility

Cluster housing: a particular type of housing development in which the houses or apartments are placed close to each other and have access to nearby common open spaces

Common area: a portion of a building or development that is available for the use of all the tenants or unit owners. Typically, common areas are owned by the property owners in the development or homeowners' association, and property owners subsequently pay the maintenance fees.

Conditional use permit (CUP): a permit given by a city or other zoning jurisdiction for a proposed use that would otherwise not be allowed in a particular zoning district. The conditional use permit provides the zoning jurisdiction with the means to impose special conditions on the proposed development, to ensure that the development will not adversely affect the surrounding neighborhood or the public safety and welfare.

Condominium: a development in which residents own their own living units but share common areas, which are maintained by the condominium corporation

Conveyance: the act of transferring an interest in a property to another person, or the document written to formalize such a transfer

Cooperative (or *Co-op*): a type of land ownership where the residents of individual units own an interest in the corporation that owns the entire property. Unlike the residents of a condominium, the residents of a cooperative do not own their own units directly.

Cul-de-sac: a dead-end street that has only one way in and often features a large circular turnaround space at the end

Dedication: the donation of a parcel of land by a developer for public use, such as for a park or school

Demising wall: see *Party wall*

Despoil: to remove items of value from a site

Development rights: the legal ability of a developer to develop a parcel of land

Discount rate: the rate of interest that reflects the time value of money and that is used to discount future values to present values or to calculate the future value of money invested at the discount rate

Downzoning: a change in zoning resulting in a decrease of allowable density

Easement: a portion of land of one ownership that another owner or a governmental agency has the right to use for a specific purpose

Eminent domain: the right of a governmental jurisdiction to take ownership of private property for the public good while paying fair market value compensation to the owner

Encroachment: an intrusion onto one property by the improvement to an adjoining property

Equity: the amount of money an owner of a property keeps after selling the property and paying off any mortgages; that is, the difference between the fair market value of a property and the amount of debt on the property

Escalation rate: the rate of change in the price for a particular good or service

Fair market value (or *Market value*): the value of a piece of property that a buyer would pay a seller in a free transaction for the property

Fixture: an item that is attached to a building and is typically included in the sale of the building

Ground lease: a long-term lease of a property that allows the tenant to use and improve the land, but that reverts to the owner at the end of the lease

Height zoning: restrictions on the heights of buildings and structures established by local laws

Improvement ratio: the ratio of the value of improvements on a property to the value of the property alone

Inverse condemnation: a remedy by a court for a private land owner whose land has been taken away by a governmental body. See also *Eminent domain*.

Landlocked: descriptive of a parcel of land that does not border any public road

Land sale leaseback: a legal arrangement in which the owner of a property sells the property to someone else but then immediately leases it from the purchaser

Lien: see *Mechanic's and materialman's lien*

Lien waiver: a document that gives up a person's right to claim a lien against property

Market value: see *Fair market value*

Mechanic's and materialman's lien: a claim placed against a property's deed by someone who provided work or materials to improve the property but was not paid for the work. Typically just called a *Lien*.

Minimum property standards: minimum standards for residential building required by the Federal Housing

Administration for construction or for underwriting a mortgage

Modified uniform present worth factor: a discount factor that is used to convert an annual amount, which is changing from year to year at a given escalation rate, to a time-equivalent present value

Net leasable area: the area of a building that is available for rent, which does not include common areas, structure, stairs, and the like

Occupancy permit: a document, issued by a city's building department, giving permission for a building to be occupied. More commonly called the *Certificate of occupancy*. The occupancy permit is part of the building permit process, and its cost is included in the building permit fee paid by the contractor.

Pad site: a separate location for development of retail space near (but not in) a shopping center

Party wall: the shared wall between two leased spaces or between two residential units. Often called a *Demising wall*.

Pro forma: a financial projection for a development project meant to determine if the project is feasible, given estimates on potential income and the cost of developing the project

Restriction: a limit on how the owner of a property or building can use or improve the property. Often called a *Restrictive covenant*, it is usually contained in the deed to the property.

Riparian: related to a body of water

Riparian rights: the rights of a landowner to use or control all or a portion of the water in a body of water bordering his or her property

Satellite tenant: a minor or smaller tenant in a shopping center. See also *Anchor tenant*.

Special use permit: an exemption from zoning regulations given to a jurisdiction

Spot zoning: the application of specific zoning regulations to specific properties when nearby land is under different zoning

Underimproved land: property that is not producing the maximum income it is capable of producing given its size, zoning, and so on

Uniform capital recovery: a method of calculating the future values of money to a present worth using the discount rate

Uniform present worth factor: the discount factor that is used to convert uniform annual values (costs) to a time-equivalent present value

Uniform sinking fund: the amount of money that has to be invested at today's value at a given interest rate (the discount rate) to have a specified amount of money in the future

Usury: the illegal practice of charging exorbitant interest rates on a loan

Variance: permission granted by a local jurisdiction to deviate from the literal provisions of a zoning ordinance where strict adherence would cause undue hardship because of conditions or circumstances unique to an individual property

Wetlands: land that has development restrictions placed on it because it is commonly flooded and may be environmentally sensitive

Zero lot line: part of a zoning regulation's setback requirements that allows a building to be constructed up to the property line with no setback

Zoning by-law: the set of zoning regulations established by a local jurisdiction that regulates certain building practices within the jurisdiction

3 BUILDING PROGRAMMING

Architectural programming is a process that seeks to analyze and define an architectural problem along with the requirements that must be met in its physical solution. It is a process of analysis, whereas design is a process of synthesis once the problem is clearly defined. The process can apply to an individual space or room, a building, or an entire complex of structures.

As building problems have become more complex and construction costs higher, determining the precise needs of the client has become more important than ever before. Programming helps the client understand the real problem and provides a sound basis for making design decisions. Programming is considered an additional service under the standard AIA documents.

Thorough programming includes a wide range of information. In addition to stating the goals and objectives of the client, a program report contains a site analysis, aesthetic considerations, space needs, adjacency requirements, organizing concepts, outdoor space needs, codes, budgeting demands, and scheduling limitations. Refer to Chs. 2 and 4 for a review of site analysis, including soil and climatic investigation.

FUNCTIONAL REQUIREMENTS

The amount of space needed and the relationships needed among spaces are two of the primary factors in determining building size and configuration. The primary function of a building is housing a specific use, and in addition to that there are always support spaces required that add to the overall size. These include such areas as mechanical rooms, toilet rooms, storage, and circulation space.

Determining Space and Volume Needs

Space needs are determined in a number of ways. Often, when programming is begun, the client will have a list of the required square footage for the new facility in addition to special height requirements. These may be based on the client's experience or on corporate space standards, or they may simply be a list of what currently exists. For example, space standards of a corporation may dictate that a senior manager have a 225 ft^2 (21 m^2) office while a junior manager be allotted 150 ft^2 (14 m^2).

These types of requirements may provide a valid basis for developing space needs, or they may be arbitrary and subject to review during programming. Where areas are not defined by one of these methods, space for a particular use is determined in one of three ways: by the number of people that must be accommodated, by an object or piece of equipment, or by a specific activity that has its own, clearly specified space needs.

People engaged in a particular activity most commonly define the space required. For example, a student sitting in a classroom needs about 15 ft^2 to 20 ft^2 (1.4 m^2 to 1.9 m^2). This includes space for actually sitting in a chair in addition to the space required for circulating within the classroom and space for the teacher's desk and shelving. An office worker needs from 100 ft^2 to 250 ft^2 (9.3 m^2 to 23 m^2), depending on whether the employee is housed in a private office or in part of an open office plan. This space requirement also includes room to circulate around the desk and may include space for visitors' chairs, personal files, and the like.

Through experience and detailed analysis, general guidelines for space requirements for various types of uses have been developed and are commonly used. A representative sample of these is shown in Table 3.1. Occasionally, space needs can be based on something other than the number of people but something that is directly related to the occupancy. For instance, preliminary planning of a hospital may be based on an area per bed, or library space can be estimated based on the number of books.

Table 3.1
Some Common Space Planning Guidelines

offices	100–250 ft²	net area per person	9.3–23 m²
restaurant dining	15–18 ft²	net area per seat	1.4–1.7 m²
restaurant kitchens	3.6–5 ft²	net area per seat	0.3–0.5 m²
hotel (1.5 persons/room)	550–600 ft²	gross area per room	51–56 m²
library reading room	20–35 ft²	net area per person	1.8–3.3 m²
book stacks	0.08 ft²	net area per bound volume	0.007 m²
theaters with fixed seats	7.5 ft²	net area per person	0.7 m²
assembly areas; movable seats	15 ft²	net area per person	1.4 m²
theater lobbies	30%	of seating area	
classrooms	15–20 ft²	net area per student	1.4–1.8 m²
stores	30–50 ft²	net area per person	2.8–4.6 m²

An architectural office may set benchmarks for the types of buildings it designs and use these benchmarks in programming. In programming, *benchmarking* is the establishment of common standards for rooms, spaces, and activities based on the measurement of similar facilities.

In some cases, space requirements are determined by fixed seating. Theaters, churches, and sports stadia are examples of projects that call for this type of space planning. For most fixed seating facilities, the space per person is determined by the width of the seats, their row-to-row spacing, and how much space is allocated per seat for aisles. Building codes give minimum requirements for seat spacing and aisle widths based on the occupant load and whether the seating is multiple aisle seating or continental seating. *Multiple aisle seating* uses rows of seating separated by intermediate aisles in addition to the side aisles. *Continental seating* consists of continuous rows of seats accessed by only the two side aisles. While continental seating requires fewer aisles, the row-to-row spacing must be greater to accommodate the larger number of people exiting each row.

Whichever way the planning is done, the number of people that must be accommodated is determined and is multiplied by the area per person. However, this only includes the space needed for the specific activity, not the space required to connect several rooms or spaces or for support areas such as mechanical rooms. These must be added to the basic area requirements.

The second way space needs are determined is by the size of an object or piece of equipment. The size of a printing press, for example, is part of what determines the area of a press room. Automobile sizes determine the space needs for parking garages.

The third way space needs are defined is through a built-in set of rules or customs related to the activity itself. Sports facilities are examples of such spaces. A basketball court must be a certain size regardless of the number of spectators present, although the seating capacity would add to the total space required. A courtroom is an example of a space in which the procedures and customs of a process (the trial) dictate an arrangement of human activity and the spacing of individual areas that only partially depend on the number of people using the space.

Determining Total Building Area

The individual areas determined by these methods, taken together, make up the net area of a facility. As mentioned, these areas do not include general circulation space between rooms, mechanical rooms, stairways, elevator and mechanical shafts, electrical and telephone equipment rooms, wall and structural thicknesses, and other spaces not directly housing the primary activities of the building. Sometimes the net area is referred to as the *net assignable area* and these secondary spaces are referred to as the *unassigned areas*.

The sum of the net area and the unassigned areas gives the *gross building area*. The ratio of the two figures is called the *net-to-gross ratio* and is often referred to as the *efficiency* of the building. Efficiency depends on the type of occupancy and how well it is planned. A hospital, which contains many small rooms and a great number of large corridors, will have a much lower efficiency ratio than a factory, where the majority of space is devoted to production areas and very little space is allowed for corridors and other secondary spaces.

Generally, net-to-gross ratios range from 60% to 80%, with some uses more or less efficient than these numbers. A list of some common efficiency ratios is shown in Table 3.2. In some cases, the client may dictate the net-to-gross ratio that must be met by the architect's design. This is usually the case when the efficiency is related to the amount of floor space that can be leased, such as in a retail mall or a speculative office building. Increasing the efficiency of a building is usually done by careful layout of the building's circulation plan. A corridor that serves rooms on both sides, for example, is much more efficient than one that only serves rooms on one side.

Table 3.2

Some Common Efficiency Ratios

offices	0.75-0.85
retail stores	0.75-0.90
restaurants	0.65-0.70
public libraries	0.75-0.80
museums	0.83-0.90
theaters	0.60-0.75
hospitals	0.50-0.65

Once the net area is determined and the appropriate efficiency ratio is established (or estimated), the gross area of the building is calculated by dividing the net area by the net-to-gross (efficiency) ratio.

Example 3.1

The net assignable area of a small office building has been programmed as 65,000 ft^2. If the efficiency ratio is estimated to be 73%, what gross area should be planned for?

$$\text{gross area} = \frac{65{,}000 \text{ ft}^2}{0.73} = 89{,}000 \text{ ft}^2$$

The design portion of the ARE sometimes requires the examinee to provide various unassignable spaces within the context of the problem. The areas are not given. The examinee is expected to make a reasonable allowance for mechanical rooms, toilet rooms, elevators, and the like, if they are not specifically listed in the program. Table 3.3 lists some typical space requirements for projects of the size and type normally found in the design portion of the exam.

Table 3.3

Space Requirements for Estimating Non-assignable Areas

mechanical rooms, total	5–9% of gross building area
heating, boiler rooms	3–5% of gross building area
heating, forced air	4–8% of gross building area
fan rooms	3–7% of gross building area
vertical duct space	3–4 ft^2 per 1000 ft^2 of floor space available (0.35 m^2 per 100 m^2)
toilets	50 ft^2 (4.6 m^2) per water closet
water closets	1 per 15 people up to 55;
	1 per 40 people over 55
urinals	Substitute one for each water closet, but total water closets cannot be reduced less than $^2/_3$ of the number required
lavatories	1 per 15 people for offices and public buildings up to 60 people
	1 per 100 people for public assembly use
hydraulic elevator, 2000 lbm (1000 kg)	7 ft 4 in wide by 6 ft 0 in deep (2235 by 1830)
elevator lobby space	6 ft 0 in deep (1830)
main corridors	5–7 ft (1500–2100)
exit corridors	4 ft 0 in; 44 in minimum by code (1220; 1118)
monumental stairs	5–8 ft (1500–2400)
exit stairs	4 ft 0 in, 44 in minimum by code (1220; 1118)

Determining Space Relationships

Spaces must not only be the correct size for the activity they support, but they also must be located near other spaces with which they share some functional relationship. Programming identifies these relationships and assigns a hierarchy of importance to them. The relationships are usually recorded in a matrix format or graphically as adjacency diagrams. See Fig. 3.1.

There are three basic types of adjacency needs: people, products, and information. Each type implies a different kind of physical design response. Two or more spaces may need to be physically adjacent or located very close to one another when people need face-to-face contact or when people move from one area to another as part of the building's use. For example, the entry to a theater, the lobby, and the theater space have a particular functional requirement for being arranged the way they are. Because of the normal flow of people, they must be located adjacent to one another. With other relationships, two spaces may simply need to have access to each other, but this can be accomplished with a corridor or through another intervening space rather than with direct adjacency.

Products, equipment, or other objects may move between spaces and require another type of adjacency. The spaces themselves may not have to be close to one another, but the movement of objects must be facilitated. Dumbwaiters, pneumatic tubes, assembly lines, and other types of conveying systems can connect spaces of this type.

Finally, there may be a requirement only that people in different spaces be able to exchange information. The adjacency may then be entirely electronic or be established through paper-moving systems. Although this is frequently the situation, personal, informal, human contact may be advantageous for other reasons.

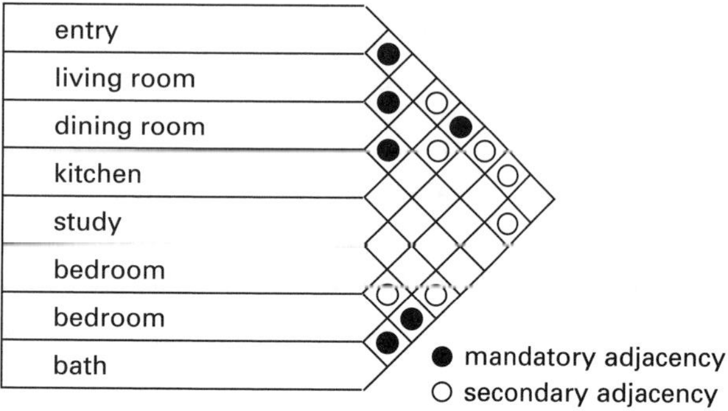

(a) adjacency matrix

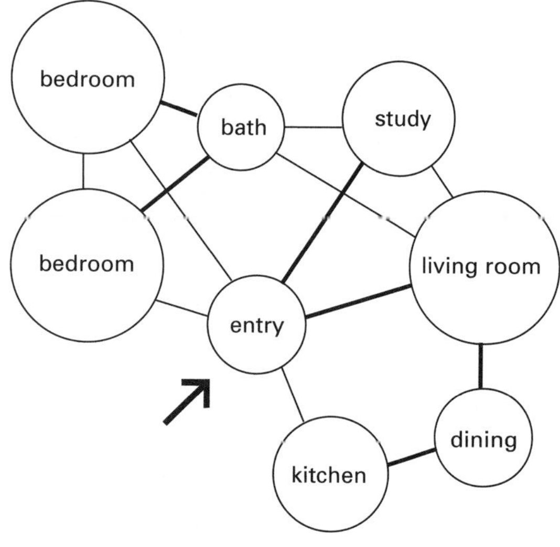

(b) adjacency diagram

Figure 3.1 Methods of Recording Space Relationships

The programmer analyzes various types of adjacency requirements and verifies them with the client. Since it is seldom possible to accommodate every desirable relationship, the ones that are mandatory need to be identified separately from the ones that are highly desirable or simply useful.

DESIGN CONSIDERATIONS

During programming, general concepts are developed as a response to the goals and needs of the client. These programmatic concepts are statements about functional solutions to the client's performance requirements. They differ from later design concepts because no attempt at actual physical solutions is made during programming; programmatic concepts guide the later development of design concepts. For example, a programmatic concept might be that a facility should be easily expandable by 20% every three years. Exactly how that would happen for a building would be developed as a design concept. It might take the form of a linear building that could be extended by a simple addition to one wing. Some of the more common design considerations that must be addressed during programming are outlined in the following sections.

Organization Concepts

The functional needs of a particular type of building most often influence how the physical environment is organized. At other times, the client's goal, the site, the desired symbolism, or additional factors suggest the organization pattern. There are six fundamental organization concepts: linear, axial, grid, central, radial, and clustered. These are shown diagrammatically in Fig. 3.2.

Linear organizations consist of a series of spaces or buildings that are placed in a single line. The spaces can be identical or of different sizes and shapes, but they always relate to a unifying line, usually a path of circulation. A linear organization is very adaptable; it can be straight, bent, or curved to meet the requirements of the client, the site, solar orientation, or construction. It is easily expandable and can be built in a modular configuration if desired.

Axial plans are variations of the linear system with two or more major linear segments about which spaces or buildings are placed. There may be additional, secondary paths growing out of the primary axes, and the major linear segments may be at right angles to each other or at some other angle.

Grid systems consist of two sets of regularly spaced parallel lines, which create one pattern that is very strong and one that is quite flexible. Within a grid, portions can be subtracted, added, or modified. The size of the grid can be changed to create different sizes of spaces or to define special areas. However, a grid can become monotonous and confusing if not used properly. Because a grid system is usually defined by circulation paths, it is more appropriate for very large buildings and building complexes where a great deal of circulation is required.

Central organization is based on one space or point about which secondary elements are placed. It is usually a very formal method of organizing spaces or buildings and inherently places the primary emphasis on the central space. Central organizations are often used in conjunction with axial or linear plans.

When more than one linear organization extends from a centralized point, it becomes a *radial organization*. Radial plans have a central focus and also have the ability to extend outward to connect with other spaces, or to expand. These types of organizing plans can be circular or assume other shapes as well.

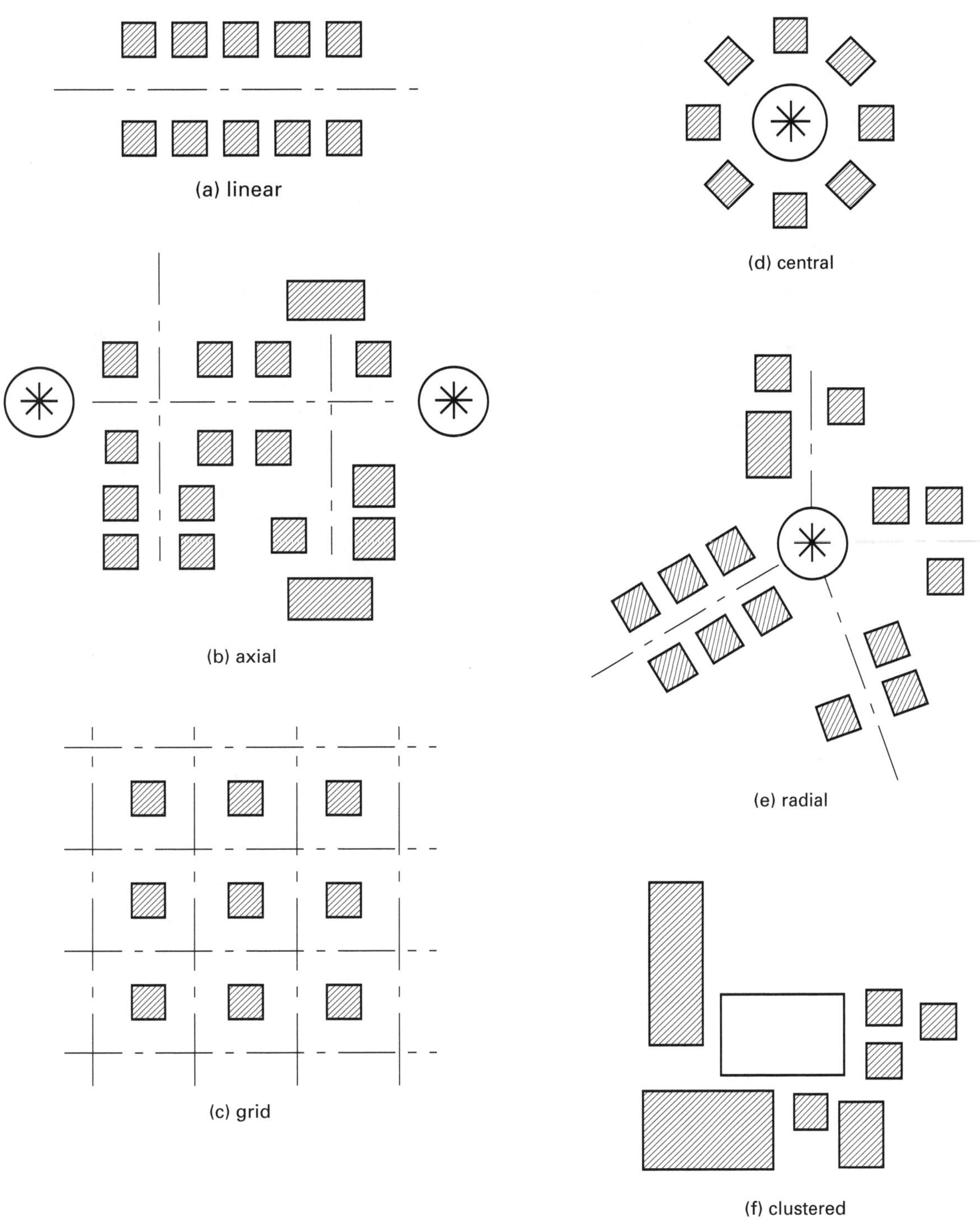

Figure 3.2 Organization Concepts

Clustered organizations are loose compositions of spaces or buildings related around a path, axis, or central space, or they are simply grouped together. The general image is one of informality. Clusters are very adaptable to requirements for different sizes of spaces and they are easy to add onto without disrupting the overall composition.

Circulation Patterns

Circulation patterns are primary ways of organizing spaces, buildings, and groups of buildings. They are vital to the efficient organization of a structure and provide people with their strongest orientation within an environment. Paths of circulation provide the means to move people, cars, products, and services.

Circulation is directly related to the organizational pattern of a building, but it does not necessarily have to mimic it. For example, a major circulation path can cut diagonally across a grid pattern. Normally there is a hierarchy of paths. Major routes connect major spaces or become spaces themselves and have secondary paths branching from them. Different sizes and types of circulation are important for accommodating varying capacities and for providing an orientation device for people using them.

Circulation for different functions may need to be separated as well. In a government building, one set of halls for the public may be separated from the internal set of corridors for the workers. A jail may have a secure passage for moving prisoners that is completely separate from other areas of public movement.

Establishing and maintaining a simple, efficient, and coherent circulation scheme is critical to successfully completing the design portion of the ARE. One of the common mistakes is to let the arranging of spaces according to the adjacency requirements take over a design and to connect the spaces with a circulation path as an afterthought. This creates a maze of awkward corridors that decreases the efficiency ratio and produces dead-end corridors and other exiting problems.

All circulation paths are linear by their very nature, but there are some common variations, many of which are similar to the organizational patterns described in the previous section. Because circulation is an important aspect of successful completion of the design portion of the examination, it is important to have a good mental picture of the various circulation concepts and the advantages and disadvantages of each. Five basic patterns are shown in Fig. 3.3, along with a hypothetical structural grid on top of them to illustrate how some patterns are better suited than others to integration of structure, adjacencies, and circulation system. Also remember that mechanical services can easily follow a logical circulation system.

The linear, *dumbbell layout* is the simplest and one of the most flexible circulation patterns. Spaces are laid out along a straight path that connects two major elements at the ends. These are usually the entrance to the building at one end and an exit at the other, although the primary entrance can occur anywhere along the path. Spaces are laid out along the spine as required. Various sizes of spaces can be easily accommodated by simply extending their length perpendicular to the path, and if outdoor spaces are required they are simply located as needed. The double-loaded corridor makes the building very efficient.

Site constraints may restrict the length of the spine, but the concept can still be used by bending the path at a right angle. With this layout, it is very easy to establish a regular, one-way structural grid perpendicular to the direction of the path. Simply extending the length of a bay can accommodate larger spaces as the program requires.

Conversely, eliminating a line or two of structure gives the location for a very large space and a long-span structural system. A two-way structural grid can also be used with this layout.

Making a complete loop results in a *doughnut configuration*. This is also very efficient because it provides a double-loaded corridor and automatically makes a continuous exitway. Building entries, exits, and stairways can be placed wherever needed. Spaces that do not need exterior exposure can be placed in the middle. Various sizes of spaces are easily accommodated on the perimeter because they can be expanded outward, just as with the dumbbell layout. A simple structural grid can be coordinated with the space layout as required. A doughnut pattern is good for square or nearly square sites and for buildings that must be compact.

A grid system is often used for very large buildings where access must be provided to many internal spaces. For the small buildings that are usually found on the ARE examination, a grid system is seldom appropriate because it results in a very inefficient layout, with single spaces being surrounded by corridors.

A radial layout is oriented on one major space with paths extending from this central area. The radial configuration generally requires a large site and is more appropriate for large buildings or building complexes. Establishing a simple structural system is more difficult with this pattern unless the circulation paths extend from the central space at 90° angles. Each corridor must also have an exit at the end if it is longer than 20 ft (6100).

Finally, a *field pattern* consists of a network of paths with no strong direction. There are major paths with secondary routes extending from or connecting the primary routes. Orientation within a field pattern is difficult, as is integrating a logical structural system.

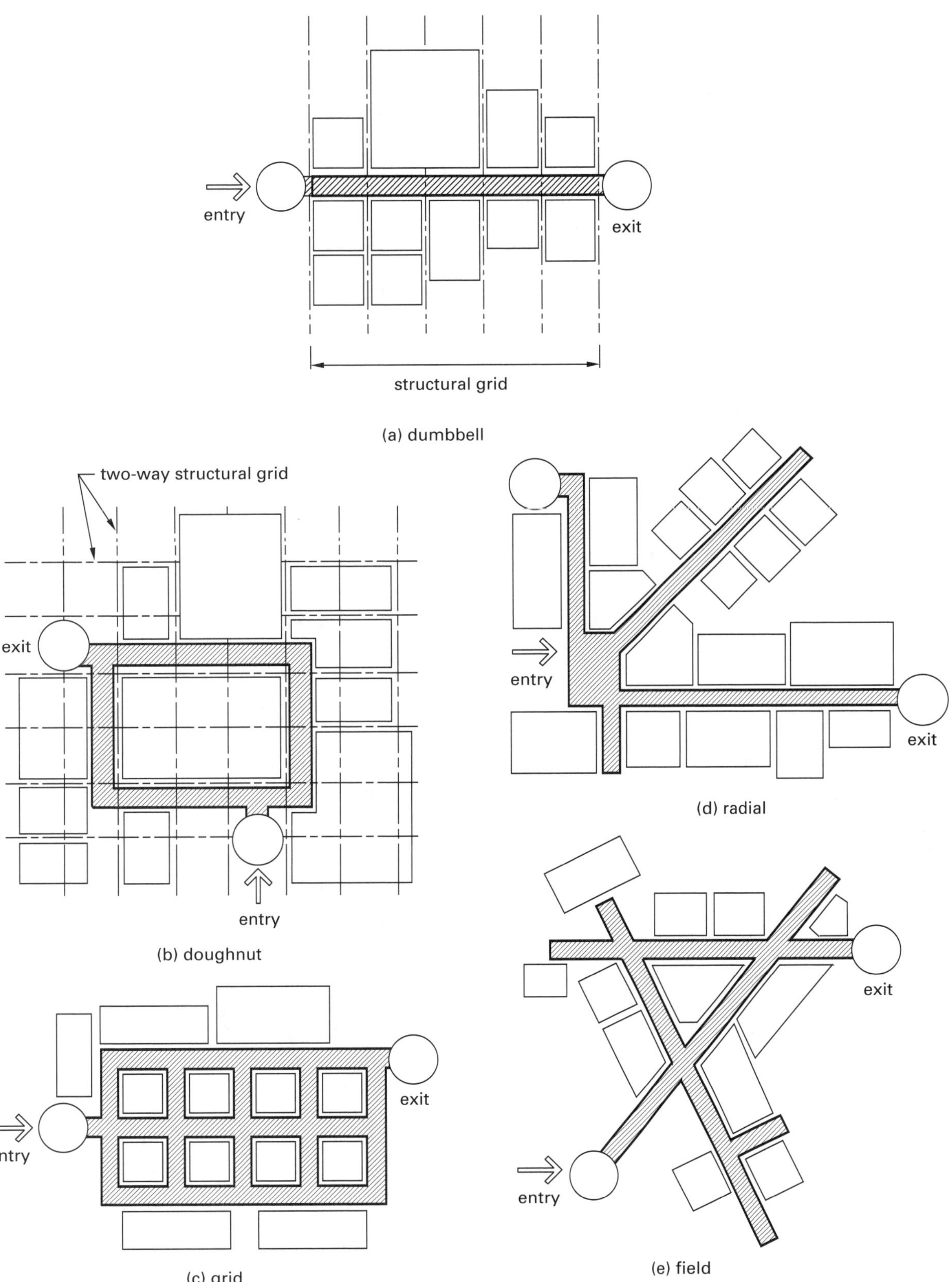

Figure 3.3 Circulation Patterns

Service Spaces

In addition to the primary programmed spaces (the net assignable area), secondary spaces such as toilet and mechanical rooms must also be planned from the start. They should not be tacked on after the majority of the design work is done.

Depending on the type of mechanical system, mechanical rooms should be centrally located to minimize lengths of duct runs and piping. This is especially true with all-air systems. Mechanical rooms usually need easy access to the outside for servicing as well as provisions for fresh-air intakes.

Toilet rooms should be located to satisfy adjacency requirements as stated in the program or in an area that has easy access to the entire floor. Men's and women's toilet rooms should be back to back to share a common plumbing wall and should be near other plumbing in the building, if possible.

Service access must also be given careful consideration. This includes service drives for trucks, the service entrance to the building, and access to mechanical rooms, storage rooms, and other functional areas as required by the program. The ARE design problem usually has a requirement for some type of service access that must be kept separate from the primary entrance and circulation paths.

Flexibility

Flexibility is a design consideration that involves a variety of concepts. *Expansibility* is the capacity of a building to be easily enlarged or added onto as needs change or growth occurs. *Convertibility* allows an existing building or space to be changed according to a new use. For example, a school gymnasium may be converted into classroom space in a second phase of construction. *Versatility* means the ability to use the same space for a variety of uses in order to make maximum use of limited space.

If a program calls for flexibility, the designer must know or determine what type of organizational and structural system is required. Expansibility may suggest one type of organizational and structural system, while convertibility may require a completely different approach.

PSYCHOLOGICAL AND SOCIAL INFLUENCES

Developing physical guidelines that respond to the psychological needs of people is one of the most difficult tasks in programming. Although there has been a great deal of research in the field of environmental psychology, predicting human behavior and designing spaces and buildings that enhance people's lives is an inexact process. However, the architect must attempt to develop a realistic model of the people who will be using the designed environment and the nature of their activities. This model can then serve as the foundation on which to base many design decisions.

During programming, a clear distinction must be made between the architect's client and the actual users. They are not always the same. For example, a public housing agency may be the client for a subsidized housing complex, but the actual users will be people who probably have an entirely different set of values and lifestyles than those helping to develop the program. Environmental psychology is a very complex subject, but a good starting point is to get familiar with the following concepts.

Proxemics

Proxemics is a term created by Edward T. Hall to describe the interrelated observations and theories of humans' use of space as a specialized elaboration of culture. It deals with the issues of spacing between people, territoriality, organization of space, and positioning of people in space, all relative to the culture of which they are a part. Some of these issues are discussed in the following sections.

Behavior Settings

A behavior setting is a useful concept for studying the effects of the environment on human activity. A *behavior setting* can be thought of as a particular place, with definable boundaries and objects within the place, in which a standing pattern of behavior occurs at a particular time.

For example, a weekly board of directors meeting in a conference room can be considered a behavior setting. The activity of the meeting follows certain procedures (call to order, reading of minutes, discussions, and so forth), it occurs in the same place (the conference room), and the room is arranged to assist the activity (chairs are arranged around a table, audio-visual facilities are present, lighting is adequate).

The concept of a behavior setting is useful for the architect because it connects the strictly behavioral aspects of human activity with the effects of the physical environment on people. Although a behavior setting is a complex system of activities, human goals, administrative requirements, physical objects, and cultural needs, it provides the architect with a definable unit of design. By knowing the people involved and the activities taking place, programmatic concepts can be developed that support the setting.

Territoriality

As mentioned in Ch. 2, *territoriality* is a fundamental aspect of human behavior. It refers to the need to lay claim to the spaces we occupy and the things we own. Although partially based on the biological imperative for protection, territoriality in humans is more related to the needs for self-identity and freedom of choice. In addition to marking out objects and larger spaces in the environment, people also protect their own personal space (also discussed in Ch. 2), that imaginary bubble of distance that varies with different circumstances.

Territoriality applies to groups as well as to individuals. A study club, school class, or street gang can claim a physical territory as their own, which helps give both the group and each individual in the group an identity. Environments should allow people to claim territory and make choices about where to be and what activities to engage in.

Personalization

One of the ways territoriality manifests itself is with the *personalization* of space. Whether it happens in one's home, at the office desk, or in a waiting lounge, people need to arrange the environment to reflect their presence and uniqueness. The most successful designs allow this to take place without major adverse effects on other people or on the environment as a whole. At home, people decorate their spaces the way they want. At the office, people bring in personal objects, family photographs, and pictures to make the space their own. In an airport lounge, people place coats and suitcases around them, not only to stake out a temporary territory but also to make the waiting time more personal and a little more comfortable.

Another way people personalize space is to modify the environment. If people using a given space find that it does not meet their needs, they can modify behavior to adapt to the environment, change their relationship to the environment (leave), or try to change the environment. The simple act of moving a chair to make viewing a screen easier is an example of modifying and personalizing a space. If the chair is attached, the design is not as adaptable to the varying needs of the people using the design.

Group Interaction

To a certain extent, the environment can either facilitate or hinder human interaction. In most behavior settings, groups are predisposed to act in a particular way. If the setting is not conducive to the activities, the people will try to modify the environment or modify their behavior to make the activity work. In extreme cases, if the setting is totally at odds with the activity taking place there, stress, anger, and other adverse reactions can occur.

Seating arrangement is one of the most common ways of facilitating group interaction. Studies have shown that people will seat themselves at a table according to the nature of their relationships with others around them. For intimate conversation, two people will sit across the corner of a table or next to each other on a sofa. For more formal situations or when people are competing, they will sit across from one another. Where social contact is not desired, two people will take chairs at opposite corners of a table.

Round tables tend to foster more cooperation and equality among those seated around them. Rectangular tables tend to make cooperation more difficult and establish the person sitting at the end in a more superior position. Strangers do not like to share the same sofa or park bench. Knowing the people and activities expected to be in a place can assist the architect in making decisions. For example, individual study carrels in a library will be more efficient than large tables because the tables will seldom be fully occupied by strangers.

In places where informal group interaction takes place, studies have shown that more than 97% of groups comprise two to four people. Designing to accommodate these sizes of groups makes more sense than anticipating groups of more people, although a plan that allows for the possibility of very large groups while preferring small groups would be the best combination. In most cases, providing a variety of spaces for interaction is the best approach.

Status

The physical environment holds a great deal of symbolism that indicates status for some human beings. Some people like colonial houses because such designs symbolize to the occupants the idea of "home." Others prefer banks of classical design with large lobbies, because that is what they think a bank should look like.

The environment can thus communicate status. In the United States, for example, someone with a corner office has more status than someone with only one exterior wall. Office size is also equated with status in many cultures. A house in an affluent neighborhood provides a higher status than one in other neighborhoods. Status can also operate at the scale of an entire building or complex. The client may want the building to symbolize some quality of the organization and to give him or her physical and psychological status in the community.

The architectural programmer should investigate the requirements or implications of status. Sometimes clients may clearly state what status-related goals they want to achieve. Other times, the programmer must raise the issue, explore it with the client, and document the response as a programmatic concept.

BUDGETING AND SCHEDULING

Establishing a budget and setting up a time frame for design and construction are two of the most important parts of programming because they influence many of the design decisions to follow and can determine whether a project is even feasible. During later stages of design, an initial budget and schedule are simply refined as more information becomes available.

Budgets may be set in several ways. For speculative or for-profit projects, the owner or developer works out a pro forma statement listing the expected income of the project and the expected costs to build it. An estimated selling price of the developed project or rent per square foot is calculated and balanced against all the various costs, one of which is the construction price. In order to make the project economically feasible, there will be a limit on the building costs. This becomes the budget within which the architect must work.

Budgets are often established through public funding or legislation. In these cases, the construction budget is often fixed without the architect's involvement, and the project must be designed and built for the fixed amount. Unfortunately, when public officials estimate the cost to build a project, they sometimes neglect to include all aspects of development, such as professional fees, furnishings, and other line items.

Budgets may also be set by the architect at the request of the owner and based on the proposed project. This is the most realistic and accurate way to establish a preliminary budget because it is based on a particular building type of a particular size on a particular site (or sites if several are being reviewed for selection).

There are four basic variables in developing any construction budget: quantity, quality, available funds, and time. There is always a balance among these four elements, and changing one or more affects the others. For instance, if an owner needs a certain amount of square footage built (quantity), needs the project built at a certain time, and has a fixed amount of money to spend, then the quality of construction will have to be adjusted to meet the other constraints. If time, quality, and the total budget are fixed, then the amount of space constructed must be adjusted. In some cases, *value engineering* can be performed during which individual systems and materials are reviewed to see if the same function can be accomplished in a less expensive way.

Cost Influences

There are many variables that affect project cost. Construction cost is only one part of the total project development budget. Other factors include such things as site acquisition, site development, fees, and financing. Table 3.4 lists most of the items commonly found in a project budget and a typical range of values based on construction cost. Not all of these are part of every development, but they illustrate the things that must be considered.

Building cost is the money required to construct the building, including structure, exterior cladding, finishes, and electrical and mechanical systems. *Site development* costs are

Table 3.4

Project Budget Line Items

	line item		example
A	site acquisition		$1,100,000
B	building costs	ft^2 times cost per ft^2	(assume) $6,800,000
C	site development	10% to 20% of B	(15%) $1,020,000
D	total construction cost	B + C	$7,820,000
E	movable equipment	5% to 10% of B	(5%) $340,000
F	furnishings		$200,000
G	total construction and furnishings	D + E + F	$8,360,000
H	professional services	5% to 10% of D	(7%) $547,400
I	inspection and testing		$15,000
J	escalation estimate	2% to 10% of G per year	(10%) $836,000
K	contingency	5% to 10% of G	(8%) $668,800
L	financing costs		$250,000
M	moving expenses		(assume) $90,000
N	Total Project Budget	G + H through M	$11,867,200

usually a separate item. They include such things as parking, drives, fences, landscaping, exterior lighting, and sprinkler systems. If the development is large and affects the surrounding area, a developer may be required to upgrade roads, extend utility lines, and do other major off-site work as a condition of getting approval from public agencies.

Movable equipment and furnishings include furniture, accessories, window coverings, and major equipment necessary to put the facility into operation. These are often listed as separate line items because the funding for them may come out of a separate budget and because they may be supplied under separate contracts.

Professional services are architectural and engineering fees as well as costs for such things as topographic surveys, soil tests, special consultants, appraisals and legal fees, and the-like. Inspection and testing involve money required for special on-site, full-time inspection (if required), and testing of such things as concrete, steel, window walls, and roofing.

Because construction takes a great deal of time, a factor for inflation should be included. Generally, the present budget estimate is escalated to a time in the future at the expected midpoint of construction. Although it is impossible to predict the future, by using past cost indexes and inflation rates and applying an estimate to the expected condition of the construction, the architect can usually make an educated guess.

A contingency should also be added to account for unforeseen changes by the client and other conditions that add to the cost. For an early project budget, the percentage of the contingency should be higher than contingencies applied to later budgets, because there are more unknowns. Normally, from 5% to 10% should be included.

Financing includes not only the long-term interest paid on permanent financing but also the immediate costs of loan origination fees, construction loan interest, and other administrative costs. On long-term loans, the cost of financing can easily exceed all of the original building and development costs. In many cases, long-term interest, called debt service, is not included in the project budget because it is an ongoing cost to the owner, as are maintenance costs.

Finally, many clients include moving costs in the development budget. For large companies and other types of clients, the money required to physically relocate, including changing stationery, installing telephones, and the like, can be a substantial amount.

Methods of Budgeting

The costs described in the previous section and shown in Table 3.4 represent a type of budget done during programming or even prior to programming to test the feasibility of a project. The numbers are preliminary, often based on sketchy information. For example, the building cost may simply be an estimated cost per square foot multiplied by the number of gross square feet needed. The square footage cost may be derived from similar buildings in the area, from experience, or from commercially available cost books.

Budgeting, however, is an ongoing activity for the architect. At each stage of the design process, there should be a revised budget reflecting the decisions made to that time.

There are five basic methods of preparing budgets and estimating costs. The method that is most appropriate depends on how much accuracy is needed and what stage of development the project is in.

In the *project comparison method*, the costs of past projects of similar scope and function are used to estimate the cost of the new project. This method is often used when setting a budget or determining a project's feasibility. Most predesign budgets are based on area alone, but other functional units can be used. For example, many companies develop rules of thumb for use in making estimates based on cost per hospital bed, cost per student, cost per hotel room, or other similar functional unit.

The project comparison method typically has an accuracy of about 15% to 25%. It requires information on projects of similar types, scope, and quality. When this estimating method is used, three budgets are often developed: low, midrange, and high.

Another way of estimating costs is the *area or volume method*. This is usually conducted when preliminary design is completed and the architect has a fairly good idea of the size of the project, its functional components, and the general level of quality or complexity. With this method of estimation, an average cost per unit of area or volume may be used, but the actual area or volume is more precisely known than in the project comparison method. The type of site development that will be required is also known at this stage. The project may also be considered as separate parts with different functions and different costs per unit of area or volume. A school, for example, may include classroom space, laboratory space, shop space, office space, and gymnasium space, each with a different cost per square foot. The area or volume method typically has an accuracy of about 5% to 15%.

A third way of estimating costs is the *assembly* or *system method*. During schematic design, when more is known about the space requirements and general configuration of the building and site, budgeting is based on major subsystems. Historical cost information on each type of subsystem can be applied to the design. At this point it is easier to see where the money is being used in the building.

Design decisions can then be based on studies of alternative systems. A typical subsystem budget is shown in Table 3.5.

Table 3.5

System Cost Budget of Office Buildings

subsystem	average cost ($/ft^2)	average cost (% of total)
foundations	3.96	5.2
floors on grade	3.08	4.0
superstructure	16.51	21.7
roofing	0.18	0.2
exterior walls	9.63	12.6
partitions	5.19	6.8
wall finishes	3.70	4.8
floor finishes	3.78	5.0
ceiling finishes	2.79	3.7
conveying systems	6.45	8.5
specialties	0.70	0.9
fixed equipment	2.74	3.6
HVAC	9.21	12.1
plumbing	3.61	4.6
electrical	4.68	6.1
	76.21	100.0

Values for low-, average-, and high-quality construction for different building types can be obtained from cost databases and published estimating manuals and applied to the structure being budgeted. The dollar amounts included in system cost budgets usually include markup for contractor's overhead and profit and other construction administrative costs. This method has an accuracy within about 10%.

A fourth way of estimating costs is the *parameter method*. This is often used during the later stages of schematic design and early stages of construction document production. It involves an expanded itemization of construction quantities and assignment of unit costs to these quantities. For example, instead of using one number for floor finishes, the cost is broken down into carpeting, vinyl tile, wood strip flooring, unfinished concrete, and so forth. Using an estimated cost per square foot, the cost of each type of flooring can be estimated based on the area.

With this type of estimating, it is possible to evaluate the cost implications of each building component and to make decisions concerning both quantity and quality in order to meet the original budget estimate. If floor finishes are over budget, the architect and the client can review the parameter estimate and decide, for example, that some wood flooring must be replaced with less expensive carpeting. Similar decisions can be made concerning any of the parameters in the budget.

Another way to compare and evaluate alternative construction components is with *matrix costing*. With this technique, a matrix is drawn showing, along one side, the various alternatives and, along the other side, the individual elements that combine to produce the total cost of the alternatives. For example, in evaluating alternatives for workstations, all of the factors that would comprise the final cost could be compared. These factors might include the cost of custom-built versus pre-manufactured workstations, task lighting that could be planned with custom-built units versus higher-wattage ambient lighting, and so on.

Parameter line items are based on commonly used units that relate to the construction element under study. For instance, a gypsum board partition would have an assigned cost per square foot of complete partition of a particular construction type rather than separate costs for metal studs, gypsum board, screws, and finishing. There would be different costs for single-layer gypsum board partitions, 1-hour rated walls, 2-hour rated walls, and other partition types.

Two additional components of construction cost are the contractor's overhead and profit. Overhead can be further divided into general overhead and project overhead. *General overhead* is the cost to run a contracting business, and involves office rent, secretarial help, heat, and other recurring costs. *Project overhead* is the money it takes to complete a particular job, not including labor, materials, or equipment. Temporary offices, project telephones, sanitary facilities, trash removal, insurance, permits, and temporary utilities are examples of project overhead. The total overhead costs, including both general and project expenses, can range from about 10% to 20% of the total costs for labor, materials, and equipment.

Profit is the last item a contractor adds onto an estimate and is listed as a percentage of the total of labor, materials, equipment, and overhead. This is one of the most highly variable parts of a budget. Profit depends on the type of project, its size, the amount of risk involved, how much money the contractor wants to make, the general market conditions, and, of course, whether or not the job is being bid.

During extremely difficult economic conditions, a contractor may cut the profit margin to almost nothing simply to get the job and keep his or her workforce employed. If the contract is being negotiated with only one contractor, the profit percentage will be much higher. In most cases, however, profit will range from 5% to 20% of the total cost of the job. Overall, overhead and profit can total about 15% to 40% of construction cost.

A fifth method of estimating costs is the *unit cost method*. The project is broken down into its individual building components and the labor required to install them. Contractors typically use this method of estimation when they are determining a bid or negotiated price for the project. It is the most accurate method, but it can only be used when the construction drawings and specifications are complete and all the requirements of the project are known. The estimate should include not only material and labor costs but also the cost of equipment, fees, and services necessary to complete the project, as well as the contractor's overhead and profit. When subcontractors or vendors will be performing work, the fixed prices of the subcontractors are added to the general contractor's costs.

Cost Information

One of the most difficult aspects of developing project budgets is obtaining current, reliable prices for the kinds of construction units being used. There is no shortage of commercially produced cost books that are published yearly. These books list costs in different ways; some are very detailed, giving the cost for labor and materials for individual construction items, while others list parameter costs and subsystem costs. The detailed price listings are of little use to architects because they are too specific and make comparison of alternate systems difficult.

There are also computerized cost estimating services that only require the architect to provide general information about the project, location, size, major materials, and so forth. The computer service then applies its current price database to the information and produces a cost budget. Many architects also work closely with general contractors to develop a realistic budget.

Commercially available cost information, however, is the average of many past construction projects from around the country. Local variations and particular conditions may affect the value of their use on a specific project.

Two conditions that must be accounted for in developing any project budget are geographical location and inflation. These variables can be adjusted by using cost indexes that are published in a variety of sources, including the major architectural and construction trade magazines. Using a base year as index 1000, for example, for selected cities around the country, new indexes are developed each year that reflect the increase in costs (both material and labor) that year.

The indexes can be used to apply costs from one part of the country to another and to escalate past costs to the expected midpoint of construction of the project being budgeted.

Example 3.2

The cost index in your city is 1257 and the cost index for another city in which you are designing a building is 1308. If the expected construction cost is $1,250,000 based on prices for your city, what will be the expected cost in the other region?

Divide the higher index by the lower index.

$$\frac{1308}{1257} = 1.041$$

Multiply this by the base cost.

$$(\$1,250,000)(1.041) = \$1,300,716$$

Scheduling

There are two major parts of a project schedule: design time and construction time. The architect has control over the scheduling of design and the production of contract documents, but practically no control over construction. However, the design professional must be able to estimate the entire project schedule so that the best course of action can be taken in order to meet the client's goals. For example, if the client must move by a certain date and normal design and construction sequences make this impossible, the architect may recommend a fast-track schedule or some other approach to meet the deadline.

The design process normally consists of several clearly defined phases, each of which must be substantially finished and approved by the client before the next one can begin. These are generally accepted in the profession and are referred to in the American Institute of Architects' Owner-Architect Agreement as well as in other documents.

Following programming, the first phase is *schematic design*. During this phase, the general layout of the project is developed along with preliminary alternate studies for materials and building systems. Once the direction of the project documented in schematic design drawings is reviewed and approved by the client, the *design development phase* starts. Here, the decisions made during the previous phase are refined and developed in more detail. Preliminary or outline specifications are written, and a more detailed cost budget is made.

Construction documents are produced as the third phase. These include the final working drawings as well as the full project manual and any bidding and contract documents required. These are used for the *bidding* or *negotiation phase*, which includes obtaining bids from several contractors and analyzing them or negotiating a contract with one contractor. The final phase is *construction administration*.

The time required for these phases is highly variable and depends on the following factors.

- The size and complexity of the project. Obviously, a 500,000 ft^2 (46 450 m^2) hospital will take much longer to design than a 30,000 ft^2 (2787 m^2) office building.
- The number of people working on the project. Although adding more people to the job can shorten the schedule, there is a point of diminishing returns. Having too many people only creates a management and coordination problem, and for some phases only a few people are needed, even for very large jobs.
- The abilities and design methodology of the project team. Younger, less-experienced designers will usually need more time to do the same amount of work than would a more senior staff.
- The type of client and the decision-making and approval processes of the client. Large corporations or public agencies are likely to have a multilayered decision-making and approval process. Getting necessary information or approval on one phase from a large client may take weeks or even months, while a small, single-authority client might make the same decision in a matter of days.

The construction schedule may be established by the contractor or construction manager, but it must often be estimated by the architect during the programming phase so that the client has some idea of the total time required from project conception to move-in. When the architect does this, it should be made very clear to the client that it is only an estimate and the architect can in no way guarantee an early (or any) estimate of the construction schedule.

Many variables can affect construction time. Most can be controlled in one way or another, but others, like weather, are independent of anyone's control. Beyond the obvious variables of size and complexity, the following is a partial list of some of the more common variables.

- the management ability of the contractor to organize his or her own forces as well as those of the subcontractors
- material delivery times
- the quality and completeness of the architect's drawings and specification
- the weather
- labor availability and labor disputes
- new construction or remodeling (remodeling generally takes more time and coordination for equal areas than new buildings take)
- site conditions (construction sites or those with subsurface problems usually take more time to build on)
- the architect (some professionals are more diligent than others in performing their duties during construction)
- lender approvals
- agency and governmental approvals

Several methods are used to schedule both design and construction. The most common and easiest is the *bar chart* or *Gantt chart*. See Fig. 3.4. The various activities of the schedule are listed along the vertical axis. Each activity is given a starting and finishing date, and overlaps are indicated by drawing the bars for each activity so that they overlap. Bar charts are simple to make and understand and are suitable for small to midsize projects. However, they cannot show all the sequences and dependencies of one activity on another.

Another scheduling tool often used is the *critical path method* (CPM). A CPM chart graphically depicts all the tasks required to complete a project, the sequence in which they must occur, their duration, the earliest or latest possible starting time, and the earliest or latest possible finishing time. It also defines the sequence of critical tasks: those tasks that must be started and finished exactly on time if the total schedule is to be met.

A CPM chart for a simple design project is shown in Fig. 3.5. Each solid arrow in the chart represents an activity with a beginning and end point (represented by the numbered circles). No activity can begin until all activities leading into a circle have been completed. The dashed arrows indicate dependency relationships that are not activities themselves, and thus they have no duration. These arrows are called *dummies* and are used to give each activity a unique beginning and ending number and to allow establishment of dependency relationships without tying in nondependent activities.

The heavier arrows in the illustration show the *critical path*, or the sequence of events that must happen as scheduled if the deadline is to be met. The numbers under the activities give the duration of each activity in days. Delaying the starting time of any of the activities in the critical path or increasing their duration will delay the whole project. The noncritical activities can begin or finish earlier or later (within limits) without affecting the final completion date. This variable time is called the *float* of each activity.

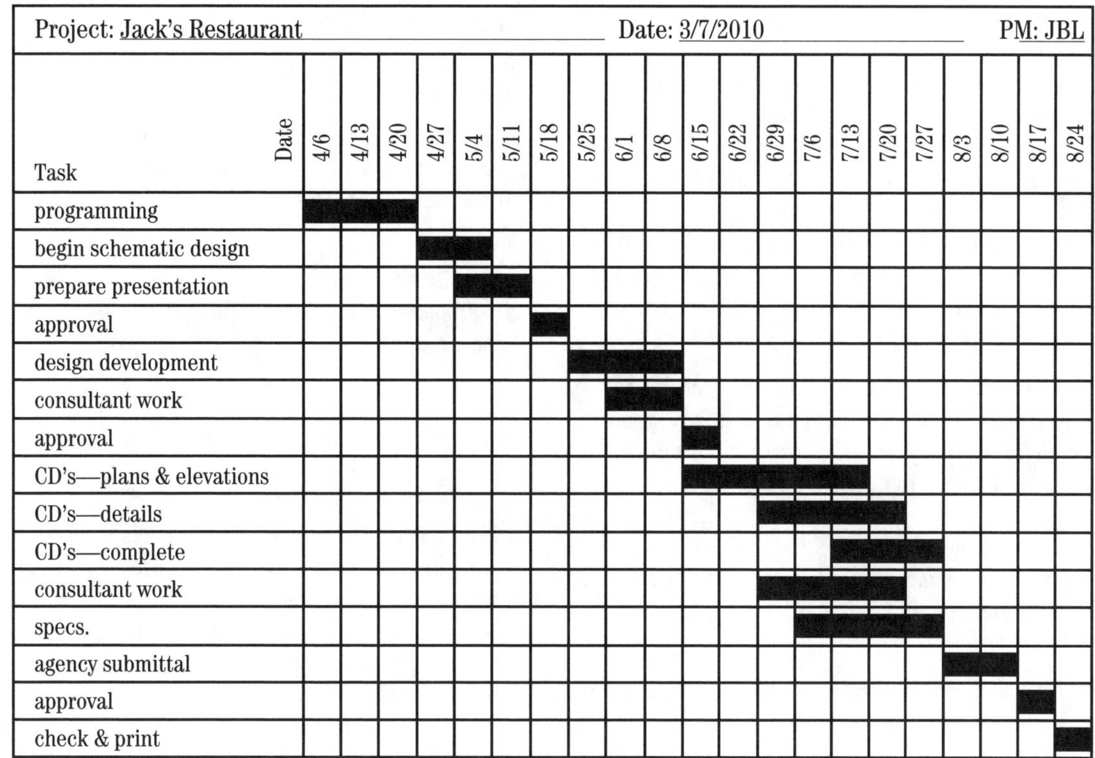

Project: Jack's Restaurant
Date: 3/7/2010
PM: JBL
Task
Date
4/6
4/13
4/20
4/27
5/4
5/11
5/18
5/25
6/1
6/8
6/15
6/22
6/29
7/6
7/13
7/20
7/27
8/3
8/10
8/17
8/24
programming
begin schematic design
prepare presentation
approval
design development
consultant work
approval
CD's—plans & elevations
CD's—details
CD's—complete
consultant work
specs.
agency submittal
approval
check & print

Figure 3.4 Gantt Chart

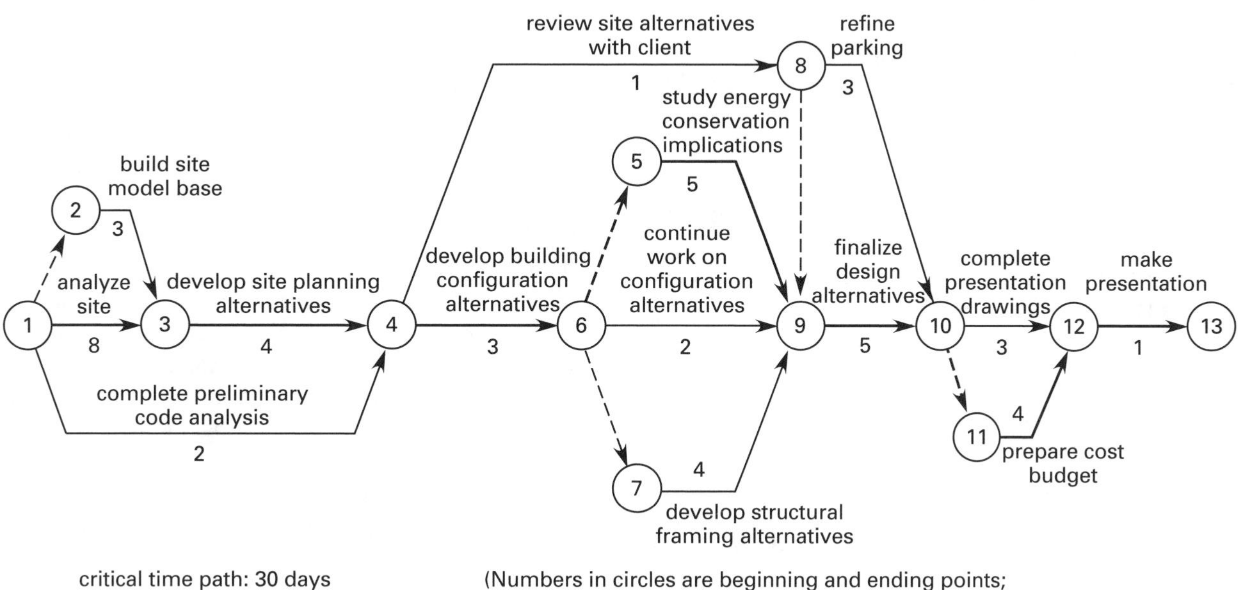

Figure 3.5 CPM Schedule

Scheduling is crucial to any project because it can have a great influence on cost. Generally, the longer a project takes the more it costs. This is due to the effect of inflation on materials and labor as well as the additional construction interest and the lost revenue a client can suffer if the job is not completed in a timely manner. For example, delayed completion of a retail store or office building delays the beginning of rental income. In other cases, quick completion of a project is required to avoid building during bad winter weather, when it costs more to build, or to meet some other fixed date set by the client's needs.

Besides efficient scheduling, construction time can be compressed with *fast-track scheduling*. This method overlaps the design and construction phases of a project. Ordering of long-lead materials and equipment can occur, and work on the site and foundations can begin before all the details of the building are completely worked out. With fast-track scheduling, separate contracts are established so that each major system can be bid and awarded by itself to avoid delaying other construction.

Although the fast-track method requires close coordination between the architect, contractor, subcontractors, owner, and others, it makes it possible to construct a high-quality building in 10% to 30% less time than with a conventional construction contract.

Refer to Ch. 53 for additional information on developing and monitoring schedules.

CODES AND REGULATIONS

A complete program for a building project will include the various legal restrictions that apply to a project. Two of the most common are zoning ordinances and building codes. Zoning is discussed in Chs. 2 and 5. Building code requirements, including provisions for making buildings accessible to the physically disabled, are reviewed in Chs. 55 and 56. In addition to zoning regulations, other land development regulations may apply. Such regulations as deed restrictions and easements are also discussed in Ch. 2.

In addition to zoning ordinances and building codes, other regulatory agency requirements that may be in force. include special rules of the local fire department, fire zones set by the local municipality, and rules of government agencies such as the Federal Housing Authority (FHA) and the Environmental Protection Agency (EPA). Additional regulations may include local health and hospital department requirements that spell out needs for restaurants and hospitals. Local and state energy conservation regulations may also be in force.

THE PROGRAMMING PROCESS

Programming is an attempt to define the problem and establish all the guidelines and needs on which the design process can be based. It is a time of analysis of all aspects of the problem and a distillation of the problem's complexity into a few clear problem statements.

One popular programming method uses a five-step process in relationship to four major considerations. It is described in *Problem Seeking* by William Peña (John Wiley & Sons). The process involves establishing goals, collecting and analyzing facts, uncovering and testing concepts, determining needs, and stating the problem. All of these steps include the considerations of form, function, economy, and time.

Establishing Goals

Goals indicate what the client wants to achieve and why. It is important to identify them because they establish the direction of programmatic concepts that ultimately suggest the physical means of achieving the goals. It is not enough to simply list the types of spaces and required areas the client needs; the client is trying to reach some objective with those spaces and areas. For example, a goal for a school administration might be to increase the daily informal interaction between students and teachers.

Collecting Facts

Facts describe the existing conditions and requirements of the problem. Facts include such things as the number of people to be accommodated, the site conditions, space adjacency needs, user characteristics, equipment to be housed, expected growth rate, money available for construction, building code requirements, and climate information. There is always a large number of facts; part of the programmer's task is not only to collect facts but also to organize them so that they are useful.

Uncovering Concepts

The programming process should develop abstract ideas that are functional solutions to the client's problems without defining the physical means that should be used to achieve them. These are programmatic concepts as discussed earlier in this chapter. They are the basis for later design concepts. To use the previous example, a programmatic concept concerning increasing the daily interaction between students and teachers might be to provide common spaces for mixed flow in circulation patterns. One possible design concept in response to this could be to provide a central court through which all circulation paths pass. Programmatic concepts are listed in the following section of this chapter.

Determining Needs

This step of the programming process balances the desires of the client against the available budget or establishes a budget based on the defined goals and needs. It is during this step that wants have to be separated from needs. Most clients want more than they can afford, so clear statements of true needs at this early stage of the process can help avoid problems later. At this stage, one or more of the four elements of cost (quantity, quality, budget, and time) may have to be adjusted to balance needs against available resources.

Stating the Problem

The previous four steps are a prelude to succinctly summarizing the essence of the problem in just a few statements. The problem statements are the bridge between programming and the design process. They are statements the client and programmer agree describe the most important aspects of the problem and serve as the basis for design and as design criteria by which the solution can be evaluated. There should be a minimum of four problem statements, one for each of the major considerations of form, function, economy, and time.

Four Major Considerations During Programming

The four major considerations of any design problem are form, function, economy, and time. *Form* relates to the site, the physical and psychological environment of the building, and the quality of construction. *Function* relates to the people and activities of the space or building and their relationships. *Economy* concerns money: the initial cost of the facility, operating costs, and life-cycle costs. Finally, *time* describes the ideas of past, present, and future as they affect the other three considerations. For example, the required schedule for construction is often a time consideration, as is the need for expansibility in the future.

Programmatic Concepts

As mentioned in the previous section, the architect must develop abstract ideas about how to view and solve the client's performance problems before attempting to solve them with three-dimensional design ideas. These abstract ideas are called *programmatic concepts*. Later in the design process, the architect develops *design concepts*, which are physical solutions to the client's problems and which reflect approaches to satisfying programmatic concepts. For example, expansibility is a programmatic concept. Two corresponding design concepts that might be used to respond to this are (1) to provide space on the site to build a future addition to the building or (2) to build a structure larger than first needed, to allow for expansion.

The book *Problem Seeking* identifies 24 programmatic concepts that tend to recur in all types of buildings, although they generally do not all occur in the same building. These include the following.

Priority establishes the order of importance of things such as size, position, and social values. For example, an entrance and reception area may have higher priority than individual offices, to reflect the goal of enhancing a company's image.

Relationships include the affinities of people and activities. This is one of the most common programming concepts established in any design problem because it most directly affects the organization of spaces and rooms.

Hierarchy relates to the idea of the exercise of authority and is expressed in physical symbols of authority. For example, to reflect the hierarchy of a traditional law firm, senior members may be given larger offices than junior members.

Character is a response to the desired image the client wants to project. This may later be expressed in design concepts using building size, shape, materials, organization, and other physical responses to project character.

Density—low, medium, or high—may relate to how a parcel of land or an individual building or space is used to respond to goals such as efficient use of land, compact use of office space, or the desired amount of interaction in a school.

Service groupings include mechanical services, such as mechanical systems, as well as other functions that support the use of the building. Storage, information, vending areas, and distribution of supplies, are examples of these types of services. For example, a goal of decentralizing access to information could be accomplished by the physical design concept of using satellite libraries throughout a facility, or by developing an electronic database accessible to all workers through computer terminals.

Activity grouping states whether activities should be integrated (or bundled together) or separated and compartmentalized. For example, compartmentalizing dining areas would respond to a goal to create an intimate dining atmosphere in a restaurant.

People grouping states the degree of massing of people derived from their physical, social, and emotional characteristics. For example, the goal of establishing work teams in a factory might suggest a concept of keeping small groups together in the same physical space.

Home base is related to the concept of territoriality and is a place where a person can maintain his or her individuality.

Communications as a concept is a response to the goal of promoting the effective exchange of information or ideas.

This concept states who communicates with whom and how they do it.

Neighbors is a concept that refers to how the project will promote or prevent sociality and how it will relate to its neighboring facilities. For example, a building may share a common entry court with another building to foster interaction and community with users of other buildings.

Accessibility relates to the idea of entry to a building and to making the facility accessible to the disabled. It answers the question of how people can find the entrance and whether or not there should be multiple entrances.

Separated flow relates to segregating the flow of people, automobiles, service access, and other activities of a building. For example, people may need to be separated from automobile traffic, or public visitors to a courthouse may need to be separated from prisoners.

Mixed flow is a concept that responds to the goal of promoting interaction among people. Mixed flow may not be a desired programmatic concept in controlled facilities.

Sequential flow is often needed for both people and objects where a specific series of events or processes is required. For example, a show at an art museum may need to direct people from a starting point to an ending point. In a factory, material must progress from one station to another in a definite sequence.

Orientation refers to providing a point of reference within a building, campus, or other group of buildings to help keep people from feeling lost within a larger context. Common examples of physical design concepts used to provide orientation include a tower among a group of lower buildings, or a central atrium or lobby within a large building.

Flexibility includes three different components. The first, expansibility, refers to how a building can accommodate growth with expansion. The second, convertibility, refers to how a building can allow for changes in function through the conversion of spaces. The third, versatility, provides for several different activities with multifunctional spaces.

Tolerance allows for extra space for a dynamic activity (one likely to change) instead of fitting the space precisely for a static activity. For example, an indoor swimming pool area can be sized to accommodate just the pool and circulation around it. Providing for tolerance would give extra room to accommodate future bleachers or extra seating areas.

Safety focuses attention on life safety and the conceptual ways to achieve it. Building codes and other safety precautions are closely tied to this concept.

Security controls are ways that both people and property can be protected based on the value of the potential loss—minimum, medium, or maximum.

Energy conservation can be achieved in several ways: by keeping the heated area to a minimum, by keeping heat flow to a minimum, by using materials produced using low amounts of energy, by using recycled materials, and by using recyclable materials.

Environmental controls are controls necessary to meet human comfort needs. These needs include levels of air temperature, light, sound, and humidity. This concept encompasses mechanical systems as well as natural means for climate control.

Phasing determines if the project must be completed in stages to meet time and cost schedules. It also states whether the project can be based on linear scheduling or must provide for concurrent scheduling to meet urgent occupancy requirements.

Cost control explores ways to establish a realistic preview of costs and a balanced budget to meet the client's available funds.

4 SOLVING THE SITE ZONING VIGNETTE

The Site Zoning vignette requires that the candidate understand the horizontal plan and vertical building area limitations of a site that are imposed by programmatic requirements and by zoning and other regulatory restrictions. Given the various limitations of a program, the candidate must draw the areas allowed for surface improvements and for buildings. Based on contour lines on a site plan, the candidate must then draw a corresponding profile of the site grade. On this site grade, the candidate must draw the maximum allowable vertical building envelope as allowed by regulatory restrictions.

TIPS FOR COMPLETING THE SITE ZONING VIGNETTE

The following guidelines are intended primarily as a study aid for the Site Zoning vignette, but they are also useful to guide study for the multiple-choice portion of the Programming, Planning, & Practice division. The Site Zoning vignette is intended to be a short test of the candidate's ability to deal with a specific design task. Time constraint is usually not a problem.

The Site Zoning vignette is fairly easy because there is only one solution. All the requirements of the problem statement must be followed exactly. The problem gives the candidate a site plan and a section grid. Based on information on the site plan and in the written description, the candidate must draw the maximum primary buildable area for both lots shown and the maximum allowable area for surface improvement. Then, the candidate must draw a profile of the ground level and the outline of the maximum buildable area above the grade.

This vignette must be completed on two different layers, one for the surface improvements area and one for the buildable area. The layers appear as two separate colors. One or more edges of both areas may or may not coincide with each other, but as a matter of procedure it is best to consider the two as separate problems. Draw the surface improvements area first and then draw the primary buildable area.

The following suggestions may help in solving the site plan portion of the problem.

- Use the sketch tools to mark setbacks and other defining elements.
- A setback is measured perpendicularly to the element that defines the setback, whether the element is a property line, easement, floodplain, or some other irregular shape.
- If a setback is required from a curved element or tree line, use the "circle sketch" tool to draw a series of circles with a diameter equal to the required setback distance. Then connect the circles at points directly opposite the property line or whatever is defining the setback. Rectangles or lines can also be used.
- In most cases, utility and other easements can be used for surface improvement areas such as parking, but read the program carefully to see whether this is allowed. For example, if the program states something like "Construction of buildings is prohibited in easement," then surface improvements are permitted in the easement.

Be careful of very small areas that may be defined by the restrictions of the problem but that would not really be considered buildable in practice. On the exam, these are important elements that the candidate must show in order to pass. There may also be a small, oddly shaped parcel that can be used for secondary construction, but not as buildable area.

The problem usually includes a property line running through the middle of the site, so there will be two outlines of two different building envelopes. Drawing the grade is simply a matter of transferring the elevation points where the contour lines cross the section cut line onto the section grid, and then connecting the dots. The maximum building envelope can be defined by any number of types of restrictions, including the following.

- setbacks from property lines, easements, water lines, and other features
- height restrictions
- view corridors and planes
- solar access planes
- stepped setbacks required to avoid a canyon effect
- limitations based on which grades the building can be built on (a floodplain, for example)
- easements
- maximum building height
- maximum floor area ratio
- landscaping that must be maintained
- airspace restrictions

Additional things to keep in mind when completing the section portion of this vignette include the following.

- Use the *sketch pad* tool to draw the various limiting lines by taking the program requirements one item at a time. In the finished drawing, the lines should all intersect to give the profile that needs to be drawn for the final solution.
- Be aware of the scale of the section grid so that an elevation taken from the site plan is correctly transferred to the corresponding horizontal line on the grid. Sometimes the horizontal grid lines may be at a different scale than the individual contour lines on the site plan.
- Solar access planes and view planes are usually diagonal lines at some specific angle. However, the trick is to be sure of the point where the sloped plane starts. For example, does a solar access plane start at a point 20 ft (6 m) above the grade at a property line or at the setback from the property line?
- Be aware of what the benchmark elevation is on the given site plan. One or more of the required height restrictions may be based on this point rather than on the elevation of the grade at any given location.

SECTION 3: SITE PLANNING & DESIGN

Chapter 5: Site Analysis and Design
Chapter 6: Solving the Site Design Vignette
Chapter 7: Solving the Site Grading Vignette

5 SITE ANALYSIS AND DESIGN

Nomenclature

A	distance from noise source to top of sound barrier	ft
B	distance from noise source to bottom of sound barrier	ft
d	line-of-sight distance from sound source to receiver	ft
f	sound frequency	Hz
H	effective height	ft
N	noise	dB

This chapter discusses the influences of a specific site on the placement and design of a building and the considerations for site development. Other pertinent topics that apply to site design are reviewed in Chs. 2 and 30.

TOPOGRAPHY

Topography affects decisions on where to place major site features such as buildings, parking areas, and drives as well as how much soil has to be moved to maintain desired slopes and drainage patterns. The topography of a site is shown with contour lines on a topographic map, as discussed in Ch. 2. Figure 5.1 shows the common conditions that contour lines represent. The examinee should be able to immediately recognize these and translate the spacing of the contour lines and the contour interval to a percentage of slope using Eq. 2.1.

When contour lines represent a ridge they "point" in the direction of the downslope, and when they represent a valley they "point" in the direction of the upslope. Equally spaced contour lines represent a uniform slope. As shown in Fig. 5.1, concave slopes have more closely spaced contour lines near the top of the slope, whereas convex slopes have more closely spaced contour lines at the bottom of the slope.

Any site requires some modification of the land, but the changes should be kept to a minimum. There are several reasons for this.

- Earth moving costs money.
- Excavating and building on steep slopes is more expensive than on gentle slopes.
- Excessive modification of the land affects drainage patterns that must be resolved with contour changes, drainage ditches, culverts, or other sitework.
- Large changes in elevations can require retaining walls, which add cost to the project.
- Removing or hauling in soil is expensive.
- Large amounts of cutting may damage existing tree roots.

When modifications are made to the contours as part of site design, the amount of material cut away should balance the amount of soil required for fill, to avoid the expense and problems related to removing or hauling in soil. Generally, it is better to orient the length of a building parallel to the direction of the contours rather than perpendicular to them in order to minimize excavation costs.

Both existing contour lines and new contour lines are shown on the same plan; the existing lines are shown dashed and the new ones solid. See Fig. 5.2. At the property lines, the contour lines must match up with the existing contours at adjacent properties or retaining walls must be built. Avoid modification of contour lines within the drip line of trees.

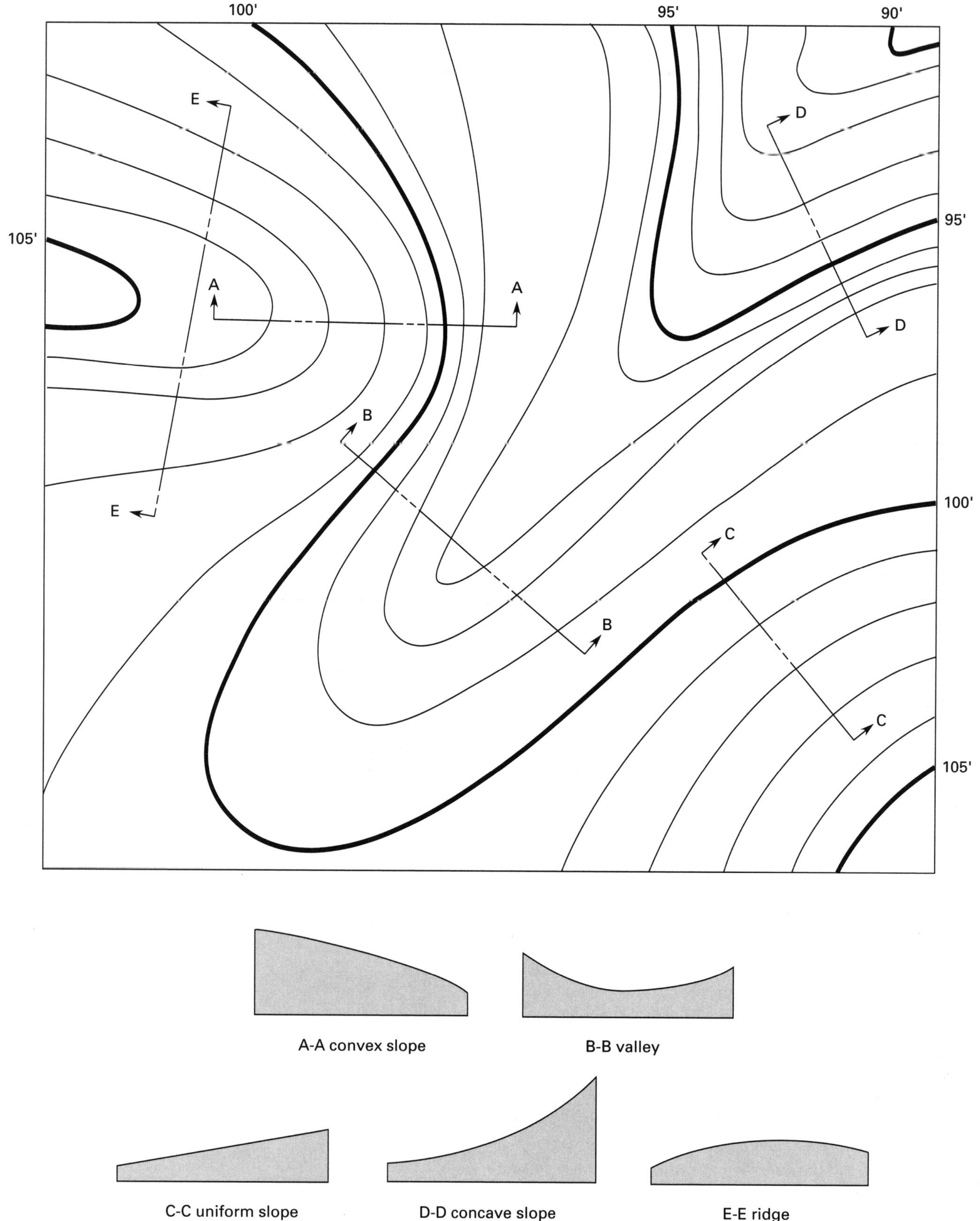

Figure 5.1 Common Contour Conditions

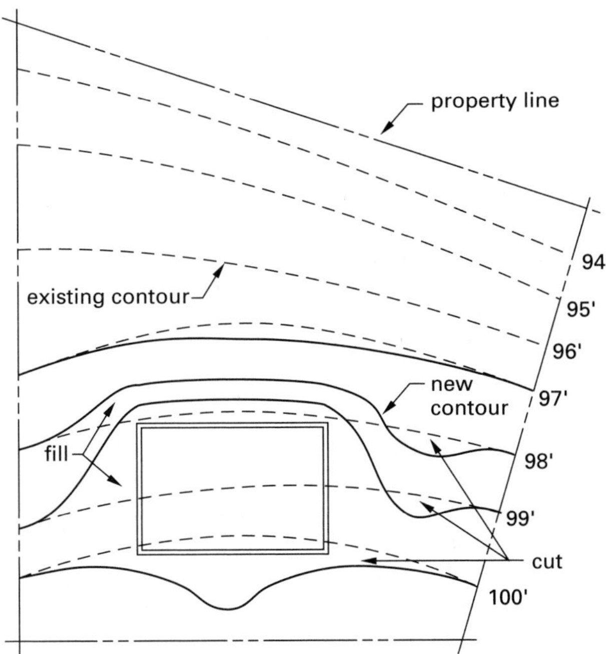

Figure 5.2 New and Existing Contour Lines

CLIMATE

Solar orientation influences three aspects of site planning: the orientation of the building to control solar heat gain or heat loss, the location of outdoor spaces and activities, and the location of building entries. Prior to design, locate the path of the sun so that you know its angle at various times of the day during the seasons. In the Northern Hemisphere, the sun's angle is lowest around December 21 and highest around June 21. In more northern latitudes, its angle is smaller all year long than in the latitudes nearer to the equator.

During the winter, the sun rises and sets south of an east-west line through the site, and, depending upon the site location, during the summer it may rise and set north of the same line. On the vernal equinox (around March 21) and the autumnal equinox (around September 21), it rises and sets directly above the equator. Some representative values for solar altitude (angle above the horizon) and azimuth (angle north or south from an east-west line) are shown in Table 5.1 for various latitudes and cities. Refer to Ch. 29 for more information on solar design.

The orientation of a building—that is, the direction its length faces, has a profound effect on energy gains and losses and on the comfort of the users. For example, for a 40° latitude, a southern exposure in the winter receives about three times the solar energy as the east and west sides, while in the summer the east and west façades of a building receive about twice the energy as the north and south combined.

For most northern hemisphere locations, the best overall orientation for a building is to have its principal facade facing south or slightly east or west of south. An orientation from 5° to 25°, depending on the climatic region, east of south is considered ideal to balance the desired heat gains in the winter months and to minimize the excessive heat gains on the east and west façades during the summer. See Fig. 29.1. Overhangs can be used to control the sun in the summer but let it strike the building and glass areas in the winter for passive solar heating. See Fig. 5.3. Deciduous trees can also be used to shield low buildings from the sun in the summer, while allowing sunlight through in the winter.

On east and west facades, however, vertical sun baffles are more effective than overhangs because the sun is at a lower angle during the morning and afternoon hours in the summer. Louvers can also be used to shield a building and its

Table 5.1

Solar Angles for Representative Latitudes and Cities
(all angles are approximate to the nearest degree)

		solar altitude/noon (degrees)			
latitude	nearest city	Dec. 21	Mar./Sept. 21	June 21	azimuth at sunrise/sunset*
30	Houston	37	60	84	27
34	Los Angeles/Atlanta	32	56	79	28
40	Denver	26	50	73	30
42	Chicago/Boston	24	48	71	32
48	Seattle	18	42	66	34

* Azimuths in this table are degrees from an east-west line. They are the same for sunrise and sunset. For sunrise on December 21, the azimuth is south of east, and for sunset it is the same angle but south of west.

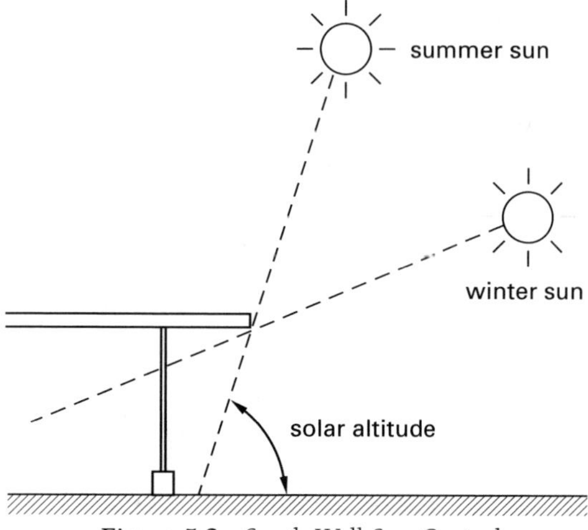

Figure 5.3 South Wall Sun Control

interior from the sun. Either exterior or interior louvers and shades are effective, but exterior louvers are more efficient since they block the sunlight before it enters the space.

Solar orientation can also influence outdoor activities. In hot, humid climates, it is better to locate patios, outdoor restaurants, and the like where they receive shade from the building or trees. In more temperate climates, the same spaces are best located where they have the advantage of the warming effects of solar radiation in the winter, spring, and fall. In cold climates, building entries are best placed on the south where direct sun can melt ice and snow in the winter.

The effects of wind on building location are reviewed in Ch. 2. In addition, the orientation of a building and locations of windows, plazas, and other elements can either take advantage of cooling breezes in hot, humid climates during the summer or shield the building and occupants from cold winds in the winter. In most temperate climates, prevailing wind patterns often change with the seasons, so a wind analysis is required to determine the direction of summer and winter winds. Shielding a building as much as possible from winter winds can reduce the heat loss through the walls, and providing for natural ventilation can help cool the building during the summer. Windbreaks can be formed with vegetation, buildings, or other manufactured site elements such as screens and fences.

Design Strategies for Climatic Regions

The four general climatic regions in the United States are cool, temperate, hot-humid, and hot-arid. The cool region includes the northern part of the United States and the Colorado Rocky Mountains. The temperate region includes the middle latitudes from coast to coast. The hot-humid region is in the southeast portion of the country, and the hot-arid region is in the southwest.

Traditionally, architects have used climate-specific design strategies based on these four regions. Knowledge of these regions is usually enough to suggest general approaches to design.

However, an architect needs more specific information on climate to respond adequately to energy conservation requirements, such as the amount of insulation and the type and position of air and water barriers in the exterior enclosure. For this reason, many building codes and standards rely on a more detailed division of the United States into climate zones. The map of climate zones used for this purpose was developed for the U.S. Department of Energy (DOE) by Pacific Northwest National Laboratory. The map has been adopted by the *International Energy Conservation Code* (IECC), the International Residential Code, and ANSI/ASHRAE/IESNA 90.1, *Energy Standard for Buildings Except Low-Rise Residential Buildings*, as well as by many states as part of their energy conservation regulations. An appendix in ANSI/ASHRAE/IESNA 90.1 gives a county-by-county listing of each zone in the United States as well as details about the climate zones of other countries.

There are eight climate zones according to this division, including four subzones of moist, dry, marine, and warm-humid. These are shown in Fig. 5.4 and numbered from zone 1 to zone 8. The curved lines overlaid on this figure (which are not part of the DOE map) indicate the approximate boundaries of the four climate regions used by many architects and promoted by Victor Olgyay in his book *Design with Climate*. Table 5.2 lists these regions by name.

The four general climatic regions can still be used as a basis for preliminary design. Design strategies for each region include the following.

Cool Climates

- Use compact forms with the smallest surface area possible relative to the volume.
- Use large, south-facing windows with small windows on the east and west and with minimal or no windows on the north.
- Use interior materials with a high thermal mass.
- Include summer shading for glazed areas.
- Use dark or medium-dark colors for the building exterior.

Temperate Climates

- Plan rectangular buildings with the long direction oriented generally along the east-west axis and facing slightly to the east. See Fig. 29.1 for suggested building orientations for various climatic regions.

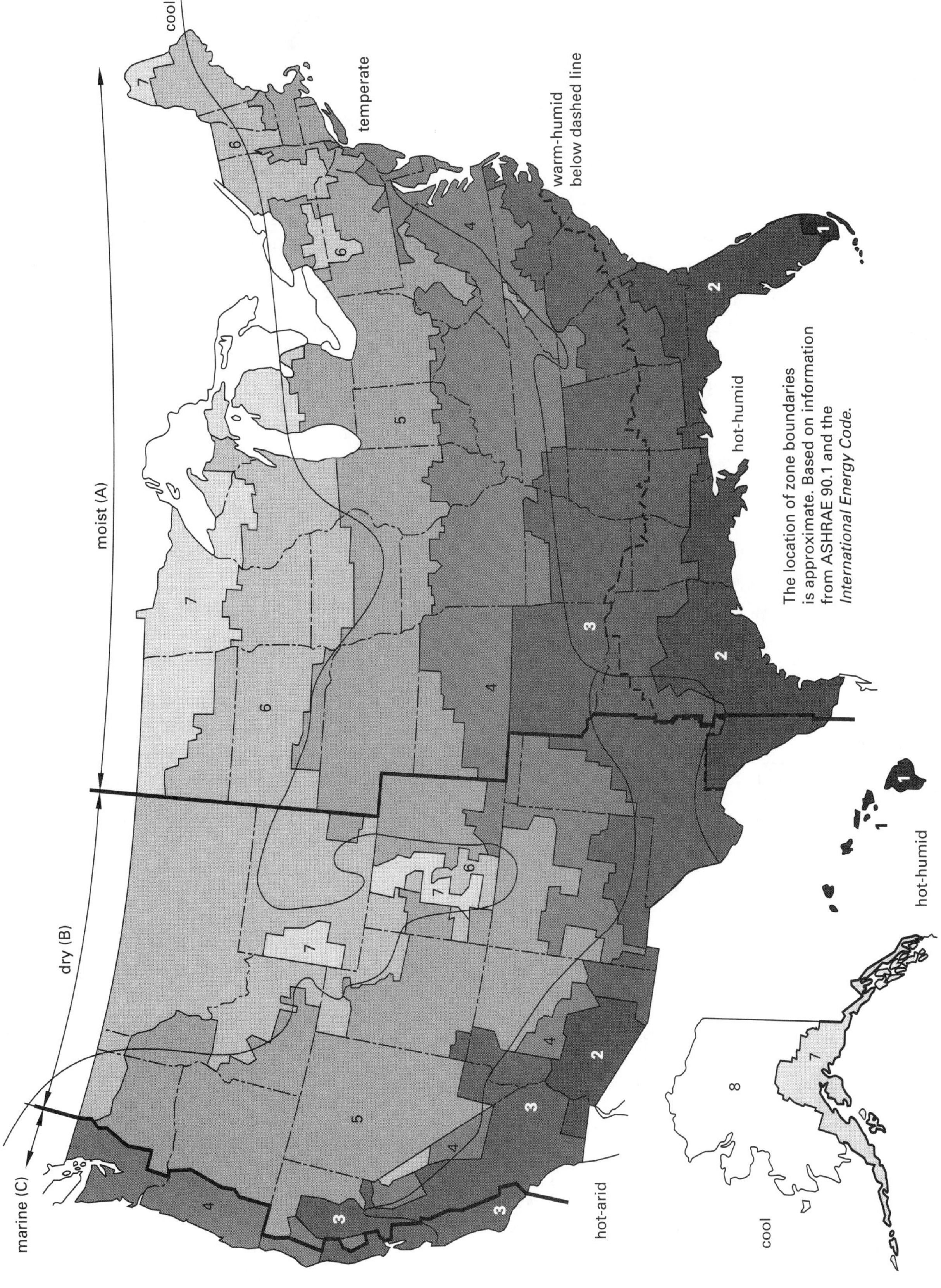

Figure 5.4 Climatic Regions of the United States

- Provide shade in the summer, and allow the sun to fall on glazing and the building in the winter.
- Use south-facing openings to capture winter sunlight.
- Plan for the cooling effects of wind in the summer; block the wind in the winter.
- Use medium colors for the building exterior.

Hot-Humid Climates

- Provide shade for all openings.
- Maximize natural ventilation with large openings, high ceilings, and cross ventilation.
- Construct buildings using light materials; minimize thermal mass.
- Use light colors for the building exterior.

Hot-Arid Climates

- Use compact forms with the smallest surface area possible relative to the volume.
- Minimize opening sizes.
- Provide shade for openings.
- Maximize thermal mass.
- Use light colors for the building exterior.

Table 5.2

Climate Zone Descriptions

zone number	description
1A, 2A, and 3A south of the warm-humid line	warm, humid
2B	warm, dry
3A north of the humid line, 4A	mixed, humid
3B, 3C, 4B	mixed, dry
4C	cool, marine
5A, 6A	cold, humid
5B, 6B	cold, dry
7	very cold
8	subarctic

Alternative Energy Systems

During the early stages of design many alternative energy systems and methods can affect the overall project concept. Such systems can affect the location, massing, shape, orientation, and primary material choice of the building as well as the configuration of other site elements like parking and landscaping. Refer to Chs. 29 and 30 for more information on both passive and active energy conservation techniques as well as sustainability principles.

Following are several brief summaries of the design strategies that can affect a project concept and overall building configuration in the early stages of project planning.

Passive Solar Heating

- If passive solar heating is to be used, orient the long axis of the building in the east-west direction so the southern collection surfaces face directly south or within approximately 15° of true south. Passive solar heating methods should be integrated with daylighting design. Both of these design strategies will result in a building that is long and relatively narrow.
- If thermal mass is used it may be featured as a design element.
- Use deciduous trees to let sunlight fall on windows during the winter months and shade the glass during the summer. Either deciduous or evergreen trees can be used on the east and west facades to block the low angle of morning and afternoon sun. However, even bare deciduous trees can block about 20% of winter solar heat gain.

Natural Cooling

- Be aware of the following natural cooling methods. *Passive solar cooling* utilizes the concepts of shading, natural ventilation, radiative cooling, evaporative cooling, and ground coupling. *Radiative cooling* uses thermal mass to store heat during the day and release heat to the outside at night. *Ground coupling* uses the stable coolness of the earth to cool a building, typically by using a ground-source heat pump.
- Use trees and other landscaping to shade windows and other surfaces, unless direct solar radiation is needed for daylighting or passive or active solar heating. If a site has existing landscaping, locate the building such that it takes advantage of shade.
- To avoid excessive heat gain, use fixed shading devices. These are typically horizontal elements when used on the south side of a building and vertical elements when used on the east and west sides. A building can also be designed wider at the upper stories than at ground level to make it self-shading.
- Minimize glazed areas on the east and west facades.
- Use water elements and wind for an evaporative cooling effect.
- Use light-colored or reflective materials to minimize radiant heat gains.
- Limit the use of paving, to avoid heat buildup around the structure. This can be done by using a pervious paving material that supports vehicles but

allows grass or other vegetation to grow through it. If extensive paving must be used, select a color that has a high reflectance. Trees can also be used to shade the paving during hot summer months.

- Use natural ventilation strategies to locate the building on the site so that it takes advantage of prevailing winds. The overall form of the building should be either narrow or spread out so that breezes can filter through the building. Courtyards may also be used.

Active Solar

- Be aware that active solar collectors on a building can make a significant adverse visual statement unless they are placed on sloped roofs or are concealed with parapets.
- Position solar collectors so that they do not reflect sunlight onto other buildings or occupied areas around the building.
- If solar collectors are used, locate them so that they avoid shade from buildings and trees. If collectors are to be mounted on the building, this factor can dictate the building's location. If collectors are mounted away from the building, an additional area on the site must be designated for the accompanying site disturbance.

Photovoltaics

- If photovoltaics (PV) are deemed to be feasible for a building project, large surfaces may be required for mounting. These can take the form of large, flat roofs or buildings designed with sloped surfaces to optimize the PV panel's exposure to the sun. New technologies are integrating PV technology with other building materials such as glass or roofing shingles. These are known as *facade-integrated photovoltaics*. Refer to Ch. 29 for more information on photovoltaics.

DRAINAGE

Any development of a site interrupts the existing drainage pattern and creates additional water flow by replacing naturally porous ground with roof area and paving. The architect must provide for any existing drainage patterns through the site and account for additional stormwater that does not seep into the ground, which is called *runoff*. The site design must also create positive drainage away from the buildings, parking areas, and walks to avoid flooding, erosion, and standing water.

The two basic types of drainage are aboveground and underground. *Aboveground* drainage involves sheet flow, gutters built into roadways and parking areas, ground swales as part of the landscaping, and channels. *Underground* drainage utilizes perforated drains and enclosed storm sewers that carry the runoff from the site to a municipal storm sewer system or to a natural drainage outlet such as a river. In a given project, combinations of several methods of drainage may be used.

Sheet flow is simply water that drains across a sloping surface, whether paved, grassy, or landscaped. In most cases, sheet flow is directed to gutters or channels, which are then emptied into a natural watercourse or storm sewer. Gutters are often used because they can be built along with the roadway or parking area and naturally follow the same slope as the paved surface. They can easily be drained into sewers, which also typically follow the path of roads.

Areas for surface drainage require minimum slopes to provide for positive drainage. Some of these are listed in Table 2.1. Although the table indicates that a slope as little as one-half of 1% may be sufficient for some drainage, this is only applicable for very smooth surfaces that have been carefully constructed. Most paved surfaces should have at least a 1% to $1^1/_2$% slope to account for paving roughness and variations in installation tolerances.

Underground systems use piping with a minimum slope of 0.3%. The storm drains collect water from roof downspouts, drain inlets, catch basins, and drain tiles surrounding the building foundation. A drain inlet simply allows

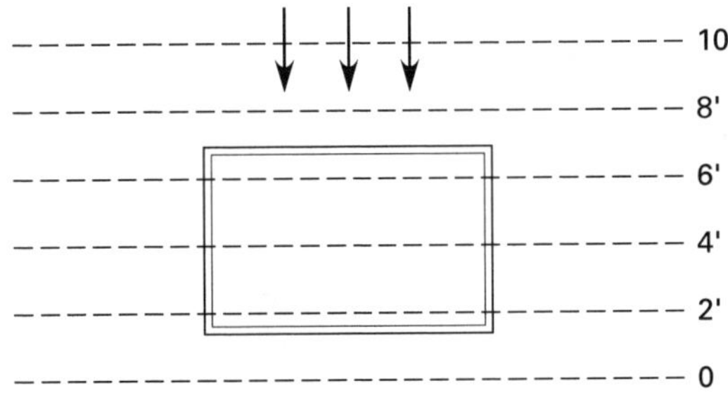

(a) drainage directly into building

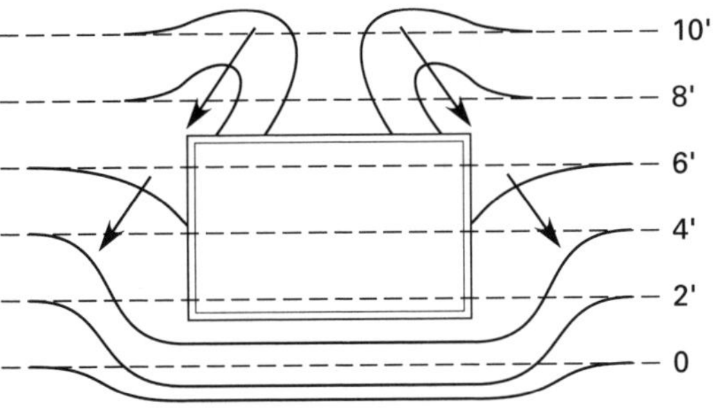

(a) drainage diverted around building

Figure 5.5 Drainage Around Buildings

stormwater to run directly into the storm sewer. A catch basin has a sump built into it so that debris will settle instead of flowing down the sewer. Periodically, the sump must be cleaned out. Large storm sewer systems require manholes for service access; these are located wherever the sewer changes direction, or a maximum of 500 ft (152 m) apart. Storm sewers are completely separate from sanitary sewers.

The capacity of a drainage system is based on the size of the area to be drained, the runoff coefficient (that fraction of water not absorbed), and the amount of water to be drained during the most severe storm anticipated in the design. Frequently, the system is planned for 25-year storms; other times a 10-year storm is used. These periods are simply the average frequency at which storms of a particular magnitude are likely to occur. If the site development creates a runoff in excess of the capacity of the existing municipal storm sewer or natural drainage course, a holding pond may be needed on the site. This collects the site runoff and releases it into the sewer system at a controlled rate without letting the excess water flood other areas.

Refer to Ch. 30 for more information on drainage as it relates to sustainability.

UTILITIES

Determine the locations of existing utilities prior to beginning design. These may include, but are not limited to, sanitary sewer lines, storm sewers, water lines, gas, electricity, steam, telephone, and cable television. If possible, the building should be located to minimize the length of utility lines between the structure and the main line.

Sanitary sewers and storm sewers usually take precedence in planning because they depend on gravity flow. The *invert*, or lowest, elevations of the existing public sewer line should be established, since the effluent must flow from the lowest point where the sewer line leaves the building to the main sewer. This portion of the horizontal piping of the sanitary sewer system outside the building is known as the *building sewer*. The actual connection of the building sewer to the main line must occur above the invert of the main line at any given point in order not to interfere with the free flow.

The minimum slope of the building sewer is 0.5% to 2.0% depending on the size of the pipe; a greater slope is required for smaller pipes. In some cases, the run of the building sewer will have to be longer than the shortest distance between the building and the main line simply to intercept the main line at a point low enough to allow for proper slope. See Fig. 5.6.

Other utilities, such as water and electricity, do not depend on gravity, so there is a little more flexibility in locating the building relative to these services. However, the total distance should still be minimized. In the case of electrical service, the location of the main electric lines may dictate the location of transformers and service entry to the building.

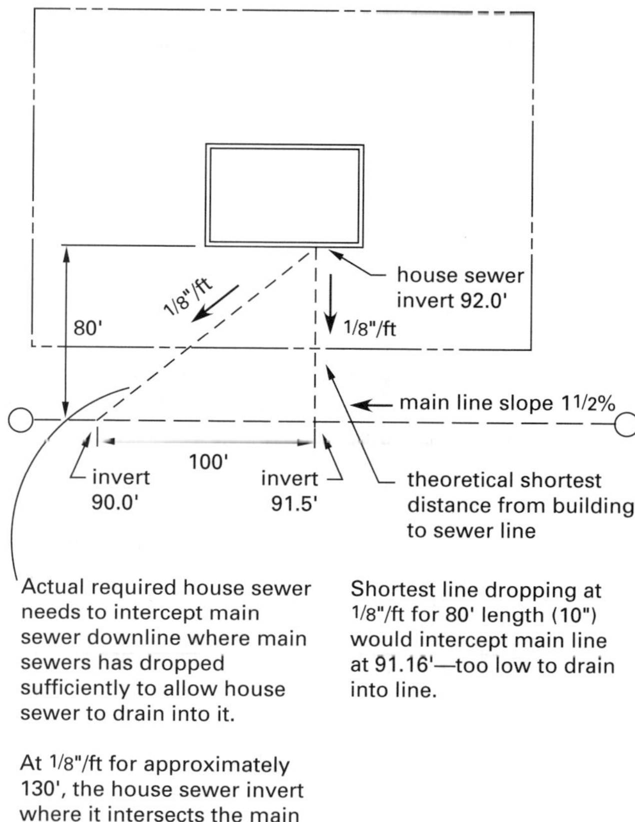

1/8"/ft
house sewer invert 92.0'
80'
1/8"/ft
main line slope 1 1/2%
100'
invert 90.0'
invert 91.5'
theoretical shortest distance from building to sewer line
Actual required house sewer needs to intercept main sewer downline where main sewers has dropped sufficiently to allow house sewer to drain into it.
At 1/8"/ft for approximately 130', the house sewer invert where it intersects the main line is about 90.7'.
Shortest line dropping at 1/8"/ft for 80' length (10") would intercept main line at 91.16'—too low to drain into line.

Figure 5.6 Sewer Layout Based on Slope Required

CIRCULATION

There are three major types of site circulation: automobile, pedestrian, and service. Both the site design and building design portions of the examination include all three.

Automobile Circulation

Planning for automobile circulation includes locating the entry drives to the site and providing on-site roads to reach the parking areas and the building drop-off point. The entire automobile circulation system should provide direct, easy access to the parking areas and building without excessive drives, turnarounds, dead ends, or conflicts with service areas and pedestrian circulation.

The size of the site, its relationship to existing public roads, and the expected traffic will help determine whether you should use a one-way loop system with two entry drives or a two-way system with one entry drive. In either case, you should lay out the roads so a driver can go directly to the parking area, drop-off point, or loading area. Forcing traffic through the parking area to get to the loading or the drop-off area should be avoided.

Figure 5.7 gives some design guidelines for on-site roads. Entry drives to the site should be as far away as possible from street intersections and other intersecting roads in order to avoid conflicts with vehicles waiting to turn and to avoid confusion about where to turn. Roads should be of sufficient width to make driving easy and to allow two vehicles to pass. Curves should be gradual, following the natural topography, and there should be no blind curves.

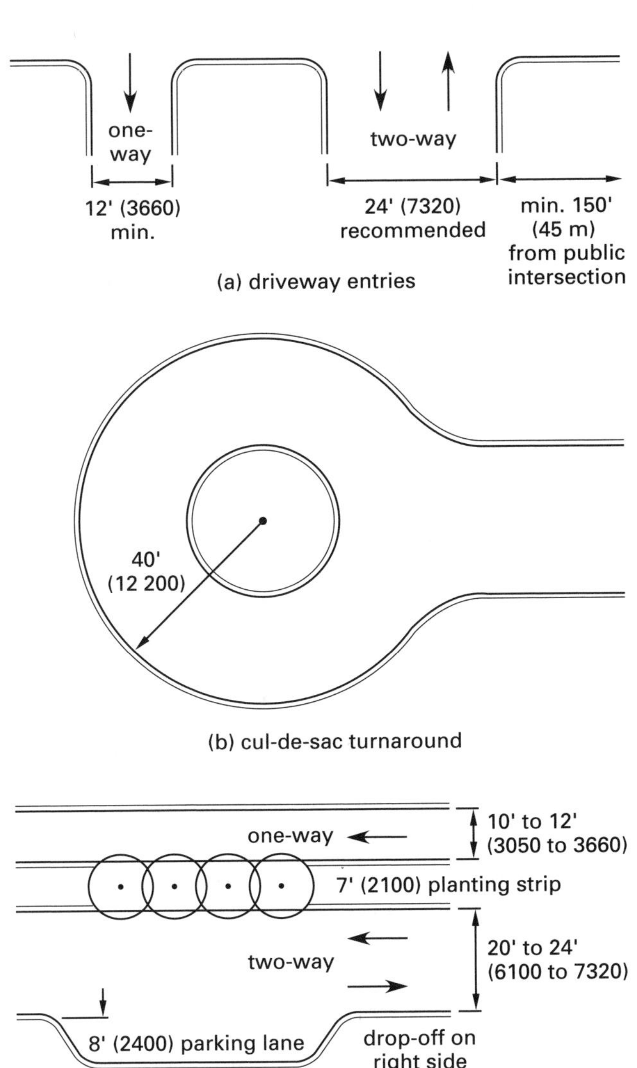

Figure 5.7 Design Guidelines for On-Site Roads

Unless the slope is very gentle, roads should not be laid out perpendicular to the slope but should be across it slightly to minimize the grade. Limit roads to a maximum slope of 15% for short distances, although 10% or less is preferable. If a road does slope more than 10%, there should be transition slopes of one-half of the maximum slope between the road and level areas. Ramps crossing sidewalks must have a level area between the ramp and the sidewalk.

Roads should have a gradual slope, a minimum of 1/4 in/ft (20 mm/m), for drainage from the center of the roadway, called the crown, to the sides. If the road has a gutter, it should be 6 in (150) high. Sometimes the representation of roads and gutters on a topographic map or site plan is confusing. Figure 5.8 shows a simple road sloping down, with a uniform pitch from the crown, and with gutters on either side. As shown in Fig. 5.1, the contours of the road point toward the direction of the slope, and the pointed contours representing the gutters point in the direction of the "valley" (in this case the gutter).

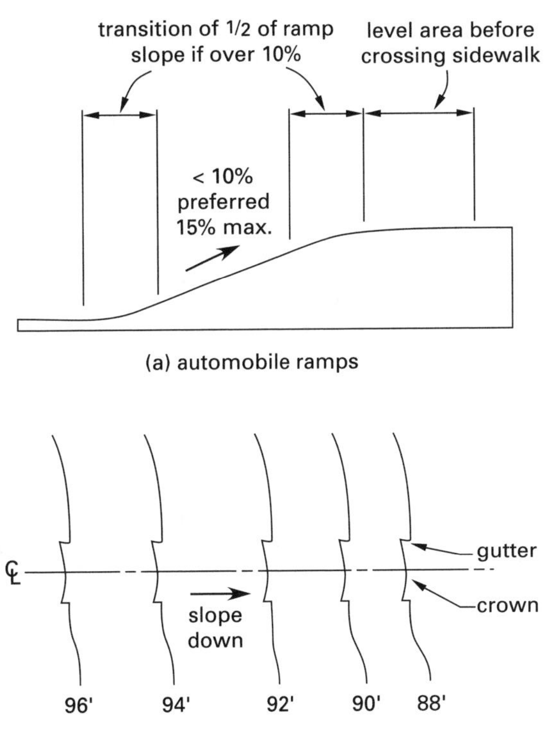

Figure 5.8 Design Guidelines for Road Grades

Pedestrian Circulation

Like roadways, pedestrian circulation should provide convenient, direct access from the various points on the site to the building entrances. If connections with adjacent buildings, public sidewalks, public transportation stops, and other off-site points are required, the circulation system must take these into account as well. Sidewalks should provide for the most direct paths from one point to another since people will generally take the shortest route possible. Pedestrian circulation paths should not cross roads, parking lots, or other areas of potential conflict. There should be collector walks next to parking areas so people can travel from their cars directly to a separate walk.

When these walks are next to parking where cars can overhang the walk, they should be a minimum of 6 ft (1800) wide. Required amenities such as seating, trash containers, and lighting should be provided. Walks should slope a minimum of 1/4 in (6) perpendicular to the direction of the paving for drainage. Figure 5.9 summarizes some of the design guidelines for exterior walks.

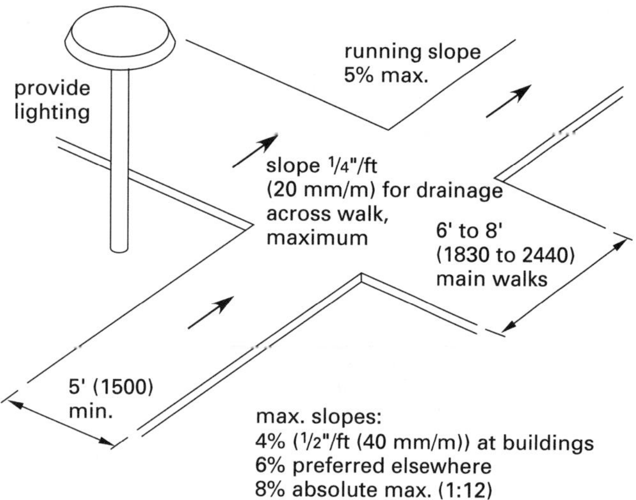

Figure 5.9 Design Guidelines for Exterior Walks

Changes in elevation are accomplished with ramps and stairs. There must be provisions for making the site accessible to the physically disabled. Requirements for curb cutouts and ramps are shown in Fig. 5.10, and general guidelines for exterior stairs are shown in Fig. 5.11. When a ramp and adjacent stairway serve the same areas, the bottom and top of the ramp and stairway should be adjacent to each other if possible. As with walks, stairways and ramps should be illuminated.

Service Circulation

Service and automobile circulation should be kept separate. This is usually stated as a specific program requirement on the ARE, but if not it should be done anyway. Service access is typically related to some space in the building program. Service trucks may use the same entry and drives as automobiles use (unless specifically stated otherwise), but the loading area should be separate. The examination does not require planning for large trucks. However, sufficient turnaround space or backing areas should be provided to allow

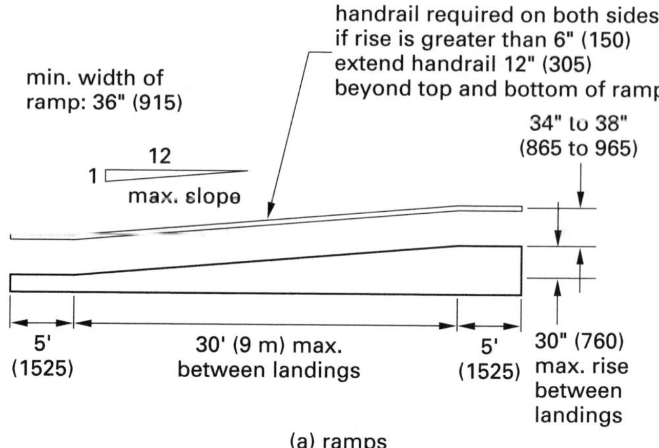

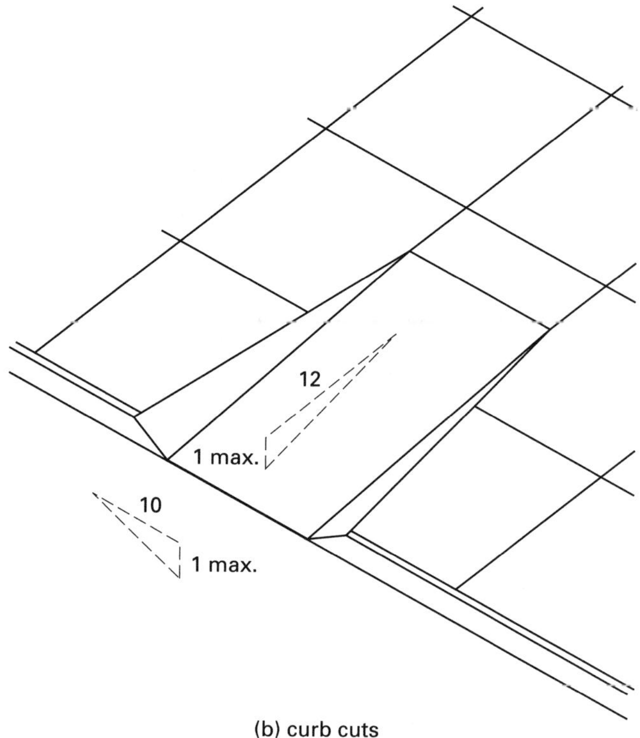

Figure 5.10 Access Requirements for the Physically Disabled

for maneuvering. Figure 5.12 shows some common guidelines for service drives for moderate-size trucks.

PARKING

Plan parking so it is efficient, convenient to the building, and separate from pedestrian circulation. The size of the site, topography, location of entry drives to the property, and relationship to the service drive and building drop-off area will determine the location of the parking area. The

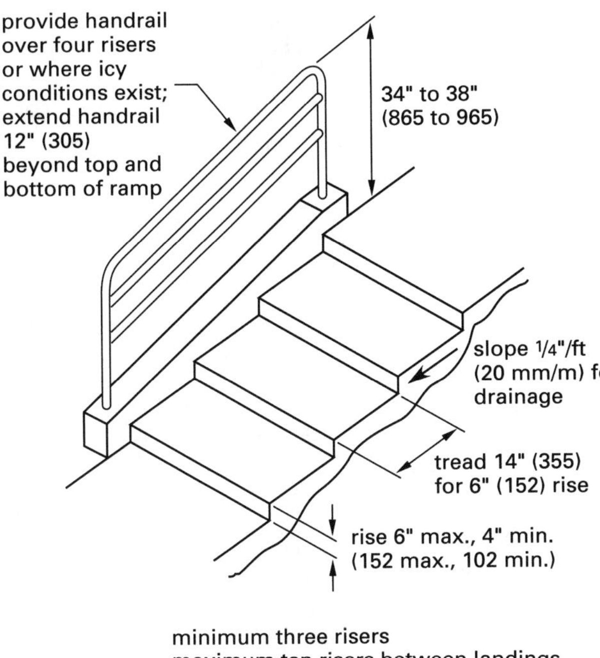

Figure 5.11 Design Guidelines for Exterior Stairs

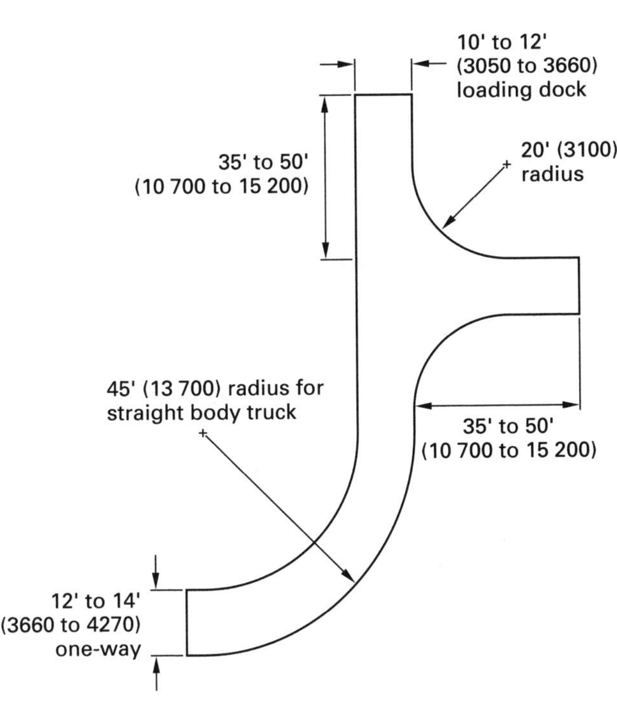

Figure 5.12 Design Guidelines for Service Drives

number of cars to be parked is determined by requirements of the zoning ordinance or by the building program.

The basic planning unit for parking is the size of a car stall. The standard size is 9 ft 0 in (2740) wide and 19 ft 0 in (5800) long for standard-size cars and 7 ft 6 in (2290) wide and 15 ft 0 in (4570) long for compact cars. Individual zoning ordinances may have slightly different requirements, so always verify particular codes; but these dimensions are good ones to use for most planning. Since a large percentage of cars today are compacts, most zoning ordinances now allow sizing of a certain percentage of required parking spaces for compact cars. However, for the purposes of the ARE, it is best to use the standard-size dimension unless otherwise stated in the problem.

Layouts for two types of parking are shown in Fig. 5.13. 90° parking is the most efficient in terms of land use, but angled parking is easier to use, forces a one-way circulation pattern, and requires less total width, for either a single- or double-loaded layout. Most parking lots should allow for continuous through circulation. Dead-end parking areas require a back-up space and are only appropriate for parking a few cars. The most efficient layouts are those that use double-loaded configurations or that utilize a drive as the back-up space.

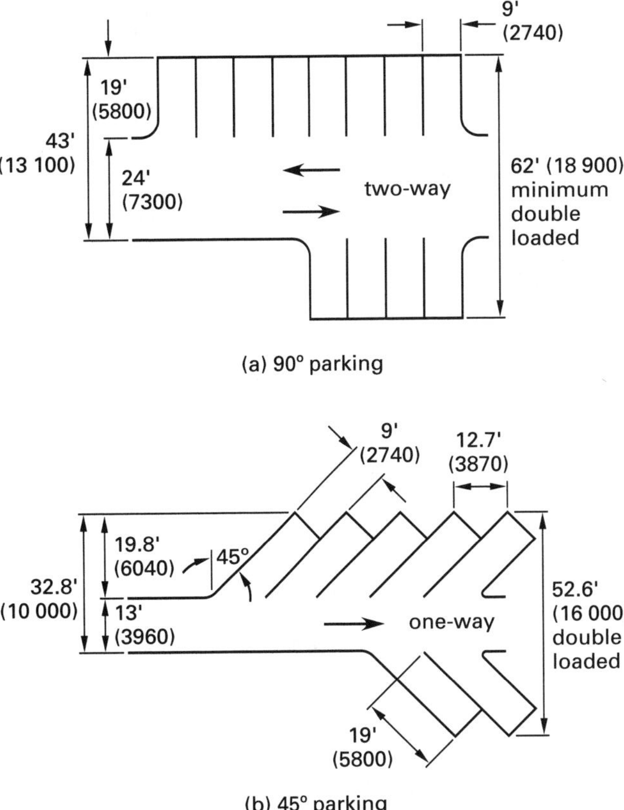

Figure 5.13 Parking Layouts

Unless otherwise required by the program, examinees must include at least one parking space for the physically disabled. Design guidelines for such a space are shown in Fig. 5.14. This space should be located close to the building entrance and should be identified with the international symbol for accessibility. If a van-accessible space is required, as it is with the Americans with Disabilities Act, the access aisle must be 96 in (2440) wide and level with the accessible route. A maximum slope of 2% ($^1/_4$ in/ft) must be maintained.

Establish drainage in parking areas as part of the site design. The minimum slope should be $1^1/_2$% with a maximum slope of 5%, but for convenience in calculating, use 2% or 3% when figuring parking slopes. Water should drain toward the edges of the parking area where it can run off into the landscaping or be collected and diverted to storm sewers or other natural water courses. Figure 5.15 shows three basic drainage patterns, depending on the orientation of the length of the lot to the contour lines. If curbs are used, there must be some way for the water to drain out, either with curb cutouts or drains to a storm sewer.

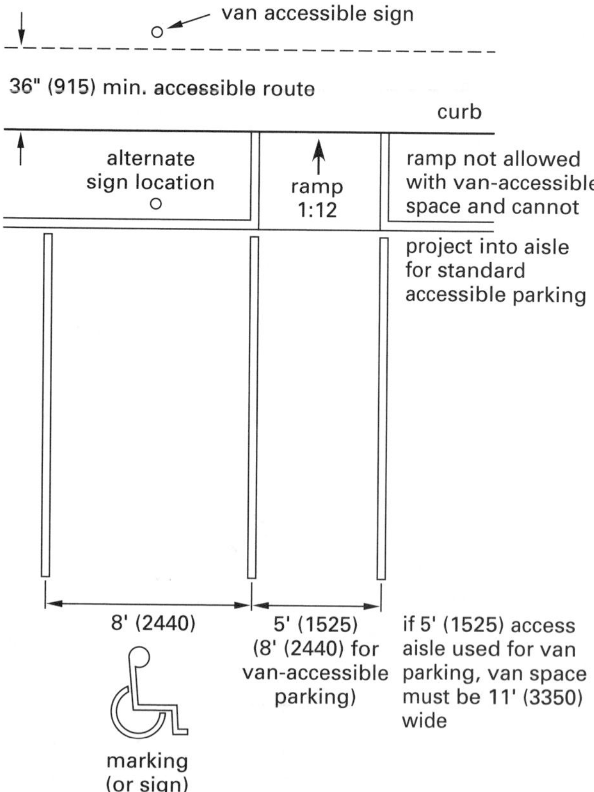

Figure 5.14 Parking for the Physically Disabled

One useful rule of thumb is that the change in elevation from one side of a double-loaded parking area to the other (62 ft [18 900]) for a minimum $1^1/_2$% slope is about 1 ft (300). With an absolute maximum of a 5% slope, the maximum change in elevation for 62 ft is about 3 ft (900). This is a useful way to quickly check new contour lines when designing a parking area.

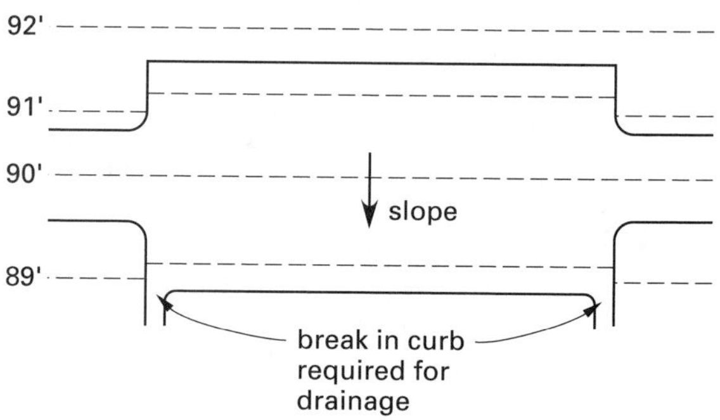

(a) drainage perpendicular to length of lot

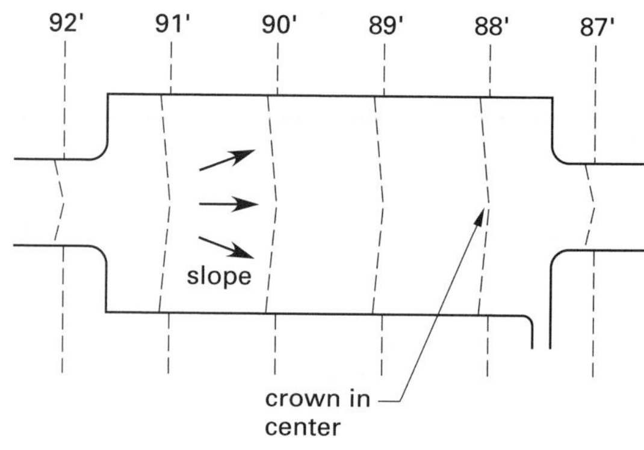

(b) drainage parallel to length

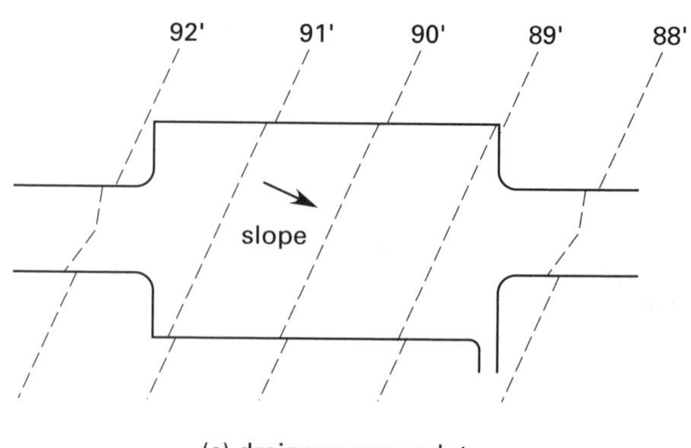

(c) drainage across lot

Figure 5.15 Drainage Patterns in Parking Lots

LANDSCAPING

Landscaping is a vital part of site development. In addition to its purely aesthetic qualities, landscaping can improve energy conservation, moderate noise, frame desirable views, block undesirable views, create privacy, fashion outdoor spaces, provide shade, retard erosion, and visually connect a building to its site. It is required in some communities.

The use of landscaping to moderate the microclimate is discussed in Ch. 2 and covers the use of deciduous trees to block sunlight in the summer while allowing it to enter a building in the winter. Trees can also moderate the wind and thereby reduce heat loss from wall surfaces. Slowing the normal wind patterns can also make outdoor spaces more pleasant to use. If trees are employed as a windbreak, evergreens should be used so they will remain effective in the winter.

Grass, shrubs, and groundcover lower the albedo of the site. *Albedo* is that portion of the radiant energy that is reflected as it falls on a surface. Combined with the low conductivity of plant materials, a well-landscaped site can reduce the daytime temperature around the building significantly and in some cases can raise the nighttime temperature slightly.

Plants are like any other design material in that they have form, size, color, texture, and other qualities that can serve the purposes of the designer and create the kind of image desired. Unlike other materials, however, plants grow.

The mature size and height of the tree or shrub must be known so adequate spacing between plants and between plants and buildings can be provided. Generally, planting strips with trees in parking areas and between other paved areas should be at least 7 ft (2130) wide, whereas landscaping strips for grass or groundcovers between paved areas should be at least 4 ft (1220) wide.

Because most trees and shrubs take so long to grow, existing healthy landscaping, especially large trees, should be saved whenever possible. The contours of the land cannot be changed around existing trees out to their drip line, so careful planning is necessary. Trees and other landscaping also need protection during construction.

PROPERTY DESCRIPTIONS

The boundaries of a site can be described in one of several ways. One of the most common is based on the United States survey system that was begun in 1784. This system laid out the majority of the United States except for those lands surveyed prior to the establishment of the control system and land based on some other system or land grant.

The system starts with a set of east-west lines called parallels that follow the lines of latitude of the earth, and with a set of north-south lines called *meridians*. There are several meridians and parallels that serve as the basis for the grid layout. These are called the *principal meridians* and *base lines*, respectively. Other meridians are called *guide meridians*, and other parallels are called *standard parallels*. They are referred to as being east or west, north or south of the base lines and principal meridians. See Fig. 5.16.

The parallels and meridians are 24 mi apart, and the squares they form are called *checks*. Since the meridian lines converge because of the shape of the earth, the south line of the first and each successive guide meridian is adjusted to be 24 mi from the principal meridian and adjacent guide meridians.

Each of the 24 mi squares is divided into 16 townships, each 6 mi on a side. The townships are referred to by a number referenced to a principal meridian and base line. The row of townships running east and west is referred to as a *township* (the same term but a different meaning), and the row of townships running north and south is referred to as a *range*.

The townships are numbered sequentially beginning at a base line. Those north of the base line are *north townships* and those south are *south townships*. Ranges are also numbered sequentially beginning at a principal meridian, either east or west. Therefore, a typical description of a township (the 6 mi^2 parcel of land) might be "township 13 north, range 7 east of the 6th principal meridian." This would typically be abbreviated to T.13N, R.7E, 6th PM.

Each township is then further divided into 36 sections, each section being a one-mile square. These are numbered sequentially starting in the northeast section, moving west, dropping down, then moving east, and so on, from sections 1 to 36 as shown in Fig. 5.16.

Sections are commonly further divided into quarter sections, and those quarter sections into four more parcels. A complete description of such a portion of a section might read: "The SE 1/4 of the NW 1/4, Section 12, T.13N, R.7E of the 6th PM, located in the County of Merrick, State of Nebraska."

Because so much urbanization has occurred in the past 100 years and subdivision of land has become common, property is often described by its particular lot number within a subdivision, the subdivision having been carefully surveyed and recorded with the city or county in which it is located. Figure 5.17 shows one such property.

In addition to the lot and subdivisions reference, a typical property description will include the bearings of the property lines and their lengths, along with any permanent corner markers set by the original subdivision surveyor. The property line bearings are referred to by the number of

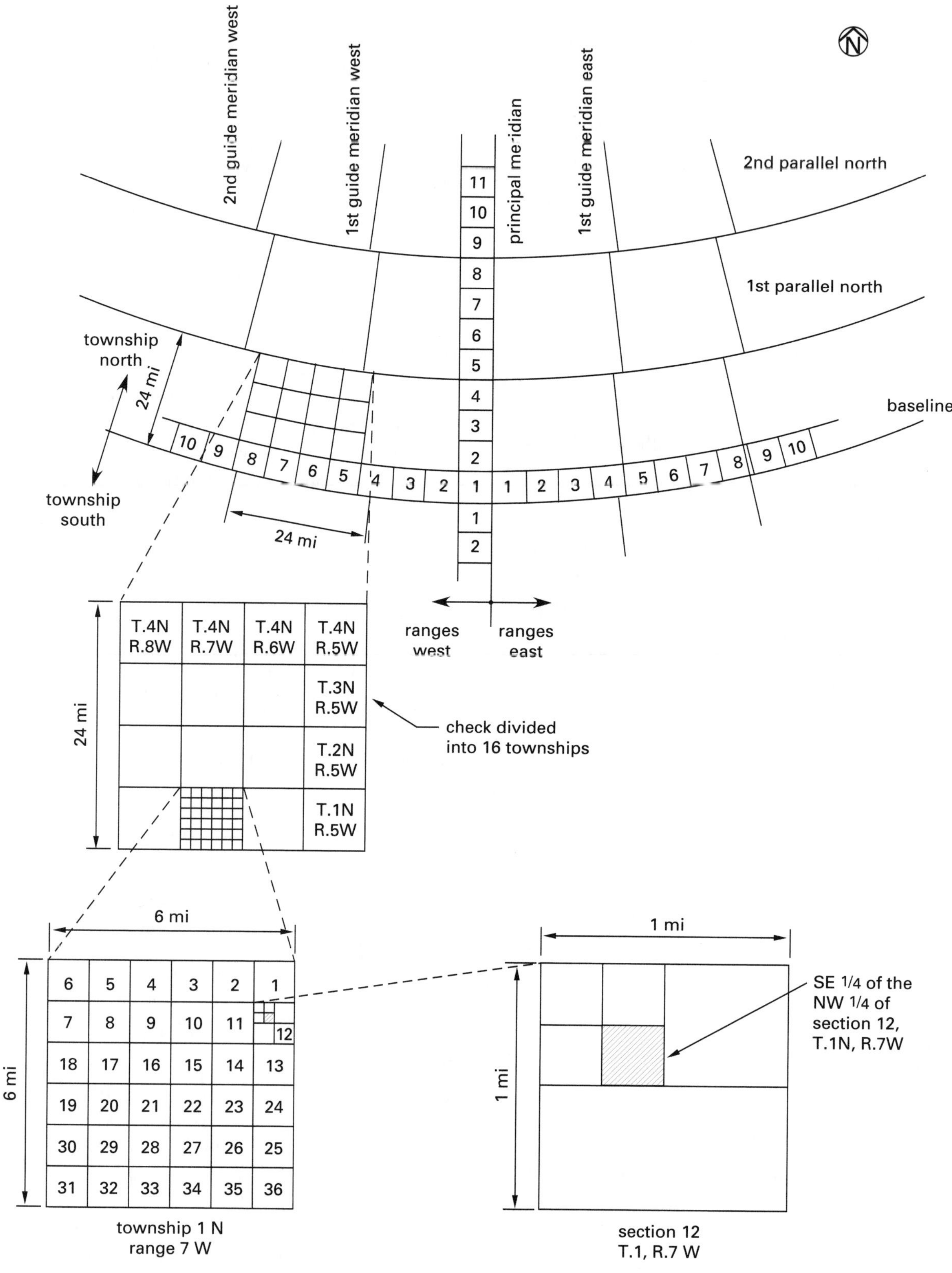

Figure 5.16 U.S. Survey System

BOUNDARY SURVEY
LOT 18, BLOCK 8, SCANLOCH SUBDIVISION GRAND COUNTY, COLORADO

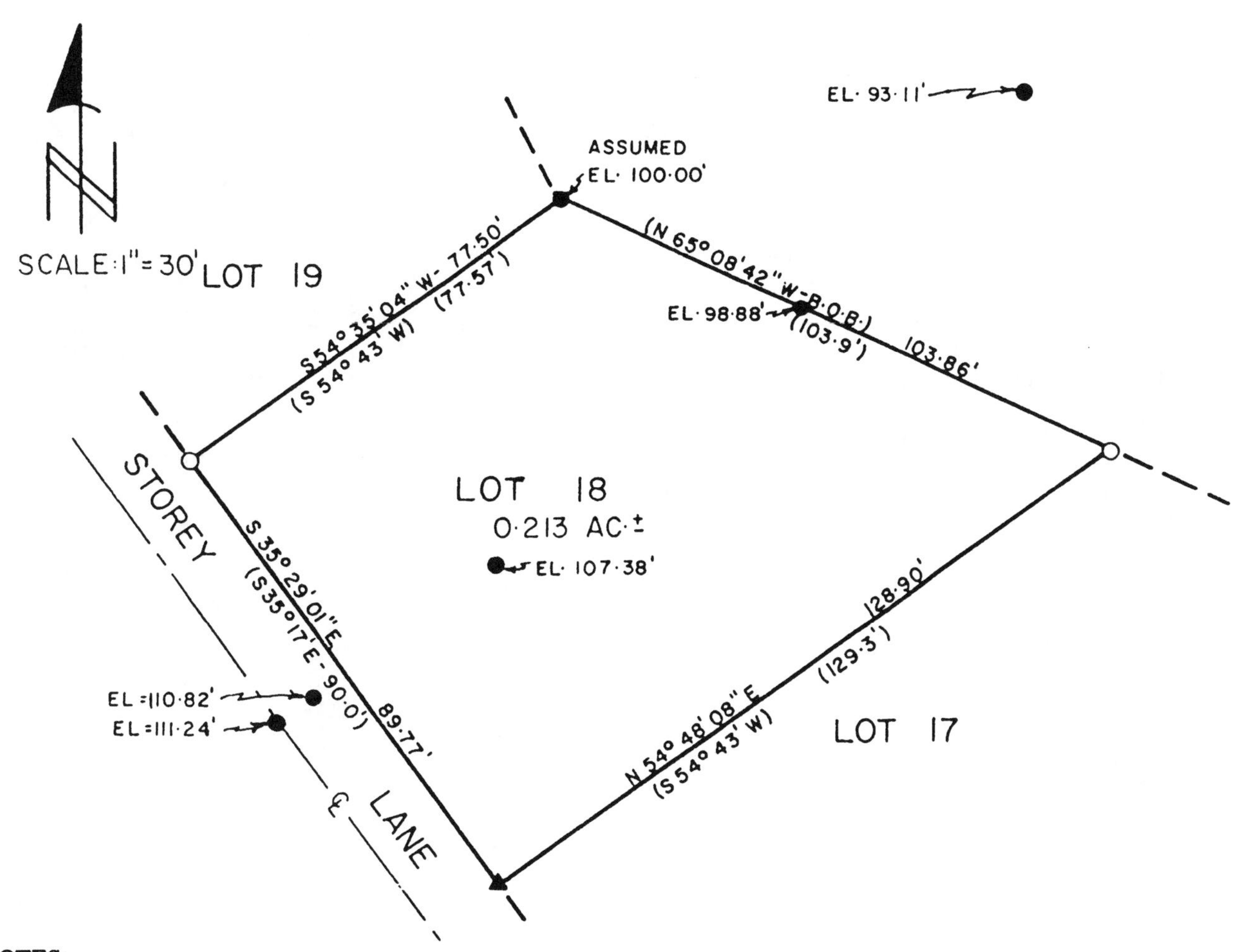

NOTES:

■ FOUND STANDARD BLM BRASS CAP MARKED AP—81 DATED 1950.

○ SET No. 4 REBAR WITH ALUMINUM CAP L. S. No. 11415.

▲ FOUND 1¼" IRON PIPE IN CONCRETE.

● CALCULATION POINT ONLY, NOTHING FOUND OR SET.

( ) BEARINGS AND DISTANCES AS PER RECORD PLAT RECEPTION No. 759621, GRAND COUNTY RECORDS, COLORADO. ALL OTHER BEARINGS AND DISTANCES ARE ACTUAL FIELD MEASUREMENTS.

B.O.B. THE BASIS OF BEARING FOR THIS SURVEY IS THE NORTHWESTERLY BOUNDARY LINE OF LOTS 17 & 18. SAID BEARING IS N65°08'42"W.

ELEVATIONS ARE ASSUMED FROM BRASS CAP NORTHEAST CORNER OF LOT 18 AP. 81—1950, ELEVATION = 100.00'.

Figure 5.17 Typical Boundary Survey Description

degrees, minutes, and seconds the line is located either east or west of a north-south line.

Another method that is sometimes used is the *metes and bounds description*. With this approach, the description is a lengthy narrative starting at one point of the property and describing the length and direction of each line around the property boundary until the point of beginning is reached.

With all types of property descriptions, the area of the parcel is also included, usually in acres (hectares), one acre containing 43,560 ft^2. Remember, too, that one section contains 640 ac, and one quarter of a quarter section contains 40 ac. A *hectare* (ha) is 10 000 m^2.

SITE ACOUSTICS

It can be useful to control site noise, both to make outdoor activities more pleasant and to reduce how much noise reaches the building interior. The architect has several design strategies available for improving site acoustics. Some are more effective than others. In general, mitigating unwanted noise is usually more successful than enhancing wanted sounds.

The most effective method of controlling site noise is the use of solid barriers. These can be either thin-wall barriers, such as of wood or concrete blocks, or earth berms. A barrier does not completely stop sound transmission; sound will travel over and around it through *diffraction*, which is the behavior of sound, light, or other waves when they encounter a barrier or pass through a small opening.

The effectiveness of a solid barrier depends on its height and position, the distance between the source and the receiver, and the frequency of the noise that the barrier is designed to block. These variables are illustrated in Fig. 5.18. When the values of these valuables are known, the reduction in noise in decibels (NR_{dB}) from a point source can be calculated with the Maekawa equation.

$$NR_{db} = 20 \log \frac{\sqrt{2\pi N}}{\tanh \sqrt{2\pi N}} + 5 \qquad 5.1$$

In this equation,

$$N = \left(\frac{f}{565}\right)(A + B - d) \qquad 5.2$$

f is the frequency of the sound (in hertz), d is the distance (in feet) of the acoustical line of sight from the source of the sound to the receiver, and $A + B$ is the length (in feet) of the shortest path around the barrier, as shown in Fig. 5.18. The Maekawa equation is empirically derived and units are not consistent.

As Eq. 5.1 and Fig. 5.18(a) indicate, the critical factor isn't the actual height of the barrier but the distance from the top of the barrier to the point where the acoustical line of sight intersects the barrier. On level ground this is usually not significant, but when the source or receiver is substantially above or below the other, the effective height can decrease. Figure 5.18(b) shows how the effective height changes when a barrier of the same overall height is located in two different positions. The Maekawa equation is for point sources; for a linear source such as a highway the noise reduction is about 20% to 25% less than that calculated by the equation.

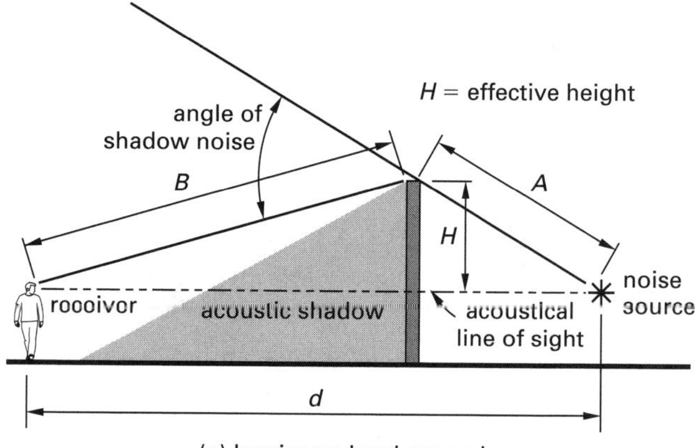

(a) barrier on level ground

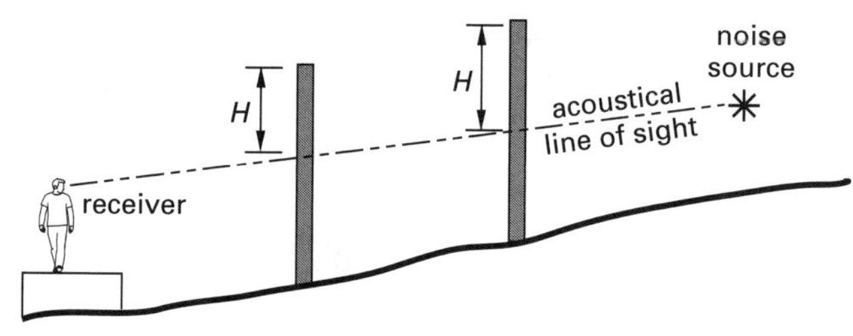

(b) barrier on sloped ground

Figure 5.18 Outdoor Sound Barriers

The following are some basic principles for designing outdoor sound barriers.

- Generally, solid barriers block high-frequency sounds better than low-frequency sounds. For high frequencies, the acoustic shadow shown in Fig. 5.18 is larger.
- The barrier is best placed as close as possible to either the source of the noise or the receiver.
- If the barrier is placed close to the noise source, it should be at least four times as high as the distance from the source to the barrier.
- The greater the effective height (the distance from the acoustic line of sight to the top of the barrier), the greater the attenuation. (See Fig. 5.18.)

- For blocking noise from a point source of noise, a short barrier should be at least four times as long as the distance from the barrier to the source or the distance from the barrier the receiver, whichever is shorter.
- A barrier should have a density of at least 5 lbm/ft^2 (25 kg/m^2) and be solid. However, greater densities than this do not increase sound attenuation significantly.

Here are some other actions that can be done to help control site noise.

- Maximize the distance between the source of the noise and the receiver. In free space, sound from a point source decreases by about 6 dB each time the distance it travels doubles. This is enough of a decrease to be noticeable but not significant; a decrease of 10 dB is needed for the noise to be perceived as half as loud. When the noise comes from a linear source, such as a highway, it will only decrease by about 3 dB for each doubling of the distance. Locating a building as far as possible from a source of loud noise, such as a busy street, can mitigate the noise that reaches the building; but on most urban and suburban sites, this will be difficult or impossible.
- Avoid hard surfaces near the source of noise. Hard surfaces reflect sound and help it travel.
- Avoid parallel hard surfaces, which can intensify the noise. Where possible, orient buildings, walls, and other hard surfaces at angles from one another.
- Use dense plantings of evergreen trees and shrubs as barriers between the noise source and the receiver. Plants have limited usefulness as sound barriers, and to be effective (a sound attenuation of around 10 dB or more) the depth must be around 100 ft (30 m) or greater. Planting is more useful when coupled with solid barriers or earth berms.
- Control sources of noise that are in or near the building. Locate mechanical equipment, service entrances, loading docks, and other noise sources away from usable outdoor spaces, building entrances, and any other areas where noise should be minimized.
- Make use of masking sounds. For example, the sound of a fountain or other source of running water in a usable outdoor space can mitigate noises at lower levels.
- Design building features to block noise. The overall shape of a building can be used to create isolated courtyards or block a source of noise. A solid balcony can block the path of a noise from outside before it strikes the glazing near the balcony. For glazing in critical areas, laminated glass can reduce how much noise penetrates the building.

Refer to Ch. 33 for more information on the basics of sound and controlling noise in buildings.

SITE SECURITY

Site security involves protecting a building or group of buildings from threats, which can range from common vandalism to intruders to vehicle-borne attacks.

Security systems for building interiors are discussed in Ch. 32. While some of these, such as microwave detectors and locking devices, can be used to protect the exterior of buildings, site security presents unique problems and design responses.

The first step in designing for site security is to define the risk and the level of protection needed. This must be done with the client, security experts, and, in the case of governmental clients, other governmental departments at the local, state, or federal level, as appropriate. As with building programming, this step determines the overall goals and objectives for site design and sets the direction of the design process with design concepts and defined constraints. Even while providing for the desired level of protection, provisions must be included for accessibility, sustainability, and usability. The visual impact of the security measures should be lessened so that the facility is sensitive to its neighborhood and does not take on the appearance of a fortress.

Design for site security can be accomplished by viewing the site at four different levels: perimeter protection, access and parking, on-site security, and building envelope protection.

Perimeter Protection

Perimeter protection is the first line of defense on a site. It is what discourages or prevents unauthorized people or vehicles, or both, from coming on the site or getting close to the building. For low-security sites, this may be as simple as a fence; for high-security buildings, it may include holding all unapproved vehicles at a required standoff distance from the building.

Fences are used more often to prevent individual intruders from entering than to keep vehicles out. They may be placed on the property line or, if enough land is available, they may be set back to lessen their visual impact. Fences are available in a variety of materials and designs and can provide a high level of security, especially if combined with camera surveillance, motion detectors, and other electronic devices. The use of solid fences should be carefully planned to maintain a clear field of view and avoid areas of concealment.

When unauthorized vehicles must be kept off the site or at a standoff distance from the building, there are various physical elements that can be used. These include walls, changes of elevation, bollards, dry moats, water features, landscaping, and hardened street furniture. These elements can be used in combination to lessen their visual impact, and combined with fences if individuals must also be prevented from entering the site. When a standoff distance is needed due to the threat of explosions, a blast analysis should be done by a competent expert to determine the distances needed from the building, building protection, and other aspects of the final building and site design.

Access and Parking

Authorized personnel, visitors, and vehicles must be allowed onto the site and into parking areas or drop-off areas. For low-security facilities, securing access may be accomplished by limiting the number of access points and by using card-controlled gates or guard stations, as well as by incorporating visual or camera surveillance of critical areas. When more protection than this is needed, these methods can be combined with guard booths, retractable bollards or other retractable devices, heavy-duty gates, or sally ports. A *sally port* is an entrance consisting of two secure gates or doors with a small area between them. The outer door or gate is opened to admit a person or vehicle into the sally port, and is then closed and secured while authorization is being checked. If the person or vehicle is cleared for entrance, the inner door or gate is opened to allow entrance to the facility. This arrangement makes it difficult for unauthorized people to gain entrance through force or by following closely behind someone authorized.

Parking lots, parking garages, loading docks, building entrances, and circulation routes on the site should be adequately illuminated, clearly signed to direct people to the proper areas, and monitored with personnel, cameras, or other electronic means as appropriate for the level of security needed.

On-Site Security

At some facilities, the outdoor area between the building (or buildings) and the site perimeter is used for other purposes than just access and parking, such as for gathering, eating lunch, recreation, public events, and landscaping. At these sites, amenities such as water fountains, pools, planters, low walls, kiosks, benches, and lighting poles can be hardened to provide protection from vehicle access without calling attention to their security purposes. Other site features like signage, landscaping, bicycle racks, and trash containers can add to the usefulness of the site while minimizing the visual impact of security measures. For sites that hold vehicles away but allow public pedestrian access up to the building, this aspect of security is especially important.

The design of the site for security should also take into account clear sight lines for supervisory personnel or cameras. Lighting must be included for both surveillance and normal safety during night hours. However, nighttime lighting must not contribute to light pollution of the neighborhood by being overused or improperly designed. Site design may also include provisions at the building entrance for queuing when entrance inspection is used.

Building Envelope Protection

The final layer of site security involves protecting the building itself and its occupants. If needed, materials may be used for the building envelope that are designed to prevent forced entry or damage by explosions. However, the need for such protection must be balanced by the need to avoid giving the building a forbidding, fortress-like look, especially if the owner wants the facility to appear open and inviting.

Exterior walls can be designed to withstand explosions and forced entry while disguising this function. Solid walls can be designed with textured surfaces, murals, water features, step-back, or decorative stone. Alternatively, the secure wall can be built as an inner wall set back from the perimeter of the building, with the visible exterior wall constructed of glass and with the space between them used for displays, waiting areas, or public use. When glass and doors are used, they can be designed, specified, and constructed to withstand forced entry and blasts.

Building entrances and egresses should be easy to use and accessible for building personnel as well as visitors. In some cases, entrances for authorized persons should be separated from visitor entrances. Egress for emergency evacuation must be adequately designed and clear space must be provided on the outside of the building for the dispersal of occupants.

Lighting and camera surveillance must be planned at the building line to provide the necessary coverage while being protected from weather and vandalism. Lighting is needed for surveillance whether by cameras or by security personnel, and is also needed for the general safety of the building occupants.

Depending on the level of threat, air intakes and HVAC equipment may need to be separated from access to the building, or otherwise protected to prevent the introduction of chemical or biological materials.

OTHER DESIGN CONSIDERATIONS

In addition to the factors already discussed, many other design considerations can influence the location, orientation, and configuration of a building, as well as other features of the site design. One of the most important is the context of the surrounding development. The design of a building should be sensitive to the scale, massing, and fenestration patterns of nearby buildings. The design should also consider any functional adjacency requirements with other structures or outdoor activities. For example, the entry to a student union building should be located near the existing, primary campus circulation routes.

Views are also an important consideration. Pleasant, desirable views can be used to advantage, as seen either from important spaces within the building or from outdoor spaces. Undesirable views can be avoided by planning the building so service spaces or less important spaces face them. Off-site sources of noise can be similarly avoided by minimizing windows near the noise source.

Quite frequently, buildings are located in order to fall on an important axis with surrounding structures or to complete the enclosure of a major outdoor space. The site-planning process should not overlook these kinds of symbolic criteria.

6 SOLVING THE SITE DESIGN VIGNETTE

The Site Design vignette requires the candidate to prepare a schematic site plan that is responsive to various programmatic, functional, orientation, and setback requirements provided in the program. A program is given along with a site plan, a conceptual building footprint for two (or possibly three) buildings, and other site factors. The candidate must understand how to site buildings, lay out parking spaces, accommodate pedestrian and vehicular circulation, and incorporate land utilization, views, existing conditions, prevailing winds, and other design considerations into the solution.

Because the problems vary from one exam to the next, to be prepared to solve any problem that may be presented, the candidate must know how to handle the following types of site design tasks.

- laying out parking
- organizing vehicular circulation
- providing for pedestrian circulation
- establishing the limits of construction (buildable area) based on setbacks, easements, rights-of-way, and other development restrictions
- planning for service and utility access to buildings
- utilizing vehicular ramps and pedestrian walkways
- satisfying criteria for accessibility, including ramps, parking, and accessible routes
- employing existing and new landscaping for energy conservation, visual barriers, and other programmatic requirements
- siting buildings and other site features to respond to climatic and programmatic influences
- relating new construction to existing design features of a building and site

TIPS FOR COMPLETING THE SITE DESIGN VIGNETTE

The following guidelines are intended primarily as a study aid for the Site Design vignette, but they are also useful to guide study for the multiple-choice portion of this division. The Site Design vignette is intended to be a short test of the candidate's ability to deal with a specific design task. Time constraint is usually not a problem.

Building Location and Orientation

- Make sure that no structure or site development other than landscaping occurs outside the limits of zoning setback lines or within easements unless the problem states otherwise. Typically, only drives and walks are allowed in these areas.
- Respect desirable views and incorporate them into the site plan. If views are a grading criterion, the problem statement will make specific mention of it. If so, be sure to comply.
- Orient the building entries as stated or implied in the program. If the program states that the entry requires shade, orient the entry toward the north; if the entry requires sun or is in a cold climate, orient it directly south. If there is a conflict with the entry orientation between climate and, for example, respecting a view, rotate the building slightly to try to get both. If a building must face south for some reason and must also be in the shade, use trees to provide the shade. Deciduous trees can be used for both shade and a view under the trees, if necessary.
- The problems usually require some major site feature other than a building or parking, such as a plaza or deck. Make sure that this feature is drawn to the correct size and positioned as required by the program. The size should be no more than 10%

larger or smaller than the program requires. A plaza may or may not be allowed as circulation to connect the other site elements. If it cannot be used for circulation, include a separate sidewalk. Be sure to read the problem to determine which is required.

- Never place a building within an easement. Also, try not to place parking lots over an easement if it can be avoided. However, unless the program prohibits it, parking lots may be located over easements without failing the problem.

Landscaping and Climate

When a vignette requires landscaping, it may call for the use of specific types of vegetation to solve the problem statement. Be familiar with the uses of deciduous trees, ornamental trees, evergreen trees, hedges, and shrubs and how these can be used for site design.

- Make every attempt to save existing trees and major vegetation. The problem usually states the maximum number of existing trees that can be removed. Do not exceed this number. Use the "check" tool to determine how many trees will be removed by the solution.
- Do not place more new trees than are necessary to meet the requirements of the problem.
- Use evergreen trees for wind control.
- Use deciduous trees for solar control in the summer and to allow solar heat gain on a building in the winter. If a view is required, deciduous trees can allow a view while providing shade.
- Use deciduous trees or ornamental trees in balanced, symmetrical patterns if the problem calls for a "formal" design.
- Hedges, shrubs, and ornamental trees can be used to direct pedestrian traffic.
- Use evergreen trees for year-round screening of loading docks, parking lots, and other service areas.
- New deciduous trees can overlap walks, parking, and plazas slightly. However, avoid placing evergreen trees so they overlap anything. Do not overlap trees themselves.
- If the problem mentions that safety is important, do not use dense landscaping close to the building or around walks. Deciduous trees provide for vegetation while allowing a clear view below the leaf canopy.
- If the problem says to assume a 45° solar altitude it means that a tree of a particular height will cast a shadow of the same length.

Vehicular Circulation and Parking

- Separate pedestrian circulation from vehicular circulation. Include walks next to parking lots whenever possible, to provide a path to the building. The problem statements are usually specific about pedestrian and vehicular circulation separation. It may be necessary only to show pedestrian access from the accessible parking to the pedestrian circulation system.
- Vehicular circulation may cross setbacks, but do not place roads within the setback if they are running parallel to the setback line.
- Know how many curb cuts are required or allowed. In most cases only one is allowed; do not show two unless required by the program.
- Plan the parking area for drive-through circulation. This is always a requirement of this vignette. Do not use dead-end parking.
- Although parking lot access and service drives may use the same entry from the street, once on the site, keep the two areas separate to avoid conflicts with cars and trucks. The program is very specific about what is required for parking and service drive separation; follow the requirements precisely. Conceal service areas from view as much as possible with vegetation or structures. The problem statement will generally give the option of using either vegetation or part of the building. For vegetation, use evergreen trees.
- Make sure the service drive connects to the service entrance of the building.
- Locate vehicular entries to the site away from intersections, because cars waiting for a stop sign or traffic light interfere with cars and trucks trying to pull into or out of the site. In most cases, the program will state a minimum distance from the driveway curb cut to the nearest intersection or some other existing site feature.
- If a driveway and a pedestrian path both need to enter a site from a street, they should be either side by side or separated by at least 60 ft (18 m), unless the problem states otherwise. See Fig. 6.1.
- 90° parking is the most efficient and is typically required by the problem statement. Most problems can be solved with this parking configuration. Double-loaded parking is generally the most efficient if the site constraints allow it. However, if single rows of parking are all that will fit, this is acceptable if the overall layout is efficient; that is, if it doesn't use up

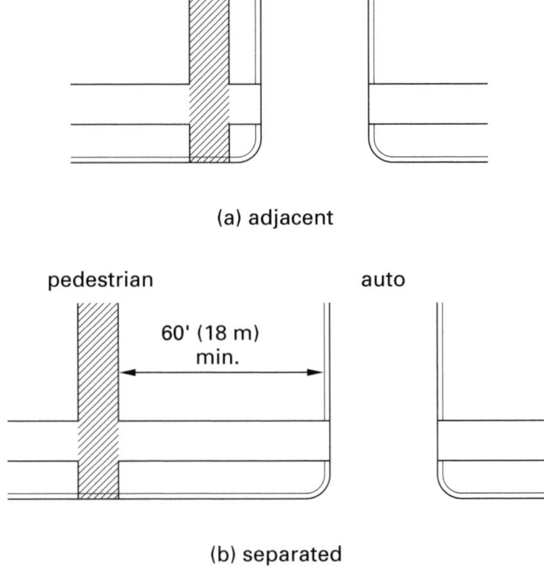

Figure 6.1 Preferred Locations of Automobile and Pedestrian Entries to Streets

too much of the site. The problem statement generally prohibits the use of angled or parallel parking.

- Do not locate drives or parking areas within the drip lines of trees. However, a minor overlap of a foot or so will probably not be enough to cause the solution to fail.
- Locate parking for the physically disabled near the main entry and in such a way that passengers do not have to cross traffic to get to the building. The program will usually state a maximum allowable distance from the accessible parking to an entrance or other site feature. This parking must be connected with walkways to the designated point.
- When starting initial planning, make liberal use of the sketch tools to define setbacks, curb cut limitations, and other restrictions. Sketch rectangles can also be drawn first, representing the rough size of the parking area, to determine if there will be any problems with existing trees, setbacks, or other restrictions.
- Use the *move group* tool to move a set of parking spaces.
- To connect one road or parking aisle to another, ensure that the dashed centerlines connect.
- Although the site elements can be drawn in any order, most candidates believe it is better to draw the parking first, then draw the roads. The parking areas can be adjusted later if necessary.

Pedestrian Circulation

- Unless otherwise required by the problem statement, use the *sidewalk* tool to create required walks. When connecting new walks to existing walks, click the tool in the center of the existing walk.
- Be sure to provide walks connecting various site features such as entrances to nearby buildings, public transportation stops, parking lots, play areas, and similar generators of pedestrian movement. The problems are usually very specific about these types of requirements, and the requirements must be satisfied.
- Pedestrian circulation may cross setbacks, but do not place walks within the setback if they are running parallel to the setback line.
- If a steep slope is part of the problem, avoid planning buildings, plazas, or parking in that area.

7 SOLVING THE SITE GRADING VIGNETTE

The Site Grading vignette tests the candidate's ability to manipulate site topography to achieve stated objectives. An existing site plan is given along with contours and a program, and the candidate must regrade the site to satisfy the requirements of the problem.

Because the problems vary from one exam to the next, to be prepared to solve any problem that may be presented, the candidate must know how to handle the following types of site grading tasks.

- manipulating contours, including minimizing (or balancing) cut and fill
- drawing contours based on spot elevations
- providing for site drainage around a constructed element

TIPS FOR COMPLETING THE SITE GRADING VIGNETTE

The following guidelines are intended primarily as a study aid for the Site Grading vignettes, but they are also useful to guide study for the multiple-choice portion of this division. The Site Grading vignette is intended to be a short test of the candidate's ability to deal with a specific design task. Time constraint is usually not a problem.

In order to pass the Site Planning & Design vignettes, the candidate must have a thorough knowledge of topography, how topograpy is represented with contour lines, and how to modify contour lines to develop drainage patterns and work around structures, parking lots, and driveways. The graphic techniques of representing topography with contour lines are shown in Fig. 5.1.

The following points are brief summaries of how contours are represented in the plan and what to remember when modifying contours.

- When contour lines represent a ridge, they "point" in the direction of the downslope as shown in section E-E of Fig. 5.1.
- When contour lines represent a valley, they "point" in the direction of the upslope as shown in section B-B of Fig. 5.1.
- Equally spaced contour lines represent a uniform slope as shown in section C-C of Fig. 5.1. Concave slopes have more closely spaced contour lines near the top of the slope. Convex slopes have more closely spaced contour lines near the bottom of the slope.
- Know how to read and indicate specific slope percentages with horizontal spacing of contour lines. The vignettes usually require that the new grading not exceed a certain percentage of slope. Percentages are based on a horizontal length of 100 ft (30 m), so a 10% slope means that the grade rises 10 ft (3 m) for every 100 ft (30 m). This example can also be reduced to a 1 ft (300 mm) rise for every 10 ft (3 m). In order to maintain a certain slope, determine the difference in elevation between contour lines shown on the site plan, and calculate how far apart contour lines must be to maintain the required slope. Then draw sketch circles of this diameter to make sure new contour lines are not drawn too close together.
- Slopes less than the maximum given in the problem statement are acceptable, but using the maximum slope allows more room for the manipulation of existing contour lines.

- Any modified contour lines on the site must match up with the contour lines at the property lines. Contour lines cannot be modified outside of the property line.
- Contour lines cannot be modified at existing vegetation, such as trees. Problem statements usually require that no contour modifications occur within the drip line of a tree (that area defined by the outside line of branches).
- Contour lines never cross. (The only exception to this is a set of contour lines representing a cave, and this will not occur on the exam.)
- One contour line never splits into two or more lines.
- Provide swales to divert water around the high sides of buildings or paved areas and away from the structure. This is one of the most common tasks on this vignette, and knowing how to do it is necessary to pass. As a guide for modifying contour lines, draw a series of sketch lines where a swale must be placed.
- Make sure water drains away from buildings or pads on all sides. This can be particularly troublesome when the building is located parallel to the contours and therefore perpendicular to the natural drainage pattern. One way of solving this problem is shown in Fig. 5.5.
- Avoid elaborate drainage patterns or systems of drainage ditches and channels. In most cases, the drainage for the site design vignettes can be accomplished directly.

Keep the following points in mind when developing contours in parking lots or on roadways and drives.

- Driveways and roads require that water be drained away from the crown, which means having a ridge in the center of the driveway or road.
- Driveways and roads should have a uniform slope, which means the contour lines must be equally spaced.
- Parking lots should also have a uniform slope and direct the water away from the center or to a collection point. Three ways of handling this are shown in Fig. 5.15.

SECTION 4: SCHEMATIC DESIGN

Chapter 8: Solving the Building Layout Vignette
Chapter 9: Solving the Interior Layout Vignette

8 SOLVING THE BUILDING LAYOUT VIGNETTE

The Building Layout vignette tests the candidate's ability to resolve program requirements, within the context of a given site plan and code requirements, into a small building. The candidate is given a site plan, a listing of the required spaces along with their required sizes and adjacencies, and generic code requirements. The problem usually consists of from 15 to 20 programmed spaces covering from approximately 6000 ft^2 to 10,000 ft^2 (560 m^2 to 930 m^2), not including circulation. A two-story solution is required, with two exit stairs, an elevator, and one first-floor space that extends above the second-floor line.

The Building Layout vignette is difficult because it asks the candidate to integrate many program requirements into a single solution, and to accomplish this within a four-hour period. This vignette tests the candidate's

- ability to locate parts of a building in relation to site elements (access, views, windows, etc.)
- ability to logically locate spaces on two floors of a building
- ability to lay out spaces to satisfy adjacency requirements and other program restrictions
- skill at organizing a building with a logical circulation plan
- knowledge of reasonable shapes for spaces
- ability to satisfy basic building code requirements related to exiting, including locations of exits, number of exits, separation of doors within a large room, direction of door swing, exit width, use of intervening rooms, vertical exit locations, and similar basic exiting requirements
- skill at keeping the areas of rooms within 10% of the programmed area
- skill at maintaining a reasonable ratio of circulation space to programmed space (25% maximum)
- ability to coordinate the upper-story perimeter walls with the first-floor perimeter walls
- ability to coordinate a two-story-high space with other spaces in the building

TIPS FOR COMPLETING THE BUILDING LAYOUT VIGNETTE

The computerized ARE requires an approach to solving the various graphic vignettes that is somewhat different from using pencil and paper. Download the sample program and vignettes from the NCARB website to use for practice before the test. This is the best way to get comfortable with using the computer to solve the problems.

This vignette is another of the difficult sections of the exam because of the number of spaces that must be planned and the coordination required between the first and second floors. Problems with completing the vignette in the allotted time can be minimized by using the following procedure.

Suggested Procedure for Solving the Building Layout Vignette

1. Read and understand the requirements of the problem and the building program. Although it is possible to switch back and forth between the program and the drawing screen, it may be easier to make notes that translate the written requirements into a graphic form for quick reference. Scratch paper is available from the proctor for this purpose, but it must be turned in at the conclusion of the exam.
2. Note the major site constraints that will influence the location of certain building spaces. These are usually

fairly simple and few in number, so a quick sketch can be made, like that shown in Fig. 8.1. Similar notations can be made on screen with the sketch tools. The only problem is that sketch lines do not allow the placement of text or graphic symbols. The advantage of a paper sketch is that it can be placed beside the computer for quick, constant reference.

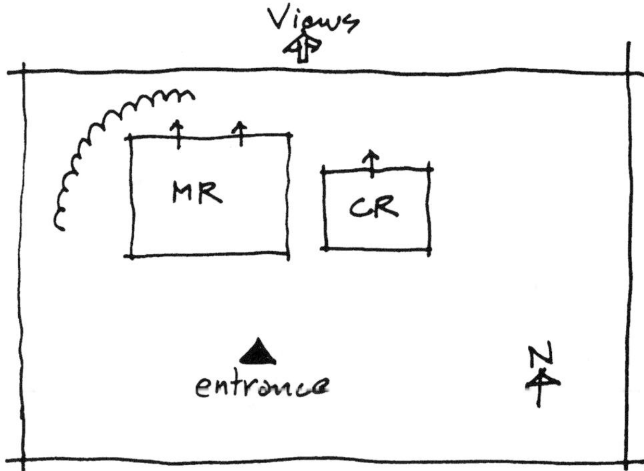

Figure 8.1 Site Constraints Notes

3. Read the program, and sketch bubble diagrams or block diagrams of groups of spaces that the program requires to be adjacent. These groupings will reduce the number of elements that have to be dealt with when planning starts, and they reduce the risk of not satisfying basic program requirements. See Fig. 8.2. Alternately, draw the spaces on the screen to their required sizes and group them, but at this early stage the best position for each space relative to the others may not be known. A quick paper sketch fixes the relationships without forcing a specific shape or configuration. Keep this sketch beside the computer for reference.

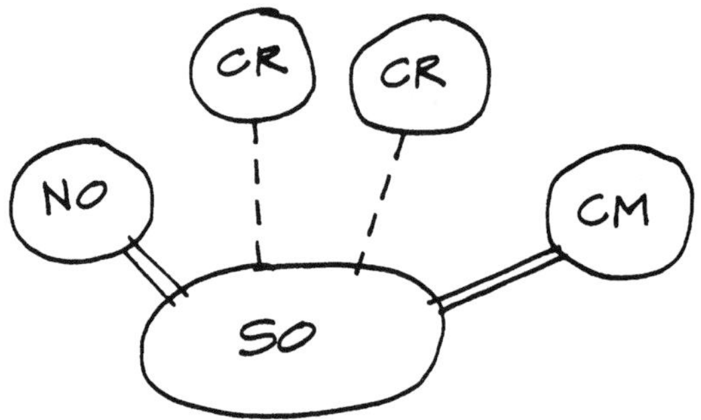

Figure 8.2 Space Groupings

4. Make a scratch paper list of which spaces must or should be on each floor. The program gives some of the specific floor location requirements; other requirements have to be logically inferred from the problem statement and the types of spaces. For example, the problem may state that one room must be on the second floor. If other rooms must be near that room, they too should be on the second floor.

5. Before starting to draw, turn on the grid and verify the spacing. It is usually best to use a grid for organization from the start, so lining up first- and second-story walls is easier as the design is refined. Working with a 5 ft (1 m) grid is helpful.

6. As drawing begins, start with the first floor, making sure the correct layer is selected. First, place the spaces that have specific site relationships stated in the program. For example, if a dining room must have a view to the west, make sure the dining room is placed on the extreme west portion of the site. The quick paper sketch can serve as a reminder not to move this space elsewhere as planning progresses.

7. In most cases, the first-floor spaces that have specific site relationships also have required adjacencies with a few other spaces. Draw these second, to the size required in the program and in a reasonable rectangular shape. Refer to the paper sketches for a quick reference to the required adjacencies. The problem always has one large, two-story-high space. Try to locate this at a corner of the building so the second floor does not have to be planned around it. After these spaces have been located, a suggested layout for the entire building should be obvious.

8. Third, draw the remaining first-floor spaces. Many of these are rooms that do not have a specific adjacency requirement and can be located anywhere. Examples of these types of spaces include mechanical rooms, toilet rooms, and storerooms. The elevator should be located centrally and near the main entrance to the building, although the elevator can be located anywhere along the corridor.

9. Finally, arrange all the first-floor rooms so they are connected with a logical circulation plan that satisfies exiting requirements. A simple, efficient circulation scheme should be a primary concern. One of the common mistakes candidates make is to work on adjacencies and locations of spaces and then string them together with a resulting maze of corridors, stairways, and lobbies. In most cases, a building of the size and complexity usually given in this vignette can be designed with a simple, straight, double-loaded corridor circulation system with stairs at each end, with the main entrance near one of the stairs or somewhere in

the middle of the corridor system. See Fig. 8.3. In the most complex case there may need to be one turn in the corridor, but more than one turn should not be necessary. Make sure that areas required to have a specific site relationship have not moved during planning. If the site happens to be basically square in shape, a double-loaded, T-shaped corridor system may be appropriate, but this is seldom the case.

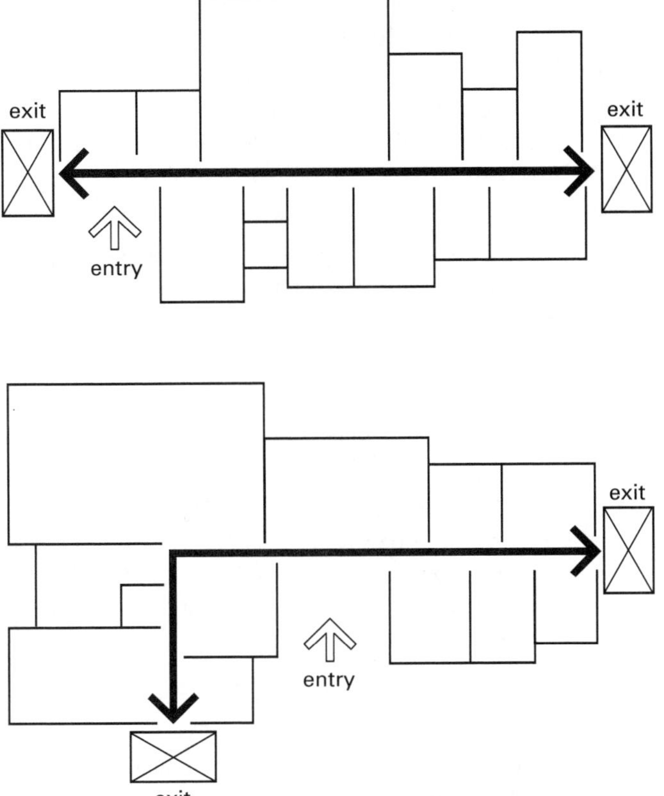

Figure 8.3 Organizing Concepts

One useful idea is to plan spaces in a modular fashion perpendicular to the corridor using a 5 ft (1 m) grid and then adjust the depth of each room or space to meet the requirements of the program. Remember, the outline of the building does not have to be regular or aligned neatly.

10. Before the spaces on the first floor become too fixed, switch layers to the second floor (with the first floor layer still turned on), and draw the required spaces. Use the list developed earlier in the process, or work directly from the program. First locate the spaces that must be directly above first-floor areas, like the stairs, the elevator, and the upper portion of the two-story space. It is helpful to stack the toilet rooms because they are the same size, but it is not critical to do so.

11. Second, using the program sketches, locate the other second-floor spaces, noting the locations of perimeter walls on the first floor. Use the corridor as the major organizing element. The exterior walls of second-floor spaces can be aligned with or inside the first-floor walls but cannot project over the first-floor walls except to provide recessed first-floor exterior doors with weather protection.

    If possible, try to plan all the spaces (with the possible exception of the corridors, janitors' rooms, elevator, and elevator equipment room) so they have at least one, and ideally two, exterior exposures. This way, when making minor adjustments in size, the exterior wall can be moved in or out to satisfy the program requirements without affecting adjacent rooms.

12. After the adjacency requirements on the second floor are satisfied and there is a reasonable layout that works with the first floor, start fine-tuning both floors to get the correct floor areas, and make sure the walls of adjacent rooms are aligned. Use the "zoom" tool to complete these tasks. Remember that the computer requires walls to align perfectly so the solution can be graded accurately. As walls are moved over others, the walls between spaces change color temporarily when properly aligned. If possible, try to maintain rectangular-shaped rooms. One or two may have to be reshaped to L-shaped spaces. Limit L-shaped rooms to secondary spaces like storerooms. Maintain reasonable shapes and minimal dimensions.

13. Once all the spaces and rooms are positioned correctly, draw in the doors and, where required by the program, the windows. If the doors and windows are drawn before the walls are adjusted, the openings may disappear and will have to be drawn again. Only draw windows if they are specifically called for in the problem statement. Make sure exit doors swing in the direction of travel. Also be sure that large spaces requiring two doors show the correct number of doors and are separated by the distance stated in the code information portion of the problem.

Checklist for Final Design Solution

The primary checklist for the design should be the problem statement itself. When finished with the layout, switch to the program screen and examine each requirement to make sure it has been satisfied.

Following is a list of some of the critical elements that should be included or considered in the final solution.

1. Program requirements and design logic
   - The solution contains all the required spaces.
   - Required spaces contain the correct amount of space, not varying by more than 10%.
   - Required adjacencies are satisfied.
   - Exterior adjacencies (e.g., entry location and view direction) are satisfied.
   - Spaces are the correct shape and proportion for the intended function.
   - Circulation is efficient, direct, and properly sized so that it does not exceed 25% of the programmed area. Corridors are labeled with "CO."
   - The elevator is centrally located and easily accessible to all users.
   - All major spaces and those required by the program have exterior exposure.
2. Code compliance
   - For each floor and large room required to have two exits, these are separated by at least one-half the diagonal distance of the building or room in which they are located.
   - Second-level egress is provided directly to the outside by the stairways or as required by the program statement.
   - Every room except the elevator equipment room connects to a corridor.
   - All exit doors swing in the direction of travel, and no door decreases the required exit width by more than the amount stated in the program.
   - Widths of exits, both corridors and stairs, are as required by the program. For example, if the program requires a 200 ft^2 (19 m^2) stair block and the code requirements state that stairs must be at least 4 ft (1220 mm) wide, draw a block at least 9 ft (2740 mm) or 10 ft (3050 mm) wide for easy area calculation.

Additional Tips and Suggestions for the Building Layout Vignette

- Draw corridors 6 ft (1800 mm) wide. Do not make them wider unless the program requires it. It is important to understand that, as spaces are drawn, the dimensions shown at the bottom of the screen are from wall centerline to wall centerline, while minimum corridor widths are graded from one edge of the corridor to the other. Measure this width, or use sketch circles to maintain the minimum required corridor width.
- "Direct access" means that one room or space must be directly adjacent to another room or space and that there must be a door or opening between the two.
- "Near" means that the doors to two rooms or spaces should be as close to each other as possible and not more than 15 ft (5 m) apart.
- Avoid using dead-end corridors. If dead-end corridors must be used, they cannot exceed 20 ft (6 m), but this dimension should be measured from the end of the corridor to 1 ft (600 mm) into the main corridor.
- Ensure that open spaces, such as entry lobbies or waiting rooms, do not exceed the 20 ft (6 m) dead-end corridor limit, because they are part of the circulation space.
- Rooms do not have to comply with the 20 ft (6 m) dead-end limit.
- Make sure that walls of adjacent circulation areas are opened with the "wall opening" tool or with doors. Wall openings can only be drawn between corridors or other circulation areas.
- Do not draw recessed alcoves for exit doors. Although an L-shaped room can be drawn to accommodate one recessed door, it is easier to draw rectangular rooms. The code information allows the doors to swing into one-half the width of the corridor.
- Limit stairs to a simple rectangle shape, approximately 10 ft by 20 ft (3 m by 6 m). L-shaped stairs cannot be drawn with the software.
- Avoid L-shaped rooms, if possible. If they must be used, use them only for storage rooms or secondary spaces.

- Carefully read the portions of the program concerning large spaces that require two exits. In most cases the code information will require that one exit discharge into the corridor and the other discharge directly to the outside. However, the program may require that both discharge into the corridor.
- When two doors from a room are required and the minimum separation between them is given as one-half the diagonal distance of the room, measure the distance between the doors from the center of one door to the center of the other door.
- Only exit doors need to swing in the direction of travel. These include the main floor entry door, the second main floor exit door, doors opening into the stairways, and the doors in large spaces when the program specifically states that two exits from the room are required.
- Show windows only when required. Do not worry about any minimum or maximum sizes for windows unless otherwise stated in the program.
- Group rooms, doors, and windows before moving a space, or the openings will disappear and have to be redrawn.
- Use the "open to below" tool to indicate the upper portion of a two-story space on a second floor. This space must be labeled with "OB."
- Toilet rooms do not necessarily have to be stacked vertically, and noncritical interior walls do not have to align on the two floors. However, spaces such as stairways, elevators, or an area on a second floor open to a large space with a high ceiling on the first floor must align.
- An elevator equipment room may be accessed from a corridor or a mechanical room. The elevator equipment room should be adjacent to the elevator, if possible. It may be located away from the elevator slightly, but if this is the case, the solution will be downgraded.
- It is not necessary to draw doors or wall openings in elevator walls.
- Keep mechanical rooms on the first floor unless the program states differently.
- The exit doors from a building may swing over the building limit line, if necessary.
- Do not add extra exterior doors that are not specifically required by the program.
- Exterior doors that are not exit doors but that are required for service (such as a kitchen service door) may open either in or out.
- If an outdoor space is required, do not cover it with a portion of the second floor.

9 SOLVING THE INTERIOR LAYOUT VIGNETTE

The Interior Layout vignette tests the candidate's ability to plan a small interior space—including furniture, room arrangement, wall locations, and doors—while satisfying program requirements and accessibility codes. The candidate is given a base plan showing the perimeter of the space, the location of the entry door, and a program, which includes the furniture required in each space. The problem requires that the candidate plan the layout of four to six spaces (usually five) within an area from approximately 1000 ft^2 to 1500 ft^2 (93 m^2 to 140 m^2). The required adjacencies and access between spaces are given, along with view and code requirements.

TIPS FOR COMPLETING THE INTERIOR LAYOUT VIGNETTE

The computerized ARE requires an approach to solving the various graphic vignettes that is somewhat different from using pencil and paper. Download the sample program and vignettes to use for practice before the test. This is the best way to get comfortable with using the computer to solve the problems.

The Interior Layout vignette is often one of the more difficult vignettes for candidates because time is limited, there are many pieces of furniture to include while maintaining accessibility, and many candidates have less experience with interior space planning than with other skills covered by the exam.

This vignette typically includes an open reception area next to the entry door, two or three private offices, a conference room, and sometimes a workroom or storage room. Generally, at least two of the spaces require an outside view (i.e., must be placed next to the windows), and two of the enclosed spaces must have direct access to each other (i.e., a doorway between them).

To solve this vignette, first estimate how large each enclosed room needs to be. Determine which rooms must be next to windows and which need to be adjacent. All of them will have to open onto the reception area or main open space. Either use the sketch paper given at the test center or use the sketch tools to draw single lines representing the approximate locations of walls. As part of a study routine before the exam, it is helpful to sketch offices and conference rooms with various types of furniture and accessibility clearances that might be on the exam, to get a feeling for about how large various rooms must be.

Because there are so few spaces and the required adjacencies and views are very explicit, the problem should almost solve itself. If the first layout doesn't work because some rooms become too narrow or the reception area is awkwardly shaped, it is easy to quickly try another scheme using the single-line approach. In most cases, if the space plan has simple rectangular or L-shaped spaces, it should be workable. There should not be any corridors.

Once a preliminary layout of walls is established, place the required furniture in each room. Zoom in as needed to accurately place the furniture, allowing for required clearances. Use sketch circles of 60 in (1525 mm) and 36 in (915 mm) as needed to check accessibility clearances. Adjust the preliminary positions of walls as necessary. However, try to keep walls aligned and the overall configuration of the walls straightforward (with few jogs or offsets, unless absolutely necessary). Place doors so they swing against walls and such that the latch jambs meet the required clearances (both push and pull sides). Placing doors in the corners of rooms, opening against the walls, is the most efficient method, if it can be done.

Code Issues Tested in the Interior Layout Vignette

The only code issues tested in this vignette are those related to accessible design. However, satisfying these codes is critical to receiving a passing score. Specifically, as listed in the problem statement, these codes include the following.

- A 60 in (1525 mm) diameter turning circle space for every room and space.
- A minimum 32 in (815 mm) clearance for doors (use a 36 in [915 mm] door in all cases).
- A 36 in (915 mm) clearance between walls and any other obstruction or piece of furniture along an aisle, corridor, or passageway.
- Maneuvering clearances on both the push and pull sides of doors according to the diagram given with the problem statement. This includes an 18 in (455 mm) distance between the latch jamb and any obstruction on the pull side of a door and a minimum 12 in (305 mm) distance between the latch jamb and any obstruction on the push side of a door. It also includes minimum distances perpendicular to the door opening. These particular requirements are often forgotten in the rush to complete the vignette, but they must be met if the candidate is to receive a passing score.

Additional Tips and Suggestions for the Interior Layout Vignette

- "Direct access" in the program statement means that there must be a door between one room and another. "Immediate access" means that two spaces or rooms must be close to each other.
- Try to put as much furniture against walls as possible. This simplifies planning and minimizes problems with providing the required access behind furniture.
- Providing less than 36 in (915 mm) clearance between the back of a secretarial chair or an executive chair and a wall is probably acceptable as long as there is not a credenza, bookcase, or other piece of furniture behind the chair. However, try to maintain 36 in (915 mm) in all cases, if possible.
- In the entry or reception area, make sure the workstations or desks face the door, for visual control.
- Make sure there is a minimum 36 in (915 mm) clearance in front of bookcases, files, credenzas, and other furniture or obstructions. Maintain a 60 in (1525 mm) clearance in front of worktables and copy machines.
- Make sure there is a minimum 36 in (915 mm) clearance between the backs of all chairs around a conference table and the walls or other obstructions or furniture.
- Provide a 36 in (915 mm) clearance in front of all desks. If there is a guest chair in front of a desk, try to place the back of the chair against a wall; otherwise, a 36 in (915 mm) clearance behind guest chairs is required.
- Provide a minimum distance of 24 in (600 mm) between the front of a desk and the front of a guest chair; 36 in (915 mm) is better.
- When a door is in the open position, make sure the full 60 in (1525 mm) clear space exists, perpendicular to the door opening. It is easy to inadvertently place a bookcase or other piece of furniture too close to the edge of a door that is in the open position.
- Do not let two door swings overlap.

SECTION 5: STRUCTURAL SYSTEMS

Chapter 10: Selection of Structural Systems

Chapter 11: Loads on Buildings

Chapter 12: Structural Fundamentals

Chapter 13: Beams and Columns

Chapter 14: Trusses

Chapter 15: Soil and Foundations

Chapter 16: Connections

Chapter 17: Building Code Requirements on Structural Design

Chapter 18: Wood Construction

Chapter 19: Steel Construction

Chapter 20: Concrete Construction

Chapter 21: Wall Construction

Chapter 22: Lateral Forces—Wind

Chapter 23: Lateral Forces—Earthquakes

Chapter 24: Long Span Structures—One-Way Systems

Chapter 25: Long Span Structures—Two-Way Systems

Chapter 26: Solving the Structural Layout Vignette

10 SELECTION OF STRUCTURAL SYSTEMS

This chapter provides a broad overview of many of the common structural systems and materials used in contemporary construction. Its purpose is to present some of the primary characteristics of structural systems and to review some of the most important criteria for their selection. For more detailed information on specific structural materials and calculation methods, refer to later chapters in this manual.

STANDARD STRUCTURAL SYSTEMS

Wood

Wood is one of the oldest and most common structural materials. It is plentiful, inexpensive, relatively strong in both compression and tension, and easy to work with and fasten. Wood is used primarily in *one-way structural systems*, where the load is transmitted through structural members in one direction at a time.

Joists are a common use of wood. They are light, closely spaced members that span between beams or bearing walls. Typical sizes are 2 × 6, 2 × 8, 2 × 10, and 2 × 12. Typical spacings are 12 in, 16 in, and 24 in on center. The typical maximum normal span is about 20 ft, but spans up to 25 ft are often used.

The space between joists is usually spanned with plywood, particleboard, or oriented strand board subflooring on which underlayment is placed in preparation for finish flooring. Sometimes, a single sheet of $^3/_4$ in subfloor/underlayment is used, although it is not as desirable. Because joists are slender, they must be laterally supported to avoid twisting or lateral displacement. The top edge is held in place by sheathing, but bridging must be used to support the bottom edge. Maximum intervals of no more than 8 ft are recommended. Either solid or cross bridging may be used. See Fig. 10.1(a).

Solid wood beams are still used to a limited degree, but their standard sizes have changed. The availability of solid beams with large cross-sectional areas in suitable lengths is limited, especially in grades that provide the desired strength. Solid wood beams for longer spans have generally been replaced with glued-laminated construction.

The most common use of solid wood beams is with *plank-and-beam framing* in which members of a 4 in or 6 in nominal width span between girders or bearing walls at spacings of 4, 6, or 8 ft. Wood decking, either solid or laminated, is used to span between the beams, with the underside of the decking being the finished ceiling. The normal maximum span for the beams in this system is about 10 ft to 20 ft. See Fig. 10.1(b).

Glued-laminated construction (glulam) is a popular method of wood construction. These structural members are made up of individual pieces of lumber $^3/_4$ in or $1^1/_2$ in thick, glued together in the factory. Standard widths are $3^1/_8$, $5^1/_8$, $6^3/_4$, and $8^3/_4$ in. Larger widths are available. Typical spans for glulam construction range from 15 ft to 60 ft.

One of the advantages of glulam construction is appearance. Structural members are usually left exposed as part of the architectural expression of the structure on the interior. In addition, glulam members can be manufactured in tapered beams, tapered and curved beams, and various types of arches.

In an effort to employ the many structural advantages of wood and increase utilization of forest products while minimizing the problems of defects and limited strength in solid wood members, several manufactured products have been developed.

One is a *lightweight I-shaped joist* consisting of a top and bottom chord of solid or laminated construction separated by a plywood or oriented strand board web. See Fig. 10.1(c). This type of joist is used in residential and light commercial

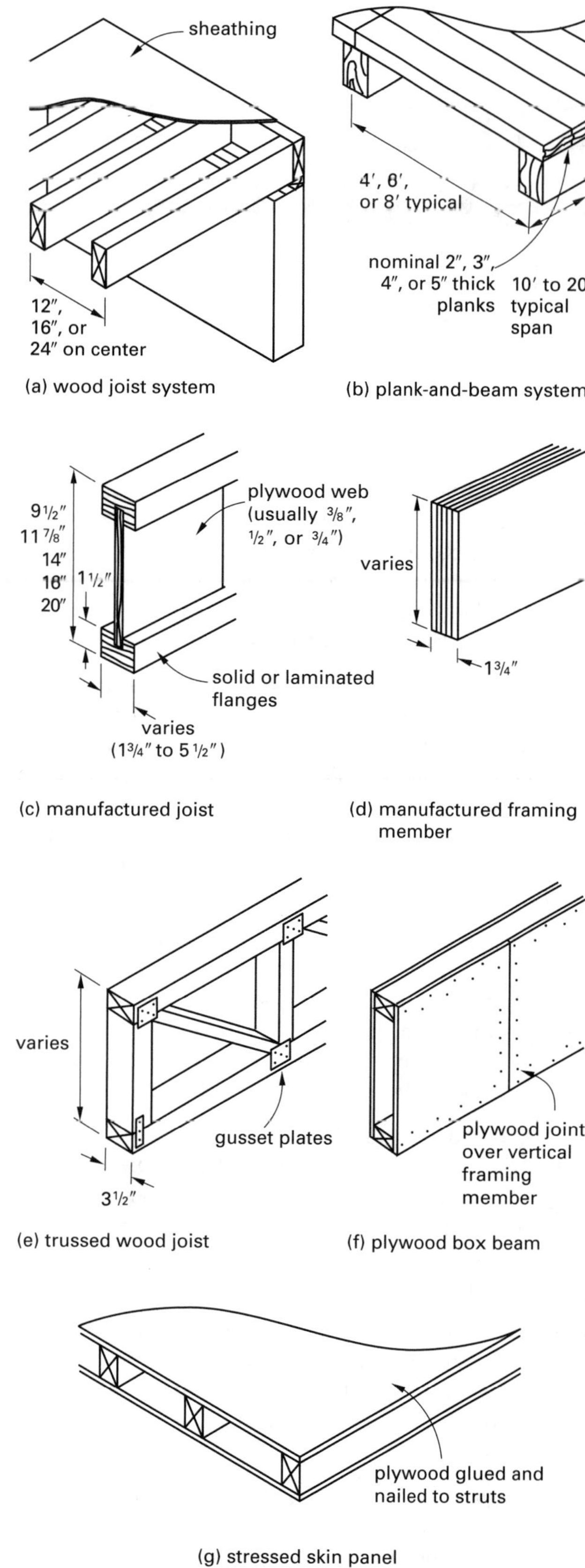

Figure 10.1 Wood Structural Systems

construction and allows longer spans than are possible with a joist system. It has a very efficient structural shape, like a steel wide flange, and because it is manufactured in a factory, problems such as warping, splits, checks, and other common wood defects are eliminated. This type of product is stronger and stiffer than a standard wood joist.

Another manufactured product is a wood member manufactured with individual layers of thin veneer glued together. See Fig. 10.1(d). It is used primarily for headers over large openings, and singly or built-up for beams. It has a higher modulus of elasticity than a standard wood joist, and its allowable stress in bending is about twice that of a Douglas-fir joist.

A third type of manufactured product is a *truss* made up of standard sized wood members connected with metal plates. See Fig. 10.1(e). Typical spans range from about 24 ft to 40 ft, and typical depths are from 12 in to 36 in. A common spacing is 24 in on center. These types of trusses are useful for residential and light commercial construction and allow easy passage of mechanical ductwork through the truss.

Two other types of wood structural members are possible, but their use is infrequent because of other product availability and the difficulty in constructing them properly since they are usually site-fabricated. One is the *box beam,* fabricated with plywood panels glued and nailed to solid wood members, usually 2 × 4 framing. See Fig. 10.1(f). Box beams are often used in locations where the depth of the member is not critical and where other types of manufactured beams cannot be brought to the building site. *Stressed skin panels* (see Fig. 10.1(g)) are the other type of built-up wood product. Like box beams, they are constructed of plywood glued and nailed to solid 2 in nominal thickness lumber and are used for floor, roof, or wall construction.

Steel

Steel is one of the most commonly used structural materials because of its high strength, availability, and ability to adapt to a wide variety of structural conditions. It is also a ductile material, which simply means that it can tolerate some deformation and return to its original shape and that it will bend before it breaks, giving warning before total collapse. Steel is particularly suited for multifloor construction because of its strength and structural continuity.

Two of the most common steel structural systems are the *beam-and-girder system* and the *open-web steel joist system.* See Fig. 10.2(a) and 10.2(b). In the beam-and-girder system, large members span between vertical supports, and smaller beams are framed into them.

The girders span the shorter distances while the beams span the longer distances. Typical spans for this system are from

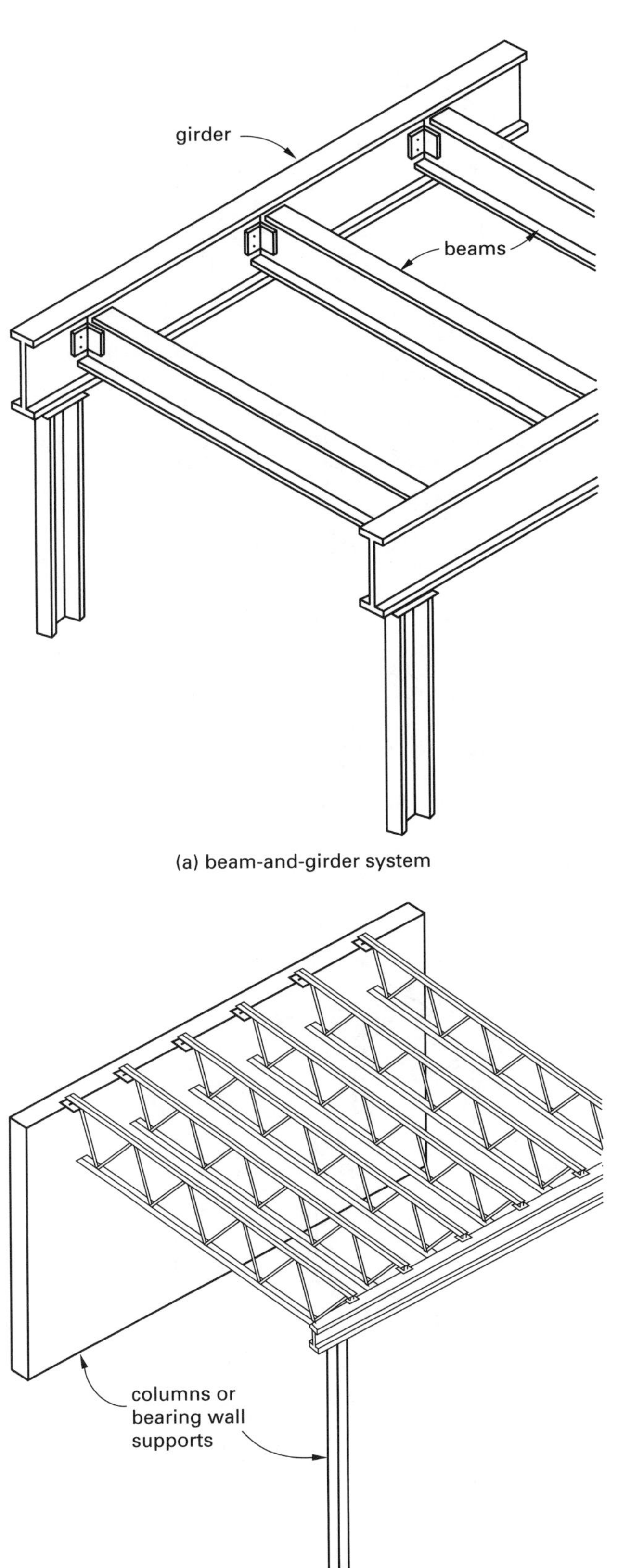

Figure 10.2 Common Steel Structural Systems

25 ft to 40 ft with the beams being spaced about 8 ft to 10 ft on center. The steel framing is usually covered with steel decking that spans between the beams. A concrete topping is then poured over the decking to complete the floor slab.

Open-web steel joists span between beams or bearing walls as shown in Fig. 10.2(b). Standard open-web joists can span up to 60 ft. Long-span joists can span up to 96 ft, and deep long-span joists are capable of spanning up to 144 ft. Depths of standard joists range from 8 in to 30 in, in increments of 2 in. Long-span joist depths range from 18 in to 72 in. Floor joists are typically placed 2 ft to 4 ft on center, while roof joists are usually placed 4 ft to 6 ft on center. Open-web steel joists used in floor construction are usually spanned with steel decking over which a concrete topping is poured. Sometimes wood decking is used, but with closer joist spacings.

Open-web steel joists are efficient structural members and are well-suited for low-rise construction where overall depth of the floor/ceiling system is not critical. They can span long distances and have a combustible construction. Because the webs are open, mechanical and electrical service pipes and ducts can easily be run between the web members.

Concrete

There are many variations of concrete structural systems, but the two primary types are *cast-in-place* and *precast*. Cast-in-place structures require formwork and generally take longer to build than precast buildings, but they can conform to an almost unlimited variety of shapes, sizes, design intentions, and structural requirements. Precast components are usually formed in a plant under strictly controlled conditions so quality control is better and erection proceeds quickly, especially if the structure is composed of numerous repetitive members.

The majority of cast-in-place concrete systems utilize only mild steel reinforcing, but in some instances post-tensioning steel is used. Precast concrete systems, on the other hand, are usually prestressed, although sometimes only mild reinforcing steel is used.

Sometimes concrete is precast on the site, but this is usually limited to wall panels (normally referred to as *tilt-up panels*) of moderate size. Lift-slab construction is still used as well. In this procedure, floor slabs of a multistory building are cast one on top of the next on the ground around the columns and then jacked into place and attached to the columns.

Cast-in-place concrete structural systems can be classified into two general types, depending on how the floors are analyzed: *one-way systems* and *two-way systems*. In one-way systems the slabs and beams are designed to transfer loads in one direction only. For example, a slab will transfer floor loads to an intermediate beam, which then transmits the load to a larger girder supported by columns.

One of the common types of one-way systems is the *beam-and-girder system*. See Fig. 10.3(a). This functions in a manner similar to a steel system in which the slab is supported by intermediate beams that are carried by larger girders. Typical spans are in the range of 15 ft to 30 ft. This system is economical for most applications, relatively easy to form, and allows penetrations and openings to be made in the slab.

A *concrete joist system*, Fig. 10.3(b), is comprised of concrete members usually spaced 24 in or 36 in apart, running in one direction, that frame into larger beams. Most spans range from 20 ft to 30 ft with joist depths ranging from 12 in to 24 in. A concrete joist system is easy to form since prefabricated metal pan forms are used. This system is good for light or medium loads where moderate distances must be spanned.

There are three principal two-way concrete systems: the flat plate, flat slab, and waffle slab. In most cases, all of these are designed for use in rectangular bays, where the distance between columns is the same, or close to the same, in both directions.

The *flat plate* is the simplest. See Fig. 10.3(c). Here, the slab is designed and reinforced to span in both directions directly into the columns. Because loads increase near the columns and there is no provision to increase the thickness of the concrete or the reinforcing at the columns, this system is limited to light loads and short spans, up to about 25 ft with slabs ranging from 6 in to 12 in. It is very useful in situations where the floor-to-floor height must be kept to a minimum or an uncluttered underfloor appearance is desired.

When the span of flat plates is large or the live loads are heavier, flat plates require drop panels (increased slab thickness around the columns) to provide greater resistance against punching shear failures. Column capitals (truncated pyramids or cones) are sometimes also used to handle punching shear as well as large bending moments in the slab in the vicinity of the columns. This type of flat plate is usually referred to as a *flat slab*. See Fig. 10.3(d). This system can accommodate fairly heavy loads with economical spans up to 30 ft.

The *waffle slab* system, Fig. 10.3(e), can provide support for heavier loads at slightly longer spans than the flat slab system. Spans up to 40 ft can be accomplished economically. Like the one-way joist system, waffle slabs are formed of prefabricated, reusable metal or fiberglass forms that allow construction to proceed faster than with custom wood

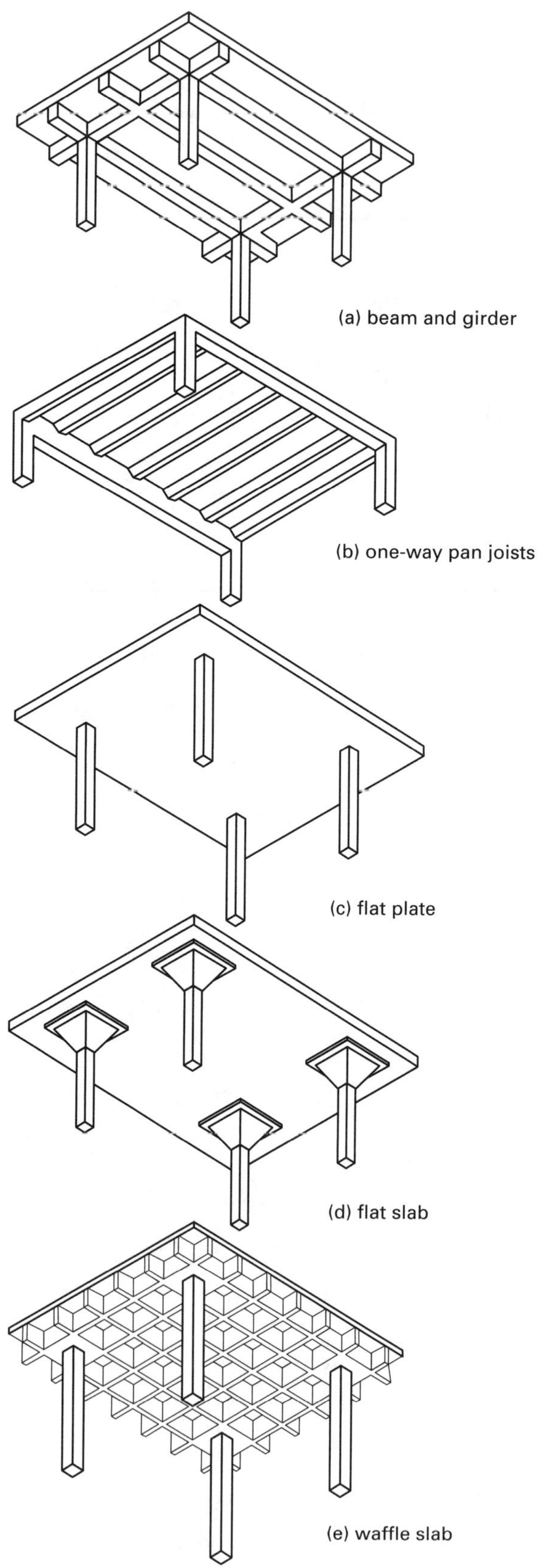

Figure 10.3 Concrete Structural Systems

forms. Waffle slabs are often left exposed with lighting integrated into the coffers.

Precast structural members come in a variety of forms for different uses. Figure 10.4 illustrates some of the more common ones. They can either be used for structural members such as beams and columns, or for enclosing elements such as wall panels. Concrete for wall panels can be cast in an almost infinite variety of forms to provide the required size, shape, architectural finish, and opening configuration needed for the job. Precast concrete members are connected in the field using welding plates that are cast into the member at the plant.

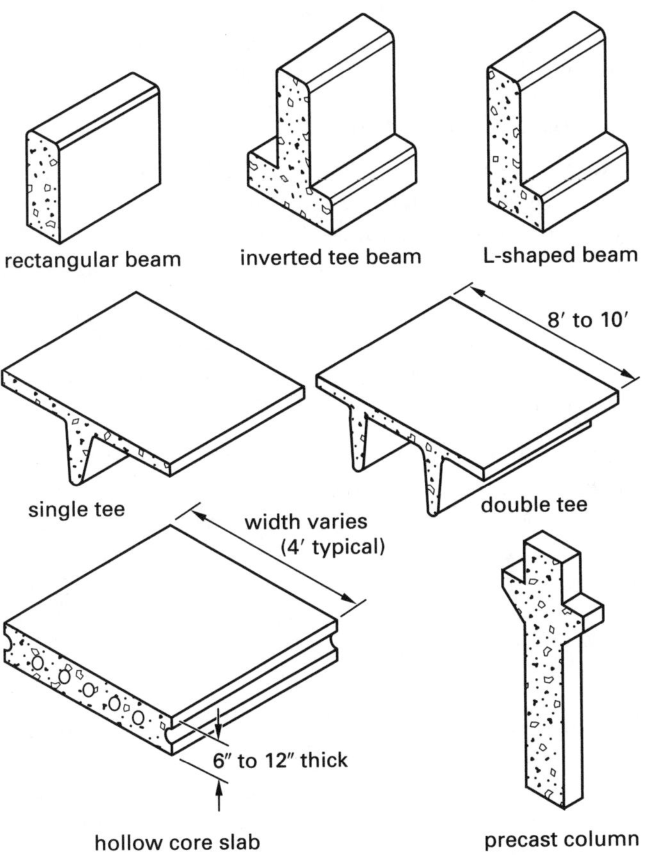

Figure 10.4 Typical Precast Concrete Shapes

When used for structure, precast concrete is typically prestressed; that is, high-strength steel cables are stretched in the precasting forms before the concrete is poured. After the concrete attains a certain minimum strength, the cables are released, and they transfer compressive stresses to the concrete. When cured, the concrete member has a built-in compressive stress that resists the tension forces caused by the member's own weight plus the live loads acting on the member.

Single tee and *double tee* beams are popular forms of precast concrete construction because they can simultaneously serve as structural supports as well as floor or roof decking, and they are easy and fast to erect. A topping of concrete (usually about 2 in thick) is placed over the tees to provide a uniform, smooth floor surface, and also to provide increased strength when the tees are designed to act as composite beams.

Because of the compressive stress in the concrete caused by the prestressing forces, unloaded beams from the prestressing plant have a camber built into them. This is the upward curvature of the structural member. The stressing in the cables is calculated to provide the correct camber and strength for the anticipated loading so that when the member is in place and live and dead loads are placed on it, the camber disappears or is greatly reduced.

Post-tensioned concrete is yet another structural system that takes advantage of the qualities of concrete and steel. In this system, the post-tensioning steel (sometimes called *tendons*) is stressed after the concrete has been poured and cured. Post-tensioning tendons can be small high-strength wires, seven-wire strands, or solid bars. They are stressed with hydraulic jacks pulling on one or both ends of the tendon with pressures of about 100 psi to 250 psi of concrete area for slabs and 200 psi to 500 psi for beams.

Post-tensioned structural systems are useful where high strength is required and where it may be too difficult to transport precast members to the job site.

Masonry

As a structural system in contemporary construction, masonry is generally limited to bearing walls. It has a high compressive strength, but its unitized nature makes it inherently weak in tension and bending. There are three basic types of masonry bearing wall construction: *single wythe*, *double wythe*, and *cavity* (see Fig. 10.5). Both of the layers in double-wythe construction may be of the same material or different materials. Cavity walls and double-wythe walls may be either grouted and reinforced or ungrouted. Single-wythe walls have no requirements for reinforcing or grouting.

Unit masonry bearing walls offer the advantages of strength, design flexibility, attractive appearance, resistance to weathering, fire resistance, and sound insulation. In addition, their mass makes them ideal for many passive solar energy applications.

The joints of masonry units must be reinforced horizontally at regular intervals. This not only strengthens the wall but also controls shrinkage cracks, ties multi-wythe walls together, and provides a way to anchor veneer facing to a structural backup wall. Horizontal joint reinforcement

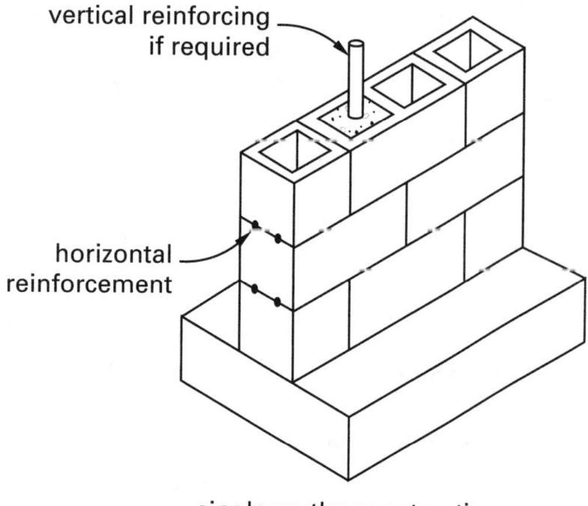

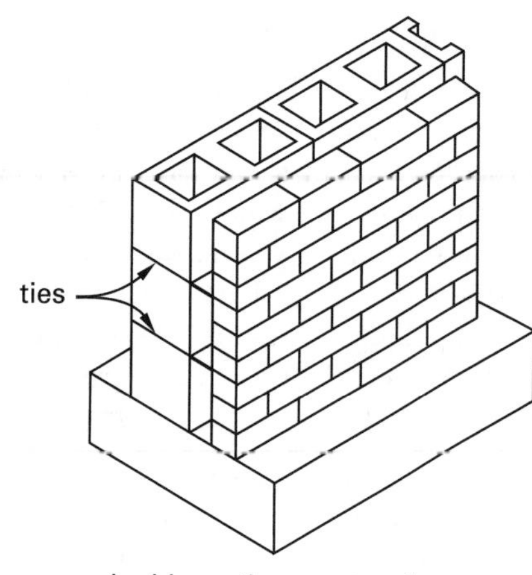

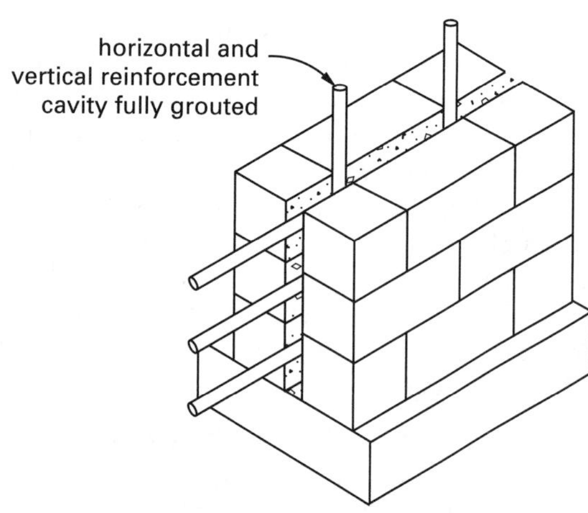

Figure 10.5 Types of Masonry Construction

comes in a variety of forms and is generally placed 16 in on center.

Vertical reinforcement is accomplished with standard reinforcing bars sized and spaced in accordance with the structural requirements of the wall. Typically, horizontal bars are also used and are tied to the vertical bars, with the entire assembly being set in a grouted cavity space. In a single-wythe concrete block wall, only vertical reinforcing is used with fully grouted wall cavities.

One important consideration in utilizing masonry walls is the thickness of the wall, which determines three important properties: the slenderness ratio, the flexural strength, and the fire-resistance rating. The *slenderness ratio* is the ratio of the wall's unsupported height to its thickness and is an indication of the ability of the wall to resist buckling when a compressive load is applied from above. The *flexural strength* is important when the wall is subjected to lateral forces such as from wind. Finally, the *fire-resistance rating* depends on both the wall's material and its thickness. These topics will be discussed in more detail in Ch. 21.

Composite Construction

Composite construction is any structural system consisting of two or more materials designed to act together to resist loads. Composite construction is employed to utilize the best characteristics of each of the individual materials.

Reinforced concrete construction is the most typical composite construction, but others include composite steel deck and concrete, concrete slab and steel beam systems, and open-web steel joists with wood chords. See Fig. 10.6.

In composite construction with concrete and steel beams, headed stud anchors are used to transfer load between the concrete and steel, making the two materials act as one unit. Composite steel deck is designed with deformations or wires welded to the deck to serve the same purpose. Composite open-web joists are used to provide a nailable surface for the floor and ceiling while using the high strength-to-weight ratio of steel for the web members.

There are many other types of composite constructions that are less frequently used. These include trusses with wood for compression members and steel rods for tension members, concrete-filled steel tube sections, and composite steel joists.

Walls and the Building Envelope

Nonbearing walls are generally not considered part of the structural system of a building, but there are two important structural considerations when deciding how to attach the exterior, nonstructural envelope to the structural frame. The first is how the weight of the envelope itself will be supported. The second is how exterior loads, primarily wind, will be transferred to the structural frame without damaging the facing.

How an exterior facing is attached depends, of course, on the specific material and the type of structural frame. Panel

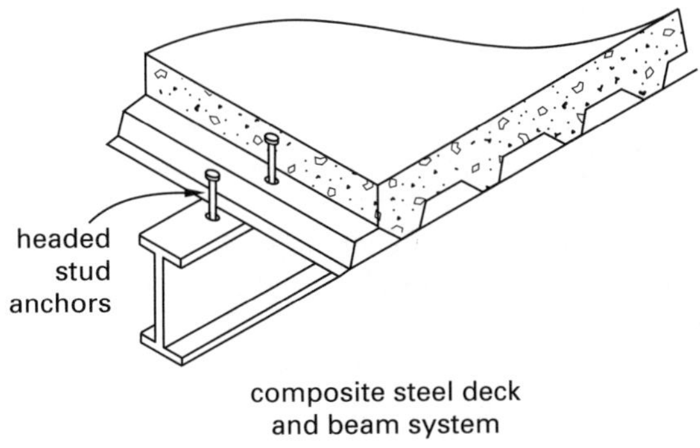

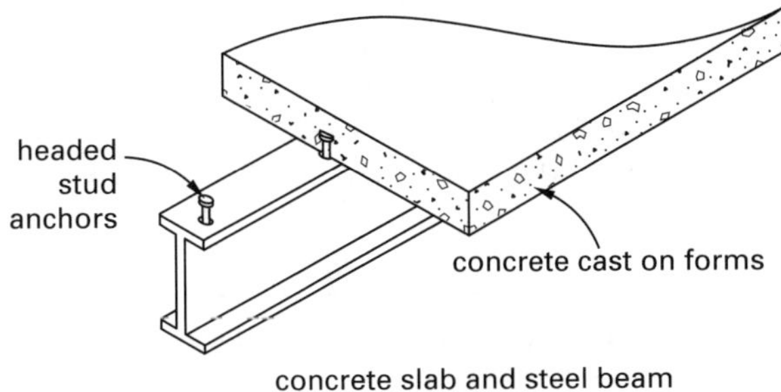

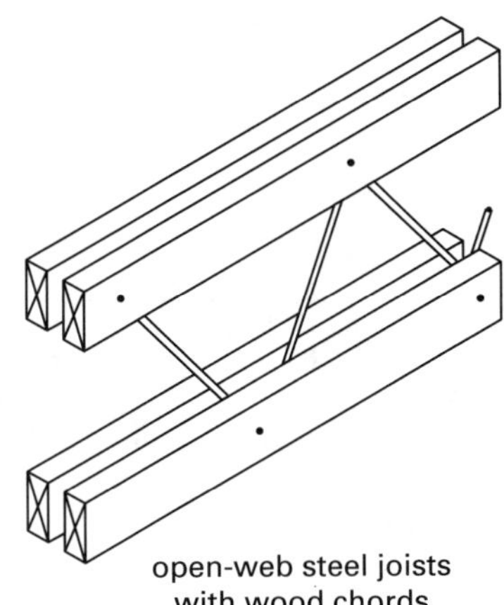

Figure 10.6 Typical Composite Construction

and curtain wall systems are attached with clips on the mullions at the structural frame. The size and spacing of the clips is determined by the structural capabilities of the curtain wall or panel system.

Stone and masonry facings are attached with clip angles, continuous angles, or special fastenings to the structural frame at the floor lines. If additional attachment is required, a grid of secondary steel framing is attached to the primary structure to serve as a framework for the facing. Lightweight facings such as wood siding, shingles, and stucco need to be applied over continuous sheathing firmly secured to the structural wall framing.

One of the most important considerations in attaching exterior facing to the structural frame is to allow for expansion and contraction due to temperature changes and slight movement of the structural frame. Materials with a high coefficient of thermal expansion, such as aluminum, require space for movement within each panel, at the connection with the structural frame, and sometimes at the perimeter of large sections of the facing. Movement can be provided for by using clip angles with slotted holes, slip joints, and flexible sealants.

Materials with a low coefficient of expansion, such as masonry, still require expansion joints at regular intervals and at changes in the plane of the wall. If these are not provided, the joints or masonry may crack or the facing itself may break away during extreme temperature changes.

Usually, steel-framed buildings do not present many problems with movement of the structural frame, but concrete and wood structures will move enough to present problems. Concrete structures are especially subject to creep, a slight deformation of the concrete over time under continuous dead load. This condition must be accounted for when designing and detailing connections. Wood structures also deform over time due to shrinkage of the wood and long-term deflection. Since most wood buildings are relatively small, this is not always a problem, but it should be considered when attaching exterior facings.

COMPLEX STRUCTURAL SYSTEMS

Trusses

Trusses are structures comprised of straight members forming a number of triangles with the connections arranged so that the stresses in the members are either in tension or compression. Trusses can be used horizontally, vertically, or diagonally to support various types of loads when it would be impossible to fabricate a single structural member to span a large distance.

Although trusses are primarily tension/compression structural systems, some amount of bending is present in many of the members. This is due to loads applied between the connections and secondary bending and shear stresses at the connections themselves caused by minor eccentric loading.

Trusses can be field-fabricated or assembled in the factory as is the case with open-web steel joists and wood-trussed rafters. The primary limiting factor is the ability to transport them from the factory to the job site.

Trusses are discussed in more detail in Ch. 14.

Arches

Arches may have hinged or fixed supports. A hinged arch is a structural shape that is primarily subjected to compressive forces. For a given set of loads, the shape of an arch to resist the loads only in compression is its *funicular shape*. This shape can be found by suspending the anticipated loads from a flexible cable and then turning the shape upside down, as Antonio Gaudi did in many of his structural studies. For a hinged arch supporting a uniform load across its span, this shape is a parabola. However, no arch is subjected to just one set of loads, so there is always a combination of compression and some bending stresses.

At the supports of a hinged arch there are two reactions: the *vertical reactions* and the *horizontal reactions*, or *thrust*, as shown in Fig. 10.7. Since the loads on the arch tend to force it to spread out, the thrust must be resisted either with tie rods that hold the two lower portions of the arch together or with foundations that prevent the spread. For a given span, the thrust is inversely proportional to the rise, or height, of the arch; if the rise is reduced by one-half, the thrust doubles.

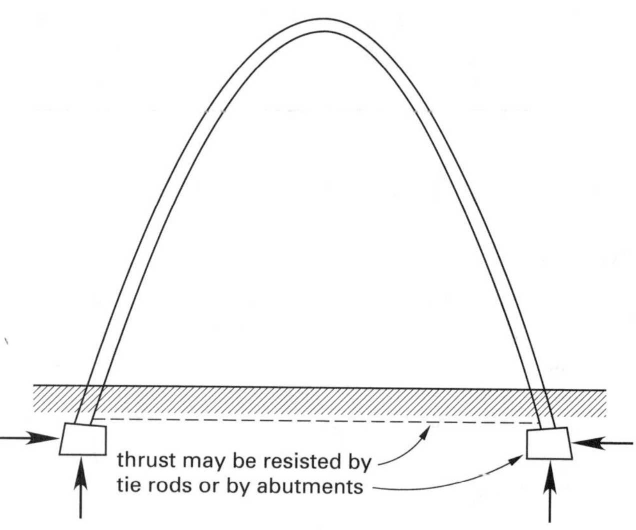

Figure 10.7 Reactions of a Hinged Arch

Arches can be constructed of any material: steel, concrete, wood, or stone, although each has its inherent limitations. Arches can also take a variety of shapes, from the classic half-round arch of the Romans, to the pointed Gothic arch, to the more decorative Arabic arches, to functional parabolic shapes. Since the shape of a building arch is often selected for its aesthetic appeal, it is not always the ideal shape and must be designed for the variety of loads it must carry in addition to simple compression. Arches typically span from 50 ft to 240 ft for wood, 20 ft to 320 ft for concrete, or 50 ft to 500 ft for steel.

Although arches may have fixed supports, they are usually hinged. This allows the arch to remain flexible and avoids developing high bending stresses under live loading and loading due to temperature changes and foundation settlement. Occasionally, an arch will have an additional hinge connection at the apex and is called a *three-hinged arch*. The addition of the third hinge makes the structure statically determinate, whereas two-hinged or fixed arches are statically indeterminate.

Rigid Frames

In contrast to a simple *post-and-beam system*, a *rigid frame* is constructed so that the vertical and horizontal members work as a single structural unit, as shown in Fig. 10.8.

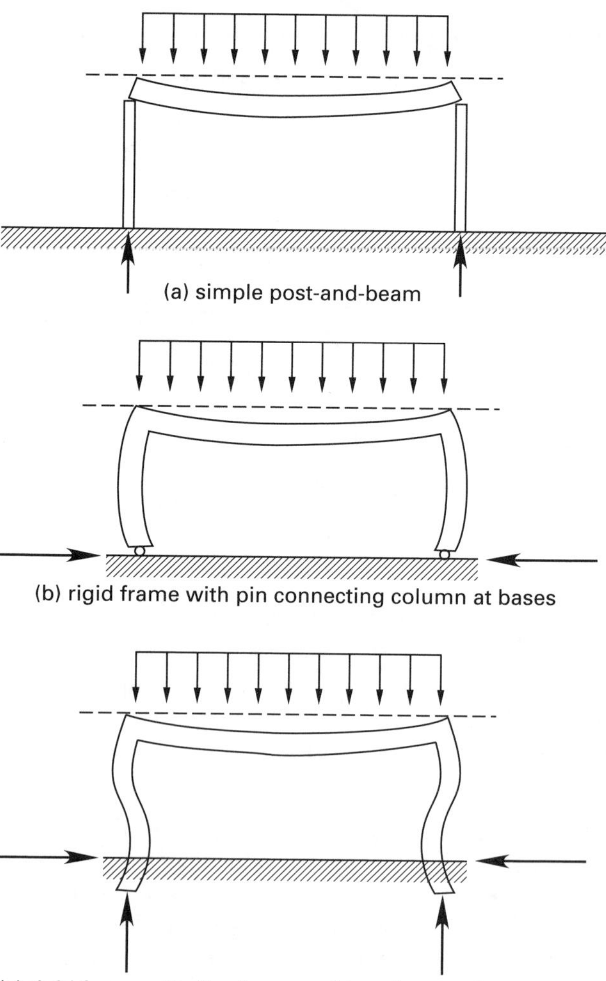

Figure 10.8 Post-and-Beam and Rigid Frames

This makes for a more efficient structure because all three members resist vertical and lateral loads together rather than singly. The beam portion is partially restrained by the columns and becomes more rigid to vertical bending forces, and both columns can resist lateral forces because they are tied together by the beam.

Because the three members are rigidly attached, there are forces and reactions in a rigid frame unlike those in a simple post-and-beam system. This is shown in Fig. 10.8(b) and 10.8(c) and results in the columns being subjected to both compressive and bending forces and a thrust, or outward force, induced by the action of the vertical loads on the beam transferred to the columns. As with an arch, this thrust must be resisted with tie rods or with appropriate foundations.

The attachment of the columns to the foundations may be rigid or hinged. This results in slightly different loads on the columns. The fixed frame as shown in Fig. 10.8(c) is stiffer than the hinged frame, and the thrust in the fixed frame is also greater.

When a horizontal beam is not required, such as in a single-story structure, a rigid frame often takes on the appearance of a *gabled frame* as shown in Fig. 10.9. This shape decreases the bending stresses in the two inclined members and increases the compression, making the configuration a more efficient structure. Because rigid frames develop a high moment (see Ch. 12) at the connections between horizontal and vertical members, the amount of material is often increased near these points as shown in the tapered columns and roof members in Fig. 10.9.

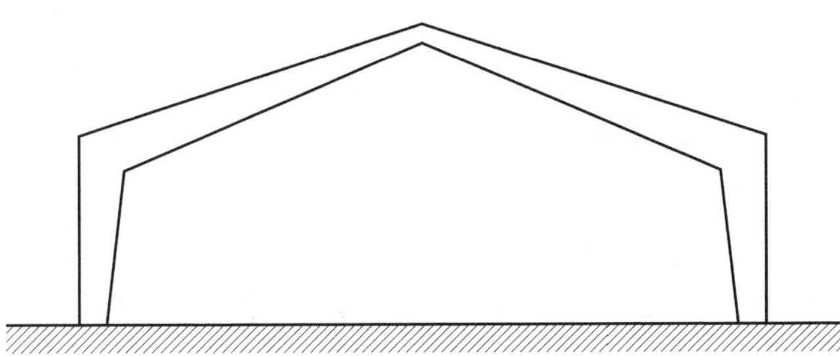

Figure 10.9 Gabled Rigid Frame

Space Frames

In simplest terms, a *space frame* is a structural system consisting of trusses in two directions rigidly connected at their intersections. With this definition it is possible to have a rectangular space frame where the top and bottom chords of the trusses are directly above and below one another. The bays created by the intersection of the two sets of trusses then form squares or rectangles. The more common type of space frame is a *triangulated space frame* where the bottom chord is offset from the top chord by half a bay, and each is connected with inclined web members. See Fig. 10.10.

Space frames are very efficient structures for enclosing large rectangular areas because of the two-way action of the components acting as a single unit. This results in a very stiff structure that may span up to 350 ft.

Span-to-depth ratios of space frames may be from 20:1 to 30:1. Other advantages include light weight and the repetitive nature of connectors and struts so that fabrication and erection time is minimized.

The structural design of space frames is complex because they are statically indeterminate structures with numerous intersections. A computer is needed for analysis and design.

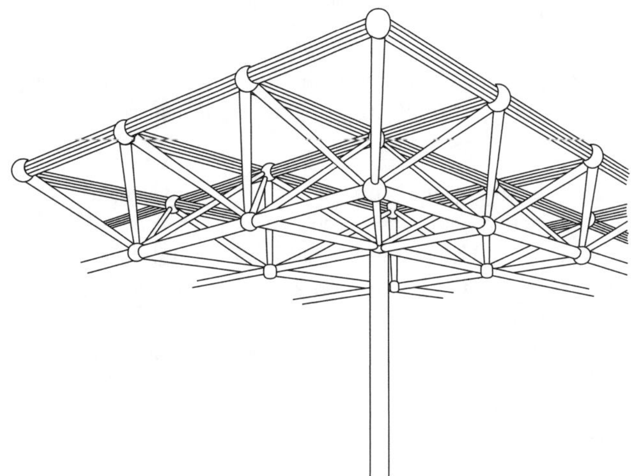

Figure 10.10 Typical Space Frame

Folded Plates

A *folded plate* structure is one in which the loads are carried in two different directions: first in the transverse direction through each plate supported by adjacent plates, and second in the longitudinal direction with each plate acting as a girder spanning between vertical supports. See Fig. 10.11. Since the plates act as beams between supports, there are compressive stresses above the neutral axis and tensile stresses below.

Folded plates are usually constructed of reinforced concrete from 3 in to 6 in thick, although structures made of wood or steel are possible. Typical longitudinal spans are 30 ft to 100 ft with longer spans possible using reinforced concrete.

Thin-Shell Structures

A *thin-shell structure* is one with a curved surface that resists loads through tension, compression, and shear in the plane of the shell only. Theoretically, there are no bending or moment stresses in a thin-shell structure. These structures

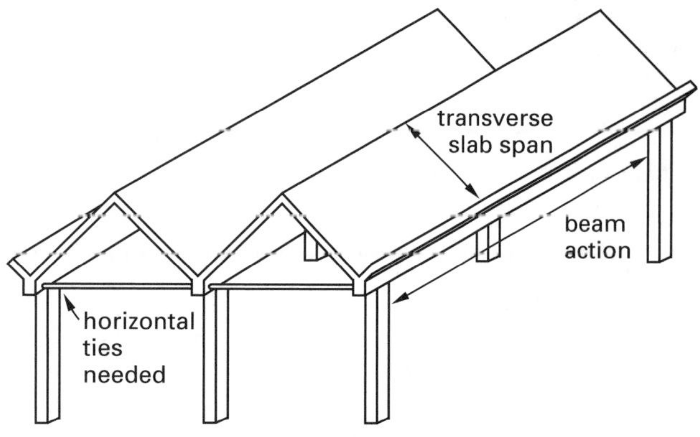

Figure 10.11 Folded Plate Construction

derive part of their name (thin) because of the method of resisting loads; a thick structure is not necessary since there are no bending stresses.

Since thin shells are composed of curved surfaces, the material is practically always reinforced concrete from about 3 in to 6 in thick. The forms can be domes, parabolas, or barrel vaults or can take on the more complex form of a saddle-shaped hyperbolic paraboloid. Thin-shell domes can span from 40 ft to over 200 ft, while hyperbolic paraboloids may span from 30 ft to 160 ft.

Stressed-Skin Structures

Stressed-skin structures comprise panels made of a sheathing material attached on one or both sides of intermediate web members in such a way that the panel acts as a series of I-beams, with the sheathing being the flange and the intermediate members being the webs. Since the panel is constructed of two or more pieces, the connection between the skin and the interior web members must transfer all the horizontal stress developed. Stressed-skin panels are typically made of wood, as shown in Fig. 10.1(g), but are also fabricated of steel and other composite materials. Although long-span steel stressed-skin panels do exist, most panels of this type span intermediate distances from 12 ft to 35 ft.

Suspension Structures

Suspension structures are most commonly seen in suspension bridges, but their use is increasing in buildings, most notably in large stadiums with suspended roofs. The suspension system was boldly used in the Federal Reserve Bank in Minneapolis, where two sets of cables were draped from towers at the ends of the building. These, in turn, support the floors and walls, leaving the space on the grade level free of columns.

Cable suspension structures are similar to arches in that the loads they support must be resisted by both vertical reactions and horizontal thrust reactions. The difference is that the vertical reactions are up and the horizontal thrust reactions are outward, since the sag tends to pull the ends together. As shown in Fig. 10.12(a), the horizontal reaction is dependent on the amount of sag in the cable. Shallow sags result in high horizontal reactions, while deep sags result in lower horizontal reactions.

Since suspension structures can only resist loads with tension, the shape of the cable used changes as the load changes. No bending stresses are possible. With a single concentrated load, the cable assumes the shape of two straight lines (not counting the intermediate sag due to the weight of the cable). With two concentrated loads, the shape is three straight lines, and so on.

If the cable is uniformly loaded horizontally, the shape of the curve is a parabola. If the cable is loaded along its length uniformly (such as when it is supporting its own weight), the shape will be a catenary curve. See Fig. 10.12(b) and 10.12(c).

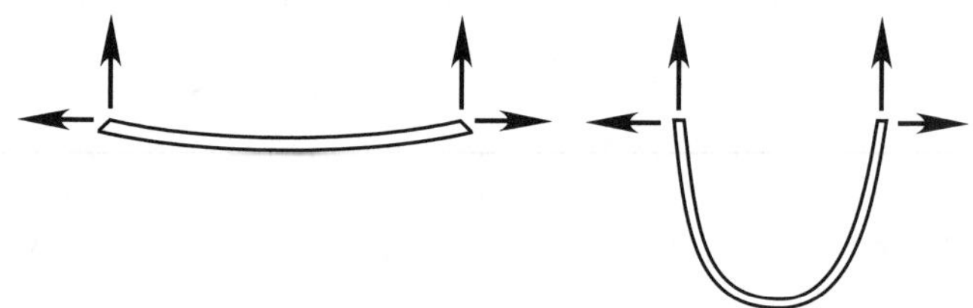

(a) horizontal reaction depends on sag

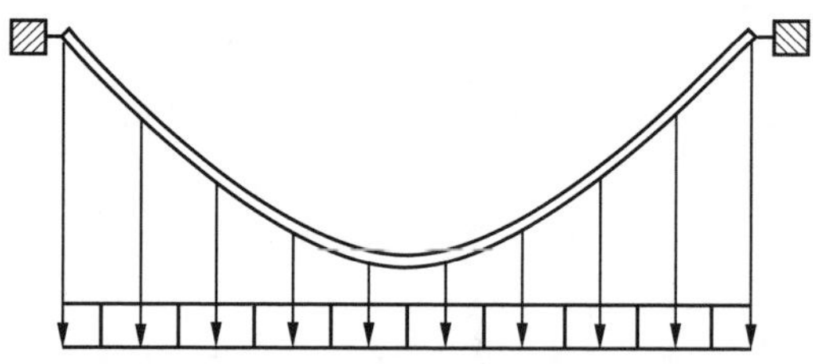

(b) uniform horizontal load results in parabolic curve

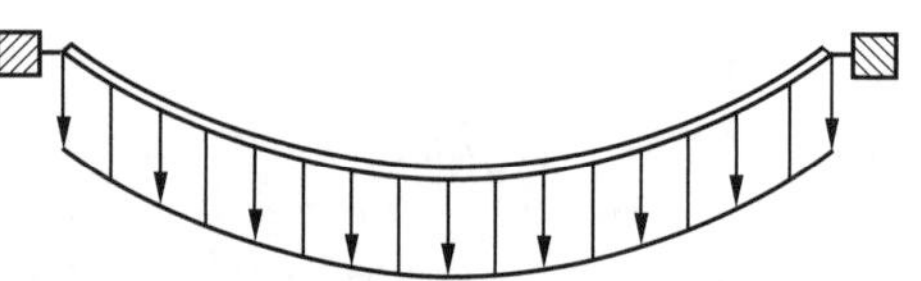

(c) uniform load on cable results in catenary curve

Figure 10.12 Cable-Supported Structures

The fact that a suspension structure can only resist loads in tension creates a disadvantage: instability due to wind and other types of loading. Suspension structures must be stabilized or stiffened with a heavy infill material, with cables attached to the ground or with a secondary grid of cables either above or below the primary set.

Inflatable Structures

Inflatable structures are similar to suspension structures in that they can only resist loads in tension. They are held in place with constant air pressure that is greater than the outside air pressure. The simplest inflatable structure is the single membrane anchored continuously at ground level and inflated.

A variation of this is the *double-skin inflatable structure* in which the structure is created by inflation of a series of voids, much like an air mattress. With this system, the need for an air lock for entry and exit is eliminated. Another variation is a double-skin structure, with only one large air pocket supported on the bottom by a cable suspension system and with the top supported by air pressure.

Like cable suspension buildings, inflatable structures are inherently unstable in the wind and cannot support concentrated loads. They are often stabilized with a network of cables over the top of the membrane. Inflatable structures are used for temporary enclosures and for large, single-space buildings such as sports arenas.

STRUCTURAL SYSTEM SELECTION CRITERIA

The selection of an optimum structural system for a building can be a complex task. In addition to the wide variety of structural systems available and their many variations and combinations, there are dozens of other considerations that must be factored into making the final selection. The architect's job is to determine the full scope of the problem and find the best balance among often conflicting requirements. This section briefly outlines some of the major selection criteria to be familiar with when analyzing possible systems.

Resistance to Loads

Of course, the primary consideration is the ability of the structural system to resist the anticipated and unanticipated loads that will be placed on it. These include the weight of the structure itself (*dead load*); loads caused by external factors such as wind, snow, and earthquakes; loads caused by building use, such as people, furniture, and equipment (*live loads*), as well as others. These are discussed in more detail in Ch. 11.

The anticipated loads can be calculated directly from known weights of materials and equipment and from requirements of building codes that set down what is statistically probable in a given situation—the load caused by people in a church, for example. Unanticipated loads are difficult to plan for but include such things as changes in the use of a building, overloading caused by extra people or equipment, unusual snow loads, ponding of water on a roof, and degradation of the structure itself.

When deciding on what material or system to use, there is always the consideration of what is reasonable for the particular circumstance. For example, wood can be made to support very heavy loads with long spans, but only at a very high cost with complex systems. A wood system does not make sense if other materials and systems, such as steel and concrete, are available.

Often, very unusual loads will be the primary determinant of the structural system and its effect on the appearance of the building. Extremely tall high-rise buildings like the Sears Tower or the John Hancock Building in Chicago, with its exterior diagonal framing, are examples of load-driven structural solutions.

Building Use and Function

The type of occupancy is one of the primary determinants of a structural system. A parking garage needs spans long enough to allow the easy movement and storage of automobiles. An office building works well with spans in the 30 ft to 40 ft range.

Sports arenas need quite large open areas. Some buildings have a fixed use over their lifespan and may work with fixed bearing walls, while others must remain flexible and require small, widely spaced columns.

These are all examples of somewhat obvious determinates of building systems. However, there are many other needs that are not so apparent. For example, in a location where building height is limited, a client may want to squeeze as many floors into a multistory building as possible. This may require the use of concrete flat-plate construction with closely spaced columns even though another system would be more economical.

In another instance, a laboratory building may need large spaces between usable floors in which to run mechanical services. This may suggest the use of deep-span, open-web trusses. If the same laboratory were to house delicate, motion-sensitive equipment, then the use of a rigid, massive concrete structure might be warranted.

Integration with Other Building Systems

Although a building's structure is an important element, it does not exist alone. The building must have exterior cladding attached to it. Ductwork and pipes run around and through it, electrical wires run among it, and interior finishes cover it. Some materials and structural systems make it easy for other services to be integrated. For instance, a steel column-and-beam system with open-web steel joists and concrete floors over metal decking yields a fairly penetrable structure for pipes, ducts, and wiring while still allowing solid attachment of ceilings, walls, and exterior cladding.

On the other hand, reinforced prestressed concrete buildings may require more consideration as to how mechanical services will be run so there is not an excess of dropped ceilings, furred-out columns, and structure-weakening penetrations. Exposed structural systems, such as glued-laminated beams and wood decking or architectural concrete, present particularly difficult integration problems.

Cost Influences

As with most contemporary construction, financial concerns drive many decisions. Structure is no exception. It is one portion of a building that is most susceptible to cost cutting because it quite often cannot be seen and the client sees no reason to spend more on it than absolutely necessary.

There are two primary elements of selecting a structural system based on cost. The first is selecting materials and systems that are most appropriate for the anticipated loads, spans required, style desired, integration needed, fire resistance called for, and all the other factors that must be considered. This generally leads to major decisions such as whether to use a concrete flat-slab construction instead of steel, or to use a steel arch system instead of glued-laminated beams.

The second part is refining the selected system so that the most economical arrangement and use of materials is selected regardless of the system used. In a typical situation, for example, a steel system is selected, but various framing options must be compared and evaluated. Changing the direction of the beams and girders or slightly altering the spacing of beams may result in a savings in the weight of steel and therefore a savings in money. Or, a concrete frame may be needed, but the one with the simplest forming will generally cost less.

Fire Resistance

Building codes dictate the fire resistance of structural systems as well as other parts of a building. These range from 1 hour to 4 hours; the time is an indication of how long the member can withstand a standard fire test before becoming dangerously weakened. The structure is, of course, the most important part of a building because it holds everything else up. As a consequence, required fire resistances are generally greater for structural members than for other components in the same occupancy type and building type.

There are two considerations in the fire resistance of a structural member. One is the combustibility of the framing itself, and the other is the loss of strength a member may experience when subjected to intense heat. Steel, for instance, will not burn but will bend and collapse when subjected to high temperatures. It must, therefore, be protected with other noncombustible materials. Heavy timber, on the other hand, will burn slightly and char, but will maintain much of its strength in a fire before it burns completely.

Some materials, such as concrete and masonry, are inherently fire resistant and are not substantially weakened when subjected to fire (assuming any steel reinforcing is adequately protected). Other materials, such as wood and steel, must be protected for the time period required by the building codes.

Since it costs money to protect structural members from fire, cost must be factored into the decision to use one material instead of another. Even though steel may be a less expensive structural material to use than concrete, it may be more expensive to fireproof and, in the long run, cost more than a concrete-framed building.

Construction Limitations

The realities of construction often are a decisive factor in choosing a structural system. Some of these include construction time, material and labor availability, and equipment availability.

Construction time is almost always a factor due to high labor costs typical in the United States. However, other things influence the need to shorten the construction period as much as possible. The cost of financing requires that the terms of construction loans be as short as feasible. This may dictate the use of large, prefabricated structural elements instead of slow, labor-intensive systems such as unit masonry. Another factor can be climate and weather. In locations with short construction seasons, buildings need to be erected as quickly as possible.

Material and labor are the two primary variables in all construction cost. Sometimes both are expensive, but usually one dominates the other. In the United States, labor costs are high in relation to materials; in many developing countries labor is extremely cheap while most modern materials are expensive or even unattainable. Even within the United States, labor and material costs for the same material or structural system in different states may vary enough to influence the structural system decision.

Related to labor costs are the skills of the workforce. A sophisticated structural system may require a technically skilled workforce that is not available in a remote region. The cost to transport and house the needed workers could very well make such a system infeasible.

Finally, equipment needed to assemble a structural system may be unavailable or prohibitively expensive. The lack of heavy cranes near the job location, for example, could suggest that large, prefabricated components not be used.

Style

Some structural systems are more appropriate as an expression of a particular style than others. One of the most obvious examples is the International Style, which could only be achieved with a steel post-and-beam system. Even when fireproofing requirements might have implied a concrete structure, steel was used.

The architect and client usually determine what style the building will be and then require that any structural solution adapt to that need. In some instances, the structural engineer may devise a structural solution that becomes the style itself. Once again, there should be a balance between what style may be desired and what is practical and reasonable from a structural point of view.

Social and Cultural Influences

Related to the style of a building are the social and cultural influences on the architecture of a geographical location and particular time period. The architect must be sensitive to these influences. For example, in a historic area where most buildings are constructed of brick, a masonry bearing wall structural system certainly should be considered. In a newly developing industrial park, more contemporary and daring structural systems might be appropriate.

11 LOADS ON BUILDINGS

Nomenclature

A	area of floor or roof	ft^2
A_t	tributary roof area supported by a structural member	ft^2
A_T	tributary floor area supported by a structural member	ft^2
D	dead load	lbf/ft^2
E	earthquake or seismic load	lbf/ft^2
f_1	floor live load occupancy combination factor	–
f_2	snow load roof shape combination factor	–
F	roof slope	in/ft
h	depth of retaining wall	ft
K_{LL}	live load element factor	–
L	floor live load	lbf/ft^2
L_O	unreduced floor live load	lbf/ft^2
L_r	roof live load	–
p	direct wind pressure	lbf/ft^2
p	maximum soil pressure on retaining wall	lbf/ft^2
P	lateral soil force	lbf/ft^2
q	lateral soil pressure	lbf/ft^2
r	rate of reduction of live load	–
R	allowable reduction of floor live load	%
R	rain load	lbf/ft^2
R_1	roof area reduction factor	–
R_2	roof slope reduction factor	–
S	snow load	lbf/ft^2
v	wind velocity	mi/hr
w	uniform total load	lbf/ft^2
W	wind load	lbf/ft^2
ω	wind load coefficient	–

Determining the loads acting on buildings is basic to structural analysis and design. An accurate determination of loads is necessary to design a safe building and satisfy building code requirements while not requiring a more costly structure than necessary. The probable magnitudes of building loads have been determined over a long period of time based on successful experience and the statistical probability that a particular situation will result in a given load. They are also based on the worst-case situation. For example, the common live load for residences of 40 psf is highly unlikely to occur on every square foot in a house, but it provides an allowance for safety and unusual circumstances.

Typically, loads are defined by building codes and by common practice. Codes, for example, give live load requirements, wind values, and earthquake values. Standard published tables provide accepted weights of building materials for dead load calculations. Occasionally, special situations may require custom load determination such as when building models are tested in a wind tunnel. Most loads on buildings are static, and those that are dynamic, such as wind, are assumed to have a static effect on the building structure so calculations are easier.

There are many types of loads on buildings. This chapter provides an overview of what the different types are, how they are determined, and their effects on buildings and architectural design. More detailed information concerning building code requirements is given in Ch. 17, while specific calculation procedures for lateral loads due to wind and earthquakes are described in Chs. 22 and 23, respectively.

GRAVITY LOADS

Dead Loads

Dead loads are the *vertical loads* due to the weight of a building and any permanent equipment. These include such things as beams, exterior and interior walls, floors, and mechanical equipment. Dead loads of structural elements cannot always be readily determined because the weight depends on the size, which in turn depends on the weight to be supported. Initially, the weight of the structure must be assumed in order to make a preliminary calculation of the size of the structural member. Then the actual weight can be used for checking the calculation.

Most dead loads are easily calculated from published lists of building material weights found in standard reference sources. Some common weights are given in Table 11.1. In addition to these, the *International Building Code* (IBC) requires that floors in office buildings and other buildings with live loads of 80 psf or less where partition locations are subject to change be design to support a minimum partition load of 20 psf. This partition load is considered part of the live load.

Table 11.1

Weights of Some Common Building Materials

material	weight
asphalt shingles	2 psf
brick, 4″ wall	40 psf
built-up roofing, 5-ply	6 psf
concrete block, 8″ heavy aggregate	55 psf
concrete, reinforced	150 pcf
concrete slab, per inch of thickness	12.5 psf
curtain wall, aluminum and glass, average	15 psf
earth, moist and packed	100 pcf
glass, 1/4″	3.3 psf
granite	170 pcf
gypsum wallboard, 1/2″	1.8 psf
hardwood floor, 7/8″	2.5 psf
marble	165 pcf
partition, 2 × 4 with 1/2″ gypsum board each side	8 psf
partition, metal stud with 5/8″ gypsum board	6 psf
plaster, 1/2″	4.5 psf
plywood, 1/2″	1.5 psf
quarry tile, 1/2″	5.8 psf
steel decking	2.5 psf
suspended acoustical ceiling	1 psf
terrazzo, 2 1/2″ sand cushion	27 psf
water	62 pcf
wood joists and subfloor, 2 × 10, 16″ o.c.	6 psf

Example 11.1

Find the uniform load on a typical interior beam supporting the floor shown. Do not include the weight of the beam.

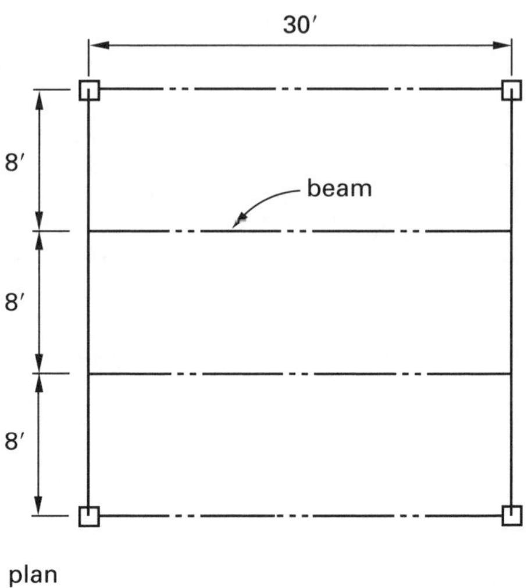

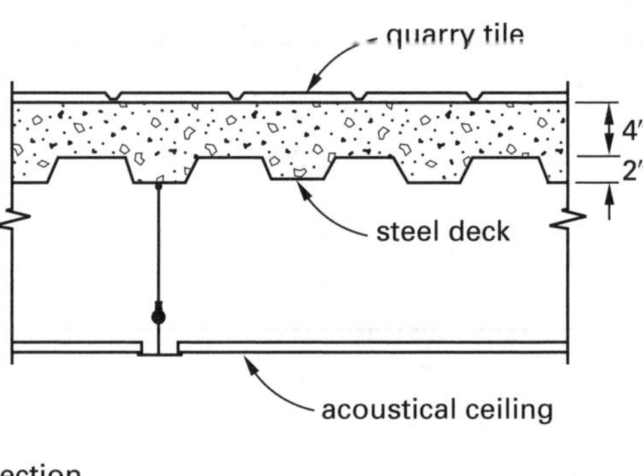

From Table 11.1, determine the weight per square foot of the materials comprising the floor. Since the concrete is on a fluted steel deck, take the average thickness of 5 in.

Therefore, the total weight is

quarry tile	5.8 psf
concrete	62.5 psf (5 × 12.5 psf)
steel deck	2.5 psf
suspended ceiling	1.0 psf
total	71.8 psf

The beam supports a portion of the floor half the distance of the beam spacing on either side of it, or 8 ft. 8 ft times 71.8 psf is 574 plf. To determine the total load, multiply by the length of the beam.

In practice, numbers such as 71.8 are rounded to the nearest whole number, so the weight in this case would be 72 psf and the load would be 576 plf.

Live Loads

Live loads are those imposed on a building by the building's particular use and occupancy and are generally considered movable or temporary. People, furniture, and movable equipment are examples of live loads. Wind, earthquake, and snow loads are not considered live loads. Snow load is often considered a special type of transient load because it is so variable. To determine snow loads, local building officials or building codes must be consulted.

Live loads are established by the building code for different occupancies. Table 11.2 gives the uniform live loads from the IBC. Roofs must also be designed for uniform live loads or any special snow loads. The snow load specification is primarily covered in ASCE/SEI Standard 7, *Minimum Design Loads for Buildings and Other Structures* (ASCE/SEI 7). The code also specifies requirements for special loads such as cranes, elevators, and fire sprinkler structural supports.

The code also requires that floors be designed to support concentrated loads if the specified load on an otherwise unloaded floor would produce stresses greater than those caused by the uniform load. The concentrated load is assumed to be located on any space 2½ ft square. The concentrated load requirements are given in the last column in Table 11.2.

The IBC allows for the live load to be reduced in most cases. The live load may not be reduced for any public assembly occupancy with a live load less than or equal to 100 psf or for any member supporting one floor of a parking garage or with a live load exceeding 100 psf. The reduced live load is given by the following formula.

$$L = L_O\left(0.25 + \frac{15}{\sqrt{K_{LL}A_T}}\right) \qquad 11.1$$

The value of L_O is the uniform live load from Table 11.2, and the value of K_{LL} is given in Table 11.3. The final value of L must not be less than $0.5L_O$ for members supporting one floor or $0.4L_O$ for members supporting more than one floor. In addition, L must not be less than $0.8L_O$ for members supporting more than one floor with a live load exceeding 100 psf or in parking garages.

The IBC allows for an alternate method to calculate live load reduction. This reduction method applies to members supporting more than 150 ft². The reduction may not be used for public assembly occupancy or live loads exceeding 100 psf.

The allowable percentage reduction from the load values shown in Table 11.2 is given by the following formula.

$$R = r(A - 150) \qquad 11.2$$

The *rate of reduction*, r, is equal to 0.08, and the tributary area uses the variable A. There are a few limitations, however. The reduction cannot exceed 40% for horizontal members or 60% for vertical members, nor can the reduction exceed the percentage determined by the following formula.

$$R = 23.1\left(1 + \frac{D}{L_O}\right) \qquad 11.3$$

Example 11.2

What live load should be used to design an interior beam that supports 225 ft² of office space, a live load of 50 psf, and a dead load of 72 psf? Calculate and compare both code methods.

Since the live load is less than 100 psf and the office is not a public assembly space or a parking garage, a reduction is permitted by either method. For each method, first determine the reduction, and then check against the limitations. Since this is an interior beam, the value of K_{LL} from Table 11.3 is 2.

$$\begin{aligned} L &= L_O\left(0.25 + \frac{15}{\sqrt{K_{LL}A_T}}\right) \\ &= \left(50\ \frac{\text{lbf}}{\text{ft}^2}\right)\left(0.25 + \frac{15}{\sqrt{(2)(225)}}\right) \\ &= 47.86\ \text{psf} \end{aligned}$$

The limiting load is $0.5L_O = (0.5)(50\ \text{psf}) = 25\ \text{psf}$, which is less than the calculated value. Use 47.9 psf. The alternate reduction yields a similar result.

$$\begin{aligned} R &= r(A - 150) \\ &= (0.08)(225 - 150) \\ &= 6\% \end{aligned}$$

The limiting reduction is 40% for horizontal members, and it cannot exceed the percentage determined by the following formula.

$$\begin{aligned} R &= 23.1\left(1 + \frac{D}{L_O}\right) \\ &= (23.1)\left(1 + \frac{72\ \frac{\text{lbf}}{\text{ft}^2}}{50\ \frac{\text{lbf}}{\text{ft}^2}}\right) \\ &= 56.36\% \end{aligned}$$

Of the three values, 6% is the least, so the reduced live load will be 50 psf − (0.06)(50 psf), or 47 psf.

Table 11.2

Uniform and Concentrated Loads[a]

occupancy or use	uniform (psf)	concentrated (lbf)
2. access floor systems		
office use	50	2000
computer use	100	2000
3. armories and drill rooms	150	–
4. assembly areas and theaters		
fixed seats (fastened to floor)	60	
lobbies	100	
movable seats	100	
stages and platforms	125	–
follow spot, projections, and control rooms	50	
catwalks	40	
8. cornices	60	–
9. corridors, except as otherwise indicated	100	–
16. garages (passenger vehicles only)	40	Note b
trucks and buses	See IBC Sec. 1607.6	
20. hospitals		
operating rooms, laboratories	60	1000
private rooms	40	1000
wards	40	1000
corridors above first floor	80	1000
22. libraries		
reading rooms	60	1000
stack rooms	150[c]	1000
corridors above first floor	80	1000
23. manufacturing		
light	125	2000
heavy	250	3000
24. marquees	75	–
25. office buildings		
file and computer rooms shall be designed for heavier loads based on anticipated occupancy		
lobbies and first-floor corridors	100	2000
offices	50	2000
corridors above first floor	80	2000
27. residential		
one- and two-family dwellings		
uninhabitable attics without storage	10	
uninhabitable attics with storage	20	–
habitable attics and sleeping areas	30	
all other areas except balconies and decks	40	
hotels and multifamily dwellings		
private rooms and corridors serving them	40	
public rooms and corridors serving them	100	
30. schools		
classrooms	40	1000
corridors above first floor	80	1000
first-floor corridors	100	1000
35. stairs and exits	100	Note d
one- and two-family dwellings	40	
all other	100	
36. storage warehouses (shall be designed for heavier loads if required for anticipated storage)		–
light	125	
heavy	250	
37. stores		
retail		
first floor	100	1000
upper floors	75	1000
wholesale, all floors	125	1000
39. walkways and elevated platforms (other than exitways)	60	–

For SI: 1 in = 25.4 mm, 1 in^2 = 645.16 mm^2, 1 psf = 0.0479 kN/m^2, 1 lbf = 0.004448 kN, 1 lbm/ft^3 = 16 kg/m^3.

[a]Where snow loads occur that are in excess of the design conditions, the structure shall be designed to support the loads due to the increased loads caused by drift buildup or a greater snow design determined by the building official (see IBC Sec. 1608). For special-purpose roofs, see IBC Sec. 1607.11.2.2.

[b]Floors in garages or portions of buildings used for the storage of motor vehicles shall be designed for the uniformly distributed live loads of IBC Table 1607.1 or the following concentrated loads: (1) for garages restricted to vehicles accommodating not more than nine passengers, 3000 lbf acting on an area of 4.5 in by 4.5 in; (2) for mechanical parking structures without slab or deck that are used for storing passenger vehicles only, 2250 lbf per wheel.

[c]The loading applies to stack room floors that support nonmobile, double-faced library bookstacks, subject to the following limitations.

1. The nominal bookstack unit height shall not exceed 90 in;
2. The nominal shelf depth shall not exceed 12 in for each face; and
3. Parallel rows of double-faced bookstacks shall be separated by aisles not less than 36 in wide.

[d]Minimum concentrated load on stair treads (on area of 4 in^2) is 300 lbf.

Note: Some rows/columns not pertinent to this text have been omitted by PPI.

Table 11.3

Live Load Element Factor, K_{LL}

element	K_{LL}
interior columns	4
exterior columns without cantilever slabs	4
edge columns with cantilever slabs	3
corner columns with cantilever slabs	2
edge beams without cantilever slabs	2
interior beams	2
all other members not identified above including edge beams with cantilever slabs cantilever beams two-way slabs members without provisions for continuous shear transfer normal to their span	1

2009 International Building Code. Copyright 2009. Washington, DC: International Code Council, Inc. Reproduced with permission. All rights reserved. www.iccsafe.org

Minimum roof live loads are prescribed by the code and act on a horizontal projected area. This *roof live load*, L_r, is given by the following formula, with a minimum value of 12 psf.

$$L_r = 20R_1R_2 \tag{11.4}$$

The value of R_1 is based on the *tributary area*, A_t, of the member. If A_t does not exceed 200 ft^2, R_1 is 1.0. If A_t exceeds 600 ft^2, R_1 is 0.6. For values of A_t between these two limits the following equation is used.

$$R_1 = 1.2 - 0.001A_t \tag{11.5}$$

The value of R_2 is based on the *roof slope*, F, in inches of rise per foot of run. If F does not exceed 4 in/ft, R_2 is 1.0. If F exceeds 12 in/ft, R_2 is 0.6. For values of F between these two limits the following equation is used.

$$R_2 = 1.2 - 0.05F \tag{11.6}$$

Example 11.3

What roof live load should be used to design a column that supports 450 ft^2 of a roof with a slope of 5 in of rise per foot of run? Calculate the reduction factors for tributary area and slope, and then find the design roof live load.

$$\begin{aligned} R_1 &= 1.2 - 0.001A_t \\ &= 1.2 - (0.001)(450) \\ &= 0.75 \end{aligned}$$

$$\begin{aligned} R_2 &= 1.2 - 0.05F \\ &= 1.2 - (0.5)(5) \\ &= 0.95 \end{aligned}$$

$$\begin{aligned} L_r &= 20R_1R_2 \\ &= \left(20\ \frac{\text{lbf}}{\text{ft}^2}\right)(0.75)(0.95) \\ &= 14.25\ \text{psf} \end{aligned}$$

Since the calculated roof live load is greater than the minimum value of 12, use 14.3 psf.

Load Combinations

It is generally agreed that when calculating the load on a building, all sources will not act at full values at once. For example, full snow load will not be present when full wind load exists because the wind will blow some of the snow away. The IBC recognizes this and requires that several combinations of load be calculated to find the most critical case. In addition some structural materials are designed using strength design while others use allowable stress design. The difference in these two methods is discussed in the appropriate structural material chapter.

The basic load combinations per IBC Sec. 1605.2.1 using strength design or load and resistance factor design are as follows.

- $1.4D$
- $1.2D + 1.6L + 0.5(L_r \text{ or } S \text{ or } R)$
- $1.2D + 1.6(L_r \text{ or } S \text{ or } R) + f_1L \text{ or } 0.8W$
- $1.2D + 1.6W + f_1L + 0.5(L_r \text{ or } S \text{ or } R)$
- $1.2D + 1.0E + f_1L + f_2S$
- $0.9D + 1.0E \text{ or } 1.6W$

The value of f_1 is 1.0 for floors in places of public assembly, parking garages, and where the live load exceeds 100 psf. For any other cases a value of 0.5 may be used for f_1. The value of f_2 is 0.7 for roof configurations that do not shed snow off the structure (such as saw tooth). For any other cases a value of 0.2 may be used for f_2.

The American Concrete Institute building code requirements allow for a slightly different set of factors, which have been used over the past few decades. These factors are given in Ch. 20.

The basic load combinations per IBC Sec. 1605.3.1 using allowable stress design are as follows.

- D
- $D + L$
- $D + L + L_r$ or S or R
- $D + W$ or $0.7E + L + L_r$ or S or R
- $0.6D + W$
- $0.6D + 0.7E$

Alternate basic load combinations per IBC Sec. 1605.3.2 using allowable stress design are as follows.

- $D + L + L_r$ or S or R
- $D + L + \omega W$
- $D + L + \omega W + S/2$
- $D + L + S + \omega W/2$
- $D + L + S + E/1.4$
- $0.9D + E/1.4$

LATERAL LOADS

Wind

Wind loading on buildings is a dynamic process. That is, the pressures, directions, and timing are constantly changing. For purposes of calculation, however, wind is considered a static force. There are several variables that affect wind loading. The first is the *wind velocity* itself. The pressure on a building varies as the square of the velocity according to the following formula.

$$p_{\text{psf}} = 0.00256 v_{\text{mph}}^2 \quad \text{[U.S.]} \quad 11.7(a)$$

$$p_{\text{N/m}^2} = 0.613 v_{\text{m/s}}^2 \quad \text{[SI]} \quad 11.7(b)$$

The second variable is the *height* of the wind above the ground. Since wind acts as any fluid where a surface causes friction and slows the fluid, wind velocity is lower near the ground and increases with height. Wind speed values are taken at a standard height of 10 m (33 ft) above the ground, so adjustments must be made when calculating pressure at different elevations.

A third variable is the nature of the building's *surroundings*. Other buildings, trees, and topography affect how the wind will finally strike the structure under consideration. Buildings in large, open areas are subject to more wind force than those in protected areas. The surroundings are taken into account along with multiplying factors found in the building codes.

Finally, there are factors like the size, shape, and surface texture of the building. Some buildings allow the wind to flow around them, while others channel or focus the wind.

A building subjected to wind forces responds in several ways. These are shown diagrammatically in Fig. 11.1. There is, of course, positive pressure on the windward side of the building. On the leeward side and roof there is often a negative

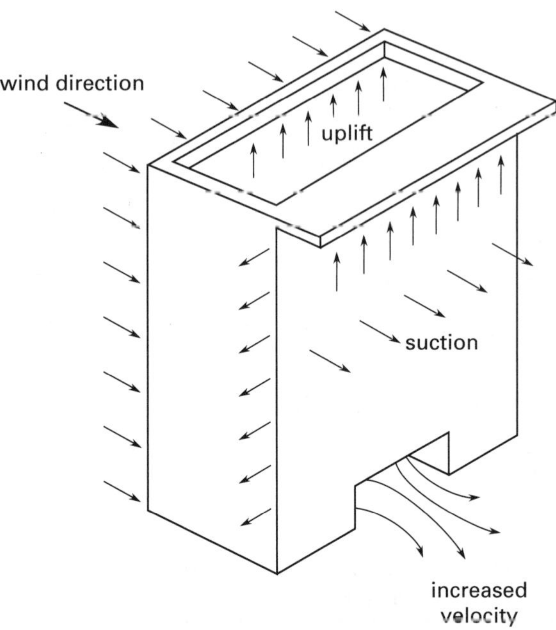

Figure 11.1 Forces on a Building Due to Wind

pressure, or suction. In addition to these, there are local areas where wind pressure is greater such as building corners, overhangs, parapets, and other projections. For complex buildings, wind tunnel tests may need to be performed. For some rectangular buildings not exceeding a height of 60 ft, simplified wind calculations are allowed. However, the code specifies an analytical method for most buildings. This analytical method is described in detail in Ch. 22.

Of particular interest to architects are building shapes and design features that may exacerbate wind problems. These include things such as closely spaced buildings or small openings at ground level that cause normally acceptable wind speeds to increase to unacceptable levels. Because wind is a fluid, forcing a given volume at a given speed into a smaller area causes the speed to increase. There have been instances, for example, where localized winds are so great that entry doors cannot be opened or an otherwise pleasant outdoor plaza is unusable.

Other potential problems include *building drift*, which is the distance a building moves from side to side in the wind. This is particularly of concern in very tall buildings where the drift may be several feet. Generally, a building should be designed to be stiff enough that the maximum drift does not exceed 1/500 of the height of the building.

Earthquake

Like wind, an earthquake produces dynamic loads on a building. During an earthquake, the ground moves both vertically and laterally, but the lateral movement is usually most significant and the vertical movement is normally ignored.

For some tall buildings or structures with complex shapes or unusual conditions, a *dynamic structural analysis* is required. With this method, a computer is used to model the building and earthquakes to study the response of the structure and what forces are developed. In most cases, however, building codes allow a static analysis of the loads produced, greatly simplifying the structural design.

With the *static analysis method*, the total horizontal shear at the base of the building is calculated according to a standard formula. Then, this total lateral force is distributed to the various floors of the building so the designer knows what force the structure must resist. Chapter 23 discusses calculation of earthquake loads in more detail.

MISCELLANEOUS LOADS

Dynamic Loads

When a load is applied suddenly or changes rapidly, it is called a *dynamic load*. When a force is only applied suddenly, it is often called an *impact load*. Examples of dynamic loads are automobiles moving in a parking garage, elevators traveling in a shaft, or a helicopter landing on the roof of a building. Dynamic loads do not occur on every building but are important to analyze and design for. The IBC specifies minimum requirements for many of these types of loads. In many cases, a dynamic load is treated as a static load value multiplied by an impact factor.

A unique type of dynamic load is a *resonant load*. This is a rhythmic application of a force to a structure with the same fundamental period as the structure itself. The *fundamental period* is the time it takes the structure to complete one full oscillation, such as a complete swing from side to side in a tall building in the wind or one up-and-down bounce of a floor. Resonant loads are usually small compared to other types of loads but slowly build over time as the load repeatedly amplifies the motion of the structure. The principle of resonant loading is what makes it possible for a few people to overturn a heavy car by bouncing it on its springs in time with the fundamental period of the springs. The rocking motion of the car eventually is great enough that a final push makes the car overturn.

Resonant loads can affect an entire structure. One example is repeated gusts of wind on a tall building or on portions of a building. A common problem is a vibrating machine attached to a floor that has the same period as the machine's vibrations. In such a situation, the floor can be subjected to forces larger than it was designed for. The problem can be alleviated by placing the machine on resilient pads or springs to dampen the vibration, or by stiffening the floor to change its fundamental period.

Occasionally, a tuned dynamic damper is placed at the top of tall buildings to dampen the effects of wind sway. This is a very heavy mass attached to the sides of the building with springs of the same period as the building. As the building oscillates in one direction, the spring-mounted mass moves in the opposite direction, effectively counteracting the action of the wind. With this approach, costly wind bracing normally required to stiffen the entire building can be minimized.

Temperature-Induced Loads

All materials expand when they are heated and contract when they are cooled. The amount of the change is dependent on the material and is expressed as the *coefficient of expansion* measured in inches per inch per degree Fahrenheit. Some materials, like wood, have a low coefficient of expansion while others, like plastic, have a high value. If a material is restrained so it cannot move and is then subjected to a temperature change, a load is introduced on the material in addition to any other applied loads.

In the worst case, temperature-induced loads can so overload a structural member that failure may occur. Most often, however, failing to account for temperature-induced loads causes other types of failures such as tight-fitting glass breaking when a metal frame contracts, or masonry walls cracking when expansion joints are not provided. In nearly all cases, the solution is fairly simple: the material or assembly of materials must be allowed to expand and contract for the expected distance. This is fairly easy to calculate, and detailed methods are described in Ch. 12.

Soil Loads

Retaining walls are required to resist the lateral pressure of the retained material in accordance with accepted engineering practice. Table 11.4 gives the minimum lateral pressures to be used in the design of retaining walls, as specified by the IBC. This is in addition to any surcharge such as vertical loads near the top of the wall or other lateral loads. In addition, retaining walls must be designed to resist sliding by at least 1.5 times the lateral force and resist overturning by at least 1.5 times the overturning moment.

To calculate the pressure at the bottom of the wall, p, simply multiply the design lateral soil pressure, q, by the depth of the wall, h, to get pounds per square foot. The active pressure specified in the table is used for free-draining backfill, while the passive pressure is used for other cases. Since the pressure varies uniformly from zero at the very top of the wall, where no earth is retained, to a maximum at the bottom, the total horizontal load per linear foot acting on the wall is found by calculating the area of the triangular distribution or the maximum earth pressure at the bottom times the height divided by two (see Fig. 11.2).

$$P = p\left(\frac{h}{2}\right)$$

Table 11.4
Soil Lateral Loads

description of backfill material[c]	unified soil classification	design lateral soil load[a] (psf/ft of depth) active pressure	at-rest pressure
well-graded, clean gravels; gravel-sand mixes	GW	30	60
poorly graded clean gravels; gravel-sand mixes	GP	30	60
silty gravels, poorly graded gravel-sand mixes	GM	40	60
clayey gravels, poorly graded gravel-and-clay mixes	GC	45	60
well-graded, clean sands; gravelly sand mixes	SW	30	60
poorly graded clean sands; sand-gravel mixes	SP	30	60
silty sands, poorly graded sand-silt mixes	SM	45	60
sand-silt clay mix with plastic fines	SM-SC	45	100
clayey sands, poorly graded sand-clay mixes	SC	60	100
inorganic silts and clayey silts	ML	45	100
mixture of inorganic silt and clay	ML-CL	60	100
inorganic clays of low to medium plasticity	CL	60	100
organic silts and silt clays, low plasticity	OL	Note b	Note b
inorganic clayey silts, elastic silts	MH	Note b	Note b
inorganic clays of high plasticity	CH	Note b	Note b
organic clays and silty clays	OH	Note b	Note b

For SI: 1 psf/ft of depth = 0.157 kPa/m, 1 ft = 304.8 mm.
[a]Design lateral soil loads are given for moist conditions for the specified soils at their optimum densities. Actual field conditions shall govern. Submerged or saturated soil pressures shall include the weight of the buoyant soil plus the hydrostatic loads.
[b]Unsuitable as backfill material.
[c]The definition and classification of soil materials shall be in accordance with ASTM D 2487.

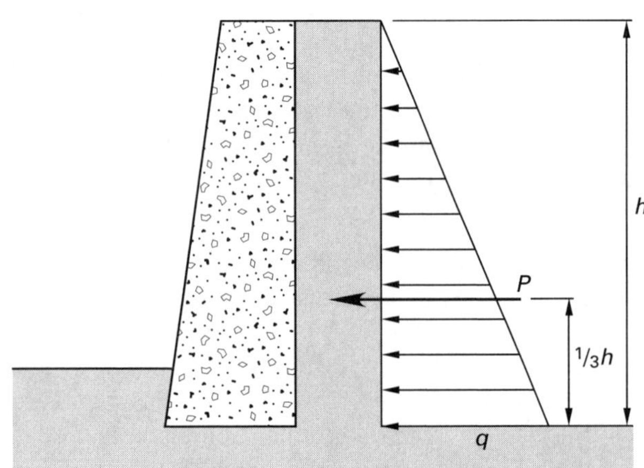

Figure 11.2 Load from Soil on Retaining Wall

Example 11.4

What is the total horizontal load exerted on a retaining wall 8 ft high? The wall is retaining free-draining silty sand. From Table 11.4 an active pressure of 45 psf may be used for the silty sand.

The pressure at the bottom is (8 ft)(45 psf), or 360 psf. The total horizontal load is (360 psf/2)(8 ft), or 1440 plf.

It will be shown that this total load acts at the centroid of a triangle, or one-third the distance from the base. Retaining-wall design is discussed in more detail in Ch. 15.

Water

Loads from water can occur in many situations: in water tanks, in swimming pools, and against retaining walls holding back groundwater. The load developed from water and other fluids is equal to the unit weight of the fluid in pounds per cubic foot multiplied by its depth. For water, the weight is about 62 lbf/ft^3, and the water force exerted on structures is called *hydrostatic pressure*.

12 STRUCTURAL FUNDAMENTALS

Nomenclature

A	area	in^2 or ft^2
b	base of rectangular section	in
d	depth of rectangular section	in
d	diameter	in
d	distance between axes	in
e	total deformation (strain)	in
E	modulus of elasticity	lbf/in^2
f	unit stress	lbf/in^2
F	force	lbf
I	moment of inertia	in^4
I_n	moment of inertia of transferred area	in^4
I_X	moment of inertia of area about neutral axis	in^4
L	original length	in
P	total force	lbf
r	radius	in
R	reaction force	lbf
T	temperature	°F
W	weight	lbf
α	coefficient of linear expansion	in/in-°F
ϵ	unit strain	decimal
θ	angle	deg

STATICS AND FORCES

Statics

Statics is the branch of mechanics that deals with bodies in a state of equilibrium. *Equilibrium* is said to exist when the resultant of any number of forces acting on a body is zero. For example, a 10 lbm object on the ground is acted on by gravity to the magnitude of 10 lbf. The ground, in turn, exerts an upward force of 10 lbf and the object is in equilibrium.

Three fundamental principles of equilibrium apply to buildings.

- The sum of all vertical forces acting on a body must equal zero (as in the preceding simple example).
- The sum of all horizontal forces acting on a body must equal zero.
- The sum of all the moments acting on a body must equal zero.

Forces

A *force* is any action applied to an object. In architecture, external forces are called *loads* and result from the weights of such things as people, wind, snow, or building materials. The internal structure of a building material must resist external loads with internal forces of their own that are equal in magnitude and of opposite sign. These external loads are called *stresses*. The structural design of buildings is primarily concerned with selecting the size, configuration, and material of components to resist, with a reasonable margin of safety, external forces acting on them.

A force has both direction and magnitude and as such is called a *vector quantity*. Direction is shown by using a line with an arrowhead, and magnitude is indicated by establishing a convenient scale. For example, at a scale of 1 in equals 2000 lbf, a line 2 in long represents a force of 4000 lbf. An 8000 lbf force would therefore be shown with a line 4 in long.

The line of action of a force is a line concurrent with the force vector. A force acting anywhere along the line of action can be considered equal or unchanged as long as the direction and magnitude do not change. This is the principle of *transmissibility*.

There are several types of forces.

- *Collinear forces* are those whose vectors lie along the same straight line. See Fig. 12.1(a). Structural members subjected to collinear forces such as tension or compression are said to be two-force members.
- *Concurrent forces* are those whose lines of action meet at a common point. See Fig. 12.1(b).
- *Nonconcurrent forces* have lines of action that do not pass through a common point. See Fig. 12.1(c). A special case of this type that is commonly found in architectural applications is a parallel force system, such as a type that may be acting on a beam. See Fig. 12.1(d).
- *Coplanar forces* are forces whose lines of action all lie within the same plane. Noncoplanar forces do not lie within the same plane.

Structural forces in buildings can be any combination of these types. For example, a truss is a collection of sets of concurrent-coplanar forces, while a space frame is an example of a combination of sets of concurrent-noncoplanar forces.

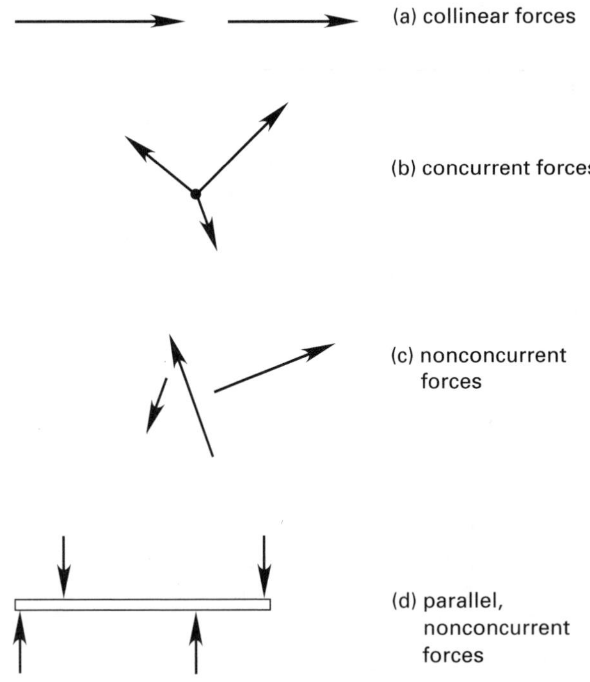

Figure 12.1 Types of Forces

It is often necessary to add two or more concurrent forces or to break down a single force into its components for purposes of structural analysis. The simplest combination of forces is represented by collinear forces. The magnitudes of the forces are added directly in the same direction of force. See Fig. 12.2.

Figure 12.2 Addition of Collinear Forces

With concurrent and nonconcurrent forces, the effect of the direction of the force must be taken into account. The methods used to find resultant forces or to break down a force into its components will be discussed in the Structural Analysis section in this chapter.

Stresses

Stress is the internal resistance to an external force. There are three basic types of stress: tension, compression, and shear. Tension and compression stresses are known as *normal stresses*. All stresses consist of these basic types or some combination thereof.

Tension is stress in which the particles of the member tend to pull apart under load.

Compression is stress in which the particles of the member are pushed together and the member tends to shorten.

Shear is stress in which the particles of a member slide past each other.

With tension and compression, the force acts *perpendicular* to the area of the material resisting the force. With shear, the force acts *parallel* to the area resisting the force.

For these three conditions, stress is expressed as force per unit area and is determined by dividing the total force applied to the total area.

$$f = \frac{P}{A} \qquad 12.1$$

Example 12.1

A balcony is partially supported from structure above by a steel rod with a $1^1/_4$ in diameter. The load on the rod is 10,000 lbf. What is the stress in the rod?

The radius of the rod is

$$r = \frac{d}{2} = \frac{1.25 \text{ in}}{2} = 0.625 \text{ in}$$

The area of the rod is

$$\begin{aligned} A &= \pi r^2 = \pi(0.625 \text{ in})^2 \\ &= 1.23 \text{ in}^2 \end{aligned}$$

From Eq. 12.1, the stress is

$$f = \frac{P}{A} = \frac{10{,}000 \text{ lbf}}{1.23 \text{ in}^2} = 8130 \text{ psi}$$

Other types of stresses consist of torsion, bending, and combined stresses. *Torsion* is a type of shear in which a member is twisted. *Bending* is a combination of tension and compression like the type that occurs in beams. This will be discussed in more detail in Ch. 13. *Combined loads* can occur in many situations. For example, a column resisting loads from above and lateral wind loads is subjected to both compression and bending.

Thermal Stress

When a material is subjected to a change in temperature, it expands if heated or contracts if cooled. For an unrestrained material, the general formula is

$$e = \alpha x \Delta T \qquad 12.2$$

Some coefficients of common materials are shown in Table 12.1.

Table 12.1

Coefficients of Linear Expansion

material	coefficient (in/in-°F)
aluminum	0.0000128
brick	0.0000034
bronze	0.0000101
concrete	0.0000055
glass	0.0000051
marble	0.0000045
plastic, acrylic	0.0000450
structural steel	0.0000065
wood, fir parallel to grain	0.0000021

If the material is restrained at both ends, a change in temperature causes an internal thermal stress. The formula for this stress is

$$f = E\alpha\Delta T \qquad 12.3$$

Notice that the unit stress is independent of the cross-sectional area of the member if there are no other loads being applied to the member while it is undergoing thermal stress.

Strain and Deformation

As a force is applied to a material, the material changes size. For example, a tensile force causes a rod to elongate and narrow, while a compressive force causes a material to shorten and widen. *Strain* is the deformation of a material caused by external forces. It is the ratio of the total change in length of a material to its original length. As a formula, it is represented as

$$\epsilon = \frac{e}{L} \qquad 12.4$$

As a force is applied to a material, the deformation (strain) is directly proportional to the stress, up to a certain point. This is known as *Hooke's law*, named after Robert Hooke, the British mathematician and physicist who first discovered it. This relationship is shown graphically in Fig. 12.3. At a certain point, however, the material will begin to change length at a faster ratio than the applied force. This point is called the *elastic limit*. At any stress up to the elastic limit, the material will return to its original size if the force is removed. Above the elastic limit there will be permanent deformation, even if the force is removed.

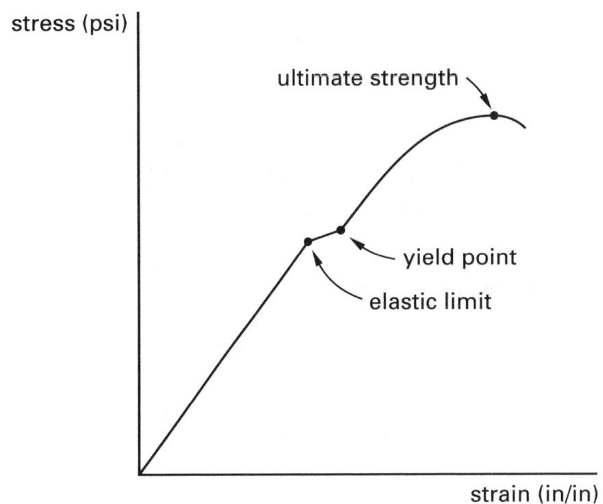

Figure 12.3 Hypothetical Stress-Strain Graph

With some materials there is also a point, slightly above the elastic limit, called the *yield point*. This is the point at which the material continues to deform with very little increase in load. Some materials, such as wood, have poorly defined elastic limits and no yield points.

If the load is continually increased, the material will ultimately rupture. The unit stress just before this occurs is called the *ultimate strength* of the material.

Although the entire range of a material's stress/strain relationship is interesting from a theoretical point of view, the most important portion from a practical standpoint is where the stress and strain are directly proportional, up to the elastic limit. Sound engineering practices and limitations set by building codes establish the working stresses to be used in calculations at some point below the yield point.

Every material has a characteristic ratio of stress to strain. This is called the *modulus of elasticity*, *E*, which is a measure of a material's resistance to deformation, or its stiffness. It can be expressed as the following formula.

$$E = \frac{f}{\epsilon} \qquad 12.5$$

Since stress was defined as total force divided by total area, $f = P/A$ (Eq. 12.1), and strain was defined as total strain divided by original length, $\epsilon = e/L$ (Eq. 12.4), the equation can be rewritten as follows.

$$E = \frac{\frac{P}{A}}{\frac{e}{L}} = \frac{PL}{Ae} \qquad 12.6$$

This equation can also be used to find the total strain (deformation) of a material under a given load by rearranging the values.

$$e = \frac{PL}{AE}$$

Example 12.2

If a load of 12,000 lbf is applied to a 3 ft, 4 × 4 Douglas fir no. 2 wood column, how much will it compress? The modulus of elasticity for Douglas fir no. 2 is 1,700,000 psi.

The actual size of a 4 × 4 is $3^1/_2$ in by $3^1/_2$ in, or 12.25 in^2. The change in length is therefore

$$e = \frac{PL}{AE} = \frac{(12{,}000 \text{ lbf})(3 \text{ ft})\left(12 \frac{\text{in}}{\text{ft}}\right)}{(12.25 \text{ in}^2)\left(1{,}700{,}000 \frac{\text{lbf}}{\text{in}^2}\right)} = 0.021 \text{ in}$$

0.0207 in is between $^1/_{64}$ in (0.01563) and $^1/_{32}$ in (0.03125).

Some representative values of E for various materials are given in Table 12.2 to show how they vary with material type. Actual values of E to be used in calculations should be derived from building codes or accepted tables of values.

Table 12.2
Modulus of Elasticity of Some Common Building Materials*

material	modulus of elasticity (psi)
structural steel	29,000,000
brass	15,000,000
aluminum	10,000,000
concrete (3000 psi)	3,200,000
lumber (Douglas fir-larch)	1,700,000
lumber (western cedar)	900,000

*These are representative values only. Exact values depend on such things as the alloy of the metal, mix of concrete, or species and grade of lumber.

Moment

Moment is a special condition of a force applied to a structure. A *moment* is the tendency of a force to cause rotation about a point. As such, it is the product of the force times the perpendicular distance to the point about which it is acting. The units are in foot-pounds, inch-pounds, or kip-feet. Figure 12.4 illustrates a simple condition of moments where two downward forces are balancing a lever on one pivot point. Even though the forces are of unequal value, they balance the lever because the distances from the pivot point result in equal moments.

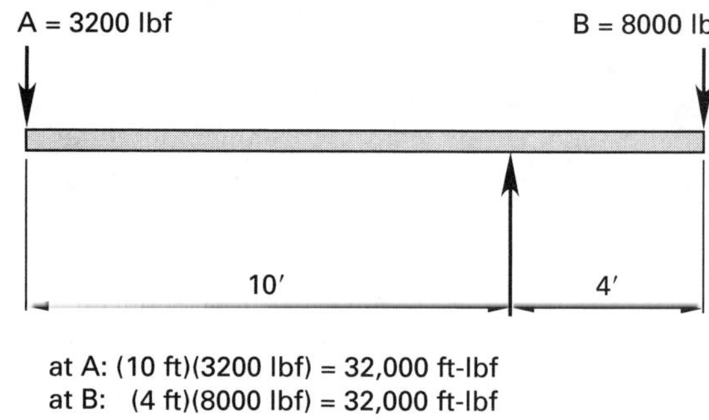

Figure 12.4 Moments in Equilibrium

Understanding the concept of moments is important in structural design because in a system in equilibrium the algebraic sum of moments about any point is zero. This concept allows an architect to analyze structures, determine support reactions, and design structural systems. When dealing with moments, it is necessary to be consistent with the values given to moments based on the directions in which they act. If a force tends to cause a clockwise rotation, the moment is said to be *positive*. If it tends to cause a counterclockwise rotation, the moment is said to be *negative*. This is a purely arbitrary convention and could be reversed, as long as the calculations are kept consistent.

Example 12.3

Consider a simply supported beam with two concentrated loads at the locations shown. Determine the reactions of the two supports, ignoring the weight of the beam itself.

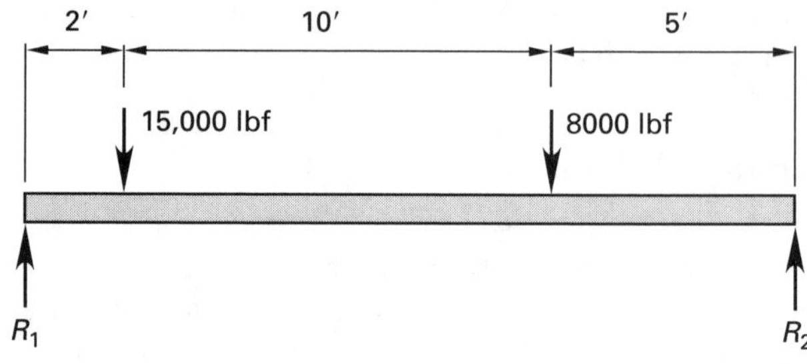

Since there are two unknowns, R_1 and R_2, select one of these points as the pivot point about which to make calculations. This eliminates one of the variables because the distance the force acts from the pivot point is zero, so the moment will be zero also. Select R_1 as the first point.

Since the algebraic sum about point R_1 is zero, the formula is as follows.

About R_1,

$$(15{,}000\ \text{lbf})(2\ \text{ft}) + (8000\ \text{lbf})(12\ \text{ft}) - R_2(17\ \text{ft}) = 0\ \text{ft-lbf}$$

The two concentrated loads tend to cause rotation in a clockwise direction (positive), while the reaction of the other beam support tends to cause a counterclockwise rotation (negative) about point R_1.

Solving for R_2 gives 7412 lbf.

Since one of the principles of equilibrium is that the sum of all vertical forces equals zero, R_1 and R_2 (upward) must equal the loads (downward). Therefore,

$$R_1 = 15{,}000\ \text{lbf} + 8000\ \text{lbf} - 7412\ \text{lbf} = 15{,}588\ \text{lbf}$$

However, you can use the same procedure of summing moments about reaction R_2 to find R_1 another way.

About R_2,

$$R_1(17\ \text{ft}) - (15{,}000\ \text{lbf})(15\ \text{ft}) - (8000\ \text{lbf})(5\ \text{ft}) = 0\ \text{ft-lbf}$$

$$R_1 = 15{,}588\ \text{lbf}$$

Moments on beams will be discussed in more detail in Ch. 13.

PROPERTIES OF SECTIONS

Regardless of material, all structural sections used to support building loads have certain properties. These properties affect how efficiently the sections can resist a load and how they are designed. The most common properties are *area*, *centroid*, *statical moment*, *moment of inertia*, *section modulus*, and *radius of gyration*. The area of a section is self-explanatory and its use in calculating stress has already been shown.

Centroid

In all solid bodies, there is a point at which the mass of the body can be considered concentrated. This is the *center of gravity*. Although technically a flat area cannot have a center of gravity because it has no mass, the point on a plane surface that corresponds to the center of gravity is called the *centroid*. In symmetrical sections, such as a rectangular wood beam or round bar, the centroid is located in the geometric center of the area as shown in Fig. 12.5.

The locations of centroids have been computed for simple nonsymmetrical areas (see Fig. 12.6).

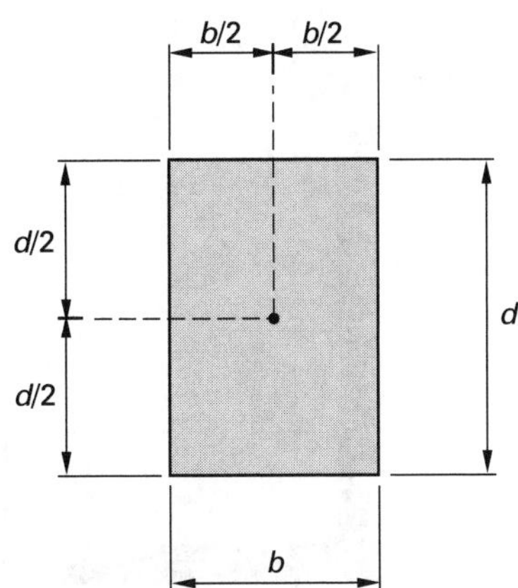

Figure 12.5 Centroid of a Symmetrical Area

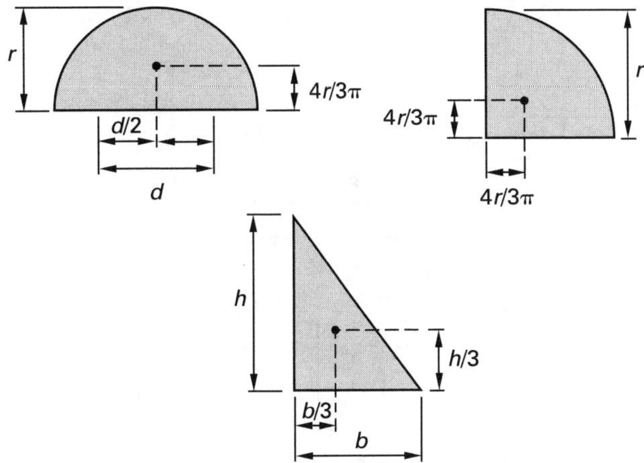

Figure 12.6 Centroids for Some Common Shapes

Manufacturers of structural members also include the location of centroids as part of their published data (see Fig. 12.7). Figure 12.7 illustrates one example of a steel section as found in the American Institute of Steel Construction *Steel Construction Manual*.

Statical Moment

To find the centroid of unsymmetrical areas, the statical moment must be used. The statical moment of a plane area with respect to an axis is the product of the area times the perpendicular distance from the centroid of the area to the axis. If a complex unsymmetrical area is divided into two or more simple parts, the statical moment of the entire area is equal to the sum of the statical moments of the parts.

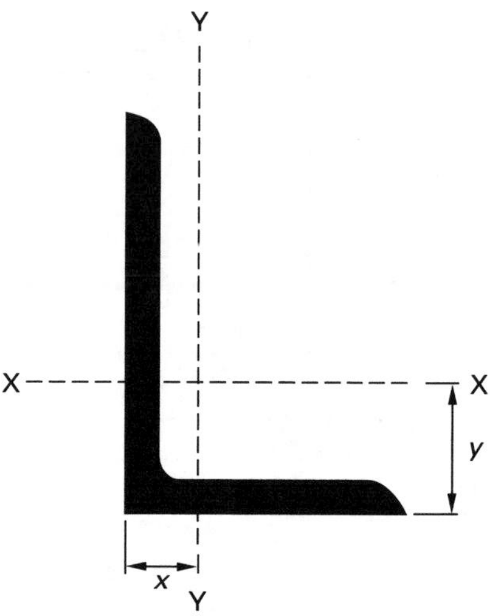

Figure 12.7 Centroidal Axes of Steel Angle with Unequal Legs

Example 12.4

Locate the centroid of the area shown.

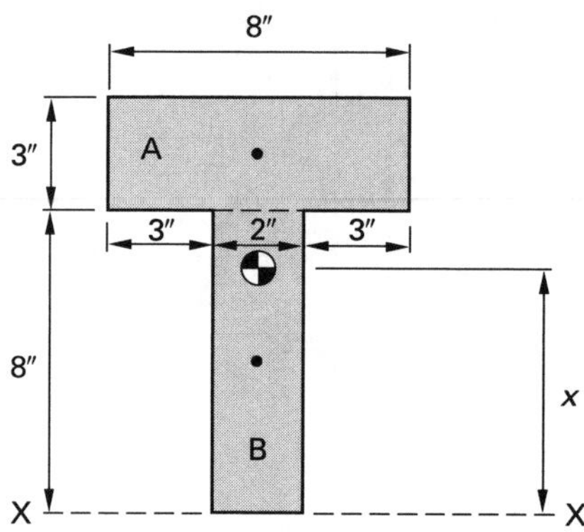

Select any convenient axis. In this case, use the X-X axis at the base of the object. Let x equal the distance from the axis to the centroid of the entire object. Divide the area into two rectangular sections, A and B, each having its centroid in the geometric center of its respective area.

The sum of the statical moments of the parts equals the statical moment of the entire section—all about the axis X-X. The distance from X-X to the centroid of area A is 9.5 in, and the distance to the centroid of area B is 4 in.

$$(9.5 \text{ in})(24 \text{ in}^2) + (4 \text{ in})(16 \text{ in}^2) = x(40 \text{ in}^2)$$

$$x = 7.3 \text{ in}$$

Since this object is symmetrical about the vertical, or Y-Y axis, the centroid will be in the center of the object between the right and left edges.

If there is a hole in the object, treat the area of the hole as a negative number.

Moment of Inertia

Another important property of structural sections is the *moment of inertia*. In general terms, this is a measure of the *bending stiffness* of a structural member's cross-sectional shape, similar to how the modulus of elasticity is a measure of the stiffness of the material of a structural member.

In more exact terms, the moment of inertia about a certain axis of a section is the summation of all the infinitely small areas of the section multiplied by the square of the distance from the axis to each of these areas. Its common designation is I, and its units are inches to the fourth power. It is most common to use the neutral axis (axis passing through the centroid) as the axis of reference, but the moment of inertia about an axis through the base of a figure is also useful when calculating I for unsymmetrical sections. See Fig. 12.8.

The derivation of the moment of inertia for a section is done with calculus, but I for common shapes can be calculated with simple equations that have been derived with calculus. In addition, most manufacturers of structural shapes give the value of the moment of inertia with respect to both vertical and horizontal axes passing through the centroid. For example, the tables of structural steel shapes give the value I for both the X-X and Y-Y centroidal axes.

For rectangular sections, the moment of inertia about the centroidal axis parallel to the base is

$$I = \frac{bd^3}{12} \qquad 12.8$$

The moment of inertia about an axis through the base of a rectangular section is

$$I = \frac{bd^3}{3} \qquad 12.9$$

Example 12.5

Find the moment of inertia of a solid wood beam 6 in wide and 13½ in deep.

$$I = \frac{(6 \text{ in})(13.5 \text{ in})^3}{12}$$

$$= 1230 \text{ in}^4$$

In order to find the moment of inertia for composite areas, transfer the moment of inertia of each section about its centroid to a new axis, typically the centroid of the composite section. The general formula for doing this, as illustrated in Fig. 12.8, is

$$I_n = I_X + Ad^2 \qquad 12.10$$

The transferred moments of inertia of the various sections are then added to get the moment of inertia for the entire section.

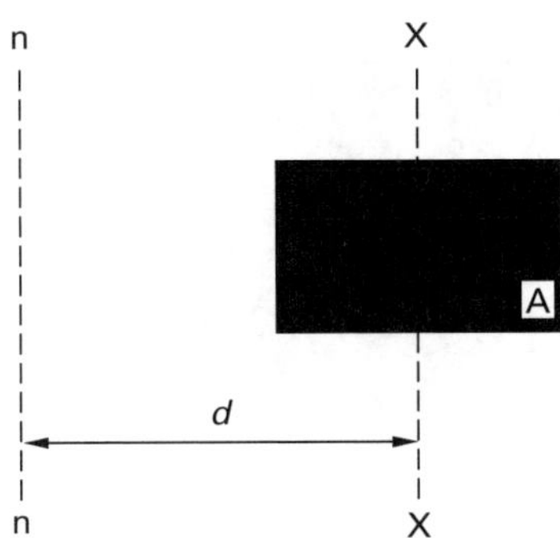

Figure 12.8 Transfer of Moment of Inertia

Example 12.6

Using the same composite section as shown in Ex. 12.4, calculate the moment of inertia.

The first step is to locate the centroid of the object. This was done in the previous example problem and was found to be 7.3 in.

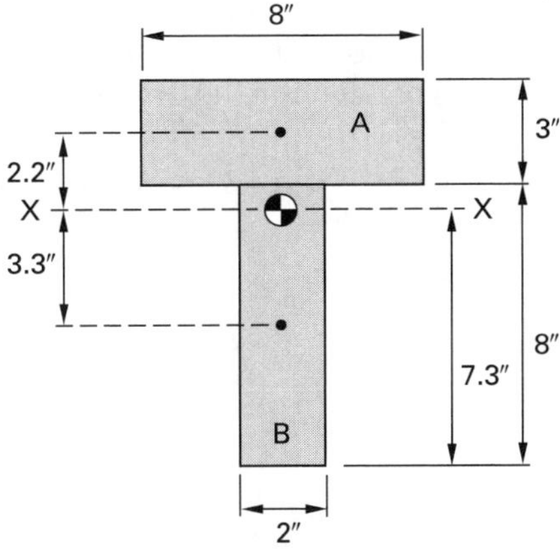

The next task is to transfer the individual moments of inertia about this centroidal axis and add them. To do this, it is helpful to set up a table so all the figures and calculations can be seen easily. This is an especially useful technique when dealing with several individual areas.

The moments of inertia of areas A and B are found with Eq. 12.8, and are denoted I_o to express the fact that these are the moments of inertia about an axis passing through the centroid of the elementary figure. d is the distance from the centroidal axis to the axes of areas A and B. Performing the calculations yields

area	I_o (in^4)	A (in^2)	d (in)	Ad^2 (in^4)	$I_o + Ad^2$ (in^4)
A	18.00	24.00	2.200	116.2	134.2
B	85.33	16.00	3.300	174.3	259.6
					I_X = 393.8 in^4

The moment of inertia is dependent on the area of a section and the distance of the area from the neutral axis, but from that statement the moment of inertia is the summation of the areas times the square of the distances of those areas from the neutral axis. From Eqs. 12.8 and 12.9, it is evident that a beam's depth has a greater bearing on the beam's resistance to bending than its width or total area. This explains why a board placed on edge between two supports is much stronger than the same board placed on its side.

There are two other important properties of sections: the *section modulus* and the *radius of gyration*. However, these are more appropriately discussed in Ch. 13. Section modulus will be explained in the sections on beams and the theory of bending, while radius of gyration will be discussed in the section on columns.

STRUCTURAL ANALYSIS

Resultant Forces

There are times when it is desirable to combine two or more concurrent forces into one force such that the one force produces the same effect on a body as the concurrent forces. This single force is called the *resultant*. If the forces are collinear, as described previously in this chapter, the resultant is simply the sum of the forces, with forces acting upward or to the right considered positive and forces acting downward or to the left considered negative. For example, in Fig. 12.9 the three forces are added to get the resultant.

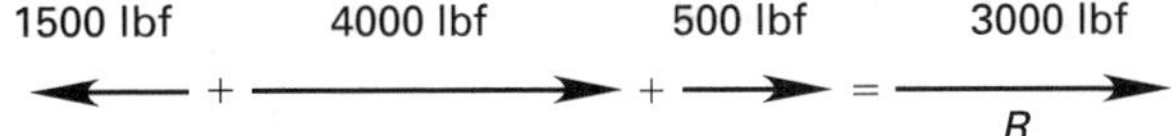

Figure 12.9 Resultant of Collinear Forces

For concurrent forces (forces whose lines of action pass through a common point), both the magnitude and direction must be taken into account. Consider the two forces shown in Fig. 12.10(a). The resultant of these forces can be found graphically or algebraically.

To find it graphically, draw the lines of force to any convenient scale, such as 1 in equals 100 lbf, and in the direction they are acting as shown in Fig. 12.10(b). Then draw a line parallel to each force, starting with the head of the force vector, to form a parallelogram. Connect the point of concurrence to the opposite corner of the parallelogram with a line. This is the resultant whose magnitude and direction can be found by scaling the length of it and measuring its angle.

To find the resultant algebraically, sketch a force triangle as shown in Fig. 12.10(c). Since the forces are in equilibrium, the triangle must close. The resultant will then be the third

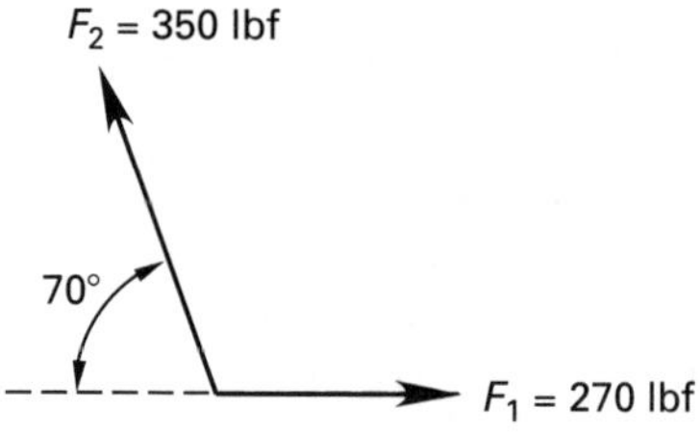

(a) concurrent, coplanar forces

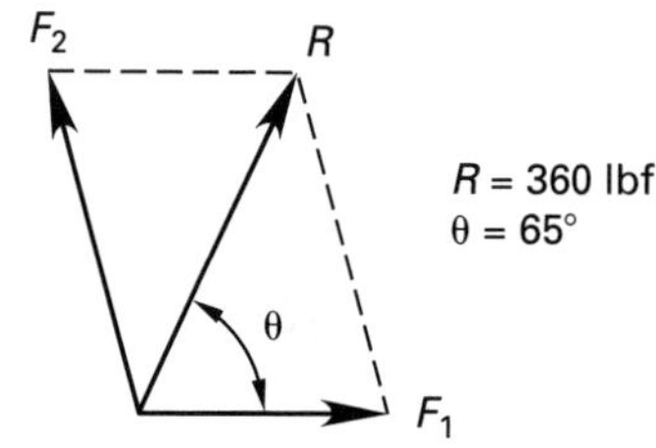

(b) graphic solution

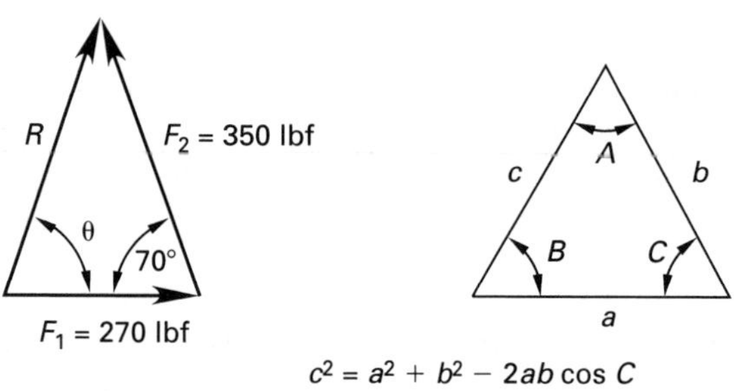

(c) algebraic solution

Figure 12.10 Finding the Resultant of Concurrent Coplanar Forces

side of the triangle. Both the magnitude and direction can be solved with trigonometry using the law of cosines and sines, or the Pythagorean theorem for a right triangle.

To find the magnitude of the resultant, use the law of cosines (see Ch. 1). From Fig.12.10(c),

$$c^2 = a^2 + b^2 - 2ab\cos C$$

$$R^2 = (350 \text{ lbf})^2 + (270 \text{ lbf})^2 - (2)(350 \text{ lbf})(270 \text{ lbf})\cos 70°$$

$$R = 361.6 \text{ lbf}$$

To find the direction of the resultant, use the law of sines.

$$\frac{a}{\sin A} = \frac{b}{\sin B} = \frac{c}{\sin C}$$

$$\frac{F_2}{\sin \theta} = \frac{R}{\sin 70°}$$

$$\sin\theta = \frac{F_2 \sin 70°}{R} = \frac{(350 \text{ lbf})\sin 70°}{361.6 \text{ lbf}} = 0.9095$$

$$\theta = \arcsin 0.9095 = 65.4°$$

Components of a Force

Just as a resultant can be found for two or more forces, so can a single force be resolved into two components. This method is often required when analyzing loads on a sloped surface (a roof, for example) and is necessary to find the horizontal and vertical reactions. As with finding resultant forces, both graphic and algebraic solutions are possible.

Example 12.7

Consider the diagonal force shown. What would be the vertical and horizontal reactions necessary to resist this force?

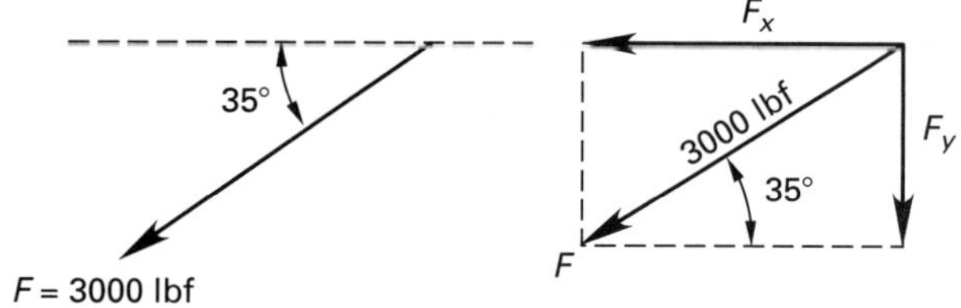

The reactions to the force would be equal in magnitude but opposite in direction to the vertical and horizontal components of the force. To solve the problem algebraically, construct a right triangle with the 3000 lbf force as the hypotenuse and the legs of the triangle as the horizontal and vertical forces.

Then,

$$\sin 35° = \frac{F_y}{3000 \text{ lbf}}$$

$$F_y = 1721 \text{ lbf}$$

$$\cos 35° = \frac{F_x}{3000 \text{ lbf}}$$

$$F_x = 2457 \text{ lbf}$$

Note that the same solution could be obtained by drawing the triangle to scale and measuring the legs of the triangle, although this method is not as accurate.

Three or more forces can be resolved by resolving each one into its horizontal and vertical components, summing these components (taking care to be consistent with positive and negative signs), and then finding the resultant of the horizontal and vertical components with the Pythagorean theorem.

Free-Body Diagrams

In analyzing structures it is sometimes convenient to extract a portion of the structure and represent the forces acting on it with force vectors. The portion then under study is called a *free-body diagram* to which the principles of equilibrium can be applied.

Consider the simple structure shown in Fig. 12.11(a) with a single load of 3000 lbf applied at the end. Find the load in member BC.

Take member BC as a free body as shown in Fig. 12.11(b). There are three forces acting on this member: the vertical load of 3000 lbf, the force in member BC (compression), and the force through member AB (tension). Since these forces act through a common point, and since the structure is in equilibrium, construct a force triangle with the force vectors as the sides of the triangle as shown in Fig. 12.11(c).

The angle, θ, can be determined from $\tan\theta = 5/8$, or 32°.

Then the force, F, in member BC is found from

$$\sin 32° = \frac{3000 \text{ lbf}}{F}$$

$$F = 5661 \text{ lbf}$$

Knowing the force in member BC, it is possible to find the horizontal and vertical components of the force using the methods described in the previous section.

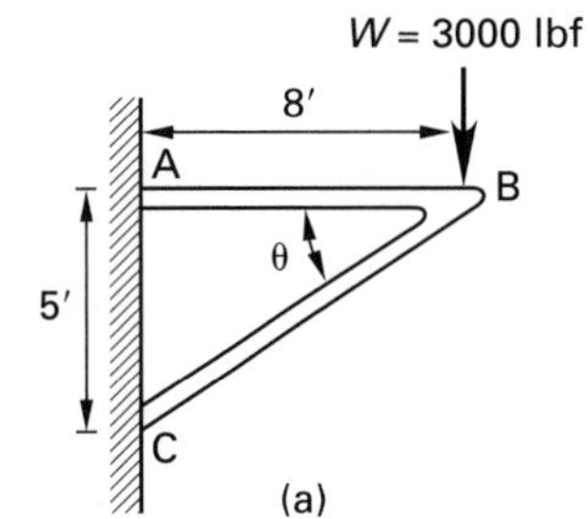

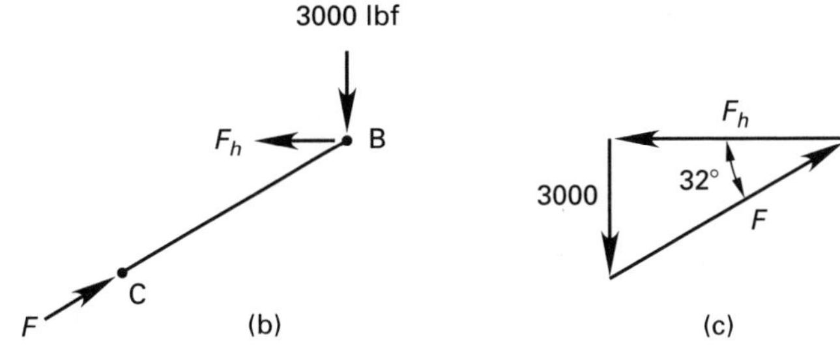

Figure 12.11 Free-Body Diagrams

13 BEAMS AND COLUMNS

Nomenclature

A	area	in^2
b	width of beam	in
c	distance from extreme fiber in bending to neutral axis	in
d	depth of beam	in
E	modulus of elasticity	lbf/in^2
f	allowable fiber stress in bending	lbf/in^2
f_b	extreme fiber stress in bending	lbf/in^2
F_a	allowable axial unit stress	lbf/in^2
I	moment of inertia	in^4
L	length	in
M	bending moment	in-lbf
P	concentrated load	lbf
Q	statical moment about neutral axis of the area above the plane under consideration	in^3
r	radius of gyration	in
S	section modulus	in^3
v_h	horizontal shear stress	lbf/in^2
V	vertical shearing force	lbf
w	uniformly distributed load	lbf/in
W	total uniformly distributed load	lbf
x	distance along a beam length	ft
σ	axial unit stress	lbf/in^2

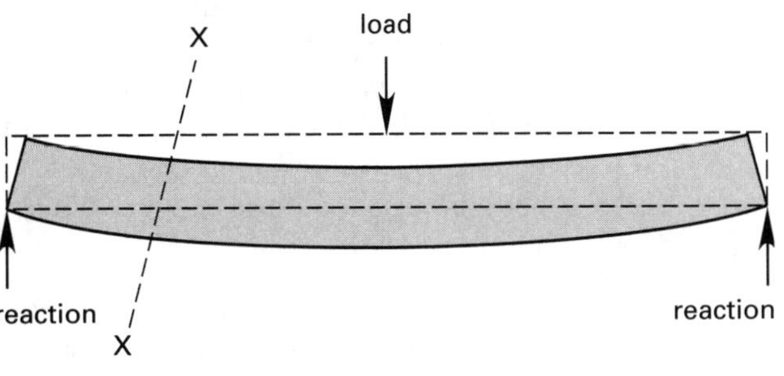

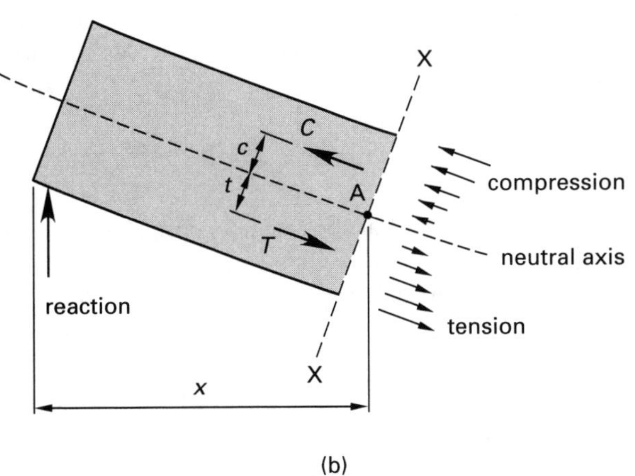

Figure 13.1 Behavior of Simply Supported Beam Under Load

BEAMS

Basic Principles

When a simply supported beam is subjected to a load, it deflects as shown in the exaggerated diagram in Fig. 13.1(a).

In order for this to happen, the top of the beam compresses and the bottom of the beam stretches, which causes compressive stresses to develop in the top half of the beam and tension stresses to develop in the bottom half. At the neutral axis, or centroid, which is in the geometric center of the beam if it is rectangular or symmetrical, the beam does not change length so no compressive or tension stresses are developed.

The actions occurring in the beam can be seen more clearly by taking an enlarged section of the beam to the left of an arbitrary cut as shown in Fig. 13.1(b).

In this diagram there are only three forces acting on the section: the reaction of the support, the compressive forces in the top of the beam, and the tensile forces in the bottom of the beam. If the beam is in equilibrium as discussed in Ch. 12, then all the moment forces must cancel out; those acting in a clockwise rotation must equal those acting in a counterclockwise rotation. Therefore, taking moments about point A in Fig. 13.1(b),

$$Rx = Cc + Tt \qquad 13.1$$

This formula represents the basic theory of bending: that the internal resisting moments at any point in a beam must equal the bending moments produced by the external loads on the beam.

As shown in Fig. 13.1(a), the moment increases as the distance from the reaction increases or as the distance from the neutral axis increases (assuming the loads stay the same). Therefore, in the case of a simply supported beam, the maximum moment occurs at the center of the span and the beam is subjected to its highest bending stresses at the extreme top and bottom fibers. (*Fibers* is the general term, regardless of the beam's material.)

Therefore, in order for a beam to support loads, the material, size, and shape of the beam must be selected to sustain the resisting moments at the point on the beam where the moment is greatest. There must be some way to relate the bending moments to the actual properties of a real beam. Although the derivation will not be given here, the final formula is simple.

$$\frac{M}{f_b} = \frac{I}{c} \qquad 13.2$$

Theoretically, Eq. 13.2 can be used to design a beam to resist bending forces, but it gets a little cumbersome with steel sections and unusual shapes. There is another property of every structural section that simplifies the formula even further. This is the *section modulus*, which is the ratio of the beam's moment of inertia to the distance from the neutral axis to the outermost part of the section (extreme fiber).

$$S = \frac{I}{c} \qquad 13.3$$

Substituting the value of S with Eq. 13.2 gives

$$S = \frac{M}{f} \qquad 13.4$$

So, knowing only the maximum moment on a beam caused by a particular loading condition and the maximum allowable fiber stress (given in tables and building codes), the required section modulus can be calculated. The minimum required section to support the bending loads can be found from reference tables or manufacturers' tables. For example, the *Steel Construction Manual* published by the American Institute of Steel Construction (AISC) gives the section modulus for all beam sections. How this formula is used will be illustrated in the sample question.

Another fundamental type of stress in beams is *shear*. This is the tendency of two adjacent portions of the beam to slide past each other in a vertical direction. See Fig. 13.2(a).

There is also *horizontal shear*, which is the tendency of two adjacent portions of a beam to slide past each other in the direction parallel to the length of the beam. This tendency can readily be seen by considering that the top portions of a beam tend to compress and the bottom portions tend to stretch. See Fig. 13.2(b).

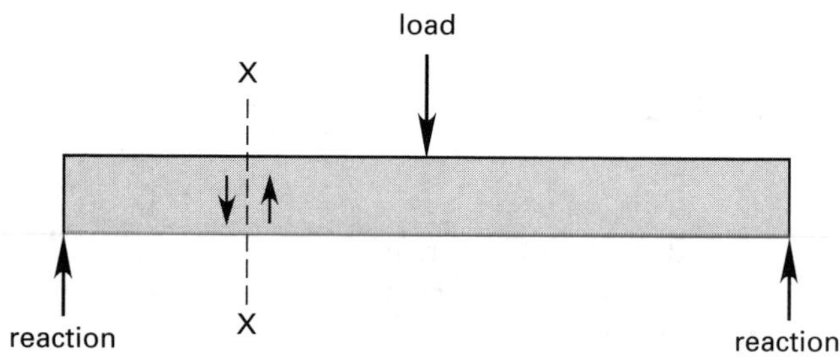

(a) vertical shear

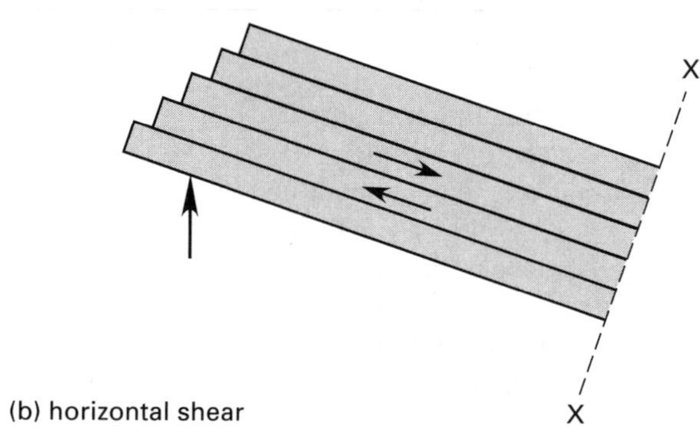

(b) horizontal shear

Figure 13.2 Shear Forces in Beams

The general equation for finding horizontal shear stress is

$$v_h = \frac{VQ}{Ib} \qquad 13.5$$

Q is the statical moment discussed in Ch. 12.

For rectangular sections, the horizontal shear stress at middepth of the beam, where the stress is a maximum, is given by

$$v_h = \frac{3V}{2bd} \quad \text{[at neutral axis of beam]} \qquad 13.6$$

This formula is obtained by substituting applicable terms in Eq. 13.5 for the specific case of a rectangular beam. Usually, horizontal shear is not a problem except in wood beams where the horizontal fibers of the wood make an ideal place for the beam to split and shear in this direction.

Another important aspect of the behavior of beams is their tendency to deflect under the action of external loads. Although beam deflection usually does not control the selection of beam size (as does bending or horizontal shear stress), it is an important factor that must be calculated. In some cases, it can be the controlling factor in determining beam size. Even though a large deflection will usually not lead to a structural collapse, excessive deflection can cause finish materials to crack, pull partitions away from the floor or ceiling, crush full-height walls, and result in a bouncy floor structure.

Types of Beams

There are several basic types of beams. These are shown in Fig. 13.3, with their typical deflections under load shown exaggerated. The simply supported, overhanging, and continuous beam all have ends that are free to rotate as the load is applied. The cantilever and fixed-end beams have one or both sides restrained against rotation. A continuous beam is one that is held up by more than two supports. Of course, there are many variations of these types, such as an overhanging beam with one end fixed, but these are the most typical situations.

There are also two typical kinds of loads on building structures: *concentrated load* and *uniformly distributed load*. Graphic representations of these loads are shown in Fig. 13.4. A concentrated load is shown with an arrow and designated P, and a uniformly distributed load is shown as w pounds per linear foot or W for the total load. Loads may either be expressed in pounds or kips (1 kip is 1000 pounds). The resultant of uniformly distributed loads is at the center of the loads. This principle is particularly useful when summing moments of partial uniform loads.

It is worth noting that simply supported, overhanging, and cantilever beams are *statically determinate*. This means that the reactions can be found using the equations of equilibrium. That is, the summation of horizontal, vertical, and moment forces equals zero as described in Ch. 12. Continuous and fixed-end beams are statically indeterminate, and other, more complex calculation methods are required to find reactions in these types of beams. The ARE will deal primarily with determinate beams, so only these types will be described here.

One of the basic requirements for the structural design of a beam is to determine the stresses due to bending moment and vertical shear caused by the particular loading conditions. Before these are determined, however, the reactions

(a) simply supported beam (statically determinate)

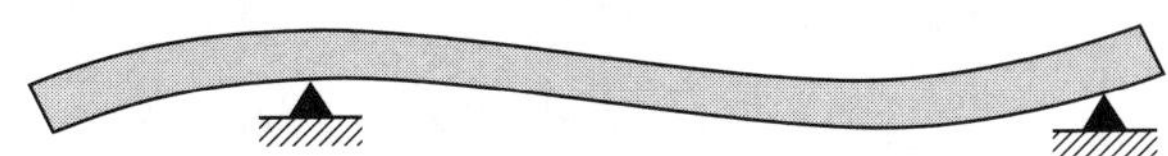

(b) overhanging beam (statically determinate)

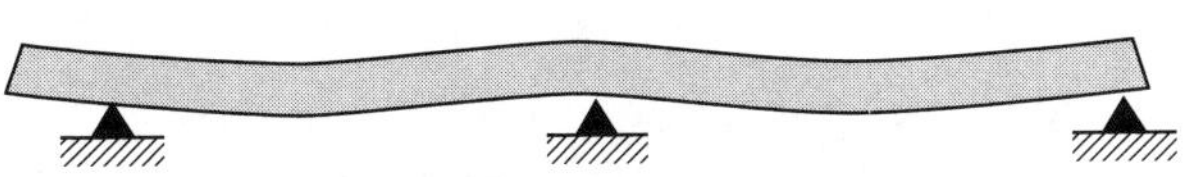

(c) continuous beam (statically indeterminate)

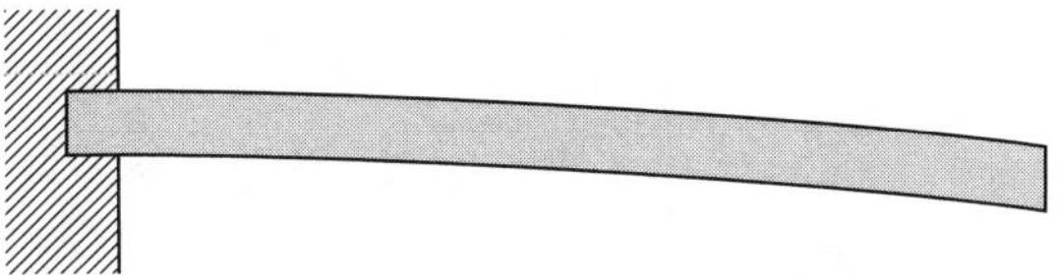

(d) cantilever beam (statically determinate)

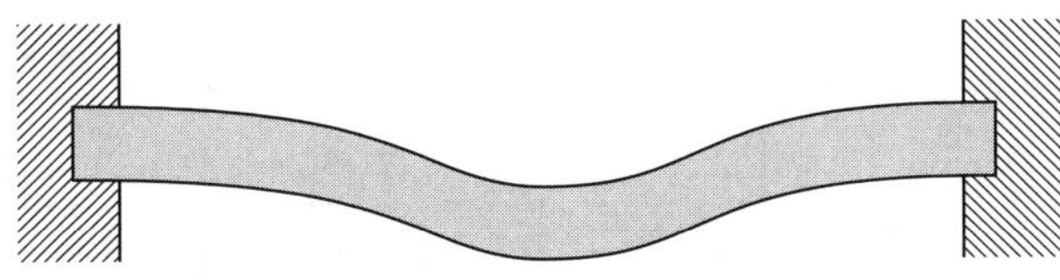

(e) fixed-end beam (statically indeterminate)

Figure 13.3 Types of Beams

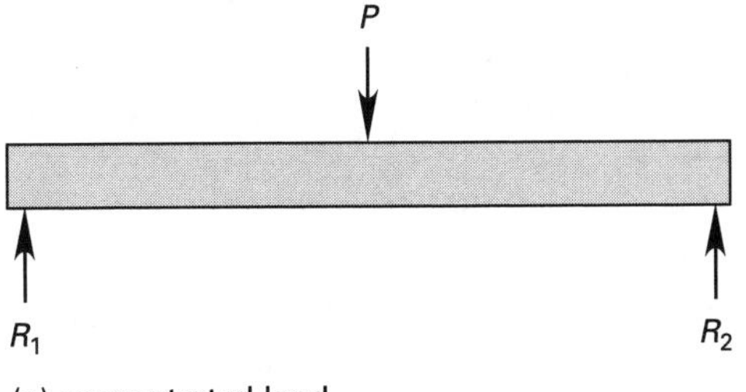

(a) concentrated load

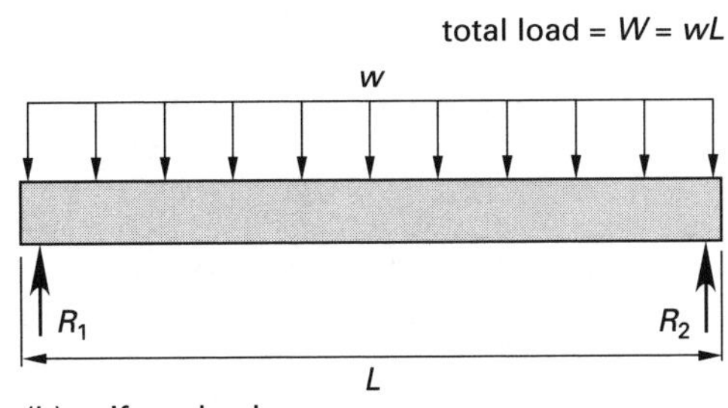

(b) uniform load

Figure 13.4 Types of Loads

of the supports must be calculated. The method of doing this for statically determinate beams was introduced in Ch. 12 but will be briefly reviewed here.

Remember the three basic principles of equilibrium.

- The sum of all vertical forces acting on a body equals zero.
- The sum of all horizontal forces acting on a body equals zero.
- The sum of all moments acting on a body or the moment of all forces about a point on the body equals zero.

Additionally, as a matter of convention, if a force tends to cause a clockwise rotation, the resulting moment is said to be positive; if it tends to cause a counterclockwise rotation, it is said to be negative.

Example 13.1

Find the reactions of the beam shown.

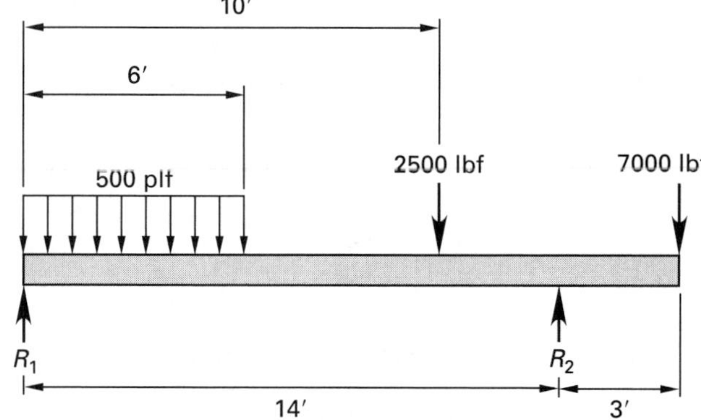

Sum the moments about R_1 to eliminate one of the unknowns. Each of the three loads tends to cause a clockwise rotation about point R_1, so these will be positive numbers; the resisting reaction, R_2, will tend to cause a counterclockwise rotation, so this will be negative. The moment sum of the loads and the resisting reaction must be zero. Remember that the total load of the uniform load is taken to act at its center, or 3 ft from R_1.

$$(3\text{ ft})\left(\left(500\ \frac{\text{lbf}}{\text{ft}}\right)(6\text{ ft})\right) + (2500\text{ lbf})(10\text{ ft}) + (7000\text{ lbf})(17\text{ ft}) - (14\text{ ft})R_2 = 0\text{ ft-lbf}$$

$$R_2 = 10{,}929\text{ lbf}$$

Since the summation of all vertical forces must also be equal, the reaction R_1 can be found by subtracting 10,929 lbf from the total of all loads acting on the beam, or

$$\left(\left(500\ \frac{\text{lbf}}{\text{ft}}\right)(6\text{ ft}) + 2500\text{ lbf} + 7000\text{ lbf}\right) - 10{,}929\text{ lbf} = 1571\text{ lbf}$$

The same answer for R_1 can be found by summing moments about reaction R_2.

Once all the loads and reactions are known, shear and moment diagrams can be drawn. These are graphic representations of the value of the shear and moment at all points on the beam.

Although it is not critical to know the values at every point on the beam, there are certain important points that are of interest in designing the beam—mainly where the shear and moment are at their maximum values and where they are zero.

Shear Diagrams

A shear diagram is a graphic representation of the values of the *vertical shear* anywhere along a beam. To find the values, take a section at any point and algebraically sum the reactions and loads to the left of the section. The same answer can be found by taking values to the right of the section, but the convention for both shear and moment is to work from left to right. Also by convention, upward forces are considered positive and downward forces are considered negative. The standard designation for shear is V.

Example 13.2

What is the vertical shear at points 4 ft and 10 ft to the right of reaction R_1 as shown?

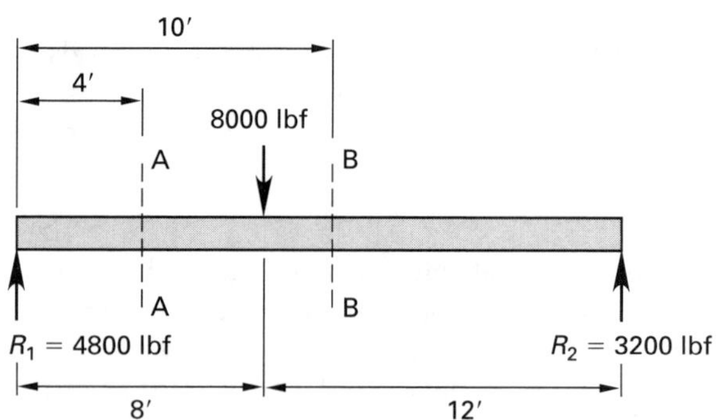

(a) beam loading and reactions

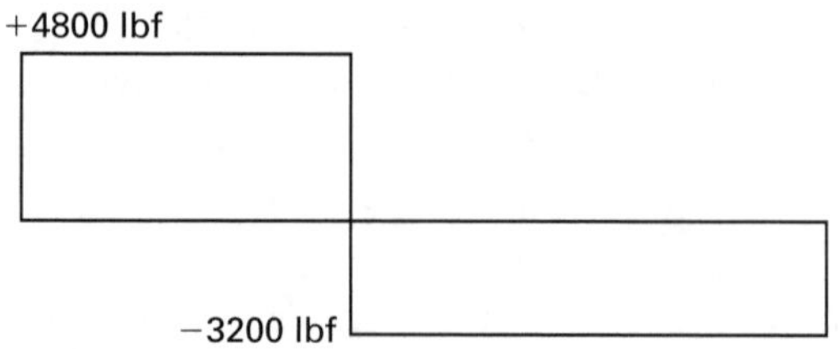

(b) shear diagram

First, compute the reaction using the summation of moments as discussed previously. R_1 is 4800 lbf, and R_2 is 3200 lbf.

Now, consider the point 4 ft from the left reaction marked as A-A in the sketch. At this point there is only the reaction of 4800 lbf acting in an upward direction, so the shear is 4800 lbf. At the point 10 ft from the reaction there are two forces to the left of the section, the reaction of +4800 lbf and the load of −8000 lbf, for a net shear of −3200 lbf. Notice that this is exactly the same as the reaction R_2. This makes sense because there are no other loads and reactions, so the summation of all vertical loads must equal zero as dictated by the principles of equilibrium.

To draw the shear diagram of a beam, first draw the beam and its loads to scale as shown in the upper portion of the sketch. Below the beam sketch, draw a horizontal line the same length as the beam and decide on a convenient vertical scale to represent the loading. Beginning from the left, the values of the shear are plotted above and below this line: the positive values above and the negative values below. The lower portion of the sketch shows the shear diagram for the beam.

Notice two things about the shear diagram. First, when there are no intervening loads between a reaction and a load (or between two loads), the portion of the shear diagram between them is a horizontal line. Second, a concentrated load or reaction causes the shear diagram to change abruptly in the vertical direction. Knowing these two facts makes it easy to draw a shear diagram by calculating shear at a few points and then just connecting the lines.

A uniformly distributed load creates a sightly different looking shear diagram. Consider the same beam loaded with a uniform load of 1500 plf. See Fig. 13.5(a). The total load is (1500 plf)(20 ft), or 30,000 lbf, which is equally distributed between the two reactions. Just at the left reaction R_1, the only force is the reaction of +15,000 lbf. Beginning here, for the remainder of the beam, the uniform load acts in a downward direction. At a point 1 ft from the reaction, the shear is 15,000 lbf − (1 ft)(1500 plf) = 13,500 lbf. At a point 3 ft from the reaction, the shear is 15,000 lbf − (3 ft)(1500 plf), or 10,500 lbf. At the midpoint of the span, the shear is zero and begins to be a negative value because the accumulating load is now larger than the reaction R_1. At reaction R_2, the positive value of the reaction brings the shear back to zero, which is consistent with the principles of equilibrium.

Once again, notice a simple fact: a uniform load creates a shear diagram with a uniformly sloping line. In the case of the example shown in Fig. 13.5(b), simply calculate the shears at the reactions, plot the one on the left as positive and the one on the right as negative, and connect the two

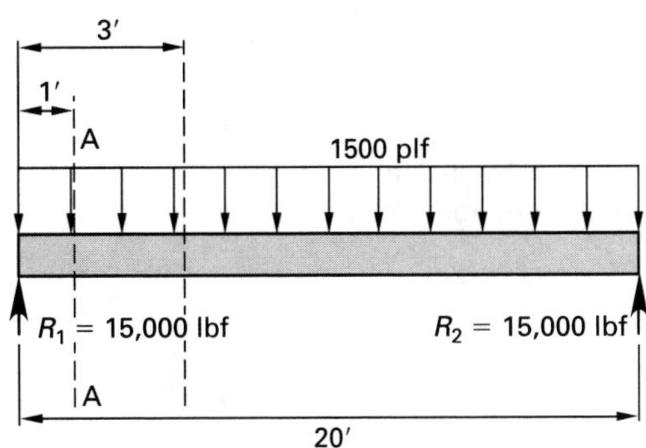

(a) beam loading and reactions

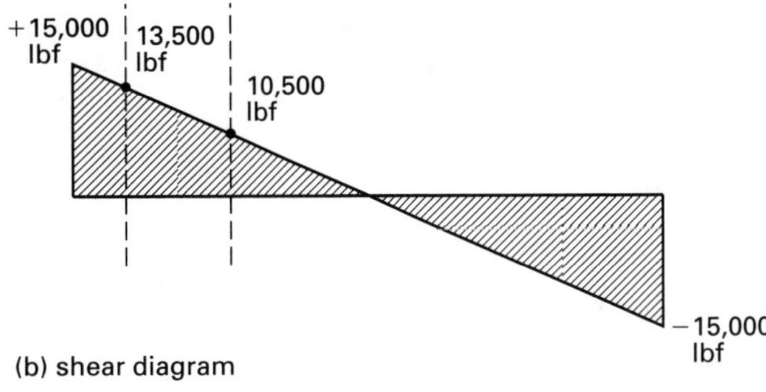

(b) shear diagram

Figure 13.5 Shear Diagram of Uniformly Loaded Beam

points with a straight line. If the diagram is drawn to scale, it is possible to find the shear at any point by simply scaling the drawing. For a more exact value, use the principle of similar triangles to find the shear at any distance along the beam.

A shear diagram provides two important pieces of information vital to designing a beam: the *maximum shear* and the point on the beam where the value of shear is zero (where maximum moment occurs and where the beam has its greatest tendency to fail in bending). In the case of Ex. 13.2, the maximum shear is 4800 lbf; in Fig. 13.5, the maximum is 15,000 lbf.

Moment Diagrams

A *moment diagram* is a graphic representation of the moment at all points along a beam. To find the moment at any point, remember that the bending moment is the algebraic sum of the moments of the forces to the left of the section under consideration and that moment is the value of force times distance. As mentioned in Ch. 12, moments tending to cause a clockwise rotation are considered positive, and those causing a counterclockwise rotation are considered negative.

Example 13.3

Using the same beam and loading as shown in Ex. 13.2, find the moments at sections A-A and B-B.

To visualize the situation a little easier, draw free-body diagrams of the two conditions. See the accompanying illustration. Of course, the moment at the reaction is zero since the moment arm distance is zero. At point A-A, 4 ft from the left reaction, the moment is

$$(4 \text{ ft})(4800 \text{ lbf}) = 19{,}200 \text{ ft-lbf}$$

At point B-B, the moment is

$$(4800 \text{ lbf})(10 \text{ ft}) - (8000 \text{ lbf})(2 \text{ ft}) = 32{,}000 \text{ ft-lbf}$$

Because the maximum moment occurs where the shear diagram crosses zero, it is wise to calculate moment at this point also. From the shear diagram shown in Ex. 13.2, this is the point where the concentrated load occurs. The moment just to the left of this point is (4800 lbf)(8 ft), or 38,400 ft-lbf. Just to the right of this point the concentrated load begins to act in a counterclockwise rotation, so the moment begins to decrease from the maximum until it is again zero at the righthand support.

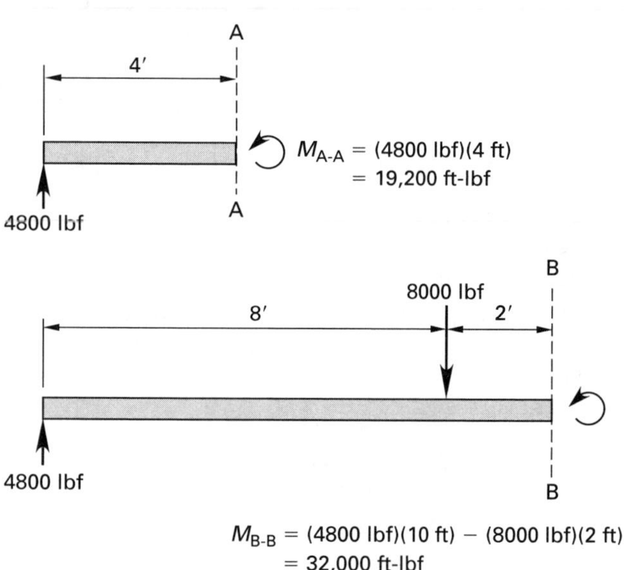

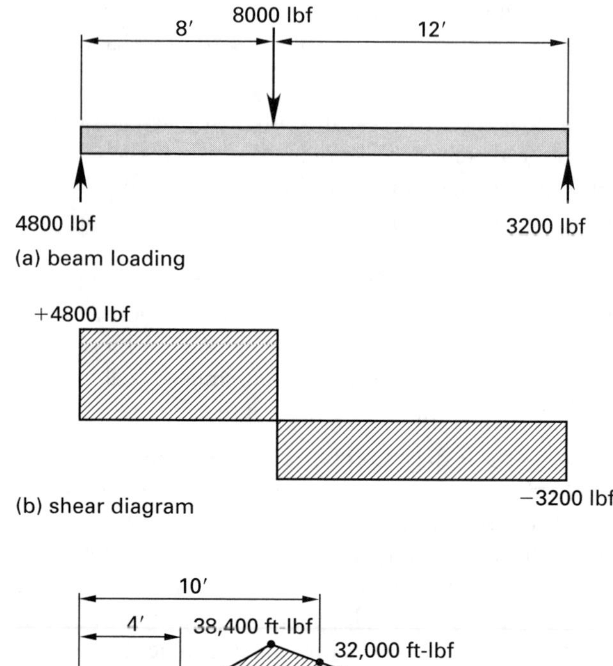

Figure 13.6 Relationship of Shear and Moment Diagrams

To draw the moment diagram, calculate moments at several points and connect them with a line in a way similar to drawing the shear diagram. This is shown in Fig. 13.6 along with the beam loading and shear diagrams from Ex. 13.2 repeated to show the relationship between the three drawings. Positive moment is shown above the base line, and negative moment (if any) is shown below the line. Negative moment will be illustrated in a later example.

As with shear diagrams, notice some important facts about the moment diagram. First, the *maximum moment* does occur where the shear diagram passes through zero, and this is indicated by the highest point of the moment diagram. Second, when the shear diagram is a constant horizontal line between two concentrated loads or reactions, the moment diagram between these two points is a straight, constant sloped line. Third, where the shear changes abruptly as shown by a vertical line, the slope of the line representing moment also changes abruptly.

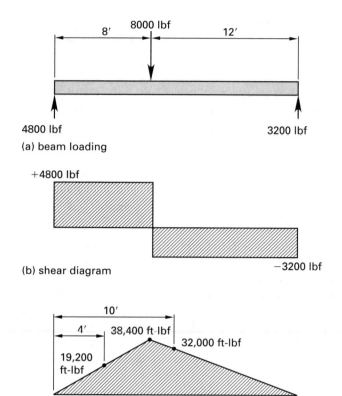

Also note, as in the next example, that when there is a uniformly distributed load and the shear diagram is a sloped line, the moment diagram will be composed of one or more parabolic curves.

Example 13.4

Draw the moment diagram of the example previously shown in Fig. 13.5.

Since the distance of the moment arm at each reaction is zero, the moment at these two points will also be zero. The maximum moment will occur where the shear diagram passes through zero, so start here. The moment is

$$\begin{aligned} M &= (15{,}000 \text{ lbf})(10 \text{ ft}) - \left(1500 \frac{\text{lbf}}{\text{ft}}\right)(10 \text{ ft})(5 \text{ ft}) \\ &= 75{,}000 \text{ ft-lbf} \end{aligned}$$

Therefore, the moment diagram is as follows. Note that the beam loading, reactions, and shear diagrams are repeated in the sketch for convenience, along with the moment diagram to illustrate the relationship among the three.

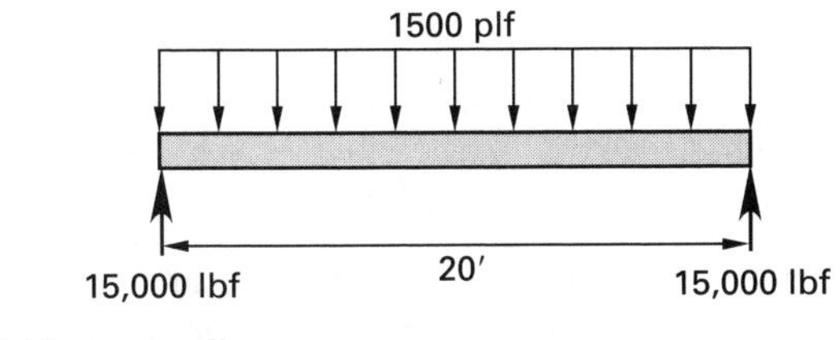

(a) beam loading

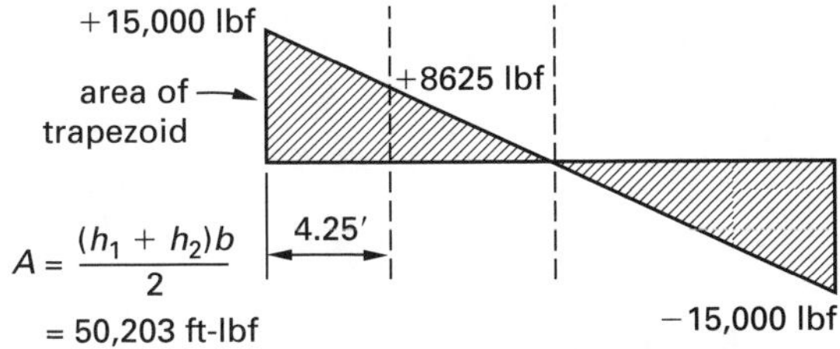

(b) shear diagram

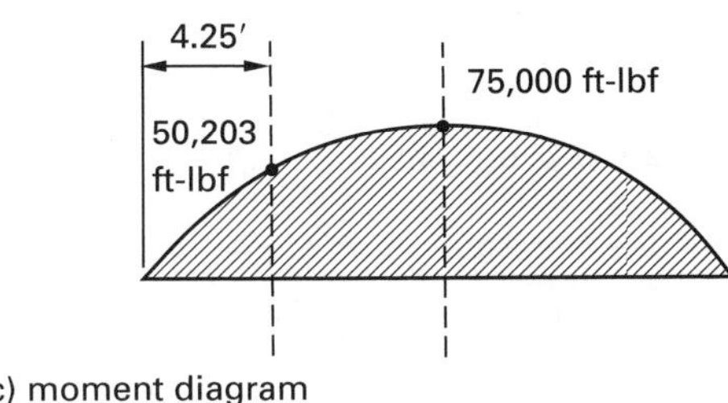

(c) moment diagram

When calculating moments due to uniform loads, remember that the moments' resultant is at the center of the loads and therefore the moment of those loads is calculated as if the total load were concentrated at the midpoints of the loads. This is why the uniform load on the beam is multiplied by 5 ft in the preceding calculation. It is recorded as a negative number because it tends to cause a counterclockwise rotation about the center of the beam where moments are taken.

To find other points of the moment diagram curve it is possible to calculate several moments and connect the points with a smooth curve, but the curve of a moment diagram of a uniformly loaded beam is parabolic so this is usually not necessary.

Note one final interesting point. The area of the shear diagram between two points along the beam is numerically equal to the change in moment of the beam between the same two points. Thus, at the midpoint of the beam as shown in the sketch, the area of the triangle is (15,000)(10)/2, or 75,000 ft-lbf, exactly the same as calculating it with moment arms. Since the shear diagram is drawn to scale in pound units in the vertical direction and foot units in the horizontal direction, the result is in foot-pounds.

In the example shown in the sketch, finding the moment at a point 4.25 ft from the left reaction would involve finding the area of the trapezoid with a height of 4.25 ft, the larger base of 15,000 lbf, and the smaller base of 8625 lbf. This latter figure can easily be found by the law of proportions of similar triangles.

Example 13.5

Find the reactions and draw the shear and moment diagrams of the beam shown.

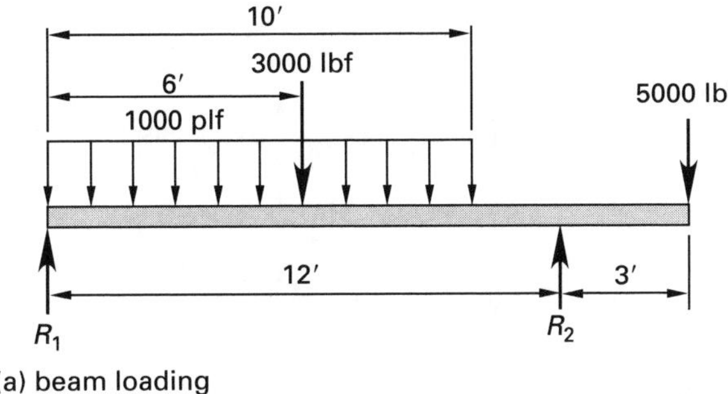

(a) beam loading

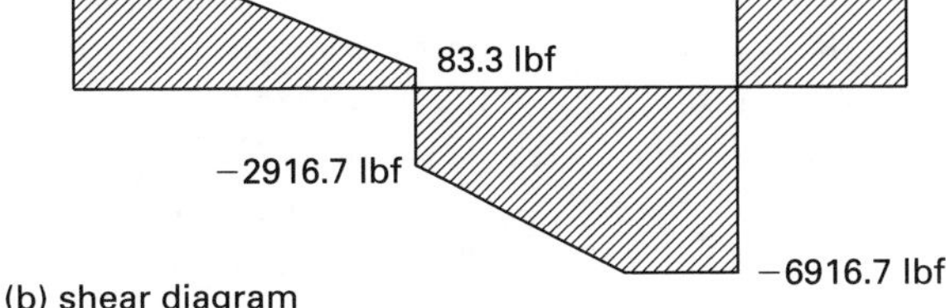

(b) shear diagram

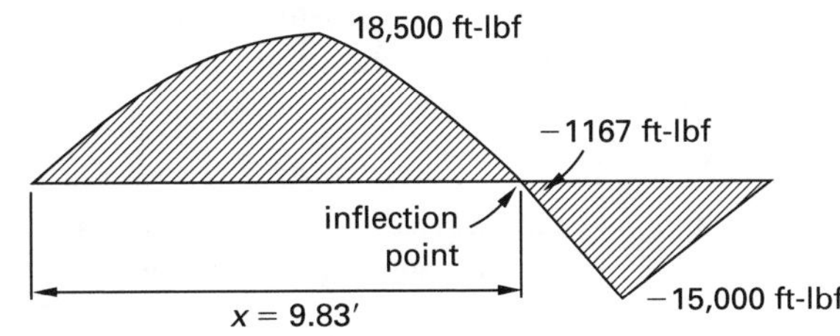

(c) moment diagram

This example is more complicated than previous ones and illustrates negative moment and combinations of load types.

First, find the reactions. As before, find the sum of moments about one of the reactions and set them equal to zero. About reaction R_1, the equation is

$$\left(1000\ \frac{\text{lbf}}{\text{ft}}\right)(10\ \text{ft})(5\ \text{ft}) + (3000\ \text{lbf})(6\ \text{ft}) - R_2(12\ \text{ft}) + (5000\ \text{lbf})(15\ \text{ft}) = 0$$

$$50{,}000\ \frac{\text{lbf}}{\text{ft}} + 18{,}000\ \frac{\text{lbf}}{\text{ft}} + 75{,}000\ \frac{\text{lbf}}{\text{ft}} = R_2(12\ \text{ft})$$

$$R_2 = 11{,}916.7\ \text{lbf}$$

R_1 is the difference between the total load and R_2, or 6083.3 lbf.

Next, find the vertical shears and draw the shear diagram.

Starting with the left reaction, the shear is 6083.3 lbf in the upward direction. The shear just to the left of the 3000 lbf load is the sum of the loads and reactions, so at this point it is

$$V = 6083.3\ \text{lbf} - \left(1000\ \frac{\text{lbf}}{\text{ft}}\right)(6\ \text{ft}) = 83.3\ \text{lbf}$$

At the 3000 lbf load, the shear is

$$V = 6083.3\ \text{lbf} - \left(1000\ \frac{\text{lbf}}{\text{ft}}\right)(6\ \text{ft}) - 3000\ \text{lbf} = -2916.7\ \text{lbf}$$

Since the load between R_1 and the 3000 lbf load is uniformly distributed, the two points connect with a sloped line as shown in the sketch. The shear at the end of the uniform load is found in the same way. From this point to the reaction R_2 there are no loads or reactions (ignoring the weight of the beam), so the line is horizontal. At the support, reaction R_2, the load changes abruptly in the magnitude of the reaction, or 11,916.7 lbf, which is added to the negative shear of 6916.7 lbf, giving a net value of +5000 lbf.

No other loads are encountered until the 5000 lbf load at the end of the overhang. Since it is in the downward direction, it is negative and brings the shear to zero at the end of the beam, which is the expected result because of the principles of equilibrium.

Finally, calculate and draw the moment diagram. In this example there are two points where the shear diagram crosses zero, so there will be two maximum moments: one positive, as in a simply supported beam, and one negative. A negative moment simply means that the beam is bending upward above a support instead of downward because of the way the loads are applied. Both moment values need to be calculated to determine which one is the greater of the two because it is not always clear from visual inspection. The highest value is the one that must be used to design the beam.

There are two ways to find the moments. One way is to draw free-body diagrams at each point of interest and take the moments about that point as was done in previous examples.

Another, sometimes simpler way is to find the area of the shear diagram between points of interest.

To find the maximum moment at the 3000 lbf load, find the area of the trapezoid with the bases of 6083.3 lbf and 83.3 lbf and the height of 6 ft.

$$\begin{aligned} A &= \frac{1}{2}(b_1 + b_2)h \\ &= \left(\frac{1}{2}\right)(6083.3\ \text{lbf} + 83.3\ \text{lbf})(6\ \text{ft}) \\ &= 18{,}500\ \text{ft-lbf} \end{aligned}$$

To find the moment 10 ft to the right of reaction, R_1, find the area of the trapezoid from the 3000 lbf load to the end of the uniform load and subtract it from the previous moment. This is because this area is below the baseline of the shear diagram and is negative.

$$A = \left(\frac{1}{2}\right)(2916.7\ \text{lbf} + 6916.7\ \text{lbf})(4\ \text{ft}) = 19{,}667\ \text{ft-lbf}$$

The moment is, therefore,

$$18{,}500\ \text{ft-lbf} - 19{,}667\ \text{ft-lbf} = -1167\ \text{ft-lbf}$$

Next, find the area of the rectangle from the end of the uniform load to the reaction R_2 (which is 13,833 ft-lbf) and subtract this from the last value. The maximum negative moment is then 15,000 ft-lbf.

Now, connect the points just found. The lines connecting points below a sloped line in the shear diagram will be sections of parabolas, and the lines below horizontal lines in the shear diagram will be straight sloped lines as shown in the moment diagram of the sketch.

Notice that the slopes of the parabolas change abruptly where the concentrated load of 3000 lbf occurs. Also notice that the curve of the moment diagram between the 6 ft point and 10 ft point crosses the zero line a little to the left of the 10 ft point. Where this occurs in a moment diagram is called the *inflection point*. Knowing where this point occurs is often important in designing beams. For instance, the inflection point is where reinforcing rods in concrete beams are bent to change from carrying positive moment to negative moment. In this example, the inflection point just happens to be very close to the end of the uniform load, but it can occur anywhere depending on the distribution of loads.

To find the inflection point, let the distance from reaction R_1 be x. Then, knowing the moment at this point is zero, draw a free-body diagram cut at this point, sum the moments to the left of this point, and set those moments equal to zero.

$$(6083\ \text{lbf})x - \left(1000\ \frac{\text{lbf}}{\text{ft}}\right)x\left(\frac{x}{2}\right) - (3000\ \text{lbf})(x - 6\ \text{ft}) = 0\ \text{ft-lbf}$$

This reduces to the quadratic equation

$$\left(500\ \frac{\text{lbf}}{\text{ft}}\right)x^2 - (3083\ \text{lbf})x - 18{,}000\ \text{ft-lbf} = 0\ \text{ft-lbf}$$

Using the general formula for the solution of a quadratic equation.

$$x = \frac{-b \pm \sqrt{b^2 - 4ac}}{2a}$$

$$= \frac{-(-3083\ \text{lbf}) \pm \sqrt{(-3083\ \text{lbf}) - (4)\left(500\ \frac{\text{lbf}}{\text{ft}}\right)(-18{,}000\ \text{ft-lbf})}}{(2)\left(500\ \frac{\text{lbf}}{\text{ft}}\right)}$$

$$= 9.83\ \text{ft}$$

Deflection

Deflection is the change in vertical position of a beam due to a load. The amount of deflection depends on the load, the beam length, the moment of inertia of the beam, and the beam's modulus of elasticity. Generally, the amount of *allowable deflection* is limited by building code requirements or practical requirements such as how much a beam can deflect before ceiling surfaces begin to crack or before the spring of the floor becomes annoying to occupants.

In many cases, the deflection due to live load is limited to $^1/_{360}$ of the beam's span, whereas the deflection due to total load (dead load plus live load) is usually limited to $^1/_{240}$ of the beam's span. If there are two or more loads on a beam, such as a uniform load and concentrated load, the deflections caused by the loads individually are added to find total deflection.

Deriving the formulas for beam deflection under various loads is a complex mathematical process. However, standard formulas for deflection as well as shear and moment are given in reference sources such as the AISC *Steel Construction Manual*. These apply to beams of any material. A few of the more common loading situations with accompanying formulas are given in Fig. 13.7.

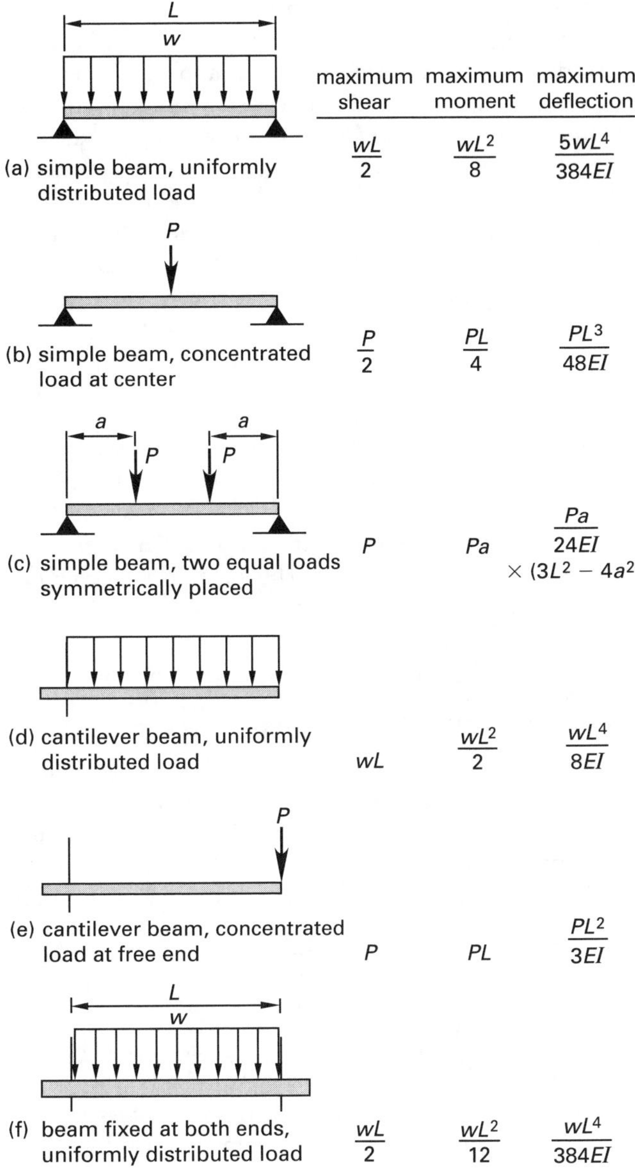

Figure 13.7 Static Formulas for Some Common Loads

COLUMNS

Basic Principles

Although columns resist axial compressive forces, there are other considerations that must be taken into account. The first is the tendency of a long, slender column to *buckle* under a load. Even though the column's material and size can withstand the load according to Eq. 13.8, the column will fail in buckling under a much smaller load.

$$F_a = \frac{P}{A} \qquad 13.8$$

The second consideration is the *combined loading* that occurs on many columns. This can be due to the normal compressive force plus lateral load, such as wind, on the column. Combined loading can also be induced by an eccentric compressive load, one that is applied off the centroidal axis of the column. In this case, the column acts a little like a beam standing on end with one face in compression and the other in tension. The compressive forces due to the eccentric load add to the normal compressive stresses on one side and subtract from the normal compressive stresses on the other. The *flexural stress* caused by eccentricity is given by the flexure formula (see Eq. 13.2).

$$f = \frac{Mc}{I} \tag{13.9}$$

Because of the inexact nature of how columns respond to loads, various column formulas have been developed and adopted for different conditions and for various materials. These have been established through experience and are standardized in building codes. The methods for designing columns in different materials will be discussed in the individual chapters on specific structural materials. This chapter focuses on the general principles of column design.

Radius of Gyration

The ability of a column to withstand a load is dependent on the column's length, cross-sectional shape and area, and moment of inertia. There is a convenient way to combine the properties of area and moment of inertia that is useful in column design. This is called the *radius of gyration* and is expressed with the following formula.

$$r = \sqrt{\frac{I}{A}} \tag{13.10}$$

For nonsymmetric sections, such as rectangular columns, there are two radii of gyration, one for each axis. The one of greater interest in column design is the lesser radius of gyration since it is in this axis that a column will fail by buckling. For example, a 4 × 8 wood column will bend under a load parallel to the 4 in dimension before it will bend in the other dimension.

Slenderness Ratio

The slenderness ratio is the most important factor in column design and is equal to

$$\text{slenderness ratio} = \frac{L}{r} \tag{13.11}$$

Example 13.6

A 4 × 6 structural steel column is 9 ft 6 in long. What is its slenderness ratio if its least radius of gyration is 1.21 in?

The slenderness ratio is

$$\frac{L}{r} = \frac{(9.5\ \text{ft})\left(12\ \frac{\text{in}}{\text{ft}}\right)}{1.21\ \text{in}} = 94.2$$

Remember, the length must be multiplied by 12 to convert to inches.

The slenderness ratio is used in a basic equation that applies to all columns and gives the maximum stress a column can resist without buckling. It is called Euler's equation and predicts the actual load just prior to failure.

$$\frac{P}{A} = \frac{\pi^2 E}{\left(\frac{L}{r}\right)^2} \tag{13.12}$$

However, because various materials behave differently, end conditions vary, and slenderness ratios affect loads, this equation is theoretical and not used without modification in actual column design. For simple wood column design, for example, the thinnest dimension of the column is used in place of the least radius of gyration.

Categories of Columns

Compression members are categorized into three groups based on their slenderness ratios: *short compressive members*, *intermediate columns*, and *slender columns*. For short compressive members, the basic stress formula $\sigma = P/A$ holds true (that is, column buckling is not a problem). For slender columns, Euler's equation generally holds true, modified to account for safety factors and end conditions. For intermediate columns, there are several formulas that attempt to predict column behavior. Building codes and sound engineering practices give the formulas used in actual design for various materials. These will be discussed in later chapters on specific materials.

End Conditions

The method by which the ends of columns are fixed affects the columns' load-carrying capacity. These methods are shown diagrammatically in Fig. 13.8. The end of any column may be in one of four states: it may be fixed against both rotation and movement from side to side (translation), it may be able to rotate but not translate, it may be able to move from side to side but not rotate, or it may be free to both rotate and translate.

The strongest type of column is one that is fixed against both rotation and translation; the weakest is one that is free to move at one end. Column formulas generally assume a condition in which both ends are fixed in translation but free to rotate. When other conditions exist, the load-carrying capacity is increased or decreased so the allowable stress must be increased or decreased or the slenderness ratio increased. For example, for steel columns, a factor, K, is used to multiply by the actual length to give an effective length. The theoretical K-values are listed in Fig. 13.8, but more conservative recommended values are often used. For steel design these are discussed in Ch. 19.

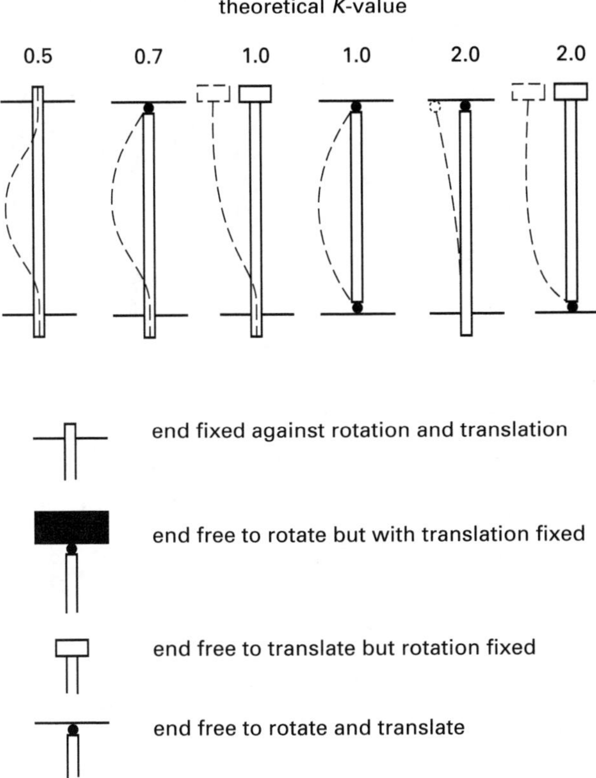

Figure 13.8 End Conditions for Columns

14 TRUSSES

BASIC PRINCIPLES

A *truss* is a structure generally composed of straight members to form a number of triangles with the connections arranged so that the stresses in the members are either in tension or compression. Trusses are very efficient structures and are used as an economical method of spanning long distances. Typical depth-to-span ratios range from 1:10 to 1:20, with flat trusses requiring less overall depth than pitched trusses. Spans generally range from 40 ft to 200 ft. However, some wood-trussed rafters are used to span shorter distances.

Some typical truss types are shown in Fig. 14.1 with nomenclature of the various parts. Generally, roof loads on a truss are transferred from the decking to purlins, which are attached to the truss at the panel points to avoid putting any bending stresses in the top chord of the truss. If concentrated loads are placed between panel points or uniform loads are applied directly to the top chords, the member must be designed for the axial loading as well as for bending.

Trusses act much like beams in that there is usually compression in the top chords and tension in the bottom chords, with the web members being either in compression or tension, depending on the loading and type of truss used. Like a beam, the forces in a parallel chord truss increase toward the center. In a bowstring truss, on the other hand, the chord forces remain fairly constant because the truss depth varies from a minimum at the supports to a maximum in the center.

In designing a trussed roof, trusses are placed from 10 ft to 40 ft on center, depending on the loads and the spanning capabilities of the purlins. In residential and light commercial construction, trussed rafters made of 2 × 4 or 2 × 6 members are often placed 2 ft on center. Open-web steel joists are usually placed 2 ft to 3 ft on center for floor construction and 4 ft to 6 ft on center for roof construction, depending on the spanning capabilities of the roof deck. Since trusses are thin and deep and subject to buckling, they must be laterally supported with bridging along the bottom chord. In some cases, diagonal bracing is required along the top chords of pitched roofs if the roof deck is not adequate to act as a diaphragm.

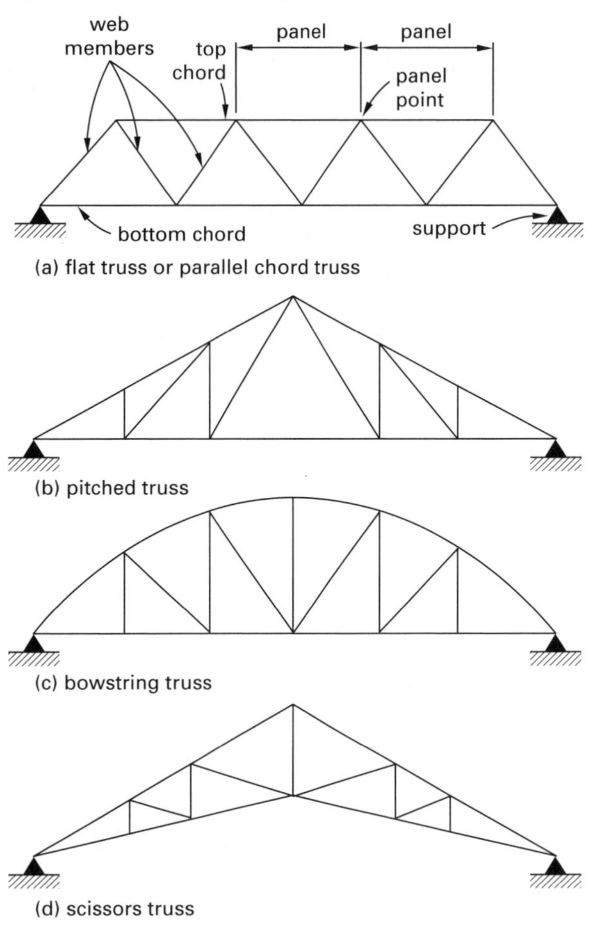

Figure 14.1 Types of Trusses

Individual truss members are designed as columns if they are in compression. If in tension, they must have adequate net area (after deducting for the area of fasteners) to resist the unit tensile stress allowed by the material being used. If concentrated loads or uniform loads are placed on any chord member between the panel points, the member must also be designed to resist bending stresses.

As with columns, the effective length of chord members in compression is important; that is, Kl in which K is determined by the restraint of the ends of the members. For steel trusses, K is usually taken as 1.0 so the effective length is the same as the actual length. Also for steel trusses, the ratio of length to least radius of gyration, l/r, should not exceed 120 for main members and 200 for secondary and bracing members.

When designing steel trusses with double angles as is usually the case, allowable concentric loads and other properties for various double-angle combinations can be found in the American Institute of Steel Construction (AISC) *Steel Construction Manual*. Given the compressive load, the length of the member, and the strength of the steel, the size and thickness of a double-angle combination can be determined.

For members in tension, the net area must be determined. This is the actual area of the member less the area of bolt holes, which is taken to be $^1/_8$ in larger than the diameter of the bolt.

Regardless of material, truss members should be designed so they are concentric; that is, so the member is symmetric on both sides of the centroid axis in the plane of the truss. To accomplish this, steel truss members are often built with two angles back-to-back separated by $^3/_8$ in or $^1/_2$ in gusset plates, with tee sections, or with wide flange sections. See Fig. 14.2.

With light loads, bars or rods can be used for tension members. Wood trusses are often constructed with web members between double top and bottom chord members or with all members in the same plane connected with steel gusset plates. See Fig. 14.3.

The centroidal axes of all intersecting members must also meet at a point to avoid eccentric loading. For steel members composed of angles, it is standard practice to have the gage lines rather than the centroidal axes meet at a common point as shown in Fig. 14.4. The *gage line* is a standard dimension from the corner edge of an angle to the centerline of the bolt hole or holes. Its value depends on the size of the angle, and the standard dimensions are published in the AISC manual.

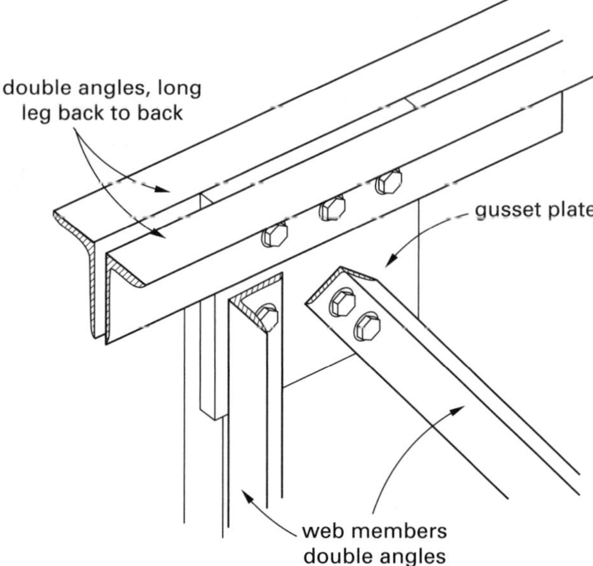

Figure 14.2 Typical Steel Truss Construction

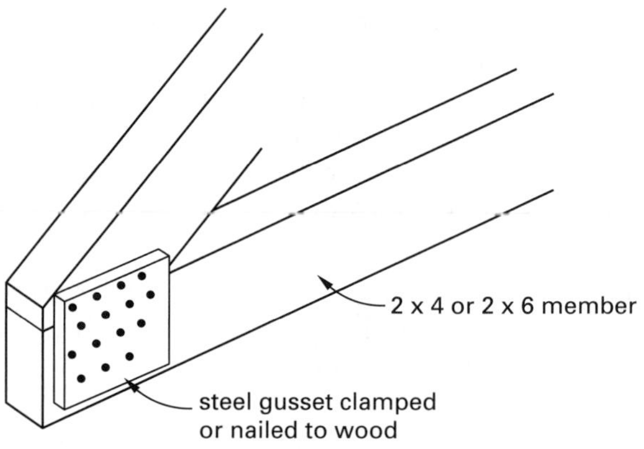

Figure 14.3 Typical Wood Trussed Rafter Construction

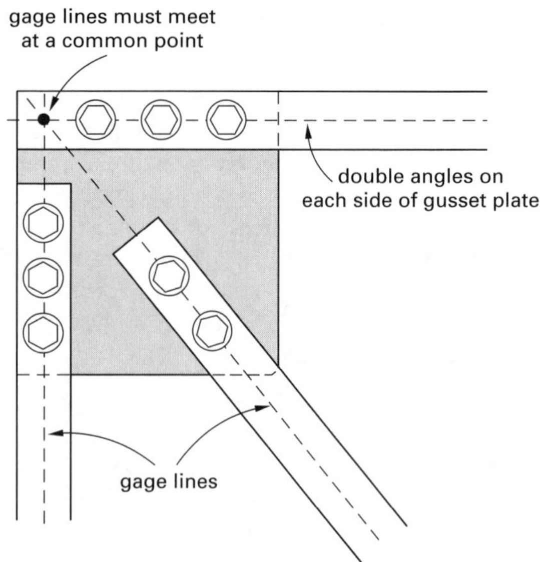

Figure 14.4 Alignment of Lines of Force in a Truss

TRUSS ANALYSIS

The first step in designing a truss is to determine the loads in the various members. Before reviewing the methods to do this, there are some general guidelines to know for truss analysis.

- The sum of vertical forces at any point equals zero.
- The sum of horizontal forces at any point equals zero.
- The sum of the moments about any point equals zero.
- Forces in each member are shown by an arrow away from a joint or cut section if in tension and toward a joint or cut section if in compression.
- Forces acting upward or to the right are considered positive (+), and forces acting downward or to the left are considered negative (−).
- All forces should be indicated acting in their known direction. If the direction is unknown when beginning the analysis, show the force in tension, acting away from the joint or cut section. If the calculation of the force is negative, this indicates that the direction is reversed.
- For analysis, trusses are assumed to have pivoting or rolling supports to avoid other stresses at these points.

Since truss analysis often involves resolving forces into their horizontal and vertical components and finding the resultant of two forces, the following guidelines will be helpful. See Fig. 14.5.

The x-component of a force (horizontal) is equal to the force times the cosine of the angle the force vector makes with the x-axis.

$$F_x = F \cos a \qquad 14.1$$

The y-component of a force (vertical) is equal to the force times the cosine of the angle the force vector makes with the y-axis.

$$F_y = F \cos b \qquad 14.2$$

Also note that the x- and y-axes can be tilted to any convenient angle if required by the problem.

There are three methods that can be used to determine the forces in truss members: the *method of joints*, the *method of sections*, and the *graphic method*. The method of joints is useful in determining the forces in all the members or when only the forces in members near the supports need to be calculated. The method of sections is convenient when it is only necessary to find the forces in a few members, particularly ones that are not at or near the supports. The graphic method is useful for complex trusses and avoids all the calculation inherent in analytic solutions but, of course, is not as accurate.

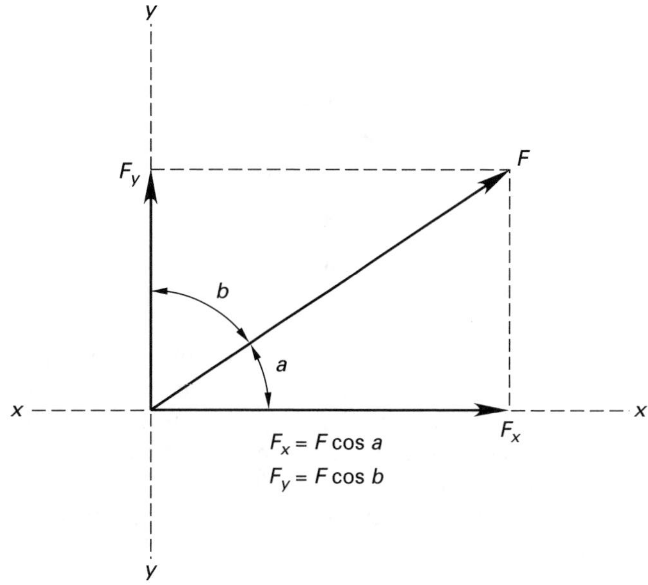

Figure 14.5 Determining Horizontal and Vertical Truss Components

Method of Joints

With this method, each joint is considered separately as a free-body diagram to which the equations of equilibrium are applied. Starting from one support, the force in each member is determined, joint by joint, until all have been calculated.

Example 14.1

Consider the simple truss shown in the sketch. Find the forces in the members using the method of joints. Neglect the weight of the structure.

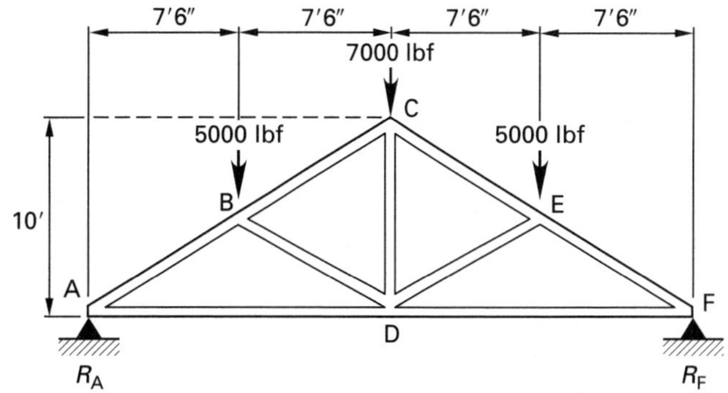

First, find the reactions. Since the loads are symmetric, $R_A = R_F = (1/2)(17{,}000\ \text{lbf}) = 8500$ lbf. If the loads were not symmetric, the reactions could be found by taking the moments about one reaction and setting the moments equal to zero.

Next, start with joint A at reaction R_A, and draw this joint as a free body diagram as shown.

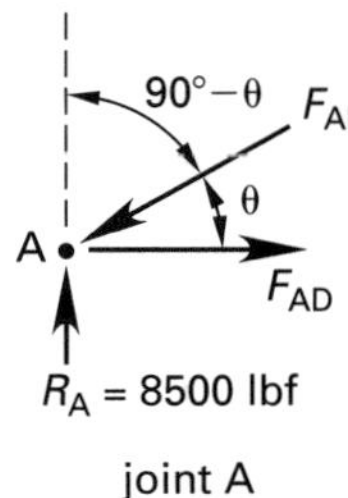

joint A

The direction of the reaction is known (upward), and the types of forces in the top chord and bottom chord can be assumed to be in compression and tension, respectively. Therefore, using the labeling convention, show force F_{AB} with an arrow toward the joint and force F_{AD} with an arrow away from the joint. Calculate the angle between member AB and AD.

$$\tan\theta = \frac{10\ \text{ft}}{15\ \text{ft}}$$

$$\theta = 33.7°$$

The complement of this angle is 56.3°.

Since the sum of vertical forces at any point equals zero, and since the vertical component of F_{AB} equals the force times the cosine of the angle with the y-axis (Eq. 14.2), then,

$$8500\ \text{lbf} - F_{AB}\cos 56.3° = 0$$

Remember, the reaction force is positive since it is acting upward, and the y-component of F_{AB} is negative since it is acting downward. Force F_{AD} has no vertical component.

Solve for F_{AB}.

$$F_{AB} = \frac{8500\ \text{lbf}}{\cos 56.3°}$$

$$= 15{,}320\ \text{lbf (compression)}$$

Since the answer is positive, the assumption that the force AB is in compression is correct.

The force in member AD is found in a similar way, knowing that the sum of the horizontal forces also equals zero.

$$F_{AD} - F_{AB}\cos 33.7° = 0$$

$$F_{AD} = 12{,}746\ \text{lbf (tension)}$$

Now, consider joint B as a free-body diagram as shown.

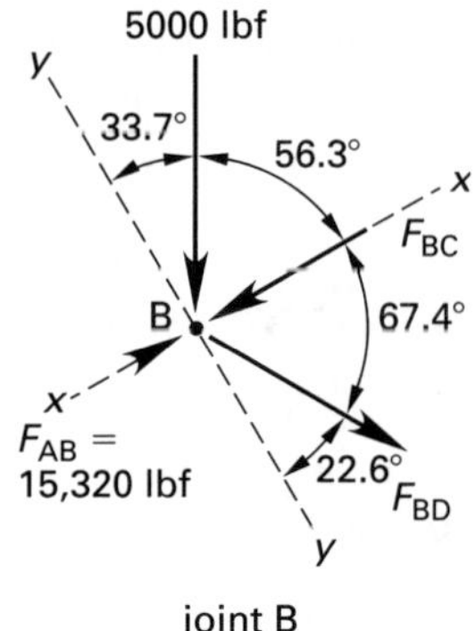

joint B

Since the direction of the force in member BD is not clear, assume it is in tension and draw it with the arrow away from the joint. (Actually, since the 5000 lbf load is acting down, there must be a force acting upward to counteract this, so member BD would have to be in compression. For purposes of illustration, however, assume it is in tension.)

In this case, tilt the x- and y-axes so the x-axis aligns with the top chord of the truss. The angles between the x- and y-axes and the forces can easily be determined by trigonometry and are shown in the joint B sketch. With the axes tilted, force F_{BC} has no vertical component in this free-body diagram, so force F_{BD} can be found easily.

$$(-5000\ \text{lbf})\cos 33.7° - F_{BD}\cos 22.6° = 0$$

(Since both forces are acting downward, they are both negative values.)

$$F_{BD} = -4506\ \text{lbf}$$

The negative number indicates that the assumption that member BD was in tension is incorrect; it is in compression.

Now, find the force in BC knowing that the sum of forces in the x-direction equals zero.

$$15{,}320\ \text{lbf} - (5000\ \text{lbf})\cos 56.3° - F_{BC} - (4506\ \text{lbf})\cos 67.4° = 0$$

$$F_{BC} = 10{,}814\ \text{lbf (compression)}$$

Finally, draw joint C as a free-body diagram.

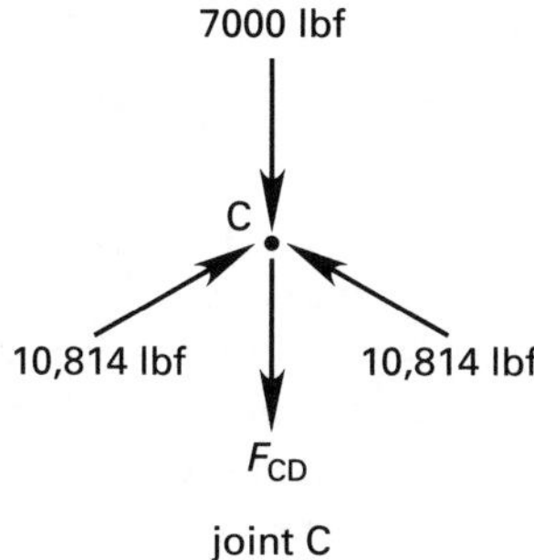

The sum of the forces in the y-direction is zero, so,

$$(10{,}814 \text{ lbf})\cos 56.3° - 7000 \text{ lbf} + (10{,}814 \text{ lbf})\cos 56.3° - F_{CD} = 0$$

$$F_{CD} = 5000 \text{ lbf (tension)}$$

Since the truss and loading are symmetric, the forces in the right half are identical to those in the left half.

Method of Sections

With this method, a portion of the truss is cut through three members, one of which is the member under analysis. The cut section is then drawn as a free-body diagram, and the force in the members is found by taking moments about the various points knowing that $\Sigma M = 0$. It is also possible to use the equations $\Sigma F_x = 0$ and $\Sigma F_y = 0$ when there is more than one unknown, but this is not usually necessary if the center of moment was selected in such a way as to eliminate two unknowns.

Example 14.2

Using the same truss as shown in Ex. 14.1, determine the forces in members BD and BC using the method of sections.

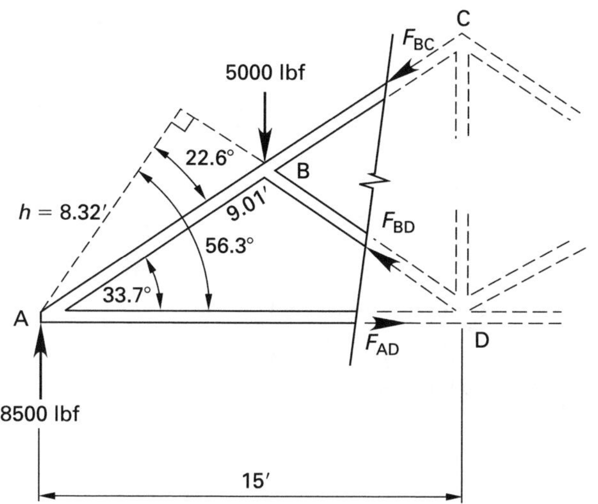

First, solve for the reactions as in the previous problem. These were determined to be 8500 lbf at each reaction.

Next, cut a section through the two members under analysis as shown in the sketch. In this free-body diagram there are five forces acting: two that are known and three that are unknown. To find the force in member BD, take moments about point A. Selecting this point eliminates the unknowns of F_{BC} and F_{AD} because their lines of action pass through the point so their moment is zero. This leaves only F_{BD} acting about A.

Remember, by convention, moments acting in a clockwise direction are positive and those acting in a counterclockwise direction are negative.

Before taking moments, find the dimension of the moment arm of BD, a line passing through A perpendicular to BD. With some simple trigonometry, the length of AB is found to be 9.01 ft and the angle between AB and the moment arm of BD is found to be 22.6°. Then,

$$\cos 22.6° = \frac{h}{9.01 \text{ ft}}$$

$$h = 8.32 \text{ ft}$$

Then, the sum of moments about A equals zero, or

$$(5000 \text{ lbf})(7.5 \text{ ft}) - F_{BD}(8.32 \text{ ft}) = 0$$

$$F_{BD} = 4507 \text{ lbf}$$

This is the same value (within 1 lbf) that was calculated by the method of joints in the previous example.

Now, find the value of F_{BC}. In this case, to eliminate two unknowns, take moments about point D. This is acceptable even though it is outside the free-body diagram because the equation of moment equilibrium holds at any point in the truss. The moment arm from D perpendicular to BC must be found. It is the same dimension as the previous moment arm calculated: 8.32 ft. Then, the sum of moments about joint D is

$$(8500 \text{ lbf})(15 \text{ ft}) - (5000 \text{ lbf})(7.5 \text{ ft}) - F_{BC}(8.32 \text{ ft}) = 0 \text{ lbf-ft}$$

$$F_{BC} = 10{,}817 \text{ lbf}$$

In both cases, the answer is a positive number, indicating that the original assumption of direction of force (compression) is correct. If either answer were negative, it would simply mean that the assumption was incorrect and the arrow or arrows should be reversed. (This answer is within 3 lbf of that found by the method of joints, allowing for some minor inaccuracies due to rounding off when calculating the length of moment arms.)

Graphic Method

Finding forces in truss members with graphics is a quick method and is particularly suited for complex trusses. However, its accuracy depends on the scale selected and the accuracy with which the diagram is drawn. A truss is analyzed graphically by drawing a stress diagram. This is a carefully drawn diagram, to scale, showing all the force polygons for each joint on one drawing.

When developing a stress diagram there are a few things to keep in mind.

- Since the truss is in equilibrium, the force polygon of each joint must close.
- When developing the force polygon for a joint, work in a clockwise direction around the joint. Do this consistently for every joint.
- To determine whether a member is in compression or tension, trace the rays of the force polygon. Imagine that the ray was transposed onto the truss diagram. If the direction of the ray is toward the joint, the member is in compression. If it is away from the joint, the member is in tension.
- There will be as many sides to each force polygon as there are truss members and forces entering a joint.

Example 14.3

Consider the same truss as used in the previous two examples. Draw a diagram of the truss, and allow room below to draw the stress diagram. Label the spaces between each load and reaction with a letter of the alphabet, A, B, C, and so on. Number each triangle of the truss. Then, each load or reaction can be identified with a two-letter combination, and each structural member can be identified with a letter/number combination.

Begin the diagram by drawing a force polygon of the loads and reactions. In the sketch, start with reaction AB. With a convenient scale, in this case 1 in = 3000 lbf, draw a line parallel to the reaction in the truss drawing (in this case vertical) to a scale of 8500 lbf. Working clockwise, the next load is the 5000 lbf load BC. Draw a line downward, parallel to a scale of 5000 lbf. Continue until you are back at point A. Since the loads and reactions are all vertical, the force polygon is a straight line, but it does close on itself.

Next, draw a force polygon for the joint at the left reaction, AB1. The load AB is already drawn, so working clockwise, draw a line parallel to B1 from point B on the stress diagram. Then, draw a line representing member 1A horizontally from point A. Where these two lines intersect is point 1. To determine the type of force, trace the lines of the polygon beginning with point A. AB is the reaction and is acting upward. B1 runs down and to the left toward point 1, which in the truss drawing is toward the joint, so B1 must be in compression. From point 1, line 1A runs to the right, which in the truss drawing is away from the joint, so 1A must be in tension.

Now, study joint BC21. Since lines 1B and BC have already been drawn, start with point C and draw a line parallel with C2. From point 1, draw a line parallel with member 12. Where these intersect is point 2, and the force polygon closes. Measuring line 12 and C2 to scale gives the magnitude of the forces in these members.

Continue the procedure until all joints have been solved. A tabulation of the forces is given in the sketch. Compare these values with those found by the method of joints and sections in the previous examples.

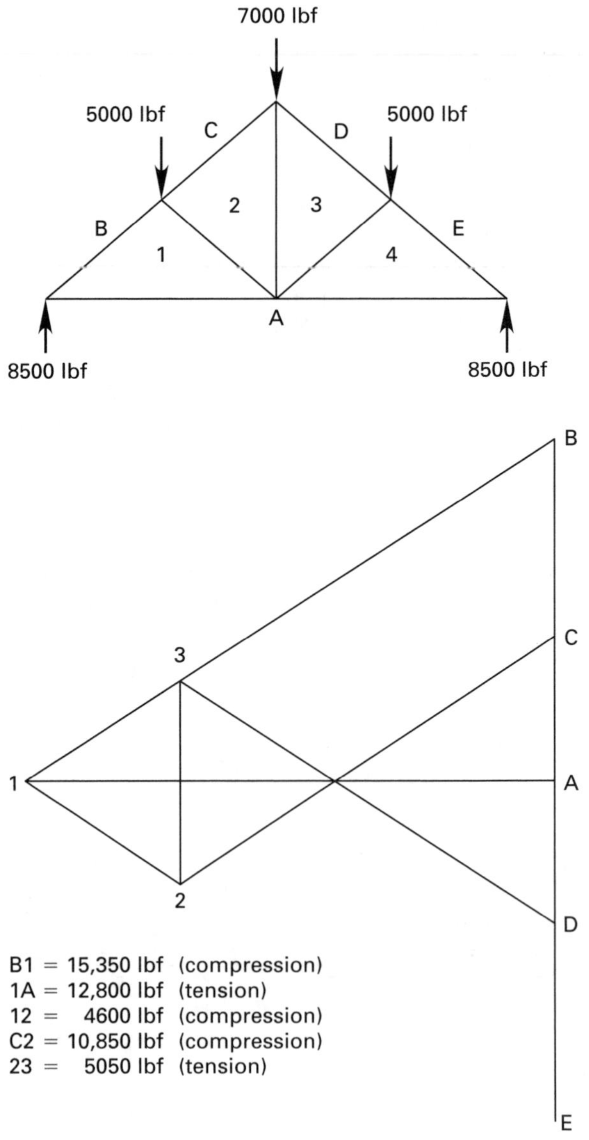

15 SOIL AND FOUNDATIONS

Nomenclature

a	depth of rectangular stress block	in
A_s	area of steel	in^2
b_w	width of footing	ft
B	bearing capacity of soil	lbf/ft^2
C_o	coefficient of earth pressure	–
d	effective depth—distance from top of footing to centroid of reinforcing steel	in
d_b	diameter of reinforcing steel	in
D	actual dead load	lbf
	specified compressive strength	lbf/in^2
f'_c	design strength of concrete	lbf/in^2
f_y	specified yield strength of reinforcing steel	lbf/in^2
h	height of retaining wall from below grade	ft
l_d	development length	in
L	actual live load	lbf
M_u	moment	ft-lbf/ft
p	earth pressure	lbf/ft
P	load	lbf/ft
q_s	design soil pressure	lbf/ft^2
U	required strength load	lbf
v	actual shear	lbf/ft
V	shear	lbf/ft
V_c	maximum allowable shear	lbf/ft
w	width of foundation wall	in
W	unit weight of soil behind retaining wall	lbf/ft^3
x	distance from face of foundation wall to edge of footing	ft
ϕ	strength reduction factor (LRFD)	–

The *foundation* is the part of the building that transmits all the gravity and lateral loads to the underlying soil. Selection and design of foundations depends on two primary elements: the required strength of the foundation to transmit the loads on it, and the ability of the soil to sustain the loads without excessive total settlement or differential settlement among different parts of the foundation.

SOIL PROPERTIES

Soil is a general term used to describe the material that supports a building. It is generally classified into four groups: sands and gravels, clays, silts, and organics. *Sands and gravels* are granular materials that are nonplastic. *Clays* are composed of smaller particles that have some cohesion, or tensile strength, and are plastic in their behavior. *Silts* are of intermediate size between clays and sands and behave as granular materials but are sometimes slightly plastic in their behavior. *Organics* are materials of vegetable or other organic matter.

In addition to these general types, there is *solid rock*, which has the highest bearing capacity of all soil types.

Subsurface Exploration

The first step in designing a foundation is to determine the bearing capacity of the underlying soil through subsurface exploration and testing. Several exploration methods are used. The two most common are *borings* and *test pits*.

With typical core borings, undisturbed samples of the soil are removed at regular intervals and the type of material recovered is recorded in a boring log. This log shows the material, the depth at which it was encountered, its standard designation, and other information such as moisture content, density, and the results of any borehole tests that might have been conducted at the bore site.

One of the most common borehole tests is the *standard penetration test* (SPT), which is a measure of the density of granular soils and consistency of some clays. In this test, a 2 in diameter sampler is driven into the bottom of the borehole by a 140 lbf hammer falling 30 in. The number of blows required to drive the cylinder 12 in is recorded. A typical boring log is shown in Fig. 15.1.

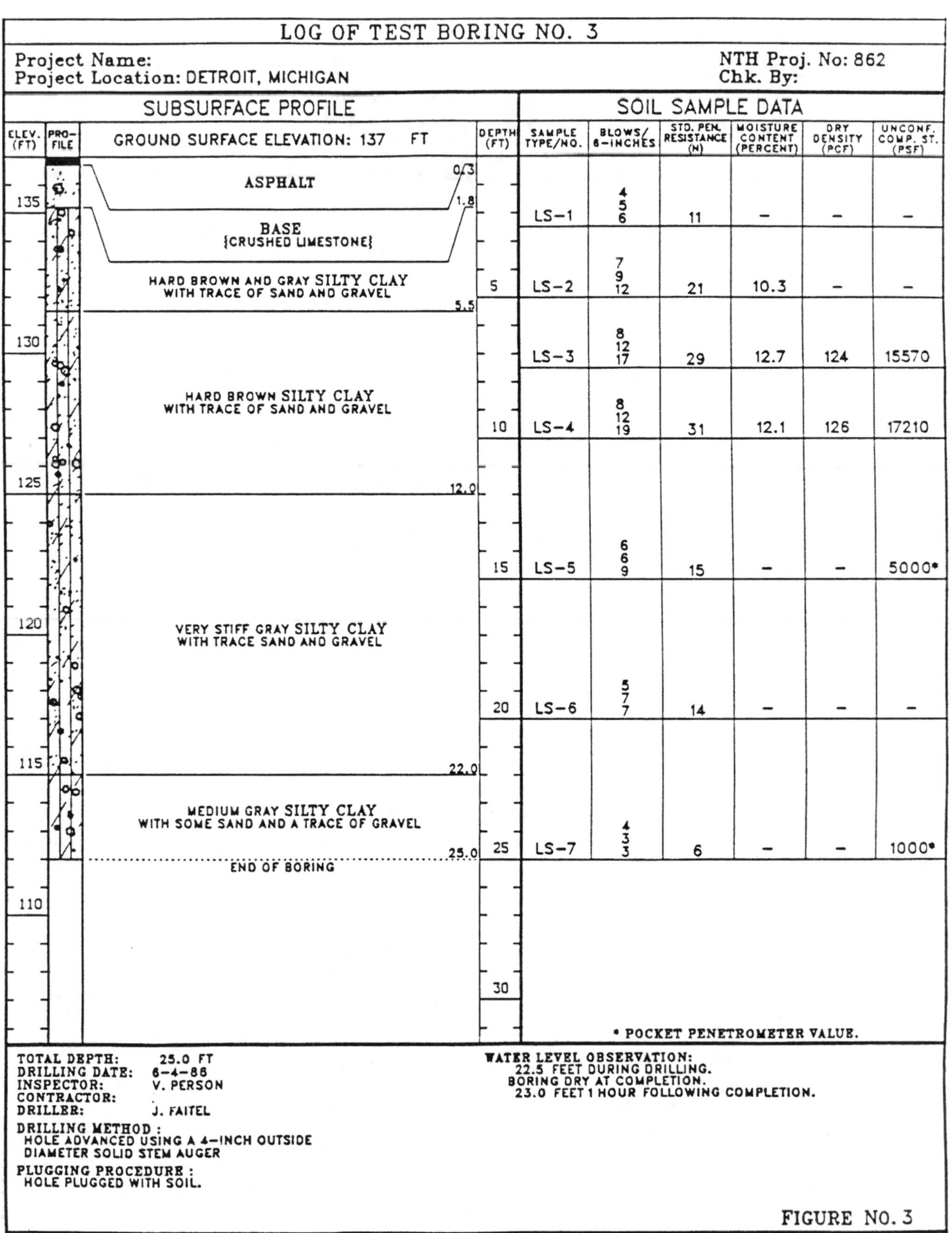
LOG OF TEST BORING NO. 3

Project Name:
Project Location: DETROIT, MICHIGAN

NTH Proj. No: 862
Chk. By:

SUBSURFACE PROFILE — GROUND SURFACE ELEVATION: 137 FT

DEPTH (FT)	DESCRIPTION
0.3	ASPHALT
1.8	BASE (CRUSHED LIMESTONE)
5.5	HARD BROWN AND GRAY SILTY CLAY WITH TRACE OF SAND AND GRAVEL
12.0	HARD BROWN SILTY CLAY WITH TRACE OF SAND AND GRAVEL
22.0	VERY STIFF GRAY SILTY CLAY WITH TRACE SAND AND GRAVEL
25.0	MEDIUM GRAY SILTY CLAY WITH SOME SAND AND A TRACE OF GRAVEL
	END OF BORING

SOIL SAMPLE DATA

DEPTH (FT)	SAMPLE TYPE/NO.	BLOWS/ 6-INCHES	STD. PEN. RESISTANCE (N)	MOISTURE CONTENT (PERCENT)	DRY DENSITY (PCF)	UNCONF. COMP. ST. (PSF)
	LS-1	4 5 6	11	–	–	–
5	LS-2	7 9 12	21	10.3	–	–
	LS-3	8 12 17	29	12.7	124	15570
10	LS-4	8 12 19	31	12.1	126	17210
15	LS-5	6 6 9	15	–	–	5000*
20	LS-6	5 7 7	14	–	–	–
25	LS-7	4 3 3	6	–	–	1000*

* POCKET PENETROMETER VALUE.

TOTAL DEPTH: 25.0 FT
DRILLING DATE: 6-4-86
INSPECTOR: V. PERSON
CONTRACTOR:
DRILLER: J. FAITEL

DRILLING METHOD: HOLE ADVANCED USING A 4-INCH OUTSIDE DIAMETER SOLID STEM AUGER

PLUGGING PROCEDURE: HOLE PLUGGED WITH SOIL.

WATER LEVEL OBSERVATION:
22.5 FEET DURING DRILLING.
BORING DRY AT COMPLETION.
23.0 FEET 1 HOUR FOLLOWING COMPLETION.

FIGURE NO. 3

Figure 15.1 Typical Boring Log

The recovered bore samples can be tested in the laboratory. Some of the tests include strength tests of bearing capacity, resistance to lateral pressure, and slope stability. In addition, compressibility tests, grain size, specific gravity, and density tests are sometimes performed. Since laboratory tests are expensive and not always necessary, they are not performed for every building project.

The number of borings taken at a building site is determined by many factors such as the size of the building, suspected subsurface geological conditions, and requirements by local codes. Usually, a minimum of four borings is taken, one near each corner of the proposed building. If wide variations are found in the initial boring logs, additional tests may be warranted.

Test pits are the second common type of subsurface exploration. These are simply trenches dug at the job site that allow visual inspection of the soil strata and direct collection of undisturbed samples. Because they are open pits, the practical limit on depth is about 10 ft so the soil below that cannot be directly examined.

The location of each test boring or test pit is shown on the plot plan and given a number corresponding to the boring log in the soil test report. Soil tests are requested by the architect but paid for by the owner. They are typically shown on the drawings for information only. However, soil tests are not part of the contract documents.

Soil Types and Bearing Capacities

Soils are classified according to the *Unified Soil Classification System* (USCS). This system divides soils into major divisions and subdivisions based on grain size and laboratory tests of physical characteristics, and provides standardized names and symbols. A summary chart of the USCS is shown in Fig. 15.2.

Bearing capacities are generally specified by code. A summary chart of the allowable bearing capacities of the *International Building Code* (IBC) is shown in Table 15.1. Other bearing capacities may be used if acceptable tests are conducted and show that higher values are appropriate.

Water In Soil

The presence of water in soil can cause several problems for foundations as well as other parts of a building. Water can reduce the load-carrying capacity of the soil in general, so larger or more expensive foundation systems may be necessary. If more moisture is present under one area of the building than another, differential settlement may occur, causing cracking and weakening of structural and nonstructural components. In the worst case, structural failure may occur.

Foundations below the groundwater line, often called the *water table*, are also subjected to hydrostatic pressure. This pressure from the force of the water-saturated soil can occur against vertical foundation walls as well as under the floor slabs. Hydrostatic pressure creates two difficulties: it puts additional loads on the structural elements, and it makes waterproofing more difficult because the pressure tends to force water into any crack or imperfection in the structure.

Even if hydrostatic pressure is not present, moisture in the soil can leak into the below-grade structure if not properly dampproofed and can cause general deterioration of materials.

There are several ways to minimize the problems caused by excess soil moisture. The first is to slope the ground away from the building sufficiently to drain away any rainwater or other surface moisture. Generally, a minimum slope of $^1/_4$ in/ft is recommended. Secondly, all water from roofs and decks should be drained away from the building with gutters, drainpipes, and other appropriate methods.

Below grade, several steps can be taken. If groundwater is a significant problem, drain tile can be laid around the footings as shown in Fig. 15.3. This tile has open joints or is perforated plastic pipe and is drained to the atmosphere, dry wells, or storm sewers. A layer of gravel is placed on top of the tile and is sometimes extended up the foundation wall to relieve the hydrostatic pressure against the wall.

An alternative method of relieving pressure against a wall is to place a continuous layer of open-web matting against the wall. Water forced against the wall loses its pressure when it encounters the matting and drips to the drain tile.

To relieve pressure against floor slabs, a layer of large gravel can be placed below the slab. If the presence of water is a significant problem, the gravel layer can be used in conjunction with a waterproofing membrane and drain tiles placed below the slab.

Soil Treatment

In order to increase bearing capacity or decrease settlement, or both, several methods of soil treatment are used.

Drainage. As mentioned in the previous section, drainage can solve several types of problems. It can increase the strength of the soil and prevent hydrostatic pressure.

Fill. If existing soil is unsuitable for building, the undesirable material is removed and new fill brought in. This may be soil, sand, gravel, or other material as appropriate. In nearly all situations, the fill must be compacted before building commences. Controlled compaction requires moisture to lubricate the particles. With all types of fill, there is an optimum relationship between the fill's density

<table>
<tr><td rowspan="8">course-grained soils
more than 50% of material is larger that no. 200 sieve</td><td rowspan="4">gravels
more than 50% of course fraction retained on no. 4 sieve</td><td rowspan="2">clean gravels
less than 5% fines</td><td>GW</td><td>well-graded gravel</td></tr>
<tr><td>GP</td><td>poorly graded gravel</td></tr>
<tr><td rowspan="2">gravels with fines
more than 12% fines</td><td>GM</td><td>silty gravel</td></tr>
<tr><td>GC</td><td>clayey gravel</td></tr>
<tr><td rowspan="4">sands
50% or more of course fraction passes no. 4 sieve</td><td rowspan="2">clean sands
less than 5% fines</td><td>SW</td><td>well-granded sand</td></tr>
<tr><td>SP</td><td>poorly graded sand</td></tr>
<tr><td rowspan="2">sands with fines
more than 12% fines</td><td>SM</td><td>silty sand</td></tr>
<tr><td>SC</td><td>clayey sand</td></tr>
<tr><td rowspan="6">fine-grained soils
50% or more passes the no. 200 sieve</td><td rowspan="3">silts and clays
liquid limit less than 50</td><td rowspan="2">inorganic</td><td>CL</td><td>lean clay</td></tr>
<tr><td>ML</td><td>silt</td></tr>
<tr><td>organic</td><td>OL</td><td>organic silty</td></tr>
<tr><td rowspan="3">silts and clays
liquid limit 50 or more</td><td rowspan="2">inorganic</td><td>CH</td><td>fat clay</td></tr>
<tr><td>MH</td><td>elastic silt</td></tr>
<tr><td>organic</td><td>OH</td><td>organic clay</td></tr>
<tr><td>highly organic soils</td><td colspan="2">primary organic matter, dark in color, and organic odor</td><td>PT</td><td>peat</td></tr>
</table>

Figure 15.2 Unified Soil Classification System

and its optimum moisture content. The method of determining this is the *Proctor test*. With the Proctor test, fill samples are tested in the laboratory to determine a standard for compaction. Specifications are then written that call for fill to be compacted between 90% to 100% of the optimum Proctor density. Higher values are necessary for heavily loaded structures, and lower values are appropriate for other loadings. Moisture contents within 2% to 4% of the optimum moisture content at the time of compaction must also be specified.

Fill is usually placed in lifts of 8 in to 12 in, with each lift being compacted before placement of the next.

Compaction. Sometimes existing soil can simply be compacted to provide the required base for construction. The same requirements for compaction of fill material apply to compaction of existing soil.

Table 15.1

IBC Allowable Foundation and Lateral Pressure

class of materials	allowable foundation pressure (psf)[d]	lateral bearing (psf/ft below natural grade)[d]	lateral sliding coefficient of friction[a]	lateral sliding resistance (psf)[b]
1. crystalline bedrock	12,000	1200	0.70	–
2. sedimentary and foliated rock	4000	400	0.35	–
3. sandy gravel and/or gravel (GW and GP)	3000	200	0.35	–
4. sand, silty sand, clayey sand, silty gravel, and clayey gravel (SW, SP, SM, SC, GM, and GC)	2000	150	0.25	–
5. clay, sandy clay, silty clay, clayey silt, silt, and sandy silt (CL, ML, MH, and CH)	1500[c]	100	–	130

For SI: 1 psf = 0.0479 kPa, 1 psf/ft = 0.157 kPa/m.

[a]Coefficient to be multiplied by the dead load.

[b]Lateral sliding resistance value to be multiplied by the contact area, as limited by IBC Sec. 1804.3.

[c]Where the building official determines that in-place soils with an allowable bearing capacity of less than 1500 psf are likely to be present at the site, the allowable bearing capacity shall be determined by a soils investigation.

[d]An increase of one-third is permitted when using the alternate load combinations in IBC Sec. 1605.3.2 that include wind or earthquake loads.

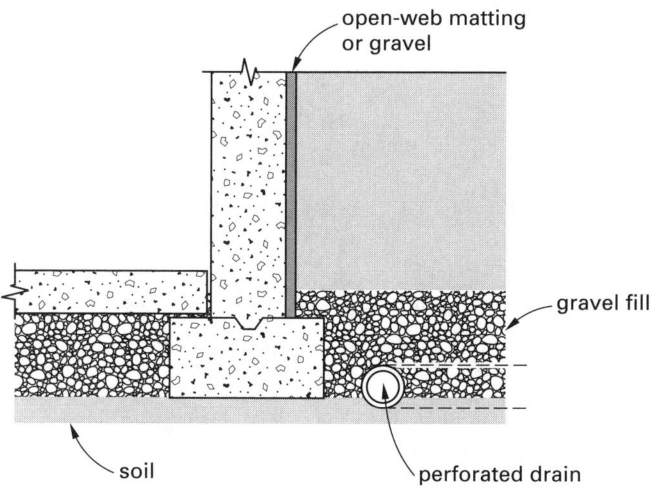

Figure 15.3 Methods of Controlling Subsurface Water

Densification. This is a type of on-site compaction of existing material using one of several techniques involving vibration, dropping of heavy weights, or pounding piles into the ground and filling the voids with sand. The specific technique used depends on the grain size of the soil.

Surcharging. Surcharging is the preloading of the ground with fill material to cause consolidation and settlement of the underlying soil before building. Once the required settlement has taken place, the fill is removed and construction begins. Although suitable for large areas, the time and cost required for sufficient settlement often preclude this method of soil improvement.

Other Considerations

Frost. Because most soils expand and heave when they freeze, footings and foundations must be placed below the frost line to prevent the structure from lifting up. The depth of the frost line varies, of course, with location and local climatic conditions. It is usually specified by the local building code or building official.

Expansive soil. Many clays, such as bentonite, expand when they get wet and shrink when they dry. If such soils are below a proposed building, the foundations must be isolated from them. One method of doing this is to use pile or caisson foundation piers that bear on material below the expansive soil. Concrete grade beams span between the piers with voids below the beams so any expansion does not cause stress on the foundation. The building walls are then built on the grade beams. The remainder of the ground level slab is usually built over select fill material, although in some instances it is suspended from beams and piers.

Repose. When sands, gravels, and other types of soils are piled up, they come to rest with a characteristic slope. The angle of the slope depends on the granular size of the material and the material's moisture content. The slope is known as the *angle of natural repose* and is the maximum practical angle for changing grades without using retaining walls or other stabilization techniques. However, even though a slope may conform to the angle of repose of a material, it may still be unsuitable to prevent erosion or allow for the desired type of landscaping.

FOUNDATION SYSTEMS

Foundations can be categorized into two broad divisions: *spread footings* and *pile* or *caisson foundations*. Spread footings do just what their name implies—they spread the load from the structure and the foundation walls over a large area, so the load-carrying capacity of the soil is not exceeded and settlement is minimized. Pile and caisson foundations (often referred to as piers) distribute the load from the building to the ends of the piles, which often bear on bedrock, or to the surrounding soil in contact with the pile through skin friction, or a combination of both.

Spread Footings

There are several types of spread footings. These are shown in Fig. 15.4. One of the most common is the *wall footing* that is placed under a continuous foundation wall that in turn supports a bearing wall. Both the footing and foundation are reinforced (except where very small loads are supported), and the joint between the footing and foundation wall is strengthened with a keyed joint (see Fig. 15.4(a)).

The *independent column footing* is similar in concept but supports only one column. The footing is usually square but may be rectangular if the column is rectangular or if there is not enough room to form a square footing.

The required size of both wall and independent column footings is found by dividing the total load on the footing by the load-carrying capacity of the soil. A safety factor is often used as well. For wall footings, design is on a linear foot basis.

Combined footings support two or more columns in situations where the columns are spaced too closely together for separate ones, or where one column is so close to the property line that a symmetrically loaded footing could not be poured. If the two columns are far apart, a variation of the combined footing is used for economy. This is the *strap footing* or *cantilever footing* (see Fig. 15.4(d)), which uses a concrete strap beam to distribute the column loads to each footing to equalize the soil pressures on each footing. The beam itself is poured on compressible material so it does not bear on the soil. Strap footings are also used where the exterior column is next to the property line but the footing cannot extend beyond the property line.

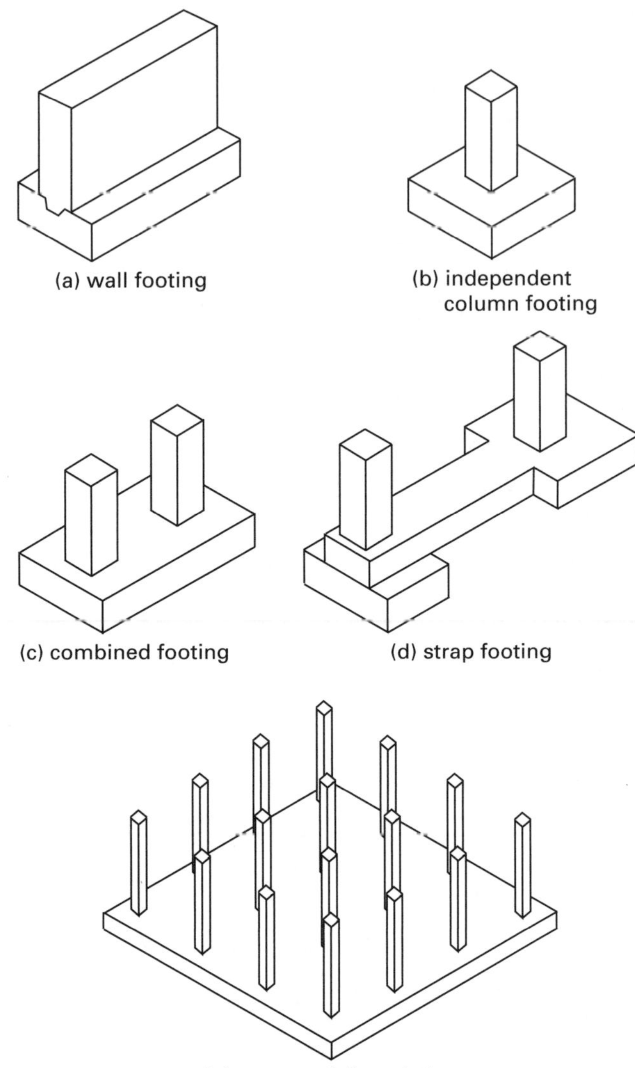

Figure 15.4 Types of Spread Footings

A *mat* or *raft foundation* (see Fig. 15.4(e)) is used when soil bearing is low or where loads are heavy in relation to soil pressures. With this type of foundation, one large footing is designed as a two-way slab and supports the columns above it. Walls or beams above the foundation are sometimes used to give added stiffness to the mat.

Pile Foundations

When soil near grade level is unsuitable for spread footings, pile foundations are used. These transmit building loads through the unsuitable soil to a more secure bearing with end bearing or side friction. Piles are either driven or drilled. Driven piles may be of timber, steel, or precast concrete and are placed with pile-driving hammers powered with drop hammers, compressed air, or diesel engines. Drilled piles or caissons are usually called *piers*. Some common types of piles are shown in Fig. 15.5.

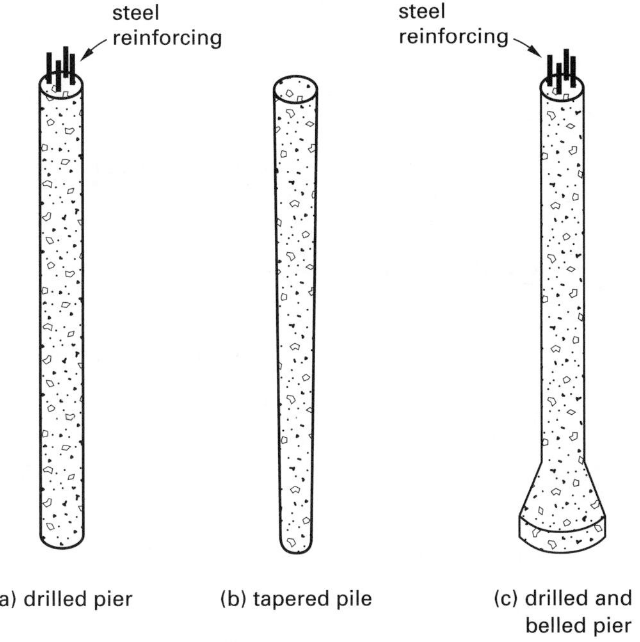

Figure 15.5 Pile Types

Drilled piers are formed by drilling out a hole to the required depth and then filling it with concrete. If the soil is soft, a metal lining is used to keep the soil from caving in during drilling. It is removed as the concrete is poured or may be left in. If the soil pressure is not sufficient for a drilled pier of normal dimensions, the bottom is "belled" out to increase the surface area for bearing (see Fig. 15.5(c)).

Piles are usually placed in groups or in a line under a bearing wall with the loads from the building transferred to them with pile caps. See Fig. 15.6. The piles are embedded from 4 in to 6 in into the pile cap, which is designed and reinforced to safely transmit the loads and resist shear and moment stresses as they develop. When two or more piles are used to support one column, the centroid of the pile group is designed to coincide with the center of gravity of the column load.

One type of pile foundation system frequently used is the *grade beam*. See Fig. 15.6(b). With this system, piles are driven or drilled in line at regular intervals and connected with a continuous grade beam. The grade beam is designed and reinforced to transfer the loads from the building wall to the piles.

This system is often used where expansive soils or clay, such as bentonite, are encountered near the surface. In this case, the grade beams are poured on carton forms that support the concrete during pouring but do not transmit any upward pressures from the soil when they expand because they disintegrate and form a void shortly thereafter.

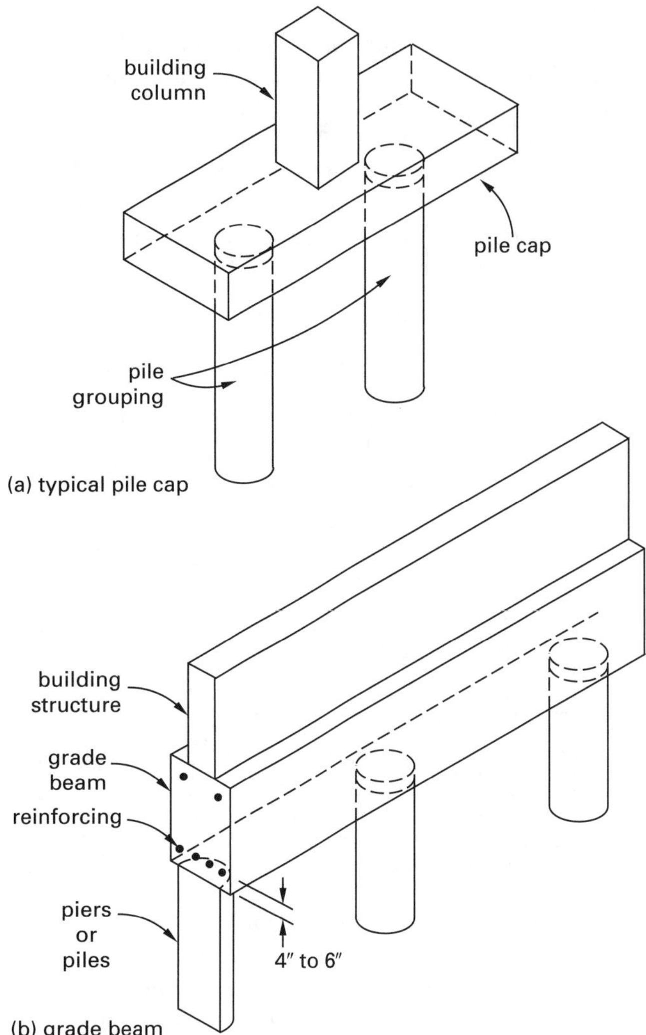

Figure 15.6 Pile Caps

Designing Footings

There are three primary factors to investigate when designing footings. The first is the *unit loading*, so that the allowable bearing pressure of the soil is not exceeded and differential settlement in various parts of the structure is eliminated as much as possible. The other two are *shear* and *bending*. There are two kinds of shear failure. A footing fails in punching or two-way shear when the column or wall load punches through the footing. A footing can also fail in flexural shear or diagonal tension the same as regular beams. Footings fail in bending when the lower surface cracks under flexural loading.

Simple spread footings act much like inverted beams with the upward soil pressure being a continuous load that is resisted by the downward column load (although in reality, the column load is the action, and the upward pressure is the reaction). See Fig. 15.7. This tends to cause bending in the upward direction, which induces compression near the top of the footing and tension near the bottom of the footing. If the tension is great enough, tension reinforcing must be added near the bottom of the footing.

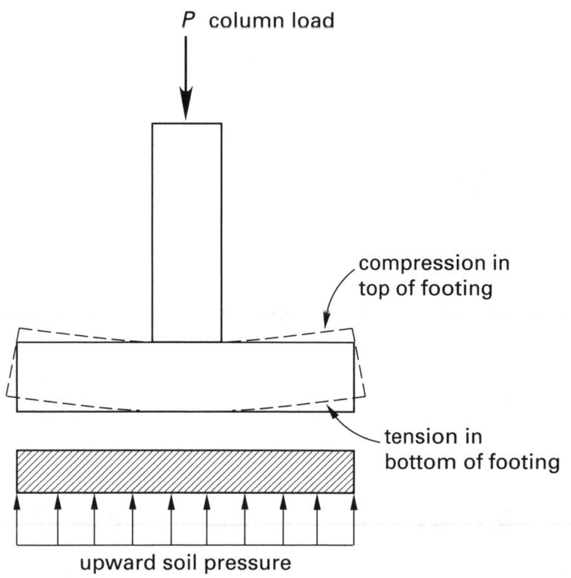

Figure 15.7 Load Action on Simple Spread Footings

The area of a spread footing is determined by dividing the total wall or column load on it plus its own weight plus any soil on top of the footing by the allowable soil bearing pressure. Then, the footing itself is designed for shear, moment, and other loads with factored loads as required by ACI 318, *Building Code Requirements for Structural Concrete* published by the American Concrete Institute (ACI). These, in effect, are safety factors to make sure the footing is of sufficient size and design to resist all loads.

There are various formulas to take into account combinations of live loads, dead loads, wind, earthquake, earth pressure, fluids, impact loads, and settlement, creep, and temperature change effects.

For foundations, the following formula is used.

$$U = 1.4D + 1.7L \qquad 15.1$$

The two most basic kinds of spread footings are the wall footing and the single column footing (see Fig. 15.4(a) and (b)). Each behaves a little differently, and each is designed based on slightly different conditions.

When designing wall footings, there are two critical sections that must be investigated. These are at the face of the wall where bending moment is greatest, and at a distance, d, from the face of the wall in wall footings where flexural shear is of most concern. These sections are shown in Fig. 15.8(a) and (b). However, the critical two-way shear section for column footings is distance $d/2$ from the face of the wall. See Fig. 15.9.

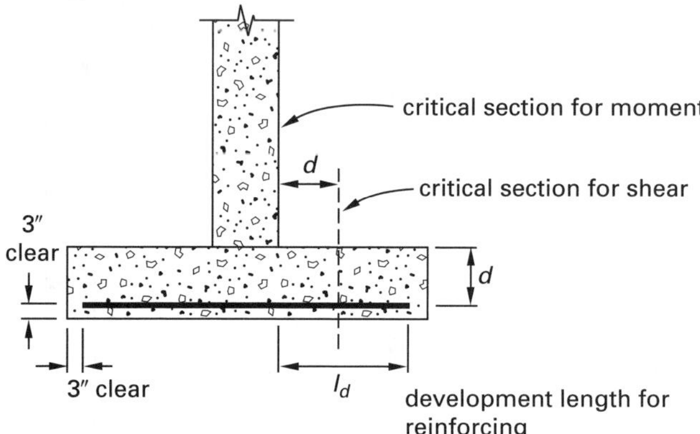

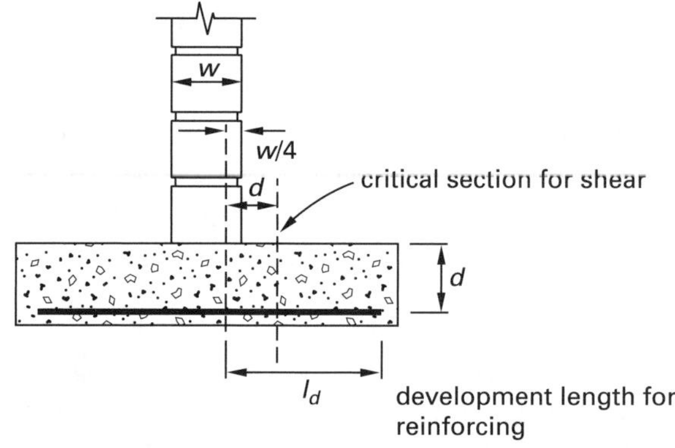

Figure 15.8 Critical Sections for Wall Footings

d is the distance from the top of the footing to the centroid of the reinforcing steel, called the *effective depth* of the footing since the concrete below the steel does not contribute any structural properties. The distance, d, for masonry and concrete foundation walls is a little different as shown in the two sketches. For concrete walls, it is measured from the face of the wall.

For lightly loaded walls where the total width of the footing is not too great, the bending action is not as critical as the shear that must be resisted by the thickness of the footing. Generally, it is not economical to provide tension reinforcement in wall footings, so the width and thickness are designed to resist the wall load and shear forces using only the strength of unreinforced concrete. Usually, however, longitudinal reinforcing is included (parallel to the length of the wall) for temperature reinforcing and to help the footing span any intermittent, weaker soil conditions.

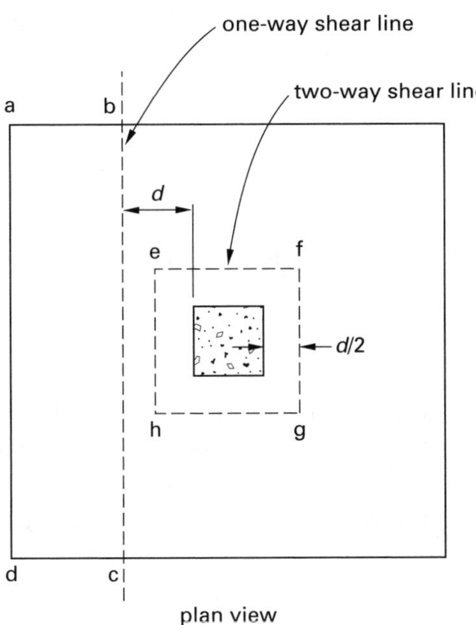

Figure 15.9 Individual Column Footings

Where heavy loads or weak soil conditions are present, the width of the footing may become great enough to require tension reinforcement. In most cases, however, maximum allowable flexural shear governs the design depth of wall footings.

Individual column footings are subject to two-way action, much like flat slabs near columns, as well as one-way shear. Because of this, both types of shear must be calculated, and the depth of the footing must be designed to resist these shear forces. When both are calculated, the greater shear value is used for design.

Figure 15.9 shows the two locations where shear must be calculated. For one-way shear at distance d from the face of the column, the factored soil design pressure is calculated over the rectangular area indicated as abcd in Fig. 15.9. For two-way shear, the soil design pressure is calculated over the area outside the square efgh indicated in Fig. 15.9.

In addition, bottom reinforcing in both directions is usually required to resist the moment forces at the face of the column.

Example 15.1

Find the required depth, width, and transverse reinforcing for the footing shown. The bottom of the footing is 5 ft below grade and carries a load per linear foot of 14,000 lbf dead load, including the wall weight, and 7000 lbf live load on a 12 in wide foundation wall. The concrete strength is 3000 psi, and the steel yield point is 60,000 psi. Soil tests have shown the allowable soil bearing pressure to be 3500 psf.

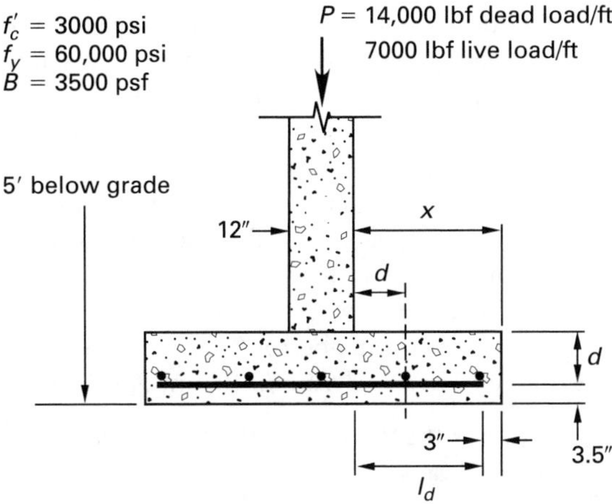

Step 1. In the design, consider a 1 ft long section of wall and footing. To find the width of the footing, divide the total load plus an allowance for the weight of the footing and an allowance for the soil on top of the footing by the allowable soil bearing pressure. Estimate the footing width as 7 ft and its depth as 12 in. With concrete weighing about 150 lbf/ft^3, a 1 ft long section of footing weighs 1050 lbf. Soil weighs about 100 psf, so the soil weight is 4 ft times 100, or 400 psf, or 1200 lbm for the 3 ft section on either side of the foundation wall.

So, the width of the footing should be

$$b_w = \frac{14{,}000\ \frac{\text{lbf}}{\text{ft}} + 7000\ \frac{\text{lbf}}{\text{ft}} + 1050\ \frac{\text{lbf}}{\text{ft}} + 2400\ \frac{\text{lbf}}{\text{ft}}}{3500\ \frac{\text{lbf}}{\text{ft}^2}}$$

$$= 6.99\ \text{ft}$$

Use a 7 ft wide footing.

Step 2. To begin the design of the footing, ACI 318 requires the design soil pressure to be calculated based on factored loads according to Eq. 15.1.

$$\begin{aligned} U &= 1.4D + 1.7L \\ &= (1.4)\left(14{,}000\ \frac{\text{lbf}}{\text{ft}}\right) + (1.7)\left(7000\ \frac{\text{lbf}}{\text{ft}}\right) \\ &= 31{,}500\ \text{plf} \end{aligned}$$

Note that this excludes the weight of the footing and the soil above the footing because they do not contribute to producing moment or shear in the footing.

The design soil pressure is then equal to the factored design load divided by the area.

$$q_s = \frac{31{,}500 \text{ plf}}{7 \text{ ft}} = 4500 \text{ psf}$$

Step 3. Assuming a footing depth of 12 in, check the flexural shear at the critical section since flexural shear almost always governs footing design. This section is at a distance, d (the effective depth of the footing), from the face of the wall (see Fig. 15.8(a)). The distance is from the top of the footing to the centroid of reinforcing steel. Since ACI 318 requires a 3 in clear dimension from steel to the bottom of a footing cast against the earth, use this plus an allowance (guess at this point) of 1/2 in for one-half the diameter of reinforcing steel. The rebars will probably be less than no. 8s, but this gives an easy number of 3 1/2 in to work with. Distance, d, is then 12 in − 3.5 in, or 8.5 in, or 0.708 ft.

Shear at this point is the distance to the end of the footing times the design soil pressure. Remember, this is a 1 ft long section of wall, so units are in feet and pounds per foot.

$$\begin{aligned} V &= (x - d)q_s \\ &= (3 \text{ ft} - 0.708 \text{ ft})\left(4500 \frac{\text{lbf}}{\text{ft}^2}\right) \end{aligned}$$

(Note: 0.708 is 8 1/2 in converted to a fraction of a foot.)

$$V = 10{,}310 \text{ plf}$$

ACI 318 limits one-way shear on plain or reinforced sections to a maximum of

$$V_c = \phi 2\sqrt{f'_c}\, b_w d \qquad 15.2$$

$$\begin{aligned} &= (0.85)(2)\sqrt{3000 \frac{\text{lbf}}{\text{ft}^2}}(12 \text{ in})(8.5 \text{ in}) \\ &= 9498 \text{ lbf/ft} \end{aligned}$$

The actual shear of 10,310 lbf is more than the allowable of 9498 lbf, so the section needs to be revised.

Try a 14 in deep footing with d = 14 in − 3.5 in, or 10.5 in.

$$\begin{aligned} V_c &= (0.85)(2)\sqrt{3000 \frac{\text{lbf}}{\text{ft}^2}}(12 \text{ in})(10.5 \text{ in}) \\ &= 11.730 \text{ lbf/ft} \end{aligned}$$

A 14 in thick footing will work since the allowable shear is now more than the actual shear of $v = (x - d)q_s = (3 \text{ ft} - 0.875 \text{ ft})(4500 \text{ lbf/ft}^2) = 9560$ plf.

Step 4. Find the moment at the face of the wall. The leg of the footing acts as an inverted cantilevered beam, so the moment is

$$M_u = \frac{q_s l}{2} = \frac{\left(4500 \frac{\text{lbf}}{\text{ft}^2}\right)(3 \text{ ft})^2}{2} = 20{,}250 \text{ ft-lbf/ft}$$

Step 5. Find the area of the steel required according to Eq. 15.3.

$$A_s = \frac{M_u}{\phi f_y\left(d - \frac{a}{2}\right)} \qquad 15.3$$

a is the depth of rectangular stress block determined by

$$a = \frac{A_s f_y}{0.85 f_c b} \qquad 15.4$$

Since steel area is not known, assume a value for a. Refer to Ch. 20 for a full discussion of this value. Try 1 in to begin with.

The strength reduction factor, ϕ, is 0.90 for flexure members.

$$\begin{aligned} A_s &= \frac{M_u}{\phi f_y\left(d - \frac{a}{2}\right)} \\ &= \frac{\left(20{,}250 \frac{\text{ft-lbf}}{\text{ft}}\right)\left(12 \frac{\text{in}}{\text{ft}}\right)}{(0.90)\left(60{,}000 \frac{\text{lbf}}{\text{in}^2}\right)\left(10.5 \text{ in} - \frac{1 \text{ in}}{2}\right)} \\ &= 0.45 \text{ in}^2\text{/ft of footing} \end{aligned}$$

There are several possible combinations of bar sizes and spacings that will satisfy this requirement. No. 5 bars at 8 in on center gives a steel area of 0.46 in²/ft, so use this. Refer to Table 20.1 for various bar/spacing combinations.

Check to see that the value of a is less than that used in the assumption by using Eq. 15.4.

$$a = \frac{A_s f_y}{0.85 f_c b} = \frac{\left(0.46 \frac{\text{in}^2}{\text{ft}}\right)\left(60{,}000 \frac{\text{lbf}}{\text{in}^2}\right)}{(0.85)\left(3000 \frac{\text{lbf}}{\text{in}^2}\right)(12 \text{ in})} = 0.90$$

This is less than the 1 in assumed in finding the area of steel, so this will work.

Step 6. Find the development length required for the steel. This is the minimum length required to develop a sufficient bond between the steel and the concrete. It is measured from the face of the wall to the end of the steel as shown in Fig. 15.8 and is found by Eq. 15.5.

$$l_d = \left(\frac{f_y \alpha \beta \lambda}{25\sqrt{f'_c}}\right) d_b \qquad 15.5$$

This equation assumes adequate concrete cover and bar spacing under normal conditions with $\alpha = \beta = \lambda = 1.0$.

From Table 20.1, the area of a no. 5 bar is 0.31 in^2, and its diameter is 0.625 in.

$$l_d = \left(\frac{f_y \alpha \beta \lambda}{25\sqrt{f'_c}} \right) d_b$$

$$= \left(\frac{\left(60{,}000 \ \frac{\text{lbf}}{\text{in}^2}\right)(1.0)(1.0)(1.0)}{25\sqrt{3000 \ \frac{\text{lbf}}{\text{in}^2}}} \right)(0.625 \text{ in})$$

$$= 27.39 \text{ in}$$

The minimum length is 12 in, so 27.39 in governs. Since the actual length is 36 in − 3 in, or 33 in, there is sufficient length of steel.

Step 7. Find the longitudinal temperature reinforcement required.

ACI 318 requires at least 0.0018 times the area of the section to be steel, so

$$A_s = (0.0018)(12 \text{ in})(14 \text{ in}) = 0.3024 \text{ in}^2$$

Number 4 bars at 7 in on center provide 0.34 in^2/ft (see Table 20.1).

RETAINING WALLS

Retaining walls are used to hold back soil or other material when the desired change in elevation between two points is greater than can be achieved by letting the soil rest at its normal angle of repose.

Types of Retaining Walls

There are three types of retaining walls: the gravity wall, the cantilever wall, and the counterfort wall. See Fig. 15.10. The *gravity wall* resists the forces on it by its own weight and by soil pressure and soil friction against its surface opposite to the earth forces. It is commonly used for low retaining walls up to about 10 ft where the forces on it are not too great.

The *cantilever wall* is the most common type and is constructed of reinforced concrete. This type resists forces by the weight of the structure as well as by the weight of the soil on the heel of the base slab. It is often constructed with a key projecting from the bottom of the slab to increase the wall's resistance to sliding as shown in Fig. 15.10(b). Occasionally, the toe is omitted if the wall is next to a property line or some other obstruction. Since the arm, heel, and toe act as cantilevered slabs, the thickness and reinforcement increase with increased length because of the larger moments developed.

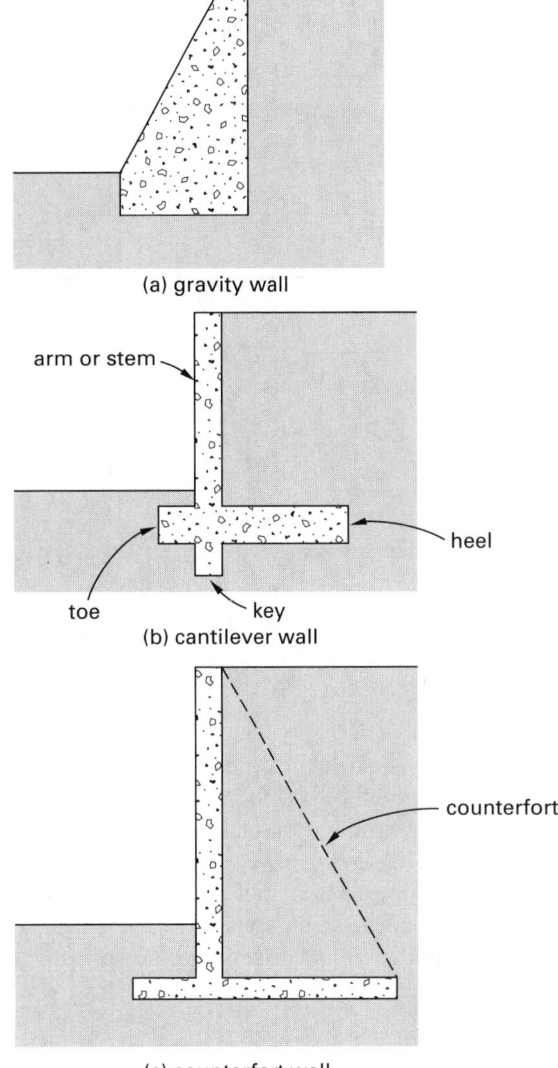

Figure 15.10 Types of Retaining Walls

Because of this, cantilevered walls are economically limited to about 20 ft to 25 ft in height.

For walls higher than 20 ft to 25 ft, the *counterfort wall* is used. This is similar to the cantilevered wall, but with counterforts placed at distances equal to or a little larger than one-half the height. The counterforts are simply reinforced concrete webs that act as diagonal bracing for the wall.

Forces on Retaining Walls

In the simplest case, the force on a retaining wall results entirely from the pressure of the earth retained acting in a horizontal direction to the wall. The earth pressure increases proportionally with the depth from the surface, ranging from zero at ground level to a maximum at the lowest depth of the wall in a triangular distribution pattern. See Fig. 15.11.

The earth pressure at any point is given by Eq. 15.6.

$$p = C_o Wh \qquad 15.6$$

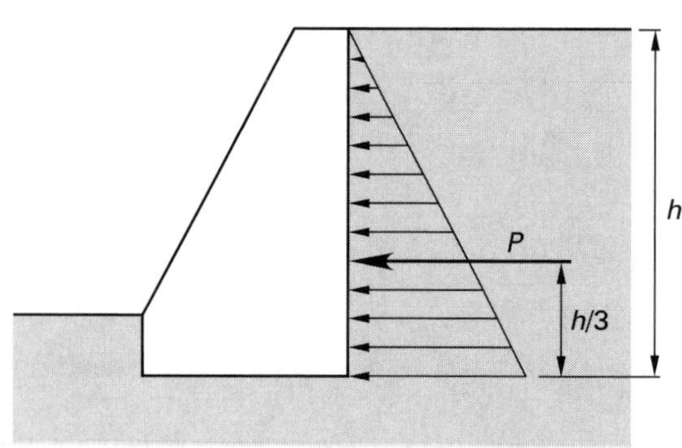

15.11 Forces Acting on a Retaining Wall

The coefficient of earth pressure, C_o, depends on the soil type and the method of backfilling and compacting it. The value may range from 0.4 for uncompacted soils like sands and gravels to 1.0 for cohesive, compacted soils. In many situations, the formula is simplified so that C_o is eliminated and the weight of the soil is considered to be equivalent to a fluid weighing 30 lbf/ft^3. Therefore, the pressure at any point is

$$p = 30h \qquad 15.7$$

In the situation shown in Fig. 15.11, since the pressure acts in a triangular form, the total lateral load against the wall can be assumed to be acting through the centroid of the triangle, or one-third the distance from the base. To find the total load, multiply the pressure at the base of the wall by the area of the triangle, $\frac{1}{2}h$. The formula for this is

$$P = (C_o Wh)\left(\frac{1}{2}h\right) = \frac{1}{2}C_o Wh^2 \qquad 15.8$$

Or, if using the 30 lbf/ft^3 assumption for the equivalent weight of the soil, the formula reduces to

$$P = 15h^2 \qquad 15.9$$

Example 15.2

Assuming the soil has an equivalent fluid weight of 30 psf per foot of height, what is the total earth pressure load on a retaining wall 9.5 ft high?

The total load acts at a point 9.5 ft/3, or 3.17 ft above the base. From Eq. 15.9, the load is

$$P = \left(15\,\frac{\text{lbf}}{\text{ft}^3}\right)(9.5\text{ ft})^2 = 1354\text{ plf}$$

Additional forces may act on retaining walls. The earth being retained may slope upward from the top of the wall, resulting in the total force acting through the centroid of the pressure triangle, but in a direction parallel to the slope of the soil. Additional loads, called surcharges, may result from driveways or other forces being imposed on the soil next to the wall. If the ground behind the wall becomes wet, there is additional pressure resulting from the water that must be added to the soil pressure.

Design Considerations

A retaining wall may fail in two ways: It may fail as a whole by overturning or by sliding, or its individual components may fail, such as when the arm or stem breaks due to excessive movement. In order to prevent failure by overturning or sliding, the resisting moment or forces that resist sliding are generally considered sufficient if there is a safety factor of 1.5. For example, the total dead load of the wall plus the weight of the earth backfill acting on the footing of a cantilevered retaining wall should be at least 1.5 times the overturning moment caused by earth pressure to be safe. See Fig. 15.12(a). To prevent sliding, the friction between the footing and surrounding soil and the earth pressure in front of the toe (and key, if any) must be 1.5 times the pressures tending to cause the wall to slide. See Fig. 15.12(b).

To prevent failure of individual components, the thickness, width, and reinforcing of the retaining wall must be designed to resist the moment and shear forces induced by soil pressures, surcharges, and any hydrostatic pressures.

Retaining walls should be designed to eliminate or reduce the buildup of water behind them. This can be accomplished by providing weep holes near the bottom of the wall and by providing a layer of gravel next to the back of the wall. In some cases, it is necessary to install a drain tile above the heel of the wall to carry away excess water.

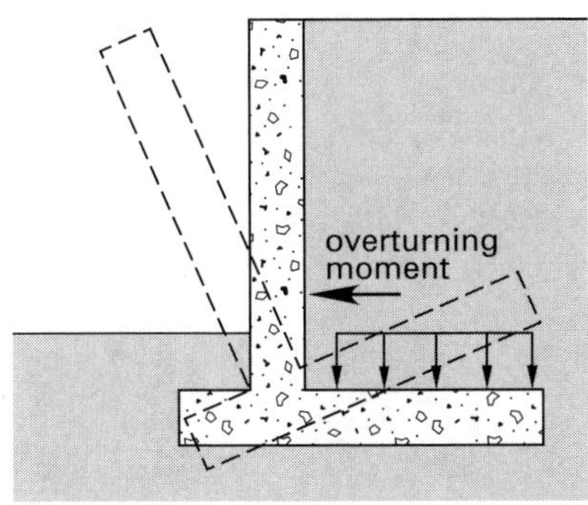

(a) overturning

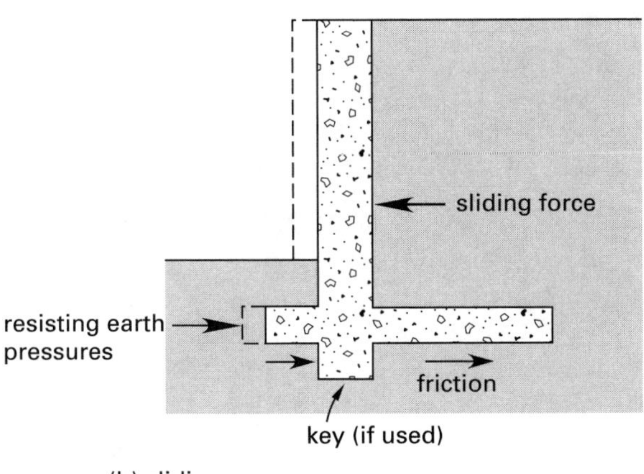

(b) sliding

Figure 15.12 Resisting Forces on Retaining Walls

16 CONNECTIONS

Nomenclature

F_c	unit stress in compression perpendicular to the grain	lbf/in^2
F_g	design value for end grain in bearing parallel to grain	lbf/in^2
F_n	unit compressive stress at inclination θ with the direction of grain	lbf/in^2
F_p	allowable bearing stress	lbf/in^2
F_t	allowable tensile stress	lbf/in^2
F_u	minimum tensile strength of steel or fastener	lbf/in^2
F_v	allowable shear stress	lbf/in^2
F_y	specified minimum yield stress of steel	lbf/in^2
G	specific gravity	–
P	tensile load	lbf
t	thickness	in
Z	nominal lateral design value for single fastener connection	lbf
θ	angle between the direction of grain and direction of load normal to face considered	deg

The majority of structural failures occur in the connections of members, not in the members themselves. Either the incorrect types of connectors are used, or the connectors are undersized, too few in number, or improperly installed. It is therefore important for ARE candidates to have a good understanding of the various types of connectors and how they are used.

WOOD CONNECTIONS

There are several variables that affect the design of wood connections. The first, of course, is the load-carrying capacity of the connector itself. Nails and screws, for example, carry relatively light loads, while timber connectors can carry large loads. Other variables that apply to all connections include the species of wood, the type of load, the condition of the wood, the service conditions, whether or not the wood is fire-retardant-treated, and the angle of the load to the grain. Additional design considerations are the critical net section, the type of shear the joint is subjected to, the spacing of the connectors, and the end and edge distances to connectors.

Species of Wood

The species and density of wood affect the holding power of connectors. Species are classified into four groups. There is one grouping for timber connectors, such as split ring connectors and shear plates, and another grouping for lag screws, nails, spikes, wood screws and metal plate connector loads. The four groups for timber connectors are designated Groups A, B, C, and D, while the grouping for other connectors are designated Groups I, II, III, and IV. Tables that give the allowable loads for connectors have separate columns for each group. Design values for connectors in a particular species apply to all grades of that species unless otherwise noted in the tables.

Type of Load

The design values for connectors can be adjusted for the duration of loading just as wood members can be (see Ch. 18). This is because wood can carry greater maximum loads for short durations than for long durations. The tables of allowable connector loads are for a normal duration of 10 years. For other conditions, the allowable values can be multiplied by the following factors.

- 0.90 for permanent loading over 10 years
- 1.15 for two months' duration (snow loading, for example)
- 1.25 for seven days' duration
- 1.60 for wind or earthquake loads
- 2.00 for impact loads

Condition of Wood

Tabulated design values found in building codes and elsewhere are for fastenings in wood seasoned to a moisture content of 19% or less. This is adequate for most use, but partially seasoned or wet wood (either at the time of fabrication or in service) reduces the holding power of the connector.

Service Conditions

Service conditions refer to the environment in which the wood joint will be used. These conditions can either be dry, wet, exposed to weather, or subject to wetting and drying. Any service conditions other than dry or continuously wet reduce the holding power of the connector.

Fire-Retardant Treatment

Wood that has been fire-retardant-treated does not hold connectors as well as wood that has not been treated. The *International Building Code* (IBC) and *National Design Specification for Wood Construction ASD/LRFD* (NDS) both specify that allowable design values for treated wood be obtained from the manufacturer.

Angle of Load

One of the most important variables affecting allowable loads carried by connectors is the angle of the load to the grain, which is defined as the angle between the direction of load acting on the member and the longitudinal axis of the member. Wood connectors can carry more load parallel to the grain than perpendicular to it, so tables of design values include both. If the load is acting other than parallel or perpendicular to the grain, it must be calculated using the *Hankinson formula* or by using one of the graphs that gives the same results.

The Hankinson formula gives the unit compressive stress at angle θ.

$$F_n = \frac{F_g F_c}{F_g \sin^2\theta + F_c \cos^2\theta} \qquad 16.1$$

Example 16.1

A 2 × 6 truss member bears on a 4 × 6 member at an angle of 40°. Both pieces of lumber are select structural Douglas fir (F_g = 1400 psi and F_c = 625 psi). What is the allowable unit compressive stress for the connection?

Using the Hankinson formula,

$$F_n = \frac{\left(1400\ \frac{\text{lbf}}{\text{in}^2}\right)\left(625\ \frac{\text{lbf}}{\text{in}^2}\right)}{\left(1400\ \frac{\text{lbf}}{\text{in}^2}\right)\sin^2 40 + \left(625\ \frac{\text{lbf}}{\text{in}^2}\right)\cos^2 40}$$

$$= \frac{875{,}000\ \frac{\text{lbf}^2}{\text{in}^4}}{\left(1400\ \frac{\text{lbf}}{\text{in}^2}\right)(0.413) + \left(625\ \frac{\text{lbf}}{\text{in}^2}\right)(0.587)}$$

$$= 926\ \text{psi}$$

Critical Net Section

When a wood member is drilled for one of the many types of connectors (except for nails and screws), there is a decrease in area of wood to carry the imposed load. The section where the most wood has been removed is called the *critical net section*. Once the size of the drilled area is known, the member must be checked for load-carrying capacity at this section. It may be necessary to increase the size of the member just to compensate for this decrease in area. See Fig. 16.1(a).

Type of Shear

Connectors such as bolts and lag screws can be in single shear, double shear, or multiple shear as shown in Fig. 16.1(b). The type of shear condition and the relative thickness of each piece to the others are especially important when designing bolted connections.

Connector Spacing

Connector spacing is the distance between centers of connectors measured along a line joining their centers as shown in Fig. 16.1(c). Minimum spacing is given for various types of connectors in building codes and in the NDS.

End and Edge Distances to Connectors

End distance is the distance measured parallel to the grain from the center of the connector to the square-cut end of the member. Edge distance is the distance from the edge of the member to the center of the connector closest to the edge of the member measured perpendicular to the edge. See Fig. 16.1(c).

For loading perpendicular to the grain, a distinction is made between the loaded and unloaded edges. The loaded edge is the edge toward which the fastener load acts, and the unloaded edge is the edge opposite from this. Minimum values for these distances are given in tables of allowable loads for the various types of connectors.

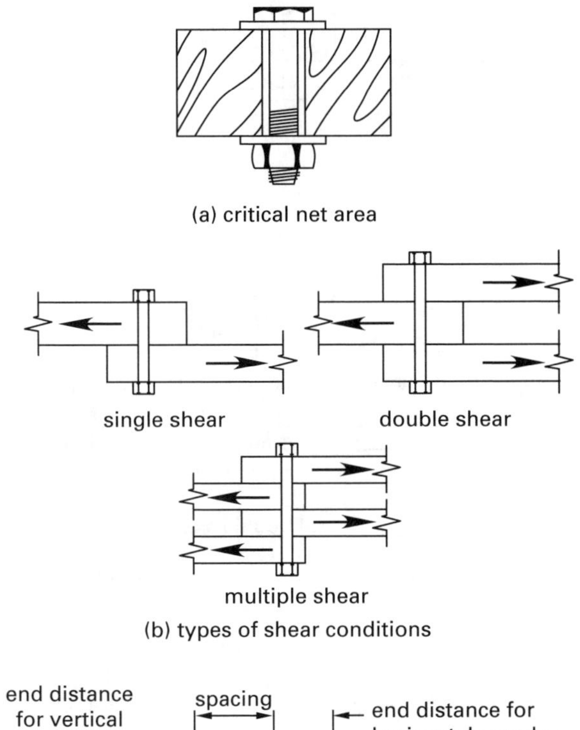

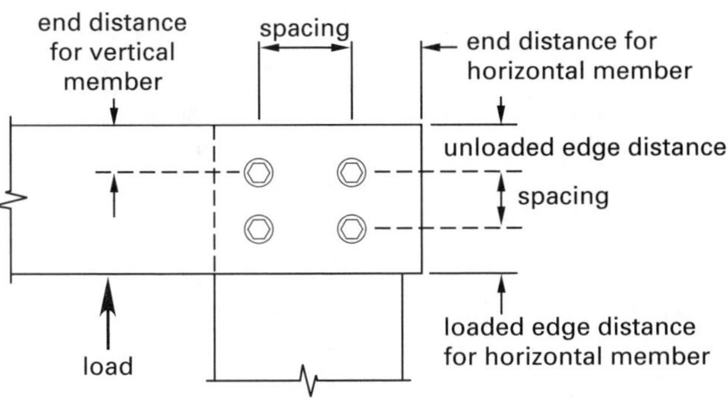

Figure 16.1 Wood Connector Design Variables

Nails

Although they are the weakest of wood connectors, nails are the most common for light frame construction. The types used most frequently for structural applications include common wire nails, box nails, and common wire spikes. Wire nails range in size from six penny (6d) to sixty penny (60d). Box nails range from 6d to 40d. 6d nails are 2 in long, while 60d nails are 6 in long. Common wire spikes range from 10d (3 in long) to $8^1/_2$ in long and $^3/_8$ in diameter. For the same pennyweight, box nails have the smallest diameter, common wire nails have the next largest diameter, and wire spikes have the greatest diameter.

For engineered applications, that is, where each nailed joint is specifically designed, there are tables of values giving the allowable withdrawal resistance and lateral load (shear) resistance for different sizes and penetrations of nails depending on the type of wood used. The typical situation of most nailed wood construction is to simply use nailing schedules found in the building code. These give the minimum size, number, and penetration of nails for specific applications such as nailing studs to sole plates, joists to headers, and so forth.

There are several orientations that nails, screws, and lag screws have with wood members. These are shown in Fig. 16.2 and affect the holding power of the fastener. The preferable orientation is to have the fastener loaded laterally in side grain where the holding power is the greatest. If one of the pieces is metal rather than wood, allowable values may be increased by 25%. For nails, the design values for shear are the same regardless of the angle of load to grain.

Fasteners may also be driven or screwed so that there is withdrawal from side grain. Fasteners loaded in withdrawal from end grain are not allowed by building codes.

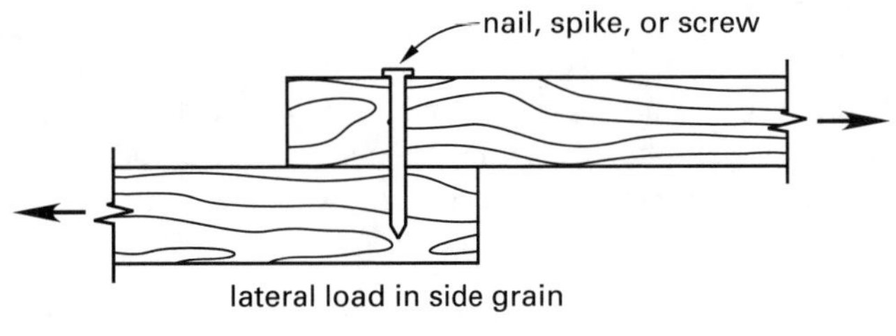

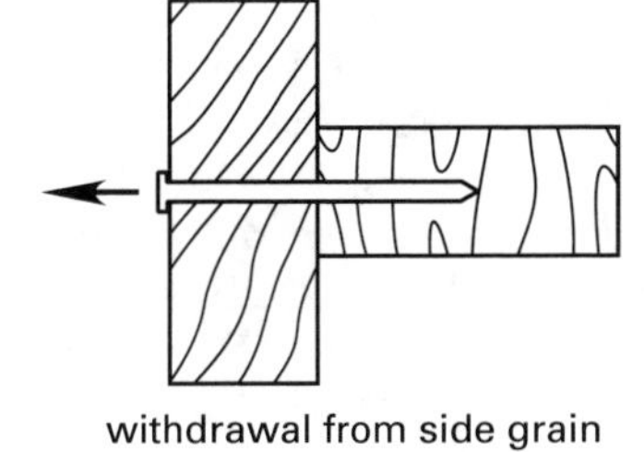

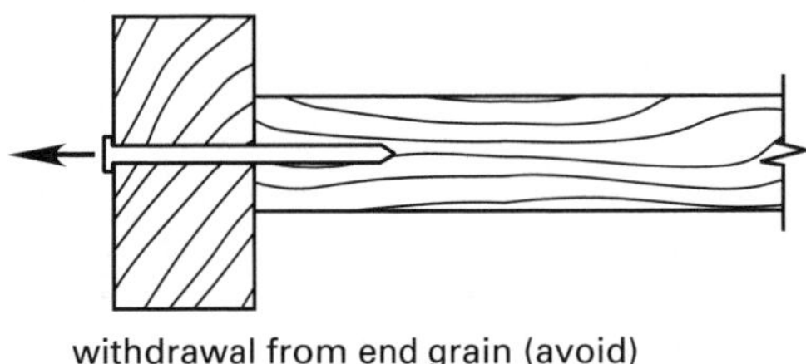

Figure 16.2 Orientation of Wood Fasteners

Screws

Wood screws used for structural purposes are available in sizes from no. 6 (0.138 in shank diameter) to no. 24 (0.372 in shank diameter) in lengths up to 5 in. The most common types are flat head and round head. As with nails, design tables give withdrawal and lateral load values for screws of different sizes, penetrations, and types of wood in which they are used. Also like nails, screws are best used laterally loaded in side grain rather than in withdrawal from side grain. Withdrawal from end is not permitted.

Design values given in the tables are for a penetration into the main member of approximately seven diameters. In no case should the penetration be less than four diameters. Like nails, design values can be increased by 25% if a metal side plate is used.

Lead holes must be drilled into the wood to permit the proper insertion of the wood screw. The recommended size of the lead hole depends on the species group of the wood being used and whether the screw is in lateral resistance or withdrawal resistance. Soap or other lubricant may be used to facilitate insertion.

Lag Screws

A lag screw is threaded with a pointed end like a wood screw but has a head like a bolt. It is inserted by drilling lead holes and screwing the fastener into the wood with a wrench. A washer is used between the head and the wood. Lag screws are also called *lag bolts*.

Sizes range from $^1/_4$ in to $1^1/_4$ in diameters and from 1 in to 12 in lengths. Diameters are measured at the nonthreaded shank portion of the screw.

The design values for lateral loading and withdrawal resistance depend on the species group, the angle of load to grain, the diameter of the lag screw, the thickness of the side member, and the length of the screw. These variables are summarized in allowable load tables for loading parallel and perpendicular to the grain. Unlike nails and spikes, if the load is other than at a 0° or 90° angle, the design value must be determined from the Hankinson formula. Spacings, end distances, and edge distance for lag screw joints are the same as for bolts of the same diameter as the shank of the lag screw.

Bolts

Bolts are one of the most common forms of wood connectors for joints of moderate to heavy loading. The design requirements for bolted joints are a little more complicated than those for screwed or nailed joints. Variables such as the thicknesses of the main and side members, ratio of bolt length in main member to bolt diameter, and the number of members joined affect the allowable design values and the spacing of the bolts.

The two typical conditions are joints in single shear and double shear as illustrated in Fig. 16.3.

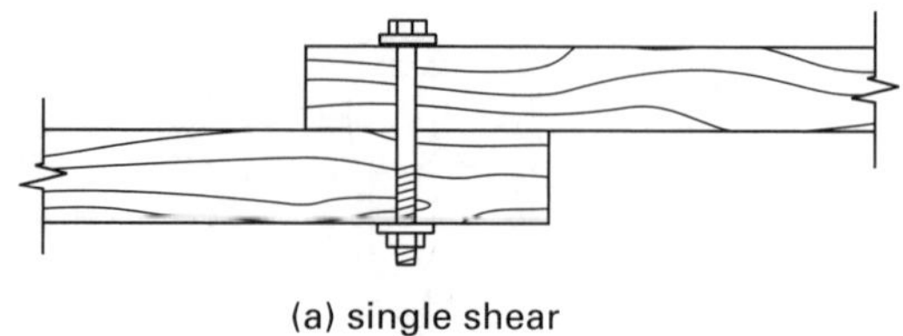

(a) single shear

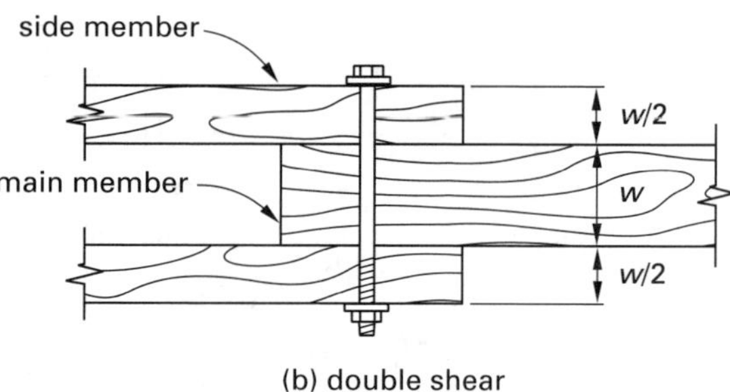

(b) double shear

Figure 16.3 Typical Bolted Connection Conditions

Design values given in tables are usually for conditions where the side members in double shear joints are one-half the thickness of the main member. If a value is given for only double shear joints, values for single shear joints of members of equal widths are taken as one-half the values for double shear joints. Tables 16.1(a) and 16.1(b) give bolt design values for single and double shear, respectively.

When $^1/_4$ in steel plates are used for side members, the design values are found in tables like Tables 16.1(a) and (b). The values must be reduced by 60% if separate side plates are not used for each row of bolts parallel to the grain or if the wood will not be dry at fabrication and service. Similar adjustments to the tabulated design values are required if adequate bolt spacing is not provided or if multiple bolts are placed in a line parallel to the load.

If loading is at an angle to the grain, the Hankinson formula must be used to determine allowable loading on a bolt. When side member dimensions vary from those shown in Fig. 16.3(b) or the bolt grouping consists of rows of multiple bolts, procedures for modifying the design values are given in the NDS.

Example 16.2

A nominal 4 × 6 southern pine beam is to be supported by two 2 × 6 members acting as a spaced column as shown in the illustration. The minimum spacing and edge distances for $^1/_2$ in bolts are shown. Assume that all normal conditions apply to the beam. How many $^1/_2$ in bolts will be required to safely carry a load of 1500 lbf?

Table 16.1(a)

Bolt Lateral Design Values (Z) for
Single Shear (Two Member) Connections[a,b]
(for sawn lumber or SCL with both members of identical specific gravity)

thickness (in) main member, t_m	thickness (in) side member, t_s	bolt diameter, D (in)	G = 0.55 mixed maple southern pine (lbf) $Z_\parallel$	$Z_{s\perp}$	$Z_{m\perp}$	$Z_\perp$	G = 0.50 Douglas fir-larch (lbf) $Z_\parallel$	$Z_{s\perp}$	$Z_{m\perp}$	$Z_\perp$	G = 0.46 Douglas fir (S) hem-fir (N) (lbf) $Z_\parallel$	$Z_{s\perp}$	$Z_{m\perp}$	$Z_\perp$
1 1/2	1 1/2	1/2	530	330	330	250	480	300	300	220	440	270	270	190
		5/8	660	400	400	280	600	360	360	240	560	320	320	220
		3/4	800	460	460	310	720	420	420	270	670	380	380	240
		7/8	930	520	520	330	850	470	470	290	780	420	420	250
		1	1060	580	580	350	970	530	530	310	890	480	480	280
3 1/2	1 1/2	1/2	660	400	470	360	610	370	430	330	580	340	400	310
		5/8	940	560	620	500	880	520	540	460	830	470	490	410
		3/4	1270	660	690	580	1200	590	610	510	1140	520	550	450
		7/8	1680	720	770	630	1590	630	680	550	1470	550	600	480
		1	2010	770	830	670	1830	680	740	590	1680	600	660	520
	3 1/2	1/2	750	520	520	460	720	490	490	430	690	460	460	410
		5/8	1170	780	780	650	1120	700	700	560	1070	650	650	500
		3/4	1690	960	960	710	1610	870	870	630	1540	800	800	560
		7/8	2170	1160	1160	780	1970	1060	1060	680	1810	980	980	590
		1	2480	1360	1360	820	2260	1230	1230	720	2070	1110	1110	640
5 1/2	1 1/2	5/8	940	560	640	500	880	520	590	460	830	470	560	430
		3/4	1270	660	850	660	1200	590	790	590	1140	520	740	520
		7/8	1680	720	1090	720	1590	630	980	630	1520	550	860	550
		1	2150	770	1190	770	2050	680	1060	680	1930	600	940	600
	3 1/2	5/8	1170	780	780	680	1120	700	730	630	1070	650	690	580
		3/4	1690	960	1090	850	1610	870	1030	780	1540	800	970	710
		7/8	2300	1160	1410	1020	2190	1060	1260	910	2060	980	1130	790
		1	2870	1390	1550	1100	2660	1290	1390	970	2500	1210	1250	860
7 1/2	1 1/2	5/8	940	560	640	500	880	520	590	460	830	470	560	430
		3/4	1270	660	850	660	1200	590	790	590	1140	520	740	520
		7/8	1680	720	1090	720	1590	630	1010	630	1520	550	950	550
		1	2150	770	1350	770	2050	680	1270	680	1930	600	1190	600
	3 1/2	5/8	1170	780	780	680	1120	700	730	630	1070	650	690	580
		3/4	1690	960	1090	850	1610	870	1030	780	1540	800	970	710
		7/8	2300	1160	1450	1020	2190	1060	1350	930	2060	980	1280	850
		1	2870	1390	1830	1210	2660	1290	1630	1110	2500	1210	1470	1030

[a]Tabulated lateral design values (Z) for bolted connections shall be multiplied by all applicable adjustment factors (see NDS Table 10.3.1).
[b]Tabulated lateral design values (Z) are for "full diameter" bolts (see NDS Appendix L) with bending yield (F_{yb}) of 45,000 psi.

Note: Some rows/columns not pertinent to this text have been omitted by PPI.

Table 16.1(b)
Bolt Lateral Design Values (Z) for
Double Shear (Three Member) Connections[a,b]
(for sawn lumber or SCL with both members of identical specific gravity)

thickness (in) main member, t_m	thickness (in) side member, t_s	bolt diameter, D (in)	$G = 0.55$ mixed maple southern pine (lbf) $Z_{\parallel}$	$Z_{s\perp}$	$Z_{m\perp}$	$G = 0.50$ Douglas fir-larch (lbf) $Z_{\parallel}$	$Z_{s\perp}$	$Z_{m\perp}$	$G = 0.46$ Douglas fir (S) hem-fir (N) (lbf) $Z_{\parallel}$	$Z_{s\perp}$	$Z_{m\perp}$
$1^1/_2$	$1^1/_2$	$^1/_2$	1150	800	550	1050	730	470	970	680	420
		$^5/_8$	1440	1130	610	1310	1040	530	1210	940	470
		$^3/_4$	1730	1330	660	1580	1170	590	1450	1040	520
		$^7/_8$	2020	1440	720	1840	1260	630	1690	1100	550
		1	2310	1530	770	2100	1350	680	1930	1200	600
$3^1/_2$	$1^1/_2$	$^1/_2$	1320	800	940	1230	730	860	1160	680	810
		$^5/_8$	1870	1130	1290	1760	1040	1190	1660	940	1090
		$^3/_4$	2550	1330	1550	2400	1170	1370	2280	1040	1210
		$^7/_8$	3360	1440	1680	3180	1260	1470	3030	1100	1290
		1	4310	1530	1790	4090	1350	1580	3860	1200	1400
	$3^1/_2$	$^1/_2$	1500	1040	1040	1430	970	970	1370	920	920
		$^5/_8$	2340	1560	1420	2240	1410	1230	2150	1290	1090
		$^3/_4$	3380	1910	1550	3220	1750	1370	3090	1610	1210
		$^7/_8$	4600	2330	1680	4290	2130	1470	3940	1960	1290
		1	5380	2780	1790	4900	2580	1580	4510	2410	1400
$5^1/_2$	$1^1/_2$	$^5/_8$	1870	1130	1290	1760	1040	1190	1660	940	1110
		$^3/_4$	2550	1330	1690	2400	1170	1580	2280	1040	1480
		$^7/_8$	3360	1440	2170	3180	1260	2030	3030	1100	1900
		1	4310	1530	2700	4090	1350	2480	3860	1200	2200
	$3^1/_2$	$^5/_8$	2340	1560	1560	2240	1410	1460	2150	1290	1390
		$^3/_4$	3380	1910	2180	3220	1750	2050	3090	1610	1900
		$^7/_8$	4600	2330	2650	4390	2130	2310	4130	1960	2020
		1	5740	2780	2810	5330	2580	2480	4990	2410	2200
$7^1/_2$	$1^1/_2$	$^5/_8$	1870	1130	1290	1760	1040	1190	1660	940	1110
		$^3/_4$	2550	1330	1690	2400	1170	1580	2280	1040	1480
		$^7/_8$	3360	1440	2170	3180	1260	2030	3030	1100	1900
		1	4310	1530	2700	4090	1350	2530	3860	1200	2390
	$3^1/_2$	$^5/_8$	2340	1560	1560	2240	1410	1460	2150	1290	1390
		$^3/_4$	3380	1910	2180	3220	1750	2050	3090	1610	1940
		$^7/_8$	4600	2330	2890	4390	2130	2720	4130	1960	2560
		1	5740	2780	3680	5330	2580	3380	4990	2410	3000

[a]Tabulated lateral design values (Z) for bolted connections shall be multiplied by all applicable adjustment factors (see NDS Table 10.3.1).
[b]Tabulated lateral design values (Z) are for "full diameter" bolts (see NDS Appendix L) with bending yield (F_{yb}) of 45,000 psi.
Note: Some rows/columns not pertinent to this text have been omitted by PPI.

Adapted from the Supplement to the National Design Specification for Wood Construction, copyright © 2005, courtesy, American Wood Council, Leesburg, VA.

This is a double shear connection, and Table 16.1(b) is appropriate. Look under the column labeled "main member." Since the length of the bolt in the main member is $3^{1}/_{2}$ in (4 in nominal width), use that row and the portion of the row labeled $1^{1}/_{2}$ in in the side members and $^{1}/_{2}$ in bolt diameter. Select the lower of the values under southern pine for $Z_{\parallel} = 1320$ lbf and $Z_m = 940$ lbf. This value is 940 lbf. Two bolts will allow for a load of (940 lbf)(2), or 1880 lbf, which is well above the 1500 lbf required.

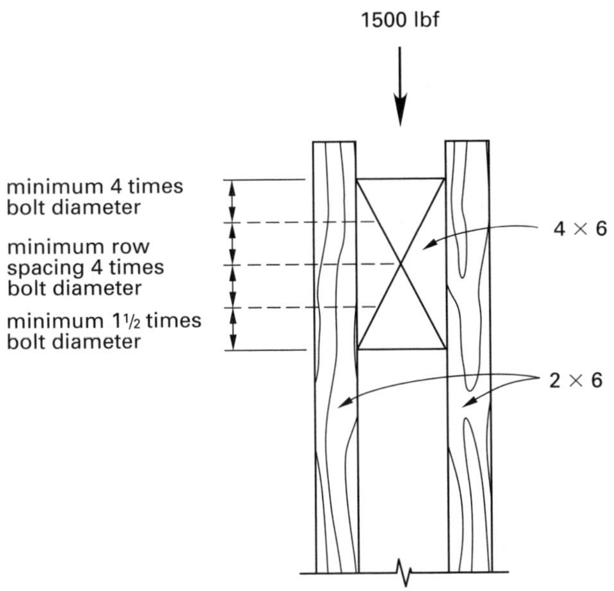

Using the spacing and edge distances given in the illustration, there must be a spacing of 2 in, a top distance of 2 in, and a bottom distance of $^{3}/_{4}$ in, for a total of $4^{3}/_{4}$ in, within the total actual depth of $5^{1}/_{2}$ in of a 4 × 6 member.

Timber Connectors

There are two types of timber connectors: split rings and shear plates. *Split rings* have either a $2^{1}/_{2}$ in or 4 in diameter and are cut through in one place in the circumference to form a tongue and slot. The ring is beveled from the central portion toward the edges. Grooves are cut in each piece of the wood members to be joined so that half the ring is in each section. The members are held together with a bolt concentric with the ring as shown in Fig. 16.4(a).

Shear plates have either a $2^{5}/_{8}$ in or 4 in diameter and are flat plates with a flange extending from the face of the plate. There is a hole in the middle through which either a $^{3}/_{4}$ in or $^{7}/_{8}$ in bolt is placed to hold the two members together. Shear plates are inserted in precut grooves in a piece of wood so that the plate is flush with one surface. See Fig. 16.4(b). Because of this configuration, shear plate connections can hold together either two pieces of wood or one piece of wood and a steel plate.

Split ring connectors and shear plates can transfer larger loads than bolts or screws alone and are often used in connecting truss members. Shear plates are particularly suited for constructions that must be disassembled. Tables of design values for loads, spacing, and end and edge distances are published by the National Forest Products Association.

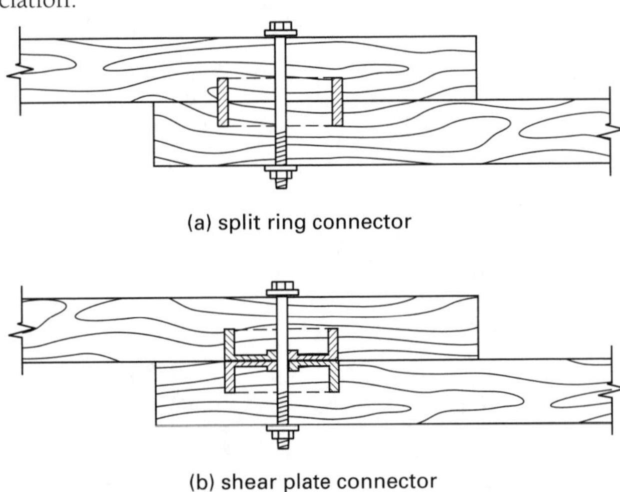

Figure 16.4 Timber Connectors

Miscellaneous Connection Hardware

Because wood is such a common building material, there are dozens of types of special connectors especially designed to make assembly easy, fast, and structurally sound. Hardware is available for standard sizes of wood members as well as for special members like wood truss joists. Manufacturers publish allowable design values for each of their pieces. Some of the common types of connection hardware are shown in Fig. 16.5.

STEEL CONNECTIONS

Bolting and *welding* are the two most common methods in use today for making steel connections. *Riveting* was once widely used but has been generally replaced with bolting because bolting is less expensive and does not take such a large crew of skilled workers to accomplish.

Bolts

There are two types of bolted connections: bearing type and slip-critical. *Bearing-type connections* resist the shear load on the bolt through friction between surfaces but may also produce direct bearing between the steel being fastened and the sides of the bolts. This is due to the fact that bolt holes are slightly larger than the bolts, and under load the two pieces of steel being connected may shift until they are bearing against the bolt.

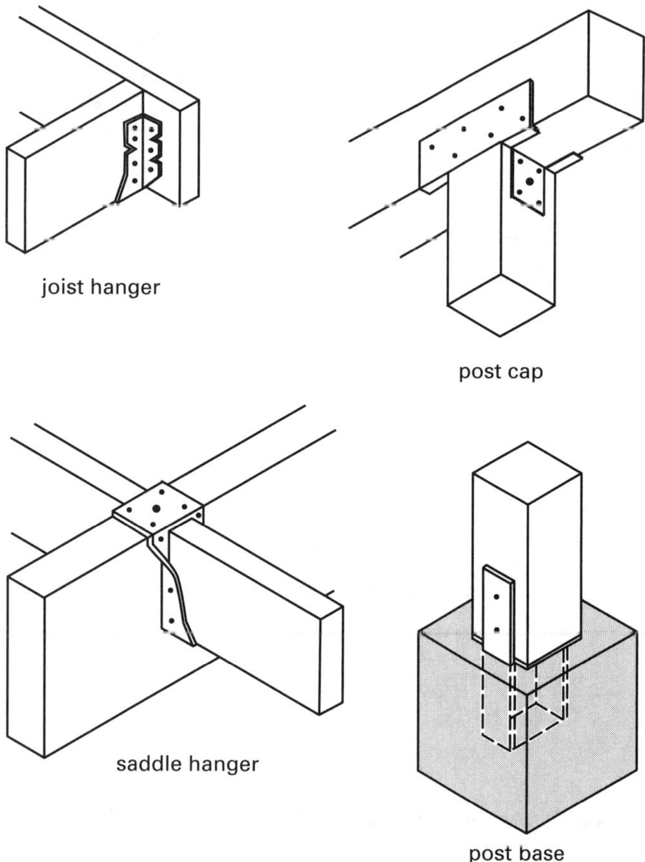

Figure 16.5 Special Connection Hardware

Slip-critical connections are those where any amount of slip would be detrimental to the serviceability of the structure, such as joints subject to fatigue loading or joints with oversized holes. With slip-critical joints, the entire load is carried by friction.

Bolts are further classified as to whether the bolt threads are included or excluded from the shear plane. This affects the strength of the connection because there is less area to resist the load through the threaded portion. See Fig. 16.6. Like wood connections, bolts may be either single shear or double shear.

There are three basic types of bolts used in modern steel construction. Bolts designated with the American Society of Testing and Materials (ASTM) number A307 are called *unfinished bolts* and have the lowest load-carrying capacity. They are used only for bearing-type connections. Bolts designated A325 and A490 are *high-strength bolts* and may be used in bearing-type connections but must be used in slip-critical connections. In slip-critical connections, the nuts are tightened to develop a high tensile stress in the bolt, thus causing the connected members to develop a high friction between them that resists the shear.

Bolts range in diameter from $^5/_8$ in to $1^1/_2$ in in $^1/_8$ in increments, but the most typically used diameters are $^3/_4$ in and $^7/_8$ in. Bolts are installed with a washer under the head and nut. In addition to the ASTM designations, there are standard codes for the conditions of use.

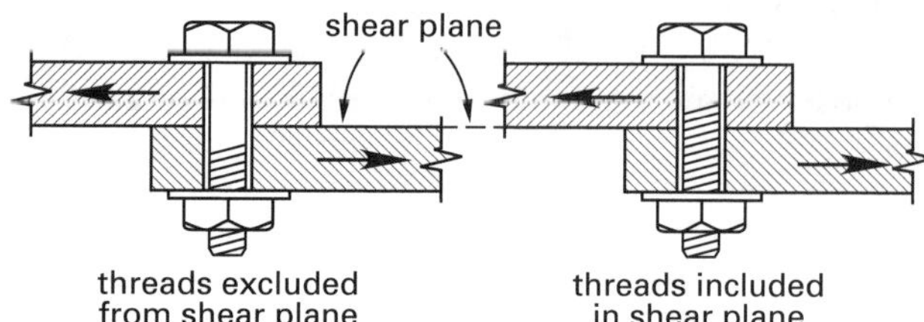

Figure 16.6 Location of Bolt Threads in Relation to Shear Plane

- SC: slip-critical connection
- N: bearing-type connection with threads included in the shear plane
- X: bearing-type connection with threads excluded from the shear plane
- S: bolt in single shear
- D: bolt in double shear

The American Institute of Steel Construction (AISC) *Steel Construction Manual* gives the allowable loads for various types of connectors in both shear and bearing. For bearing connections, different values are given based on the minimum tensile strength of the base material of the connected part. For A36 steel, this value is 58 ksi. The maximum allowable bearing stress between the bolt and the side of the hole is given by the equation

$$F_p = 1.2F_u \qquad 16.2$$

The allowable loads for shear are given in Table 16.2, and the allowable loads for bearing based on bolt spacing are given in Table 16.3. Similar tables for bearing strength are given in the *Steel Construction Manual* based on bolt edge distance. To use the tables, the bolt's diameter and designation must be known, as well as the type of hole being used, the connection type, and the loading condition. Procedures for using these tables will be shown in following examples.

There are several types of holes for bolted connections. *Standard round holes* are $^1/_{16}$ in larger than the diameter of the bolt. Other kinds of holes may be used with high-strength bolts having $^5/_8$ in and larger diameters.

Oversized holes may have nominal diameters up to $^3/_{16}$ in larger than bolts $^7/_8$ in and less in diameter, $^1/_4$ in larger than 1 in bolts, and $^5/_{16}$ in larger than bolts $1^1/_8$ in and greater in diameter. These holes may only be used in slip-critical connections.

Table 16.2

Available Shear Strength of Bolts

Available Shear Strength of Bolts, kips

Nominal Bolt Diameter d_b, in.					5/8		3/4		7/8		1	
Nominal Bolt Area, in.^{2}					0.307		0.442		0.601		0.785	
ASTM Desig.	Thread Cond.	F_{nv}/Ω (ksi)	ϕF_{nv} (ksi)	Loading	r_n/Ω_v	$\phi_v r_n$	r_n/Ω_v	$\phi_v r_n$	r_n/Ω_v	$\phi_v r_n$	r_n/Ω_v	$\phi_v r_n$
		ASD	LRFD		ASD	LRFD	ASD	LRFD	ASD	LRFD	ASD	LRFD
A325 F1852	N	24.0	36.0	S	7.36	11.0	10.6	15.9	14.4	21.6	18.8	28.3
				D	14.7	22.1	21.2	31.8	28.9	43.3	37.7	56.5
	X	30.0	45.0	S	9.20	13.8	13.3	19.9	18.0	27.1	23.6	35.3
				D	18.4	27.6	26.5	39.8	36.1	54.1	47.1	70.7
A490	N	30.0	45.0	S	9.20	13.8	13.3	19.9	18.0	27.1	23.6	35.3
				D	18.4	27.6	26.5	39.8	36.1	54.1	47.1	70.7
	X	37.5	56.3	S	11.5	17.3	16.6	24.9	22.5	33.8	29.5	44.2
				D	23.0	34.5	33.1	49.7	45.1	67.6	58.9	88.4
A307	–	12.0	18.0	S	3.68	5.52	5.30	7.95	7.22	10.8	9.42	14.1
				D	7.36	11.0	10.6	15.9	14.4	21.6	18.8	28.3

Nominal Bolt Diameter d_b, in.					1 1/8		1 1/4		1 3/8		1 1/2	
Nominal Bolt Area, in.^{2}					0.994		1.23		1.48		1.77	
ASTM Desig.	Thread Cond.	F_{nv}/Ω (ksi)	ϕF_{nv} (ksi)	Loading	r_n/Ω_v	$\phi_v r_n$	r_n/Ω_v	$\phi_v r_n$	r_n/Ω_v	$\phi_v r_n$	r_n/Ω_v	$\phi_v r_n$
		ASD	LRFD		ASD	LRFD	ASD	LRFD	ASD	LRFD	ASD	LRFD
A325 F1852	N	24.0	36.0	S	23.9	35.8	29.5	44.2	35.6	53.5	42.4	63.6
				D	47.7	71.6	58.9	88.4	71.3	107	84.8	127
	X	30.0	45.0	S	29.8	44.7	36.8	55.2	44.5	66.8	53.0	79.5
				D	59.6	89.5	73.6	110	89.1	134	106	159
A490	N	30.0	45.0	S	29.8	44.7	36.8	55.2	44.5	66.8	53.0	79.5
				D	59.6	89.5	73.6	110	89.1	134	106	159
	X	37.5	56.3	S	37.3	55.9	46.0	69.0	55.7	83.5	66.3	99.4
				D	74.6	112	92.0	138	111	167	133	199
A307	–	12.0	18.0	S	11.9	17.9	14.7	22.1	17.8	26.7	21.2	31.8
				D	23.9	35.8	29.5	44.2	35.6	53.5	42.4	63.6

ASD	LRFD
$\Omega_v = 2.00$	$\phi_v = 0.75$

Table 16.3

Available Bearing Strength at Bolt Holes Based on Bolt Spacing

Available Bearing Strength at Bolt Holes Based on Bolt Spacing

kips/in. thickness

Hole Type	Bolt Spacing, s, in.	F_u, ksi	Nominal Bolt Diameter d_b, in.							
			5/8		3/4		7/8		1	
			r_n/Ω_v ASD	$\phi_v r_n$ LRFD	r_n/Ω_v ASD	$\phi_v r_n$ LRFD	r_n/Ω_v ASD	$\phi_v r_n$ LRFD	r_n/Ω_v ASD	$\phi_v r_n$ LRFD
STD SSLT	$2^2/_3\ d_b$	58	34.1	51.1	41.3	62.0	48.6	72.9	55.8	83.7
		65	38.2	57.3	46.3	69.5	54.4	81.7	62.6	93.8
	3 in.	58	43.5	65.3	52.2	78.3	60.9	91.4	67.4	101
		65	48.8	73.1	58.5	87.8	68.3	102	75.6	113
SSLP	$2^2/_3\ d_b$	58	27.6	41.3	34.8	52.2	42.1	63.1	47.1	70.7
		65	30.9	46.3	39.0	58.5	47.1	70.7	52.8	79.2
	3 in.	58	43.5	65.3	52.2	78.3	60.9	91.4	58.7	88.1
		65	48.8	73.1	58.5	87.8	68.3	102	65.8	98.7
OVS	$2^2/_3\ d_b$	58	29.7	44.6	37.0	55.5	44.2	66.3	49.3	74.0
		65	33.3	50.0	41.4	62.2	49.6	74.3	55.3	82.9
	3 in.	58	43.5	65.3	52.2	78.3	60.9	91.4	60.9	91.4
		65	48.8	73.1	58.5	87.8	68.3	102	68.3	102
LSLP	$2^2/_3\ d_b$	58	3.62	5.44	4.35	6.53	5.08	7.61	5.80	8.70
		65	4.06	6.09	4.88	7.31	5.69	8.53	6.50	9.75
	3 in.	58	43.5	65.3	39.2	58.7	28.3	42.4	17.4	26.1
		65	48.8	73.1	43.9	65.8	31.7	47.5	19.5	29.3
LSLT	$2^2/_3\ d_b$	58	28.4	42.6	34.4	51.7	40.5	60.7	46.5	69.8
		65	31.8	47.7	38.6	57.9	45.4	68.0	52.1	78.2
	3 in.	58	36.3	54.4	43.5	65.3	50.8	76.1	56.2	84.3
		65	40.6	60.9	48.8	73.1	56.9	85.3	63.0	94.5
STD, SSLT, SSLP, OVS, LSLP	$s \geq s_{full}$	58	43.5	65.3	52.2	78.3	60.9	91.4	69.6	104
		65	48.8	73.1	58.5	87.8	68.3	102	78.0	117
LSLT	$s \geq s_{full}$	58	36.3	54.4	43.5	65.3	50.8	76.1	58.0	87.0
		65	40.6	60.9	48.8	73.1	56.9	85.3	65.0	97.5

		5/8	3/4	7/8	1
Spacing for full bearing strength s_{full}[a], in.	STD, SSLT, LSLT	$1^{15}/_{16}$	$2^5/_{16}$	$2^{11}/_{16}$	$3^1/_{16}$
	OVS	$2^1/_{16}$	$2^7/_{16}$	$2^{13}/_{16}$	$3^1/_4$
	SSLP	$2^1/_8$	$2^1/_2$	$2^7/_8$	$3^5/_{16}$
	LSLP	$2^{13}/_{16}$	$3^3/_8$	$3^{15}/_{16}$	$4^1/_2$
Minimum Spacing[a] $= 2^2/_3\ d_b$, in.		$1^{11}/_{16}$	2	$2^5/_{16}$	$2^{11}/_{16}$

STD = Standard Hole
SSLT = Short-Slotted Hole oriented transverse to the line of force
SSLP = Short-Slotted Hole oriented parallel to the line of force
OVS = Oversized Hole
LSLP = Long-Slotted Hole oriented parallel to the line of force
LSLT = Long-Slotted Hole oriented transverse to the line of force

ASD	LRFD
$\Omega_v = 2.00$	$\phi_v = 0.75$

Note: Spacing indicated is from the center of the hole or slot to the center of the adjacent hole or slot in the line of force. Hole deformation is considered. When hole deformation is not considered, see AISC Specification Section J3.10.

[a] Decimal value has been rounded to the nearest sixteenth of an inch.

Short slotted holes are $1/16$ in wider than the bolt diameter and have a length that does not exceed the oversized hole dimensions by more than $1/16$ in. They may be used in either bearing or slip-critical connections, but if used in bearing, the slots have to be perpendicular to the direction of the load.

Long slotted holes are $1/16$ in wider than the bolt diameter and a have length not exceeding $2^1/2$ times the bolt diameter. They may be used in slip-critical connections without regard to direction of load, but must be perpendicular to the load direction in bearing-type connections.

Slotted holes are used where some amount of adjustment is needed. Long slotted holes can only be used in one of the connected parts of a joint. The other part must use standard round holes or be welded.

In addition to the load-carrying capacities of the bolts, the effect of reducing the cross-sectional area of the members must be checked. Figure 16.7 shows a typical example of this. In this case, a beam is framed into a girder with an angle welded to the girder and bolted to the beam. With a load applied to the beam, there is a tendency for the web of the beam to tear where the area of the web has been reduced by the bolt holes. This area is known as the *net area*. As shown, there is both shear failure parallel to the load and tension failure perpendicular to the load.

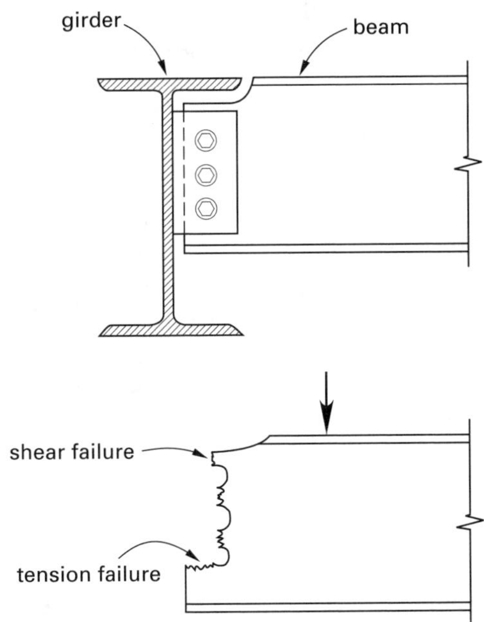

Figure 16.7 Tearing Failures at Bolted Connection

The AISC manual limits the allowable stress on the net tension area to

$$F_t = 0.50F_u \qquad 16.3$$

The allowable stress on the net shear area is limited to

$$F_v = 0.30F_u \qquad 16.4$$

For A36 steel, $F_u = 58$ ksi and $F_y = 36$ ksi.

The total tearing force is the sum required to cause both forms of failure.

The stress on net tension area must be compared with the allowable stress on the gross section, which is

$$F_t = 0.60F_y \qquad 16.5$$

Example 16.3

A $3/8$ in A36 steel plate is suspended from a $1/2$ in plate with three $3/4$ in A325 bolts in standard holes spaced as shown. The threads are excluded from the shear plane, and the connection is bearing type. Assuming full bearing capacity, what is the maximum load-carrying capacity of the $3/8$ in plate?

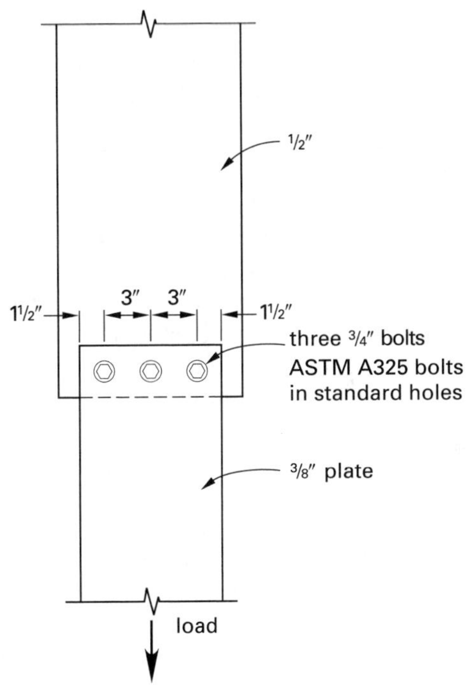

First, check the shear capacity of the bolts. From Table 16.2, one bolt can carry a load of 13.3 kips, or three bolts can carry (3)(13.3 kips), or 39.9 kips.

Next, check bearing capacity. The thinner material governs, which is $3/8$ in. In Table 16.3, read from the STD and $s > s_{full}$ row under the $3/4$ in diameter column (with $F_u = 58$ and ASD). The available strength is 52.2 kips/in thickness. Multiply this value by the $3/8$ in thickness to get 19.6 kips. Three bolts will then carry (3)(19.6 kips) = 58 kips.

Finally, determine the maximum stress on the net section through the holes. Once again, the thinner material is the most critical component. The allowable unit stress is

$$F_t = 0.50F_u = (0.50)(58\ \text{kips}) = 29\ \text{ksi}$$

The diameter of each hole is 1/8 in larger than the bolt for net sections, 1/8 or 7/8 in, which is 0.875 in. The net width of the 3/8 in plate is

$$9\ \text{in} - (3)(0.875\ \text{in}) = 6.375\ \text{in}$$

The allowable load on the net section is

$$P = (6.375\ \text{in})(0.375\ \text{in})\left(29\ \frac{\text{kips}}{\text{in}^2}\right) = 69.33\ \text{kips}$$

The allowable stress on the gross section is

$$\begin{aligned} P &= (0.6)\left(36\ \frac{\text{kips}}{\text{in}^2}\right)(9\ \text{in})(0.375\ \text{in}) \\ &= 72.9\ \text{kips} \end{aligned}$$

From these four loads, the minimum governs, which is the shear capacity of the bolts, or 39.9 kips.

There are many kinds of framed connections depending on the type of connector being used, the size and shape of the connected members, and the magnitude of the loads that must be transferred. Figure 16.8 illustrates some of the more typical kinds of steel connections. In most cases, the angle used to connect one piece with another is welded to one member in the shop and bolted to the other member during field erection. Slotted holes are sometimes used to allow for minor field adjustments.

If the top flange of one beam needs to be flush with another, the web is coped as shown in Fig. 16.8(b).

Simple beam-to-column connections are often made as illustrated in Fig. 16.8(c). The seat angle carries most of the gravity load, and the clip angle is used to provide stability from rotation. If a moment connection is required, a detail similar to Fig. 16.8(d) is used, although welding is more suitable for moment connections. For tubes and round columns, a single plate can be welded to the column and connected with beams as shown in Fig. 16.8(f). When the loads are heavy, some engineers prefer to slot the column and run the shear plate through, welding it at the front and back of the column.

Since connecting beams to columns and other beams with angles and bolts is such a common method of steel framing, the AISC manual gives tables of allowable loads for various types and diameters of bolts and lengths and thicknesses of angles. Two such tables are reproduced in Tables 16.4 and 16.5. The first is for 3/4 in bolts, and the second is for 7/8 in bolts.

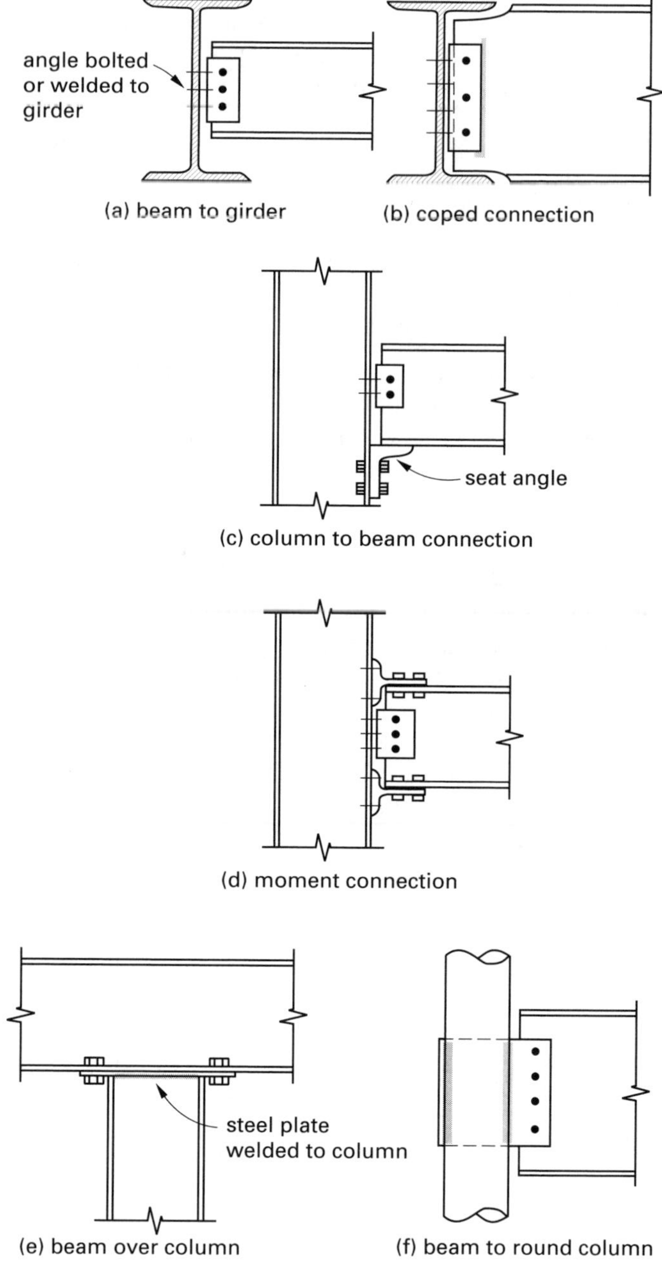

Figure 16.8 Typical Steel Framing Connections

One of the important considerations in bolted steel connections, just as in wood connections, is the spacing of bolts and the edge distance from the last bolt to the edge of the member. The AISC manual specifies minimum dimensions. The absolute minimum spacing is 2 2/3 times the diameter of the bolt being used, with 3 times the diameter being the preferred dimension. Many times, a dimension of 3 in is used for all sizes of bolts up to 1 in diameter.

Table 16.4

All-Bolted Double-Angle Connections—$^3/_4$ in Bolts

Beam F_y = 50 ksi, F_u = 65 ksi
Angle F_y = 36 ksi, F_u = 58 ksi

All-Bolted Double-Angle Connections

$^3/_4$-in. Bolts

Bolt and Angle Available Strength, kips

5 Rows W30, 27, 24, 21, 18	ASTM Desig.	Thread Cond.	Hole Type	Angle Thickness $^1/_4$ ASD	$^1/_4$ LRFD	$^5/_{16}$ ASD	$^5/_{16}$ LRFD	$^3/_8$ ASD	$^3/_8$ LRFD	$^1/_2$ ASD	$^1/_2$ LRFD
	A325/F1852	N	—	83.3	125	104	156	106	159	106	159
		X	—	83.3	125	104	156	125	187	133	199
		SC Class A	STD	73.8	111	73.8	111	73.8	111	73.8	111
			OVS	53.3	80.0	53.3	80.0	53.3	80.0	53.3	80.0
			SSLT	62.8	94.1	62.8	94.1	62.8	94.1	62.8	94.1
		SC Class B	STD	83.3	125	104	156	105	158	105	158
			OVS	76.2	114	76.2	114	76.2	114	76.2	114
			SSLT	82.0	123	89.6	134	89.6	134	89.6	134
	A490	N	—	83.3	125	104	156	125	187	133	199
		X	—	83.3	125	104	156	125	187	166	249
		SC Class A	STD	83.3	125	92.3	138	92.3	138	92.3	138
			OVS	66.7	100	66.7	100	66.7	100	66.7	100
			SSLT	78.4	118	78.4	118	78.4	118	78.4	118
		SC Class B	STD	83.3	125	104	156	125	187	132	198
			OVS	82.4	124	95.2	143	95.2	143	95.2	143
			SSLT	82.0	123	102	154	112	168	112	168

Beam Web Available Strength per Inch Thickness, kips/in.

Hole Type		STD				OVS				SSLT			
L_{eh}*		$1^1/_2$		$1^3/_4$		$1^1/_2$		$1^3/_4$		$1^1/_2$		$1^3/_4$	
L_{ev}, in.		ASD	LRFD	ASD	LRFD	ASD	LRFD	ASD	LRFD	ASD	LRFD	ASD	LRFD
Coped at Top Flange Only	$1^1/_4$	208	312	216	324	195	293	203	305	205	307	213	320
	$1^3/_8$	210	316	219	328	197	296	206	308	207	311	216	323
	$1^1/_2$	213	319	221	332	200	300	208	312	210	315	218	327
	$1^5/_8$	215	323	223	335	202	303	210	316	212	318	220	331
	2	223	334	231	346	210	314	218	327	220	329	228	342
	3	242	363	250	375	229	344	237	356	239	359	247	371
Coped at Both Flanges	$1^1/_4$	197	296	197	296	185	278	185	278	197	296	197	296
	$1^3/_8$	202	303	202	303	190	285	190	285	202	303	202	303
	$1^1/_2$	207	311	207	311	195	293	195	293	207	311	207	311
	$1^5/_8$	212	318	212	318	200	300	200	300	212	318	212	318
	2	223	334	227	340	210	314	215	322	220	329	227	340
	3	242	363	250	375	229	344	237	356	239	359	247	371
Uncoped		293	439	293	439	293	439	293	439	293	439	293	439

Support Available Strength per Inch Thickness, kips/in.

Hole Type	ASD	LRFD
STD/OVS/SSLT	585	878

Notes:
STD = Standard holes
OVS = Oversized holes
SSLT = Short-slotted holes transverse to direction of load
N = Threads included
X = Threads excluded
SC = Slip critical

* Tabulated values include $^1/_4$-in. reduction in end distance L_{eh} to account for possible underrun in beam length.

Table 16.5

All-Bolted Double-Angle Connections—7/8 in Bolts

Beam	F_y = 50 ksi, F_u = 65 ksi
Angle	F_y = 36 ksi, F_u = 58 ksi

All-Bolted Double-Angle Connections — 7/8-in. Bolts

Bolt and Angle Available Strength, kips

5 Rows — W30, 27, 24, 21, 18

ASTM Desig.	Thread Cond.	Hole Type	1/4 ASD	1/4 LRFD	5/16 ASD	5/16 LRFD	3/8 ASD	3/8 LRFD	1/2 ASD	1/2 LRFD
A325/F1852	N	—	82.4	124	103	155	124	185	144	216
	X	—	82.4	124	103	155	124	185	165	247
	SC Class A	STD	82.4	124	103	154	103	154	103	154
		OVS	74.3	111	74.3	111	74.3	111	74.3	111
		SSLT	81.1	122	87.4	131	87.4	131	87.4	131
	SC Class B	STD	82.4	124	103	155	124	185	144	216
		OVS	77.2	116	96.5	145	106	159	106	159
		SSLT	81.1	122	101	152	122	182	125	187
A490	N	—	82.4	124	103	155	124	185	165	247
	X	—	82.4	124	103	155	124	185	165	247
	SC Class A	STD	82.4	124	103	155	124	185	129	194
		OVS	77.2	116	93.3	140	93.3	140	93.3	140
		SSLT	81.1	122	101	152	110	165	110	165
	SC Class B	STD	82.4	124	103	155	124	185	165	247
		OVS	77.2	116	96.5	145	116	174	133	200
		SSLT	81.1	122	101	152	122	182	157	235

Beam Web Available Strength per Inch Thickness, kips/in.

Hole Type		STD				OVS				SSLT			
L_{ev}, in.	L_{eh}*	1 1/2		1 3/4		1 1/2		1 3/4		1 1/2		1 3/4	
		ASD	LRFD	ASD	LRFD	ASD	LRFD	ASD	LRFD	ASD	LRFD	ASD	LRFD
Coped at Top Flange Only	1 1/4	195	293	203	305	182	273	190	285	192	288	200	300
	1 3/8	197	296	206	308	184	277	193	289	194	292	203	304
	1 1/2	200	300	208	312	187	280	195	293	197	295	205	307
	1 5/8	202	303	210	316	189	284	197	296	199	299	207	311
	2	210	314	218	327	197	295	205	307	207	310	215	322
	3	229	344	237	356	216	324	224	336	226	339	234	351
Coped at Both Flanges	1 1/4	185	278	185	278	173	260	173	260	185	278	185	278
	1 3/8	190	285	190	285	178	267	178	267	190	285	190	285
	1 1/2	195	293	195	293	183	274	183	274	195	293	195	293
	1 5/8	200	300	200	300	188	282	188	282	199	299	200	300
	2	210	314	215	322	197	295	202	303	207	310	215	322
	3	229	344	237	356	216	324	224	336	226	339	234	351
Uncoped		341	512	341	512	341	512	341	512	341	512	341	512

Support Available Strength per Inch Thickness, kips/in.

Hole Type	ASD	LRFD
STD/OVS/SSLT	683	1020

Notes:
STD = Standard holes
OVS = Oversized holes
SSLT = Short-slotted holes transverse to direction of load
N = Threads included
X = Threads excluded
SC = Slip critical

* Tabulated values include 1/4-in. reduction in end distance L_{eh} to account for possible underrun in beam length.

The required edge distance varies with the diameter of the bolt being used: at the edges of plates, shapes, or bars, the dimension is 1 in for a 3/4 in bolt and 1.25 in for a 1 in bolt. To simplify detailing and tabulated values, a dimension of 1.25 in is often used for all bolts having a diameter up to 1 in.

Example 16.4

A W24 × 104 girder supports a W18 × 55 beam with two 3 1/2 × 3 1/2 × 5/16 × 14 1/2 in long angles. The connection is made with 7/8 in, A325 bolts in a slip-critical Class B connection. What is the maximum allowable load that can be supported?

Since 7/8 in bolts are being used, look in Table 16.5 in the row for A325-SC Class B bolts with standard (STD) holes. Find the column corresponding to the angle thickness of 5/16 in. Read the allowable load directly as 103 kips for ASD.

Welds

Welded connections are quite frequently used in lieu of bolts for several reasons.

- The gross cross section of the members can be used instead of the net section.
- Construction is often more efficient because there are no angles, bolts, or washers to deal with and no clearance problems with wrenches.
- Welding is more practical for moment connections.

Since members must be held in place until welding is completed, welding is often used in combination with bolting. Connection angles and other pieces are welded to one member in the shop with the outreach leg punched or slotted for field connection with bolts.

There are several types of welding processes, but the one most commonly used in building construction is the *electric arc process*. One electrode from the power source is attached to the steel members being joined, and the other electrode is the welding rod the welder holds in his or her hand. The intense heat generated by the electric arc formed when the welding rod is brought close to the members causes some of the base metal and the end of the electrode to melt into the joint, so the material of the electrode and both pieces of the joint are fused together. *Penetration* refers to the depth from the surface of the base metal to the point where fusion stops.

Two types of electrodes are in common use today: the E60 and the E70. The allowable shear stress for E60 electrodes is 18 kips per square inch (ksi), and for E70 electrodes it is 21 ksi.

There are many types of welds. Which one to use depends on the configuration of the joint, the magnitude and direction of the load, the cost of preparing the joint, and what the erection process will be. The three most common types of welded joints are the *lap*, the *butt*, and the *tee*. Some of the common welding conditions for these joints are shown in Fig. 16.9 along with the standard welding symbol used on drawings. In addition to the welds shown, plug or slot welds are frequently used to join two pieces. In these welds, a hole is cut or punched in one of the members, and the area is filled with the weld.

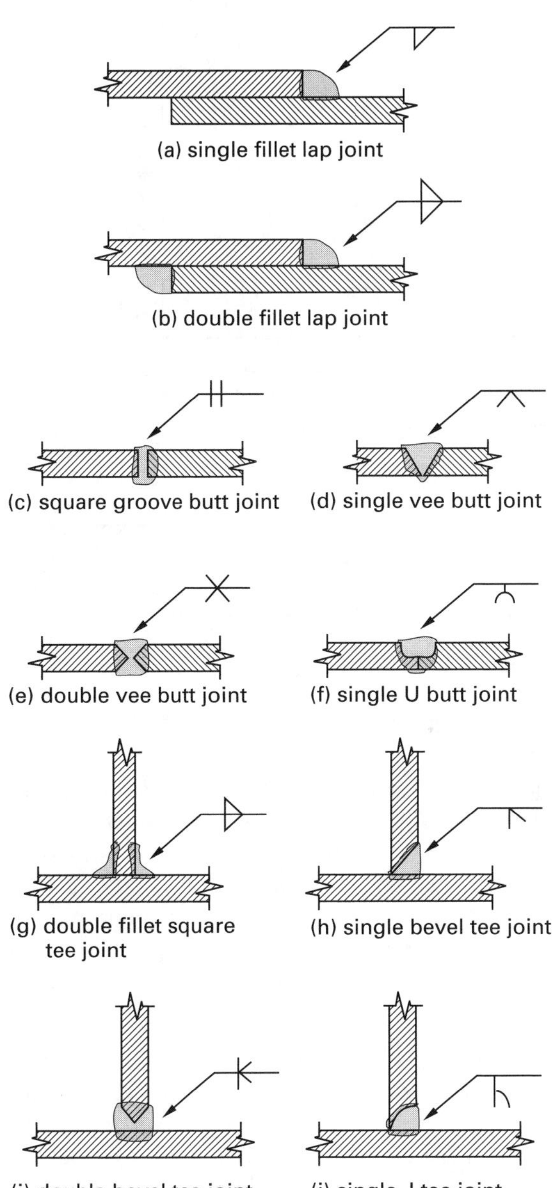

Figure 16.9 Types of Welded Connections

The fillet weld is one of the most common types. In section, its form is an isosceles triangle with the two equal legs of the triangle being the size of the weld. The perpendicular distance from the 90° corner to the hypotenuse of the triangle is called the *throat*. See Fig. 16.10(a). Because the angles are

45°, the dimension of the throat is 0.707 times the leg dimension.

For a butt joint, the throat dimension is the thickness of the material if both pieces are the same thickness, or the size of the thinner of two materials if they are unequal as shown in Fig. 16.10(b).

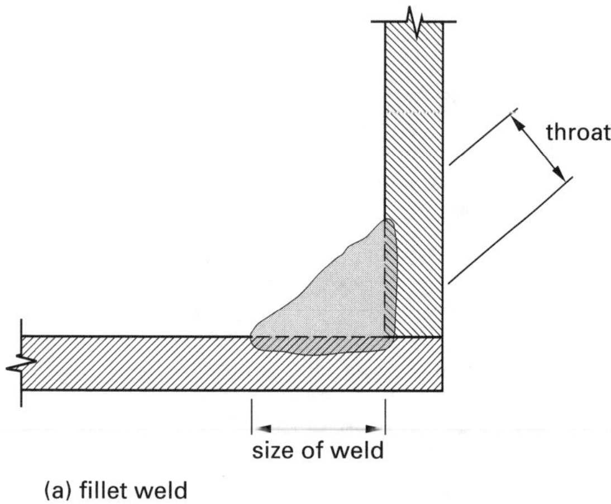

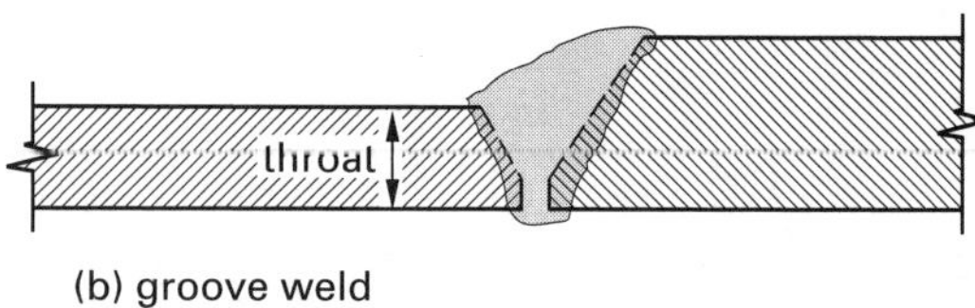

Figure 16.10 Weld Dimensions

There are common symbols used for welding. These are listed in the AISC *Steel Construction Manual*. A few are reproduced in Fig. 16.11(a). The full range of symbols gives information regarding the type, size, location, finish, welding process, angle for grooves, and other information. To indicate information about a weld, a horizontal line is connected to an arrowhead line that points to the weld. This is shown in Fig. 16.11(b).

The type of weld is indicated with one of the standard symbols and placed below the line if the weld is on the side near the arrow and above the line if it is on the side away from the arrow. If the members are to be welded on both sides, the symbol is repeated above and below the line. Other data placed with the weld symbol are the size, length of weld, and spacing, in that order, reading from left to right. Field welds are indicated with a flag placed at the junction of the horizontal line and the arrowhead line and pointing toward the tail of the reference line. A circle at the same point indicates that the weld should be made all around. The perpendicular legs of the fillet, bevel, J, and flare bevel welds must be at the left.

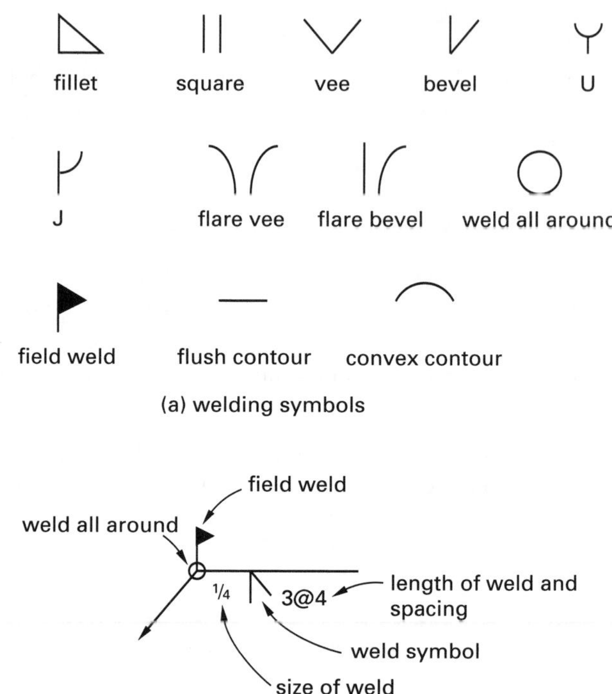

Figure 16.11 Welding Symbols

Designing a welded joint requires knowledge of the load to be resisted and the allowable stress in the weld. For fillet welds, the stress is considered as shear on the throat regardless of the direction of the load. For butt welds, the allowable stress is the same as for the base metal. As previously mentioned, the allowable stress for fillet welds of E60 electrodes is 18 ksi, and for E70 electrodes it is 21 ksi. These stresses apply to A36 steel. For any size fillet weld it is possible to multiply the size by 0.707 and by the allowable stress to get the allowable working strength per linear inch of weld, but these values have been tabulated for quicker calculations. The allowable strengths are listed in Table 16.6.

Table 16.6

Allowable Working Strengths of Fillet Welds

size of weld	allowable load (kips/in)	
(in)	E60 electrodes	E70 electrodes
3/16	2.4	2.8
1/4	3.2	3.7
5/16	4.0	4.6
3/8	4.8	5.6
1/2	6.4	7.4
5/8	8.0	9.3
3/4	9.5	11.1

Source: Steel Construction Manual, 13th ed., American Institute of Steel Construction

In addition to knowing the allowable stresses, some AISC code provisions apply to weld design. The following are some of the requirements.

- The maximum size of a fillet weld is $^1/_{16}$ in less than the nominal thickness of the material being joined if it is $^1/_4$ in thick or more. If the material is less than $^1/_4$ in thick, the maximum size is the same as the material.
- The minimum size of fillet welds is shown in Table 16.7.
- The minimum length of fillet welds must not be less than 4 times the weld size plus $^1/_4$ in for starting and stopping the arc.
- For two or more welds parallel to each other, the length must be at least equal to the perpendicular distance between them.
- For intermittent welds, the length must be at least $1^1/_2$ in.

Table 16.7

Minimum Size of Fillet Welds

material thickness of the thicker part joined (in)	minimum size of fillet weld (in)
to $^1/_4$ inclusive	$^1/_8$
over $^1/_4$ to $^1/_2$	$^3/_{16}$
over $^1/_2$ to $^3/_4$	$^1/_4$
over $^3/_4$	$^5/_{16}$

Source: Steel Construction Manual, 13th ed., American Institute of Steel Construction

Example 16.5

An A36 steel bar, $^3/_8 \times 4$, is welded to a tube section with E70 electrodes as shown. What is the maximum load-carrying capacity if the maximum size of weld is used?

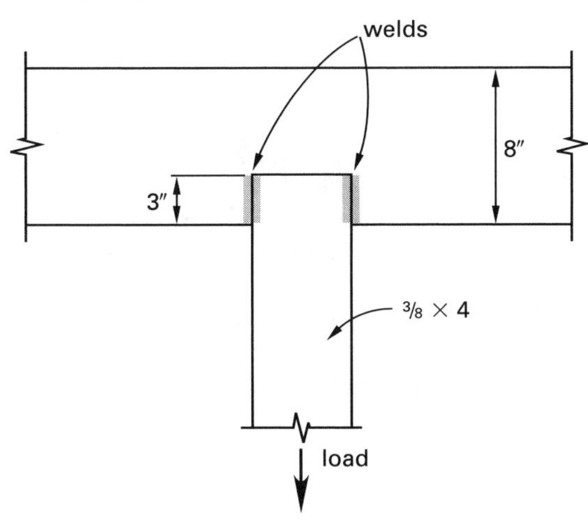

Since the maximum weld size is $^1/_{16}$ in less than the member being joined, a weld of $^5/_{16}$ in will be used. From Table 16.6, the allowable load is 4.6 kips/in. The total load is therefore

$$(2)(3\text{ in})\left(4.6\ \frac{\text{kips}}{\text{in}}\right) = 27.6\text{ kips}$$

Example 16.6

A $3 \times 3 \times {}^1/_4$ angle (area of 1.44 in^2) is to be welded to a gusset plate to serve as a tension member as shown. If A36 steel and E60 electrodes are used, what are the required size and length of weld on both sides of the angle if the full load-carrying capacity of the angle is to be developed?

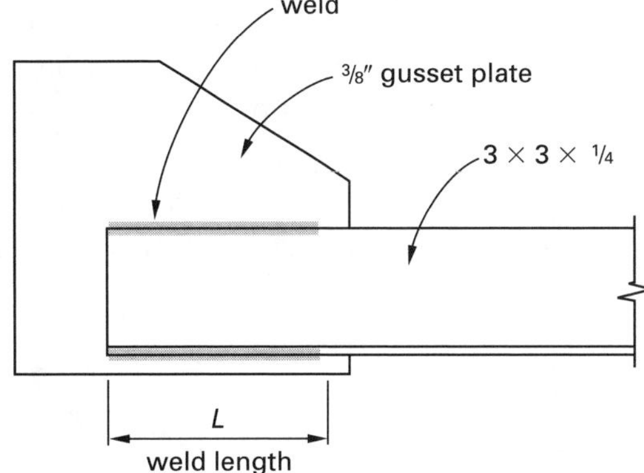

First, the maximum allowable capacity of the angle must be determined. The allowable unit stress is 0.60 times the minimum yield point of steel (Eq. 16.5). The total maximum capacity is the unit stress times the area of the angle.

$$(0.60)\left(36\ \frac{\text{kips}}{\text{in}^2}\right)(1.44\text{ in}^2) = 31.1\text{ kips}$$

For a $^1/_4$ in angle, the maximum size of weld is $^3/_{16}$ in which, from Table 16.6, has a load-carrying capacity of 2.4 kips/in with E60 electrodes. The total length of weld is

$$\frac{31.1\text{ kips}}{2.4\ \frac{\text{kips}}{\text{in}}} = 12.96\text{ in}$$

Round up to 13 in. Since the welding will be on both sides of the angle, each weld should be at least $6^1/_2$ in long.

CONCRETE CONNECTIONS

In most cast-in-place concrete construction there are generally no connectors as with wood or steel. Different pours of concrete are tied together with reinforcing bars or with keyed sections. For precast concrete construction, however, there must be some way of rigidly attaching one piece to another. This is accomplished with weld plates.

Rebars and Keyed Sections

The most typical type of cast-in-place concrete joint is one where the reinforcing bars are allowed to extend past the formwork to become part of the next pour. Continuity is achieved through the bonding of the two pours of concrete with the rebars that extend through the joint. These types of joints are found in many situations: footing to foundation wall, walls to slabs, beams to beams, columns to beams, and several others. When the reinforcing is only for the purpose of tying two pours of concrete together rather than transmitting large loads, they are called *dowels*. Some typical conditions are shown in Fig. 16.12. The length of the dowels or extensions of rebar from one section of concrete to the next is determined by the minimum development length required to transmit the loads or by ACI 318.

Keyed sections are used either alone or with rebars to provide a stronger joint between two pours of concrete. Keyed sections are often used in footings and floor slabs as shown in Fig. 16.13.

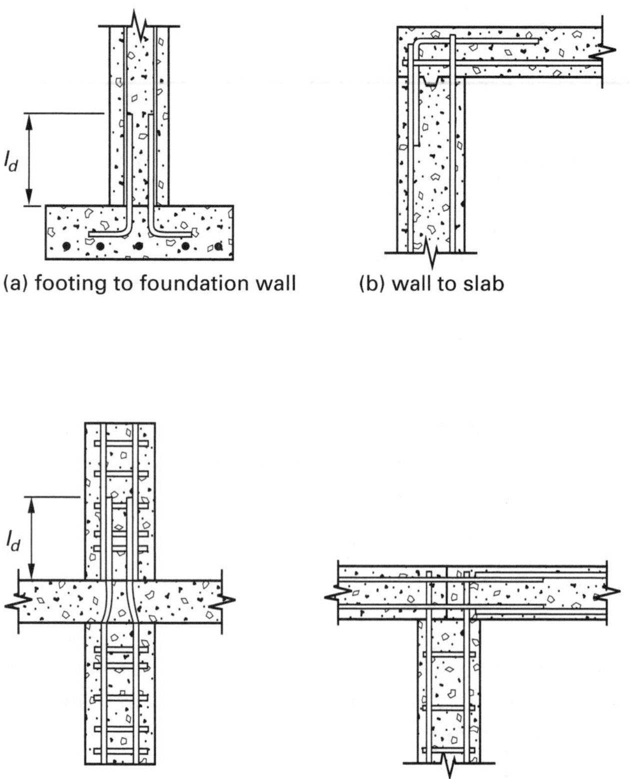

Figure 16.12 Concrete Joints Tied with Rebars

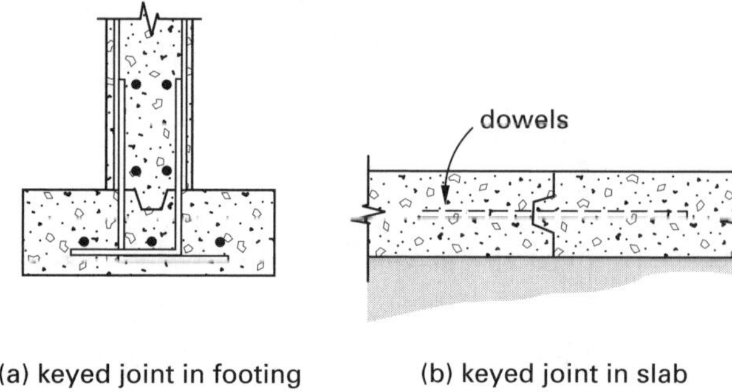

Figure 16.13 Keyed Concrete Connections

Weld Plates

Because precast structures are built in sections, there must be some way to transmit horizontal, vertical, and moment forces from one piece to the next. This is usually accomplished by casting weld plates, angles, and other types of steel pieces into the concrete members at the factory. At the site, the members are placed in position, and corresponding plates are welded together. When allowance must be made for horizontal movement due to temperature changes, concrete shrinkage, and the like, precast members often bear on elastomeric pads rather than being rigidly fastened. Figure 16.14 shows two of the many possible types of precast connections.

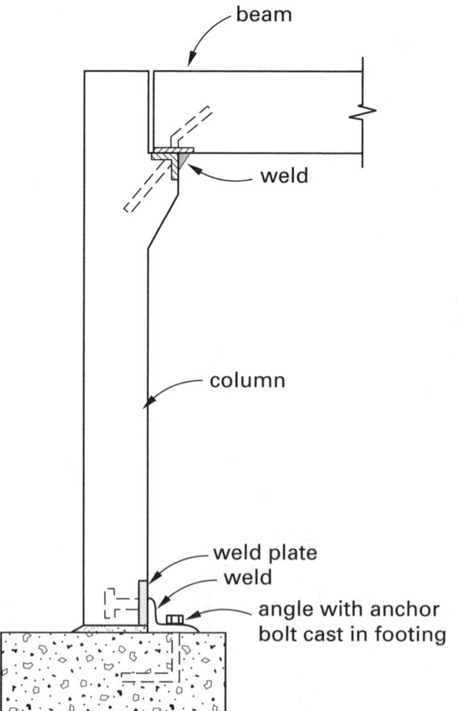

Figure 16.14 Precast Concrete Connections

Shear Connectors

Shear connectors are not really connectors in the usual sense, but are used to tie steel and concrete together in composite sections so forces are transmitted from one to the other. They are available in diameters of $^{5}/_{8}$ in, $^{3}/_{4}$ in, and $^{7}/_{8}$ in. One of the typical applications of shear connectors is with concrete slab/steel beam composite sections as shown in Fig. 16.15. Here, the connectors are welded to the top of the steel beam in the fabricating shop at a fairly close spacing, which is determined by engineering calculations to transmit the forces created by the applied loads.

When the beam is erected, forms are placed and the concrete is poured around the connectors (along with any tensile and temperature steel). The enlarged head of the connector is provided to give extra bearing surface. These are often called *headed anchor studs* and abbreviated HAS on the drawings.

Figure 16.15 shows a single row of studs, but two rows may be used if required. Metal decking instead of removable forms is often used for forming the concrete.

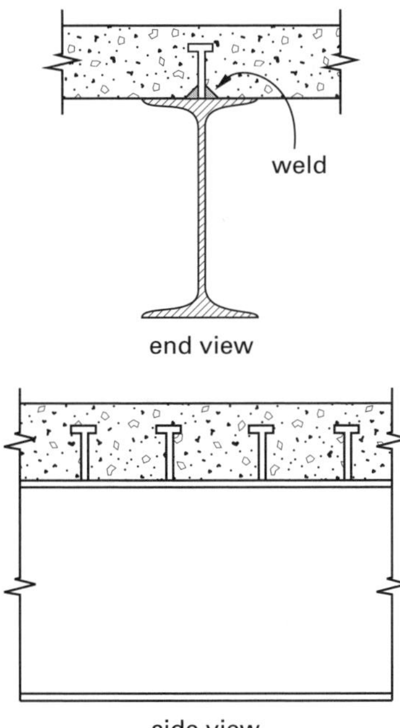

Figure 16.15 Shear Connectors

17 BUILDING CODE REQUIREMENTS ON STRUCTURAL DESIGN

Nomenclature

C_F	size factor	–
d	depth of beam	in
D	dead load	lbf/ft^2
E	earthquake or seismic load	lbf/ft^2
f_1	floor live load occupancy combination factor	–
f_2	snow load roof shape combination factor	–
f'_c	compressive strength	lbf/in^2
F_b	allowable bending stress	lbf/in^2
F_t	allowable axial tensile stress	lbf/in^2
F_v	allowable shear stress	lbf/in^2
F_y	specified minimum yield stress of the type of steel being used	lbf/in^2
L	live load	lbf/ft^2
L_r	roof live load	–
R	rain load	lbf/ft^2
S	snow load	lbf/ft^2
W	wind load	lbf/ft^2
ω	wind load coefficient	–
Ω	safety factor (ASD)	–

Building code provisions related to structural design deal with how loads must be determined, what stresses are allowed in structural members, formulas for designing members of various materials, and miscellaneous requirements for construction. This chapter provides an overview of the requirements with which the candidate should be familiar. Specific provisions and calculation methods are presented in other chapters. Loads on buildings are covered in Ch. 11, wind loading and calculation methods in Ch. 22, and seismic design methods are reviewed in Ch. 23. The code provisions outlined here are based on the *International Building Code* (IBC).

LOADING

Chapter 16 of the IBC details how loads must be calculated. In general terms, the code requires that any construction method be based on a rational analysis in accordance with well-established principles of mechanics, and that such an analysis provide a path for all loads and forces from their point of origin to the load-resisting elements. The analysis must include distribution of horizontal shear, horizontal torsional moments, stability against overturning, and anchorage. Horizontal torsional moment results from torsion due to eccentricity between the center of application of a lateral force and the center of rigidity of the force-resisting system. Anchorage resists the uplift and sliding forces on a structure.

When the building design is based on allowable stress or working stress design, each component must be designed to resist the most critical effect resulting from the combination of loads listed. When other design methods are used for concrete or steel, each component must be designed to resist the most critical effects of load combinations as prescribed in each chapter of the code related to the specific material used.

The basic load combinations per IBC Sec. 1605.2.1 using strength design or load and resistance factor design are as follows.

- $1.4D$
- $1.2D + 1.6L + 0.5(L_r \text{ or } S \text{ or } R)$
- $1.2D + 1.6(L_r \text{ or } S \text{ or } R) + f_1L \text{ or } 0.8W$
- $1.2D + 1.6W + f_1L + 0.5(L_r \text{ or } S \text{ or } R)$
- $1.2D + 1.0E + f_1L + f_2S$
- $0.9D + 1.0E \text{ or } 1.6W$

The value of f_1 is 1.0 for floors in places of public assembly, parking garages, and where the live load exceeds 100 psf. For any other cases a value of 0.5 may be used for f_1. The value of f_2 is 0.7 for roof configurations that do not shed snow off the structure (such as saw tooth). For any other cases a value of 0.2 may be used for f_2.

The ACI 318 requirements allow for a slightly different set of factors, which have been used over the past few decades. These factors are given in Ch. 20.

The basic load combinations per IBC Sec. 1605.3.1 using allowable stress design are as follows.

- D
- $D + L$
- $D + L + L_r$ or S or R
- $D + W$ or $0.7E + L + L_r$ or S or R
- $0.6D + W$
- $0.6D + 0.7E$

Alternate basic load combinations per IBC Sec. 1605.3.2 using allowable stress design are as follows.

- $D + L + L_r$ or S or R
- $D + L + \omega W$
- $D + L + \omega W + S/2$
- $D + L + S + \omega W/2$
- $D + L + S + E/1.4$
- $0.9D + E/1.4$

In addition, lateral earth pressure must be included in the design when it results in a more critical case.

Live Loads

Required floor live loads are given in IBC Table 1607.1, which is reproduced in Table 11.2. The IBC allows for the live load to be reduced in most cases. The live load may not be reduced for any public assembly occupancy with a live load less than or equal to 100 psf or for any member supporting one floor of a parking garage or with a live load exceeding 100 psf. The reduced live load is determined using Eq. 11.1 and Table 11.3. Chapter 11 contains examples of floor and roof live load calculations.

Additional code provisions related to live loads include the following.

- Provisions must be made for designing floors to accommodate concentrated loads as shown in Table 11.2. If these loads, acting on any space $2^1/_2$ ft square on an otherwise unloaded floor, would result in stresses greater than those caused by the uniform load, then the floor must be designed accordingly.
- Where uniform live floor and roof loads are involved, the design may be limited to full dead load on all spans in combination with full live load on adjacent spans and on alternate spans. This is particularly important where structural continuity of adjacent spans is involved. In any case, the code requires the investigation of loading conditions that would cause maximum shear and bending moments along continuous members.
- Live loads for each floor or portion thereof in commercial or industrial buildings must be conspicuously posted.
- Interior walls, permanent partitions, and temporary partitions over 6 ft high must be designed to resist all loads on them but in no case less than a force of 5 psf applied perpendicular to the wall.

Dead Loads

The IBC defines dead load as the vertical load due to the weight of all permanent structural and nonstructural components of a building, such as walls, floors, roofs, and fixed service equipment. The code does not specifically state required dead loads; rather, the designer must use standard unit weights for various building materials published in standard reference sources.

However, two specific provisions are mentioned. First, floors in office buildings where partition locations are subject to change must be designed to support a uniformly distributed live load equal to 20 psf. Second, access floor systems may be designed to support an additional 10 psf of uniformly distributed dead load over all other loads.

Lateral Loads

Lateral loads include wind loads and seismic loads. Wind is assumed to come from any direction, and the design wind pressure used for calculations is dependent on the height of the structure above the ground, the exposure of the structure, a wind stagnation pressure at a standard height of 33 ft above the ground, the portion of the structure under consideration, and a factor related to the importance of the building during an emergency, such as a fire station. These are established as values and coefficients given in tables at the end of Ch. 16 of the IBC. The formula for determining design wind pressure and a full explanation of the factors involved are given in Ch. 22.

When special conditions exist, such as structures sensitive to dynamic effects, structures sensitive to wind-excited oscillations, and buildings over 400 ft in height, the buildings must be designed in accordance with approved national standards. This basically means using accepted wind tunnel testing procedures to determine the actual wind forces on the structure.

For earthquake loads, the code requires that stresses be calculated as the effect of a force applied horizontally at each floor or roof level above the base. The designer must assume that the force can come from any direction. Although the IBC gives detailed methods and concepts for designing structures to resist seismic forces, it does allow that other methods can be approved by the local building official if it can be shown that equivalent ductility and energy absorption can be provided. In the event that wind loads produce higher stresses, they must be used in place of those resulting from earthquake forces.

Seismic forces and methods of design are discussed in more detail in Ch. 23.

ALLOWABLE STRESSES

The IBC establishes basic allowable stresses for various types of construction materials. The design of any structural member must be such that these stresses are not exceeded. Although some provisions of the code are extremely complex (such as with concrete), this section outlines some of the more important provisions to be familiar with.

Wood

Tables 2A, 4A, 4B, 4C, 4D, 4E, 5A, 5B, and 5C of the *National Design Specification for Wood Construction, ASD/ LRFD* (NDS) give allowable unit stresses in structural lumber and glued-laminated timber. Examples of these tables are shown in Ch. 18. These include allowable stresses for extreme fiber in bending, tension parallel to the grain, horizontal shear, and compression perpendicular and parallel to the grain. The stresses given are for normal loading and must be adjusted according to various conditions of use as follows.

Repetitive use: A factor (C_r) equal to 1.15 is used when several beam members, such as joists or rafters, are used together. In order to use the repetitive factor C_r, the members cannot be over 4 in thick (nominal), cannot be spaced more than 24 in on center, and must be joined by transverse load-distributing elements (such as bridging or decking), and there must be at least three members in a group.

Duration of load: The amount of stress a wood member can withstand is dependent on the time during which the load producing the stress acts. This relation of strength to duration of load is shown graphically in Fig. 17.1. Allowable design loads are based on what is called *normal duration of load*, which is assumed to be 10 years. For duration of loads shorter than this, the allowable stress may be increased according to the following percentages.

- 15% for two months' duration, as for snow
- 25% for seven days' duration, as for roof loads
- 60% for wind or earthquake loads
- 100% for impact loads

If a structural member is fully stressed to the maximum allowable stress for more than 10 years under conditions of maximum design load, the allowable stress cannot exceed 90% of those listed in the tables.

Fire-retardant treatment: The NDS states that the effect of fire retardant chemical treatments on strength must be considered. Allowable design values, including connection design values, for lumber and structural glued-laminated timber pressure treated with fire-retardant chemicals must be obtained from the company providing the treatment and redrying service.

Size factor adjustment: Design values for bending, tension, and compression parallel to the grain for visually graded dimension lumber 2 in to 4 in thick must be multiplied by size factors given at the beginning of NDS Tables 4A, 4B, and 4E. When the depth of a rectangular sawn bending member 5 in or thicker exceeds 12 in, the bending design values, F_b, must be multiplied by a size factor determined by Eq. 17.1.

$$C = \left(\frac{12}{d}\right)^{1/9} \qquad 17.1$$

There is also a slenderness factor adjustment for unsupported beams. However, most wood members are supported either with bridging or with continuous decking material, so this adjustment is not usually required.

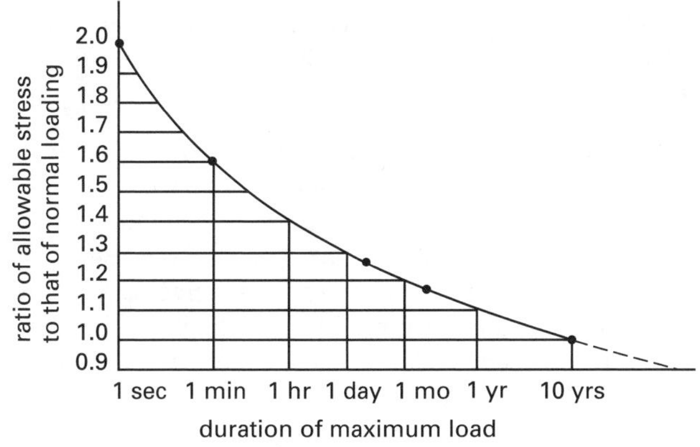

Figure 17.1 Relation of Strength to Duration of Load for Wood Structural Members

Steel

Using the ASD method of design, the allowable stress for a steel member is expressed as the yield stress of the steel divided by a safety factor, Ω. This factor varies with the type of stress the member is under (shear, compression, bending, or tension) and with conditions such as unsupported lengths and geometry of the section. Some of the more common code requirements for allowable stress are as follows.

For tension on the gross area, $\Omega = 1.67$.

$$F_t = F_y/\Omega = 0.60F_y \quad 17.2$$

For tension on the net effective area, $\Omega = 2.00$.

$$F_t = F_u/\Omega = 0.50F_u \quad 17.3$$

For shear on gross sections, $\Omega = 1.50$.

$$F_v = 0.6F_y/\Omega = 0.40F_y \quad 17.4$$

At beam end connections where the top flange is coped, and similar conditions where failure might occur along a plane through the fasteners, $\Omega = 2.00$.

$$F_v = 0.6F_u/\Omega = 0.30F_u \quad 17.5$$

For bending where the beam is laterally supported and the section meets the requirements of a compact section and is loaded in the plane of the minor axis, $\Omega = 1.67$.

$$F_b = F_y/\Omega = 0.60F_y \quad 17.6$$

For bending where the beam is not a compact section but where it is supported laterally, the stress will be less.

Allowable stresses for bolts, rivets, and threaded parts are based on the type of load placed on them and are given as values in kips per square inch based on the ASTM designation of the fastener or as a fraction of the minimum tensile strength of the type of fastener. These are shown in Tables 16.2 and 16.3 in Ch. 16.

Allowable stresses for welds are based either on the yield strength of the base metal or on the nominal tensile strength of the weld metal. The allowable stress is then multiplied by the area of the weld. IBC Ch. 22, and the AISC *Steel Construction Manual* both describe the requirements for welds in great detail. Table 16.6 in Ch. 16 summarizes the allowable working strengths for welds of various sizes.

Concrete

Building code requirements for reinforced concrete are very complex and detailed and cover all aspects of formwork, reinforcing, mixing, placing, and curing. IBC Ch. 19 concerns concrete construction. It contains specific requirements too numerous to mention here. In addition, it makes reference to ACI 318, as well as to other ACI publications.

The candidate is not expected to know all the code provisions for concrete design, but to have a general understanding of the more important limitations. Two of the most important concepts are the safety factors of increased ultimate load above the calculated dead and live loads, and the strength reduction factor. These are discussed in detail in Ch. 20 along with other code requirements.

Concrete construction is based on the specified compressive strength, f'_c, expressed in pounds per square inch. Many of the formulas for concrete design use this as a part of the equation.

Because concrete is a highly variable material, the IBC goes to great lengths to specify how concrete is to be mixed and then how quality control is to be maintained. This is to ensure that a building is actually constructed of concrete that meets or exceeds the original design strength.

The IBC requires that samples for strength tests are taken for each class of concrete placed. Samples must be taken not less than once per day, nor less than once for each 150 yd^3 of concrete, nor less than once for each 5000 ft^2 of surface area for slabs or wall. The average of all sets of three consecutive strength tests must equal or exceed f'_c, and no individual test can be less than 500 psi below the f'_c value.

CONSTRUCTION REQUIREMENTS

In addition to allowable stresses and other requirements related to structural calculations, the IBC places many restrictions on how various materials may be used. The following sections outline some of the more important ones with which ARE candidates should be familiar.

Wood

Since the structural integrity of wood is dependent on such factors as moisture, fire, insect attack, and connections, the IBC goes to great lengths to specify wood construction techniques. Be familiar with the following requirements.

- The bottom of wood joists must be at least 18 in above exposed ground, and the bottom of wood girders must be at least 12 in above ground, unless they are treated or made of a species with a natural resistance to decay.
- Ends of wood girders entering masonry or concrete walls must be provided with a $^1/_2$ in airspace on top, sides, and end, unless the wood is of natural resistance to decay or it is treated.
- Foundation plates and sills must be treated or made of foundation redwood.
- Under-floor areas such as crawl spaces must be ventilated with openings having a net area of not less than 1 ft^2 for each 150 ft^2 of under-floor area, and they must be placed to provide cross ventilation.
- Wood used for construction of permanent structures located nearer than 6 in to earth must be treated or wood of natural resistance to decay.

- All wood used as structural members must be protected from exposure to the weather and water with approved protection.
- Fire stops are required in walls at the ceiling and floor levels and at 10 ft intervals both vertical and horizontal.
- Fire stops are required at interconnections between concealed vertical and horizontal spaces such as soffits and dropped ceilings.
- Fire stops are required in concealed spaces in stairway construction and in vertical openings between floors and the roof that could afford a passage for fire.

Steel

Two provisions in the IBC relate to an important consideration in steel design. The first requires that roof systems without sufficient slope for drainage be investigated to ensure stability under ponding conditions. This is to prevent failure when an amount of water collects on a roof causing it to deflect, which allows a further accumulation of water, which leads to further deflection.

The second provision requires that horizontal framing members be designed for deflection criteria and ponding requirements. It also requires that trusses longer than 80 ft be cambered for the dead load deflection.

Concrete

In addition to allowable stresses, the IBC and ACI 318 set forth highly detailed requirements for other aspects of concrete use. In addition to those mentioned in Ch. 20, some of the more important ones include the following.

- Construction loads cannot be supported nor any shoring removed until the concrete has sufficient strength to safely support its weight and loads placed on it. However, some formwork can be removed if the structure in combination with remaining formwork can support the loads.
- There are limitations on the amount and placement of conduits and other pipes embedded in concrete so as not to decrease the load-resisting area. Aluminum conduits cannot be embedded unless effectively coated or covered to prevent aluminum-concrete reaction or electrolytic action between steel and aluminum. Pipes carrying fluids or gases must be pressure-tested prior to placement of concrete.
- The size and bending of reinforcement are clearly spelled out to ensure that a sufficient bond is developed between the concrete and steel and that all reinforcement acts together.
- Minimum concrete cover over reinforcing is specified. This is to protect the steel from rusting and to ensure proper bonding of the concrete to the steel. Concrete exposed to the weather or in direct contact with the ground requires more cover than do concrete members in a protected area.

FIREPROOFING

One of the primary purposes of any building code is to ensure that buildings are adequately protected from fire and that if a fire does occur, structural members are sufficiently protected. Chapter 6 of the IBC defines fire-resistance requirements for various building elements based on types of construction. Chapter 7 and Table 7-A of the IBC define the minimum protection of structural portions of a building based on time periods for various noncombustible insulating materials.

Although steel is noncombustible, it loses strength at high temperatures and must be protected with approved insulating materials, such as sprayed-on fireproofing or gypsum wallboard. The exception to this is for roof framing, other than the structural frame, that is more than 25 ft above the floor. This framing may be of unprotected noncombustible materials.

Wood framing, of course, is combustible but may be used in certain types of construction if adequately protected. A unique property of wood is that while it is combustible, thick pieces of wood exposed to fire will char but not immediately loose structural integrity. The IBC recognizes this by having a separate type of construction, Type IV, for heavy timber construction. In this type of construction, columns must be at least 8 in in any dimension, beams and girders must be at least 6 in wide and 10 in deep, and floor decking must be at least 3 in thick.

18 WOOD CONSTRUCTION

Nomenclature

A	area of a member	in^2
b	width of beam	in
C_D	load duration factor	–
C_F	size factor	–
C_{fu}	flat use factor	–
C_M	wet service factor	–
C_r	repetitive member factor	–
d	depth of beam	in
d'	depth of beam remaining at a notch	in
E	modulus of elasticity	lbf/in^2
f_b	actual value for extreme fiber in bending stress	lbf/in^2
f_t	actual unit stress in tension parallel to the grain	lbf/in^2
f_v	actual unit stress in horizontal shear	lbf/in^2
F_b	design value for extreme fiber in bending	lbf/in^2
F_b'	allowable bending stress	lbf/in^2
F_c	design value for compression parallel to grain	lbf/in^2
F_c'	design value for compression parallel to grain, adjusted for l/d ratio	lbf/in^2
$F_{c\perp}$	design value for compression perpendicular to grain	lbf/in^2
F_t	design value for tension parallel to grain	lbf/in^2
F_v	design value for horizontal shear	lbf/in^2
I	moment of inertia	in^4
K	largest slenderness ratio, l/d, at which intermediate column formula applies	–
K_e	effective buckling length factor	–
l	span of bending member or effective length of column	in
L	span of bending member	ft
M	moment of inertia	in-lbf
P	total concentrated load or total axial load	lbf
S	section modulus	in^3
V	vertical shear	lbf
w	uniform load per foot	lbf/ft
W	total uniformly distributed load	lbf
Δ	deflection	in

PROPERTIES OF STRUCTURAL LUMBER

Sizes

Structural lumber is referred to by its nominal dimension in inches such as 2 × 4 or 2 × 10. However, after surfacing at the mill and drying, its actual dimension is somewhat less.

Table 18.1 gives the actual dimensions for various nominal sizes of sawn lumber. Also shown in Table 18.1 are the actual areas, section modulus, and moment of inertia, which are all based on the actual size. The majority of structural lumber used is surfaced and dried to the actual sizes listed in Table 18.1, so these are the values that must be used in structural calculations.

Grading

Since a log yields lumber of varying quality, the individual sawn pieces must be categorized to allow selection of the quality that best suits the purpose. For structural lumber, the primary concern is the amount of stress that a particular grade of lumber of a species will carry. The load-carrying ability is affected by such things as size and number of knots, splits, and other defects, as well as the direction of grain and the specific gravity of the wood.

Grading of structural lumber is done under standard rules established by several different agencies certified by the American Lumber Standards Committee. The grading is done at the sawmill either by visual inspection or by machine. The resulting allowable stress values are published in tables referred to as design values for visually

Table 18.1

Sectional Properties of Standard Dressed Lumber

nominal size	standard dressed size, $b \times d$ (in)	area, A (in^2)	moment of inertia, I (in^4)	section modulus, S (in^3)
2 × 3	$1^1/_2 \times 2^1/_2$	3.750	1.953	1.563
2 × 4	$1^1/_2 \times 3^1/_2$	5.250	5.359	3.063
2 × 6	$1^1/_2 \times 5^1/_2$	8.250	20.797	7.563
2 × 8	$1^1/_2 \times 7^1/_4$	10.875	47.635	13.141
2 × 10	$1^1/_2 \times 9^1/_4$	13.875	98.932	21.391
2 × 12	$1^1/_2 \times 11^1/_4$	16.875	177.979	31.641
4 × 4	$3^1/_2 \times 3^1/_2$	12.250	12.505	7.146
4 × 6	$3^1/_2 \times 5^1/_2$	19.250	48.526	17.646
4 × 8	$3^1/_2 \times 7^1/_4$	25.375	111.148	30.661
4 × 10	$3^1/_2 \times 9^1/_4$	32.375	230.840	49.911
4 × 12	$3^1/_2 \times 11^1/_4$	39.375	415.283	73.828
4 × 14	$3^1/_2 \times 13^1/_4$	46.375	678.475	102.411
6 × 6	$5^1/_2 \times 5^1/_2$	30.250	76.255	27.729
6 × 8	$5^1/_2 \times 7^1/_2$	41.250	193.359	51.563
6 × 10	$5^1/_2 \times 9^1/_2$	52.250	392.963	82.729
6 × 12	$5^1/_2 \times 11^1/_2$	63.250	697.068	121.229
6 × 14	$5^1/_2 \times 12^1/_2$	74.250	1127.672	167.063
6 × 16	$5^1/_2 \times 15^1/_2$	85.250	1706.776	220.229
8 × 8	$7^1/_2 \times 7^1/_2$	56.250	263.672	70.313
8 × 10	$7^1/_2 \times 9^1/_2$	71.250	535.859	112.813
8 × 12	$7^1/_2 \times 11^1/_2$	86.250	950.547	165.313

graded structural lumber and design values for machine-stress-rated structural lumber.

Visually graded lumber is divided into categories based on nominal size, so the same grade of lumber in a species may have different allowable stresses depending on which category it is in. This can be confusing, but is critical in selecting the correct allowable stress for a particular design condition. For example, one of the most common categories is 2 in to 4 in thick, 5 in and wider. This includes wood members like 2 × 6s, 2 × 8s, and the like, but not 2 × 4s. 2 × 4 members are in two separate categories: 2 in to 4 in thick, 2 in to 4 in wide; and 2 in to 4 in thick, 4 in wide. The first category is based on structural grades, and the second category is based on appearance grades.

There are also categories for beams and stringers, and posts and timbers. *Beams and stringers* are defined as members 5 in and wider, having a depth more than 2 in greater than the width. *Posts and timbers* are defined as members 5 in by 5 in and larger, with a depth not more than 2 in greater than the width.

Machine-stress-rated lumber is based on grade designations, which depend on the allowable bending stress and modulus of elasticity of the wood.

Design Values

For visually graded lumber, allowable design values are based on the species of wood, the size category, the grade, and the direction of loading. Different values are required based on the direction of loading because wood is not an isostropic material. The tables give values for extreme fiber stress in bending, F_b; tension parallel to the grain, F_t; horizontal shear, F_v; compression perpendicular to grain, ; and compression parallel to grain, F_c. Table 18.2(a) shows a portion of a table of design values as published by the National Forest Products Association.

One additional variable for selecting the extreme fiber in bending stress is whether or not the member is being used

Table 18.2(a)

Design Values for Visually Graded Dimension Lumber (use with Table 18.2(b) adjustment factors)

species and commercial grade	size classification	bending, F_b	tension parallel to grain, F_t	shear parallel to grain, F_v	compression perpendicular to grain, $F_{c\perp}$	compression parallel to grain, F_c	modulus of elasticity, E	grading rules agency
aspen								
select structural		875	500	120	265	725	1,100,000	
no. 1		625	375	120	265	600	1,100,000	
no. 2	2″ & wider	600	350	120	265	450	1,000,000	NELMA
no. 3		350	200	120	265	275	900,000	NSLB
stud	2″ & wider	475	275	120	265	300	900,000	WWPA
construction		700	400	120	265	625	900,000	
standard	2″–4″ wide	375	225	120	265	475	900,000	
utility		175	100	120	265	300	800,000	
beech-birch-hickory								
select structural		1450	850	195	715	1200	1,700,000	
no. 1		1050	600	195	715	950	1,600,000	
no. 2	2″ & wider	1000	600	195	715	750	1,500,000	
no. 3		575	350	195	715	425	1,300,000	NELMA
stud	2″ & wider	775	450	195	715	475	1,300,000	
construction		1150	675	195	715	1000	1,400,000	
standard	2″–4″ wide	650	375	195	715	775	1,300,000	
utility		300	175	195	715	500	1,200,000	
cottonwood								
select structural		875	525	125	320	775	1,200,000	
no. 1		625	375	125	320	625	1,200,000	
no. 2	2″ & wider	625	350	125	320	475	1,100,000	
no. 3		350	200	125	320	275	1,000,000	NSLB
stud	2″ & wider	475	275	125	320	300	1,000,000	
construction		700	400	125	320	650	1,000,000	
standard	2″–4″ wide	400	225	125	320	500	900,000	
utility		175	100	125	320	325	900,000	
Douglas fir-larch								
select structural		1500	1000	180	625	1700	1,900,000	
no. 1 & btr		1200	800	180	625	1550	1,800,000	
no. 1		1000	675	180	625	1500	1,700,000	
no. 2	2″ & wider	900	575	180	625	1350	1,600,000	WCLIB
no. 3		525	325	180	625	775	1,400,000	WWPA
stud	2″ & wider	700	450	180	625	850	1,400,000	
construction		1000	650	180	625	1650	1,500,000	
standard	2″–4″ wide	575	375	180	625	1400	1,400,000	
utility		275	175	180	625	900	1,300,000	
Douglas fir-larch (north)								
select structural		1350	825	180	625	1900	1,900,000	
no. 1 & btr		1150	750	180	625	1800	1,800,000	
no. 1/no. 2	2″ & wider	850	500	180	625	1400	1,600,000	
no. 3		475	300	180	625	825	1,400,000	NLGA
stud	2″ & wider	650	400	180	625	900	1,400,000	
construction		950	575	180	625	1800	1,500,000	
standard	2″–4″ wide	525	325	180	625	1450	1,400,000	
utility		250	150	180	625	950	1,300,000	
Douglas fir-south								
select structural		1350	900	180	520	1600	1,400,000	
no. 1		925	600	180	520	1450	1,300,000	
no. 2	2″ & wider	850	525	180	520	1350	1,200,000	
no. 3		500	300	180	520	775	1,100,000	WWPA
stud	2″ & wider	675	425	180	520	850	1,100,000	
construction		975	600	180	520	1650	1,200,000	
standard	2″–4″ wide	550	350	180	520	1400	1,100,000	
utility		250	150	180	520	900	1,000,000	

Adapted from National Design Specification for Wood Construction, copyright © 2005, courtesy, American Wood Council, Leesburg, VA.

Table 18.2(b)

Adjustment Factors

Repetitive Member Factor, C_r

Bending design values, F_b, for dimension lumber 2 in to 4 in thick shall be multiplied by the repetitive member factor, C_r = 1.15 when such members are used as joists, truss chords, rafters, studs, planks, decking, or similar members that are in contact or spaced not more than 24 in on centers, are not less than 3 in number and are joined by floor, roof, or other load distributing elements adequate to support the design load.

Wet Service Factor, C_M

When dimension lumber is used where moisture content will exceed 19% for an extended time period, design values shall be multiplied by the appropriate wet service factors from the following table.

Wet Service Factors, C_M

F_b	F_t	F_v	$F_{c\perp}$	F_c	E
0.85*	1.0	0.97	0.67	0.8**	0.9

*when $F_bC_F \leq 1150$ psi, $C_M = 1.0$
**when $F_cC_F \leq 750$ psi, $C_M = 1.0$

Flat Use Factor, C_{fu}

Bending design values adjusted by size factors are based on edgewise use (load applied to narrow face). When dimension lumber is used flatwise (load applied to wide face), the bending design value, F_b, shall also be multiplied by the following flat use factors.

Flat Use Factors, C_{fu}

width	thickness (breadth)	
(depth)	2″ & 3″	4″
2″ & 3″	1.0	–
4″	1.1	1.0
5″	1.1	1.05
6″	1.15	1.05
8″	1.15	1.05
10″ & wider	1.2	1.1

NOTE

To facilitate the use of Table 18.2(a), shading has been employed to distinguish design values based on a 4 in nominal width (Construction, Standard and Utility grades) or a 6 in nominal width (Stud grade) from design values based on a 12 in nominal width (Select Structural, no. 1 & btr, no. 1, no. 2, and no. 3 grades).

Size Factor, C_F

Tabulated bending, tension and compression parallel to grain design values for dimensional lumber 2″ to 4″ thick shall be multiplied by the following size factors:

Size Factors, C_F

		F_b		F_t	F_c
		thickness (breadth)			
grades	width (depth)	2″ & 3″	4″		
select structural, no. 1 & btr, no. 1, no. 2, no. 3	2″, 3″ & 4″	1.5	1.5	1.5	1.15
	5″	1.4	1.4	1.4	1.1
	6″	1.3	1.3	1.3	1.1
	8″	1.2	1.3	1.2	1.05
	10″	1.1	1.2	1.1	1.0
	12″	1.0	1.1	1.0	1.0
	14″ & wider	0.9	1.0	0.9	0.9
stud	2″, 3″ & 4″	1.1	1.1	1.1	1.05
	5″ & 6″	1.0	1.0	1.0	1.0
	8″ & wider	Use no. 3 grade tabulated design values and size factors			
construction, standard	2″, 3″ & 4″	1.0	1.0	1.0	1.0
utility	4″	1.0	1.0	1.0	1.0
	2″ & 3″	0.4	–	0.4	0.6

Adapted from National Design Specification for Wood Construction, copyright © 2005, courtesy, American Wood Council, Leesburg, VA.

alone or with other members such as a row of joists. In order to qualify for repetitive member use, there must be at least three members spaced not more than 24 in apart, and there must be some method to distribute the load among them such as bridging or sheathing.

As mentioned in Ch. 17, the amount of stress a wood member can withstand is also dependent on the length of time the load acts on the member. Design values given in the tables are based on what is considered a normal duration of loading—10 years. However, for a shorter loading duration, the allowable unit stresses may be increased as follows.

- 15% for two months' duration, as for snow
- 25% for seven days' duration, as for roof loading
- 60% for wind or earthquake loading
- 100% for impact loads

Moisture Content

Moisture content is defined as the weight of water in wood as a fraction of the weight of oven-dry wood. Moisture content is an important variable because it affects the amount of shrinkage, weight, strength, and withdrawal resistance of nails.

Moisture exists in wood both in the individual cell cavities and bound chemically within cell walls. When the cell walls are completely saturated but no water exists in the cell cavities, the wood is said to have reached its *fiber saturation point*. This point averages about 30% moisture content in all woods. Above this point, the wood is dimensionally stable, but as the wood dries below this point it begins to shrink.

When wood is used for structural framing and other construction purposes, it tends to absorb or lose moisture in response to the temperature and humidity of the surrounding air. As it loses moisture it shrinks, and as it gains moisture it swells. Ideally, the moisture content of wood when it is installed should be the same as the prevailing humidity to which it will be exposed. However, this is seldom possible, so lumber needs to be dried—either air-dried or kiln-dried—to reduce the moisture content to acceptable levels.

To be considered dry lumber, moisture content cannot exceed 19%. To be grademarked *kiln dry*, the maximum moisture content permitted is 15%. Design values found in tables assume that the maximum moisture content will not exceed 19%. If it does, the allowable stresses must be decreased slightly.

Wood shrinks most in the direction perpendicular to the grain and very little parallel to the grain. Perpendicular to the grain wood shrinks most in the direction of the annual growth rings (tangentially) and about half as much across the rings (radially).

In developing wood details, an allowance must be made for the fact that wood will shrink and swell during use regardless of its initial moisture content. Of particular importance is the accumulated change in dimension of a series of wood members placed one on top of the next. The shrinkage of an individual member may not be significant, but the total shrinkage of several may result in problems such as sagging floors, cracked plaster, distortion of door openings, and nail pops in gypsum board walls.

WOOD BEAMS

The design of wood beams is a fairly simple procedure. First, the loads and stresses on the beam are determined as described in Ch. 13. This includes finding the support reactions, vertical shear forces, and bending moments. Then, the basic flexure formula is used to find the required section modulus needed to resist the bending moment. A beam size is then selected that has the required section modulus. Second, horizontal shear stresses are calculated and compared with the allowable horizontal shear for the species and grade of lumber being used. This is especially important because wood beams have a tendency to fail parallel to the grain where their strength is lowest. Finally, deflection is checked to see if it is within acceptable limits. This, too, is important because wood is not as stiff as steel or concrete. Even though a beam may be strong enough to resist bending moment, the deflection may be outside of tolerable limits.

Design for Bending

To design wood beams for bending, the basic flexure formula is used.

$$S = \frac{M}{F'_b} \qquad 18.1$$

The basic allowable extreme fiber stress in bending, F_b, is found in Table 18.2(a) or similar tables in the building code or other referenced sources, and the section modulus is found in Table 18.1. This value must be modified for many factors, including those shown in Table 18.2(b). For sawn lumber under major axis bending, the following formula is used.

$$F'_b = F_b C_D C_M C_t C_L C_F C_i C_r \qquad 18.2$$

The definitions of C_M, C_F, and C_r are given in Table 18.2(b). Values of C_D are used to include the duration of load. In any combination of loads the largest value of C_D is used. This corresponds to the shortest load duration. The durations of load factors are as follows.

permanent duration, dead load = 0.90
normal, 10-year duration, floor live load = 1.00
two-month duration, snow load = 1.15
seven-day duration, roof live load = 1.25
10-minute duration,
wind or earthquake load = 1.60
impact duration = 2.00

The other values are for special cases of high temperature, C_t; laterally unbraced beams, C_L; and incised members, C_i. For laterally braced beams under normal usage, these values, along with C_M, may all be taken as 1.0. The examples presented in this chapter will assume this is the case.

Example 18.1

A simply supported wood beam spans 12 ft and carries a combined dead and roof live load of 350 plf. If the beam is Douglas fir-larch, no. 2, what size beam should be used?

First, find the maximum bending moment. From Fig. 13.7, the moment for a uniformly loaded beam is $wL^2/8$. The moment is

$$M = \frac{wL^2}{8} = \frac{\left(350\ \frac{\text{lbf}}{\text{ft}}\right)(12\ \text{ft})^2}{8}$$

$$= 6300\ \text{ft-lbf}$$

Using Table 18.2(a), find the column labeled "bending." For Douglas fir-larch no. 2, the tabulated value of F_b is 900 psi. All appropriate adjustments must be made to this value. The load is due to dead and roof live load, so the value of C_D should be 1.25. Since the beam size is unknown, a value of C_F must be assumed. A reasonable assumption would be 1.1. The allowable bending stress is then found by multiplying the tabulated values by the appropriated factor, using Eq. 18.2.

$$F_b' = C_D C_F F_b = (1.25)(1.1)\left(900\ \frac{\text{lbf}}{\text{in}^2}\right)$$

$$= 1237\ \text{psi}$$

The required section modulus is then found from the basic flexure formula, Eq. 18.1.

$$S = \frac{M}{F_b'} = \frac{(6300\ \text{ft-lbf})\left(12\ \frac{\text{in}}{\text{ft}}\right)}{1237\ \frac{\text{lbf}}{\text{in}^2}}$$

$$= 61.11\ \text{in}^3$$

Remember to multiply the moment by a factor of 12 to convert foot-pounds to inch-pounds.

Looking in Table 18.1, the smallest beam that will provide this section modulus is a 4 × 12 with an S of 73.828 in^3. Notice that a 6 × 10 would also provide the required value (82.729), but this has more area and therefore costs more than the 4 × 12. In addition, if a 6 in wide beam were used, a different value for F_b may have to be used in the beams and stringer category. The adjustment factors would also be different for a beam and stringer.

The assumed value for C_F of 1.1 is correct. This value is given in Table 18.2(b) for a no. 2 grade, 12 in wide and 4 in thick. The 4 × 12 is the most appropriate selection to support the load.

Example 18.2

What is the maximum moment-carrying capacity, in foot-pounds, of a 2 × 10 select structural Douglas fir-larch beam with applied dead and floor live load?

Rearranging Eq. 18.1 gives

$$M = SF_b'$$

The allowable tabulated unit stress, F_b, from Table 18.2(a) is 1500 psi, and the section modulus (from Table 18.1) of a 2 × 10 is 21.391 in^3. The load duration factor, C_D, for combined dead and floor live load is 1.0. The size factor, C_F, from Table 18.2(b) is 1.1.

$$F_b' = C_D C_F F_b = (1.00)(1.1)\left(1500\ \frac{\text{lbf}}{\text{in}^2}\right)$$

$$= 1650\ \text{psi}$$

$$M = SF_b' = \frac{(21.391\ \text{in}^3)\left(1650\ \frac{\text{lbf}}{\text{in}^2}\right)}{12\ \frac{\text{in}}{\text{ft}}}$$

$$= 2941\ \text{ft-lbf}$$

Sometimes, either the width or depth of a beam is established by some limiting factor (such as ceiling clearance), and the other dimension must be found. This is easy to calculate, recalling that the section modulus of a rectangular beam is

$$S = \frac{bd^2}{6} \qquad 18.3$$

Example 18.3

A wood beam spanning 10 ft must be designed to support a concentrated load of 2900 lbf in the center of the span, but there is only enough room for a nominal 8 in deep beam. If the beam can be dense select structural Douglas fir-larch with an allowable unit stress of 1900 psi, what beam width is necessary?

The moment of a beam with a concentrated load is $PL/4$ (from Fig. 13.7). The moment is

$$M = \frac{PL}{4} = \frac{(2900\ \text{lbf})(10\ \text{ft})\left(12\ \frac{\text{in}}{\text{ft}}\right)}{4}$$

$$= 87{,}000\ \text{in-lbf}$$

The required modulus from Eq. 18.1 is

$$S = \frac{M}{F'_b} = \frac{87{,}000\ \text{in-lbf}}{1900\ \frac{\text{lbf}}{\text{in}^2}}$$

$$= 45.79\ \text{in}^3$$

If there were no limitation on the depth of the beam, a 4×10 would work with a section modulus of 49.911. However, if the maximum depth is 7.5 in (the actual depth of a nominal 8 in beam and stringer), then the required width, from Eq. 18.3, is

$$S = \frac{bd^2}{6}$$

Rearranging the formula gives

$$b = \frac{6S}{d^2} = \frac{(6)(45.79\ \text{in}^3)}{(7.5\ \text{in})^2}$$

$$= 4.88\ \text{in}$$

A nominal 6 in wide beam will work with an actual width of 5.50 in.

Example 18.4

A Douglas fir-larch no. 1 beam supports a roof with a dead load of 100 plf and a snow load of 150 plf. If the beam must span 8 ft, what is the most economical size to use?

For the snow load, a load duration factor of 1.15 is multiplied by the tabulated allowable stress. However, when there are loads of different durations on wood members, each load combination should be checked. For the dead load, a load duration of 0.9 is used. From Fig. 13.7, for a uniformly loaded beam, the moment due to dead loads is

$$M = \frac{wL^2}{8} = \frac{\left(100\ \frac{\text{lbf}}{\text{ft}}\right)(8\ \text{ft})^2\left(12\ \frac{\text{in}}{\text{ft}}\right)}{8}$$

$$= 9600\ \text{in-lbf}$$

The moment due to dead load and snow load is

$$M = \frac{\left(250\ \frac{\text{lbf}}{\text{ft}}\right)(8\ \text{ft})^2\left(12\ \frac{\text{in}}{\text{ft}}\right)}{8}$$

$$= 24{,}000\ \text{in-lbf}$$

Remember, the factor of 12 must be used to convert foot-pounds to inch-pounds.

Since the beam size is unknown, the size factor will be assumed to be 1.1. The tabulated bending stress from Table 18.2(a) for Douglas fir-larch no. 1 is 1000 psi. The required section modulus for dead load only is

$$S = \frac{M}{F'_b} = \frac{M}{C_D C_F F_b} = \frac{9600\ \text{in-lbf}}{(0.9)(1.1)\left(1000\ \frac{\text{lbf}}{\text{in}^2}\right)}$$

$$= 9.70\ \text{in}^3$$

The required section modulus for the combined load is

$$S = \frac{24{,}000\ \text{in-lbf}}{(1.15)(1.1)\left(1000\ \frac{\text{lbf}}{\text{in}^2}\right)}$$

$$= 18.97\ \text{in}^3$$

Use the greater of the calculated section moduli—a 2×10 with a section modulus of 21.391 (from Table 18.1). The assumed value for C_F of 1.1 is correct. This value is given in Table 18.2(b) for a no. 1 grade, 10 in wide and 2 in thick. The 2×10 is the most appropriate selection to support the loads.

Design for Horizontal Shear

Because it is easy for wood to shear along the lines of the grain, actual horizontal shear must always be checked against the allowable unit shear stress, F_v. This is especially important for short spans with large loads. Frequently, a beam that is sufficient in size to resist bending stresses must be made larger to resist horizontal shear stresses.

Because horizontal shear failure will always occur before vertical shear failure, it is not necessary to check for vertical shear except for beams notched at their supports.

For rectangular beams, the maximum unit horizontal shear stress is

$$f_v = \frac{3V}{2bd} \qquad 18.4$$

The basic allowable stress in shear, F_v, is found in Table 18.2(a), and the sizes are found in Table 18.1. This value must be modified for five factors, including those shown in

Table 18.2(b). The following formula is used for allowable shear stress.

$$F_v' = F_v C_D C_M C_t C_i C_H \tag{18.5}$$

The values of C_D, C_M, C_t, and C_i are found in a manner similar to that for finding the values applied to bending stress. Values of C_H are omitted from Table 18.2(b). This value should only be used if the architect or engineer will verify the extent of cracking in the wood member.

When calculating the vertical shear, V, the loads within a distance from the supports equal to the depth of the member may be neglected.

Example 18.5

Check the beam found in Ex. 18.1 for horizontal shear.

The load is 350 plf for 12 ft, or 4200 lbf total. The vertical shear at each reaction is 2100 lbf. Subtract the load within a distance equal to the depth of the beam, $11^1/_4$ in.

$$V = 2100\text{ lbf} - \left(\frac{11.25\text{ in}}{12\,\frac{\text{in}}{\text{ft}}}\right)\left(350\,\frac{\text{lbf}}{\text{ft}}\right) = 1772\text{ lbf}$$

The value of bd is the area, found in Table 18.1 to be 39.375 in^2.

The actual horizontal shear is found from Eq. 18.4.

$$f_v = \frac{3V}{2bd} = \frac{(3)(1772\text{ lbf})}{(2)(39.375\text{ in}^2)} = 67.50\text{ psi}$$

From Table 18.2(a), the allowable tabulated horizontal shear, F_v, is 180 psi for Douglas fir-larch no. 2. This must be multiplied times the duration of load factor of 1.25. The allowable shear stress, F_v', is 225 psi and is larger than the actual stress, so the beam is adequate to resist horizontal shear. If the actual value were greater than the allowable, a larger beam would be needed.

Design for Deflection

Since wood is not as stiff as steel or concrete, deflection is always a concern. Detrimental effects of deflection can include nail popping in gypsum ceilings, cracking of plaster, bouncy floors, and visible sagging. In many cases, a wood member can be selected that will satisfy bending requirements but will not satisfy deflection criteria. Therefore, the design of wood beams must always include a check for deflection.

The formulas for deflection are the same ones used for other materials and are outlined in Fig. 13.7. The criteria for maximum deflection is given in the *International Building Code* (IBC) and requires that two different conditions of loading be checked. The first limits deflection due to live load only to L/360 of the span. The second limits deflection due to live load and dead load for unseasoned wood to L/240 of the span. In both cases, the units of deflection will be the same as the units used for the value of L.

The IBC does allow a reduction by one-half of the dead load for the condition of the live load and dead load if seasoned wood is used. *Seasoned wood* is defined as wood with a moisture content of less than 16% at the time of installation and used under dry conditions. This is typically the case, but since wood will deflect under long-term use beyond its initial deflection, it is common practice to use the full value of dead load and live load when checking deflection against the L/240 criterion. This provides for the extra stiffness necessary to limit deflection under long-term loading.

The basic modulus of elasticity, E, is found in Table 18.2(a). This value must be modified for four factors, including those shown in Table 18.2(b). The following formula is used for allowable modulus of elasticity.

$$E' = EC_M C_t C_i C_T \tag{18.6}$$

The values of C_M, C_t, and C_i are found in a manner similar to that for finding the values applied to bending stress. Values of C_T only apply to small truss members in compression. All of these values are 1.0 under normal conditions.

Example 18.6

Using the same beam found in Ex. 18.1, check to see that its deflection is within allowable limits. Assume that of the total load of 350 plf, dead load is 150 lbf and live load is 200 plf.

From Fig. 13.7, the deflection for a uniformly loaded beam is

$$\Delta = \frac{5wL^4}{384EI} \tag{18.7}$$

The modulus of elasticity of Douglas fir-larch no. 2 is 1,600,000 psi as found in Table 18.2(a), and the moment of inertia of a 4 × 12 is 415.283 as found in Table 18.1.

In this case, it is important to keep units consistent in order for the answer to be in inches. Remember that in Eq. 18.7, w is the load per unit length and L is the length. If L is in inches, the load must be in pounds per inch, not feet. For calculating the total dead and live load, 350 plf is 350/12, or 29.167 lbf/in. The beam length of 12 ft must be converted to inches and then raised to the fourth power.

$$\Delta = \frac{(5)\left(29.167\ \frac{\text{lbf}}{\text{ft}}\right)\left((12\ \text{ft})\left(12\ \frac{\text{in}}{\text{ft}}\right)\right)^4}{(384)\left(1{,}600{,}000\ \frac{\text{lbf}}{\text{in}^2}\right)(415.283\ \text{in}^4)}$$

$$= 0.25\ \text{in}$$

Another way to arrive at the same answer is to remember that Eq. 18.7 can also take the form

$$\Delta = \frac{5wL^3}{384EI} \qquad 18.8$$

W is the total uniformly distributed load on the beam. The length still needs to be converted to inches and then raised to the third power, so the calculation is

$$\Delta = \frac{5WL^3}{384EI} = \frac{(5)\left(\left(350\ \frac{\text{lbf}}{\text{ft}}\right)(12\ \text{ft})\right)\left((12\ \text{ft})\left(12\ \frac{\text{in}}{\text{ft}}\right)\right)^3}{(384)\left(1{,}600{,}000\ \frac{\text{lbf}}{\text{in}^2}\right)(415.283\ \text{in}^4)}$$

$$= 0.25\ \text{in for dead and live loads}$$

For deflection due to the live load only,

$$\Delta = \frac{5WL^3}{384EI} = \frac{(5)\left(\left(200\ \frac{\text{lbf}}{\text{ft}}\right)(12\ \text{ft})\left((12\ \text{ft})\left(12\ \frac{\text{in}}{\text{ft}}\right)\right)^3}{(384)\left(1{,}600{,}000\ \frac{\text{lbf}}{\text{in}^2}\right)(415.283\ \text{in}^4)}$$

$$= 0.14\ \text{in}$$

Next, determine the allowable deflection limits. For the live load only,

$$\frac{L}{360} = \frac{(12\ \text{ft})\left(12\ \frac{\text{in}}{\text{ft}}\right)}{360} = 0.40\ \text{in}$$

This is more than the actual deflection under the live load only of 0.14, so this is acceptable. For the total load,

$$\frac{L}{240} = \frac{(12\ \text{ft})\left(12\ \frac{\text{in}}{\text{ft}}\right)}{240} = 0.60\ \text{in}$$

This is also more than the actual deflection under the total load of 0.25 in, so the 4 × 12 beam is acceptable for deflection requirements.

MISCELLANEOUS PROVISIONS

Notched Beams

Notching of beams should be avoided, but if it is done, the IBC states that notches in sawn lumber bending members cannot exceed one-sixth the depth of the member and cannot be located in the middle third of the span. When the notches are at the supports as shown in Fig. 18.1, the depth cannot exceed one-fourth of the beam depth.

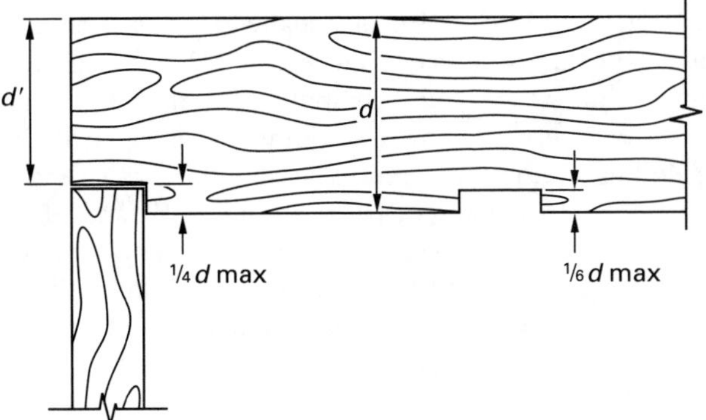

Figure 18.1 Notching of Beams

If beams are notched, the vertical shear cannot exceed the value determined by the formula

$$V = \left(\frac{2bd'F'_v}{3}\right)\left(\frac{d'}{d}\right) \qquad 18.9$$

Example 18.7

If the beam in Ex. 18.1 is notched 2 in, is it still an acceptable size?

The beam found in Ex. 18.1 is a 4 × 12, so its actual width is 3.5 in and its actual depth is 11.25 in. Subtracting 2 in from the depth gives a d' value of 9.25 in. From Ex. 18.5, the allowable horizontal shear for Douglas fir-larch no. 2 is 225 psi. Applying Eq. 18.9, the vertical shear is

$$V = \left(\frac{2bd'F'_v}{3}\right)\left(\frac{d'}{d}\right)$$

$$= \left(\frac{(2)(3.5\ \text{in})(9.25\ \text{in})\left(225\ \frac{\text{lbf}}{\text{in}^2}\right)}{3}\right)\left(\frac{9.25\ \text{in}}{11.25\ \text{in}}\right)$$

$$= 3993\ \text{lbf}$$

From Ex. 18.5, the vertical shear at each reaction was found to be 2100 lbf, so this beam could be notched 2 in without exceeding the allowable vertical shear limitation.

Size Factor

As the depth of a beam increases, there is a slight decrease in bending strength. The IBC requires that the allowable unit stress in bending, F_b, be decreased by a size factor as determined by the formula

$$C_F = \left(\frac{12}{d}\right)^{1/9} \qquad 18.10$$

This applies only to rectangular sawn bending members that are visually graded timber or visually graded southern pine dimension lumber exceeding a depth of 12 in. Design values for bending, tension, and compression parallel to the grain for visually graded dimension lumber 2 in to 4 in thick, excluding southern pine, must be multiplied by size factors given at the beginning of NDS Tables 4A, 4B, and 4E. The size factor does not affect the allowable strength to any great amount. C_F for a 14 in deep beam, for example, is only 0.987, and for a 16 in deep beam, it is 0.972.

Lateral Support

When a wood beam is loaded in bending, there is a tendency for it to buckle laterally. The IBC provides that a decrease in allowable bending strength be made if certain conditions are not met. For the vast majority of wood construction, this is not required if proper lateral support is provided. This amounts to providing continuous support at the compression edge, such as with sheathing or subflooring, and providing restraint against rotation at the ends of the members and at intervals with bridging. Most wood construction meets these conditions, so adjustments are not required.

Bearing

The load on a wood beam compresses the fibers where the weight is concentrated at the supports. To determine the required bearing area, the total reaction load is divided by the allowable compression perpendicular to grain, $F_{c\perp}$, found in Table 18.2(a). For joists, the IBC states that there must be at least $1^1/_2$ in bearing on wood or metal, and at least 3 in bearing on masonry. Beams or girders supported on masonry must have at least 3 in of bearing surface.

Example 18.8

What is the required bearing area on a masonry wall for the beam selected in Ex. 18.1?

The total reaction of the beam is

$$R = \frac{\left(350\ \frac{\text{lbf}}{\text{ft}}\right)(12\ \text{ft})}{2} = 2100\ \text{lbf}$$

The required bearing area is

$$A = \frac{2100\ \text{lbf}}{625\ \frac{\text{lbf}}{\text{in}^2}} = 3.36\ \text{in}^2$$

Since the beam is $3^1/_2$ in wide, the required length of bearing is 3.36/3.5, or 0.96 in. However, since this is less than the code requirement of 3 in, 3 in must be used.

WOOD COLUMNS

As discussed in Ch. 13, columns have a tendency to buckle under a load, so even though a column may have enough cross-sectional area to resist the unit compressive forces, it may fail in buckling. For wood columns, the ratio of the column length to its width is just as important as it is for concrete and steel columns. However, for wood columns, the slenderness ratio is defined as the laterally unsupported length in in divided by the least dimension of the column. This is a little different than the length divided by the radius of gyration as discussed in Ch. 13, but the same principles apply.

Wood columns can be solid members of rectangular, round, or other shapes, or spaced columns built up from two or more individual solid members separated by blocking. Since almost all wood columns are solid rectangular sections, the method of design in this section will be limited to these types.

As mentioned in Ch. 13, the load-carrying capacity of a wood column depends on the way the ends of the column are fixed. For design, the *effective length* must be determined. This is the total unsupported length multiplied by an effective buckling length factor, K_e. These factors for various end conditions are shown in Fig. 18.2. Notice that this diagram is very similar to Fig. 13.8, but the values are slightly different.

Because of the way most wood construction is detailed, columns are usually fixed in translation but free to rotate, so the K-value is taken as 1, and the effective length is taken as the actual unsupported length.

The allowable unit stress in pounds per square inch of cross-sectional area of square or rectangular solid columns is determined according to a complex formula that considers the effective length; whether the wood is visually graded or machine graded; and whether the wood is sawn lumber, round timber piles, or glued-laminated timber. Because of the complexity of the formula, it is unlikely that the test will ask for specific values to be calculated.

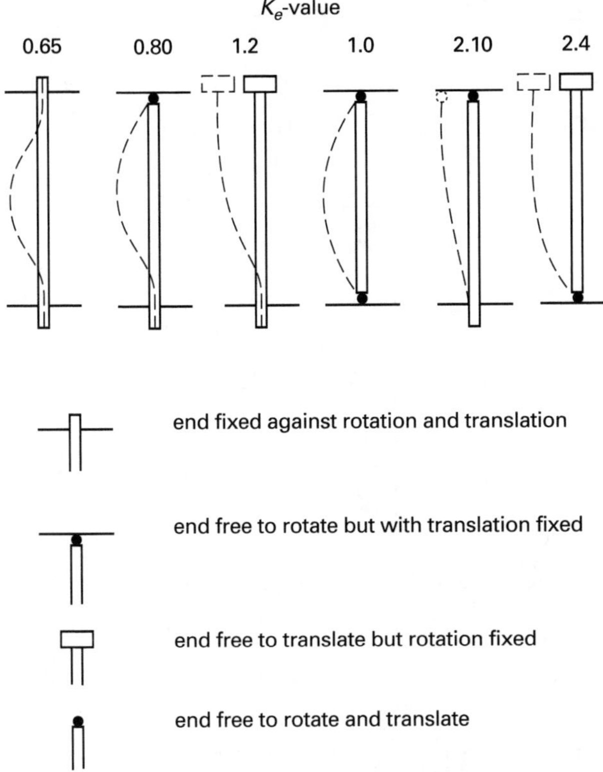

Figure 18.2 K_e-Values for Wood Columns

JOISTS

Joists are a very common type of wood construction. They are small, closely spaced members used to support floor, ceiling, and roof loads, and are usually lumber nominally 2 in wide by 6, 8, 10, and 12 in deep, spaced 12, 16, or 24 in on center. Of course, they are beams and can be designed using the methods described earlier in this section, but since they are used so frequently, their size and spacing is usually selected from tables. When they are designed as beams, the design value of F_b from Table 18.2(a) should be multiplied by the repetitive use factor, C_r, from Table 18.2(b). The design value is slightly larger for multiple member use than for single members.

Table 18.3 shows one joist table from the IBC. Similar tables are published by the National Forest Products Association, the Southern Forest Products Association, other trade groups, and reference sources. For a given joist size and spacing and a given modulus of elasticity, the table gives the maximum allowable span when the bending and deflection are the limiting factors. Most tables are established for typical floor and roof loads, so in unusual circumstances the required size and spacing will have to be calculated using the methods of beam design.

To use the table, either begin with a known span and lumber species and find the required size and spacing of joists, or begin with the span and joist design and determine what design values are required to satisfy the requirements. Then specify a lumber species and grade that have the design values needed. The design values are found in Table 18.2(a).

Example 18.9

A floor must be designed to support a live load of 40 psf and a dead load of 20 psf. The joists will span 13 ft. If the most readily available grade of wood joist is Douglas fir-larch no. 2, what size and spacing is required?

Table 18.3 gives span values based on lumber species, joist spacing, dead load, and joist size for a live load of 40 psf. For Douglas fir-larch no. 2 joists spaced 12 in on center, the first size that will carry 20 psf of dead load for at least a 13 ft span is a 2 × 8. These 2 × 8 joists spaced 12 in on center will span 13 ft 3 in as indicated in Table 18.3. Additionally, 2 × 10 joists spaced 16 in on center will span 14 ft 1 in. A 24 in spacing would require 2 × 12 joists.

GLUED-LAMINATED CONSTRUCTION

Glued-laminated wood members consist of a number of individual pieces of lumber glued together and finished under factory conditions for use as beams, columns, purlins, and other structural uses. Glued-laminated construction, or *glulam* as it is usually referred to, is used when larger wood members are required for heavy loads or long spans and simple sawn timber pieces are not available or cannot meet the strength requirements. Glulam construction is also used where unusual structural shapes are required and appearance is a consideration. In addition to being fabricated in simple rectangular shapes, glulam members can be formed into arches, tapered forms, and pitched shapes.

Glulam members are manufactured in standard sizes of width and depth. In most cases, $1^1/_2$ in actual depth pieces are used, so the overall depth is some multiple of $1^1/_2$ depending on how many laminations are used. $^3/_4$ in thick pieces are used if a tight curve must be formed. Standard widths and depths are shown in Fig. 18.3.

Because individual pieces can be selected free from certain defects and seasoned to the proper moisture content, and the entire manufacturing process is conducted under carefully controlled conditions, the allowable stresses for glulam construction are higher than for solid, sawn lumber. Although glulam beams are usually loaded in the direction perpendicular to the laminations, they can be loaded in either direction to suit the requirements of the design. Tables of design values give allowable stresses about both axes.

For structural purposes, glulams are designated by size and a commonly used symbol that specifies its stress rating. For design purposes, glulams are available in three appearance

Table 18.3

Floor Joist Spans for Common Lumber Species
(Residential Living Area, Live Load = 40 psf, L/Δ = 360)

joist spacing (in)	species and grade		maximum floor joist spans (ft-in)							
			dead load = 10 psf				dead load = 20 psf			
			2 × 6	2 × 8	2 × 10	2 × 12	2 × 6	2 × 8	2 × 10	2 × 12
12	Douglas fir-larch	SS	11-4	15-0	19-1	23-3	11-4	15-0	19-1	23-3
	Douglas fir-larch	no. 1	10-11	14-5	18-5	22-0	10-11	14-2	17-4	20-1
	Douglas fir-larch	no. 2	10-9	14-2	17-9	20-7	10-6	13-3	16-3	18-10
	Douglas fir-larch	no. 3	8-8	11-0	13-5	15-7	7-11	10-0	12-3	14-3
	southern pine	SS	11-2	14-8	18-9	22-10	11-2	14-8	18-9	22-10
	southern pine	no. 1	10-11	14-5	18-5	22-5	10-11	14-5	18-5	22-5
	southern pine	no. 2	10-9	14-2	18-0	21-9	10-9	14-2	16-11	19-10
	southern pine	no. 3	9-4	11-11	14-0	16-8	8-6	10-10	12-10	15-3
16	Douglas fir-larch	SS	10-4	13-7	17-4	21-1	10-4	13-7	17-4	21-0
	Douglas fir-larch	no. 1	9-11	13-1	16-5	19-1	9-8	12-4	15-0	17-5
	Douglas fir-larch	no. 2	9-9	12-7	15-5	17-10	9-1	11-6	14-1	16-3
	Douglas fir-larch	no. 3	7-6	9-6	11-8	13-6	6-10	8-8	10-7	12-4
	southern pine	SS	10-2	13-4	17-0	20-9	10-2	13-4	17-0	20-9
	southern pine	no. 1	9-11	13-1	16-9	20-4	9-11	13-1	16-4	19-6
	southern pine	no. 2	9-9	12-10	16-1	18-10	9-6	12-4	14-8	17-2
	southern pine	no. 3	8-1	10-3	12-2	14-6	7-4	9-5	11-1	13-2
19.2	Douglas fir-larch	SS	9-8	12-10	16-4	19-10	9-8	12-10	16-4	19-2
	Douglas fir-larch	no. 1	9-4	12-4	15-0	17-5	8-10	11-3	13-8	15-11
	Douglas fir-larch	no. 2	9-1	11-6	14-1	16-3	8-3	10-6	12-10	14-10
	Douglas fir-larch	no. 3	6-10	8-8	10-7	12-4	6-3	7-11	9-8	11-3
	southern pine	SS	9-6	12-7	16-0	19-6	9-6	12-7	16-0	19-6
	southern pine	no. 1	9-4	12-4	15-9	19-2	9-4	12-4	14-11	17-9
	southern pine	no. 2	9-2	12-1	14-8	17-2	8-8	11-3	13-5	15-8
	southern pine	no. 3	7-4	9-5	11-1	13-2	6-9	8-7	10-1	12-1
24	Douglas fir-larch	SS	9-0	11-11	15-2	18-5	9-0	11-11	14-9	17-1
	Douglas fir-larch	no. 1	8-8	11-0	13-5	15-7	7-11	10-0	12-3	14-3
	Douglas fir-larch	no. 2	8-1	10-3	12-7	14-7	7-5	9-5	11-6	13-4
	Douglas fir-larch	no. 3	6-2	7-9	9-6	11-0	5-7	7-1	8-8	10-1
	southern pine	SS	8-10	11-8	14-11	18-1	8-10	11-8	14-11	18-1
	southern pine	no. 1	8-8	11-5	14-7	17-5	8-8	11-3	13-4	15-11
	southern pine	no. 2	8-6	11-0	13-1	15-5	7-9	10-0	12-0	14-0
	southern pine	no. 3	6-7	8-5	9-11	11-10	6-0	7-8	9-1	10-9

Check sources for availability of lumber in lengths greater than 20 ft.
For SI: 1 in = 25.4 mm, 1 ft = 304.8 mm, 1 psf = 47.8 N/m^2.
Note: Some rows/columns not pertinent to this text have been omitted by PPI.

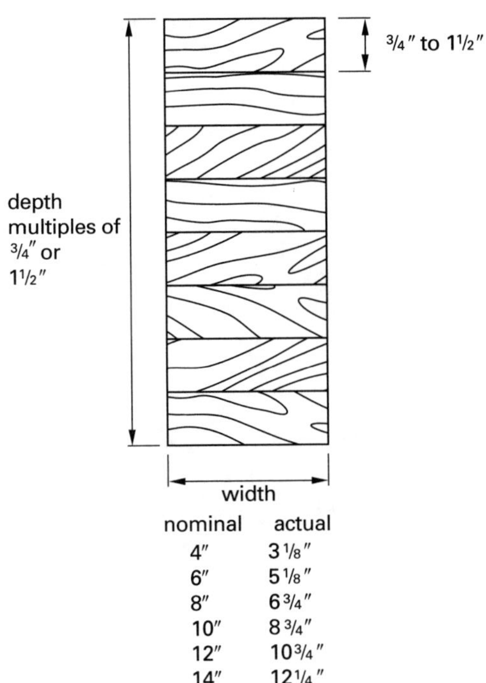

Figure 18.3 Glued-Laminated Beam

grades: *industrial*, *architectural*, and *premium*. These do not affect the structural properties but only designate the final look and finishing of the member. Industrial is used where appearance is not a primary concern, while premium is used where the finest appearance is important. Architectural grade is used where appearance is a factor but the best grade is not required.

PLANKING

Wood planking, or *decking* as it is often called, is solid or laminated lumber laid on its face spanning between beams. Planking is available in nominal thicknesses of 2, 3, 4, and 5 in with actual sizes varying with manufacturer and whether the piece is solid or laminated. All planking has some type of tongue-and-groove edging, so the pieces fit solidly together and load can be distributed among adjacent pieces.

The allowable span depends on the thickness of the planking and load to be supported, and ranges from 4 ft to 20 ft. Planking is often used in heavy timber construction with glued-laminated beams and purlins. Planking has the advantages of easy installation, attractive appearance, and efficient use of material since the planking serves as floor structure, finish floor, and finish ceiling below. Its primary disadvantages are that there is no place to put additional insulation or conceal mechanical and electrical services.

19 STEEL CONSTRUCTION

Nomenclature

A	cross-sectional area	in^2
BF	factor used in calculating glexural strength (Eq. 19.3)	–
d	actual depth of beam	in
E	modulus of elasticity	lbf/in^2
f_b	computed bending stress	lbf/in^2
f_v	unit shear stress	lbf/in^2
f_v	shear stress on gross sections	lbf/in^2
F_a	allowable axial compressive stress	lbf/in^2
F_{cr}	allowable axial buckling stress	lbf/in^2
F_y	specified minimum yield stress of the type of steel being used	lbf/in^2
I	moment of inertia	in^4
K	effective length factor	
l	unbraced span or column length	ft
L	span or column length	ft
L_b	unbraced length of bending compression flange	ft
L_p	maximum unbraced length of the compression flange at which the allowable bending strength may be taken at M_p	ft
L_r	maximum unbraced length of the compression flange at which the allowable bending strength may be taken at Eq. 19.3	ft
M	moment	ft-lbf
M_n	nominal resisting moment	ft-lbf
M_p	maximum bending strength permitted in a member in the absence of axial force	ft-lbf
P	concentrated load	lbf
P_n	allowable tensile strength	lbf
r	governing radius of gyration	in
R	end beam reaction	lbf
S	section modulus	in^3
t_w	thickness of web	in
V	maximum web shear	lbf
V_n	allowable shear strength	lbf
w	weight per foot	lbf
W	total uniform load on a beam	lbf
W_c	uniform load constant	ft-lbf
Z	plastic section modulus	in^3
Δ	deflection	in
Ω	safety factor (ASD)	–

There are currently two accepted methods of structural steel design in the United States: the *allowable stress design* (ASD) method and the *load and resistance factor design* (LRFD) method. The use of either method is allowed by the *International Building Code* (IBC), but the IBC is based on the ASD method. The material in this chapter is also based on the ASD method.

PROPERTIES OF STRUCTURAL STEEL

Steel is one of the most widely used structural materials because of its many advantages, which include high strength, ductility, uniformity of manufacture, variety of shapes and sizes, and ease and speed of erection. Steel has a high strength-to-weight ratio. This makes it possible to reduce a building's dead load and to minimize the space taken up by structural elements. In addition, steel has a high modulus of elasticity, which means it is very stiff.

Ductility is a property that allows steel to withstand excessive deformations, due to high tensile stresses, without failure. This property makes steel useful for earthquake-resistant structures.

Because steel is manufactured under carefully controlled conditions, the composition, size, and strength of steel members can be uniformly predicted. Unlike concrete structures, structures made of steel do not have to be overdesigned to allow for unpredictable variations in manufacturing or erection.

The variety of available sizes and shapes of steel also allows the designer to select a member that is the most efficient for the job and that is not larger than it needs to be. These properties make possible a wide range of cost-efficient structures.

Finally, because most of the cutting and preparation of members can occur in the fabricating plant, steel structures can be erected very quickly and easily, thus reducing overall construction time.

In spite of its advantages, however, steel does have negative properties that must be allowed for. Most notable are its reduction in strength when subjected to fire and its tendency to corrode in the presence of moisture. Steel itself does not burn, but it deforms at high temperatures. As a result, steel must be protected with fire-resistant materials such as sprayed-on cementitious material or gypsum board, or it must be encased in concrete.

As with any ferrous material, steel will rust and otherwise corrode if not protected. This can be accomplished by including alloys in the steel to protect it (e.g., stainless steel), or by covering it with paint or other protective coatings.

Types and Composition of Steel

Steel is composed primarily of iron with small amounts of carbon and other elements that are part of the alloy, either as impurities left over from manufacturing or deliberately added to impart certain desired qualities to the alloy. In *medium-carbon steel* used in construction, these other elements include manganese (from 0.5% to 1.0%), silicon (from 0.25% to 0.75%), and smaller amounts of phosphorus and sulfur. Phosphorus and sulfur in excessive amounts are harmful in that they affect weldability and make steel brittle, but sulfur is difficult to remove completely, and a very small amount of phosphorus improves strength and hardness.

The percentage of carbon present affects the strength and ductility of steel. As carbon is added, the strength increases but the ductility decreases. Percentages of carbon range from about 0.15% for very mild steel to 0.70% for high-carbon steel. Standard structural steel has from 0.20% to 0.50% carbon.

The most common type of steel for structural use is ASTM A992, which means that the steel is manufactured according to ASTM International specification number A572. The yield point for this steel is 50 kips per square inch (ksi). Other high-strength steels include A242, A440, A441, and A572 steel, which have yield points of 46 ksi or 50 ksi.

Shapes and Sizes of Structural Steel

Structural steel comes in a variety of shapes, sizes, and weights. This gives the designer a great deal of flexibility in selecting an economical member that is geometrically correct for any given situation. Figure 19.1 shows the most common shapes of structural steel.

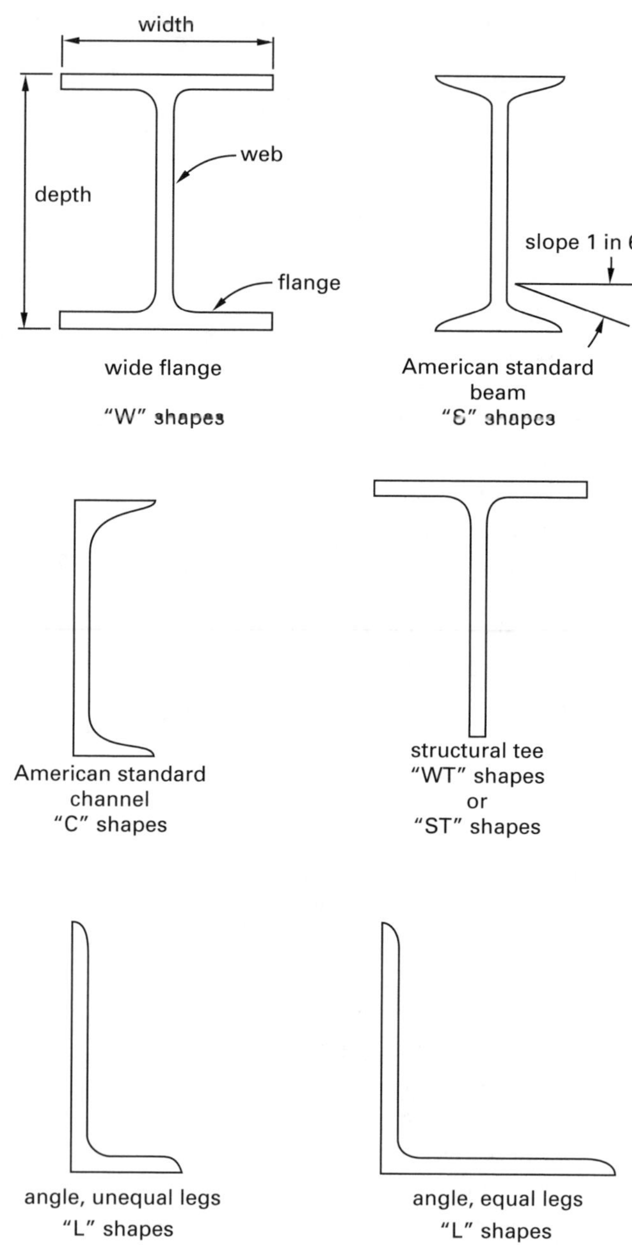

Figure 19.1 Structural Steel Shapes

Wide-flange members are H-shaped sections used for both beams and columns. They are called "wide flange" because the width of the flange is greater than that of standard I-beams. The outside and inside faces of the flanges are parallel. Many of the wide-flange shapes are particularly suited for columns because the width of the flange is very nearly equal to the depth of the section, so they have about the same rigidity in both axes. 14 in deep wide-flange sections are often used for columns in high-rise multistory structures. In low-rise and mid-rise multistory buildings, usually the smallest column used is an 8 in deep wide flange.

Wide-flange sections are designated with the letter W followed by the nominal depth in inches and the weight in pounds per linear foot (plf). For example, a W18 × 86 is a wide flange nominally 18 in deep and weighing 86 plf. Because of the way these sections are rolled in the mill, the actual depth varies slightly from the nominal depth.

American standard I-beams have a relatively narrow flange width in relation to their depth, and the inside face of the flanges have a slope of $16^2/_3$%, or $^1/_6$. Unlike wide-flange members, the actual depth of an I-beam in any size group is also its nominal depth. Heavier sections are made by adding thickness to the flanges on the inside face only. The designation of depth and weight per foot for these sections is preceded with the letter S. These sections are usually used for beams only.

American standard channel sections have a flange on one side of the web only and are designated with the letter C followed by the depth and the weight per foot. Like the American standard I-beams, the depth is constant for any size group. Extra weight is added by increasing the thickness of the web and the inside face of the flanges. Channel sections are typically used to frame openings, to form stair stringers, and in other applications where a flush side is required. They are seldom used by themselves as beams or columns because they tend to buckle due to their asymmetrical shape.

Structural tees are made by cutting either a wide-flange section or I-beam in half. If cut from a wide-flange section, a tee is given the prefix designation WT, and if cut from an American standard I-beam, it is given the designation ST. A WT9 × 65, for example, is cut from a W18 × 130. Because they are symmetrical about one axis and have an open flange, tees are often used for chords of steel trusses.

Steel angles are available with either equal or unequal legs. They are designated by the letter L followed by the lengths of the two legs and their thickness. Angles are used in pairs for members for steel trusses or singly as lintels in a variety of applications. They are also used for miscellaneous bracing of other structural members.

Square tube sections, *rectangular tube sections*, and *round pipe* are also available. These are often used for light columns and as members of large trusses or space frames. Structural tubing of various sizes is available in several different wall thicknesses, while structural pipe is available in standard weight, extra strong, and double-extra strong. Each of the three weights has a standard wall thickness depending on the size. Pipe is designated by its nominal diameter, but the actual outside dimension is slightly larger, while the size designation for square or rectangular tubing refers to its actual outside dimensions.

Finally, steel is available in bars and plates. A *bar* is considered any rectangular section 6 in or less in width with a thickness of 0.203 in or greater, or a section 6 in to 8 in in width with a thickness of 0.230 or greater.

A *plate* is considered any section over 8 in wide with a thickness of 0.230 in and over, or a section over 48 in wide with a thickness of 0.180 in and over.

Table 19.1 gives examples of the standard designations for structural steel shapes.

Table 19.1

Standard Designations for Structural Shapes

wide-flange shapes	W12 × 22
American standard beams	S12 × 35
miscellaneous shapes	M12 × 11.8
American standard channels	C15 × 40
miscellaneous channels	MC12 × 35
angles, equal legs	L3 × 3 × $^3/_8$
angles, unequal legs	L4 × 3 × $^1/_2$
structural tees—cut from wide flange shapes	WT7 × 15
structural tees—cut from American standard beams	ST9 × 35
plates	PL10″ × $^1/_2$″ × 0′10″
structural tubing, square	HSS8 × 8 × $^3/_8$
pipe	pipe 4 std.

Allowable Stresses

Allowable unit stresses for structural steel are expressed as percentages of the minimum specified yield point of the grade of steel used. For A992 steel, the yield point is 50 ksi. The percentages used depend on the type of stress, the condition of use, and other factors. Allowable strengths are established by the American Institute of Steel Construction (AISC) and are commonly adopted by reference by model codes such as the IBC and by local codes. Table 19.2 summarizes some of the more common AISC values for 50 ksi steel.

STEEL BEAMS

The design of steel beams involves finding the lightest weight section (and therefore the least expensive) that will resist bending and shear forces within allowable limits of stress, and one that will not have excessive deflection for the

Table 19.2

Selected Allowable Strengths for 50 ksi Steel

type of stress and condition	strength nomenclature	AISC safety factor	stress value for A992 steel (ksi)
bending			
tension and compression on extreme fibers of laterally supported compact sections symmetrical about and loaded in the plane of their minor axes	M_p	1.67	30
compression on axially loaded compact section	P_n	$F_{cr}/1.67$	varies
shear on gross sections	V_n	$0.60F_y/1.50$	20
tension			
on net section	P_n	$F_y/1.67$	30
on effective net area, except at pinholes	P_n	$F_u/2.00$	29

condition of use. Beam design can be accomplished either through the use of the standard formulas for flexure, shear, and deflection, or by using tables in the *Steel Construction Manual* published by the AISC. Both methods will be reviewed in the following sections.

Lateral Support and Compact Sections

Before proceeding with methods for steel beam design, gain a firm understanding of two important concepts: lateral support and compact sections. When a simply supported beam is subjected to a load, the top flange is in compression and the bottom flange is in tension as discussed in Ch. 13. At the compression flange, there is a tendency for the beam to buckle under load, just as a column can buckle under an axial load. For overhanging beams, when the bottom flange is in compression the same potential problem exists.

To resist this tendency, either the compression flange needs to be supported or the beam needs to be made larger. In many cases, steel beams are automatically laterally supported because of standard construction methods. This occurs with beams supporting steel decking welded to the beams, beams with the top flange embedded in a concrete slab, or composite construction. In some instances, a girder is only supported laterally with intermittent beams.

If a beam is continuously supported or supported at intervals no greater than L_p, the full allowable strength of M_p may be used. If the support is greater than L_p but not greater than L_r, then the allowable strength must be reduced to the value in Eq. 19.3. The values of L_p and L_r are given in tables in the AISC manual and will be illustrated in later example problems.

Sections are determined to be either *compact* or *noncompact* based on the yield strength of the steel and the width-to-thickness ratios of the web and flanges. If a section is noncompact, a lower allowable bending stress must be used. Identification of noncompact sections and the reduced stresses are incorporated into the design tables in the AISC manual.

Design for Bending

There are two approaches to designing steel beams: with the flexure formula as discussed in Ch. 13 and with the tables found in the AISC manual. Both will be discussed here.

The basic flexure formula is

$$Z = \frac{M}{F_y} \qquad 19.1$$

This formula from Ch. 13 is the same for steel design, except that the AISC uses the nomenclature M_n for the allowable moment strength instead of f_b, which it reserves for computed bending stress.

The basic formula is used in two forms either to select a beam by finding the required section plastic modulus, Z, or to calculate the maximum resisting moment, M, when a beam is being analyzed. These two forms are Eqs. 19.1 and 19.2.

$$M_n = ZF_y \qquad 19.2$$

The following equation is used when the unbraced length of the compression flanges is between L_p and L_r. The values are given in Table 19.4.

$$M_n = M_p - BF(F_b - L_p) \qquad 19.3$$

Moments are calculated using the static formulas for various types of loading conditions as shown in Fig. 13.7, or by using the methods described in Chs. 12 and 13 with shear and moment diagrams, or with the summation of moments method.

It is important to keep the units consistent. It is typical in steel design to use the units of kips (thousands of pounds) instead of pounds, and feet instead of inches. However, allowable stresses are often listed in kips per square inch, so it is often necessary to convert between inch-kips and foot-kips. In addition, many of the tables used in the AISC manual are in kips while problems are often given in pounds. The best way to avoid difficulty is to adopt a consistent procedure of using kips and feet in all problems. If a problem is stated in pounds or inches, the first step should be to convert the units. The following example problems will illustrate this point.

Example 19.1

An A992 steel beam that is laterally supported is to span 26 ft, supporting a uniform load of 1500 plf not including its own weight. What is the most economical wide-flange section that can be used?

The weight of a beam can be accounted for in one of two ways. Either assume a weight and add it to the load and then calculate moment, or ignore it, solve the problem to find the actual weight of the beam, and then recheck the work. Since the weight of a steel beam is usually a very small percentage of the total load, it can usually be ignored for preliminary calculations. For example, the heaviest wide-flange section used for a beam is a W44 × 335, so the most additional weight possible is 0.335 klf.

Find the maximum moment, ignoring the weight of the beam.

From Fig. 13.7, the formula for moment is

$$M = \frac{wL^2}{8}$$

Converting 1500 plf to 1.5 klf,

$$M = \frac{\left(1.5\ \frac{\text{kips}}{\text{ft}}\right)(26\ \text{ft})^2}{8}$$

$$= 127\ \text{ft-kips}$$

For A992 steel, the allowable bending stress is 30 ksi (Table 19.2). Use Eq. 19.1 to find the required section modulus.

$$Z = \frac{(127\ \text{ft-kips})\left(12\ \frac{\text{in}}{\text{ft}}\right)}{30\ \frac{\text{kips}}{\text{in}^2}}$$

$$= 50.8\ \text{in}^3$$

The value of 127 ft-kips had to be converted to inch-kips to work with the value of 30 ksi and yield an answer in cubic inches for the section modulus.

To find the most economical section (the lightest weight), look in the various AISC tables showing properties of sections (Table 19.3, for example), or look in the section modulus table in the AISC manual. A portion of this table is reproduced in Table 19.4. This table lists the various sections in the order of descending section modulus value with the lightest member in a group shown in boldface type. For this problem, the lightest section that satisfies the required section modulus is a W16 × 31 with a Z of 54.0 in^3.

Table 19.4 also lists the maximum resisting moment that the beam can carry and the length limits, L_p and L_r, for unsupported sections. The columns on the right are for calculating M_n. The maximum moment this beam can resist, assuming L_b is less than L_p, is 135 ft-kips. If an additional 40 lbf (0.040 kips) of beam weight is added to the load and the moment is recalculated, the resulting moment is 130.1 ft-kips. This is less than the maximum allowable of 135 ft-kips, and the selection is okay.

The other way to select the beam is to use the Maximum Total Uniform Load tables in the AISC manual. One page is reproduced in Table 19.5. These tables make it very easy to calculate allowable loads for a given size beam, select a beam for a given span and loading, find deflections and shear values, and check for unbraced lengths. The tables take into account the weight of the beams, but these should be deducted to determine the net load that the beam will support.

The tables are for uniformly loaded beams, but they can be used for concentrated loads by using the table of concentrated load equivalents in the AISC manual, which give factors for converting concentrated loads to uniform loads. In Table 19.5, the notation L_p is used to denote the maximum unbraced length of the compression flange, in feet, for which the allowable loads for compact symmetrical shapes are calculated with an allowable strength of M_p. The tables are not applicable for beams with an unbraced length greater than L_r.

Table 19.3
Properties of Wide Flange Shapes

W Shapes — Dimensions

Shape	Area, A	Depth, d		Web Thickness, t_w		$\frac{t_w}{2}$	Flange Width, b_f		Flange Thickness, t_f		Distance k, k_{des}	Distance k, k_{det}	k_1	T	Workable Gage
	in.^{2}	in.		in.		in.	in.		in.		in.	in.	in.	in.	in.
W12×58	17.0	12.2	12 1/4	0.360	3/8	3/16	10.0	10	0.640	5/8	1.24	1 1/2	15/16	9 1/4	5 1/2
×53	15.6	12.1	12	0.345	3/8	3/16	10.0	10	0.575	9/16	1.18	1 3/8	15/16	9 1/4	5 1/2
W12×50	14.6	12.2	12 1/4	0.370	3/8	3/16	8.08	8 1/8	0.640	5/8	1.14	1 1/2	15/16	9 1/4	5 1/2
×45	13.1	12.1	12	0.335	5/16	3/16	8.05	8	0.575	9/16	1.08	1 3/8	15/16	↓	↓
×40	11.7	11.9	12	0.295	5/16	3/16	8.01	8	0.515	1/2	1.02	1 3/8	7/8	↓	↓
W12×35[c]	10.3	12.5	12 1/2	0.300	5/16	3/16	6.56	6 1/2	0.520	1/2	0.820	1 3/16	3/4	10 1/8	3 1/2
×30[c]	8.79	12.3	12 3/8	0.260	1/4	1/8	6.52	6 1/2	0.440	7/16	0.740	1 1/8	3/4	↓	↓
×26[c]	7.65	12.2	12 1/4	0.230	1/4	1/8	6.49	6 1/2	0.380	3/8	0.680	1 1/16	3/4	↓	↓
W12×22[c]	6.48	12.3	12 1/4	0.260	1/4	1/8	4.03	4	0.425	7/16	0.725	15/16	5/8	10 3/8	2 1/4[g]
×19[c]	5.57	12.2	12 1/8	0.235	1/4	1/8	4.01	4	0.350	3/8	0.650	7/8	9/16	↓	↓
×16[c]	4.71	12.0	12	0.220	1/4	1/8	3.99	4	0.265	1/4	0.565	13/16	9/16	↓	↓
×14[c,v]	4.16	11.9	11 7/8	0.200	3/16	1/8	3.97	4	0.225	1/4	0.525	3/4	9/16	↓	↓
W10×112	32.9	11.4	11 3/8	0.755	3/4	3/8	10.4	10 3/8	1.25	1 1/4	1.75	1 15/16	1	7 1/2	5 1/2
×100	29.4	11.1	11 1/8	0.680	11/16	3/8	10.3	10 3/8	1.12	1 1/8	1.62	1 13/16	1	↓	↓
×88	25.9	10.8	10 7/8	0.605	5/8	5/16	10.3	10 1/4	0.990	1	1.49	1 11/16	15/16	↓	↓
×77	22.6	10.6	10 5/8	0.530	1/2	1/4	10.2	10 1/4	0.870	7/8	1.37	1 9/16	7/8	↓	↓
×68	20.0	10.4	10 3/8	0.470	1/2	1/4	10.1	10 1/8	0.770	3/4	1.27	1 7/16	7/8	↓	↓
×60	17.6	10.2	10 1/4	0.420	7/16	1/4	10.1	10 1/8	0.680	11/16	1.18	1 3/8	13/16	↓	↓
×54	15.8	10.1	10 1/8	0.370	3/8	3/16	10.0	10	0.615	5/8	1.12	1 5/16	13/16	↓	↓
×49	14.4	10.0	10	0.340	5/16	3/16	10.0	10	0.560	9/16	1.06	1 1/4	13/16	↓	↓
W10×45	13.3	10.1	10 1/8	0.350	3/8	3/16	8.02	8	0.620	5/8	1.12	1 5/16	13/16	7 1/2	5 1/2
×39	11.5	9.92	9 7/8	0.315	5/16	3/16	7.99	8	0.530	1/2	1.03	1 3/16	13/16	↓	↓
×33	9.71	9.73	9 3/4	0.290	5/16	3/16	7.96	8	0.435	7/16	0.935	1 1/8	3/4	↓	↓
W10×30	8.84	10.5	10 1/2	0.300	5/16	3/16	5.81	5 3/4	0.510	1/2	0.810	1 1/8	11/16	8 1/4	2 3/4[g]
×26	7.61	10.3	10 3/8	0.260	1/4	1/8	5.77	5 3/4	0.440	7/16	0.740	1 1/16	11/16	↓	↓
×22[c]	6.49	10.2	10 1/8	0.240	1/4	1/8	5.75	5 3/4	0.360	3/8	0.660	15/16	5/8	↓	↓
W10×19	5.62	10.2	10 1/4	0.250	1/4	1/8	4.02	4	0.395	3/8	0.695	15/16	5/8	8 3/8	2 1/4[g]
×17[c]	4.99	10.1	10 1/8	0.240	1/4	1/8	4.01	4	0.330	5/16	0.630	7/8	9/16	↓	↓
×15[c]	4.41	10.0	10	0.230	1/4	1/8	4.00	4	0.270	1/4	0.570	13/16	9/16	↓	↓
×12[c,f]	3.54	9.87	9 7/8	0.190	3/16	1/8	3.96	4	0.210	3/16	0.510	3/4	9/16	↓	↓

[c] Shape is slender for compression with $F_y = 50$ ksi.
[f] Shape exceeds compact limit for flexure with $F_y = 50$ ksi.
[g] The actual size, combination, and orientation of fastener components should be compared with the geometry of the cross-section to ensure compatibility.
[v] Shape does not meet the h/t_w limit for shear in Specification Section G2.1a with $F_y = 50$ ksi.

W Shapes — Properties (W12 – W10)

Nominal Wt.	Compact Section Criteria $\frac{b_f}{2t_f}$	$\frac{h}{t_w}$	Axis X-X I	S	r	Z	Axis Y-Y I	S	r	Z	r_{ts}	h_o	Torsional Properties J	C_w
lb/ft			in.^{4}	in.^{3}	in.	in.^{3}	in.^{4}	in.^{3}	in.	in.^{3}	in.	in.	in.^{4}	in.^{6}
58	7.82	27.0	475	78.0	5.28	86.4	107	21.4	2.51	32.5	2.82	11.6	2.10	3570
53	8.69	28.1	425	70.6	5.23	77.9	95.8	19.2	2.48	29.1	2.79	11.5	1.58	3160
50	6.31	26.8	391	64.2	5.18	71.9	56.3	13.9	1.96	21.3	2.25	11.6	1.71	1880
45	7.00	29.6	348	57.7	5.15	64.2	50.0	12.4	1.95	19.0	2.23	11.5	1.26	1650
40	7.77	33.6	307	51.5	5.13	57.0	44.1	11.0	1.94	16.8	2.21	11.4	0.906	1440
35	6.31	36.2	285	45.6	5.25	51.2	24.5	7.47	1.54	11.5	1.79	12.0	0.741	879
30	7.41	41.8	238	38.6	5.21	43.1	20.3	6.24	1.52	9.56	1.77	11.9	0.457	720
26	8.54	47.2	204	33.4	5.17	37.2	17.3	5.34	1.51	8.17	1.75	11.8	0.300	607
22	4.74	41.8	156	25.4	4.91	29.3	4.66	2.31	0.848	3.66	1.04	11.9	0.293	164
19	5.72	46.2	130	21.3	4.82	24.7	3.76	1.88	0.822	2.98	1.02	11.8	0.180	131
16	7.53	49.4	103	17.1	4.67	20.1	2.82	1.41	0.773	2.26	0.982	11.7	0.103	96.9
14	8.82	54.3	88.6	14.9	4.62	17.4	2.36	1.19	0.753	1.90	0.962	11.7	0.0704	80.4
112	4.17	10.4	716	126	4.66	147	236	45.3	2.68	69.2	3.07	10.1	15.1	6020
100	4.62	11.6	623	112	4.60	130	207	40.0	2.65	61.0	3.03	10.0	10.9	5150
88	5.18	13.0	534	98.5	4.54	113	179	34.8	2.63	53.1	2.99	9.85	7.53	4330
77	5.86	14.8	455	85.9	4.49	97.6	154	30.1	2.60	45.9	2.95	9.73	5.11	3630
68	6.58	16.7	394	75.7	4.44	85.3	134	26.4	2.59	40.1	2.91	9.63	3.56	3100
60	7.41	18.7	341	66.7	4.39	74.6	116	23.0	2.57	35.0	2.88	9.54	2.48	2640
54	8.15	21.2	303	60.0	4.37	66.6	103	20.6	2.56	31.3	2.86	9.48	1.32	2320
49	8.93	23.1	272	54.6	4.35	60.4	93.4	18.7	2.54	28.3	2.84	9.42	1.39	2070
45	6.47	22.5	248	49.1	4.32	54.9	53.4	13.3	2.01	20.3	2.27	9.48	1.51	1200
39	7.53	25.0	209	42.1	4.27	46.8	45.0	11.3	1.98	17.2	2.24	9.39	0.976	992
33	9.15	27.1	171	35.0	4.19	38.8	36.6	9.20	1.94	14.0	2.20	9.30	0.583	791
30	5.70	29.5	170	32.4	4.38	36.6	16.7	5.75	1.37	8.84	1.60	10.0	0.622	414
26	6.56	34.0	144	27.9	4.35	31.3	14.1	4.89	1.36	7.50	1.58	9.89	0.402	345
22	7.99	36.9	118	23.2	4.27	26.0	11.4	3.97	1.33	6.10	1.55	9.81	0.239	275
19	5.09	35.4	96.3	18.8	4.14	21.6	4.29	2.14	0.874	3.35	1.06	9.85	0.233	104
17	6.08	36.9	81.9	16.2	4.05	18.7	3.56	1.78	0.845	2.80	1.04	9.78	0.156	85.1
15	7.41	38.5	68.9	13.8	3.95	16.0	2.89	1.45	0.810	2.30	1.01	9.72	0.104	68.3
12	9.43	46.6	53.8	10.9	3.90	12.6	2.18	1.10	0.785	1.74	0.983	9.66	0.0547	50.9

Table 19.4
Section Modulus and Moment of Resistance
of Selected Structural Shapes

Z_x W Shapes

Selection by Z_x

F_y = 50 ksi

Shape	Z_x	M_{px}/Ω_b	$\phi_b M_{px}$	M_{rx}/Ω_b	$\phi_b M_{rx}$	BF		L_p	L_r	I_x	V_{nx}/Ω_v	$\phi_v V_{nx}$
		kip-ft	kip-ft	kip-ft	kip-ft	kips	kips				kips	kips
	in.^{3}	ASD	LRFD	ASD	LRFD	ASD	LRFD	ft	ft	in.^{4}	ASD	LRFD
W18×35	**66.5**	**166**	249	**101**	151	**8.07**	12.1	**4.31**	**12.4**	**510**	**106**	159
W12×45	64.2	160	241	101	151	3.83	5.75	6.89	22.4	348	80.8	121
W16×36	64.0	160	240	98.7	148	6.19	9.31	5.37	15.2	448	93.6	140
W14×38	61.5	153	231	95.4	143	5.39	8.10	5.47	16.2	385	87.4	131
W10×49	60.4	151	227	95.4	143	2.44	3.67	8.97	31.6	272	68.0	102
W8×58	59.8	149	224	90.8	137	1.70	2.56	7.42	41.7	228	89.3	134
W12×40	57.0	142	214	89.9	135	3.66	5.50	6.85	21.1	307	70.4	106
W10×45	54.9	137	206	85.8	129	2.59	3.89	7.10	26.9	248	70.7	106
W14×34	**54.6**	**136**	205	**84.9**	128	**5.05**	7.59	**5.40**	**15.6**	**340**	**79.7**	120
W16×31	**54.0**	**135**	203	**82.4**	124	**6.76**	10.2	**4.13**	**11.9**	**375**	**87.3**	131
W12×35	51.2	128	192	79.6	120	4.28	6.43	5.44	16.7	285	75.0	113
W8×48	49.0	122	184	75.4	113	1.68	2.53	7.35	35.2	184	68.0	102
W14×30	**47.3**	**118**	177	**73.4**	110	**4.65**	6.99	**5.26**	**14.9**	**291**	**74.7**	112
W10×39	46.8	117	176	73.5	111	2.51	3.77	6.99	24.2	209	62.5	93.7
W16×26[v]	**44.2**	**110**	166	**67.1**	101	**5.96**	8.96	**3.96**	**11.2**	**301**	**70.5**	106
W12×30	43.1	108	162	67.4	101	3.92	5.89	5.37	15.6	238	64.2	96.3
W14×26	**40.2**	**100**	151	**61.7**	92.7	**5.32**	7.99	**3.81**	**11.1**	**245**	**70.9**	106
W8×40	39.8	99.3	149	62.0	93.2	1.64	2.47	7.21	29.9	146	59.4	89.1
W10×33	38.8	96.8	146	61.1	91.9	2.39	3.59	6.85	21.8	171	56.4	84.7
W12×26	**37.2**	**92.8**	140	**58.3**	87.7	**3.61**	5.42	**5.33**	**14.9**	**204**	**56.2**	84.3
W10×30	36.6	91.3	137	56.6	85.0	3.08	4.62	4.84	16.1	170	62.8	94.2
W8×35	34.7	86.6	130	54.5	81.9	1.62	2.43	7.17	27.0	127	50.3	75.5
W14×22	**33.2**	**82.8**	125	**50.6**	76.1	**4.75**	7.14	**3.67**	**10.4**	**199**	**63.2**	94.8
W10×26	31.3	78.1	117	48.7	73.2	2.90	4.36	4.80	14.9	144	53.7	80.6
W8×31[f]	30.4	75.8	114	48.0	72.2	1.58	2.37	7.18	24.8	110	45.6	68.4
W12×22	**29.3**	**73.1**	110	**44.4**	66.7	**4.65**	6.99	**3.00**	**9.17**	**156**	**64.0**	96.0
W8×28	27.2	67.9	102	42.4	63.8	1.66	2.50	5.72	21.0	98.0	45.9	68.9
W10×22	**26.0**	**64.9**	97.5	**40.5**	60.9	**2.68**	4.02	**4.70**	**13.8**	**118**	**48.8**	73.2
W12×19	**24.7**	**61.6**	92.6	**37.2**	55.9	**4.27**	6.43	**2.90**	**8.62**	**130**	**57.2**	85.7
W8x24	23.1	57.6	86.6	36.5	54.9	1.59	2.39	5.69	19.0	82.7	38.9	58.3
W10×19	**21.6**	**53.9**	81.0	**32.8**	49.3	**3.17**	4.77	**3.09**	**9.72**	**96.3**	**51.2**	76.8
W8×21	20.4	50.9	76.5	31.8	47.8	1.86	2.79	4.45	14.8	75.3	41.4	62.1

ASD	LRFD
$\Omega_b = 1.67$	$\phi_b = 0.90$
$\Omega_v = 1.50$	$\phi_v = 1.00$

[f] Shape exceeds compact limit for flexure with F_y = 50 ksi.
[v] Shape does not meet the h/t_w limit for shear in Specification Section G2.1a with F_y = 50 ksi, $\Omega_v = 1.67$, $\phi_v = 0.90$.

(continued)

Table 19.4 *(continued)*
Section Modulus and Moment of Resistance
of Selected Structural Shapes

F_y = 50 ksi

W Shapes
Selection by Z_x

Z_x

Shape	Z_x	M_{px}/Ω_b	$\phi_b M_{px}$	M_{rx}/Ω_b	$\phi_b M_{rx}$	*BF*		L_p	L_r	I_x	V_{nx}/Ω_v	$\phi_v V_{nx}$
		kip-ft	kip-ft	kip-ft	kip-ft	kips	kips				kips	kips
	in.^{3}	ASD	LRFD	ASD	LRFD	ASD	LRFD	ft	ft	in.^{4}	ASD	LRFD
W21×55	126	314	473	192	289	10.8	16.3	6.11	17.4	1140	156	234
W14×74	126	314	473	196	294	5.34	8.03	8.76	31.0	795	128	191
W18×60	123	307	461	189	284	9.64	14.5	5.93	18.2	984	151	227
W12×79	119	297	446	187	281	3.77	5.67	10.8	39.9	662	116	175
W14×68	115	287	431	180	270	5.20	7.81	8.69	29.3	722	117	175
W10×88	113	282	424	172	259	2.63	3.95	9.29	51.1	534	131	197
W18×55	112	279	420	172	258	9.26	13.9	5.90	17.5	890	141	212
W21×50	110	274	413	165	248	12.2	18.3	4.59	13.6	984	158	237
W12×72	108	269	405	170	256	3.72	5.59	10.7	37.4	597	105	158
W21×48[f]	107	265	398	162	244	9.78	14.7	6.09	16.6	959	144	217
W16×57	105	262	394	161	242	7.98	12.0	5.65	18.3	758	141	212
W14×61	102	254	383	161	242	4.90	7.46	8.65	27.5	640	104	156
W18×50	101	252	379	155	233	8.69	13.1	5.83	17.0	800	128	192
W10×77	97.6	244	366	150	225	2.59	3.90	9.18	45.2	455	112	169
W12×65[f]	96.8	237	356	154	231	3.60	5.41	11.9	35.1	533	94.5	142
W21×44	95.4	238	358	143	214	11.2	16.8	4.45	13.0	843	145	217
W16×50	92.0	230	345	141	213	7.59	11.4	5.62	17.2	659	124	185
W18×46	90.7	226	340	138	207	9.71	14.6	4.56	13.7	712	130	195
W14×53	87.1	217	327	136	204	5.27	7.93	6.78	22.2	541	103	155
W12×58	86.4	216	324	136	205	3.76	5.66	8.87	29.9	475	87.8	132
W10×68	85.3	213	320	132	199	2.57	3.86	9.15	40.6	394	97.8	147
W16×45	82.3	205	309	127	191	7.16	10.8	5.55	16.5	586	111	167
W18×40	78.4	196	294	119	180	8.86	13.3	4.49	13.1	612	113	169
W14×48	78.4	196	294	123	184	5.10	7.66	6.75	21.1	484	93.8	141
W12×53	77.9	194	292	123	185	3.65	5.48	8.76	28.2	425	83.2	125
W10×60	74.6	186	280	116	175	2.53	3.80	9.08	36.6	341	85.8	129
W16×40	73.0	182	274	113	170	6.69	10.1	5.55	15.9	518	97.7	146
W12×50	71.9	179	270	112	169	3.97	5.97	6.92	23.9	391	90.2	135
W8×67	70.1	175	263	105	159	1.73	2.60	7.49	47.7	272	103	154
W14×43	69.6	174	261	109	164	4.82	7.24	6.68	20.0	428	83.3	125
W10×54	66.6	166	250	105	158	2.49	3.74	9.04	33.7	303	74.7	112

ASD	LRFD
$\Omega_b = 1.67$	$\phi_b = 0.90$
$\Omega_v = 1.50$	$\phi_v = 1.00$

[f] Shape exceeds compact limit for flexure with F_y = 50 ksi.

Table 19.5

Maximum Total Uniform Load

F_y = 50 ksi

Maximum Total Uniform Load, kips

W Shapes

W12

Shape		W12×											
		53		50		45		40		35		30	
Design		ASD	LRFD	ASD	LRFD	ASD	LRFD	ASD	LRFD	ASD	LRFD	ASD	LRFD
Span, ft	6									150	225	128	193
	7			180	271	162	242			146	219	123	185
	8			179	270	160	241	141	211	128	192	108	162
	9	166	250	159	240	142	214	126	190	114	171	95.6	144
	10	155	234	144	216	128	193	114	171	102	154	86.0	129
	11	141	212	130	196	116	175	103	155	92.9	140	78.2	118
	12	130	195	120	180	107	161	94.8	143	85.2	128	71.7	108
	13	120	180	110	166	98.6	148	87.5	132	78.6	118	66.2	99.5
	14	111	167	103	154	91.5	138	81.3	122	73.0	110	61.4	92.4
	15	104	156	95.7	144	85.4	128	75.8	114	68.1	102	57.4	86.2
	16	97.2	146	89.7	135	80.1	120	71.1	107	63.9	96.0	53.8	80.8
	17	91.5	137	84.4	127	75.4	113	66.9	101	60.1	90.4	50.6	76.1
	18	86.4	130	79.7	120	71.2	107	63.2	95.0	56.8	85.3	47.8	71.8
	19	81.8	123	75.5	114	67.4	101	59.9	90.0	53.8	80.8	45.3	68.1
	20	77.7	117	71.8	108	64.1	96.3	56.9	85.5	51.1	76.8	43.0	64.7
	21	74.0	111	68.3	103	61.0	91.7	54.2	81.4	48.7	73.1	41.0	61.6
	22	70.7	106	65.2	98.0	58.2	87.5	51.7	77.7	46.5	69.8	39.1	58.8
	23	67.6	102	62.4	93.8	55.7	83.7	49.5	74.3	44.4	66.8	37.4	56.2
	24	64.8	97.4	59.8	89.9	53.4	80.3	47.4	71.3	42.6	64.0	35.8	53.9
	25	62.2	93.5	57.4	86.3	51.3	77.0	45.5	68.4	40.9	61.4	34.4	51.7
	26	59.8	89.9	55.2	83.0	49.3	74.1	43.8	65.8	39.3	59.1	33.1	49.7
	27	57.6	86.6	53.2	79.9	47.5	71.3	42.1	63.3	37.9	56.9	31.9	47.9
	28	55.5	83.5	51.3	77.0	45.8	68.8	40.6	61.1	36.5	54.9	30.7	46.2
	29	53.6	80.6	49.5	74.4	44.2	66.4	39.2	59.0	35.2	53.0	29.7	44.6
	30	51.8	77.9	47.8	71.9	42.7	64.2			34.1	51.2	28.7	43.1
	31									33.0	49.5		
Beam Properties													
W_c/Ω_b	$\phi_b W_c$, kip-ft	1550	2340	1440	2160	1280	1930	1140	1710	1020	1540	860	1290
M_p/Ω_b	$\phi_b M_p$, kip-ft	194	292	179	270	160	241	142	214	128	192	108	162
M_r/Ω_b	$\phi_b M_r$, kip-ft	123	185	112	169	101	151	89.9	135	79.6	120	67.4	101
BF	BF, kips	3.65	5.48	3.97	5.97	3.83	5.75	3.66	5.50	4.28	6.43	3.92	5.89
V_n/Ω_v	$\phi_v V_n$, kips	83.2	125	90.2	135	80.8	121	70.4	106	75.0	113	64.2	96.3
Z_x, in.^{3}		77.9		71.9		64.2		57.0		51.2		43.1	
L_p, ft		8.76		6.92		6.89		6.85		5.44		5.37	
L_r, ft		28.2		23.9		22.4		21.1		16.7		15.6	

ASD	LRFD	
$\Omega_b = 1.67$ $\Omega_v = 1.50$	$\phi_b = 0.90$ $\phi_v = 1.00$	Note: For beams laterally unsupported, see Table 3–10. Available strength tabulated above heavy line is limited by available shear strength.

For relatively short spans, the allowable loads for beams may be limited by the shear stress in the web instead of by the maximum bending stress. Loads above the heavy line in the tables are limited by the maximum allowable web shear.

When the spacing of lateral bracing exceeds L_p, but is less than L_r, the tabulated loads must be reduced by the ratio of M_p to the value of M_n as derived from Eq. 19.3.

Example 19.2

An A992 beam, fully laterally supported, spans 20 ft and carries a uniform load of 2700 plf. If there is only space for a 12 in deep beam, what size section should be used? If the beam is only laterally supported at its third points, could the same beam be used?

2700 plf is 2.7 klf, so the total load on the beam is 2.7 klf times 20 ft, or 54.0 kips.

From Table 19.5, the lightest 12 in section that can support 54.0 kips is a W12 × 40 (which has a uniform load value of 56.9 kips).

If the beam is only supported at its third points (every 6.67 ft), this distance is less than the L_p value for a W12 × 40 (6.85 ft, from Table 19.5). Because the unsupported length is less than 6.85 ft, the beam is adequate. Therefore, this beam is acceptable.

Example 19.3

A W12 × 45 beam of A992 steel spans 21 ft. What is the maximum load per foot this beam can carry?

From Table 19.5 for a W12 × 45 beam, the total allowable load for a 21 ft span is 61 kips. Dividing by 21, the allowable load per foot is

$$w = \frac{61 \text{ kips}}{21 \text{ ft}} = 2.9 \text{ kips/ft}$$

Design for Shear

In most cases, shear is not a factor when designing steel beams. The section selected to resist the required bending stresses is typically more than adequate to resist shear. However, shear should be checked, especially for short, heavily loaded beams or beams with heavy loads near the supports. In these cases, shear may govern the design of the beam.

Because shearing stresses are not distributed evenly over the cross section and are zero at the extreme fibers, the flanges are discounted in calculating resistance to shear; only the area of the web is used. The unit shearing stress is given by the formula

$$f_v = \frac{V}{dt_w} \qquad 19.4$$

Example 19.4

Check the shear in the beam in Ex. 19.2.

Since the total load on the beam is 54.0 kips, the maximum vertical shear at one support is one-half this, or 27.0 kips. From Table 19.3 for a W12 × 40 beam, the actual depth is 11.90 in, and the web thickness is 0.295 in. The actual unit shear stress is

$$f_v = \frac{27.0 \text{ kips}}{(11.90 \text{ in})(0.295 \text{ in})} = 7.69 \text{ ksi}$$

From Table 19.2, the allowable shear on gross sections is 20 ksi. The area of the web is (11.90 in)(0.295 in), or 3.51 in^2. The allowable shear force is

$$V = \left(20 \frac{\text{kips}}{\text{in}^2}\right)(3.51 \text{ in}^2) = 70.2 \text{ kips}$$

This allowable shear can also be found at the bottom of Table 19.5 under the row labeled V. In this case it is rounded to 70.4 kips.

Design for Deflection

Steel beams need to be checked for deflection. Although a beam may be sufficient to resist bending stresses, it may sag enough to be objectionable or create problems such as cracking of finished ceilings or ponding of water on a roof. The maximum allowable deflection is determined partly by codes and partly by design judgment. For example, the AISC limits the live load deflection of beams supporting plaster ceilings to $1/360$ of the span.

Deflection can be calculated in one of two ways: by using the deflection formulas for various static loads as given in Fig. 13.7 and in the AISC manual, or by using tables. Both methods will be illustrated here.

Example 19.5

Find the actual deflection of the W12 × 40 beam used in Ex. 19.2.

Using the formula for maximum deflection of a uniformly loaded beam as given in Fig. 13.7,

$$\Delta = \frac{5wl^4}{384EI}$$

All units must be consistent. In this example, all feet must be converted to inches. Since the load in Ex. 19.2 is 2700 plf and the weight of the beam is 40 plf, the total load is 2740 plf, or 228.3 lbf/in (2740 lfb/ft divided by 12 in/ft). The span must also be converted to inches. From Table 19.3, the moment of inertia for a W12 × 40 beam is 307 in^4. The modulus of elasticity for steel is 29,000,000 psi.

$$\Delta = \frac{(5)\left(228.3\ \frac{\text{lbf}}{\text{in}}\right)\left((20\ \text{ft})\left(12\ \frac{\text{in}}{\text{ft}}\right)\right)^4}{(384)\left(29{,}000{,}000\ \frac{\text{lbf}}{\text{in}^2}\right)\left(307\ \text{in}^4\right)}$$

$$= 1.108\ \text{in}$$

If deflection were limited to $^1/_{360}$ of the span, the maximum allowable deflection would be

$$\Delta = \frac{(20\ \text{ft})\left(12\ \frac{\text{in}}{\text{ft}}\right)}{360}$$

$$= 0.67\ \text{in}$$

The actual deflection in this example is more than the maximum, so the selected beam would be inadequate in deflection.

STEEL COLUMNS

As with columns of any material, the amount of load a steel column can support depends not only on its area and allowable unit stress, but also the unbraced length of the column. As discussed in Ch. 13, columns of moderate to long length tend to fail first by buckling under load. The properties of a column that resist buckling are the area and the moment of inertia. These are mathematically combined into a single value, the radius of gyration. For a nonsymmetrical column, the radius of gyration is different for each axis. Review the section on columns in Ch. 13 for a further explanation.

The effect of a column's unbraced length and radius of gyration is combined in the slenderness ratio, which is defined for steel columns as the ratio of a column's length in inches to the radius of gyration.

$$\text{slenderness ratio} = \frac{l}{r} \qquad 19.5$$

In general, the greater the slenderness ratio, the greater the tendency for the column to fail under buckling, and therefore the smaller the load the column can carry. Because most steel columns are not symmetrical about both axes (such as with a wide-flange shape), the least radius of gyration governs for design purposes because it is about this axis that the column will fail first. The radii of gyration, r, about both axes are given in the AISC manual, and some representative values are shown in Table 19.3.

Ideally, for the most efficient column, the radius of gyration should be the same in each direction such as with a pipe column or a square tube column. For light to moderate loads, these types of sections are often used as columns for this reason. However, they are not appropriate for heavy loads and where many beam connections must be made. Wide-flange sections are most often used because the radius of gyration in the Y-Y axis is close to the radius of gyration in the X-X axis. There are special wide-flange sections specifically manufactured to provide nearly symmetrical columns with large load-carrying capacities. Most of these are 12 in and 14 in in nominal depth.

The allowable axial compressive stress, F_a, in steel columns depends on the slenderness ratio and the allowable yield stress of steel. The exact value of the allowable stress is calculated with several rather complex equations based on the Euler equation discussed in Ch. 13. The specific equation to be used depends on the slenderness ratio of the column. Once the allowable stress is determined, the basic equation for axial loading can be used.

$$P_n = F_{cr}A \qquad 19.6$$

End Conditions

There is one additional variable that affects steel column design: the method in which the ends of the columns are fixed. Column ends can be in one of four states: They can be fixed against both rotation and translation (side-to-side movement) such as with a column embedded in concrete or with a moment-resisting connection. They can be fixed in rotation but free in translation. They can be fixed in translation but free to rotate. Finally, they can be free to both rotate and move side to side like the top of a flagpole.

How the ends are fixed affects the ability of a column to resist axial loads, so the AISC introduces a value, K, to modify the unbraced length of a column when calculating the slenderness ratio. Multiplying the K-value by the actual unbraced length gives the effective length of the column. The entire formula for slenderness ratio then becomes

$$\text{slenderness ratio} = \frac{Kl}{r} \qquad 19.7$$

Values for the various end conditions are given in Fig. 19.2. For most building conditions, the value of K is taken as 1.0.

Example 19.6

A W12 × 50 column 13 ft high is fixed at the top and bottom in both rotation and translation. What is the effective slenderness ratio?

From Table 19.3, the radius of gyration for a W12 × 50 section is 5.18 in the X-X axis and 1.96 in the Y-Y axis. Figure 19.2 gives the recommended K-value for fixed top and bottom ends as 0.65. The slenderness ratio is

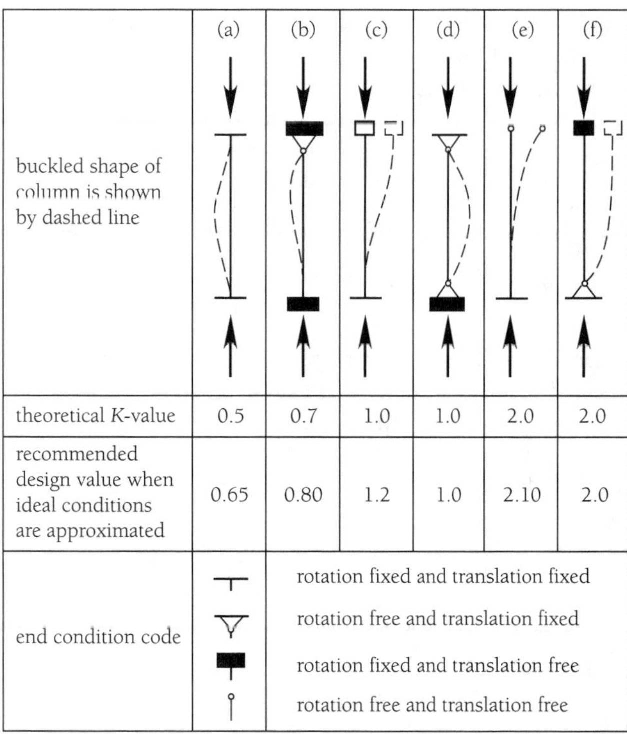

(a)
(b)
(c)
(d)
(e)
(f)
buckled shape of column is shown by dashed line
theoretical K-value
0.5
0.7
1.0
1.0
2.0
2.0
recommended design value when ideal conditions are approximated
0.65
0.80
1.2
1.0
2.10
2.0
end condition code
rotation fixed and translation fixed
rotation free and translation fixed
rotation fixed and translation free
rotation free and translation free

Figure 19.2 *K*-Values for Various End Conditions

$$\frac{Kl}{r} = \frac{(0.65)\,(13\text{ ft})\left(12\,\frac{\text{in}}{\text{ft}}\right)}{1.96\text{ in}} = 51.7$$

The length must be converted to inches and the least radius of gyration must be used.

Design for Axial Compression

As with most steel design, calculation can be done with formulas or with tables in the AISC manual. Both will be illustrated here. Even though the column formulas to determine allowable axial stress are complicated, the AISC manual has tabulated allowable stress values based on the slenderness ratio and the allowable yield stress of the steel being used. One page of these tables is shown in Table 19.6 for *Kl*/*r* values of 1 to 200. *Kl*/*r* values over 200 are not allowed.

Example 19.7

A W12 × 26 column of A992 steel has an unsupported length of 18 ft. If it is free to rotate but fixed in translation at both ends, what is the column's maximum load-carrying capacity?

From Table 19.3, a W12 × 26 section has an area of 7.65 in^2 and a least radius of gyration of 1.51 in.

The *K*-value for this type of column is 1.0, so the slenderness ratio is

$$\frac{Kl}{r} = \frac{(1.0)(18\text{ ft})\left(12\,\frac{\text{in}}{\text{ft}}\right)}{1.51\text{ in}} = 143$$

From Table 19.6, the allowable axial stress, F_a, is 7.35 ksi. Using Eq. 19.10, the maximum load is then

$$P_n = F_{cr}A = \left(7.35\,\frac{\text{kips}}{\text{in}^2}\right)(7.65\text{ in}^2)$$
$$= 56.23\text{ kips}$$

The other design method involves the use of tables of allowable column loads in the AISC manual. These give allowable axial loads in kips for various wide flange shapes, pipe columns, and square structural tubing of steel with yield values for both ASD and LRFD. Table 19.7 shows one page of the AISC tables. The loads are arranged according to effective length, *Kl*. Load values are omitted when *Kl*/*r* exceeds 200. For wide-flange sections, the values are calculated with respect to the minor axis.

Example 19.8

Select the lightest 12 in wide-flange shape of A992 steel to support a concentric axial load of 250 kips if the unbraced length is 12 ft and the *K*-value is 1.0.

In Table 19.7, find the row for *Kl* equal to 12. Look in the ASD columns for the allowable loads for various sections.

W12 × 58	401 kips
W12 × 53	364 kips
W12 × 50	294 kips
W12 × 45	264 kips
W12 × 40	234 kips

The W12 × 45 is the lightest section with an allowable load greater than 250 kips, so this is the best choice.

The same design procedures apply for columns of allowable loads for pipe and tube columns.

BUILT-UP SECTIONS

There are many times when standard rolled sections are inadequate or uneconomical to support heavy loads or exceptionally long spans. In these cases, special built-up sections can be fabricated to meet the special needs of the structure. One of the most typical is a *plate girder section*, which consists of a steel plate as a web and steel plates

Table 19.6

Available Critical Stress for Compression Members

Available Critical Stress for Compression Members

$F_y = 35$ksi			$F_y = 36$ksi			$F_y = 42$ksi			$F_y = 46$ksi			$F_y = 50$ksi		
$\frac{Kl}{r}$	F_{cr}/Ω_c ksi ASD	$\phi_c F_{cr}$ ksi LRFD	$\frac{Kl}{r}$	F_{cr}/Ω_c ksi ASD	$\phi_c F_{cr}$ ksi LRFD	$\frac{Kl}{r}$	F_{cr}/Ω_c ksi ASD	$\phi_c F_{cr}$ ksi LRFD	$\frac{Kl}{r}$	F_{cr}/Ω_c ksi ASD	$\phi_c F_{cr}$ ksi LRFD	$\frac{Kl}{r}$	F_{cr}/Ω_c ksi ASD	$\phi_c F_{cr}$ ksi LRFD
121	9.91	14.9	121	10.0	15.0	121	10.2	15.4	121	10.3	15.4	121	10.3	15.4
122	9.79	14.7	122	9.85	14.8	122	10.1	15.2	122	10.1	15.2	122	10.1	15.2
123	9.67	14.5	123	9.72	14.6	123	9.93	14.9	123	9.94	14.9	123	9.94	14.9
124	9.55	14.3	124	9.59	14.4	124	9.78	14.7	124	9.78	14.7	124	9.78	14.7
125	9.43	14.2	125	9.47	14.2	125	9.62	14.5	125	9.62	14.5	125	9.62	14.5
126	9.31	14.0	126	9.35	14.0	126	9.47	14.2	126	9.47	14.2	126	9.47	14.2
127	9.19	13.8	127	9.22	13.9	127	9.32	14.0	127	9.32	14.0	127	9.32	14.0
128	9.07	13.6	128	9.10	13.7	128	9.17	13.8	128	9.17	13.8	128	9.17	13.8
129	8.95	13.4	129	8.98	13.5	129	9.03	13.6	129	9.03	13.6	129	9.03	13.6
130	8.83	13.3	130	8.86	13.3	130	8.89	13.4	130	8.89	13.4	130	8.89	13.4
131	8.71	13.1	131	8.73	13.1	131	8.76	13.2	131	8.76	13.2	131	8.76	13.2
132	8.60	12.9	132	8.61	12.9	132	8.63	13.0	132	8.63	13.0	132	8.63	13.0
133	8.48	12.7	133	8.49	12.8	133	8.50	12.8	133	8.50	12.8	133	8.50	12.8
134	8.37	12.6	134	8.37	12.6	134	8.37	12.6	134	8.37	12.6	134	8.37	12.6
135	8.25	12.4	135	8.25	12.4	135	8.25	12.4	135	8.25	12.4	135	8.25	12.4
136	8.13	12.2	136	8.13	12.2	136	8.13	12.2	136	8.13	12.2	136	8.13	12.2
137	8.01	12.0	137	8.01	12.0	137	8.01	12.0	137	8.01	12.0	137	8.01	12.0
138	7.89	11.9	138	7.89	11.9	138	7.89	11.9	138	7.89	11.9	138	7.89	11.9
139	7.78	11.7	139	7.78	11.7	139	7.78	11.7	139	7.78	11.7	139	7.78	11.7
140	7.67	11.5	140	7.67	11.5	140	7.67	11.5	140	7.67	11.5	140	7.67	11.5
141	7.56	11.4	141	7.56	11.4	141	7.56	11.4	141	7.56	11.4	141	7.56	11.4
142	7.45	11.2	142	7.45	11.2	142	7.45	11.2	142	7.45	11.2	142	7.45	11.2
143	7.35	11.0	143	7.35	11.0	143	7.35	11.0	143	7.35	11.0	143	7.35	11.0
144	7.25	10.9	144	7.25	10.9	144	7.25	10.9	144	7.25	10.9	144	7.25	10.9
145	7.15	10.7	145	7.15	10.7	145	7.15	10.7	145	7.15	10.7	145	7.15	10.7
146	7.05	10.6	146	7.05	10.6	146	7.05	10.6	146	7.05	10.6	146	7.05	10.6
147	6.96	10.5	147	6.96	10.5	147	6.96	10.5	147	6.96	10.5	147	6.96	10.5
148	6.86	10.3	148	6.86	10.3	148	6.86	10.3	148	6.86	10.3	148	6.86	10.3
149	6.77	10.2	149	6.77	10.2	149	6.77	10.2	149	6.77	10.2	149	6.77	10.2
150	6.68	10.0	150	6.68	10.0	150	6.68	10.0	150	6.68	10.0	150	6.68	10.0
151	6.59	9.91	151	6.59	9.91	151	6.59	9.91	151	6.59	9.91	151	6.59	9.91
152	6.51	9.78	152	6.51	9.78	152	6.51	9.78	152	6.51	9.78	152	6.51	9.78
153	6.42	9.65	153	6.42	9.65	153	6.42	9.65	153	6.42	9.65	153	6.42	9.65
154	6.34	9.53	154	6.34	9.53	154	6.34	9.53	154	6.34	9.53	154	6.34	9.53
155	6.26	9.40	155	6.26	9.40	155	6.26	9.40	155	6.26	9.40	155	6.26	9.40
156	6.18	9.28	156	6.18	9.28	156	6.18	9.28	156	6.18	9.28	156	6.18	9.28
157	6.10	9.17	157	6.10	9.17	157	6.10	9.17	157	6.10	9.17	157	6.10	9.17
158	6.02	9.05	158	6.02	9.05	158	6.02	9.05	158	6.02	9.05	158	6.02	9.05
159	5.95	8.94	159	5.95	8.94	159	5.95	8.94	159	5.95	8.94	159	5.95	8.94
160	5.87	8.82	160	5.87	8.82	160	5.87	8.82	160	5.87	8.82	160	5.87	8.82

ASD	LRFD
$\Omega_c = 1.67$	$\phi_c = 0.90$

Table 19.7

Available Strength in Axial Compression

Available Strength in Axial Compression, kips

W Shapes

W12

F_y = 50 ksi

Shape	W12×									
Wt/ft	58		53		50		45		40	
Design	P_n/Ω_c	$\phi_c P_n$	P_n/Ω_c	$\phi_c P_n$	P_n/Ω_c	$\phi_c P_n$	P_n/Ω_c	$\phi_c P_n$	P_n/Ω_c	$\phi_c P_n$
	ASD	LRFD	ASD	LRFD	ASD	LRFD	ASD	LRFD	ASD	LRFD
Effective length *KL* (ft) with respect to least radius of gyration r_y										
0	510	767	466	701	437	657	393	590	350	526
6	481	722	438	659	396	595	356	534	316	475
7	470	707	429	644	382	574	343	516	305	458
8	459	689	418	628	367	551	329	495	292	439
9	446	670	406	610	350	526	314	472	279	419
10	432	649	393	590	332	499	298	448	264	397
11	417	627	379	569	314	471	281	422	249	375
12	401	603	364	547	294	443	264	396	234	351
13	385	578	349	525	275	413	246	370	218	328
14	368	553	333	501	255	384	228	343	202	304
15	350	527	317	477	236	354	211	317	186	280
16	333	500	301	452	217	326	193	291	171	257
17	315	473	284	427	198	297	176	265	156	234
18	297	446	268	402	180	270	160	241	141	212
19	279	420	251	378	162	244	144	217	127	191
20	262	393	235	353	146	220	130	196	115	172
22	227	342	204	306	121	182	108	162	94.8	142
24	195	293	174	261	102	153	90.4	136	79.6	120
26	166	249	148	222	86.6	130	77.0	116	67.9	102
28	143	215	127	192	74.6	112	66.4	99.8	58.5	88.0
30	125	187	111	167	65.0	97.7	57.9	87.0	51.0	76.6
32	109	165	97.6	147	57.1	85.9	50.9	76.4	44.8	67.3
34	97.0	146	86.5	130						
36	86.5	130	77.1	116						
38	77.6	117	69.2	104						
40	70.1	105	62.5	93.9						

Properties

	58		53		50		45		40	
P_{wo} (kips)	74.4	112	67.6	101	70.3	105	60.0	90.0	49.9	74.9
P_{wi} (kips/in.)	12.0	18.0	11.5	17.3	12.3	18.5	11.2	16.8	9.83	14.8
P_{wb} (kips)	83.2	125	73.2	110	88.5	133	65.7	98.7	44.8	67.4
P_{fb} (kips)	76.6	115	61.9	93.0	76.6	115	61.9	93.0	49.6	74.6
L_p (ft)	8.87		8.76		6.92		6.89		6.85	
L_r (ft)	29.9		28.2		23.9		22.4		21.1	
A_g (in.^{2})	17.0		15.6		14.6		13.1		11.7	
I_x (in.^{4})	475		425		391		348		307	
I_y (in.^{4})	107		95.8		56.3		50.0		44.1	
r_y (in.)	2.51		2.48		1.96		1.95		1.94	
Ratio r_x/r_y	2.10		2.11		2.64		2.64		2.64	
$P_{ex}(KL^2)/10^4$ (k-in.^{2})	13600		12200		11200		9960		8790	
$P_{ey}(KL^2)/10^4$ (k-in.^{2})	3060		2740		1610		1430		1260	

ASD	LRFD	
$\Omega_c = 1.67$	$\phi_c = 0.90$	Note: Heavy line indicates Kl/r equal to or greater than 200.

welded to it for flanges. It is similar to a wide-flange or I-section in shape but is much heavier. These can easily be fabricated deeper than the maximum 44 in deep rolled section available in the United States.

Because the web of a plate girder is thin relative to the girder's depth, it must usually be reinforced with vertical stiffeners to prevent buckling. These are usually angle sections welded to the web perpendicular to the depth of the section as shown in Fig. 19.3.

Another common built-up section is a *standard rolled section* with cover plates welded to the top and bottom flanges to provide additional cross-sectional area where the bending moment is the greatest. This combines the advantages of using a standard section with minimizing total weight of the beam. Cover plates can also be welded to columns to provide extra cross-sectional area or to equalize the radius of gyration in one axis with that of the other axis.

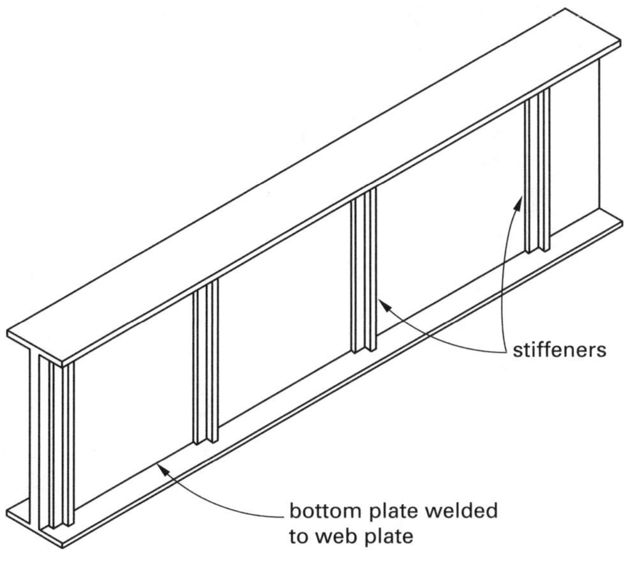

Figure 19.3 Plate Girder

OPEN-WEB STEEL JOISTS

Open-web steel joists are standardized, shop-fabricated trusses with webs that comprise linear members and with chords that are typically parallel. However, some types have top chords that are pitched for roof drainage. See Fig. 19.4.

There are three standard series of open-web joists: the *K-series*, *LH-series*, and *DLH-series*, with properties as summarized in Table 19.8. The standard depths in the K-series are multiples of 2 in, and the standard depths in the LH- and DLH-series are multiples of 4 in; LH-series joists are also available with a depth of 18 in. The standard designation for an open-web joist consists of the depth, the series designation, and the particular type of chord used. For

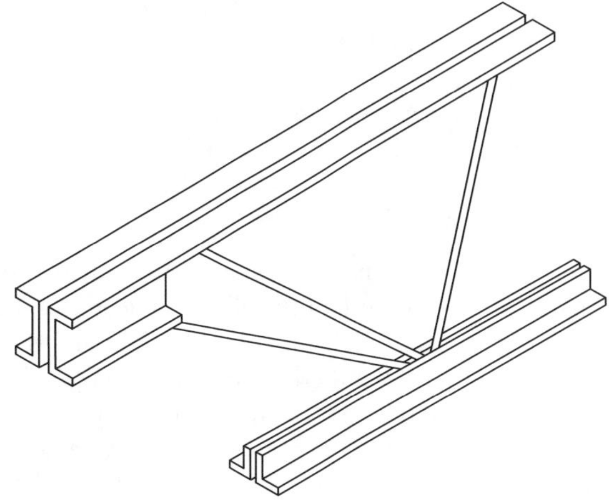

Figure 19.4 Open-Web Steel Joist

example, a 36LH13 joist is a 36 in deep joist of the LH-series with a number 13 chord type. Within any size group, the chord type number increases as the load-carrying capacity of that depth joist increases.

Open-web steel joists have many advantages for spanning medium to long distances. They are lightweight and efficient structural members, easy and quick to erect, and the open webbing allows for ductwork and other building services to be run through the joists rather than under them. In addition, a variety of floor decking types can be used, from wood systems to steel and concrete deck systems. They can easily be supported by steel beams, masonry or concrete bearing walls, or heavier open-web joist girders.

Table 19.8

Open-Web Steel Joist Series

series	name	span limits (ft)	depths in series (in)
K	standard	8 to 60	8 to 30
LH	long span	25 to 96	18 to 48
DLH	deep long span	89 to 144	52 to 72

Because open-web joists are deep and slender, they are subject to buckling and must be laterally supported both at the top and bottom chords. All the tables are based on the assumption that there is continuous lateral support at the top chord. The Steel Joist Institute gives minimum requirements for horizontal or diagonal bridging based on the span length and chord size.

Exact configurations of open-web joists vary with manufacturers, but certain standards have been established by the Steel Joist Institute, which also publishes standard load tables for design purposes. The design tables give the load-carrying capacities in pounds per linear foot of the various joist designations based on span. In the tables, two numbers are given: The top number gives the total safe uniformly distributed load-carrying capacity. The bottom number gives the live load per linear foot of joist, which will produce an approximate deflection of 1/360 of the span. Live loads that will produce a deflection of 1/240 of the span may be obtained by multiplying the bottom number by 1.5.

When using the tables, both the total load and live load must be determined so both of the allowable load numbers can be compared with actual loads. To use the tables, determine the span in feet and the live load and total load per linear foot. Look at the row of the required span in the table, and read across until a load equal to or greater than the required total load is reached. Then look at the bottom number to determine if the allowable live load is greater than the actual live load. If either of these conditions is not met, look for a heavier joist in the same depth group or use a deeper section.

A portion of the design tables for the K-series is shown in Table 19.9. For the K-series, there is also an economy table that lists the various sections in order of increasing weight, so it is easier to select the most economical section in this series.

Example 19.9

Open-web joists spaced 2 ft on center span 30 ft. They support a dead load of 50 psf including an allowance for their own weight and a live load of 60 psf. If the maximum allowable deflection due to live load is $^1/_{360}$ of the span, what is the most economical section to use?

First, the load must be converted to load per linear foot of joist. Since the joists are 2 ft on center, the dead load is (50 psf)(2 ft), or 100 plf, and the live load is (60 psf)(2 ft), or 120 plf, for a total load of 220 plf.

Looking in Table 19.9 across the row of 30 ft spans, there is an 18K4 that will support 245 lbf total load and 144 lbf live load. There is also a 20K3 that will support 227 lbf total load and 153 lbf live load. Both of these will work, but looking at the weight per foot it can be seen that the first section weighs 7.2 plf, and the second section weighs 6.7 plf. Therefore, the 20K3 is the more economical section. (There is also a 16K5 joist that will work, but it is not shown in Table 19.9.)

Table 19.9
Standard Load Table for Open-Web Steel Joists, K-Series
(based on a maximum allowable tensile stress of 50,000 psi; loads in pounds per linear foot)

Joist Designation	18K3	18K4	18K5	18K6	18K7	18K9	18K10
Depth (In.)	18	18	18	18	18	18	18
Approx. Wt. (lbs./ft.)	6.6	7.2	7.7	8.5	9.0	10.2	11.7
Span (ft.) ↓							
18	550 550	550 550	550 550	550 550	550 550	550 550	550 550
19	514 494	550 523	550 523	550 523	550 523	550 523	550 523
20	463 423	550 490	550 490	550 490	550 490	550 490	550 490
21	420 364	506 426	550 460	550 460	550 460	550 460	550 460
22	382 316	460 370	518 414	550 438	550 438	550 438	550 438
23	349 276	420 323	473 362	516 393	550 418	550 418	550 418
24	320 242	385 284	434 318	473 345	526 382	550 396	550 396
25	294 214	355 250	400 281	435 305	485 337	550 377	550 377
26	272 190	328 222	369 249	402 271	448 299	538 354	550 361
27	252 169	303 198	342 222	372 241	415 267	498 315	550 347
28	234 151	282 177	318 199	346 216	385 239	463 282	548 331
29	218 136	263 159	296 179	322 194	359 215	431 254	511 298
30	203 123	245 144	276 161	301 175	335 194	402 229	477 269
31	190 111	229 130	258 146	281 158	313 175	376 207	446 243
32	178 101	215 118	242 132	264 144	294 159	353 188	418 221
33	168 92	202 108	228 121	248 131	276 145	332 171	393 201
34	158 84	190 98	214 110	233 120	260 132	312 156	370 184
35	149 77	179 90	202 101	220 110	245 121	294 143	349 168
36	141 70	169 82	191 92	208 101	232 111	278 132	330 154

Joist Designation	20K3	20K4	20K5	20K6	20K7	20K9	20K10
Depth (In.)	20	20	20	20	20	20	20
Approx. Wt. (lbs./ft.)	6.7	7.6	8.2	8.9	9.3	10.8	12.2
Span (ft.) ↓							
20	517 517	550 550	550 550	550 550	550 550	550 550	550 550
21	468 453	550 520	550 520	550 520	550 520	550 520	550 520
22	426 393	514 461	550 490	550 490	550 490	550 490	550 490
23	389 344	469 402	529 451	550 468	550 468	550 468	550 468
24	357 302	430 353	485 396	528 430	550 448	550 448	550 448
25	329 266	396 312	446 350	486 380	541 421	550 426	550 426
26	304 236	366 277	412 310	449 337	500 373	550 405	550 405
27	281 211	339 247	382 277	416 301	463 333	550 389	550 389
28	261 189	315 221	355 248	386 269	430 298	517 353	550 375
29	243 170	293 199	330 223	360 242	401 268	482 317	550 359
30	227 153	274 179	308 201	336 218	374 242	450 286	533 336
31	212 138	256 162	289 182	314 198	350 219	421 259	499 304
32	199 126	240 147	271 165	295 179	328 199	395 235	468 276
33	187 114	226 134	254 150	277 163	309 181	371 214	440 251
34	176 105	212 122	239 137	261 149	290 165	349 195	414 229
35	166 96	200 112	226 126	246 137	274 151	329 179	390 210
36	157 88	189 103	213 115	232 125	259 139	311 164	369 193
37	148 81	179 95	202 106	220 115	245 128	294 151	349 178
38	141 74	170 87	191 98	208 106	232 118	279 139	331 164
39	133 69	161 81	181 90	198 98	220 109	265 129	314 151
40	127 64	153 75	172 84	188 91	209 101	251 119	298 140

Joist Designation	22K4	22K5	22K6	22K7	22K9	22K10	22K11
Depth (In.)	22	22	22	22	22	22	22
Approx. Wt. (lbs./ft.)	8.0	8.8	9.2	9.7	11.3	12.6	13.8
Span (ft.) ↓							
22	550 548	550 548	550 548	550 548	550 548	550 548	550 548
23	518 491	550 518	550 518	550 518	550 518	550 518	550 518
24	475 431	536 483	550 495	550 495	550 495	550 495	550 495
25	438 381	493 427	537 464	550 474	550 474	550 474	550 474
26	404 338	455 379	496 411	550 454	550 454	550 454	550 454
27	374 301	422 337	459 367	512 406	550 432	550 432	550 432
28	348 270	392 302	427 328	475 364	550 413	550 413	550 413
29	324 242	365 272	398 295	443 327	532 387	550 399	550 399
30	302 219	341 245	371 266	413 295	497 349	550 385	550 385
31	283 198	319 222	347 241	387 267	465 316	550 369	550 369
32	265 180	299 201	326 219	363 242	436 287	517 337	549 355
33	249 164	281 183	306 199	341 221	410 261	486 307	532 334
34	235 149	265 167	288 182	321 202	386 239	458 280	516 314
35	221 137	249 153	272 167	303 185	364 219	432 257	494 292
36	209 126	236 141	257 153	286 169	344 201	408 236	467 269
37	198 116	223 130	243 141	271 156	325 185	386 217	442 247
38	187 107	211 119	230 130	256 144	308 170	366 200	419 228
39	178 98	200 110	218 120	243 133	292 157	347 185	397 211
40	169 91	190 102	207 111	231 123	278 146	330 171	377 195
41	161 85	181 95	197 103	220 114	264 135	314 159	359 181
42	153 79	173 83	188 96	209 106	252 126	299 148	342 168
43	146 73	165 82	179 89	200 99	240 117	285 138	326 157
44	139 68	157 76	171 83	191 92	229 109	272 128	311 146

Reproduced with permission from Standard Specifications, Load Tables, and Weight Tables for Steel Joists and Joist Girders,

20 CONCRETE CONSTRUCTION

Nomenclature

a	height of rectangular stress block	in
A_s	area of steel reinforcing	in^2
A_v	area of web reinforcement	in^2
b	width of beam	in
b_w	width of beam web, rectangular or T-beam	in
C	resultant of compressive forces	lbf
d	effective depth of beam	in
d_b	diameter of reinforcing bar	in
D	calculated dead load	lbf/ft^2 or lbf/ft
E	earthquake or seismic load	lbf/ft^2 or lbf/ft^2
f'_c	design strength of concrete	lbf/in^2
f_y	yield strength of steel	lbf/in^2
l_d	minimum development length	in
l_n	clear span length	ft
L	calculated live load	lbf/ft^2 or lbf/ft
M_u	ultimate moment capacity	ft-lbf
s	spacing of web reinforcement	in
T	resultant of tension forces	lbf
U	factored load	lbf/ft^2 or lbf/ft
V_c	design shear strength of concrete	lbf
V_u	required shear strength	lbf
W	wind load	lbf/ft^2 or lbf/ft
α	reinforcement location factor	–
β	coating factor	–
β_c	distance from top of beam to resultant of compressive force	in
β_1	constant for finding percentage of steel	–
λ	lightweight aggregate factor	–
ρ_b	percentage of steel for balanced design	decimal
ρ_s	percentage of steel	decimal
ρ_{max}	maximum allowable percentage of steel	decimal
ρ_{min}	minimum allowable percentage of steel	decimal
ϕ	strength reduction factor	–

Structural design of concrete is more complicated than design with steel or wood because there are more variables and the choices depend on the experience and trained judgment of the designer. In modern construction, concrete is always reinforced. This results in a nonhomogeneous section with two materials of differing strengths and in structural shapes that are not symmetrical about the neutral axis. Because of these facts, concrete design is an iterative process; certain design assumptions have to be made and then tested to see if they work. If not, the assumption must be changed and new calculations made.

The strength design method is used for concrete. Although the working stress method is still allowed by some building inspection departments in some instances, it has generally been supplanted by the newer procedure. The *Building Code Requirements for Structural Concrete* (ACI 318), published by the American Concrete Institute (ACI), is based on the strength design method.

This chapter will discuss some of the basic principles of structural reinforced concrete design and show how to make some common, fairly simple design calculations.

CONCRETE MATERIALS AND PLACEMENT

Composition of Concrete

Concrete is a combination of cement, aggregates, and water mixed in the proper portions and allowed to cure to form a hard, durable material. As a construction material, it is a mixture of portland cement, sand, gravel, and water. In addition, *admixtures* are used to impart particular qualities to the mix. Since the strength of concrete depends on the materials and their proportions, it is important to understand the relationship between the constituent parts.

Cement is the binding agent in concrete. It chemically interacts with water to form a paste that binds the other aggregate particles together in a solid mass. *Portland cement* is a finely powdered material manufactured primarily from limestones and clays or shales. It is supplied in bulk or in 94 lbm bags containing one cubic foot.

Although water is required for hydration (the chemical hardening of concrete) and to make it possible to mix the concrete and place it into forms, too much water can decrease concrete's strength. This is because excess water not used in the chemical process remains in the paste and causes pores to form, which cannot resist compressive forces. Generally, for complete hydration to occur, an amount of water equal to 25% of the weight of the cement is required. An extra 10% to 15% or more is required to make a workable mix. The water itself must be potable, or drinkable, to ensure that it is free of any foreign matter that could interfere with adhesion of the aggregates to the cement paste.

For most concrete mixes, the minimum water-cement ratio is about 0.35 to 0.40 by weight. Based on the weight of water, this works out to about 4 to 4.5 gallons of water per 94 lbm sack of cement. Because of the way water and cement interact, the water-cement ratio is the most critical factor in determining the strength of concrete. For a given mix, there should be just enough water to give a workable mix without being excessive.

Aggregates consist of coarse and fine aggregates. *Fine aggregates* are those that pass through a no. 4 sieve (one with four openings per linear inch). Since cement is the most expensive component of concrete, the best mix is one that uses a combination of aggregate sizes that fill most of the volume with a minimum amount of cement while still achieving the desired strength. Typically, aggregates occupy about 70% to 75% of the total volume of the concrete.

Generally, aggregates are sand and gravel, but others are used. Materials such as expanded clays, slags, and shales are used for lightweight structural concrete. Pumice or cinders are used for insulating concretes. While standard reinforced stone concrete weighs about 150 lbm/ft^3, lightweight mixes can range from 50 lbm/ft^3 for insulating concretes to 120 lbm/ft^3 for lightweight reinforced structural concrete.

The size of *coarse aggregates* is determined by the size of the forms and the spacing between the reinforcing. In most instances, it should not be larger than three-fourths of the smallest distance between reinforcing bars, nor larger than one-fifth of the smallest dimension of forms, nor more than one-third of the depth of slabs.

Several methods are used to specify the proportions of the concrete mix. One is to define the ratio of cement to sand to gravel by weight using three numbers such as 1:2:4, which means 1 part cement, 2 parts sand, and 4 parts gravel. In addition, the amount of water must also be specified. Another method is to specify the weight of materials, including water, per 94 lbm bag of cement. Yet another method is to define the weight of the materials needed to make up one cubic yard of concrete. This is useful for large batch quantities.

The strength of the final mix is specified by the compressive strength of the concrete after it has cured and hardened for 28 days—this is known as the *design strength of concrete*. Typical specified design strengths, indicated with the symbol f'_c, are 2000 psi, 3000 psi (one of the most common), and 4000 psi. Higher strengths up to 12,000 psi are available for special applications, but these are more expensive than the standard mixes.

Admixtures

Admixtures are chemicals and other materials added to concrete to impart certain qualities. Admixtures are used to speed hydration, retard hardening, improve workability, add color, and improve durability, and for a variety of other purposes. The following are some of the more common admixtures.

Air-entraining agents form tiny dispersed bubbles in the concrete. These agents increase the concrete's workability and durability and improve its resistance to freezing and thawing cycles. They also help reduce segregation of the components during placing of the mix into forms.

Accelerators speed up the hydration of the cement so the concrete achieves strength faster. This allows for faster construction and reduces the length of time needed for protection in cold weather.

Plasticizers are used to reduce the amount of water needed while maintaining the consistency needed for correct placement and compaction. Reducing the water, of course, makes it possible to mix higher-strength concrete.

Reinforcing Steel

There are three forms of reinforcing steel: bars for standard cast-in-place concrete, wire or strands for prestressing and post-tensioning, and welded wire fabric for reinforcement of slabs. Reinforcing bars, often called *rebars*, are available in diameters from $^3/_8$ in to $2^1/_4$ in, in $^1/_8$ in increments up to $1^3/_8$ in, and then in two special large sizes of $1^3/_4$ in and $2^1/_4$ in. Bars are designated by numbers that represent the number of $^1/_8$ in increments in the nominal diameter of the bar. Thus, a no. 6 bar is $^6/_8$ in in diameter, or $^3/_4$ in. A listing of the available bars and their dimensional properties is shown in the first part of Table 20.1.

Because reinforcing steel and concrete must bond together to provide maximum strength, rebars are deformed to create a mechanical interlocking of the two materials. Additional bonding is provided by the chemical adhesion of the concrete to steel and by the normal roughness of the steel. There are several different types of deformation patterns depending on the mill that manufactures the bar, but they all serve the same purpose. So that bars can be clearly identified on the job site, standard designations have been developed for marking bars at the mill. These are shown in Fig. 20.1.

Table 20.1
Properties of Reinforcing Bars

dimensional properties of individual bars

bar no.	diameter	area (in²)	perimeter (in)	weight (lbm/ft)
3	0.375	0.11	1.18	0.376
4	0.500	0.20	1.57	0.668
5	0.625	0.31	1.96	1.043
6	0.750	0.44	2.36	1.502
7	0.875	0.60	2.75	2.044
8	1.000	0.79	3.14	2.670
9	1.128	1.00	3.54	3.400
10	1.270	1.27	3.99	4.303
11	1.410	1.56	4.43	5.313
14	1.693	2.25	5.32	7.650
18	2.257	4.00	7.09	13.600

areas of bars in reinforced concrete

spacing	bar size (in²/ft)								
(in)	3	4	5	6	7	8	9	10	11
3	0.44	0.80	1.24	1.76	2.40	3.16	4.00	5.08	6.25
$3^1/_2$	0.38	0.69	1.06	1.51	2.06	2.71	3.43	4.35	5.35
4	0.33	0.60	0.93	1.32	1.80	2.37	3.00	3.81	4.68
$4^1/_2$	0.29	0.53	0.83	1.17	1.60	2.11	2.67	3.39	4.16
5	0.26	0.48	0.74	1.06	1.44	1.90	2.40	3.05	3.74
$5^1/_2$	0.24	0.44	0.68	0.96	1.31	1.72	2.18	2.77	3.40
6	0.22	0.40	0.62	0.88	1.20	1.58	2.00	2.54	3.12
$6^1/_2$	0.20	0.37	0.57	0.81	1.11	1.46	1.85	2.34	2.88
7	0.19	0.34	0.53	0.75	1.03	1.35	1.71	2.18	2.67
$7^1/_2$	0.18	0.32	0.50	0.70	0.96	1.26	1.60	2.03	2.50
8	0.17	0.30	0.46	0.66	0.90	1.18	1.50	1.90	2.34
9	0.15	0.27	0.41	0.59	0.80	1.05	1.33	1.69	2.08
10	0.13	0.24	0.37	0.53	0.72	0.94	1.20	1.52	1.87
12	0.11	0.20	0.31	0.44	0.60	0.79	1.00	1.27	1.56

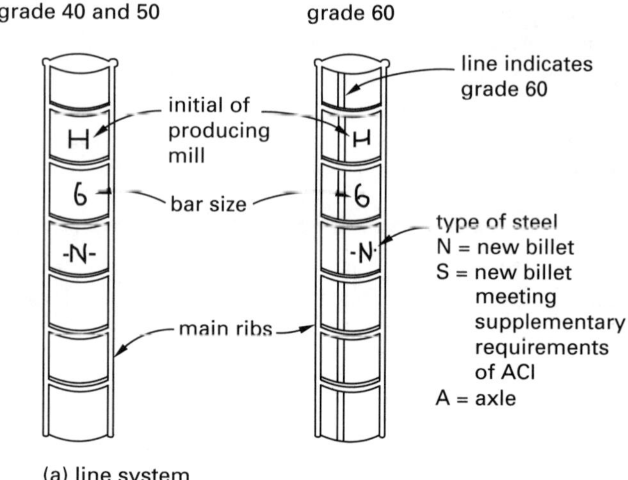

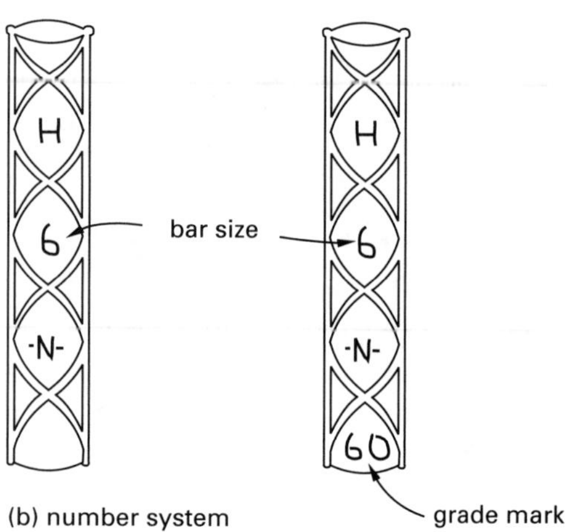

Figure 20.1 Reinforcing Bar Identification

Rebars come in two common grades: grade 40 and grade 60. Grades 50 and 75 are also sometimes available. These numbers refer to the yield strengths in kips per square inch. Grade 60 is the type most used in construction. Wire for prestressing has a much higher tensile strength—up to 250 ksi or 270 ksi.

Welded wire fabric is used for temperature reinforcement in slabs and consists of cold-drawn steel wires at right angles to each other that are welded at their intersections. The wires are usually in a square pattern with spacings of 4 in and 6 in. Designations for welded wire fabric consist of the size first and then the gage.

A new system is currently replacing the old system, but both are in use. The old system uses a designation grid size and gage. For example, 6 × 6-10/10 means the grid is 6 in by 6 in and both wires are 10 gage. The new designation for the same material is 6 × 6-W1.4 × 1.4 (152 × 152-MW9 × MW9). The first part is still the grid size, but the gage designation has been replaced with a letter, either W or D, to indicate smooth (W) or deformed (D), and a number that gives the cross-sectional wire area in hundredths of a square inch (square millimeters). The 1.4 in the example means that the area is 0.014 in^2. (The 9 in MW9 indicates 9 mm^2).

Placing and Curing

Two important parts of the entire process of concrete design and construction are getting the concrete to the forms and ensuring that it is allowed to cure properly. Transporting the material from the truck or mixer actually involves several steps. First it must be conveyed to the formwork. This is done with bottom-dump buckets, by pumping, or in small buggies or wheelbarrows.

Then the concrete must be placed in the formwork in such a way as to avoid segregation, which is the separation of the aggregates, water, and sand from each other because of their inherent dissimilarity. Dropping concrete long distances from the conveying device to the forms is one of the typical ways segregation can occur. Excessive lateral movement of the concrete in forms or slab work is another practice that should be minimized.

Finally, the concrete must be compacted to make sure the wet material has flowed around all the forms and rebars, that it has made complete contact with the steel, and to prevent *honeycombing*, which is the formation of air pockets within the concrete and next to the forms. For small jobs, hand compaction can be used. More typically, various types of vibrators are used.

Since concrete hardens and gains strength by curing through chemical reaction between the water and the cement rather than by drying, it is critical that the proper conditions of moisture and temperature be maintained for at least seven days and up to two weeks for critical work. If concrete dries out too fast, it can lose strength—up to 30% or more in some instances. With high-early-strength cements, of course, the time can be reduced. This is because concrete gains about 70% of its strength during the first week of curing, and final 28-day design strength depends on the initial curing conditions.

There are many techniques for maintaining proper moisture levels, including covering with plastic, using sealing compound, or continually sprinkling the surfaces with water.

Concrete must also be kept from freezing while curing or it will also lose strength, sometimes as much as half. Since concrete produces heat while it cures (known as *heat of hydration*), it is often sufficient to cover the fresh material with insulated plastic sheets for a few days. In very cold conditions, external heat may need to be supplied or other construction techniques employed.

Testing Concrete

Because there are so many variables in concrete construction, the material must be continually tested at various stages to maintain quality. There are three tests that the architect must be familiar with: the *slump test*, the *cylinder test*, and the *core cylinder test*.

The slump test measures the consistency of the concrete, usually at the job site. In this test, concrete is placed in a 12 in high truncated cone, 8 in at the base and 4 in at the top. It is compacted by hand with a rod, and then the mold is removed from the concrete and placed next to it. The distance the concrete slumps from the original 12 in height is then measured in inches. The amount of slump desired depends on how the concrete is going to be used, but is typically in the range of 2 in to 6 in. Too great a slump indicates excessive water in the mix, and a very small slump indicates the mixture will be too difficult to place properly.

The cylinder test measures compressive strength. As the concrete is being placed, samples are put in cylinder molds, 6 in in diameter and 12 in high, and are moist-cured for 28 days at which time they are laboratory-tested according to standardized procedures. The compressive strength in pounds per square inch is calculated and compared with the value used in the design of the structure. Almost always, cylinders are tested at seven days when their strength is about 60% to 70% of the 28-day strength.

The core cylinder test is used when a portion of the structure is in place and cured, but needs to be tested. Usually, if regular cylinder tests do not come up to the specified design strength, core cylinder tests are requested by the architect or structural engineer. A cylinder is drilled out of the concrete and then tested in the laboratory to determine its compressive strength. Drilled core cylinders are about $2^1/_2$ in in diameter, and their length varies depending on the location they are drilled from, but usually they are about 6 in long.

SAFETY FACTORS

Because of the many variables with reinforced concrete and the loads applied to concrete structures, there are two fundamental ways that safety provisions are built into ACI 318. The first is the recognition that the structure should be designed to support the loads that would cause it to fail. However, since these are not known with certainty, load factors are applied to the calculated loads to increase them to values that in all probability would never be reached, but which represent an acceptable factor of safety.

ACI 318 gives a variety of load factor formulas to account for various combinations of dead loads, live loads, wind, earthquake, earth pressure, fluids, impact, settlement, creep, shrinkage, and temperature change effects. The most basic alternate load and strength reduction factors are

- $U = 1.4D + 1.7L$ 20.1(a)
- $U = 0.75(1.4D + 1.7L) + 1.6W$ or $1.0E$ 20.1(b)
- $U = 0.9D + 1.6W$ or $1.0E$ 20.1(c)

This formula accounts for the concept that dead loads can be calculated with more accuracy than live loads, so the dead load needs to be increased less than the potential live load. Other formulas are used for other loading situations.

The second safety provision is known as the *strength reduction factor*, commonly symbolized by the Greek letter ϕ. The calculated strength of each member is reduced by multiplying it by ϕ. This factor is always less than one, but varies to reflect the limitations on how accurately strength can be calculated for different kinds of structural members, the quality control achievable with concrete, and the importance of various kinds of structural members. For example, columns are more important than beams in preventing catastrophic collapse, so ϕ generally has lower values for columns than for beams. The strength reduction factors for various types of loading are given in Table 20.2.

This combination of load factors and strength reduction factors is designed to reduce the probability of failure to about 1 in 100,000.

Table 20.2

Strength Reduction Factors

type of loading	strength reduction factor, ϕ
flexure and axial tension (tension controls)	0.90
shear and torsion	0.85
bearing on concrete	0.65
spirally reinforced columns	0.75
tied columns	0.70
flexure in plain concrete	0.65

CONCRETE BEAMS

Candidates for the ARE need to have a general understanding of the particular requirements of reinforced concrete construction and how it differs from building with other materials such as steel or timber. Since beams are one of the many common uses of concrete, they will be used to illustrate some of the unique aspects of concrete design.

Basic Concepts of Design

Concrete design is complex because of the many variables involved. Some of these variables include the strength of concrete, the strength of the reinforcing steel, the amount of reinforcing used, and the size of the member. In addition, building code conditions change depending on the type of structural member being designed, its condition of use, and the strength of the basic materials.

Because of the many combinations possible with these variables, there is usually no single structural solution to a concrete design problem. Many combinations of design elements can support the same loading conditions. In most cases, concrete design is an iterative process where the designer must make some assumptions to start the process, work through the calculations, and then check the results against code requirements and cost efficiency. If the initial assumptions yield a less than optimum result, they are modified and new calculations are made. Fortunately, design aids such as graphs, tables, and computers make the process easier than it once was.

As discussed in Ch. 13, when a load is applied to a simply supported rectangular beam there are compression forces in the top half and tension forces in the lower half. If the beam is constructed from a homogeneous material such as timber, the neutral axis is at the center of the beam where no compression or tension forces exist. These forces increase in proportion to the distance from the neutral axis until they reach their maximum value at the extreme fibers of the beam.

In a simply supported concrete beam, the same general action occurs. However, because the beam is nonhomogeneous, that is, composed of two materials, concrete and steel, the neutral axis is not at the midpoint of the beam's depth. In fact, the location of the neutral axis changes as the load on the beam is increased.

In concrete design, it is assumed that the concrete resists only compressive forces and the reinforcing steel resists only the tension forces. Because of this assumption, none of the concrete on the tension side (lower side) of the beam below the centroid of the steel is assumed to have any structural value—it only serves to protect the steel from moisture and fire. Therefore, the *effective depth of the beam*, commonly referred to as d in formulas, is the distance from the top of the beam to the centroid of the steel. See Fig. 20.2(a).

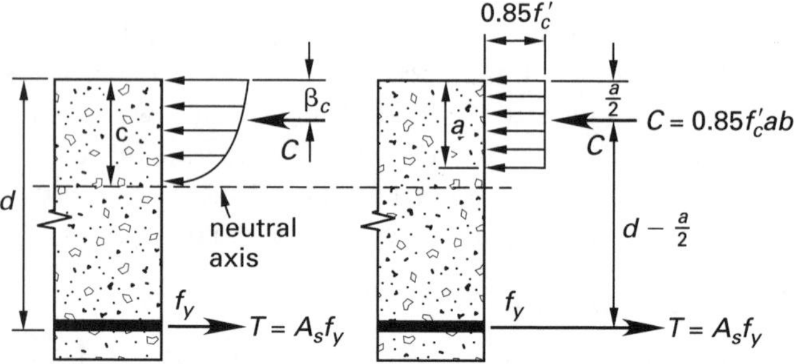

Figure 20.2 Stress Distribution in Concrete Beams

In order to resist bending moments in a beam, the internal compressive and tension forces form a couple with the resultant of the tension forces, T, at the centroid of the steel and the resultant of the compressive forces, C, at some fraction of the distance from the top of the beam to the neutral axis, β_c. See Fig. 20.2(a). The shape of the distribution of the compressive forces varies considerably, with one of the many possible shapes shown in Fig. 20.2(a). However, the stress distribution curve can be replaced with a more regular shape in which the resultant C acts in the same position.

The assumed distribution pattern that is used is called the *Whitney stress block* as shown in Fig. 20.2(b), and although its resultant still acts at a distance β_c from the top of the beam, its height is somewhat less than the distance to the neutral axis and is referred to as a, while its width is the width of the beam, or b. Through extensive testing of concrete beams it has been determined that the compressive force that a beam can resist is

$$C = 0.85f'_cab \qquad 20.2$$

The 0.85 value is a stress intensity factor that has been determined through testing to be independent of f'_c.

The tensile force, T, that a beam can resist is simply the strength of the steel, f_y, times the area of the steel, A_s.

$$T = A_sf_y \qquad 20.3$$

These two values of T and C, shown in the preceding formulas, give the forces in the steel and concrete just as the beam is about to fail. This is part of the current theoretical approach to concrete design known as the *strength method*. In order to resist the bending moment caused by a load, the values of T and C created in the beam will be equal but, of course, will act in opposite directions.

However, if a beam was designed to resist equal values of T and C, the concrete would be designed to fail (crush) at the same time the steel failed (yielded). This is what is known as balanced design. This is not desirable since concrete fails by crushing without warning, and rather explosively, resulting in immediate collapse of the member. Steel, on the other hand, fails in a concrete beam more slowly, giving advance warning with excessive cracking of the concrete on the tension side and excessive deflection. Therefore, current building codes require that the reinforcing steel should fail before the concrete crushes so building occupants have some advance warning.

In order to do this, the amount of steel needed for balanced design in a given beam to support a given load must be determined. Then, ACI 318 requires that the actual maximum amount of steel that can be used is equal to three-fourths of that. The amount of steel for balanced design is expressed in terms of percentage of the area of the concrete according to the formula

$$\rho_b = \frac{A_s}{bd} \qquad 20.4$$

The maximum amount of steel is given by the formula

$$\rho_{\text{max}} = 0.75\rho_b \qquad 20.5$$

This results in a beam that is actually under-reinforced.

The formula for finding the percentage of steel for a balanced design is given by

$$\rho_b = 0.85\beta_1 \left(\frac{f'_c}{f_y}\right)\left(\frac{87{,}000}{87{,}000 + f_y}\right) \qquad 20.6$$

β_1 is a constant that is 0.85 for concrete equal to or less than 4000 psi strength.

There are, however, limits to the minimum amount of steel. ACI 318 sets this minimum at

$$\rho_{\text{min}} = \frac{200}{f_y} \leq \frac{3\sqrt{f'_c}}{f_y} \qquad 20.7$$

Even though the steel may be designed to yield first, the actual design cannot be based on the assumption that the resisting forces, T and C, will be reached under the expected design load. Factors of safety must be included. These are the load factors and the strength reduction factor, ϕ, as discussed in the previous section. The idea is to find out what the design of the beam must be at failure under increased loads, which will likely never be reached, and at a reduced strength, which is probably less than what the designed member will actually provide.

Design for Flexure

Since the design of simple concrete members can be complex and time consuming, it is unlikely that problems will be given on the test that require detailed calculations. However, this section shows how to design a simple concrete beam to illustrate the iterative process and how the formulas are used.

For design, a few additional formulas are needed. The moment-carrying capacity of a beam is given by the formula

$$M_u = \phi A_s f_y \left(d - \frac{a}{2}\right) \qquad 20.8$$

ϕ is 0.90 for flexure.

In Eq. 20.8, a is found with the formula

$$a = \frac{A_s f_y}{0.85 f'_c b} \qquad 20.9$$

With substitutions, and using the percentage of steel instead of the area, Eq. 20.8 can be rewritten as follows.

$$M_u = \phi\rho f_y bd^2\left(1 - (0.59)\left(\frac{\rho f_y}{f'_c}\right)\right) \qquad 20.10$$

Example 20.1

Design a reinforced concrete beam to support a live load of 3.4 klf and a dead load of 1.5 klf. The beam is simply supported and 20 ft long. Concrete strength is 4000 psi, and steel strength is $f_y = 60{,}000$ psi.

Step 1. Determine the factored load from Eq. 20.1(a).

$$\begin{aligned} U &= 1.4D + 1.7L \\ &= (1.4)\left(1.5\ \frac{\text{kips}}{\text{ft}}\right) + (1.7)\left(3.4\ \frac{\text{kips}}{\text{ft}}\right) \\ &= 7.88 \text{ klf} \end{aligned}$$

Step 2. Determine the amount to be carried.

$$\begin{aligned} M_u &= \frac{wl^2}{8} \\ &= \frac{\left(7.88\ \frac{\text{kip}}{\text{ft}}\right)(20 \text{ ft})^2\left(12\ \frac{\text{in}}{\text{ft}}\right)}{8} \\ &= 4728 \text{ in-kips} \end{aligned}$$

Step 3. At this point, there are three unknowns: the beam width, beam depth, and steel area. Using the formulas previously given, assume a value for one or two unknowns and find the others. Since there are minimum and maximum guidelines for finding the percentage of steel, begin with that.

The maximum percentage allowed is $0.75\rho_b$.

From Eq 20.6, the balanced steel percentage is

$$\begin{aligned} \rho_b &= (0.85)(0.85) \\ &\quad \times \left(\frac{4000\ \frac{\text{lbf}}{\text{in}^2}}{60{,}000\ \frac{\text{lbf}}{\text{in}^2}}\right)\left(\frac{87{,}000\ \frac{\text{lbf}}{\text{in}^2}}{87{,}000\ \frac{\text{lbf}}{\text{in}^2} + 60{,}000\ \frac{\text{lbf}}{\text{in}^2}}\right) \\ &= 0.0285 \end{aligned}$$

$$\begin{aligned} \rho_{\text{max}} &= (0.75)(0.0285) \\ &= 0.0214 \end{aligned}$$

This percentage can be used to design an adequate beam but will result in a beam that is shallower than necessary since the steel is at its maximum. If there are no functional or architectural needs for a shallow beam, reducing the steel percentage and increasing the beam depth generally results in a more economical design and may reduce deflection. For economy of material, a concrete beam with a depth 2 to 3 times the width is desirable.

The minimum steel percentage is $\rho_{min} = 200/f_y$, or 0.0033. As a starting point, try a percentage of 0.0180, which is a little less than ρ_{max} calculated above.

Step 4. Find the dimensions of the beam using the assumed steel percentage and Eq. 20.10. With this formula, assume a beam width and solve for d, the effective depth. Or solve for the quantity bd^2 to more easily try different width-to-depth proportions. Reduce pounds per square inch to kips per square inch to keep units consistent.

$$M_u = \phi\rho f_y bd^2\left(1 - (0.59)\left(\frac{\rho f_y}{f'_c}\right)\right)$$

$$4728 \text{ in-kips} = (0.90)(0.0180)\left(60 \frac{\text{kips}}{\text{in}^2}\right)bd^2 \times \left(1 - (0.59)\left((0.0180)\left(\frac{60}{4}\right)\right)\right)$$

$$bd^2 = 5786 \text{ in}^3$$

Assume a 12 in wide beam. Then,

$$d = 21.96 \text{ in}$$

Round up to 22 in. With a cover below the centroid of the steel of about $2^1/_2$ in, this will give an overall beam depth of $24^1/_2$ in minimum. At this point, such a beam would seem reasonable.

Step 5. Find the actual area of steel using the minimum dimensions.

$$A_s = \rho bd = (0.0180)(12 \text{ in})(21.96 \text{ in}) = 4.74 \text{ in}^2$$

Using Table 20.1, six no. 8 bars will give exactly 4.74 in^2, or five no. 9 bars will give 5.00 in^2.

Unfortunately, this number of bars will not fit in a single layer in a 12 in wide beam. This is because of the minimum cover and spacing requirement of ACI 318, which requires a minimum of $1^1/_2$ in clear between the steel and exterior of concrete in beams and columns. It also requires a minimum clear dimension of one inch or one bar diameter (whichever is greater) between bars to allow proper placement of the concrete. For a 12 in beam (assuming no. 4 bars for shear reinforcement) the clearance requirements leave a width of only 8 in for the tension steel. This only leaves room for four no. 8 bars; an additional 3 in would be needed to accommodate six no. 8 bars. Actually, the beam would probably be made 16 in wide rather than 15 in, because widths are usually multiples of 2 in.

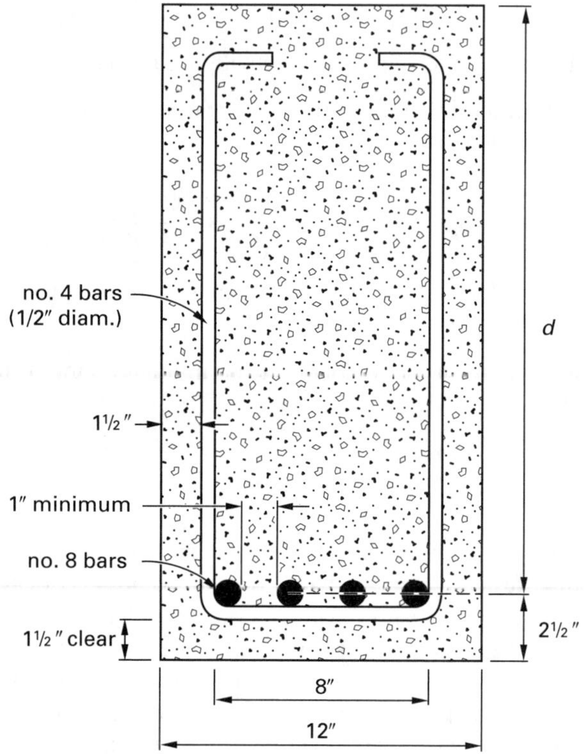

Either the beam must be increased in width, or the percentage of steel must be reduced. It would be more economical to reduce the steel percentage and increase the depth of the beam, so try a new percentage of 0.0130 and recalculate.

$$4728 \text{ in-kips} = (0.90)(0.0130)\left(60 \frac{\text{kips}}{\text{in}^2}\right)bd^2 \times \left(1 - (0.59)\left((0.0130)\left(\frac{60 \frac{\text{kips}}{\text{in}^2}}{4 \frac{\text{kips}}{\text{in}^2}}\right)\right)\right)$$

$$bd^2 = 7611 \text{ in}^3$$

Since at this point it is known that the width of the beam is important simply to accommodate the steel, try a width of 14 in this time.

$$(14 \text{ in})d^2 = 7611 \text{ in}^3$$
$$d = 23.32 \text{ in}$$

Rounding up to 23½ in and assuming a cover of 2½ gives a total beam depth of 26 in. A 14 × 26 beam seems reasonable, so use this.

Find the actual area of steel with this new size and new assumed percentage of steel.

$$A_s = (0.0130)(14 \text{ in})(23.5 \text{ in}) = 4.28 \text{ in}^2$$

This can be satisfied with four no. 10 bars ($A = 5.08$ in^2) or five no. 9 bars ($A = 5.00$ in^2). However, once again, five bars will not quite fit in a 14 in wide beam (required minimum width 14.15 in), so use four no. 10 bars in a 14 × 26 beam.

Shear

In the previous section, only stresses due to bending were discussed. However, forces caused by shear can also be significant and must be checked and provided for with additional reinforcement if the concrete itself is not capable of resisting them. It is especially important that concrete beams be adequately designed for shear, because, like compressive failure, shear collapse occurs suddenly and without warning.

Actually, what is commonly referred to as shear stress is really *diagonal tension stress* caused by the combination of shear and longitudinal flexural stress. The result is a characteristic diagonal cracking of the concrete beam in the areas of high shear forces, usually close to the beam supports as shown in Fig. 20.3.

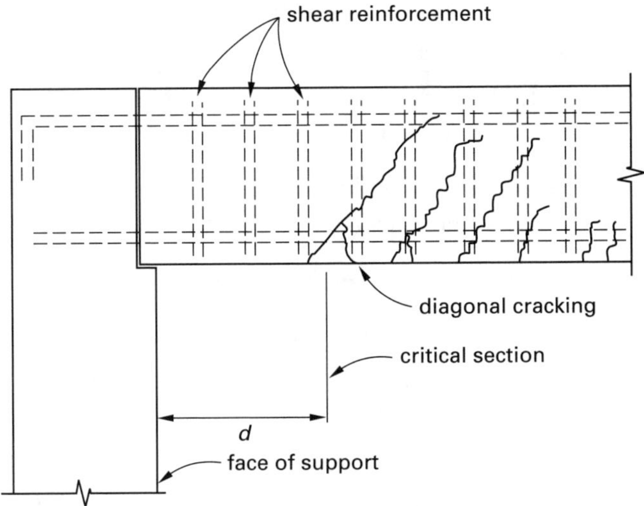

Figure 20.3 Typical Shear Cracking Pattern near End of Beam

When calculating for shear forces, the critical section is usually taken at the distance, d, from the support. This is because the reactions from the supports or from a monolithic column introduce vertical compression into the beam, which mitigates excessive shear in that area.

There are two ways shear reinforcement, correctly called *web reinforcement*, is provided for. One way is to bend up some of the tension steel near the supports at a 45° angle as shown in Fig. 20.4(a). This is possible since most of the tension steel is required in the center of the beam where the moment is the greatest. The other, more common way, is to use vertical stirrups as shown in Fig. 20.4(b). These are small diameter bars (usually no. 3, no. 4, or no. 5 bars) that form a U-shaped cage around the tension steel.

The theories behind shear and diagonal tension in beams are still not completely understood. Exact, rational-analysis formulas do not exist. The existing formulas are based on tests, experience, and some mathematical analysis, and can become quite complicated.

The following formulas are a few of the basic ones with which ARE candidates should be familiar.

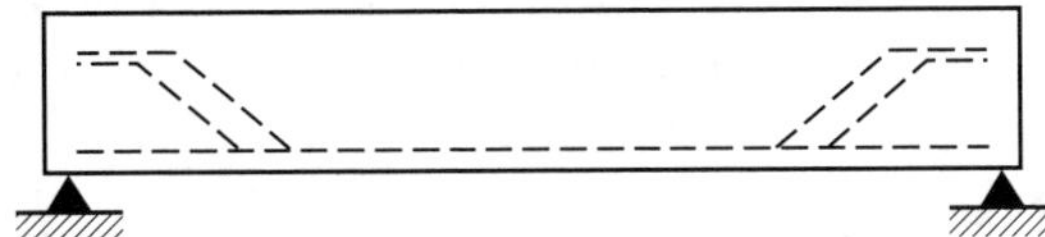

(a) inclined web reinforcement

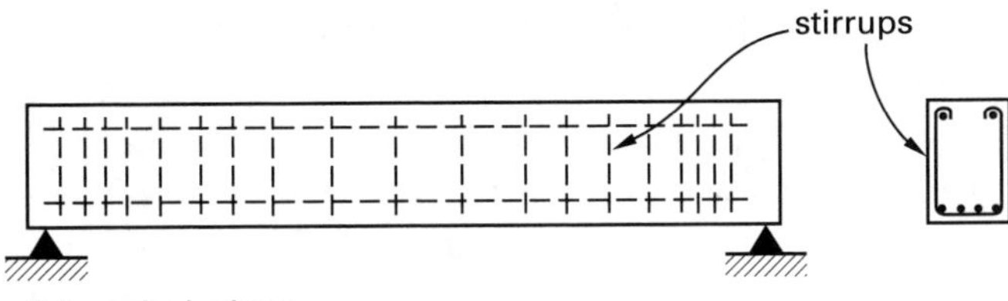

(b) vertical stirrup

Figure 20.4 Methods of Providing Web Reinforcement

$$V_c = 2\sqrt{f'_c}\, b_w d \qquad 20.11$$

The minimum area of web reinforcement required by the ACI 318 is given by the formula

$$A_v = (50)\left(\frac{b_w s}{f_y}\right) \qquad 20.12$$

This formula must be used if the required shear strength, V_u, is more than one-half of the shear capacity, which is V_c times the strength reduction factor, ϕ. For shear, ϕ is 0.85.

To design the area of steel required for vertical stirrups the following formula is used.

$$s = \frac{\phi A_v f_y d}{V_u - \phi V_c} \qquad 20.13$$

Compression Steel

In most reinforced concrete construction, reinforcement is added to the top side of a beam, compression side of a beam, or some other section. Such beams are often called *doubly reinforced beams*. There are several reasons for this. First, the concrete alone may not be able to resist the compressive forces. This is especially true if the concrete is of low strength or if the cross-sectional area is small in proportion to the applied loads. Second, compression steel reduces long-term deflections caused by concrete creep. Third, steel in the compression zone may simply be used to support stirrups before the concrete is poured. Finally, it may be included to provide for expected or unexpected negative moment in a member normally stressed with only positive moment. This can happen when an imposed load on one portion of a continuous span causes an adjacent unloaded span to bend upward.

If the member is designed for compression, the steel must be restrained to prevent its buckling outward just as with a column. Lateral ties are used for this purpose and must encircle the compression and tension steel on all four sides and be spaced for the entire length of the member. The shear reinforcement can serve part of this purpose, but instead of being U-shaped bars, it must continue across the top of the compression reinforcement to form a secure tie.

Development Length and Reinforcement Anchorage

In order for concrete reinforcement to do its job, there must be a firm bond between the two materials so that they act together to resist loads. As mentioned earlier, this is accomplished by mechanical bonding due to the deformations of the rebars and through chemical bonding between the two materials. One of the primary requirements for safety is that there is a sufficient length of steel bar from any point of stress to the end of the bar to develop the necessary bond.

The required tension development length is primarily dependent on the strength of concrete, the strength of steel, the size of bar, the amount of concrete surrounding the bar, and the amount of transverse reinforcement surround the bar. ACI 318 allows the development length to be calculated by two separate means. Both methods include the dependent factors, but one is more detailed in calculation. The first method will be presented, as it is more simply applied.

The choice of which equation to use is based on the amount of concrete clear cover on the bar, the clear spacing between bars, and whether the transverse reinforcing is at least minimum in terms of stirrups or ties. Case I may be used if either of the following conditions applies. First the clear cover is not less than the bar diameter, and the clear spacing is not less than two times the bar diameter. Second, the clear cover is not less than the bar diameter, the clear spacing is not less than the bar diameter, and the transverse reinforcing meets the minimum for ties or stirrups. Case II applies if neither of the Case I conditions are met.

The following are the tension development length equations for each case.

Case I for no. 6 bars and smaller:

$$l_d = \left(\frac{f_y\alpha\beta\lambda}{25\sqrt{f'_c}}\right)d_b \qquad 20.14$$

for no. 7 bars and larger:

$$l_d = \left(\frac{f_y\alpha\beta\lambda}{20\sqrt{f'_c}}\right)d_b \qquad 20.15$$

Case II for no. 6 bars and smaller:

$$l_d = \left(\frac{3f_y\alpha\beta\lambda}{50\sqrt{f'_c}}\right)d_b \qquad 20.16$$

for no. 7 bars and larger:

$$l_d = \left(\frac{3f_y\alpha\beta\lambda}{40\sqrt{f'_c}}\right)d_b \qquad 20.17$$

However, ACI 318 requires that the length not be less than 12 in.

The variables of α, β, and λ are used to account for bar location, coating, and lightweight concrete, respectively. The values of each are as follows.

α = reinforcement location factor
= 1.3 for horizontal reinforcement with more than 12 in of fresh concrete placed below the bar
= 1.0 for other reinforcement

β = coating factor
= 1.5 for epoxy-coated bars with clear cover $< 3d_b$ and clear spacing $< 6d_b$
= 1.2 all other epoxy-coated bars
= 1.0 for uncoated reinforcement

However, the product $\alpha\beta$ need not exceed 1.7.

λ = lightweight aggregate factor
= 1.3 for lightweight aggregate used and f_{ct} (splitting tensile strength) is not specified
= 1.0 for normal weight
= as follows if f_{ct} is specified, but not less than 1.0

$$\lambda = 6.7\left(\frac{\sqrt{f'_c}}{f_{ct}}\right) \le 1.0 \qquad 20.18$$

Deflections

Although concrete may seem to be a very stiff material and not subject to much deflection, this is not the case. This is true because the strength design method of design, and higher strength concretes and steels, both result in smaller structural members that are less stiff than in the past.

Controlling deflection in concrete structures is important to avoid cracking partitions, glass, and other building components attached to the concrete, to avoid sagging of roofs and subsequent ponding of water, and to prevent noticeable deflection of visible members.

As with other aspects of concrete design, predicting deflection is not as easy as it is with homogeneous materials such as steel and wood. Design is further complicated by the fact that concrete has two phases of deflection: *immediate deflection* caused by normal dead and live loads, and *long-term deflection* caused by shrinkage and creep. Long-term deflection may be two or more times the initial deflection.

There are formulas and procedures that give the approximate initial and long-term deflections. These deflections can then be compared with deflection limitations in ACI 318 for various types of members and conditions of deflection. These limitations are expressed in terms of fractions of the total span. See Table 20.3.

If certain conditions are met, ACI 318 gives minimum depths of members in the form of span-to-depth ratios for various conditions. These are shown in Table 20.4.

Table 20.4

Minimum Thickness of Nonprestressed Beams or One-Way Slabs Unless Deflections Are Computed

member	maximum thickness, *h*			
	simply supported	one end continuous	both ends continuous	cantilever
	members not supporting or attached to partitions or other construction likely to be damaged by large deflections			
solid one-way slabs	$\ell/20$	$\ell/24$	$\ell/28$	$\ell/10$
beams or ribbed one-way slabs	$\ell/16$	$\ell/18.5$	$\ell/21$	$\ell/8$

*Span length ℓ is in inches.

Values given shall be used directly for members with normal weight concrete (w_c = 145 pcf) and Grade 60 reinforcement. For other conditions, the values shall be modified as follows:

(a) For structural lightweight concrete having unit weights in the range 90–120 lbm/ft^3, the values shall be multiplied by $(1.65 - 0.005w_c)$ but not less than 1.09, where w_c is the unit weight in lbm/ft^3.

(b) For f_y other than 60,000 psi, the values shall be multiplied by $(0.4 + f_y/100{,}000)$.

Reprinted with permission from the ACI 318-08, by American Concrete Institute, copyright 2008.

Table 20.3

Maximum Computed Deflections

type of member	deflection to be considered	deflection limitation
flat roofs not supporting or attached to nonstructural elements likely to be damaged by large deflections	immediate deflection due to live load *L*	$\frac{\ell^{a}}{180}$
floors not supporting or attached to nonstructural elements likely to be damaged by large deflections	immediate deflection due to live load *L*	$\frac{\ell}{360}$
roof or floor construction supporting or attached to nonstructural elements likely to be damaged by large deflections	that part of the total deflection occurring after attachment of nonstructural elements (sum of the long-time deflection due to all sustained loads and the immediate deflection due to any additional live load)[c]	$\frac{\ell^{b}}{480}$
roof or floor construction supporting or attached to nonstructural elements not likely to be damaged by large deflections		$\frac{\ell^{d}}{240}$

[a]Limit not intended to safeguard against ponding. Ponding should be checked by suitable calculations of deflection, including added deflections due to ponded water, and considering long-time effects of all sustained loads, camber, construction tolerances, and reliability of provisions for drainage.
[b]Limit may be exceeded if adequate measures are taken to prevent damage to supported or attached elements.
[c]Long-time deflection shall be determined in accordance with ACI Sec. 9.5.2.5 or 9.5.4.2 but may be reduced by amount of deflection calculated to occur before attachment of nonstructural elements. This amount shall be determined on basis of accepted engineering data relating to time-deflection characteristics of members similar to those being considered.
[d]But not greater than tolerance provided for nonstructural elements. Limit may be exceeded if camber is provided so that total deflection minus camber does not exceed limit.

Reprinted with permission from the ACI 318-08, by American Concrete Institute, copyright 2008.

Continuity

Since continuity is such a typical condition in concrete construction, ARE candidates should be familiar with its basic principles. *Continuity* is an extension of a structural member over one or more supports. An example of a continuous member is placing a 30 ft steel beam over four supports, each 10 ft on center. Since concrete is typically poured in forms extending across several columns (or a slab extending over several beams), concrete structures are inherently continuous. Concrete structures are typically continuous in the vertical direction as well as in the horizontal direction.

A portion of an exaggerated concrete structure is shown in Fig. 20.5(a) with deflections due to vertical load also shown exaggerated. In the midspans of the beams, there is positive moment as discussed in Ch. 12. Over the center column support, however, the loads tend to cause the beam to bend upward with negative moment, while at the outer columns, the beam is fixed.

Continuous beams and columns are statically indeterminate, meaning that they cannot be solved with the principles or equations of equilibrium discussed in Ch. 12. A few of the typical conditions for shear, moment, and deflection for beams are shown in Fig. 13.7. Continuous beams are more efficient than simply supported beams because the maximum moment for a given load and span is less than the moment for the corresponding simple beam. This is because the loads in adjacent spans effectively counteract each other to a certain extent.

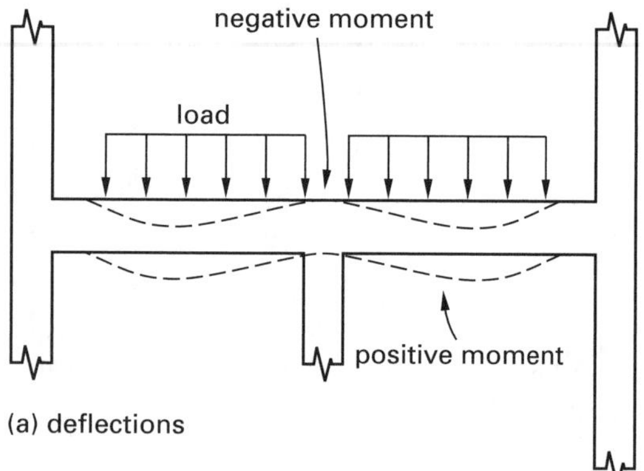

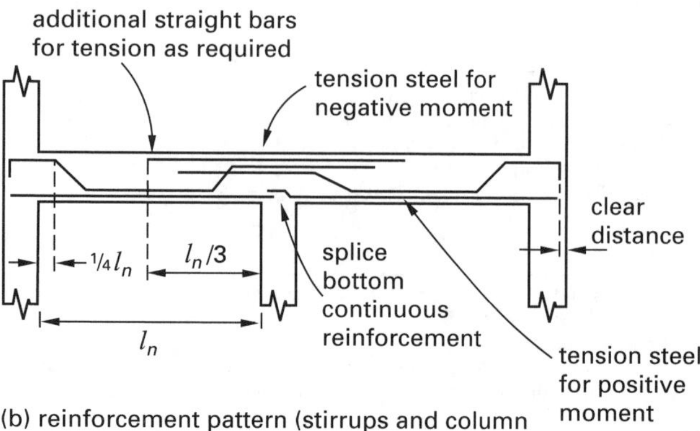

Figure 20.5 Continuity in Concrete Construction

For concrete structures, the negative moment causes the top of the beam to experience tension rather than the usual compression, so reinforcing steel must be added to counteract the forces just as in the bottom of a simply supported beam. In some cases, straight rebars are added over the supports to act as tension reinforcement. In other cases, some of the bottom tension steel is bent upward at the point of inflection to serve as negative reinforcement. See Fig. 20.5(b).

T-Beams

Since floor and roof slabs are always poured with the beams that support them, the two elements act integrally, with a portion of the slab acting as the top portion of the beam. In effect, then, what looks like a simple rectangular beam becomes a T-beam with a part of the slab resisting compressive forces. The horizontal portion is called the *flange*, and the vertical portion below the flange is called the *web* or *stem*. For an isolated T-section, the entire top flange acts in compression. However, for stems that are in the middle of slabs or edge beams, the effective flange width is smaller than what is actually available. The various conditions are shown in Fig. 20.6. ACI 318 limits the effective flange widths as shown in Fig. 20.6.

For isolated beams, the flange thickness shall not be less than one-half the width of the web, and the total flange width shall not be more than four times the web width. See Fig. 20.6(a).

For symmetrical T-beams (such as interior beams poured with the slab), the smallest of three conditions determines the effective width. This width shall not exceed one-fourth of the span of the beam, nor shall the overhanging slab width on either side of the beam web exceed eight times the thickness of the slab, nor shall it exceed one-half the clear distance to the next beam. See Fig. 20.6(b).

For edge beams, the effective overhanging slab portion shall not exceed $1/12$ the span of the beam, nor shall the overhanging slab exceed six times the thickness of the slab, nor shall it exceed one-half the clear distance to the next beam. See Fig. 20.6(c).

If the neutral axis is equal to or less than the slab thickness, the section is designed as though it were a solid beam with a width equal to the effective width of the flange. If the neutral axis is in the web, special T-beam analysis is required.

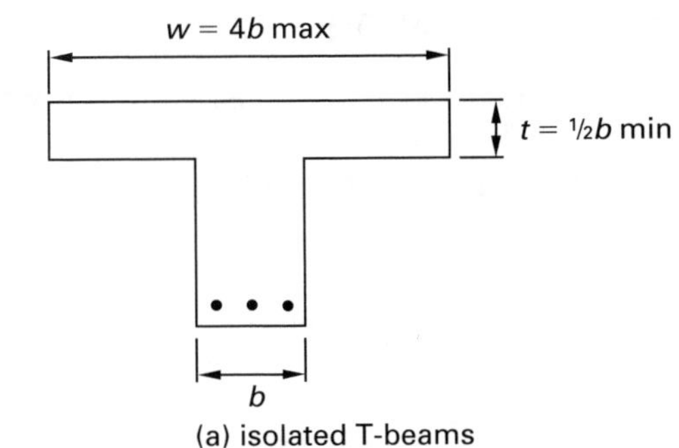

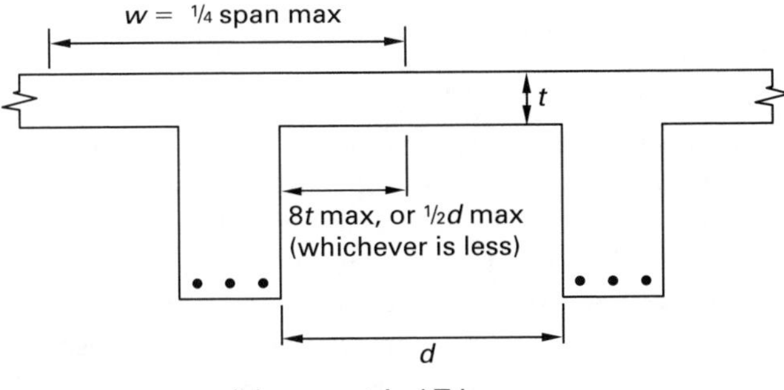

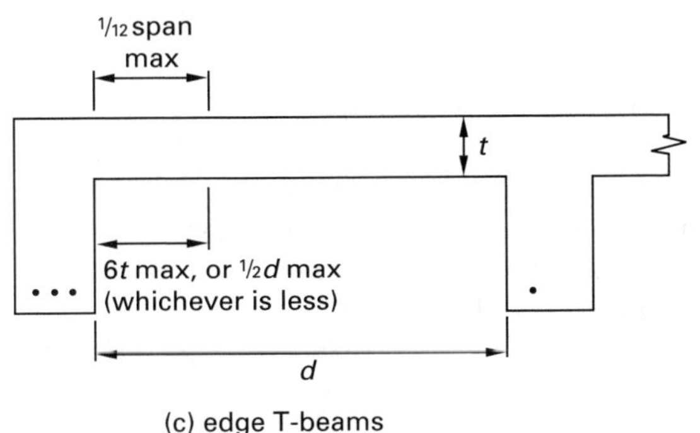

Figure 20.6 T-Beams

CONCRETE SLABS

As part of a structural system of columns and beams, slabs can either span (structurally) in one direction or two directions. The former is called a *one-way slab* and the latter is called a *two-way slab*.

In a one-way slab, reinforcement is run in one direction perpendicular to the beams supporting the slab. Two-way slabs have rebars in both directions and are more efficient because the applied loads are distributed in all directions. However, in order for two-way slabs to work as intended, the column bays supporting them should be square or nearly square. When the ratio of length to width of one slab bay approaches 2:1, the slab begins to act as a one-way slab regardless of the reinforcement or edge supports.

One-way slabs need extra reinforcement to counteract the effects of shrinkage and temperature changes. Often called *temperature steel*, the minimum amount of reinforcement is set by ACI code by percentage as tension steel is, but in no case can the rebars be placed farther apart than five times the slab thickness or more than 18 in. The minimum steel ratio, based on gross concrete area, is 0.0018 for f_y = 60 ksi or 0.0020 for f_y = 40 ksi or 50 ksi.

CONCRETE COLUMNS

Columns are the most typical of several types of concrete compressive members, including arch ribs, compressive members of trusses, and portions of rigid frames. The design of concrete compressive members is complex, especially when eccentric loading is involved or when the member supports both axial and bending stresses. This section will cover the basics of the two most typical types of concrete compressive members: *tied columns* and *spiral columns*. Composite compressive members, which consist of concrete reinforced with structural steel shapes, are sometimes used, but are not included here.

As with other types of columns, one of the primary considerations in design is the effect of buckling of the column caused by the axial load. The overall size of concrete columns usually results in length-to-width ratios of from 8 to 12, so slenderness is often not a critical consideration. However, since the steel reinforcement is very slender, it tends to fail by buckling and pushing out the concrete cover at the faces of the column. To prevent this, lateral ties are required, either as individual tied bars or a continuous spiral as discussed in the next two sections. Ties also hold the longitudinal steel in place before the concrete is poured. If columns are slender, either by design or by using higher strength concretes and reinforcement, then special calculations are required.

ACI 318 limits the percentage of longitudinal steel to from 0.01 minimum to 0.08 maximum of the gross concrete cross section. It further requires there be at least four bars for tied columns and six for spiral columns. One reason for a limited percentage of steel is that large numbers of bars create a congested column form and make proper placing of the concrete difficult.

Tied Columns

Tied columns consist of vertical steel running parallel to the length of the column near its faces, with lateral reinforcement consisting of individual rebars tied to the vertical reinforcement at regular intervals. See Fig. 20.7(a). ACI 318 requires that the lateral ties be at least no. 3 rebars for longitudinal bars up to no. 10 and at least no. 4 rebars for no. 11, no. 14, and no. 18 bars. No. 4 rebars must also be used for bundled reinforcement. Tied columns are most often used for square or rectangular shapes.

The spacing of the ties cannot exceed 16 diameters of vertical bars, 48 diameters of tie bars, or the least dimension of the column. The ties must be arranged so that every corner and alternate vertical bar has lateral support in both directions. No bar can be more than 6 in clear from such a laterally supported bar.

The strength reduction factor, ϕ, is 0.70 for tied columns.

Spiral Columns

Spiral columns have a continuous spiral of steel in lieu of individual lateral ties as shown in Fig. 20.7(b). The spiral must be at least $^3/_8$ in in diameter, and the clear spacing between turns cannot be less than 1 in or more than 3 in. The distance between the center lines of the turns is called the *pitch of the spiral*. Figure 20.7 shows a square spiral column, but they may also be round.

The strength reduction factor, ϕ, for spiral columns is 0.75, reflecting the fact that spiral columns are slightly stronger than tied columns of the same size and reinforcement. Another important difference to note is that spiral columns are more ductile, meaning that they fail in a gradual manner with the outer covering of concrete spalling before the column fails. Tied columns tend to fail suddenly without warning.

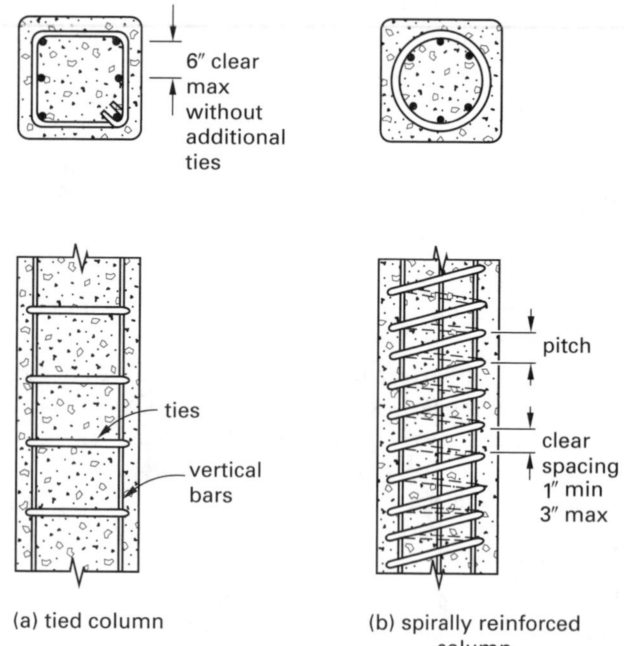

Figure 20.7 Concrete Columns

PRESTRESSED CONCRETE

Prestressed concrete consists of members that have internal stresses applied to them before they are subjected to service loads. The prestressing consists of compressive forces applied where normally the member would be in tension, which effectively eliminates or greatly reduces tensile forces that the member is not capable of carrying. In addition to making a more efficient and economical structural section, prestressing reduces cracking and deflection, increases shear strength, and allows longer spans and greater loads. Prestressing is accomplished in one of two ways: *pretensioning* or *post-tensioning*.

Precast, Pretensioned

With this system, concrete members are produced in a precasting plant. High-strength pretensioning stranded cable or wire is draped in forms according to the required stress pattern needed, and a tensile force is applied. The concrete is then poured and allowed to cure. Once cured, the cables are cut, and the resulting compressive force is transmitted to the concrete through the bond between cable and concrete.

Post-tensioned

For post-tensioning, hollow sleeves or conduit are placed in the forms on the site, and concrete is poured around them. Within the conduit is the prestressing steel, called *tendons*, which are stressed with hydraulic jacks or other means after the concrete has cured. In some cases, the space between the tendons and the conduit is grouted. The resulting stress is transferred to the concrete through end plates in the concrete member.

21 WALL CONSTRUCTION

Nomenclature

A_g	gross area of concrete wall	in^2
A_s	area of reinforcing	in^2
f'_c	specified compressive strength of concrete	lbf/in^2
f'_m	compressive strength of masonry at 28 days	lbf/in^2
F_a	allowable average axial compressive stress for centroidally applied axial load	lbf/in^2
h	height of wall	in
h'	effective wall height (kh)	in
k	effective length factor	
l_c	vertical distance between supports	in
P_n	nominal axial load strength	lbf
r	radius of gyration	in
t	effective thickness of wythe or wall	in
ϕ	strength reduction factor (0.70 for concrete bearing walls)	–

The two primary classifications of walls are *load-bearing* and *non-load-bearing*. Load-bearing walls support their own weight in addition to vertical and lateral loads. They can be further classified into *vertical load-bearing walls*, *shear walls*, and *retaining walls*. Vertical load-bearing walls support the weight of other walls above, in addition to floor and roof loads. Shear walls are structural walls that resist lateral loads acting in the plane of the wall. Retaining walls, as discussed in Ch. 15, are structural walls that resist the movement of soil.

Non-load-bearing walls support only their own weight and are used to enclose a building or to divide space within a building. When used for a building enclosure, they do serve to transfer wind forces to the primary structural frame. A non-load-bearing exterior wall is called a *curtain wall*.

Although the primary focus of this chapter is the structural design of walls, there are other considerations in selecting the optimum wall for a particular circumstance. In addition to load-carrying ability, a wall must provide for openings, keep out the weather, be cost effective, satisfy the aesthetic requirement of the job, resist heat loss and gain, and be easy to maintain. The architect must exercise judgment in selecting the wall system to best satisfy all the requirements of a project.

MASONRY WALLS

There are many varieties of masonry walls, both non-load-bearing and load-bearing, consisting of single or multiple wythes, either reinforced or unreinforced. A *wythe* is a continuous vertical section of a wall one masonry unit in thickness. For structural purposes, the two primary masonry materials are brick and concrete block.

Masonry walls can be engineered or designed by empirical requirements given in building codes and generally accepted rules of thumb. The model codes differ in some areas concerning requirements for masonry walls; the ones given here are based on the *International Building Code* (IBC). Requirements also vary depending on which seismic zone the building is in. Structures in zones subject to more frequent and severe earthquakes, of course, require additional reinforcement, and there are limitations on the types of mortar and masonry units that can be used.

The specified compressive stress in masonry walls depends on the strength of the masonry unit as well as the strength of the mortar. Because the quality of a masonry wall is highly dependent on the workmanship, the formulas for allowable stress given by the building code assume that special inspection will be made during the construction of the wall. If this inspection is not made, the allowable stresses must be reduced by one-half.

The compressive strength of a masonry wall, f'_m, can be based on tests of actual wall samples; on field experience based on similar mortar, masonry, and construction combinations; or on assumed values given in the IBC. Tables 21.1(a) and (b) give the assumed designed strength of clay and concrete masonry, respectively, for three mortar types.

The allowable axial compressive stress for reinforced and unreinforced walls is determined by the following formula.

$$F_a = 0.25f'_m\left(1 - \left(\frac{h'}{140r}\right)^2\right) \quad \left[\text{where } \frac{h'}{r} \leq 99\right] \qquad 21.1$$

$$F_a = 0.25f'_m\left(\frac{70r}{h'}\right) \quad \left[\text{where } \frac{h'}{r} > 99\right] \qquad 21.2$$

As indicated in this formula, the allowable stress is determined not only by the masonry strength but also by the slenderness ratio of the wall, just as with column design. There are five basic types of masonry walls: veneered, single-wythe, reinforced hollow unit masonry, cavity, and reinforced grouted masonry. These are illustrated in Fig. 21.1.

A *veneered wall* is a non-load-bearing wall having a facing of a single wythe of masonry, usually brick, anchored to a backing. The masonry is primarily for decorative and weatherproofing purposes such as a brick veneer wall over a wood stud backing wall.

Single-Wythe Walls

A *single wythe* consists of a single unit of unreinforced masonry that can act as either a bearing or nonloadbearing wall. Since it is unreinforced vertically, there are limits to the amount of load that can bear on this type of wall, and building codes limit the maximum ratio of unsupported height or length to thickness. For solid masonry walls or bearing partitions designed according to the IBC, the ratio cannot exceed 20. For hollow masonry or cavity walls, the ratio cannot exceed 18.

Example 21.1

What is the maximum unsupported height for a solid brick wall 8 in thick?

The nominal thickness, t, of the wall is used in the calculation, so the maximum height is (8 in)(20), or 160 in, or 13 ft 4 in.

Even though single-wythe walls are not reinforced vertically, they must have a minimum amount of horizontal reinforcement, just as multi-wythe walls must. The most commonly used reinforcements are prefabricated assemblies consisting of minimum nine-gage steel laid every 16 in. See Fig. 21.2.

Reinforced Hollow Unit Masonry

This type of wall construction consists of a single wythe of concrete block with vertical reinforcing rods placed in the cells of the block, which are filled with grout. See Fig. 21.1(c). Grout may be placed in every cell or just in those cells containing the reinforcing. Since concrete block is

Table 21.1(a)

Compressive Strength of Clay Masonry

net area compressive strength of clay masonry units (psi)		net area compressive strength of masonry (psi)
Type M or S mortar	Type N mortar	
1700	2100	1000
3350	4150	1500
4950	6200	2000
6600	8250	2500
8250	10,300	3000
9900	–	3500
13,200	–	4000

For SI: 1 psi = 0.00689 MPa.

Table 21.1(b)

Compressive Strength of Concrete Masonry

net area compressive strength of concrete masonry units (psi)		net area compressive strength of masonry (psi)[a]
Type M or S mortar	Type N mortar	
1250	1300	1000
1900	2150	1500
2800	3050	2000
3750	4050	2500
4800	5250	3000

For SI: 1 in = 25.4 mm, 1 psi 5 0.00689 MPa.

[a]For units less than 4 in in height, 85% of the values listed.

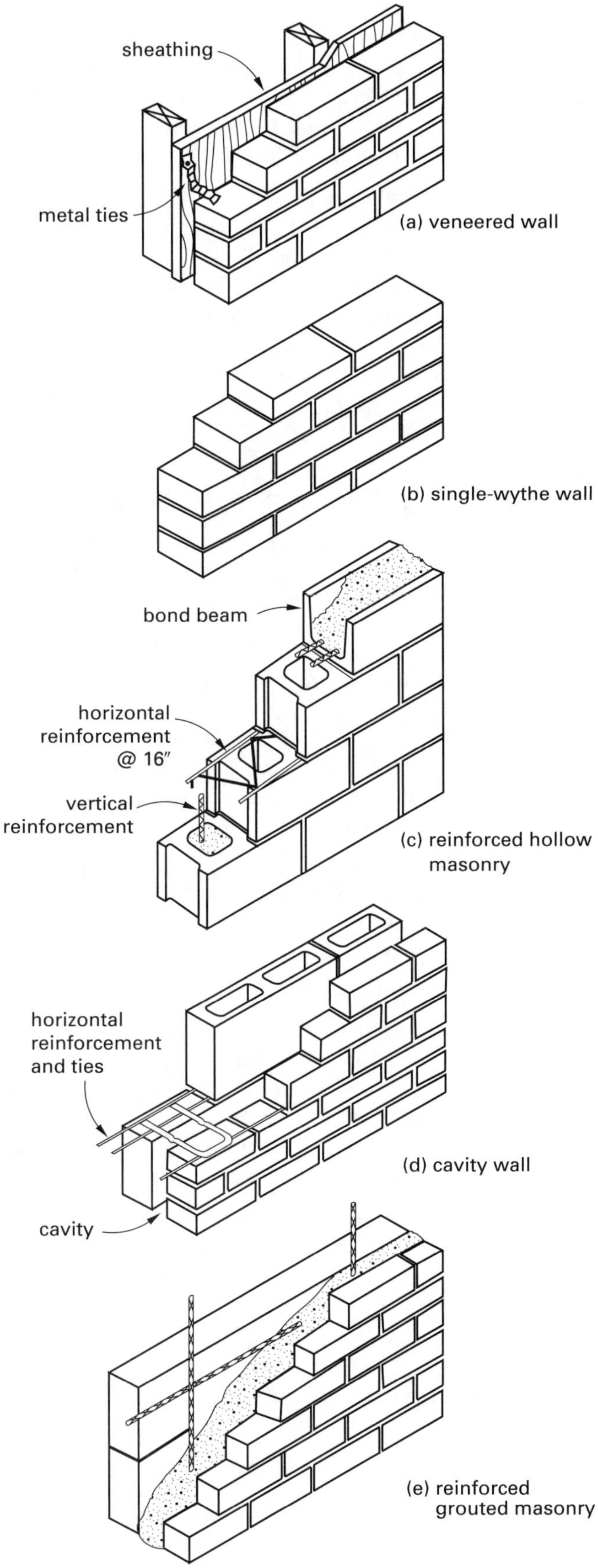

Figure 21.1 Masonry Wall Types

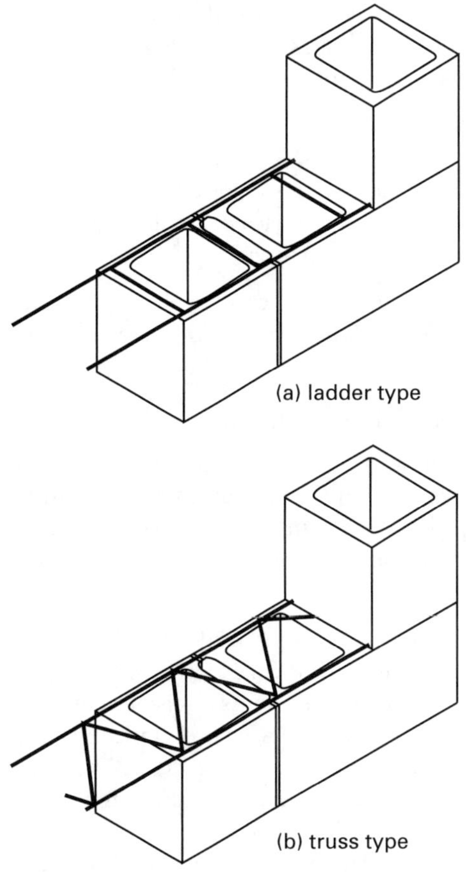

Figure 21.2 Horizontal Joint Reinforcement

based on an 8 in module, the spacing of the vertical reinforcing bars is a multiple of 8 in.

Horizontal reinforcement is provided by prefabricated units as shown in Fig. 21.2. When additional horizontal reinforcement is needed over openings or at the top of the wall, a U-shaped block, called a *bond beam*, is used with rebar placed in the bottom and filled with grout. The minimum nominal thickness of a reinforced masonry bearing wall is 6 in.

Cavity Walls

Cavity walls consist of two wythes of masonry, separated by an air space normally 2 in wide. See Fig. 21.1(d). Cavity walls have the advantages of providing extra protection against water penetration and additional insulation value because of the air. The cavity is often filled with insulation to enhance the insulation value of the wall. Both wythes may be of the same masonry type, or they may be mixed. A common type of cavity wall is a backing of 4 in or 8 in concrete block with an exterior wythe of brick.

The wythes of a cavity wall must be tied together with a corrosion-resistant metal tie at least $^3/_{16}$ in in diameter for every $4^{1}/_{2}$ ft^2 of wall area, or with other approved horizontal joint reinforcement as shown in Fig. 21.2. Metal ties are normally spaced every 16 in vertically.

Example 21.2

What is the maximum unsupported height for a cavity wall consisting of a 4 in brick facing and an 8 in concrete block wall separated by a 1 in space?

In computing the ratio for cavity walls, the thickness is the sum of the nominal thicknesses of the wythes. The maximum height is (4 in + 8 in)(18), or 216 in, or 18 ft.

Reinforced Grouted Masonry

Reinforced grouted masonry is used where additional load-carrying capacity is required, for lateral loads such as wind or earthquake. Reinforcing bars are installed in the cavity of the wall, and then the cavity is filled with grout. See Fig. 21.1(e).

Reinforcement is usually installed both vertically and horizontally, especially in seismic design categories E and F where it is required. For these seismic zones, the code requires that the sum of the areas of horizontal and vertical reinforcement be at least 0.002 times the gross cross-sectional area of the wall, and that the minimum area of reinforcement in either direction be at least 0.0007 times the gross cross-sectional area of the wall. The spacing of the reinforcement cannot exceed 4 ft and must have at least a $^{3}/_{8}$ in diameter.

Example 21.3

What reinforcing should be provided for a masonry cavity wall consisting of an 8 in concrete block backup wythe separated by a 2 in space from a 4 in brick facing wythe?

The IBC defines the gross cross-sectional area as that encompassed by the outer periphery of any section, so the actual width of the above wall assembly is the sum of the actual width of the block ($7^{5}/_{8}$ in) plus the cavity plus the actual width of the brick ($3^{5}/_{8}$ in), or a total of 13.25 in.

The required horizontal and vertical reinforcing per foot of height or length is

$$\begin{aligned} A_s &= (0.0007)(13.25 \text{ in})\left(12 \frac{\text{in}}{\text{ft}}\right) \\ &= 0.1113 \text{ in}^2/\text{ft} \end{aligned}$$

The minimum sum of vertical and horizontal reinforcing is

$$\begin{aligned} A_s &= (0.002)(13.25 \text{ in})\left(12 \frac{\text{in}}{\text{ft}}\right) \\ &= 0.318 \text{ in}^2/\text{ft} \end{aligned}$$

When deciding on the size and spacing of the reinforcing bars, use standard bar sizes while minimizing the amount of steel used (and therefore the cost) and the number of bars placed (more bars placed generally increases the labor cost). The area of rebars is given in Table 20.1 in Ch. 20.

Decide on horizontal reinforcing first. 0.1113 in^2/ft means a minimum steel area of (0.1113 in^2/ft)(4), or 0.445 in^2 per 4 ft (48 in) of height. One option is to use a no. 7 bar every 4 ft (area = 0.60 in^2), but this size bar would be heavy and awkward to place and make it difficult to grout the cavity. Try a spacing of 16 in instead, or three bars per 4 ft of height. The steel area needed is

$$\frac{0.45 \text{ in}^2}{3} = 0.15 \text{ in}^2$$

A no. 4 bar (A = 0.20 in^2) spaced every 16 in would work.

Next, determine the size and spacing of vertical reinforcement. The total area required per 4 ft length is (0.318 in^2/ft)(4 ft), less the actual area of the horizontal reinforcement.

$$\left(0.318 \frac{\text{in}^2}{\text{ft}}\right)(4 \text{ ft}) - (0.20 \text{ in}^2)(3) = 0.672 \text{ in}^2$$

Once again, try a spacing of 16 in. Each bar would need a minimum area of 0.672 in^2/3, or 0.224 in^2. A no. 4 bar spaced every 16 in will not work, but a no. 5 bar spaced every 16 in would be satisfactory.

The grout used for reinforced masonry walls is a mixture of portland cement, hydrated lime, and aggregate. It may either be fine grout or course grout. Course grout has a higher percentage of larger aggregates.

A wall may be grouted in one of two ways. The first is called *low-lift grouting*, which is accomplished by laying up no more than 8 in of masonry and then placing the grout. The second method is *high-lift grouting*. A larger portion of the wall, no more than 6 ft in height, is laid up and the reinforcing placed. Grout is then pumped into the cavity and mechanically vibrated to ensure that all voids are filled.

The building code specifies the minimum clear dimensions of the cavity less the width of horizontal reinforcing based on the height of the grout pour and whether fine or course grout is used. For low-lift grouting with fine grout, the minimum grout space is $^{3}/_{4}$ in plus the width of the reinforcing. For coarse grout, it is $1^{1}/_{2}$ in. Mortar projections must be kept to a minimum of $^{1}/_{2}$ in, and the cavity space must be kept clear of loose mortar and other foreign material.

Openings

Regardless of the type of lintel used to span an opening, there is always arch action over an opening, provided the masonry has a running bond. This is shown diagrammatically in

Fig. 21.3. Unless a concentrated load or a floor load is near the top of the opening, the lintel only carries the weight of the wall above the opening in a triangular area defined by a 45° angle from each side of the opening. If a floor line is within a distance equal to the top of this imaginary triangle, the lintel carries the weight of the wall and the weight of the floor load as wide as the opening.

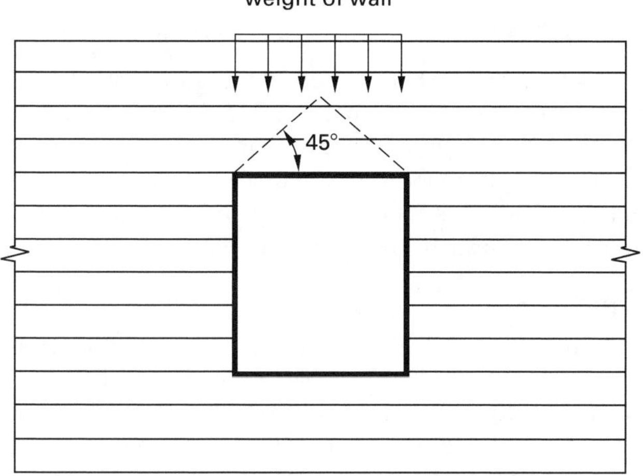

Figure 21.3 Arch Action in a Masonry Wall over an Opening

Openings in masonry walls may be spanned with masonry arches, steel lintels, precast reinforced concrete lintels, or precast masonry lintels reinforced with rebars and filled with grout. See Fig. 21.4.

Steel lintels are often used because they are inexpensive and simple to install and the size and thickness can be varied to suit the span of the opening. Lintels should bear on each end of the supporting masonry such that the bearing capacity is not exceeded, but in no case should the bearing length be less than 6 in.

STUD WALLS

Stud wall systems are one of the most common types of structural systems for residential and light commercial buildings. Stud walls are relatively small members, closely spaced and tied together with exterior and interior sheathing. The sheathing is necessary to brace the small members against buckling and to resist lateral loads.

Stud wall systems have many advantages. They are easy to erect by a small construction crew, relatively inexpensive, and lightweight; their materials are readily available; they are adaptable to a variety of designs; and the space between the studs can be used for insulation and electrical service.

Stud wall systems allow for many types of exterior finish materials such as wood or aluminum siding, stucco, and brick veneer.

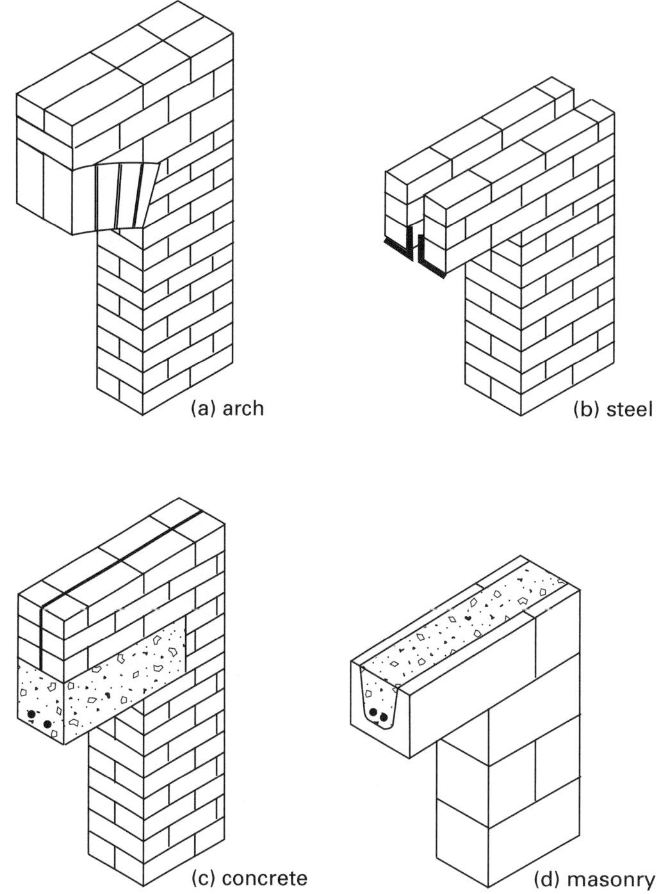

Figure 21.4 Masonry Lintels

Wood Studs

Wood studs are the most common type of material used for stud wall systems. They are typically 2 × 4 members spaced 16 in or 24 in on center, covered with plywood or particle board sheathing on the exterior and gypsum board on the interior. 2 × 4 and 2 × 6 studs can be used for bearing walls up to 10 ft high. If the studs support one floor, roof, and ceiling, the maximum spacing is 16 in for 2 × 4s and 24 in for 2 × 6s.

The most common type of wood stud construction is *platform framing* as illustrated in Fig. 21.5. With this method, wood studs one story high are placed on a sole plate at the bottom and spanned with a double top plate at the ceiling level. The second floor joists bear on the top plate and, when the second floor sheathing is in place, serve as a platform on which to erect the second-story stud walls.

The other method of stud construction is *balloon framing*, in which the studs run the full height from the first floor to the top of the second floor. The second-floor joists bear on a continuous 1 × 4 ribbon let into the studs, and are also

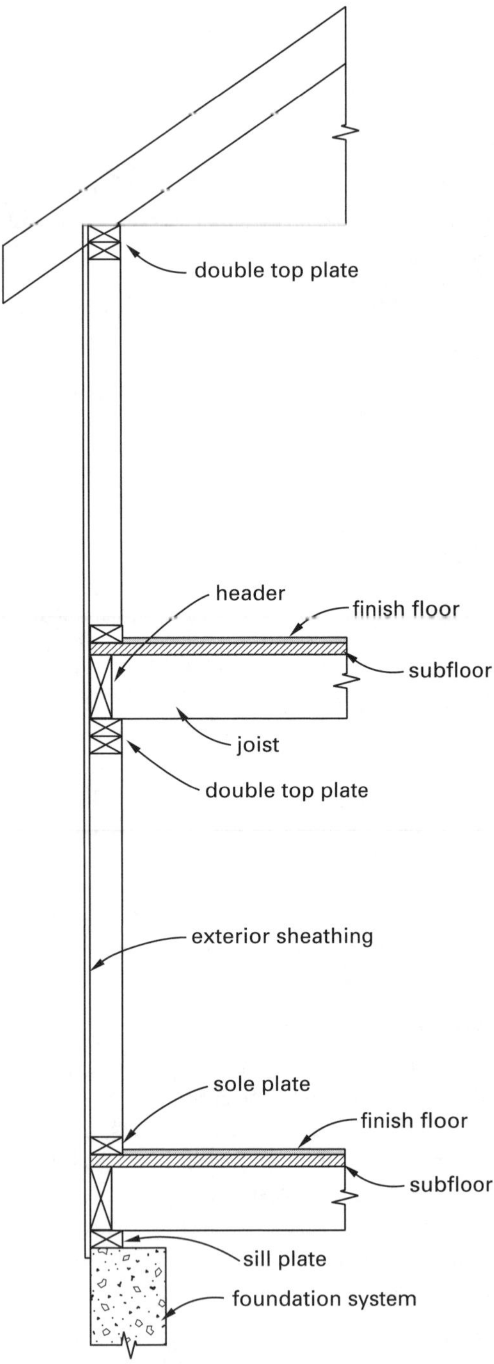

Figure 21.5 Platform Construction

nailed into the sides of the studs. This method of construction is seldom used, although its advantage is that it minimizes the overall shrinkage of the vertical dimension of the wall because the majority of the lumber is oriented parallel to the grain of the wood.

Metal Studs

Metal stud systems are similar in concept to wood stud systems except that light-gage C-shaped metal members are used instead of wood. Standard sizes of exterior metal studs are $3^1/_2$, $3^5/_8$, 4, and 6 in in depth, in thicknesses of 14, 16, and 18 gage. Deeper studs are also available. Metal studs are usually placed 24 in on center rather than 16 in. If the entire building is being framed in light-gage metal, floor joists and rafters are constructed of steel members as well.

Metal stud wall systems may be used with other structural framing systems. For example, a building may have a steel or concrete primary structural frame with light-gage steel studs used for nonbearing exterior and interior walls. The exterior stud walls are then faced with brick, siding, tile, or some other weatherproof finish material.

Openings

Openings in stud walls are framed in the same material as the stud wall itself. Openings in wood stud walls are spanned with headers consisting of nominal 2 in thick lumber placed on edge as shown in Fig. 21.6. The width of the header depends on the width of the opening. Double 2 × 4s can be used on openings up to 3 ft, 2 × 6s can be used on openings up to 4 ft, and 2 × 8s can be used on openings up to 5 ft.

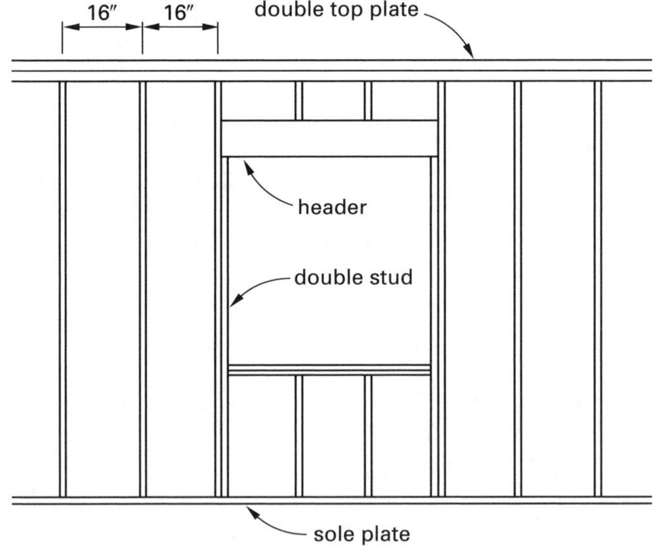

Figure 21.6 Typical Wood Stud Wall Framing

The headers are supported by short studs that are doubled next to the full-height studs and next to the space above and below the opening framed with cripple studs. Openings in metal stud walls are framed in a similar manner.

CONCRETE WALLS

Concrete walls are ideal where high strength, durability, and fire resistance are required. Although concrete walls can be designed just as bearing walls, they usually also act as shear walls and sometimes as deep beams spanning between footings. Having them serve more than one function makes more efficient use of the material and labor required for their construction.

Building codes and the American Concrete Institute detail the many requirements that concrete bearing walls must meet, and like other aspects of concrete construction, they are quite complicated and depend on iterative design processes. However, the following guidelines are a useful summary.

Cast-in-Place

When certain conditions are met, the IBC allows an empirical design method to be used. With this method, the design axial load strength can be computed with the formula

$$\phi P_n = 0.55\phi f_c' A_g\left(1 - \left(\frac{kl_c}{32t}\right)^2\right) \qquad 21.3$$

The effective length factor, k, is taken as 0.8 for walls restrained against rotation at the top or bottom or both, and as 1.0 for walls unrestrained against rotation at both ends. The strength reduction factor, ϕ, is taken as 0.7 for walls in compression. Additional loads such as seismic and wind loading may require extra reinforcing.

The conditions that must be met in order to use Eq. 21.3 include the following.

- Walls must be anchored to intersecting elements such as floors, roofs, columns, and intersecting walls and footings.
- The minimum ratio of vertical reinforcement area to gross concrete area must be 0.0012 for deformed bars not larger than no. 5 with a yield strength of not less than 60 ksi. For other bars, the ratio is 0.0015.
- The minimum ratio of horizontal reinforcement area to gross concrete area must be 0.0020 for deformed bars not larger than no. 5 with a yield strength of not less than 60 ksi. For other bars, the ratio is 0.0025.
- Walls more than 10 in thick, except basement walls, must have the reinforcement placed in two layers with the layer next to the exterior face containing not less than one-half and not more than two-thirds of the total reinforcement required.
- Reinforcement cannot be spaced farther apart than three times the wall thickness, or 18 in.
- Not less than two no. 5 bars must be provided around all window and door openings, and these must be extended past the corners of the openings not less than 24 in.
- The minimum thickness of bearing walls cannot be less than $^1/_{25}$ of the unsupported height or length, whichever is shorter, nor less than 4 in.
- The resultant of the loads must fall within the middle one-third of the wall thickness to avoid eccentricity.

Precast Concrete Walls

Precast bearing walls are required to be designed in the same way as cast-in-place walls, including the effects of temperature and shrinkage. Often, extra reinforcing is needed simply to protect the integrity of the panels against the stresses of transportation and erection.

Precast walls are an economical way to enclose a building and provide for bearing if there is sufficient repetition in the panel sizes and configurations to make mass production possible. Rather than serving as a bearing member, precast walls are often nonbearing and attached to a structural framework of steel or precast concrete.

Precast bearing walls are most often connected by field welding steel plates that have been cast into the panel at the precasting plant. Figure 21.7 illustrates some of the typical connections used.

BUILDING ENVELOPE

The design of the walls that enclose a building is one of the most difficult detailing problems in building construction because not only does the exterior wall have to be structurally sound, but it must also accommodate various kinds of movement that occur in all structures. In addition, connections between the cladding and the structure must be designed to allow for on-site adjustments during erection, so the final wall will be within proper tolerances. These requirements exist whether the exterior wall is bearing or nonbearing. However, this section will only discuss the attachment of nonbearing exterior cladding to the primary structural frame.

Attachment to Structural Members

Exterior cladding and its attachment to the primary structural frame must resist three basic types of loads: the *dead load* of the wall system itself, *horizontal wind loads*, and *seismic loads*.

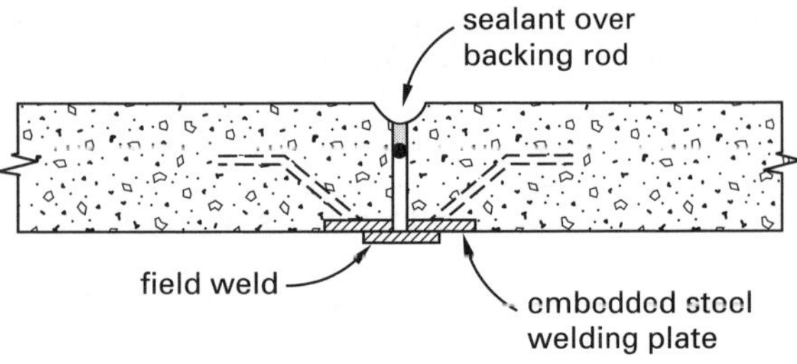

(a) wall panel connection

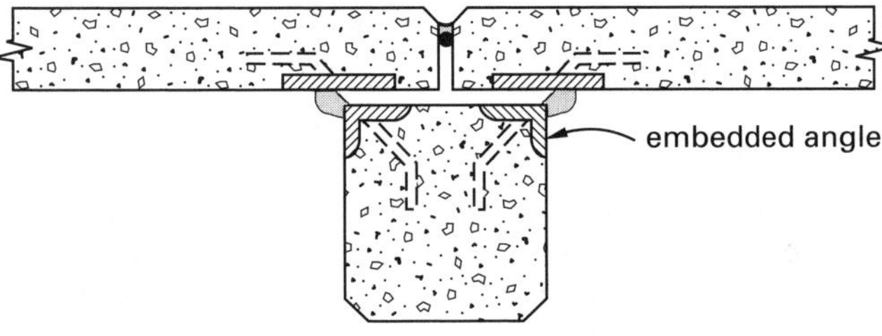

(b) connection to column

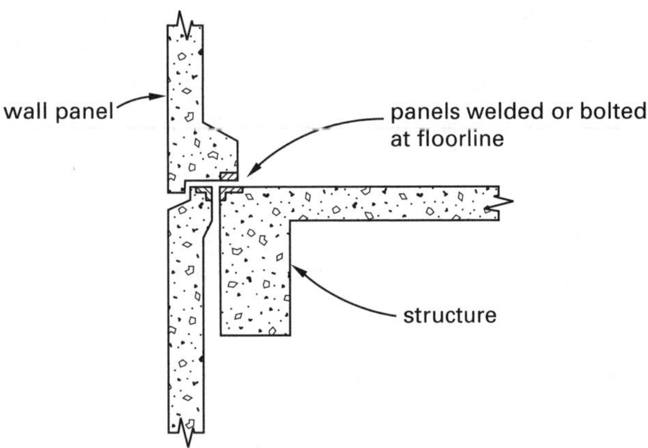

(c) exterior nonbearing walls

Figure 21.7 Precast Concrete Wall Panel Connections

The method of providing dead load support depends on the material used and the structural frame. For example, heavy materials, such as brick and concrete block used in one- or two-story buildings, usually rest directly on the foundation. In taller buildings, the load must be carried at intermediate floor levels because the strength of a panel or portion of a wall is not sufficient to carry any weight beyond its own dead load.

Figure 21.8 illustrates a typical method of supporting masonry in a multistory building. In this case, the weight of the masonry is carried on a continuous steel angle bolted to the structural frame. Horizontal ties provide for attachment of the exterior wall to the frame and help in the transfer of

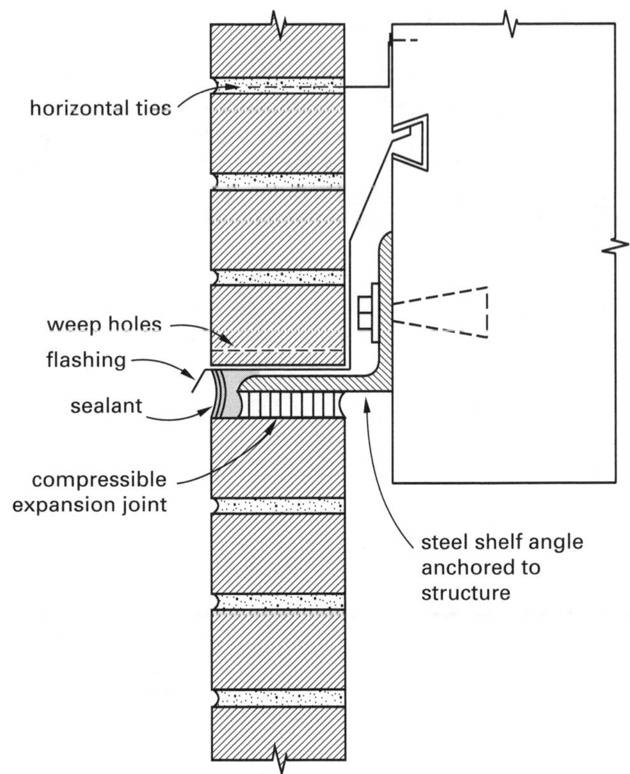

Figure 21.8 Typical Attachment of Brick Facing at Intermediate Floor

wind loads as well. The attachment of veneer stone is accomplished in a similar manner, although individual details are somewhat different.

Precast concrete panels are also attached at every floor or every other floor using various combinations of embedded steel angles and plates that are field-welded or bolted together as shown in Fig. 21.7(c).

With metal curtain wall systems, the provision for both dead loads and wind load is made with various types of clip attachment of the curtain wall system to the structural frame. There are many possible ways this can be accomplished depending on the type of curtain wall system, its fabrication, the loads that must be resisted, and the type and configuration of the primary structural frame, as well as other variables.

In most cases, some type of steel anchor is firmly attached to the structure at floor and column lines. The support system for the curtain wall is then attached to these anchors using shims and slotted bolt holes to provide for precise alignment of the exterior wall. One system of this type is shown in Fig. 21.9.

In resisting wind loading, the cladding must maintain its own structural integrity and transfer the wind loads to the

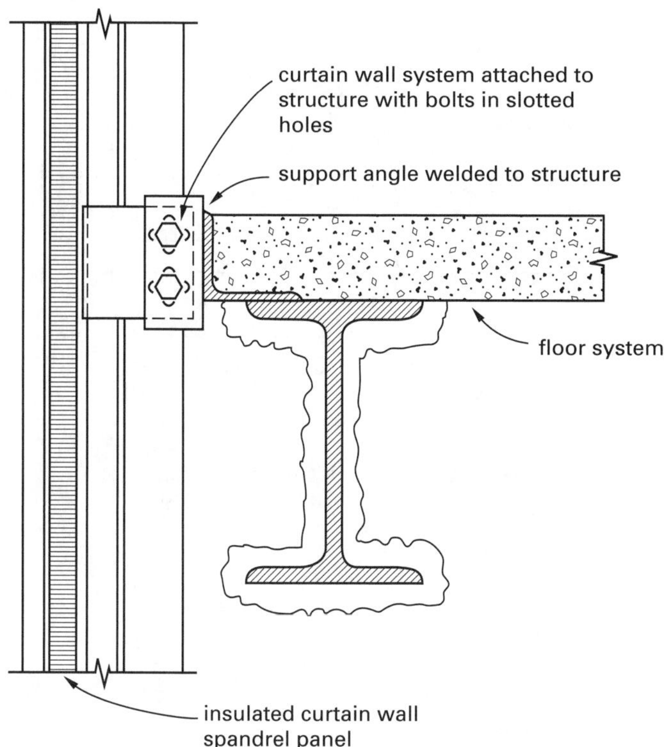

Figure 21.9 Typical Attachment of Curtain Wall

structural frame. Wind can either produce a positive or negative load on a component. Quite often, the suction on an exterior wall can be greater than the inward pressure caused by wind. In most cases, however, nonbearing exterior walls are designed to span between supports, so intermediate connections for the transfer of wind loads are not required. One exception is brick masonry, which may require intermittent horizontal ties because of its low flexural strength.

Nonbearing, exterior wall systems in areas of frequent seismic activity must be designed primarily to maintain their integrity and connection to the building to avoid injury caused by falling debris. Although it is desirable to provide for movement and absorption of energy during an earthquake to avoid cracking and damage of the wall material, this is usually not practical for severe earthquakes. Instead, connections and joints should accommodate movement to avoid buildup of stresses that could dislocate the wall from the structure.

The design of curtain wall systems is especially important in resisting seismic loads. Of course, the panels must withstand the force of an earthquake, but most of the load is concentrated in the connections to the primary structural system. In severe earthquake zones, additional connections may be required above those needed for gravity and wind loading. Much of the earthquake energy in a curtain wall system can be dissipated by providing joints that can move slightly in several directions with such details as slip joints or flexible bushings between bolt and steel members.

To minimize the possibility of damage to nonbearing panels during an earthquake, the panels should be anchored vertically at column lines and horizontally at floor lines. It is at these points where the seismic forces are concentrated, so curtain wall panels should not span across these points.

Movement

All buildings move. There are a variety of causes of building movement, and the exterior walls must accommodate all of them. Movement can be a result of wind loads, temperature changes, moisture, earthquakes, differential movement of building materials, and deflection of the structure, both immediate and long term.

Building materials expand and contract with changes in temperature as noted in Ch. 11. The amount of movement is dependent on the material's coefficient of thermal expansion and length. An aluminum curtain wall system will change dimension to a much greater degree than a masonry wall.

Moisture can cause some material to change size to such an extent that if the change is not accounted for, damage can occur. Wood, of course, swells when wet, so siding or a structure exposed to the weather must be protected with coatings, or an allowance must be made for the amount of movement expected. Even changes in humidity levels can cause wood members to expand and contract.

Differential movement of materials is another important concern. Brick will swell and expand at a different rate than a concrete block backing wall. Metal windows will move in response to wind and temperature changes more than the concrete wall they are anchored to. An aluminum curtain wall will change size much more than the steel frame it is attached to. These examples are just a few of the many situations where differential movement can cause problems.

The deflection of both the structure and the attached exterior wall is often overlooked. For example, a masonry wall laid up to the underside of a beam or floor can buckle under dead loading or long-term deflection. There should always be some method of providing for this kind of movement. The compressible expansion joint shown in Fig. 21.8, for example, allows for minor deflection of the steel angle above as well as provides for expansion of the brick below.

The methods of dealing with all the types of building movement mentioned here are varied, depending on the material and the type and amount of movement expected. Following are a few general guidelines.

First, there must be *through-building expansion joints* to accommodate large-scale movement of portions of the entire building. These are needed in large buildings where there is a change in height, structural system, or major materials, or where differential movement might be expected between various parts of the building. For example, a parking structure connected to an office tower would probably require a building expansion joint between the two structures.

Second, there must be *through-wall expansion joints* to allow for movement in wall sections caused by temperature, moisture, differential movement, and other forces. These are usually made by separating the materials structurally, but providing for weatherproofing.

One example of a vertical masonry expansion joint is shown in Fig. 21.10. The individual brick walls are securely anchored to the concrete structural frame, but the joint allows each to move independently in the direction parallel to the wall. The dovetail anchors allow for minor movement in the direction perpendicular to the wall. The joint filler and sealant accommodate expansion and contraction while providing a tight seal.

Third, *construction joints* must be used to separate one type of material from another. These joints allow for differential movement as well as provide for clearance when one building component is installed within another. For example, the caulked joint between a wood door frame and a brick wall allows the frame to shrink and swell and allows the brick to move slightly without causing damage to either material.

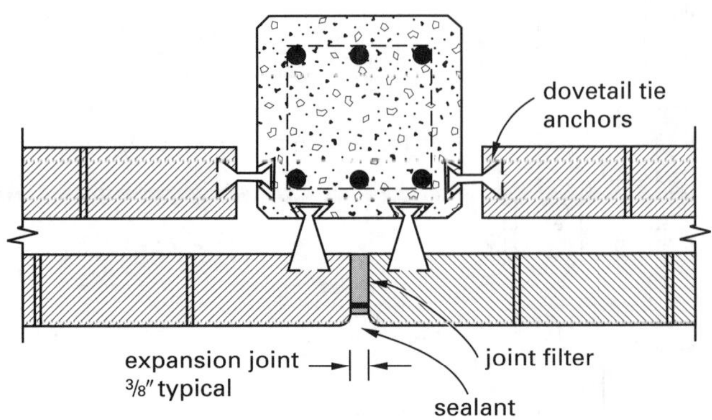

Figure 21.10 Typical Horizontal Attachment of Masonry to Primary Structure

22 LATERAL FORCES—WIND

Nomenclature

C	chord force	lbf
C_p	external pressure coefficient	–
C_{pi}	internal pressure coefficient	–
d	depth of building	ft
f	load on individual building element	lbf/ft
G	gust effect factor	–
I	importance factor	–
K_d	directionality factor	–
K_h	exposure coefficient at mean roof height	–
K_z	exposure coefficient at any height z	–
K_{zt}	topographic factor	–
L	length of building	ft
M	diaphragm moment	ft-lbf
P	design wind pressure	lbf/ft^2
q	wind pressure	lbf/ft^2
q	wind stagnation at height z	lbf/ft^2
q_h	wind pressure at mean roof height	lbf/ft^2
q_i	wind pressure for internal component	lbf/ft^2
v	diaphragm shear stress	lbf/ft^2
v	unit shear stress	lbf/ft
v	wind speed (velocity)	mph
V_s	total shear	lbf
ω	wind load coefficient	–

BASIC PRINCIPLES

Wind is air in motion. The movement of the atmosphere is caused by differences in the temperature of air over various parts of the globe. These temperature differences are produced by the uneven absorption and reradiation of heat from the sun as it strikes the air, water vapor, and different earth surfaces.

As warm air rises near the equator, it forms jet streams that move toward the colder, denser air of the polar regions. Some of the air descends in the temperate regions, forming high pressure systems, and then splits, some of it moving north and south closer to the earth. On a global scale, the winds caused by these temperature differences are further affected by the rotation of the earth, resulting in a worldwide wind pattern that is generally predictable from season to season.

On a smaller scale, wind is affected by topography and local climatic conditions. For example, the shores of the Great Lakes have unusual winds, unlike the surrounding country, as do the areas along the eastern front range of the Rocky Mountains in Colorado.

The Effect of Wind on Buildings

The primary effects of wind on buildings are the lateral forces it places on the exterior cladding and lateral forces on the entire structure. As mentioned in Ch. 11, wind can cause a direct, positive pressure as well as a suction, or negative pressure. The exact location of the negative pressure depends on the configuration of the building but most often occurs on the leeward side and frequently occurs on the sides parallel to the wind direction. See Fig. 22.1. It also occurs on the roof, whether flat or sloped.

Smaller, localized areas on a building are also subject to specific pressures that can exceed the pressure on the main body of the structure. This occurs at the building corners, under eaves, on parapets, and elsewhere.

A building's shape or the locations of several buildings in a group can be subject to unusual wind forces that may not affect the structural design as much as the comfort of people and use of the building. Figure 22.1, for example, shows the funneling effect of a small opening. Similar conditions can be produced by two or more buildings placed near one

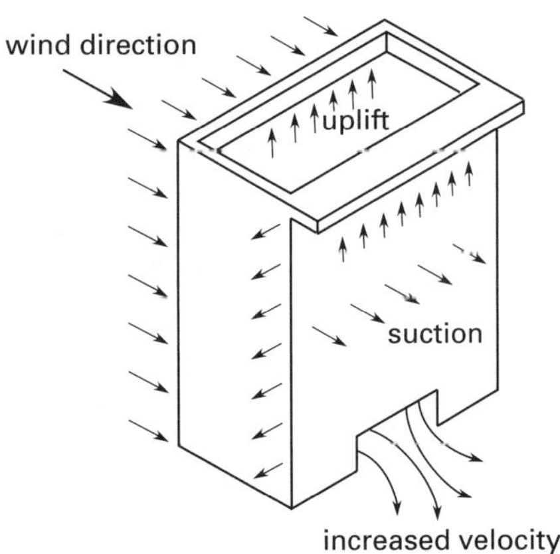

Figure 22.1 Forces on a Building Due to Wind

another. The high-speed, localized winds produced can make outdoor plazas and building entries unpleasant at best and unusable at worst. In many cases, wind tunnel testing is required to determine the precise nature of wind around buildings.

Another effect of concern to architects is the drift, or lateral displacement, of a building when subjected to wind forces. Excessive drift can damage brittle or tightly attached exterior materials and can affect the comfort of the occupants near the top of a tall building, and so it must be minimized. Maximum drift should be limited to $^1/_{500}$ of the building's height, and drift between adjacent stories should be limited to 0.0025 times the story height.

Wind can cause a potentially damaging dynamic load on a building, called a *resonant load* or *oscillating load*, and can result in the building oscillating side to side perpendicular to the direction of the wind. Dynamic loads can also be induced when repeated gusts of wind strike a building at the same rate as the fundamental period of the building. The *fundamental period* is the time it takes the structure to complete one full swing from side to side. The American Society of Civil Engineers code *Minimum Design Loads for Buildings and Other Structures* (ASCE/SEI 7) recognizes these potential problems and requires that structures sensitive to dynamic effects be designed in accordance with approved national standards, which usually means wind tunnel testing.

Wind Measurement

Wind speed is measured in several different forms. One of the most common methods is called the *fastest-mile wind*. This is the average speed of a column of air 1 mi long that passes over a given point. Using this method eliminates the effect of sudden, short-term gusts. This type of wind speed is measured with an anemometer.

The value used in designing buildings and other structures is the *three-second peak gust wind*. This is the maximum 3 sec peak gust speed recorded at 33 ft above the ground. The ASCE/SEI 7 wind speed corresponds to an ultimate wind speed that would occur approximately every 700 years. The basic wind speeds used for determining wind pressures on buildings are given in Fig. 22.2. Because friction against the ground affects wind speed, in order to establish some uniformity in measurement and reporting, the values shown are taken at 10 m above the ground. Linear interpolation between wind speed contours is acceptable.

Some areas on the map in Fig. 22.2 are designated as special wind regions. These are locales where topography and conditions are so variable that wind speeds are determined by local records and experience or are individually set by the building official.

Variables Affecting Wind Loading

One of the primary factors affecting wind speed is the friction caused by the ground. Since wind acts like water or any other fluid, its speed is reduced when it is in contact with or near other surfaces. There are three basic surface conditions for the purpose of building design: *open country*, *suburban areas*, and *metropolitan areas*. Open country results in the most severe wind conditions because there is nothing to slow the movement of air.

In each of three cases, wind speed is slowest right at ground level and gradually increases with height until its gradient height is reached. *Gradient height* is that height above which the friction from the ground and other obstructions no longer affects wind speed. This height is 900 ft for open country, 1200 ft for suburban areas, and 1500 ft for metropolitan areas. See Fig. 22.3.

Below the gradient height, wind speed can be calculated at any given elevation according to a formula that includes the factors of wind pressure at 10 m elevation, a velocity pressure coefficient, and a gust response factor. However, for most building design purposes, ASCE/SEI 7 simplifies the effects of height and surface exposure into one factor. The use of this factor, K_z, will be discussed in more detail later in this chapter.

Surrounding buildings also affect the wind speed, by either reducing it with shielding effects or increasing it by funneling it between narrow openings. ASCE/SEI 7 does not allow for any reduction in wind pressure due to the shielding effect of adjacent structures. However, if wind tunnel tests are conducted on a model of a proposed building, any increases in wind pressure on the building due to adjacent conditions would be taken into account.

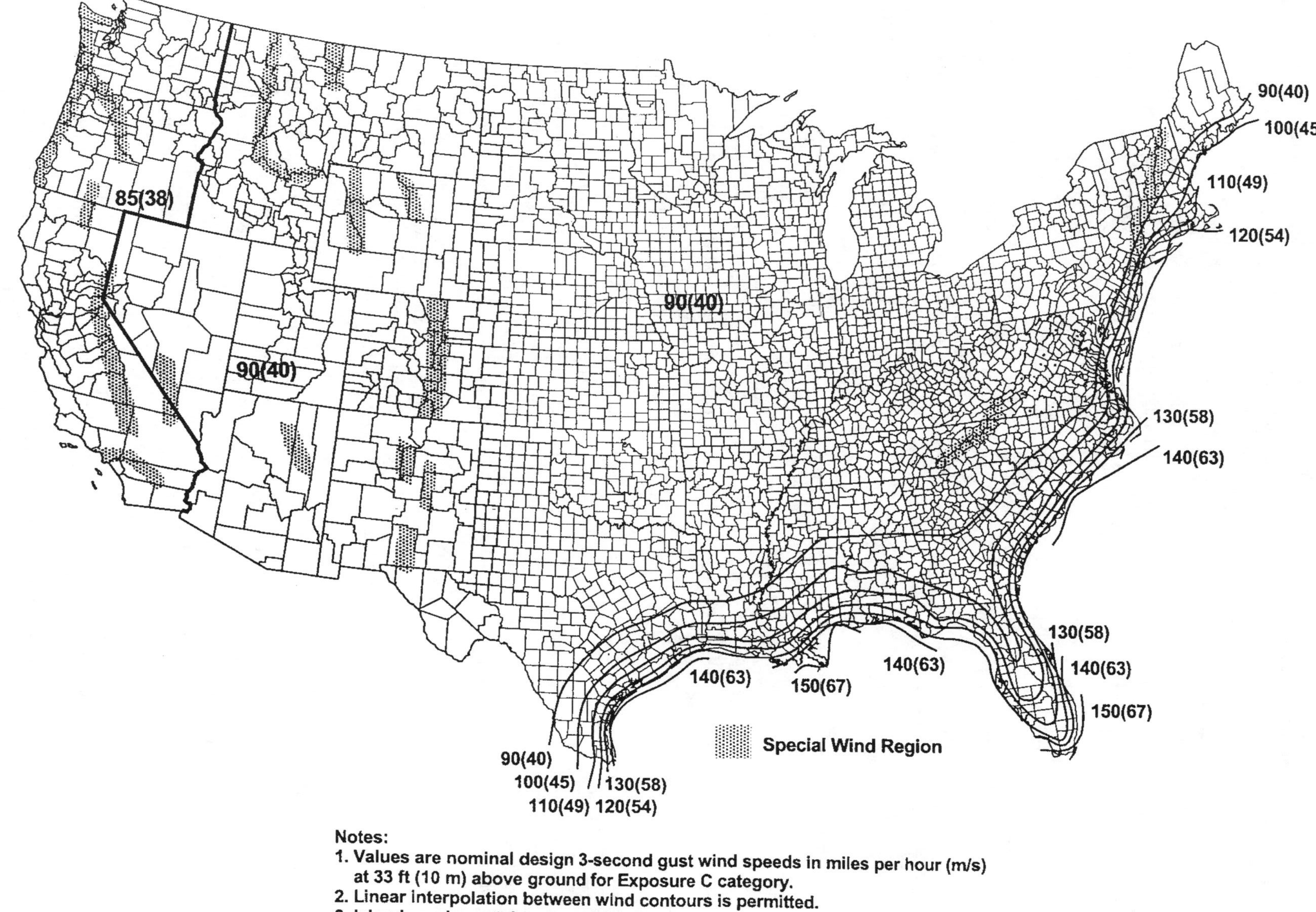
85(38)
90(40)
90(40)
90(40)
100(45)
110(49)
120(54)
130(58)
140(63)
130(58)
140(63)
150(67)
140(63)
150(67)
140(63)
90(40)
100(45)
110(49)
120(54)
130(58)
Special Wind Region
Notes:
1. Values are nominal design 3-second gust wind speeds in miles per hour (m/s) at 33 ft (10 m) above ground for Exposure C category.
2. Linear interpolation between wind contours is permitted.
3. Islands and coastal areas outside the last contour shall use the last wind speed contour of the coastal area.
4. Mountainous terrain, gorges, ocean promontories, and special wind regions shall be examined for unusual wind conditions.

Reproduced from the 2005 edition of Minimum Design Loads for Buildings and Other Structures, copyright © 2006, with permission from the publisher, the American Society of Civil Engineers.

Figure 22.2 Basic Wind Speeds

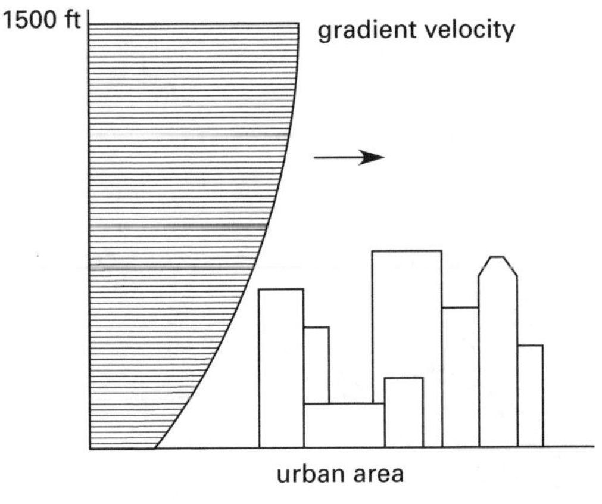

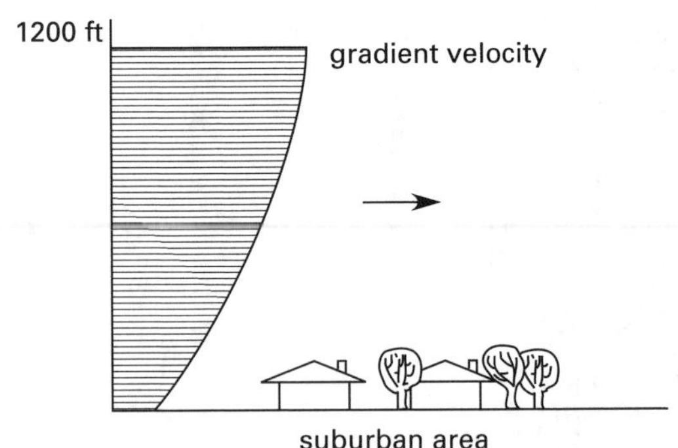

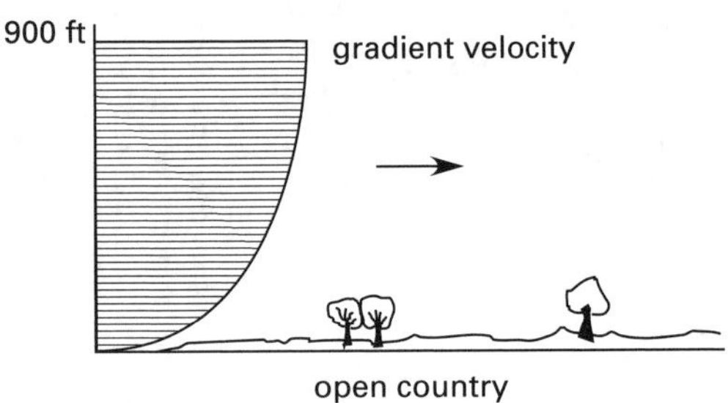

Figure 22.3 Wind Velocity as a Function of Terrain

ANALYSIS OF WIND LOADING

The first step in designing a building to resist wind load is, of course, to determine the forces acting on the structure as a whole and on the individual elements. Then, shear walls, diaphragms, reinforcing, connections, and other components can be selected and sized accordingly. The pressure acting on the building and individual elements depends on many variables. Complex and lengthy design formulas are available to account for all the variables, and wind tunnel testing may be used to design any building, but ASCE/SEI 7 simplifies the procedure somewhat by requiring that the design wind pressure be determined for most buildings by the following formula.

$$P = qGC_p - q_i(GC_{pi}) \qquad 22.1$$

The G factor takes into account both atmospheric and aerodynamic effects. The value of G may be taken as 0.85 for rigid structures. Flexible or dynamically sensitive structures require a more detailed approach to calculating the gust factor. The values q and C_p are discussed elsewhere in this chapter.

However, for structures over 400 ft high, buildings subject to dynamic effects, such as those with a height-to-width ratio more than 5 or those sensitive to wind-excited oscillations, must be designed in accordance with approved national standards. These involve more complex and lengthy calculations and, frequently, wind tunnel testing.

K_z Factor

ASCE/SEI 7 combines the effects of height, exposure, and wind gusting into one factor labeled K_z. Table 22.1 gives these factors and is based on Table 6-3 of ASCE 7. There are three exposure categories: Exposure D is the most severe and represents areas where the terrain is flat and unobstructed facing large bodies of water of at least 5000 ft or 10 times the building height, excluding hurricane-prone areas. This exposure extends inland 660 ft or 10 times the building height, whichever is greater. Exposure C has open terrain with scattered obstructions less than 30 ft in height and includes all hurricane-prone areas. Exposure B includes urban and suburban wooded areas or other terrain that has closely spaced obstructions upwind for at least 2630 ft or 10 times the building height, whichever is greater.

The value K_z varies with height on the windward side of a building. For the leeward wall and roof the value K_h is used over the entire surface. This value, K_h, is the value of K_z evaluated at the mean roof height.

C_p Factor

The C_p factor takes into account the differing effect of the wind on various parts of the building. For instance, there is negative pressure on the leeward side, uplift on the roof, and so forth. These factors are shown in Table 22.2. There are two general parts to this table: one for determining loads on the walls and the other for determining loads on the roof.

Similar procedures are required for calculating pressures on individual elements and special areas. The value GC_{pi} is used to evaluate internal pressures and may be taken as ± 0.18 for enclosed buildings. For symmetric buildings, the internal pressures on opposing walls will cancel out on the main

Table 22.1

K_z Values

height above ground level, z		exposure			
		B		C	D
ft	m	Case 1	Case 2	Cases 1 & 2	Cases 1 & 2
0–15	0–4.6	0.70	0.57	0.85	1.03
20	6.1	0.70	0.62	0.90	1.08
25	7.6	0.70	0.66	0.94	1.12
30	9.1	0.70	0.70	0.98	1.16
40	12.2	0.76	0.76	1.04	1.22
50	15.2	0.81	0.81	1.09	1.27
60	18	0.85	0.85	1.13	1.31
70	21.3	0.89	0.89	1.17	1.34
80	24.4	0.93	0.93	1.21	1.38
90	27.4	0.96	0.96	1.24	1.40
100	30.5	0.99	0.99	1.26	1.43
120	36.6	1.04	1.04	1.31	1.48
140	42.7	1.09	1.09	1.36	1.52
160	48.8	1.13	1.13	1.39	1.55
180	54.9	1.17	1.17	1.43	1.58
200	61.0	1.20	1.20	1.46	1.61
250	76.2	1.28	1.28	1.53	1.68
300	91.4	1.35	1.35	1.59	1.73
350	106.7	1.41	1.41	1.64	1.78
400	121.9	1.47	1.47	1.69	1.82
450	137.2	1.52	1.52	1.73	1.86
500	152.4	1.56	1.56	1.77	1.89

Case 1: a. All components and cladding.
b. Main wind force resisting system in low-rise buildings designed using Fig. 6-10 in ASCE/SEI 7.

Case 2: a. All main wind force resisting systems in buildings except those in low-rise buildings designed using Fig. 6-10 in ASCE/SEI 7.
b. All main wind force resisting systems in other structures.

wind resisting system. For partially enclosed buildings, a much higher value of $C_{pi} = \pm 0.55$ must be used.

Table 22.2 also reflects one of the two methods by which ASCE/SEI 7 requires pressures to be calculated for various types of buildings. Method 1, called the *projected area method*, assumes that horizontal pressures act on the full vertical projected area of the structure and that vertical pressures act simultaneously on the full horizontal projected area. Method 2 is called the *normal force method*. With this method, the wind pressures are assumed to act simultaneously normal to all exterior surfaces. For pressures on the leeward side, the height is taken at the mean roof height and is constant for the full height of the building.

Method 1 may be used for structures less than 60 ft high. The building must be approximately symmetric and be a simple diaphragm structure. The building must not be subject to any special wind considerations. The wind pressures for this simplified and limited method are taken directly from tables in ASCE/SEI 7. ASCE/SEI 7 calls this the *simplified method* and calls Method 2 the *analytical method*. Method 2 must be used for gabled rigid frames and may be used for any structure. Figure 22.4 graphically illustrates these two methods for calculating wind pressure with wind normal to the ridge on a sloped roof. Similar distributions are used for buildings with wind parallel to a ridge or on flat roof, but the pressure on the windward roof will vary similarly to that on the windward wall.

q Factor

The effect of wind speed on pressure is accounted for in the *wind stagnation factor*. The pressures are based on the three-second peak gust wind at a standard height of 33 ft and are calculated with the formula

$$q = 0.00256 K_z K_{zt} K_d v^2 I \qquad 22.2$$

The topographic factor, K_{zt}, takes into account hills and escarpments close to the building. The value for level ground may be taken as 1.0. The directionality factor, K_d, takes into account the type of structure being analyzed. The value for buildings may be taken as 0.85. The factors K_z and I are discussed elsewhere in this chapter. The wind speed that must be used, v, is determined from Fig. 22.2, from local records, or from local building department requirements if the location is in one of the special wind regions.

Importance Factor (*I*)

The importance factor, *I*, in Eq. 22.2 represents a safety factor for essential facilities that must be safe and usable for emergency purposes during and after a windstorm. The occupancy categories of various facility types are shown in Table 23.4 with earthquake design. The corresponding importance factors are also given in Tables 22.3 and 23.4.

Table 22.2

C_p Values

wall pressure coefficients, C_p			
surface	L/B	C_p	use with
windward wall	all values	0.8	q_z
	0–1	−0.5	
leeward wall	2	−0.3	q_h
	≥4	−0.2	
side wall	all values	−0.7	q_h

roof pressure coefficients, C_p, for use with q_h

wind direction	h/L	windward angle, θ (degrees) 10	15	20	25	30	35	45	≥60	leeward angle, θ (degrees) 10	15	≥20
normal to ridge for θ ≥ 10°	≤0.25	−0.7	−0.5	−0.3	−0.2	−0.2	0.0*			−0.3	−0.5	−0.6
		−0.18	0.0*	0.2	0.3	0.3	0.4	0.4	0.01 θ			
	0.5	−0.9	−0.7	−0.4	−0.3	−0.2	−0.2	0.0*		−0.5	−0.5	−0.6
		−0.18	−0.18	0.0*	0.2	0.2	0.3	0.4	0.01 θ			
	≥1.0	−1.3**	−1.0	−0.7	−0.5	−0.3	−0.2	0.0*		−0.7	−0.6	−0.6
		−0.18	−0.18	−0.18	0.0*	0.2	0.2	0.3	0.01 θ			

wind direction	h/L	horiz. distance from windward edge	C_p
normal to ridge for θ < 10 and parallel to ridge for all θ	≤0.5	0 to $h/2$	−0.9, −0.18
		$h/2$ to h	−0.9, −0.18
		h to $2h$	−0.5, −0.18
		>$2h$	−0.3, −0.18
	≥1.0	0 to $h/2$	−1.3**, −0.18
		> $h/2$	−0.7, −0.18

*Value is provided for interpolation purposes.

**Value can be reduced linearly with area over which it is applicable as follows.

area (ft^2)	reduction factor
≤100 (9.3 m^2)	1.0
200 (23.2 m^2)	0.9
≥1000 (92.9 m^2)	0.8

1. Plus and minus signs signify pressures acting toward and away from the surfaces, respectively.
2. Linear interpolation is permitted for values of L/B, h/L, and θ other than shown. Interpolation shall only be carried out between values of the same sign. Where no value of the same sign is given, assume 0.0 for interpolation purposes.
3. Where two values of C_p are listed, this indicates that the windward roof slope is subjected to either positive or negative pressures and the roof structure shall be designed for both conditions. Interpolation for intermediate ratios of h/L in this case shall only be carried out between C_p values of like sign.
4. For monoslope roofs, entire roof surface is either a windward or leeward surface.
5. For flexible buildings use appropriate G_f as determined by Sec. 6.5.8.
6. Refer to Fig. 6-7 for domes and Fig. 6-8 for arched roofs.
7. Notation:
   B: Horizontal dimension of building, in feet (meters), measured normal to wind direction.
   L: Horizontal dimension of building, in feet (meters), measured parallel to wind direction.
   h: Mean roof height in feet (meters), except that eave height shall be used for θ ≤ 10°.
   z: Height above ground, in feet (meters).
   G: Gust effect factor.
   q_z, q_h: Velocity pressure, in psf (N/m^2), evaluated at respective height.
   θ: Angle of plane of roof from horizontal, in degrees.
8. For mansard roofs, the top horizontal surface and leeward inclined surface shall be treated as leeward surface from the table.
9. Except for MWFRSs at the roof consisting of moment resisting frames, the total horizontal shear shall not be less than that determined by neglecting wind forces on roof surfaces.

For roof slopes greater than 80°, use C_p = 0.8.

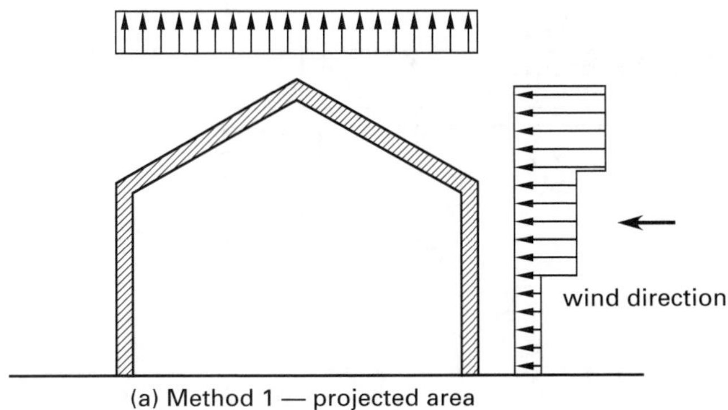

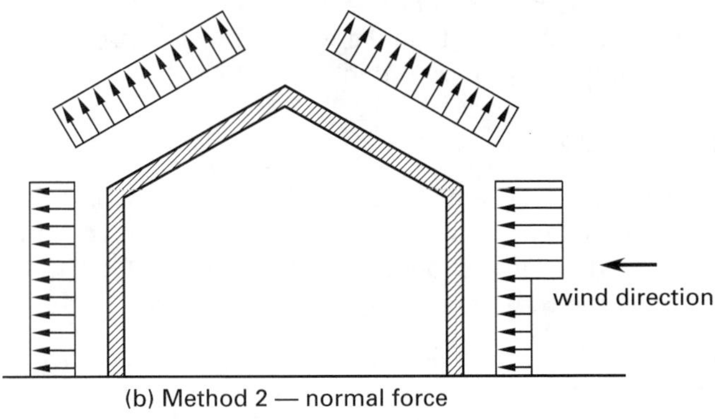

Figure 22.4 Methods for Calculating Pressures

Table 22.3

I Values

category	non-hurricane-prone regions and hurricane-prone regions with v = 85–100 mph and Alaska	hurricane-prone regions with v > 100 mph
I	0.87	0.77
II	1.00	1.00
III	1.15	1.15
IV	1.15	1.15

Reproduced from the 2005 edition of Minimum Design Loads for Buildings and Other Structures, copyright © 2006, with permission from the publisher, the American Society of Civil Engineers.

Example 22.1

A one-story office building 13 ft high is being designed for downtown Rapid City, South Dakota. The building will have a flat roof and a 75 ft square plan. Using Method 1, what are the design wind pressures, in pounds per square foot, for the windward and leeward walls and the roof?

First, Eq. 22.2 is used to determine the basic velocity pressure. From Table 22.1, the K_z value is 0.57 for a building in a downtown area with exposure B (Method 1, Case 2). This is the value that may be used up to 15 ft and therefore applies to both the walls and roof. The values for K_{zt} and K_d are taken as 1.0 and 0.85, respectively, for a flat site and a building structure. From the map in Fig. 22.2, the basic wind speed is 90 mph for Rapid City. From Table 23.4, the importance factor is 1.00 for a category II occupancy. This is the appropriate category for an office building. The calculated basic pressure is as follows.

$$\begin{aligned} q &= 0.00256 K_z K_{zt} K_d \text{v}^2 I \\ &= (0.00256)(0.57)(1.00)(0.85)(90)^2(1.00) \\ &= 10.05 \text{ psf} \end{aligned}$$

Using Method 1, from Table 22.2, the pressure coefficients, C_p, are 0.8 (inward) for the windward wall and 0.5 (outward) for the leeward wall with a square plan ($L/B = 1$). For a flat roof with $h/L = 13/75$ ($h/L < 0.5$), there are three values: 0.9, 0.5, and 0.3 in this case. The first value, h, applies for the first 13 ft, and the second value, $2h$, applies for the next 13 ft from the windward edge. The value for G is taken as 0.85 for a rigid structure. The internal pressure contributions may be ignored, since the building section is symmetric, and Eq. 22.1 becomes $P = qGC_p$.

Windward wall:

$$P = \left(10.05 \frac{\text{lbf}}{\text{ft}^2}\right)(0.85)(0.8) = 6.83 \text{ psf, inward}$$

Leeward wall:

$$P = \left(10.05 \frac{\text{lbf}}{\text{ft}^2}\right)(0.85)(0.5) = 4.27 \text{ psf, outward}$$

Roof:

$$P = \left(10.05 \frac{\text{lbf}}{\text{ft}^2}\right)(0.85)(0.9) = 7.69 \text{ psf, outward for first 13 ft}$$

$$P = \left(10.05 \frac{\text{lbf}}{\text{ft}^2}\right)(0.85)(0.5) = 4.27 \text{ psf, outward for first 13 ft}$$

$$P = \left(10.05 \frac{\text{lbf}}{\text{ft}^2}\right)(0.85)(0.3) = 2.56 \text{ psf, outward for the remainder}$$

The pressures are summarized in the following illustration.

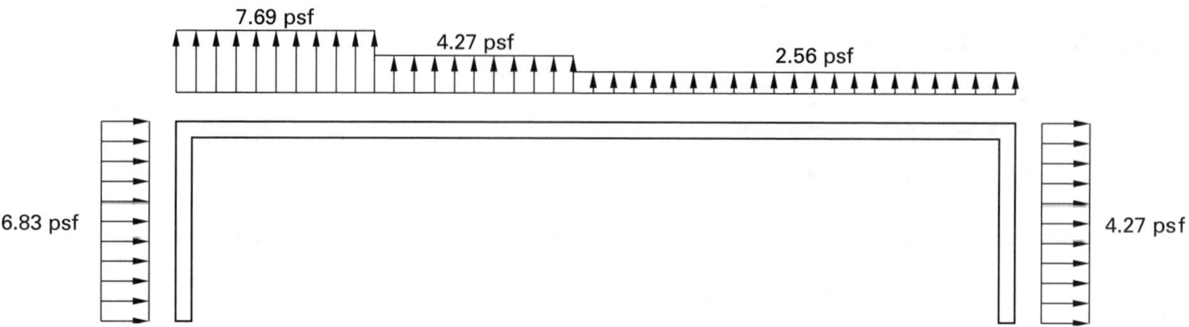

Load Combinations

As discussed in Ch. 11, the code requires that buildings be designed to resist the most critical effects caused by combinations of loads. The load combinations that involve buildings designed for wind per IBC Sec. 1605.2.1 using strength design or load and resistance factor design are as follows.

- $1.4D$
- $1.2D + 1.6(L_r \text{ or } S \text{ or } R) + 0.8W$
- $1.2D + 1.6W + f_1L + 0.5(L_r \text{ or } S \text{ or } R)$
- $0.9D + 1.6W$

The basic load combinations that involve buildings designed for wind per IBC Sec. 1605.3.1 using allowable stress design are as follows.

- D
- $D + W + L + L_r$ or S or R
- $0.6D + W$

Alternate basic load combinations per IBC Sec. 1605.3.2 using allowable stress design are as follows.

- $D + L + \omega W$
- $D + L + \omega W + S/2$
- $D + L + S + \omega W/2$

The value of ω should be taken as 1.3 for wind loads calculated in accordance with the IBC or ASCE/SEI 7 codes. For other wind loads it may be taken as 1.0.

Special Areas and Components

In addition to finding the pressures on the primary structural frame, individual areas need to be analyzed. This is because higher pressures are experienced on elements such as parapets and building corners than on the building as a whole. The pressure coefficients given in the IBC reflect this fact and provide the method by which these greater forces are calculated.

The process and formulas to calculate wind pressures on components and cladding of a building are the same as those for the wind resisting system. The only difference is that the values of GC_p are higher and are dependent on the tributary area supported by the component. The internal pressure coefficients must be considered for all components and cladding. Parapets must be design for the worst case of combined coefficients from the wall and roof. These values are given in many tables within ASCE/SEI 7.

Example 22.2

Find the wind pressures needed to design the wall of the building in Ex. 22.1 if the combined gust coefficients are ±0.9 for the interior portion of the wall and $+0.9$ and -1.8 for the corners of the wall.

Each portion of the wall is design for a positive and negative pressure. The basic velocity pressure taken at the mean roof height was 10.05 psf for all cases here, since $h < 15$ ft. The wall pressure coefficients are combined with the interior pressure coefficients to determine the final pressure. The combined interior pressure coefficient is $GC_{pi} = \pm0.18$ for enclosed buildings.

Interior portion of wall:

$$P = \left(10.05\ \frac{\text{lbf}}{\text{ft}^2}\right)(0.9) + \left(10.05\ \frac{\text{lbf}}{\text{ft}^2}\right)(0.18)$$

$$= 10.85\ \text{psf, inward}$$

$$P = \left(10.05\ \frac{\text{lbf}}{\text{ft}^2}\right)(-0.9) + \left(10.05\ \frac{\text{lbf}}{\text{ft}^2}\right)(-0.18)$$

$$= -10.85\ \text{psf, outward}$$

Corner portion of wall:

$$P = \left(10.05\ \frac{\text{lbf}}{\text{ft}^2}\right)(0.9) + \left(10.05\ \frac{\text{lbf}}{\text{ft}^2}\right)(0.18)$$

$$= 10.85\ \text{psf, inward}$$

$$P = \left(10.05\ \frac{\text{lbf}}{\text{ft}^2}\right)(-1.8) + \left(10.05\ \frac{\text{lbf}}{\text{ft}^2}\right)(-0.18)$$

$$= -19.90\ \text{psf, outward}$$

Example 22.3

If the building in Ex. 22.1 had a 2 ft high parapet at the roof and the roof combined gust coefficient is −2.8 for the interior zone, what moment would have to be designed for at the point where the parapet was attached to the roof?

Parapets must be designed for the worst case of combined coefficients from the wall and roof. In this case the +0.9 wall coefficient on the front is combined with a −2.8 roof coefficient on the back of the parapet. These are combined with the interior pressure coefficients to determine the final pressure.

$$P = \left(10.05 \ \frac{\text{lbf}}{\text{ft}^2}\right)(0.9 + 2.8) + \left(10.05 \ \frac{\text{lbf}}{\text{ft}^2}\right)(0.18)$$

$$= 38.99 \text{ psf, inward}$$

The moment is found just like it would be for a cantilever beam, with the uniform wind pressure assumed to be acting at the midpoint of the span, or in this case 1 ft above the roof. The moment acting on 1 ft of parapet wall is

$$M = \left(38.99 \ \frac{\text{lbf}}{\text{ft}^2}\right)(2 \text{ ft})(1 \text{ ft})$$

$$= 77.98 \text{ ft-lbf per foot of parapet}$$

DESIGN OF WIND-RESISTING STRUCTURES

Once the wind forces have been calculated for the various surfaces and components of a building, their distribution to the structural elements must be determined, and then suitable sizes and connections of the structure must be designed to resist the wind forces. Before reviewing some of the specific design methods, it is necessary to understand the basics of lateral load distribution and some of the concepts of shape and framing methods used to resist both wind and earthquake forces.

Lateral Force Distribution

When wind strikes the sides of a building, the pressures are transferred through the exterior cladding to the points of connections with the floors and roof. The horizontal surfaces of floors and roof act as diaphragms to transfer the forces to the lateral-force-resisting elements, which can be the side walls of the building, interior walls, or the structural frame. Walls designed to carry lateral loads are called *shear walls* because they transfer the horizontal shear to the foundations of the building. Column and beam lines designed to carry wind loads are called *bents*. Figure 22.5 shows a simplified diagram of the transfer of lateral forces using shear walls.

It is helpful to conceptualize the diaphragm as a beam laid on its side, viewing the floor or roof as the web of the beam and the windward and leeward edges as the top and bottom flanges of the beam. The beam spans between the two end walls (or intermediate shear walls), which can be imagined as columns that carry the load to the foundations. Just as with a beam, there is compression in the top (the side facing the wind) and tension in the bottom (the side away from the wind). These edges, called the *chords*, will be discussed in more detail in a later section.

When designing a building to resist lateral forces, all of these components must be examined: the shear in the diaphragm, the chord forces, the shear walls, and all of the connections.

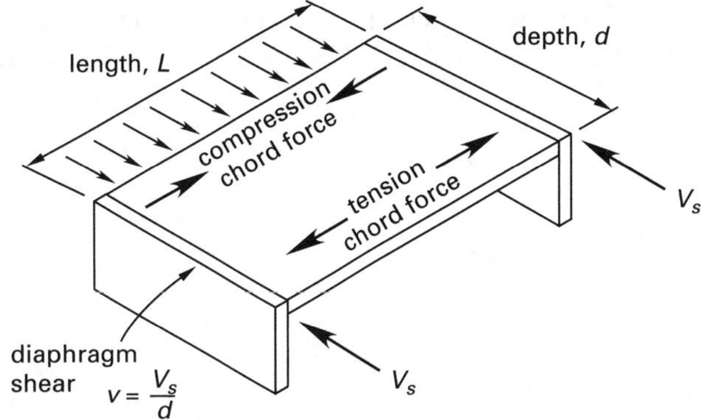

(a) diaphragm loads

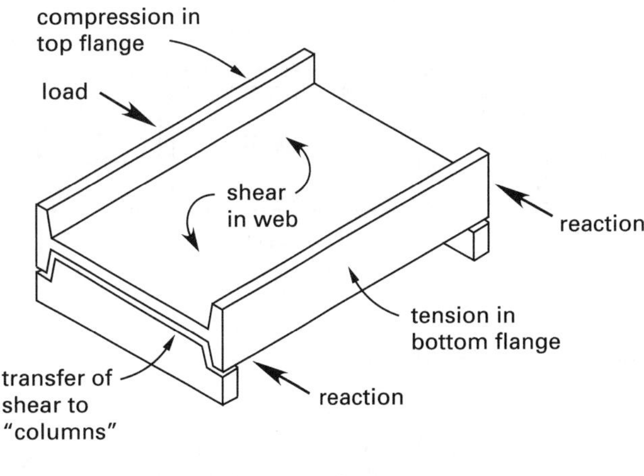

(b) beam analogy

Figure 22.5 Diaphragm Loading

Example 22.4

Assume the building used in Ex. 22.1 is 150 ft long and 75 ft wide and that the two 75 ft end walls will act as shear walls. Assuming the wind force is applied perpendicular to the length of the building and using Method 1, determine the total force each shear wall must resist and the stress per linear foot along the shear walls that the roof diaphragm must transfer to the shear walls.

The building and a wall section are shown diagrammatically in the accompanying sketches. The wind load on the roof results from the wind pressure from the midpoint of the wall to the top of the roof.

From Ex. 22.1, the wind pressure was calculated to be 6.83 psf on the windward side of the building. Because Method 1 is used, the negative pressure on the leeward side must be included. This was calculated as 4.27 psf in the previous example problem. These pressures are also shown in the sketch of the wall section. The load per foot of length on the roof is the pressure multiplied by one-half the height of the building.

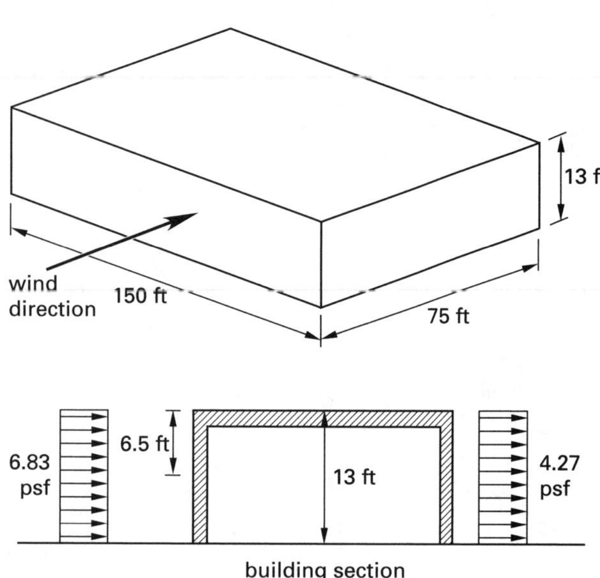

Roof load, windward:

$$\left(6.83\ \frac{\text{lbf}}{\text{ft}^2}\right)(6.5\ \text{ft}) = 44.4\ \text{plf}$$

Roof load, leeward:

$$\left(4.27\ \frac{\text{lbf}}{\text{ft}^2}\right)(6.5\ \text{ft}) = 27.8\ \text{plf}$$

This is a total of 72.2 plf.

The total shear force each wall must resist is found by taking the total load per foot times the length of the building and dividing by two because there are only two walls.

$$\begin{aligned} V_s &= \frac{fL}{2} \\ &= \frac{\left(72.2\ \frac{\text{lbf}}{\text{ft}}\right)(150\ \text{ft})}{2} \\ &= 5415\ \text{lbf} \end{aligned}$$

The unit shear stress is the total shear distributed along the depth of the building.

$$\begin{aligned} v &= \frac{V_s}{d} = \frac{5415\ \text{lbf}}{75\ \text{ft}} \\ &= 72.2\ \text{plf} \end{aligned}$$

Building Shape and Framing Methods

Some building shapes and framing systems are more resistant to wind forces than others. The first consideration in designing a structure to resist wind is the plan shape of the building. Rectangular shapes have a tendency to block more wind than round and tapered shapes, but they are also usually more functional in terms of space planning and are generally less expensive to construct.

Rectangular shapes, however, do allow for some adjustment in planning to make them more efficient. Consider the two building shapes shown diagrammatically in Fig. 22.6 with the wind coming from an assumed direction. Building A is rectangular in plan, while building B is square in plan. Both buildings have the same height and floor area, but building B is more efficient in resisting wind for two reasons.

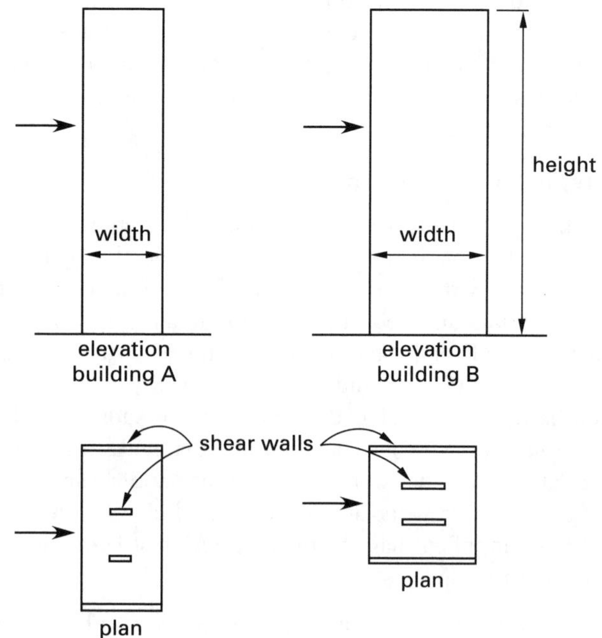

Figure 22.6 Effect of Building Shape on Efficiency

First, the surface area of building B facing the wind is less than that of building A, so the total force on the structural system will be less. Secondly, building B's increased width allows for deeper shear walls and a reduction in the height-to-width ratio. Since shear walls act as beams cantilevered out of the ground, the deeper section is more efficient and requires less structural material to resist the forces.

However, if the length-to-width ratio is increased enough, the basic rigidity in the long dimension will distribute the wind forces among the normal structural elements enough so that special wind bracing will not be required; it will only be necessary in the short dimension.

Framing methods are the second consideration that determines a building's inherent resistance to lateral loads. The sketches in Fig. 22.7 show some of the basic types of steel framing systems that are used to resist both wind and earthquake loads.

The simplest is the *moment-resisting frame*. See Fig. 22.7(a). With this system, moment-resisting connections are used between columns and beams as discussed in the section on connections. The connections may consist of simple welded joints or may include small brackets when larger loads are involved. This system is useful for low-rise buildings and high-rise buildings under 30 stories. Above this height, the wind loads cannot be efficiently resisted without additional types of bracing.

Knee bracing, as shown in Fig. 22.7(b), is an economical way to provide rigidity to a steel frame, whether it is a one-story industrial building or a large high-rise. The bracing struts are usually short enough that they can be concealed above a suspended ceiling if appearance is a concern.

Two of the most common types of lateral bracing for tall structures are the *X-brace* and the *K-brace* or *chevron brace*. See Figs. 22.7(c) and (d). They are usually placed in a central set of bays in a building's structural framework and act as vertical trusses cantilevered out of the ground. The diagonal members can be designed primarily as tension members to minimize their size. With this approach, it is assumed that when the wind loads the building from one side, one of the braces is in tension and the other is not stressed. When the building is loaded from the opposite side, the stresses in the diagonal members reverse. Although both systems are very efficient, the K-bracing system results in less horizontal drift because the diagonal members are shorter and therefore elongate less under stress.

The *portal frame* system illustrated in Fig. 22.7(e) is composed of trusses at each floor level with knee braces connecting the truss to the columns. It is not used very much unless the trusses are also used to support the vertical loads of the floor system or the roof of a one-story building.

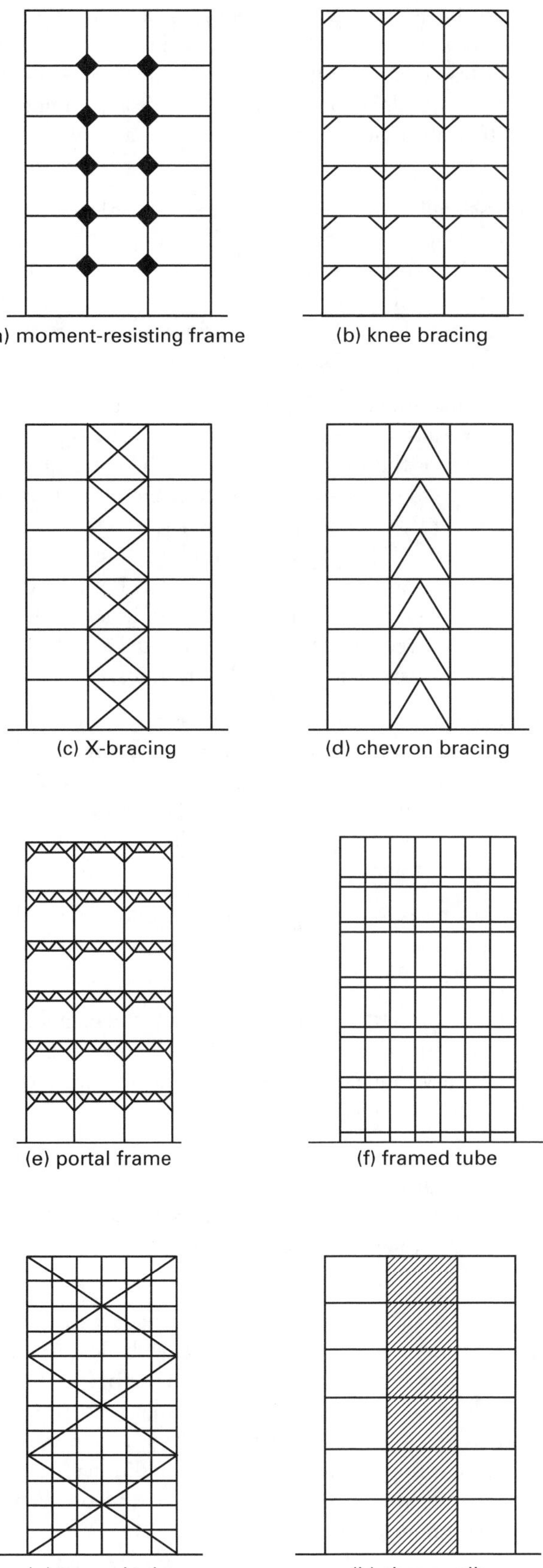

Figure 22.7 Framing Systems to Resist Lateral Loads

As lateral loads increase and buildings become taller, the *framed tube* system (see Fig. 22.7(f)) is often used. This system creates a large, hollow tube cantilevered from the ground. It is built of closely spaced exterior columns and beams that are rigidly connected to form a very efficient, stiff structure.

The *trussed tube* concept shown in Fig. 22.7(g) uses a combination of rigid frame and diagonal braces on the exterior wall. The X-braces span from 5 to 10 floors and result in a structure very resistant to lateral loads. For additional strength and reduced drift, the exterior walls can be sloped slightly like the John Hancock Tower in Chicago.

Finally, a steel frame can be used in conjunction with concrete *shear walls* as shown in Fig. 22.7(h). The steel frame carries most of the vertical loads while the concrete shear walls transmit the lateral forces to the foundation. This system is frequently used because the concrete shear walls can easily be a part of the core of the building, enclosing elevators, stairways, and mechanical duct space. For added efficiency, the shape of the concrete walls can be varied to suit the structural needs of the building, forming H- or T-shaped sections so there is rigidity in both directions.

There are many variations to these basic types of framing systems. The bundled tube concept used for the Sears Tower in Chicago, for example, extends the framed tube idea by grouping nine tubes together. Other systems include belt trusses at intermediate floors and buildings with tapered profiles.

Framing systems for concrete structures follow some of the same approaches as steel with a few variations owing to the nature of the material.

Rigid frame structures can be built out of concrete, but moment-resisting connections between columns and beams are not as easy to make, so these building systems are limited to 20 to 30 stories.

For greater resistance, rigid frames are combined with concrete shear walls that are designed to take the majority of the lateral forces. Frame walls can also be used with shear walls so the two act together in resisting wind and earthquake loads.

Framed tubes can be built out of concrete as well as steel. Like steel structures, these are buildings with closely spaced exterior columns rigidly connected with the beams. Such a building also acts as a large tube cantilevered from the ground. When this idea is extended, the system becomes a tube-within-a-tube system where an additional tube of closely spaced interior columns is attached to the exterior grouping with a rigid floor at each level. This is one of the most efficient kinds of high-rise concrete structures, exemplified by Water Tower Place in Chicago.

Diaphragm Design

A diaphragm must be able to resist the lateral loads placed on it without excessive deformation or failure. It must be designed to act as a unit so the forces can be transferred to the shear walls. Horizontal diaphragms can be constructed of plywood, particleboard, concrete, steel decking, and combinations of these materials. Each material or combination has its own load-carrying capacity as a diaphragm member.

For example, allowable shear for horizontal diaphragms of plywood and particleboard and allowable shear for plywood and particleboard shear walls are given in IBC Table 2306.2.1(1). The table for wood structural panel diaphragms is reproduced in Table 22.4. These tables give the allowable shear in pounds per foot based on the grade of material, material thickness, nail sizes, nail spacing, and framing member size, and based on whether the material is blocked or unblocked. Blocked diaphragms are those with solid framing members at each edge of the plywood or particleboard.

Example 22.5

Select a plywood diaphragm system for the loads calculated in Ex. 22.4.

The unit stress in the roof was found to be 72.2 plf. Any of the combinations listed in Table 22.4 will work because the unit stress is so low in this example. Depending on the spacing of the joists, a $^3/_8$ in thickness of plywood would probably be the minimum thickness for practical use. Any of the combinations using 8d nails at the maximum allowable spacing of 6 in would work in this instance.

Chord Force

As shown in Fig. 22.5, wind loading along a floor or roof of a building produces a compression and tension force in the diaphragm, just like in the top and bottom flanges of a beam. This force, distributed along the depth of the diaphragm, is known as the *chord force* and is used to determine the kind of connection that is needed between the diaphragm and the shear walls in order to transfer the lateral load.

Since the diaphragm acts like a simple, uniformly loaded beam when it is between two shear walls, the chord force can be found by first determining the moment at the edges of the diaphragm using the formula found in Fig. 4.7: $M = wl^2/8$. Then, the chord force is the moment divided by the depth of the diaphragm.

$$C = \frac{M}{d} \qquad 22.3$$

Table 22.4

Allowable Shear for Wood Structural Diaphragms[a]

panel grade	common nail size or staple[f] length and gage	minimum fastener penetration in framing (in)	minimum nominal panel thickness (in)	minimum nominal width of framing member (in)	blocked diaphragms: fastener spacing (in) at diaphragm boundaries (all cases) at continuous panel edges parallel to load (Cases 3, 4), and at all panel edges (Cases 5 and 6)[b] 6; fastener spacing (in) at other panel edges (Cases 1, 2, 3 and 4)[b] 6	4; 6	$2\frac{1}{2}$[c]; 4	2[c]; 3	unblocked diaphragms: fasteners spaced 6 in max. at supported edges[b] Case 1 (no unblocked edges or continuous joints parallel to load)	all other configurations (Cases 2, 3, 4, 5, and 6)
structural I grades	6d[e]	$1\frac{1}{4}$	$\frac{5}{16}$	2	185	250	375	420	165	125
				3	210	280	420	475	185	140
	8d	$1\frac{3}{8}$	$\frac{3}{8}$	2	270	360	530	600	240	180
				3	300	400	600	675	265	200
	10d[d]	$1\frac{1}{2}$	$\frac{15}{32}$	2	320	425	640	730	285	215
				3	360	480	720	820	320	240
sheathing, single floor and other grades covered in DOC PS 1 and PS 2	6d[e]	$1\frac{1}{4}$	$\frac{5}{16}$	2	170	225	335	380	150	110
				3	190	250	380	430	170	125
	6d[e]	$1\frac{1}{4}$	$\frac{3}{8}$	2	185	250	375	420	165	125
				3	210	280	420	475	185	140
	8d	$1\frac{3}{8}$	$\frac{3}{8}$	2	240	320	480	545	215	160
				3	270	360	540	610	240	180
	8d	$1\frac{3}{8}$	$\frac{7}{16}$	2	255	340	505	575	230	170
				3	285	380	570	645	255	190
	8d	$1\frac{3}{8}$	$\frac{15}{32}$	2	270	360	530	600	240	180
				3	300	400	600	675	265	200
	10d[d]	$1\frac{1}{2}$	$\frac{15}{32}$	2	290	385	575	655	255	190
				3	325	430	650	735	290	215
	10d[d]	$1\frac{1}{2}$	$\frac{19}{32}$	2	320	425	640	730	285	215
				3	360	480	720	820	320	240

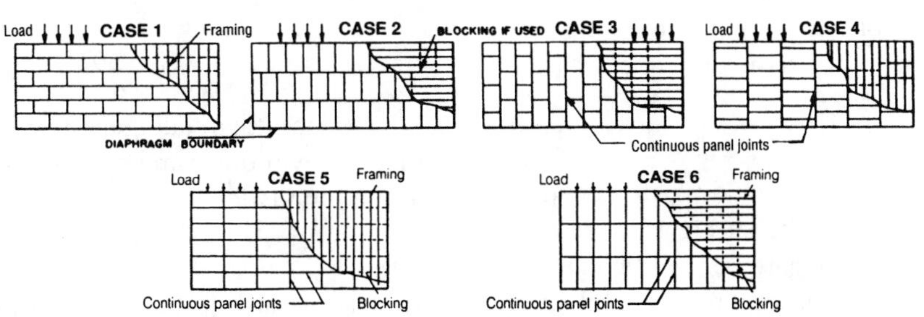

For SI: 1 in = 25.4 mm, 1 plf = 14.5939 N/m.

[a]For framing of other species: (1) Find specific gravity for species of lumber in the AFPA National Design Specification. (2) For staples find shear value from table above for Structural I panels (regardless of actual grade) and multiply value by 0.82 for species with specific gravity of 0.42 or greater, or 0.65 for all other species. (3) For nails find shear value from table above for nail size for actual grade and multiply value by the following adjustment factor: Specific Gravity Adjustment Factor = (1 − (0.5 − SG)), where SG = Specific Gravity of the framing lumber. This adjustment factor shall not be greater than 1.

[b]Space fasteners maximum 12 in o.c. along intermediate framing members (6 in o.c. where supports are spaced 48 in o.c.).

[c]Framing at adjoining panel edges shall be 3 in nominal or wider, and nails shall be staggered where nails are spaced 2 in o.c. or $2\frac{1}{2}$ in o.c.

[d]Framing at adjoining panel edges shall be 3 in nominal or wider, and nails shall be staggered where both of the following conditions are met: (1) 10d nails having penetration into framing of more than $1\frac{1}{2}$ in and (2) nails are spaced 3 in o.c. or less.

[e]8d is recommended minimum for roofs due to negative pressures of high winds.

[f]Staples shall have a minimum crown width of $\frac{7}{16}$ in.

Note: Some rows/columns not pertinent to this text have been omitted by PPI.

Example 22.6

Find the chord force for the roof in Ex. 22.4.

As calculated in Ex. 22.4, the total force on the roof is 72.2 plf, the length of the building is 150 ft, and the building depth is 75 ft.

The moment is

$$M = \frac{\left(72.2 \ \frac{\text{lbf}}{\text{ft}}\right)(150 \text{ ft})^2}{8} = 203{,}060 \text{ ft-lbf}$$

The chord force, using Eq. 22.5, is

$$C = \frac{203{,}060 \text{ ft-lbf}}{75 \text{ ft}} = 2707 \text{ lbf}$$

Shear Walls and Overturning

Once the wind forces have been transferred through the diaphragm and chords into the shear wall, the shear wall must transfer the forces to the foundation. In addition, the shear walls and the entire building must resist the tendency for the structure to overturn due to the moment caused by the lateral force. Finally, the shear wall must be attached to the foundation and footings in such a way as to prevent the entire building from sliding, and the footings and foundation system must be designed to resist the additional loads (caused by the overturning moment), which are added to the simple vertical forces of dead and live loads.

The methods of analysis and design for shear walls are complex and beyond the scope of this book, but the following example will illustrate some of the basic principles.

Example 22.7

Considering the same hypothetical building discussed in the previous examples, assuming the shear walls are constructed of 8 in lightweight aggregate concrete block (35 psf) with 30% open area for windows, find the total shear forces in one of the end walls and the overturning moment.

The accompanying sketch summarizes the loads on the shear wall. The load on the roof is the load per linear foot times the length divided by 2.

$$f = \frac{\left(72.2 \ \frac{\text{lbf}}{\text{ft}}\right)(150 \text{ ft})}{2} = 5415 \text{ lbf}$$

The loads on the shear wall are shown in the sketch. These are the loads that would be used to design the structure of the shear wall, regardless of what material was used.

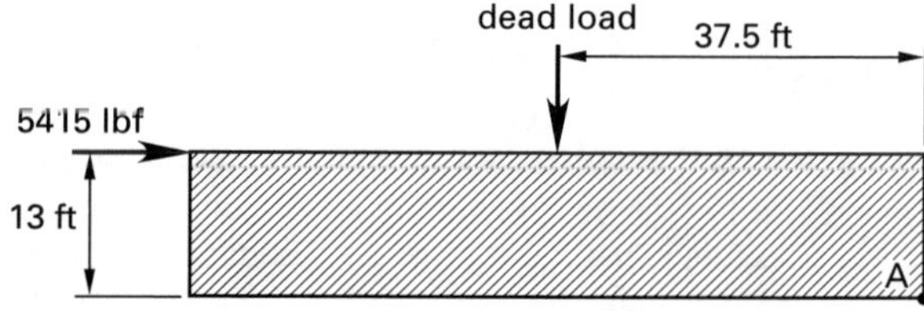

The overturning moment is important to calculate because the building code requires that the resisting moment developed by the dead load on the shear wall be 1.5 times the overturning moment caused by the wind. In this example, the overturning moment is the force at the roof multiplied by the length of the moment arm.

$$M = (5415 \text{ lbf})(13 \text{ ft}) = 70{,}395 \text{ ft-lbf}$$

The required dead load moment must be

$$(1.5)(70{,}395 \text{ ft-lbf}) = 105{,}590 \text{ ft-lbf}$$

The actual weight of the wall allowing for 30% void is

$$(75 \text{ ft})(13 \text{ ft})\left(35 \ \frac{\text{lbf}}{\text{ft}^2}\right)(0.7) = 23{,}887 \text{ lbf}$$

This weight is assumed to act at the midpoint of the wall, so the moment arm is 37.5 ft. The resisting moment is

$$M = (23{,}887 \text{ lbf})(37.5 \text{ ft}) = 895{,}781 \text{ ft-lbf}$$

This is more than adequate to resist the wind overturning moment without using special anchors attaching the walls to the foundation.

Drift

Drift is the lateral displacement of a building caused by a lateral load from a true vertical line. For wind loading, the maximum permissible drift of one story relative to an adjacent story is 0.0025 times the story height. In the previous example, if the story height is 13 ft, the maximum drift is

$$(0.0025)(13 \text{ ft})\left(12 \ \frac{\text{in}}{\text{ft}}\right) = 0.39 \text{ in}$$

Connections

Connections are a critical part of any structural frame that resists lateral loads. These include connections of curtain wall to frame, beams to columns, diaphragm to shear wall, and primary structural frame to the foundation, among others. Moment-resisting connections are fairly common because they occur somewhere in practically any structure designed for lateral forces. Four of the more common types of connections used in steel framed buildings are shown in Fig. 22.8. In all connections, the resisting moment increases with increased distance between the centroids of the top and bottom portions of the connection.

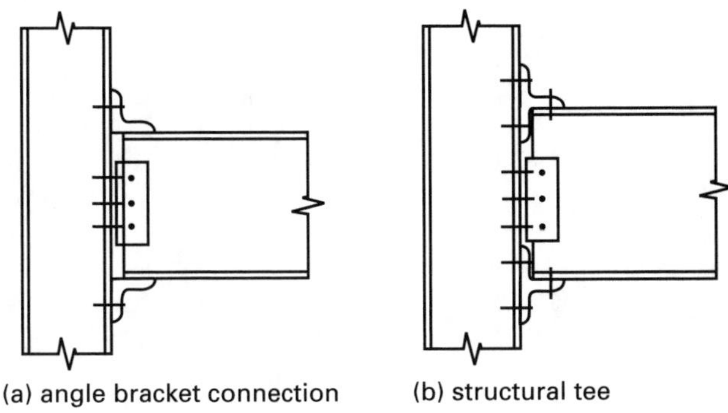

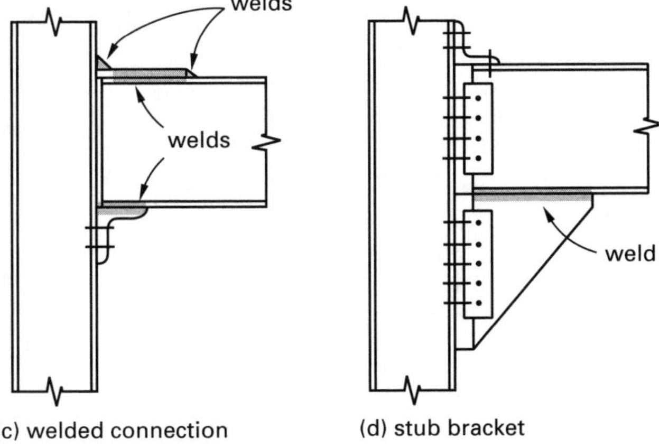

Figure 22.8 Beam-to-Column Connections

One type of connection that has little moment resistance is the angle bracket connection, shown in Fig. 22.8(a). This is a typical steel frame semirigid connection. Because the angles are relatively flexible, very little moment can be transferred from beam to column. The structural tee connection shown in Fig. 22.8(b) is sometimes used instead. The increased rigidity of the structural tees can provide a moment-resisting joint.

In order to minimize the number of pieces and ensure a good moment-resisting joint, beams and columns are often welded as shown in Fig. 22.8(c). There is usually an angle seat to hold the beam in place during erection and to carry the shear loads, but the welded plates transfer the moment.

For an even more rigid connection, a small stub bracket as shown in Fig. 22.8(d) can be used. The triangular shape is structurally efficient and usually can be concealed by the finish column cover or within a suspended ceiling. There are many variations of this connection detail; usually, it includes a combination of bolted and welded joints.

23 LATERAL FORCES—EARTHQUAKES

Nomenclature

a_p	component amplification factor	–
C_s	seismic response coefficient	–
C_t	approximate period coefficient	–
C_U	period upper-limit coefficient	–
C_{vx}	vertical distribution factor	–
F_p	lateral force on part of a structure	lbf
F_v	velocity-based site coefficient	–
F_x	lateral force applied to level x	lbf
F_α	acceleration-based site coefficient	–
h_n	total height of building	ft
h_x	height above base to level x	ft
I	component occupancy importance factor	–
I_p	component importance factor	–
k	seismic distribution exponent	–
R	response modification coefficient	–
R_p	component response modification factor	–
S_1	mapped spectral response at period of 1 sec for site class B	–
S_{D1}	design spectral response at period of 1 sec	–
S_{DS}	design spectral response at short period	–
S_{M1}	spectral response at period of 1 sec for given site class	–
S_{MS}	spectral response at short period for given site class	–
S_S	mapped spectral response at short period for site class B	–
T	fundamental period of vibration	sec
T_a	approximate fundamental period	sec
T_L	long-period transition period	sec
T_s	ratio of S_{D1}/S_{DS}	–
V	total design lateral force or base shear	lbf
w_x	the portion of W that is located at level x	lbf
W	weight	lbf
W_p	weight of a portion of a structure	lbf
x	approximate period exponent	–
Δ_M	story deflection modified for response and importance	–
Δ_S	story deflection determined by elastic analysis	–

Although a great deal has been learned about earthquakes and their effects on buildings during the last 50 years, seismic design is still an inexact science. Because seismic design deals with dynamic forces rather than static forces, and because of the many variables involved, it is often difficult to precisely predict the performance of a building in an earthquake and provide the best possible design to resist the resulting lateral forces.

Another difficulty with seismic design is that the forces produced by an earthquake are so great that no building can economically and reasonably be designed to completely resist all loads in a major earthquake without damage. Building codes and analytical methods of design are, therefore, a compromise between what could resist all earthquakes and what is reasonable. Because of this, the current approach in designing earthquake-resistant structures is that they should first of all not collapse during major seismic activity. Additionally, the components of buildings should not cause other damage or personal injury even though they may be structurally damaged themselves. Finally, structures should be able to withstand minor earthquakes without significant damage.

The analytic methods of analysis and design of earthquake-resistant structures are complex, even with the equivalent lateral force method allowed by the *International Building Code* (IBC). However, a great deal of resistance is provided by the basic configuration and structural system of a building. The design of buildings for earthquake loads requires an early and close collaboration between the architect and engineer to arrive at the optimum structural design while still satisfying the functional and aesthetic needs of the client.

This chapter will discuss some of the basic principles of earthquakes and the primary design and planning guidelines with which ARE candidates should be familiar. In addition, a basic review of the static analysis method will be presented along with some simplified problems to help explain the design concepts.

BASIC PRINCIPLES

The IBC provides for many methods of design for seismic forces. These may be categorized into three types of procedures: simplified analysis, equivalent lateral force, and dynamic analysis. The equivalent lateral force method treats the seismic loads as equivalent lateral loads acting on various levels of the building. The total base shear is calculated and then distributed along the height of the building. The dynamic method uses a computer to mathematically model the building so the response of the structure can be studied at each moment in time using an actual or simulated earthquake accelerogram. The dynamic method is very complex and its details are not covered in the ARE. The equivalent lateral force method is reviewed later in this chapter.

The IBC is specific about which analysis method may or must be used. The use of each method is based on the seismic design category and the seismic use group of the structure. These will be discussed in later sections. The simplified analysis can only be used in seismic design category A and in category B for three-story light-framed buildings and other two-story buildings of use group 1. Any structure may be designed using one of the dynamic methods of analysis. The equivalent lateral force method may be used for buildings in seismic design categories A, B, and C. In the following cases, it may also be used for buildings in seismic design categories D, E, and F.

- regular structures with $T < 3.5T_s$
- irregular structures with $T < 3.5T_s$ and having only plan irregularities 2, 3, 4, or 5 or vertical irregularities 4 or 5

The value of T is discussed in the T Factor section, and T_s is the ratio of S_{D1}/S_{DS} given in the Analysis of Earthquake Loading section. All other structures must be designed using a dynamic method of analysis.

Characteristics of Earthquakes

Earthquakes are caused by the slippage of adjacent plates of the earth's crust and the subsequent release of energy in the form of ground waves. Seismology is based on the science of plate tectonics, which proposes that the earth is composed of several very large plates of hard crust many miles thick, riding on a layer of molten rock closer to the earth's core. These plates are slowly moving relative to one another, and over time tremendous stress is built up by friction. Occasionally the two plates slip, releasing the energy we know as earthquakes. One of the best-known boundaries between two plates occurs between the Pacific plate and the North American plate along the coast of California. Earthquakes also occur in midplates, but the exact mechanism, other than fault slippage, is not fully understood.

The plates slip where the stress is at a maximum, usually several miles below the surface of the earth, at a location called the *hypocenter* of the earthquake. The term heard more often is the *epicenter*, which is the point on the earth's surface directly above the hypocenter.

When an earthquake occurs, complex actions are set up. One result is the development of waves that ultimately produce the shaking experienced in a building. There are three types of waves: *P* or *pressure waves*, *S* or *shear waves*, and *surface waves*. Pressure waves cause a relatively small movement in the direction of wave travel. Shear waves produce a sideways or up-and-down motion that shakes the ground in three directions. These are the waves that cause the most damage to buildings. Surface waves travel at or near the surface and can cause both vertical and horizontal earth movement.

The ground movement can be measured in three ways: by acceleration, velocity, and displacement. All three occur over time, with most earthquakes lasting only a few seconds. It is the acceleration of the ground that induces forces on a structure.

The interaction of the various waves and ground movement is complex. Not only does the earth move in three directions, but each direction has a different, random acceleration and amplitude. In addition, the movement reverses, creating a vibrating action. Even though there is vertical movement, the IBC allows these forces to be neglected under certain types of seismic design. The weight of a structure is usually enough to resist vertical forces. It is side-to-side movement that causes the most damage.

Measurement of Earthquakes

Earthquake strength is commonly measured in two ways: with the Richter scale and with the modified Mercalli intensity scale. The *Richter scale* measures magnitude as an indirect measure of released energy based on instrument recordings according to certain defined procedures. The scale runs from zero at the low end and is open at the upper end, although the largest earthquake ever recorded had a Richter magnitude of nine.

The scale is logarithmic; each whole number value on the scale represents a tenfold increase in amplitude. In terms of energy released, each scale number represents about 32 times the amount of energy below it.

The *modified Mercalli intensity scale* is a measure of an earthquake's intensity. It is an entirely subjective rating based on the observed damage to structures and other physical effects. The scale ranges from I to XII, with the upper rating being the most severe. Each scale includes a verbal description of the effects and damage of an earthquake.

The modified Mercalli scale is imprecise because it depends on people's observations, but it does provide information on how an earthquake affects structures and how the same earthquake affects areas at different distances from the epicenter, both of which cannot be accounted for with the Richter scale.

Unfortunately for building design, neither scale is useful. This is because neither provides any information on the acceleration or duration of an earthquake, both of which are critical in the analysis and design of structures. However, they are used for risk analysis and determination of seismic zones.

Objective, quantified data useful for building design is provided by the *strong motion accelerograph*. This machine measures the acceleration of the ground or a building. The IBC requires that in seismic design categories D, E, and F every building over 6 stories with an aggregate floor area of 60,000 ft^2 or more, and every building over 10 stories regardless of floor area, be provided with not less than three accelerographs. These must be placed in the basement, midportion, and near the top of the building. Some jurisdictions may have additional requirements.

The records obtained by these instruments provide valuable data for research and design of similar buildings in the same geographical area. The acceleration they measure is usually expressed as a fraction of the acceleration of gravity, g, which is 32 ft/sec^2. Thus, an earthquake may be recorded as having an acceleration of 0.55g.

Seismic Design Categories

Based on seismic records, experience, and research, some areas of the United States are determined to have a greater probability of earthquakes than others, and some areas have more severe earthquakes (areas where two major plates abut, for example). This is taken into account by dividing the country into different zones that represent estimates of future earthquake occurrence and strength.

The maps used by the IBC, shown in Figs. 23.2(a) and (b), give the mapped spectral response acceleration at a period of 0.2 sec and 1.0 sec. These values are for the maximum considered earthquake, under site class B, and are used in the analysis procedure. The 0.2 sec period is considered a short period of vibration, and the 1.0 sec period is considered long. They are given as percents and should be divided by 100 for use in formulas.

The Effect of Earthquakes on Buildings

When an earthquake occurs, the first response of a building is to not move at all due to the inertia of the structure's mass. Almost instantaneously, however, the acceleration of the ground causes the building to move sideways at the base, causing a lateral load on the building and a shear force at the base, as though forces were being applied in opposite directions. See Fig. 23.1(a). As the direction of the acceleration changes, the building begins to vibrate back and forth.

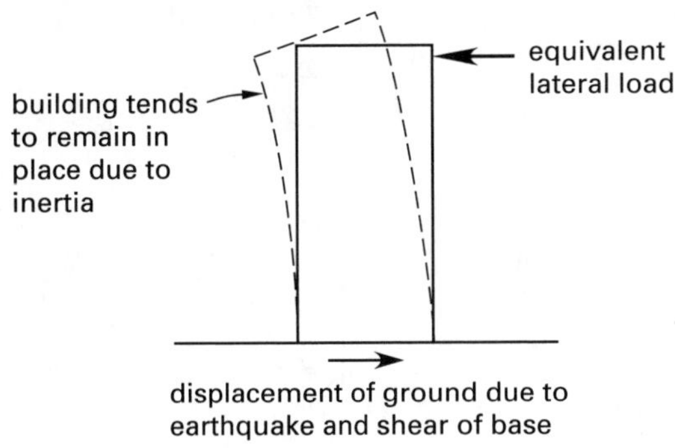

(a) response of a building to earthquake

period is time for one complete oscillation of the building

(b) period of a building

Figure 23.1 Building Motion During an Earthquake

Theoretically, the force on the building can be found by using Newton's law, which states that force equals mass times acceleration. Since the acceleration is established by the given earthquake, the greater the mass of the building, the greater the force acting on it. However, the acceleration of the building depends on another property of the structure—its natural period.

If a building is deflected by a lateral force such as the wind or an earthquake, it moves from side to side. The period is the time in seconds it takes for a building to complete one

Figure 23.2(a) Maximum Considered Earthquake Ground Motion of 0.2 sec Spectral Response Acceleration

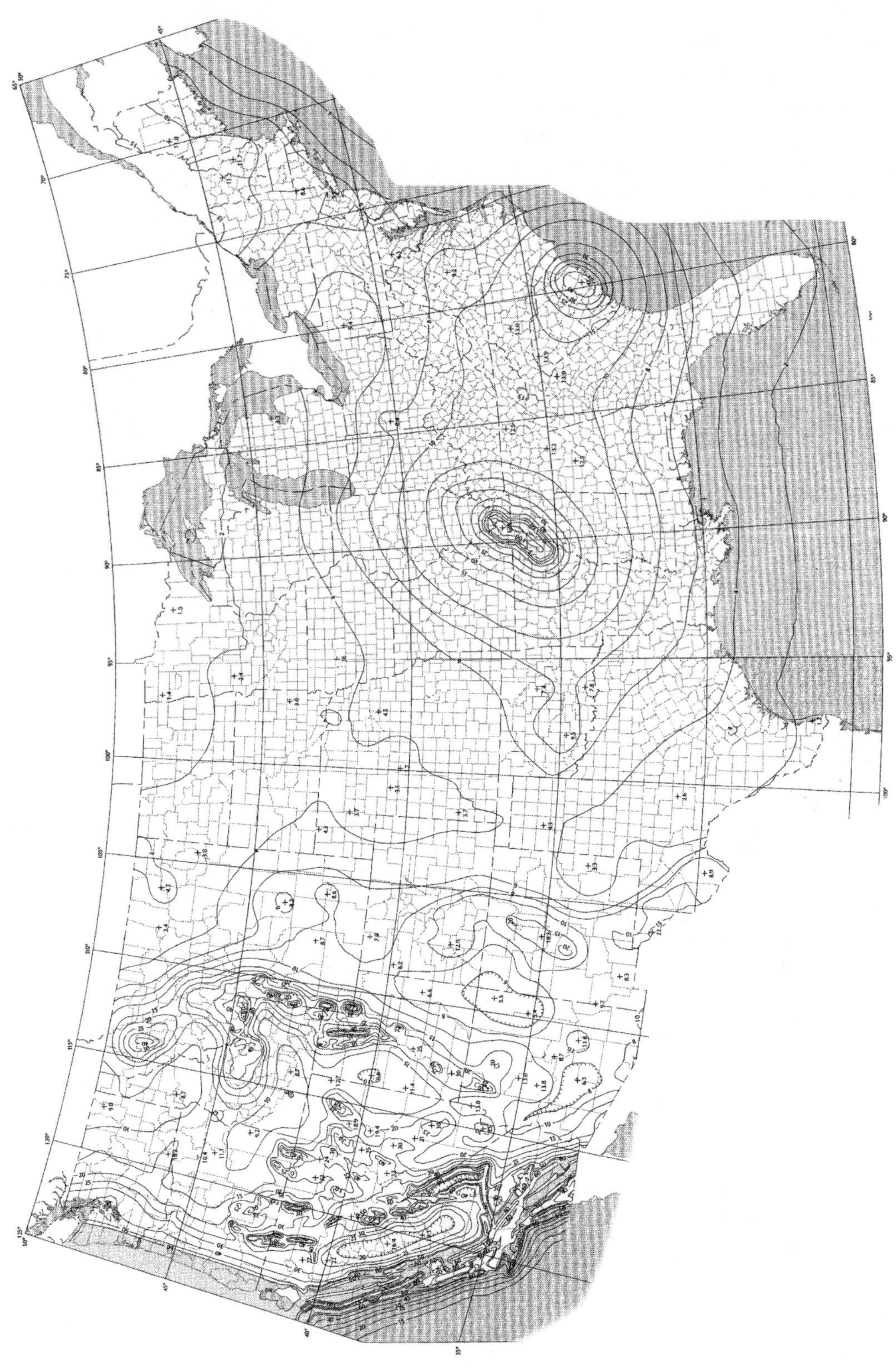

Figure 23.2(b) Maximum Considered Earthquake Ground Motion of 1.0 sec Spectral Response Acceleration

full side-to-side oscillation. See Fig. 23.1(b). The period is dependent on the mass and the stiffness of the building.

In a theoretical, completely stiff building, there is no movement, and the natural period is zero. The acceleration of such an infinitely rigid building is the same as the ground. As the building becomes more flexible, its period increases and the corresponding acceleration decreases. As mentioned previously, as the acceleration decreases, so does the force on the building. Therefore, flexible, long-period buildings have less lateral force induced, and stiff, short-period buildings have more lateral force induced.

As the building moves, the forces applied to it are either transmitted through the structure to the foundation, absorbed by the building components, or released in other ways such as collapse of structural elements.

The goal of seismic design is to build a structure that can safely transfer the loads to the foundation and back to the ground and absorb some of the energy present rather than suffering damage.

The ability of a structure to absorb some of the energy is known as *ductility*, which occurs when the building deflects in the inelastic range without failing or collapsing. The elastic limit, as discussed in Ch. 12, is the limit beyond which the structure sustains permanent deformation. The greater the ductility of a building, the greater is its capacity to absorb energy.

Ductility varies with the material. Steel is a very ductile material because of its ability to deform under a load above the elastic limit without collapsing. Concrete and masonry, on the other hand, are brittle materials. When they are stressed beyond the elastic limit, they break suddenly and without warning. Concrete can be made more ductile with reinforcement, but at a higher cost.

STRUCTURAL SYSTEMS TO RESIST LATERAL LOADS

The IBC specifies the types of structural systems used to resist seismic loads. The code requires that structural systems be classified as one of the types listed in ACI 318 Table 12.2-1. (See Table 23.1.) In addition to outlining the various types of structural systems, this table gives the R factor used in calculations and the maximum height of each type of structural system. There are four broad categories of systems.

Bearing Wall System

A bearing wall system is a structural system without a complete vertical load-carrying space frame in which the lateral loads are resisted by shear walls or braced frames. Bearing walls or bracing systems provide support for all or most gravity loads. Remember that a space frame is defined as a three-dimensional structural system, without bearing walls, that is comprised of members interconnected such that it functions as a complete, self contained unit.

A *shear wall* is a vertical structural element that resists lateral forces in the plane of the wall through shear and bending. Such a wall acts as a beam cantilevered out of the ground or foundation, and just as with a beam, part of its strength derives from its depth. Figure 23.3 shows two examples of a shear wall, one in a simple one-story building and another in a multistory building.

In Fig. 23.3(a), the shear walls are oriented in one direction, so only lateral forces in this direction can be resisted. The roof serves as the horizontal diaphragm and must also be designed to resist the lateral loads and transfer them to the shear walls.

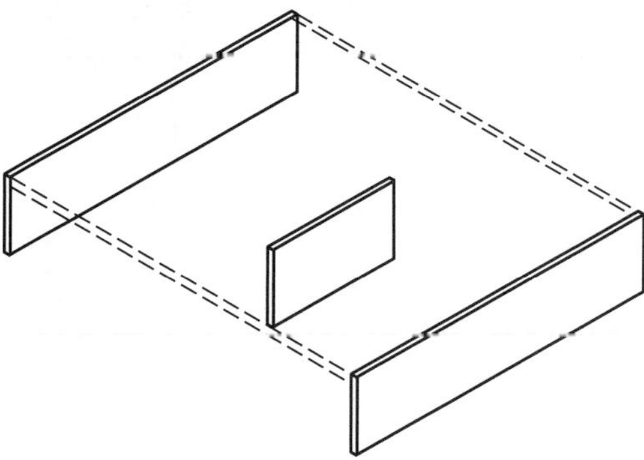

(a) end shear walls and interior shear wall

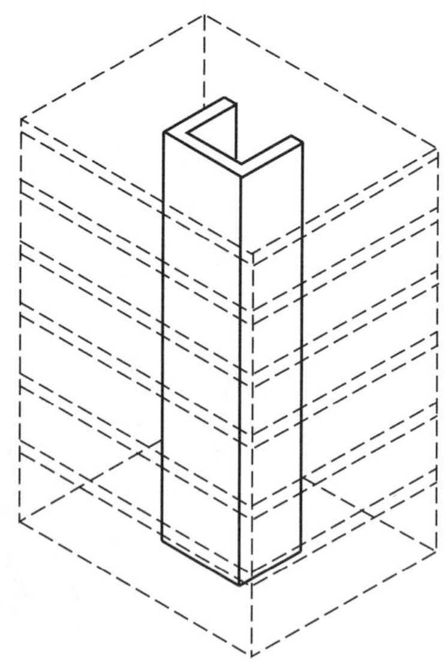

(b) interior shear walls for bracing in two directions

Figure 23.3 Shear Walls

Table 23.1

Seismic Force Resisting Systems

Seismic Force–Resisting System	ASCE 7 Section where Detailing Requirements are Specified	Response Modification Coefficient, R^a	System Overstrength Factor, $\Omega_0{}^g$	Deflection Amplification Factor, $C_d{}^b$	Structural System Limitations and Building Height (ft) Limit[c]				
					Seismic Design Category				
					B	C	D^d	E^d	F^e
A. BEARING WALL SYSTEMS									
1. Special reinforced concrete shear walls	14.2 and 14.2.3.6	5	2½	5	NL	NL	160	160	100
2. Ordinary reinforced concrete shear walls	14.2 and 14.2.3.4	4	2½	4	NL	NL	NP	NP	NP
3. Detailed plain concrete shear walls	14.2 and 14.2.3.2	2	2½	2	NL	NP	NP	NP	NP
4. Ordinary plain concrete shear walls	14.2 and 14.2.3.1	1½	2½	1½	NL	NP	NP	NP	NP
5. Intermediate precast shear walls	14.2 and 14.2.3.5	4	2½	4	NL	NL	40^k	40^k	40^k
6. Ordinary precast shear walls	14.2 and 14.2.3.3	3	2½	3	NL	NP	NP	NP	NP
7. Special reinforced masonry shear walls	14.4 and 14.4.3	5	2½	3½	NL	NL	160	160	100
8. Intermediate reinforced masonry shear walls	14.4 and 14.4.3	3½	2½	2¼	NL	NL	NP	NP	NP
9. Ordinary reinforced masonry shear walls	14.4	2	2½	1¾	NL	160	NP	NP	NP
10. Detailed plain masonry shear walls	14.4	2	2½	1¾	NL	NP	NP	NP	NP
11. Ordinary plain masonry shear walls	14.4	1½	2½	1¼	NL	NP	NP	NP	NP
12. Prestressed masonry shear walls	14.4	1½	2½	1¾	NL	NP	NP	NP	NP
13. Light-framed walls sheathed with wood structural panels rated for shear resistance or steel sheets	14.1, 14.1.4.2, and 14.5	6½	3	4	NL	NL	65	65	65
14. Light-framed walls with shear panels of all other materials	14.1, 14.1.4.2, and 14.5	2	2½	2	NL	NL	35	NP	NP
15. Light-framed wall systems using flat strap bracing	14.1, 14.1.4.2, and 14.5	4	2	3½	NL	NL	65	65	65
B. BUILDING FRAME SYSTEMS									
1. Steel eccentrically braced frames, moment resisting connections at columns away from links	14.1	8	2	4	NL	NL	160	160	100
2. Steel eccentrically braced frames, non-moment-resisting, connections at columns away from links	14.1	7	2	4	NL	NL	160	160	100
3. Special steel concentrically braced frames	14.1	6	2	5	NL	NL	160	160	100
4. Ordinary steel concentrically braced frames	14.1	3¼	2	3¼	NL	NL	35^j	35^j	NP^j
5. Special reinforced concrete shear walls	14.2 and 14.2.3.6	6	2½	5	NL	NL	160	160	100
6. Ordinary reinforced concrete shear walls	14.2 and 14.2.3.4	5	2½	4½	NL	NL	NP	NP	NP
7. Detailed plain concrete shear walls	14.2 and 14.2.3.2	2	2½	2	NL	NP	NP	NP	NP
8. Ordinary plain concrete shear walls	14.2 and 14.2.3.1	1½	2½	1½	NL	NP	NP	NP	NP
9. Intermediate precast shear walls	14.2 and 14.2.3.5	5	2½	4½	NL	NL	40^k	40^k	40^k
10. Ordinary precast shear walls	14.2 and 14.2.3.3	4	2½	4	NL	NP	NP	NP	NP
11. Composite steel and concrete eccentrically braced frames	14.3	8	2	4	NL	NL	160	160	100
12. Composite steel and concrete concentrically braced frames	14.3	5	2	4½	NL	NL	160	160	100
13. Ordinary composite steel and concrete braced frames	14.3	3	2	3	NL	NL	NP	NP	NP
14. Composite steel plate shear walls	14.3	6½	2½	5½	NL	NL	160	160	100
15. Special composite reinforced concrete shear walls with steel elements	14.3	6	2½	5	NL	NL	160	160	100
16. Ordinary composite reinforced concrete shear walls with steel elements	14.3	5	2½	4½	NL	NL	NP	NP	NP
17. Special reinforced masonry shear walls	14.4	5½	2½	4	NL	NL	160	160	100
18. Intermediate reinforced masonry shear walls	14.4	4	2½	4	NL	NL	NP	NP	NP
19. Ordinary reinforced masonry shear walls	14.4	2	2½	2	NL	160	NP	NP	NP
20. Detailed plain masonry shear walls	14.4	2	2½	2	NL	NP	NP	NP	NP
21. Ordinary plain masonry shear walls	14.4	1½	2½	1¼	NL	NP	NP	NP	NP

(continued)

Table 23.1 *(continued)*

Seismic Force Resisting Systems

Seismic Force–Resisting System	ASCE 7 Section where Detailing Requirements are Specified	Response Modification Coefficient, R^a	System Overstrength Factor, $\Omega_0{}^g$	Deflection Amplification Factor, $C_d{}^b$	Structural System Limitations and Building Height (ft) Limit[c] Seismic Design Category				
					B	C	D[d]	E[d]	F[e]
22. Prestressed masonry shear walls	14.4	1½	2½	1¾	NL	NP	NP	NP	NP
23. Light-framed walls sheathed with wood structural panels rated for shear resistance or steel sheets	14.1, 14.1.4.2, and 14.5	7	2½	4½	NL	NL	65	65	65
24. Light-framed walls with shear panels of all other materials	14.1, 14.1.4.2, and 14.5	2½	2½	2½	NL	NL	35	NP	NP
25. Buckling-restrained braced frames, non-moment-resisting beam-column connections	14.1	7	2	5½	NL	NL	160	160	100
26. Buckling-restrained braced frames, moment-resisting beam-column connections	14.1	8	2½	5	NL	NL	160	160	100
27. Special steel plate shear wall	14.1	7	2	6	NL	NL	160	160	100
C. MOMENT-RESISTING FRAME SYSTEMS									
1. Special steel moment frames	14.1 and 12.2.5.5	8	3	5½	NL	NL	NL	NL	NL
2. Special steel truss moment frames	14.1	7	3	5½	NL	NL	160	100	NP
3. Intermediate steel moment frames	12.2.5.6, 12.2.5.7, 12.2.5.8, 12.2.5.9, and 14.1	4.5	3	4	NL	NL	35[h,i]	NP[h]	NP[i]
4. Ordinary steel moment frames	12.2.5.6, 12.2.5.7, 12.2.5.8, and 14.1	3.5	3	3	NL	NL	NP[h]	NP[h]	NP[i]
5. Special reinforced concrete moment frames	12.2.5.5 and 14.2	8	3	5½	NL	NL	NL	NL	NL
6. Intermediate reinforced concrete moment frames	14.2	5	3	4½	NL	NL	NP	NP	NP
7. Ordinary reinforced concrete moment frames	14.2	3	3	2½	NL	NP	NP	NP	NP
8. Special composite steel and concrete moment frames	12.2.5.5 and 14.3	8	3	5½	NL	NL	NL	NL	NL
9. Intermediate composite moment frames	14.3	5	3	4½	NL	NL	NP	NP	NP
10. Composite partially restrained moment frames	14.3	6	3	5½	160	160	100	NP	NP
11. Ordinary composite moment frames	14.3	3	3	2½	NL	NP	NP	NP	NP
D. DUAL SYSTEMS WITH SPECIAL MOMENT FRAMES CAPABLE OF RESISTING AT LEAST 25% OF PRESCRIBED SEISMIC FORCES	12.2.5.1								
1. Steel eccentrically braced frames	14.1	8	2½	4	NL	NL	NL	NL	NL
2. Special steel concentrically braced frames	14.1	7	2½	5½	NL	NL	NL	NL	NL
3. Special reinforced concrete shear walls	14.2	7	2½	5½	NL	NL	NL	NL	NL
4. Ordinary reinforced concrete shear walls	14.2	6	2½	5	NL	NL	NP	NP	NP
5. Composite steel and concrete eccentrically braced frames	14.3	8	2½	4	NL	NL	NL	NL	NL
6. Composite steel and concrete concentrically braced frames	14.3	6	2½	5	NL	NL	NL	NL	NL
7. Composite steel plate shear walls	14.3	7½	2½	6	NL	NL	NL	NL	NL
8. Special composite reinforced concrete shear walls with steel elements	14.3	7	2½	6	NL	NL	NL	NL	NL
9. Ordinary composite reinforced concrete shear walls with steel elements	14.3	6	2½	5	NL	NL	NP	NP	NP
10. Special reinforced masonry shear walls	14.4	5½	3	5	NL	NL	NL	NL	NL
11. Intermediate reinforced masonry shear walls	14.4	4	3	3½	NL	NL	NP	NP	NP
12. Buckling-restrained braced frame	14.1	8	2½	5	NL	NL	NL	NL	NL
13. Special steel plate shear walls	14.1	8	2½	6½	NL	NL	NL	NL	NL

(continued)

Table 23.1 *(continued)*

Seismic Force Resisting Systems

Seismic Force-Resisting System	ASCE 7 Section where Detailing Requirements are Specified	Response Modification Coefficient, R[a]	System Overstrength Factor, Ω_0[g]	Deflection Amplification Factor, C_d[b]	Structural System Limitations and Building Height (ft) Limit[c]				
					Seismic Design Category				
					B	C	D[d]	E[d]	F[e]
E. DUAL SYSTEMS WITH INTERMEDIATE MOMENT FRAMES CAPABLE OF RESISTING AT LEAST 25% OF PRESCRIBED SEISMIC FORCES	12.2.5.1								
1. Special steel concentrically braced frames[f]	14.1	6	2½	5	NL	NL	35	NP	NP[h,k]
2. Special reinforced concrete shear walls	14.2	6½	2½	5	NL	NL	160	100	100
3. Ordinary reinforced masonry shear walls	14.4	3	3	2½	NL	160	NP	NP	NP
4. Intermediate reinforced masonry shear walls	14.4	3½	3	3	NL	NL	NP	NP	NP
5. Composite steel and concrete concentrically braced frames	14.3	5½	2½	4½	NL	NL	160	100	NP
6. Ordinary composite braced frames	14.3	3½	2½	3	NL	NL	NP	NP	NP
7. Ordinary composite reinforced concrete shear walls with steel elements	14.3	5	3	4½	NL	NL	NP	NP	NP
8. Ordinary reinforced concrete shear walls	14.2	5½	2½	4½	NL	NL	NP	NP	NP
F. SHEAR WALL-FRAME INTERACTIVE SYSTEM WITH ORDINARY REINFORCED CONCRETE MOMENT FRAMES AND ORDINARY REINFORCED CONCRETE SHEAR WALLS	12.2.5.10 and 14.2	4½	2½	4	NL	NP	NP	NP	NP
G. CANTILEVERED COLUMN SYSTEMS DETAILED TO CONFORM TO THE REQUIREMENTS FOR:	12.2.5.2								
1. Special steel moment frames	12.2.5.5 and 14.1	2½	1¼	2½	35	35	35	35	35
2. Intermediate steel moment frames	14.1	1½	1¼	1½	35	35	35[h]	NP[h,i]	NP[h,i]
3. Ordinary steel moment frames	14.1	1¼	1¼	1¼	35	35	NP	NP[h,i]	NP[h,i]
4. Special reinforced concrete moment frames	12.2.5.5 and 14.2	2½	1¼	2½	35	35	35	35	35
5. Intermediate concrete moment frames	14.2	1½	1¼	1½	35	35	NP	NP	NP
6. Ordinary concrete moment frames	14.2	1	1¼	1	35	NP	NP	NP	NP
7. Timber frames	14.5	1½	1½	1½	35	35	35	NP	NP
H. STEEL SYSTEMS NOT SPECIFICALLY DETAILED FOR SEISMIC RESISTANCE, EXCLUDING CANTILEVER COLUMN SYSTEMS	14.1	3	3	3	NL	NL	NP	NP	NP

[a] Response modification coefficient, R, for use throughout the standard. Note R reduces forces to a strength level, not an allowable stress level.

[b] Reflection amplification factor, C_d, for use in Sections 12.8.6, 12.8.7, and 12.9.2

[c] NL = Not Limited and NP = Not Permitted. For metric units use 30.5 m for 100 ft and use 48.8 m for 160 ft. Heights are measured from the base of the structure as defined in Section 11.2.

[d] See Section 12.2.5.4 for a description of building systems limited to buildings with a height of 240 ft (73.2 m) or less.

[e] See Section 12.2.5.4 for building systems limited to buildings with a height of 160 ft (48.8 m) or less.

[f] Ordinary moment frame is permitted to be used in lieu of intermediate moment frame for Seismic Design Categories B or C.

[g] The tabulated value of the overstrength factor, Ω_0, is permitted to be reduced by subtracting one-half for structures with flexible diaphragms, but shall not be taken as less than 2.0 for any structure.

[h] See Sections 12.2.5.6 and 12.2.5.7 for limitations for steel OMFs and IMFs in structures assigned to Seismic Design Category D or E.

[i] See Sections 12.2.5.8 and 12.2.5.9 for limitations for steel OMFs and IMFs in structures assigned to Seismic Design Category F.

[j] Steel ordinary concentrically braced frames are permitted in single-story buildings up to a height of 60 ft (18.3 m) where the dead load of the roof does not exceed 20 psf (0.96 kN/m^2) and in penthouse structures.

[k] Increase in height to 45 ft (13.7 m) is permitted for single story storage warehouse facilities.

Figure 23.3(a) also shows an important aspect of shear walls in particular and vertical elements in general. This is the aspect of symmetry that has a bearing on whether torsional effects will be produced. The shear walls in Fig. 23.3(a) show the shear walls symmetrical in the plane of loading. Torsion will be discussed in a later section.

Figure 23.3(b) illustrates a common use of shear walls at the interior of a multistory building. Because walls enclosing stairways, elevator shafts, and mechanical chases are mostly solid and run the entire height of the building, they are often used for shear walls. Although not as efficient from a strictly structural point of view, interior shear walls do leave the exterior of the building open for windows.

Notice that in Fig. 23.3(b) there are shear walls in both directions, which is a more realistic situation because both wind and earthquake forces need to be resisted in both directions. In this diagram, the two shear walls are symmetrical in one direction, but the single shear wall produces a nonsymmetric condition in the other since it is off center. Shear walls do not need to be symmetrical in a building, but symmetry is preferred to avoid torsional effects.

Shear walls can be constructed from a variety of materials, but the most common are plywood on wood framing for residential and small commercial buildings, and concrete for larger buildings. Reinforced masonry walls can also be used. Shear walls may have openings in them, but the calculations are more difficult, and a wall's ability to resist lateral loads is reduced depending on the percentage of open area.

Building Frame Systems

A *building frame system* is an essentially complete space frame that provides support for gravity loads in which the lateral loads are resisted by shear walls or braced frames. A *braced frame* is a truss system of the concentric or eccentric type in which the lateral forces are resisted through axial stresses in the members. Just as with a truss, the braced frame depends on diagonal members to provide a load path for lateral forces from each building element to the foundation. Figure 23.4(a) shows a simple one-story braced frame. At one end of the building two bays are braced, and at the other end only one bay is braced. As with Fig. 23.3, this building is only braced in one direction and uses compression braces because the diagonal member may be either in tension or compression, depending on which way the force is applied.

Figure 23.4(b) shows two methods of bracing a multistory building. A single diagonal compression member in one bay can be used to brace against lateral loads coming from either direction. Alternately, tension diagonals can be used to accomplish the same result, but they must be run both ways to account for the load coming from either direction.

Braced framing can be placed on the exterior or interior of a building and may be placed in one structural bay or several. In a trussed tube building, the diagonals span between several floors of the building. Obviously, a braced frame can present design problems for windows and doorways, but it is a very efficient and rigid lateral force resisting system.

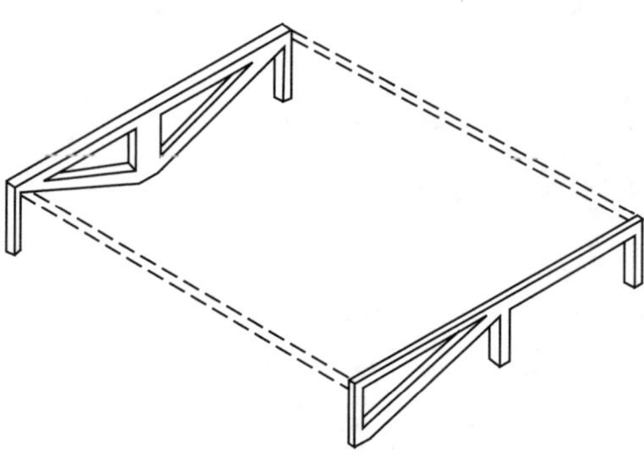

(a) single-story braced frame

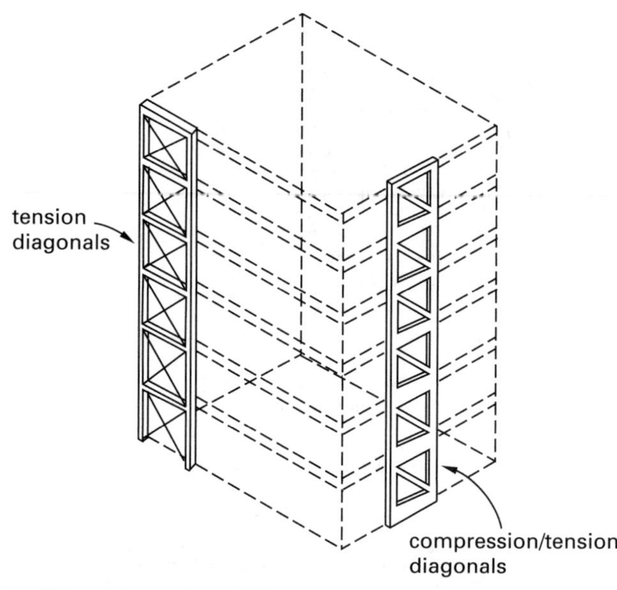

(b) multistory braced frame

Figure 23.4 Braced Frames

Moment-Resisting Frame Systems

Moment-resisting frames carry lateral loads primarily by flexure in the members and joints. Joints are designed and constructed so they are theoretically completely rigid, and therefore any lateral deflection of the frame occurs from the bending of columns and beams. The IBC differentiates between three types of moment-resisting frames.

The first type is the special moment-resisting frame, which must be specifically detailed to provide ductile behavior and comply with the provisions of Chs. 19 and 22 (Concrete and Steel) of the IBC.

The second type is the intermediate moment-resisting frame, which has fewer restrictive requirements than special moment-resisting frames. These cannot be used in seismic design category D, E, or F; however, steel intermediate moment-resisting frames up to 35 ft high may be used in category D.

The third type is the ordinary moment-resisting frame. This is a steel or concrete moment-resisting frame that does not meet the special detailing requirements for ductile behavior. Ordinary steel frames may only be used in seismic design categories A, B, and C, while ordinary concrete frames cannot be used in category A or B.

Moment-resisting frames are more flexible than shear wall structures or braced frames; the horizontal deflection, or drift, is greater. Adjacent buildings cannot be located too close to each other, and special attention must be paid to the eccentricity developed in columns, which increases the column bending stresses.

Two types of moment-resisting frames are shown in Fig. 23.5.

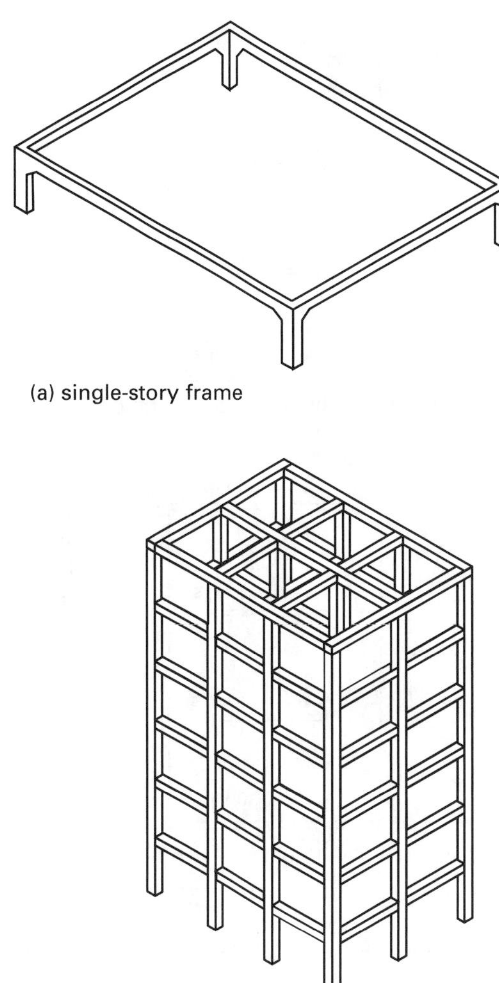

Figure 23.5 Moment-Resisting Frames

Dual Systems

A *dual system* is a structural system in which an essentially complete frame provides support for gravity loads, and resistance to lateral loads is provided by a specially detailed moment-resisting frame and shear walls or braced frames. The moment-resisting frame must be capable of resisting at least 25% of the base shear, and the two systems must be designed to resist the total lateral load in proportion to their relative rigidities. The moment-resisting frame may be either steel or concrete. Other types of dual systems include the use of eccentrically braced frames and shear wall-frame interactive systems.

Horizontal Elements

In all lateral-force-resisting systems, there must be a way to transmit lateral forces to the vertical resisting elements. This is done with several types of structures, the most common of which is the *diaphragm*. As discussed in Ch. 22, a diaphragm acts as a horizontal beam resisting forces with shear and bending action. Refer to Fig. 22.5.

Other types of horizontal elements include horizontal trussed frames and horizontal moment-resisting frames. There are two types of diaphragms: flexible and rigid. Although no horizontal element is completely flexible or rigid, a distinction is made between the two types because the type affects the way in which lateral forces are distributed.

A *flexible diaphragm* is one that has a maximum lateral deformation more than two times the average story drift of that story. This deformation can be determined by comparing the midpoint in-plane deflection of the diaphragm with the story drift of the adjoining vertical resisting elements under equivalent tributary load. The lateral load is distributed according to tributary areas as shown in Fig. 23.6(a).

With a *rigid diaphragm*, the shear forces transmitted from the diaphragm to the vertical elements will be in proportion to the relative stiffness of the vertical elements (assuming there is no torsion). See Fig. 23.6(b). If the end walls in the diagram are twice as stiff as the interior walls, then one-third of the load is distributed to each end wall and one-third is distributed to the two interior walls and equally divided between them. Figure 23.6(b) shows symmetrically placed shear walls, so the distribution is equal. However, if the vertical resisting elements are asymmetric, the shearing forces are unequal.

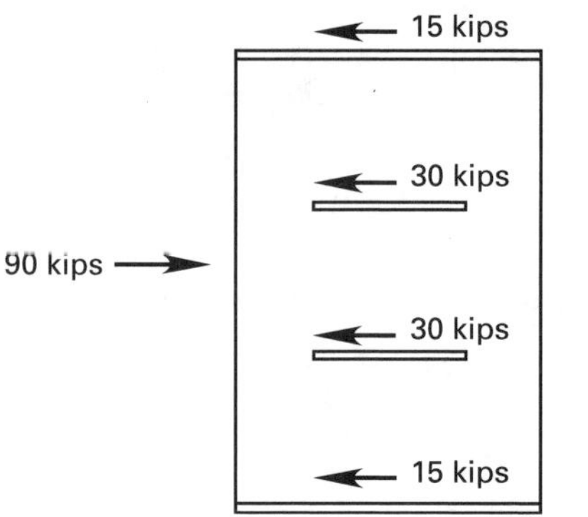

(a) flexible diaphragm load distribution

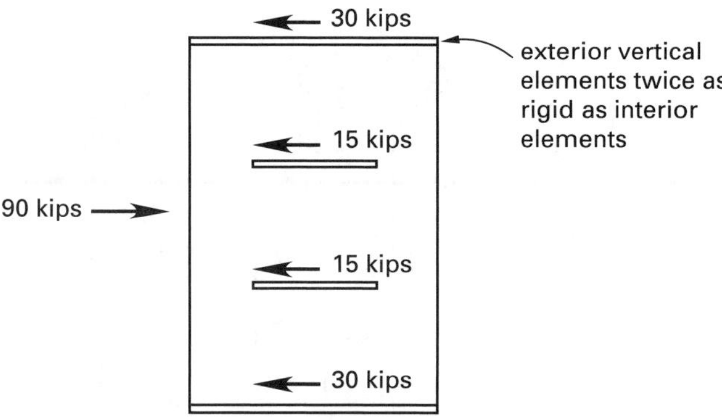

(b) rigid diaphragm load distribution

Figure 23.6 Diaphragm Load Distribution

Concrete floors are considered rigid diaphragms, as are steel and concrete composite deck construction. Steel decks may be either flexible or rigid, depending on the details of their construction. Wood decks are considered flexible diaphragms.

BUILDING CONFIGURATION

In recent years, there has been increased emphasis on the importance of a building's configuration in resisting seismic forces. Early decisions concerning size, shape, arrangement, and location of major elements can have a significant influence on the performance of a structure. Since the design professional plays a large role in these early decisions, it is imperative that the architect thoroughly understand the concepts involved.

Building configuration refers to the overall building size and shape and the size and arrangement of the primary structural frame, as well as the size and location of the nonstructural components of the building that may affect its structural performance. Significant nonstructural components include such things as heavy nonbearing partitions, exterior cladding, and large weights like equipment or swimming pools.

In ASCE/SEI 7, elements that constitute both horizontal and vertical irregularities are specifically defined, so it is clear which structures must be designed with the dynamic method and which structures may be designed using the static analysis method.

The code states that all buildings must be classified as either regular or irregular. Whether a building is regular or not helps determine if the static method may be used. Irregular structures generally require design by the dynamic method (with exceptions mentioned in the Basic Principles section), and additional detailed design requirements are imposed depending on what type of irregularity exists.

Table 23.2 lists and defines five types of vertical structural irregularities along with references to the specific code sections that give specific design requirements. Table 23.3 lists and defines five types of horizontal structural irregularities along with their code references. Note that the definition of torsional irregularity (Horizontal Structural Irregularity Type 1 in Table 23.3) mentions diaphragms that are not flexible. Flexible diaphragms are defined in the Horizontal Elements section.

Also note that the definition of nonparallel systems (Horizontal Structural Irregularity Type 5 in Table 23.3) includes buildings in which a column forms part of two or more intersecting lateral-force-resisting systems, unless the axial load due to seismic forces acting in either direction is less than 20% of the column allowable axial load.

The following sections describe some of the important aspects of building configuration.

Torsion

Lateral forces on a portion of a building are assumed to be uniformly distributed and can be resolved into a single line of action acting on a building. In a similar way, the shear reaction forces produced by the vertical resisting elements can be resolved into a single line of action. For symmetric buildings with vertical resisting elements of equal rigidity, these lines of action pass through the same point as shown diagrammatically in Fig. 23.7(a).

If the shear walls or other vertical elements are not symmetric or are of unequal rigidity, the resultant of their shear resisting forces, the center of rigidity, does not coincide with the applied lateral force. This is shown in Fig. 23.7(b). Since the forces are acting in opposite directions with an eccentricity, torsion force is developed, which is in addition to the lateral load alone.

When the force on a vertical element caused by the eccentricity acts in the same direction as the force caused by the

Table 23.2

Vertical Structural Irregularities

	Irregularity Type and Description	Reference Section	Seismic Design Category Application
1a.	**Stiffness-Soft Story Irregularity** is defined to exist where there is a story in which the lateral stiffness is less than 70% of that in the story above or less than 80% of the average stiffness of the three stories above.	Table 12.6-1	D, E, and F
1b.	**Stiffness-Extreme Soft Story Irregularity** is defined to exist where there is a story in which the lateral stiffness is less than 60% of that in the story above or less than 70% of the average stiffness of the three stories above.	12.3.3.1 Table 12.6-1	E and F D, E, and F
2.	**Weight (Mass) Irregularity** is defined to exist where the effective mass of any story is more than 150% of the effective mass of an adjacent story. A roof that is lighter than the floor below need not be considered.	Table 12.6-1	D, E, and F
3.	**Vertical Geometric Irregularity** is defined to exist where the horizontal dimension of the seismic force–resisting system in any story is more than 130% of that in an adjacent story.	Table 12.6-1	D, E, and F
4.	**In-Plane Discontinuity in Vertical Lateral Force-Resisting Element Irregularity** is defined to exist where an in-plane offset of the lateral force-resisting elements is greater than the length of those elements or there exists a reduction in stiffness of the resisting element in the story below.	12.3.3.3 12.3.3.4 Table 12.6-1	B, C, D, E, and F D, E, and F D, E, and F
5a.	**Discontinuity in Lateral Strength–Weak Story Irregularity** is defined to exist where the story lateral strength is less than 80% of that in the story above. The story lateral strength is the total lateral strength of all seismic-resisting elements sharing the story shear for the direction under consideration.	12.3.3.1 Table 12.6-1	E and F D, E, and F
5b.	**Discontinuity in Lateral Strength–Extreme Weak Story Irregularity** is defined to exist where the story lateral strength is less than 65% of that in the story above. The story strength is the total strength of all seismic-resisting elements sharing the story shear for the direction under consideration.	12.3.3.1 12.3.3.2 Table 12.6-1	D, E, and F B and C D, E, and F

Table 23.3

Horizontal Structural Irregularities

	Irregularity Type and Description	Reference Section	Seismic Design Category Application
1a.	**Torsional Irregularity** is defined to exist where the maximum story drift, computed including accidental torsion, at one end of the structure transverse to an axis is more than 1.2 times the average of the story drifts at the two ends of the structure. Torsional irregularity requirements in the reference sections apply only to structures in which the diaphragms are rigid or semirigid.	12.3.3.4 12.8.4.3 12.7.3 12.12.1 Table 12.6-1 Section 16.2.2	D, E, and F C, D, E, and F B, C, D, E, and F C, D, E, and F D, E, and F B, C, D, E, and F
1b.	**Extreme Torsional Irregularity** is defined to exist where the maximum story drift, computed including accidental torsion, at one end of the structure transverse to an axis is more than 1.4 times the average of the story drifts at the two ends of the structure. Extreme torsional irregularity requirements in the reference sections apply only to structures in which the diaphragms are rigid or semirigid.	12.3.3.1 12.3.3.4 12.7.3 12.8.4.3 12.12.1 Table 12.6-1 Section 16.2.2	E and F D B, C, and D C and D C and D D B, C, and D
2.	**Reentrant Corner Irregularity** is defined to exist where both plan projections of the structure beyond a reentrant corner are greater than 15% of the plan dimension of the structure in the given direction.	12.3.3.4 Table 12.6-1	D, E, and F D, E, and F
3.	**Diaphragm Discontinuity Irregularity** is defined to exist where there are diaphragms with abrupt discontinuities or variations in stiffness, including those having cutout or open areas greater than 50% of the gross enclosed diaphragm area, or changes in effective diaphragm stiffness of more than 50% from one story to the next.	12.3.3.4 Table 12.6-1	D, E, and F D, E, and F
4.	**Out-of-Plane Offsets Irregularity** is defined to exist where there are discontinuities in a lateral force-resistance path, such as out-of-plane offsets of the vertical elements.	12.3.3.4 12.3.3.3 12.7.3 Table 12.6-1 16.2.2	D, E, and F B, C, D, E, and F B, C, D, E, and F D, E, and F B, C, D, E, and F
5.	**Nonparallel Systems-Irregularity** is defined to exist where the vertical lateral force-resisting elements are not parallel to or symmetric about the major orthogonal axes of the seismic force–resisting system.	12.5.3 12.7.3 Table 12.6-1 Section 16.2.2	C, D, E, and F B, C, D, E, and F D, E, and F B, C, D, E, and F

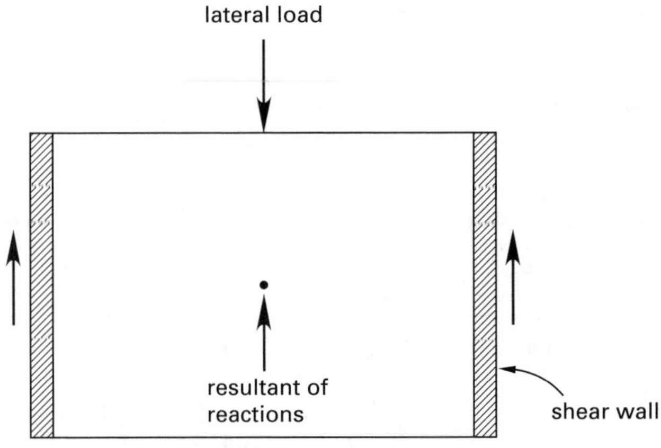

(a) symmetric building

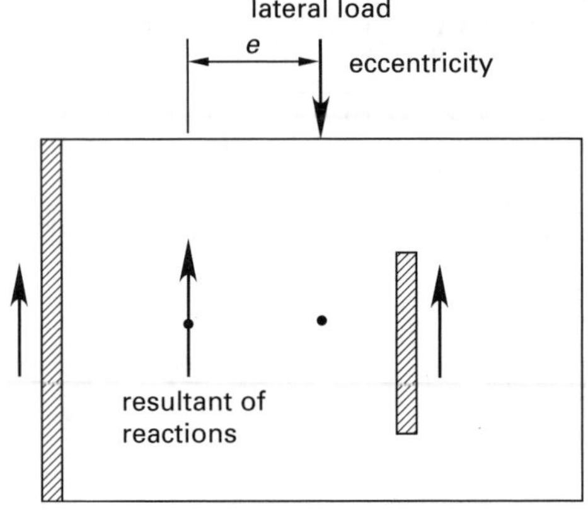

(b) nonsymmetric vertical load-resisting elements

Figure 23.7 Development of Torsion

lateral load directly, the forces must be added. However, when the torsional force acts in the opposite direction, one force cannot be subtracted from the other.

The IBC requires that even in symmetrical buildings a certain amount of accidental torsion be planned for. This accounts for the fact that the positions of loads in an occupied building cannot be known for certain. The code requires that the mass at each level is assumed to be displaced from the calculated center of mass in each direction by a distance equal to 5% of the building dimension at that level perpendicular to the direction of the force under consideration. For example, for a building 50 ft wide and 100 ft long, the center of mass for forces acting perpendicular to the 100 ft dimension is offset 5 ft. For forces acting in the other direction, the center of mass is offset $2^1/_2$ ft.

The importance of understanding the concept of torsion will become apparent in the following sections.

Plan Shape

Irregularities in plan shape can create torsion and concentrations of stress, both of which should be avoided whenever possible. One of the most common and troublesome plan shapes is the reentrant corner. Figure 23.8(a) shows some common varieties of this shape. During an earthquake, the ground motion causes the structure to move in such a way that stress concentrations are developed at the inside corners. See Fig. 23.8(b).

In addition, since the center of mass and the center of rigidity do not coincide, there is an eccentricity established that results in a twisting of the entire structure as discussed in the previous section and shown in Fig. 23.7(b).

Of course, building shape is often dictated by the site, the program, or other requirements beyond the control of the architect or engineer. In the cases where such shapes are unavoidable, there are ways to minimize the problem. The portions of the building can be separated with a seismic joint, they can be tied together across the connection, or the inside corner can be splayed. These design approaches are shown in Fig. 23.9.

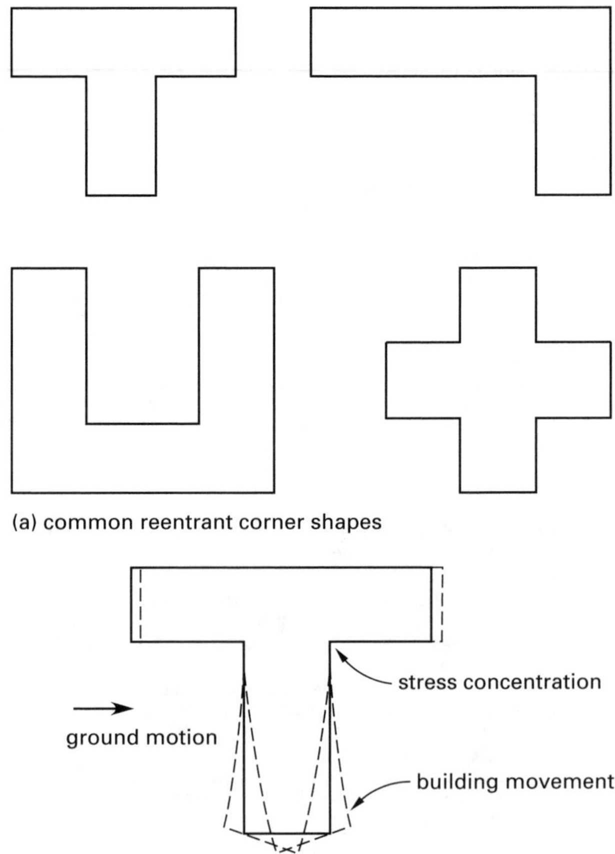

Figure 23.8 Problem Plan Shapes

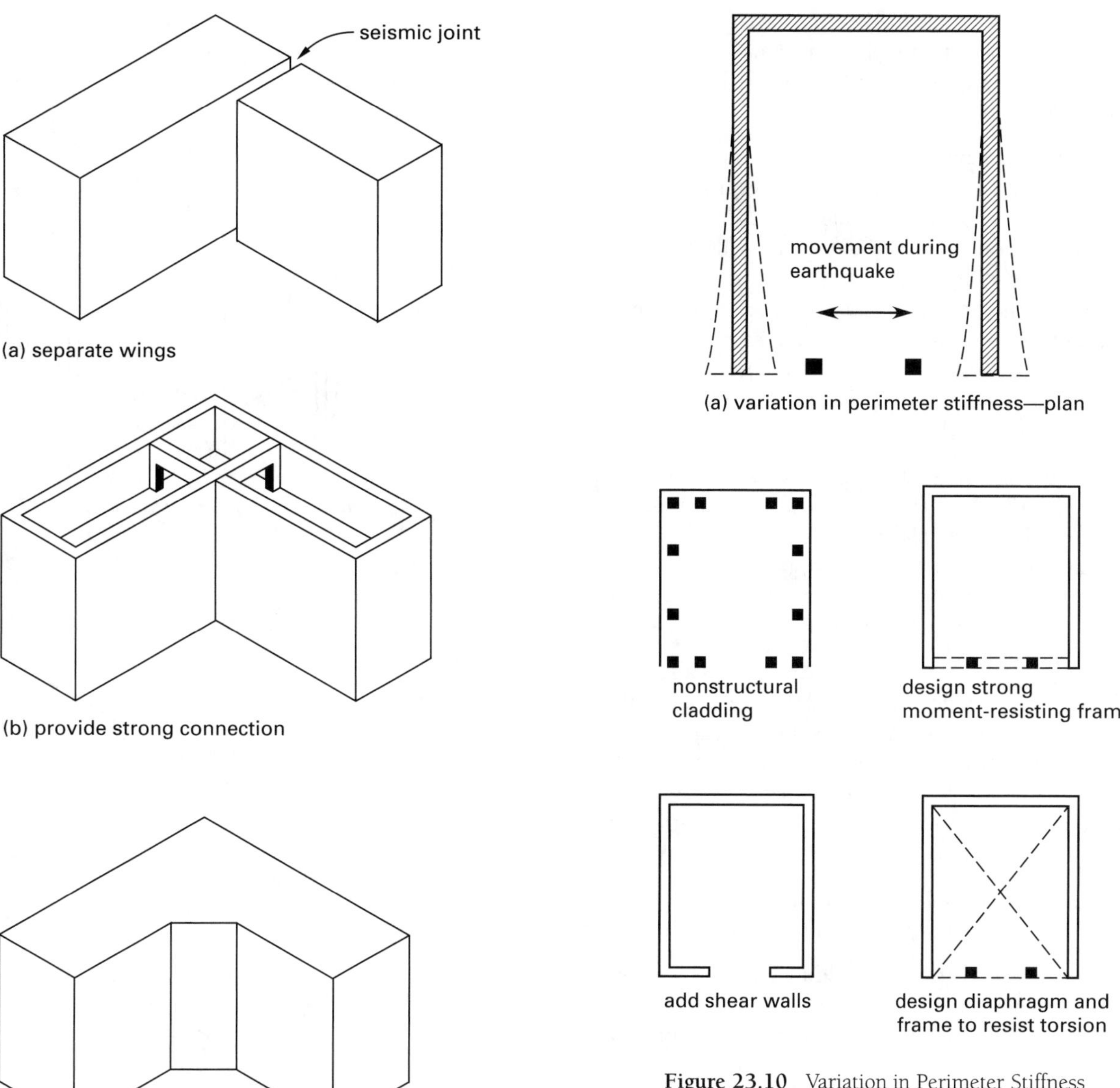

Figure 23.9 Solutions to Reentrant Corners

Figure 23.10 Variation in Perimeter Stiffness

A second common problem that arises with building plans is a variation in the stiffness and strength of the perimeter. Even though a building may be symmetric, the distribution of mass and lateral resisting elements may place the centers of mass and rigidity in such a way that torsion is developed. One example of this is shown diagrammatically in Fig. 23.10(a), where a building has rigid shear walls on three sides but is open in the front.

During an earthquake, the open end of the building acts as a cantilevered beam causing lateral displacement and torsion. There are four possible ways to alleviate the problem. These are shown in Fig. 23.10.

In the first instance, a rigid frame can be constructed with symmetric rigidity, and then the cladding can be made nonstructural. Secondly, a strong, moment-resisting or braced frame can be added that has a stiffness similar to the other walls. Third, shear walls can be added to the front if this does not compromise the function of the building. Finally, for small buildings, the structure can simply be designed to resist the expected torsion forces.

Elevation Design

The ideal elevation from a seismic design standpoint is one that is regular, symmetrical, continuous, and matches the other elevations in configuration and seismic resistance. Setbacks and offsets should be avoided for the same reason as reentrant corners in plan should be avoided—to avoid areas of stress concentration. Of course, perfect symmetry is not always possible due to the functional and aesthetic requirements of the building, but there are two basic configurations that should (and can) be avoided by the architect early in the design process.

The first problem configuration is a discontinuous shear wall. This is a major mistake and should never happen. Discontinuities can occur when a shear wall is given a large opening, stops short of the foundation, or is altered in some other way. Since the entire purpose of a shear wall is to carry lateral loads to the foundation and act as a beam cantilevered out of the foundation, any interruption of this is counterproductive. Of course, small openings like doors and small windows can be placed in shear walls if proper reinforcement is provided.

Two common examples of discontinuous shear walls are shown in Fig. 23.11. In the first, the shear wall is stopped at the second floor level and supported by columns. This is often done to open up the first floor, but it creates a situation where stress concentrations are so great that even extra reinforcing cannot always resist the build-up of stress.

The second example, shown in Fig. 23.11(b), is also a common design feature where the second floor and floors above are cantilevered slightly from the first floor shear wall. Even though the shear wall continues, the offset also creates an undesirable situation because the direct load path for the lateral loads is interrupted, and the floor structure has to carry the transfer of forces from one shear wall to the next.

In all cases of discontinuous shear walls, the solution is simple: shear walls should run continuously to the foundation.

Another serious problem with building configuration is the soft story. This occurs when the ground floor is weaker than the floors above. Although a soft story can occur at any floor, it is most serious at grade level because this is where the lateral loads are the greatest. The discontinuous shear wall discussed in the previous section is a special case of the soft story. Others can occur when all columns do not extend to the ground or when the first story is high compared with the other floors of the structure. See Fig. 23.12.

A soft story can also be created when there is heavy exterior cladding above the first story and the ground level is open. Of course, there are usually valid reasons for all of these situations to occur. For example, a hotel may need a high first story but shorter floors above for the guest rooms.

When earthquake loads occur, the forces and deformations are concentrated at the weak floor instead of being uniformly distributed among all the floors and structural members.

There are several ways to solve the problem of a soft story. The first, of course, is to eliminate it and try to work the architectural solution around the extra columns or lower

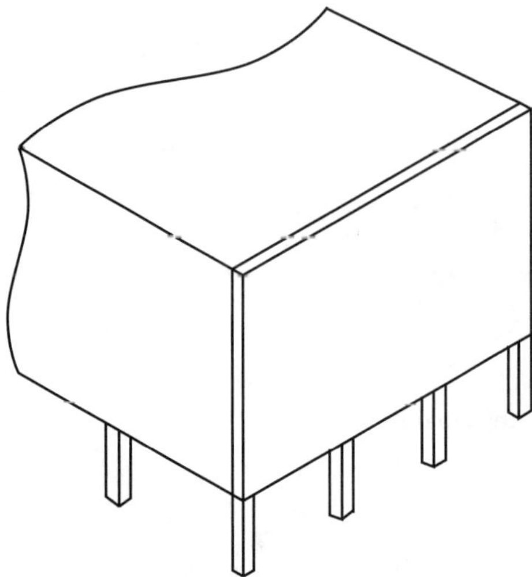

(a) shear wall to column transition

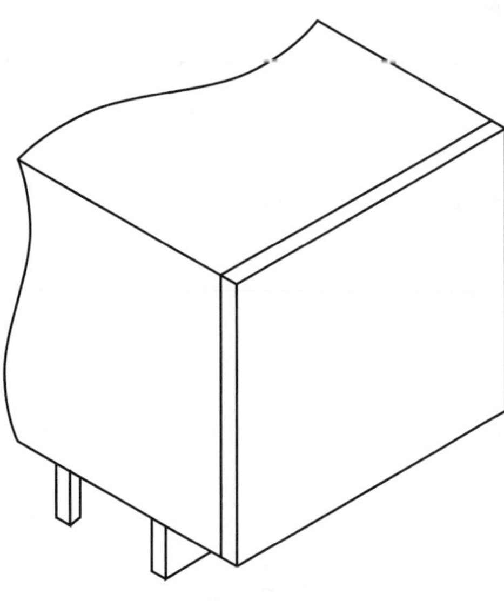

(b) offset shear walls

Figure 23.11 Discontinuous Shear Walls

height. If height is critical, extra columns can be added at the first floor. Another solution is to add extra horizontal and diagonal bracing. Finally, the framing of the upper stories can be made the same as the first story. The entire structure then has a uniform stiffness. Lighter, intermediate floors can be added above the first between the larger bays so they do not affect the behavior of the primary structural system.

ANALYSIS OF EARTHQUAKE LOADING

This section discusses the equivalent lateral force procedure for determining the base shear, or total lateral force, on a building. Except for structures required to be designed

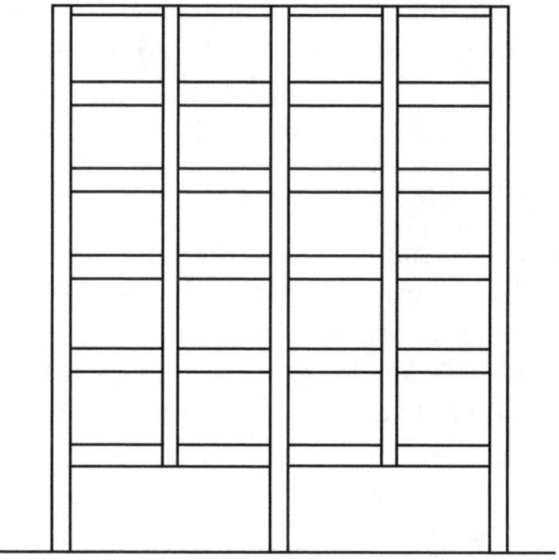
(a) discontinuous columns

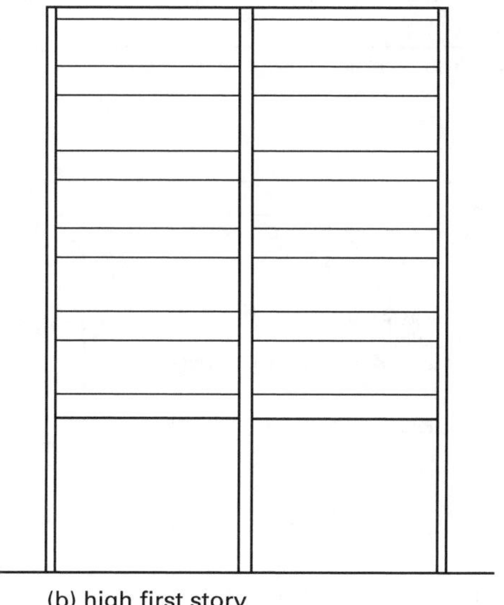
(b) high first story

Figure 23.12 Soft First Stories

according to dynamic analysis as previously mentioned, ASCE/SEI 7 allows the total seismic force on the main structural frame to be calculated according to a simplified formula. When using this formula, the base shear in each of the main axes of the building must be determined, and the structural system must be designed to resist the forces.

In addition, the code requires that forces on elements of structures and nonstructural components be calculated according to a different formula. This will be reviewed in a later section.

When a structure meets the requirements listed in the Basic Principles section earlier in this chapter, the equivalent lateral force procedure may be used. The formula for finding the total lateral force or shear at the base of the structure is

$$V = C_s W \qquad 23.1$$

The value C_s is the seismic response coefficient and is dependent on many building characteristics, which are discussed in the following sections. The weight of the building, W, is given in the W Factor section. The formula for the seismic response coefficient is

$$C_s = \frac{S_{DS}}{\frac{R}{I}} \qquad 23.2$$

The value S_{DS} is the design spectral response at the short period of 0.2 sec and is discussed in the S_S Factor section. The response modification coefficient, R, is given in Table 23.1 based on the type of seismic force resisting system. The importance factor, I, is given in the I Factor section. The IBC code places upper and lower limits on the seismic response coefficient. The upper limit that C_s need not exceed is one of the following.

$$C_{s,\max} = \frac{S_{D1}}{T\left(\frac{R}{I}\right)} \quad [\text{for } T \leqslant T_L] \qquad 23.3(a)$$

$$C_{s,\max} = \frac{S_{D1}T_L}{T^2\left(\frac{R}{I}\right)} \quad [\text{for } T > T_L] \qquad 23.3(b)$$

The value T_L is the long-period transition period of the structure found in maps in ASCE/SEI 7 Fig. 22-15 through Fig. 22-20. T is normally less than T_L for low-rise buildings. The value S_{D1} is the design spectral response at the long period of 1.0 sec and is discussed in the S_S Factor section. The building period, T, is given in the T Factor section. The lower limit below which C_s shall not be taken is

$$C_{s,\min} = 0.01 \qquad 23.4$$

If the building is where S_1 is greater than 0.6g (60% of gravity) then the additional lower limit is

$$C_s = \frac{0.5S_1}{\frac{R}{I}} \qquad 23.5$$

The value S_1 is the mapped design spectral response at the long period of 1.0 sec and is found from Fig. 23.2(b). Once the lateral base shear is determined, it is used to determine the forces on the various horizontal and vertical elements. The distribution of this base shear to the different levels of the building is discussed in the Distribution of Base Shear section.

I Factor

The importance factor, I, varies from 1.0 to 1.5, depending on the occupancy category of the structure. These factors are listed in Table 23.4, along with the values for wind and snow. The description of the nature of each occupancy category is also given in this table.

F_α Factor/F_v Factor

The site coefficients, F_α and F_v, represent both the seismicity of a region and the characteristics of the soil. These two coefficients correspond to the short and long period site values. Tables 23.5 and 23.6 give these coefficients based on the mapped spectral response values and the site class. The site classes are given in Table 23.7 based on the soil profile at the building site. These coefficients are used to determine the design spectral response factors in the S_S Factor section.

S_S Factor/S_1 Factor

The amount of seismic risk and the intensity of the maximum considered earthquake in a given geographical location are represented by the S_S and S_1 in Figs. 23.2(a) and (b), respectively. They are given as percentages of gravity (g) and should be divided by 100 for use in formulas. The value S_S is acceleration based and is for an acceleration

Table 23.4(a)

Occupancy Categories and Requirements

Nature of Occupancy	Occupancy Category
Buildings and other structures that represent a low hazard to human life in the event of failure, including, but not limited to: • Agricultural facilities • Certain temporary facilities • Minor storage facilities	I
All buildings and other structures except those listed in Occupancy Categories I, III, and IV	II
Buildings and other structures that represent a substantial hazard to human life in the event of failure, including, but not limited to: • Buildings and other structures where more than 300 people congregate in one area • Buildings and other structures with daycare facilities with a capacity greater than 150 • Buildings and other structures with elementary school or secondary school facilities with a capacity greater than 250 • Buildings and other structures with a capacity greater than 500 for colleges or adult education facilities • Health care facilities with a capacity of 50 or more resident patients, but not having surgery or emergency treatment facilities • Jails and detention facilities Buildings and other structures, not included in Occupancy Category IV, with potential to cause a substantial economic impact and/or mass disruption of day-to-day civilian life in the event of failure, including, but not limited to: • Power generating stations[a] • Water treatment facilities • Sewage treatment facilities • Telecommunication centers Buildings and other structures not included in Occupancy Category IV (including, but not limited to, facilities that manufacture, process, handle, store, use, or dispose of such substances as hazardous fuels, hazardous chemicals, hazardous waste, or explosives) containing sufficient quantities of toxic or explosive substances to be dangerous to the public if released. Buildings and other structures containing toxic or explosive substances shall be eligible for classification as Occupancy Category II structures if it can be demonstrated to the satisfaction of the authority having jurisdiction by a hazard assessment as described in Section 1.5.2 that a release of the toxic or explosive substances does not pose a threat to the public.	III
Buildings and other structures designated as essential facilities, including, but not limited to: • Hospitals and other health care facilities having surgery or emergency treatment facilities • Fire, rescue, ambulance, and police stations and emergency vehicle garages • Designated earthquake, hurricane, or other emergency shelters • Designated emergency preparedness, communication, and operation centers and other facilities required for emergency response • Power generating stations and other public utility facilities required in an emergency • Ancillary structures (including, but not limited to, communication towers, fuel storage tanks, cooling towers, electrical substation structures, fire water storage tanks or other structures housing or supporting water, or other fire-suppression material or equipment) required for operation of Occupancy Category IV structures during an emergency • Aviation control towers, air traffic control centers, and emergency aircraft hangars • Water storage facilities and pump structures required to maintain water pressure for fire suppression • Buildings and other structures having critical national defense functions Buildings and other structures (including, but not limited to, facilities that manufacture, process, handle, store, use, or dispose of such substances as hazardous fuels, hazardous chemicals, or hazardous waste) containing highly toxic substances where the quantity of the material exceeds a threshold quantity established by the authority having jurisdiction. Buildings and other structures containing highly toxic substances shall be eligible for classification as Occupancy Category II structures if it can be demonstrated to the satisfaction of the authority having jurisdiction by a hazard assessment as described in Section 1.5.2 that a release of the highly toxic substances does not pose a threat to the public. This reduced classification shall not be permitted if the buildings or other structures also function as essential facilities.	IV

[a]Cogeneration power plants that do not supply power on the national grid shall be designated Occupancy Category II.

Table 23.4(b)

Importance Factor, I

Occupancy Category	I
I or II	1.0
III	1.25
IV	1.5

Table 23.4(c)

Importance Factor, I (snow loads)

Category	I
I	0.8
II	1.0
III	1.1
IV	1.2

Table 23.4(d)

Importance Factor, I (wind loads)

Category	Non-Hurricane Prone Regions and Hurricane Prone Regions with V = 85-100 mph and Alaska	Hurricane Prone Regions with V > 100 mph
I	0.87	0.77
II	1.00	1.00
III	1.15	1.15
IV	1.15	1.15

Table 23.5

Seismic Site Coefficient F_α[a]

site class	mapped spectral response acceleration at short periods				
	$S_S \leq 0.25$	$S_S = 0.50$	$S_S = 0.75$	$S_S = 1.00$	$S_S \geq 1.25$
A	0.8	0.8	0.8	0.8	0.8
B	1.0	1.0	1.0	1.0	1.0
C	1.2	1.2	1.1	1.0	1.0
D	1.6	1.4	1.2	1.1	1.0
E	2.5	1.7	1.2	0.9	0.9
F	Note b	Note b	Note b	Note b	Note b

a. Use straight-line interpolation for intermediate values of mapped spectral response acceleration at short period, S_S.

b. Site-specific geotechnical investigation and dynamic site response analyses shall be performed to determine appropriate values, except that for structures with periods of vibration equal to or less than 0.5 sec, values of F_a for liquefiable soils are permitted to be taken equal to the values for the site class determined without regard to liquefaction in Sec. 1615.1.5.1.

Table 23.6

Seismic Site Coefficient F_v[a]

site class	mapped spectral response acceleration at 1 sec periods				
	$S_1 \leq 0.1$	$S_1 = 0.2$	$S_1 = 0.3$	$S_1 = 0.4$	$S_1 \geq 0.5$
A	0.8	0.8	0.8	0.8	0.8
B	1.0	1.0	1.0	1.0	1.0
C	1.7	1.6	1.5	1.4	1.3
D	2.4	2.0	1.8	1.6	1.5
E	3.5	3.2	2.8	2.4	2.4
F	Note b	Note b	Note b	Note b	Note b

a. Use straight-line interpolation for intermediate values of mapped spectral response acceleration at 1 sec period, S_1.

b. Site-specific geotechnical investigation and dynamic site response analyses shall be performed to determine appropriate values, except that for structures with periods of vibration equal to or less than 0.5 sec, values of F_v for liquefiable soils are permitted to be taken equal to the values for the site class determined without regard to liquefaction in Sec. 1615.1.5.1.

Table 23.7

Site Class Definitions

site class	soil profile name	average properties in top 100 ft, as per Sec. 1615.1.5 soil shear wave velocity, (ft/sec)	standard penetration resistance,	soil undrained shear strength, (psf)
A	hard rock		n/a	n/a
B	rock		n/a	n/a
C	very dense soil and soft rock			
D	stiff soil profile			
E	soft soil profile			
E	–	Any profile with more than 10 ft of soil having the following characteristics: 1. plasticity index $PI > 20$, 2. moisture content $w \geq 40\%$, and 3. undrained shear strength psf		
F	–	Any profile containing soils having one or more of the following characteristics: 1. soils vulnerable to potential failure or collapse under seismic loading such as liquefiable soils, quick and highly sensitive clays, collapsible weakly cemented soils 2. peats and/or highly organic clays ($H > 10$ ft of peat and/or highly organic clay where H = thickness of soil) 3. very high plasticity clays ($H > 25$ ft with plasticity index $PI > 75$) 4. very thick soft/medium stiff clays ($H > 120$ ft)		

For SI: 1 ft = 304.8 mm, 1 ft^2 = 0.0929 m^2, 1 psf = 0.0479 kPa, n/a = not applicable.

period of 0.2 sec. The value S_1 is velocity based for a period of 1.0 sec. These mapped values are for site class B and must be adjusted for a specific site class as discussed in the F_α/F_v Factor section. The design spectral response coefficients, S_{DS} and S_{D1}, are given by the following two formulas.

$$S_{DS} = \tfrac{2}{3} F_\alpha S_S \qquad 23.6(a)$$

$$S_{D1} = \tfrac{2}{3} F_v S_1 \qquad 23.6(b)$$

These design values are used in Eqs. 23.2, 23.3, and 23.4 to calculate the response coefficient. They are also used to determine the seismic design category for the building. The building's seismic design category is found in Tables 23.8 and 23.9 based on the design spectral response values and the seismic use group.

Table 23.8

Seismic Design Categories for Short-Period Response

value of S_{DS}	seismic use group I	II	III
$S_{DS} < 0.167g$	A	A	A
$0.167g \leq S_{DS} < 0.33g$	B	B	C
$0.33g \leq S_{DS} < 0.50g$	C	C	D
$0.50g \leq S_{DS}$	D[a]	D[a]	D[a]

a. Seismic use group I and II structures located on sites with mapped maximum considered earthquake spectral response acceleration at 1 sec period, S_1, equal to or greater than 0.75g, shall be assigned to seismic design category E, and seismic use group III structures located on such sites shall be assigned to seismic design category F.

Table 23.9

Seismic Design Categories for
1 sec Period Response

value of S_{D1}	seismic use group I	II	III
$S_{D1} < 0.067g$	A	A	A
$0.067g \le S_{D1} < 0.133g$	B	B	C
$0.133g \le S_{D1} < 0.20g$	C	C	D
$0.20g \le S_{D1}$	D[a]	D[a]	D[a]

a. Seismic use group I and II structures located on sites with mapped maximum considered earthquake spectral response acceleration at 1 sec period, S_1, equal to or greater than 0.75g, shall be assigned to seismic design category E, and seismic use group III structures located on such sites shall be assigned to seismic design category F.

Reproduced from the 2009 edition of the 2009 International Building Code, copyright © 2009, with permission of the publisher, the International Code Council.

Table 23.11

Approximate Period Parameters, C_t and x

Structure Type	C_t	x
Moment-resisting frame systems in which the frames resist 100% of the required seismic force and are not enclosed or adjoined by components that are more rigid and will prevent the frames from deflecting where subjected to seismic forces:		
Steel moment-resisting frames	0.028 (0.0724)[a]	0.8
Concrete moment-resisting frames	0.016 (0.0466)[a]	0.9
Eccentrically braced steel frames	0.03 (0.0731)[a]	0.75
All other structural systems	0.02 (0.0488)[a]	0.75

[a]Metric equivalents are shown in parentheses.

Reproduced from the 2005 edition of Minimum Design Loads for Buildings and Other Structures, copyright © 2005, with permission from the publisher, the American Society of Civil Engineers.

T Factor

The IBC gives two methods of determining T: an approximate method that can be used for all buildings, and a more complex method based on the deformational characteristics of the resisting elements in the building. The formula for approximating T is

$$T_a = C_t h_n^x \qquad 23.7$$

In Eq. 23.7, the values of C_t and x are given in Table 23.11 based on the structure type. The value h_n is the height of the highest point of the structure measured from the base. The period, T, used in Eq. 23.3 is the product of the approximate period and the coefficient, C_U, given in Table 23.10 as follows.

$$T = C_U T_a \qquad 23.8$$

Table 23.10

Upper Limit Period Coefficient, C_U

Design Spectral Response Acceleration Parameter at 1 s, S_{D1}	Coefficient C_u
≥ 0.4	1.4
0.3	1.4
0.2	1.5
0.15	1.6
≤ 0.1	1.7

Reproduced from the 2005 edition of Minimum Design Loads for Buildings and Other Structures, copyright © 2005, with permission from the publisher, the American Society of Civil Engineers.

R Factor

The R factor is based on the type of structural system used. These factors are given in Table 23.1 as previously discussed. For nonbuilding structures, the R factor is given in similar tables in the ASCE/SEI 7.

The R factor reflects the energy-absorbing capabilities of various types of structural systems. Notice that systems with high ductility, such as steel special moment-resisting space frames, have a higher R-value than systems with less ductility. Because the R-value is now placed in the denominator of Eqs. 23.2, 23.3(a), 23(b), and 23.5, a higher value results in a lower value of V, the design seismic force.

W Factor

The W factor is the total dead load of the building. Other applicable loads listed here must also be added.

- In warehouses and storage occupancies, a minimum of 25% of the floor live load must be added.
- When partition loads are used in the design of the floor, not less than 10 psf must be included.
- 20% of a flat roof snow load must be added where the snow load exceeds 30 psf.
- The total weight of permanent equipment must be included.

Example 23.1

A small, three-story hospital is being planned for Denver, Colorado. The structure is to be 45 ft high, and preliminary soils reports indicate 50 ft of soft clay. If a bearing wall system with concrete shear walls is planned and the estimated weight is 3500 kips, what is the base shear?

From Figs. 23.2 (a) and (b), the mapped spectral response values, S_S and S_1, are found for Denver as approximately 20% and 6%. Table 23.7 gives the site class as E for soft soil. For site class E with the 0.20 and 0.06 values, the coefficients F_α and F_v can be found in Tables 23.5 and 23.6 as 2.5 and 3.5, respectively. The design spectral response values can then be calculated from Eqs. 23.6(a) and (b).

$$S_{DS} = \tfrac{2}{3} F_\alpha S_S = \left(\tfrac{2}{3}\right)(2.5)(0.20) = 0.333$$

$$S_{D1} = \tfrac{2}{3} F_v S_1 = \left(\tfrac{2}{3}\right)(3.5)(0.06) = 0.140$$

From Table 23.11, the approximate parameters for a bearing wall system, C_t and x, are 0.02 and 0.75, respectively. This corresponds to all other structural systems. The approximate building period for a 45 ft tall structure can be calculated from Eq. 23.7.

$$T_a = C_t h_n^x = (0.02)(45)^{0.75} = 0.3475$$

For an S_{D1} value of 0.140, Table 23.10 gives the coefficient, C_U, as 1.62 by interpolation. The building period is calculated by Eq. 23.8 as follows.

$$T = C_U T_a = (1.62)(0.3475) = 0.563$$

The importance factor for a hospital is found in Table 23.4 as 1.50 for a category IV building. Assuming that emergency or surgical care will be provided in this facility, the corresponding seismic use group is found in the footnotes as III for category IV. For seismic use group III with the 0.333 and 0.140 values, the seismic design categories can be found in Tables 23.8 and 23.9 as D and D, respectively. The response modification factor for a bearing wall system with concrete shear walls can be found in Table 23.1 as $5^1/_2$. It should be noted that a special reinforced concrete shear wall system is required in seismic design category D. The seismic response coefficient can now be calculated from Eqs. 23.2, 23.3, and 23.4. The later two equations are the maximum and minimum values.

$$C_s = \frac{S_{DS}}{\frac{R}{I}} = \frac{0.333}{\frac{5.5}{1.5}} = 0.0908$$

$$C_{s,\max} = \frac{S_{D1}}{T\left(\frac{R}{I}\right)} = \frac{0.140}{(0.563)\left(\frac{5.5}{1.5}\right)} = 0.0678$$

$$C_{s,\min} = 0.01$$

Since the calculated value is greater than the maximum value, the maximum value of 0.0678 may be used. The base shear can be calculated from Eq. 23.1.

$$V = C_s W = (0.0678)(3500 \text{ kips}) = 237 \text{ kips}$$

Distribution of Base Shear

Once the total base shear is known, it is used to determine the forces on the various building elements. For single-story buildings, this is fairly straightforward. For multistory buildings, the forces must be distributed according to the displacement that occurs during an earthquake. Although structural movement under seismic forces is complex, the static lateral force procedure uses the most pronounced displacement that takes place, which results in an inverted force triangle varying from zero at the base to the maximum at the top. See Fig. 23.13(a).

With this simplified approach, it is assumed that there is uniform mass distribution and equal floor heights, but the code does provide for variations as will be shown in Eq. 23.9. The sum of the loads at each level equals the total base shear. Also note that while the greatest force is at the top of the building, the shear increases from zero at the top to its maximum at the base. Each floor shear is successively added to the sum from above. This method for the distribution of loads is only for the design of vertical lateral load-resisting elements. There is another formula for determining the force on the diaphragm at each level of a multistory building.

To account for tall buildings that do not have a uniform triangular distribution, the IBC requires that the height variable in the distribution equation be raise to an exponential power. This power, k, is a function of the building period. For structures with a period less than or equal to $T = 0.5$, $k = 1$, and for periods greater than $T = 2.5$, $k = 2$. For periods from 0.5 to 2.5, linear interpolation is allowed between k or 1 and 2, respectively. The equation for the fraction of the base shear, C_{vx}, applied at any height, h_x, is given as follows in Eq. 23.9, with w_x corresponding to the weight of that level.

$$C = \frac{w_x h_x^k}{\sum_{i-1}^{n} w_i h_i^k} \qquad 23.9$$

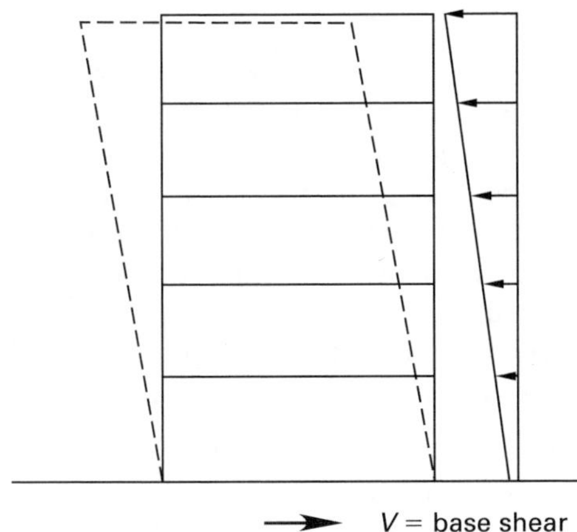

(a) distribution of forces using the equivalent static load method

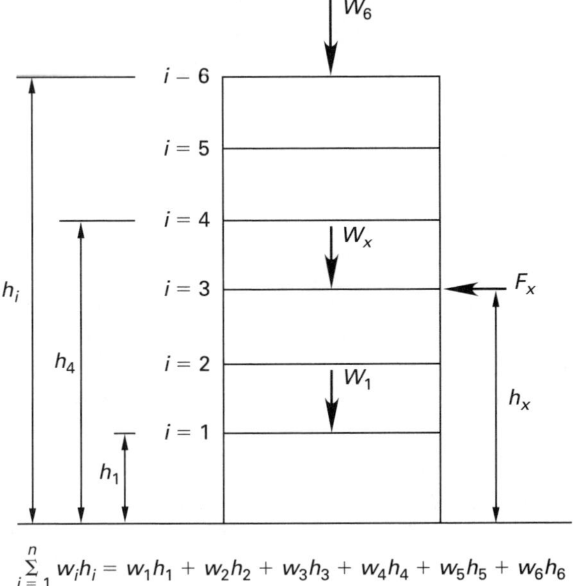

Figure 23.13 Distribution of Base Shear

The value in the denominator is the sum of all the floor weights times the height at each floor raised to the appropriated exponent. The formula can be easily solved using a tabular approach as shown in Ex. 23.2. The values included in Eq. 23.9 are shown graphically in Fig. 23.13. The lateral force applied to each level is simply the fraction calculated in Eq. 23.9 times the total base shear.

$$F_x = C_{vx} V \qquad 23.10$$

Example 23.2

A three-story office building located in Gary, Indiana, is 40 ft by 80 ft. Each story is 12 ft high, and the building is wood frame construction with plywood shear walls at each end. Building weights are as follows.

roof	15 psf
floors	20 psf
exterior walls	18 psf
partitions	8 psf

Determine the distribution of shear in the transverse direction.

Step 1. Determine the weight at each level and the total weight. This is done by taking the area of the floor or roof times the corresponding weight of that component. The partition load is added, and so is the floor load. The exterior wall load is calculated by taking the tributary height at each level times the perimeter times the weight of the wall.

$$\begin{aligned} w_{\text{roof}} &= (40 \text{ ft})(80 \text{ ft})(15 \text{ lbf/ft}^2) \\ &\quad + (6 \text{ ft})(2)(40 \text{ ft} + 80 \text{ ft})(18 \text{ lbf/ft}^2) \\ &= 73{,}920 \text{ lbf} \end{aligned}$$

$$\begin{aligned} w_{\text{floor}} &= (40 \text{ ft})(80 \text{ ft})(20 \text{ lbf/ft}^2 + 8 \text{ lbf/ft}^2) \\ &\quad + (12 \text{ ft})(2)(40 \text{ ft} + 80 \text{ ft})(18 \text{ lbf/ft}^2) \\ &= 141{,}440 \text{ lbf} \end{aligned}$$

For simplicity these weights will be rounded up to the next 1000 lbf. The roof weight is 74 kips, and the second and third floor weights are 142 kips, for a total weight of 358 kips.

Step 2. Determine all the seismic factors and calculate the base shear. From Figs. 23.2 (a) and (b), the mapped spectral response valves, S_S and S_1, are found for Gary as approximately 18% and 7%, respectively. Since no soil information is provided, use a conservative assumption of site class E. For site class E with the 0.18 and 0.07 values, the coefficients F_α and F_v can be found in Tables 23.5 and 23.6 as 2.5 and 3.5, respectively. The design spectral response values can then be calculated from Eqs. 23.6(a) and (b).

$$S_{DS} = \tfrac{2}{3} F_\alpha S_S = \left(\tfrac{2}{3}\right)(2.5)(0.18) = 0.300$$

$$S_{D1} = \tfrac{2}{3} F_v S_1 = \left(\tfrac{2}{3}\right)(3.5)(0.07) = 0.163$$

From Table 23.11, the approximate parameters for wood frame construction with plywood shear wall systems, C_t and x, are 0.02 and 0.75, respectively. This corresponds to all other structural systems. The approximate building period for a 36 ft tall structure can be calculated from Eq. 23.7.

$$T_a = C_t h_n^x = (0.02)(36)^{0.75} = 0.294$$

For an S_{D1} value of 0.163, Table 23.10 gives the coefficient, C_U, as 1.57 by interpolation. The building period is calculated by Eq. 23.8 as follows.

$$T = C_U T_a = (1.57)(0.294) = 0.462$$

The importance factor for an office is found in Table 23.4 as 1.00 for a category II building. The corresponding seismic use group is found in the footnotes as I for category II. For seismic use group I with the 0.300 and 0.163 values, the seismic design categories can be found in Tables 23.8 and 23.9 as B and C, respectively. The response modification factor for wood frame construction with plywood shear walls can be found in Table 23.1 as 6½. The seismic response coefficient can now be calculated from Eqs. 23.2, 23.3, and 23.4. The latter two equations are the maximum and minimum values.

$$C_s = \frac{S_{DS}}{\frac{R}{I}} = \frac{0.300}{\frac{6.5}{1.0}} = 0.0462$$

$$C_{s,\text{max}} = \frac{S_{D1}}{T\left(\frac{R}{I}\right)} = \frac{0.163}{(0.462)\left(\frac{6.5}{1.0}\right)} = 0.0543$$

$$C_{s,\text{min}} = 0.01$$

The calculated value falls between the maximum and minimum values and will be used. The base shear can be calculated from Eq. 23.1.

$$V = C_s W = (0.0462)(358 \text{ kips}) = 16.5 \text{ kips}$$

And since the calculated period of 0.462 is less than 0.5, the distribution exponent in Eq. 23.9 is 1.0.

Step 3. Determine the distribution of the base shear. This is done by tabulating the values needed for solving Eq. 23.9 and calculating the results.

1	2	3	4	5	6
level	w_x	h_x^k	$w_x h_x^k$	C_{vx}	F_x
	(kips)	(ft)	(ft-kips)		(kips)
roof	74	36	2664	0.343	5.69
3	142	24	3408	0.438	7.27
2	142	12	1704	0.219	3.64
Σ	358	–	7776	1.000	16.60

The values in column 5 are those calculated from Eq. 23.9. The values in column 6 are from Eq. 23.10 and represent the final forces applied to each level in kips.

Parts of Buildings

The code requires that in addition to the primary structural frame, individual elements of structures, nonstructural components, and their connections be designed to withstand seismic forces. Of particular importance are connections of the floors and roof to the walls and columns, walls to the structural frame, partitions to floors and ceilings, ceilings to boundary walls, millwork to floors and walls, equipment and fixtures to floors, piping and ducts to the structure, and suspended lights to the ceilings.

The force on structural and architectural components is determined in a similar way as the lateral force resisting system. The basic component force is given by Eq. 23.11. The maximum is given in Eq. 23.12 and the minimum is given in Eq. 23.13.

$$F_p = \left(\frac{0.4a_p S_{DS} W_p}{\frac{R_p}{I_p}}\right)\left(1 + 2\frac{z}{h}\right) \qquad 23.11$$

$$F_{p,\text{max}} = 1.6 S_{DS} I_p W_p \qquad 23.12$$

$$F_{p,\text{min}} = 0.3 S_{DS} I_p W_p \qquad 23.13$$

The values of a_p, I_p, and R_p are similar to those for the lateral force resisting system. They may be found in a table contained in ASCE/SEI 7. In general the values for rigid components like walls and floors are $a_p = 1$ and $R_p = 1.0$. The values for flexible components like cantilevers and parapets are $a_p = 2.5$ and $R_p = 2.5$. The value of I_p is 1.5 for life safety, storage, and hazardous elements, but 1.0 for most elements. The value of z is the height of attachment of the component above the base.

There are two types of elements: rigid and nonrigid. *Rigid elements* are defined as those having a fixed base period less than or equal to 0.06 sec. *Nonrigid elements*, or flexibly supported items, have a fixed base period greater than 0.06 sec.

Example 23.3

It is decided that the building in Ex. 23.2 is to have an 8 in masonry exterior and a 3 ft high parapet. Determine the load on the parapet if the parapet weighs 55 psf.

From Ex. 23.2, $S_{DS} = 0.300$. Consider the parapet to be flexible. The values of a_p, I_p, and R_p are thus 2.5, 1.0, and 2.5, respectively. The parapet is attached at roof height, so both z and h are 36 ft. The calculations based on Eqs. 23.10, 23.11, and 23.12 are

$$F_p = \left(\frac{0.4a_pS_{DS}W_p}{\frac{R_p}{I_p}}\right)\left(1 + 2\frac{z}{h}\right)$$

$$= \left(\frac{(0.4)(2.5)(0.30)\left(55\ \frac{\text{lbf}}{\text{ft}^2}\right)}{\frac{2.5}{1.0}}\right)\left(1 + (2)\left(\frac{36\ \text{ft}}{36\ \text{ft}}\right)\right)$$

$$= 19.8\ \text{psf}$$

$$F_{p,\max} = 1.6S_{DS}I_pW_p = (1.6)(0.30)(1.0)\left(55\ \frac{\text{lbf}}{\text{ft}^2}\right)$$

$$= 26.4\ \text{psf}$$

$$F_{p,\min} = 0.3S_{DS}I_pW_p = (0.3)(0.30)(1.0)\left(55\ \frac{\text{lbf}}{\text{ft}^2}\right)$$

$$= 4.95\ \text{psf}$$

The calculated value falls between the maximum and minimum values and will be used. The force on the parapet is 19.8 psf. This value can be used to determine the moment on the parapet and the required reinforcing.

Load Combinations Required

The IBC requires that buildings be designed to resist the most critical effects caused by combinations of loads. The load combinations that involve buildings designed for earthquakes per IBC Sec. 1605.2.1 using strength design or load and resistance factor design are as follows.

- $1.4D$
- $1.2D + 1.0E + f_1L + f_2S$
- $0.9D + 1.0E$

The value of f_1 is 1.0 for floors in places of public assembly, parking garages, and where the live load exceeds 100 psf. For any other cases a value of 0.5 may be used for f_1. The value of f_2 is 0.7 for roof configurations that do not shed snow off the structure (such as saw tooth). For any other cases a value of 0.2 may be used for f_2.

ACI 318 allows for a slightly different set of factors, which have been used over the past few decades. These factors are given in Ch. 20.

The basic load combinations per IBC Sec. 1605.3.1 using allowable stress design are as follows.

- D
- $D + 0.7E + L +$ (L_r or S or R)
- $0.6D + 0.7E$

Alternate basic load combinations per IBC Sec. 1605.3.2 using allowable stress design are as follows.

- $D + L + S + E/1.4$
- $0.9D + E/1.4$

ADDITIONAL CONSIDERATIONS

The complete and detailed design of earthquake-resistant structures is a complex procedure and beyond the scope of this book. However, this section outlines some additional concepts with which ARE candidates should be familiar.

Overturning Moment

Because the inertial force created by an earthquake acts through the center of mass of a building, there is a tendency for the moment created by this force acting above the base to overturn the structure. This overturning force must be counteracted in some way. Normally, the dead weight of the building, also acting through the center of mass, is sufficient to resist the overturning force, but it must always be checked. However, only 90% of the dead load may be used to resist uplift. Figure 23.14 shows these two forces and the resulting moments diagrammatically.

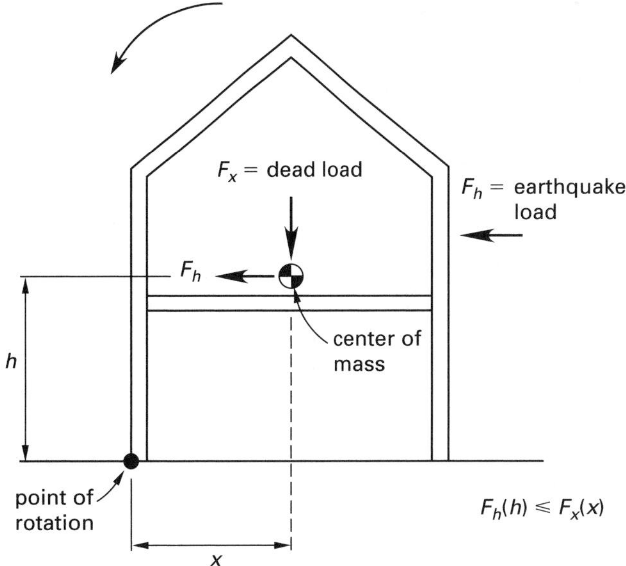

Figure 23.14 Overturning Moment

Drift

Drift is the lateral movement of a building under the influence of earthquake- or wind-induced vibrations. Story drift is the displacement of one level relative to the level above or below. ASCE/SEI 7 gives stringent limitations on story drift. A static analysis shall be used to determine the design level response displacement, Δ_S. The maximum inelastic response displacement, Δ_M, shall be computed as follows.

$$\Delta_M = \frac{C_d \Delta_S}{I} \qquad 23.14$$

The deflection amplification factor, C_d, is given in Table 23.1. The code also gives the limiting values of story drift that Δ_M may not exceed. These limits are more stringent for the higher seismic use groups. For example, the value for a normal frame structure is 0.02 times the story height for use group I and 0.01 times the story height for use group III.

Drift as a limiting factor is important in order to ensure that exterior facades do not break off or crack excessively. When two buildings or portions of buildings are isolated by a seismic joint, they must be separated by at least the sum of the drifts to avoid pounding during an earthquake.

24 LONG SPAN STRUCTURES—ONE-WAY SYSTEMS

A *long span* is generally considered to be one over 60 ft in length. The study of long spans as distinct structural entities is important because of the unique design problems that arise when structures cover long distances. These problems include such things as temperature expansion and contraction, shipping, and deflection, among others. These will be discussed in detail in later sections.

One of the most important characteristics of long span structures is their lack of redundancy. In structures with many separate, small bays, the collapse of one beam would be damaging, but the majority of the building would remain standing supported by other parts of the framing system. With a long span structure, failure of one portion affects a much greater area and can even cause collapse of the entire building. The potential for catastrophic loss of life and property is much greater.

Long span structures can be categorized into two broad divisions: one-way and two-way systems. *One-way systems* are characterized by linear members that span in one direction and resist loads primarily by beam action, or bending. A one-way long span generally consists of primary members that bridge the long distance, and a series of secondary members that span between the primary one, also with simple beam action, and support the floor or roof system. *Two-way systems* distribute loads to supports in both directions and involve complex, three-dimensional methods of resisting loads. Two-way systems will be covered in the next chapter.

TYPES OF ONE-WAY SYSTEMS

The following sections outline some of the more typical long span, one-way systems. Most of these use steel or concrete as their primary material because of the high strength-to-weight ratio of steel and concrete. Wood is used for long span construction in trusses and glued-laminated beams.

Many variables determine the exact size and configurations of a member that is to span a particular distance, such as loading and the allowable stress of the material. Table 24.1 summarizes several of the one-way systems along with typical span ranges, depths, and depth-to-span ratios.

Table 24.1

One-Way Long Span Systems

system	typical spans (ft)	typical depths (ft)	typical depth-to-span ratios
steel girders	10–72	$^2/_3$–3	1/20
steel rigid frames	30–150	2–5	1/20–1/30
glued laminated rigid frames	30–120	$1^1/_2$–4	1/20–1/30
flat wood trusses	40–120	4–12	1/10
pitched wood trusses	40–100	7–17	1/6
flat steel trusses	40–300	4–30	1/10–1/12
pitched steel trusses	40–150	5–20	1/6–1/8
long span joists	25–96	$1^1/_2$–4	1/20–1/24
deep, long span joists	90–144	$1^1/_3$–6	1/20–1/24
joist girders	20–100	2–10	1/10–1/12
glued laminated beams	10–60	1–4	1/24
prestressed single tee concrete	20–120	1–4	1/20–1/30
prestressed double tee concrete	20–60	1–$2^1/_2$	1/20–1/30
prestressed concrete girders	40–120	3–6	1/15–1/20
steel arches	50–500	1–5	1/100
concrete arches	40–320	1–7	1/50
wood arches	50–240	$1^1/_2$–6	1/40

Steel Girders

Rolled steel members are sometimes used for long spans if the loads are not excessive. The largest rolled section available is 44 in deep, and its practical span length is about 72 ft. If additional moment-carrying capacity is required, cover plates can be welded to the top or bottom flanges as shown in Fig. 24.1(a).

If longer spans are required for steel sections, they must be fabricated from individual components. The most common type of section is the plate girder, which is composed of sheet steel for the web and either steel bars or angles for the flanges. Figure 24.1(b) shows a plate girder built up of angles. Figure 19.3 illustrates a welded plate girder. Plate girders are efficient long span members because most of the material is in the flanges separated by a large distance, which results in a high moment of inertia.

In order to minimize the amount of steel required (and, therefore, the weight and cost), plate girders used as roof beams can be tapered toward the middle of the span where the moment is the greatest. See Fig. 24.1(c).

Plate girders are often 8 ft deep or more. They are sometimes used to transfer the load of a column to two wider spaced columns to create a clear span below as shown in Fig. 24.2. This is often required in buildings such as hotels, where the lobby requires a more open space than the rooms above. In most cases, because the web is relatively thin compared with its length, intermediate stiffeners are required to prevent buckling of the web. These are usually angles welded perpendicular to the length of the web.

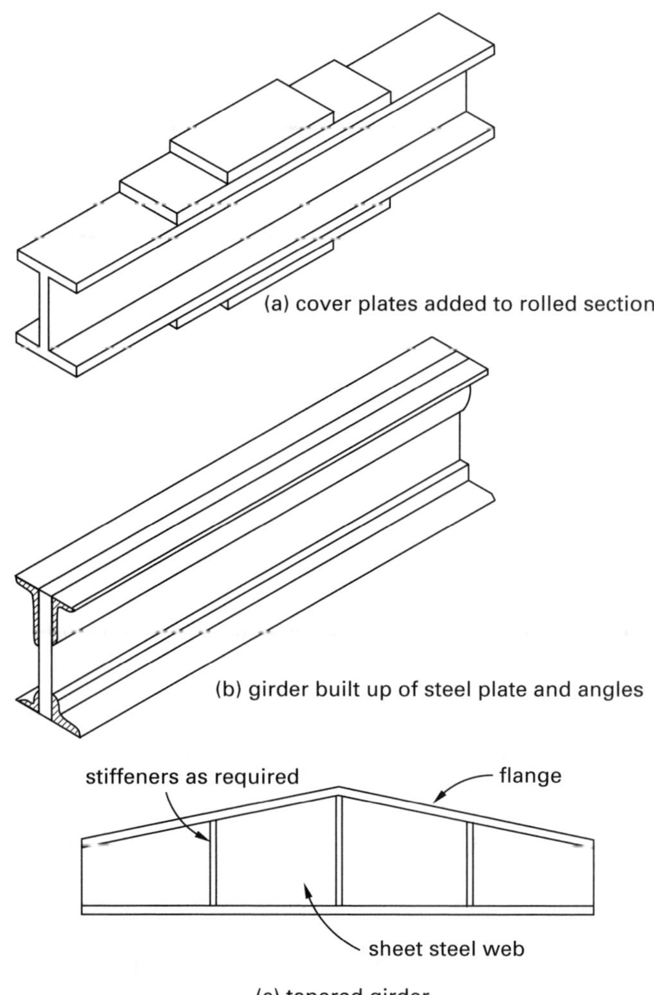

Figure 24.1 Built-Up Steel Sections

Rigid Frames

A *rigid frame* is a structural system in which the vertical and horizontal members and joints resist loads primarily by flexure, and in which moments are transferred from beams to columns. When discussing long span structures, a rigid frame has a sloped roof with a rigid, moment-resisting connection between the columns and the roof structure, or the column/roof structure is one continuous member. See Fig. 24.3. A rigid frame may have fixed connections between the columns and foundation and between the two halves, or it may have pinned connections at these points. With pinned connections, the structure is determinate and does not develop secondary stresses caused by temperature differences. If the entire frame is rigidly connected, it is an indeterminate structure.

Part of the spanning capability of a rigid frame comes from the arch action of the sloping beams, through which vertical loads are transferred to the columns through compression as well as bending. In addition, since the two columns are tied together, lateral loads are transferred to both columns, resulting in a more efficient structure. As shown

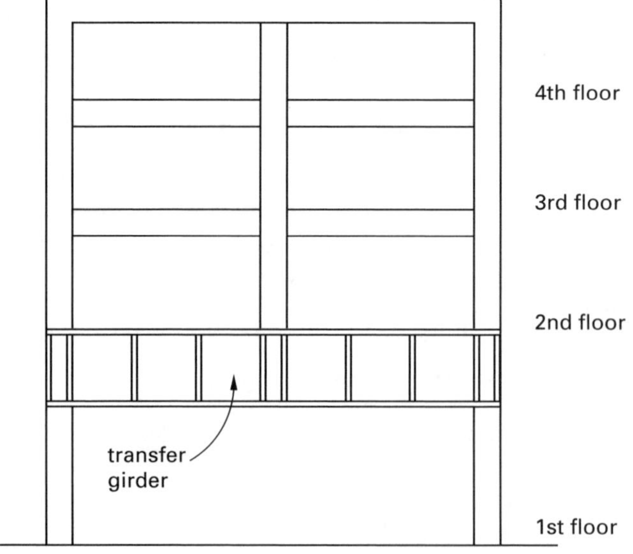

Figure 24.2 Transfer Girder

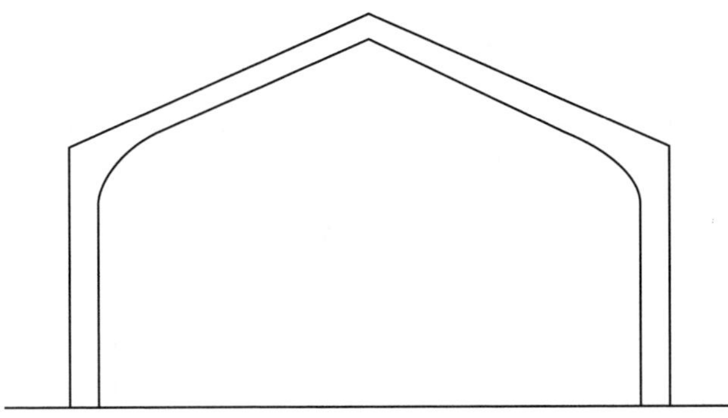

Figure 24.3 Rigid Frame

in the illustration, the column and beam are often tapered toward the foundation and ridge. This reflects the fact that the moment is greatest at the junction where more material is needed to resist the forces in the structure.

Rigid frames are used for industrial facilities, warehouses, manufacturing plants, and other instances where a simple, rectangular open space is required. They are primarily constructed of steel, but are also made of glued laminated lumber because each half can be easily fabricated as a single, continuous unit.

Trusses

As stated in Ch. 14, a *truss* is a structure comprised of straight members that form a number of triangles, with the connections arranged so that the stresses in the members are either in compression or tension. Trusses are very efficient structures to span long distances because of their primary reliance on compression and tension to resist forces, rather than bending, and their high strength-to-weight ratios. Trusses are usually constructed of steel or wood, and sometimes a combination of materials.

Trusses offer many advantages in bridging large spaces. They are relatively lightweight, the space between the members can be used for mechanical services, they can be partially prefabricated for fast erection, they make efficient use of material, and they can theoretically be made as deep and large as needed to span most any distance, although there are practical limits to the span. One disadvantage of a truss, however, is the number of connections, which can increase fabrication or erection time.

Trusses are usually spaced from 10 ft to 40 ft on center with intermediate purlins spanning between them and bearing on the *panel points*, those points where the web members intersect the top chord. Roof or floor decking then spans between the purlins.

The typical spans and depths of the various types of trusses are shown in Table 24.1. Some of the more common truss configurations are shown in Fig. 24.4. Refer to Ch. 14 for more information on truss analysis.

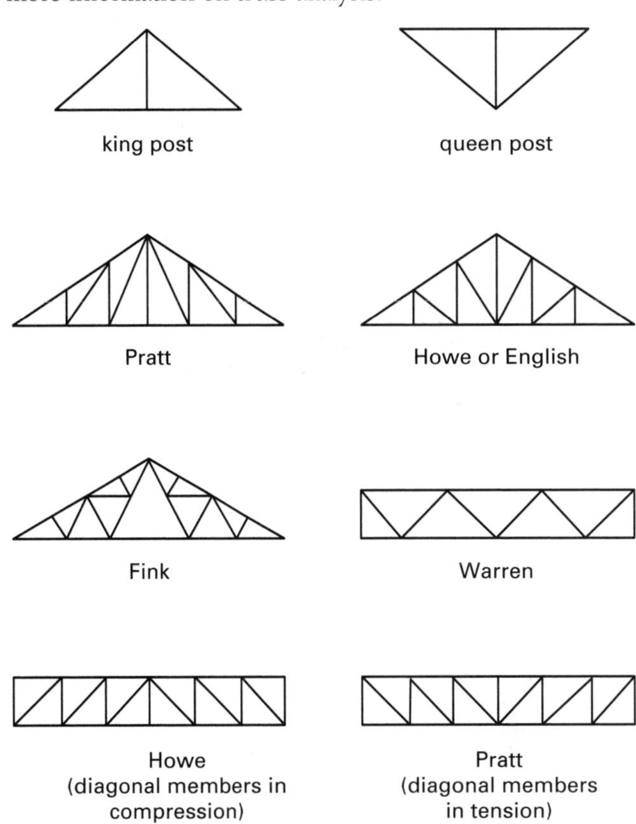

Figure 24.4 Truss Configurations

Open-Web Steel Joists and Joist Girders

Open-web joists are prefabricated truss members using hot-rolled or cold-formed steel members. These joists have been standardized into three major groups: K-series, LH-series, and DLH-series. The K-series spans up to 60 ft, so the LH- and DLH-series are considered long span. The LH-series is suitable for the direct support of floors and roof decks, and the DLH-series is suitable for direct support of roof decks.

Even though each manufacturer has its own chord and web profiles, the sizes and specifications for the manufacturing have been standardized by the Steel Joist Institute. Long span joists, the LH-series, come in depths from 18 in to 48 in and span up to 96 ft. The deep, long span joists, the DLH-series, come in depths from 52 in to 72 in and span up to 144 ft. The depths increase in 2 in or 4 in increments.

Open-web joists typically bear on the top chord and have underslung ends. However, square end trusses can be purchased that bear on the bottom chord. The depth of the bearing portion is standardized at 5 in for the LH-series and for chord sizes through 17 in the DLH-series. For chord sizes of 18 and 19 in the DLH-series, the standard bearing depth is $7^1/_2$ in.

There are a number of standard chord configurations. These are illustrated in Fig. 24.5. Of course, parallel chord trusses are required for floor systems, but the pitched top chord configuration is useful for roof structures to provide for positive drainage. In addition, there are a number of accessories such as bottom chord ceiling extensions, extended ends for the top chord, and various types of anchoring devices.

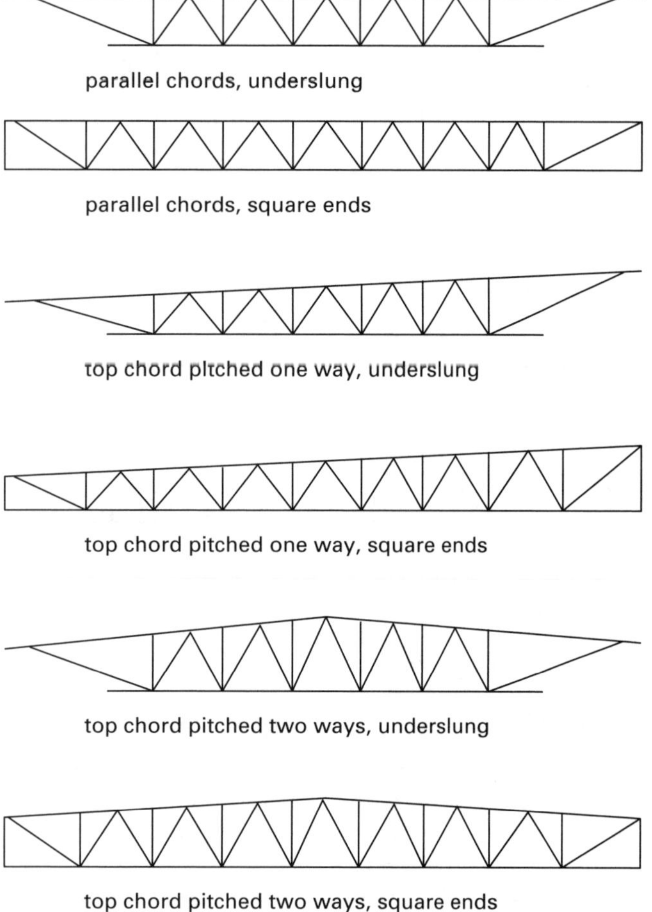

Figure 24.5 Open-Web Steel Joist Configurations

Both LH-series and DLH-series joists are manufactured with camber, the amount depending on the length of the top chord. *Camber* is the rise in a beam to compensate for deflection. The cambers range from $^1/_4$ in for a 20 ft length to $8^1/_2$ in for the longest, 144 ft span.

Open-web joists are very flexible. By varying the spacing, depth, and chord size, a wide variety of floor and roof loads and spans can be accommodated. They can bear on steel beams, masonry walls, concrete walls, and joist girders. The top chord can likewise support a variety of flooring and roofing systems. Because they are lightweight and prefabricated, erection is quick and simple. For more information, including design methods, refer to the section on open-web joists in Ch. 19.

Joist girders are designed to serve as primary structural members that support evenly spaced open-web joists. Joist girders are available in depths of 20 in to 120 in and can span up to 100 ft. They are manufactured with steel angle sections. Although each manufacturer may have its own particular configuration, there is a standard way of designating a joist girder. For example, in the designation 48G8N8.8K, the 48G indicates the depth in inches, the 8N indicates the number of joist spaces, and the 8.8K indicates the required design load in kips at each panel point.

Vierendeel Trusses

A *Vierendeel truss* is a structure composed of a series of rigid rectangular frames. However, it is not a true truss because there are no triangles and the members must resist bending as well as tension and compression. See Fig. 24.6. A Vierendeel truss is used when diagonal members are undesirable, and in many instances will occupy an entire story height when used to transfer loads from closely spaced columns above to column-free spaces below.

The top and bottom chords of a Vierendeel truss are in compression and tension, respectively, just as with any beam or true truss. However, there is bending moment in the chords as well as in the vertical members. As a result, all portions of a Vierendeel truss must be designed with larger members than would be necessary with a regular truss, and the joints must be capable of resisting moments as well. This is why these trusses often have triangular brackets or short knee braces as shown in Fig. 24.6.

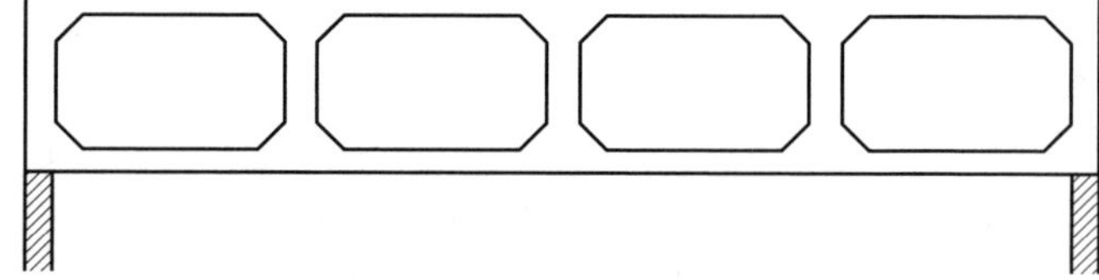

Figure 24.6 Vierendeel Truss

Glued-Laminated Beams

Although glued-laminated construction seldom exceeds the 60 ft distance arbitrarily considered long span, it is included here because it is used for spans and loads that regular sawn timber is incapable of supporting, and because many of the special considerations of long spans apply to this type of construction. Long distances are spanned by glued-laminated members in two primary ways: with straight, rectangular beams and with rigid frame arches.

As mentioned in Ch. 18, glued-laminated members consist of a number of individual pieces of lumber, either 3/4 in or 1 1/2 in thick, glued together and finished in a factory. See Fig. 18.3. Because the individual pieces can be hand-selected free from major defects and the entire member can be properly seasoned, gluelams, as they are called, have higher stress ratings than standard sawn lumber sections. In addition, much larger sizes are possible, so the span and load-carrying capabilities are much greater for gluelam construction than for standard wood frame buildings.

Glulam beams are designed with the same formulas used for other wood construction, except a few additional formulas are required to account for modifications in stress ratings when curved members are used. As with sawn members, there are load tables that make selection easier by giving the allowable load per foot based on span and size of beam.

Prestressed Concrete

When concrete is used for one-way systems to span long distances, it is nearly always prestressed or post-tensioned. Prestressed concrete consists of a member that has had an internal stress applied before it is subjected to service loads. This stress is applied by stressing high-strength steel strands in a form into which concrete is poured. When the concrete cures, the external stress is removed and it is transferred to the concrete. This process effectively counteracts the tension that concrete is not capable of carrying. The prestressing process also reduces cracking and deflection, and permits concrete to span longer distances with smaller sections than is possible with reinforced, cast-in-place construction.

There are several types of precast sections suitable for long span concrete sections. The three most common ones are shown in Fig. 24.7 and include the single tee, the double tee, and the AASHTO (American Associations of State Highway and Transportation Officials) girder.

Single tees are typically 4, 6, or 8 ft wide with an 8 in to 12 in thick web. Depths range from 1 ft to 4 ft with span capabilities up to about 120 ft.

Double tees are usually 8 ft or 10 ft wide with a 2 in flange thickness and depths ranging from 8 in to 32 in. Span distances are less than with single tees; the maximum span is 60 ft to 80 ft. Double tees typically have a 2 in thick concrete topping that covers the joints, smooths out any irregularities between adjacent panels, and strengthens the floor or roof assembly.

Double tees are used frequently because of their many advantages. They function both as a structure and a decking, are relatively inexpensive to produce, can be erected quickly, and can be used either as horizontal or vertical

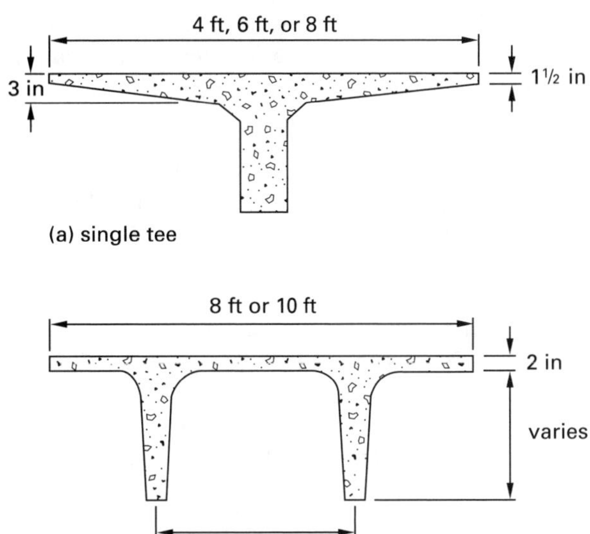

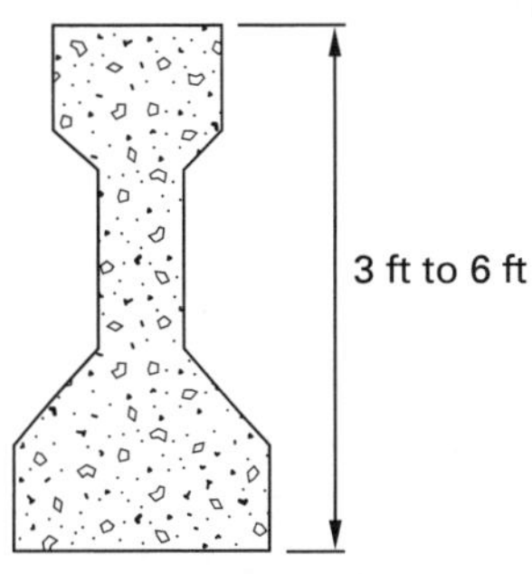

Figure 24.7 Typical Prestressed Concrete Shapes

members. In addition, the space between the webs can be used for mechanical and electrical service runs.

AASHTO girders are not used very often in building construction; their use is generally limited to highway bridges. However, similar rectangular beams can be precast to span long distances, with lengths up to 120 ft possible.

Other precast shapes include box girders and channel slabs, but these are not used for building as frequently as the sections shown in Fig. 24.7.

Post-tensioned Concrete

With post-tensioned concrete construction, the concrete member is cast with hollow sleeves embedded in it. High-strength steel cables, called *tendons*, are placed in the hollow sleeves, and after the concrete has cured, tension is applied to the tendons by hydraulic jacks. When the design stress is reached, the cables are anchored to the ends of the concrete member with steel plates or by grouting the space between the tendon and the sleeve. The post-tensioning equipment is removed, and the resulting member functions in a way similar to prestressed concrete.

Post-tensioning can be used in beams, floor slabs, or other sections to increase the load-carrying capacity of the member and to allow for longer spans.

Arches

Arches are one of the oldest long span structural systems used by man. This is because an arch depends primarily on compression to resist loads, and ancient materials like stone were very strong in compression. In a true arch, all of the load is carried in compression. For a given set of loads, the shape of an arch that acts in this way is its funicular shape. For an arch supporting a uniform load across its span, this shape is a parabola.

However, in practical terms, there is no such thing as a true arch, because there are always combinations of loads that place both compressive and bending stresses in an arch. For a good working definition, an *arch* is a structure that resists imposed loads primarily by compression with some bending stresses involved.

There are several arch shapes. Some of the more common ones are shown in Fig. 24.8. The A frame and gabled frame are not immediately apparent as arches, but they represent the concept of arch action, in which there is some compression in the spanning member as well as bending. As the slope of the arch approaches vertical, there is more compression and less bending.

As was discussed in Ch. 10, internal loads tend to cause an arch to spread out unless it is restrained with foundations or a tie rod. For a given span, this tendency to spread, or the *thrust* of the arch, is inversely proportional to the rise, or height, of the arch. As the rise increases, the thrust decreases.

Arches can be constructed with wood, concrete, and steel, and some spans have reached over 1000 ft. For most purposes, however, the typical spans for arches range from 50 ft to 240 ft for wood; 40 ft to 320 ft for concrete; and 50 ft to 500 ft for steel. Typical depth-to-span ratios are about 1:40 for wood arches and up to 1:100 for steel arches.

Arches can be either fixed or hinged. If the arch is hinged at the supports, it can move slightly under loads caused by temperature, soil settlement, and wind without developing high bending stresses.

When used in one-way structural systems, arches are the primary structural member, and the space between is spanned with secondary members that in turn support the roofing system.

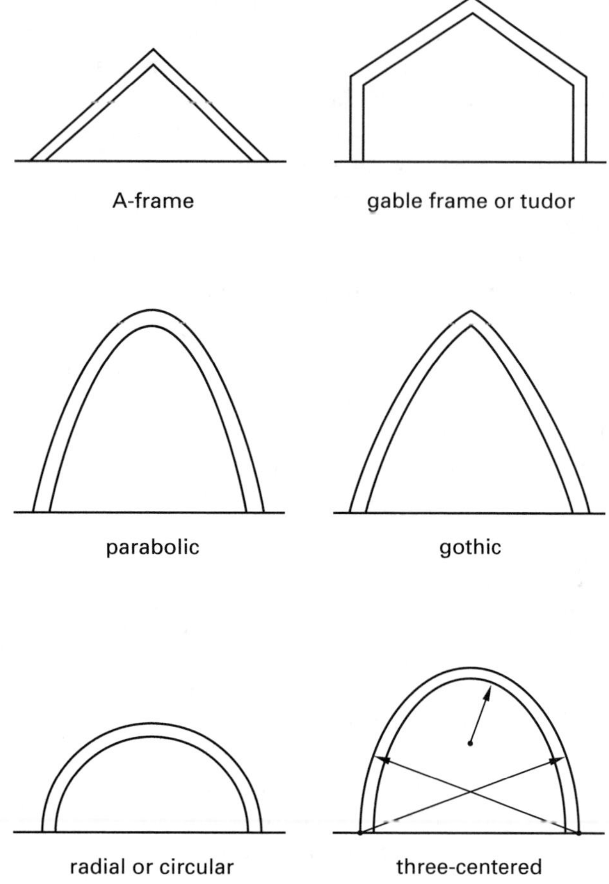

Figure 24.8 Types of Arches

DESIGN AND SELECTION CONSIDERATIONS

The selection of the most appropriate long span system for a particular project involves finding a balance between many different factors. This section and the next will outline some of the more important factors for both one-way and two-way systems.

Function

All structural systems must meet the functional needs of the building being designed. An auditorium may need a clear span of 150 ft, a sports arena may require an open area large enough for hockey and thousands of spectators, or a manufacturing plant may simply need narrow, but very long, unobstructed bays. A system appropriate for one use may not be the best choice for another use. For example, it would not make sense to use a steel arch capable of spanning 400 ft if long span open-web joists clearing 60 ft would do just as well.

Cost and Economy

Selecting and designing an economical long span structural system for a particular project requires that the architect and engineer balance many interrelated factors. There are six general considerations that affect the cost of any structure.

- structural system
- material
- labor
- equipment
- construction time
- integration with other building systems

Regardless of the relative efficiency of a long span structural system, bridging great lengths always comes at a cost. The first determinant, therefore, is the structural system itself. Generally speaking, it is less costly to build more columns to decrease spans as much as possible than it is to provide deeper and heavier beams or complex two- or three-dimensional systems. All other things being equal, the most economical structure will be the one that spans just the required distance and no farther without stretching the limits of the system.

Since most materials are more efficiently used in compression and tension than in bending, a system that reflects this fact will often cost less than one that relies on flexure. X-braced buildings, for example, may use less steel than moment-resisting frames, or trusses may require less weight than comparable solid beams. However, material use may be offset by higher fabricating costs or labor required for assembly.

Finally, deeper bending members are more efficient and require less material than shallow ones. A deep steel beam will weigh less (and cost less) than a shallow one that supports the same load. If other considerations allow it, the architect should provide as much space as possible for structural members.

Material is the second consideration affecting cost. In addition to the size and amount required by the system selected, cost can be affected by the availability of material. For instance, in some parts of the country, steel may be more readily available and at a lower cost than concrete, or a job site may be quite remote from a precasting plant, which would rule out prestressed concrete.

The choice of material may also have repercussions for other materials. Steel will require fireproofing while concrete will not, or masonry walls in cold climates may require more complex insulating systems than simple steel stud cavity walls.

One of the major determinates of cost is labor. This is especially true in the United States. Generally, any structural system that minimizes the amount of labor, especially on-site labor, will have an economic advantage. This is why precast concrete is often preferred over cast-in-place concrete.

The other aspect of labor cost is the availability of skilled labor to perform certain building tasks. A brick structure needs skilled masons, and a welded steel frame requires competent welders, for example. In metropolitan areas, this may not be a problem. In more remote areas, the best structural system may be one that is prefabricated and requires simple site assembly.

Equipment required for the erection of long span structures is usually large and expensive. Here, there is a balance between the cost of equipment, and speed and ease of construction. Larger cranes may cost more to rent than smaller ones, but may allow the use of larger, prefabricated members and therefore reduce construction time and the number of connections required.

Construction time has become very important in many building situations due to the high cost of financing. Anything that reduces the building period has the effect of saving money. Therefore, such things as readily available material, prefabrication, simple long span systems, and easy on-site labor can significantly affect the economy of a building.

Finally, any long span structure must be selected so that it integrates with other building systems and components. There must be room for mechanical ductwork without excessive floor-to-floor heights, the exterior configuration must work with the fenestration system, and there must be provisions for easy installation of partitions and finishes.

Shipping

Because of their very nature, most long span structures, especially one-way systems, require large components to be shipped to the job site. There are many advantages to prefabricating structural members in sizes as large as possible, but these must be weighed against the practical limits of the transportation system serving the site. For instance, with precast concrete, the largest size possible should be shipped in order to reduce the number of field connections required and to speed erection. However, this goal must be balanced with the practical limits of weight and truck size.

In most cases, the maximum length is 60 ft for truck shipment and 80 ft for railroad shipment. Maximum height for truck shipment is 14 ft. In some special situations, these dimensions are exceeded, but only at greater cost and with unusual provisions for transportation.

Access to the site must also be considered. In constricted urban locations, it may be impossible to maneuver a large truck into proper position for unloading.

Acoustics

Acoustics can be a factor in the selection of a long span structural system if the system's shape is one that concentrates sound reflections. Barrel vaults, domes, and some polygonal shapes can increase the noise level or produce undesirable echoes. This can be a critical concern in sports arenas, manufacturing plants, and other buildings where the normal noise level is usually high. Adding a false ceiling or making other provisions for acoustical control can add to the cost of the structure.

Assembly and Erection

There are several things to consider about the assembly and erection of long span structures. The first, of course, is the speed and ease of construction, both of which can affect the cost of the building. In addition, the equipment required for erection must be taken into account, as previously mentioned. More important, in many instances, are the structural and safety requirements of long span construction. Because long span members are usually large, correspondingly large erection stresses can be developed. Sometimes these stresses are greater than those the member will encounter in use, and the piece must be designed and sized accordingly.

Due to the lack of redundant members to support the structure, materials, and workers during erection, it is critical that correct procedures and sequences of construction be followed to avoid instability or overstressing until the entire building is complete and all bracing components are in place.

For example, when open-web steel joists are erected, several procedures must be followed. The hoisting cables must not be removed until bolted diagonal bridging near the midspan is installed. The number of bridging lines that must be installed before the hoisting cables are released depends on the span. If the joist is bottom bearing, the ends must be restrained and bridging must be installed before the hoisting cables are released. Further, all bridging and bridging anchors must be completely installed before construction loads are placed on the joists.

During erection of joist girders, it is recommended that a loose connection of the lower chord be made to the column, or that some other support is provided to stabilize the lower chord laterally and help brace the joist girder against possible overturning. For both open-web joists and joist girders, concentrated construction loads must not be placed so as to exceed the load-carrying capacity of any member.

Precast concrete presents special problems with erection because of its weight. While it is desirable to fabricate large members to speed construction and minimize joints and field connections, the practical limits of crane capacities need to be considered, as well as the space available around the building site to maneuver trucks, cranes, and large precast sections. Additionally, each individual member must be properly braced until the complete system is assembled.

Fire Protection

As mentioned previously, the requirement for fire protection of structural members may influence the selection of a particular system. In some instances, the cost and difficulty of installing fire-resistant covering may offset the initial economy of an otherwise efficient material. Steel, of course, is especially vulnerable to weakening when exposed to high temperatures.

The *International Building Code* (IBC) allows an exception to the fire protection of structural steel in some instances. In Group A (assembly) and E (educational) occupancies, if the structural framework of the roof is more than 25 ft above the floor, fire protection may be omitted. This is why there is no fire protection in many sports stadiums, exhibition halls, and concert halls.

TECHNICAL CONSIDERATIONS

Long span structures pose special problems that are not present, or at least not significant, with standard structural systems. For example, a 30 ft long steel beam will expand so slightly with an increase in temperature that it is of little consequence. The expanson of a 120 ft truss, however, can be significant. Because of the nonredundant nature of long span structures and the potential for catastrophic failure, the following considerations are especially important.

Connections

Many of the failures of long span structures (as well as standard structures) occur not with the primary spanning members but with the connections. As with other aspects of long span structures, there is less redundancy with connections. If one fails, it can lead to a progressive failure of others when they are overstressed.

In addition to building code requirements, it is often wise to build in extra connections. Shop drawings should also be carefully reviewed to make sure changes were not made by the fabricator, and this should be followed up by meticulous field observation to verify that the connections are properly installed and in the proper sequence for the type of material and system being used.

For example, if a rigid connection is made between a joist girder and a column, it must be made only after the application of the dead loads. In such a case, the girder must be investigated for continuous frame action because the girder is no longer a simply supported beam.

Envelope Attachment

The connection of roofing and exterior wall materials to long span structures requires special attention. This is due to the larger movements experienced by both the structural system and the building envelope. Expansion and contraction of the primary frame caused by temperature differentials can exert unusual stresses on cladding, so expansion joints need to be designed to accommodate this type of movement.

Deflection of a long span floor or roof is also significant in terms of weatherproof attachment of the roofing material and flooring and ceiling finish.

For simple, one-way structural systems, the end rotation of a beam or girder can be significant for a long span member where it is of little consequence in normal span construction. There must be enough room at the end of the beam to allow for this type of movement without stressing or dislodging the exterior envelope.

Ponding

Ponding is potentially one of the most dangerous conditions with long span roofs. It occurs when a roof deflects enough to prevent normal water runoff. Instead, some water collects in the middle of the span. With the added weight, the roof deflects a little more, which allows additional water to collect, which in turn causes the roof to deflect more. The cycle continues until structural damage or collapse occurs.

The IBC specifically requires that all roofs be designed with sufficient slope or camber to ensure adequate drainage after long-term deflection, or that roofs be designed to support maximum roof loads, including possible ponding.

For glued-laminated construction, the IBC requires that the roof slope provide a positive slope not less than $^1/_4$ in/ft between the level of the drain and the highest point of the roof. This slope must be in addition to the camber provided by the beams, which must be $1^1/_2$ times the calculated dead load deflection.

The best design approach is to plan roofs so that there is more than enough slope to provide positive drainage while allowing for the usual construction variances. Instead of $^1/_4$ in/ft, provide at least $^1/_2$ in/ft. In addition, pay particular attention to situations that can create ponding. If a roof area depends on drains, some kind of provision must be made for drainage if the primary drain is clogged.

Temperature Movement and Stresses

The greater length of long span structures over standard length members means that any movement caused by temperature differentials will be increased in proportion to the length of the member. Where an expansion of one-tenth of an inch in the length of a short steel beam may not pose any particular problem, an increase of three-tenths of an inch may overstress a connection or crack an attached brick wall.

Particular attention needs to be paid to detailing long span structures to account for these kinds of movement. The situation is even more critical if the structure is exposed to the weather; temperature differentials and movement will be even greater than for interior structural members. Temperature stresses can be avoided by using flexible joints, providing clearance for the anticipated movement, providing slip joints, and so on.

Tolerances

Just as with temperature-induced movement, fabrication and erection tolerances are greater for long span structures. Details and connections must be designed to accommodate a member whose length or depth may vary by an inch or more from what is designed and shown on the drawings. Hinged connections, slotted bolt holes, shims, and similar devices are often used to allow for tolerance variations.

Stability

Many long span structures depend on secondary framing and horizontal or vertical diaphragms for complete rigidity. During erection, the primary elements, such as arches and rigid frames, need to be braced temporarily until enough of the remainder of the structure can be built to make the entire assembly self-supporting. Although the contractor is responsible for construction methods, the drawings and specifications need to be clear in their instructions. In all cases, industry standards and the recommendations of the manufacturer or fabricator should be followed.

Shop Drawing Review

Minor changes in the preparation of shop drawings are a fact of life in the design and construction industry. However, where a slight change from the original details or specifications may be acceptable in a normal structure, such a change can have disastrous consequences in long span construction. The architect should fulfill his or her role in the shop drawing review process and verify that the structural engineer, contractor, and erection subcontractor have thoroughly reviewed the shop drawings, and that any deviation from the original design is completely studied and approved by all parties.

Construction Observation

The final step in the correct design and construction of a long span structure is the thorough observation of the erection sequence. Both the architect and structural engineer must be involved in this process to verify that construction is in accordance with the plans and specifications.

25 LONG SPAN STRUCTURES—TWO-WAY SYSTEMS

Two-way structural systems distribute loads in two or more directions and consist of members that are all considered to be primary. Because the load is shared by many members in the system and generally distributed to more supports, two-way systems are structurally more efficient than one-way systems. This can be seen by comparing a simple one-way system with a two-way system. See Fig. 25.1.

Figure 25.1(a) shows a single concentrated load on a flexure member. The beam carries the entire load with one-half of the load carried by each support. With a two-way system, as shown in Fig. 25.1(b), the same load is distributed to two flexure members with each support only having to carry one-fourth of the load.

With this type of two-way system, the structure is most efficient if the shape is square so the loads are equally distributed. If the shape becomes rectangular, more and more of the load is carried in the short dimension and less in the long dimension. When the proportion becomes 2:1, nearly all the load is carried in the short dimension. This is why systems such as a waffle slab and flat plate construction are most efficient when the bays are square.

Some two-way systems also offer the advantage of redundancy, which, as noted in Ch. 24, is lacking in most of the one-way systems. For example, the failure of one joint or member of a space frame will not cause the entire structure to collapse.

Two-way systems are more efficient in use of material and can span farther and carry heavier loads than comparable one-way systems. However, one disadvantage is that they are more complicated to design and build. The design work is a minor problem today because of computer programs that can calculate highly indeterminate structures. The problem of complex construction still remains, however. Most two-way systems require a large number of pieces and connections, which require a great deal of fabrication time.

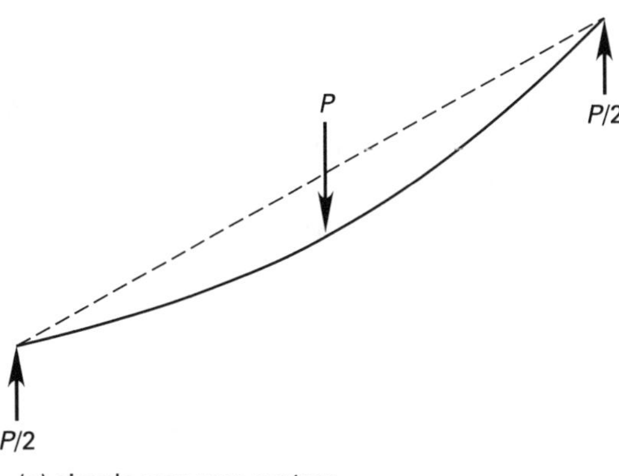

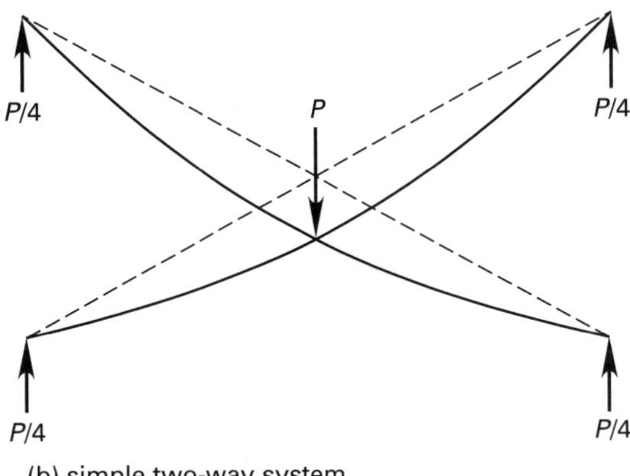

Figure 25.1 One-Way and Two-Way Systems

An additional limitation of long span, two-way systems is that nearly all of them can only be used for roof structures due to their basic shape. Space frames are the one exception, but even these are almost always used only for roofs and occasionally wall systems. Note that this limitation applies only to long span structures. Other two-way systems, like flat slabs and stressed skin floor panels, do utilize the efficiency of two-way action.

TYPES OF TWO-WAY LONG SPAN SYSTEMS

As with one-way systems, there are many types and variations of two-way, long span structural systems. This section discusses the major ones with some of the most used variations. Table 25.1 summarizes the typical two-way systems, giving typical span ranges, thicknesses, and height-to-span ratios. With the exception of space frames, the height-to-span ratio is not the same as the depth-to-span ratio used with one-way structures. Since all of the systems listed are three-dimensional, they all have an optimum total height that is different from the size or thickness of individual members.

Table 25.1

Two-Way Long Span Systems

system	typical spans (ft)	typical thickness (in)	typical height-to-span ratios
space frames	80–220	–	1/15–1/25
geodesic domes	50–400	–	1/3–1/5
thin shell domes	40–240	3–6	1/5–1/8
hyperbolic paraboloids	30–160	3–6	1/6–1/10
barrel vaults	30–180	3–5	1/10–1/15
lamella arches	40–150	–	1/4–1/6
folded plates	50–100	3–6	1/6–1/10
suspended cable structures	50–450	–	1/8–1/15

Space Frames

A space frame is a three-dimensional structural system that transfers loads through a network of members attached to each other at nodal connection points. Space frames are very efficient structures because of the large number of members and the fact that they resist loads primarily in compression or tension.

One of the unique features of a space frame that is uncharacteristic of many other long span structures is redundancy. Buckling of one member under a concentrated load does not lead to the collapse of the whole structure. This is because the system distributes concentrated loads evenly throughout the entire frame.

There are many configurations for space frames. They all have a top chord grid and a bottom chord grid connected with diagonal bracing. The two grids can be identical and run in the same direction, or run in different directions while still forming a regular pattern. Grids can be square or triangular, although the square grid is more common.

The simplest type of space frame is a two-way truss system. With this, trusses spanning two directions are interconnected and form a grid of square openings. The diagonal members are vertical and in the plane of each truss, just as with a one-way truss system. See Fig. 25.2.

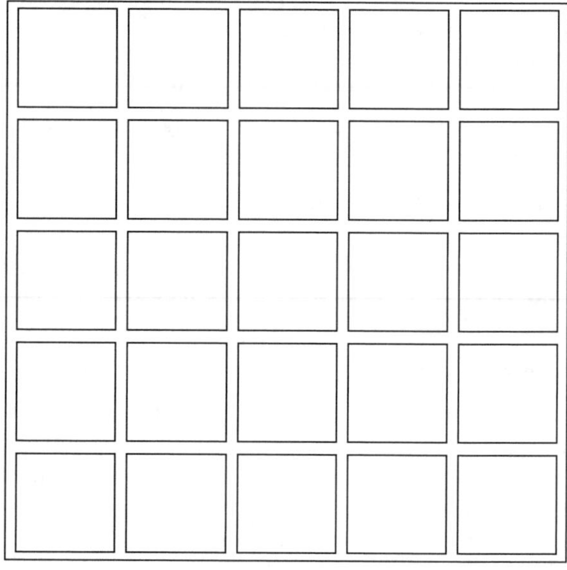

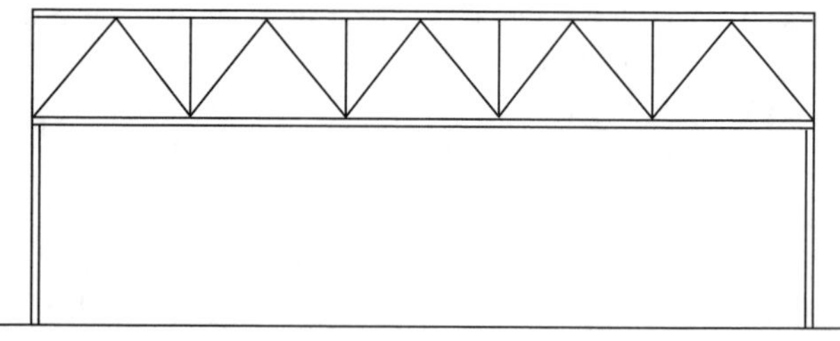

Figure 25.2 Two-Way Truss Space Frame

A more common type of space frame is the offset grid as illustrated in Fig. 25.3. Here, the top and bottom grids consist of identical squares, but the bottom one is offset from

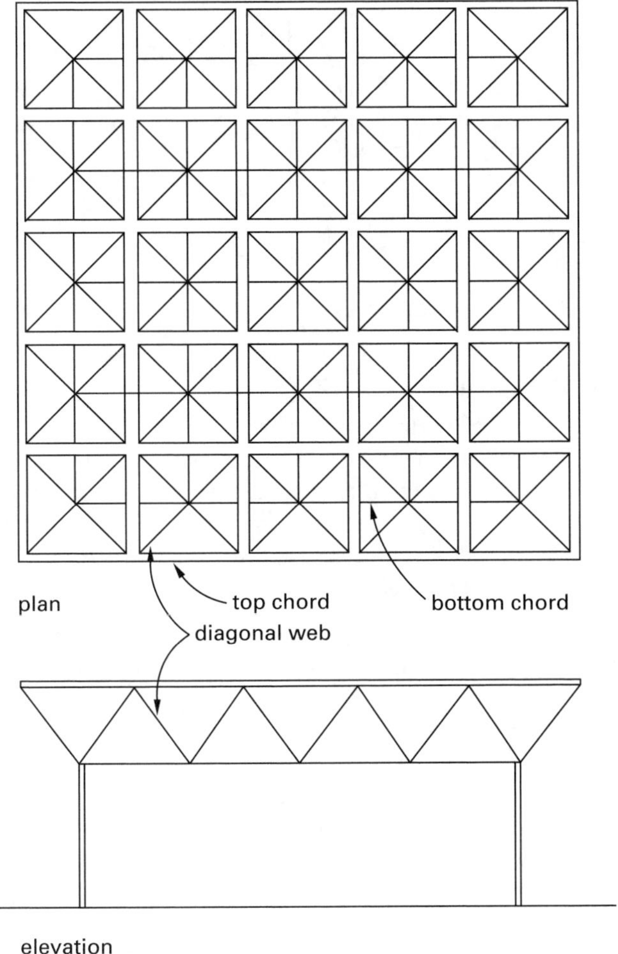

Figure 25.3 Offset Grid Space Frame

the top by one half grid. The two grids are connected with skewed diagonal members.

The module size of a space frame can be varied to suit the functional needs of the building and the structural limitations of the grid members. The depth of the grid can also be varied as necessary, but the most economical depth-to-module ratio is about 0.707. Of course, the larger the module size, the fewer the number of connections, which is desirable in order to save fabrication and erection time and money.

There are many types of connections. They may be formed of hollow or solid sections with tapped holes for screw attachment of the members. They may be bent plates to which the members are bolted or welded, or prefabricated units that are slipped over the spanning members. Whatever type is used, the connection must provide for attaching the supporting structure and for attaching the roofing and sidewall system to the primary frame. Some of the typical methods of support are shown in Fig. 25.4.

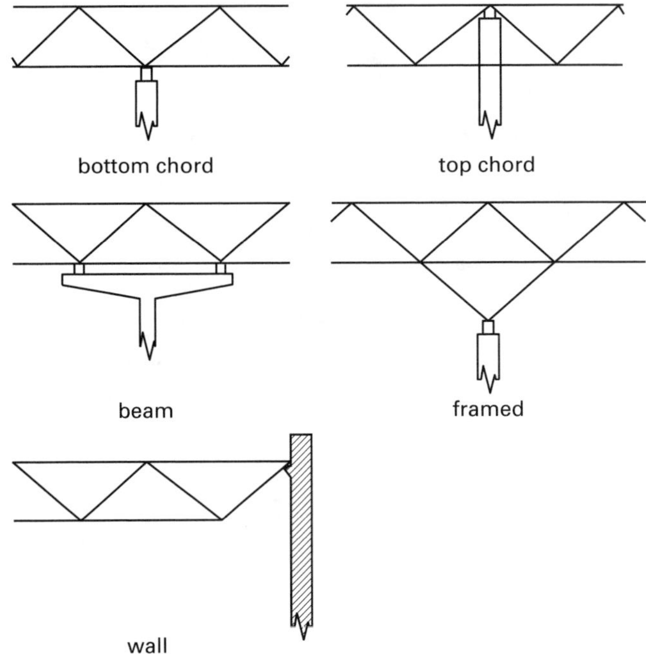

Figure 25.4 Methods of Space Frame Support

The supports for a space frame can be located at any node, but for greatest efficiency they are usually spaced symmetrically. Cantilevers of 15% to 30% of the span are possible and even desirable since less chord material is required.

Domes

Domes are one of the most efficient structural systems known. This is because the shape of the structure itself helps resist loads placed on it primarily through compression and tension, and in the case of thin-shell structures, shear. There are three basic variations of domes: the *frame dome*, the *geodesic dome*, and the *thin-shell dome*.

The forces in all domes can be visualized by viewing a simple circular frame dome as shown in Fig. 25.5(a). The meridian lines act as individual arches, transferring loads to the ground through compression. The meridians are supported laterally by the hoops, those lines running parallel to the horizontal.

For very shallow, or low-rise domes, the entire structure can be placed in compression, without any tensile stresses at all. The vertical load at the bottom of the dome must then be resisted by the ground or a foundation.

For high-rise domes (the most typical situation) when the dome is under a uniform load, such as from its own weight or from a snow load, each meridian tends to compress in the upper part of the dome and expand in the lower part. See Fig. 25.5(b). This deflection is held in check, however, by the hoops. But because of the deflection, the hoops in

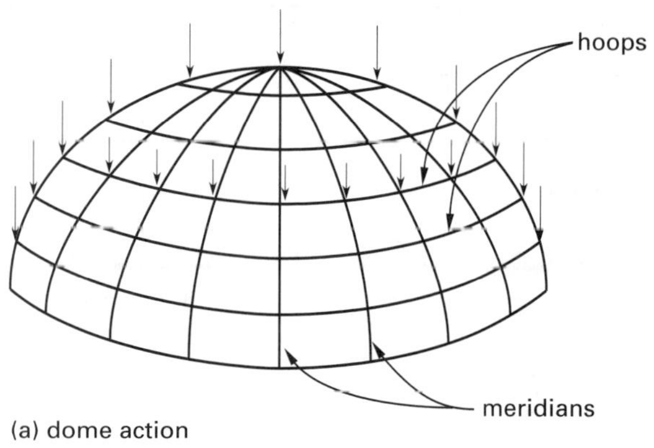

(a) dome action

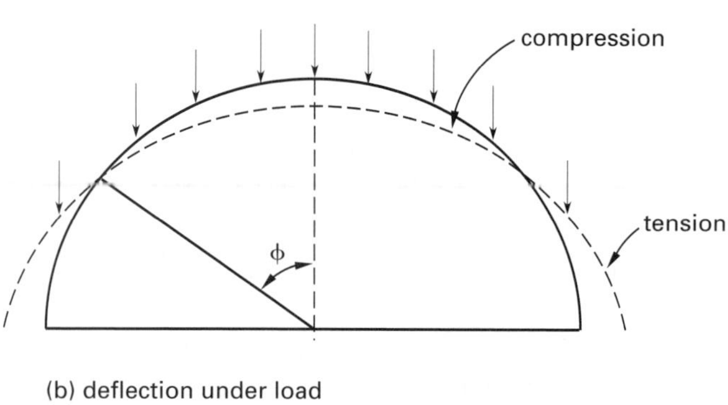

(b) deflection under load

Figure 25.5 Dome Structural Behavior

the upper part of the dome compress, and the hoops in the lower part are placed in tension. If there is sufficient hoop material at the base of the dome that can resist the tensile forces, the dome is self-supporting without the need for a foundation to carry the thrust. The foundation only needs to carry the vertical component of dead and live loads.

The point at which the stresses change from compression to tension varies with the load. Under dead load the angle ϕ, as shown in Fig. 25.5(b), is about 52°; under snow load the angle is 45°.

As a consequence of all the stresses being in compression or tension, the strains are relatively small. This is why a dome is a very stiff structure with very little deflection.

There are several variations of the framed dome. All are approximations of a true dome because only straight members are used. One of the common types of framed domes is the Schwedler dome as shown in Fig. 25.6. The areas between the meridians and the hoops are braced with single or double diagonals and spanned with purlins or directly with the roofing.

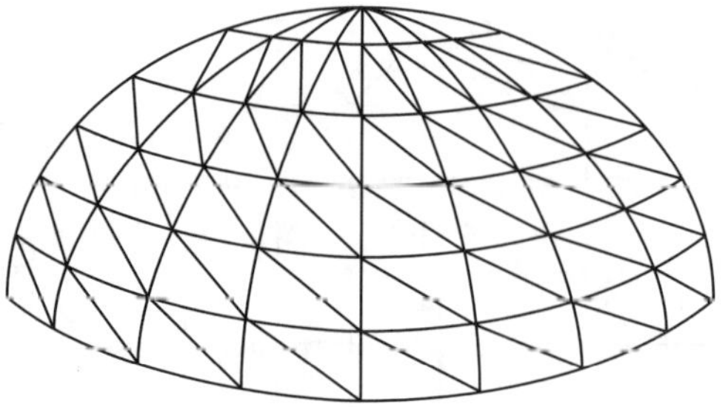

Figure 25.6 Schwedler Dome

Geodesic Domes

Geodesic domes, invented by Buckminster Fuller, are like space frames formed in the shape of a sphere. The grid of a geodesic dome is based on great circle arcs and is composed of spherical polyhedrons, usually formed of equilateral triangles. A geodesic dome can be constructed with a single or double layer of struts.

Geodesic domes are extremely strong, stiff, and lightweight, and they enclose the greatest volume with the least surface area. They can easily span 400 ft or more.

Thin-Shell Structures

Thin-shell structures are a class of form-resistant structures whose strength is a result of their ability to support loads through compression, tension, and shear in the plane of the shell because of their basic shape. The other broad category of form-resistant structure is the membrane, which can only support loads through tension. Membranes will be discussed in the next section.

Shells are classified as either singly curved or doubly curved. The most common example of a singly curved thin shell structure is the *barrel vault* as shown in Fig. 25.7. Barrel vaults with end frames act as curved beams, with the upper portion in compression and the lower portion in tension. Beam action carries the loads to the two ends where it is transferred by shear action to the end frames.

This structural condition is true only for a long barrel; that is, a barrel whose length is larger than its radius. It is also only true for a barrel supported by end frames and end supports. With such a barrel, there is a tendency for the longitudinal edges of the barrel to deform inward. This is usually counteracted by an adjacent vault or with longitudinal stiffeners. If a barrel vault is only supported by its longitudinal edges, arch action develops along with the corresponding thrust common to arches. If the shape of the barrel is not the funicular shape for the loads, some bending stresses will also be present. Such a barrel vault will have to be thicker than an end-supported vault to account for these additional loads.

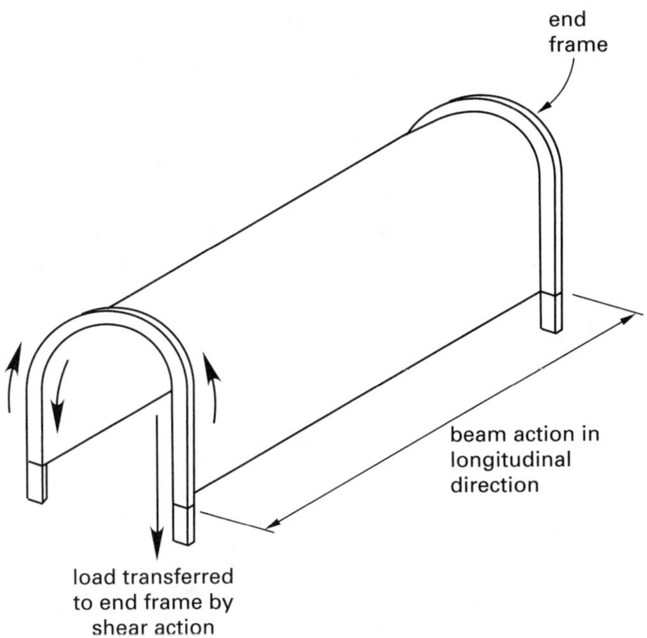

Figure 25.7 Thin-Shell Barrel Vault

A barrel vault shape with rounded hip ends can also be created with a *lamella roof*. This is a structure formed by two intersecting grids of parallel skewed arches covering a rectangular area. Lamella arches are very efficient because of the interaction between the beams of the two grids and because the short lengths of the beams near the corners have small spans, thus reducing the length of the span of the beams framed into them.

The second class of thin-shell structures is the doubly curved shell. There are two types of doubly curved shells. *Synclastic shells* are those with curves on the same side of the surface. *Anticlastic shells* are those with the main curves on opposite sides of the surface. See Fig. 25.8. A dome is an example of a synclastic shell, and a hyperbolic paraboloid is an anticlastic shell.

Thin-shell domes are very rigid and efficient structures. They are stable for either symmetric or asymmetric loads. In theory, they behave like the frame domes discussed in a previous section, but because they consist of one continuous surface, each infinitesimal portion is resisting compression, tension, and shear. See Fig. 25.9. Compression is acting in the lines of the meridian, and either tension or compression is acting in the hoop direction. Shear is therefore developed in any section to keep the structure in equilibrium.

Another common thin shell is the *hyperbolic paraboloid*. This anticlastic shell is formed by moving a vertical parabola with downward curvature along an upward curving parabola that is perpendicular to it. The resulting form is

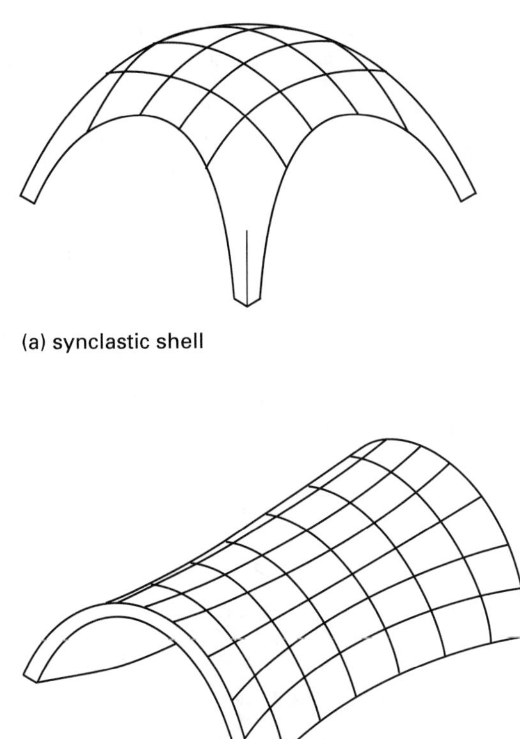

Figure 25.8 Types of Thin-Shell Surfaces

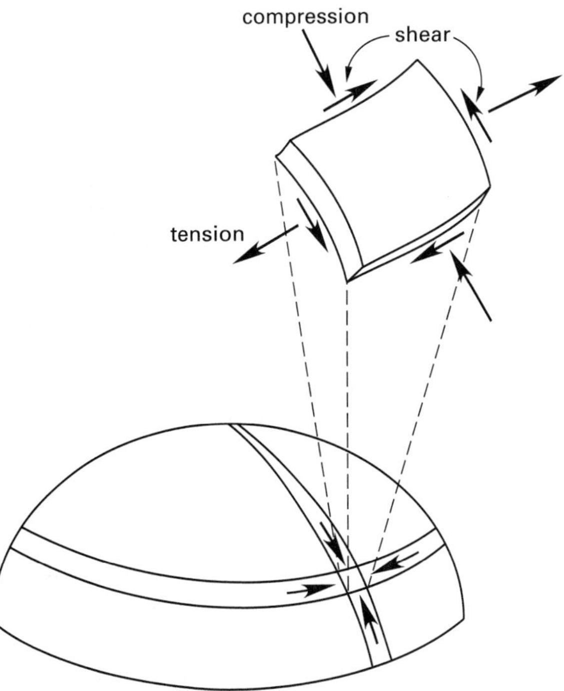

Figure 25.9 Shear Stresses in Domes

that shown in Fig. 25.8(b). The shape that a horizontal plane makes with the curve is a hyperbola.

Hyperbolic paraboloids can also be formed by straight lines moving along two nonparallel lines. There are many variations of this method of generating these thin-shell forms, but one of the most common is shown in Fig. 25.10. This form is actually four separate hyperbolic paraboloids arranged to cover a square. In this form, the loads are resisted in the plane of the shell and transferred to the boundaries of the hyperbolic paraboloids, where they become compression forces in the edge stiffeners and are transmitted to the foundations. There is an outward thrust caused by this arch action that must be resisted by the tie rods or suitable foundations.

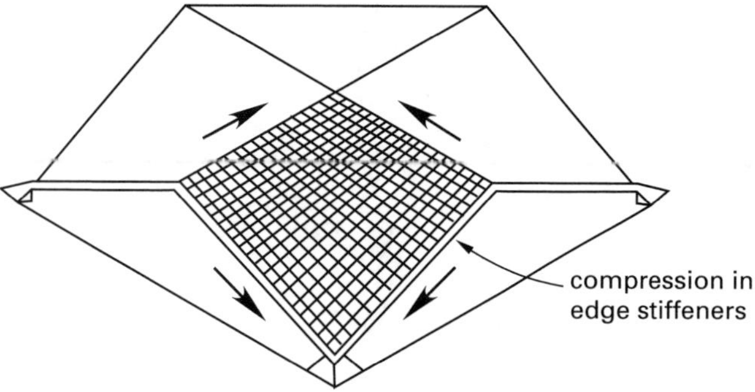

Figure 25.10 Four-Section Hyperbolic Paraboloid Roof

In most cases, thin shells can be made only a few inches thick and still be structurally stable, but the minimum thickness is usually determined by the space required for reinforcing steel, minimum cover distances over the steel, and a sufficient thickness to allow for placing the concrete by machine. Building codes also limit the minimum thickness in order to provide for possible bending moments that may be induced in the structure from concentrated loads.

Although thin shells are very efficient in their minimal use of material and have great strength and stiffness, they are often not the structural system of choice in the United States because they are labor-intensive structures to construct. It is typically less expensive to pay for more, less-efficient structural material if it can be erected quickly with as little on-site labor as possible.

Membrane Structures

Membranes are the second class of form-resistant structures. Unlike shells, membranes can only resist loads in tension. As such, the membrane must be anchored between elements that can be placed in compression like the poles of a tent. Although membranes are very efficient in the amount of material they require, their biggest disadvantage is that they move and change shape in response to varying loads. They also flutter in the wind.

These problems can be counteracted to a great degree by prestressing the membrane with anticlastic shapes. Figure 25.11(a) shows a simple membrane draped between two horizontal supports. Figure 25.11(b) shows the same configuration except that a cable perpendicular to the transverse drape has been pulled tightly over the membrane, resulting in a doubly curved surface. The resulting shape is much more stable.

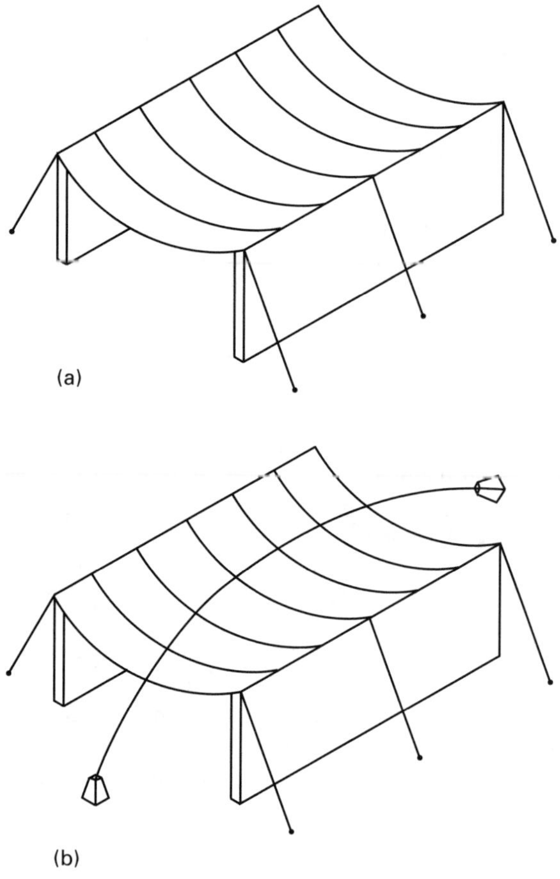

Figure 25.11 Membrane Structures

Air-Supported Structures

Another form of the membrane structure is the air-supported or pneumatic roof. The membrane can still only support loads through tension but the membrane is held in place by air pressure rather than by cables and compression members. The simplest type of air-supported structure is the single membrane inflated like a balloon. Very little air pressure above the atmospheric air pressure is needed to keep a pneumatic structure inflated, but the interior does have to be kept closed to the outside.

Air-supported structures suffer from the same problems as other types of membrane roofs. Specifically, they are unstable under concentrated and varying loads and flutter in the wind. To minimize these problems, they need to be stabilized. One way of doing this is to run cables over the top of the structure so that it is stiffened both from within by the pressure and on the outside by tension in the cables.

Other methods of stabilization include using a double skin structure inflated like a large pillow or with a large number of individual air pockets like an air mattress. These kinds of pneumatic structures also eliminate the need for air lock doors and the continuous pumping of air into the building to maintain the required pressure.

Folded Plates

A folded plate structure consists of thin slabs bent to increase the load-carrying capacity. A typical folded plate roof is illustrated in Fig. 10.11. Folded plate structures are stronger than simple horizontal flat plates because instead of having a structural depth just the thickness of the slab, the structural depth is as deep as the fold of the plate. Additionally, the span is much less, only the distance from one edge of the slab to the other. See Fig. 25.12(a).

Folded plates resist loads with a combination of slab action in the transverse direction and beam action in the longitudinal direction. However, as shown in Fig. 25.12(a), the slab only has to support loads within the distance from one

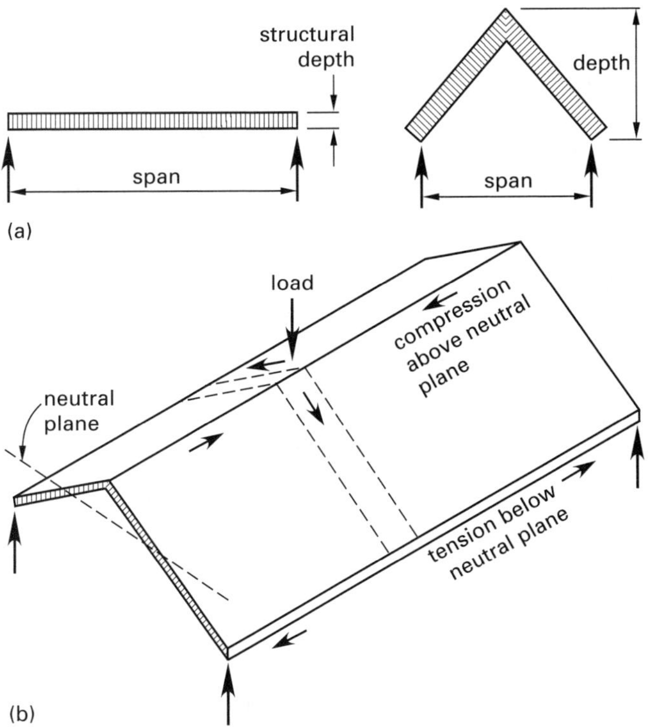

Figure 25.12 Folded Plate Structure

fold to the next, and the load at the apex of each fold is divided into two components, half transferred to one plate and half to the other. In the longitudinal direction, the entire plate assembly acts as a beam with compressive stresses above the neutral plane and tensile stress below. See Fig. 25.12(b).

Folded plate structures can span up to about 100 ft in the longitudinal direction and about 25 ft to 35 ft between outer folds of each plate assembly. They are most commonly built of concrete but can be constructed of plywood, steel, or aluminum as well. One of their primary advantages is that the shapes are simple flat pieces so they can be prefabricated, or if cast in place, the formwork is easy to build.

Since the exterior slabs of any flat slab construction are more highly stressed than interior slabs, a short stiffening slab is usually placed at both edge boundaries to compensate for the additional stress. An example of such a stiffening slab is shown in Fig. 10.11.

Suspension Structures

Suspension structures are similar to membranes in that they can only resist loads by tension. However, this is also one of their great advantages since any given cross section of cable is uniformly stressed because no variable bending stresses can be developed. This results in the material being utilized to its fullest unit stress capability.

Because a cable structure is not inherently rigid, it assumes its funicular shape for any given set of loads. A simple cable supporting one load in midspan will assume a symmetrical triangular shape. If the load is shifted to one side, the shape of the cable changes.

In cable structures, the amount of tensile force is inversely related to the sag of the cable: the greater the sag, the less the tension in the cable. This can be visualized by examining two cables with different sags supporting the same amount of weight in the middle of the cable. See Fig. 25.13(a). If the load is weight P, each of the vertical components of the reaction must be one-half of the weight as dictated by the laws of equilibrium. However, the resultant of the vertical and horizontal forces acts in the direction opposite from the direction of the cable so a simple force polygon as discussed in Ch. 14 can be constructed.

For a cable with a small sag, the resultant (tension) and corresponding horizontal component are large. For a large sag, the resultant and horizontal component are small. In the extreme case of maximum sag, the cable would hang vertically and there would be no horizontal component.

Of course, as the sag increases, the tensile force and hence the amount of cable cross-sectional area required decreases, but the length of the cable increases. If the efficiency and cost of the structure is dependent on the amount of cable

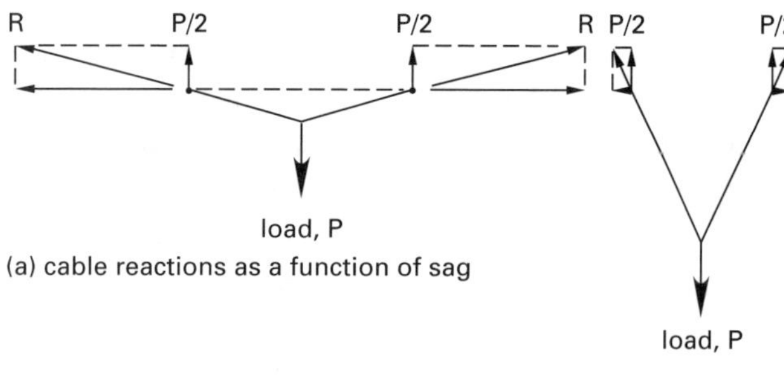

(a) cable reactions as a function of sag

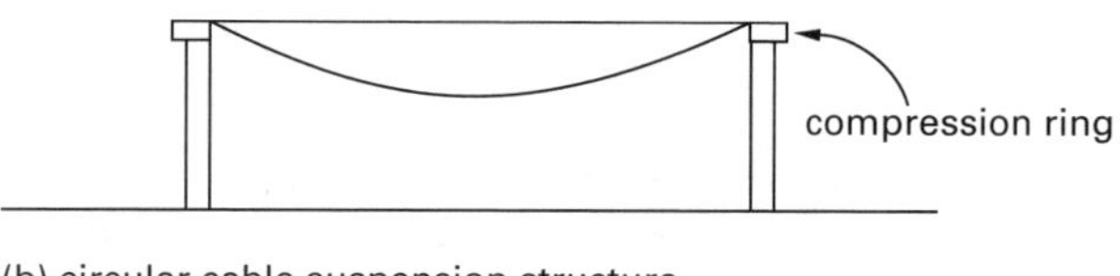

(b) circular cable suspension structure

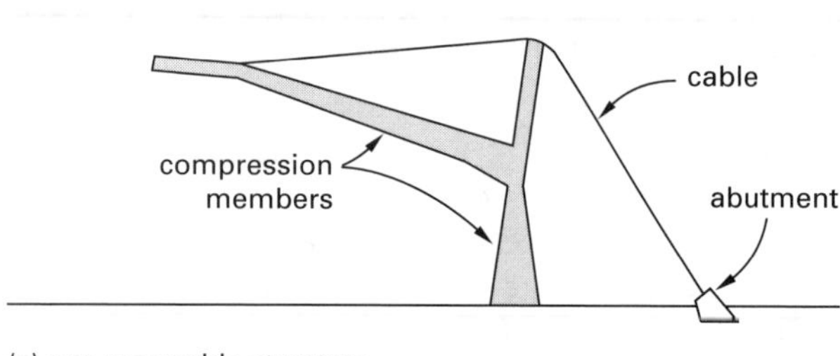

(c) one-way cable structure

Figure 25.13 Cable Structures

material, then there must be some optimum sag that balances cable length with cable cross section. For a cable supporting a single load in the middle, the ideal proportion is that the sag should be one-half the span so that the cable is at a 45° angle.

In building situations, however, single concentrated loads are the exception. A cable structure supports uniform loads. As discussed in Ch. 10, there are two typical uniform loading conditions for cable structures: where the load is uniformly applied on the horizontal projection of the cable and where the load is uniformly applied along the length of the cable. See Fig. 10.12(b) and (c). A uniform horizontal load results in the cable assuming the shape of a parabola, and a uniform load along the length of the cable (such as supporting its own weight) results in a catenary curve.

For these loading conditions, the optimum sag for a parabolic cable is three-tenths of the span, and for a catenary curve the optimum sag is one-third of the span. In practice, however, these sags are not achieved because the low sags would interfere with the function of the building.

For cable-supported structures, there must always be some way of balancing the tensile forces in the cable. This is done with compression members or by extending the cable across a support to a foundation that holds the cable in place, or with some combination of both.

For circular buildings, the tensile forces can be balanced with a continuous compression ring at the perimeter of the roof as shown in Fig. 25.13(b). If the building is not circular, the cable can be draped over a compression member and anchored to a massive foundation. See Fig. 25.13(c). Circular buildings with cable roofs pose a particular problem, however, because the lowest point of the roof for drainage is in the middle of the span.

Cable-suspended structures have the same problem as membrane structures. Because they can only resist loads in tension, they are inherently unstable in the wind and with concentrated loads or other types of changing loads. Sometimes the flexibility of the cable structure can be stabilized simply with the weight of the roof or other structure. More often, additional cables and a stiffening structure need to be included.

DESIGN AND SELECTION CONSIDERATIONS

Many of the design considerations discussed in the last chapter concerning one-way long span systems apply to two-way systems as well. There are, however, a few additional factors that need to be taken into account.

Function

As illustrated in the first part of this chapter, most two-way systems are used exclusively for roofs because of their three-dimensional configuration. Two-way, long span systems are also used primarily for enclosing large, open, single-use spaces such as sports arenas and auditoriums. Therefore, the size and use of the building is the first consideration in deciding on the type of two-way system to use.

Additional functional considerations include provisions for drainage, insulation, and waterproofing. Of course, some shapes, such as domes, some thin-shell structures, and air-supported roofs, are well suited for positive drainage. Others, such as cable-suspended roofs with their low point in the center, membrane structures that drain toward the interior, and some folded plates that trap water in their folds, present definite problems.

Insulating a long span, two-way structure can be a problem since such structures are often selected because of their appearance and architectural drama, in addition to their ability to bridge large distances. Adding insulation to the interior may be difficult or impossible, or may mar the internal appearance. Placing insulation on the exterior may be equally difficult, especially if the shape is complex.

Waterproofing presents similar problems for some types of systems. Structures such as space frames, frame domes, and cable-suspended structures have many parts and facets, resulting in a large number of joints that are always difficult to waterproof easily. Other forms, such as domes and folded plates, can easily be covered with liquid-applied waterproofing membranes.

Cost and Economy

Most two-way structures are very efficient in their use of material and can easily span long distances. However, other factors mitigate these advantages. The most notable disadvantage with many two-way systems is the increased labor cost required for either their fabrication or erection, or both. A space frame is an example of one such framing type with a great number of connections. The problem can be minimized somewhat by using large module sizes, which reduces the number of connections. This means a lower labor cost and lower material costs for the nodes, which are usually the most expensive material part of a space frame.

Likewise, thin-shell structures are very efficient in material use, but are often prohibitively expensive to form because of all the complex curves and careful placement of concrete required.

Occasionally, some prefabrication of shells, folded plates, and space frames is possible to save money. Shot concrete can also be used to speed up concrete placement on thin shells.

For some two-way systems, the attachment of roofing and glazing to the structure may be uneconomical. For example, a geodesic dome must have provisions for attaching the nonstructural, somewhat flexible skin to the rigid framing members. Then, each joint between the panels must be sealed against the weather. For a large dome, this process can be very expensive.

Shipping

Shipping is less of a problem with two-way systems than it is with one-way systems, because most of the assembly is done on site. Components such as connectors and members of a geodesic dome, or the cable for a cable-suspended structure, can easily be shipped to the site.

Acoustics

Some shell configurations and membrane structures can focus sounds as discussed in Ch. 24. If the use of the building requires a good acoustical environment, the choice of a two-way system should be carefully evaluated since adding acoustical control can be difficult and expensive to achieve.

Assembly and Erection

Since most of the construction of a two-way system is done on site, either by casting concrete or assembling small pieces, shipping large members to a job site or building in remote areas is usually not a problem. However, this advantage is often offset by the higher erection costs due to more labor components.

TECHNICAL CONSIDERATIONS

The technical considerations reviewed in Ch. 24 also apply to two-way systems, so they will not be repeated here.

26 SOLVING THE STRUCTURAL LAYOUT VIGNETTE

The Structural Layout vignette presents a floor plan of a small building with two levels and requires that the candidate sketch a structural system using given graphic conventions in order to meet the problem requirements. The structural system includes columns, bearing walls, and roof structure, and may include simple foundation indications. The candidate must indicate an appropriate structural system with reasonable spacing of beams and joists, given the spans and layout of the building. The elements necessary for structural continuity, such that all loads are carried from the roof through all structural elements to the foundation, must be shown.

TIPS FOR COMPLETING THE STRUCTURAL LAYOUT VIGNETTE

This vignette requires the candidate to lay out a basic structural concept using columns, bearing walls, beams, joists, and decking based on a background floor plan and specific program requirements. The problem generally requires framing a high ceiling and a low ceiling (or two levels of some type) while accommodating openings and a change in roof height. Although the problem is fairly straightforward, there are generally several possible solutions that will provide a passing grade. No lateral loads are involved; all the solutions require simple gravity loads in an orthogonal direction. There is usually a clerestory window between the lower roof and the upper roof. A beam is required to support the roof over the clerestory.

The following suggestions can improve the solution.

- In most cases the best solution will be one with a combination of bearing walls and columns, but some vignettes can be solved with columns alone.
- It is usually best to think of the solution starting with the upper roof and working toward the first-floor level.
- The solution must be efficient and cost effective, so use the maximum possible joist spacing, avoid redundant supports (i.e., bearing walls and columns), and do not exceed the span lengths of beams and joists. Try not to exceed a 30 ft (9 m) span for joists or a 40 ft (12 m) span for beams. Generally, joists should span the short direction over a rectangular space.
- Do not show a bearing wall if one is not needed.
- To determine the roof joist spacing, use the maximum span of the roof decking as stated in the program.
- Be sure to show support for decking on all four sides of a roof area. If joists are spanning parallel to a bearing wall (although unlikely) or a nonbearing wall, be sure to place a joist immediately adjacent to the wall. It is possible to center a joist on a wall, but then there should be a beam shown above it—an awkward solution at best.
- Columns can rest on the lowest part of the plan or on bearing walls.
- Beams should not support bearing walls or columns. However, lintels may support bearing walls (and usually do).
- Beams should not support other beams. In any case, the problems are not so complex that this would be required.
- Both ends of joists and beams must be supported and clearly shown. Cantilevers are not allowed. Ends of joists must be supported on beams or bearing walls, or on a combination of the two. Beams must be supported on both ends by columns or bearing walls, or by a combination of the two.

- Use the *layers* tool to view both layers at once and verify that all structural elements drawn on the upper framing plan are supported by appropriate elements on the lower framing plan.
- When drawing joists, extend them to the center of a bearing wall or beam. When drawing beams, extend them to the center of a column.
- Be sure to put lintels over all openings in bearing walls. If openings get larger than 5 ft or 6 ft (1520 mm or 1830 mm), show a beam supported by columns rather than a bearing wall with lintels. Normally, double doors can be handled with lintels; larger openings require beams. The same tool is used to draw both lintels and beams.

SECTION 6: BUILDING SYSTEMS

Chapter 27: Human Comfort and Mechanical System Fundamentals

Chapter 28: HVAC Systems

Chapter 29: Energy Efficiency and Alternative Energy Sources

Chapter 30: Sustainable Design

Chapter 31: Plumbing Systems

Chapter 32: Electrical Systems

Chapter 33: Acoustics

Chapter 34: Solving the Mechanical and Electrical Plan Vignette

27 HUMAN COMFORT AND MECHANICAL SYSTEM FUNDAMENTALS

Nomenclature

A	area of a building assembly	ft^2	m^2
C	conductance	Btu/hr-ft^2-°F	W/m^2·K
e	emittance	hr-ft^2-°F/Btu	m^2·K/W
k	conductivity (for 1 in (25) thickness)	Btu/hr-ft^2-°F	W/m·K
q	total heat loss through a building assembly	Btu/hr	W
q_v	sensible heat loss or gain due to infiltration or ventilation	Btu/hr	W
R	resistance	hr-ft^2-°F/Btu	m^2·K/W
ΔT	temperature difference between indoor and outdoor air	°F	°C
U	coefficient of heat transmission	Btu/hr-ft^2-°F	W/m^2·K
V	volume flow rate of outside air	ft^3/min	L/s
ϵ	emissivity	–	–

DEFINITIONS

British thermal unit (Btu): the amount of heat required to raise the temperature of 1 lbm of water by 1°F. In SI units, energy is measured in joules, J. One joule is a newton-meter, or the force of 1 N acting through a distance of 1 m. One joule is $^1/_{4.184}$ of the amount of heat required to raise the temperature of a gram of water by 1°C. One Btu equals about 1.055 kJ.

Coefficient of heat transmission: the overall rate of heat flow through any combination of materials, including airspaces and air layers on the interior and exterior of a building assembly. It is the reciprocal of the sum of all the resistances in the building assembly.

Conductance: the number of British thermal units per hour that pass through 1 ft^2 of homogeneous material of a given thickness when the temperature differential is 1°F. In SI units, conductance is the rate in watts at which heat passes through 1 m^2 of material when the temperature differential is 1K (Celsius).

Conductivity: the number of British thermal units per hour that pass through 1 ft^2 of homogeneous material 1 in thick when the temperature differential is 1°F. In SI units, conductivity is the rate in watts at which heat flows through 1 m^2 of material 1 m thick when the temperature differential is 1K (Celsius).

Dew point: the temperature at which water vapor in the air becomes saturated and begins to condense to drops of water

Dry-bulb temperature: the temperature of the air-water mixture as measured with a standard dry-bulb thermometer

Enthalpy: the total heat in a substance, including latent heat and sensible heat

Latent heat: heat that causes a change of state of a substance, such as the heat required to change water into steam. The amount of heat required to change the state of a substance is much greater than the heat required to raise the temperature of the substance (sensible heat). The average value of latent heat per pound of moisture is 1061 Btu (1120 kJ).

Resistance: the number of hours needed for 1 Btu to pass through 1 ft^2 of material or assembly of a given thickness when the temperature differential is 1°F. It is the reciprocal of conductance. In SI units, resistance is the number of seconds needed for 1 J to pass through 1 m^2 of material or assembly of a given thickness when the temperature differential is 1K (Celsius).

Sensible heat: heat that causes a change in temperature of a substance but not a change of state. For example, the sensible heat required to raise the temperature of 1 lbm of water from 50°F to 100°F (10°C to 38°C) is 50 Btu (53 kJ). In contrast, the latent heat required to change water at 212°F (100°C) to steam at the same temperature is 1061 Btu (1120 kJ).

Specific heat: the number of Btus (joules) required to raise the temperature of a specific material by 1°F (1K). Specific heat is a measure of a material's capacity to store heat as compared with the storage capacity of water.

Wet-bulb temperature: the temperature of the air as measured with a sling psychrometer. The wet-bulb temperature is a more critical measure of heat in high humidity because it is an indicator of stress when the human body is near the upper limits of temperature regulation by perspiration.

HUMAN COMFORT

Human comfort is based on the quality of the following primary environmental factors: temperature, humidity, air movement, temperature radiation to and from surrounding surfaces, air quality, sound, vibration, and light. For each of these factors there are certain levels within which people are comfortable and can function most efficiently. Acoustics and lighting are reviewed in later chapters. This section discusses human comfort relative to the thermal environment. Chapter 28 deals with the mechanical systems used to modify internal environments to maintain human comfort.

Human Metabolism

The human body is a heat-producing machine. It takes in food and water and, through the metabolic process, converts these to mechanical energy and other bodily processes necessary to maintain life. Because the body is not very efficient in this conversion, it must give off excess heat in order to maintain a stable body temperature. The body's heat production is measured in metabolic units, or *mets*. A met is the energy produced per unit of surface area per hour by a seated person at rest. One met is 18.4 Btu/hr-ft^2 (58.2 W/m^2). Given the average surface area of an adult, this means that at rest the human body gives off about 400 Btu/hr (117 W). This increases to around 700 Btu/hr to 800 Btu/hr (205 W to 235 W) for moderate activities like walking and work, and up to 2000 Btu/hr (586 W) for strenuous exercise.

The body loses heat in three primary ways: convection, evaporation, and radiation. It can also lose heat by conduction, but this accounts for a very small portion of total body heat loss. *Convection* is the transfer of heat through the movement of a fluid, either a gas or liquid. This occurs when the air temperature surrounding a person is less than the body's skin temperature, around 85°F (29°C). The body heats the surrounding air, which rises and is replaced with cooler air. Heat loss through *evaporation* occurs when moisture changes to a vapor as a person perspires or breathes. *Radiation* is the transfer of heat energy through electromagnetic waves from one surface to a colder surface. The body can lose heat to a cooler atmosphere or to a cooler surface. *Conduction* is the transfer of heat through direct contact between two objects of different temperatures.

The body loses heat (or is prevented from losing heat) through these four processes in various proportions depending on the environmental conditions. If the body cannot lose heat one way it must lose it another. For example, when the air temperature is above the body temperature of 98.6°F (37°C), there can be no convection transfer because heat always flows from a higher level to a lower level. (This is the second law of thermodynamics.) The body must then lose its heat by evaporation. Figure 27.1 illustrates how the total amount of heat generated at rest is transferred depending on the surrounding temperature.

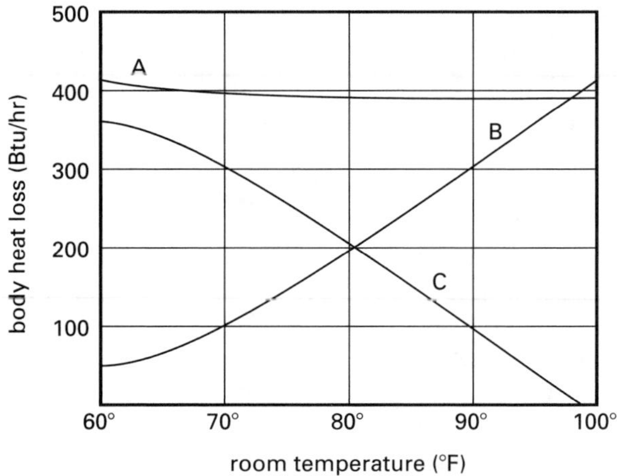

Figure 27.1 Body Heat Generated and Lost at Rest

The body maintains its proper temperature by regulating physiological processes, mainly the control of blood flow to the various parts of the body. This is done by the hypothalamus in the brain. When the body is too hot, the hypothalamus signals the sweat glands to increase secretion and sends more blood to the skin surface, a process called *vasodilation*. This carries body heat to the skin, where the heat energy is lost to the atmosphere through evaporation, or sweating. When the body is too cold, the hypothalamus signals the body to decrease blood flow to the skin surface and to the extremities, a process called *vasoconstriction*.

The sensation of thermal comfort depends on the interrelationship of many factors. Some of these include air temperature, humidity, air movement, surface temperature, clothing, and ventilation. These are discussed in the following sections. Other factors that are more difficult to quantify objectively include personal metabolic rate, age, and psychological variables such as light, color, and aroma.

Air Temperature

Temperature is the primary determinant of comfort. It is difficult to precisely state a normal range of comfortable temperature limits because the range depends on many factors including the humidity levels, radiant temperatures, air movement, clothing, cultural factors, age, and sex. However, a general comfortable range is between 69°F and 80°F (20°C to 27°C), with a tolerable range from 60°F to 85°F (16°C to 29°C), depending on relative humidity. The *International Mechanical Code* (IMC) and the IBC both require that any space intended for human occupancy be provided with an active or passive space-heating system capable of maintaining a minimum indoor temperature of 68°F (20°C) at a point 3 ft (914) above the floor on the design heating day.

A value called the *effective temperature* (ET) has been developed that attempts to combine the effects of air temperature, humidity, and air movement.

Dry-bulb temperature is measured with a standard thermometer. Wet-bulb temperature is measured with a *sling psychrometer*, a device that consists of a thermometer with a moist cloth around the bulb. The thermometer is swung rapidly in the air, causing the moisture in the cloth to evaporate. In dry air, the moisture evaporates rapidly and acquires latent heat, which produces a low wet-bulb temperature. A large difference between the wet-bulb temperature and the dry-bulb temperature indicates low relative humidity. In moist air, less moisture evaporates from the cloth, so the wet-bulb temperature is higher.

Humidity

Relative humidity is the ratio of the percentage of moisture in the air to the maximum amount the air can hold at a given temperature without condensing. Comfortable relative humidity ranges are between 30% and 65%, with tolerable ranges between 20% and 70%. Relative humidity is particularly important in the summer months because as the air temperature rises, the body can lose less heat through convection and must rely mostly on evaporation. However, as the humidity rises, it is more difficult for perspiration to evaporate; hence, a person feels much hotter than the air temperature would indicate.

Air Movement

Air movement tends to increase evaporation and heat loss through convection. This is why a person will feel comfortable in high temperatures and humidities if there is a breeze. It also explains the windchill effect when a tolerable cold air temperature becomes unbearable in a wind. Wind speeds from 50 ft/min to about 200 ft/min (0.25 to 1.02 m/s) are generally acceptable for cooling without causing annoying drafts.

Surface Temperature

Because the body gains or loses heat through radiation, the temperature of the surrounding surfaces is an important factor in determining human comfort. If the surface temperatures of the surroundings are colder than the surface temperature of the skin, about 85°F (29°C), the body loses heat through radiation; if the surrounding surfaces are warmer than the skin, the body gains heat. The rate at which radiation occurs depends on the surface temperatures of the body and the nearby object, the viewed angle, and the emissivity.

The *viewed angle* is the solid angle formed between the measuring position and the outer edges of the object. For example, when sitting close to a fireplace, a person experiences relatively high radiant heat because the fireplace occupies a large angle of view relative to the body. When the person sits across the room, the same fireplace occupies a much smaller angle of view, so it will not feel as warm.

The *emissivity* (ϵ) of an object is a measure of its ability to absorb and then radiate heat. Technically, the emittance of an object is the ratio of the radiation emitted by a given object or material to that emitted by a black body at the same temperature. Shiny objects or materials have very low emissivity, so they do not absorb or radiate heat as well as black objects. The shiny foil on many insulation materials is an example of the use of emissivity to reduce heat transfer.

To determine the effects of surface temperatures on comfort, all room surfaces and their temperatures and positions must be taken into account. The value used to calculate these factors is the *mean radiant temperature* (MRT). The MRT is a weighted average of the various surface temperatures in a room and the angle of exposure of the occupant to these surfaces, as well as of any sunlight present.

The MRT is an important comfort factor in cold rooms or in the winter because as the air temperature decreases, the body loses more heat through radiation than by evaporation, as shown in Fig. 27.1. Even a room with an adequate temperature will feel cool if the surfaces are cold. Warming these surfaces and providing radiant heating panels are two ways to counteract this effect.

Another way to factor in the effects of surface temperatures on human comfort is with operative temperature. *Operative temperature* is an average of the air temperature of a space and the mean radiant temperature (MRT) of the space. It can be measured with a *globe thermometer*, which is a thermometer inside a black globe. This type of thermometer can account for both the air temperature and radiant effects from surrounding surfaces.

Clothing

Clothing acts as an insulator, moderating the effects of conduction, convection, and radiation. Nearly all measurements and standards for human comfort are based on wearing clothing. To quantify the effects of clothing the unit of the *clo* was developed. One clo is about equal to the typical American man's business suit or about 0.15 clo/lbm (0.35 clo/kg) of clothing.

Ventilation

There are two basic types of ventilation requirements, one for unoccupied spaces such as attics and crawl spaces, and one for occupied spaces. See Ch. 55 for ventilation requirements for attics and crawl spaces.

Ventilation is needed for occupied spaces for many reasons: to provide oxygen and remove carbon dioxide, to remove odors, to carry away contaminants, and to remove unwanted moisture. The *International Mechanical Code* (IMC) requires that every occupied space be provided with either natural or mechanical ventilation. In addition, certain spaces and uses are required to have a separate exhaust system to remove contaminants, odors, and moisture. These spaces and uses include toilet rooms, clothes dryers, cooking appliances, refuse conveyor systems, and laboratories.

Where natural ventilation is used, the IMC (and the IBC as well) requires that the area openable to the outdoors be equal to at least 4% of the floor area being ventilated. When a room or space without outside openings is ventilated through an adjoining room, the opening to the adjoining room must have an unobstructed area of at least 8% of the floor area of the interior room or space, and not less than 25 ft^2 (2.3 m^2). In this case, the minimum area openable to the outdoors is calculated based on the total floor area being ventilated.

Where mechanical ventilation is used, the rate of supply air brought into the room or space must be approximately equal to the rate of return air, or exhaust air, carried out of it. However, the development of positive or negative pressure is allowed when it is needed for the use of the space. The amount of outdoor ventilation air that must be brought in depends on the type of use and the occupant load. A table in the IMC gives the minimum ventilation rates in both cubic feet per minute per person (cfm/person) and cubic feet per minute per square foot of area (cfm/ft^2), based on the occupancy classification. The table also gives the occupant density in number of people per unit area (per square foot or square meter) that must be used when calculating the occupant load.

The occupancy classifications and the occupant density used in these calculations are not the same as those used in the IBC for calculation of egress requirements. The IMC table assumes that smoking is not present. If smoking is expected in a space other than a smoking lounge, the ventilation system must be designed to provide more ventilation than what is required by the table. Smoking lounges have a separate ventilation and exhaust requirement in the table. Once the ventilation rates are known from the IMC table, a series of complex calculations is required to design a specific mechanical system to meet the requirements.

This same table also gives required exhaust airflow rates, in cubic feet per minute per square foot of area, for spaces that require a separate exhaust system. Refer to Ch. 28 for more information on exhaust systems.

MEASUREMENT SYSTEMS

Because the relationships between temperature, humidity, radiation, and other factors are complex, various methods have been developed to show these relationships and to assist in designing mechanical systems. Two of the more common methods are discussed in the following sections.

Comfort Charts

Comfort charts show the relationships among temperature, humidity, and other comfort factors. A simplified version is shown in Fig. 27.2. It shows the comfort zones for both winter and summer for temperature zones in the United States (about 40° latitude) for elevations below 1000 ft (300 m) above sea level, and for people normally engaged in sedentary or light work.

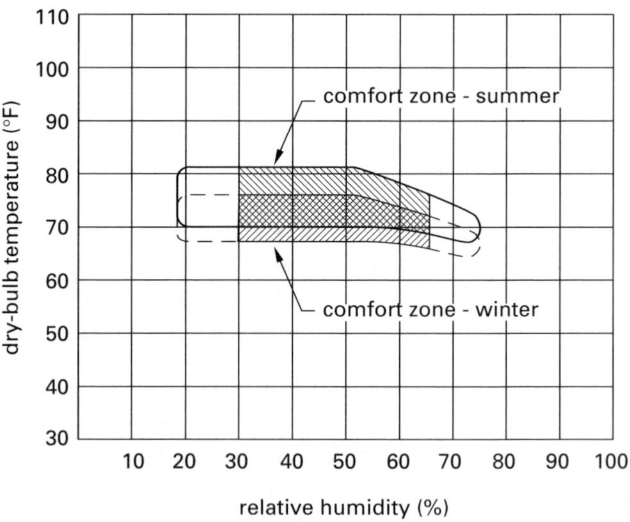

Figure 27.2 Comfort Chart for Temperate Zones

The tolerable humidity limits of about 20% and 75% are shown, but limits between 30% and 65% are preferred. The chart shows that as humidity increases, the air temperature must decrease to provide the same amount of comfort as is felt with lower humidity levels.

As the temperature drops below the recommended levels, radiation in the form of sunshine or mechanical radiation is needed to maintain comfort. The lower the temperature, the more radiation is required. As the humidity and temperature increase, air movement is required to maintain comfort levels.

Psychrometric Chart

The psychrometric chart is a graphical representation of the complex interactions between heat, air, and moisture. The study of the water vapor content of air is known as *psychrometry*. Because warm air can hold more moisture than cold air can, and because the amount of moisture in the air (humidity) affects human comfort, especially at high temperatures, there must be a way to calculate the amount of heat and moisture that must be either added or removed by HVAC systems. The psychrometric chart is the tool used to make the necessary calculations.

Figure 27.3 shows a simplified version of the psychrometric chart. For illustrative purposes, it does not show all the graph lines that are present on the full chart. The vertical lines show dry-bulb temperatures, while the lines sloping from upper left to lower right show wet-bulb temperatures. The curved lines represent relative humidity from 0% to 100%. The 100% line is also known as the *saturation line* or *dew-point line*. This shows when water vapor will form when saturated air comes in contact with any surface at or below the air's dew-point temperature. At 100% relative humidity, the wet-bulb and dry-bulb temperatures are the same.

Along the upper-left side of the chart is a scale representing *enthalpy*, or the total amount of both sensible and latent heat in the air-moisture mixture. Its lines run approximately parallel to the wet-bulb temperature lines and are in units of Btu/lbm (kJ/kg) of dry air. The *enthalpy line* is used to determine the total amount of heat that must be either removed (in cooling) or added (in heating) from conditioned air. This is more than just the heat represented by air temperature (sensible heat), because the latent heat contained in the moisture in the air must also be removed or added.

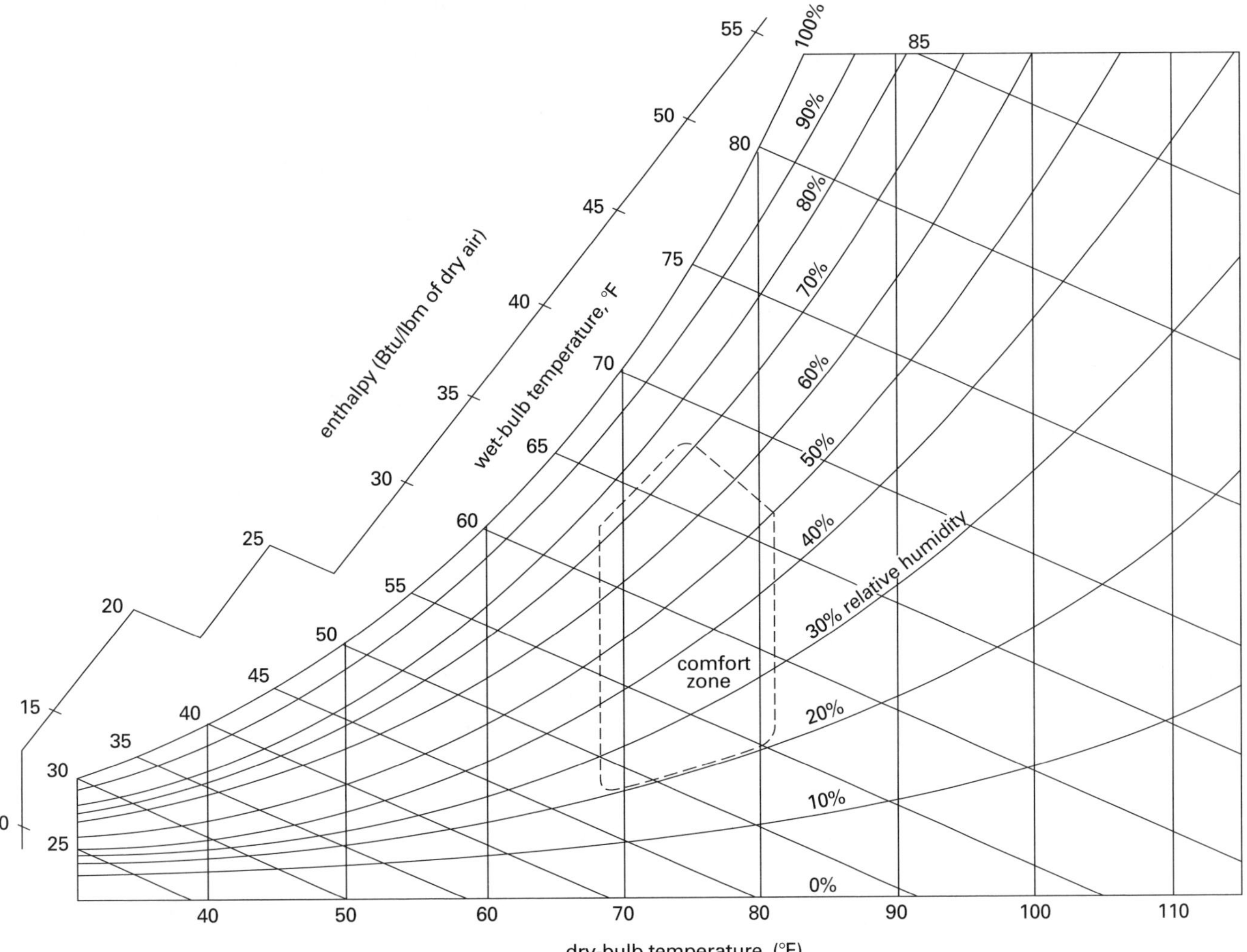

Figure 27.3 Psychrometric Chart

The amount of moisture that must be removed or added can also be read along a horizontal scale at the right side of the chart. These lines are not shown in the simplified version of Fig. 27.3, but represent the *humidity ratio*, or the amount of moisture by weight within a given weight of air.

The psychrometric chart illustrates why evaporative coolers only work in hot, dry climates. An *evaporative cooler* (swamp cooler) reduces the temperature of the air but does not reduce the enthalpy (total heat). For example, select the wet-bulb temperature line of 70°F (which is nearly parallel to the enthalpy lines) where it crosses the vertical dry-bulb temperature line of 90°F. Follow it up and to the left until it crosses the vertical 80°F dry-bulb temperature line. The chart shows that without changing the enthalpy and dropping the air temperature 10°F, the humidity has increased from about 40% to more than 60%.

In addition to providing a wide range of information for HVAC design, the psychrometric chart can also be used to plot the comfort zone based on combinations of temperature and humidity. This also is shown in Fig. 27.3.

EXTERNAL AND INTERNAL LOADS

In order to maintain human comfort, a building must resist either the loss of heat to the outside during cold weather or the gain of heat during hot weather. Any excess heat gain or loss must be compensated for with passive energy conservation measures or with mechanical heating and cooling systems.

External factors that cause heat loss include air temperature and wind. External factors that cause heat gain include air temperature and sunlight. Internal factors that produce heat loads include people, lights, and equipment.

Heat is transferred between the outside and inside of a building through conduction, convection, and radiation. *Conduction* is the transfer of heat through direct contact between molecules. *Convection* is the transfer of heat through the movement of air. *Radiation* is the transfer of heat energy through electromagnetic waves from one surface to a colder surface.

Heat Loss Calculations

In order to determine the size of a heating system for a building, the total amount of heat lost per hour must be calculated. Heat is lost in two basic ways: through the building envelope and through air infiltration. The *building envelope* consists of the walls, roof, doors, windows, and foundation. Each of the materials or groups of materials comprising these building elements resists the transfer of heat that occurs through the processes of conduction, convection, and radiation.

Every material has a unique property known as its *conductivity*, k, which is the amount of heat lost through 1 ft^2 of a 1 in thickness of the material when the temperature differential is 1°F. *Conductance*, C, is the same property, but when the material is a thickness other than 1 in. The *resistance*, R, of a material, is the number of hours needed for 1 Btu to pass through a material of a given thickness when the temperature differential is 1°F. In SI units conductivity, k, is the rate in watts at which heat flow through 1 m^2 of material when the temperature differential is 1K (Celsius). Resistance, R, in SI units is the number of secondss needed for 1 J to pass through 1 m^2 of material or assembly of a given thickness when the temperature differential is 1K (Celsius).

Conductance and resistance are related by the formula

$$R = \frac{1}{C} \qquad 27.1$$

Values for k, C, and R for various materials are given in standard reference texts as well as in the American Society of Heating, Refrigerating and Air-Conditioning Engineers (ASHRAE) *Handbook of Fundamentals*. If any heat loss calculations are required on the exam, the necessary tables will be included with the online reference materials.

When a building assembly consists of more than one material, the value used to calculate heat loss is the coefficient of heat transmission, U. However, the value of U is not simply the sum of all the conductances of the individual materials. Instead, the coefficient of heat loss must be calculated according to the formula

$$U = \frac{1}{\Sigma R} \qquad 27.2$$

The amount of heat loss through one unit of area of building material or assembly is dependent on the coefficient of heat transmission of the material or assembly and the temperature differential between the inside and outside. For an entire area of one type of material, this value is multiplied by the total area to get the total heat loss. The formula is

$$q = UA\Delta t \qquad 27.3$$

In order to calculate the heat loss for an entire room or building, the heat losses of all the different types of assemblies—walls, windows, roofs, and so forth—must be determined and then added together.

Example 27.1

Find the coefficient of heat transmission for the wall assembly shown.

The R- and C-values for the various components are given. However, they must all be converted to conductances for the thicknesses used. Remember that air spaces and the thin

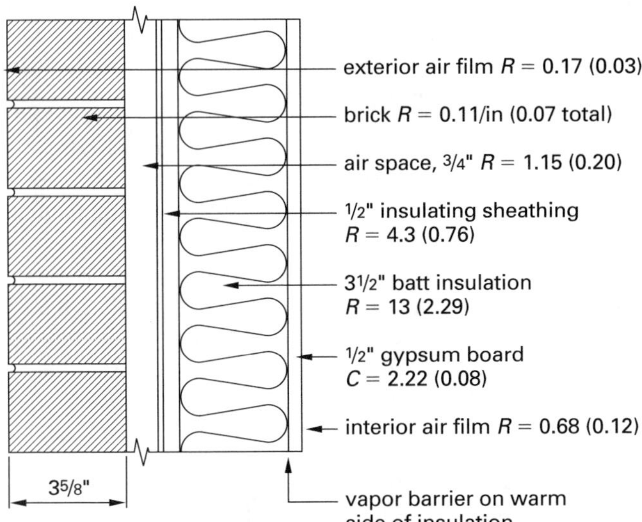

layer of air on the exteriors and interiors of buildings have some thermal resistance. If the brick has an *R*-value of 0.11 hr-ft^2-°F/Btu per inch and is $3^5/_8$ in thick (3.625), then its total R-value is 0.40 hr-ft^2-°F/Btu. The conductance of the gypsum board is 2.22 hr-ft^2-°F/Btu, so its resistance is $^1/_{2.22}$, or 0.45.

The summation of the *R*-values of the assembly is

	R-value	
	(hr-ft^2-°F/Btu)	(m^2·K/W)
exterior air film	0.17	0.03
brick	0.40	0.07
airspace	1.15	0.20
sheathing	4.30	0.76
insulation	13.00	2.29
gypsum board	0.45	0.08
interior air film	0.68	0.12
ΣR	20.15	3.55

The overall coefficient of transmission is then

$$\begin{aligned} U &= \frac{1}{\Sigma R} \\ &= \frac{1}{20.15}\ \text{Btu/hr-ft}^2\text{-°F} \quad \left(\frac{1}{3.55}\ \text{W/m}^2\text{·K}\right) \\ &= 0.05\ \text{Btu/hr-ft}^2\text{-°F} \quad \left(0.28\ \text{W/m}^2\text{·K}\right) \end{aligned}$$

The value for ΔT is determined by subtracting the outdoor design temperature from the desired indoor temperature in the winter, usually 70°F (21°C). Outdoor design temperatures vary with geographical region and are found in the ASHRAE Handbook or are set by local building codes.

One important aspect of heat loss calculations and the use of the psychrometric chart is to determine the dew point of the moisture in the air to avoid condensation on interior surfaces and especially inside building construction. For example, air at 70°F (21°C) and 35% relative humidity has a dew point of 41°F (5°C). Moisture will condense on surfaces at or below this temperature.

In Ex. 27.1, if the outdoor temperature is 0°F (−18°C) and the indoor temperature 70°F (21°C), somewhere inside the wall assembly the temperature is 41°F (5°C) or less. Water vapor from inside the building permeating the construction would condense on this surface, damaging the wood construction and possibly negating the effectiveness of the insulation. To avoid this problem, a vapor barrier must be placed on the warm side of the insulation, as shown in Ex. 27.1. Vapor barriers can be thin plastic films, or they can be a part of sheathing or insulation batts.

Heat loss through infiltration will be discussed in a separate section.

Heat Gain Calculations

There are several sources of heat gain in buildings. There is, of course, heat gain produced when the outside temperature is high and heat is transferred by conduction, convection, and radiation, just as with heat loss. Heat gain through infiltration is also a factor when outside temperatures are high. In addition, heat is produced by the radiation of the sun on glazing, by the building's occupants, by lighting, and by equipment such as motors.

The percentage of heat generated by each of these factors varies with the occupancy of the building. For example, a residence is dominated by gains from the building envelope and through glazing. The number of occupants and lighting is negligible. A large office building, however, has a great many occupants, each producing a minimum of 400 Btu/hr (117 W) at rest, a large number of light fixtures, and a significant amount of equipment. The ratio of room and wall surface may be quite low for such an office building compared with a residence. Because of these types of conditions, it is not unusual in many occupancies for air conditioning to be required even in the winter months.

Heat gain through the building envelope is calculated in a manner similar to heat loss, using the overall coefficient of heat transmission and the area of the building assembly (as shown in Eq. 27.3), but the temperature differential is not used directly. Instead, a value known as the *design equivalent temperature difference* (DETD) must be used. This value, calculated through complex formulas, takes into account the air temperature differences, effects of the sun, thermal mass storage effects of materials, colors of finishes exposed to the sun, and the daily temperature range. These values are published in tables produced by ASHRAE.

Another way to combine the effects of solar radiation with air temperature is by using the sol-air temperature in calculations. The *sol-air temperature* is an outdoor temperature that combines the effects of temperature difference with solar radiation. The calculated value can be used as the ΔT value in heat gain calculations. The basic formula for calculating the sol-air temperature is

$$T_e = T_o + \frac{\alpha l}{h_o} - 7°\text{F} \qquad \text{[U.S.]} \quad 27.4(a)$$

$$T_e = T_o + \frac{\alpha l}{h_o} - 3.9°\text{C} \qquad \text{[SI]} \quad 27.4(b)$$

In Eq. 27.4, T_e is the sol-air temperature and T_o is the outdoor dry-bulb temperature. α is the surface's absorptance for solar radiation. Light-colored surfaces are usually assumed to be 0.45; dark surfaces are assumed to be 0.90. Detailed values are given in the *ASHRAE Handbook*. l is the total solar radiation incident on the surface, given in units of Btu/hr-ft^2 (W/m^2); solar heat gain factors are given in the *ASHRAE Handbook*. h_o is the coefficient of heat transfer by long-wave radiation and convection at the surface; this is usually assumed to be 3.0 Btu/hr-ft^2-°F (17.0 W/m^2·K).

As Eq. 27.4 illustrates, heat flow through construction assemblies is strongly affected both by the amount of solar radiation and by the color of the surface, with dark surfaces resulting in much greater heat flow than light surfaces.

Heat gain through glazing can be a very significant factor. It is calculated by multiplying the area of the glazing by the *design cooling load factor* (DCLF). Like the design equivalent temperature difference, the DCLF takes into account several variables that affect how solar heat gain occurs, including the type of glazing, the type of interior shading, and the outdoor design temperature. Design cooling load factors are also published by ASHRAE.

The occupants of a building produce two kinds of heat: sensible heat and latent heat in the form of moisture from breathing and perspiration. Sensible heat gain from occupants can be assumed to be about 225 Btu/hr (66 W), although this varies slightly with occupancy type. Total sensible heat is calculated by multiplying the number of occupants by 225 Btu/hr (66 W).

Heat gains from lighting can be found by using the fact that one watt equals 3.41 Btu/hr. Simply multiply the total wattage load of the building's lighting by 3.41. For fluorescent and other discharge lights, the energy used by the ballast must also be included. A rule of thumb is to multiply the Btu/hr generated by these types of fixtures by 1.25. In SI units, watts can be used directly.

Heat generated by equipment such as motors, elevators, appliances, water heaters, and cooking equipment can be a significant factor in commercial buildings. The methods of calculating such heat are complex and depend on variables such as horsepower ratings and efficiencies of motors, load factors, and any latent heat produced.

Latent heat must be accounted for in calculating heat gains because, for cooling purposes, moisture in the air (latent heat) must be removed to maintain a comfortable relative humidity level while the sensible heat level is being reduced. In heat gain calculations, latent heat gain is either accounted for separately or by multiplying the total sensible heat gain in a building by a certain percentage derived through experience. Latent heat gain in residential and many other occupancies is about 30% of the sensible heat gain.

One effective passive method to mitigate the effects of heat gain from solar radiation and air temperature is to use building materials with high mass. Materials such as masonry, concrete, and tile slow the transmission of heat into a building. During the day, these materials absorb the heat energy and store it. During the night, when the air temperature is cooler than the surface of the mass, much of this energy is lost to the atmosphere instead of being transmitted into the building.

Infiltration

Infiltration is the transfer of air into and out of a building through open doors, through cracks around windows and other openings, through flues and vents, and through other gaps in the exterior construction. Unless a building is well sealed, infiltration can account for more heat loss than does transmission through the walls and roof. However, no building is perfectly sealed; there is always some infiltration.

Heat loss through infiltration is calculated by the formula

$$q_v = V(1.08)\Delta T \qquad 27.5$$

The factor of 1.08 Btu-min/ft^3-°F-hr accounts for the specific heat of air; that is, the amount of heat that air at a certain density can hold. The value of V can be calculated in detail based on the air lost through cracks, doors, and other openings, or it can be estimated with the use of tables that give air changes per hour based on certain criteria.

In SI units, the formula is

$$q_v = V(1200)\Delta T \qquad 27.6$$

q_v is in watts, V is liters per second, and ΔT is in degrees Kelvin (or Celsius). The factor of 1200 J·s/m^3·°C · h accounts for the specific heat of air.

Calculating sensible heat gain through infiltration is similar to calculating heat loss. The total heat gain is found by multiplying the total area by an infiltration factor. If a building is being mechanically ventilated, however, the volume of air being introduced into the building is multiplied by the amount of heat that must be extracted both to cool the air and to remove excess humidity (latent heat). In humid climates, the energy required to do this can be substantial.

CLIMATIC TYPES AND DESIGN RESPONSES

From the standpoint of human comfort, buildings are designed to moderate the effects of climate. When passive design strategies cannot maintain conditions of temperature and humidity within the comfort zone, additional active or mechanical means are used.

With today's technology, HVAC systems can provide comfort regardless of how a building is designed. However, relying only on mechanical systems without regard to passive design strategies appropriate to the local climate increases costs, wastes energy, contributes to pollution, and ignores the often desirable regional characteristics of architecture.

As discussed in Ch. 5, architects have traditionally used four very basic climatic regions to develop both passive and active design responses to climate. These regions are cool, temperate, hot-humid, and hot-arid. Code-writing organizations now use eight climate zones to set standards for insulation, air barriers, water barriers, and other energy conservation features. These climate zones are shown in Fig. 5.4 with the rough boundaries of the four climatic regions overlaid on the map. An architect should determine what climatic zone is applicable and follow code-regulated guidelines. The following describes the general location of the four basic climatic regions and suggested design responses.

The *cool zone* includes all of Canada, the northern part of the middle United States, and the mountainous regions of Wyoming and Colorado. The *temperate zone* includes most of the middle latitudes of the United States, including the northwest and northeast areas of the country. The *hot-humid zone* includes the southeastern parts of the country, and the *hot-arid zone* stretches from Southern California across the desert Southwest to portions of southern Texas.

In cold climates, buildings should ideally minimize the exposed surface area to reduce heat loss. This generally suggests buildings with cubical shapes and those built partially underground. Northern exposure should be minimized, as should door and window openings. Entries should have air locks, and landscaping and building design should block winter winds. Because of extremes of temperature and little direct sunlight in the winter, passive solar heating is usually not appropriate. Mechanical heating and active solar heating are required.

In temperate climate zones, heat loss in the winter can be significant, so northern exposure should be minimized and winter winds should be blocked to reduce heat loss. However, solar heat gain is desirable in the winter, so building lengths should be oriented east and west to maximize southern exposure. In the summer, the same south-facing sides of buildings should be shaded with deciduous trees and mechanical devices like awnings to protect from unwanted heat gain. To mitigate the effects of daytime heating, it is best to provide for nighttime ventilation for the exhaust of hot air. Solar heating, both active and passive, works well in many locations without excessive cloud cover.

Hot-humid climates are the most difficult to design for without mechanical cooling. Buildings should be planned for the maximum amount of natural ventilation using narrow floor plans with cross ventilation; large, open windows; porches; and breezeways. Shading with vegetation (without blocking ventilation) or with double roofs is required. Building materials should be thermally lightweight so they do not store daytime heat and release it at night.

In hot-arid climates, shading from direct sunlight is also required, but the wide variations between day and night temperatures can be used to advantage by employing materials with high thermal mass so daytime heat is released at night. The same mass cools at night for daytime comfort. Night ventilation is very useful to remove heat built up during the day. If sufficient water is available, pools can reduce local air temperature through evaporation. Roof ponds for one- or two-story buildings provide this type of evaporative cooling as well as high thermal mass. Evaporative coolers work well in arid climates because an increase in humidity with a decrease in air temperature is desirable.

28 HVAC SYSTEMS

ENERGY SOURCES

Regardless of what energy conservation measures are adopted for a building, either the primary or backup energy source will be one of the conventional fuels. The selection of fuel type depends on the fuel's availability and dependability of supply, its cost, cleanliness, convenience of storage, and requirements of the equipment needed to use it. For example, in an urban area steam may be readily available as a by-product of a local utility company, whereas in a suburban area oil may have to be the energy source. In some parts of the country electricity is inexpensive and readily available; in other locations its use for heating is cost prohibitive.

Natural Gas

Of all the fossil fuels, natural gas is the most efficient. It is clean burning and relatively low in cost. Depending on geographic location and local market conditions, however, it may not always be available, or the price may fluctuate widely. In remote locations it may not be available at all. It has a heating value of about 1050 Btu/ft^3 (39 100 kJ/m^3).

Propane is one type of gas that can be used in areas where natural gas is not available. It is delivered and stored in pressurized tanks and has a heating value of about 21,560 Btu/lbm, or 2500 Btu/ft^3 (93 150 kJ/m^3).

Oil

Oil is widely used in some parts of the country, but because it is a petroleum product, its cost and availability are dependent on world and local market conditions. It must be stored in or near the building where it is used, and the equipment needed for burning it is subject to more maintenance than that used for gas-fired boilers.

Oil is produced in six grades for residential and commercial heating use: no. 1, no. 2, no. 4, no. 5 light, no. 5 heavy, and no. 6. The lower the number, the more refined and the more expensive the oil. No. 2 fuel oil is the grade most commonly used in residential and light commercial boilers, whereas no. 4 and no. 5 grades are used in larger commercial applications. The heat value for no. 2 oil is from 137,000 Btu/gal to 141,000 Btu/gal (38 200 kJ/L to 39 300 kJ/L), and that for no. 5 is from 146,800 Btu/gal to 152,000 Btu/gal (40 900 kJ/L to 42 400 kJ/L).

Electricity

Electricity has the advantages of being easy to install, low in installation cost, simple to operate, easy to control, and flexible in zoning; and it does not require storage facilities, exhaust flues, or supply air. Its primary disadvantage is its cost in most parts of the country compared with other fuels. Because most electric utilities now charge more for peak use as well as total electricity consumed, heating during a cold period can be very expensive.

Electricity is ideal for radiant heating, either in a ceiling or in individual panels. It can be used in baseboard units as well as to operate electric furnaces for forced air systems. One of its most prevalent uses is for supplemental space heating. Electricity has an equivalent heating value of 3413 Btu/kW (3600 kJ/kW).

Steam

Steam is not considered a basic fuel as are gas and oil, but in many urban locations it is available from a central plant or as a by-product of the generation of electricity. Once piped into a building, it is not used directly for heating but can be used to heat water for water or air heating systems and to drive absorption-type water chillers for air conditioning.

Heat Pumps

A *heat pump* is a device that can either heat in the winter or cool in the summer. It works by transferring heat from one place to another, using the principles of refrigeration as discussed in a later section. In the summer a heat pump acts as a standard air conditioner, pumping refrigerant to the condenser, where it loses heat, and then to the evaporator indoors, where it absorbs heat. By means of a special valve, the refrigerant flow is reversed in the winter so that the heat pump absorbs available heat from the air outside and transfers it to the indoor space.

Because of this process, however, the efficiency of a heat pump for heating decreases as the outdoor air temperature decreases. Below about 40°F (4°C), a heat pump is not competitive with oil or gas as an energy source. It is more effective in mild climates where winter temperatures are usually moderate. For supplemental heating, electrical resistance coils are often placed in supply ductwork.

To extend its efficiency, a heat pump can be connected to a solar energy system. With this approach, solar energy provides heat when the outdoor temperature is between 47°F and 65°F (8°C and 18°C). Below the lower extreme, a heat pump automatically turns on and provides heat until the temperature becomes too cold for its efficient use. Then both systems are used: the heat pump to preheat air and the solar energy system to raise the temperature high enough for space heating. Electrical resistance heating is also available for very cold or cloudy days.

Natural Energy Sources

Other energy sources include solar (either passive or active), photovoltaic, geothermal, wind, and tidal. These are described in Ch. 29. Of these, solar energy is the one that has been developed to the point where it is readily available and efficient for residential and some commercial uses.

Photovoltaic panels are available, but the cost per kilowatt-hour is high, and their general use is limited. This is changing as more research is conducted and more efficient panels are manufactured. Refer to Ch. 29 for more information on photovoltaics.

Use of the other natural energy sources is still in the research and development stage and is limited to large-scale generation rather than use with individual buildings.

Selection of Fuel Sources

In addition to the considerations mentioned previously in regard to the selection of a fuel source, the number of degree days in a building's location and the efficiency of the fuel must be taken into account.

Degree days are a measure of the approximate average yearly temperature difference between the outside and the inside in a particular location. The number of degree days for a day is found by taking the difference between an indoor temperature of 65°F (18°C) and the average outside temperature for a 24-hour period. For example, if the 24-hour average is 36°F, then the number of degree days is 65 − 36 = 29. The values for each day of the year are added to get the total number of degree days for the year. Degree days are used to calculate yearly fuel consumption, to size some passive solar energy systems, and to factor into other heating computations.

Because different fuel types convert energy into heat with varying levels of efficiency, efficiency is an important consideration in the selection of fuel, assuming all fuels are available. Table 28.1 shows the typical efficiency ranges of several fuels.

Table 28.1

Approximate Efficiencies of Fuels

fuel	efficiency (%)
natural gas	70–80
propane	70–90
no. 2 oil	65–85
anthracite coal	65–75
electricity	95–100

ENERGY CONVERSION

Whatever type of fuel is selected for heating and cooling, it must be converted into a useful form for distribution throughout a building. This usually requires additional energy, such as electricity, to operate fans, motors, and other components of the system. This fact applies to conventional fuels as well as to natural energy sources such as active solar energy systems.

Heat Generation Equipment

Two of the most common devices for converting fuel to heat are the furnace and the boiler. *Furnaces* burn either gas or oil to heat air, which is then distributed throughout the building. *Boilers* use fuel to heat water, and the steam or hot water is used to distribute heat.

A furnace burns fuel inside a combustion chamber around which air is circulated by a fan. As the cool air from return air ducts passes over the combustion chamber, it is heated for distribution to the building. The hot exhaust gases pass through a flue that is vented to the outside. Replaceable filters are used on the return air side of the furnace to trap dust and dirt in the system.

Forced air furnaces may be of the upflow, downflow, or horizontal type. In an *upflow furnace*, the return air is supplied at the bottom of the unit and the heated air is delivered to the bonnet above the furnace where it is distributed through ductwork. A *downflow furnace* operates in exactly the opposite way and is used in cases where ductwork is located in a basement or crawl space and the furnace is located on the first floor. A *horizontal furnace* is designed to be used in areas where headroom is limited, such as in crawl spaces.

Boilers use fuel to create hot water or steam. The fuel source can be gas, oil, electricity, or steam. In the typical boiler, tubes containing the water to be heated are situated within the combustion chamber where the heat exchange takes place. As with furnaces, the gases and other products of combustion are carried away through breeching into the flue or chimney. Of course, if the primary fuel source is electricity or steam, there is no need for an exhaust flue.

Principles of Refrigeration

There are two types of refrigeration processes that can produce chilled air or water: compressive refrigeration and absorption. A third type, evaporative cooling, can be used to produce cool air in some climates.

Compressive refrigeration is based on the transfer of heat during the liquefaction and evaporation of a refrigerant. As a refrigerant in a gaseous form is compressed, it liquefies and releases latent heat as it changes state. As the same liquid expands and vaporizes back to a gas, it absorbs latent heat from the surroundings into the gas. These principles are used in the basic refrigeration cycle shown in Fig. 28.1.

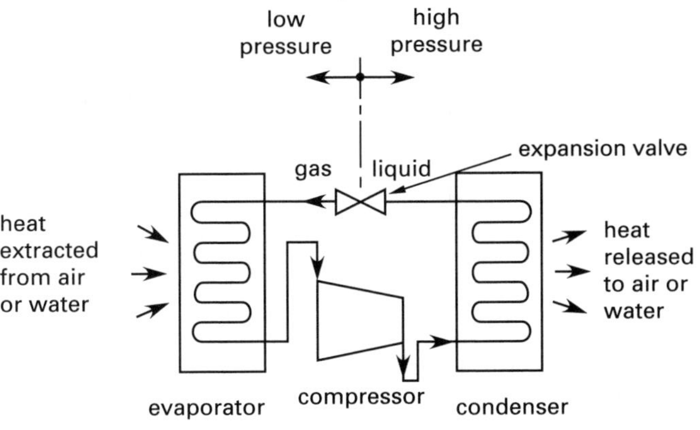

Figure 28.1 Compressive Refrigeration

In the past, refrigerants such as Freon were used in compressive refrigeration. However, these compounds contain chlorofluorocarbons (CFCs) that contribute to the depletion of the earth's ozone layer when leaked into the atmosphere. As a consequence, new refrigerants such as hydrofluorocarbons (HFCs) have replaced CFCs.

There are three basic components of a compressive refrigeration cycle: the compressor, the condenser, and the evaporator. The *compressor* takes the refrigerant in a gaseous form and compresses it to a liquid. The liquid refrigerant then passes through the *condenser* where the latent heat is released. This is usually on the outside of the building, and the heat is released to the outside air or to water. The refrigerant flows out of the condenser into the *evaporator* where it is allowed to expand. As it expands, it vaporizes back to a gas. In the process of vaporizing, it absorbs heat from the surroundings (either air or water) and then enters the compressor where it is cycled through the process again.

For many small cooling units, air is forced over the evaporator coils with a fan, and it is this cool air that is circulated through the space. However, water is a much more efficient medium to carry heat than is air. In larger units and in large buildings, water is pumped over the evaporator coils to produce chilled water, which is then pumped to remote cooling units where air is circulated over the chilled water pipes. On the condenser side, water is used to extract the heat from condenser pipes and carry it to remote cooling towers where the heat is released to the air.

Refrigeration by absorption produces chilled water and is accomplished by the loss of heat when water evaporates. This evaporation is produced in a closed system by a salt solution that draws water vapor from the evaporator. See Fig. 28.2.

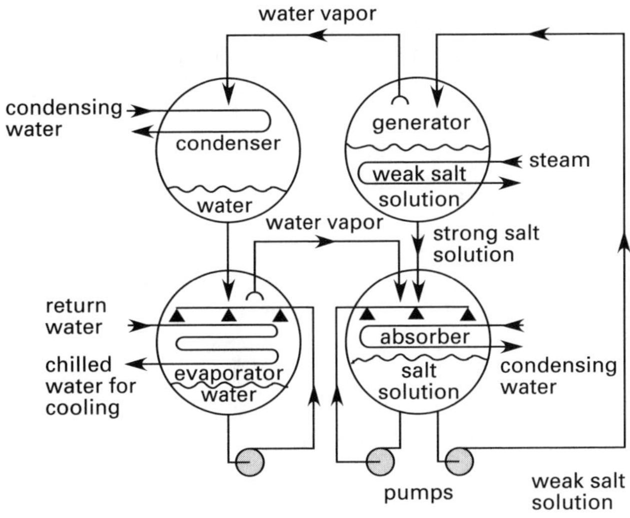

Figure 28.2 Absorption Cooling

As the salt solution absorbs water, it dilutes and must be regenerated by boiling off the water and returning the strong salt solution to the absorber. This is most often done with steam, but it can also be done with high-temperature water produced by solar collectors. The water boiled off in the generator is returned to a liquid state in the condenser and then returned to the evaporator. Both the condenser and absorber require condensing water, which removes the waste heat and carries it to cooling towers. Absorption systems are less efficient than compressive systems and are most often used when waste heat is available for energy input to the generator.

A third type of conditioning is *evaporative cooling*. Water is dropped over pads or fin tubes through which outdoor air or water is circulated. As the free water is evaporated to vapor, heat is drawn from the air or circulating water, which is then distributed to the indoor spaces. This type of cooling only works in hot-arid climates where the outdoor air has a low enough humidity level to allow the moistened air to evaporate. It is more economical than refrigeration cooling in some instances because it uses only one motor instead of three. An evaporative cooler is also simpler in construction and operation because it needs no refrigerant line and uses fewer parts.

A *ton of refrigeration* is a unit used to describe the capacity of a refrigeration system. It is the cooling effect obtained when 1 ton of 32°F ice melts to water at 32°F in 24 hours. This is equivalent to 12,000 Btu/hr (3516 W). In general, the required capacity of a refrigeration machine can be determined by dividing the total heat gain in Btu/hr by 12,000.

HVAC SYSTEMS

HVAC systems can be categorized by the medium used to heat or cool a building. The two primary methods of transporting heat are air and water. Electricity can also be used directly for heating. Some systems use a combination of media. This section outlines some of the more common systems with which an examinee should be familiar.

Direct Expansion

The simplest type of system is the *direct expansion*, or *DX, system* (DX), also known as an *incremental unit*. This is a self-contained unit that passes nonducted air, which is to be cooled, over the evaporator and back into the room. The condenser uses outdoor air directly, so DX systems are typically placed in an exterior wall.

Smaller units with 1/3 ton to 2 ton capacities are adequate for individual rooms, whereas larger units with more than a 2 ton capacity can serve several rooms in a single zone. With the addition of a heating coil, a DX system can serve both heating and cooling functions. Ventilation comes directly from the outside. Direct expansion units can be through-wall types, roof mounted, or packaged.

All-Air Systems

All-air systems cool or heat spaces by conditioned air alone. Heat is transported to the space with supply and return air ducts. The most basic type of all-air system is the constant-volume *single-duct system*. This is typically used in residential and small commercial applications. Air is heated (and cooled, if required) in a central furnace (and air conditioner) and is distributed throughout the building in ductwork at a constant volume. One centrally located thermostat controls the operation of the furnace. Return air ducts collect cooler air and return it to the furnace for reheating.

This type of system is simple and easy to operate, but it cannot be zoned so that different rooms or areas of the building receive varying amounts of heat (or cooling). The only control possible is by adjusting dampers on each supply air register to adjust the amount of heated (or cooled) air coming into a room. The need for individual zone or room control is one reason many homes use hydronic, or all-water systems.

For larger buildings there are four basic types of all-air systems.

Variable air volume system. For large buildings and situations where temperature regulation is required, humidity control is needed, and energy conservation is a concern, a variable air volume (VAV) system is often used. See Fig. 28.3.

With this system, air is heated or cooled as required in a central plant and distributed to the building at a constant

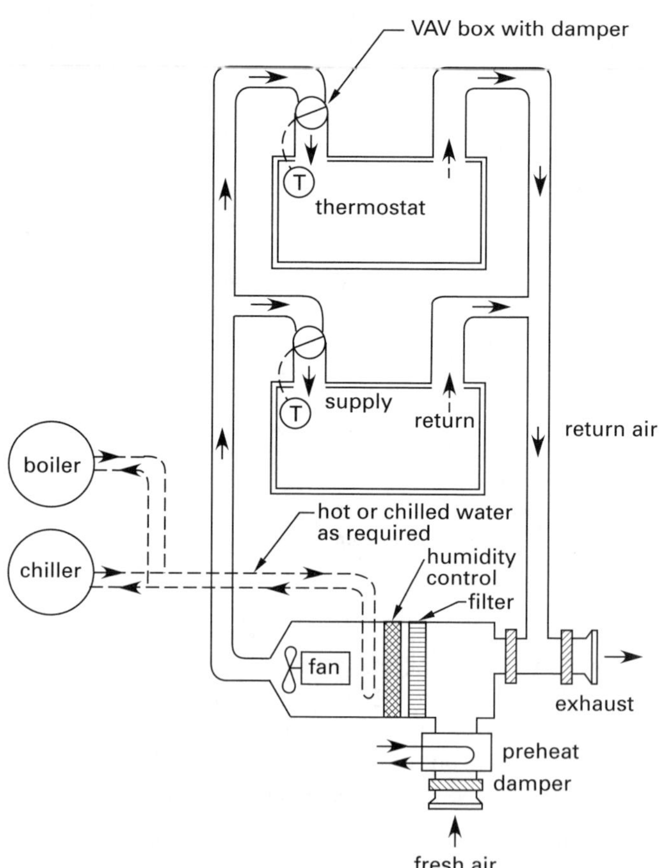

Figure 28.3 Variable Air Volume System

temperature through a single duct. At each zone, a thermostat controls a damper that varies the volume of conditioned air entering the space to respond to the user's needs. Dampers on the return air side of the system allow variable amounts of fresh air (up to 100%) to be introduced into the building for ventilation and for cooling when outdoor conditions make it unnecessary to mechanically condition the air. This system is somewhat limited in its ability to compensate for extremes in simultaneous heating and cooling demands in a building, but it offers a very efficient means of air conditioning large internal load dominated buildings.

Dual-duct (high-velocity) system. Where more flexibility is required, a high-velocity dual-duct system can be used. This system provides two parallel ducts, one with hot air and one with cool air. These two streams of air are joined in a mixing box in proportions to suit the temperature requirements of the conditioned space. A thermostat controls pneumatic valves in the mixing box to create the proper mixture. Figure 28.4 shows a simplified diagram of this type of system.

Because both hot and cool air is available anywhere in the building, a dual-duct system can respond to varying requirements. For example, during a cold day on the north side of a structure with a high percentage of glazing, heating may be required. On the south side of the same building the combination of solar heat gain, lighting, and occupancy may create a need for cooling. Because the air travels at a high velocity, about 3000 ft/min (15 m/s), the ducts can be smaller, which saves space in high-rise buildings.

In spite of these advantages, a high-velocity dual-duct system has some disadvantages. It is inherently inefficient because both hot and cool air have to be supplied winter or summer, and previously cooled air may need to be heated or previously heated air may need to be cooled. In addition, the high velocity requires larger, more powerful fans to move the air, which requires more energy. Finally, the high velocity can cause noise problems in the ductwork. Initial cost is high because of the quantity of ductwork.

Reheat (constant volume) system. A reheat system takes return air and fresh outdoor air and cools and dehumidifies the mixture, which is then distributed in a constant volume at low temperature throughout the building. At or near the spaces to be conditioned, the air is reheated as required by the cooling load of the space. See Fig. 28.5.

Reheating of the air is accomplished most often with heated water, but it can also be done with electricity. If the reheating equipment is located near the conditioned space, the unit is called a *terminal reheat system*. If the reheating coils are located in ductwork to serve an entire zone, the unit is

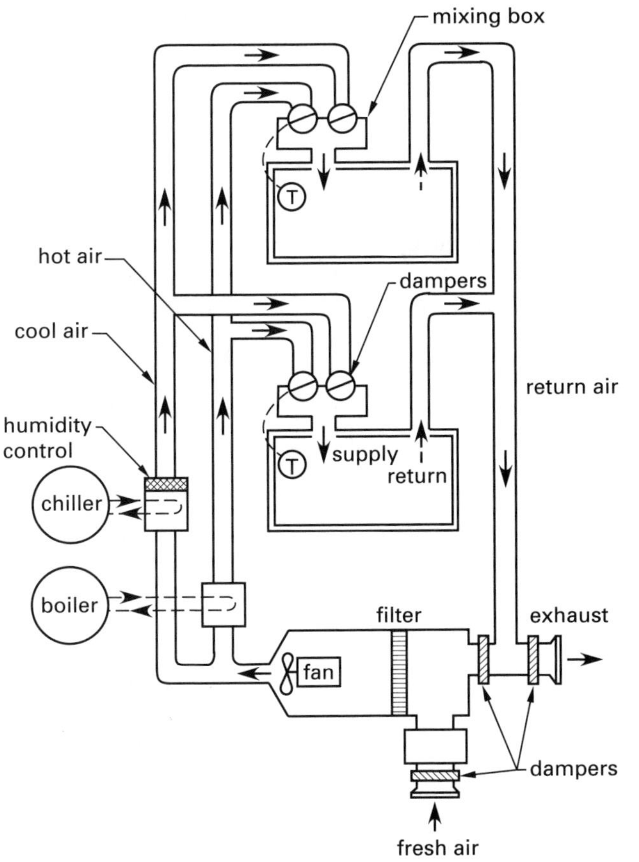

Figure 28.4 High-Velocity Dual-Duct System

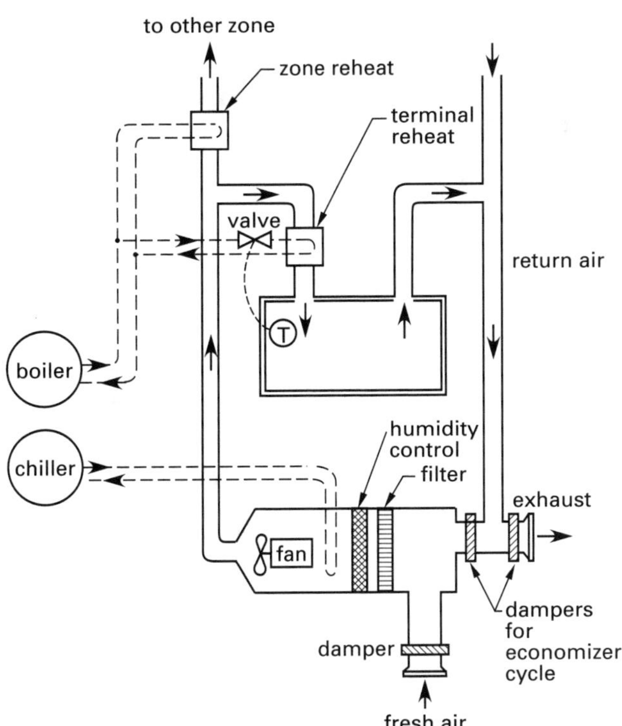

Figure 28.5 Constant Volume with Reheat

called a *zone reheat system*. Thermostats control valves in the water supply line to regulate the temperature.

In many cases, an *economizer cycle* is used. This allows outdoor air to be used for cooling when temperatures are low enough. The economizer works by adjusting dampers on the return air ducts and fresh air intakes.

The advantages of the reheat system are that humidity and temperature can be carefully controlled, and that the low supply temperature equates to smaller duct sizes and lower fan horsepower. However, a reheat system does use more energy than some systems because the primary air volume must be cooled most of the time, then reheated.

Multizone system. A multizone system (Fig. 28.6) supplies air to a central mixing unit where separate heating and cooling coils produce hot and cold air streams. These are mixed with dampers controlled by zone thermostats, and the resulting tempered air is delivered to the zones.

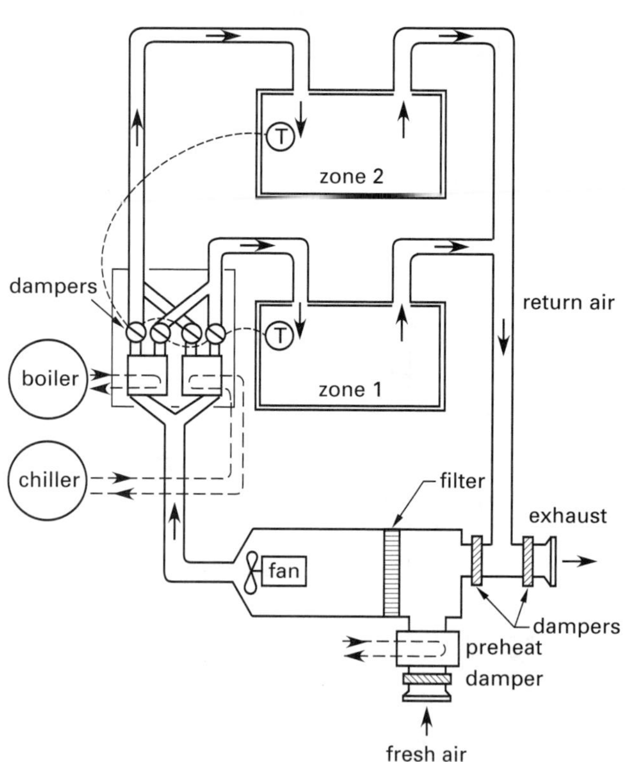

Figure 28.6 Multizone System

Multizone units offer the same advantage as dual-duct systems in that simultaneous cooling and heating of different zones can be accommodated. The main disadvantage is that the amount of duct space increases rapidly as more zones are added. This system is usually only used for medium-sized buildings or where a central mixing unit is located on each floor.

All-Water Systems

An *all-water system* uses a fan coil unit in each conditioned space. The fan coils are connected to one or two water circuits. Ventilation is provided with openings through the wall where the fan coil unit is located, from interior zone air heating, or by simple infiltration. In a two-pipe system, either hot or chilled water is pumped through one pipe and returned in another. In a four-pipe system, as shown in Fig. 28.7, one circuit is provided for chilled water and one for hot water. There are two supply pipes and two return pipes. A three-pipe system uses a single return pipe for both hot and cold water.

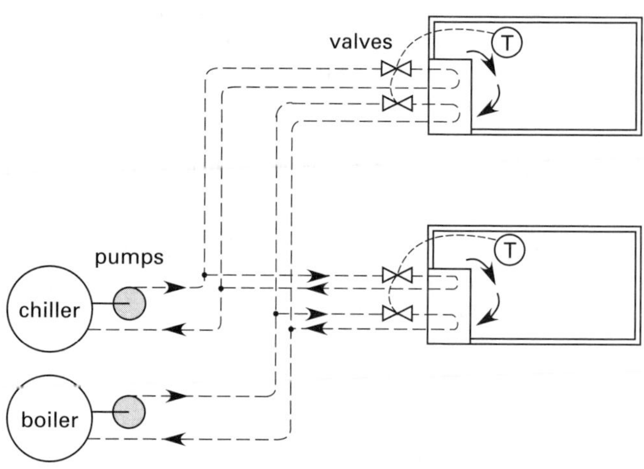

Figure 28.7 Four-Pipe All-Water System

All-water systems are an efficient way to transfer heat and are easily controlled, with a thermostat in each room regulating the amount of water flowing through the coils. However, humidity control is not possible at the central unit.

Air-Water Systems

Air-water systems rely on a central air system to provide humidity control and ventilation air to conditioned spaces. However, the majority of the heating and cooling is provided by fan coil units in each space. Air-water systems are often used where return air cannot be recirculated, such as in hospitals and laboratories. In these cases, 100% outside air is supplied, and return air is completely exhausted to the exterior.

With an induction system, shown in Fig. 28.8, air is supplied throughout the building under high pressure and velocity to each induction unit, where the velocity and noise are attenuated before the air passes over the coils and is heated or cooled as required. The water supply system may be either a two- or four-pipe system. Thermostatic control is provided by regulating the amount of water flowing through the coils. Another type of air-water system uses a fan-coiled unit for primary heating and cooling but has a separate air supply to provide humidity control and ventilation. See Fig. 28.9.

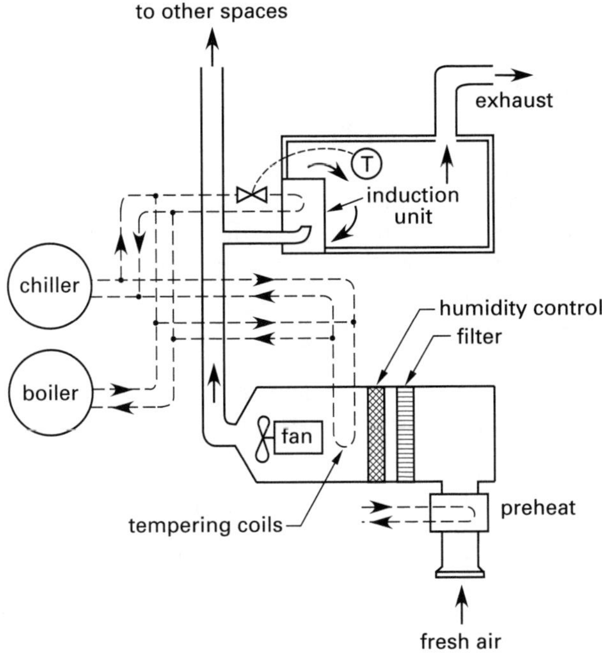

Figure 28.8 Air-Water Induction System

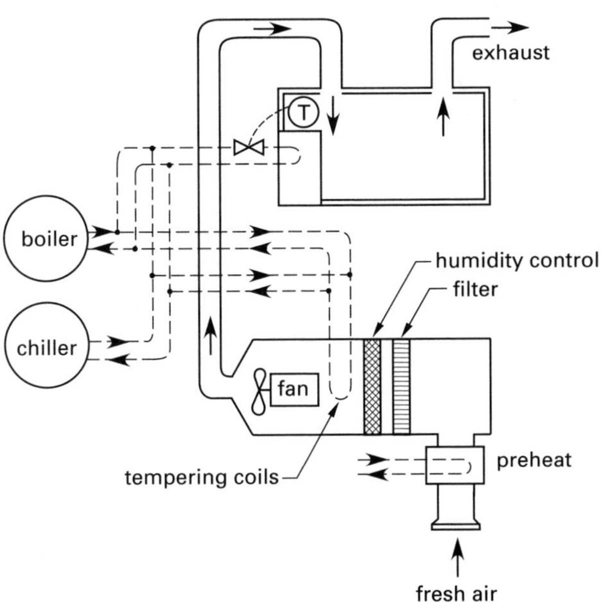

Figure 28.9 Fan Coil with Supplementary Air

Electric Systems

Electric heating is most often accomplished by laying a grid of wires in the ceiling of a room to provide radiant heating. Electric baseboard radiators are also available. This type of system provides a uniform, clean, inconspicuous form of heating that can easily be controlled with a separate thermostat in each room. No space is required for piping or ductwork. The big disadvantage is that electric heat is generally not economical except in areas where electricity is inexpensive. Most often, electric heat is used for supplemental heating in localized radiant panels or where water or air systems need a boost in temperature.

Selection of Systems

Selecting the most appropriate HVAC system for a building depends on several interrelated variables. These include the following.

- use profile of the building
- building scale
- control requirements
- fuels available
- climatic zone
- integration with building structure and systems
- flexibility required
- economics

The first consideration in selecting an HVAC system is the anticipated use and occupancy of the building. Some occupancies, such as office buildings or retail stores, need a flexible system to account for changes during the life of the building and for different requirements of multiple tenants. Variable air volume or induction systems satisfy this requirement. Buildings with multiple uses or that are subject to simultaneous variations in heating or cooling loads may require a dual-duct system or multizone system. Occupancies such as hospitals and laboratories will require systems like induction or fan coils with supplementary air so that all air supply is 100% fresh with complete exhaust to the outside.

The size of the building helps determine whether to use a central system or individual units. If the air conditioning load is under about 25 tons, direct expansion units or heat pumps can usually be used, either rooftop mounted or the through-wall variety. For larger cooling needs, a central station is more economical and provides the required flexibility.

The third consideration is the kind of control that is required. Hotels, motels, apartments, and some office buildings need the ability for individual room or area thermostatic control, whereas other buildings such as theaters need less individual control.

Although chillers, boilers, and furnaces that operate with a variety of fuels are available, the designer will likely select an HVAC system according to which system is most readily and economically available. If steam is adjacent to the building site, for example, absorption-type chillers may be more appropriate than refrigeration equipment.

The climatic zone will also affect the system selection. If the proposed building is in a hot-arid climate, the requirement for dehumidification will not be as great, so an all-water system may be appropriate. Locations that experience a wide swing in temperatures during the day may need a dual-duct system or four-pipe system to provide flexibility and quick response as outdoor conditions change.

The consideration of integrating the mechanical system with other building systems is one with which the architect is most closely involved. The system must work with the building's structure; the location of the mechanical equipment room; provisions for piping and duct runs; the location and appearance of terminal units, such as fan coils or induction boxes; the choice of return air methods, either ducted or above a suspended ceiling; the means of air supply and location of supply air diffusers; and the locations and appearances of air intakes or exhaust grills on the exterior of the building.

In addition, the mechanical system may have to be integrated with the method of fire protection and smoke control required for the structure. For example, smoke control in a high-rise building can be accomplished by providing a separate fan room on each floor. In the event of fire, the air supply on the fire floor can be switched off and all return air can be exhausted to the outside. At the same time, the dampers on the floors above and below the fire floor can be switched to provide full pressurization, keeping the occupants safe and preventing the spread of smoke.

Flexibility is another important selection consideration for buildings that must change internally or that will be added onto in the future. All-water systems or air-water systems can be sized to accommodate the ultimate capacity of the building. Expansion is then a simple matter of extending the piping runs from the central heating and cooling plant.

Economic decisions involve initial costs of an HVAC system, its long-term maintenance, and the cost of operating the system. Speculative developers may want a low initial-cost system, whereas people owning and occupying a structure will be more concerned with the long-term energy efficiency of the system, including the cost of fuel. Usually, a life-cycle cost analysis of several alternatives is required in order to make an informed decision.

Summary of System Selection

Buildings have different HVAC needs because of differences in size, zoning, economics, need for individual control, need for humidity control, and so on. An apartment building, for example, needs a system that allows each tenant to adjust heating and cooling levels individually. Some common types of HVAC systems and the kinds of buildings they are often used in are summarized in Table 28.2.

Exhaust

In addition to the ventilation requirements discussed in Ch. 27 and the exhaust components of standard HVAC systems shown in Figs. 28.3 through 28.9, the IMC devotes a separate chapter to requirements for mechanical exhaust systems. This is distinct from the requirements for ventilation discussed in Ch. 27. Exhaust systems include systems handling hazardous and nonhazardous exhaust, as well as those systems necessary for specific equipment operations, and those exhausting away from sources of contamination. This includes the following systems and equipment.

- equipment and processes that produce or throw off dust or particles sufficiently light to float in the air
- equipment and processes that emit heat, odors, fumes, spray, gas, or smoke in such quantities so as to be irritating or injurious to health or safety
- hazardous production materials
- garages and motor vehicle repair facilities
- clothes dryers
- domestic kitchen exhaust
- commercial kitchen hoods and grease ducts
- laboratories
- dust, stock, and refuse conveying systems
- subslab soil exhaust systems
- smoke control systems (see Ch. 31)
- energy recovery ventilation systems (see Energy Conservation section later in this chapter)

Exhaust air must be discharged outdoors at a place where it will not cause a nuisance and from which it cannot be drawn in again by a ventilating system. A *nuisance* in this case is a legal term meaning that which is dangerous to human life or detrimental to health. The IMC does not specify exact distances from general HVAC exhaust outlets and air intakes, leaving that determination to the local code official. Exhaust air cannot be discharged into an attic or crawl space. The IMC also details the minimum distances from the termination points of exhaust air and other building elements. These are shown in Table 28.3.

Table 28.2

HVAC Systems for Building Types

	direct expansion	constant volume, single duct	variable air volume	dual duct, high velocity	constant volume, terminal reheat	constant volume, zone reheat	multizone	all-water system	air-water induction	closed loop heat pumps	fan coil	electric
apartments										•	•	
auditoriums/theaters		•	•				•					
churches		•	•				•					
commercial—small			•				•	•				•
hospitals		•		•	•	•	•		•		•	
hotels/motels		•								•	•	
laboratories		•	•	•	•	•						
libraries			•				•					
office buildings			•				•		•		•	
residential—single family	•	•						•				•
schools			•								•	
shopping centers		•	•									

Table 28.3

Location of Exhaust Outlets

	distance in ft (mm) from					
exhaust type	property lines	operable openings	exterior walls and roofs	combustible walls and operable openings in the direction of the exhaust discharge	above adjoining grade	mechanical air intakes
ducts conveying explosive or flammable vapors, fumes, or dusts	30 (9144)	10 (3048)	6 (1829)	30 (9144)	10 (3048)	
other product-conveying outlets	10 (9144)	10 (3048)	3 (1829)		10 (3048)	
environmental air exhaust (domestic kitchen, bath, and clothes dryers)	3 (9144)	1 (3048)				10 (3048)
clothes dryers, kitchen hoods, dust stock systems, subslab soil exhaust systems, smoke control, refrigerant discharge, machinery room discharge	requirements specified in individual sections of the IMC					

SYSTEM SIZING

Calculating the size of an HVAC system involves determining the required capacity of the heating and cooling equipment, determining the size of the mechanical spaces to house the equipment, and figuring the space needs and layout of the distribution system of pipes and ducts.

System Capacity

The primary determinants in sizing equipment are the total heat gains and losses the building will experience in the most extreme conditions. These are calculated according to the procedures discussed in Ch. 27, and then equipment is selected to offset these gains or losses. In some cases, cooling equipment is undersized slightly to lower initial costs, with the knowledge that some occasional minor extremes in indoor design temperature will be tolerated.

Mechanical Room Space Requirements

For preliminary sizing of mechanical rooms for medium- to large-sized buildings using all-air or air-water systems, allow from 3% to 9% of the gross building area. This includes space for boilers, chillers, fans, and related pumps and piping. All-water systems will require about 1% to 3% of the total gross area.

Boilers and chillers require rooms long enough to allow for the removal of the tubes, so the room has to be slightly longer than twice the length of the equipment. Equipment rooms need to be from 12 ft to 18 ft (4 m to 6 m) high.

Ductwork Distribution and Sizing

Supply ductwork for all-air and air-water systems must run from the central air handling unit to each terminal unit or supply air diffuser. Because ductwork can occupy a significant amount of space, a logical, simple, and direct route must be planned and coordinated with the other building systems. Either round or rectangular ducts are used. Round ducts are the most efficient and produce the least amount of pressure loss for air delivered, but rectangular ducts make better use of available space above ceilings and in vertical duct chases.

In most cases, main trunk ducts can follow the path of circulation systems because these must serve every space just as hallways do. The ductwork can be located above the ceiling in the corridors or between structural beams. Some structural systems, such as open-web steel joists, allow ductwork to run both parallel and perpendicular to the direction of the structure.

In air ducts, there is a loss of pressure due to the friction of the air moving through the ducts, fittings, registers, and other components. The pressure required to overcome this friction loss is called the *static head* and is measured in inches (millimeters) of water. As this pressure increases, larger ducts and fans are required to overcome it, resulting in higher initial costs as well as higher operating costs.

For preliminary sizing of low-pressure duct space, allow about 3 ft^2 to 6 ft^2 for every 1000 ft^2 (0.3 m^2 to 0.6 m^2 for every 100 m^2) of floor space served for both vertical and horizontal duct runs. This figure includes supply and return ducts. Of course, high-pressure supply ducts will require less space.

ENERGY CONSERVATION

In many cases, it is possible to minimize reliance on HVAC systems by applying various mechanical techniques. These techniques can involve mechanical system components, heat transfer methods, building automation systems, or building commissioning.

Mechanical System Components

The amount of energy used by HVAC systems in buildings ranges from 40% to 60% of the overall energy consumption in the building, depending on the building type, climate, design, and other variables. Because some type of mechanical system is always required in large buildings and most small buildings, it is reasonable to include energy-efficient mechanical systems in an overall strategy for energy conservation and sustainability.

In order to make standard HVAC equipment described in previous sections more efficient, the National Appliance Energy Conservation Act of 1987 established minimum efficiency standards for both small and large heating and cooling equipment. The performance of this equipment is rated based on various standards including annual fuel utilization efficiency, the coefficient of performance, the energy efficiency ratio, the integrated part load value, and the seasonal energy efficiency ratio. These standards are defined in the Definitions section at the end of this chapter.

In addition to using more efficient equipment, reliance on standard HVAC systems can be minimized by the application of various mechanical techniques and devices to conserve energy. Following are some of the commonly used methods, many of which involve various methods of heat transfer.

Economizer Cycle

An *economizer cycle* uses outdoor air when it is cool enough to mix with recirculated indoor air. This reduces the energy required for refrigeration and is useful when the outdoor air temperature is about 60°F (16°C). An economizer cycle is basically a mechanical substitute for the open window, with the advantages of filtering the air and providing more even distribution. It has the added advantage of providing fresh air into the building to improve indoor air quality. As the temperature drops, less outdoor air is introduced because it would need to be heated. The control system balances the need for fresh air intake with the outdoor temperature and other variables of the heating system. For large, commercial buildings where internal loads and heat gain require cooling even in winter months, an economizer cycle can save significant amounts of energy.

Dual-Condenser Chillers

For refrigeration equipment, two condensers are used instead of one. When building heating is not needed, a heat rejection condenser sends heat to the cooling towers. When heat is needed, a separate heat recovery condenser sends excess heat to fan coil units or other devices. The building automation system controls how the system operates based on outdoor temperature and heating and cooling needs of the building. Another option is to use multiple chillers with units of varying sizes instead on one large chiller. This option allows the system to operate more efficiently by using the best sized chiller for the load.

Gas-Fired Absorption-Based Chillers

Conventional air-conditioning chillers of the centrifugal or reciprocating type are powered by electricity and use the compressive method (with HCFCs or other refrigerants) as described earlier in this chapter. Absorption-type chillers do not rely on ozone-depleting refrigerants. They are commonly powered by natural gas, which is generally a lower-cost fuel than electricity. Where potential power sources such as steam or high-temperature water from an industrial process are available, these may be used instead of natural gas. Although absorption chillers are not as efficient as electrically driven chillers, have a higher initial cost, and reject more heat to cooling towers, they may be more efficient for large buildings, especially in areas where electricity costs are high and where low-cost heat sources from steam or industrial processes are available. As an added benefit, equipment can be selected to provide hot water for heating.

Solar-Powered Absorption Cooling

Absorption chillers can be even more efficient (and sustainable) if they are powered by hot water from solar collectors. Standard flat-plate solar collectors can supply water from 175°F to 195°F (79°C to 91°C), which may prove less costly than running compressive-type chillers with electricity, even though the efficiency is low. Efficiency can be increased by using parabolic concentrating solar collectors to provide higher-temperature water.

Solar-Powered Desiccant Cooling

Another type of solar-powered cooling system uses desiccants to dehumidify and cool air by means of evaporative cooling. A *desiccant* is a material, either liquid or solid, that absorbs water. Designs vary, but a typical system passes incoming air over a desiccant, which is usually mounted on a wheel rotating in the airstream. As the air passes over the desiccant, it is cooled and dehumidified. Thermal energy from solar collectors is used to dry out the desiccant so it can be used again in the cycle. Desiccants used in these systems include silica gel, zeolite, lithium bromide, and monoethylene glycol.

Direct-Contact Water Heaters

A *direct-contact water heater* heats water by passing hot gases directly through the water. Natural gas is burned to provide the flue gases that transfer sensible and latent heat to the water. As a further efficiency, a heat exchanger on the combustion chamber reclaims any heat lost from the chamber. Although the gases are in direct contact with the water, the water is considered safe for human consumption. These types of heaters can be up to 99% efficient when the inlet water temperature is below 59°F (15°C). They have the added advantage of producing low emissions of carbon monoxide and nitrous oxides. Because direct-contact water heaters are a high-cost alternative, they are best used where there is a continuous demand for hot water, such as for food processing, laundries, and industrial purposes.

Recuperative Gas Boilers/ Boiler Fuel Economizers

A *recuperative gas boiler* recovers the sensible and latent heat from the high heat of exhaust flue gases that would normally be discharged to the atmosphere. Recuperative gas boilers are designed to cool flue gas temperatures enough to achieve condensation. The reclaimed heat is used to preheat the cold water entering the boiler or to preheat combustion air. Efficiencies can be increased from a high of only 83%, with standard gas boilers, up to 95%. Some systems also have reduced emissions of carbon monoxide and nitrous oxides. Installation is also easier than with standard flues because, since the final emitted flue gases are cool, plastic vent pipe can be used.

Displacement Ventilation

Displacement ventilation is an air distribution system in which supply air originates at floor level and rises to return air grilles in the ceiling as shown in Fig. 28.10. Because the supply air is delivered close to users, it does not have to be cooled as much, resulting in energy savings. Displacement ventilation is a good system for removing heat generated by ceiling-level lights and for improving indoor air quality, because these systems typically use a high percentage of outdoor air. This system can also be used in conjunction with personal temperature control and flexible underfloor wiring.

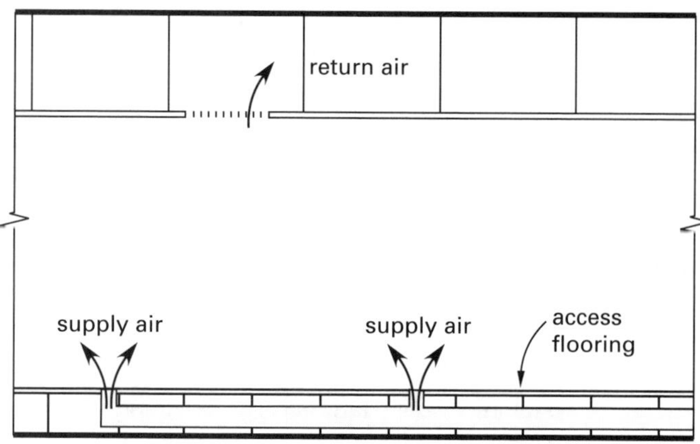

Figure 28.10 Displacement Ventilation

Most displacement ventilation systems use an access flooring system to provide space for underfloor ducting and to allow rearrangement of supply air outlets as the space layout changes. However, this makes displacement ventilation appropriate only for new construction, where the additional floor-to-floor height can be set to accommodate the 12 in (300) or more required for ductwork and where the elevations of stairway landings and elevator stops can match the elevation of the access floor.

A variation of this system uses supply air outlets located low on exterior walls, but this system only works for spaces next to the exterior wall to a depth of about 16 ft (5 m).

Water-Loop Heat Pumps

Water-loop heat pumps compose a heating and cooling system that uses a series of heat pumps (described earlier in this chapter) for different zones of a building, which are all connected to the same piping system of circulating water. See Fig. 28.11. The water loop is maintained at a temperature between 60°F and 90°F (between 15°C and 32°C). When some zones are cooling and dumping heat into the loop and other zones are heating and extracting heat from the loop, no additional energy has to be added or removed. Only when most of the units are in the same mode does the water in the loop have to be cooled or heated with a cooling tower or boiler. Automatic valves at the cooling tower and boiler direct the water as required.

This system is very efficient where there is a simultaneous need for heating and cooling in different parts of the building. It also reduces piping costs over two or four pipe water heating systems. It is not appropriate for buildings where cooling loads are small.

Thermal Energy Storage

Thermal energy storage uses water, ice, or rock beds to store excess heat or coolness for use at a later time. Thermal storage makes it possible to manage a building's energy needs over climatic temperature swings throughout the day or week, and it allows the use of less expensive, off-peak energy costs to cool. For example, in the summer, chillers can cool water at night when utility rates are typically lower and the cooling needs of the building are not as great as they are during the day. During the next day, the stored coolness can be used to minimize the energy required for cooling. Heat and coolness can be stored in water, rocks, or other appropriate thermal masses. Coolness can also be stored in ice. Ice has the advantage of being able to store sensible heat as well as the latent heat of fusion of ice. So, for a given amount of heat capacity (coolness), ice will occupy about one-eighth as much space as water.

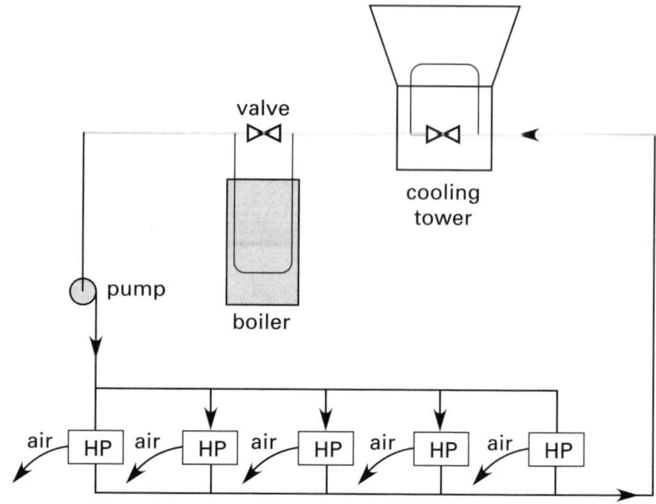

Figure 28.11 Water-Loop Heat Pump System

Heat Transfer

The desire for energy conservation is not always compatible with the need for indoor air quality (IAQ). Historically, initial efforts at increasing energy conservation resulted in tightly sealed buildings with reduced infiltration of fresh air and reuse of conditioned air. This led to problems with human comfort, sick building syndrome, and other building-related illnesses. One of the ways to alleviate some indoor air quality problems is to introduce more outdoor air through the ventilation system while exhausting used, conditioned air. However, heating or cooling incoming air requires energy. The solutions to these incompatible requirements for energy conservation and IAQ involve various methods of heat transfer. The following are all based on the concept of heat exchange from a source where heat (or coolness) is not wanted to a place where it is desirable.

Energy Recovery Ventilators

Energy recovery ventilators, also called *air-to-air heat exchangers*, reclaim waste energy from the exhaust air stream and use it to condition the incoming fresh air. The energy required to condition the incoming air can be reduced from 60% to 70%. Energy recovery ventilators are especially efficient in very cold, hot, or humid climates, where the temperature differential between indoor and outdoor air is high. They are generally not justified in temperate climates. They are also most efficient in buildings with continuous occupancy, such as hotels, hospitals, and others that operate more than eight hours a day.

Although the IMC generally prohibits recirculation of outdoor air introduced into a mechanical system, it does allow up to 10% of recirculated air to be used. This is to allow the use of energy recovery ventilator technology, which does not completely eliminate leakage between the exhaust and supply airstreams. However, energy recovery ventilators cannot be used in hazardous exhaust systems, in dust, stock, and refuse systems that convey explosive or flammable vapors, in smoke control systems, in commercial kitchen exhaust systems, or in clothes dryer exhaust systems.

Three common devices are used to make air-to-air heat exchange: flat-plate heat recovery units, energy transfer wheels, and heat pipes. Energy transfer wheels and heat pipes are described in the following separate sections. *Flat-plate heat recovery units* have two separate ducts of various designs—one for incoming air and one for exhaust air of various designs—separated by a thin wall that facilitates the heat transfer. These types of recovery ventilators can only exchange sensible heat and offer no humidity control themselves.

Three conditions should be met when using energy recovery ventilators. First, the fresh air intake must be kept as far away from the exhaust outlet as possible, to avoid sucking contaminated indoor air back into the building. Second, exhaust air that contains excessive moisture, grease, or other contaminants should be separated from the heat-exchanger air. Third, in cold winter conditions, a defroster in the device may be needed to prevent the condensate in the exhaust air from freezing.

Energy Transfer Wheels

Energy transfer wheels, also called *enthalpy heat exchangers*, transfer heat between two air streams through the use of a heat exchanger wheel consisting of small openings through which the air passes. The wheels are impregnated with lithium chloride or other proprietary substances. They are typically used in commercial buildings. The advantage of energy transfer wheels over other types of heat exchangers is that they can transfer latent heat (humidity) as well as sensible heat. In winter operation, warm, humidified exhaust air is transferred to the cool, dry incoming air. In summer operation, the cool exhaust air removes some of the heat from the hot incoming air. In addition, the humidity in the hot incoming air is transferred to the exhaust stream before the incoming air enters the building. See Fig. 28.12.

Energy transfer wheels conserve energy, reduce the cooling load, and minimize the need to humidify indoor air during the winter. Some units have a transfer efficiency up to 80%.

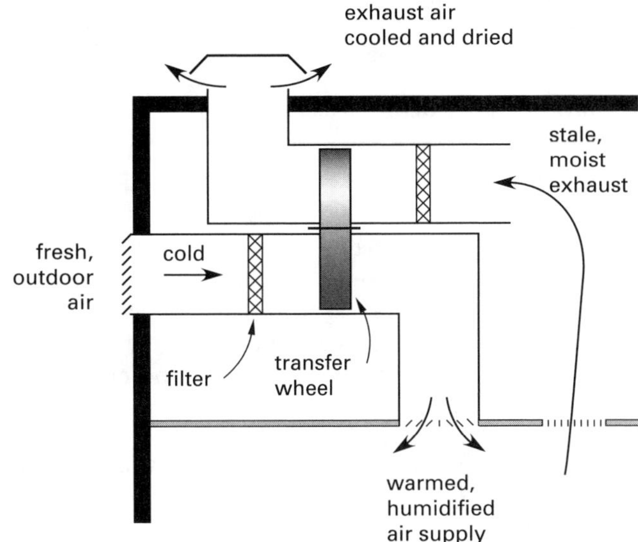

Figure 28.12 Energy Transfer Wheel

Heat Pipes

A *heat pipe* is a self-contained device that transfers sensible heat energy from hot exhaust air to cool outdoor air. As the hot exhaust air passes over the heat pipe, it vaporizes a refrigerant inside the pipe, which passes to the area of cool incoming air. As the refrigerant condenses, it gives off heat to the incoming air, warming it. The refrigerant then passes back to the hot side by capillary action through a wick material in the heat pipe. For heat pipes to work, the incoming and outgoing air streams must be adjacent.

Water-to-Water Heat Exchangers

Water-to-water heat exchangers, sometimes called *runaround coils*, use water or some other liquid transfer medium to exchange heat. The main advantage of this type of system is that the incoming and exhaust air streams do not have to be adjacent. In winter operations, this type of system simply pumps a heat transfer fluid from coils over which the hot exhaust air passes to coils over which the cool incoming air passes. In summer, the flow uses the cooled indoor air to reduce the temperature of the hot incoming air. These types of systems are commonly used in large buildings and eliminate the possibility that incoming air could be contaminated with exhaust air. The efficiency of water-to-water heat exchangers ranges from 50% to 70%.

Extract-Air Windows

An *extract-air window* uses a double-paned insulated glass unit over which another pane of glass is placed on the inside of the building. Air is drawn up between the inside pane and the main window unit and is extracted into the return air system. This has the effect of warming the glass in winter and cooling it in summer to maintain a comfortable radiant temperature and eliminate the need for a separate perimeter heating system.

Ground-Coupled Heat Exchangers

Ground-coupled heat exchangers heat or cool outside air by circulating it through pipes buried in the ground. In the summer the air can be used directly if the outdoor air is higher than the ground temperature. In the winter the system can preheat air for an energy recovery ventilator (to prevent frosting) or for a standard fan-coil heating unit. Ground-coupled heat exchangers are typically only suitable for low-rise buildings. Their disadvantage is the long runs of pipes they require for efficient operation. Because the air is forced through the pipes, the energy saved with the system must outweigh the energy required to run the fans. An alternative to this type of system that uses geothermal energy is the ground-source heat pump, described in Ch. 29.

Chilled Beams

A *chilled beam* is a ceiling-mounted unit that uses water to provide cooling and heating. There are two types of chilled beams, passive and active.

A passive chilled beam system relies on natural convection and can provide only cooling. The unit is usually installed above a suspended ceiling. Cool water is circulated through piping attached to aluminum fins, much as fin tube radiators operate in domestic heating. Warm room air, rising by natural convection, enters the unit and comes into contact with the fin tubes. The air is cooled by this contact, and the cool air sinks naturally back into the room. Because no ventilation air is used, separate ventilation ducts are required. However, because heating and cooling are not involved with the ventilation, air ducts and fans can be smaller, reducing energy consumption.

With passive chilled beams, the temperature of the water must be a little over the room's dew point to avoid condensation. Because this temperature range is higher than the standard chilled water supplied to HVAC units, the building's central chillers can be smaller than is usual, further saving energy. The humidity level of the ventilation air must also be controlled.

An active chilled beam system is integrated with a ventilation system, and can provide both heating and cooling. Fresh air is drawn into the unit, where it is either cooled or warmed by water, and is then forced out of the unit and into the room. In this way temperature control and ventilation are handled at the same time.

Multiservice beams combine an active chilled beam system with other building services such as lighting, sprinklers, data cabling, and building management system sensors.

Although chilled beams currently have a high initial cost, they offer significant energy savings over traditional all air and air/water HVAC systems. Because they have fewer parts, they also offer lower maintenance, more compact design, and quieter operation.

Building Automation Systems

A *building automation system* (BAS) is a computer-based integrated system used to monitor and control building systems. The systems included in a BAS will vary depending on the complexity of the building and the needs of the owner, but they typically include HVAC, energy management, lighting control, life safety, and security. Other systems that may be part of a BAS include vertical transportation, communications, material handling, and landscape irrigation. A BAS reduces energy costs through better systems management, allows for monitoring of large, complex buildings, reduces the number of personnel needed to supervise a large building, improves occupant comfort, and provides detailed documentation of all aspects of the building's subsystems. If problems arise, the BAS notifies the building systems manager and outside authorities, if necessary.

The energy conservation component of a BAS, the energy management system (EMS), detects environmental conditions both inside and outside the building, monitors the status of all equipment (including temperature, humidity, and flow rates), and optimizes the control of the equipment (including start and stop times and operational adjustments).

Building Commissioning

Building commissioning is the process of inspecting, testing, starting up, and adjusting building systems and then verifying and documenting that they are operating as intended and meet the design criteria of the contract documents. Commissioning is an expansion of the traditional testing, adjusting, and balancing (TAB) that is commonly performed on mechanical systems, but with a greatly broadened scope over a longer time period.

Building commissioning begins during the design phase with the determination of which systems will be commissioned and what the criteria will be for acceptance, and the preparation of specifications to precisely outline the requirements for subsequent phases. The most important part of commissioning occurs during the construction phase when the various building systems are started up and tested to see if they meet the design criteria. Incorrectly functioning equipment is adjusted, corrected, or repaired as required. The operation and maintenance of the controls and equipment are demonstrated, and training is conducted for the building operators (owner). During this phase a commissioning report is also prepared to summarize the results of the construction-phase commissioning and to provide detailed operation and maintenance manuals for each of the systems. Finally, commissioning should be carried through a post-occupancy phase. Ideally, this should occur one year after initial occupancy to again verify that the systems are operating as intended under normal occupancy and operating conditions. Adjustments and corrections should take place at this time if necessary.

The building systems that require commissioning depend on the complexity of the building and the needs of the owner. They may include some or all of the following.

- mechanical systems (including heating and cooling equipment, air handling equipment, distribution systems, pumps, sensors and controls, dampers, and cooling tower operation)
- electrical systems (including switchgear, controls, emergency generators, fire management systems, and safety systems)
- plumbing systems (including tanks, pumps, water heaters, compressors, and fixtures)
- sprinkler systems (including standpipes, alarms, hose cabinets, and controls)
- fire management and life safety systems (including alarms and detectors, air handling equipment, smoke dampers, and building communications)
- vertical transportation (including elevator controls and escalators)
- telecommunication and computer networks

Because commissioning a large building is a complex process, a knowledgeable person should be assigned responsibility for coordinating the efforts of everyone on the team. This may be the building contractor, the construction manager, or an independent commissioning agent. The people who should participate in building commissioning include

- the architect
- the mechanical, electrical, and plumbing engineers as well as other design consultants as appropriate
- the general contractor
- the various subcontractors for mechanical, electrical, fire protection, and so on
- the owner, owner's operation personnel, and owner's maintenance personnel
- others directly involved with the process, including the owner's agent, code officials, and construction manager

DEFINITIONS

Actuator: a device in a building control system that receives commands from a controller and activates a piece of equipment

Annual fuel utilization efficiency (AFUE): the ratio of annual fuel output energy to annual input energy. This includes nonseasonal pilot light input losses.

Coefficient of performance (COP): a unitless number that is a rating of the efficiency of heating or cooling equipment. It is derived by dividing the steady-state rate of energy output (or the rate of heat removal, in the case of cooling equipment) of the equipment by the steady-state rate of energy input to the equipment. The output and input values must be in equivalent units, such as watts out to watts in.

Controller: a device that measures, analyzes, and initiates actions in a building control system

Deadband: in a building control system, the range of temperature within which neither heating nor cooling is called for

Energy efficiency ratio (EER): the ratio of net cooling capacity in Btu/hr to the total rate of electrical input in watts under designated operating conditions

Energy management system (EMS): a computer-based system used to monitor and control facility energy use. An EMS is typically part of a building automation system.

Ground-coupled cooling: a method of cooling a building by direct contact with the earth or by circulating air through underground tunnels to cool it

Heating seasonal performance factor (HSPF): a measure of the performance of a heat pump operating in the heating cycle. See also *Seasonal energy efficiency ratio.*

Home energy rating system (HERS): a standardized system for rating the energy efficiency of residential buildings using the HERS Council Guidelines and the Mortgage Industry HERS Accreditation Procedures. A HERS score is a numeric value between 0 and 100 indicating the relative energy efficiency of a given home as compared with the HERS Energy-Efficient Reference Home.

Integrated part load value (IPLV): the single-number figure of merit based on part-load EER or COP expressing part-load efficiency for air conditioning and heat pump equipment on the basis of weighted operation at various load capacities for the equipment, as determined using the applicable test method in the Appliance Efficiency Regulations

Relative solar heat gain (RSHG): the ratio of solar heat gain through a window, corrected for external shading, to the incident solar radiation. This heat gain includes directly transmitted solar heat and absorbed solar radiation, which are conducted or convected into the space.

Seasonal energy efficiency ratio (SEER): the total cooling output of a central air conditioning system or heat pump in the cooling mode, measured in Btu/hr (W), during its normal usage period for cooling divided by the total electrical input in watt-hours, as determined by specific test procedures. The higher the SEER, the more efficient the equipment performance. The minimum SEER for residential air conditioning equipment in the United States is 13.

ENERGY EFFICIENCY AND ALTERNATIVE ENERGY SOURCES

29

This chapter covers passive design methods for energy efficiency and the use of alternative energy sources. The careful use of both these strategies can greatly reduce reliance on mechanical systems, reduce operating costs, improve human comfort, and reduce the use of fossil fuels.

Additional sustainable design issues and building techniques are discussed in Ch. 30. Sustainable design techniques that can be employed during the pre-design and site planning processes are discussed in Chs. 2 and 5. Energy conservation techniques that incorporate features into HVAC systems to make them more efficient are discussed in Ch. 28. Refer to Ch. 32 for information on energy efficiency in electrical systems.

PART 1: ENERGY EFFICIENCY

BUILDING ORIENTATION

By orienting a building correctly, an architect can maximize solar heat gain in the winter (if desired), reduce solar heat gain in the summer, encourage cooling with prevailing winds, minimize exposure to cold winter winds, and optimize daily use of the prevailing climate. Preliminary siting decisions based on climatic influences are discussed in Ch. 5.

Selecting the optimum building orientation for energy efficiency is often difficult because of the interrelated and sometimes conflicting requirements for factors such as heat gain, protection from overheating, daylighting, use of photovoltaic and solar heating panels, use of beneficial cooling breezes, protection from cold winds, and the practical aspects of site topography and the building program. However, all other constraints being equal, building orientation for energy conservation attempts to balance the overheated and underheated periods during the year while also considering daily temperature fluctuations.

Many studies have been done to determine optimum building orientation. While they differ in the exact angle, they all recommend that rectangular buildings be oriented with the long direction generally east-west to minimize the intense east and west solar radiation while taking advantage of the heating potential of south-facing surfaces in the winter. During the summer months the sun is higher in the sky and strikes south-facing walls higher, so there is less incident radiation, and what incident radiation there is can be shaded easily. Considering the slightly lower morning temperatures, a rectangular building is best oriented slightly east of south as shown in Fig. 29.1. The exact angle of the south face varies slightly depending on the climatic region

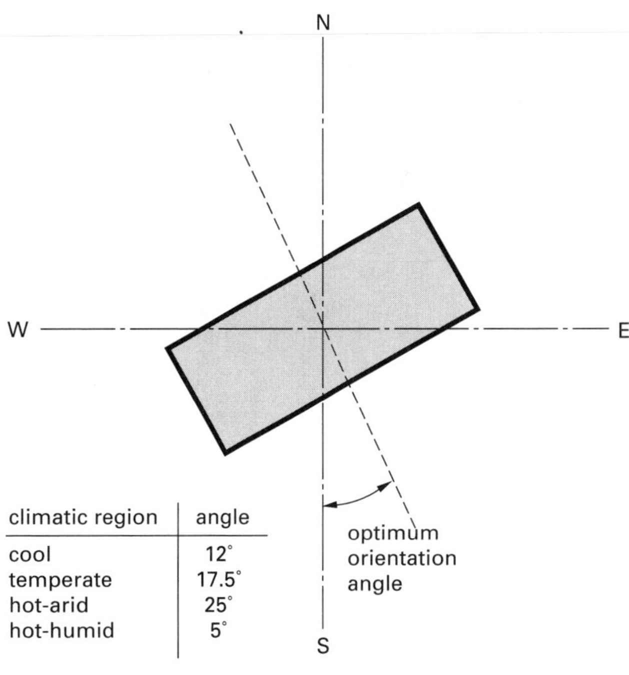

climatic region	angle
cool	12°
temperate	17.5°
hot-arid	25°
hot-humid	5°

Figure 29.1 Optimum Building Orientation

but is approximately 15° east of south. In hot-arid and hot-humid climates the building may have to be rotated slightly off this angle to pick up the cooling breezes of the local climate.

In cold climates, a building's entrance can be located on the leeward side to avoid winter winds. In temperate climates, entrances should be located on the south side to make them more inviting and capitalize on the natural snow-melting effects of the sun. In hot climates, the long side of a building can be oriented to catch cooling breezes.

BUILDING SHAPE

As with building orientation, building shape is the result of many interrelated and sometimes conflicting requirements and programmatic needs. However, considering just the aspect of energy conservation, some general guidelines for building shape can be established.

Building shape can affect energy use in a number of ways. Because both heating and cooling loads depend on the thermal conductance of the walls and roof and the areas of those surfaces, any building that minimizes the total area will generally use less energy. A cubic building has the least surface for the volume contained. See Fig. 29.2(a). (A sphere is the ideal shape because it encloses the most volume for the least surface area, but it is not practical for buildings.) A two-story building is better than a one-story building of the same floor area. However, the goal of minimal surface area must be balanced with the gains provided by other building shapes that utilize solar heating, natural ventilation, and similar techniques. Minimizing surface area generally works best in cold climates.

As described in the previous section, the advantage of a rectangular building is that its long face can be oriented toward the south, for solar heating and to minimize heat gain on the east and west. Long, thin buildings also make it easier to utilize daylighting and to capture prevailing winds for natural ventilation. Larger buildings may require courtyards and rambling shapes for daylighting and ventilation. See Fig. 29.2(b).

Looking at energy efficiency in greater detail, the ideal shape of a building will depend on its climatic region and whether it is an external load dominated building or an internal load dominated building.

External load dominated buildings (also known as *skin-load dominated buildings*) are those whose energy use is determined mainly by heat loss or gain through the exterior envelope (or skin). These types of buildings generally have few occupants per unit area and a small amount of heat gain from lighting, equipment, and people. Examples of these types of buildings include houses, apartments, condominiums, and warehouses.

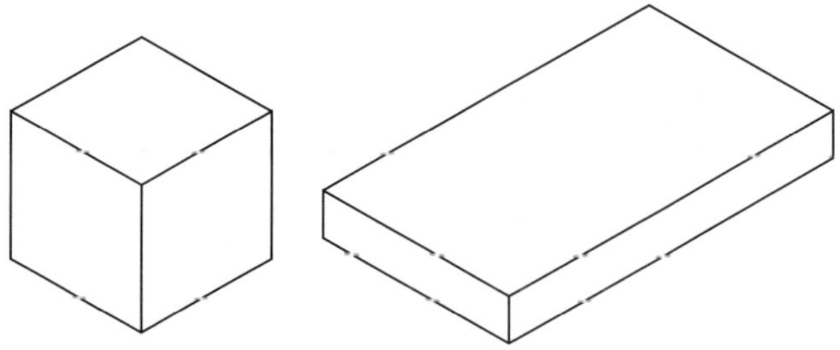

(a) For same floor area, cubic buildings have less surface area.

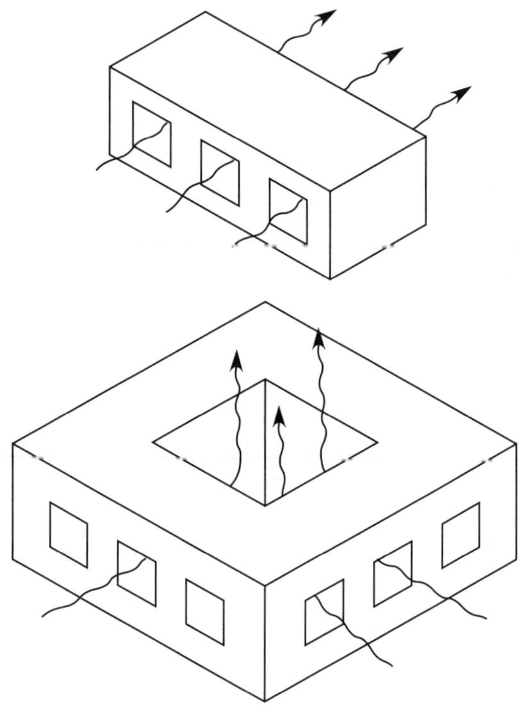

(b) Thin sections are best for natural ventilation and daylighting.

Figure 29.2 Building Shape Affects Energy Use

Internal load dominated buildings are those whose energy use is driven by high heat gain from occupants, lighting, and equipment. Examples of these types of buildings include office buildings, hospitals, retail stores, schools, and laboratories. In most cases, building shape for internal load dominated buildings influences the energy efficiency less than it would for external load dominated buildings. The exception would be if the building shape were being used for extensive daylighting or other passive or active energy conservation techniques.

Figure 29.3 illustrates a generalized summary of the optimum building shapes, based on type of load, for each of the four climatic regions of the United States. See Fig. 5.4 for a map of the climatic regions in the United States.

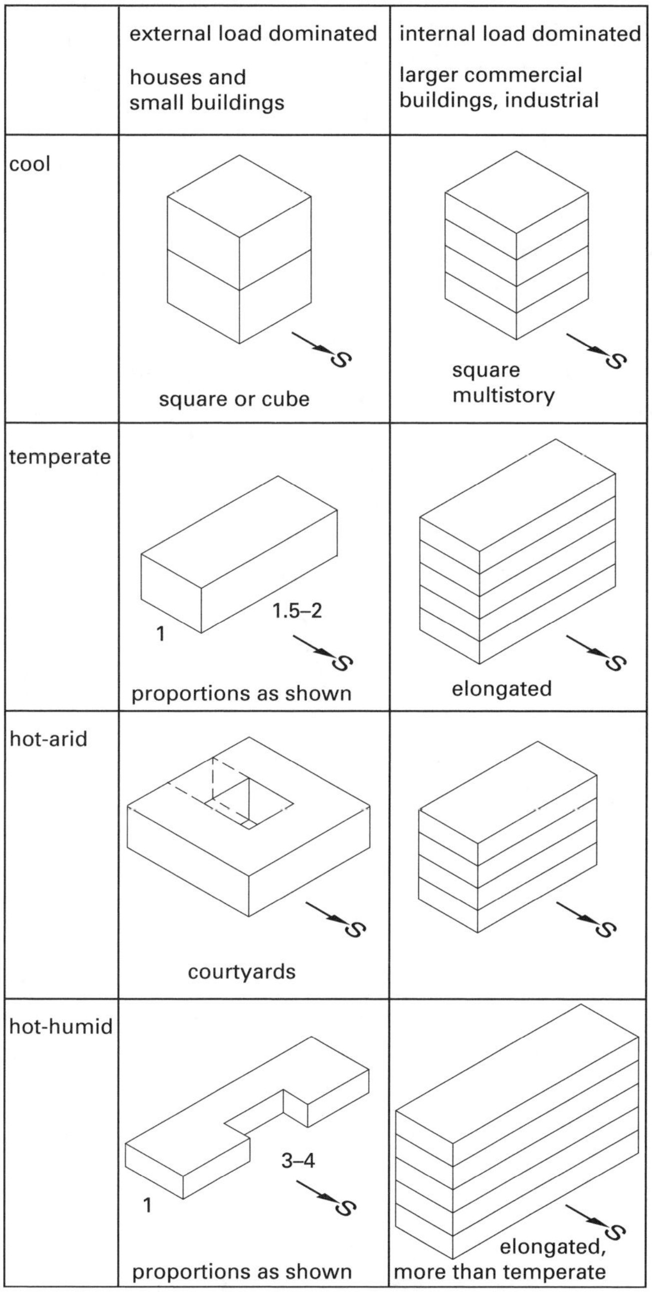

	external load dominated houses and small buildings	internal load dominated larger commercial buildings, industrial
cool	S square or cube	S square multistory
temperate	1.5–2 1 S proportions as shown	S elongated
hot-arid	S courtyards	S
hot-humid	3–4 1 S proportions as shown	S elongated, more than temperate

Figure 29.3 Building Shapes Based on Climate Type and Type of Load

For the cool and cold regions a square or cubic shape generally works best because the extremes of winter temperature suggest the skin area should be minimized in both types of load dominated buildings. For the same floor area, a two-story house is better than a one-story house.

For temperate climates shape has less of an effect, but a building elongated in the east-west direction has some advantages for winter solar heat gain, daylighting, and minimum heat gain in the summer.

For hot-arid regions a more square shape is best, but the plan should include open courtyards for external load dominated buildings or massive, multistory buildings for internal load dominated buildings.

For hot-humid regions shapes elongated in the east-west direction are preferable to allow breezes, provide natural cooling, and minimize severe heat gain from the east and west directions. Courtyards and broad overhangs are also useful.

LANDSCAPING

Trees and shrubs should be located such that they moderate the microclimate and maximize the energy efficiency of the building. For example, simply protecting a house or other external load dominated building from the effects of a cold wind can reduce the heating load substantially, sometimes up to one half.

Deciduous trees can be used on the south side of a building to provide the building with shade in the summer and allow solar heating in the winter. However, because even a deciduous tree will block some solar radiation in the winter, a building that depends on passive solar heating or solar panels may need to be exposed on the south side.

The effect of using trees to shield a building from undesirable winds is highly variable depending on the types of trees, the width of the row, how densely the trees are planted, and tree height. As mentioned in Ch. 2, a very deep row of trees can reduce wind velocities substantially. However, most site designs only have space for a single or double row of trees. In general, a row of trees of a certain height will decrease the velocity of the wind between 30% and 40% at a distance about five times the height of the trees. Trees planted next to a building may reduce wind velocity between 20% and 60%, depending on the density of the trees. The effect of trees on reducing wind velocity decreases greatly at about 10 times the tree height and is negligible beyond 20 times the tree height. In most cases evergreen trees are more effective at blocking wind than are deciduous trees. Evergreens should certainly be used for blocking winter winds.

Trees can also be used to direct desirable cooling breezes. Refer to Chs. 2 and 5 for more information on using landscaping to improve energy efficiency.

BUILDING SHADING

Building shading should be used selectively to minimize unwanted solar heat gain in the summer and maximize heat gains in the winter. This can be done naturally with deciduous trees or with horizontal or vertical shading devices. The shading devices can be either fixed or moveable. If daylighting is used, horizontal blinds can both shade glass and provide reflective surfaces to direct sunlight into a building.

The orientation of a building's facade determines the most effective type of shading device. South-facing facades require moderate overhangs or horizontal louvers, while east- and west-facing facades should be protected with vertical louvers. Southeast- and southwest-facing facades may require either a very wide overhang or vertical louvers, or both. Of course, fixed exterior shading devices will usually be supplemented with interior window coverings. See Fig. 29.4.

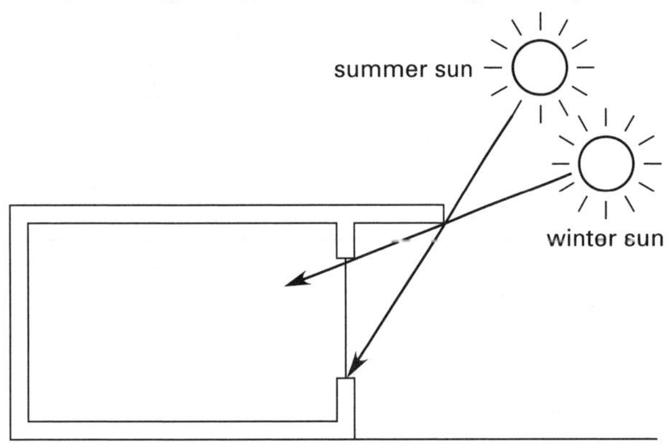

(a) horizontal shading on south

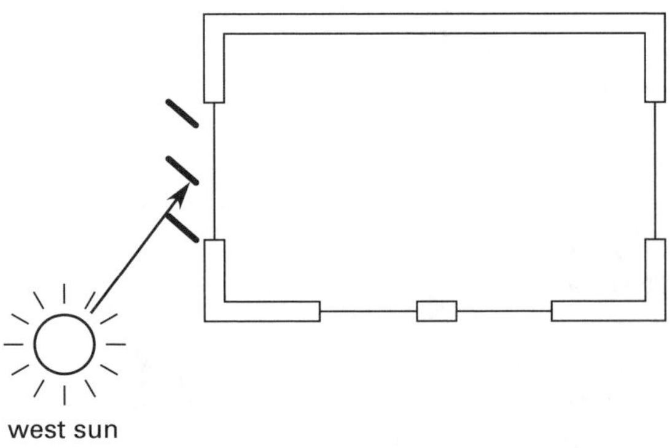

(b) vertical shading on west

Figure 29.4 Building Shading

EARTH SHELTERING

Burying a portion of a building underground has several advantages. Below a few feet the temperature of the earth is fairly stable. It is cooler in the summer and warmer in the winter than is the air aboveground. Therefore, heat gain and heat loss are minimized, and the impact of extreme outdoor air temperatures is lessened. Earth sheltering also protects a structure from cold winter winds. Additional advantages include natural soundproofing, less outside maintenance, and better protection from high winds, hail, and tornados.

There are three variations on the earth-sheltered design. The first design type is built aboveground and has earth bermed against the walls on one or more sides. The second design is similar to the first, but is built into the side of a hill, ideally with the north side built into the hill and the south side exposed for solar heating, views, and daylight. The east and west sides may be partially or completely buried. In either of these first two designs, the roof may also be covered with earth. The third type of earth-sheltered design is completely buried below grade with a courtyard in the middle to allow for access, daylight, an outdoor living area, and ventilation.

Usually, earth sheltering is only used on a portion of a building while the south side of the building is exposed. This approach combines the advantages of earth sheltering with the need to permit desirable heat gain and admit light.

Some of the practical considerations of earth-sheltered designs include the following.

- Ideally, there should be a natural slope to the land so earthmoving can be minimized.
- The soil should be granular. Gravel, sand, and sandy loam are all appropriate soils. Clay soils are not appropriate for earth-sheltered designs because they do not drain well and can expand with moisture. The site should be tested for radon concentrations.
- The groundwater level must be below the building, and positive drainage away from the building should be maintained.
- Extra care must be taken to waterproof the underground portions adequately.
- Even though earth-sheltered designs do not require much insulation, the insulation must be correctly designed to keep the indoor temperature comfortable and prevent condensation from forming on cool inside walls in a humid environment.
- With fewer windows on all sides, the building will need adequate ventilation to control humidity and maintain good air quality.

GREEN ROOFS

A *green roof*, also called a *vegetated roof cover*, *garden roof*, or *eco-roof*, is a thin layer of vegetation installed on the top of a roof. The advantages of a green roof can include the following.

- conserving energy by reducing cooling and heating loads
- reducing storm runoff
- absorbing carbon dioxide
- reducing ambient air temperatures
- filtering the air and binds dust particles
- reducing the heat island effect normally caused by roofing
- protecting the roofing from ultraviolet light degradation, temperature extremes, wind, and hail
- adding acoustical insulation
- adding aesthetic appeal to the roof

A variety of types of green roofs can be designed—from simple low-growing grasses and flowers in a thin layer of soil to complex groupings of grass, flowers, shrubs, and trees in a layer of growing media 12 in (300) or more deep. Green roofs are generally divided into two major types: extensive and intensive. *Extensive green roofs* use soil less than 6 in (150) deep supporting meadow grasses, sedums, herbs, and perennials. *Intensive green roofs* use thicker soil and support complex landscapes, including shrubs and small trees along with ponds and fountains. If required by the climate, a subsurface irrigation system is installed.

Most green roofs include a continuous layer of growth medium. Alternatively, the plants can be placed in modular plastic containers. In most cases the modular systems weigh less, are more flexible, and can be easily removed to replace plants or make roof repairs.

Although there are many variations in design and detailing, a typical intensive roof over a concrete deck is constructed as shown in Fig. 29.5. All green roofs must be constructed over a structural deck strong enough to hold the wet weight of the assembly. Depending on the type of system used, green roofs may weigh from 12 psf to 300 psf (60 kg/m^2 to 1470 kg/m^2). This means that green roofs should typically be used only in new buildings where the structure can be designed correctly from the beginning. However, it may be possible to place lighter green roof systems over existing structures without additional support.

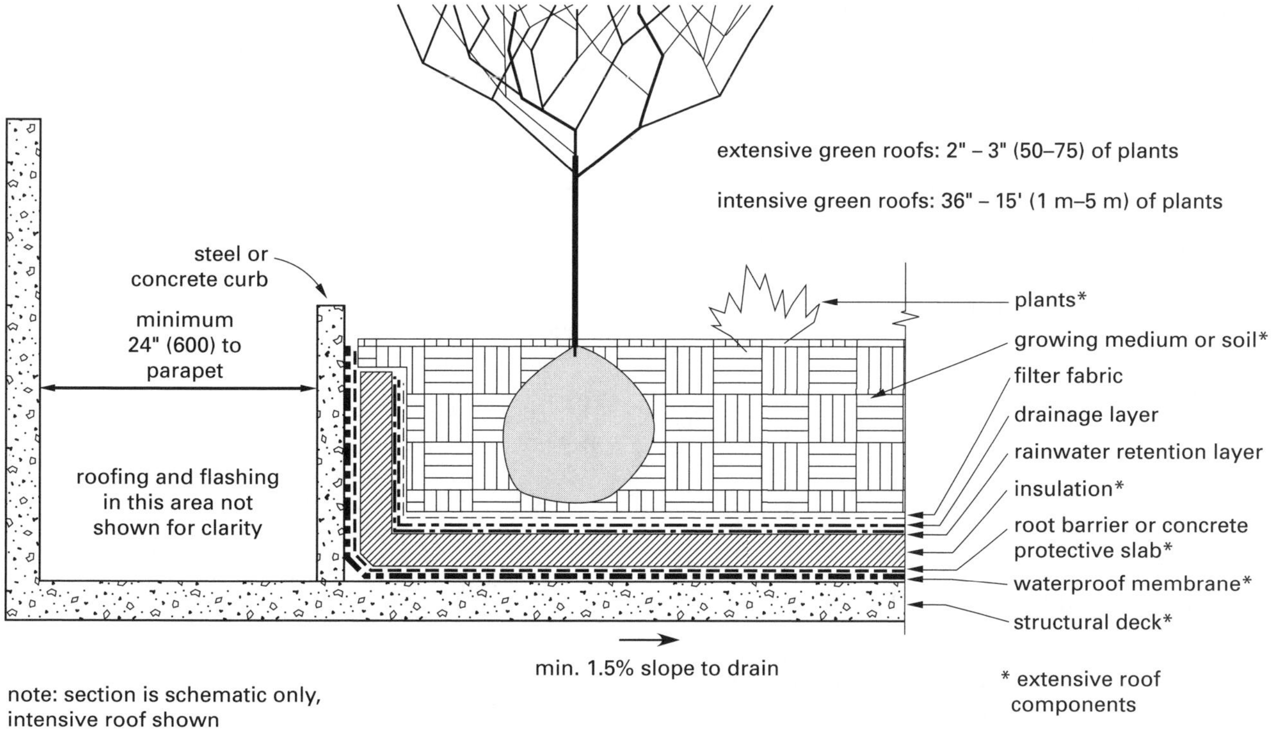

Figure 29.5 Green Roof Construction

The steps involved in constructing a green roof over a concrete deck are as follows.

1. A waterproof membrane is placed over the structural deck. This may be made of one of a variety of materials and may include polyvinyl chloride (PVC), ethylene propylene diene monomer (EPDM), thermoplastic polyolefin (TPO), or a polymer modified bituminous membrane.
2. If required, a root barrier is placed over the waterproofing. Some materials, such as PVC, EPDM, and TPO, are inherently root resistant.
3. Insulation is placed over the root barrier. Insulation helps prevent water stored in the growth media from extracting heat in the winter, and it adds thermal insulation. Some systems use a retention layer over the insulation to provide a long-term water supply.
4. A drainage layer is installed over the insulation to allow water that is not absorbed to flow to drains or scuppers. Green roofs should be constructed on decks with a minimum 1.5% slope. The maximum recommended slope is 30%, but on steep slopes stabilization panels, battens, and other devices must be used to prevent the growing medium from shifting.
5. A filter fabric above the drainage layer prevents the fine particles of the soil or growing medium from entering and clogging the drainage layer. Materials used for filter fabric include polypropylene or polyethylene mats or water-resistant polyester fiber mats.
6. Finally, the growth medium is placed in thicknesses from 2 in (50) to 12 in (300) or more. The growth medium is not just soil but an engineered mixture of soil plus organic and mineral additives, such as peat, sand, lava, expanded clay, and others. The growth medium is designed for the types of plants that will be used.

The construction of a green roof over a metal deck is a little different and is typically accomplished as follows.

1. A thermal barrier is placed over the metal deck to protect the insulation from heat transfer. This is required by the IBC and most local codes, and can consist of $^1/_2$ in (13) of gypsum sheathing or other approved material.
2. Rigid insulation is placed over the thermal barrier in a thickness appropriate for the climate and as required by the local code. Extruded polystyrene (XPS) is typically used because it is resistant to moisture and has a high compressive strength. Polyisocyanurate insulation can also be used and, if allowed by the local code, does not need a thermal barrier. However, it has a lower compressive strength than XPS and needs to be covered with a protection board to protect it from damage during subsequent construction operations.
3. The waterproofing membrane is placed over the insulation. If required by the manufacturer, a separation layer is placed between the waterproofing and the insulation. As with membranes over concrete decks, the membrane may be PVC, TPO, or EPDM.
4. If required by the membrane manufacturer, a root barrier is placed over the membrane.
5. A drainage layer is placed over the membrane (or root barrier). Types of drainage layers include those made from entangled filaments, thermoformed dimpled cups, and geonets.
6. Finally, the growth medium is placed on the drainage layer.

Because the waterproofing layer is such a critical part of any green roof system, quality control measures must be taken to ensure a watertight system. This can be done in several ways. A *flood test* is a common way to verify watertightness. The area is flooded with 2 in (51) of water for 48 hours and the interior of the building is inspected for leaks. An independent inspection company can also be hired to view the installation of the waterproofing membrane and other components. An alternate to the flood test is *electric field vector mapping* (EFVM). EFVM is a method of detecting the precise location of leaks in a waterproofing membrane by using the small electrical potential between the grounded roof deck and the growing medium. In this method, the growing medium is wetted to provide an electrically conductive layer, and the deck is grounded. A leak will cause electric flow from the growing medium to the deck below. Using probes connected to a potentiometer, a technician can walk the roof and detect the direction of any electric current.

The actual plant material varies widely depending on whether an extensive or intensive system is planned, the local climate, the maintenance that will be available, and the aesthetic needs of the project. A drip irrigation system is usually recommended instead of a spray system.

A project can receive LEED® credit for having a green roof if it covers at least 50% of the total roof area. LEED is an acronym for Leadership in Energy and Environmental Design, a program of the U.S. Green Building Council designed to encourage the implementation of sustainable building practices. Buildings receive credits for various sustainable design practices and are then awarded a LEED certificate if they accumulate enough points. Refer to the section on Building Rating Systems in Ch. 30 for more information on LEED.

AIR LOCKS

A vestibule entry system is desirable in cold and temperate climates and can be beneficial in hot climates where a building is mechanically cooled. In addition to preventing cold drafts from entering when an exterior door is opened, air locks minimize heat loss when people enter and leave a building. In lieu of a vestibule, revolving doors can be used.

INSULATION AND WEATHER SEALING

One of the most basic passive energy conservation techniques is to adequately insulate and seal a building against air infiltration. How much insulation to use, in terms of cost considerations, depends on the climate. But the money spent on insulation, weatherstripping, and caulking is generally recovered within a few years in the majority of buildings. In addition to reducing heat flow, adequate insulation also keeps wall and ceiling surfaces warmer, raises the mean radiant temperature so the comfort level is increased, and improves acoustic qualities.

Insulation

Insulation is made from a variety of materials and is available in several forms. Commonly used materials include fiberglass, mineral wool, polystyrene, polyisocyanurate, polyurethane, and cellulose. Other materials that have not been traditionally used include cementitious foam, autoclaved aerated concrete, straw panels, straw-bale construction, and plastic fiber. Insulation is available as loose fill, batts, rigid foam boards, spray-on foam, and as part of other construction assemblies, like structural insulated panels.

Prior to selecting the type and form of insulation, the required *R*-value must be determined. The local or state building codes will either prescribe *R*-values or reference their locations in a model energy code, such as the *International Energy Conservation Code*, or in ASHRAE Standard 90.1. For example, the *International Residential Code* provides a prescriptive table that gives building envelope thermal component criteria for ceilings, walls, floors, basement walls, perimeter slabs, and crawl space walls based on the climatic zone (shown in Fig. 5.4) and the number of heating degree days. Commercial buildings may be subject to energy budgets.

However, for increased energy savings, a life-cycle analysis can be made comparing the initial cost of installing more insulation of various types (and costs) with the long-term energy savings based on local fuel costs and other factors. Most insulation types also require a vapor barrier to be effective.

Insulation that requires chlorofluorocarbons (CFCs) or hydrochlorofluorocarbons (HCFCs) in its production should not be used, because CFCs are ozone-depleting compounds. However, today all closed-cell polyurethane foam insulation made is produced with a non-CFC gas as the blowing agent. When possible, use foamed-in-place insulations that use carbon dioxide (rather than pentane or hydrochlorofluorocarbons) in the manufacturing process.

Refer to Ch. 30 for more information on insulation and sustainability and Ch. 41 for more information on specific insulation types.

Superinsulation

Superinsulation is simply the technique of providing higher levels of insulation than normally used, tightly sealing all joints and cracks, and preventing any thermal bridges between the outside and inside, such as through studs. All portions of the building are carefully detailed so that every piece is insulated. Gaps, such as electrical outlets on exterior walls, are avoided or placed inside the insulation. In many cases, exterior walls have to be made thicker than required to accommodate the added insulation. For homes this means using 2 × 6 studs instead of 2 × 4 studs.

Transparent Insulation

Transparent insulation consists of a relatively thick layer of polycarbonate honeycomb material, acrylic foam, or fiberglass sandwiched between layers of glazing. It is used to admit light while providing a high degree of insulation. It can also be used over another thermal mass material to trap solar heat and then slow the loss of the stored heat back into the atmosphere. Although good for diffusing light, transparent insulation cannot be used where a view is desired.

Movable Insulation

Movable insulation is typically used on windows that provide passive solar heating. The insulation is removed during sunlight hours and replaced at night or during cloudy weather to prevent heat loss. This type of insulation can be manually operated, power operated, or set to work automatically. Common types of movable insulation include roll-down shutters, insulated shades, swinging panels of insulation, and expanded polystyrene beads blown between panes of glass.

Air Barriers

An *air barrier* is the part of a building envelope system that controls the movement of air into and out of a building (infiltration and exfiltration). An effective air barrier is important for three reasons. First, it conserves energy because unwanted infiltrating air has to be conditioned to meet indoor requirements and conditioned air is not lost to exfiltration. From 25% to 40% of the heating energy used by buildings is lost due to infiltration. Second, it blocks out infiltrating air, which may contain pollutants. Third, by controlling air movement an air barrier helps minimize the migration of moisture, which can condense and contribute to mold growth and degradation of building materials.

Vapor transmission can be caused by diffusion through materials, as is further discussed in Ch. 41. However, vapor transmission by air movement is a larger problem. It is estimated that the water vapor carried by air infiltration is 10 to 200 times greater than that carried by diffusion through materials. Air movement is caused by pressure differentials, which in turn are caused by wind, by the stack effect, by the mechanical system in the building, or by a combination. The *stack effect* (or *chimney effect*) is caused by differences in pressure at the top and bottom of a building due to temperature differentials. The effect is most pronounced in high-rise buildings. In a cold climate, air will be warmer in the upper part of the building and cooler at the bottom, causing infiltration of air near the ground and exfiltration at the top.

The solution to air leakage is to provide a continuous barrier around the conditioned spaces in the building. This is done by using air barrier materials, components, and assemblies to provide a complete air barrier system on all vertical and horizontal surfaces exposed to the exterior. Air barrier materials are the primary elements used to provide an air barrier system, and they include both vapor-permeable barriers and vapor-impermeable barriers. Vapor-impermeable barriers provide both an air barrier and a vapor retarder in the same material. Types of vapor-permeable barriers include relatively thin sheets of spunbonded polyolefin, various types of sheathing, self-adhered membranes, and fluid-applied products. If the air barrier is vapor permeable, it should have a permeance rating of 5 to 10 perms (285 ng/s·m^2·Pa to 570 ng/s·m^2·Pa) or greater.

Permeance is the property of a material that prevents water vapor from diffusing through it. The unit of permeance is the *perm*, which is one grain of moisture per hour per square foot per inch of mercury difference in vapor pressure. In customary U.S. units, 1 perm is equal to 1 g/hr-ft^2-in Hg. In SI units, permeance is given in nanograms of water per second per square meter per pascal of vapor pressure. 1 perm expressed in SI units equals an approximate flow rate of 57 ng/s·m^2·Pa.

The maximum permeance of an air barrier material should be 0.004 cfm/ft^2 at 1.57 lbf/ft^2 (0.02 L/s·m^2 at 75 Pa) when tested according to ASTM E2178. (1.57 lbf/ft^2 is equal to 0.3 in wg at 68°F.) This value is approximately the permeance of a sheet of $^1/_2$ in (13) unpainted gypsum wallboard.

ANSI/ASHRAE/IESNA 90.1, *Energy Standard for Buildings Except Low-Rise Residential Buildings,* requires that one of the following three options be used for many commercial buildings.

1. Individual air barrier material cannot exceed 0.004 cfm/ft^2 at 0.30 in wg (0.02 L/s·m^2 at 75 Pa).
2. Air barrier assemblies cannot exceed 0.04 cfm/ft^2 at 0.30 in wg (0.2 L/s·m^2 at 75 Pa) when tested according to ASTM E1677.
3. Whole-building air barriers cannot exceed 0.4 cfm/ft^2 at 0.30 in wg (2.0 L/s·m^2 at 75 Pa) when tested according to ASTM E779.

For individual projects, the requirements of the local building code regarding air and vapor barriers must be determined.

In order for an air barrier system to function properly, the following conditions must be met.

- The air barrier, assemblies, and whole building must meet the minimum permeance ratings listed above or as prescribed by the local building code.
- The air barrier must be continuous around the conditioned spaces including walls, roof, foundation walls, and slabs on grade.
- All joints between materials, components, and assemblies must be sealed.
- The air barrier must be securely and tightly joined at other building components such as windows, doors, the roof air barrier component, and foundations.
- All penetrations for pipes, ducts, and similar elements must be sealed.
- The barrier must be securely attached to the structure to prevent billowing, tearing, or breaking away from attachments and other building components. It must resist the loads on it caused by wind, stack effect, and HVAC systems, both as positive and negative air pressure.
- The air barrier at movement joints must be capable of moving with the joint without breaking or tearing.
- The air barrier must be durable and last the life of the building or be able to be maintained.
- If both a vapor retarder and air barrier are used and they are separate membranes, the air barrier should be 10 to 20 times more permeable to water vapor diffusion than the vapor retarder, to prevent trapping moisture between the two layers.

The location of an air barrier within the wall or roof assembly is not important. However, for ease of construction and durability the air barrier generally should be located behind the exterior cladding and outside the sheathing. This makes it easier to install, seal, join to other building components, and properly support. If the same material performs the functions of both air barrier and vapor retarder, it is usually placed on the outside of the structure and sheathing and behind the cladding. If the air barrier and vapor retarder are different materials, their locations within the building envelope depend on the climatic region, interior environmental conditions, and the specific construction of the envelope.

Common air barriers include spunbonded polyolefin (house wrap), polyethylene, elastomeric coatings, liquid-applied spray-on or trowel-on materials, self-adhesive membranes, sheathing sealed with tape, silicon-based materials, and combinations of these materials.

GLAZING

Historically, glazing has been one of the weak points in constructing energy-efficient buildings. Glazing materials were limited to double-paned glass, tinted glass, reflective glass, and a few other glass types. Today, however, there are numerous glazing products that can balance the often conflicting requirements that glass must offer views, admit daylight, provide for solar heating, and insulate against extremes of temperature. For example, glass that will admit more than 70% of visible light while blocking nearly 95% of the infrared spectrum is available for daylighting use. Refer to Ch. 42 for more information on glazing types.

Glass can be a major source of heat loss and heat gain in a building. This is true because heat movement through glass occurs by both convection and radiation, and standard float glass has little resistance to either. In the winter the low insulative value of float glass results in large heat losses, whereas in summer the same glass can be a significant source of heat gain by radiation unless it is shaded. A single pane of glass has a *U*-value of about 1.11 Btu/ft^2-hr-°F (6.3 W/m^2·K).

Insulating glass is one product used to control heat loss through glazing. This is glass with two or, in some cases, three panes of glass separating a sealed airspace or partially evacuated space that acts as an insulator. *U*-values decrease to about 0.57 Btu/ft^2-hr-°F (3.2 W/m^2·K) for a $^1/_4$ in (6) air space. However, air currents within the airspace still allow heat loss by convection. In addition, some of the desired solar heat gain through the glass is lost by radiation as objects in the building get warm and begin to emit infrared radiation that passes back outside.

Double glazing can be made more efficient at stopping heat transfer by convection by using an inert gas fill instead of a vacuum. Typically, argon gas is used because is offers good thermal performance at a low cost. Alternately, krypton gas can be used, but it costs about 200 times more than argon. Krypton is more efficient than argon when the space between glass panes is small, around $^3/_8$ in (9). A double-glazed unit with argon gas in a $^1/_4$ in (6) space has a *U*-value of about 0.52 Btu/ft^2-hr-°F (2.9 W/m^2·K). However, the gas can leak out over time at a rate of approximately 0.5% to 1% per year.

Historically, heat gain was first controlled with tinted, reflective, or heat-absorbing glass that lowered the shading coefficient (SC) and solar heat gain coefficient (SHGC), thereby reducing the solar heat gain. Refer to the Definitions section at the end of this chapter for a description of SC and SHGC. However, because about 50% of the incident solar radiation on glass is in the visible spectrum and about 50% is in the infrared spectrum, tinted and reflective glass also reduced the visible light transmittance. This reduced or eliminated the use of daylighting to conserve energy, darkened the view out, and generally resulted in darker-appearing interiors, especially on cloudy days. These glass types also eliminated the use of solar heat gain when it was desirable.

Some of the more effective glazing types developed for heat gain control are described in the following sections.

Low-ε Glazing

Another glazing type is *low-emittance glass*, or *low-ε glass*. This is double glazing with a thin film or coating placed somewhere in the glazing cavity. The film or coating allows both visible and near-infrared radiation to be transmitted through the glass. However, as objects in the room are heated and emit long-wave radiation, the film or coating prevents the loss of this heat; instead, the heat is reflected back into the room. When used with an argon gas fill to reduce convection, low-ε window units provide a very efficient fenestration. For example, a double-glazed unit with argon gas in a $^1/_4$ in (6) space with a low-ε coating ($\varepsilon = 0.15$) has a *U*-value of about 0.36 Btu/ft^2-hr-°F (2.0 W/m^2·K). With a $^1/_2$ in (13) space, the *U*-value drops to approximately 0.28 Btu/ft^2-hr-°F (1.6 W/m^2·K).

Spectrally Selective Glazing

Spectrally selective glazing transmits a high proportion of the visible solar spectrum while blocking heat from the infrared portion of the spectrum, up to 80%. Used with a low-ε coating, a double-glazed window can achieve an SHGC of approximately 0.25. These types of glazing materials are especially good for buildings that have a long cooling season and that require high light levels.

Super Windows

Super windows are glazing units that combine two low-ε coatings with gas-filled cavities between three layers of glass. With a *U*-value of 0.15 Btu/ft^2-hr-°F (0.8 W/m^2·K) or less, these units can actually gain more thermal energy than they lose over a 24-hour period in winter.

Other glazing technologies are currently being developed that allow glazing to serve the multiple functions of daylighting, view, maximizing heat gain when wanted, and minimizing heat loss in winter. For example, thermochromic glass becomes translucent when it reaches a certain temperature.

Switchable Glazings

Switchable glazings are chromogenic fenestration products that change their characteristics based on particular environmental conditions or through human intervention. They include the following types of products.

Electrochromic glazing consists of a multilayered thin film, applied to glass, that changes continuously from dark to clear as low-voltage electrical current is applied. This type of glazing allows variable transmittance in the visible portion of the spectrum while reflecting in the infrared spectrum, thereby reducing solar heat gain. The voltage can be controlled manually or automatically. Refer to Ch. 42 for more information on this type of glazing.

Photochromic glazing darkens under the direct action of sunlight, in the same way that some sunglasses do. As the light intensity increases, the window becomes darker. Although offering the advantage of automatic action, this type of glazing does not offer the control of electrochromic glazing. For example, there could be times when clear glazing is desirable, such as on a cold, sunny day.

Thermochromic glazing changes darkness in response to temperature. Like photochromic glazing, this technique offers less control than electrochromic glazing does.

Transition-metal hydride electrochromics make it possible to have a glazing material that changes from transparent to reflective. These products are based on coatings of nickel-magnesium instead of the oxides used in other electrochromic materials.

DOUBLE ENVELOPE

The double envelope concept involves constructing two glazed layers as the outer skin of a building. In a double envelope system these two glazed layers are typically separated by about 2 ft to 3 ft (600 to 1000) and incorporate some type of sun control (louvers, blinds, or shades) and either a passive or active ventilation system. Sometimes the system may include devices to redirect sunlight and thus enhance daylighting of the interior spaces.

The outer shell moderates the effects of the environment and provides a cavity between itself and the inner shell, which can be passively heated or not, depending on the climate and needs of the overall building design. Air flowing between the layers can exhaust excessive heat buildup directly to the outside in hot weather or can be redirected to a heat exchanger to warm incoming air in cold weather.

Although the cost is significantly more than that of a single envelope facade, the advantages of a double envelope system include reduced cooling loads, enhanced sun control, reduced operating costs, optimized daylighting, and enhanced air quality when natural ventilation is used.

When a new outer layer of glazing is built around an existing building, the system is known as a *dynamic buffer zone*. These types of systems are constructed primarily to prevent and control condensation that may result from remodeling and upgrading the existing building with higher humidity levels. In this type of system the space between the existing building and the new facade is ventilated with dry, preheated air during winter months.

DAYLIGHTING

Electric lighting and the cooling it requires typically account for 30% to 40% of a commercial building's total energy use and can sometimes range as high as 50%. In addition to providing energy savings and a sustainable design, daylighting can increase occupant satisfaction and increase productivity. Well-daylighted spaces can make it easier to lease space and reduce tenant turnover.

In order to make daylighting feasible and cost effective, several conditions must be met. First, there must be sufficient views of the sky. This may preclude the use of daylighting in dense urban sites or for houses or small buildings nestled among tall trees. Second, glazing must transmit enough light. This is usually not a problem in new building design, but it may be problematic in remodeling or historic building renovations where glazing cannot be changed. Finally, the daylighting design must be coordinated with artificial lighting control and mechanical systems design.

One concept often used in daylighting calculations is the *daylight factor* (DF). This is the ratio, expressed as a percentage, of the indoor illuminance at a point on a horizontal surface to the unobstructed exterior horizontal illuminance. Direct sunlight is excluded. The daylight factor can be calculated and compared with recommended daylight factors for various tasks. These range from about 1.5% for ordinary visual tasks to about 4% for difficult visual tasks such as drafting.

Daylighting Variables

Many variables must be accounted for in designing for daylighting. These include the compass orientations of the facades utilizing daylight, the brightness of the sky (which is affected by solar altitude, cloud conditions, and time of day), the area of the glass, the height of the head of the glass, the transmittance of the glass, the reflectance of both room surfaces and nearby outdoor surfaces, and obstructions such as overhangs and trees. Figure 29.6 illustrates some of the variables of daylighting design.

The advantages of daylighting must be weighed against the potential problems. These include unwanted heat gain or loss as glass area is increased, glare, and imbalanced lighting if side lighting is too strong. The issue of control must also be addressed because daylighting does not conserve energy if electric lights are not switched off. Normally, automatic switching is used to overcome this problem as discussed in Ch. 32.

Building Design

The preliminary design of a building can have a significant impact on daylighting. Generally, buildings or portions of buildings where daylighting is to be optimized should be long and narrow and oriented with the long dimension in the east-west direction. Buildings with deep facades can provide a space for shading devices and light shelves. If the building is one or two stories, the glazed areas should be located away from tall trees or other obstructions. Light-colored surfaces on the exterior of the building should be used to reflect more daylight. Within the limits of cost, the building should also have high ceilings. This increases the penetration of daylight into the interior and makes it easier to incorporate light shelves into the design.

Window Design

Two of the most important variables to consider when designing windows for daylighting are the height of the window head above the floor and the effective aperture (EA). The head of the window should be as high above the floor line as possible. With a standard window having no overhang protection or light shelf, the effective daylighted zone extends about 1.5 times the window head height into the room. With a light shelf, the effective daylighted zone is from 2.0 to 2.5 times the window head height.

The *effective aperture* combines the variables of light transmittance and window-to-wall ratio. The *visible light transmittance* (VLT) is the percentage of light that passes through a glazing material. The *window-to-wall ratio* (WWR) is the net glazing area in a room or space divided by the gross exterior wall area. It does not include window frames or mullions.

Small, punched windows have low WWRs while large, continuous windows have high WWRs. Generally, an EA of between 0.20 and 0.30 provides good daylighting. Thus, if the glazing has a low VLT, the size of the window should be increased.

For best uniform light distribution, use continuous windows (instead of punched windows) with solid wall between them.

Light Shelves

One of the problems with large, high windows for daylighting on the south side of a building is the resultant glare and heat gain of direct sun. One of the most effective ways to solve this problem is by using a light shelf. A *light shelf* is simply a horizontal surface placed above eye level that reflects direct daylight onto the ceiling while shading the lower portions of the window and the interior of the room. A light shelf also has the desirable effect of distributing the light more evenly from the window to the back of the room. This is diagrammed in Fig. 29.7.

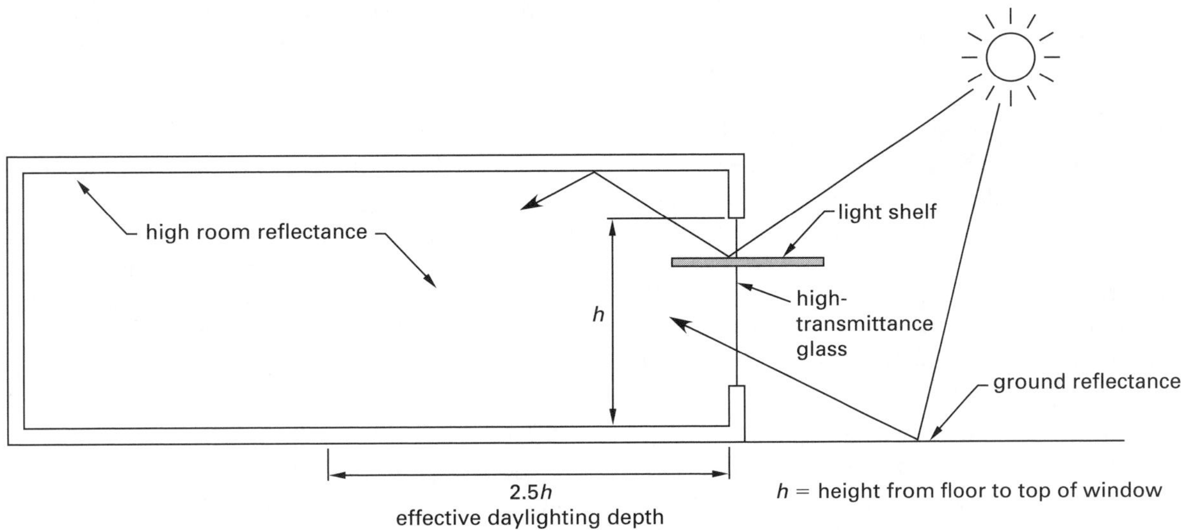

Figure 29.6 Daylighting Variables

Light shelves also provide a practical dividing point for using glass with a higher VLT above the shelf while using a tinted glass below for glare control. However they are designed, light shelves should have a diffuse or highly reflective surface.

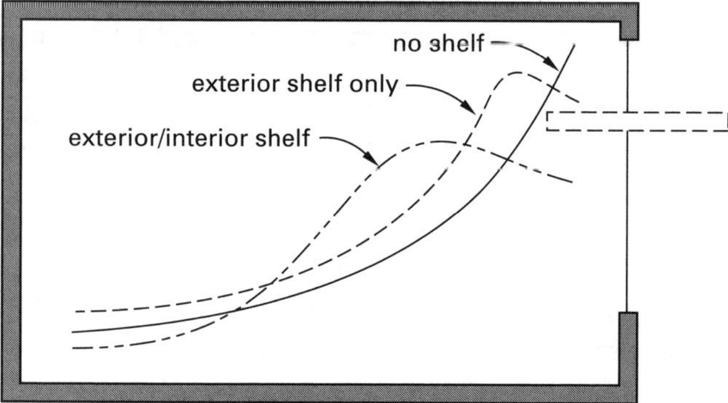

Figure 29.7 Effect of Light Shelf

Glazing Selection

Historically, one of the biggest problems with daylighting has been trying to balance the need for a high VLT against the need for glare control and unwanted heat gain. To control heat loss through convection, a glazing unit with a low U-value is desirable. To control gain from the sun's radiation, a low SHGC is desired. Generally, some type of tinted glass has been used. Today, however, spectrally selective glazing can be used, which gives a fairly high VLT with a good SHGC.

For glare control, a glass with a VLT value from 50% to 70% with the lowest possible SHGC is a good choice. If glare control is critical and if the size of the glazing area can be increased to achieve an EA between 0.20 and 0.30, a glazing product with a lower VLT can be selected.

Shading

As mentioned in a previous section, some type of shading is always required on windows, regardless of the compass orientation of the facade under consideration. Exterior shading devices are generally more effective than interior systems at blocking solar heat gain, although some type of interior window covering is usually required for occupant control and for those times when glare is excessive or the inside space needs to be darkened. Interior shading by itself has limited ability to control solar heat gain.

For daylighting applications, horizontal shading above the window on the south side of a building provides effective control. If a sufficient projection cannot be provided, a series of horizontal shades can be provided along the height of the glazing, but this is often expensive and blocks views. If light shelves are used they should be partially inside and partially outside the building.

Room Design

In addition to requiring shading and the correct size, position, and type of glazing, effective daylighting requires considerations related to room design. The reflectance of interior surfaces should be as high as possible. Minimum reflectances should be 80% for ceilings, 50% to 70% for walls, and 20% to 40% for floors. The wall facing the window should always be as light as possible to improve light distribution.

Furniture and equipment placement must be coordinated to make optimum use of the daylight. Low furniture should be used to ensure that light is not blocked from reaching the farther reaches of the space. Tasks that required higher light levels should be located closer to the windows. Computer monitors should be positioned such that they avoid reflected glare; that is, away from windows, with the screen oriented approximately perpendicular to and tilted slightly away from the window. Partial partitions can also be used to darken the area immediately around the screen.

Top Lighting

Top lighting with daylight involves using light pipes, skylights, roof monitors, sawtoothed roofs, or sloped glazing. Providing another source of daylight is advantageous because it is easier to evenly distribute the light, and because daylight can be provided to a larger portion of the building. Obviously, top lighting only works in one-story buildings, low-rise stepped-back buildings, or on the top floor of a multistory building.

Control of direct sunlight is often more difficult using these types of devices. One good product for providing light without direct sunlight is an insulated glazing panel or transparent insulation as described previously. These diffuse the light and keep heat loss to a minimum.

Light Pipes

Light pipes are round or square tubes with highly reflective interior coatings that extend from the roof to the space to be lighted. Sunlight is captured through a clear plastic dome and directed down to a translucent diffusing plate at the bottom. Light pipes are available in diameters from 10 in to 16 in (250 to 400). These devices are a relatively inexpensive way to bring natural light to the interior of a building, but their obvious limitation is that they only work in a space near the roof.

A project can receive LEED credit for achieving a minimum glazing factor of 2% in 75% of all space occupied or by meeting other requirements. Refer to the LEED rating systems for exact requirements. Additional credit is given if 90% of spaces have views to the outside.

PART 2: ALTERNATIVE ENERGY SOURCES

Using alternative energy sources is one of the best ways to improve a building's sustainability while decreasing the building's life-cycle costs. Although most buildings designed to use alternative energy sources have a higher initial cost, they have relatively short payback periods. In addition, a project can receive LEED credit for supplying at least 5% of the building's total energy use with on-site renewable energy systems, such as solar energy, geothermal, wind, biomass, and bio-gas strategies. Another credit is given for supplying 10% of the building's total energy use, and yet another for reaching 20%.

SOLAR DESIGN

Good solar design can have a tremendous impact on energy conservation because of the vast amount of solar energy that strikes the earth every hour. In addition to providing energy for building heating and cooling and for water heating, the sun's light can be used for daylighting and electrical generation via photovoltaic cells.

Design Basics

Like most natural phenomena, daylighting is highly variable, and using it for building design requires an understanding of how it varies during different times of the year and day and in different geographical locations.

The sun's position varies by season because of the relationship between it and the earth. In fact, the seasons are a result of the change in angle between the earth and sun. The north-south axis of the earth is tilted at an angle of 23.5° relative to the north-south axis of the sun. This is called the *declination angle* (or simply the declination) of the earth and remains constant as the earth revolves around the sun during a one-year period.

As shown in Fig. 29.8, when the axis of the earth is tilted toward the sun it is summer in the Northern Hemisphere. This is when the rays of the sun are closest to perpendicular in relation to the surface of much of the northern part of the earth—when we consider the sun "highest" in the sky and when the Northern Hemisphere receives the most solar radiation. During the winter months the earth is tilted away from the sun, decreasing its angle relative to the horizon and reducing the amount of solar energy striking the earth. The times of maximum tilt are approximately December 21 for the *winter solstice* and June 21 for the *summer solstice*. On about March 21 and September 21, the tilt of the earth is sideways in relation to the sun, and day and night are of equal length. These times are called the *spring equinox* and *fall equinox*, respectively.

Seasonal variation determines how high above the horizon the sun is at any given time during the day. The other variable that determines the apparent height of the sun above the horizon is the latitude of the observer on the earth. At the equator, or 0° latitude, the surface of the earth is closer to perpendicular than at 90° latitude, or at the North Pole.

The position of the sun as viewed from the earth is described by two angles, the azimuth and the altitude. See Fig. 29.9. The *azimuth* angle is the compass orientation of the sun. For solar design purposes this is usually the number of degrees either east or west of due south. For example, if the sun is halfway between south and west, the azimuth is 45° west of south. Sometimes, azimuth angle is measured in a 360° circle with due north being 0°, due east being 90°, south at 180°, and west at 270°. The *altitude* angle is the apparent height of the sun as measured from the horizon (which is 0° to directly overhead, which is 90°).

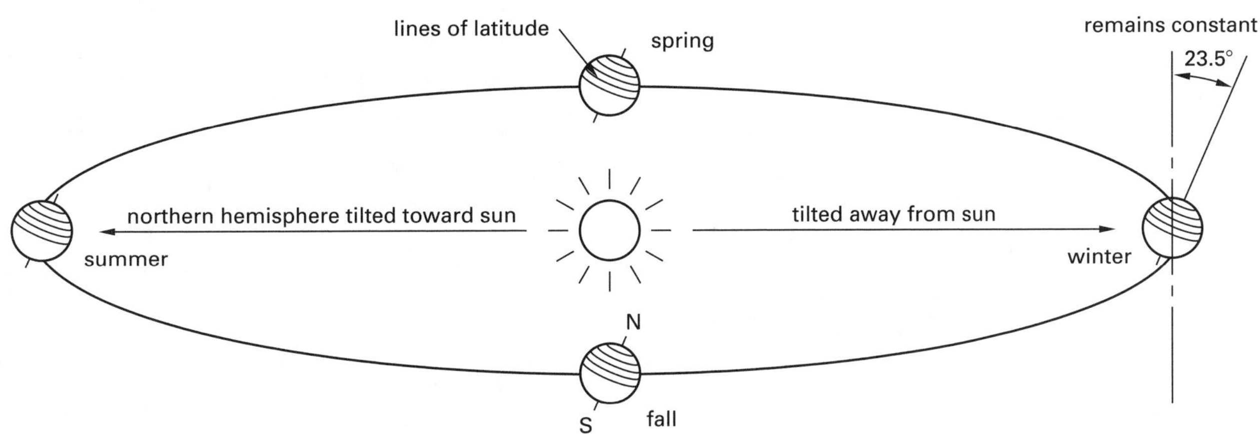

Figure 29.8 Seasonal Variation of Sun Angle

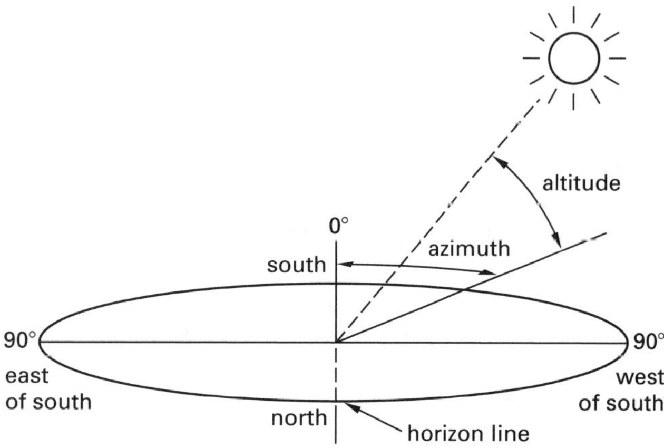

Figure 29.9 Sun Angles

Because the earth follows a repetitive pattern around the sun during a year, the position of the sun at any location on earth on any given day and at any given time can be calculated with various formulas. A simpler and quicker method is to use sun charts or solar plots similar to that shown in Fig. 29.10. Sun charts plot the altitude and azimuth at different times during a day.

The sun chart shown in Fig. 29.10 is known as a *rectilinear projection*. In this kind of chart, the solar azimuth is plotted along the horizontal axis and the solar altitude along the vertical axis. Several lines represent the sun at yearly time intervals (usually the 21st day of each month).

Solar altitude varies with latitude, and in theory a different sun chart could be plotted for every fraction of a degree of latitude. In practice, sun charts are usually plotted for every 2°, 5°, or 10° of latitude, depending on what level of accuracy is wanted. Data for dates and latitudes between the plotted lines can be interpolated.

Three other types of sun charts, or sunpath projections, are the equidistant horizontal projection, the gnomonic

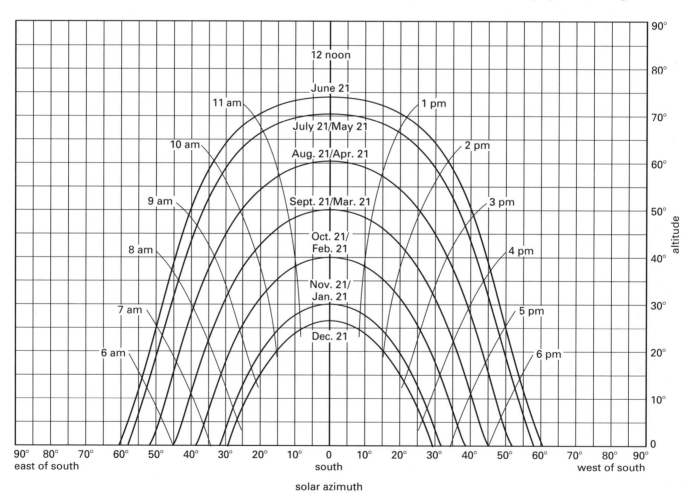

Figure 29.10 Typical Sun Chart

projection, and the stereographic projection (also known as the *fish-eye projection*).

The *equidistant horizontal projection* (also known as the *horizontal polar projection*) is a sun chart that plots the path of the sun at various times of the year on a circular chart. Fig. 29.11(a) shows a simplified version of this type of chart. The spokes of the chart represent the azimuth angles. Curved lines overlaid on the chart show the path of the sun on different dates based on the latitude. Intersecting lines represent the time of day.

The *gnomonic projection* (also called a *sun peg chart*) is derived from a sundial projection. At low angles of the sun, the lines extend to infinity, as shown in Fig. 29.11(b). A gnomonic projection is less useful as a solar chart than the other types are, but it can be used for shadow studies. As with the other charts, a separate projection is required for each latitude. To use the chart, place the chart next to the building model to be studied, and place a small peg perpendicular to the chart in the location shown. Tilt the model and chart in sunlight until the tip of the shadow cast by the peg intersects the selected date and time. The shadows on the model are then the same as they would be in the actual building at that time and date.

Using any type of sun chart depends on knowing the direction of *solar south*, the direction of the geographic south pole. Solar south is not necessarily the same as *magnetic south*, south as determined by a compass. The earth's magnetic field is irregular and not aligned with its geographic north and south poles, and so in most places on earth a compass does not point toward the true north pole; due to regional irregularities in the magnetic field, a compass may not even point directly toward the north magnetic pole. Magnetic north, then, may be easterly or westerly from true north, and this difference varies with the compass's location on the earth.

To determine the direction of true north, the *magnetic declination*—the angle of difference between magnetic north and true north—must be known for that location. The compass reading is adjusted by the magnetic declination to give the direction of true north. True south, or solar south, is then the opposite direction.

Another way to determine solar south is to place a vertical stake in the ground. Determine the time of sunrise and sunset for the location and find the time exactly halfway between them. This is solar noon. The shadow cast by the stake at solar noon will point toward solar north or south.

Sun charts can be used to determine the best design for overhangs and other shading devices and to plot the shading effects of surrounding structures and vegetation on a building using solar heating or daylighting. Such a plot is called a *shadow mask*. Although sun charts and shadow masks are useful for preliminary design and quick studies, there are computer programs that can quickly give exact data based on a project's location. Many three-dimensional design programs also can calculate sun position and show accurate shadows on the 3-D model.

Charts and tables are also available that give the amount of solar radiation in Btu/ft^2-day (W/m^2·d) for different geographical locations for use in designing passive and active solar energy systems.

Passive Solar Design

There are several generic types of passive solar heating systems. A *passive solar energy system* simply means that solar energy is collected, stored, and distributed without the use of mechanical equipment. The following general categories describe the most commonly used passive solar design techniques. See Fig. 29.12.

Direct gain systems collect heat through south-facing glass and store the heat in high-mass materials such as concrete floors, masonry walls, tile, stone, or terrazzo. See Fig. 29.12(a). During nighttime hours the high-mass materials slowly release the heat gained during the day. To make this system effective, the glass area must be well insulated at night or the glazing must be low-ε glass. In order to be efficient, glazing used for passive solar heating should have a *U*-factor of less than 0.35 Btu/ft^2-hr-°F (2.0 W/m^2·K). Because moveable, nighttime insulation is not very efficient and requires human intervention, newer glazing materials can be used instead. The mass areas should be dark colored and free of rugs, wall hangings, and other materials that would interfere with the storage and release of heat.

Indirect gain systems are similar to direct gain systems except that the thermal mass is not in direct sunlight. Rather, the mass is heated during the day by room air temperature and reflected sunlight. Indirect gain systems are less efficient than direct gain systems; they require about four times the amount of mass. However, they can be used in conjunction with direct gain systems to even out the temperature variations in different parts of the building.

A *thermal storage wall* is placed directly behind a south-facing glass wall and collects solar energy during the day for release at night, similar to a direct gain system. Most thermal storage walls are vented, which allows cool air to circulate in the space between the glass and wall, become heated, and travel by convection up and over the wall and back into the space. A common form of thermal storage wall as diagrammed in Fig. 29.12(b) is the *Trombe wall*, which is constructed of masonry with vents at the top and bottom to allow thermocirculation. Thermal storage walls can also be constructed of water containers or phase change materials. Water is better than concrete or masonry because it has a higher specific heat and can store more energy than

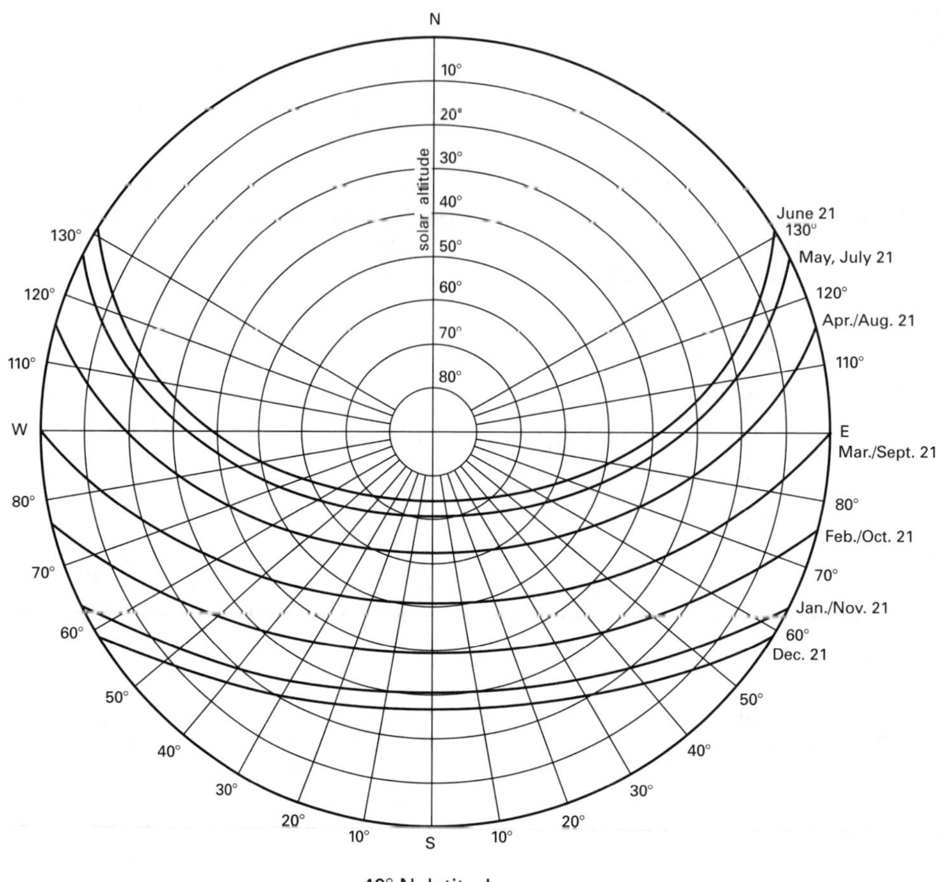

40° N. latitude

(a) equidistant horizontal projection

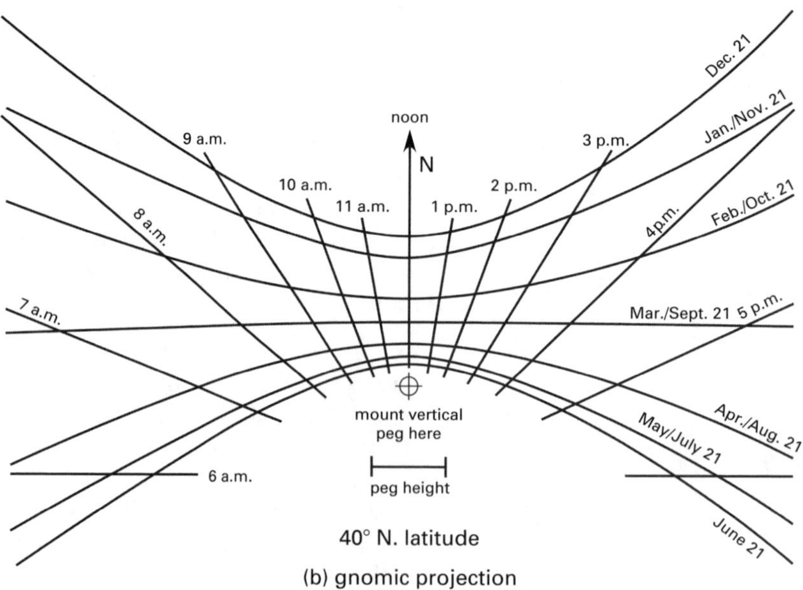

40° N. latitude

(b) gnomic projection

Figure 29.11 Sun Path Projections

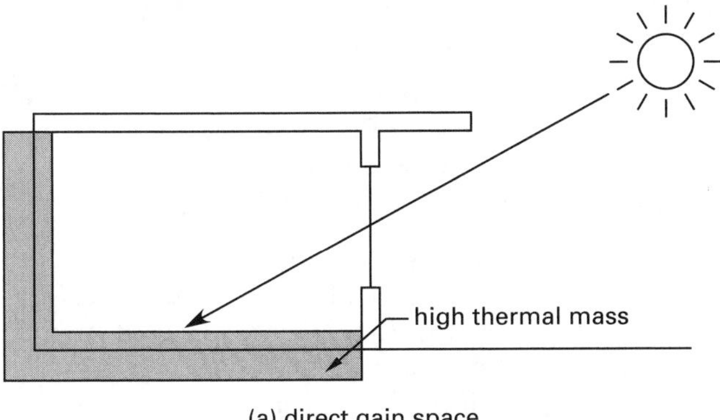

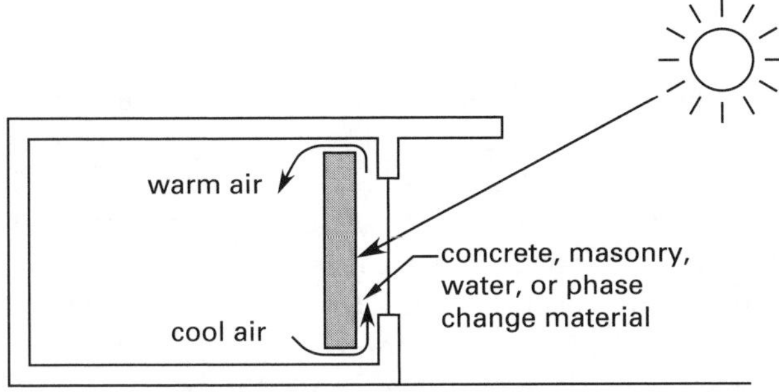

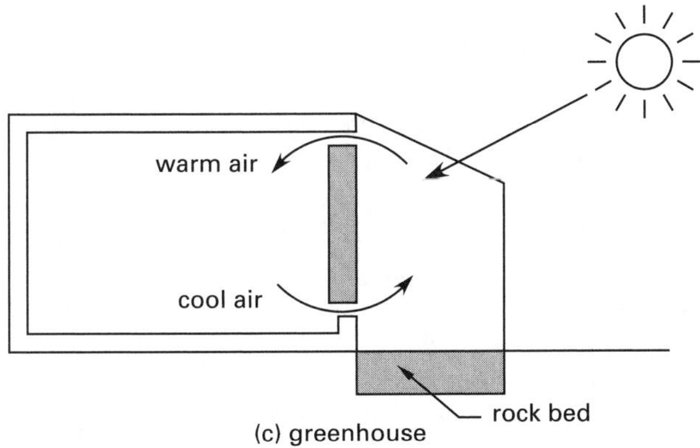

Figure 29.12 Passive Solar Heating Types

masonry. *Phase change materials* are used to prevent overheating and wide swings in temperatures that can occur with concrete, masonry, and water. Phase change materials are typically eutectic salts that change from a solid to a liquid at a fairly low temperature, around 70°F (21°C). They store large amounts of heat because they store latent heat as they undergo the phase change from solid to liquid. At night, the heat is released as they change state from liquid to solid.

Greenhouse designs include large glazed areas on the south side of the building with a heavy thermal mass wall separating the greenhouse and the remainder of the structure. A rock bed or high thermal mass floor is built in the greenhouse. While the greenhouse often overheats and is subject to heat loss at night, the stored heat thermocirculates into the rest of the building at night. See Fig. 29.12(c).

Roof ponds store heat in large water-filled bags on the roof of a building. In winter during the day, the bags heat up. At night, insulation is moved over the roof pond, which loses its heat downward into the building. The same system can be reversed in the summer to cool the building by radiation. During the night the insulation is removed from the pond, so the heat collected from the building during the day is lost upward, away from the building.

Convective loop systems place the solar collector below the space so that air is circulated by natural convection as the warm air rises and cool air falls back to the collector. Convective loop systems are often used to circulate water.

Active Solar Design

Active solar energy systems use pumps, fans, ducts, pipes, and other mechanical equipment to collect, store, and distribute solar energy. In order of use, active solar systems are used for domestic and process water heating, space heating, space cooling, and electricity generation, although generation of electricity is still limited due to the expense of photovoltaic cells. One of the most common categories of active systems, which may be thought of as a "passive system with active assist," is when one of the types of passive systems described previously is used with ductwork and fans to distribute the heated air without relying solely on natural convection.

For a typical active solar system, three components are required: the collector, a storage device, and a distribution system.

Collectors may be either flat-plate collectors or focusing collectors. *Flat-plate collectors* consist of a network of pipes located on an absorptive black surface with low emissivity below a covering of glass or plastic. The pipes carry the heat transfer fluid, which is generally water with antifreeze but can also be air or other liquids. *Focusing collectors* are parabolic-shaped reflectors that focus the incoming radiation to a single pipe that carries the heat-transfer medium. Because the reflectors focus the sun's energy, focusing collectors operate at a much higher temperature than do flat-plate collectors. However, they must be continuously aimed at the sun for maximum benefit, so they are usually attached to mechanisms that automatically track the path of the sun.

Storage devices are usually water for water systems or rock beds for air systems. Phase change materials can also be used, but are more expensive.

Distribution components are the same as for standard HVAC systems: ducts for air, pipes for water, and associated fans, pumps, registers, and control devices.

When solar energy is used for water heating it may be in either an open loop or closed loop. In an open loop, the water to be used is heated directly in the solar collector. In a closed loop, water or some other transfer medium is heated in the collector and circulated to a heat exchanger where the actual water to be used is heated by the transfer medium. A closed loop is often employed because antifreeze can be added to the water that circulates through the collectors. Refer to Ch. 31 for more information on solar water heating.

When solar energy is used for space heating, either air or water can be used for the transfer medium. If air is used, the heated air is circulated to a rock bed, normally under the building, where the heat is stored. At night, fans circulate cool air over the rock bed, where the air warms and is distributed to the building. If water is used as the transfer medium, it is stored in a large tank and then, when needed, it is pumped to baseboard heaters, radiant panels, or a heat exchanger in a forced air furnace.

Solar energy can be used for cooling if high enough temperatures are reached in the transfer medium. The heated water is used as the energy source for absorptive cooling, as diagrammed in Fig. 28.2.

WIND

Wind power offers an extremely sustainable method of generating electricity from a renewable and free source. There are many commercial wind farms across the United States and Canada that help reduce the need for fossil-fuel-burning power plants. However, wind energy is generally not appropriate for individual building use. Wind machines are costly, and most jurisdictions will not allow their use on urban or suburban sites. Of course, they are only appropriate for windy locations.

Even where a wind generating system can be installed, in most cases, the electricity must be used as it is generated. Using wind energy to charge batteries has limited use for most building sites. Some power companies will purchase excess electricity when it is placed back in the utility power grid.

GEOTHERMAL

Broadly speaking, geothermal alternate energy sources encompass a broad range of heat sources from the earth, including hot springs. Practically, geothermal energy involves the use of *ground-source heat pumps* (GSHPs) that use the relatively constant temperature of the earth. These are electrically powered systems that work like air-source heat pumps by either extracting heat from the ground in winter or giving off excess heat to the ground in summer. The heat from the ground is increased through the use of a vapor-compressor refrigeration cycle.

GSHPs can be used for space heating and cooling and for preheating water for domestic hot water. They can save from 20% to 50% on energy consumption for space heating and cooling and up to 50% on water heating.

Although the initial cost is higher than that of conventional equipment, long-term costs are lower, and they reduce the need for fossil fuel-based energy. They can be used for both residential and commercial buildings; however, they are most effectively used in buildings that require significant space and water heating and cooling over extended hours of operation. These include homes, multifamily buildings, schools, and similar uses.

The main feature of a GSHP is the assemblage of durable plastic pipes buried in the ground, either vertically or horizontally, depending on the space available and the geology of the site. About 400 ft (120 m) of pipe are required for every 12,000 Btu/hr (3500 W) of heating or cooling capacity needed. In the heating mode, water is pumped through the plastic tubing in the earth to the heat pump, where the water's heat is increased. The GSHP can then be used to preheat water or exchange heat in a water-water or water-air heat exchanger. The cycle is reversed for cooling.

PHOTOVOLTAICS

Photovoltaics is the direct conversion of sunlight into electricity. Photovoltaic (PV) cells are made from various types of semiconductor materials and deposited or arranged on a variety of materials in flat panels. There are also concentrator systems that focus sunlight on cells, but these are generally limited for use in large-scale power generation. The cells convert the sunlight into direct current (DC), which is converted into alternating current (AC). The electricity is used immediately, stored in batteries, or sold back to the power utility if the system is connected to the power grid.

Photovoltaics has many advantages. It reduces the demand on nonrenewable energy sources, such as coal- or gas-fired power plants. It can reduce energy costs because the power is generated on site and the excess can, in many states, be sold back to the utility. It produces electricity with no pollution and comes from a free resource. Disadvantages include a higher initial cost, the need for solar access, low winter production, no production during night hours, and sometimes the requirement for storage batteries. In addition, some local jurisdictions, especially homeowners' associations, may limit the use of photovoltaics.

The development of PV technology is ongoing, and the efficiency is increasing while the cost is decreasing. Manufacturers now provide 20-year warranties for PV cells. The use of this technology continues to grow, with some states offering tax rebates or other financial incentives to make their use more feasible.

There are three types of photovoltaic cells in use: crystalline, polycrystalline, and thin-film. Crystalline cells are the most widely used. Polycrystalline cells are less expensive than crystalline but produce less power. Thin-film cells can be deposited onto other materials such as glass, metal, and plastic, and are ideal when the cells need to be integrated with other building materials. However, thin-film cells only produce as little as one-third the power of crystalline PV cells.

Photovoltaic cells are assembled into arrays and can be placed on a building in one of two ways. The PV arrays can be constructed in frames and attached to the roof, walls, or elsewhere as a distinct visual element. Alternatively, newer technology now allows the cells to be built into other building materials, such as shingles, metal roofing, membrane roofing, and glass. When a PV array is used on a roof, its ideal angle is determined by the latitude of the building site. For maximum year-round energy generation, the tilt angle should be the same as the latitude of the building site. For maximum energy generation in the winter, the tilt angle should be 10° to 15° greater than the latitude.

DEFINITIONS

Analemma: the figure-eight curve that represents the angular offset of the sun from its mean position as viewed from the earth. At any given point on the earth, if the position of the sun is noted at the same time every day for a year, the figure of the analemma is produced.

Balance-point temperature: the outdoor temperature at which a building makes a transition from a heating need to a cooling need

Daylight factor (DF): the ratio, expressed as a percentage, of the indoor illuminance at a point on a horizontal surface to the unobstructed exterior horizontal illuminance. Direct sunlight is excluded.

Effective aperture: the product of visible transmittance multiplied by the window-to-wall ratio

Equation of time: the factor used to account for the difference between solar time and clock time. Solar time is based on the position of the sun. Its basic unit is the solar day, the time it takes for the earth to make one complete rotation on its axis. A solar day may be slightly more than or less than 24 hours by clock time; its exact length changes from day to day due to the earth's elliptical orbit around the sun and the tilt of the earth's axis. Depending on the time of year, then, solar days may be passing more quickly or more slowly than days on the clock. As the small differences accumulate, solar time can be ahead or behind clock time by as much as about $16^1/_2$ minutes. The equation of time is also expressed in the analemma. (The difference between solar time and clock time is also affected by one's position east or west within a time zone; this is a separate factor from the equation of time.)

Glazing factor: a LEED-based number calculated by taking into account window area, floor area, a window geometry factor, light transmission, and a window height factor

Ground light: visible light from the sun and sky, reflected by exterior surfaces below the plane of the horizon

Light shelf: a horizontal element positioned above eye level and designed to reflect daylight on the ceiling for improved daylighting effectiveness

Net metering: the requirement that a utility pay and charge equal rates regardless of which way electricity flows as part of the utility grid. Thus, excess electricity generated with photovoltaics or wind systems can be sold back to the utility.

Radiation spectrum: the entire range of electromagnetic radiation extending from 0 Hz to about 10^{23} Hz. This includes visible light as well as infrared radiation, radio waves, and gamma rays, among others.

Radiative cooling (or *Nocturnal cooling* or *Night-cooled mass*): a passive or active design strategy that uses thermal mass to collect and store heat during the day for release at night. This works best in climates where there is a significant difference between daytime and nighttime temperatures, such as the Southwest or in temperate climates.

Shading coefficient (SC): the ratio of the solar heat gain through a glazing product to the solar heat gain through an unshaded $^1/_8$ in thick (3), clear, double-strength glass under the same set of conditions. This is a value for the glass only and does not include the frame. The SC is a value between 0.0 and 1.0. Because this rating includes only the glass, the solar heat gain coefficient is considered a more accurate rating.

Solar constant: the amount of solar energy that falls in a unit time on a unit area that is 93,000,000 miles (149 669 000 km) from the sun and oriented on a plane perpendicular to the sun's rays. The mean value of the solar constant is 433 Btu/hr-ft^2 (1.37 kW/m^2). Some of this energy is lost as the energy travels through the earth's atmosphere.

Solar heat gain coefficient (SHGC): the ratio of the solar heat gain through a fenestration to the total solar radiation incident on the glazing. Solar heat gain includes directly transmitted solar heat and absorbed solar radiation, which is then reradiated, conducted, or convected into the space. This rating includes the effects of the frame and glass spacer. The SHGC is a value between 0.0 and 0.87.

Solar savings fraction: the fraction of the total energy required by a system that is provided by a solar technology. The solar savings fraction, represented by the variable f, ranges from zero where no solar energy is used to 1.0 where all energy used by a system is solar energy.

Solar time: the time as defined by the sun and its position relative to the earth. Because the length of the solar day varies, most references use the *mean solar day* as a basis for timekeeping. This is the average length of a solar day.

Visible light transmittance (VLT): the fraction of visible light that passes through a glazing material

Window-to-wall ratio: the net glazing area (glass only, not including frame or mullions) in a room or space divided by the gross exterior wall area

Workplane: the assumed height at which work is performed, usually considered to be at desk height, 30 in (760) above the floor

30 SUSTAINABLE DESIGN

Sustainability encompasses a wide range of concepts and strategies. Although specifics vary, a general definition of *sustainability* includes meeting the needs and wants of the present generation without harming or compromising the ability of future generations to meet their needs.

For architecture, *sustainable design* (also called *green building*, *environmental design*, or *ecological design*, among other terms) involves many planning, design, operational, and reuse concepts that together can create functional, healthy, nonpolluting, and environmentally friendly buildings without compromising practical requirements or human comfort. In addition, the long-term costs are no greater, and are often less, than those of comparable buildings designed without sustainability in mind.

This chapter reviews the sustainable design issues that have not been covered elsewhere.

SITE DEVELOPMENT

The first step in developing a sustainable building project is to disturb the natural site as little as possible, by minimizing the building footprint, parking, and other development. The natural topography must be respected, and climatic conditions must be considered. All of these will affect the final building form. Additionally, development should take place to make the best use of community services such as public transportation, utilities, and pedestrian paths. Buildings should not be developed on sites designated as prime farmland, in floodplains, on or within 100 ft (30 m) of wetlands, on land designated as habitat for threatened species, or on land that was previously public parkland. A project can receive LEED® credit for meeting these requirements. LEED is an acronym for Leadership in Energy and Environmental Design, a program of the U.S. Green Building Council designed to encourage the implementation of sustainable building practices. Buildings receive credits for using various sustainable design practices and are then awarded a LEED certificate if they accumulate enough points. See the section on Building Rating Systems later in this chapter for more information on LEED.

Refer to Ch. 2 for more information on how sustainability practices affect project concepts. Refer to Ch. 5 for more information on how topography, utilities, climate, and alternative energy systems and new material technologies affect project concepts. See Ch. 29 for information on energy efficiency and alternative energy sources.

WATER USE

Water use in sustainable design involves a variety of issues. These include controlling and directing stormwater runoff, preventing erosion and contamination of runoff, using rainwater, employing graywater, and practicing general water conservation through a variety of strategies, including low-flow plumbing fixtures.

When discussing water use for sustainability in architectural design there are four classifications: potable water, rainwater, graywater, and blackwater. *Potable water* is treated and is suitable for drinking. *Graywater* is wastewater not from toilets or urinals. *Blackwater* is water containing toilet or urinal waste, although some jurisdictions may include water from kitchen sinks and laundry facilities in the category of blackwater.

In an ideal situation, each of these types of water would be kept separate, and rainwater and graywater would be used for irrigation and for flushing toilets. With suitable treatment, blackwater could be used for irrigation. Both graywater and blackwater could be run through heat exchangers to preheat cold water for final heating in a water heater. However, because of high initial costs and strict local and state health regulations, making extensive use of graywater and blackwater is seldom feasible, especially in an urban or suburban setting.

Storm Runoff and Erosion Control

The first consideration in sustainable design of water use should be to protect existing watersheds on a site and on the surrounding areas and waterways. Improper water control during and after construction can create one or more of the following problems.

- increased load on local storm sewer systems
- increased potential for flooding
- pollution of waterways with sediment, road salts, petroleum products, fertilizers, heavy metals, and pathogenic bacteria
- erosion of sites and waterways
- erosion of stream banks
- accelerated soil creep or landslides
- stream warming
- loss of aquatic biodiversity

All development sites should have a stormwater management plan. *Stormwater management* is the use of structural or nonstructural practices designed to reduce stormwater runoff pollutant loads, discharge volumes, and peak flow discharge rates.

During construction, erosion must be controlled while natural surfaces are stripped and subjected to building conditions. Most states and local municipalities have regulations to control erosion and sediment. Silt fences, sediment traps or basins, vegetated buffer strips, hay bales, and other methods are used to control water flow and pollutants onto adjacent property and ultimately into natural waterways.

The final constructed site should minimize the impervious coverage of development, utilize the natural filtration and cleansing action of soils and plants, and capture and control excessive runoff. Some of the common ways of doing this are to use pervious paving, develop constructed wetlands, and build grass-lined swales. *Pervious paving* can be manufactured grids of concrete, plastic, or other materials that allow grass or other ground covers to grow through, or it can be porous asphalt or concrete.

Refer to the definitions at the end of this chapter for additional terms related to stormwater management. Additional guidelines for sustainable site design are given in Ch. 2.

Rainwater Collection

If local regulations allow, rainwater can be collected and used for irrigation and, in some cases, for nonpotable uses such as flushing toilets. Rainwater collection also reduces the amount of site runoff that can burden a storm sewer system. The effectiveness of a rainwater collection system is limited by the amount of rain some geographic regions receive and the quality of rainwater in air-polluted locations. 1 in of rain per square foot of roof area is about 0.6 gal (25 mm/m^2 is about 2.3 L).

A *rainwater collection system* is composed of a water collection system, a storage cistern, and a water distribution system. The water collection system is commonly the roof area of the building. If a roof is used, the materials should be selected to avoid contamination of the water or the addition of sediment. Good choices are metal, clay, and concrete tile. Avoid using asphalt shingles or lead-containing materials such as flashing. Steep roofs are better than low-sloped roofs because they are scoured by winds and collect less dust and debris. Devices can be used to divert the first flush of water during a rainfall, to prevent it from entering the cistern.

For irrigation use, the runoff can be filtered first with screens on the gutters and then with simple graded screens, paper filters, or sand filters. Additional treatment may be needed for use in flushing toilets and similar nonpotable applications.

After the rainwater is collected it is stored in a *cistern*. Cisterns can be made from fiberglass, steel, or concrete. They must be watertight and covered to prevent contamination. If cisterns can be located above the area of use, water can flow by gravity; otherwise, small pumps are used to distribute the water.

To calculate the amount of rainwater available, the horizontal area of the catchment area is multiplied by the average annual rainfall for a region and reduced by some amount, typically 75%, to account for evaporation and other losses.

Graywater and Blackwater Systems

Graywater recycling is the collection, treatment, storage and distribution of wastewater from sources that do not contain human waste, such as showers and sinks. Depending on the treatment methods and local health regulations, graywater may be used for irrigation, toilet flushing, vehicle washing, janitorial cleaning, cooling, and similar uses.

Graywater systems are generally only cost effective in new construction where separate piping can easily be installed and where the ratio of the demand for nonpotable to potable water is relatively high, such as for laundries and car washes. Other cost considerations include the net reduction in water consumption, the price of potable water, and economies of scale.

Even if graywater is only used for irrigation, health regulations may require that it be filtered and be applied subsurface, using drip or other methods rather than sprinklers. Any type of graywater system should have interceptors to prevent the flow of grease and hair into the system.

If graywater is not reused directly, the heat it carries can be run through heat exchangers to preheat potable water flowing to a water heater. This can reduce energy demand, increase the availability of hot water, allow downsizing of heated water storage, and lower energy costs. Heat recovery systems are best for buildings that have large domestic hot water needs such as restaurants, laundries, apartments, and arenas. Heat exchangers can either be a *direct system*, where the graywater flows past a coil of cold water, or a *tank system*, where the graywater is held around coils of incoming cold water. The tank system has the ability to extract more heat from the graywater, but requires periodic maintenance. Both systems require protection against contamination of the potable water supply. One way of doing this is with a double-walled heat exchanger. Building officials and health departments must be consulted to determine the local requirements for these types of systems.

Blackwater recycling is the collection, treatment, storage and distribution of wastewater from nearly any source, including from toilets and urinals. Because of the obvious contamination, blackwater requires more extensive treatment before use. Generally, blackwater recycling is not cost effective except on a large scale, although commercial systems are available for single-building use.

Plumbing Fixtures

The simplest method of water conservation for sustainable design is to reduce the amount of treated water used. This can easily be accomplished with low-flow toilets, showerheads, and faucets. Currently, 1.6 gal (6 L) toilets are the largest permitted by law in the United States, and toilets that use even less water are available. Using various designs with air pressure tanks or vacuum systems, some toilets use as little as 1.5 qt (1.4 L) of water with each flush. Low-consumption appliances are also available that reduce water use without compromising function. For example, a front-loading washing machine uses less water than does a top-loading model.

ALTERNATIVE ENERGY SOURCES AND ENERGY EFFICIENCY

Alternative energy sources refer to renewable sources such as solar or wind power. While it is seldom possible to use only alternative energy sources in all buildings or for all of a building's energy needs, using them can substantially reduce reliance on depletable sources, such as fossil fuels, and can reduce pollution. Energy efficiency refers to a reduction in the consumption of energy. Both of these topics are discussed in Ch. 29. Energy efficiency using conventional fuels and mechanical systems is discussed in Ch. 28. Refer to Ch. 32 for more information on how sustainability can be improved with electrical and lighting systems.

MATERIALS

The selection and use of materials in a building represents a significant part of the total sustainability of a building project. As with energy consumption and other sustainability issues, material selection must be made with consideration of the entire life cycle of the building. However, sustainability issues must be considered along with the traditional concerns of function, cost, appearance, and performance.

Life-Cycle Assessment

A *life-cycle assessment* (LCA) provides the methodology to evaluate the environmental impact of using a particular material or product in a building. There are commonly four phases to an LCA. These are

- defining the goals and scope of the study
- performing an inventory analysis
- performing an impact assessment
- performing an improvement analysis, or interpretation, and reporting the results of the study

The first step in the process is to determine the purpose and goals of doing the study. Limits of the study and the units for study must also be established so alternatives can be compared and the framework for data acquisition can be developed.

The *inventory analysis* is often the most difficult part because it involves determining and quantifying all the inputs and outputs of the product under study. These might include the energy required to obtain the raw materials and process or manufacture them, the energy of transportation, the need for ancillary materials, and the pollution or waste disposal involved in the manufacturing, use, and disposal processes. The ability to recycle the material is also considered. Some of the criteria used for evaluating building materials are given in the next section.

The *impact assessment* attempts to characterize the effects of the processes found in the inventory analysis in terms of their impacts on the environment. The analysis may include such things as resource depletion, generation of pollution, health impacts, and effects on social welfare. For example, the energy required to produce a product may necessitate the addition of electrical generating capacity, which in turn may produce both waterborne and airborne pollution.

Finally, the *improvement analysis* is a way to suggest how to reduce the environmental impact of all the raw materials, energy, and processing required to produce the product or construction activity.

There are four main stages of a product's life cycle: raw material acquisition, manufacturing, use in the building, and disposal or reuse. The potential individual elements of each stage are as follows.

Raw Material Acquisition

- acquisition of raw materials and energy from mining, drilling, or other activities
- processing of raw materials
- transportation of raw materials to processing points

Manufacturing

- conversion of processed raw materials into useful products
- manufacturing or fabrication of materials into the final product
- packaging of the product
- transportation of the finished product to the job site

Use and Maintenance

- installation or construction of the product into the building
- long-term use of the product throughout its life or the life of the building
- maintenance and repair of the product throughout its life

Disposal

- demolition of the product used in the building
- conversion of the waste into other useful products
- waste disposal of the product
- reuse or recycling of the product if not disposed or converted

At any point in the life cycle of a building material or product (but most commonly during inventory analysis) consideration must be given to all the inputs and outputs of the material or product under study. These include the energy and other resources required to acquire, process, or use the product and the materials released to the air, water, and land as a result of its use. A model for analyzing these effects is shown in Fig. 30.1.

This model is helpful in directing the required collection of data. Inputs for energy are typically in units such as British thermal units or megajoules, inputs for raw materials are in pounds or kilograms, and water is commonly in gallons or liters. Output is typically given by weight, in pounds or kilograms.

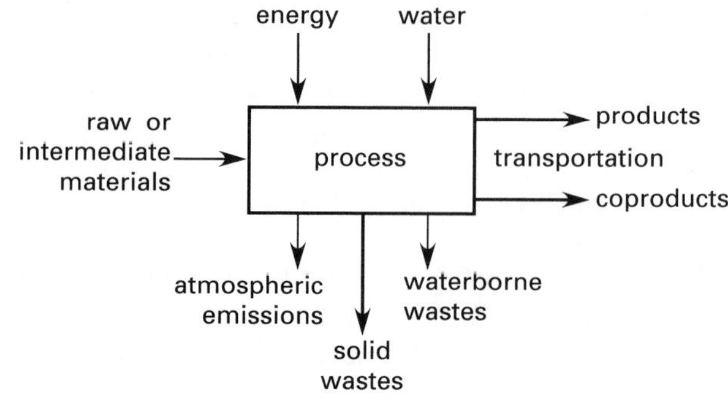

Figure 30.1 Life-Cycle Inventory Model

Criteria for Evaluating Building Materials

Some of the criteria for evaluating how sustainable a product or construction process is include the following. Of course, not all the criteria will apply to every product.

- *Embodied energy*. The material or product should require as little energy as possible for its extraction as a raw material, initial processing, and subsequent manufacture or fabrication into a finished building product. This includes the energy required for transportation of the materials and products during their life cycle. The production of the material should also generate as little waste or pollution as possible. Table 30.1 lists the approximate embodied energy of some common building materials.
- *Renewable materials*. A material is sustainable if it comes from sources that can renew themselves within a fairly short time. LEED credits are given for using rapidly renewable building materials and products for 5% of the total value of all building materials and products used in the project. These include products typically made from plants that are harvested within a 10-year cycle or shorter. Products that meet this criterion include wool carpets, bamboo flooring and paneling, straw board, cotton batt insulation, linoleum flooring, poplar OSB, sunflower seed board, and wheatgrass cabinetry.
- *Recycled content*. The more recycled content a material has, the less raw materials and energy are required to process the raw materials into a final product. Each of the three types of recycled content should be considered: post-consumer materials, post-industrial materials, and recovered materials.
- *Energy efficiency*. Materials, products, and assemblies should reduce the energy consumption in a building.

Table 30.1

Embodied Energy in Common Building Materials

material	embodied energy Btu/lbm	embodied energy MJ/kg
stone (local)	340	0.79
clay brick	1080	2.5
lumber	1080	2.5
gypsum wallboard	2630	6.1
stone (imported)	2930	6.8
particleboard	3450	8.0
aluminum (recycled)	3490	8.1
steel (recycled)	3830	8.9
plywood	4480	10.4
MDF	5130	11.9
glass	6850	15.9
ceramic tile	8390	19.5
tempered glass	11,290	26.2
steel (virgin)	13,790	32.0
zinc	21,980	51.0
brass	26,720	62.0
PVC	30,170	70.0
copper	30,430	70.6
vinyl flooring	34,090	79.1
paint	40,210	93.3
wool carpet	45,690	106.0
linoleum	49,990	116.0
nylon carpet	63,790	148.0
aluminum (virgin)	82,320	191.0

All information should be viewed as approximate due to different sources, different methods of calculating values, varying assumptions, and what factors may have been used in the calculations. It is best to view the information in terms of relative differences in magnitude and what other sustainable factors may be involved in the decision to use a particular material. For example, a material with a high embodied energy may otherwise be desirable because it has a long life span, can be recycled, is very durable, and reduces energy consumption in the building during occupancy.

Sources: *Environmental Resource Guide*, American Institute of Architects; *The Energy Embodied in Building Materials—Updated New Zealand Coefficients and Their Significance*, George Baird; Environmental Building News, July 1, 2001; United States Gypsum.

- *Use of local materials*. Using locally produced materials reduces transportation costs and can add to the regional character of a design. A building can receive LEED credit for using 20% of building materials and products that are manufactured regionally within a radius of 500 mi. Additional credit is available for using 50% or more of local materials and products.
- *Durability*. Durable materials will last longer and generally require less maintenance over the life of a product or building. Even though initial costs may be higher, the life cycle costs may be less.
- *Low volatile organic compounds* (VOC) *content*.
- *Low toxicity*. Materials should be selected that emit little or no harmful gasses such as chlorofluorocarbons (CFCs), formaldehyde, and others listed on the EPA's list of hazardous substances.
- *Moisture problems*. If possible, materials should be selected that prevent or resist the growth of biological contaminants.
- *Water conservation*. Products should reduce water consumption in a building and in landscaping.
- *Maintainability*. Materials and products should be able to be cleaned and otherwise maintained with only nontoxic or low-VOC substances.
- *Potential for reuse and recycling*. Some materials and products are more readily recycled than others. Steel, for example, can usually be separated and melted down to make new steel products. On the other hand, plastics used in construction are difficult to remove and separate.
- *Reusability*. A product should be reusable after it has served its purpose in the original building. This type of product becomes a salvaged material in the life cycle of another building.

Use of Salvaged Materials

Salvaged materials should be used as much as possible. This includes items such as doors, window units, cabinetry, furnishings, and equipment. There may be extra costs involved in preparing salvaged materials for reuse, but these costs can be offset by savings on new materials and the costs associated with their production or disposal. Reusing materials, such as brick or timber from old buildings, can even add to the aesthetic appeal of a new building.

Concrete

Concrete is generally not a sustainable material, because the manufacture and production of portland cement requires substantial energy and raw material consumption and produces environmental emissions. However, when properly constructed, concrete does have a long life, and it can be recycled as crushed aggregate for highway base, fill, and subsequent concrete manufacture. By itself, concrete does not emit any appreciable air pollutants. However, some concrete admixtures (such as superplasticizers and water reducing agents) and form-release agents can produce odors and emissions.

The sustainability of concrete can be improved by incorporating fly ash admixtures, using recycled aggregates when possible, and using low-waste formwork. *Fly ash* is a waste material obtained from coal-fired power plants. It is used to increase concrete strength, decrease permeability, reduce temperature rise during placement, increase sulfate resistance, and improve the workability of concrete. It can be used to reduce the total amount of cement needed. In high-volume fly ash concrete, between 40% and 50%, and sometimes as much as 65% of the portland cement can be replaced by fly ash. Recycled aggregate can be used in some applications when its strength is sufficient for the purpose. Using lightweight aggregates such as pumice or perlite can lessen the need for standard aggregates, reduce the structural load, and improve insulation values. Finally, using steel forms or permanent rigid plastic foam forms can reduce the waste associated with standard wood forms. Rigid plastic foam forms have the additional advantage of improving the thermal resistance of foundation walls.

Autoclaved aerated concrete (AAC) is a lightweight, precast concrete made with aluminum powder as an extra ingredient, hardened in molds, and cured in an autoclave. It is formed into blocks, typically 10 in by 25 in (250 by 635) in thicknesses of 4 in, 8 in, or 10 in (100, 200, or 250). It can easily be cut and shaped with normal woodworking tools. ACC is used for non-load-bearing residential and light commercial walls. It provides excellent insulation value, reduced air infiltration, and improved acoustic qualities. ACC also requires less cement than does standard concrete.

Masonry

As with concrete, masonry (either concrete or clay based) and mortar require large amounts of energy and raw materials in their production. However, brick is a natural material and is generally manufactured close to the place of use and from locally quarried clay, reducing transportation costs. It is also a durable material with a long life. Like concrete, masonry produces no pollution or emissions once in place and provides excellent thermal mass. It can be recycled and, when placed in landfills, produces no toxic substances. Environmental impacts can be minimized by using fly ash, recycled aggregates (such as ground granulated blast furnace slag) and lightweight aggregates.

Metals

Although metals require large amounts of embodied energy for their production, they have a high potential for recycling. Steel is the most common metal used in buildings and is often recycled as scrap to produce more steel. Steel with a recycled content up to 30% or more is readily available. Aluminum is also widely used and is available with a recycled content of 20% or more. Copper has great value as a recycled material, and brass, bronze, and stainless steel can also be recycled, if separated.

Problems can arise with some metals that are plated or coated with chemicals. Electroplating processes produce high levels of pollution and by-products. Alternatives to these processes include powder coatings and plastic polymer coatings. Whatever finish is applied, it should be readily removable to facilitate recycling.

Wood and Plastic

Lumber and wood products represent a large portion of both residential and commercial construction, from rough framing to furniture. This includes both softwoods and hardwoods from domestic and foreign sources. Deforestation, processing, and the manufacture of wood products represent a large ecological problem, but architects can minimize this by applying three sustainable strategies. These include using reclaimed wood, specifying sustainable or alternate materials, and using certified wood products.

Reclaimed wood is basically recycled wood from old buildings or structures that has been salvaged and prepared for a new use. Preparation may include removing nails and other fasteners, drying, and cutting or planing. In addition to being ecologically sound, reclaimed wood members have a unique visual character than many architects and clients find desirable.

Sustainable materials (or *alternate materials*) include a wide range of products. Standard solid-wood framing products can be replaced with engineered wood products such as wood I-joists, laminated veneer lumber, and structural insulated panels (SIPs). These products are discussed in Ch. 16. Panel products that use waste material, such as particleboard and medium-density fiberboard, are good sustainable products but often require adhesives and resins that outgas formaldehyde or other pollutants. These panels are typically made from urea formaldehyde. However, formaldehyde-free MDF or low-emission panels that use phenol-formaldehyde or urethane adhesives are available. These have a formaldehyde level of 0.04 ppm (parts per million) or less, which is below the commonly accepted level of 0.05 ppm. Another alternative to urea formaldehyde is methylene-diphenyl isocyanate (MDI). This resin does not emit toxic gases during use and requires less dryer energy and lower press temperatures than do traditional binders.

Other innovative products can be used in some instances to replace rough lumber. Straw particleboard, for example, is made from wheat straw, a waste product from farming. The straw is milled into fine particles and hot pressed together with formaldehyde-free resins. It can be used for both construction and furniture making. Other agricultural products used are rice straw and bagasse, the residue from the processing of sugar cane. Some products also use post-consumer recycled waste paper for making building panels.

A building can receive a LEED credit for using low-emitting materials such as wood and agrifiber products that contain no added urea-formaldehyde resins.

For finish carpentry and architectural woodwork many alternate products exist. Molding can be made from medium-density fiberboard or molded high-density polyurethane foam. Composite wood veneers are manufactured from readily available and fast-growing trees by slicing veneers, dying them, and gluing them back into an artificial "log." The manufactured log is then sliced. By varying the dye colors and how the artificial log is cut, a wide variety of veneers is possible, from those that look like standard wood to highly figured and colored products.

Certified wood products are those that use wood obtained through sustainable forest management practices. While there are many forest certification groups in North America, the most well known is the Forest Stewardship Council (FSC). This organization is an international body that oversees the development of national and regional standards based on basic forest management principles and criteria. It accredits certifying organizations that comply with its principles. The three groups the FSC accredits in the United States are the SmartWood Program of the Rainforest Alliance, the Forest Conservation Program of Scientific Certification Systems (SCS), and SGS Systems and Services Certification, Inc.

The FSC has 10 basic principles and 56 individual criteria it uses to evaluate organizations for accreditation. It has also established additional regional criteria for different parts of the United States. The 10 principles are as follows.

- Forest management must respect all applicable laws of the country in which they occur and must comply with FSC Principles and Criteria.
- Long-term tenure and use rights to the land and forests must be defined, documented, and legally established.
- The rights of indigenous peoples to own, use, and manage their land must be recognized and respected.
- Forest management practices and operations must maintain or enhance the long-term social and economic well-being of workers and local communities.
- Forest management must encourage the efficient use of the forest's products to ensure economic viability and environmental and social benefits.
- Forest management must conserve biological diversity, water resources, soils, ecosystems, and landscapes to maintain the ecological functions of the forest.
- A management plan must be written, implemented, and maintained.
- Monitoring must be conducted to assess the condition of the forest, yields, chain of custody, and management activities and their social and environmental impacts.
- Management activities in high-conservation-value forests must maintain or enhance the attributes that define such forests.
- Plantations must follow the first nine principles and the criteria that apply to plantations. Plantations should complement the management of, reduce pressures on, and promote the restoration and conservation of natural forests.

A building can receive a LEED credit for using at least 50% wood-based materials and products, certified in accordance with the FSC's Principles and Criteria. However, even though only a very small fraction of forests comply with FSC criteria, there are many other well-managed forests in North American and elsewhere.

Plastics identified as recyclable should be reserved and recycled. If possible, compostable plastics should be separated and identified as such. Recycled plastics have many uses. Polyethylene terephthalate (PET) from soft drink containers, for example, can be used to manufacture carpet with properties similar to polyesters.

Plastic lumber is being used for decking, fencing, and other outdoor applications. This material may be either all plastic (a mixture of recycled plastic and pure high-density polyethylene (HDPE)), or a wood-plastic composite that is a mixture of recycled plastic resin (usually polyethylene) combined with wood fiber, which can be also be recycled material.

In addition to providing a use for post-consumer and post-industrial materials, plastic lumber is also an alternative to using chromated copper arsenate (CCA) pressure-treated wood, which can pose an environmental risk during disposal. Plastic lumber is durable, will not rot, absorb water, or crack, and can be worked with standard woodworking saws and carbide blades. However, it is not suitable for load-bearing applications. Some wood-plastic composite lumber, on the other hand, has been graded for structural use.

Two new developments in plastic may improve the sustainability of this material type. The first is *bio-plastics*, specifically *polylactide* (PLA). This is a plastic derived from harvested corn that is biodegradable. It is currently used in fibers for carpet manufacture. The second is the development of *metallocene polyolefins*. This type of plastic allows polyolefins to be precisely manufactured to have specific properties. These may be a replacement for PVC and other plastics that are more harmful to the environment. They may be used for window frames, membrane roofing, siding, and wire sheathing.

Thermal Insulation and Moisture Protection

Materials for insulation and moisture protection are some of the most important for energy efficiency and the control of mold and other water-related problems. Very efficient plastic-based insulations with high thermal resistance are available, but these may cause problems with manufacturing (use of petroleum products and pollution), use (outgassing), and disposal. Because chlorofluorocarbons (CFCs) and hydrochlorofluorocarbons (HCFCs) have been phased out and replaced with other agents, the problem with ozone depletion has been reduced. Note than when CFCs were banned they were replaced with HCFCs, but these were phased out by the EPA in January of 2003.

Other types of insulation that are resource efficient and pose little danger for indoor air quality include the following. The conductivity of each is given in Table 41.1.

- *Cellulose insulation* containing at least 70% post-consumer paper waste is available in loose-fill form. More commonly, cellulose insulation is made from 80% to 100% recycled paper combined with a fire-retardant additive. It also has a low embodied energy.
- *Compressed straw* can be used as infill in structural insulated panels.
- *Cotton insulation* is made from pre-consumer recycled cotton denim scrap material with a small amount of polyester for binding and stability. It also has a low embodied energy.
- *Glass fiber insulation* containing at least 30% post-consumer recycled glass is available in rigid boards, batts, and loose-fill form.
- *Mineral-fiber insulation*, which is made from steel mill slag or basalt rock, is available in rigid boards, batts, and loose-fill form. Most manufacturers use from 50% to 95% recycled material with 75% post-industrial content being about average.
- *Perlite*, which is made from volcanic rock expanded by heat, is used as a lightweight aggregate for plaster and concrete and as loose-fill insulation.
- *Spray-on cellulose* is manufactured as loose-fill insulation with about the same recycled content. The EPA recommends that spray-on cellulose insulation contain at least 75% post-consumer recovered paper.
- *Vermiculite*, which is made from mica expanded by heat, is used for loose-fill applications. See the section on hazardous material mitigation later in this chapter for information on asbestos-containing vermiculite.

Refer to Ch. 41 for more information on insulation types.

Doors and Windows

Windows provide one of the best resources for sustainable design when they are used for daylighting, solar heat gain, and ventilation while maintaining good insulation qualities. New glazing products provide a variety of options to suit the individual needs of each building. In addition to controlling solar heat gain, glazing can have very high *R*-values.

In using any type of glazing, special consideration should also be given to the framing. If aluminum or steel is used, there should be a thermal break between the inside and outside surfaces. The energy efficiency of windows, doors, and skylights should be certified by an independent laboratory according to the standards of the National Fenestration Rating Council (NFRC) for *U*-factor (*U*-value), solar heat gain coefficient (SHGC), and visible light transmittance (VLT) coefficients. Windows may be certified with the Green Seal label if they meet the criteria given in Green Seal's Standard GS-13.

Refer to Ch. 42 for more information on windows and glazing products.

Finishes

Interior finish materials provide a primary method of improving a building's sustainability because they are one of the main sources of potential indoor air pollution and they are typically replaced several times over the life of a building. Finish types are grouped according to the categories of adhesives, flooring, wall finishes, and ceiling finishes. The following sections give some of the more traditional finish materials as well as some alternative sustainable materials that are being used more frequently for both residential and commercial construction.

Adhesives

With many types of finishes, the potential problem is due to adhesives or coatings and not the finish material itself. Most adhesives emit gases because they contain plastic resins and other materials that can outgas. Three types of low-emission and zero-VOC adhesives can be used for installing carpet, resilient flooring, plastic laminates, sheet metal, wood veneers, and some types of wall coverings: dry adhesives that contain resins stored in capsules released by pressure, water-based adhesives containing latex or polyvinyl acetate, and natural adhesives containing plant resins in a water dispersion system. A building can receive a LEED credit for using adhesives and sealants with a VOC content less than that defined in the California South Coast Air Quality Management District (SCAQMD) Rule 1168, which is among the lowest VOC content standards in the country.

Flooring

When using carpet, there are three major considerations for sustainability: raw-material use, raw-material disposal, and indoor air quality. Good raw materials include polyester and nylon-blended carpet made from recycled soft drink containers (PET) or wool. Although wool has a higher initial cost, it is a renewable resource, wears well, and may have a lower life-cycle cost when compared to less expensive carpet that typically needs to be replaced more frequently. Carpet cushions made from recycled materials, such as tire rubber or synthetic and natural fiber from textile mill waste, should also be selected.

Disposal of carpet is a problem because of the total quantity that is placed in landfills, the fact that it does not decompose easily, the difficulty of separating the various components for recycling, and the costs of recycling compared with landfill disposal. Nylon 6, one type of nylon fiber, can be recycled easily. Although some manufacturers have made efforts to recycle used carpet, the amount is just a fraction of the total amount of carpet disposed. Generally, carpet tiles are more sustainable than broadloom carpet. This is because only a small number need to be replaced when they are damaged or worn, the adhesives used to apply them tend to offgas less than do broadloom adhesives, and several manufactures have programs to recycle the tiles.

Carpet can affect indoor air quality because of its construction and the adhesives used in direct-glue applications. Most carpet is made by bonding the face fiber to a backing with a synthetic latex resin. The latex can be replaced with fusion bonding, in which the face fiber is heat-welded to a sponge plastic backing. Carpets made with a needlepunching process also avoid the use of latex bonding. The Carpet and Rug Institute (CRI) has a voluntary testing program under which manufacturers have their carpet tested by an independent agency for four emissions: total volatile organic compounds, styrene, formaldehyde, and 4-phenylcyclohexene (4-PC). Carpet that passes the test criteria is allowed to carry the CRI IAQ carpet testing program label, or the "Green Label." The CRI also recommends that the ventilation system be operated at maximum capacity during and after installation for 48 to 72 hours. A building can receive a LEED credit for using carpet systems that meet or exceed the requirements of the CRI IAQ carpet testing program.

Vinyl flooring provides many benefits, including durability, easy cleaning, a wide choice of patterns and colors, and relatively low cost. However, it requires highly refined petrochemicals for its manufacture and contains a large percentage of polyvinyl chloride (PVC) that can cause environmental problems during manufacture and disposal. Because of the high concentration of chlorine in the tile, hazardous substances can be given off if vinyl flooring is incinerated. Some vinyl tile is manufactured from recycled PVC, and one brand is made without chlorine. As with carpet, low-VOC adhesives should be specified for laying vinyl flooring.

Rubber flooring, both tile and sheet goods, made from recycled tires is available. This flooring is durable, slip-resistant, and resilient. However, because of the methods of manufacture and the binders that are used, recycled rubber flooring may give off indoor pollutants. This type of flooring should only be used where there is adequate ventilation, such as in outdoor sports areas, locker rooms, and other utility spaces.

Linoleum is available in tile or sheet form and can also be used for baseboards. Linoleum is made from natural, renewable products, including linseed oil, rosin, cork powder, and pigments. It is a durable floor material and is biodegradable, waterproof, fire resistant, naturally antibacterial, and does not generate static electricity. When used with low-VOC adhesives it emits only low levels of contaminants, less than those of vinyl flooring.

Cork flooring is made from a renewable resource, the bark of cork oak trees, which regenerates every nine to ten years. Cork forests are well managed and protected by the countries that have them. The only disadvantage to using cork as a natural material is that it must be imported from Mediterranean countries, increasing the transportation energy required. Although cork requires binders to hold the individual pieces together, the binders used today are phenol-formaldehyde, polyurethane, or all-natural protein products. Cork flooring using urea-formaldehyde should not be used. Cork can be finished with water-based urethanes with very low VOCs that provide durability along with water and chemical resistance. It should be installed with a water-based, low-VOC latex adhesive. Cork flooring is also an excellent absorber of sound.

Wood flooring offers many options for sustainable use. First, wood originating from well-managed forests can be selected. Both domestic and tropical hardwood is available from sustainable, FSC-accredited, certified sources. Second, veneered and laminated products using a plywood or MDF core can be used. Finally, salvaged solid-wood flooring is available. Whenever possible, prefinished flooring should be used to eliminate the need for sanding and finishing on the job site, which could create indoor air quality problems. If adhesives are required they should be low-VOC content types. On-site finishing should only use water-dispersed urethanes. Varnishes, acid-cured varnishes, or hardening oils for on-site finishing should be avoided.

As an alternate to standard wood floors, bamboo or palm wood can be used. Bamboo is a fast-growing grass that reaches maturity in three to four years. It is almost as hard and twice as stable as red oak or maple and is sold in tongue-and-groove strips prefinished with a durable polyurethane coating. Palm wood is harvested as a byproduct of commercial coconut plantations. It is harder than maple or oak and is also sold in tongue-and-groove strips and prefinished with polyurethane.

Ceramic tile is generally considered a sustainable material in spite of the high embodied energy required to produce it and the transportation costs to get it from the factory to the job site. It uses readily available natural materials, is very durable, produces practically no harmful emissions, and requires very little maintenance. Some tile is made from post-consumer or post-industrial waste products using from 25% to 100% recycled material. Cement mortars and grouts are also environmentally friendly and produce very few emissions. Avoid epoxy-modified grout, plastic adhesives with solvents, and sealers that contain VOCs.

Wall Finishes

Gypsum wallboard is manufactured with 100% recycled content for its paper faces and with some recycled content for the core. Some manufacturers mix recycled newspaper with gypsum as the core material. In addition, about 7% of the industry's total use of gypsum is synthetic gypsum. Synthetic gypsum is chemically identical to natural, mined gypsum but is a by-product of various manufacturing, industrial, or chemical processes. The main source of synthetic gypsum in North America is *flue-gas desulfurization*. This is the process whereby power-generating plants (and similar plants) remove polluting gases from their stacks to reduce emission of harmful materials into the atmosphere. Synthetic gypsum represents an efficient application for refuse material. By itself, gypsum wallboard does not contribute in any significant way to indoor air pollution. However, adhesives, paints, and caulking can be pollution sources and should be specified carefully.

Disposal of gypsum wallboard is problematic because wallboard taken out of an old building cannot be reused. Some gypsum wallboard plants are recycling old wallboard. However, the wallboard must be separated from other materials and be free of screws, nails, and lead paint, and the cost of collecting and transporting the old wallboard is a disincentive for recycling. If the wallboard can be recycled, it is pulverized and can be worked into the ground as a soil additive.

Sisal wall covering is a natural material made from the fiber of the henequen plant. The branches are harvested and the fiber extracted, dyed, and spun into yarn. Although fairly rough and not suitable for wet areas, sisal wall covering (and floor covering) is durable, low maintenance, and reduces sound reflection and transmission. It should be applied with a zero-VOC adhesive and detailed to allow slight expansion and contraction with absorption and release of humidity.

Paints and other coatings require careful consideration in their selection and use. Although federal, state, and local regulations have eliminated coatings containing dangerous components such as lead and cadmium and have limited the use of volatile organic compounds, some commercial coatings may still contain them. Generally, paint sold now must conform to VOC limits set by the Environmental Protection Agency (EPA) as required by the Clean Air Act. The limits are set in the National Volatile Organic Compound Emission Standards for Architectural Coatings, 40 CFR Part 59. Many types of coatings are listed in the standard. For example, the VOC content of flat interior paint cannot exceed 250 g/L (2.1 lbm/gal), while non-flat interior paint cannot exceed 380 g/L (3.2 lbm/gal). (Enforcement of the rule is based on SI units.) California has stricter standards, limiting paint to 100 g/L (0.84 lbm/gal) for flat paint and 150 g/L (1.3 lbm/gal) for non-flat coatings. In the future these limits in California will be reduced even further.

A building can receive a LEED credit for using interior paints and coatings that comply with the VOC and chemical component limits of the Green Seal Standard GS-11. However, these standards are stricter for flat paint than are the EPA standards. Green Seal standards state that flat interior paint cannot exceed 50 g/L (0.42 lbm/gal).

Ceilings

Acoustical ceiling tile that uses recycled content of old tiles, newsprint, or perlite is available. Other materials, such as clay and wood fibers, may also be used. Fiberglass ceiling panels are also available with recycled content. Recycled content varies but can be up to 95%, depending on the manufacturer and the product type. Old tile can be repainted if the correct type of paint and procedures are used. One manufacturer offers a recycling program that allows customers to ship old tile to their plant if the manufacturers' own tile is to be used as a replacement. The cost to recycle is typically less than the cost of sending the material to a landfill. The grid itself can be recycled as scrap steel.

However, tile may shed fiber if it is damaged or as it ages. This fiber can be collected by the HVAC system if the plenum is used as a return air space. Using separate ducts for return air or regular cleaning of the plenum with vacuums can alleviate some of the problem.

Furnishings

In addition to other sustainability issues, furnishings can be a significant source of formaldehyde in residential and commercial settings because of the particleboard, MDF, and coatings used in their construction. The following strategies can be used to improve sustainability through the selection and specification of furnishings.

- Use refurbished or reused office furniture.
- Consider using furniture made from steel, solid wood, and glass, which are all materials that can readily be recycled.
- Specify that furnishings can be fabricated with wood certified under standards established by the Forest Stewardship Council (FSC) or with reclaimed wood.
- Require that furnishings be fabricated with formaldehyde-free medium-density fiberboard or strawboard.
- Use furniture with cushions, workstation panels, and fabrics made with recycled PET (polyethylene terephthalate) from soda bottles.
- Look for fabrics with biodegradable and nontoxic dyes.
- Use finish coverings for furniture made of cotton, wool, ramie, blends, or other natural materials. Use chemical-free organic cotton fabrics.
- Use low-VOC finishes.
- Use powder coatings for finishes instead of standard paint.
- Require that cushions be foamed with CO_2-injected foam or other environmentally friendly materials.

INDOOR AIR QUALITY

Maintaining health is an important aspect of sustainable design, and one of the basic requirements of health is good indoor air quality (IAQ). In addition to simply maintaining health, the quality of indoor air affects a person's sense of well-being and can affect absenteeism, productivity, creativity, and motivation. Indoor air quality is a complex subject because there are hundreds of different contaminants, dozens of causes of poor IAQ, many possible symptoms building occupants may experience, and a wide variety of potential strategies for maintaining good IAQ. This section outlines some of the more important areas of knowledge with which you should be familiar. Because IAQ has become such an important topic in building design, there is no shortage of laws and standards devoted to regulating indoor air quality. Some of these are given at the end of this section.

Indoor Air Contaminants

Indoor air contaminants can be broadly classified into two groups: chemical contaminants and biological contaminants. Chemical contaminants include things such as volatile organic compounds, inorganic chemicals, tobacco smoke, and dozens of others, while biological contaminants include mold, pollen, bacteria, and viruses.

Volatile organic compounds (VOCs) are chemicals that contain carbon and hydrogen and that vaporize at room temperature and pressure. They are found in many indoor sources, including building materials and common household products. Common sources of VOCs in building materials include paint, stains, adhesives, sealants, water repellents and sealers, particleboard, furniture, upholstery, and carpeting. Other sources include copy machines, cleaning agents, and pesticides.

The Environmental Protection Agency has established regulations for VOCs in coatings. The final regulation on volatile organic compounds (VOCs) in architectural, industrial, and maintenance coatings was issued on September 13, 1998. This regulation listed the maximum content of VOCs in the various types of coatings. The maximum VOC levels of some common coatings were listed in the previous section. However, state laws also regulate VOCs, and each state may permit a different level. For example, the California South Coast Air Quality Management District has very strict limits on the volatile organic content of paints.

Formaldehyde is a colorless gas with a pungent odor. It is used in the preparation of resins and adhesives most commonly found in particleboard, wall paneling, furniture, carpet adhesives, and other glues used in the construction and furnishings industry. Formaldehyde is designated as a probable human carcinogen and causes irritant effects of the eyes and respiratory tract.

The maximum suggested or allowable exposure rates vary depending on the agency. ASHRAE recommends a maximum continuous indoor air concentration of 0.1 parts per million (ppm). OSHA specifies concentrations not to exceed 0.75 ppm in an 8-hour time period with a 2 ppm 15-minute short-term exposure. In order to qualify as Greenguard certified, a product cannot emit more than 0.05 ppm.

The problems associated with formaldehyde can most easily be solved by minimizing the source, using two or three coats of sealants, or airing out the building before occupancy.

There are potentially hundreds of organic and inorganic chemicals that may be harmful to humans. The California Office of Environmental Health Hazard Assessment has a list of 76 chemicals (at the time of this writing) that the state regulates along with the chronic inhalation reference exposure level (REL) for each, in micrograms per cubic meter (μg/m^3). These were developed as a result of California's Proposition 65, which was passed in 1986. Proposition 65 required businesses to provide a clear and reasonable warning before knowingly and intentionally exposing anyone to a listed chemical.

The Greenguard Environmental Institute also produces a list of products, chemicals in those products, and allowable maximum emission levels. Some of the common chemicals include VOCs, formaldehyde, aldehydes, 4-phenylcyclohexene, and styrene, as well as particulates and biological contaminates. In order to be certified by Greenguard, a product must meet these standards after being tested according to ASTM D5116 and D6670, the State of Washington's protocol for interior furnishings and construction materials, and the EPA's testing protocol for furniture.

Tobacco Smoke

Secondhand smoke, also called environmental tobacco smoke (ETS), is a mixture of the smoke given off by the burning end of a cigarette, pipe, or cigar and the smoke exhaled from the lungs of smokers. Secondhand smoke has been found to contain over 4000 substances, more than 40 of which are known to cause cancer in humans and many of which are strong irritants. The EPA and the California EPA have found that exposure to secondhand smoke causes increased risk for cancer and other serious health effects. In order to improve indoor air quality, smoking should either be banned completely from buildings and near entrances, or isolated smoking rooms should be constructed that have a separate ventilation system that vents directly to the outside.

Biological Contaminants

Potential biological contaminants in a building include the common problem of mold and mildew in addition to bacteria, viruses, mites, pollen, animal dander, dust, and insects. Even protein in urine from rats and mice is an allergen.

Molds and mildew are microscopic organisms, a type of fungi, that produce enzymes to digest organic matter. Their reproductive spores are present nearly everywhere. When exposed to the spores, people sensitive to molds and mildew may experience eye irritation, skin rash, running nose, nausea, headaches, and similar symptoms.

Mold spores require three conditions to grow: moisture, a nutrient, and a temperature range from 40°F to 100°F (4°C to 38°C). Nutrients are simply organic materials—which can include wood, carpet, the paper coating of gypsum wallboard, paint, wallpaper, insulation, and ceiling tile, among others—that serve as a nourishing food source for organisms. Because nutrients and a suitable temperature are always present in buildings, the only way to prevent and control mold is to prevent and control moisture in places where mold growth should be prevented.

Causes of Poor Indoor Air Quality

There are four basic causes of poor indoor air quality. These include chemical contaminants from indoor sources, chemical contaminants from outdoor sources, biological contaminants, and poor ventilation. These factors may be present alone or combined with one or more of the others to produce the various symptoms of poor indoor air quality.

One of the most common sources of poor indoor air quality is chemical contaminants from indoor sources. These sources include all of the contaminants previously mentioned—VOCs, environmental tobacco smoke, respirable particles, carbon monoxide, and nitrogen dioxide, and so on. Lists of harmful chemicals can be found at one of the following sources.

- *Hazardous Chemicals Desk Reference*, Richard J. Lewis. New York: Van Nostrand Reinhold.
- National Toxicology Program. (Lists chemicals known to be carcinogenic.)
- International Agency for Research of Cancer (IARC). (Classifies chemicals that are known to be carcinogenic.)
- Chronic Reference Exposure Levels. California Office of Environmental Health Hazard Assessment. (Lists hazardous chemicals recognized by this office, with links to more information about each chemical.)
- California Health and Welfare Agency, Safe Drinking Water and Toxic Enforcement Act of 1986 (Proposition 65). (Lists chemicals known to cause cancer and reproductive toxicity.)
- California Air Toxics. California Environmental Protection Agency, Air Resources Board (ARB).

Chemical contaminants from outdoor sources are introduced to a building when air intake vents, windows, or doors from parking garages are improperly located, allowing pollutants from the outside (carbon monoxide, for example) to be drawn into the building. Indoor pollutants from exhausts and plumbing vents can also be sucked back into the building through improperly located air intakes.

Biological contaminants such as mold, bacteria, and viruses may develop from moisture infiltration, standing water, stagnant water in mechanical equipment, and even from insects or bird droppings that find their way into the building. These were discussed in the previous section.

Poor ventilation allows indoor pollutants to accumulate to unpleasant or even unhealthy levels and affects the general sense of well-being of building occupants. One of the most difficult aspects of providing proper ventilation is balancing the requirement for energy conservation. However, this problem can be solved by using heat exchangers and other methods described in Ch. 28. Some of the minimum levels of ventilation are given the following section on strategies for maintaining good IAQ.

Symptoms of Poor Indoor Air Quality

There are many symptoms of poor indoor air quality, from temporary, minor irritations to serious, life-threatening illnesses. They are generally grouped into three classifications: sick building syndrome, building-related illnesses, and multiple chemical sensitivities. Problems with asbestos, lead, and radon are serious, long-term problems and are generally not grouped with these three classifications.

Sick building syndrome (SBS) describes a condition in which building occupants experience a variety of health-related symptoms that cannot be directly linked to any particular cause. Generally, symptoms disappear after the occupants leave the building. Symptoms may include irritation of the eyes, nose, and throat; dry mucous membranes and skin; erythema (redness of the skin); mental fatigue and headache; respiratory infections and cough; hoarseness of voice and wheezing; hypersensitivity reactions; and nausea and dizziness.

Building-related illness (BRI) describes a condition in which the health-related symptom or symptoms of a building's occupants are identified and can be directly attributed to certain building contaminants. In the case of BRI, the symptoms do not immediately improve when the occupant leaves the building. Legionnaires' disease is an example of BRI.

Multiple chemical sensitivity (MCS) is a condition brought on by exposure to volatile organic compounds (VOCs) or other chemicals. People with MCS may develop acute, long-term sensitivity that shows symptoms each time they are exposed to the chemicals. These sensitivities can remain with some people for the rest of their lives. In many cases only a slight exposure to the chemical can be enough to produce symptoms.

Strategies for Maintaining Good Indoor Air Quality

Methods of maintaining good indoor air quality that the architect can use or suggest to the building owner can be classified into five broad categories: eliminate or reduce the sources of pollution, control the ventilation of the building, establish good maintenance procedures, control occupant activity as it affects IAQ, and provide appropriate filtration.

Eliminate or Reduce Sources of Pollution

- Establish the owner's criteria for indoor air quality early in the project. This may be part of the programming process and should include the budget available.
- Select and specify building materials and furnishings with low emissions and VOCs. The standards listed in the next section provide guidance on choosing materials. Because it is not always possible to eliminate all sources of pollutants, set priorities by identifying materials that are the most volatile and that represent large quantities.
- Specify materials that are resistant to the growth of mold and mildew, especially in areas that may become wet or damp.
- Request emissions test data from manufacturers. This can be the material safety data sheets (MSDSs) from the manufacturer, or other data provided by the manufacturer. However, OSHA regulations require all manufacturers to develop and supply MSDSs for their products if they contain chemicals.
- Design the building envelope to properly control moisture.
- Prior to occupancy, the HVAC system in a new building or occupied space should be operated at full capacity for two weeks to reduce the emissions due to outgassing chemicals and moisture.

Control Ventilation

- During the programming phase, determine the owners' and occupants' requirements for ventilation. Also determine the energy conservation code requirements.
- Provide the minimum outdoor air ventilation as recommended by the American Society of Heating, Refrigerating and Air-Conditioning Engineers for the specific activity of the building or individual space. These minimums, as given in ASHRAE Standard 62, range from 15 cfm/person to 60 cfm/person (8 L/s/person to 30 L/s/person). The absolute minimum now recommended is 15 cfm/person (8 L/s/person). 20 cfm/person (10 L/s/person) is recommended for office spaces. The high range of 60 cfm/person (30 L/s/person) is used for smoking lounges.
- Locate fresh-air intakes away from loading docks, bus stops, or parking garages where carbon monoxide, carbon dioxide, nitrous-oxides, and odors can be drawn into the building.

- Avoid fresh-air vents near landscaped areas where irrigation moisture could be drawn into the building.
- Provide separate rooms and ventilation for equipment that emits high concentrations of pollutants. In an office, a high-volume copier might require a separate room. Health clubs, laboratories, and kitchens are other common locations for such equipment.
- When thermal insulation is required, place it on the outside of ductwork. Use acoustical insulation that is encapsulated for the inside of ducts.
- Design the HVAC system with local controls so building maintenance personnel can correct heating, cooling, and ventilating problems.
- Specify independent building commissioning and testing, adjusting, and balancing (TAB) of the HVAC system.

Establish Good Maintenance Procedures

Once a building is completed it is important that it be properly maintained. Of course, the architect has little control over this aspect of indoor air quality, but through the proper selection of materials, development of maintenance manuals, and establishment of operating guidelines, the architect, mechanical engineer, interior designer, and other design professionals can provide the building owner with the basis for proper maintenance.

- Select and specify building materials and finishes that are easy to clean and maintain.
- In the specifications, include requirements for warranties and maintenance contracts.
- Suggest that the building owner conduct post-occupancy evaluations at regular intervals to review procedures for maintaining good IAQ.
- In the specifications, require that the contractor assemble an operation and maintenance manual from the various suppliers of HVAC and electrical equipment giving performance criteria, operation requirements, cleaning instructions, and maintenance procedures.
- In the maintenance manual, include materials and procedures for regular cleaning of specified products, including furnishings. These should be low-emission products recommended by the manufacturer of each product or finish.

Control Occupant Activity

As with maintenance procedures, the architect has little control over occupant activity once the building is completed. However, the architect can suggest to the building owner methods of controlling occupant activity as it affects IAQ. The architect can also add long-term occupancy IAQ suggestions to the operation and maintenance manual.

- Suggest a no smoking policy for the building.
- Suggest that the building owner or manager monitor individual space use to determine if major changes to occupant load, activities, or equipment occur. The building HVAC system may need to be adjusted accordingly.
- Install sensors for carbon dioxide (CO_2), carbon monoxide (CO), VOCs, and other products, which are connected to the building management system.

Provide Appropriate Filtration

Filtration is an effective way to keep indoor air free of particle air pollutants. The selection of filtering methods should be based on the needs of the type of occupancy. There are three basic types of filters that can be incorporated into an HVAC system.

- *Particulate filters* remove larger particles, such as dust and lint, from the air and trap them in the filter. Particulate filters must be cleaned or replaced frequently. *Panel filters* trap only the largest particles, while *media filters* use a finer filter paper. The most efficient filter is the *high-efficiency particulate arrestance* (HEPA) filter. Particulate filters, except HEPA filters, are commonly located in front of the HVAC equipment to clean the air before it enters the unit.
- *Adsorption filters* are used to remove unwanted gases from the air and make use of various chemicals as needed for the type of gas being filtered. A common type of adsorption filter is the activated-charcoal filter. As with particulate filters, adsorption filters must be replaced or regenerated to remain effective. Adsorption filters are typically located downstream from the HVAC unit to trap microbiological contaminants.
- *Electronic filters* trap particles by creating different electrostatic charges between the particles and the filter.

Indoor Air Quality Standards

The last few decades have seen the development of many laws, regulations, and standards enacted at the federal, state, and local level that attempt to control and improve indoor air quality. The Occupational Safety and Health

Administration (OSHA) has also proposed rules for IAQ. Some of the more important laws and regulations with which architects should be familiar are listed here.

For a listing of additional regulations and industry standards related to sustainability, refer to the section later in this chapter.

- Clean Air Act (CAA) of 1970. This law regulates air emissions from area, stationary, and mobile sources. The law authorized the EPA to establish the National Ambient Air Quality Standards to protect public health and the environment. It has been amended several times since 1970 to extend deadlines for compliance and add other provisions.
- National Ambient Air Quality Standard. U.S. Environmental Protection Agency, 40 CFR 50. This standard implements part of the Clean Air Act.
- ASHRAE Standard 62.1, *Ventilation for Acceptable Indoor Air Quality*. This is an industry standard and, as such, compliance with it is voluntary. However, most building codes incorporate all or a part of this standard by reference, thereby giving it the force of law. In addition to setting minimum outdoor air requirements for ventilation, the standard includes provisions for managing sources of contamination, controlling indoor humidity, and filtering building air, as well as requirements for HVAC system construction and startup, and operation and maintenance of systems.
- ASHRAE Standard 62.2, *Ventilation and Acceptable Indoor Air Quality in Low-Rise Residential Buildings*. This is also a voluntary industry standard. The standard applies to single-family houses and multifamily buildings of three stories or less, including manufactured and modular houses. It defines the roles of and minimum requirements for mechanical and natural ventilation systems as well as the building envelope.
- National VOC Emission Standards for Architectural Coatings (40 CFR Part 59). This rule implements part of the Clean Air Act and sets limits on the amount of volatile organic compounds that manufacturers and importers of architectural coatings can put into their products.
- South Coast Air Quality Management District (SCAQMD) Rule 1113, Architectural Coatings. This rule limits the VOC content of architectural coatings used in the South Coast Air Quality Management District in California. The limits it sets are more restrictive than the national VOC emission standard published by the EPA. Rule 1168 limits the VOC content of adhesives and sealants.
- California Safe Drinking Water and Toxic Enforcement Act of 1986 (Proposition 65). This law prohibits businesses from discharging chemicals that cause cancer or reproductive toxicity into sources of drinking water and requires that warning be given to individuals exposed to such chemicals. The California Environmental Protection Agency's Office of Environmental Health Hazard Assessment (OEHHA) is the lead agency for the implementation of Proposition 65.
- Greenguard Environmental Institute. The Greenguard Environmental Institute (described later in this chapter) tests products following ASTM Standards D5116 and D6670, the EPA's testing protocol for furniture, and the State of Washington's protocol for interior furnishings and construction materials. Greenguard has a list of the emission levels that products must meet before they are certified by the organization.
- *Threshold Limit Values* and *Biological Exposure Indices*. American Conference of Governmental Industrial Hygienists (ACGIH). This document gives exposure limits for chemicals in the workplace called threshold limit values (TLV).
- ASTM D5116, *Standard Guide for Small-Scale Environmental Chamber Determinations of Organic Emissions from Indoor Materials/Products*. This guide describes the equipment and techniques suitable for determining organic emissions from small samples of indoor materials. It cannot be used for testing complete assemblages or coatings. Another standard, ASTM D6803, is used for testing paint using small environmental chambers.
- ASTM D6670, *Standard Practice for Full-Scale Chamber Determination of Volatile Organic Emissions from Indoor Materials/Products*. This practice details the method to be used to determine the VOC emissions from building materials, furniture, consumer products, and equipment under environmental and product usage conditions that are typical of those found in office and residential buildings. It is referenced by other standards or laws as a standard way to determine the level of VOC emissions.
- ASTM E1333, *Standard Test Method for Determining Formaldehyde Concentrations in Air and Emission Rates from Wood Products Using a Large Chamber*. This test method measures the formaldehyde concentration in air and the emission rate from wood products in a large chamber under conditions designed to simulate product use.

RECYCLING AND REUSE

Recycling and reuse of materials and products is an important part of the total life cycle of a building. As many materials as possible should be recycled into other products or reused for their original purpose. In turn, new buildings should incorporate as many recycled and reused materials as possible to provide a market for those products. Ideally, all materials should be durable, biodegradable, or recyclable.

Adaptive Reuse

Adaptive reuse begins with reusing as much of the existing building stock as possible instead of constructing new buildings. Buildings can be either updated to conform to their original use or adapted to a new use. Turning an old warehouse into residences is a common example of adaptive reuse. A project can receive LEED credit for maintaining at least 75% of the existing building structure and shell, excluding window assemblies and nonstructural roofing material. Additional credit is also given for using at least 50% of the non-shell areas such as walls, doors, floor coverings, and ceiling systems.

On a smaller scale, individual products can be reused in new buildings. These include building elements such as plumbing fixtures, doors, timber, and bricks. For example, heavy timber can be reused by resawing and planing. In most cases, using these old materials adds to the architectural character of the new building. A project can receive LEED credit for using salvaged, refurbished, or reused materials, products, and furnishings for at least 5% of the total of all building materials. Additional credit is given for using 10%.

Reuse conserves natural resources, reduces the energy required to construct new buildings or products, lessens air and water pollution due to burning or dumping, and keeps materials from entering the waste stream.

Recycled Materials

Recyclability is the ability of a previously used material to be used as a resource in the manufacturer of a new product. Melting down old steel to manufacture new steel is an example of recyclability. Recycling materials is often difficult because of the problem of separating different substances so that they can be individually marketed. Most of this separating must be done by hand, and in some cases, such as with gypsum wallboard, the cost of separating all the component parts may be more than the cost of sending the material to a landfill.

Before selecting and specifying materials, the architect should ask product suppliers about the recycled content of their product. A project can receive LEED credit for using recycled materials if the sum of the post-consumer recycled content plus half of the post-industrial content constitutes at least 5% of the total value of the materials in the project. Additional credit is given for using 10%.

Recycling of consumer products can be encouraged by providing bins, recycling rooms, and other provisions as part of the building design. In some areas of the country local codes require that a portion of the trash area be reserved for recycling bins.

Building Disposal

If old products and materials cannot be reused or recycled, they must be burned or placed in a landfill for disposal. If a material is biodegradable it can break down quickly and return to the earth. Some materials, such as aluminum, most plastics, and steel, take a very long time to decompose naturally. A project can receive LEED credit for diverting at least 50% of construction, demolition, and land-clearing debris from landfill disposal to recycling or donation of usable materials to charitable organizations.

Biobased products may be used to minimize disposal problems while saving depletable raw materials. Biobased products are primarily made from plant or animal materials. Using biobased products also helps maintain good indoor air quality and provides a market for the rural economy. Some examples of biobased products are adhesives, composite panels, gypsum wallboard substitutes, ceiling tiles, and carpet backing. A project can receive LEED credit for using rapidly renewable building materials made from plants that are typically harvested within a 10-year cycle or shorter for 5% of the total value of all building materials used.

HAZARDOUS MATERIAL MITIGATION

Hazardous materials are chemicals or other biological substances that pose a threat to the environment or to human health if released or misused. There are thousands of products and substances that can be defined as hazardous. A few of the more common ones found in buildings are described in the following sections.

In many cases, building sites or existing buildings may be contaminated with harmful chemicals, mold, mildew, and so on. These contaminants need to be identified and removed in accordance with best practices and in compliance with federal, state, or local regulations.

Asbestos

Asbestos is a naturally occurring fibrous mineral found in certain types of rock formations. After mining and processing, asbestos consists of very fine fibers. Asbestos is known to cause lung cancer, asbestosis (a scarring of the lungs), and mesothelioma (a cancer of the lining of the chest or abdominal cavity). Oral exposure may be associated with cancer of the esophagus, stomach, and intestines. In buildings, exposure generally comes from asbestos that has become friable (easily crumbled) or that has been disturbed accidentally or by construction activities. Although generally not a problem in new construction, asbestos can be found in many types of existing building materials, including pipe and blown-in insulation, asphalt flooring, vinyl sheet and tile flooring, construction mastics, ceiling tiles, textured paints, roofing shingles, cement siding, caulking, vinyl wall coverings, and many other products.

Asbestos is regulated under two federal laws and one federal agency restriction: the Clean Air Act (CAA) of 1970, the Toxic Substances Control Act (TSCA) of 1976, and the U.S. Consumer Product Safety Commission (CPSC). Under authority of the TSCA, in 1989 the EPA issued a ban on asbestos. However, much of the original rule was vacated by the U.S. Fifth Circuit Court of Appeals in 1991. Products still banned include flooring felt, corrugated or specialty paper, commercial paper, and rollboard. The ban also prevents the use of asbestos in products that have not historically contained asbestos. Under authority of the CAA, the National Emission Standards for Hazardous Air Pollutants (NESHAP) rules for asbestos ban the use of sprayed-on or wet-applied asbestos-containing materials (ACM) for fireproofing and insulation. These rules took effect in 1973. NESHAP also bans the use of ACMs for decorative purposes. This took effect in 1978. The CPSC bans the use of asbestos in certain consumer products such as textured paint and wall patching compounds.

Testing for asbestos and mitigation efforts must be done by an accredited company following strict procedures. In many cases, if the asbestos has not been disturbed it can be left in place because the EPA and NIOSH (National Institute for Occupational Safety and Health) have determined that intact and undisturbed asbestos materials do not pose a health risk. The asbestos may be encapsulated to protect it from becoming friable or from accidental damage. During building demolition or renovation, however, the EPA does require asbestos removal. This must be done by a licensed contractor certified for this type of work.

Vermiculite

Vermiculite is a hydrated laminar magnesium-aluminum-ironsilicate that resembles mica. It is separated from mineral ore that contains other materials, including the possibility of asbestos. When heated during processing, vermiculite expands into worm-like pieces. In construction, it is used for pour-in insulation, acoustic finishes, fire protection, and sound-deadening compounds. Vermiculite obtained from a mine in Montana is known to contain some amount of asbestos. The mine was closed in 1990. It is still mined at other locations, but those have low levels of contamination. The current concern is with loose, pour-in insulation used in attics and concrete blocks.

The EPA recommends that attic insulation that may contain asbestos-contaminated vermiculite not be disturbed, and that any cracks in the ceiling be sealed. If the insulation must be removed, only a trained and certified professional contractor should perform the work.

Lead

Lead is a highly toxic metal that was once used in a variety of consumer and industrial products. Exposure to lead can cause serious health problems, especially to children, including damage to the brain and nervous system, slowed growth, behavior problems, seizures, and even death. In adults it can cause digestive and reproductive problems, nerve disorders, muscle and joint pain, and difficulties during pregnancy. Most exposure from lead comes from paint in homes built before 1978 and from soil and household dust that has picked up lead from deteriorating lead-based paint. The federal government banned lead-based paint from housing in 1978.

Federal law requires that anyone conducting lead-based paint removal be certified and that lead-based paint be removed from some types of residential occupancies and child-occupied facilities by a certified company using approved methods for removal and disposal. Removal of lead-based paint should not be done by sanding, propane torch, heat gun, or dry scraping. Sometimes, covering the wall with a new layer of gypsum wallboard or simply repainting is an acceptable alternative. Also, lead-coated copper used in flashing, sheet metal panels, gutters, and downspouts is no longer used due to the potential for soil contamination.

Radon

Radon is a colorless, odorless, tasteless, naturally occurring radioactive gas found in soils, rock, and water throughout the world. Radon causes lung cancer, with most of the risk coming from breathing air contaminated with radon and its decay products. Most radon exposure occurs in places where it accumulates, such as homes, schools, and office buildings, so most remedial work is done in existing buildings. Testing for radon is easy and can be done by a trained contractor or by homeowners with kits available in hardware stores or through the mail. The Environmental Protection Agency recommends that remedial action be taken if a radon level over 4 picocuries per liter (pCi/L) is found.

Remedial work should follow the radon mitigation standards of the EPA and ASTM E2121 and can include any or a combination of the following.

- sealing cracks in floors, walls, and foundations
- venting the soil outside the foundation wall

- depressurizing the voids within a block wall foundation (block wall depressurization)
- ventilating the crawl space with a fan (crawl space depressurization)
- using a vent pipe without a fan to draw air from under a slab to the outside (passive sub-slab depressurization)
- using a fan-powered vent to draw air from below the slab (active sub-slab depressurization)
- using a fan-powered vent to draw air from below a membrane laid on the crawl space floor (sub-membrane depressurization)

Polychlorinated Biphenyls (PCBs)

Polychlorinated biphenyls (PCBs) are mixtures of synthetic organic chemicals with physical properties ranging from oily liquids to waxy solids. PCBs were used in many commercial and industrial applications, including building transformers, fluorescent light transformers, paints, coatings, and plastic and rubber products. PCBs are known to cause cancer and other adverse health effects afflicting the immune system, reproductive system, nervous system, and endocrine system. Because of concerns regarding the toxicity and persistence of PCBs in the environment, their manufacture and importation were banned in 1977 under the Toxic Substances Control Act (TSCA) of 1976. While there are some exceptions on the use of PCBs, the TSCA strictly regulates manufacturing, processing, distribution, and disposal.

If PCBs are discovered in building components or on site, they must be handled by a certified contractor and disposed of by incineration, dechlorination, or placement in an approved chemical waste landfill.

LIFE-CYCLE COST ANALYSIS

Life-cycle cost analysis (LCC) is a method for determining the total cost of a building or building component or system. It takes into account the initial cost of the element or system under consideration as well as the cost of financing, operation, maintenance, and disposal. Any residual value of the components is subtracted from the other costs. The costs are estimated over a length of time called the *study period*. The duration of the study period varies with the needs of the client and the useful life of the material or system. For example, investors in a building may be interested in comparing various alternate materials over the expected investment time frame, while a city government may be interested in a longer time frame representing the expected life of the building. All future costs are discounted back to a common time, usually the base date, to account for the time value of money. The *discount rate* is used to convert future costs to their equivalent present values.

Using life-cycle cost analysis allows two or more alternatives to be evaluated and their total costs to be compared. This is especially useful when evaluating energy conservation measures where one design alternative may have a higher initial cost than another, but a lower overall cost because of energy savings. Some of the specific costs involved in an LCC of a building element include the following.

- initial costs, which include the cost of acquiring and installing the element
- operational costs for electricity, water, and other utilities
- maintenance costs for the element over the length of the study period, including any repair costs
- replacement costs, if any, during the length of the study period
- finance costs required during the length of the study period
- taxes, if any, for initial costs and operating costs

The residual value is the remaining value of the element at the end of the study period based on resale value, salvage value, value in place, or scrap value. All of the costs listed are estimated, discounted to their present value, and added together. Any residual value is discounted to its present value and then subtracted from the total to get the final life-cycle cost of the element.

Note that a life-cycle cost analysis is not the same as a life-cycle assessment (LCA), described earlier in this chapter. An LCA analyzes the environmental impact of a product or building system over the entire life of the product or system.

SUSTAINABLE BUILDING PROGRAMS, RATING SYSTEMS, AND STANDARDS

Throughout the United States, Canada, and Great Britain, several organizations have emerged that provide industry-recognized ratings and standards for environmental design. These organizations develop objective criteria that designers must follow in order for a building or interior build-out to adhere to a particular standard or receive a particular rating. Although conforming to the criteria that these organizations establish is not mandatory by any building code, some governmental entities and large corporations may require that their designers follow an organization's guidelines. The following are the major programs, rating systems, and standards used in the United States, Canada, and Great Britain.

Building Research Establishment Environmental Assessment Method (BREEAM)

The BRE Environmental Assessment Method (BREEAM) is a certified environmental assessment method offered by the Building Research Establishment (BRE), a British organization that provides research-based consultancy, testing, and certification services covering all aspects of the built environment and associated industries.

BREEAM measures the environmental performance of building materials and products by evaluating buildings—including offices, industrial buildings, retail buildings, and homes—in the areas of management, energy use, health and well-being, pollution, transportation, land use, ecology, materials, and water use. Credits are awarded in each area and are added to produce a total score. The building is then given a rating of pass, good, very good, or excellent, and awarded a certificate. For more information, visit the BREEAM website at www.breeam.org.

Collaborative for High Performance Schools (CHPS)

The Collaborative for High Performance Schools is a membership organization composed of public, private, and nonprofit organizations. Its goal is to increase the energy efficiency of schools in California and improve the quality of education. CHPS publishes several manuals on best practices, holds training seminars, and maintains a list of low-emitting materials meeting the criteria of California's *Special Environmental Requirements, Specifications Section 01350* governing indoor air quality in buildings.

Section 01350 was developed by the state of California to cover key environmental performance issues related to the selection and handling of building materials. It gives specifications for testing emissions from interior finish materials and other elements that affect indoor air quality, screening building materials for hazardous content, and avoiding mold and mildew from construction. It is a good source of information and is being incorporated into other specification programs.

CHPS provides resources, including assessment tools and criteria for recognition that are used by California and ten other states. For new construction and major modernizations, CHPS provides two different recognition programs: CHPS Designed is self-monitored, while CHPS Verified involves an independent review. Depending on the state in which it is located, a project may be eligible for either program or just one. For more information, go to the CHPS website at www.chps.net.

Energy Star® for Buildings and Manufacturing Plants

The Energy Star for Buildings and Manufacturing Plants is part of the U.S. Environmental Protection Agency's Energy Star program, which began in 1992. To achieve an Energy Star label, buildings and plants must record a year's worth of energy performance, which is then compared with other similar types of facilities and given a rating between 1 and 100. Facilities scoring 75 or higher are eligible for the Energy Star label. For more information, visit the Energy Star website at www.energystar.gov.

Green Globes™

Green Globes is a green building guidance and assessment program available in Canada and the United States that was developed by the Green Building Initiative (GBI), a nonprofit organization promoting practical green building approaches for residential and commercial construction. Green Globes uses a 1000-point scale to assess a building in categories such as energy, indoor environment, site, water, resources, emissions, and project management. After the initial assessment, third-party assessors review the building and documentation and may grant certification and award a rating of one to four globes. For more information, visit the GBI website at www.thegbi.org.

Leadership in Energy and Environmental Design® (LEED®)

The Leadership in Energy and Environmental Design (LEED) Green Building Rating System™ is a consensus-based building rating system designed to accelerate the development and implementation of green building practices in the United States. It was developed by the U.S. Green Building Council (USGBC), which is a national coalition of leaders from all aspects of the building industry working to promote buildings that are environmentally responsible and profitable and that provide healthy places to live and work.

There are several rating systems for different building types, including new construction, existing buildings, operations and maintenance, commercial interiors, core and shell, schools, retail, health care, homes, and neighborhood development. In order for a building to be LEED certified, certain prerequisites must be achieved and enough points must be earned to meet or exceed the program's technical requirements. Points add up to a final score that relates to one of four possible certification levels: certified, silver, gold, and platinum.

LEED for New Construction was the first rating system developed by USGBC. This rating system is divided into seven categories, each containing a number of possible points that can be earned, for a total of 110 points, as shown in Table 30.2.

Table 30.2

LEED for New Construction Point Categories

category	possible points	percent of total
sustainable sites	26	24%
water efficiency	10	9%
energy and atmosphere	35	32%
materials and resources	14	13%
indoor environmental quality	15	13%
innovation in design	6	5%
regional priority	4	4%

Out of 100 base points, with an additional 10 points possible for innovation in design and regional priority (for meeting criteria that are of particular regional concern), the different certification levels are as follows.

Certified: 40 to 49 points
Silver: 50 to 59 points
Gold: 60 to 79 points
Platinum: 80 points and above

For more information about LEED, visit the USGBC website at www.usgbc.org.

Leadership in Energy and Environmental Design Canada (LEED Canada)

The Canada Green Building Council (CaGBC) has adopted the United States' LEED program for use in Canada and Canadian climates. The requirements are essentially the same, the only major modifications being that SI units are used, reference is made to Canadian standards and regulations, protection of fish habitats is recognized, and a few definitions are changed. For more information, visit the CaGBC website at www.cagbc.org.

National Green Building Standard

The National Association of Home Builders (NAHB) and the International Code Council (ICC) developed the *National Green Building Standard*, along with companion publications, to provide guidance for builders engaged in or interested in green building products and practices for residential design, development, and construction. The standard covers seven areas: lot and site development, resource efficiency, energy efficiency, water efficiency, indoor environmental quality, and homeowner education. After a home is constructed, the builder can request a third-party inspection and review. A successful project can be awarded a bronze, silver, gold, or emerald rating. For more information, visit the NAHB website at www.nahbgreen.org.

PRODUCT CERTIFICATION

There are a number of organizations and programs that will certify certain kinds of products as environmentally sound. The following are some of the most notable.

BIFMA International

The Business and Institutional Furniture Manufacturer's Association (BIFMA) maintains two ANSI-approved standards for limiting volatile organic compound emissions from office furniture. These are ANSI/BIFMA M7.1, *Standard Test Method for Determining VOC Emissions from Office Furniture Systems, Components, and Seating,* and ANSI/BIFMA X7.1, *Standard for Formaldehyde and TVOC Emissions of Low-Emitting Office Furniture Systems and Seating.*

BIFMA has also developed BIFMA e3, *Furniture Sustainability Standard.* This standard establishes criteria in the four areas of materials, energy and atmosphere, human and ecosystem health, and social responsibility. A product that goes through the process of certification by one of two accredited third-party certifiers, NSF International and Scientific Certification Systems, can earn level certification and a rating of silver, gold, or platinum. For more information, visit the BIFMA website at www.bifma.org.

Cradle to Cradle (C2C)

The Cradle to Cradle program of McDonough Braungart Design Chemistry (MBDC) certifies products that use environmentally safe materials, are designed so that their materials that can be recovered and reused, use water and energy efficiently in their manufacturing, and are manufactured by socially responsible organizations. Acceptable materials are classed as technical nutrients, which are synthetic materials that can be reused without a loss in quality, and biological nutrients, which are organic materials that will safely decompose into the natural environment after use. Levels of certification are basic, silver, gold, and platinum. For more information, visit the MBDC website at www.mbdc.com.

Energy Star

In addition to the building rating system discussed earlier in this chapter, Energy Star also offers a voluntary labeling program designed to promote energy-efficient products such as consumer appliances, office equipment, residential furnaces and air conditioning equipment, lighting, and consumer electronics. Products that qualify may place the Energy Star label on their products with their energy-saving features noted. For more information, visit the Energy Star website at www.energystar.gov.

FloorScore

The FloorScore program of the Resilient Floor Covering Institute (RFCI) tests and certifies hard-surface flooring products that comply with strict indoor air quality requirements in California and qualify for use in high-performance schools and office buildings in California. Products bearing the FloorScore seal have been certified by Scientific Certification Systems as meeting the requirements. For more information, visit the RFCI website at www.rfci.com.

Forest Stewardship Council (FSC)

The Forest Stewardship Council is an international organization that oversees the development of national and regional standards for responsible forest management based on its *FSC Principles and Criteria for Forest Stewardship*. It accredits certifying organizations that comply with these principles. The FSC logo on a wood product ensures that materials have come from environmentally conscious management and have followed the other FSC principles. Refer to the section on wood later in this chapter for more information on the FSC, or visit the FSC website at www.fsc.org.

Green Label Plus

The Green Label Plus program of the Carpet and Rug Institute (CRI) is a voluntary testing program for carpet, cushion, and adhesive that conforms to California's high-performance schools program. Carpet carrying the Green Label Plus mark is certified as being low-emitting and meets the CHPS requirements as defined in California's *Section 01350* specification. For more information, visit the CRI website at www.carpet-rug.org.

Green Seal

Green Seal is an independent, nonprofit organization that strives to achieve a more sustainable world by promoting environmentally responsible production, purchasing, and products. Among other programs, Green Seal develops environmental standards for products in specific categories and certifies products that meet these standards. The organization meets the criteria of the International Organization for Standardization's ISO 14020 and ISO 14024 for ecolabeling. Green Seal's product evaluations are conducted by third-party organizations using a life-cycle approach that considers energy, resource use, and emissions to air, water, and land, as well as other effects on health and the environment. The Green Seal is awarded to products that meet the high standards of the program. For more information, visit the Green Seal website at www.greenseal.org.

GreenFormat

GreenFormat™ is a web-based database developed by the Construction Specifications Institute (CSI) to allow manufacturers to self-report sustainability properties of their products using a standard questionnaire format. The information is reported in five categories: background information, product details, product lifecycle, additional information, and authorization. Designers, contractors, and others can search the database through the standard format. Although the information is self reported, sustainability claims are verified by relating questions on the questionnaire to standards and certifications. For more information, visit the GreenFormat website at www.greenformat.com.

Greenguard Environmental Institute

The Greenguard Environmental Institute is a nonprofit, industry-independent organization that oversees the Greenguard Certification Program. This program tests indoor products for emissions to ensure that they meet guidelines and standards for pollutants affecting indoor air quality. Products are tested for emissions of total volatile organic compounds (VOCs), formaldehyde, total aldehydes, respirable particles, carbon monoxide, nitrogen oxide, and carbon dioxide.

If a product meets the standards of Greenguard, it is added to the Greenguard Registry. Products listed on the registry include building materials, furnishings, furniture, cleaning and maintenance products, electronic equipment, and personal care products. Greenguard also sets allowable emission levels for testing these products, using the lowest level among those established by the Environmental Protection Agency's procurement specifications, the state of Washington's indoor air quality program, the World Health Organization, and Germany's Blue Angel Program for electronic equipment. For more information, visit the Greenguard Environmental Institute website at www.greenguard.org.

International Organization for Standardization (ISO)

The International Organization for Standardization is a nongovernmental organization comprising national standards bodies from over 120 countries. ISO 14000 is a collection of standards and guidelines covering issues such as performance, product standards, labeling, environmental management, and life-cycle assessment as these relate to the environment. Several of the individual standards and guidelines are applicable to building products.

ISO 14020 describes a set of principles that should be followed by any practitioner of environmental labeling. ISO 14024 covers labeling programs and specifies the procedures and principles that third-party certifiers, or ecolabelers, should follow. For example, an organization should not have any financial interest in the products it certifies, it should conduct scientific evaluations using internationally accepted methodologies, and it should use a life-cycle approach when evaluating products. The ISO 14040 series of standards covers requirements for life-cycle assessments. For more information, visit the ISO website at www.iso.org.

Scientific Certification Systems (SCS)

Scientific Certification Systems is a private organization established to advance both public and private sectors toward more environmentally sustainable policies. Under its Environmental Claims Certification program, the SCS certifies specific product attributes such as biodegradability and recycled content. It also certifies environmentally preferable products, which are products that have a reduced environmental impact when compared to similar products performing the same function. SCS's work is based on scientifically defensible, field-verifiable, performance measurement systems. Building products that are certified include carpet, nonwoven flooring, composite panel products, adhesives and sealants, furniture, paints, casework, ceiling tiles, and other wall coverings. SCS also certifies qualifying forests under their Forest Certification Program. For more information, visit the SCS's website at www.scscertified.com.

SMaRT

The Institute for Market Transformation to Sustainability (MTS) oversees the Sustainable Materials Rating Technology (SMaRT) program, among others. SMaRT identifies sustainable products based on awarding points in the areas of safety for public health and environment; energy reduction and renewable energy materials; company and facility requirements including social equity; use of biobased or recycled materials; and reuse, reclamation, and end-of-life management of products. Products are certified at one of four levels: sustainable, sustainable silver, sustainable gold, and sustainable platinum. For more information, visit the MTS website at mts.sustainableproducts.com.

Sustainable Forestry Initiative (SFI)

The Sustainable Forestry Initiative is an independent charitable organization dedicated to promoting sustainable forest management. The SFI includes forest certification, chain-of-custody certification, fiber sourcing requirements, and SFI labels. It has developed a sustainable forestry initiative standard (SFIS) that includes nine principles and 13 objectives in the areas of land management, procurement, forestry research, training and education, legal and regulatory compliance, public and landowner involvement, and management review and continual improvement. The FSI label on a product indicates that it has come from a certified forest.

The SFI program gives four different product labels to participating companies that meet the SFI requirements based on both environmental and market demands. For more information, visit the SFI website is at www.sfiprogram.org.

UL Environment

UL Environment is a program of Underwriters Laboratories that helps support the growth and development of sustainable products, services, and organizations in the global marketplace. It provides independent green claims validation, product certification, training, and advisory services and standards development. Among the claims UL Environment can validate are recycled content, rapidly renewable materials, regional materials, volatile organic compound emissions, volatile organic compound content, energy efficiency, water efficiency, hazardous or toxic substances, reclamation programs, mold resistance, manufacturing energy audits, degradability, and compostability. UL Environment maintains a database of products it has certified. For more information, visit the UL Environment website at www.ulenvironment.com.

WaterSense

WaterSense is a program of the U.S. Environmental Protection Agency (EPA) that helps consumers identify water-efficient programs and products with the WaterSense label. Products are certified by independent, third-party licensed certifying bodies based on EPA criteria for water efficiency and performance by following testing and certification protocols specific to each product category. For more information, visit the WaterSense website at www.epa.gov/watersense.

REGULATIONS AND INDUSTRY STANDARDS RELATED TO SUSTAINABILITY

For a listing of standards and regulations that govern indoor air quality, refer to the previous section in this chapter.

- ANSI/ASHRAE/IESNA Standard 90.1, *Energy Standard for Buildings Except Low-Rise Residential Buildings*. This is a voluntary industry standard that gives information on minimum energy efficiency standards, building envelope requirements, zone isolation, floor, ceiling, and roof insulation, and power allowance calculation. It is written in mandatory enforceable language suitable for code adoption.
- ANSI/ASHRAE/USGBC/IES Standard 189.1, *Standard for the Design of High-Performance Green Buildings Except Low-Rise Residential Buildings*. This is a voluntary standard developed by the American Society of Heating, Refrigerating and Air-Conditioning Engineers (ASHRAE), in conjunction with the American National Standards Institute (ANSI), the U.S. Green Building Council (USGBC), and the Illuminating Engineering Society (IES). Although voluntary, it is written in such a way that it can be adopted by building code organizations or local

jurisdictions. It covers a wide range of requirements including site sustainability, water use efficiency, energy efficiency, indoor environmental quality, and the building's impact on the atmosphere, materials, and resources.

- ASTM E1991, *Standard Guide for Environmental Life Cycle Assessment of Building Materials/Products*
- ASTM E2114, *Standard Terminology for Sustainability Relative to the Performance of Buildings*
- ASTM E2129, *Standard Practice for Data Collection for Sustainability Assessment of Building Products*
- Green Seal, GS-11, product standard for paints
- Green Seal, GS-13, product standard for windows
- *International Energy Conservation Code* (IECC). This model code was developed by the International Code Council to regulate minimum energy conservation requirements for new buildings. It addresses requirements for all aspects of energy uses in both commercial and residential construction, including heating and ventilating, lighting, water heating, and power usage for appliances and building systems.
- Toxic Substances Control Act (TSCA) of 1976. This law was enacted to give the Environmental Protection Agency the authority to track and regulate over 75,000 industrial chemicals produced or imported into the United States. It allows the EPA to ban the manufacture and import of those chemicals that pose an unreasonable risk.

DEFINITIONS

Coproduct: a marketable by-product from a process. Materials traditionally considered to be waste but that can be used as raw materials in a different manufacturing process are considered coproducts.

Demand control ventilation: a system designed to adjust the amount of ventilation air provided to a space based on the extent of occupancy. The system normally uses carbon dioxide sensors but may also use occupancy sensors or air quality sensors.

Detention: the temporary storage of storm runoff in a detention facility to control peak discharge rates and to provide gravity settling of pollutants. The detention facility is designed to provide for a gradual release of stored water at a controlled rate.

Drainage easement: the legal right granted by a landowner to a grantee, commonly a governmental entity, allowing the use of private land for stormwater management

Embodied energy: the total energy required to extract, produce, fabricate, and deliver a material to a job site, including the collection of raw materials, the energy used to extract and process the raw materials, transportation from the original site to the processing plant or factory, the energy required to turn the raw materials into a finished product, and the energy required to transport the material to the job site

Fee in lieu: payment of money by a developer in place of meeting all or part of stormwater performance standards

Hydrologic soil group (HSG): a classification system developed by the Natural Resource Conservation Service in which soils are categorized into four runoff potential groups. These groups range from A soils, with high permeability and little runoff production, to D soils, which have a high runoff potential

Infiltration: the process of percolating stormwater into the subsoil

Post-consumer: referring to a material or product that has served its intended use and has been diverted or recovered from waste destined for disposal, having completed its life as a consumer item.

Post-industrial: referring to materials generated in manufacturing processes, such as trimmings or scrap, that have been recovered or diverted from solid waste. Also called *Pre-consumer*.

Pre-consumer: see *Post-industrial*

Recovered materials: waste or by-products that have been recovered or diverted from solid waste disposal. (Note: This term does not apply to materials that are generated from or reused within an original manufacturing process.)

Renewable product: a product that can be grown or naturally replenished or cleansed at a rate that exceeds human depletion of the resource

Sustainable: the condition of being able to meet the needs of the present generation without compromising the needs of future generations

Watercourse: any body of water including, but not limited to, lakes, ponds, rivers, and streams

Waterway: a channel that directs surface runoff to a watercourse or to a public storm drain

31 PLUMBING SYSTEMS

WATER SUPPLY

Depending on geographic location, water is available from a variety of sources. It comes from rivers, lakes, wells, surface runoff, oceans, and even recycled wastewater. In some cases, water may be pure enough in its natural state for immediate human use. In most instances, however, it must be treated to remove impurities. Water suitable for human drinking is called *potable water*. If it is not suitable for drinking, it is called *nonpotable*, but this type of water may be used for irrigation, flushing toilets, and the like.

Two of the most common sources of large water supplies for cities are surface water and groundwater. Surface water comes from rain and snow that runs off into rivers and lakes. Groundwater is that which seeps into the ground until it hits an impervious layer of rock or soil. It then forms a water table that is tapped by drilling. Large regions of subsurface water are called *aquifers*.

Generally, the best sources for water are those that require little or no treatment, including water from deep wells, relatively clean rivers, and surface runoff. This type of water can be easily treated in most cases and can be made available in large quantities. However, with increasing pollution and the scarcity of water in some locations, greater use of treated seawater or recycled wastewater will be necessary. The means are available to do this, but the processing is more expensive than it is for other methods.

Water has many characteristics and can contain many types of chemical, biological, and physical contaminants. One common characteristic of all water is its pH level. The *pH level* is a measure of the relative acidity or alkalinity of water. It is based on a scale of 0 to 14, with a pH of 7 being neutral. Anything below 7 is considered acidic and can be corrosive; anything above 7 is considered alkaline. Knowing the pH of water is useful in determining necessary water treatment for corrosion, chemicals, and disinfection. For example, acidic water, along with entrained oxygen, can cause iron and steel pipes to rust. The problem can be corrected by adding a neutralizer to the washer. This raises the water's alkaline content.

Rainwater is slightly acidic in its natural state, but in many industrialized areas the acid level is greater due to sulfur and nitrogen compounds in the atmosphere. The compounds combine to form sulfuric or nitric acid and fall as "acid rain."

Another common characteristic of water is its hardness. *Hardness* is caused by calcium and magnesium salts in water. If untreated, hard water can cause clogged pipes and corrosion of boilers. It also makes laundry and other types of washing difficult because it inhibits the cleaning action of soaps and detergents. Treatment methods for hardness are discussed in the next section.

Other common water quality problems include turbidity, color, odor, biological contamination, and chemical contamination. *Turbidity* is caused by suspended material in the water—such as silt, clay, and organic material. Although it is not hazardous, turbidity is unpleasant and can be treated by filtration.

Color and odor problems are caused by organic matter, inorganic salts, or dissolved gases. Odor problems can be corrected with filtration through activated carbon. Color problems can be corrected with fine filtration or chlorination.

Biological contamination in water can be caused by bacteria, viruses, and protozoa, all of which can be dangerous to health. The bacteria in the coliform group are one of the most common kinds found in water supplies, especially well water. *Escherichia coli* or E. coli, is the most well known of this group. Water tests commonly check for this bacterium. Another bacterium of concern to building designers is *Legionella pneumophila*, the bacterium that causes Legionnaires' disease. Although usually not a problem in drinking water, these types of bacteria grow in warm water such as that found in cooling towers, air conditioning systems, large plumbing systems, and hot tubs.

Two types of protozoa that can cause diarrheal illness are *Giardia* and *Cryptosporidium*. These protozoa exist in cyst form, like microscopic eggs, and are transmitted through improperly treated drinking water. Slow sand filters can remove nearly all *Giardia* cysts.

Chemical contamination includes hundreds of hazardous materials including chemicals from industrial processes, mining, and pesticides. Some chemicals affect only the color and taste of water, but others are deadly. Treatment includes filtration, when possible, and other complex processes.

Water Treatment Methods

There are a variety of methods used for the treatment of water used for drinking, as well as water for other uses. They are often used in combination to filter and disinfect the various types of contaminants found in natural water sources. Water treatment methods can be categorized into four general groups: pretreatment, filtration, demineralization, and disinfection. Additional methods include distillation and aeration.

Pretreatment

Pretreatment is often required before other treatment methods can be used. This step of water management is designed to remove suspended matter and large particles from the water.

- *Sedimentation* uses gravity and still water, allowing heavy particles to sink to the bottom of a holding basin or tank. The clear water is then piped out into a secondary filtration system or treatment facility. Sedimentation can take place with or without coagulation and flocculation.
- *Coagulation* is the process of getting particles in the water to stick together by adding alum or other chemicals.
- *Flocculation* is the next step after coagulation. The mix of water and alum is sent to still water, where the particles and alum form a loosely aggregated mass called *floc*, and are heavy enough for sedimentation to take place.

Filtration

- *Slow sand filtration* allows water to seep through a bed of fine sand about 3 ft to 4 ft (1 m to 1.2 m) deep. As a biological slime forms on the sand filter, it traps small particles and degrades organic matter. Sand filters do not require coagulation or flocculation. Slow sand filters are excellent at filtering out *Giardia* and particulates, but they are not good for water with high turbidity.
- *Direct filtration* passes water under pressure through a filter medium. This process always includes coagulation and filtration, and may require a flocculation tank. Direct filtration is good for eliminating nearly all *Giardia* and most viruses.
- *Packaged filtration* is the same as direct filtration except that all the elements used are placed in a single unit for direct hookup to a water supply.
- *Diatomaceous earth filtration* uses a thin layer of diatomaceous earth from $^1/_8$ in to $^1/_5$ in (3 mm to 5 mm) thick placed on a septum or filter element. Diatomaceous earth is a light-colored, soft sedimentary rock formed mainly of the siliceous shells of diatoms. This filtration method is good for removing cysts, algae, and asbestos, but not as good at removing bacteria and turbidity.
- *Membrane filtration* forces water at high pressure through a thin membrane that removes particles 0.2 μm and larger, as well as *Giardia*, other bacteria, some viruses, and other microorganisms.
- *Cartridge filtration* uses self-contained units placed along the water supply line to filter out particles 0.2 μm and larger. The cartridges must be replaced as they get fouled, but are useful for individual faucets as well as on small supply systems.

Demineralization

Demineralization removes dissolved solids and the chemicals that cause hard water.

- *Ion exchange* is used in water softeners to treat hard water and to remove cadmium, chromium silver, radium, and other chemicals. Hard water is piped into the softener, which contains zeolite. The calcium or magnesium ions are exchanged for the sodium ions in the zeolite. The water softener must be recharged periodically by passing a brine solution through the zeolite; this is done automatically by the water softening equipment. Water run through an ion exchange unit must be pretreated to reduce suspended solids.
- *Reverse osmosis* (RO) removes contaminants by using a semipermeable membrane that allows only water to pass through and not dissolved ions. RO is useful for removing inorganic chemicals, bacteria, and suspended particles. The unit is cleaned by forcing clear water through the membrane, which

leaves the contaminants behind in a brine that must be carefully disposed of.

- *Electrodialysis* places charged membranes at the inflow stream of water to attract counterions. Electrodialysis can remove barium, cadmium, selenium, fluoride, and nitrates. Electrodialysis systems are expensive to buy and operate, and they require high water pressure and a source of direct current power.

Disinfection

Disinfection is needed to destroy microorganisms that can cause disease in humans. As with the other water treatment processes, there are several methods used to disinfect water. The EPA Surface Water Treatment Rule (SWTR) requires disinfection of water supply systems that get their water either from surface water or from groundwater under the direct influence of surface water.

- *Chlorination*, the most common form of treatment, kills organisms by introducing chlorine into the water stream. The chlorine may be in the form of a gas, liquid, or solid, depending on the type of system used.

- *Chloramine* is used in a way similar to chlorination, but it is a weaker disinfectant than chlorine. Chloramine is produced by adding ammonia to water than contains chlorine, or by chlorinating water that contains ammonia. Chloramine is generally used as a secondary disinfectant to prevent bacterial regrowth in a distribution system.

- *Ozonation* disinfects water through the use of ozone, a powerful oxidizing and disinfecting agent. Ozonation is used mainly as a primary disinfectant and typically requires a secondary disinfectant for water supplies. It is typically used for treating cooling tower water to prevent *Legionella pneumophila*, scale, and algae.

- *Ultraviolet light* (UV) destroys a cell's ability to reproduce and is effective against bacteria and viruses. It is not effective with *Giardia* or *Cryptosporidium* and is not useful for water that contains high levels of turbidity, suspended solids, or soluble organic matter. UV light must be used with a secondary disinfectant to prevent regrowth of microorganisms.

- *Nanofiltration* uses filter membranes that are capable of trapping particles as small as one nanometer (one billionth of a meter, or 10^{-9} m) in size. At this scale the filter can remove bacteria, viruses, pesticides, and organic material. Because of the small size of the filter medium, the water must be forced through at high pressure.

Distillation is another method of treating water, by boiling it and then condensing the vapors. It results in very clean water with all solids, bacteria, salts, and other material removed. It is often used to treat seawater.

Aeration (oxidation) is used to improve the taste and color of water. It also aids in the removal of iron and manganese by oxidizing them so they can be more easily removed by filtration. It is a simple process by which as much water as possible is exposed to air through sprays, fountains, or waterfalls. For drinking water treatment, the water should be aerated in an enclosed space or in a tank.

Private Water Supply

Private water supplies include wells, springs, and collected rainwater. The most common type, however, is the well, which is used for residences and small buildings where a municipal supply is not available. Wells are most commonly drilled or bored. A rotary bit is used for drilled wells, which is the only method possible for going through rock, and a bored well uses a rotary auger to make the hole.

Two of the most important considerations in drilling a well are depth and yield. The depth of a well may range from less than 25 ft (7.6 m), known as a *shallow well*, to several hundred feet. Of course, the depth affects the cost of the well, and there is no sure way of knowing prior to drilling how deep the well may have to be. Before drilling, the architect should talk to neighbors, local well drillers, and geologists in the area to see what their experience has been.

The *yield* of a well is the number of gallons per minute (gpm) it provides. A yield from 5 gpm to 10 gpm (0.3 L/s to 0.6 L/s) is about the minimum required for a private residence. If a yield is too low for the project, the system may need to include a large storage tank that can be filled during periods of low use, such as during the night, so enough water is available during peak periods.

As a well is drilled or bored, a pipe casing is lowered into the hole to prevent the hole from caving in and to prevent seepage of surface contamination into the well. The casing is a steel pipe from 4 in to 6 in (100 to 150) in diameter. Lower in the well, perforated casings are used to allow the water to seep into the well from which it is pumped out.

Pumps

Several kinds of pumps are used in wells, including suction, deep-well jet, turbine, and submersible. *Suction pumps* are only suitable for water tables less than 25 ft (7.6 m), while *deep-well jet pumps* can operate at depths from 25 ft to over 100 ft (7.6 m to over 30 m). *Turbine pumps* are used for high-capacity systems with deep wells. One of the most common types for moderate to deep wells serving private residences or small buildings is the *submersible pump*. This type has a waterproof motor and pump that are placed below the water line and pump water to a pressure tank.

Jet pumps have the pump and motor aboveground and lift water by the venturi principle. Water is forced through a pipe in the well where a jet stream of small diameter is created in another pipe. The low pressure sucks up the well water and drives it to the surface. In both types of pumps, water is pumped to a pressure tank where air pressure circulates the water and operates fixtures.

In addition to the well itself and the pump, most well systems require some type of storage tank or pressure tank. Pressure tanks are required to maintain a constant pressure for use in the building and to compensate for brief peak use demand that exceeds the capacity of the pump. Pressure tanks also reduce the amount of time the pump must be running because small quantities of water can be used from the tank without the need for the pump to operate. As the pressure tank is emptied, a pressure gauge senses the loss and activates the pump. In a *jet (venturi) pump* system, an air volume control senses the depletion of the tank. When the yield of a well is too low to meet the demand, a larger storage tank may be used to provide water for normal use. During nighttime or low periods of use the pump slowly fills the tank.

Municipal Water Supply

Most cities get their water from rivers, lakes, or snow melt. In addition to the methods described earlier, water treatment typically involves first settling out heavy materials and coagulation (or flocculation) with a chemical such as alum. Suspended particles combine with the alum and settle out. The water is then filtered and treated with chlorine or some other chemical to kill organic materials. The water may also be aerated to improve its taste, and fluoride may be added to help prevent tooth decay. Other treatments can adjust the pH level.

Once the water is treated, it is piped through water mains at a pressure of about 50 psi (345 kPa), although this can vary from 40 psi to 80 psi (275 kPa to 550 kPa) depending on location and other factors. If the pressure is too high, a pressure-reducing valve is used between the water main and the building meter.

One of the first tasks in a building project is to determine the location of the water main, its size, its pressure, and the cost for tapping it. This information is available from the local water company. If a main is not adjacent to the property, the property owner is often required to extend the line at his or her own cost. If the water main is a substantial distance from the proposed building, the cost impact can be significant. The pressure in the line is needed to determine what kind of supply system can be used, as described in a later section.

WATER SUPPLY DESIGN

Designing a water supply system involves selecting the type of system; deciding on the type of piping, fittings, and fixtures of the system; and sizing the pipe. Each of these will be discussed in turn. Hot water supply system design is outlined in a later section.

Supply Systems

There are two primary types of water supply systems: the upfeed and the downfeed. The choice between the two is usually based on the height of the building and the pressure required to operate the fixtures.

Water supplied from a city main or from a pressure tank with a private well comes from the pipe under a certain pressure; in city mains it is about 50 psi (345 kPa). This pressure must be sufficient to overcome friction in the piping, fittings, meter, and static head, and still be high enough to operate fixtures. A flush valve, for example, requires from 10 psi to 20 psi (70 kPa to 140 kPa) to operate properly; a shower needs about 12 psi (80 kPa).

The static head is the pressure required to push water vertically, or the pressure caused at the bottom of a column of water. It requires 0.433 psi to lift up water 1 ft. Viewed another way, 1 psi will lift water 2.3 ft. In SI units, 1 m of head equals 10 kPa.

Example 31.1

How much pressure is lost in static head at a fixture 40 ft (12 m) above a water main with a pressure of 45 psi (310 kPa)? Ignoring friction loss, how much pressure is available to operate a fixture at this level?

If 0.434 psi is equivalent to 1 ft (10 kPa is equivalent to 1 m), then the pressure loss is

$$(40\text{ ft})\left(0.433\,\frac{\frac{\text{lbf}}{\text{in}^2}}{\text{ft}}\right) = 17.32\text{ psi} \qquad \text{[U.S.]}$$

$$(12\text{ m})\left(10\,\frac{\text{kPa}}{\text{m}}\right) = 120\text{ kPa} \qquad \text{[SI]}$$

Ignoring friction loss, the remaining pressure at the 40 ft (12 m) level is

$$45\text{ psi} - 17.32\text{ psi} = 27.68\text{ psi} \qquad \text{[U.S.]}$$

$$310\text{ kPa} - 120\text{ kPa} = 190\text{ kPa} \qquad \text{[SI]}$$

An *upfeed system* uses pressure in the water main directly to supply the fixtures. See Fig. 31.1(a). Because there is always some friction in the system and some pressure must be available to work the highest fixtures, the practical limit is about 40 ft to 60 ft (12 m to 18 m).

If the building is too tall for an upfeed system, a *downfeed system* is most often used. In this case, water from the main is pumped to storage tanks near the top of the building or at the top of the zone served and flows by gravity to the fixtures. See Fig. 31.1(b). The pressure at any fixture or point in the system is determined by the distance from the outlet of the tank to the fixture, using the equivalency of 0.433 psi for every foot (10 kPa for every meter).

The height of the zone served by a downfeed system is determined by the maximum allowable pressure on the fixtures at the bottom of the zone, allowing for friction loss in the piping. Depending on the fixture and manufacturer, this maximum pressure is from 45 psi to 60 psi (310 kPa to 415 kPa). Therefore, the maximum height of a zone is 60 divided by 0.433 psi, or about 138 ft ($^{415}/_{10}$ kPa, or about 41.5 m). Beyond this, pressure-reducing valves are required.

Conversely, the pressure at the fixtures at the top of a downfeed system is also of concern because there must be a minimum pressure to make fixtures work properly. For example, if a flush toilet needs 15 psi (100 kPa), then the water tank must be a minimum of $^{15}/_{0.434}$, or about 35 ft above the fixture ($^{100}/_{10}$, or about 10 m). Actually, the distance would have to be slightly greater to overcome friction loss in the piping.

In some cases, the lower floors of a high-rise building are served by an upfeed system and the upper floors are served by a downfeed system.

Another type of supply system that can be used for medium-sized buildings is the *direct upfeed pumping system*, or *tankless system*. Several pumps are used together controlled by a pressure sensor. When demand is light, only one pump operates to supply the needed pressure. As demand increases and is detected by the pressure sensor, another pump automatically starts.

Components and Materials

A water supply system is comprised of piping, fittings, valves, and other specialized components. Piping can be copper, steel, plastic, or brass. Copper is most commonly used because of its corrosion resistance, strength, low friction loss, and small outside diameter. Where the water is not corrosive, steel or galvanized steel pipe can be used, but these materials are more difficult to assemble because of their screw fittings. Steel pipe is available in different wall thicknesses that are indicated by schedule numbers. Schedule 40 pipe is the most commonly used.

Copper is available in three grades: K, L, and M. DWV copper is also used for drainage, waste, and vent piping that is not subject to pressure as supply pipe is, but it is rarely used. Type K has the thickest walls and comes in straight lengths (hard temper) or in coils (soft temper). It is used for underground supply pipe where greater strength is required. Type L has thinner walls than type K and also comes in straight lengths or coils. It is the grade most commonly used for the majority of the plumbing system in a building. Type M is the thinnest of the three types and is available in straight lengths (hard temper) only. It is only used where low pressure is involved, such as branch supply lines, chilled water systems, exposed lines in heating systems, and drainage piping.

Plastic pipe has generally gained acceptance as a material suitable for supply piping, although some codes still restrict its use.

Local codes should be consulted to determine what type of plastic pipe may be used and in what types of buildings; some kinds of pipe are allowed in Type III, IV, and V buildings, but not allowed in certain locations in Type I and II buildings.

Plastic pipe has many advantages over rigid copper or steel piping. These include light weight, corrosion resistance, fast and easy installation, flexibility, and flameless installation (unlike copper). However, plastics can be flammable or may emit smoke and toxic gas if burned, and require petroleum products for manufacture. Table 31.1 gives a summary of the types of plastic pipe in use.

A new pipe material gaining wider use is cross-linked polyethylene (PEX). PEX is manufactured as continuous flexible tubing for use with both hot and cold water supply under pressure as well as for hydronic heating. Unlike a standard plumbing system, PEX is generally run directly from each fixture back to a manifold that connects to the main hot or cold supply piping. This avoids the need for fittings and makes installation faster. PEX has many advantages over other types of plastic piping including the following.

- It is flexible and can be run around obstructions in walls and ceilings.
- It is manufactured in continuous lengths, so it can be run from fixtures directly to the supply manifold without the need for fittings.
- It is lightweight, making it easier to ship, handle, and install than rigid pipe.
- It conserves energy because of its low thermal conductivity.
- It is resistant to freezing and is less prone to breakage if a building loses heat.
- It is resistant to scale buildup.
- It has a lower installed cost than rigid piping or other types of plastic.
- It eliminates water hammer and allows water to flow quietly through it.

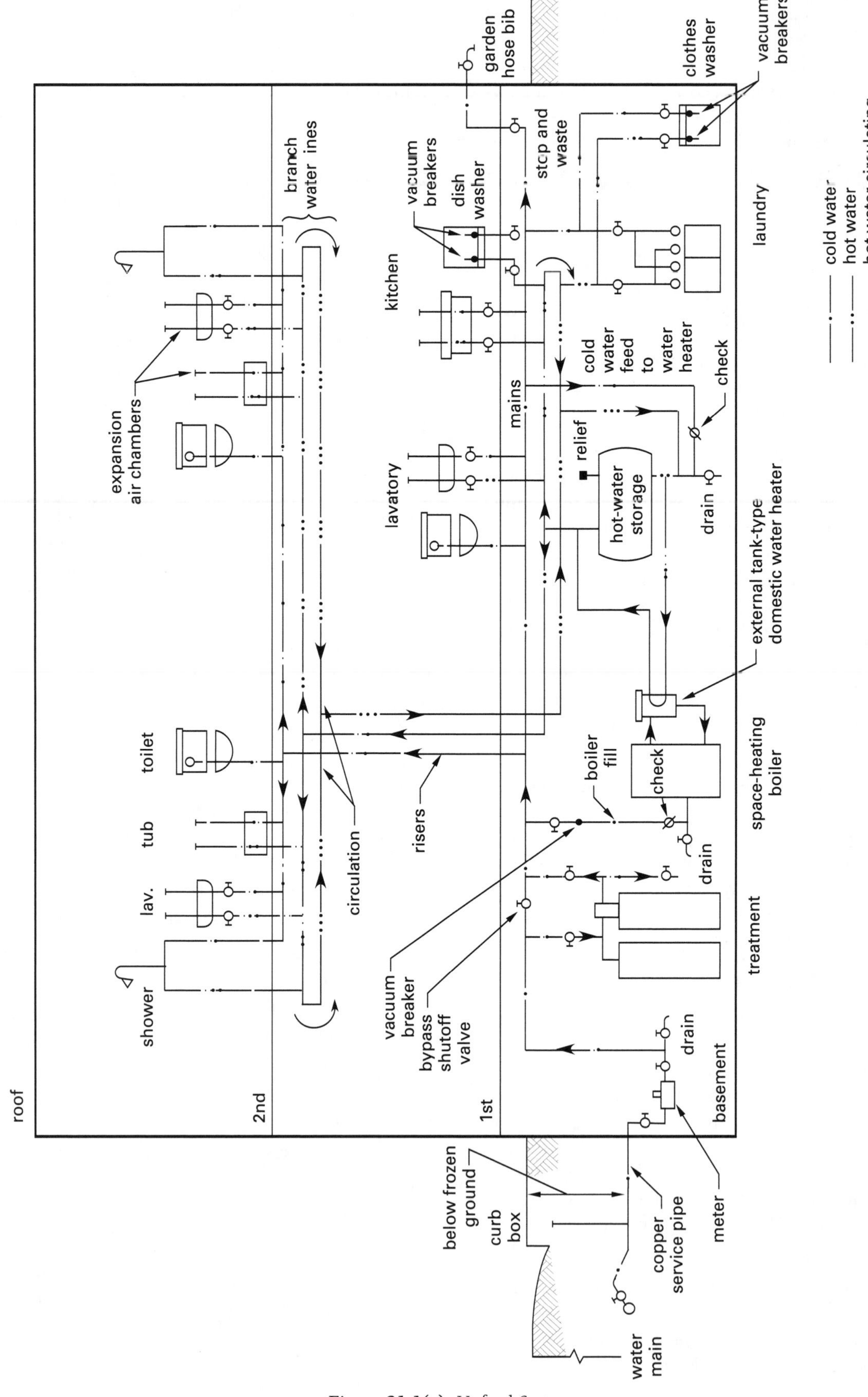

Figure 31.1(a) Upfeed System

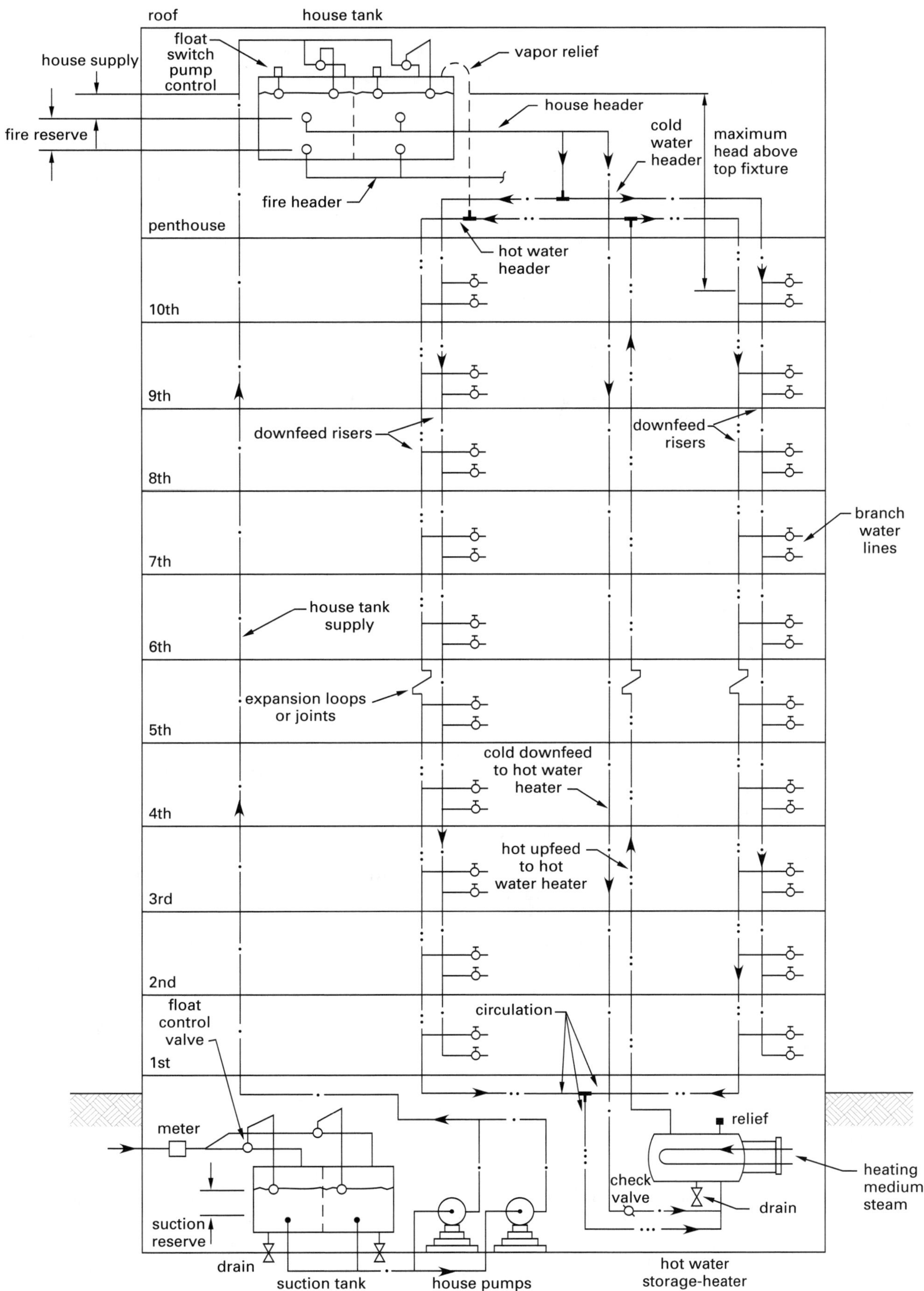

Figure 31.1(b) Downfeed System

Table 31.1

Plastic Pipe Types and Uses

abbreviation	uses	rigidity	connections
ABS	drainage	rigid	hub and clamps, solvent
CPVC	hot and cold supply, sprinklers	rigid	solvent welded, heat fused
HDPE	exterior water supply	rigid/flexible	heat fused, solvent welded
PE	water supply, irrigation sprinklers, exterior drainage	flexible	clamps, heat fused
PEX	hot and cold supply, hydronic heating	flexible	expansion fittings, compressing, crimping
PEX-AL-PEX	water supply, compressed air and gas	flexible	expansion fittings, compressing, crimping
PP	industrial supply and waste for chemical resistance and high heat	rigid	compression, solvent weld
PVC	cold water supply only, drainage	rigid	solvent welded, threaded for schedule 80

ABS: acrylonitrile butadiene styrene
CPVC: chlorinated polyvinyl chloride
HDPE: high-density polyethylene
PE: polyethylene
PEX: cross-linked polyethylene
PEX-AL-PEX: PEX/aluminum/PEX
PP: polypropylene
PVC: polyvinyl chloride

Because of its environmentally intensive extraction and manufacturing processes, PEX is more environmentally friendly than copper, even though copper is highly recyclable. PEX is also more environmentally friendly than CPVC, because the manufacturing process for CPVC is toxic, the solvents used in joining CPVC pipe are hazardous, and CPVC can release toxins when burned.

Supply piping is connected with a variety of fittings, valves, and other components to form a complete system. Fittings connect pipes where lengths must be joined, where a change in direction occurs, where three pipes join, or where a change in size occurs. Figure 31.2 shows some common fittings for rigid piping.

A *union* is a special fitting that connects two rigid sections of pipe and that can be easily unscrewed to allow for repairs or additions to the piping system. Unions are also used between piping and devices that may need to be replaced, such as water heaters. Adapters are also available that allow two different piping materials to be joined.

Fittings for steel and brass are made from malleable iron, cast iron, and brass and are threaded to receive the threaded pipe. Pipe compound or pipe tape is used to produce a watertight seal when the two are joined. Copper and plastic fittings are slightly larger than the pipe, to allow them to be slipped in. Copper joints are sealed by soldering, sometimes called sweating, and plastic pipes are sealed by using a solvent that "melts" the plastic together.

The connections between small-diameter pipes connecting bath and kitchen fixtures to supply line valves are often made with compression fittings. To make these types of connections, a flare nut is slipped over the copper tubing. Then, the copper end is flared slightly and fit onto a mating flange on the valve or faucet. The flare nut is then screwed onto the threads of the valve or faucet fitting, compressing the flanged tubing tightly against the mating flange.

Valves are used to control water flow. They are located at risers, horizontal branch lines, and pipe connections to fixtures and equipment, such as water heaters and sinks. Valves allow selective shutdown of the system for repairs without affecting the entire building. Four common valve types are shown in Fig. 31.3.

The *globe valve* is used where water flow is variably and frequently controlled, such as with faucets or hose bibbs. A handle operates a stem that compresses a washer against a metal seat. Because the water must make two 90° turns, the friction loss in this type of valve is high. A *gate valve* seats a

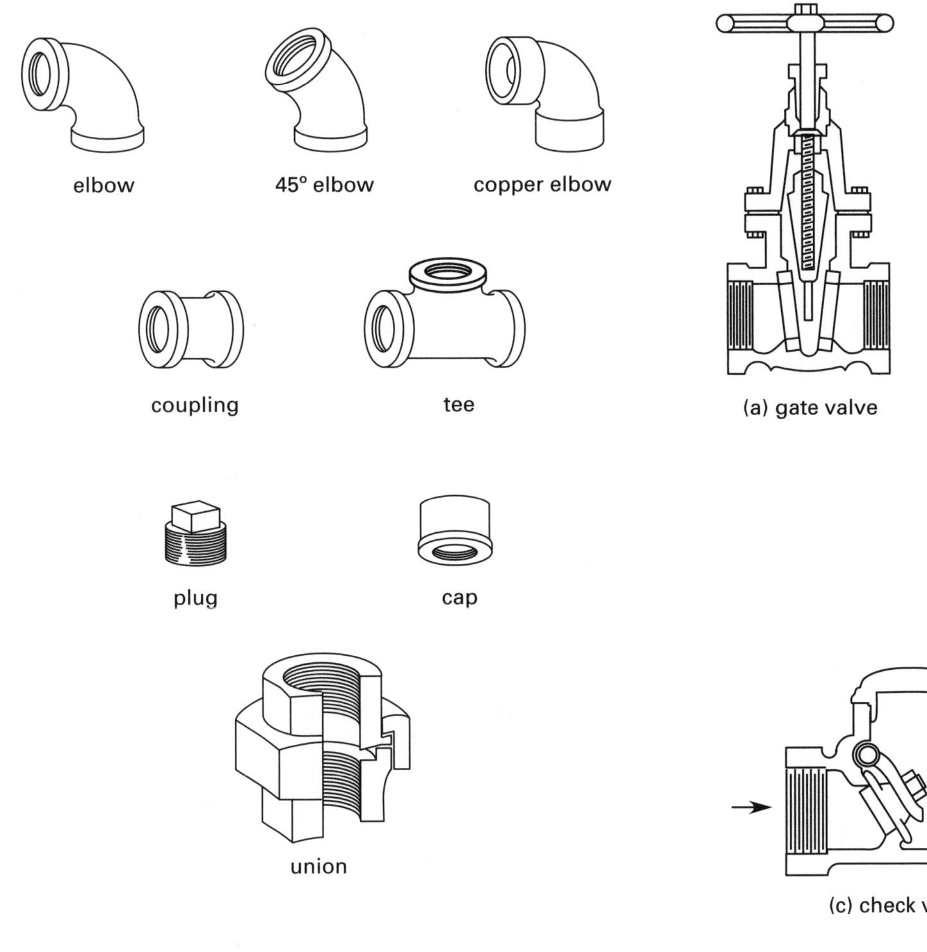

Figure 31.2 Plumbing Fittings

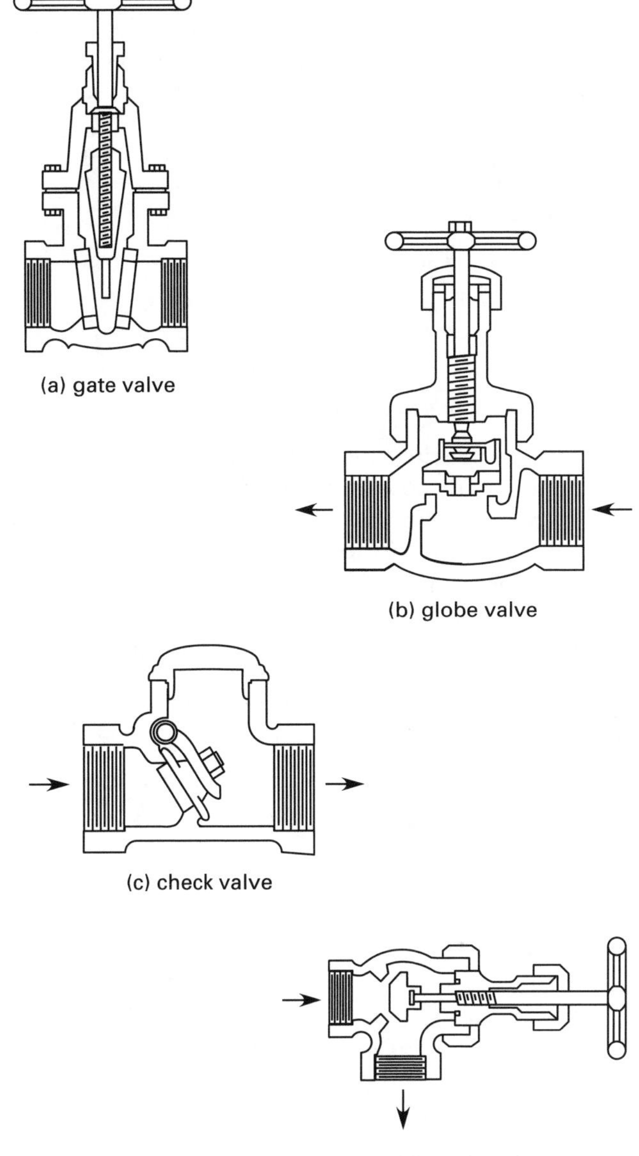

Figure 31.3 Valves

metal wedge against two metal parts of the valve. It is used where control is either completely on or off. Because there are no turns, it has a low friction loss. A *check valve* works automatically and allows water flow in only one direction where, for example, backflow might contaminate a potable water supply.

For water control at sinks and lavatories, a single-handle faucet is most commonly used. One handle controls both the hot and cold water supply and mixes the water to suit the temperature needs of the user. Valves are also available that control temperature to prevent scalding and restrict flow to conserve water.

Other types of components include air chambers, shock absorbers, pressure reducers, and flow restrictors. Air chambers and shock absorbers are used to prevent *water hammer*. This is the noise caused when a valve or faucet is closed quickly, causing the water moving in the system to stop abruptly and the pipes to rattle. An *air chamber* is a length of pipe installed above the connection to the faucet that cushions the surge of water. A *shock absorber* performs the same function with a manufactured expansion device.

Pressure reducers, sometimes called *pressure regulators*, are required on fixtures if the supply pressure is too high, over about 60 psi (415 kPa). Because most fixtures only require from 5 psi to 15 psi (35 kPa to 100 kPa) to operate, higher pressures can cause excessive wear on the fixture. Pressure relief valves, on the other hand, are safety devices designed to open when pressure exceeds some predetermined maximum. They are used on water heaters and similar equipment where excessively high pressures could cause damage or explosion.

System Design

Designing a plumbing system involves sizing the pipes and laying out the required fittings, valves, and other components. As previously mentioned, there must be adequate pressure at the most remote fixture after deducting various pressure losses from the available pressure at the water main. Stated another way, the sum of all these values must be equal to or less than the water main pressure.

	pressure at most remote fixture
+	pressure loss from static head
+	pressure loss by friction in piping and fittings
+	pressure loss through water meter
=	total street water main pressure

The pressure required for fixtures can be found in Table 31.2. The pressure loss from static head is found by multiplying the total height by 0.434. (In SI units, multiply the height in meters by 10.) The water main pressure is found by consulting the local water company. What remains is to determine the pressure losses through the piping and water meter, which is most often a process of trial and error.

Table 31.2

Minimum Flow Pressure for Various Fixtures

	minimum pressure	
fixture	(psi)	(kPa)
standard lavatory	8	55
self-closing faucet	12	80
sink faucet, $^3/_8$ in	10	70
kitchen sink	8	55
service sink	8	55
flush-tank toilet	8	55
flush-valve toilet	15	100
flush-valve urinal	15	100
bathtub	8	55
shower	8	55
dishwasher	8	55
clothes washer	8	55
drinking fountain	8	55
hose bibb	8	55
fire hose	30	200

Pressure loss in pipes depend on the diameter of the pipe and the flow in gallons per minute. Pressure loss is due to friction within the pipe. For the same flow rate, the smaller the diameter of the pipe, the greater the friction. Likewise, for the same diameter pipe, the greater the flow rate, the greater the friction. The probable demand flow is found by first determining the demand load of the entire system or individual parts of the system. Probable demand is defined by fixture units; a fixture unit is a unit flow rate approximately equal to 1 ft^3/min. Fixture units for various fixtures have been established and are listed in Table 31.3.

Because it is unlikely that all the fixtures in a building would be in use at the same time, tables or graphs are available that relate load (i.e., fixture units) to flow in gallons per minute (liters per second). The *International Plumbing Code* (IPC) uses a table. In these tables or graphs, two sets of values are available, one for systems that primarily use flush-tank toilets and one for systems that use flush valves (which use more water). Table 31.4 shows a portion of the table used in the IPC for estimating demands. The values are based on experience and illustrate that flow does not increase in direct proportion to an increase in load.

Example 31.2

What is the flow rate for a group of plumbing fixtures in a small office building consisting of five flush-valve toilets, two $^3/_4$ in flush-valve urinals, four lavatories, two service sinks, and a drinking fountain?

From Table 31.3, the fixture units are calculated as follows.

toilets	(5)(10)	= 50
urinals	(2)(5)	= 10
lavatories	(4)(1.5)	= 6
sinks	(2)(2.25)	= 4.5
fountain	(1)(0.25)	= 0.25
total		70.75 fixture units

In Table 31.4, locate the demand for predominately flush valves, with a load of 70 fixture units. The demand is found to be about 58 gpm. Round up to 60 gpm.

Once the probable flow rate is known, other charts are used to relate flow, pipe size, and friction loss in static head in pounds per square inch per 100 ft length of pipe. The goal in pipe sizing is to select the smallest size that will do the job within the pressure loss limits. The smallest possible pipe size is desired because cost increases with pipe size. Several charts are available for different types of pipe. One such chart is shown in Fig. 31.4.

To use the chart, find the flow in gallons per minute determined from the fixture unit demand, and then read across to the intersection with one of the pipe diameter lines. If necessary, assume a pipe size at first, and then determine the total friction loss. If the total friction loss is too great, select a larger pipe size and perform the calculation again. Using Ex. 31.2, the pressure loss for 60 gpm in a $1^1/_2$ in pipe is about 12 psi per 100 ft.

In this example, if a $1^1/_2$ in pipe is used, the flow rate will be about 10 ft/sec (3 m/s). This, combined with the relatively high pressure drop of 12 psi per 100 ft (83 kPa per 30 m), would suggest that at least a 2 in (50) pipe should be used instead of a $1^1/_2$ in pipe.

Table 31.3
Load Values Assigned to Fixtures

fixture	occupancy	type of supply control	load values, in water supply fixture units (wsfu) cold	hot	total
bathroom group	private	flush tank	2.7	1.5	3.6
bathroom group	private	flush valve	6.0	3.0	8.0
bathtub	private	faucet	1.0	1.0	1.4
bathtub	public	faucet	3.0	3.0	4.0
bidet	private	faucet	1.5	1.5	2.0
combination fixture	private	faucet	2.25	2.25	3.0
dishwashing machine	private	automatic		1.4	1.4
drinking fountain	offices, etc.	3/8″ valve	0.25		0.25
kitchen sink	private	faucet	1.0	1.0	1.4
kitchen sink	hotel, restaurant	faucet	3.0	3.0	4.0
laundry trays (1 to 3)	private	faucet	1.0	1.0	1.4
lavatory	private	faucet	0.5	0.5	0.7
lavatory	public	faucet	1.5	1.5	2.0
service sink	offices, etc.	faucet	2.25	2.25	3.0
shower head	public	mixing valve	3.0	3.0	4.0
shower head	private	mixing valve	1.0	1.0	1.4
urinal	public	1″ flush valve	10.0		10.0
urinal	public	3/4″ flush valve	5.0		5.0
urinal	public	flush tank	3.0		3.0
washing machine (8 lbs)	private	automatic	1.0	1.0	1.4
washing machine (8 lbs)	public	automatic	2.25	2.25	3.0
washing machine (15 lbs)	public	automatic	3.0	3.0	4.0
water closet	private	flush valve	6.0		6.0
water closet	private	flush tank	2.2		2.2
water closet	public	flush valve	10.0		10.0
water closet	public	flush tank	5.0		5.0
water closet	public or private	flushometer tank	2.0		2.0

For SI: 1 inch = 25.4 mm, 1 pound = 0.454 kg
For fixtures not listed, loads should be assumed by comparing the fixture to one listed using water in similar quantities and at similar rates. The assigned loads for fixtures with both hot and cold water supplies are given for separate hot and cold water loads and for total load, the separate hot and cold water loads being three-fourths of the total load for the fixture in each case.

When using a chart like the one shown in Fig. 31.4, the velocity must be considered when selecting a pipe size. Above about 10 ft/sec (3 m/s) water in pipes is too noisy. In sound-sensitive situations anything above about 6 ft/sec (1.8 m/s) may be too noisy. The additional diagonal lines shown in Fig. 31.4 show the velocity, so this variable can be checked.

To find the total friction loss in the piping and fittings, calculate the total length of piping from the meter to the fixture under consideration. Friction loss in fittings is calculated by referring to tables that give the losses for various diameter fittings in equivalent lengths of pipe. Table 31.5 is one such table.

If the layout of the plumbing system has not been completely determined, it may be necessary to estimate the number and locations of fittings. Friction losses for pipes and fittings are then added together to get the total loss in pounds per square inch.

The final step is to calculate the loss through the water meter. Charts that relate pressure loss to meter size and flow rate in gallons per minute are also available for this. When the supply main is $1^1/_2$ in (38) or greater, the typical meter size is one pipe size smaller than the main.

One critical part of plumbing design in large buildings is allowance for the expansion of piping. This is especially

Table 31.4
Table for Estimating Demand

supply systems predominantly for flush tanks			supply systems predominantly for flush valves		
load	demand		load	demand	
(water supply fixture units)	(gallons per minute)	(cubic feet per minute)	(water supply fixture units)	(gallons per minute)	(cubic feet per minute)
1	3.0	0.04104			
2	5.0	0.0684			
3	6.5	0.86892			
4	8.0	1.06944			
5	9.4	1.256592	5	15.0	2.0052
6	10.7	1.430376	6	17.4	2.326032
7	11.8	1.577424	7	19.8	2.646364
8	12.8	1.711104	8	22.2	2.967696
9	13.7	1.831416	9	24.6	3.288528
10	14.6	1.951728	10	27.0	3.60936
11	15.4	2.058672	11	27.8	3.716304
12	16.0	2.13888	12	28.6	3.823248
13	16.5	2.20572	13	29.4	3.930192
14	17.0	2.27256	14	30.2	4.037136
15	17.5	2.3394	15	31.0	4.14408
16	18.0	2.90624	16	31.8	4.241024
17	18.4	2.459712	17	32.6	4.357968
18	18.8	2.513184	18	33.4	4.464912
19	19.2	2.566656	19	34.2	4.571856
20	19.6	2.620128	20	35.0	4.6788
25	21.5	2.87412	25	38.0	5.07984
30	23.3	3.114744	30	42.0	5.61356
35	24.9	3.328632	35	44.0	5.88192
40	26.3	3.515784	40	46.0	6.14928
45	27.7	3.702936	45	48.0	6.41664
50	29.1	3.890088	50	50.0	6.684
60	32.0	4.27776	60	54.0	7.21872
70	35.0	4.6788	70	58.0	7.75344
80	38.0	5.07984	80	61.2	8.181216
90	41.0	5.48088	90	64.3	8.595624
100	43.5	5.81508	100	67.5	9.0234
120	48.0	6.41664	120	73.0	9.75864
140	52.5	7.0182	140	77.0	10.29336
160	57.0	7.61976	160	81.0	10.82808
180	61.0	8.15448	180	85.5	11.42964
200	65.0	8.6892	200	90.0	12.0312
225	70.0	9.3576	225	95.5	12.76644
250	75.0	10.0260	250	101.0	13.50168
275	80.0	10.6944	275	104.5	13.96956
300	85.0	11.3628	300	108.0	14.43744
400	105.0	14.0364	400	127.0	16.97736
500	124.0	16.57632	500	143.0	19.11624
750	170.0	22.7256	750	177.0	23.66136
1,000	208.0	27.80544	1,000	208.0	27.80544
1,250	239.0	31.94952	1,250	239.0	31.94952
1,500	269.0	35.95992	1,500	269.0	35.95992
1,750	297.0	39.70296	1,750	297.0	39.70296

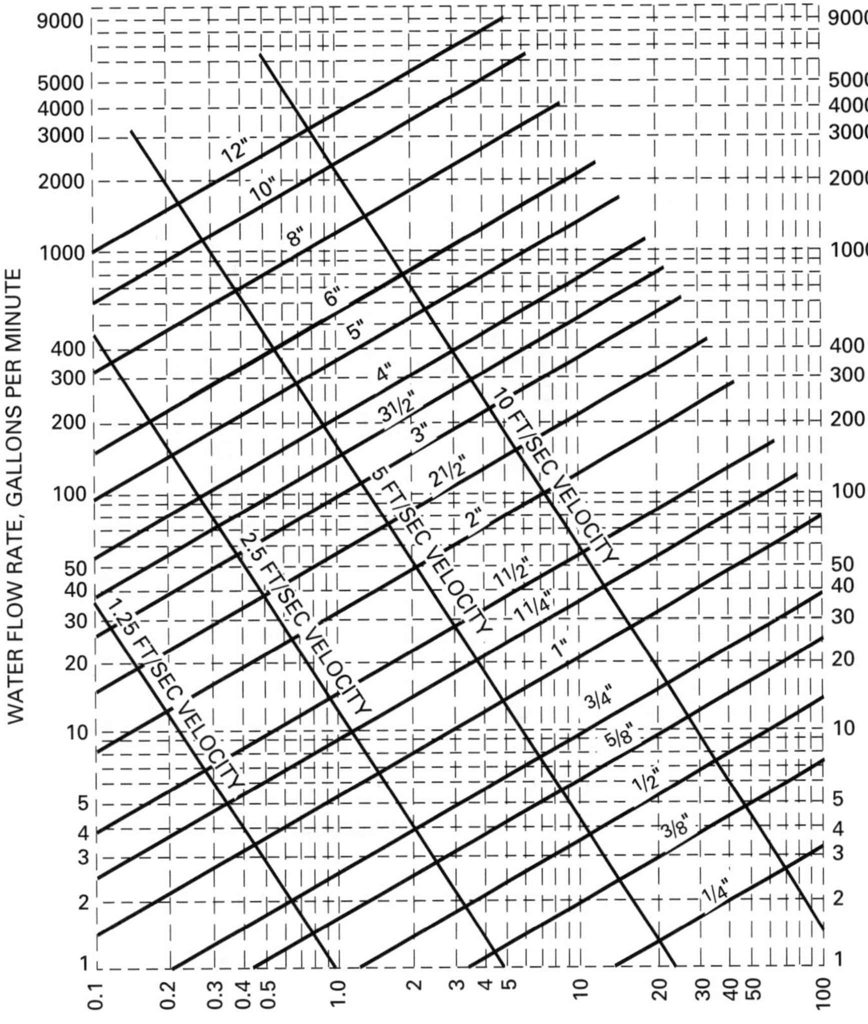

Note: Fluid velocities in excess of 5 to 8 feet/second are not usually recommended.

FIGURE E103A.2
FRICTION LOSS IN SMOOTH PIPE[a]
(TYPE L, ASTM B 88 COPPER TUBING)

For SI: 1 inch = 25.4 mm, 1 foot = 304.8 mm, 1 gpm = 3.785 L/m, 1 psi = 6.895 kPa, 1 foot per second = 0.305 m/s

a. This chart applies to smooth new copper tubing with recessed (Streamline) soldered joints and to the actual sizes of types indicated on the diagram.

Figure 31.4 Flow Chart for Type L Copper Pipe

Table 31.5
Allowance in Equivalent Length of Pipe for Friction Loss in Valves and Threaded Fittings

fitting or valve	pipe sizes (in) 1/2	3/4	1	1 1/4	1 1/2	2	2 1/2	3
45-degree elbow	1.2	1.5	1.8	2.4	3.0	4.0	5.0	6.0
90-degree elbow	2.0	2.5	3.0	4.0	5.0	7.0	8.0	10.0
tee, run	0.6	0.8	0.9	1.2	1.5	2.0	2.5	3.0
tee, branch	3.0	4.0	5.0	6.0	7.0	10.0	12.0	15.0
gate valve	0.4	0.5	0.6	0.8	1.0	1.3	1.6	2.0
balancing valve	0.8	1.1	1.5	1.9	2.2	3.0	3.7	4.5
plug-type cock	0.8	1.1	1.5	1.9	2.2	3.0	3.7	4.5
check valve, swing	5.6	8.4	11.2	14.0	16.8	22.4	28.0	33.6
globe valve	15.0	20.0	25.0	35.0	45.0	55.0	65.0	80.0
angle valve	8.0	12.0	15.0	18.0	22.0	28.0	34.0	40.0

For SI: 1 inch = 25.4 mm, 1 foot = 304.8 mm, 1 degree = 0.0175 rad.

important in high-rise buildings where long lengths of piping are encountered. For example, a 100 ft length of copper pipe can expand well over 1/2 in with a 60° temperature change. PVC pipe expands 3.5 times more than copper pipe. Figure 31.5 shows two common methods of providing for expansion.

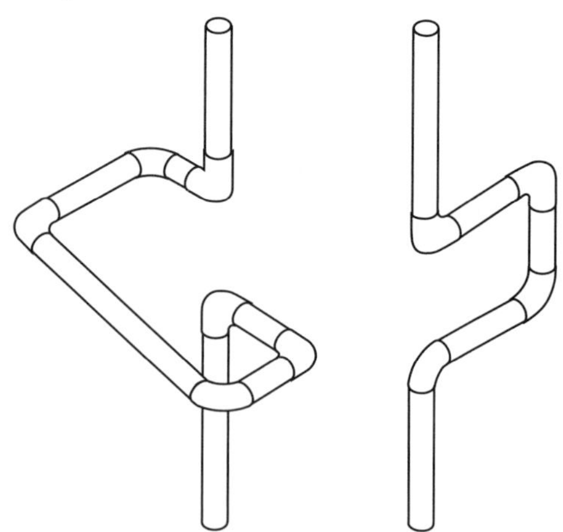

Figure 31.5 Expansion Devices for Hot Water Piping

Irrigation Systems

Irrigation is required for most landscape watering. However, to reduce potable water use and plan more sustainable buildings, irrigation must be designed efficiently or significantly reduced. This can be done in two ways: by landscaping with native plants that require little or no artificial watering and by using efficient irrigation systems. A building project can receive from two to four points in the LEED rating system by incorporating water-efficient landscaping.

The simplest way to reduce irrigation requirements is to use plants that can grow with the climate's natural precipitation. This is possible in all climates, including desert regions. If some landscaping is needed that does need irrigation, it can be limited to certain areas, and the remainder of the site can be planted with plants that need little or no additional water.

If irrigation is used, it should be designed as efficiently as possible. Timers can be used to limit sprinkler watering to early mornings or evenings, which will reduce evaporation. Rain sensors can be installed to stop the watering when there is rain. *Tensiometers*, which measure the moisture content of the soil at the plant's root zone, can be used so that no more water is used than needed. For small trees, shrubs, and individual plants, a *drip irrigation* system is more efficient than sprinklers. This type of system slowly releases water only in the area of the plant and can also be controlled with timers and rain sensors.

Hot Water Supply

Hot water is supplied by tank-type water heaters or boilers in which water is heated with gas, oil, electricity, or steam. In residences and small buildings, a single supply pipe is provided from the heater to the fixtures. This minimizes the cost of piping but can result in long waits for hot water when the fixture has not been turned on for a while. The water in the pipes cools and must be run until fresh hot water from the heater travels the distance to the fixture.

This problem can be solved with a two-pipe circulating system. All fixtures needing hot water are connected with a supply pipe and a return pipe. The natural convection in the system keeps the water slowly circulating; hot water rises to the uppermost fixtures and, as it cools, falls down to the water heater to be reheated. When a circulating system is used in long, low buildings or buildings where natural convection may not provide enough circulation, pumps are used.

The size of the water heater is based on the total daily and peak hourly hot water demands of a building. The peak hourly demand can range from 0.4 gal (1.52 L) per person in a peak hour for an office building to 12 gal (45.5 L) per unit for a small apartment building. The peak hourly demand is used because at certain times of the day it is likely that most occupants will want hot water at the same time. For residences and small buildings, the capacity for the peak hourly demand will be the size of the water heater. For large buildings, a separate storage tank is required to meet demand, while a smaller boiler actually heats the water.

In addition to storage capacity, the *recovery rate* of a water heater is important. This is the number of gallons (liters) per hour of cold water that the heater can raise to the desired temperature.

The size of hot water piping is determined in a manner similar to that used for cold water piping except that only the fixtures requiring hot water are used to calculate load. This value is multiplied by 0.75 (75%) and then looked up in Table 31.4 to find the flow rate. In no case can the pipe size be less than the minimum sizes given in the plumbing codes.

Water heaters are set to keep the water at any desired temperature. Generally, this setting is the highest temperature that is required at the point of use. Recommended point-of-use temperatures range from 95°F (35.0°C) for therapeutic baths to 180°F (82.2°C) for commercial and institutional laundries and for sanitizing rinses for commercial dishwashers. Other common temperatures include 105°F (40.6°C) for hand washing, 110°F (43.3°C) for showers and baths, and 140°F (60.0°C) for residential dish washing and laundry. Above about 110°F (43.3°C), water becomes uncomfortable to the touch.

Water heaters are available in several configurations and heating methods as diagrammed in Fig. 31.6. First, there are two basic heating methods, direct and indirect. *Direct heating* brings the water directly into contact with heated surfaces that are warmed with flame, hot gases, electricity, or solar radiation. This is the method used for the typical residential tank-type water heater. *Indirect heating* uses an intermediary transfer medium to heat the water. For example, in commercial applications where central steam is available, the steam can be piped to tubes within a tank containing the domestic hot water.

With either direct or indirect heating there are three basic types of equipment: storage tank, tankless, and circulating. Diagrams of these types of units using both direct and indirect heating are shown in Fig. 31.6. With the *storage tank system*, the same tank is used to both heat the water and store it for use. In the *tankless system*, water is quickly heated as it is needed and sent to where it is needed. One of the common variations of the diagram shown in Fig. 31.6 is the electric instantaneous water heater. These units are often used in remote locations where it is impractical or uneconomical to pipe hot water continuously. As the hot-water faucet is turned on, a high-capacity electric coil instantaneously heats cold water. With the *circulating system*, the water is heated in one place and stored in a separate tank until it is needed. This method is commonly used in solar-powered water heating systems and in many commercial applications.

In some cases it is impractical or very inefficient to use an indirect, tankless system. For example, heating domestic hot water in a furnace or boiler whose primary purpose is to provide space heating only works when the furnace or boiler is functioning. This means that the heating plant would have to work in the summer. In these cases, the heating plant provides only supplemental heating, and there is another source of heat for water heating only.

Solar Water Heating

Solar energy is commonly used to heat water for domestic use, industrial use, and swimming pools. Nearly all solar heating systems have certain components in common. These include some type of solar collector, a storage tank, associated piping to move the fluids, and a backup heater. If it is an active system it will use pumps and associated controls and sensors. The collectors are usually flat plate, but they can also be focusing collectors, or in the case of batch systems, they can be simply a black tank behind glass or plastic.

Many types of solar water heating systems exist, but they can be broadly classified by how the heat transfer occurs, how the heating fluid is circulated, and their means of protection from freezing.

Solar heat is transferred either directly or indirectly. In a *direct system*, or *open-loop system*, the water used in the building is the same water that is heated in the solar collectors. An *indirect system*, or *closed-loop system*, uses a separate fluid for collecting heat, which is then transferred to the domestic hot water. Direct systems have the advantages of simple design and operation and high efficiency, but they are subject to freezing. Indirect systems are easier to protect

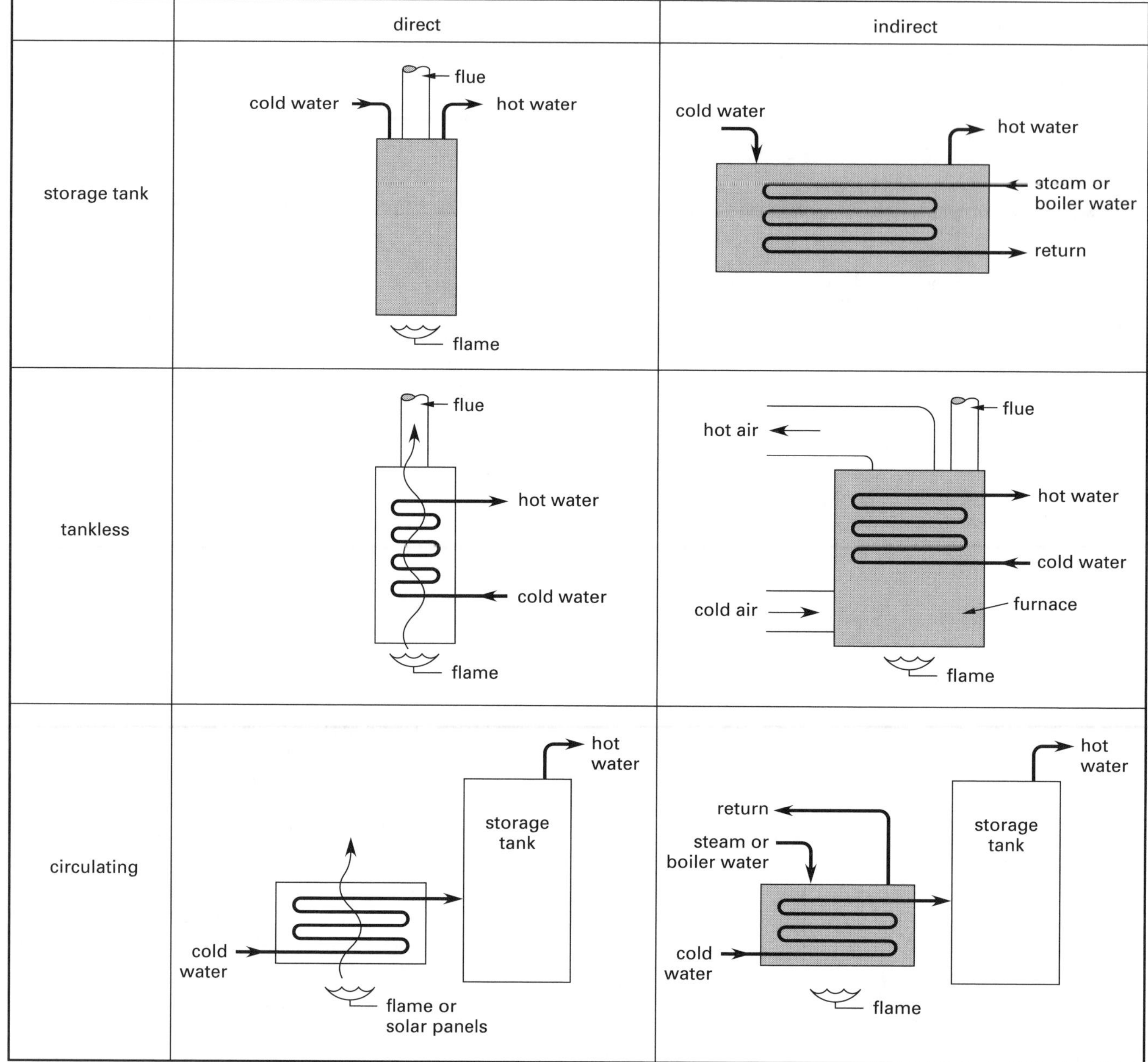

Figure 31.6 Water Heater Types

from freezing because the heat-collecting fluid can contain antifreeze, and these systems can also operate at a lower pressure than that required for the domestic hot water. However, a heat exchanger is required, which reduces efficiency.

The heating fluid is circulated either passively or actively. *Passive circulation systems* rely on gravity and the thermosiphoning action of heated water. They are simple and low-cost systems, but their storage tanks must be placed above the solar collectors, and the points of use must be close to the storage tanks. *Active circulation systems* use pumps to circulate the heat-collecting fluid. These systems are much more flexible and reliable but add costs for equipment and operation.

Protection from freezing is provided either by using a non-freezing medium (antifreeze solution or phase-change material) or by draining the fluid at night and during cloudy weather. Of course, direct or open-loop systems must use some type of drainage system.

Some of the common types of solar heating systems with which examinees should be familiar are listed here.

Batch system. A batch system (also known as a *breadbox heater*) heats water directly in a black-painted tank inside a glazed box. This passive system is simple, but it is subject to freezing and nighttime heat loss.

Thermosiphon system. A thermosiphon system relies on the natural movement of heated water to circulate the water in a passive, open-loop system. This system is also simple, but the storage tanks must be located above the collectors, and the piping must be kept simple to minimize pipe friction. To address the problem of freezing, a variation of this method uses a closed-loop system with antifreeze fluid.

Closed-loop active system. This is one of the most common types of systems for both residential and commercial applications. A separate, nonfreezing fluid is circulated by pumps through the solar collectors and into a heat exchanger where the domestic hot water is heated. A differential controller senses when the temperature of the collector is lower than that of the stored water and turns the pumps off. This system is flexible and provides control but suffers from some loss in efficiency because of the need for a heat exchanger.

Drain-down system. A drain-down system is a direct (open-loop), active system that solves the problem of freezing by automatically draining the water from the collectors when the outside temperature is near freezing. Because water is wasted whenever the system is drained, this method is best for climates with mild winters where the draining process would not occur frequently.

Drain-back system. The drain-back system is an indirect (closed-loop), active system that uses water as the heat-collector fluid. The heated water is pumped to a heat exchanger where a coil of domestic hot water is heated. When the controller senses the temperature is too low, it turns off the pump, and the collector water drains back into the solar storage tank.

Phase-change system. Hot water systems can also take advantage of phase-change materials as the collector fluid. As discussed in the previous chapter, phase-change materials store large amounts of latent heat as well as sensible heat.

SANITARY DRAINAGE AND VENTING

Drainage is separated into sanitary and storm drainage. *Sanitary drainage* comprises any drainage that may include human waste, whereas *storm drainage* involves only runoff from roof drains, landscaped areas, and the like. The two types of drainage are separated because storm drainage does not have to be treated. It can also easily overload the lines of a sanitary sewage disposal system and cause sewage to back up into a building. This section will discuss sanitary drainage only.

Sanitary drainage systems are sometimes further divided into the categories of graywater and blackwater. *Blackwater* is sewage including human waste, and *graywater* is sewage not including human waste, such as from kitchen sinks, dishwashers, and lavatories. In some conservation systems this distinction is made because gray water can often be recycled directly or with very little treatment for use in irrigation and for other purposes, whereas blackwater needs more extensive treatment prior to recycling or disposal.

Drainage Systems

A drainage system consists of a number of components designed to safely carry away sewage to a private or municipal disposal system. Beginning with an individual fixture, there are a number of components with which examinees should be familiar.

The first is the *trap*. With few exceptions, traps are located at every fixture and are designed to catch and hold a quantity of water to provide a seal that prevents sewage system gases from entering the building. When fixtures, such as toilets, have traps as an integral part of their design or where adjacent fixtures, such as a double kitchen sink, are connected, traps need not be installed. Traps are usually installed within 2 ft (600) of the fixture but may be installed at slightly greater distances depending on the size of the pipe. Occasionally, a house trap is installed at the point where the house drain leaves the building, but this is not always mandatory.

Traps are connected, of course, to the actual drainage piping, but they must also be connected to vents. *Vents* are pipes connected to the drainage system in various ways, vented to outside air, and designed to serve two primary purposes. First, they allow built-up sewage gases to escape instead of bubble through the water in the traps. Second, they allow pressure in the system to equalize so that discharging waste does not create a siphon that would drain the water out of the traps.

Air gaps are also used as a safety feature in sanitary drainage systems. If the potable water outlet was below the highest level of the overflow of a sink or tub, contaminated water in the sink could be siphoned back into the potable water supply lines. To prevent this, faucets are always mounted with their outlets at least 2 in above the highest possible level of waste water.

On fixtures where the water supply is below the rim of the fixture (on a flush-valve toilet, for example) a device called a *vacuum breaker* is used to prevent siphonage by closing when backward water pressure is present.

Figure 31.7 shows a simplified diagram of a typical drainage and vent system. From the trap, sewage travels in fixture branch lines to a vertical stack. If the stack carries human waste from toilets, it is called a *soil stack*. If the stack carries wastes other than human waste, it is known as a *waste stack*.

Vents from individual fixtures are connected above the fixtures in two ways. If a vent connects to a soil or waste stack above the highest fixture in the system, the portion of the stack above this point is known as a *stack vent*. The stack vent extends through the roof. Multistory buildings use a separate pipe for venting. This is called a *vent stack* and either extends through the roof or connects with the stack vent above the highest fixture, as shown in Fig. 31.7.

The stacks connect at the bottom of the building to a horizontal drain. Within the building and to a point 3 ft (1 m) outside the building this is the *house drain* (also known as the *building drain*). From a point 3 ft (1 m) outside the building to the main sewer line or private disposal system, the horizontal pipe is the *house sewer* (also known as the *building sewer*). Cleanouts are provided at the intersections of the stacks and house drain to allow for maintenance of the drain.

Horizontal drains must be sloped to allow for gravity drainage. The usual minimum for branch lines of house drains and sewers is $^1/_4$ in/ft (20 mm/m), but for pipes larger than 3 in (76), $^1/_8$ in/ft (10 mm/m) is sometimes allowed. Changes in direction must be made with easy bends rather than right-angle fittings.

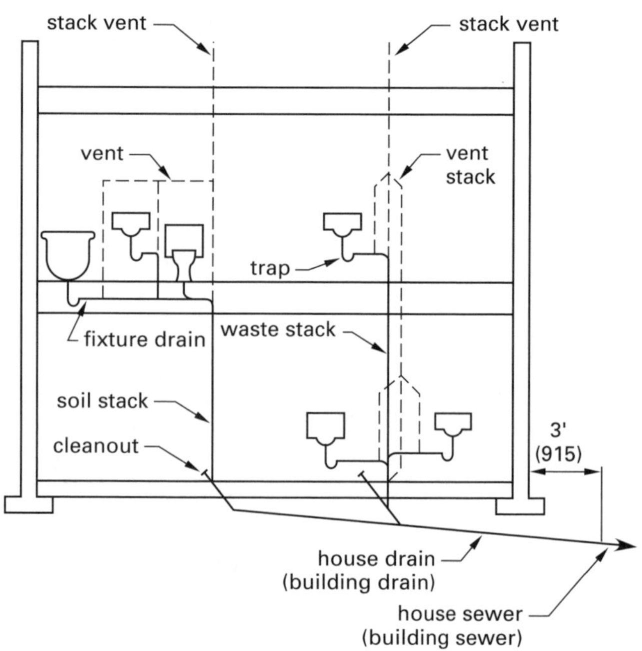

Figure 31.7 Drainage and Vent System

Components and Materials

Piping for drainage systems may be DWV (drainage, waste, and vent) copper, cast iron, or plastic. Plastic has become very popular because it is less expensive and less labor intensive to install than other types. Polyvinyl chloride (PVC) and acrilylonitrile-butadiene styrene (ABS) plastic are suitable for DWV systems. Occasionally, vitrified clay tile may be used for building sewers if allowed by the local code, but the joints in these pipes allow tree roots to grow into them, so they are seldom used.

Cast-iron piping can be connected with hub and spigot joints or with hubless joints. In the hub and spigot fitting, the end of one pipe is slipped into an enlarged hub of another pipe, and the joint is sealed with a gasket. A hubless joint uses a gasket held in place with a stainless steel retaining clamp. Cast-iron pipe is required for the house sewer. Copper and plastic piping are joined, as is supply water piping.

Other parts of a drainage system may include the following components.

Backflow preventers or *backwater valves* prevent sewage from upper stories or from the building sewer from reversing flow and backing up into fixtures set at a lower elevation.

When plumbing fixtures must be below the level of the house drain and house sewer, a *sump pit* and *sump pump* (sometimes called an *ejector pump*) are installed. This device collects the sewage and pumps it to a higher level where it can flow by gravity into the sewer.

Floor drains collect water in shower rooms or in places where overflow is likely. Because some floor drains are seldom used, special care must be taken so that the water seal does not evaporate and allow sewer gases to penetrate the building. The traps of floor drains are usually required to have deeper seals than other types of traps.

Interceptors are devices that collect foreign matter at the source instead of allowing it to enter the sewer system. Some of the more common types include grease traps, plaster traps, and lubricating oil traps. Interceptors have provisions for periodic cleanout of the foreign matter. However, interceptors cannot trap toxic liquids.

System Design

The sizing of drainage pipes is based on the idea of drainage fixture units (just as water supply piping is), although with different values of fixture units for each type of fixture. For example, a lavatory is assigned a drainage fixture unit of 1, and a public water closet is considered to have 6 fixture units. There are also certain minimum sizes of trap arms for individual fixtures: a single lavatory must have at least a $1^1/_4$ in (32) drain and a single toilet must have at least a 3 in

(76) trap arm. The minimum size for a vent is $1^1/_4$ in (32). These values are given in tables from the plumbing code.

Design of a drainage system begins with the individual fixtures and branch lines and proceeds to the sizing of stacks and building drains. Tables in the plumbing code give the maximum number of fixture units and the maximum vertical and horizontal lengths of piping based on pipe diameter. It is thus a simple matter to accumulate fixture units served by a particular stack or drain and increase the size as needed as more fixtures are added to it.

The plumbing code also states the minimum sizes and lengths of vents based on fixture units connected. It also gives the maximum horizontal distance of trap arms based on size.

WASTE DISPOSAL AND TREATMENT

Once sewage leaves a building, it is transported by the house sewer to either a municipal collection system or a private disposal system. Private systems generally consist of a septic tank and a leaching field. The *septic tank* collects the sewage and allows the solid matter to settle to the bottom and the effluent (liquid portion) to drain into the distribution system, where it seeps into the ground. See Fig. 31.8.

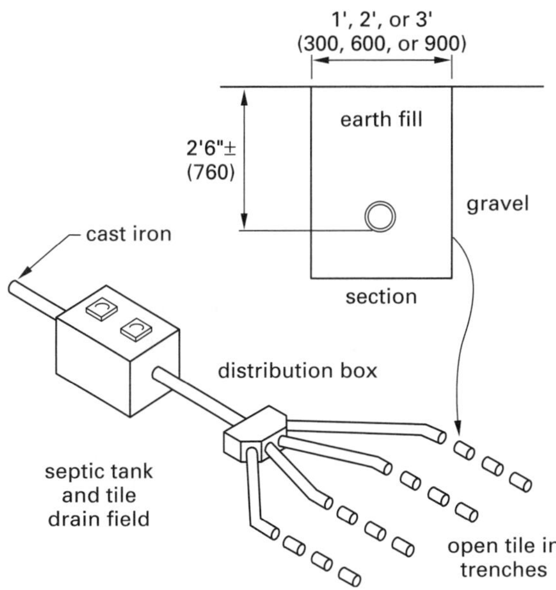

Figure 31.8 Private Sewage Disposal

The size of the septic tank is determined by the amount of daily flow. For residences this is usually based on the number of bedrooms and baths. For larger installations, it is based on the calculated sewage flow in gallons per day. The size and length of the leaching field system are based on the ability of the soil to absorb the effluent. A *leaching field* is an area where effluent seeps from the drain tiles into the soil. This is determined by a percolation test, which measures the amount of time it takes water in a test hole to drop 1 in. Tables give the minimum length of piping in leaching fields based on percolation and volume handled.

Because there is the potential for septic tanks and leaching fields to contaminate potable water supplies—mainly wells—plumbing codes give minimum required distances between various parts of the system and other features of the site, such as wells, property lines, rivers, and buildings. For example, there must be a minimum of 100 ft (30.5 m) between a leaching field and a well, 50 ft (15 m) between a septic tank and a well, and 10 ft (3 m) between a leaching field and a building.

Where sewage is transported from a building to public sewer lines, the building sewer connects to a line in the street or other public right of way. From there, branch lines connect to larger main lines that eventually reach a sewage treatment facility. Manholes are provided for maintenance and inspection of the lines. They are located at every change in direction and at intervals of 150 ft (46 m).

Another method of treating wastewater is with *waste stabilization ponds* (WSP). These ponds, which are typically 4 ft to 8 ft (1.2 m to 2.4 m) deep, act as holding basins for secondary wastewater treatment. The wastewater is directed through a series of ponds, sitting in each one for between three weeks and six months; the process takes longer in colder locations. In the ponds, sewage decomposes biologically through aerobic and anaerobic processes.

One type of WSP system is the *advanced integrated wastewater pond system* (AIWPS). As the wastewater makes its way through the four separate ponds in the system, it is exposed to different conditions to encourage the breakdown and removal of organic matter. The first pond is a facultative pond, in which the wastewater is exposed to aerobic activity near the surface and anaerobic activity near the bottom. The anaerobic activity ferments and consumes sludge, while the aerobic activity oxidizes gases that rise from the fermentation.

The second pond contains a high level of algae, which produce oxygen that promotes further aerobic activity, breaking down dissolved organic matter. Next is a settling pond in which more than half of the algae settle out. Finally, in the maturation pond the water rests to allow pathogenic bacteria of human origin to die. The effluent can then be reused for agricultural or landscape irrigation.

STORM DRAINAGE

Water drainage from rain and snow melt is kept separate from sanitary drainage, as outlined in the previous section. This is to avoid overloading the sanitary drainage system, causing possible backup of sanitary sewer lines. In sparsely populated areas, storm drainage normally soaks into the ground or finds its way to rivers and lakes. In more populated areas with a higher percentage of roofed area and paved streets and parking lots, artificial systems are necessary to safely carry away storm water.

Private Systems

There are several methods for draining water from a private home. The first is the simplest and consists of collecting water from the roof in roof drains or gutters and leaders and simply letting it run onto the ground surrounding the house, where it soaks in. Splash blocks and other devices are used to carry the water far enough from the building to avoid excess water seeping into the foundation or eroding soil around the foundations.

If this is not adequate, drywells are connected to the drain leaders with underground pipes. A *drywell* is a large, porous, underground container where water collects and seeps into the soil. If a drywell is not adequate or the ground is not sufficiently porous, a *drain field*, similar to a leaching field, can be used. In addition to draining water from the roof, the land around the building must be graded to divert water away from the foundation.

Some communities require roof drains to be directly connected to the public sewer system.

Municipal Systems

A municipal storm sewer system is laid out in a manner similar to the sanitary sewage system, collecting runoff from street gutters, catch basins, and individual taps from private buildings and land developments. The system carries the water by gravity to natural drainage areas such as rivers, lakes, or oceans.

In some areas the potential runoff of rainwater from a storm may be too great for the storm system to handle. In this case, building regulations may required private owners to include a retention pond in their site plan. A *retention pond* is designed to contain the maximum expected runoff and then slowly release the water to the storm sewer system. Retention ponds may have a small outlet at one end, like a dam or drain to a low point in the middle of the pond, where a catch basin, or grate, covers the entrance to a pipe. This pipe transports the water to a storm sewer system or other natural drainage area.

Drains, Gutters, and Downspout Sizing

The sizes of horizontal drain pipes, gutters, and downspouts are determined based on the area of the roof or paved area drained and the maximum hourly rainfall. For gutters and horizontal piping, the slope of the pipe is also a factor, lower slopes requiring a greater size. Gutter slopes range from $^1/_{16}$ in/ft (5 mm/m) to $^1/_2$ in/ft (40 mm/m).

Rainfall rates are available from the local weather service or from published maps of the United States and Canada. When calculating the roof area of a sloped roof, the projected area is used. This is the horizontal area defined by the edges of the roof without regard to the slope. Based on the maximum hourly rainfall rate, roof area, and proposed slope of gutter, tables are created that give the minimum required diameter of gutter or roof leader.

FIRE PROTECTION AND LIFE SAFETY

Fire protection and life safety in buildings addresses three major objectives: the protection of life, the protection of property, and the restoration and continued use of the building after the fire. Life safety also involves the protection of people during emergencies other than fire, such as earthquakes, floods, terrorist threats, and similar disasters. However, this section only deals with life safety during fires.

Fire protection in buildings is accomplished in several ways.

- by preventing fires
- by early fire detection and alarm
- by providing for quick exiting of building occupants
- by containing the fire
- by suppressing the fire

Fire prevention includes limiting the products of combustion and other hazardous situations that could lead to starting a fire. Building codes address these concerns in a number of ways that include setting forth minimum flame-spread ratings and establishing flammability standards and similar constraints. These issues and those of exiting are outlined in Ch. 55.

Fire detection systems and alarms are critical, to provide sufficient warning for occupants to leave the building and to alert firefighters so that extinguishing efforts can begin before the fire spreads. Fire detection and alarms are covered in Ch. 32.

Fire containment is achieved through building materials, compartmentation, and smoke control. Fire suppression is achieved through sprinkler systems, standpipes, and other methods. These topics are reviewed in the following sections.

Compartmentation

Compartmentation is a critical concept in fire and life safety. The basic idea is to contain a fire and limit its spread, both to allow building occupants to escape and to protect other parts of the building that are not initially subject to the fire. In high-rise buildings, where it may not be practical to evacuate the building immediately, compartmentation can provide places of refuge where occupants can wait until the fire is extinguished or until they can exit safely. Compartmentation provides time for fire suppression, either by automatic sprinklers or by fire fighting personnel.

Compartmentation has been integral to building codes for a long time. Codes require fire separation between different occupancies, between use areas and exits, and between parts of a building when the maximum allowable area is exceeded. Separation is required both vertically, with fire-resistive floor-ceiling assemblies, and horizontally, with fire-rated walls. Any openings through fire assemblies must also provide protection for the spread of fire and smoke. These topics are covered in Ch. 55.

On a larger scale, the concept of compartmentation also applies to an entire building, so fire does not spread to adjacent structures. This is why building codes require certain fire ratings for exterior walls, limit the locations of buildings on a piece of property, and limit the size of or require protection of exterior openings when a building is near other structures or property lines. These requirements are also reviewed in Ch. 55.

On a smaller scale, structural members are isolated to protect them from the effects of fire and prevent structural collapse. In addition, the sizes of concealed areas above ceilings, in attics, in pipe chases, and under floors are limited to prevent the spread of fire, since a fire in these parts of a building would be especially difficult to extinguish. Fire stops in stud spaces between the first and second floors of a house are one important example of this kind of small-scale compartmentation.

Smoke Control

Because more deaths and injuries occur in fires due to inhalation of smoke and other gases rather than due to flame and heat exposure, *smoke control* is one of the most important aspects of fire protection. Smoke is particularly troublesome because many factors cause it to move rapidly through a building, well beyond the location of the fire. Smoke moves by the natural convection forces caused by differential air pressure between cool and warm air. In multistoried buildings, especially tall ones, the stack effect also pulls smoke through any vertical penetration such as stairways, elevator shafts, mechanical shafts, and atriums. Smoke spread is exacerbated by HVAC systems that can potentially distribute smoke a great distance from the original source.

There are several elements to smoke control. These include containment, exhaust, and, to a lesser degree, dilution. The same compartmentation that is used to contain fires is also used to contain the spread of smoke. Devices such as fire dampers, gaskets on fire doors, and automatic closing fire doors seal openings in fire walls. By containing smoke to one area of the building, places of refuge can be established. However, containment alone is not enough.

Because smoke is so deadly, it is always desirable to remove it from a building as quickly as possible. This helps keep it out of refuge areas, removes toxic smoke and gases, makes it easier to fight the fire, and helps control the path of the fire.

Some building codes provide for two types of control: passive and active. A *passive smoke control system* is one with a system of smoke barriers arranged to limit the migration of smoke. An *active smoke control system* is an engineered system that uses mechanical fans to produce pressure differentials across smoke barriers or to establish airflows to limit and direct smoke movement.

Passive smoke barriers can be partitions, doors with smoke seals, or curtain boards. A *curtain board* is a piece of construction suspended a minimum of 6 ft (1829) from the ceiling that restricts the passage of smoke and flame during a fire's initial stages. Curtain boards are commonly used in vented buildings and around escalator enclosures in conjunction with sprinkler systems to protect floor openings.

In one-story buildings of group F and S occupancies over 50,000 ft^2 (4645 m^2) and in Group H occupancies over 15,000 ft^2 (1394 m^2) in a single-floor area, automatic smoke and heat vents must be installed. These open automatically when their fusible links are subjected to excessive heat. Smoke vents must also be provided over stages more than 1000 ft^2 (93 m^2) in area, in atria, and in other locations specified by the code.

The concept of active smoke control combined with compartmentation is illustrated in Fig. 31.9, which shows a diagrammatic plan of one floor of a high-rise building. A *high-rise* is defined as a building with a floor area more than 75 ft (22 860) above the lowest level of fire department vehicle access. When a fire starts in one zone and activates an alarm, several events take place. All open doors connected to automatic closing devices that provide communication between the two zones, such as those leading to the elevator lobby close. The supply air and return air ducts to the fire zone shut down, and exhaust to outside air is turned on, creating a negative pressure in the fire zone. In the other zone, return and exhaust air ducts are closed, and supply air is forced into the safe area. This creates a slight positive pressure in the refuge zone and prevents smoke from migrating in, even if doors are opened momentarily.

Stairways are also pressurized to prevent smoke from entering them. Vestibules are also pressurized at a level slightly higher than that of the fire floor but slightly less than that

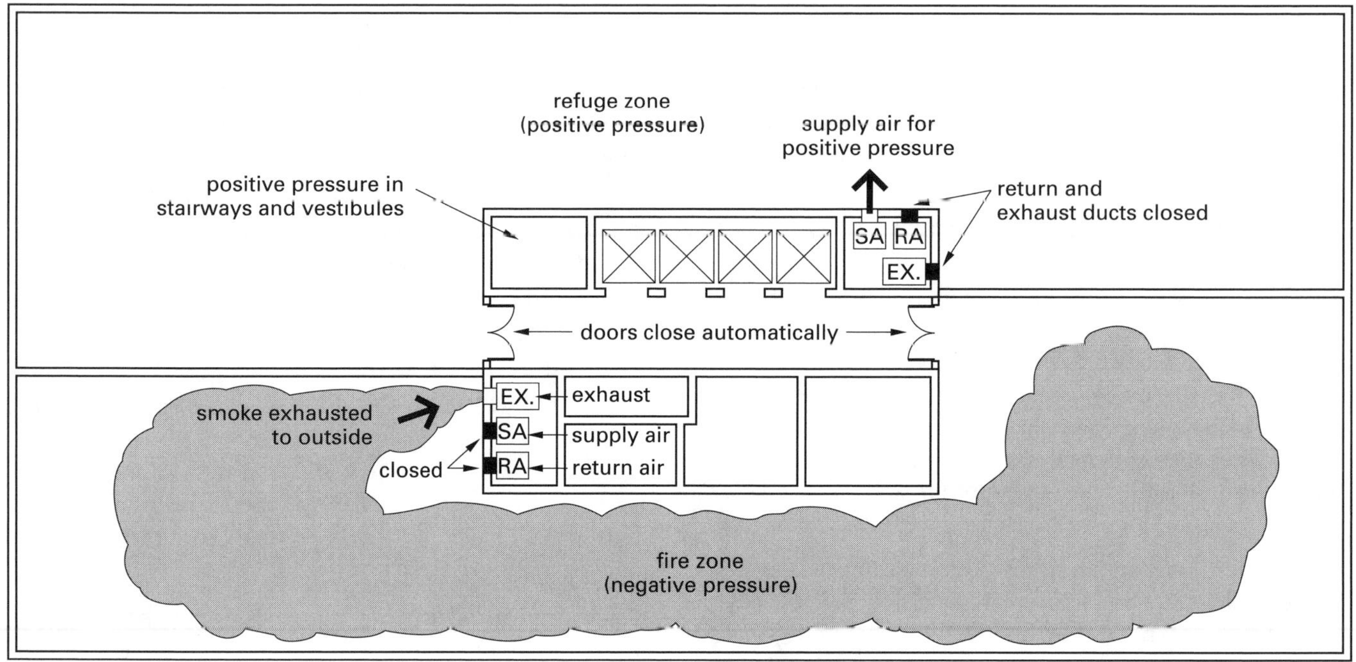

Figure 31.9 Smoke Control in High-Rise Buildings

of the stairway. This arrangement provides a double protection of the stairway and also keeps smoke out of the vestibules, where the areas of refuge for wheelchair occupants are located and where the standpipe connections and fire department communication devices are located. This system of protection for stairways replaces the former "smokeproof enclosures" of previous codes.

Similar systems can be used for other building types, such as large shopping malls, buildings with atria, and large industrial buildings. The building code prescribes where smoke control must be installed and whether it must be active or passive.

Sprinkler Systems

Fire sprinkler systems are becoming more prevalent in construction because of increasingly more stringent building code regulations and because of the awareness of owners and insurance companies of the systems' ability to minimize property damage and improve life safety. For example, the IBC requires sprinklers in buildings over 75 ft (22 860) high.

There are four types of sprinkler systems: wet-pipe, dry-pipe, preaction, and deluge. *Wet-pipe systems* are the most common. They are constantly filled with water and respond immediately to a rise in temperature at any sprinkler head of from 135°F to 170°F (57°C to 77°C). The exact temperature trigger point depends on the normal temperature at the ceiling; fusible links are available for a range of temperatures. In most wet-pipe systems, flow detectors are placed on each zone of sprinkler piping. When a sprinkler head opens, the detector senses movement of water and sends a signal to an annunciator panel or fire control center so that fire fighting personnel know where the fire is.

Dry-pipe systems are used in areas subject to freezing. The pipes are filled with compressed air or nitrogen until one or more heads are activated, allowing water to flow. Alternately, a dry-pipe system can be activated by a valve connected to a fire alarm.

Preaction systems are similar to dry-pipe systems except that water is allowed into the system before any sprinkler head has opened. At the same time an alarm is activated. This system is used where damage from water might result. The early alarm allows the fire to be put out before any sprinkler head opens.

Deluge systems activate all the sprinkler heads in an area at once, regardless of where the fire is. All the sprinkler heads are open and the pipes are empty. Upon activation of an alarm, valves automatically open, flooding the space. Deluge systems are used in high-hazard areas where fire is likely to spread rapidly.

In tall buildings, water for a sprinkler system can either be supplied in a tank near the top of the building or zone, just as the water supply is, or can be supplied with pumps connected to an emergency power supply. When tanks are used, they are designed to provide fire fighting capability for a certain percentage of sprinklers for a given time until firefighters can arrive. Siamese connections are provided on the exterior of the building so the fire department can connect hose pumps to the sprinkler system.

The installation of fire sprinkler systems is governed by each local building code, but most codes refer to NFPA 13, Standard for the Installation of Sprinkler Systems, published by the National Fire Protection Association. This standard classifies the relative fire hazard of buildings into three groups: light, ordinary, and extra hazard. Each hazard classification is further divided into groups. The hazard classification determines the required spacing of sprinklers and other regulations.

For example, light hazard includes occupancies such as residences, offices, hospitals, schools, and restaurants. In these occupancies there must be one sprinkler for each 200 ft^2 (18.6 m^2), or 225 ft^2 (20.9 m^2) if the design of the system is hydraulically calculated. For open-wood joist ceilings, the area drops to 130 ft^2 (12.1 m^2). Maximum spacing between sprinkler heads is 15 ft (4.6 m) for the 225 ft^2 coverage requirement, with the maximum distance from a wall being one-half the required spacing.

Sprinkler Heads

Several styles of sprinkler heads are available, including upright, sidewall, and pendant. *Upright heads* sit above the sprinkler pipe and are used where plumbing is exposed and ceilings are high and unfinished. *Sidewall heads* are used for corridors and small rooms when only one row of sprinklers will provide adequate coverage for small spaces. Sidewall heads also can be plumbed from the walls instead of from the ceiling, which makes them useful for remodeling work.

A *pendant head* is located below the sprinkler pipe, and there are several variations. One of the most common is fully exposed below the ceiling. A *recessed head* is partially recessed above the ceiling, with its deflector below the ceiling. A *flush head* has only its thermosensitive element below the ceiling. A *concealed head* has a smooth cover that is flush with the ceiling. When there is a fire, the cover falls away and the sprinkler head activates.

Every sprinkler head has some type of restraining device that keeps the head closed until activated by high temperature. Older heads used a fusible metal link, but contemporary heads use a glass bulb filled with a colored liquid and an air bubble. The color of the liquid indicates at what temperature the head is designed to activate.

There are different types of sprinkler activation devices, and the one used depends on the level of hazard, the specific type of occupancy, and the contents of the space being protected. *Standard residential sprinklers* are fast-response devices sensitive to both heat and smoldering. *Quick-response sprinklers* are more sensitive to heat than standard sprinklers, so that it takes less time for the device to reach the heat required to open the sprinkler. *Early-suppression fast-response* (ESFR) sprinklers spray water at high pressure and at a higher rate of flow than most sprinklers, and are for use in more hazardous locations. While most sprinklers are designed to keep a fire from spreading until the fire department arrives to extinguish it, ESFR sprinklers are designed to extinguish the fire while it is small. In addition to spraying greater amounts of water under high pressure, ESFR sprinkler heads are more sensitive to heat and produce large droplets that penetrate plumes of fire.

Quick-response early-suppression (QRES) sprinklers are similar to ESFR sprinklers, but have a smaller orifice and are designed for light-hazard occupancies. *Extended coverage* (EC) sprinklers cover a larger area per sprinkler than most sprinklers, but may only be used in light-hazard occupancies and under smooth, flat ceilings.

Standpipes

Standpipes are pipes that run the height of a building and provide water outlets at each floor to which fire fighting hoses can be connected. They are located within the stairway or, in the case of pressurized enclosures, within the vestibule.

The IBC defines three classes of standpipes. Class I is a dry-standpipe system without a directly connected water supply and equipped with $2^1/_2$ in (63.5) outlets for use by fire department personnel. Class II is a wet-standpipe system directly connected to a water supply and equipped with $1^1/_2$ in (38.1) outlets and hoses intended for use by building occupants. Class III is a combination system directly connected to a water supply and equipped with both $1^1/_2$ in (38.1) and $2^1/_2$ in (63.5) outlets.

The IBC defines where each class of standpipe is required. Class III standpipes must be installed in buildings where the floor level of the highest story is more than 30 ft (9144) above the lowest level of fire department vehicle access, or where the floor level of the lowest story is located more than 30 ft (9144) below the highest level of fire department access. However, four exceptions allow Class I standpipes to be used. These include buildings equipped with a sprinkler system, open parking garages less than 150 ft (45 720) high, open parking garages subject to freezing temperatures, and basements that are sprinklered.

In buildings over 10,000 ft^2 (929 m^2) per story, Class I automatic wet or manual wet standpipes must be used where any portion of the building's interior area is more than 200 ft (60 960) of travel, vertically or horizontally, from the nearest point of fire department vehicle access. However, exceptions to this requirement include fully sprinklered buildings, Group A-4, A-5, F-2, R-2, S-2, or U occupancies, and cases where automatic dry and semiautomatic dry standpipes are allowed as provided for in NFPA 14, *Standpipe and Hose System*.

Other requirements given in the IBC cover Group A buildings, covered mall buildings, stages, and underground buildings.

Class I standpipes must be located at every level of a building within stairway enclosures or within the vestibule if the exit enclosures are pressurized. They are also required on each side of the wall adjacent to the exit opening of horizontal exits. Class II and III standpipes must be accessible and located so all portions of a building are within 30 ft (9144) of a nozzle attached to 100 ft (30 480) of hose.

Water is supplied in two ways: from storage tanks and through siamese connections at ground level for connection with fire department apparatus pumps.

Like a sprinkler system, the standpipes can be either dry or wet. In a wet system, the standpipes are constantly filled with water and are connected to a tank of water at the top of the building that provides a supply of water for immediate use. Once firefighters arrive, water is pumped from fire hydrants through the fire truck pumps to the standpipes. In a dry system, there is no water standing in the pipe. In the event of a fire, water must be charged with pumps in the building or by the fire department through siamese connections.

Other Extinguishing Agents

Although sprinkler systems are the most common type of automatic extinguishing system, others are available.

Portable fire extinguishers are helpful for stopping small fires in the early stages of development. There are four general classes of extinguisher: A, B, C, and D. These classes correspond to the four fire types. Fires of type A involve ordinary combustibles of paper, wood, and cloth. Fire extinguishers for these fires contain water or water-based agents. B fires involve flammable liquids such as gasoline, solvents, and paints. B extinguishers contain smothering types of chemicals like carbon dioxide, foam, and halogenated agents. C fires involve electrical equipment, and the corresponding extinguisher contains nonconductive agents. Finally, class D fires involve combustible metals. Each type of fire must be fought with a suitable extinguisher. Combination extinguishers are also available for type A, B, and C fires.

Halogenated agents, commonly referred to as *halon*, are used where water might damage the contents of a room, like in computer installations. Halon is a gas that chemically inhibits the spread of fire. However, halon is a CFC gas that can damage the ozone layer, so alternate extinguishing agents will be used in the future.

Various types of foam can also be used to smother fires. Foam is commonly used where flammable liquid fires might occur, for example, in industrial plants or aircraft hangars.

Another type of extinguishing agent is actually a building material and acts passively in reaction to a fire. *Intumescent materials* respond to fire by expanding rapidly, insulating the surface they protect or filling gaps to prevent the passage of fire, heat, and smoke. They are available in the form of strips, caulk, paint, and spreadable putty. For example, a strip of intumescent material placed along the edge of one of a pair of fire doors will expand and seal the crack, substituting for an astragal that would otherwise be required. Intumescent paints can be applied to protect normally flammable wood.

32 ELECTRICAL SYSTEMS

Nomenclature

d	distance	ft	m
E	illumination	fc	lux
I	current (electrical circuits)	A	A
I	luminous intensity (lighting design)	candlepower	cd
pf	power factor		
R	resistance	Ω	Ω
t	time	hr	h
V	voltage	V	V
W	power	W	W
Z	impedance	Ω	Ω
θ	angle	degrees	degrees

ELECTRICAL FUNDAMENTALS

Definitions

Ampere: the unit flow of electrons in a conductor equal to 6.251×10^{18} electrons passing a given section in 1 sec

Energy: the product of power and time, also called *work*

Impedance: the resistance in an alternating current (AC) circuit, measured in ohms

Ohm: the unit of resistance in an electrical circuit

Power factor: the phase difference between voltage and current in an alternating current circuit

Reactance: part of the electrical resistance in an alternating current circuit, caused by inductance and capacitance

Volt: the unit of electromotive force or potential difference that will cause a current of 1 A to flow through a conductor whose resistance is 1 Ω

Watt: the unit of electrical power

Basic Relationships

Electricity is the energy caused by the flow of electrons. A basic electric circuit consists of a conductor, the actual flow of electrons (current), an electric potential difference to cause the electrons to move (voltage), and some type of resistance to the flow of electrons. The circuit can be interrupted with a switch. These basic components are shown in Fig. 32.1.

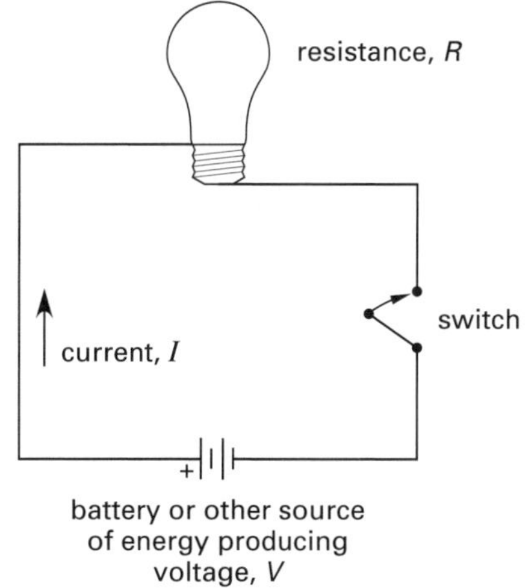

Figure 32.1 Basic Electric Current

Ohm's law relates current, voltage, and resistance in direct current (DC) circuits according to the formula

$$I = \frac{V}{R} \qquad 32.1$$

This states that the current in a circuit is directly proportional to the voltage and inversely proportional to the resistance.

In physics, power is the rate at which work is done or the rate at which energy is used. In electric circuits, power is expressed in watts. Wattage, in DC circuits, is the product of voltage and current, or

$$W = VI \qquad 32.2$$

Although this is the standard formula, a useful mnemonic way of remembering it is to think of PIE, or $P = IE$, power (wattage) equals current (I) times electromotive force (E), which is voltage.

Electrical circuits for alternating current are slightly different due to how alternating current is generated; they operate according to the principle of electromagnetic induction. This principle was discovered by Michael Faraday in 1831 and states that when a conductor is moved in a magnetic field, a voltage is induced. The direction of the movement determines the polarity of the voltage, either positive or negative. When a coil of conductor, or wire, is rotated within a magnetic field (or when the magnetic field is rotated around a fixed coil), a voltage of alternating polarity is produced. AC voltage is represented graphically with a sine wave as shown in Fig. 32.2. The *amplitude* of the wave represents the voltage, and the distance between peaks is one cycle. In the United States, alternating current is produced at a frequency of 60 cycles per second, or 60 Hz. In Europe and other countries the frequency is 50 Hz.

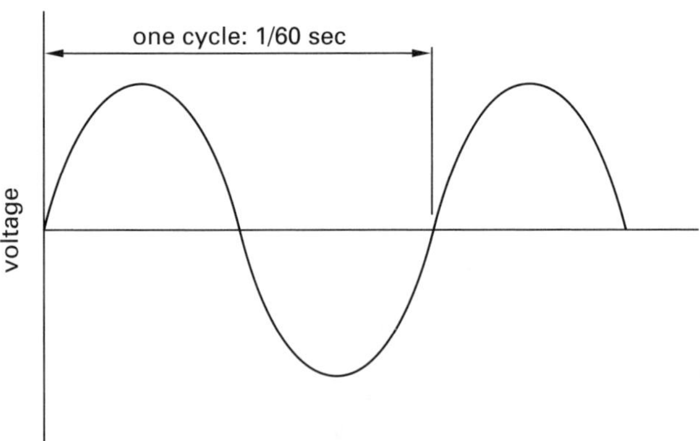

Figure 32.2 Sine Wave of Alternating Current

In AC circuits, resistance is known as *impedance*, which comprises resistance and reactance and causes a phase-change difference between voltage and current. The difference is represented by the power factor (pf) and can be a significant factor in calculating power in an AC circuit. For circuits with only resistive loads, such as incandescent lights or electric heating elements, the power factor is 1.0. Sometimes capacitors are used to improve the power factor.

For AC circuits, Ohm's law is similar to formula 32.1.

$$I = \frac{V}{Z} \qquad 32.3$$

Power in AC circuits is similar to formula 32.2 but with the power factor added.

$$W = VI(\text{pf}) \qquad 32.4$$

Example 32.1

Find the current in a 120 V circuit serving nine 150 W downlights.

Using formula 32.4 and rearranging,

$$I = \frac{W}{V(\text{pf})}$$

Because the power factor is 1.0 in this case,

$$I = \frac{(9)(150\ \text{W})}{(120\ \text{V})(1.0)} = 11.25\ \text{A}$$

To determine the energy used in a system, simply multiply power times time, or

$$E = Wt \qquad 32.5$$

Energy can be measured in watt-hours but is more commonly measured in thousands of watt-hours, or kilowatt-hours, kWh.

There are two basic types of electric circuits: series and parallel. These are shown diagrammatically in Fig. 32.3. In *series circuits*, the loads (represented in the diagrams by zigzag lines) are placed in the circuit one after another. The current, I, remains constant throughout the circuit, but the voltage potential changes, or drops, across each load. In a *parallel circuit*, the loads are placed between the same two points. The voltage remains the same, but the current is different across each load. However, adding up the individual currents results in a total current that is applied to the circuit as a whole.

Notice that if one load is removed in a series circuit (a lightbulb burned out) then the entire circuit is opened. This fact and the problem of voltage drops across individual loads are two reasons series circuits are not used in building construction.

Materials

The basic material of electrical systems is the conductor. Sizes of conductors are based on American Wire Gauge (AWG) and thousand circular mil (MCM) designations. AWG sizes range from 16 gauge to 0000 (4/0) gauge. Actual

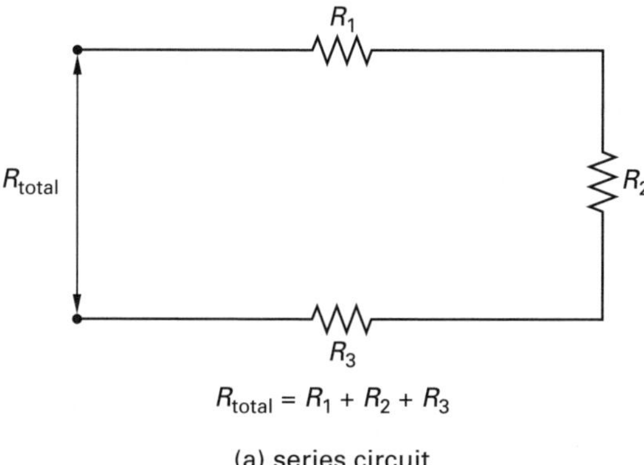

(a) series circuit

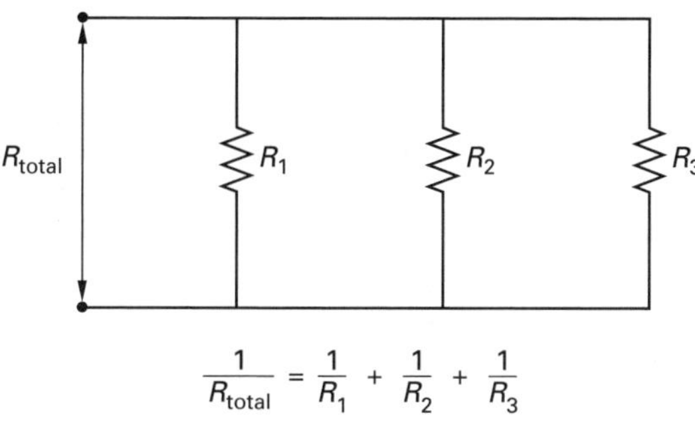

(b) parallel circuit

Figure 32.3 Basic Circuit Types

size of the conductor increases as the number designation decreases, so 16 gauge is the smallest at a 0.0508 in diameter, and 4/0 is the largest at a 0.460 in diameter. A single insulated conductor no. 6 AWG or larger, or several conductors assembled into a single unit, is referred to as *cable*. Conductors no. 8 AWG or smaller are called *wire*.

Cable larger than 4/0 gauge is designated with the MCM nomenclature. A circular mil is a derived area measurement representing the square of the cable diameter in thousandths of an inch (mils). The MCM cable sizes are 250, 300, 400, and 500. The current-carrying capacity (or *ampacity*) of a conductor is dependent on its size, the type of insulation around it, and the surrounding temperature.

There are many different types of conductors and insulating materials. The two basic conductors are copper and aluminum. Aluminum conductors must be larger than copper ones to carry the same amperage, but they are lighter and generally have a lower installation cost in large sizes. Copper is more cost effective in small- and medium-sized wire and cable. Aluminum conductors require special care in installation because joints can loosen and oxides can form, causing resistance and overheating. Because of these potential problems, aluminum is limited to primary circuits that are installed by skilled workers.

Some of the common cables, based on the type of insulation they use, are as follows.

Nonmetallic sheathed cable, also known by the trade name Romex™, consists of two or more plastic-insulated conductors and ground wire surrounded by a moisture-resistant plastic jacket. This type of cable can be used in wood-frame residential buildings and those not exceeding three stories, as long as it is used with wood studs and protected from damage by being concealed behind walls and ceilings. Because it does not require conduit, it is inexpensive to install.

Flexible metal-clad cable, also known by the trade name BX™, consists of two or more plastic-insulated conductors encased in a continuous spiral-wound strip of steel tape. It is often used in remodeling work because it can be pulled through existing spaces within a building.

The most common type of wire and cable is a single conductor covered with thermoplastic or rubber insulation. Several different types are available for different voltages and service conditions. This cable must be placed in metal conduit or other approved types of carriers.

When high currents are involved, the use of very large cables becomes expensive and awkward to tap into for transformers and branch circuits. Instead, rectangular bars of copper, called busbars, are used. When several busbars are assembled in a special metal housing, it is called a *busduct* or *busway*.

For commercial construction and large residential construction, individual conductors must be placed in metal conduit or other approved carriers. Conduit supports and protects the wiring, serves as a system ground, and protects surrounding construction from fire if the wire overheats or shorts.

There are three types of rigid steel conduit: rigid steel conduit, intermediate metal conduit, and electric metallic tubing. *Rigid steel conduit* is the heaviest and is connected to junction boxes and other devices with threaded fittings. *Intermediate metal conduit* (IMC) has thinner walls but the same outside diameter as rigid steel conduit. It is also installed with threaded fittings. *Electric metallic tubing* (EMT) is the lightest of the three and is installed with special pressure fittings because it is too thin to thread. It is easier and faster to install but cannot be used in hazardous areas. Flexible metal conduit is also available to minimize vibration transmission from equipment to the structure and for areas where installation of rigid conduit is not possible. It is commonly referred to as *flex*.

The number of conductors that can be placed in a conduit depends on the conductor type, the conductor size, and the size of the conduit. The purpose of limiting the number of conductors is to prevent damage from trying to pull too many conductors through a small space and to control the heat buildup inside the conduit. The *National Electrical Code* places certain limits on the length, number, and radius of bends in a conduit between pull boxes, to prevent damage to the conductors and make pulling the conductors easier. In most cases, there can be no more than four 90° bends between pull boxes.

Two additional types of power distribution that are often used in office buildings and wherever outlets must be changed frequently are underfloor raceways and undercarpet cable.

There are two varieties of underfloor raceways: underfloor ducts and cellular metal floors. *Underfloor ducts* are proprietary steel raceways cast into a concrete floor at regular spacing, usually about 4, 5, or 6 ft (1200, 1500, or 1800). Feeder ducts run perpendicular to the distribution ducts and carry power and signal wiring from the main electrical closet to each distribution duct. Preset inserts are placed along the distribution ducts at close intervals, and these are tapped wherever an outlet or telephone connection is required.

Cellular metal floors use the same basic concept but are actually part of the structural floor. They are essentially metal decking designed for use as cable raceways. Cellular floors differ from underfloor ducts in that the cells are closer together. Alternating cells can be used for power, telephone, and signal cabling. Cellular floors also have preset locations that can be easily tapped to install electrical outlets, telephone jacks, and computer outlets.

Under-carpet wiring is thin, flat, protected wire that can be laid under carpet without protruding. Cable for both 120 V circuits and telephone and signal lines is available. However, it must be used with carpet tiles so that it is readily accessible. Under-carpet wiring connects pedestals in the middle of the room that contain electrical outlets and telephone connections to junction boxes in nearby walls, where the wiring is connected to standard conduit-enclosed cable.

POWER SUPPLY

The most common form of electrical energy used in buildings is alternating current (AC). Direct current (DC) is used for some types of elevator motors and for low-voltage applications such as signal systems, controls, and similar equipment. Electricity is supplied by the local power company and distributed as described in the following sections. For emergency power, generators and batteries are used. These systems are also described in a later section.

Primary Service

Electrical service is provided by the utility company at the property line. It is the owner's responsibility to install and pay for wiring, metering, transformers, and distribution beyond that point, although most utility companies will, for a charge, extend the power supply from the line to the building's service entrance.

Service may be either overhead or underground. Underground service is more expensive but avoids the clutter of overhead wires and protects the lines from snow, wind, and other potentially damaging conditions. When overhead service is provided to smaller projects, the service cable is connected to a weatherhead at least 12 ft (4 m) above the ground. This is part of the conduit that leads to the meter and distribution panel.

There are several voltages that may be supplied to a building. Which one is used depends on what is available from the utility company at the property, what the electrical loads of the building are, and what types of transformers the owner may want to provide. In some cases, it is less expensive for the owner of a large commercial building to buy power from the utility company at higher voltages and supply the transformer than to pay a higher charge for lower voltages.

Power is supplied to buildings in several different voltages. The most common for residences and very small buildings is a 120/240 V, single-phase, three-wire system. It is used where the actual load does not exceed 80 A, although minimum service is considered 100 A. Figure 32.4(a) diagrams this system type, which consists of two hot wires, each carrying 120 V, and one neutral wire. Appliances, such as electric ranges and dryers, that need 240 V use the two hot wires, whereas 120 V service is obtained by tapping one hot wire and the neutral wire.

A system often used for larger buildings is the 120/208 V, three-phase, four-wire system. It is frequently used because it allows use of a variety of electrical loads. This system is shown schematically in Fig. 32.4(b).

For larger buildings, a 277/480 V, three-phase, four-wire system is used. It is the same as the 120/208 V system except for the higher voltages. The advantages to this system include smaller feeders, smaller conduit, and smaller switchgear. This is possible because of the higher voltages used and therefore the smaller currents the equipment has to carry. Buildings with this system have predominantly 277 V fluorescent lighting, which requires smaller wiring. Small, step-down transformers are used where 120 V service is needed for receptacles and other equipment.

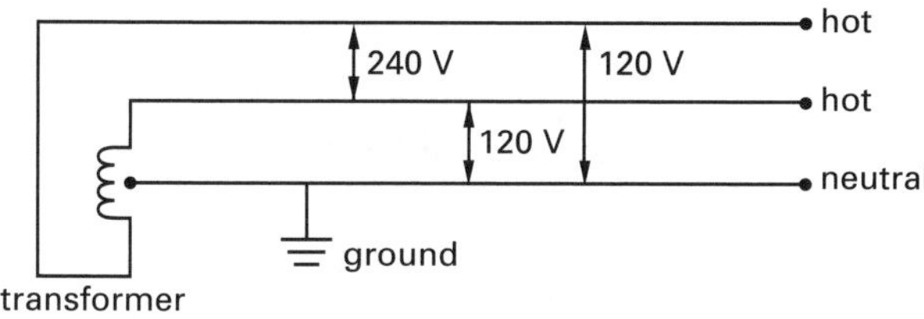

(a) 120/240 V, single-phase, 3-wire system

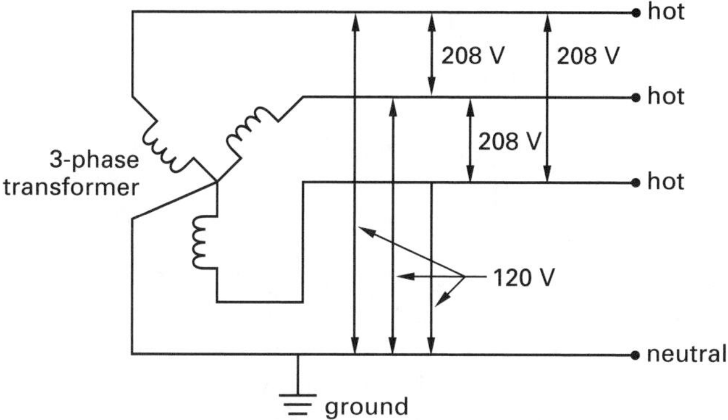

(b) 120/208 V, 3-phase, 4-wire system

Figure 32.4 Electrical Service Types

For very large commercial buildings and factories with a great deal of machinery, 2400/4160 V, three-phase, four-wire systems are available.

Transformers

Transformers are used to change alternating current voltages, either up or down. In most cases, power is supplied to a building at high voltage because the lines can be smaller and there is less voltage drop. The building owner must supply the transformer to provide one of the types of service described in the previous section. For residences and very small buildings, the utility company usually supplies step-down transformers to serve a small group of houses with 120/240 V service.

Transformers are rated on their kilovolt-amperes capacity (kVa) and described by their type, phase, voltage, method of cooling, insulation, and noise level. For cooling, transformers are either dry, oil filled, or silicone filled. When there is a possibility of fire, as with oil-filled transformers, the equipment must be placed in a fire-resistive transformer vault room. Because transformers generate a great deal of heat, the vault must be at an exterior wall and vented to the outside. Locating a transformer vault near the exterior wall also makes it easier to move the large, heavy device into place and replace it when necessary.

Metering and Load Control

Metering must be provided at a building's service entrance to allow the utility company to charge for energy used. For residences and other single-use buildings, one meter is typically used. For multiple-occupancy buildings, such as shopping centers and apartments, banks of meters are installed so that each unit can be metered independently. One of the reasons for this is to encourage energy conservation, because every tenant must pay for the energy used.

The most common meter is the watt-hour meter. This registers the use of power over time in kilowatt-hours. The meter is placed on the incoming power line in front of any master service switch so that it can operate continuously.

In order to encourage the conservation of energy and pay for the cost of providing power to customers, many energy companies levy energy charges based not only on the total amount of energy used (kilowatt-hours) but also on peak demand. The reasoning behind this is that if a customer uses a nominal amount of energy (power multiplied by time) over a billing period, but uses a great deal of energy only at certain times, the utility company must still provide facilities to supply the peak demand. The total amount of energy used can be relatively low even though the utility company must be ready to supply the occasional maximum amount.

To compensate for this, most utility companies make charges based on the maximum interval demand, the average amount of energy used in a certain time period, such as 15 min or 30 min. The ratio of the average power used to the maximum power demand is called the *load factor*. A low load factor implies an inefficient use of energy and a high demand charge.

From the user's standpoint, a building's electrical system should be designed to avoid peak electricity use. There are several methods of doing this, which are called *load control*. Other terms used include *load shedding*, *peak demand control*, and *peak load regulation*.

Manual and automatic devices are available to accomplish load control. With automatic load shedding, for example, a device automatically monitors the use of energy, and when a certain point is reached the device shuts off nonessential electrical loads. Such loads can include nonessential lighting, water heating, and space heating. Load scheduling can also be used if the energy consumption characteristics of the building are known. With this method, different electrical loads are automatically scheduled to operate at different times to control the peak demand.

Primary Distribution

For large buildings, a central electrical distribution center is required. Called the *switchgear*, this center consists of an assembly of switches, circuit breakers, and cables or busducts that distribute power to other parts of the building. A transformer and metering are also often included with the switchgear. The equipment is usually housed in a separate room, depending on the type of transformer used and the security required.

Power coming through the meter and transformer is split into separate circuits, each with a master switch and circuit breaker to protect the circuit from overload or short circuits. From the switchgear, power is distributed to substations for further transforming and distribution, to motor control centers, to elevator controls, and to individual panel boxes as part of the secondary distribution system.

Power Quality

The power supplied by an electric utility is not always at a steady, regulated voltage. There can be power surges and voltage variations from various causes. Building use and equipment such as electronic devices, lighting dimmers, and motor controls can cause these and other problems, including radio frequency interference and overheating. Individual problems can be corrected with specific pieces of equipment such as voltage regulators, surge suppressors, and filters. For example, an individual computer can be protected with a plug-in surge suppressor. For larger installations such as computer rooms and other sensitive electronic equipment, one-piece units called *power conditioning units* can be used.

Harmonic currents are a problem for many buildings with computers and other electronic equipment. A *harmonic current* is a voltage or current at a frequency that is a multiple of the fundamental frequency. In the case of U.S. power supply at 60 Hz, for example, a harmonic current could be at 120 Hz, 180 Hz, and so on. Harmonic currents are produced by electrical loads that are nonlinear, which includes almost any load other than simple resistive loads such as incandescent lights, heaters, and motors. In large buildings with many nonlinear loads such as computers, copiers, electronic ballasts, variable-speed motors, and other solid-state equipment, harmonic currents can create significant problems. These problems can include overheating of the neutral conductor wiring, nuisance tripping of circuit breakers, overheated transformers, and telephone interference.

In some cases, the problem can be solved by oversizing the neutral conductor and adding passive harmonic filters in the electric distribution system. More commonly, active line conditioning is used. A variable power conditioning unit, controlled by computer, continuously analyzes the harmonics of the line voltage and adds an equal but out-of-phase voltage to cancel the harmonics.

Secondary Distribution and Branch Circuits

Power from the main switchgear is distributed to individual panelboards where it is further split into individual branch circuits used for power, lighting, motors, and other electrical needs of the building. Secondary distribution involves the typical lower voltages of 120 V, 240 V, and 277 V. Secondary distribution is made with wires in conduit, various types of underfloor raceways, or flexible cabling systems.

Each circuit is protected with circuit breakers in the panelboard. These are rated for the amperage the circuit is expected to carry, ranging from 15 A and 20 A circuits for general lighting and power circuits to 100 amps or more for main disconnect switches or large loads.

There are three important kinds of protection for electric circuits: grounding, ground-fault protection, and arc-fault protection. All new construction is grounded with a separate wire in addition to the hot and neutral wiring of each circuit. One of the primary purposes for providing a ground is to prevent a dangerous shock if someone touches an appliance with a short circuit and simultaneously touches a ground path such as a water pipe. The ground provides a path for the fault. The ground wire and the neutral wire are both grounded at the building service entrance to either a grounding electrode buried in the earth or in the foundation, or to a buried cold water pipe.

A ground fault, however, can create other problems, because the current required to trip a circuit breaker is high and small current leaks can continue unnoticed until someone receives a dangerous shock or a fire develops. *Ground fault circuit interrupters* (GFCIs), often also called *ground fault interrupters* (GFIs), are devices that can detect small current leaks. If a leak is detected, the device immediately disconnects the power to the circuit or appliance.

A GFCI can be a part of a circuit breaker or installed as an outlet. In dwelling units, GFCIs are required in bathrooms, garages, accessory buildings at or below grade, crawl spaces, unfinished basements, countertop receptacles in kitchens, laundry and utility rooms, and boathouses, as well as outdoors and within 6 ft (1.8 m) of the outside edge of a wet bar. They are also required for receptacles in bathrooms in commercial (non-dwelling) occupancies, and in other locations specified in the *National Electrical Code* (NEC).

The third type of protection is the *arc-fault circuit interrupter* (AFCI). This device helps protect against the effects of arc faults by recognizing characteristics that are unique to arcing and by de-energizing the circuit when an arc fault is detected. In some jurisdictions, AFCIs are required in bedroom branch circuits that serve both receptacles and lighting, as well as in other locations. The bedroom branch circuits must be run separately from all other circuits in the dwelling. The NEC also requires AFCIs on 15 A and 20 A branch circuits that supply outlets in family rooms, dining rooms, living rooms, libraries, dens, sunrooms, recreation rooms, closets, hallways, and similar rooms.

Wiring Devices

Wiring devices include those normally installed in outlet boxes such as receptacles, switches, and pilot lights. The most common receptacle for normal power distribution is the *duplex receptacle*, or *duplex outlet* as it is often called. It is also called a *convenience outlet* because it is designed for normal use by building occupants for portable lamps, clocks, electronic devices, appliances, and similar devices that operate at 120 V. Special receptacles are used for appliances and equipment that require higher voltages, such as electric ranges, dryers, and large copy machines. In addition, GFI outlets are provided for safety as described in the previous sections. These are sometimes called *ground fault circuit interrupters* (GFCI). Electrical devices that are not plugged in but are connected to the building circuits in junction boxes are said to be *hardwired*.

A convenience outlet has two holes to receive the prongs of the plug supplying power and a third hole for the grounding prong. The grounding pole is connected to a green wire that is part of the wiring in the conduit. Alternately, the grounding pole of the outlet may be connected to the metal conduit that acts as the system ground. *Split-wired receptacles* can be installed so that one outlet is always energized but the other is controlled from a wall switch. This allows floor lamps and other devices that normally plug in to be controlled with a switch.

Outlets are normally mounted vertically from 12 in to 18 in (305 to 455) above the floor, although a minimum 15 in (380) mounting height is required for forward reach accessibility for persons in wheelchairs. In residential construction, outlets must be located no more than 12 ft (3660) apart, or such that no point is more than 6 ft (1830) from an outlet.

Most residential convenience outlet circuits are 15 A, but at least two 20 A appliance circuits must be provided for the kitchen, pantry, breakfast room, and dining room. The outlets serving the kitchen countertop area must be supplied from at least two different circuits, with no more than four outlets per 20 A circuit. The outlets in the kitchen must be located so that no point on a wall above a countertop is more than 24 in (610) from an outlet. There must also be at least one outlet between appliances and the sink so that no cord has to be draped across an appliance or the sink. Outlets within 6 ft (1830) of a sink must be of the GFCI type.

Switching

Switches are used to control power to lights, receptacles, and other electric devices. The most common is the toggle type, which simply switches on or off with a toggle, or lever. Other types that perform the same function include the rocker, push, and key. When one switch controls a light or other device it is called a *two-way switch*. When two switches are used to control the same device they are *three-way switches*. *Four-way switches* are used to control the same device from three or more locations. Other types of switches include dimmer switches, automatic timer switches, and programmable switches.

Low-voltage switching is also available. With this system, individual switches are operated on a 24 V circuit and control relays that provide the 120 V switching. Although more costly to install, low-voltage switching has several advantages over line-voltage switching. First, the same light or device can be controlled from several positions that are remote from each other. Second, a central control station can be set up to monitor the entire system and override local control. For example, pilot lights at the central station in a house can show which lights are on and which are off and allow switching from that station. Third, control devices such as timers and energy management systems can be wired to override local control. Finally, for large installations that require flexibility of control, low-voltage wiring and switches are a less expensive alternative to installing the same scope of line-voltage wiring and devices.

Another approach to remotely controlling line-voltage lighting and outlets is the use of a *power line carrier* (PLC) system. A PLC system uses the power lines to carry control signals, which are low-voltage, high-frequency coded signals. Each control device, such as a light switch, can respond to its unique code. These systems have the advantage that no additional wiring is required.

Traditionally, individual switching and dimming controls have been used for most lighting situations. However, current energy conservation codes and building rating systems, such as the LEED rating systems, generally require the use of more sophisticated controls that can reduce a building's total energy use. This can be done with a variety of lighting controls and switching methods.

The most basic approach is to provide individual switches for each use area, instead of one switch to control several areas. When an area is not in use, the lighting can be turned off. This basic type of control is now required by model codes and energy conservation codes, as described in more detail below.

Alternatively, one luminaire can be controlled with two switches. For example, two switches can control a four-lamp fluorescent luminaire, providing two levels of illumination.

Other methods can be used to provide more than two levels of illuminance. *Multilevel lighting control* is a variation of this idea that allows lighting power to be reduced in steps, while maintaining a reasonably uniform level of illuminance through the area controlled.

Dimmers make it possible to reduce light levels when the maximum light output of the luminaires is not required. However, neither individual switching nor dimmers will reduce energy usage unless they are consciously used to do so, and studies have shown that this is not an effective approach. To conserve energy, automatic lighting controls are needed. The following are some of the methods used.

The most common type of automatic control is a programmable *time-of-day controller*. This device simply turns off the power at designated times. A single device can be simply mounted in an individual switch box, or many devices can be integrated into a complex building management system. They can be programmed to turn off lights in response to the normal time schedules of the users, while still providing egress lighting or dimmed lighting for after-hours building maintenance. The ability to override a controller can be incorporated into the system for use when an occupant needs to work overtime.

Occupant sensors can turn lights on and off in response to the presence of people in a room or area. These sensors can be passive infrared, ultrasonic, or a mix of both. Manually operated switches can override the sensor function.

Daylight compensation controls use photocells to dim lights or turn lights on and off automatically as the level of daylight changes. Of course, how effectively and economically daylighting can be used varies with the latitude, climate, surrounding buildings and landscaping, direction of window exposure, and type, size, and configuration of glazing. In most cases, these types of controls can be used in a perimeter zone to the depth at which the zone receives at least one-half of its illuminance from daylight for several hours a day. Daylighting studies can be done manually or with available computer programs to determine if daylight compensation controls are economically feasible.

Well-designed daylighting compensation controls can reduce energy use along the inside perimeter of a building by up to 60%, depending on the climate, effectiveness of the daylighting design, hours of building use, and other variables. Refer to Ch. 29 for more information on daylighting design.

Although the specific requirements for switching and other lighting control may vary by jurisdiction and what version of a particular code that jurisdiction is using, most requirements are very similar, if not identical, to ANSI/ASHRAE/IESNA Standard 90.1, *Energy Standard for Buildings Except Low-Rise Residential Buildings*. This standard requires that automatic lighting shutoff be used in most buildings larger than 5000 ft^2 (464 m^2). Three methods are acceptable.

- Time-of-day controllers may be used that are programmed to shut off lighting at specific times. Each controller may govern an area of up to 25,000 ft^2 (2320 m^2) and no more than one floor.
- Occupant sensors may be used that turn off lighting within 30 minutes of an area becoming unoccupied.
- A separate control or alarm system, such as a building security system, may be set up to send a signal to a lighting control device when an area is unoccupied.

There are exceptions for 24-hour operations, spaces where patient care is rendered, and spaces where automatic shutoff would endanger the safety or security of the room or building occupants.

Standard 90.1 also requires that every space enclosed by ceiling-height partitions must have at least one device that controls the general lighting in that space. This device must automatically turn lighting off within 30 minutes of the space becoming unoccupied. In classrooms, conference/meeting rooms, and employee lunch/break rooms, a manual switch is not required. In all other spaces, the control device must also have an easily accessible manual switch that can override any time-of-day scheduled shutoff, but not for more than four hours. Depending on the size of the space, two or more devices may be required. The area that each device controls may not be more than 2500 ft^2 (232 m^2) if the enclosed space is 10,000 ft^2 (930 m^2) or less, or more than 10,000 ft^2 if the enclosed space is greater than 10,000 ft^2.

Control devices are also required for exterior lighting except where required for safety and security; these devices must operate by photosensors or a programmable time switch with astronomic correction.

Additional controls are required for the following uses.

- Display and accent lighting must have separate control devices.
- Hotel and motel guest rooms must have a master control device at the main room entry that controls all permanently installed luminaires and switched receptacles.
- Supplemental task lighting, including undercabinet lighting, must have a control device integral to the luminaires or be controlled by a wall-mounted device.
- Nonvisual lighting, like food warming, must have a separate control device.
- Lighting equipment that is for sale or used in demonstrations must have a separate control device.

The type of control required can affect how lights must be circuited. When many lights are connected to a single dimmer switch, they must be on their own circuit. Both incandescent and fluorescent lights can be dimmed, but fluorescent dimmers are more expensive, and special fixtures are needed to minimize flicker when they are dimmed. Generally, a single circuit should not include both incandescent and fluorescent lights. In many large commercial installations, 277 V circuits are used for fluorescent lights for greater efficiency, while incandescent lights are on 120 V circuits, so that the two kinds of lights must be on separate circuits in any case.

Emergency Power Supply

Emergency power is required for electrical systems that relate to the safety of occupants or community needs. This includes systems for exit lighting, alarms, elevators, telephones, and fire pumps, as well as equipment that could have life-threatening implications if power were lost, such as some medical equipment. Standby power, on the other hand, provides electricity for functions that the building owner requires to avoid an interruption in business. This often includes computer operations or industrial processes.

Emergency power is supplied by generators or batteries. Generators provide the capacity for large electrical loads for long periods of time, limited only by the available emergency fuel supply. However, they are expensive to install and must be maintained and checked periodically for proper operation.

Batteries are used for smaller loads for shorter time periods. Emergency lighting often consists of separate lighting packs with their own batteries, placed in strategic locations such as corridors and stairways. Large installations have racks of batteries in separate rooms connected to lights and other equipment with wiring.

LIGHTING FUNDAMENTALS

Light and Vision

Light is defined as visually evaluated radiant energy. Visible light is a form of electromagnetic radiation with wavelengths that range from about 400 nm (10^{-9} m) for violet light to about 700 nm for red light. White light is produced when a source emits approximately equal quantities of energy over the entire visible spectrum.

When light strikes a surface it can be transmitted, reflected, or absorbed. If a material is transparent, such as window glass, most of the light is transmitted. The ratio of the total transmitted light to the total incident light is the *transmittance* or *coefficient of transmission*, expressed as a percentage. Clear glass has a transmittance of about 85%, whereas frosted glass has a transmittance between 70% and 85%. The remainder of the light is either reflected or absorbed. Material that allows the transmittance of light but not of a clear image is said to be *translucent*. In clear materials, light is *refracted*, or bent slightly, as it passes through the material. Refraction is the principle on which lenses are made, so light passing through the lens is bent toward the thicker part of the lens.

If a material allows no light to pass through, it is opaque, and all incident light is either reflected or absorbed. A flat, black material, for example, absorbs most of the incident light. A white material reflects most of the incident light. As with transmittance, the ratio of the total reflected light to the total incident light is the *reflectance* or *reflectance coefficient*, also expressed as a percentage. How light is reflected depends on the finish of the material it is striking. As shown in Fig. 32.5, reflection is specular, combined specular and diffuse, or diffuse. *Specular reflection* results from a smooth, polished surface, such as a mirror. The angle of incidence equals the angle of reflection. *Diffuse reflection* results from a uniformly rough surface. It appears uniformly bright, and the image of the source cannot be seen. *Combined specular and diffuse reflection* makes surfaces appear to be brighter at the point where the source is shining than in the surrounding areas.

Light is perceived through the eye and with the brain. In the process of seeing, light enters the eye through the pupil. See Fig. 32.6. The amount of light entering the eye is controlled by the iris. The lens focuses the image (upside down) on the retina, where the light stimulates cells that send messages to the brain for interpretation. The retina contains two types of cells: cones and rods. *Cones* are cells located near the fovea, or central portion of the retina. They are shaped like cones and are extremely sensitive to detail and color. However, they are located within only a 2° cone of vision around the line of sight. On the remainder of the retina are the cells shaped like rods. *Rods* are extremely sensitive to light and motion. On the other hand, they are not as good as the cones at discriminating color or detail. That is why in dim light people lose their sense of color vision; objects appear in varying shades of gray.

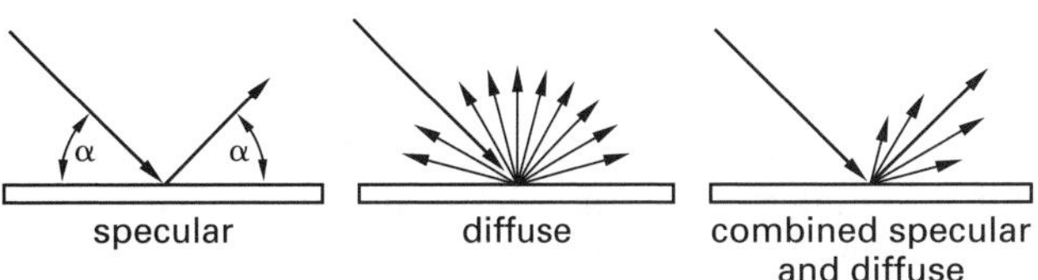

Figure 32.5 Light Reflections

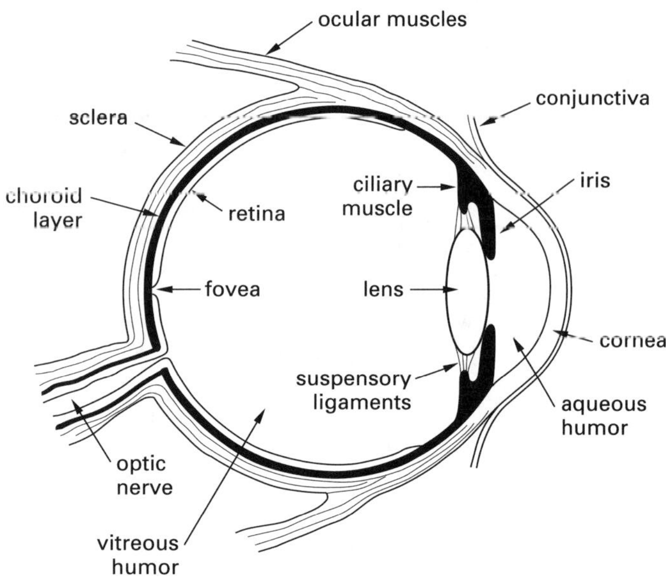

Figure 32.6 Human Eye

Measuring Light

Examinees should be familiar with the relationships between several illumination definitions. Figure 32.7 shows these units of light.

Candlepower: the unit of luminous intensity approximately equal to the horizontal light output from an ordinary wax candle. In the SI system of measurement, this unit is the *candela*.

Illuminance: the density of luminous flux incident on a surface in lumens per unit area. One lumen uniformly incident on 1 ft^2 of area produces an illuminance of 1 fc. In SI units, 1 lumen incident on 1 m^2 of spherical surface 1 m away produces 1 lux of illuminance.

Lumen: the unit of luminous flux equal to the flux in a unit solid angle of 1 steradian from a uniform point source of 1 candlepower. On a unit sphere (1 ft radius), an area of 1 ft^2 will subtend an angle of 1 steradian. Because the area of a unit sphere is 4π, a source of 1 candlepower produces 12.57 lm.

Luminance: the luminous flux per unit of projected (apparent) area and unit solid angle leaving a surface, either reflected or transmitted. By definition, the unit (in SI measurements now commonly used) is the candela per square meter (cd/m^2), also called the *nit*. In the older inch-pound system, the unit is the *footlambert*, where 1 footlambert is $^1/_\pi$ candlepower per square foot. Luminance takes into account the reflectance and transmittance properties of materials and the directions in which they are viewed. Thus, 100 lux striking a 1 m^2 surface with 50% reflectance would result in a luminance of 50 candelas per square meter. (In inch-pounds units, 100 fc striking a surface with 50% reflectance would result in a luminance of 50 footlamberts.) Luminance is sometimes called *brightness*, although brightness includes the physiological sensation of the adaptation of the eye, whereas luminance is the measurable state of object luminosity.

Luminous intensity: the solid angular flux density in a given direction measured in candlepower or candelas

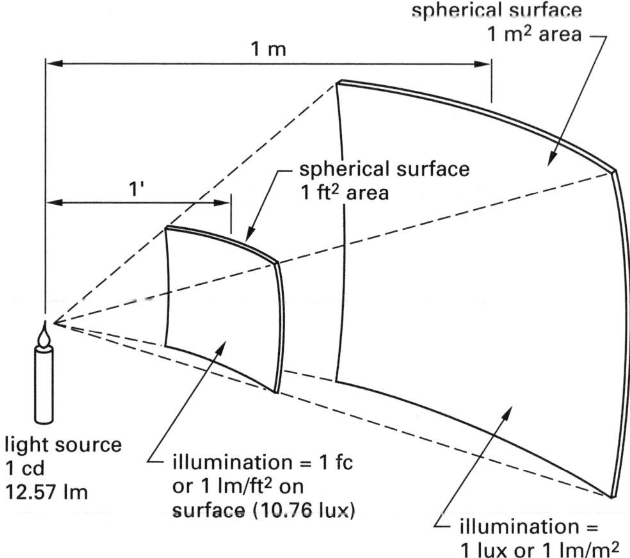

Figure 32.7 Relationship of Light Source and Illumination

Light Levels

Good lighting design involves providing both the proper quantity and proper quality of light to perform a task. This section discusses quantity; the next section discusses quality. Different visual tasks under different conditions require varying levels of illumination. The variables involved include the nature of the task itself, the age of the person performing the task, the reflectances of the room, and the demand for speed and accuracy in performing the task.

The Illuminating Engineering Society of North America (IESNA) has established a method for determining a range of illumination levels in footcandles (lux) appropriate to particular design conditions. Various areas and activities are assigned an illuminance category, and these categories are used with other variables to establish the recommended task and background illuminances.

The required illumination level for an individual task, room, or area must be balanced with requirements for energy conservation. ASHRAE Standard 90.1 and other energy conservation codes and standards now set a maximum limit on the total power that may be used for lighting a building or space. This limit is given in units of watts per square foot (square meter) and is based on the type of building or individual space. It takes careful design and the use of high-efficacy lamps and luminaires to light the building or space effectively while staying under the limit. Refer to the section on energy conservation later in this chapter for a discussion of lighting power densities.

Design Considerations

The quality of light is just as important as the amount of light provided. Important considerations are glare, contrast, uniformity, and color.

There are two types of glare: direct and reflected. *Direct glare* results when a light source in the field of vision causes discomfort and interference with the visual task. Not all visible light sources cause direct glare problems. The extent of the problem depends on the brightness of the source, its position, the background illumination, and the adaptation of the eye to the environment.

In order to evaluate the direct glare problem, the visual comfort probability (VCP) factor was developed. This factor is the percentage of normal observers who may be expected to experience visual comfort in a particular environment with a particular lighting situation. Although the calculations are complex, some simplifications are made, and many manufacturers publish the VCP rating for their light fixtures when it is used under certain conditions.

For most situations, the critical zone for direct glare is in the area above a 45° angle from the light source. See Fig. 32.8. This is because the field of vision (when looking straight ahead) includes an area approximately 45° above a horizontal line. Many direct glare problems can be solved by using a luminaire with a 45° cutoff angle or by moving the luminaire out of the offending field of view.

Reflected glare occurs when a light source is reflected from a viewed surface into the eye. If it interferes with the viewing task, it is also called *veiling reflection*. The effect of reflected glare is to decrease the contrast of the task and its background. For example, a strong light on paper with pencil writing can bounce off the relatively reflective graphite, making it almost as bright as the paper, and effectively obscuring the writing.

Veiling reflections are a complex interaction of light source and brightness, position of the task, reflectivity of the task, and position of the eye. One of the simplest ways to correct veiling reflections is to move the position of the task or the

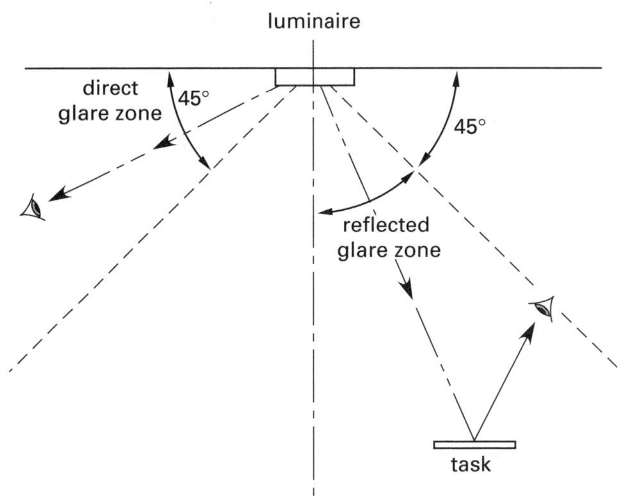

Figure 32.8 Glare Zones

light source. Because the angle of incidence is equal to the angle of reflection, this is easy to calculate. It is not always possible to calculate, however, because the exact use of a room and its furniture arrangement are not always known. Another approach is to provide general background illumination and specific task lighting, the position of which can be controlled by the user.

Contrast is the difference in illumination level between one point and nearby points. Because contrast is the means by which people see, it is vital to the quality of an environment. A printed word on a page is only visible because it contrasts with the brightness of the surrounding paper. However, too much contrast can be detrimental. It is difficult to see fine detail on a small, dark object when the object is viewed against a bright background because the eye has adapted (the iris of the eye is smaller) to the brighter background and cannot admit enough light to see the darker object. The eye adapts by opening and closing the iris, but this causes eye strain and fatigue.

In most situations, brightness ratios should be limited to $1{:}^1/_3$ between the task and adjacent surroundings, to $1{:}^1/_5$ between the task and more remote darker surfaces, and to 1:10 between the task and more remote lighter surfaces.

Uniformity of lighting affects a person's perception of a space as being comfortable and pleasant. Complete uniformity is usually not desirable except for certain tasks like drafting or machine shop work. Because people see by contrast, some amount of shade and shadow provides highlight and interest to a space.

Color in lighting is an interaction between the color of the light source (lamp or daylighting) and the color of the objects that reflect the light. Color in lighting is a complex subject but one that can affect people's comfort and impressions of an environment. For example, most people think of reds and yellows as "warm" colors and greens and blues as "cool" colors. Colors of light sources will be discussed in the next section, and the use of color in lighting design is covered in the following section. Refer to Ch. 43 for a discussion of color systems.

LIGHT SOURCES

In addition to daylight, there are four types of light sources: incandescent, fluorescent, high-intensity discharge, and light-emitting diodes. Some of the considerations that influence the type of light source used are its color rendition characteristics, initial cost, operating cost, efficacy, size, operating life, and ability to control its output from a luminaire. *Efficacy* is the ratio of luminous flux emitted to the total power input to the source and is measured in lumens per watt. It is an important measure of the energy efficiency of a light source. The amount of heat generated by a light source is also an important selection consideration because waste heat usually needs to be removed or compensated for with the air conditioning system, which can add to the total energy load of a building. Some characteristics of common light sources are shown in Table 32.1. These are described in more detail in the following sections.

Some types of incandescent and fluorescent lamps that have traditionally been used in architectural applications are no longer manufactured in or imported into the United States. This is a result of the Energy Policy Act (EPACT) of 1992, which, among other things, set minimum standards for energy efficiency of these two sources of light. The deadline for final implementation was October 31, 1995. After this date certain classes of incandescent and fluorescent lamps had to meet minimum efficacy standards based on their wattage (minimum lumens per watt). These are described in more detail in the following two sections.

Incandescent

An *incandescent* lamp consists of a tungsten filament placed within a sealed bulb containing an inert gas. When electricity is passed through the lamp the filament glows, producing light. Incandescent lamps are produced in a wide variety of shapes, sizes, and wattages for different applications. Some of the more common shapes are shown in Fig. 32.9. A typical designation of an incandescent lamp is a letter followed by a number, such as A-21. This means that the shape is the standard arbitrary shape and the diameter of the bulb at its widest point is 21/8 in, or 2 5/8 in.

Incandescent lamps are inexpensive, compact, easy to dim, can be repeatedly started without a decrease in lamp life, and have a warm color rendition. In addition, their light output can be easily controlled with reflectors and lenses. Their disadvantages include low efficacy, short lamp life, and high heat output. The combination of low efficacy and heat production makes incandescent lamps undesirable for large, energy-efficient installations. For example, a standard 150 W lamp produces less than 20 lm per watt, whereas a 40 W cool white fluorescent lamp has an efficacy of about 80 lm/W with much less heat output.

Table 32.1
Characteristics of Common Light Sources

lamp description	efficacy (lm/W)	color temperature (K)	CRI	approx. lamp life (h)
incandescent	5–20	2700–2800	100	750–4000
tungsten-halogen	18–22	3000–3100	100	1000–4000
fluorescent (T12 and T8)	65–105	2700–7500	55–98	6000–24,000
fluorescent (T5)	95–105	3000–4100	75–95	6000–16,000
compact fluorescent	25–48	2700–4100	82	10,000
mercury-vapor	20–60	5500–5900	15–52	14,000–25,000
metal-halide	35–95	3200–4300	65–85	5000–20,000
ceramic metal-halide	80–100	3000–4100	80–90	15,000
high-pressure sodium	80–140	1800–2800	22–70	10,000–24,000
GU-24	40–70	varies	84	10,000–30,000
LED	40–100+	varies	varies	10,000

Note: The values listed in the table are approximate and representative only. Individual manufacturers and lamps may provide different values.

*Values for the efficacy of LEDs are difficult to compare with other sources because as yet there are no industry standard test procedures for rating the luminous flux of LED devices and arrays. Values are also expected to increase rapidly as improvements in LEDs take place.

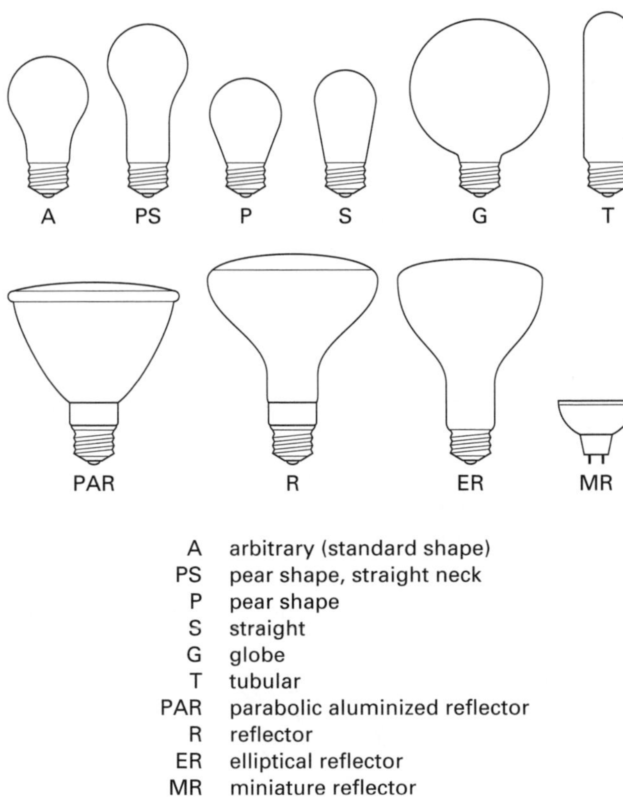

Figure 32.9 Incandescent Lamp Shapes

Another type of incandescent lamp is the *tungsten halogen*. Light is produced by the incandescence of the filament, but there is a small amount of a halogen, such as iodine or bromine, in the bulb with the inert gas. Through a recurring cycle, part of the tungsten filament is burned off as the lamp operates, but it mixes with the halogen and is redeposited on the filament instead of on the wall of the bulb as in standard incandescent lamps. This results in longer bulb life, low lumen depreciation over the life of the bulb, and a more uniform light color. Because the filament burns under higher pressure and temperature, the bulb is made from quartz and is much smaller than standard incandescent lamps. These lamps are often referred to as quartz-halogen. Both standard-voltage (120 V) and low-voltage tungsten-halogen lamps are available.

In addition to their other advantages, tungsten-halogen lamps are compact and have a greater efficacy than standard incandescent lamps. Their higher operating temperature gives more light in the blue end of the spectrum, resulting in a light that looks whiter.

However, because they operate at high temperatures and pressures, failures result in an explosive shattering of the lamp. For this reason, halogen lamps are enclosed in another bulb or are covered with a piece of glass or a screen.

Reflector (R) and *parabolic aluminized reflector* (PAR) lamps contain a reflective coating built into the lamp. This increases the efficiency of the lamp and allows more precise beam control. Both are available in *flood* (wide) and *narrow* (spot) beam dispersal patterns. PAR lamps are made with heavier glass and are also suitable for outdoor use.

Elliptical reflector (ER) lamps are an improved version of R lamps. They provide a more efficient throw of light from a fixture by focusing the light beam at a point slightly in front of the lamp before it spreads out. Its spread is slightly smaller than that of an R lamp. The design is used for downlights with deep baffles or with small openings so that less of the light's output is trapped in the fixture.

Low-voltage miniature reflector (MR) lamps are small tungsten-halogen lamps that are available in a wide variety of wattages (20 W to 75 W) and beam spreads. The regenerative halogen cycle provides consistently high output and a lamp life of from 2000 hr to 3000 hr. Typical color temperatures range from 2000K to 3400K, which makes many of them whiter than standard incandescent lights. MR lamps are available as MR-11 and MR-16. The numbers designate the diameter of the reflector in eighths of an inch. Therefore, an MR-16 is 2 in (50) across. MR-16 lamps are also available for use in 120 V circuits where they can be screwed directly into a socket without the need for a transformer.

Effective October 31, 1995, the Energy Policy Act of 1992 prohibits the manufacture or importation of several types of incandescent lamps that do not meet minimum energy standards. These include all medium-base PAR and R lamps of 40 W and higher. In place of these, some types of ER lamps and lower-wattage lamps can be used. Low-voltage and tungsten-halogen lamps can also be used in place of the old lamps.

Fluorescent

Fluorescent lamps contain a mixture of an inert gas and low-pressure mercury vapor. When the lamp is energized, a mercury arc is formed that creates ultraviolet light. This invisible light, in turn, strikes the phosphor-coated bulb, causing the bulb to fluoresce and produce visible light. The three types of fluorescent lamps are preheat, rapid start, and instant start, according to their circuitry. Preheat lamps have been supplanted by rapid-start types. These lamps maintain a constant low current in the cathode that allows them to start within about 2 sec. Instant-start lamps use a voltage high enough to start the arc in the tube directly without preheating of the cathode.

Every gaseous discharge lamp, including fluorescent lamps, has a *ballast*. This is a device that supplies the proper starting and operating voltages to the lamp and limits the current once the lamp has started. There are several types of ballasts. The *magnetic ballast*, which is generally obsolete but may still be found in older luminaires, is constructed from laminated steel plates wrapped with copper windings. It operates at 60 Hz.

Most luminaires use a solid-state *electronic ballast*. Electronic ballasts operate at much higher frequencies (from 25 kHz to 60 kHz) and use much less power than the older magnetic ballasts. In addition, they operate without noise or flicker, generate less heat, and can allow dimming over a continuous range of levels from 1% to 100%.

Other types of ballasts include low-current and high-current ballasts designed to be matched with specific lamp types. *Multilevel ballasts*, either two-level or three-level, are used to change lighting levels evenly to conserve energy. *Energy-saving ballasts* reduce the total wattage of the lamp-ballast combination by the use of a lower current, by efficient design of the ballast, and by disconnecting the lamp filaments after the lamp starts.

All ballasts are rated for their efficiency by various factors. The *ballast factor* (BF) is the ratio of the light output of a lamp when operated on a tested ballast to the light output when the lamp is operated by a standard reference ballast according to a standard testing procedure; that is, to a "perfect" ballast. Although the ballast factor is not a measure of energy efficiency, matching a ballast factor with a particular lamp for a particular application can reduce energy usage.

The *ballast efficacy factor* (BEF) is the ratio of the ballast factor multiplied by 100 (for example, a 0.75 ballast factor would be 75 as used in the ratio) to the power in watts. The BEF gives a way to compare the efficacy of different ballasts when used with the same kind and number of lamps, even when the wattages used by the different lamp-ballast combinations are different. The BEF does not give a valid comparison, however, when comparing different kinds or different numbers of lamps.

The *power factor* of a ballast is a measure of how effectively the ballast converts the power supplied into usable power (watts) for the lamps. In most cases, ballasts with higher power factors cost more but are more energy efficient. A power factor of 0.90 or above is considered to be high. A *power factor corrected* ballast has a power factor from 0.80 to 0.90.

Some electronic ballasts and all magnetic ballasts produce noise. Because of this they are rated for sound, using letters from A to F. An A-rated ballast is the quietest and is appropriate for spaces with the lowest ambient noise levels. Class F is suitable only for noisy environments.

Lamps are produced in tubular shapes. They are normally straight, but U-shaped and circular lamps are also produced. They are designated according to their type, wattage, diameter, color, and method of starting. Thus, F40T12WW/RS describes a fluorescent lamp, 40 W, tubular, $^{12}/_{8}$ in in diameter ($1^{1}/_{2}$ in [38]), warm white color, with a rapid start circuit. Like incandescent lamps, size is designated in eighths of an inch. A T8 lamp has a 1 in (25.4) diameter, for example. Fluorescent lamps come in a variety of lengths, 4 ft being the most common. 2, 3, and 8 ft lengths are also available as well as special U-shaped sizes. Compact fluorescent (CF) lamps have either a T-4 (10 mm) or T-5 (15 mm) glass envelope bent into a U shape or double U shape and mounted on a special base that houses the ballast and allows the lamp to be screwed into existing incandescent luminaires. Other CF lamps require luminaires specifically designed for them.

A relatively new type of fluorescent lamp and luminaire is the GU-24. A *GU-24 lamp* is a high-efficacy compact fluorescent with a two-pin base that makes it impossible to use any other type of lamp in a GU-24 luminaire. The GU-24 is becoming the most common type of energy-efficient lamp. It is available in a spiral CFL shape or a spiral squat version and for use in 120 V or 277 V circuits. A variety of color temperatures are available with a CRI of 80 or higher. GU-24 lamps have efficacies from 40 W/lm to 70 W/lm, depending on wattage and the specific manufacturer. Rated lamp life ranges from 10,000 hr up to 30,000 hr.

The GU-24 socket and base system is designed to replace the standard Edison screw base. The *Energy Star Program Requirements for Residential Light Fixtures* require that residential lighting fixtures do not use the standard Edison screw base.

In the past, one of the objections to fluorescent lighting was that it was too "cold." Actually, lamps are available in a wide range of color temperatures, ranging from a "cool" FL/D (daylight) lamp of 6500K color temperature to a WWD (warm white deluxe) with a color temperature of 2800K, which has a large percentage of red in its spectral output.

Fluorescent lamps have a high efficacy (about 80 lm/W), relatively low initial cost, and long life. They come in a variety of color temperatures. They can also be dimmed, although fluorescent lamp dimmers are more expensive than their incandescent counterparts. Because fluorescent lamps are larger than incandescents, it is more difficult to control them precisely, so they are usually more suitable for general illumination. However, with developments of smaller and brighter compact fluorescent lamps, several manufacturers now produce downlights with reflector designs for compact fluorescents that can replace traditional incandescent downlights.

The Energy Policy Act of 1992 prohibits the manufacture or importation of several types of fluorescent lamps that do not meet minimum energy standards. These include the standard F40T12 lamp, U-shaped lamps, and other full-wattage lamps. The F40T12 lamp has been replaced with a 32 W, T-8 lamp. This lamp has a higher efficacy and better color rendering than the old lamp. However, it requires an electronic ballast, so retrofitted fixtures have to include this as well as lamp replacement. The new T-8 fixtures also include relatively new triphosphor coatings, which give the lamps improved color rendering.

High-Intensity Discharge

High-intensity discharge (HID) lamps include mercury vapor, metal halide, and high- and low-pressure sodium. In the mercury vapor lamp, an electric arc is passed through high-pressure mercury vapor, which causes it to produce both ultraviolet light and visible light, primarily in the blue-green band. For improved color rendition, various phosphors can be applied to the inside of the lamp to produce more light in the yellow and red bands. Mercury lamps have a moderately high efficacy, in the range of 30 lm/W to 50 lm/W, depending on voltage and the type of color correction included.

A *metal halide lamp* is similar to a mercury lamp except that a combination of metal halides has been added to the arc tube. This increases the efficacy and improves the color rendition, but also shortens the life of the lamp. Among the HID lamps, metal halide lamps provide the best combination of features for many purposes. They have color rendering indexes between 60 and 90, high efficacy, and relatively long life.

The main disadvantage of a metal halide lamp is that its apparent color temperature shifts significantly over its life. (See the section on lighting design for a discussion of color temperature.) Like all HID lamps, a metal halide lamp has an outer bulb to protect the arc tube and to protect people from dangerous ultraviolet light. There are three types of outer bulbs: clear, phosphor-coated, and diffuse. *Clear bulbs* are used when optical control is required. *Phosphor-coated bulbs* are used for better color rendition. *Diffuse bulbs* are specified in recessed downlight fixtures installed in low ceilings.

A new type of metal-halide is the *ceramic metal halide* (CMH) lamp. A CMH lamp uses a ceramic arc tube rather than a quartz tube, which allows the lamp to burn at a higher temperature, improving color rendition and light control. The efficacy of CMH lamps is better than the older metal halide lamps, and there is better color consistency over the lamp's lifetime. Disadvantages of CMH lamps include higher initial costs, difficulty in dimming, and the requirement for a ballast. They are useful in high-ceilinged spaces where long life and high efficacy are desirable, and in retail uses where point source control and excellent color rendition are needed.

High-pressure sodium (HPS) lamps produce light by passing an electric arc through hot sodium vapor. The arc tube must be made of a special ceramic material to resist attack by the hot sodium. HPS lamps have efficacies from 80 lm/W to 140 lm/W, making them among the most efficient lamps available. They also have extremely long lives, about 10,000 hr for the improved-color lamps and up to 24,000 hr for other types. Unfortunately, standard HPS lamps produce a very yellow light. However, HPS lamps are also available with color correction, and their color rendition is acceptable for some interior applications. It is possible to get HPS lamps with color rendering indexes of up to 70.

Low-pressure sodium lamps have even higher efficacies, about 150 lm/W, but they produce a monochromatic light of a deep yellow color. Therefore, they are suitable only when color rendition is not important, such as for street lighting.

All HID lamps need time to restart after being shut off or in case of a power failure. The lamp must cool first and then warm up again. Mercury-vapor lamps need about 3 min to 10 min to relight, metal halide lamps need about 10 min to 20 min, and high-pressure sodium lamps need about 1 min.

Light-Emitting Diodes (LEDs)

A *light-emitting diode* (LED) is a semiconductor device that uses solid-state electronics to create light. LEDs are a class of solid-state lighting that also includes organic light-emitting diodes and light-emitting polymers. LEDs have been used for many years as indicator panel lights and in other small electronic devices. Recent technological developments have made it feasible to use LEDs in traffic signal lights, signage lights, outdoor decorative lighting, and railroad and automotive applications. More efficient LEDs are now being used for general building lighting.

The advantages of LED lamps include brightness, long life, no heat production, and low power consumption. Lamp life ranges from 50,000 hr to 100,000 hr. LEDs can be directly controlled by a digital interface. They can be manufactured to produce a number of colors or white light. Their main disadvantages are their low efficacy (lumens per watt) and high cost. However, as the technology improves, LEDs are being used in an increasing number of architectural and interior design applications. Currently, LED lighting can be used for decorative purposes, exit lights, emergency lighting, and anywhere where a life-cycle cost analysis shows that their low power consumption and long life justifies the higher initial cost. Recent developments in the technology have produced lamps that have efficacies of 50 lm/W to 70 lm/W in a variety of configurations, including reflector lamps and 2 ft × 2 ft (600 mm × 600 mm) luminaires designed to replace standard fluorescent recessed troffers.

In addition to the four basic types of lamps, there are neon lamps, cold-cathode lamps, and fiber optic luminaires. *Neon lamps* can be formed into an unlimited number of shapes and are used for signs and specialty accent lighting. By varying the gases within the tube, a variety of colors can be produced. *Cold-cathode lamps* are similar to neon in that they can be produced in long runs of thin tubing and bent to shape, but they have a higher efficacy, are slightly larger (with about a 1 in diameter), and can produce several shades of white as well as many colors.

A *fiber optic luminaire* carries light from a remote light source to the area or object to be illuminated. Bundled optical fibers deliver light to the ends of the fibers with little or no loss. Fiber optic systems are often used where ultraviolet radiation and heat must be kept away from the illuminated object, such as in a museum display of delicate objects. Other uses include lighting swimming pools, spas, storage areas for highly flammable materials, and other areas where electrical wiring could be a hazard, and bringing light to hard-to-reach areas while locating the light source where it can be easily accessed for maintenance.

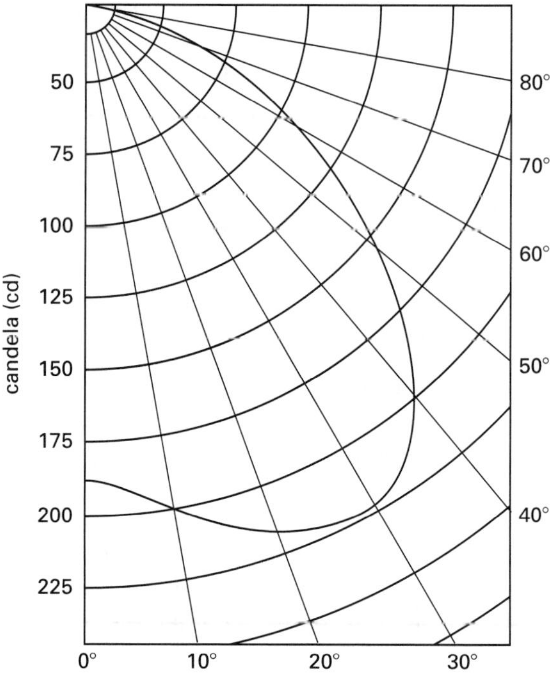

Figure 32.10 Candlepower Distribution Curve

LIGHTING DESIGN

Lighting design is both an art and a science. There must be a sufficient amount of light to perform a task without glare and other discomfort, but the lighting should also enhance the architectural design of the space or landscaping. Lighting must also be designed to minimize energy use, work with the HVAC design, and be cost efficient.

Lighting design is dependent on the fixtures, or luminaires, that are available to provide light. Thousands of different types of luminaires are available from hundreds of manufacturers, and each uses a different lamp in its own proprietary fixture to satisfy a wide range of needs. One of the basic elements of every luminaire is the way it delivers light to the space. This is shown graphically with a candlepower distribution curve, which shows how much light is output at all angles from the luminaire. A typical curve is shown in Fig. 32.10. In this example only one curve is shown for a downlight luminaire where the distribution is the same at all angles to the fixture. In contrast, a rectangular fluorescent luminaire typically distributes light differently in the direction parallel to the fixture and perpendicular to the fixture. In this case the candlepower distribution curve graph would have two slightly different curves. In some cases three curves are shown, the third being the distribution at a 45° angle to the fixture.

Lighting Systems

There are several general types of lighting systems. The terms used to describe them can refer to individual luminaires or to the entire lighting installation. They are broadly described as direct, semidirect, direct-indirect, semi-indirect, and indirect. See Fig. 32.11.

Direct lighting systems provide all light output on the task. A recessed fluorescent luminaire is an example of direct lighting. *Semidirect lighting* systems put a majority of the light down and a small percentage toward the ceiling. Obviously, fixtures for this type of system must be surface mounted or suspended. *Indirect lighting* systems throw all the light toward a reflective ceiling where it illuminates the room by reflection.

Another common system is *task-ambient lighting*. This approach to lighting design recognizes that it is inefficient to try to illuminate an entire room to the level required for individual tasks scattered around the room. Instead, a general background level of illumination is provided, and separate light fixtures are used to increase the light levels at individual workstations. This can be done with desk lamps, directed spotlights, or more fixtures near the tasks requiring more illumination. In addition to being energy efficient and responding to individual lighting needs, task-ambient systems usually create a more pleasant work environment.

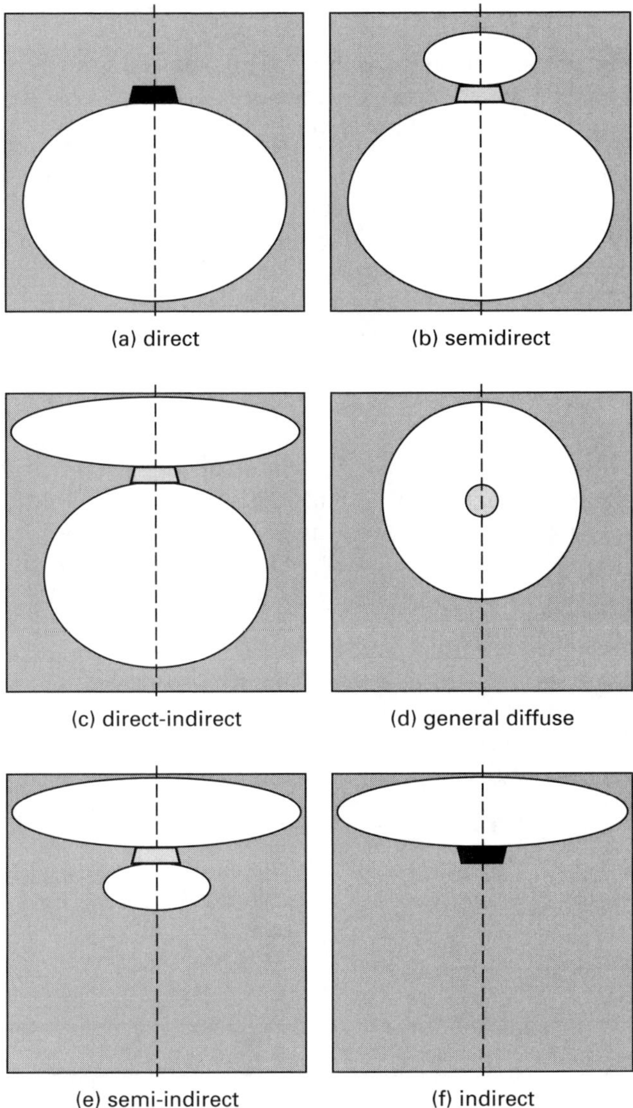

Figure 32.11 Lighting Systems

Luminaire Types

Several general types of luminaires are available for lighting design. These are surface-mounted, recessed, suspended, wall-mounted, furniture-mounted, and freestanding fixtures, as well as accessory lighting.

Surface-mounted fixtures are among the most commonly used types for residential and commercial buildings. As the name implies, the luminaire is directly attached to the finished surface of the ceiling, directing all or a majority of the light into the room. These fixtures are used where there is not sufficient space above the ceiling to recess a fixture, or where fixtures are added after the ceiling has been constructed.

Recessed fixtures are used in both residential and commercial construction and include both incandescent and fluorescent lights. When the entire ceiling is made up of lighting, a luminous ceiling is formed. Recessed incandescents can be general downlights for overall illumination or wallwashers, which aim light in one direction only. Continuous, narrow strips of fluorescent luminaires can also be recessed next to a wall to wash the wall uniformly with light.

Luminaires dropped below the level of the ceiling are called *suspended fixtures*. These include direct incandescent or fluorescent fixtures, track lighting, indirect systems, chandeliers, and other types of specialty lights. Suspended mounting is required for indirect lighting systems. The fixture must be located far enough below the ceiling to allow for the proper spread of light to bounce off the surface. Suspended mounting is also used when the architect needs to get the source of light closer to the task area in a high-ceilinged room.

Wall-mounted luminaires can provide indirect, direct-indirect, or direct lighting. For general illumination, sconces direct most of the light toward the ceiling. Various types of adjustable and nonadjustable direct lighting fixtures are available that serve as task lighting, such as bed lamps. Cove lighting can also be mounted on a wall near the ceiling and will indirectly light either the ceiling or the wall depending on how it is shielded.

Furniture-mounted lighting is common with task-ambient systems. Individual lights are built into the furniture above the work surface to provide sufficient task illumination, whereas uplighting is provided by lights either built into the upper portions of the furniture or designed as freestanding elements.

Freestanding light fixtures include items such as floor lamps. These are available in thousands of different styles and sizes and can be custom designed and manufactured if needed. A freestanding light that directs most of its output to the ceiling is a *torchère*. For task-ambient lighting systems, freestanding kiosks contain high-wattage lights that provide indirect lighting by illuminating the ceiling.

Accessory lighting includes table lights, reading lamps, and fixtures that are intended for strictly decorative lighting rather than for task or ambient lighting.

Quality of Light

Lighting design requires the selection of luminaires, lamps, and fixture arrangement to provide the correct quantity of light. However, quality of light is just as important. (The topics of glare and contrast were discussed in a previous section.) Color quality depends on the color of the light source and its interaction with objects.

Every lamp has a characteristic *spectral energy distribution*. This is a measure of the energy output at different wavelengths, or colors. One such energy distribution curve is shown in Fig. 32.12.

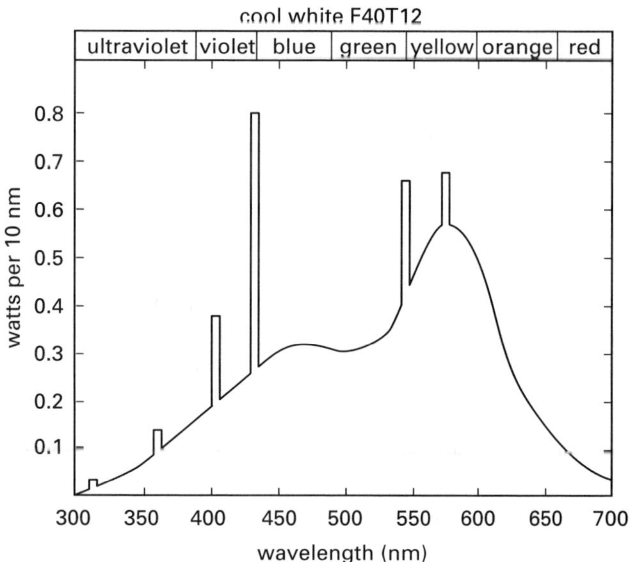

Figure 32.12 Spectral Energy Distribution Curve

Sources are also given a single number rating of their dominant color based on the temperature in degrees Kelvin to which a black-body radiator would have to be heated to produce that color. Lower temperatures, such as 3100K, are relatively warm colors like that of a warm white fluorescent light. Higher color temperatures, such as 5000K to 6000K, are cool colors with a high percentage of blue. A daylight fluorescent lamp has a color temperature of 6500K, for example.

Sources are also rated with a number known as the *color rendering index* (CRI). This is a measure of how closely the perceived colors of an object illuminated with a test source match the colors of the object when it is illuminated with daylight of the same color temperature. The maximum CRI rating is 100, so a light source with a rating of 85 or more is very good.

It is important to know the color characteristics of a light source when designing a lighting system because the light color can affect the colors of objects. For example, using a lamp with a high complement of blue and violet will make finishes and furniture of the warmer colors of red appear dull and washed out. Where color appearance is important, finishes and materials should be selected under the same lighting as will be used in the finished space.

Lighting Calculations

Lighting calculations involve determining the quantity of light in a space. These calculations can be complex because illumination is a result of several variables.

For point sources of light, the illumination on a surface varies directly with the luminous intensity of the source and inversely with the square of the distance between the source and the point. If the surface is perpendicular to the direction of the source, the illumination is determined by the formula

$$E = \frac{I}{d^2} \quad (32.6)$$

For surfaces that are not perpendicular to the source, the inverse square law of formula 32.6 must be adjusted to account for the angle. This relationship is shown in Fig. 32.13. The formula for finding the illumination on the horizontal surface is

$$E = \frac{I \cos\theta}{d^2} \quad (32.7)$$

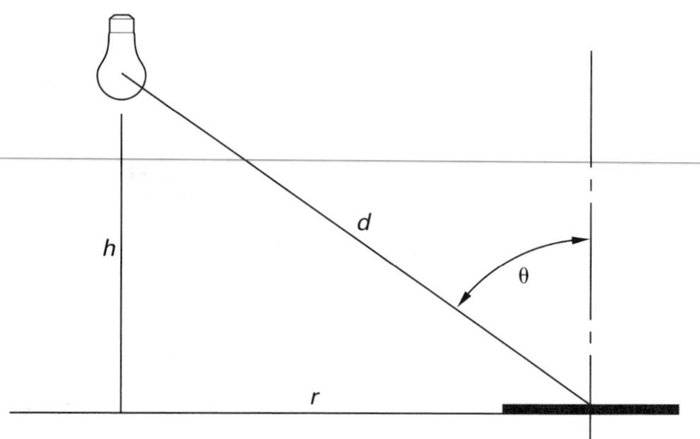

Figure 32.13 Illumination at an Angle to a Point Source

For spaces with several luminaires, other methods are used to calculate the illumination on the work surface or, knowing the desired illumination level, to determine the number of luminaires required. One of the most common is the zonal cavity method. This procedure takes into account several variables. They are

- the lumen output of the lamps used
- the number of lamps in each luminaire
- the efficiency of the luminaire in a particular space. The rating given a particular luminaire is known as the *coefficient of utilization* (CU) and represents the fact that not all of the lumens produced by the lamps reach the work surface. The CU is a number from 0.01 to 1.00 that depends on the design of the

light fixture as well as the characteristics of the room in which the fixture is placed, including the room size and surface reflectances. Manufacturers publish tables that give the CU for each of their luminaires under various conditions.

- the *light loss factor* (LLF). This is a fraction that represents the amount of light that will be lost due to several additional factors. Among these are lamp *lumen depreciation*, which is light loss with age, and *luminaire dirt depreciation*, which is light loss due to accumulated dirt on lamps based on the kind of environment in which they operate. Additional factors are lamp burnout, room surface dirt, operating voltage of the lamps, ambient operating temperature of the lamps, and accumulated dirt on the luminaire.

To calculate the number of luminaires required in a room to maintain a given illumination level, the following formula is used.

$$\text{number of luminaires} = \frac{(\text{footcandles})(\text{area of room})}{(\text{number of lamps})(\text{lumen per lamp})(\text{CU})(\text{LLF})} \qquad 32.8$$

For complex spaces, manual calculation can be time consuming and error prone. Other tools are available. One is the *isolux chart* (sometimes called an *isofootcandle chart*), a diagram showing lines of equal illumination produced by a specific luminaire from a particular manufacturer. The chart is produced either by full-scale mock-ups of the luminaire or by computer simulation. If several fixtures are used, they can be moved around on a floor plan, and the illumination levels can be added to determine the total illumination at any given point.

Another calculation tool commonly used is computer simulation. Lighting design by computer is accurate and fast, and it allows the designer to try many alternatives that would not be possible with manual calculations. In addition, the computer gives more information than is common with manual calculation.

The coefficient of utilization takes into account the characteristics of both the luminaire and the room it is used in, but the efficacy of a luminaire can also be evaluated by itself. The *luminaire efficacy rating* (LER) is the ratio of the luminaire's light output to the input power, expressed in lumens per watt. In practical terms, the LER measures how efficiently a particular luminaire can get the available light from the lamps out of a fixture. It takes into account the luminaire's efficiency and lumen output, as well as the total power it uses, including the ballast. The LER is calculated using Eq. 32.9.

$$\text{LER} = \frac{(\text{EFF})(\text{TLL})(\text{BF})}{W} \qquad 32.9$$

In Eq. 32.9, EFF is the luminaire's efficiency expressed as a two-place decimal fraction; this is a measure, based on photometric testing, of how efficiently the luminaire distributes light. TLL is total lamp lumens, the number of lamps multiplied by the rated lumens output of each lamp. BF is the ballast factor expressed as a two-place decimal fraction. W is the total power input expressed in watts.

The LER applies to fluorescent luminaires, high-intensity discharge luminaires, and commercial downlights. With fluorescent lights, the LER applies to five different types of luminaires, and when comparing one luminaire with another, only similar types should be compared. The five types are FL, fluorescent lensed, FP, fluorescent parabolic, FW, fluorescent wraparound, FI, fluorescent industrial, and FS, fluorescent strip light.

Energy Conservation

Nearly all building code jurisdictions in the United States require energy conservation measures for electric use in buildings. They may adopt the *International Energy Conservation Code* (IECC), ANSI/ASHRAE/IESNA Standard 90.1, or some other standard. The IECC itself adopts, by reference, Standard 90.1. The LEED rating systems also give points for optimizing energy performance. In addition to setting requirements for switching and other lighting controls, as discussed previously in this chapter, Standard 90.1 limits the total amount of power that can be used for lighting. The architect and electrical engineer may comply with the requirements in one of three ways: the building area method, the space-by-space method, or the energy cost budget method.

The *building area method* limits the total power used in a building by giving a maximum allowable power in watts per square foot (square meter) of building area, based on the building type. This is the *lighting power density* (LPD) and varies with the type of facility. In Standard 90.1, the LPD is given in a simple table. For example, a courthouse is allowed 1.2 W/ft^2 (0.11 W/m^2), while a hotel is allowed 1.0 W/ft^2 (0.09 W/m^2). The gross lighted floor area of the building is multiplied by the LPD. If there are different area types in the building, the area of each type is multiplied by the appropriate LPD to get the *lighting power allowance* (LPA) for that area. The LPAs for the individual areas are summed to get the total LPA for the building. Trade-offs are permitted, so if one area uses less power, the unused allowance can be assigned to another area.

The *space-by-space method* assigns LPDs to common space types. The designer must determine the gross area of each space type in the building, and multiply each area by the allowable watts per square foot (square meter). For example, a dining area for a hotel is allowed 1.3 W/ft^2 (0.12 W/m^2) while a family dining area is allowed 2.1 W/ft^2 (0.19 w/m^2). The LPAs for all areas are added to arrive at a total LPA for the building.

When the space-by-space method is used, additional lighting power is allowed for certain functions. This includes an increase of 1.0 W/ft^2 (0.09 W/m^2) for decorative lighting in the space used. Decorative lighting includes things such as chandeliers, wall sconces, and lighting for art or exhibits.

When lighting is installed in retail spaces specifically to highlight merchandise, an additional allowance of 1000 watts is given, plus an allowance per unit area depending on what type of merchandise is being displayed. This ranges from 1.0 W/ft^2 (0.09 W/m^2) to 4.2 W/ft^2 (0.39 W/m^2).

Lighting power densities for various exterior applications are also given in Standard 90.1 for use with both the building area and the space-by-space method. Internally illuminated exit signs cannot exceed 5 W per face.

Both these methods provide for many exceptions to the lighting power allowance, as long as the lighting is controlled by an independent control device. Some of these exceptions include

- exhibit displays for museums, monuments, and galleries
- lighting that is integral to equipment and instrumentation installed by the manufacturer
- medical and dental procedures
- open and glass-enclosed refrigerator and freezer cases
- equipment for food warming and food preparation
- growth and maintenance of plants
- areas specifically designed for the visually impaired
- retail display windows, provided that the display is enclosed by ceiling-height partitions
- interior spaces specifically designated as registered interior historic landmarks
- lighting that is an integral part of advertising or directional signage
- exit signs
- demonstration systems used in selling or teaching about lighting equipment
- theatrical, stage, film, and video production
- television broadcasting in sports activity areas
- casino gaming areas
- furniture-mounted supplemental task lighting controlled by automatic shutoff

The *energy cost budget method* is a complex way to determine the energy cost budget for a specific building design. The budget is calculated by means of a computer simulation of hourly energy use over the course of a year, using appropriate climatic data, approved envelope design, a baseline building, and other aspects as defined in Standard 90.1. In this method, lighting power allowances are only one aspect of the building's total energy use. The designer can make trade-offs between energy needs for lighting and those for other buildings systems.

Although it is a complex procedure, the energy cost budget method is the only way to deal with unique designs, renewable energy, high-efficiency equipment, and other unique aspects of a building's design. This method is also used to verify compliance with LEED requirements. In addition, any building that is complying with Standard 90.1 by this method must still meet the mandatory requirements of all sections of the standard.

Another energy conservation measure is *lighting system tuning*, which is the adjustment of the lighting installation after construction is complete. It is common for many changes to be made in the lighting design between the time it is first executed and when the client is ready to move in. During tuning, lamps are replaced with lower (or higher if really necessary) wattage units, adjustable luminaries are aimed for their optimal positions, ballasts are adjusted for maximum efficiency, and switches are replaced with dimmer controls or time-out units.

Emergency Lighting

The IBC, *National Electrical Code*, and *Life Safety Code* all include provisions for emergency lighting. Because each jurisdiction differs slightly in its requirements, the local codes in force must be reviewed. Generally, however, all codes require that in the event of a power failure, sufficient lighting be available to safely evacuate building occupants.

Emergency and standby power systems are required to provide electricity for emergency egress illumination, exit signs, smoke control systems, horizontal sliding doors, and means of egress elevators. In some occupancies, voice communication systems and other items must also be powered. The power systems may include batteries, generators, or both.

Building codes require that the means of egress be illuminated whenever the building is occupied. In the event of a power failure, the emergency power system must provide illumination to

- exit access corridors and aisles in rooms and spaces required to have two or more exits
- exit access corridors and exit stairways in buildings required to have two or more exits

- interior exit discharge elements when permitted, such as building lobbies where 50% of the exit capacity may egress through the ground-floor lobby

The means-of-egress illumination level must be a minimum of 1 fc (10.8 lx) measured at the floor level and must be maintained for not less than 90 min.

With some exceptions, exit signs are required at exits and exit access doors, positioned in such a way that no point in an exit access corridor is more than 100 ft (30 480) from an exit sign. Directional exit signs are required at corridor intersections or where a corridor changes direction so that it is always evident to the occupants where the exits are. Exit signs may be either externally or internally illuminated. If the sign is externally illuminated, the minimum light level cannot be less than 5 fc (54 lx). Internally illuminated signs must be lit at all times and must be listed and labeled. Illuminated exit signs, whether illuminated internally or externally, must be connected to an emergency power circuit.

Self-luminous and photoluminescent exit signs may be used if approved by the local jurisdiction. *Self-luminous* exit signs are "glow-in-the-dark" signs that do not require external power or batteries. They are illuminated by tritium, which is a self-luminous isotope of hydrogen. *Photoluminescent* exit signs are charged with energy absorbed from the ambient lighting during normal building operation. When the ambient lighting is gone, the signs give off the stored energy and glow in the dark, but their glow slowly dims as the darkness continues.

SIGNAL AND SAFETY ALARM SYSTEMS

Contemporary buildings contain a complex variety of signal and communication systems. These are low-voltage circuits connecting various types of devices that make it possible for the building to function properly and that protect the occupants. In addition to communication systems such as telephone lines, building automation systems control the mechanical, electrical, and security systems from one central station and continuously monitor their operation.

Communication Systems

Communication systems include telephone systems, intercom systems, paging and sound systems, television, closed circuit television (CCTV), and most recently, computer systems, as well as local area networks (LANs) that allow the sharing of data on several computers within one building or in a complex of buildings.

Telephone systems are the most prevalent type of communication system. In most buildings, main telephone lines enter the structure in a main cable and connect to the terminal room where they are split into riser cables. These risers are generally located near the core and connect telephone equipment rooms on each floor. From these equipment rooms the lines branch out to serve individual spaces.

In the past, each floor would have one telephone equipment room that contained relay panels and other equipment. With the proliferation of separate telephone companies in recent years, each tenant space in a large building usually needs its own equipment room. The size of the room is dependent on the type of equipment used and the number of telephone lines connected.

Other types of communication systems are typically wired as the building is constructed. Cabling terminates at electrical boxes in the wall or floor with a jack into which individual equipment can be connected. Most signal cabling is run in metal conduit, such as electrical cable, unless the local building code allows it to be exposed. Conduit protects the cable and prevents it from burning in a fire and giving off dangerous gases.

Security Systems

Security systems include methods for detecting intruders, preventing entry, controlling access to secure areas, and notifying authorities in the event of unauthorized entry or other emergencies. The types of hardware and electronic devices that are used depend on the nature of the threat, the level of security desired, and the amount of money that can be devoted to the system. Following are some of the more common devices with which examinees should be familiar.

Intrusion detection. Security derived from intrusion detection devices can be classified into three types: perimeter protection, area or room protection, and object protection.

Perimeter protection secures the entry points to a space or building. These include doors, windows, skylights, and even ducts, tunnels, and other service entrances. Some of the more common types of perimeter protection are the following.

- *Magnetic contacts* are used on doors and windows to either sound an alarm when the contact is broken (door or window opened) or send a signal to a central monitoring and control station. These can be surface mounted, recessed into the door and frame, or concealed in special hinges.

- *Glass break detectors* sense when a window has been broken or cut by using either metallic foil or a small vibration detector mounted on the glass.

- *Window screens* in which fine wires are embedded can be used to set off an alarm when they are cut or broken.

- *Photoelectric cells* detect when the beam has been broken, by either a door opening or someone's passing through an opening. These can be surface mounted, but they are more secure and look better if provisions are made to recess them in the partition or other construction.

Area or room protection senses when someone is in a room or area within the device's field of coverage. These devices provide the advantage of warning of unauthorized entry when perimeter sensors have not been activated. Area intrusion devices include the following.

- *Photoelectric beams* warn of intrusion by sending a pulsed infrared beam across a space. If the beam is broken it can sound an alarm or send a signal to a monitoring station. Photoelectric beams can be focused in large and small areas alike.
- *Infrared detectors* sense sources of infrared radiation, such as the human body, compared with the normal room radiation. They are unobtrusive, but must have a clear field of view of the area they are protecting.
- *Audio detectors* identify unusual sounds in a space at levels above what is normally encountered. When that level is exceeded an alarm is sounded. Microphones can also be used to continuously monitor all sounds in a space through a speaker at a central monitoring station.
- *Pressure sensors* detect weight on a floor or other surface. Sensor mats can be separate fixtures laid over the existing floor finish or they can be placed under carpet or other building materials.
- *Ultrasonic detectors* emit a very high-frequency sound wave. When this is interrupted by an intruder, an alarm signal is activated. The range of ultrasonic detectors is limited to a space of about 12 ft (3.6 m) in height and 20 ft by 30 ft (6.1 m by 9.1 m) in area.
- *Microwave detectors* sense interruptions in the field of microwave radiation that these detectors emit. Their use is limited in interior construction, however, because the microwave radiation can penetrate most building materials and can be reflected by metal.

Object protection is used to sense movement or tampering with individual objects such as safes, artwork, file cabinets, or other equipment. Capacitance proximity detectors sense touch on metal objects; vibration detectors sense a disturbance of an object; and infrared motion detectors can determine if the space around an object is violated.

Access control. Access to secure areas can be controlled with a number of devices. The simplest is the traditional mechanical lock. High-security locksets are available that provide an additional level of security through the use of key types that are difficult to duplicate, special tumbler mechanisms, and long-throw dead bolts.

Because access and duplication of keys can be a problem even for the most secure mechanical lock, various types of electronic locks are available. These can not only selectively control access better than keys, but they can also monitor who enters and exits a door and record when the access was made.

Card readers are common electronic access control devices. When a valid card is passed through the reader, the plastic card's coded magnetic strip unlocks the door. Card readers can be connected to a central monitoring computer that keeps a log of which person's card was used to open the door and when the door was opened. The computer can be programmed to allow only certain cards to operate certain doors. Operation can be further limited to specific hours during the day and specific days of the week. If a card is lost or stolen, its access code can be quickly and easily removed from the system.

Numbered keypads operate in the same way by unlocking a door when the user enters the correct numerical code. However, numbered keypads do not provide the same flexibility as do magnetic cards. Numbered keypads can also include the keypad and knob or lever handle in one unit. These are not connected to a central station, but they do eliminate the key-control problem of standard locksets.

Card readers and other devices control the operation of one of several types of locking mechanisms. One type is the *electric lock*, which retracts the bolt when activated from the secure side of the door. Unlatching from the inside is done by a button or switch or by mechanical retraction of the bolt with the lever handle. Electric locks require an electric hinge or other power-transfer device to carry the low-voltage wiring from the control device to the door and then to the lock.

Electric strikes are also used. These replace the standard door strike and consist of a movable mechanism that is mortised into the frame. The latch bolt is fixed from the secure side of the door. On activation, the electric strike retracts, allowing the door to be opened. On the inside, the latch bolt can be retracted by mechanical means with the lever handle.

Doors can also be secured with *electromagnetic locks*. When activated, the lock holds the door closed with a powerful magnetic force. Card readers, keypads, buttons, or other devices deactivate the electromagnet. These can be designed to open on activation of a fire alarm or power failure.

New *biometric devices* are now available that can read individual biological features such as the iris or retina of the eye or a handprint, providing a counterfeit-proof method of identification. These devices are expensive but may be worth the cost when a very high level of security is required. Work is continuing on developing commercially available devices that can recognize voiceprints and fingerprints.

Notification systems. When intrusion is detected an alarm signal is triggered. This signal can activate an alarm such as a bell or horn, turn on lights, alert an attendant at a central control station, or be relayed over phone lines to a central security service. Combinations of all three notifications are also possible. If an office building has a central station, a building tenant may be able to connect special lease space security with the central station. When a central station is notified, the alarms are automatically recorded in the system.

Fire Detection and Alarms

There are four basic types of fire detection devices. The first is the *ionization detector*, which responds to products of combustion-ionized particles rather than to smoke. Ionization detectors are not appropriate where fires may produce a lot of smoke but few particles. Because they can detect particles from a smoldering fire before it bursts into flames, these devices are considered early warning detectors.

Photoelectric detectors respond to smoke, which obscures a light beam in the device. These are useful where potential fires may produce a great deal of smoke before bursting into flames.

Rise-of-temperature detectors sense the presence of heat and can be set to trip an alarm when a particular temperature is reached in the room. The major disadvantage is that flames must usually be present before the alarm temperature is reached. By that time it may be too late, because a fire can smolder and produce deadly smoke long before it reaches the flame stage.

There are also flame detectors that respond to infrared or ultraviolet radiation given off by flames. However, like rise-of-temperature detectors, they do not give an early warning of smoldering fires.

In many buildings, a combination of fire-detection devices must be used depending on the particular type of space in which they are placed. For example, an ionization device would not operate properly where air currents or other circumstances would prevent the products of combustion from entering the device.

The building code states the required types and locations of fire detectors. Detectors are required near fire doors, in exit corridors, in individual hotel rooms, in bedrooms, and in places of public assembly. They are also often required in main-supply and return-air ducts. Codes usually require them in other spaces based on a given area coverage.

When activated, fire detectors can be wired to trigger a general audible alarm as well as visual alarm lights for the deaf. They can also activate a central monitoring station or a municipal fire station. In large buildings with a central station, the detection of a fire also activates fire dampers, exhaust systems, the closing of fire doors, and other preventive measures as the alarm is being signaled to fire officials.

33 ACOUSTICS

Nomenclature

a	coefficient of absorption	–
A	total acoustical absorption	sabins
c	velocity of sound	ft/sec (m/s)
f	frequency of sound	Hz
I	sound intensity	W/cm^2
I_o	minimum sound intensity audible to the average human ear	10^{-16} W/cm^2
IL	sound intensity level	dB
NR	noise reduction	dB
P	acoustic power	W
r	distance from the source	cm
S	area of barrier or component between rooms	ft^2 (m^2)
t	coefficient of transmission	
T	reverberation time	sec
TL	transmission loss	dB
V	room volume	ft^3 (m^3)
w	wavelength	ft (m)
W	power	W

DEFINITIONS

Amplification: the increased intensity of sound by mechanical or electrical means

Articulation index: a measure of speech intelligibility calculated from the number of words read from a selected list that are understood by an audience. A low articulation index (less than 0.15) is desirable for speech privacy, whereas a high articulation index (above 0.6) is desired for good communication.

Attenuation: the reduction of sound

Decibel: 10 times the common logarithm of the ratio of a quantity to a reference quantity of the same kind, such as power, intensity, or energy density. It is often used as the unit of sound intensity according to Eq. 33.5.

dBA: the unit of sound intensity measurement that is weighted to account for the response of the human ear to various frequencies

Frequency: the number of pressure fluctuations or cycles occurring in 1 sec, expressed in hertz (Hz)

Hertz: the unit of frequency; one cycle per second equals 1 Hz

Impact insulation class (IIC): a single-number rating of a floor-ceiling's impact sound transmission performance at various frequencies

Intensity: the amount of sound energy per second across a unit area

Intensity level: 10 times the common logarithm of the ratio of a sound intensity to a reference intensity. See *Decibel*.

Noise: any unwanted sound

Noise criteria (NC): a set of single-number ratings of acceptable background noise corresponding to a set of curves specifying sound pressure levels across octave bands. Noise criteria curves can be used to specify continuous background noise, achieve sound isolation, and evaluate existing noise situations.

Noise insulation class (NIC): a single-number rating of noise reduction

Noise reduction (NR): the arithmetic difference, in decibels, between the intensity levels in two rooms separated by a barrier of a given transmission loss. Noise reduction is dependent on the transmission loss of the barrier, the area of the barrier, and the absorption of the surfaces of the receiving room.

Noise reduction coefficient (NRC): the average sound absorption coefficient to the nearest 0.05, measured at the four one-third octave band center frequencies of 250, 500, 1000, and 2000 Hz

Octave band: a range of frequencies in which the upper frequency is twice that of the lower

Phon: a unit of loudness level of a sound equal to the sound pressure level of a 1000 Hz tone judged to be as loud

Reverberation: the persistence of a sound in a room after the source has stopped producing the sound

Reverberation time: the time it takes the sound level to decrease 60 dB after the source has stopped producing the sound

Sabin: the unit of absorption; theoretically, 1 ft^2 of surface having an absorption coefficient of 1.00 (1 m^2 of surface having an absorption of 1.00)

Sabin formula: the formula that relates reverberation time to a room's volume and total acoustical absorption. See Eq. 33.11.

Sound: a small compressional disturbance of equilibrium in an elastic medium, which causes the sensation of hearing

Sound absorption coefficient: the ratio of the sound intensity absorbed by a material to the total intensity reaching the material. Theoretically, 1.00 is the maximum possible value of the sound absorption coefficient.

Sound power: the total sound energy radiated by a source per second, in watts

Sound transmission class (STC): a single-number average over several frequency bands of a barrier's ability to reduce sound. The higher the STC rating, the better the barrier's ability to control sound transmission.

Transmission loss (TL): the difference, in decibels, between the sound power incident on a barrier in a source room and the sound power radiated into a receiving room on the opposite side of the barrier. The transmission loss varies with the frequency being tested.

FUNDAMENTALS OF SOUND AND HUMAN HEARING

Qualities of Sound

Sound has three basic qualities: velocity, frequency, and power.

The *velocity* of sound depends on the medium in which it is traveling and the temperature of the medium. In air at sea level the velocity of sound is approximately 1130 ft/sec (344 m/s). For acoustical purposes in buildings, the temperature effect on velocity is not significant.

Frequency is the number of cycles completed per second; it is measured in hertz (Hz). One hertz equals one cycle per second.

Frequency and velocity are related by the following formula.

$$f = \frac{c}{w} \qquad 33.1$$

Power is the quality of acoustical energy as measured in watts. Because a point source emits waves in a spherical shape in free space, the sound intensity (watts per unit area) is given by the following formula.

$$I = \frac{P}{4\pi r^2} \qquad 33.2$$

Because 1 ft^2 equals 930 cm^2, the formula can be rewritten for English units as

$$I = \frac{P}{(930 \text{ cm}^2)(4\pi r^2)} \qquad 33.3$$

Inverse Square Law

The basic inverse square law is derived from formula 33.3 where sound intensity is inversely proportional to the square of the distance from the source.

$$\frac{I_1}{I_2} = \frac{r_2^2}{r_1^2} \qquad 33.4$$

Sound Intensity

The sensitivity of the human ear covers a vast range (from 10^{-16} W/cm^2 to 10^{-3} W/cm^2). Because of this and the fact that the sensation of hearing is proportional to the logarithm of the source intensity, the decibel is used in acoustical descriptions and calculations. The decibel conveniently relates actual sound intensity to the way humans experience sound. By definition, zero decibels is the threshold of human hearing and 130 dB is the threshold of pain.

In mathematical terms, this relationship is expressed by the following formula.

$$\text{IL} = 10 \log \frac{I}{I_0} \qquad 33.5$$

Some common sound intensity levels and their subjective evaluations are shown in Table 33.1.

Loudness

The sensation of loudness is subjective, but some common guidelines are shown in Table 33.2. These are useful in evaluating the effects of increased or decreased decibel levels in architectural situations. For example, spending money to modify a partition to increase its sound transmission class by 3 dB probably would not be worth the expense because it would hardly be noticeable.

Addition of Decibels of Uncorrelated Sounds

Because decibels are logarithmic, they cannot be added directly. A detailed calculation can be performed, but a convenient rule of thumb gives results accurate to within 1%. Given two decibel values, use the values in Table 33.3 to add decibels.

For three or more sources, first add two, then add the result to the third number, and so on.

Example 33.1

Find the combined intensity level of two office machines, one generating 70 dB and the other generating 76 dB.

Use the rule of thumb shown in Table 33.3. The difference between 76 and 70 is 6; therefore, add 1 dB to 76, which gives 77 dB.

For the addition of several sources of identical value, use Eq. 33.8.

$$IL_{\text{total}} = IL_{\text{source}} + 10 \log(\text{number of sources}) \qquad 33.8$$

Example 33.2

What would the sound level be in a room of eight typewriters, each producing 73 dB?

$$\begin{aligned} IL_{\text{total}} &= 73 \text{ dB} + 10 \log 8 \\ &= 82 \text{ dB} \end{aligned}$$

Human Sensitivity to Sound

Although human response to sound is subjective and varies with age, physical condition of the ear, background, and other factors, some common guidelines are useful to remember.

Table 33.1
Common Sound Intensity Levels

IL (dB)	example	subjective evaluation	intensity (W/cm^2)
140	jet plane takeoff		
130	gun fire	threshold of pain	10^{-3}
120	hard rock band, siren at 100 ft	deafening	10^{-4}
110	accelerating motorcycle	sound can be felt	10^{-5}
100	auto horn at 10 ft	conversation difficult to hear	10^{-6}
90	loud street noise, kitchen blender	very loud	10^{-7}
80	noisy office, average factory	difficult to use phone	10^{-8}
70	average street noise, quiet typewriter, average radio	loud	10^{-9}
60	average office, noisy home	usual background	10^{-10}
50	average conversation, quiet radio	moderate	10^{-11}
40	quiet home, private office	noticeably quiet	10^{-12}
30	quiet conversation	faint	10^{-13}
20	whisper		10^{-14}
10	rustling leaves, soundproof room	very faint	10^{-15}
0	threshold of hearing		10^{-16}

Table 33.2
Subjective Change in Loudness Based on Decibel Level Change

change in intensity level (dB)	change in apparent loudness
1	almost imperceptible
3	just perceptible
5	clearly noticeable
6	change when distance to source in a free field is doubled or halved
10	twice or half as loud
18	very much louder or quieter
20	four times or one-fourth as loud

Table 33.3
Addition of Decibels

when difference between the two values is:	add this value to the higher value:
0 or 1 dB	3 dB
2 or 3 dB	2 dB
4 to 8 dB	1 dB
9 dB or more	0 dB

The normal human ear of a healthy young person can hear sounds in the range of 20 Hz to 20,000 Hz and is most sensitive to frequencies in the 3000 Hz to 4000 Hz range. Speech is composed of sounds primarily in the range of 125 Hz to 8000 Hz, with most energy in the range of 100 Hz to 600 Hz.

The human ear is less sensitive to low frequencies than to middle and high frequencies for sounds of equal energy.

Most common sound sources contain energy over a wide range of frequencies. Because frequency is an important variable in how a sound is transmitted or absorbed, it must be taken into account in building acoustics. For convenience, measurement and analysis is often divided into eight octave frequency bands identified by the center frequency. These are 63, 125, 250, 500, 1000, 2000, 4000, and 8000 Hz. For detailed purposes, smaller bands are often used.

Because the human ear is less sensitive to low frequencies (around 500 Hz and below), a modified decibel scale, called the dBA scale, is used to predict human response to sounds and for acoustical design when low frequencies are part of the sound.

SOUND TRANSMISSION

Transmission Loss and Noise Reduction

One of the primary objectives of architectural acoustics is to reduce the transmission of sound from one space to another. Transmission of sound is primarily retarded by the mass of the barrier. In addition, the stiffness of the barrier is also important. Given two barriers of the same weight per unit area, the one that is less stiff will perform better than the other.

There are two important concepts in noise reduction: transmission loss and actual noise reduction. *Transmission loss* (TL) is the difference (in decibels) between the sound power incident on a barrier in a source room and the sound power radiated into a receiving room on the opposite side of the barrier. This is the measurement typically derived in a testing laboratory.

Noise reduction (NR) is the arithmetic difference (in decibels) between the intensity levels in two rooms separated by a barrier of a given transmission loss. Noise reduction is dependent on the transmission loss of the barrier, the area of the barrier, and the absorption of the surfaces in the receiving room.

Noise reduction is calculated by the following formula.

$$\text{NR} = \text{TL} + 10 \log \frac{A}{S} \qquad 33.6$$

In SI units, A is in metric sabins and S is in m^2. One metric sabin equals 10.76 English sabins.

This formula shows that noise reduction can be increased by increasing the transmission loss of the barrier, by increasing the absorption in the receiving room, by decreasing the area of the barrier separating the two rooms, or by some combination of the three.

The actual transmission loss of a barrier varies with the frequencies of the sounds being tested. Test reports, often published with manufacturers' literature, include the transmission loss over six or more octave bands. A single-number rating that is often used is the *sound transmission class* (STC). The higher the STC rating, the better the barrier (theoretically) in stopping sound.

There are many times when a partition will comprise two or more types of constructions, for example, a door in a wall or a glass panel in a wall. The combined transmission loss can be found by the following formula.

$$\text{TL}_{\text{composite}} = 10 \log \frac{\text{total area}}{\Sigma tS} \qquad 33.7$$

In finding the value of t, if the value of the transmission loss of individual materials is known, the following formula can be used.

$$t = 10^{-(\mathrm{TL}/10)} \qquad 33.8$$

Example 33.3

A conference room and an office are separated by a common wall 13 ft long and 9 ft high with an STC rating of 54. The total absorption of the office has been calculated to be 220 sabins. What is the total noise reduction from the conference room to the office?

$$\begin{aligned} \mathrm{NR} &= 54 + 10 \log \frac{220 \text{ sabins}}{(9 \text{ ft})(13 \text{ ft})} \\ &= 54 + 10 \log 1.88 \\ &= 54 + 2.7 \\ &= 57 \text{ dB} \end{aligned}$$

Notice that the second term of Eq. 33.6 can be a negative number, resulting in a noise reduction less than the transmission loss of the wall.

Example 33.4

What is the combined transmission loss of a wall 9 ft high and 15 ft long with a 3 ft by 7 ft door in it? Assume the TL of the wall is 54 dB and that the door, with full perimeter seals, is 29 dB.

total wall area: $(9 \text{ ft})(15 \text{ ft}) = 135 \text{ ft}^2$

area of door: 21 ft^2

area of partition: $135 \text{ ft} - 21 \text{ ft} = 114 \text{ ft}^2$

t of partition $= 10^{-5.4}$

t of door $= 10^{-2.9}$

$$\begin{aligned} \mathrm{TL}_{\text{composite}} &= 10 \log \frac{135}{(10^{-5.4})(114) + (10^{-2.9})(21)} \\ &= 10 \log 5012 \\ &= 37 \text{ dB} \end{aligned}$$

Remember that STC ratings represent the ideal loss under laboratory conditions. Walls, partitions, and floors built in the field are seldom constructed as well as those in the laboratory. Also, breaks in the barrier such as cracks, electrical outlets, doors, and the like will significantly reduce the overall noise reduction.

In critical situations, transmission loss and selection of barriers should be calculated using the values for the various frequencies rather than the single STC average value. Some materials may allow an acoustical "hole," stopping most frequencies but allowing transmission of a certain range of frequencies. This often happens with very low or very high frequencies. However, for preliminary design purposes in typical situations the STC value is adequate.

Noise Criteria Curves

All normally occupied spaces have some amount of background noise. This is not undesirable, because some noise is necessary to avoid the feeling of a "dead" space and to help mask other sounds. However, the acceptable amount of background noise varies with the type of space and the frequency of sound. For example, people are generally less tolerant of background noise in bedrooms than they are in public lobbies, and they are generally more tolerant of higher levels of low-frequency sound than of high-frequency sound.

These variables have been consolidated into a set of noise criteria (NC) curves relating frequency in eight octave bands to noise level. See Fig. 33.1. Accompanying these curves are noise criteria ratings for various types of space and listening requirements. A representative sampling is shown in Table 33.4. Noise criteria curves can be used to specify the maximum amount of continuous background noise allowable in a space, to establish a minimum amount of noise desired to help mask sounds, and to evaluate an existing condition.

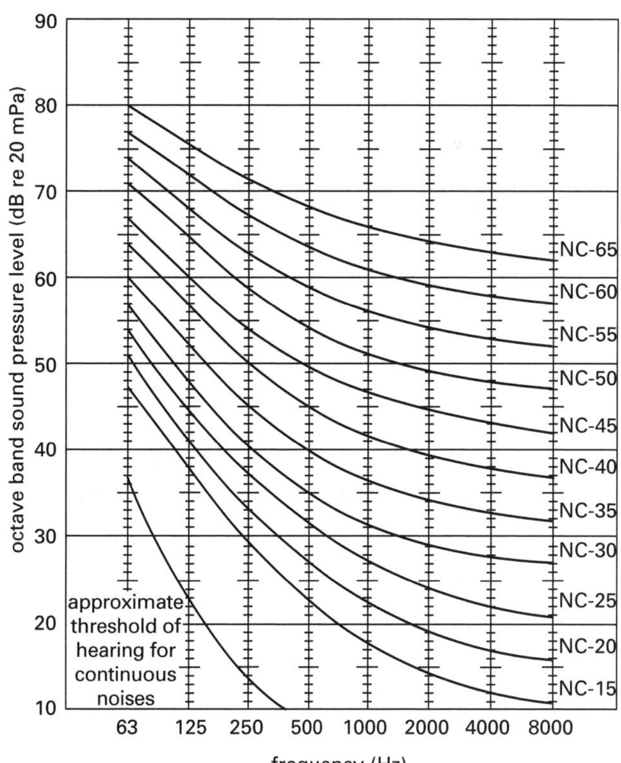

Figure 33.1 NC (Noise Criteria) Curves

Table 33.4

Some Representative Noise Criteria

type of space	preferred NC (dB)
concert halls, opera houses, recording studios	15–20
bedrooms, apartments, hospitals	20–30
private offices, small conference rooms	30–35
large offices, retail stores, restaurants	35–40
lobbies, drafting rooms, laboratory work spaces	40–45
kitchens, computer rooms, light maintenance shops	45–55

For example, if the noise spectrum of an air conditioning system was plotted on the NC chart, as shown in Fig. 33.1, the noise criteria rating would be defined by that curve that was not exceeded by the air conditioning spectrum curve at any frequency.

When background noise conforms to a noise criteria curve, it usually still contains too many low-frequency and high-frequency sounds for comfort. A modification of the NC curves, called the *preferred noise criteria* (PNC), has been established that has sound-pressure levels lower than the NC curves on the low- and high-frequency ends of the chart.

Rules of Thumb

In addition to using calculations for acoustical design, many rules of thumb can be used for preliminary estimating and for noncritical situations.

- In general, transmission loss through a barrier tends to increase with the frequency of sound.
- A wall with 0.1% open area (from cracks, holes, undercut doors, etc.) will have a maximum transmission loss of about 30 dB. A wall with 1% open area will have a maximum of about 20 dB.
- A hairline crack will decrease a partition's transmission loss by about 6 dB. A 1 in^2 opening in a 100 ft^2 gypsum board partition can transmit as much sound as the entire partition.
- Although placing fibrous insulation in a wall cavity increases its STC rating, the density of the insulation is not a significant variable.
- In determining the required STC rating of a barrier, the guidelines in Table 33.5 may be used.

Table 33.5

Effect of Barrier STC on Hearing

STC	effect on hearing
25	normal speech can clearly be heard through barrier
30	loud speech can be heard and understood fairly well; normal speech can be heard but barely understood
35	loud speech is not intelligible but can be heard
42–45	loud speech can only be faintly heard; normal speech cannot be heard
46–50	loud speech is not audible; loud sounds other than speech can only be heard faintly, if at all

SOUND ABSORPTION

Fundamentals

Controlling sound transmission is only part of good acoustical design. The proper amount of sound absorption must also be included. Although sound intensity level decreases about 6 dB for each doubling of distance from the source in free space, this is not the case in a room or semi-enclosed outdoor area. In a room, sound level decreases very near the source as it does in free space, but then it begins to reflect, and it levels out at a particular intensity.

In addition to reducing this intensity level of sound within a space, sound absorption is used to control unwanted sound reflections, improve speech privacy, and decrease or enhance reverberation.

The absorption of a material is defined by the coefficient of absorption, a, which is the ratio of the sound intensity absorbed by the material to the total intensity reaching the material. Therefore, the maximum absorption possible is 1—that of free space. Generally, a material with a coefficient below 0.2 is considered reflective, and one with a coefficient above 0.2 is considered sound absorbing.

The coefficient of absorption varies with the frequency of the sound, and some materials are better at absorbing some frequencies than others. For critical applications all frequencies should be checked, but for convenience the single-number noise reduction coefficient (NRC) is used. The NRC is the average of a material's absorption coefficients at the four frequencies of 250, 500, 1000, and 2000 Hz, rounded to the nearest multiple of 0.05.

Although most product literature still gives NRC ratings, the NRC has been superseded by the sound absorption average (SAA). The two are similar and each provides a single number rating. The SAA is the average of the absorption coefficients for the 12 one-third-octave bands from 200 Hz to 2500 Hz when tested in accordance with ASTM C423.

The total absorption of a material is dependent on its coefficient of absorption and the area of the material.

$$A = Sa \qquad 33.9$$

Because most rooms have several materials of different areas, the total absorption in a room is the sum of the various individual material absorptions.

Noise Reduction Within a Space

Increasing sound absorption within a space will result in a noise reduction according to the following formula.

$$\text{NR} = 10 \log \frac{A_2}{A_1} \qquad 33.10$$

A_1 = total original room absorption in sabins

A_2 = total room absorption after increase of absorption

This formula relates to overall reverberant noise level in a room and does not affect noise level very near the source.

Example 33.5

A room 15 ft by 20 ft with a 9 ft ceiling has a carpeted floor with a 44 oz carpet on pad ($a = 0.40$), gypsum board walls, and a gypsum board ceiling ($a = 0.05$). What would be the noise reduction achieved by directly attaching acoustical tile with a given NRC of 0.70 to the ceiling?

The original total absorption of the room is

$$\begin{aligned} \text{floor:}\quad & (15 \text{ ft})(20 \text{ ft}) &&= (300 \text{ ft}^2)(0.40) = 120 \text{ sabins} \\ \text{walls:}\quad & (2 \text{ ft})(15 \text{ ft})(9 \text{ ft}) &&= (270 \text{ ft}^2)(0.05) = 14 \text{ sabins} \\ & (2 \text{ ft})(20 \text{ ft})(9 \text{ ft}) &&= (360 \text{ ft}^2)(0.05) = 18 \text{ sabins} \\ \text{ceiling:}\quad & (15 \text{ ft})(20 \text{ ft}) &&= (300 \text{ ft}^2)(0.05) = 15 \text{ sabins} \\ & && \text{total} = 167 \text{ sabins} \end{aligned}$$

The absorption after treatment is

$$\text{ceiling: } (15 \text{ ft}^2)(20 \text{ ft}^2) = (300 \text{ ft}^2)(0.70) = 210 \text{ sabins}$$

Subtracting 15 from the old value and adding 210 as a new value, the net total is 362 sabins.

$$\begin{aligned} \text{NR} &= 10 \log \frac{362}{167} \\ &= 10 \log 2.17 \\ &= 3.4 \text{ dB} \end{aligned}$$

Increasing the absorption by this amount helps a little, but the difference would be just perceptible (see Table 33.2). Tripling the absorption would be clearly noticeable.

Rules of Thumb

There are several rules of thumb related to sound absorption that are useful to remember.

- The average absorption coefficient of a room should be at least 0.20. An average absorption above 0.50 is usually not desirable, nor is it economically justified. A lower value is suitable for large rooms, while higher values are suitable for small or noisy rooms.
- Each doubling of the amount of absorption in a room results in a noise reduction of only 3 dB.
- If additional absorptive material is being added to a room, the total absorption should be increased at least three times (amounting to a change of about 5 dB, which is clearly noticeable). The increase may need to be more or less than three times to bring absorption to between 0.20 and 0.50.
- In adding extra absorption, an increase of 10 times is about the practical limit. Beyond this (representing a reverberant noise reduction of 10 dB), more absorption results in a decreasing amount of noise reduction and reaching the practical limit of 0.50 total average absorption coefficient.
- Each doubling of the absorption in a room reduces reverberation time by one-half.
- Although absorptive materials can be placed anywhere, ceiling treatment for sound absorption is more effective in large rooms, whereas wall treatment is more effective in small rooms.
- Generally, absorption increases with an increase in thickness of a porous absorber, except for low-frequency situations that require special design treatment.
- The amount of absorption of a porous type of sound absorber such as fiberglass or mineral wool is dependent on (1) the material's thickness, (2) the material's density, (3) the material's porosity, and (4) the orientation of the fibers in the material. A porous sound absorber should be composed of open, interconnected voids.

Reverberation

Reverberation is an important quality of the acoustical environment of a space. It is the one quality that affects the intelligibility of speech and the quality of conditions for music of all types. *Reverberation time* is the time it takes the sound level to decrease 60 dB after the source has stopped producing the sound. Reverberation time is found by the following formula.

$$T = 0.05\left(\frac{V}{A}\right) \qquad 33.11$$

In SI units,

$$T = 0.16\left(\frac{V}{A}\right)$$

Each type of use has its own preferred range of reverberation time, shorter times being best for smaller spaces and longer times working best for larger spaces. See Table 33.6.

Table 33.6

Recommended Reverberation Times

space	time (sec)
auditoriums (speech and music)	1.5–1.8
broadcast studios (speech only)	0.4–0.6
churches	1.4–3.4
elementary classrooms	0.6–0.8
lecture/conference rooms	0.9–1.1
movie theaters	0.8–1.2
offices, small rooms for speech	0.3–0.6
opera halls	1.5–1.8
symphony concert halls	1.6–2.1
theaters (small dramatic)	0.9–1.4

SOUND CONTROL

Control of Room Noise

There are three primary ways sound can be controlled within a space: by reducing the level of the sound source, by modifying the absorption in the space, and by introducing nonintrusive background sound to mask the sound.

Reducing the level of the sound source is not always possible if the source is a fixed piece of machinery, if people are talking, or in similar situations. However, if the source is noise from the outside or an adjacent room, the transmission loss of the enclosing walls can be improved. If a machine is producing the noise, it can often be enclosed or modified to reduce its noise output.

Modifying the absorption of the space can achieve some noise reduction, but there are practical limits to adding absorptive materials. This approach is most useful when the problem room has a large percentage of hard, reflective surfaces.

In most cases, introducing nonintrusive background sound is desirable because it can mask unwanted noise. Some amount of background noise is always present. This may come from the steady hum of HVAC systems, business machines, traffic, conversation, or other sources. For example, in an office, if the sound level on one side of a partition with an STC rating of 45 is 75 dB and the background noise on the other side of the partition is 35 dB, the noise will not be heard (theoretically) on the "quiet" side of the wall. See Fig. 33.2. If the background noise level is decreased to 25 dB, then sounds will be heard.

This phenomenon is used to purposely introduce carefully controlled sound—often called *white sound*, *random noise*, or *acoustical perfume*—into a space rather than rely only on random background noise. Speakers are placed in the ceiling of a space and connected to a sound generator that produces a continuous, unnoticeable sound at particular levels across the frequency spectrum. The sound generator can be tuned to produce the frequencies and sound levels appropriate to mask the undesired sounds. White sound is often used in open offices to provide speech privacy and to help mask office machine noise.

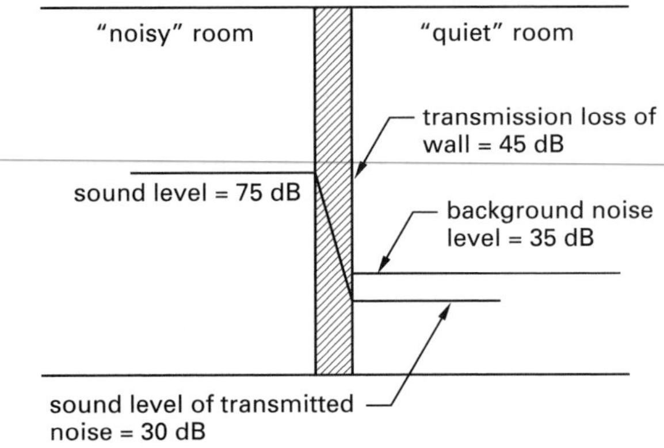

If transmitted sound level is below the background level, the sound is not perceptible.

Figure 33.2 Noise Reduction

Room noise can be reduced by adding absorption in the space. This is usually accomplished by adding some type of acoustic panels or upholstered walls. However, these types of panels are only effective for the higher frequencies and for speech. Controlling low-frequency and very high-frequency sounds within a room requires construction elements that can trap the longer, low-frequency wavelengths or control the very short high-frequency wavelengths.

Low-frequency control usually requires an allowance for thicker partitions or more space to apply detailing that absorbs low-frequency sound. Two typical methods for doing this include panel resonators and cavity resonators (also called *Helmholtz resonators*). See Fig. 33.3. The panel

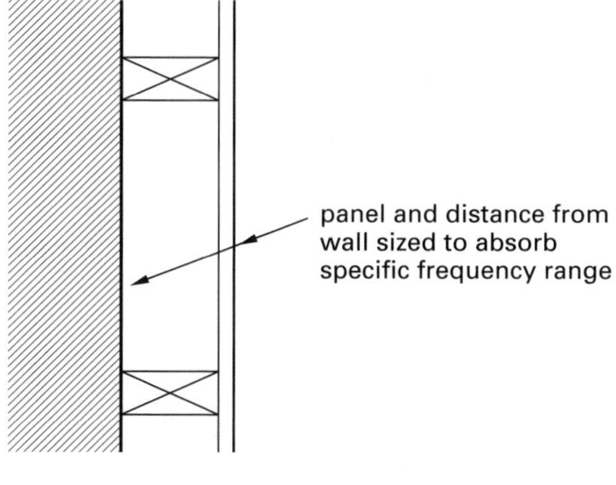

(a) vibrating panel

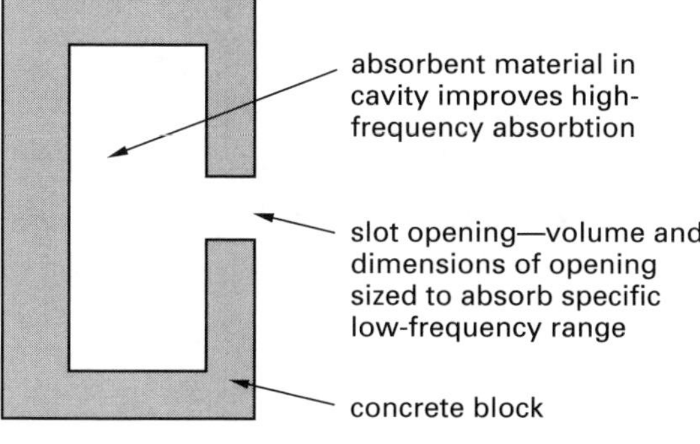

(b) volume resonator (Helmholtz resonator)

Figure 33.3 Details for Low-Frequency Sound Absorption

resonator absorbs low-frequency energy while reflecting mid- and high-frequency energy. Helmholtz resonators consist of a large air space with a small opening. As the sound strikes the resonator, the air mass inside the construction resonates at a particular frequency where the absorption is very great. However, the amount of absorption above and below the particular frequency drops off rapidly at higher and lower frequencies. A common type of cavity resonator is a concrete block wall constructed of special masonry units with narrow slits opening into the cavity of the block.

Control of Sound Transmission

As mentioned previously, control of sound transmission through barriers is primarily dependent on the mass of the barrier, and to a lesser extent on its stiffness. Walls and floors are generally rated with their STC value; the higher the STC rating, the better the barrier in reducing transmitted sound. Manufacturers' literature, testing laboratories, and reference literature typically give the transmission loss at different frequencies.

In addition to the construction of the barrier itself, other variables are critical for control of sound transmission. See Fig. 33.4.

Gaps in the barrier must be sealed. Edges at the floor, ceiling, and intersecting walls should be caulked. Penetrations of the barrier should be avoided, but if absolutely necessary they can be sealed as well. For example, electrical outlets should not be placed back to back; rather, they should be staggered in separate stud spaces and caulked.

Penetrations of the barrier should be avoided. Pipes, ducts, and similar penetrations provide a path for both airborne sound and mechanical vibration. If they are unavoidable, they should not be rigidly connected to the barrier, and any gaps should be sealed and caulked.

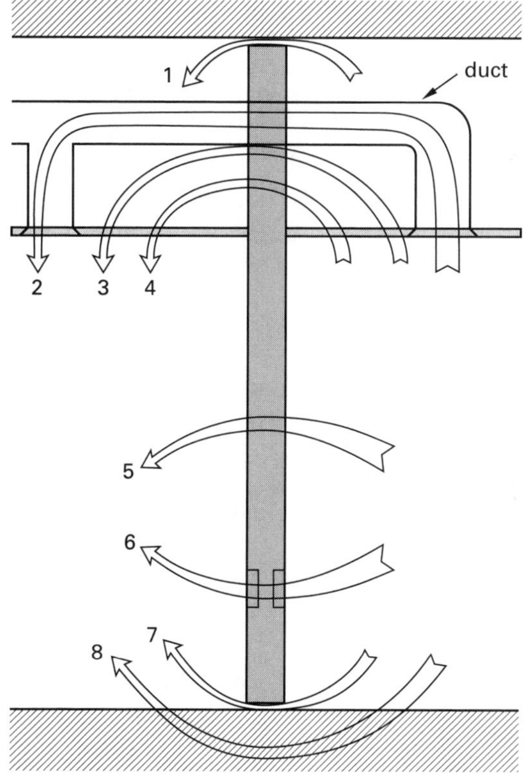

1 leaks between adjacent construction
2 flanking loss through duct
3 leaks at partition penetrations
4 flanking loss through ceiling into plenum
5 transmission and impact loss through partition
6 loss through outlets and other openings
7 leaks at floor/wall intersection
8 impact sounds through floor

Figure 33.4 Potential Sources of Sound Leaks Through Partitions

"Weaker" construction within the barrier should be avoided or given special treatment. Construction with a lower STC rating than the barrier itself will decrease the overall rating of the barrier. Doors placed in an otherwise well-built sound wall are a common problem and can be dealt with in several ways. The perimeter should be completely sealed with weatherstripping specifically designed for sound sealing at the jamb and head and with a threshold or automatic door bottom at the sill. The door itself should be as heavy as possible, preferably a solid-core wood door. Often, two doors are used, separated by a small air gap. See Fig. 33.5.

Interior glass lights can be designed with laminated glass set in resilient framing. Laminated glass provides more mass, and the plastic interlayer improves the damping characteristics of the barrier. If additional transmission loss is required, two or more layers can be installed with an air gap between them. See Fig. 33.6.

Flanking paths for sound to travel should be eliminated or treated appropriately, including air conditioning ducts, plenum spaces above ceilings, hallways, and open windows in adjacent rooms.

Unusual sound conditions or frequencies must be given special consideration and design. Low-frequency rumbling or high frequencies are often not stopped, even with a wall with a high STC rating.

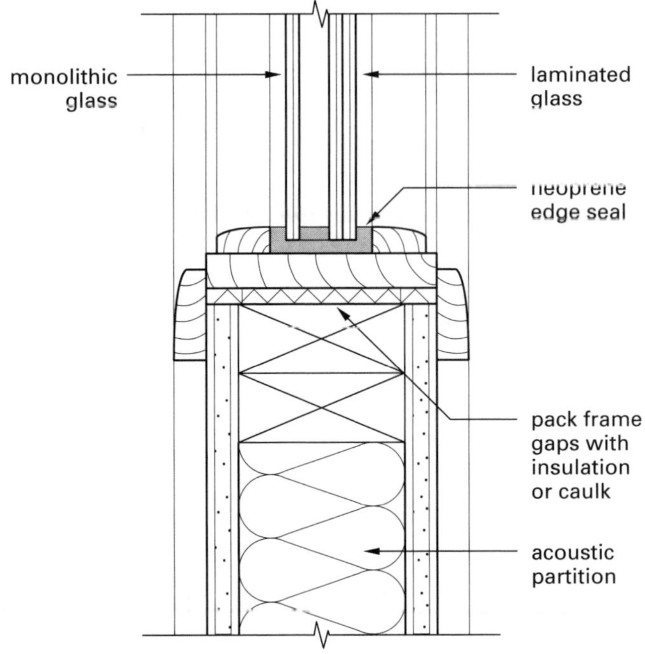

Figure 33.6 Glazing Assembly for Sound Control

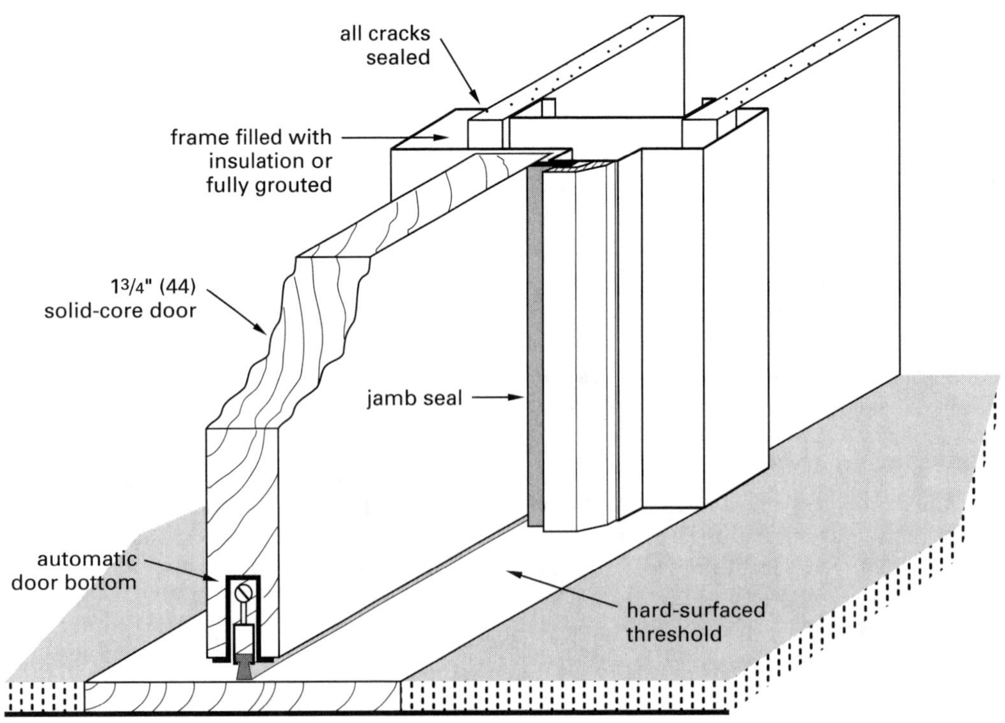

Figure 33.5 Principles of Acoustic Control for Doors

Speech Privacy

In many architectural situations, the critical acoustical concern is not eliminating all noise or designing a room for music, but providing for a certain level of privacy while still allowing people to talk at a normal level. In many cases, speech privacy is regarded as a condition in which talking may be heard as a general background sound but not easily understood.

Of course, speech privacy is subjective and depends on circumstances. People involved in highly confidential conversations may need greater privacy than those conducting normal, nonconfidential business in an open office. Also, one person may be annoyed by adjacent conversations more than another person.

Speech privacy is usually of greatest concern in office planning, and especially in open office planning. Because speech privacy in open offices depends on a complex interaction of many variables, two measures are used to evaluate open office acoustics: the articulation class (AC) and the articulation index (AI). Both of these test methods and rating systems have replaced the Speech Privacy Noise Isolation Class (NIC) and the Speech Privacy Potential (SPP) that were formerly used.

The *articulation class* (AC) gives a rating of system component performance and does not account for masking sound. The *articulation index* (AI) measures the performance of all the elements of a particular configuration working together: ceiling absorption, space dividers, furniture, light fixtures, partitions, background masking systems, and HVAC systems. It is used to objectively test speech privacy of open office spaces, either in the actual space or in a laboratory mock-up of the space.

The articulation index can be used to (1) compare the relative privacy between different pairs of workstations or areas, (2) evaluate how changes in open office components affect speech privacy, and (3) measure speech privacy objectively for correlation with subjective responses. The articulation index predicts the intelligibility of speech for a group of talkers and listeners, and the result of the test is a single number rating. The AI rating can range from 0.00 to 1.00, with 0.00 being complete privacy and 1.00 being absolutely no privacy where all individual spoken words can be understood. Confidential speech privacy exists when speech cannot be understood and occurs when the articulation index is at or below 0.05. Normal speech privacy means concentrated effort is required to understand intruding speech and exists when the AI is between 0.05 and 0.20. Above an AI of 0.20, speech becomes readily understood. Privacy no longer exists when the AI is above 0.30.

Both the articulation index and articulation class are intended only for open office situations with speech as the sound source of concern. However, the articulation index can be adapted for other open plans (like schools) and can be applied to measure speech privacy between enclosed and open spaces and between two enclosed rooms.

Another way to evaluate design conditions and predict the intelligibility of speech is with the *speech interference level* (SIL). The SIL, in decibels, is the average of the sound pressure levels (above a reference pressure level) of the interfering noise in the four one-octave bands centered on the frequencies of 500, 1000, 2000, and 4000 Hz. The SIL is a useful measure of the effect of background noise on spoken communications, such as is described in Table 33.7. Charts and graphs have also been developed to relate the SIL to various types of communications at different distances.

Speech privacy in areas divided by full-height partitions is usually achieved by sound loss through the partitions and, to a lesser extent, by the proper use of sound-absorbing surfaces. In open areas, such as an open-plan office, speech privacy is more difficult to achieve. There are five important factors in designing for speech privacy in an open area. All of these must be present to achieve an optimal acoustical environment.

1. The ceiling must be highly absorptive. The idea is to create a "clear sky" condition so that sounds are not reflected from their source to other parts of the environment.
2. There must be space dividers that reduce the transmission of sound from one space to the adjacent space. The dividers should have a combination of absorptive surfaces to minimize sound reflections placed over a solid liner (septum).
3. Other surfaces, such as the floor, furniture, windows, and light fixtures, must be designed or arranged to minimize sound reflections. A window, for example, can provide a clear path for reflected noise around a partial height partition.
4. If possible, activities should be distanced to take advantage of the normal attenuation of sound with distance.
5. There must be a properly designed background masking system. If the right number of sound-absorbing surfaces is provided, the surfaces will absorb all sounds in the space, not just the unwanted sounds. Background sound must then be reintroduced to maintain the right balance between speech sound and the background noise. This is referred to as the *signal-to-noise ratio*. If the signal-to-noise ratio is too great (as a result of either loud talking or minimal background noise), speech privacy will be compromised.

Table 33.7

Effect of SIL on Communication

speech interference level (dB)	effect on communication
30–40	communication in normal voice possible
40–50	communication in normal voice satisfactory at 3 ft to 6 ft (1 m to 2 m) need to raise voice at 6 ft to 13 ft (2 m to 4 m) telephone use satisfactory
50–60	communication in normal voice satisfactory at 1 ft to 2 ft (300 mm to 600 mm) need to raise voice at 3 ft to 6 ft (1 m to 2 m) telephone use slightly difficult
60–70	communication with raised voice satisfactory at 1 ft to 2 ft (300 mm to 600 mm) telephone difficult to use
70–80	communication slightly difficult with raised voice at 1 ft to 2 ft (300 mm to 600 mm) communication slightly difficult with shouting at 3 ft to 6 ft (1 m to 2 m) telephone use very difficult
80–85	communication slightly difficult with shouting at 1 ft to 2 ft (300 mm to 600 mm) telephone use unsatisfactory

Control of Impact Noise

Impact noise, or sound resulting from direct contact of an object with a sound barrier, can occur on any surface, but it generally occurs on a floor and ceiling assembly. It is usually caused by footfalls, shuffled furniture, or dropped objects.

Impact noise is quantified by the *Impact Insulation Class* (IIC) number, a single-number rating of a floor-ceiling's impact on sound performance. A given construction is analyzed in accordance with a standardized test over 16 third-octave bands, and the results are compared with a reference plot much as noise criteria ratings are established. The higher the IIC rating, the better the floor's performance in reducing impact sounds in the test frequency range.

The IIC value of a floor can be increased by adding carpet, by providing a resiliently suspended ceiling below, by floating a finished floor on resilient pads over the structural floor, and by providing sound-absorbing material in the air space between the floor and the finished ceiling.

Control of Mechanical Noise

Mechanical noise is similar to impact noise in that the cause is due to direct contact with the barrier. However, mechanical noise occurs when a vibrating device is in continuous direct contact with the structure. There are several ways mechanical noise can be transmitted.

- Rigidly attached equipment can vibrate the building structure or pipes, which in turn radiate sound into occupied spaces.
- The airborne noise of equipment can be transmitted through walls and floors to occupied spaces.
- Noise can be transmitted through ductwork.
- The movement of air or water through ducts and pipes can cause undesirable noise. This is especially true of high-velocity air systems or situations where the air or water changes velocity rapidly.

Depending on the circumstances, mechanical noise can be controlled in several ways.

- Mechanical equipment should be mounted on springs or resilient pads (isolators).
- Connections between equipment and ducts and pipes should be made with flexible connectors.
- Where noise control is critical, ducts should be lined or provided with mufflers.
- Noise-producing equipment can be located away from quiet, occupied spaces.
- Walls, ceilings, and floors of mechanical rooms should be designed to attenuate airborne noise.
- Mechanical and plumbing systems should be designed to minimize high-velocity flow and sudden changes in fluid velocity.

ROOM ACOUSTICS

Reflection, Diffusion, and Diffraction

Reflection is the return of sound waves from a surface. If a surface is greater than or equal to four times the wavelength of a sound striking it, the angle of incidence will equal the angle of reflection. Wavelength, of course, varies with frequency according to Eq. 33.1. Assuming a velocity of 1130 ft/sec (344 m/s), Table 33.8 gives wavelengths of certain frequencies.

Table 33.8
Wavelengths Based on Frequency

	wavelength	
frequency (Hz)	(ft)	(m)
50	23.0	6.8
100	11.0	3.4
250	4.5	1.4
500	2.25	0.7
1000	1.13	0.34
2000	0.57	0.17
5000	0.23	0.07
10,000	0.11	0.034

Reflection can be useful for reinforcing sound in lecture rooms and concert halls and for directing sound where it is wanted. It can be annoying, however, if it produces echoes, which occur when a reflected sound reaches a listener later than about $^1/_{17}$ sec after the direct sound. Assuming a sound speed of 1130 ft/sec (344 m/s), an echo will occur whenever the reflected sound path exceeds the direct sound path by 70 ft (21.3 m) or more.

Diffusion is the random distribution of sound from a surface. It occurs when the surface dimension equals the wavelength of the sound striking it.

Diffraction is the bending of sound waves around an object or through an opening. Diffraction explains why sounds can be heard around corners and why even small holes in partitions allow so much sound to be heard. Refer to Ch. 5 for a discussion of diffraction around site barriers.

Room Geometry and Planning Concepts

There are many ways the acoustical performance of a building or individual room can be affected by floor plan layout and the size and shape of the room itself. In addition to designing walls and floors to retard sound transmission and for proper use of sound absorption, use the following suggestions to help minimize acoustical problems.

- Plan similar use areas next to each other. For example, placing bedrooms next to each other in an apartment complex is better than placing a bedroom next to the adjacent unit's kitchen. This concept is applicable for vertical organization as well as horizontal (plan) organization.
- Use buffer spaces such as closets and hallways to separate noise-producing spaces whenever possible. Using closets between bedrooms at a common wall is one example of this method.
- Locate noise-producing areas such as mechanical rooms, laundries, and playrooms away from "quiet" areas.
- Stagger doorways in halls and other areas to avoid providing a straight-line path for noise.
- Locate operable windows as far from each other as possible.
- If possible, locate furniture and other potential noise-producing objects away from the wall separating spaces.
- Minimize the area of the common walls between two rooms where a reduction in sound transmission is desired.
- Avoid room shapes that reflect or focus sound. Barrel-vaulted hallways and circular rooms, for example, produce undesirable focused sounds. Rooms that focus sound also deprive some listeners of useful reflections.
- Avoid parallel walls with hard surfaces in small rooms. In such situations, repeated echoes, called *flutter echoes*, can be generated that result in a perceived "buzzing" sound of higher frequencies. This is why small music practice rooms have splayed walls. Standing waves can also be produced in small rooms, when parallel walls are some integral multiple of one-half wavelength apart and a steady tone is introduced in the room.

SOLVING THE MECHANICAL AND ELECTRICAL PLAN VIGNETTE

34

The Mechanical and Electrical Plan vignette presents a background drawing, a program, code requirements, and a lighting diagram. It requires that the candidate complete a reflected ceiling plan by placing the ceiling grid and arranging the mechanical and electrical system components within it. The problem can include considerations for structural element sizes, duct sizes and types, footcandle levels, fire dampers, rated vertical shafts, placement of diffusers, and other mechanical system requirements.

TIPS FOR COMPLETING THE MECHANICAL AND ELECTRICAL PLAN VIGNETTE

In this vignette the candidate must demonstrate an ability to integrate the layout of mechanical, lighting, and ceiling systems with given building components. The candidate must also be able to read and apply a candlepower distribution curve (lighting diagram) to determine correct spacing of luminaires. One of the most difficult aspects of this vignette is reading the lighting diagrams correctly and providing the correct illumination level. This can be one of the more difficult vignettes because of the large number of requirements that have to be satisfied.

The following suggestions may be used to complete this vignette successfully.

- Lay out the ceiling grids first, centering them in the rooms so that the luminaires can be arranged equally and provide uniform illumination. The spacing between luminaires should be the same in both directions. The direction and position of the grid will be suggested by the requirement for uniform illumination. Check the lighting diagrams first to determine the required spacing, and then draw the grid to allow for symmetric spacing of luminaires.
- If the grid is already drawn in a space and needs to be adjusted to accommodate a symmetric lighting layout, use the *move, adjust* tool, and click anywhere within the grid to shift the grid. The *rotate* tool can be used to change the grid orientation.
- When determining the required spacing of light fixtures, consult the lighting diagrams. They will probably show the line of the required footcandle level crossing the horizontal line representing the position of the lighting plane at a point below the ceiling, fairly close to a vertical line representing the distance from the fixture that would be half the required spacing. This is to minimize the need for interpolating between lines on the graph. Refer to the lighting diagrams in the sample problem for an example of this. In the lighting diagram for fluorescent fixtures the required 70 fc (700 lux) line crosses the 6 ft 6 in (165 mm) point at 2 ft (610 mm) from the fixture, giving a spacing between fixtures of 4 ft (1220 mm). Remember, to find which horizontal line to use on the lighting diagrams, take the ceiling height given in the program and subtract the height of the desk level, also given in the program (typically 30 in or 36 in [760 mm or 915 mm]). The desk height may or may not be the same for the rooms where the incandescent and fluorescent fixtures are to be located, so read the program carefully.
- Because a 2 ft by 4 ft (600 mm by 1200 mm) grid is used and the grid cannot be cut, the spacing between edges of fluorescent lights will probably be 4 ft (1200 mm) or some multiple of 2 ft (600 mm). This should coincide with the spacing derived from the lighting diagrams.
- Keep recessed incandescent lights a reasonable minimum distance from walls; 18 in (460 mm) is a good

minimum dimension. Do not locate them more than 4 ft (1200 mm) from any wall.

- Do not mix luminaire types unless specifically required to do so by the program.
- Study the program and the base plan carefully to determine where the rigid ducts can be placed when they need to be perpendicular to the joists. Because flexible ducts can only be 10 ft (3 m) long (or as stated in the program), locating the rigid ducts is critical to successfully completing the problem. Rigid ducts can run between joists and parallel to them.
- In most cases only the supply registers are required to be connected with ductwork. However, the program may state that the return air grilles must also be connected with ductwork. Otherwise, the return air grilles just open into the plenum.
- Remember that even if supply diffusers touch or overlap rigid ducts they must still be connected with a flexible duct, no matter how short.
- For rooms along the exterior window wall, place the supply air registers near the windows and the return air grilles near the inside walls.
- If a return air riser is shown in a chase, be sure to show a short section of duct with a fire damper from the riser to the plenum space. This is easy to forget.
- Keep the amount of ductwork to a minimum. Try to use one run of rigid ductwork with flexible ducts taking off from either side.
- If a room or space exceeds the required area for one supply air register, it may be difficult to determine whether or not two registers should be included. If the area of the room exceeds the area required for a single register by more than 10 ft^2 (1 m^2), consider rounding up and using two registers. If it is possible and can be easily done, consider reducing the size of the room slightly.
- Be sure to separate the supply air registers and the return air grilles as much as possible and at least as much as required by the program.

SECTION 7: BUILDING DESIGN & CONSTRUCTION SYSTEMS

Chapter 35: Site Work

Chapter 36: Concrete

Chapter 37: Masonry

Chapter 38: Metals

Chapter 39: Structural and Rough Carpentry

Chapter 40: Finish Carpentry and Architectural Woodwork

Chapter 41: Moisture Protection and Thermal Insulation

Chapter 42: Doors, Windows, and Glazing

Chapter 43: Finish Materials

Chapter 44: Vertical Transportation

Chapter 45: Solving the Accessibility/Ramp Vignette

Chapter 46: Solving the Stair Design Vignette

Chapter 47: Solving the Roof Plan Vignette

35 SITE WORK

Site work includes demolition and clearing of land, earthwork, installation of piles and caissons, paving and other types of surfacing, drainage, site improvements, and landscaping. Included in this chapter are those aspects of site work encountered on almost any architectural project.

SOIL

Because all aspects of site work depend on the nature of the soil, the architect must have a basic understanding of this element. *Soil* is the general term used to describe the material that supports a building. It is generally classified into four groups: sands and gravels, silts, clays, and organics.

Sands and gravels are granular materials that are low in plasticity. *Sand* consists of particles from about 0.002 in to $^1/_4$ in (0.05 to 6) in size. *Gravel* consists of rock particles from $^1/_4$ in to $3^1/_2$ in (6 to 89) in size. Both sands and gravels are very good bases for building foundations. In addition, they provide good drainage because of the voids between the individual particles.

Silt is fine-grained sedimentary soil composed of material smaller than sand but larger than clay. Silts behave as granular materials, but they are sometimes slightly plastic in their behavior.

Clays are composed of smaller particles than silts. Clays have some cohesion, or tensile strength, and are plastic in their behavior when wet. Clay is very unpredictable because it swells when it absorbs water and shrinks when it dries. In some cases silts and clays can provide an adequate base for foundations if soil investigations show they are stable. Generally, they make better foundations if they are mixed with other types of soil.

Organics are materials of vegetable or other organic matter and make poor bases for foundations.

In addition to these general types there are other commonly used terms for various types of soil. *Hardpan* refers to an unbroken mixture of clay, sand, and gravel. It is a good base for building foundations. *Shale* and *slate* are soft rocks with a fine texture. *Boulders* describe rocks that have broken off of bedrock. Finally, *bedrock* is the solid rock that forms the earth's crust. Bedrock has the highest bearing capacity of all soil types. Shale and slate make up the group with the second highest bearing capacity.

Soil Tests

Prior to design and construction, the exact nature of the soil must be determined. This is done with one of a variety of soil tests used to determine such things as the bearing capacity, water table level, and porosity. Porosity must be known if the land is to be used for private sewage disposal systems. Two of the most common soil tests for bearing capacity are borings and test pits.

With typical core borings, undisturbed samples of the soil are removed at regular intervals and the type of material recovered is recorded in a *boring log*. This log shows the material, the depth at which it was encountered, its standard designation, and other information, such as moisture content, density, and the results of any borehole tests that might have been conducted at the bore site. A typical boring log is shown in Fig. 35.1.

One of the most common borehole tests is the *standard penetration test* (SPT), which is a measure of the density of granular soils and the consistency of some clays. In this test, a 2 in (51) diameter sampler is driven into the bottom of the borehole by a 140 lbm (63 kg) hammer falling 30 in (760). The number of blows, N, required to drive the cylinder 12 in (305) is recorded.

The recovered bore samples can be tested in the laboratory. Some of the tests include strength tests of bearing capacity, resistance to lateral pressure, and slope stability. In addition,

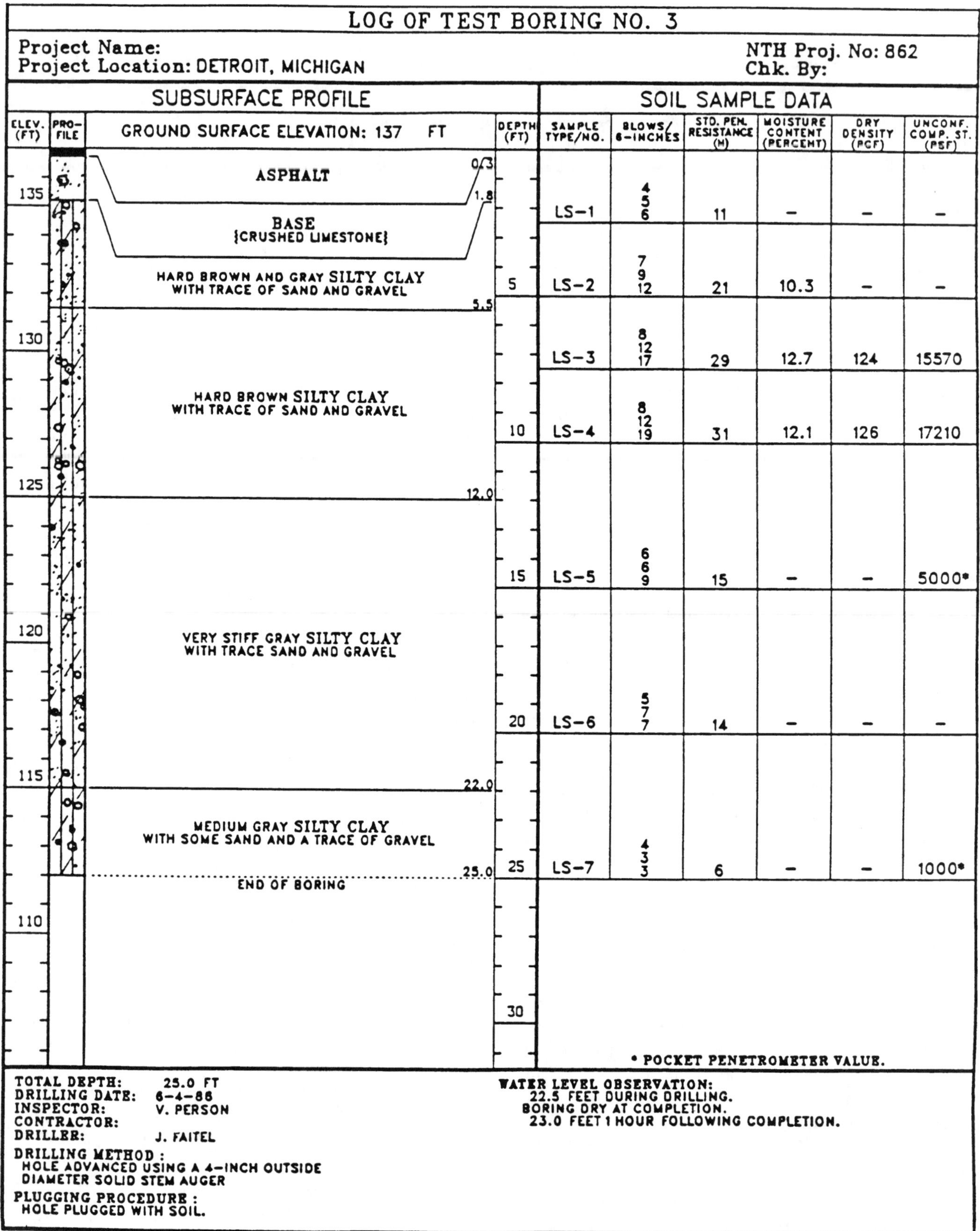

LOG OF TEST BORING NO. 3

Project Name:
Project Location: DETROIT, MICHIGAN

NTH Proj. No: 862
Chk. By:

SUBSURFACE PROFILE

GROUND SURFACE ELEVATION: 137 FT

DEPTH (FT)	DESCRIPTION
0.3	ASPHALT
1.8	BASE {CRUSHED LIMESTONE}
5.5	HARD BROWN AND GRAY SILTY CLAY WITH TRACE OF SAND AND GRAVEL
12.0	HARD BROWN SILTY CLAY WITH TRACE OF SAND AND GRAVEL
22.0	VERY STIFF GRAY SILTY CLAY WITH TRACE SAND AND GRAVEL
25.0	MEDIUM GRAY SILTY CLAY WITH SOME SAND AND A TRACE OF GRAVEL
	END OF BORING

SOIL SAMPLE DATA

DEPTH (FT)	SAMPLE TYPE/NO.	BLOWS/ 6-INCHES	STD. PEN. RESISTANCE (N)	MOISTURE CONTENT (PERCENT)	DRY DENSITY (PCF)	UNCONF. COMP. ST. (PSF)
	LS-1	4 5 6	11	–	–	–
5	LS-2	7 9 12	21	10.3	–	–
	LS-3	8 12 17	29	12.7	124	15570
10	LS-4	8 12 19	31	12.1	126	17210
15	LS-5	6 6 9	15	–	–	5000*
20	LS-6	5 7 7	14	–	–	–
25	LS-7	4 3 3	6	–	–	1000*

* POCKET PENETROMETER VALUE.

TOTAL DEPTH: 25.0 FT
DRILLING DATE: 6-4-86
INSPECTOR: V. PERSON
CONTRACTOR:
DRILLER: J. FAITEL

DRILLING METHOD:
HOLE ADVANCED USING A 4-INCH OUTSIDE DIAMETER SOLID STEM AUGER

PLUGGING PROCEDURE:
HOLE PLUGGED WITH SOIL.

WATER LEVEL OBSERVATION:
22.5 FEET DURING DRILLING.
BORING DRY AT COMPLETION.
23.0 FEET 1 HOUR FOLLOWING COMPLETION.

Figure 35.1 Typical Boring Log

compressibility, grain size, specific gravity, and density tests are sometimes performed. Because laboratory tests are expensive and not always necessary, they are not performed for every building project.

The number of borings taken at a building site is determined by many factors, such as the size of the building, suspected subsurface geological conditions, and requirements by local codes. Usually, a minimum of four borings is taken, one near each corner of the proposed building. If wide variations are found in the initial boring logs, additional tests may be warranted.

Test pits are the second common type of subsurface exploration. These are trenches dug at the job site that allow visual inspection of the soil strata and direct collection of undisturbed samples. Because they are open pits, the practical limit on depth is about 10 ft (3 m), so the soil below that depth cannot be directly examined.

The location of each test boring or test pit is shown on the plot plan and given a number corresponding to the boring log in the soil test report. Soil tests are usually requested by the architect but paid for by the owner. They are typically referred to in the specifications for information only. However, soil tests are not part of the contract documents.

Other types of tests include auger borings, wash borings, dry sample borings, and soil load tests. *Auger borings* raise samples of the soil by using a standard auger bit. The test is best used in sand or clay for shallow or intermediate depths because the auger cannot penetrate hard obstructions such as bedrock or hardpan soil.

Wash borings are made with a 2 in to 4 in diameter (50 to 100) pipe through which a water jet is maintained to force up the soil material. The resulting samples are so thoroughly mixed that analysis is difficult, but the test is useful for soils too hard for an auger test. Wash borings can extend down about 100 ft (30 m) or more.

Dry sample borings extract material by driving a pipe with a split sampling pipe on the leading edge about 5 in (125) into the soil. The pipe is lifted out, and the samples are removed for analysis. Subsequent samples are taken in approximately 5 in (125) increments.

Soil load tests involve building a platform on the site, placing incremental loads on it, and observing the amount of settlement during given time periods until settlement becomes regular after repeated loading. The design load is usually half the test load.

After the field sampling is done, the soil is tested in a laboratory and the soils engineer issues a report stating the results of the testing. From this the soils engineer gives the allowable soil bearing pressure and recommends a foundation type to use. Some of the properties that can be tested include the following.

Grain size and shape. These determine (for granular soil) the shear strength of the soil, its permeability, the likely result of frost action, and compaction ability.

Liquid and plastic limits. These values give the compaction and compressibility values for cohesive soil.

Specific gravity. This is used to determine void ratio, which determines compressibility of the soil.

Unconfined compression. The shear strength for cohesive soil is measured from this value.

Water content. This number is used to get the compressibility and compaction values for cohesive soil.

Soil Types

Soils are classified according to the *Unified Soil Classification System* (USCS). This system divides soils into major divisions and subdivisions based on grain size and laboratory tests of physical characteristics and provides standardized names and symbols. A summary chart of the USCS is shown in Fig. 35.2.

Bearing capacities are generally specified by the building code based on the soil type. Other bearing capacities may be used if acceptable tests are conducted that show higher values are appropriate.

Water in Soil

The presence of water in soil can cause several problems for foundations as well as other parts of the site. Water can reduce the load-carrying capacity of the soil in general, so larger or more expensive foundation systems may be necessary. If more moisture is present under one area of the building than another, differential settlement may occur, causing cracking and weakening of structural and nonstructural components. In the worst case, structural failure may occur. Improperly prepared soil can also cause heaving or settling of paving, fences, and other parts of the site.

Foundations below the groundwater line, often called the *water table*, are also subjected to hydrostatic pressure. This pressure from the force of water-saturated soil can occur against vertical foundation walls as well as under the floor slabs. Hydrostatic pressure creates two difficulties: it puts additional loads on the structural elements, and it makes waterproofing more difficult because the pressure tends to force water into any crack or imperfection in the structure. See Fig. 41.1 for a typical method of waterproofing a foundation.

<table>
<tr><td rowspan="8">course-grained soils
more than 50% of material is larger that no. 200 sieve</td><td rowspan="4">gravels
more than 50% of course fraction retained on No. 4 sieve</td><td rowspan="2">clean gravels
less than 5% fines</td><td>GW</td><td>well-graded gravel</td></tr>
<tr><td>GP</td><td>poorly graded gravel</td></tr>
<tr><td rowspan="2">gravels with fines
more than 12% fines</td><td>GM</td><td>silty gravel</td></tr>
<tr><td>GC</td><td>clayey gravel</td></tr>
<tr><td rowspan="4">sands
50% or more of course fraction passes No. 4 sieve</td><td rowspan="2">clean sands
less than 5% fines</td><td>SW</td><td>well-graded sand</td></tr>
<tr><td>SP</td><td>poorly graded sand</td></tr>
<tr><td rowspan="2">sands with fines
more than 12% fines</td><td>SM</td><td>silty sand</td></tr>
<tr><td>SC</td><td>clayey sand</td></tr>
<tr><td rowspan="6">fine-grained soils
50% or more passes the no. 200 sieve</td><td rowspan="3">silts and clays
liquid limit less than 50</td><td rowspan="2">inorganic</td><td>CL</td><td>lean clay</td></tr>
<tr><td>ML</td><td>silt</td></tr>
<tr><td>organic</td><td>OL</td><td>organic silt</td></tr>
<tr><td rowspan="3">silts and clays
liquid limit 50 or more</td><td rowspan="2">inorganic</td><td>CH</td><td>fat clay</td></tr>
<tr><td>MH</td><td>elastic silt</td></tr>
<tr><td>organic</td><td>OH</td><td>organic clay</td></tr>
<tr><td>highly organic soils</td><td colspan="2">primary organic matter, dark in color, and organic odor</td><td>PT</td><td>peat</td></tr>
</table>

Figure 35.2 Unified Soil Classification System

Even if hydrostatic pressure is not present, moisture in the soil can leak into the below-grade structure if not properly dampproofed and can cause general deterioration of materials.

Soil Treatment

In order to increase bearing capacity, decrease settlement, or do both, several methods of soil treatment are used.

- *Drainage*. As mentioned in the previous section, proper drainage can solve several types of problems. It can increase the strength of the soil and prevent hydrostatic pressure.
- *Fill*. If existing soil is unsuitable for building, the undesirable material is removed and new engineered fill is brought in. This may be soil, sand, gravel, or other material as appropriate. In nearly all

situations, the engineered fill must be compacted before building commences. Controlled compaction requires moisture to lubricate the particles. With all types of fill, there is an optimum relationship between the fill's density and its optimum moisture content. The method for determining this is the Proctor test, in which fill samples are tested in the laboratory to determine a standard for compaction. Specifications are then written that call for fill to be compacted between 90% and 100% of the optimum Proctor density; higher values are necessary for heavily loaded structures, and lower values are appropriate for other loadings. Moisture contents within 2% to 4% of the optimum moisture content at the time of compaction must also be specified. Fill is usually placed in lifts of 8 in to 12 in (200 to 300), with each lift compacted before placement of the next.

- *Compaction*. Sometimes existing soil can simply be compacted to provide the required base for construction. The same requirements for compaction of fill material apply to compaction of existing soil. One device used to compact large areas is the *sheepsfoot roller*.
- *Densification*. This is a type of on-site compaction of existing material using one of several techniques involving vibration, dropping of heavy weights, or pounding piles into the ground and filling the voids with sand. The specific technique used depends on the grain size of the soil.
- *Surcharging*. Surcharging is the preloading of the ground with fill material to cause consolidation and settlement of the underlying soil before building. Once the required settlement has taken place, the fill is removed and construction begins. Although suitable for large areas, the time and cost required for sufficient settlement often preclude this method of soil improvement.
- *Mixing*. In lieu of complete replacement of the soil, a layer of sand or gravel can be placed on less stable soil and mixed in, thus improving the soil's bearing capacity. By varying the type of added material, a soil with required properties can be created.

EARTHWORK

Earthwork includes excavating soil for the construction of a building foundation, water and sewer lines, and other buried items as well as modifying the site's land contours.

Excavation

Excavation is the removal of soil to allow construction of foundations and other permanent features below the finished level of the grade. It is usually done with machinery, although small areas may be excavated by hand. When a relatively narrow, long excavation is done for piping or for narrow footings and foundation walls, it is called *trenching*.

Because excavations can pose a hazard to workers, unshored sides of soil should be no steeper than their natural angle of repose or not greater than a slope of $1^1/_2$ horizontal to 1 vertical. Where this is not possible, the earth must be temporarily shored as discussed in the next section.

For large excavations, excess soil has to be removed from the site. However, to minimize cost, it is best to use the soil elsewhere on the site for backfill or in contour modification.

Grading

Grading is the modification of the contours of the site according to the grading plan. Rough grading involves the moving of soil prior to construction to approximate levels of the final grades. It also includes adding or removing soil after construction to the approximate final grades. In both of these operations, the grade is usually within about 6 in to 1 ft (150 to 300) of the desired level. Often, excavating is part of the rough grading as soil removed from the building is placed in low spots where the grade must be built up.

Finish grading is the final moving of soil prior to landscaping or paving, where the level of the earth is brought to within 1 in (25) of the desired grades. This operation is done with machines and by hand and often includes the placement of topsoil.

SHORING AND BRACING

For shallow excavations in open areas, the sides of the excavation can be sloped without the need for some supporting structure. However, if the depth increases or the excavation walls need to be vertical in confined locations, temporary support is required. There are two common methods of doing this.

The first method employs a system of vertical beams and horizontal timbers. See Fig. 35.3(a). Prior to excavation, steel wide-flange soldier beams are driven at 6 ft to 10 ft (1830 to 3050) intervals to a length slightly deeper than the anticipated excavation. As soil is removed, horizontal timbers 2 in to 4 in (50 to 100) thick, called *breast boards* or *cribbing*, are placed between the soldier beams so they bear against the inside face of the flange.

When the excavation reaches a certain point, holes are drilled diagonally into the earth or deeper rock. Rods or tendons are inserted into the holes and grouted into place.

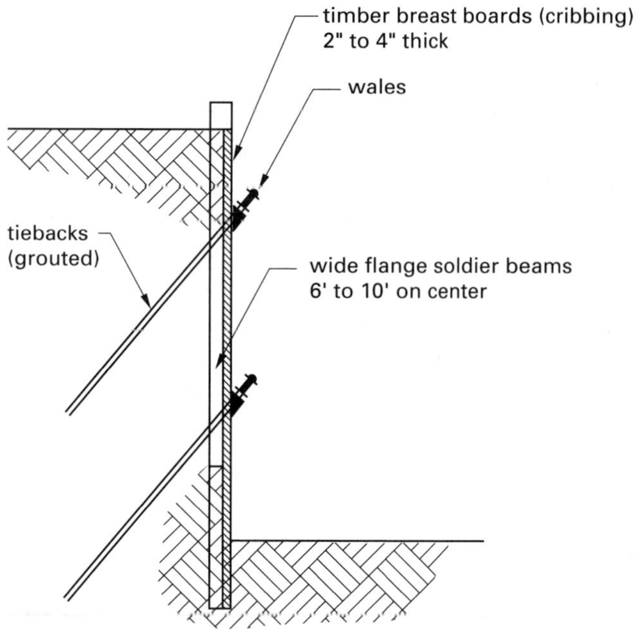

(a) soldier beams and breast boards

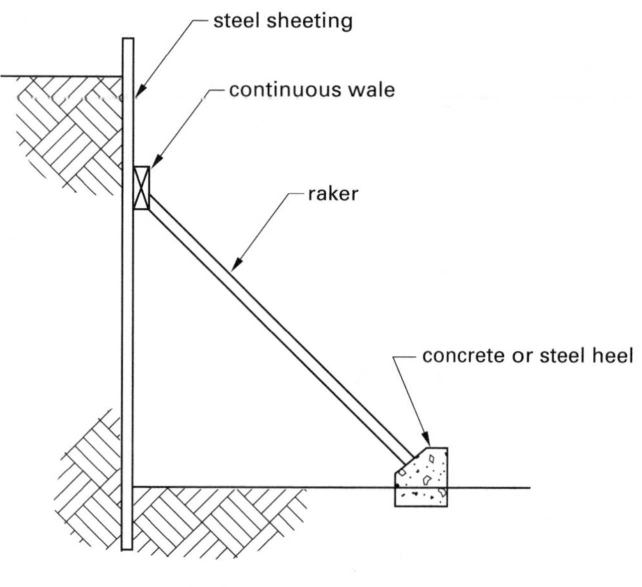

(b) braced excavation

Figure 35.3 Excavation Shoring

These tiebacks are connected to horizontal wales that hold the soldier beams back against the pressure of the excavation. As the excavation proceeds, more breast boards and tiebacks are added. The advantage of this method of shoring is that the excavation is free from bracing and allows drilling of piers, forming of foundation walls, and other construction to proceed unimpeded.

The second method uses vertical sheeting, either wood or steel, supported by diagonal braces, as shown in Fig. 35.3(b). Steel sheeting is composed of interlocking Z-shaped sections supported by continuous horizontal members called *wales*. The wales, in turn, are supported by diagonal rakers that are anchored to the bottom of the excavation with steel or concrete heels. For very small excavations, the diagonal rakers can be replaced with horizontal braces connecting opposite sides of the excavation.

Shoring and bracing are used to temporarily support adjacent buildings and other construction with posts, timbers, and beams when excavation is proceeding and to temporarily support the sides of an excavation.

Underpinning is a method to temporarily support existing foundations while they are being repaired or strengthened or when they are being extended to a lower level. Needle beams supported by the adjacent grade and hydraulic jacks are used to temporarily support the building while the new foundation is constructed.

SITE DRAINAGE

Water must be properly drained from a site to carry off excess rain and other surface water, to avoid leakage into the building, and to make other parts of the site, such as walks, parking areas, and outdoor activity areas, usable. There are two primary types of drainage to consider: subsurface and surface.

Subsurface Drainage

Water below ground can reduce the load-carrying capacity of the soil, cause differential settlement, and leak into a building. For these reasons, the site for a building must be examined and tested for potential water problems, and steps must be taken to drain excess water.

A small amount of moisture in the soil normally does not pose significant problems. However, if there is a high percentage of water in the soil or if the water table is high, these problems must be dealt with. The *water table* is the level below which the soil is saturated with groundwater. If any part of a structure is below this level, it is subject to hydrostatic pressure, putting additional loads on the structural elements of the foundation and making waterproofing more difficult.

In order to minimize subsurface water, the land around the building must be sloped to drain surface water before it soaks into the ground near the structure. A minimum slope of $^1/_4$ in/ft (6/305) is recommended. All water from roofs and decks should also be drained away from the building with gutters and drain pipes.

Below ground, perforated drain tile should be laid around the footings at least 6 in (150) below the floor slab to collect water and carry it away to a storm sewer system, drywell, or some natural drainage area. The drain tile is set in a gravel setting bed, and more gravel is placed above the drain. This is commonly known as a "French drain" or subdrain.

If hydrostatic pressure against the wall is a problem, a layer of gravel can be placed next to the wall. Open-web matting (geotextile material) can also be used. With either of these methods, when water is forced against gravel or matting, it loses its pressure and drips through the gravel or matting into the drain tile.

To relieve pressure against floor slabs, a layer of large gravel is placed below the slab. If the presence of water is a significant problem, the gravel layer is used in conjunction with a waterproofing membrane, and drain tiles are placed below the slab. See also Ch. 41.

Surface Water Drainage

Surface water should be drained away from a building by sloping the land and otherwise modifying the finish contours to divert water into natural drainage patterns or artificial drains. Gutters can be built into curbing to collect water from paved areas. In some cases, large paved or landscaped areas need to be sloped to drain inlets or catch basins that connect with storm sewers.

A drain inlet allows stormwater to run directly into the storm sewer. A catch basin has a sump built into it so that debris will settle instead of flowing down the sewer. The sump can be cleaned out periodically. Large storm sewer systems require manholes for service access, located wherever the sewer changes direction, or a maximum of 500 ft (152 m) apart.

Refer to Chs. 2 and 5 for more information on sustainable design during the site analysis and design phases.

SITE IMPROVEMENTS

Site improvements include items not connected to the building, such as parking areas, walks, paving, landscaping, sprinkler systems, outdoor lighting, fences, retaining walls, and various types of outdoor furnishings.

Paving

Paving is used for parking areas, driveways, and large, hard-surfaced activity areas. Paving is normally constructed of concrete, asphaltic concrete, or unit pavers.

Concrete paving is placed on compacted soil or a gravel bed and is normally reinforced with welded wire fabric to resist temperature stresses. If heavy loading is anticipated, the concrete is often reinforced with standard reinforcing bars. Concrete paving should be a minimum of 5 in (127) thick, but the actual thickness required depends on the anticipated loading. Concrete paving is poured in sections, with joints between the sections. Expansion joints should be located every 20 ft (6100) separated with a $^1/_2$ in (13) premolded joint filler. Construction joints or control joints are placed where separate sections of concrete are poured, and they are intended to control the locations of the inevitable minor cracking that occurs in concrete.

Asphaltic concrete paving is a general term that includes several types of bituminous paving. The most common type of asphaltic concrete consists of asphalt cement and graded aggregates. This is laid on the base and rolled and compacted while still hot. Cold-laid asphalt is the same except that cold liquid asphalt is used. Before the asphalt is applied, a subbase of coarse gravel is overlaid with finer aggregate and compacted and rolled to the desired grade. The asphalt is laid over this base to a depth of 2 or 3 in.

Unit pavers can be any of a number of types of materials, including concrete, brick, granite, and flagstone. Unit pavers should be laid on a level, compacted base of sand over crushed gravel. For greater stability they may also be laid on a bituminous setting bed over a poured concrete slab. Figure 35.4 shows a typical unit paver section, and Fig. 35.5 shows common paving patterns.

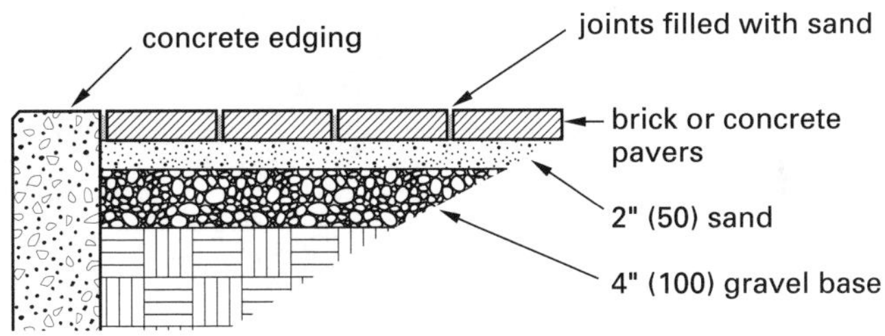

Figure 35.4 Unit Paving

Walks

Walks are common site improvements. Like paving, walks can be constructed of a number of materials, such as asphalt or brick, but the most common is concrete because of its strength and durability. Concrete walks should be laid over a gravel subbase with control joints every 5 ft (1500) and expansion joints every 20 ft (6100). Walks are usually 4 in (100) thick. Additionally, expansion joints should be located where walks abut buildings, curbs, paving, and other permanent structures.

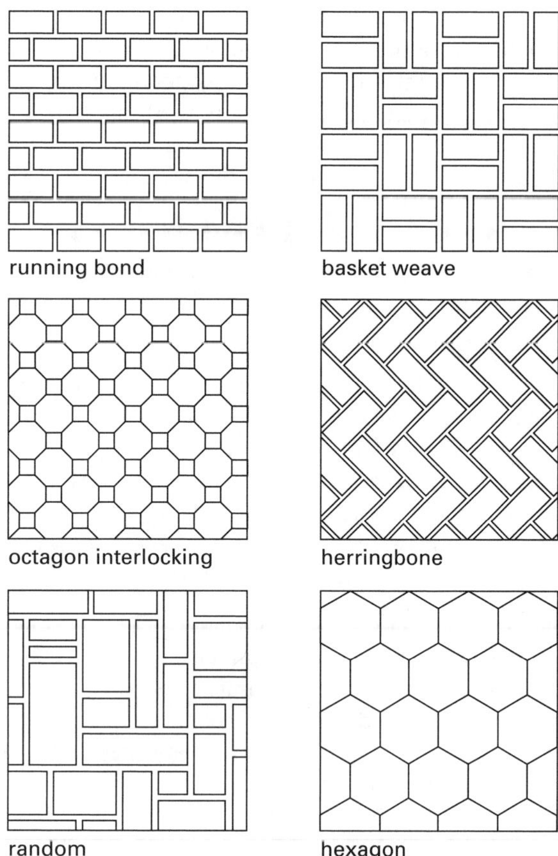

Figure 35.5 Unit Paving Patterns

Low Retaining Walls

The IBC requires that retaining walls be designed for lateral loads, overturning, sliding, and water uplift. Some of the types of retaining walls and how they are designed are discussed in Ch. 15. In some cases, such as residential or small commercial site work, a low retaining wall with no surcharge may be constructed of interlocking concrete or stone blocks designed for that use, large treated timbers, or similar materials, without engineering analysis. These walls are usually limited to approximately three or four feet high depending on the requirements of the local authority having jurisdiction. When timbers or large blocks are used, the retaining wall may be anchored back to the earth with a deadman. *A deadman* is a timber, plate, or similar object placed perpendicular to the face of the retaining wall and that serves to anchor the wall by means of earth friction or pressure. Deadmen may also be used in larger, engineered walls, such as those discussed in Ch. 15.

36 CONCRETE

Concrete is one of the most versatile basic building materials. It is durable, strong, and weather resistant, and it can be formed into a wide variety of shapes and finished in a number of ways. It can be used in structural or nonstructural applications. Although concrete has many advantages, its use requires a knowledge of many variables and construction steps. These include formwork, reinforcing, placing, curing, testing, and finishing.

HISTORY OF CONCRETE

Concrete was first discovered by the Romans. As early as the third century B.C., Roman builders were using a mortar of lime and sand. Later, they discovered that by mixing pozzolana (a volcanic ash) with lime and water they would get a mixture that would set underwater. They mixed their new cement with stone and brick rubble to form walls, and cast it in wooden forms for vaults, arches, and domes.

Concrete was forgotten until the late eighteenth century when John Smeaton found that quicklime containing clay would harden under water. He used a primitive form of this mortar for a stone lighthouse. In 1824, Joseph Aspdin developed portland cement, the first manufactured hydraulic (able to set underwater) binding material. Reinforced concrete, or ferroconcrete as it was first known, was developed in the latter part of the century when both wire and bars were used to strengthen the construction.

Although some experimenting was done with concrete during the nineteenth century (the Paris Exhibition of 1867 used concrete in portions of the main building), it was not until the first two decades of the twentieth century that engineers and architects began to fully exploit the possibilities of the material.

The Swiss engineer Robert Maillart used concrete extensively in his bridges and industrial buildings. One of his best known works was Cement Hall, completed in 1939 in Zurich. It was a thinshell parabolic vault that fully exploited the possibilities of reinforced concrete.

Auguste Perret was another innovator with concrete. However, he used the material for structural frames in simple rectangular constructions. The area between the concrete frame was frequently filled in with other materials. A contemporary of Perret, Tony Garnier, envisioned using ferroconcrete as the basis for the buildings in his proposed town plan, the *cité industrielle*, designed between 1901 and 1904.

The engineer Pier Luigi Nervi used reinforced concrete for many of his most innovative structures. His stadiums at Florence, bridges, and airplane hangars use exposed concrete in daring and innovative forms. His most famous works include the Exhibition Building in Turin (1948) and the sports palace in Rome (1957). Nervi also experimented and used precast reinforced concrete units in many of his buildings.

Le Corbusier used concrete extensively in many of his later buildings. The apartment block at Marseilles (1946–1952), Ronchamp (1950–1954), and the Palace of Justice in Chandigarh (1953) are all examples of a master architect exploiting all the plastic possibilities of the material. Even Frank Lloyd Wright used reinforced concrete in many of his famous buildings such as Fallingwater, the Johnson Wax Company, and the Guggenheim Museum. Wright also experimented with concrete masonry units in his California concrete block houses in the 1920s.

FORMWORK

Formwork refers to the system of boards, ties, and bracing required to construct the mold in which wet concrete is placed. Formwork must be strong enough to withstand the weight and pressure created by the wet concrete and must be easy to erect and remove.

Types of Forms

Forms are constructed out of a variety of materials. Unless the concrete is finished in some way, the shape and pattern of the formwork will affect the appearance of the final product. Wood grain, knotholes, joints, and other imperfections in the form will show in their negative image when the form is removed.

Plywood is the most common forming material. It is usually $^3/_4$ in (19) thick and is coated on one side with oil, a water-resistant glue, or plastic to prevent water from penetrating the wood and to increase the reusability of the form. Oil on forms also prevents adhesion of the concrete so the forms are easier to remove. The plywood is supported with solid wood framing, which is braced or shored as required. Figure 36.1 shows two typical wood-framed forms.

Prefabricated steel forms are often used because of their strength and reusability. They are often employed for forming one-way joist systems, waffle slabs, round columns, and other special shapes.

Other types of forms include glass-fiber reinforced plastic, hardboard, and various kinds of proprietary systems. Plastic forms are manufactured with a variety of patterns embedded in them. These patterns are transferred to the concrete and constitute the final surface. Special form liners can also be used to impart a deeply embossed pattern.

For exposed architectural surfaces, a great deal of consideration must be given to the method and design of the formwork because the pattern of joints and form ties will be visible. Joints are often emphasized with rustication strips, continuous pieces of neoprene, wood, or other material that when removed shows a deep reveal in the concrete.

Form ties are metal wires or rods used to hold opposite sides of the form together and also to prevent their collapse. When the forms are removed, the wire remains in the concrete, and the excess is twisted or cut off. Some form ties are threaded rods that can be unscrewed and reused. Tie holes are made with cone-shaped heads placed against the concrete form. When these are removed, a deep, round hole is left that allows the tie to be cut off below the surface of the concrete. These holes can remain exposed as a design feature or can be patched with grout.

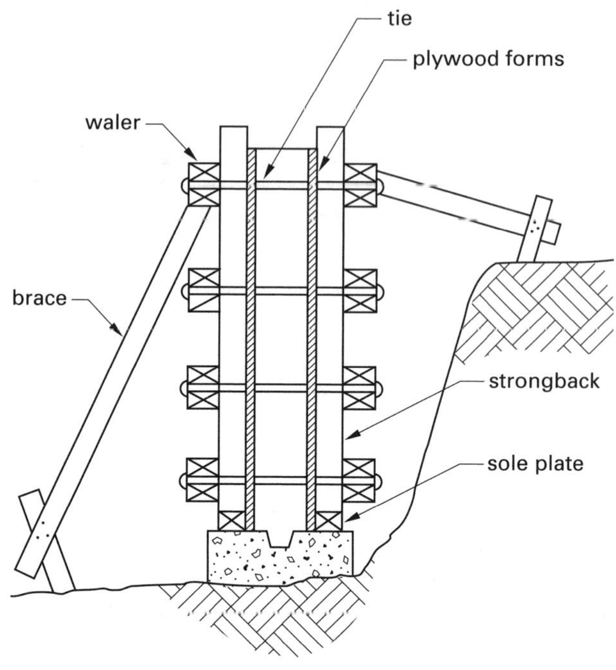

(a) wall formwork

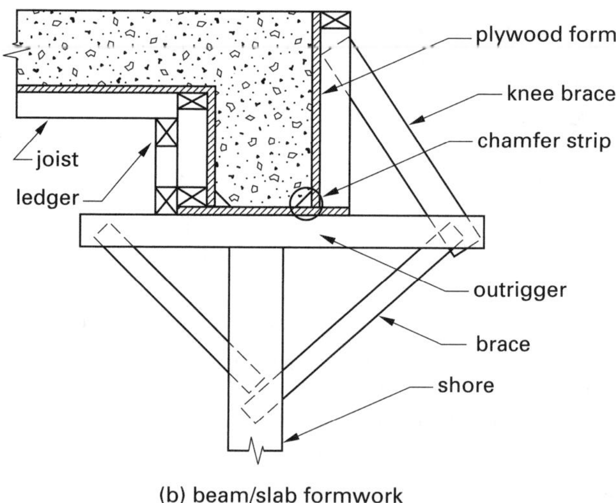

(b) beam/slab formwork

Figure 36.1 Concrete Formwork

Special Forms

Most formwork is designed and constructed to remain in place until the concrete cures sufficiently to stand on its own. However, one method, called *slip forming*, moves as the concrete cures. Slip forming is used to form continuous surfaces such as tunnels and high-rise building cores. The entire form is constructed along with working platforms and supports for the jacking assembly. The form moves continuously at about 6 in to 12 in (150 to 300) per hour. Various types of jacking systems are used to support the form as it moves upward.

Flying forms are large fabricated sections of framework that are removed, once the concrete has cured, to be reused in forming an identical section above. They are often used in buildings with highly repetitive units, such as hotels and apartments. After forming the floor for a hotel, for example, the form assembly is slid outside the edge of the building where it is lifted by crane to the story above. Once that floor is poured, the process is repeated.

Insulating Concrete Forms

Insulating concrete forms (ICFs) are polystyrene foam forms that provide the formwork for poured concrete and then remain in place after the concrete cures. Finish materials are applied directly to plastic or metal ties that are part of the forms. ICFs speed construction and provide insulation, all in one operation. When used for above-grade walls, they produce a strong exterior wall with significant sound attenuation and less air infiltration.

There are three basic varieties of ICF systems: block, plank, and panel. Block systems use foam blocks about the size of concrete blocks; they have interlocking edges and integral ties and can be stacked like simple building blocks. The ties that hold the two sides of the block together are attached to the plastic or metal strips that are used for the attachment of finishes. Plank systems use large, flat foam panels up to 4 ft × 12 ft (1220 × 3660). Panel systems use flat forms up to 12 in high and from 4 ft to 8 ft long (305 high and from 1220 to 2440 long). In all systems, reinforcement is placed in the forms as required by the structural requirements of the project.

ICFs are used primarily for single- and two-family houses and small commercial construction. They can be used for basements alone or for basements and one or two stories above grade.

Depending on the type of system used and the wall height, ICFs usually reduce how much bracing is needed. For block forms, the concrete is usually placed in lifts to prevent blowout of the forms. In all cases, codes require that both sides of the wall be protected from fire and exposure to sunlight and weather. Gypsum wallboard of a minimum 1/2 in (13) thickness may be applied directly to the interior for finish and fire protection, or furring may be attached for application of other materials. Below grade, the exterior of the wall must be protected from moisture with dampproofing or waterproofing as required by the soil conditions.

Economy in Formwork

Because one of the biggest expenses for cast-in-place concrete is formwork, the architect can minimize overall cost by following some basic guidelines. To begin with, forms should be reusable as much as possible. This implies uniform bay sizes, beam depths, column widths, opening sizes, and other major elements. Slab thicknesses should be kept constant without offsets, as should walls. Of course, structural requirements will necessitate variations in many elements, but it is often less expensive to use a little more concrete to maintain a uniform dimension than to form offsets.

Tolerances

Because of the nature of the material and forming methods, concrete construction cannot be perfect; there are certain tolerances that are industry standards. Construction attached to concrete must be capable of accommodating these tolerances. For columns, piers, and walls, the maximum variation in plumb will be plus or minus 1/4 in (6) in any 10 ft (3050) length. The same tolerance applies for horizontal elements such as ceilings, beam soffits, and slab soffits.

The maximum variation out of plumb for the total height of the structure is 1 in (25) for interior columns and 1/2 in (13) for corner columns for buildings up to 100 ft (30 m) tall, while the maximum variation for the total length of the building is plus or minus 1 in (25). Elevation control points for slabs on grade can vary up to 1/2 in (13) in any 10 ft (3050) bay and plus or minus 3/4 in (19) for the total length of the structure.

For elevated, formed slabs the tolerance is plus or minus 3/4 in (19). Finished concrete floors can be specified anywhere from plus or minus 1/8 in in 10 ft (3 mm in 3 m) for very flat slabs to plus or minus 1/2 in (13) for bullfloated slabs.

MOISTURE MIGRATION AND VAPOR BARRIERS

In all construction, water and moisture can cause a variety of problems. For concrete construction the potential problem of water migration through slabs on grade is one of the most significant. The problem of moisture is not as significant for suspended slabs; that is, those with an airspace below them.

Moisture Migration Through Slabs on Grade

Moisture can migrate through slabs by capillary action or by movement of water vapor. Capillary action causes water to be drawn up through the slab through the forces of adhesion, surface tension, and cohesion. Water vapor moves from areas of high vapor pressure to areas of lower vapor pressure by the process of diffusion, which can occur in concrete and soil when water changes from a liquid to a vapor as it evaporates.

For slabs on grade, a vapor barrier is necessary to prevent the migration of moisture through the slab onto the surface of the slab or into the space above the slab. Moisture can cause damage to water-sensitive floor finishes, such as vinyl tile, and can create indoor air quality problems by supplying one of the necessary components of mold and mildew growth.

In addition to providing a vapor barrier, water problems inside the building can be minimized by specifying a low water-cement (w/c) ratio and, if possible, scheduling construction so that slabs have as much time as possible to cure and dry before any sealing or floor finishes are applied. Because it takes so long for the free water (that not used in the curing process) to evaporate out of the slab it is recommended that a maximum w/c ratio be set at 0.45 to 0.50. Ideally, concrete slabs should be allowed to cure and dry for a minimum of six weeks before resilient flooring is installed.

Vapor Barriers

The best way to stop the migration of moisture is with a vapor barrier placed directly below the concrete slab and on top of any sand cushion layer or subbase. This most recent recommendation is contrary to the traditional method of placing the vapor barrier under the sand cushion. However, the traditional method is no longer recommended, because the sand acts as a sponge to hold any water present during construction.

A *vapor barrier* is a thin sheet material, generally plastic, designed to prevent water vapor from passing through it. A *vapor retarder*, on the other hand, only slows the rate of water vapor transmission. A vapor barrier should have a permeance not exceeding 0.04 perm and be at least 10 mils thick. *Permeance* is a measure of a material's resistance to water-vapor transmission, expressed in perms. As discussed in Ch. 29, a *perm* is the passage of one grain of water vapor per hour through one square foot of material at a pressure differential of one inch of mercury between the two sides of the material (one nanogram per second per square meter per pascal of pressure difference).

REINFORCEMENT

Concrete is very strong in compression but weak in tension. As a result, reinforcing is required to resist the tensile stresses in beams, slabs, and columns, and to reduce the size of columns. There are two types of reinforcing steel for cast-in-place concrete: deformed bars and welded wire fabric for reinforcement of slabs.

Reinforcing Bars

Reinforcing bars, often called *rebar*, are available in diameters from $^3/_8$ in to $2^1/_4$ in (9.5 to 57), with $^1/_8$ in (3.2) increments up to $1^3/_8$ in (35). There are also two special large sizes of $1^3/_4$ in and $2^1/_4$ in (44.5 and 57). Bars are designated by numbers that represent the number of $^1/_8$ in increments in the nominal diameter of the bar. Thus, a no. 6 bar has a diameter of $^6/_8$ in, or $^3/_4$ in (19).

Because reinforcing steel and concrete must be bonded together to provide maximum strength, rebars are deformed to provide a mechanical interlocking of the two materials. Additional bonding is provided by the chemical adhesion of the concrete to steel and by the normal roughness of the steel. There are several different types of deformation patterns depending on the mill that manufactures the bar, but they all serve the same purpose. In order to clearly identify bars on the job site, standard designations have been developed for marking bars at the mill. These are shown in Fig. 36.2.

Rebars come in two common grades: grade 40 and grade 60. Grades 50 and 75 are also sometimes available. These numbers refer to the yield strengths in kips per square inch. Grade 60 is the type most used in construction. Wire for prestressing has a much higher tensile strength, up to 250 or 270 kips/in^2 (1724 or 1862 MPa). Rebars are classified as axle, rail, and billet; billet is the most commonly used.

In order to protect the reinforcing, there are certain minimum clearances between the steel and the exposed face of the concrete under various conditions. These are listed in Table 36.1. There are also minimum clearances between rebars to allow the coarse aggregate to pass through as the

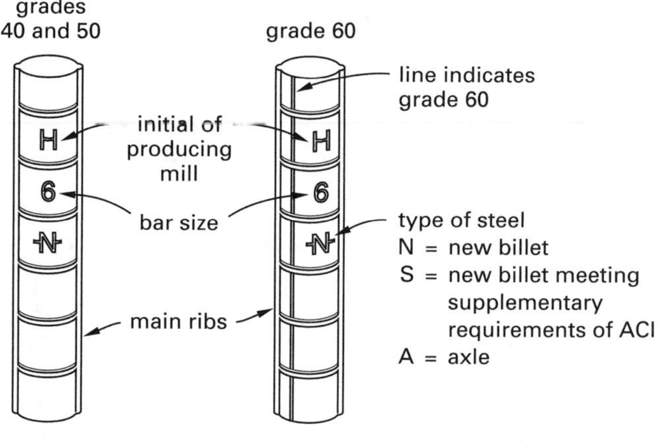

(a) line system

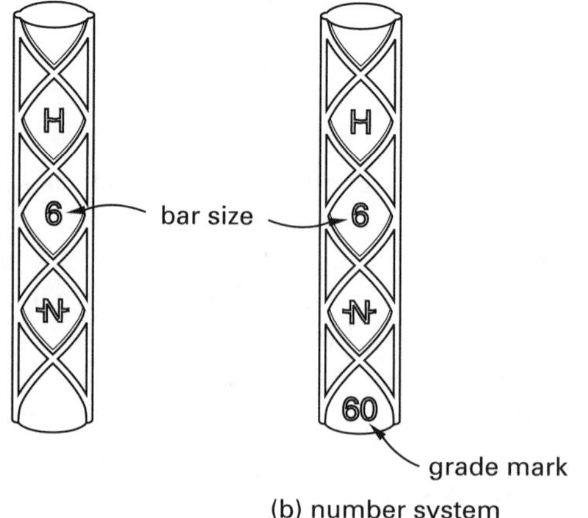

(b) number system

Figure 36.2 Reinforcing Bar Identification

concrete is poured. If the concrete will be exposed to corrosive environments, specifically chlorides, in seawater or deicing salts, the rebars are coated with an epoxy compound or are galvanized.

Table 36.1

Minimum Concrete Protection for Reinforcement
(distance from edge of rebar to face of concrete)

location	distance (in)	distance (mm)
surfaces not exposed directly to the weather or ground:		
slabs and walls	3/4	19
beams and columns	1 1/2	38
surfaces exposed to the weather or in contact with the ground:		
no. 5 bars and smaller	1 1/2	38
larger than no. 5 bars	2	51
concrete poured directly on the ground	3	76

Welded Wire Fabric

Welded wire fabric is used for temperature reinforcement in slabs and consists of cold-drawn steel wires, at right angles to each other, that are welded at their intersections. The wires are usually in a square pattern with spacings of 4 in or 6 in (102 to 152).

The system used to designate welded wire fabric consists of the size first and then the gage. The size is in inches and the gage is given in cross-sectional area in hundredths of a square inch. For example, 6 × 6–W1.4 × 1.4 means that the grid is 6 in by 6 in (150 m by 150 m), and the size of the wire is 1.4 hundredths of a square, or 0.014 in^2. The letter preceding the gage is either W for smooth wire or D for deformed wire. Refer to the next section for information on carbon fiber mesh.

Accessories

Before concrete is poured into the forms, various types of embedded items must be placed in addition to the reinforcing. These include welding plates for attachment of steel and other structural members, electrical boxes and conduit, sleeves for pipes to pass through the concrete, and other types of anchoring devices for suspended components and finish walls. Embedded items must be accurately placed and are temporarily held in position by wiring to the reinforcing, with nails, or with other proprietary devices until secured by the concrete.

Other accessories are used to hold the reinforcing bars in their proper locations. Intersecting reinforcing bars are wired together and held in place with spacers in walls and chairs in slabs. *Chairs* are metal wire devices placed on the form to hold the rebars above the bottom of the form at the proper distance.

CONCRETE MATERIALS

Basic Components

Concrete is a combination of cement, fine and course aggregates, and water mixed in the proper portions and allowed to cure to form a hard, durable material. In addition, admixtures are used to impart particular qualities to the mix. Because the strength of concrete depends on the materials and their proportions, it is important to understand the relationship between the constituent parts.

Portland cement is the binding agent in concrete. It is made from lime, silica, iron oxide, and alumina under strictly controlled conditions. It chemically interacts with water to form a paste that binds the other aggregate particles together in a solid mass. Cement is supplied in bulk or in 94 lbm bags containing one cubic foot.

There are five different types of cement, all used for specific purposes. Type I is called *standard cement*, or *normal cement*, and it is used for most general construction where the other types are not needed. Type II is called *modified cement*, and it is used in places where a modest amount of sulfate resistance is needed and where the heat of hydration needs to be controlled, such as in dams or other massive structures. Type III is *high-early-strength cement* and is used where a quick set is needed. Type III also has a higher heat of hydration, so it is suitable for cold-weather concreting. Type IV, used in massive structures to minimize cracking, is called *low-heat cement*, and it is very slow setting. Type V is *sulfate-resisting cement* and is used for structures that will be exposed to water or soil with a high alkaline content.

Although water is required for *hydration* (the chemical hardening of concrete) and to make it possible to mix and place the concrete into forms, too much water can decrease the concrete's strength. This is because excess water not used in the chemical process remains in the paste and forms pores that cannot resist compressive forces. Generally, for complete hydration to occur, an amount of water equal to 25% of the weight of the cement is required. An extra 10% to 15% or more is required to make a workable mix. The water itself must be potable, or drinkable, to ensure that it is free of any foreign matter that could interfere with adhesion of the aggregates to the cement paste.

For most concrete mixes the minimum water-cement ratio is about 0.35 to 0.40 by weight. Based on the weight of water, this works out to about 4 gal to 4.5 gal of water per 94 lbm sack of cement (15.1 L to 17 L per 42.7 kg sack). Because of the way water and cement interact, the water-cement ratio is the most critical factor in determining the strength of concrete. For a given mix, there should be just enough water to give a workable mix without being excessive. If too much water is added, *laitance* may develop. This is a chalky surface deposit of low-strength concrete. If additional concrete will be poured, the laitance must be removed in order for the new concrete to bond.

Aggregates consist of coarse and fine aggregates; fine aggregates are those that pass through a no. 4 sieve (one with four openings per linear inch [25 mm]). Because cement is the most expensive component of concrete, the best mix is one that uses a combination of aggregate sizes that fill most of the volume with a minimum amount of cement while still achieving the desired strength. Typically, aggregates occupy about 70% to 75% of the total volume of the concrete.

Generally, aggregates are sand and gravel, but others are used. Materials such as expanded clays, slags, and shales are used for lightweight structural concrete. Pumice or cinders are used for insulating concretes. Whereas standard concrete weighs about 150 lbm/ft^3 (2400 kg/m^3), lightweight mixes can range from 50 lbm/ft^3 for insulating concretes to 120 lbm/ft^3 for lightweight structural concrete (800 kg/m^3 to 1920 kg/m^3).

The size of coarse aggregates is determined by the size of the forms and the spacing between the reinforcing. In most instances, the size should not be more than three-fourths of the smallest distance between reinforcing bars, one-fifth of the smallest dimension of forms, or one-third of the depth of slabs, whichever is smallest.

Proportioning

Several methods are used to specify the proportions of the concrete mix. One is to define the ratio of cement to sand to gravel by weight using three numbers such as 1:2:4, which means one part cement, two parts sand, and four parts gravel. In addition, the amount of water must also be specified. Another method is to specify the weight of materials, including water, per 94 lbm bag of cement. Yet another method, useful for large batch quantities, is to define the weight of the materials needed to make up one cubic yard of concrete.

The strength of the final mix is specified by the compressive strength of the concrete after it has cured and hardened for 28 days. This is known as the *design strength* of concrete. Typical specified design strengths, indicated with the symbol , are 2000 psi, 3000 psi (one of the most common), and 4000 psi (13790, 20680, and 25580 kPa). Higher strengths, up to 12,000 psi (82700 kPa), are now available for special applications but are more expensive than the standard mixes.

Admixtures

Admixtures are chemicals or other materials added to concrete to impart certain qualities. Admixtures are used to speed hydration, retard hardening, improve workability, add color, improve durability, and serve a variety of other purposes. Some of the more common admixtures are the following.

- *Air-entraining agents* form tiny, dispersed bubbles in the concrete. These agents increase the workability and durability of the concrete and improve its resistance to freezing and thawing cycles. They also help reduce segregation of the components during placing of the mix into forms.

- *Accelerators* speed up the hydration of the cement so that the concrete achieves strength faster. This allows faster construction and reduces the length of time needed for protection in cold weather.

- *Plasticizers* reduce the amount of water needed while maintaining the necessary consistency for correct placement and compaction. Reducing the water, of course, makes it possible to mix higher-strength concrete.

- *Retarders* slow down the setting time to help reduce the heat of hydration.

- *Waterproofing* agents decrease the permeability of the concrete.

Supplementary Cementitious Materials

Supplementary cementitious materials (SCMs) are added to concrete as part of the total cementitious system and also impart other desirable qualities to a concrete mix. Unlike admixtures, SCMs have cementing properties, like portland cement, and are often used as a partial replacement of portland cement.

- *Fly ash* is a waste material obtained from coal-fired power plants. Fly ash in concrete improves workability, reduces temperature rise, minimizes bleeding, reduces permeability, inhibits alkali-silica reaction (ASR), and enhances sulfate resistance. Refer to the section on testing concrete for more information on ASR. Like other SCMs, fly ash can also be used to decrease the total amount of cement needed. Refer to Ch. 30 for more information on how fly ash is used to make concrete a more sustainable material.

- *Ground-granulated blast-furnace slag* (GGBFS) is produced from the material formed from molten slag as a by-product of iron and steel manufacturing. The material is dried and ground to a fine powder to produce a hydraulic cementing material that is substituted for portland cement at various ratios; a 50% substitution is common. Slag in concrete provides many benefits. It improves workability, decreases the need for water, and increases setting time, which can be a benefit in large pours and during hot weather. It also reduces bleeding, improves resistance to sulfate and chloride attack, and can prevent damage from ASR. Concrete that contains slag develops strength more slowly than standard concrete, particularly in the first seven days, but it continues to gain strength beyond 28 days and has a higher ultimate strength than standard portland cement concrete.
- *Silica fume* is collected by filtering the smoke created during the production of silicon and ferrosilicon metals. It consists mostly of particles of silicon dioxide about 1/100th the size of cement grains. Silica fume is also available in liquid form. It is added to concrete in a proportion of 7% to 10% by weight of the cement. Silica fume decreases permeability, increases compressive strength, improves abrasion resistance, and reduces bleeding.
- A *pozzolan* is a siliceous or aluminosiliceous material that, in finely divided form and in the presence of moisture, reacts chemically with the calcium hydroxide released by the hydration of portland cement to form various cementitious compounds. Pozzolans are used as a partial replacement for portland cement and to decrease permeability, increase strength, and improve resistance to ASR and sulfate attack. Natural pozzolans, which are formed from clay, shale, and other materials that have cementitious properties, include calcined shale, calcined clay, and metakaolin. The ancient Romans used volcanic ash, another natural pozzolan, to mix the earliest form of concrete.

NEW CONCRETE PRODUCTS

Concrete continues to be improved through the use of new materials, admixtures, equipment, and construction techniques. Following are some innovations that are beginning to be adopted in mainstream construction practices.

Autoclaved Aerated Concrete

Autoclaved aerated concrete (AAC) is a precast concrete product manufactured by adding aluminum powder to concrete, hardening it in molds, and then curing the molds in a pressurized steam chamber (autoclave). The resultant blocks have about one-fifth the density of conventional concrete. They are typically manufactured in blocks 10 in (250) high by 25 in (635) long and in thicknesses of 4 in, 8 in, and 10 in (100, 200, and 250). The blocks are laid with a thin-set mortar and can be cut and shaped with woodworking tools. Unreinforced and reinforced panels of ACC are also produced for use as floor, roof, and wall panels.

As a sustainable material, AAC requires less material than does normal concrete and results in less construction site waste than does building with standard concrete block. It has very good sound control qualities and thermal mass and has greater air tightness than do wood stud walls. It is resistant to insects, rodents, and mold. However, it does not have the strength of standard concrete, so construction is limited to nonloadbearing walls and low-rise structures. It must also be protected from the exterior environment with plaster, masonry, or some other exterior finish.

Self-Consolidating Concrete

Self-consolidating concrete (SCC) is a concrete mixture that can be placed purely by means of its own weight without the use of vibration. SCC is made possible with the use of a superplasticizer admixture called a polycarboxylate polymer. Because no vibration is required, SCC placement is accelerated, less labor is required, and productivity is increased. The concrete flows easily around dense reinforcement and provides a more uniform and smooth surface than does standard concrete, so less time is required to make minor cosmetic repairs. Because the concrete develops strength faster than conventional concrete, forms can be stripped sooner.

Carbon Fiber Concrete

Carbon fiber concrete uses epoxy-coated carbon fiber mesh in place of standard steel mesh for secondary steel reinforcement. It is used for precast panels, to make them thinner and lighter. Because carbon fiber is noncorrosive, less concrete cover is required. The resulting panels, in turn, require smaller foundations and support structures, reduce transportation costs, and speed the erection process.

The carbon fiber is manufactured by using industrial-grade carbon fiber and extruding it into ultrathin fibers. The fibers are bundled together to form pieces resembling yarn, called tows. The tows are laid perpendicular to each other in a grid, with the intersecting tows bound together by a heat-cured epoxy resin. The resulting grid is about 0.04 in (1) thick. The various components of the grid can be modified to meet different strength requirements, with a typical grid having nearly seven times the tensile strength of standard steel mesh.

Poured Gypsum Decks

Poured gypsum decks are used for roofs and are similar to concrete in that a liquid mixture is poured on reinforcing material. In typical gypsum deck construction, purlins support fiber plank or rigid insulation. Wire mesh reinforcing is placed over this and gypsum poured on the assembly to a minimum depth of $2^1/_2$ in (64). Gypsum provides a highly fire-resistant roof deck.

Precast gypsum planks with tongue-and-groove edges are also available in 2 in and 4 in (50 and 100) thicknesses. They are reinforced with wire fabric and span up to 10 ft (3050).

CURING AND TESTING

Curing Concrete

Because concrete hardens and gains strength by curing through chemical reaction between the water and the cement rather than by drying, it is critical that the proper conditions of moisture and temperature be maintained for at least seven days and up to two weeks for critical work. If concrete dries out too fast, it can lose strength, up to 30% or more in some instances. With high-early-strength cements, of course, the time can be reduced. This is because concrete gains about 70% of its strength during the first week of curing, and the final 28-day design strength depends on the initial curing conditions.

There are many techniques for maintaining proper moisture levels, including covering with plastic, using sealing compounds, or continually sprinkling the surfaces with water.

Concrete must also be kept from freezing while curing or it will lose strength, sometimes as much as half. Because concrete produces heat while it cures (known as *heat of hydration*) it is often sufficient to cover the fresh material with insulated plastic sheets for a few days. In very cold conditions, Type III cement may be used and external heat supplied. In addition, the water and aggregate may be heated prior to mixing.

Testing Concrete

Because there are so many variables in concrete construction, the material must be continually tested at various stages to maintain quality. There are several tests with which the architect must be familiar: the slump test, the cylinder test, the core cylinder test, the Kelly ball test, the impact hammer test, and the K-slump test.

The *slump test* measures the consistency of the concrete, usually at the job site. In this test, concrete is placed in a 12 in high (305) truncated cone, 8 in (203) at the base and 4 in (102) at the top. It is compacted by hand with a rod, and then the mold is removed from the concrete and placed next to it. The distance the concrete slumps from the original 12 in (305) height is then measured in inches (mm). The amount of slump desired depends on how the concrete is going to be used, but it is typically in the range of 2 in to 6 in (51 to 152). Too much slump indicates excessive water in the mix, and a very small slump indicates that the mixture will be difficult to place properly.

The *cylinder test* measures compressive strength. As the concrete is being placed, samples are put in cylinder molds that are 6 in (152) in diameter and 12 in (305) high, and are moist-cured and tested in the laboratory according to standardized procedures. The compressive strength in pounds per square inch is calculated and compared with the value used in the design of the structure. Cylinders are tested at a specified number of days, normally 7 and 28 days. Seven-day tests are usually about 60% to 70%of the 28-day strength.

The *core cylinder test* is used when a portion of the structure is in place and cured but needs to be tested. A cylinder is drilled out of the concrete and tested in the laboratory to determine its compressive strength.

In the *Kelly ball test*, also known as the *ball penetration test*, a hemispheric mass of steel with a calibrated stem is dropped onto a slab of freshly laid concrete. The amount of penetration of the ball into the concrete is measured and compared to one-half the values of the slump test.

The *impact hammer test* is a nondestructive way to test concrete strength after it has hardened. A spring-loaded plunger is snapped against a concrete surface, and the amount of rebound is measured. The amount of rebound gives an approximate reading of the concrete strength. If this test is not accurate enough, then cylinder cores can be cut from hardened concrete and tested in the laboratory.

The *K-slump test* uses a $^3/_4$ in (19) tube that contains a floating scale. The tube is placed on the wet concrete, and the scale is pushed into the mixture and released. The distance the scale floats out is read directly and is a measure of the consistency of the concrete, comparable to the slump.

Testing Concrete for Moisture Content and Alkalinity

Because unwanted moisture in a slab on grade can create so many problems, as mentioned previously, the concrete should be tested for moisture level prior to the application of any critical finishes such as vinyl, rubber, linoleum, urethane, or wood. The flooring industry generally recommends that these types of flooring not be installed until the moisture emission from the concrete has reached a certain level. This maximum limit for moisture emission is 3.0 lbm per 1000 ft^2 per 24 hr (1.4 kg per 42 m^2 per 24 h) when exposed to 73°F and 50% relative humidity. There are several tests by which moisture level can be determined.

The *calcium chloride test* (sometimes called the *moisture dome test*) is one of the most common tests for moisture in concrete and is inexpensive and easy to complete. It also gives results in the same form that many flooring manufacturers use to determine if their products can be successfully installed. This test is made by placing a standard mass of calcium chloride below a plastic cover and sealing it to the concrete floor. After 60 to 72 hours, the calcium chloride is weighed to compare it with its pre-test weight. Through a mathematical formula, the amount of moisture the calcium chloride absorbed is converted to the standard measure of pounds per 1000 ft^2 per 24-hour period. One test should be conducted for every 500 ft^2 to 1000 ft^2 (46 m^2 to 93 m^2) of slab area.

The *hygrometer test* (sometimes called the *relative humidity test*) determines the moisture emission by measuring the relative humidity (RH) of the atmosphere confined adjacent to the concrete floor. In this test a pocket of air is trapped below a vapor-impermeable box, and a probe in the device measures the RH. Test standards recommend that moisture-sensitive flooring not be installed unless the RH is 75% or less.

The *polyethylene sheet test* is a qualitative test conducted by sealing an 18 in by 18 in (460 by 460) sheet of plastic to the floor to trap excessive moisture. After a minimum of 16 hours a visual inspection is made of the floor and the sheet. The presence of visible water indicates the concrete is insufficiently dry for the application of finishes.

Similar to the sheet test is the *mat test*. This is also a qualitative method that uses a 24 in by 24 in (600 by 600) sample of vapor-retardant floor finish. The sample is applied with adhesive, and the edges are sealed with tape. After 72 hours a visual inspection is made. If the mat is firmly bonded or if removal of the mat is difficult, the level of moisture present is considered to be sufficiently low for installation of the flooring material.

The *electrical impedance test* uses proprietary meters to determine the moisture content of the concrete by measuring conductance and capacitance. Probes of the meter are placed on the concrete, and the percentage of moisture content in the slab is read out directly.

In addition to testing for moisture, the slab should be tested for pH level and alkalinity. *pH level* is a measure of the acidity or alkalinity of a material rated on a scale from 0 to 14 with 7 being neutral. Materials with a pH less than 7 are considered acidic while those above 7 are considered alkaline. The scale is logarithmic, so a material with a pH of 12 is actually ten times more alkaline than one with a pH of 11. Concrete normally has a pH of about 12.0 to 13.3. In addition to the alkalis within the concrete, excess alkalinity can also be carried from the soil below the slab through the migration of water vapor. This is another reason why vapor barriers are important. Although pH level is an indication of the presence of alkalinity, pH level and alkalinity are not synonymous. Two slabs can have the same pH level, but one can have a much higher alkalinity. Alkalinity cannot exist without moisture because the moisture causes the soluble alkalis in the concrete to enter into the solution. This is why it is important to first control moisture in slabs, as described previously.

Alkalinity in concrete can cause problems in two ways. High alkalinity on the surface of a slab can damage a tile installation by causing the adhesive to re-emulsify, or revert to its original liquid state. It can also cause problems with other coatings. At a level of about 9 or 10, most tile adhesives may begin to experience problems, although professional-grade adhesives can sometimes be used with a pH of 11. Surface alkalinity can be controlled with various proprietary coatings.

Alkalinity is also responsible for the phenomenon known as *alkali-silica reaction* (ASR). In this process strongly alkaline cement begins to dissolve sand and rock within the concrete. The chemical reaction produces a gel-like material that creates tremendous pressures in the pores of the concrete surface. These pressures, in turn, can buckle or blister floor finishes. The risk for ASR can be reduced by specifying aggregates that are not susceptible to ASR, by using low-lime cement, by proper curing, or by not finishing the concrete with a hard trowel surface. Resistance to ASR can also be improved by using SCMs as discussed in the previous section.

A *pH test* is used to test the surface of concrete that will come in contact with flooring adhesives or other critical floor coatings. It is a simple test that uses a coated paper strip or a small pH meter. Once the pH level is known, it can be compared with the maximum pH recommended by the flooring manufacturer. A pH of 8.5 is considered ideal and about the minimum that concrete can have, with values up to 9.0 being acceptable.

In addition to the pH test, a *titration test* can be used to determine the level of alkalinity in concrete. This involves grinding portions of the concrete, mixing the resulting powder with demineralized water, and performing laboratory chemical analysis. A testing laboratory must perform this test.

PLACING AND FINISHING

Concrete Placement

Placing concrete involves several steps, from transporting the material from the truck or mixer to using the forms. First, the concrete must be conveyed to the formwork. This is done with bottom-dump buckets, by pumping, or in small buggies or wheelbarrows. Which method is used depends on the available equipment, the quantity of concrete, and the physical size and layout of the job. Concrete can even be placed underwater with a long, cylindrical steel chute called a *tremie*.

Once at the formwork, the concrete must be placed in such a way as to avoid *segregation*, which is the separation of the aggregates, water, and sand from each other. Dropping concrete long distances from the conveying device to the forms is one of the typical causes of segregation. Typically, 5 ft (1500) is the maximum distance that concrete should be dropped. Excessive lateral movement of the concrete in forms or slab work is another practice that should be minimized.

After placement, the concrete must be compacted to make sure the wet material has flowed into all the forms and around all the rebar, to make sure that it has made complete contact with the steel, and to prevent *honeycombing*, the formation of air pockets within the concrete and next to the forms. For small jobs, hand compaction can be used. More typically, it is done with vibrators.

As-Cast Finishes

Concrete can be finished in a variety of ways. The simplest is to leave the concrete as it is when the forms are removed. A *rough form finish* shows the pattern of the formwork and joints between forms. Defects and tie holes may be left unfinished or finished. This is the roughest finish and is usually used for concrete that will not be visible.

A *smooth form finish* is similar, but smooth forms of wood, metal, or hardboard are used, and joints and tie holes are planned so that they are symmetrical. Any fins left from concrete seeping into joints between forms are removed.

Architectural Finishes

Architectural finishes are used where concrete will be exposed and appearance is a consideration. There are several varieties of these finishes.

- *Form liner*. The concrete is shaped with liners of plastic, wood, or metal. Parallel rib liners are a common type. Joints and form tie holes are treated as desired—either left exposed or patched.
- *Scrubbed*. The surface of the concrete is wetted and scrubbed with a wire or fiber brush to remove some of the surface mortar and expose the coarse aggregate.
- *Acid wash*. The surface of the concrete is wetted with muriatic acid to expose and bring out the full color of the aggregate.
- *Water jet*. A high-pressure water jet mixed with air is used to remove some of the mortar and expose the aggregate.

Tooled and Sandblasted Finishes

Tooled finishes are produced by mechanically modifying the concrete surface.

- *Bush hammering*. A bush-hammered finish gives a rugged, heavy texture by removing a portion of the surface made with form liners. The type of texture depends on the form liner used.
- *Grinding*. This finishing technique smoothes out the surface of the concrete. It is similar to terrazzo in appearance.
- *Applied*. Applied finishes include the application of other materials, such as stucco, to the concrete.
- *Sandblasted finishes*. These are produced by removing surface material from the concrete. This exposes the fine and coarse aggregate to varying degrees, depending on whether the sandblasted finish is specified as light, medium, or heavy.

Rubbed Finishes

- *Smooth*. The surface of the concrete is wetted and rubbed with a carborundum brick to produce a smooth, uniform color and texture.
- *Grout cleaned*. Grout is applied over the concrete and smoothed out. This results in a uniform surface with defects concealed.

Concrete Slab Finishes

After a concrete slab is poured, the first finishing operation is to *strike off* the concrete by drawing a straightedge (metal or wood) across the forms to give a roughly level surface. If a smooth surface is required, the slab is then floated. This operation brings cement paste to the surface, where it is consolidated and smoothed over the coarse aggregate. *Floating* can be done with a wood or magnesium float or a bull float. *Floats* are simply handheld wood or magnesium trowels. A *bull float* is similar to a standard float, but is wider and is attached to a long handle that allows finishers to smooth large concrete surfaces while standing away from the fresh concrete. At this point in the finishing operation the following finishes are available.

- If no further work is done after floating, the finish is called a *float finish*. It gives a sandpaper-like texture and is appropriate for exterior surfaces or where smooth surfaces are not required for other finish materials. A wood float gives a rougher finish texture than does a magnesium float.
- A *light steel troweled finish* is achieved by using a steel trowel several hours after floating. This further consolidates the concrete. Either hand trowels or large, mechanically driven rotary trowels may be used.
- A *hard steel troweled finish* continues the consolidation of the concrete and greatly densifies the top $^{1}/_{8}$ in (3) of the concrete, making a very smooth surface.
- After floating, a *broom finish* is created by running an industrial broom with medium bristles over the surface of the concrete. This process dislodges fine aggregate and products a rough-textured surface useful for slip-resistance on outdoor slabs.
- A *superflat floor finish* typically has a hard steel troweled finish, but mainly refers to the smoothness and levelness of a concrete slab. A superflat floor is commonly used in industrial warehouses where automated or special forklift vehicles are used to rapidly locate and retrieve materials from high-rack storage. Because of the small distances between the storage racks and the vehicles and the high reach of the lifts, the vehicle must travel on a very smooth, level floor.

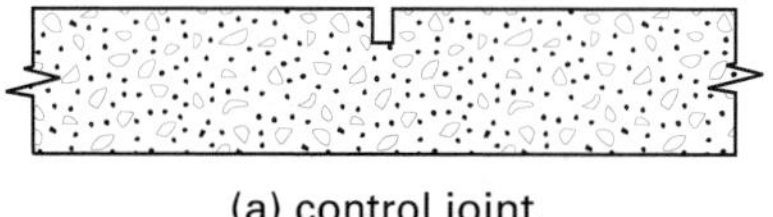
(a) control joint

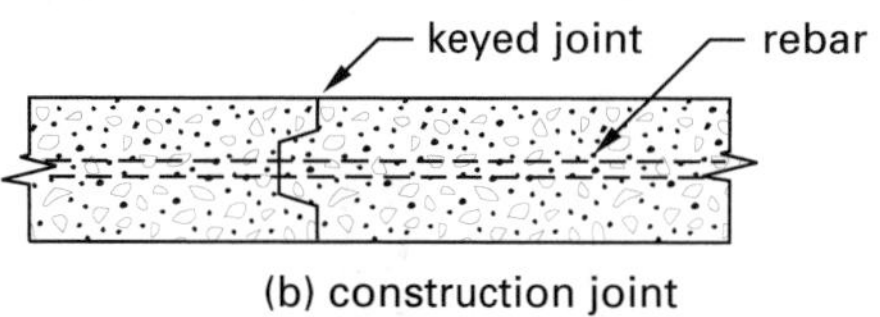

(b) construction joint

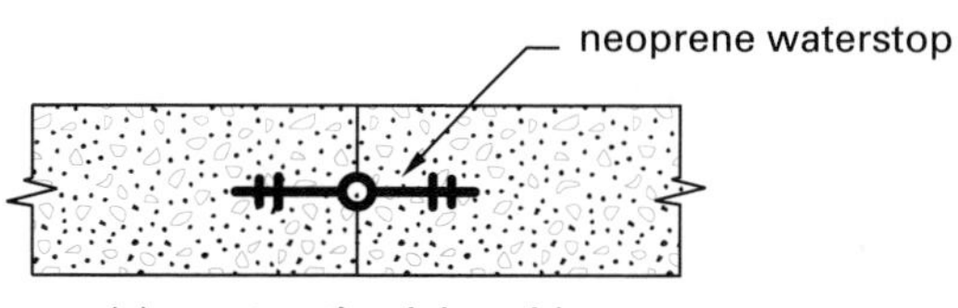

(c) construction joint with waterstop

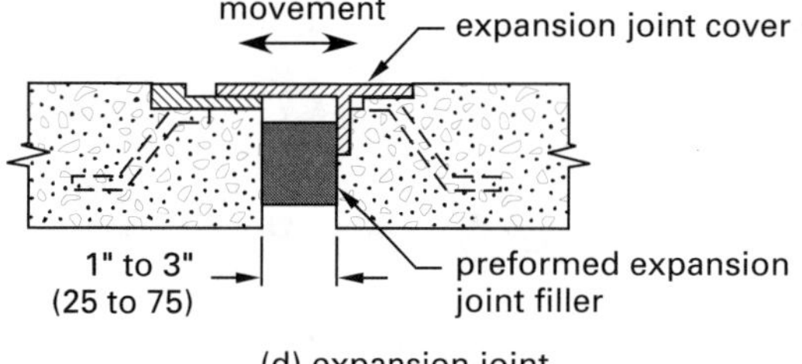

(d) expansion joint

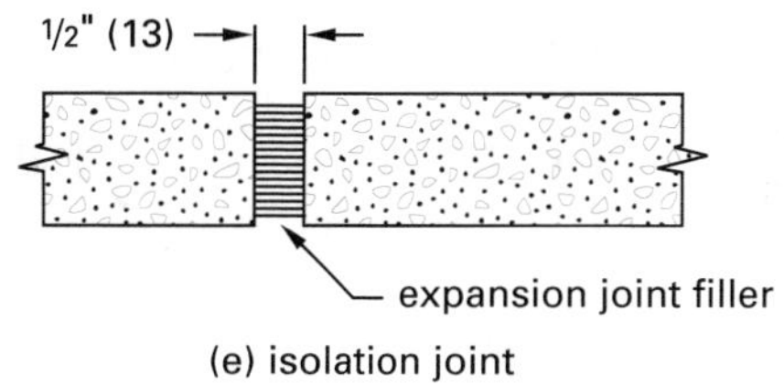

(e) isolation joint

Figure 36.3 Concrete Joints

JOINTS AND ACCESSORIES

Purposes and Types of Concrete Joints

There are four primary types of concrete joints: control, construction, expansion, and isolation. They all serve different functions and are constructed differently. See Fig. 36.3.

Control joints create a weak section so that normal temperature and stress cracking occurs along the joint instead of at random. Control joints are normally formed by tooling when the concrete is still wet, by sawcutting, or by using premolded sections in the formwork. They are cut to a depth of one-fourth the slab thickness.

Construction joints occur wherever there are two successive pours; that is, wherever there is a new pour against a cured section of concrete. Because a construction joint creates a plane of weakness, it should be located at points of minimum shear. Normally, reinforcing extends from one pour to another to tie the two sections together. Construction joints are also a point where water leakage can occur. To prevent this, prefabricated waterstops can be inserted in the first pour that extend into the second pour, as shown in Fig. 36.3.

Expansion joints allow entire sections of a concrete structure to move independently of one another. The movement can be caused by shrinkage of the concrete or temperature changes. Because the movement can be cyclical, the expansion joint must be capable of moving in two directions. Expansion joints are complex fabrications, portions of which are embedded in the concrete and portions of which are exposed. In most instances, the expansion joint extends through the entire structure so there is no rigid connection between any two components of adjacent building sections.

Isolation joints also allow two adjacent sections to move independently of one another, but they are not as complex as expansion joints. Typically, they simply consist of two separate pours of concrete separated with a premolded joint material. They are often used to separate columns from slabs and slabs from foundations and other types of walls.

Inserts

Concrete inserts include a wide range of anchoring devices used to attach other materials and components to concrete construction. For example, *weld plates* are steel plates cast flush with the surface of concrete, to which steel members are welded. The weld plate is attached to a steel anchor that extends into the concrete for positive anchorage. In some cases, the anchors are welded to the reinforcing bars.

Concrete Sealers

Concrete sealers are proprietary products applied to concrete to protect against weather and water penetration, provide resistance to chemicals, to prevent dusting of the surface, or harden the surface. Other coatings are applied for decorative purposes. Some products help cure the concrete while sealing it.

There are two general types of concrete sealers: coating types and penetrating types. The coating types dry as a surface film and are made from a variety of materials including acrylics, urethanes, and epoxies. The penetrating types seep into the tiny pores of the concrete and include proprietary products made with silicones, silanes, and siloxanes. Because of the way they work, penetrating sealers do not wear off as some surface sealers do. Some proprietary formulations can be used to stop moisture and alkaline migration through an existing concrete slab.

PRECAST CONCRETE

Precast concrete consists of components cast in separate forms in a place other than their final position. Precast concrete can be cast on site or in fabricating plants where conditions can be more carefully controlled and where work can proceed regardless of the weather.

Beams and Columns

Precast concrete beams for buildings are usually rectangular, T-shaped, or L-shaped, as shown in Fig. 36.4. T-shaped and L-shaped beams allow the floor structure to be flush with the top of the beam and minimize the total depth needed for the structure. Two very efficient sections that are widely used are the single-T and double-T. These combine a deep section for efficient beam action and a wide flange for the floor structure. When T-sections are used, a topping slab is poured to cover the joints and provide a level floor. T-sections are often used with T-shaped and L-shaped beams in precast buildings.

Precast columns are usually rectangular in shape and cast with welding plates at the top and bottom. They are often cast with haunches that support beams, as shown in Fig. 36.4.

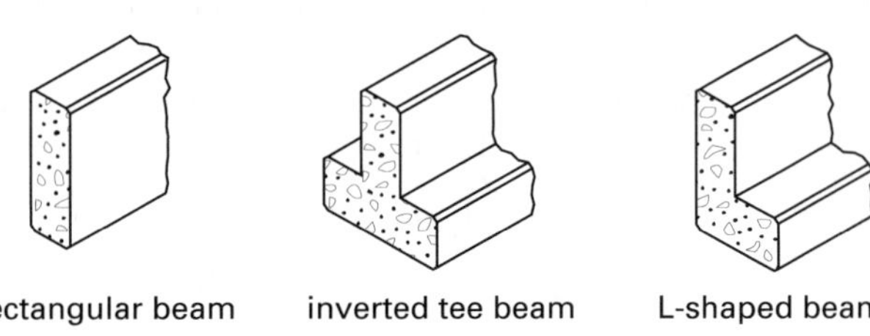

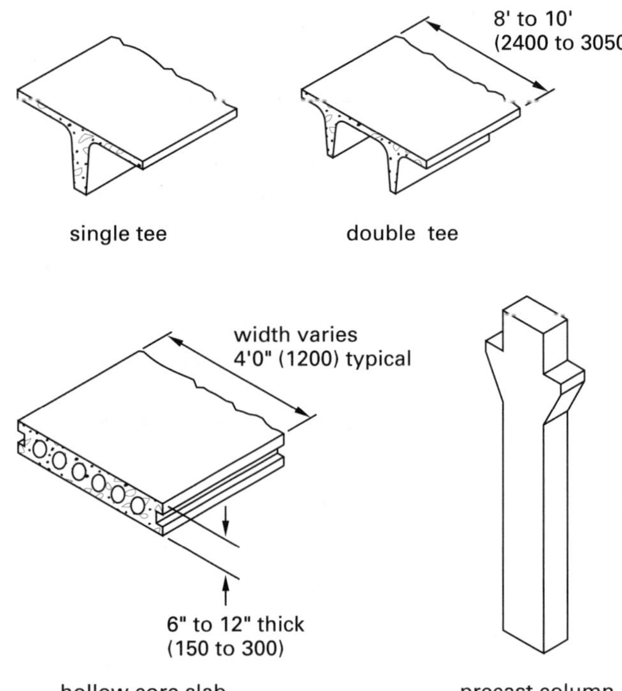

Figure 36.4 Typical Precast Concrete Shapes

Floor and Roof Panels

In addition to precast T-sections that serve as floor and roof structures, simple reinforced concrete slabs are cast for this purpose. For light loads and short spans, the slabs may be solid; for heavier loads and longer spans, hollow, cored slabs are used. These allow the depth of the slab to be increased for more efficient load-carrying capability while still minimizing weight. Cored slabs are 6 in to 12 in (150 to 300) thick and normally 4 ft (1200) wide. They can span up to 36 ft (11 m).

Lift-slab construction is a technique for multistory construction in which entire floor sections are cast on the ground, one on top of another around pre-erected columns. The slabs are poured with a bond breaker between successive pours. Once cured, the slabs are lifted into place with jacks attached to the columns. The slabs are connected to the columns with weld plates. This type of construction minimizes the amount of formwork required and generally reduces total construction time.

Wall Panels

Wall panels can be cast in a variety of sizes and shapes. For greatest economy, the number of types of panels and openings should be minimized. Wall panels are generally 5 in to 8 in (125 to 200) thick (although they can be thicker) and long enough to span columns or beams. If the panels span beams, greater cost savings can be achieved in multistory buildings by casting panels to span two floors.

Wall panels can be cast in a precasting plant or on site. A typical method of building is with tilt-up construction. With this procedure the panels are cast in a horizontal position near their final location and lifted into place when sufficiently cured. In many cases the panels are cast directly on the building's floor slab with temporary boards forming the edges. A bond breaker is used to prevent the wall panel from sticking to the casting surface. A bond breaker may be a liquid solution or a sheet of plastic, but liquids result in a better finish.

PRECAST, PRESTRESSED CONCRETE

Prestressed concrete consists of members that have internal stresses applied to them before they are subjected to service loads. The prestressing consists of compressive forces applied where the member would normally be in tension. This effectively eliminates or greatly reduces tensile forces that the member is not capable of carrying. In addition to making a more efficient and economical structural section, prestressing reduces cracking and deflection, increases shear strength, and allows longer spans and greater loads. Prestressing is accomplished in one of two ways: pretensioning and post-tensioning.

Pretensioning

With this system, concrete members are produced in a precasting plant. High-strength pretensioning stranded cable or wire is draped in forms according to the required stress pattern, and a tensile force is applied. The concrete is then poured and allowed to cure. Once the concrete cures, the cables are cut and the resulting compressive force is transferred to the concrete through the bond between cable and concrete.

Post-tensioning

In post-tensioned construction, hollow sleeves or conduits are placed in the forms on the site, and concrete is poured around them. Within the sleeves are high-strength steel tendons, which are stressed with hydraulic jacks after the concrete has cured. Once the desired stress has been applied, the ends of the cables are secured to the concrete and the jacks are removed. If the tendons are to be unbonded, no further action is taken. In bonded construction, the sleeves are removed and grout is forced into the space between the tendons and the concrete.

Unbonded systems typically use monostrand tendons, which are typically composed of seven wire strands wound together and coated with corrosion-inhibiting grease. Monostrand, unbonded post-tensioning is commonly used in slabs and beams for buildings, in parking structures, and in slabs on grade. Bonded systems typically use multistrand tendons, which are composed of two or more tendons stressed with a large, multistrand jack and anchored in a common anchorage device. Multistrand systems are typically used in bridges and in heavily loaded beams in buildings.

37 MASONRY

Masonry construction is one of the oldest building techniques known. It has survived through the centuries because of its many advantages: masonry is durable and strong, it can be formed into a variety of building shapes, and the raw materials are available in most parts of the world. Combined with modern materials such as improved mortars, reinforcing, and flashing, brick and stone remain timeless materials.

In simplest terms, masonry consists of an assembly of relatively small units of stone, burned clay, or other manufactured material held in place with mortar. Traditionally, masonry has been considered a material to be used to support loads in compression because stone, brick, and mortar have negligible resistance to tensile or bending forces. Horizontal spanning with masonry was always accomplished with some form of arch.

However, with steel reinforcing, high-strength mortars, steel lintels, and the like, brick and unit masonry can be used in an ever wider variety of situations, both horizontally and vertically. Philosophically, however, many designers still feel that since masonry is compressive by nature, it should be used in the traditional way.

MORTAR

Mortar is the cementitious material used to hold masonry units together. It must be compatible with the masonry units being used, the strength required, and the environmental conditions.

Components of Mortar

Mortar is a mixture of cement, lime, sand, and water. Normally, portland cement is used. Lime is added to plasticize the cement so that it is more workable, to add resilience, and to increase the water retention of the mortar. Resilience is important to accommodate movement caused by temperature change and brick swell. Water retention is important to improve the hydration of the cement as it sets.

Masonry cement is a prepared mixture of portland cement and pulverized limestone. It is not as strong or expensive as portland cement, but it has greater plasticity. It is suitable for low-rise building veneers and for interior, nonloadbearing applications.

Various other types of cements are available for special applications. One of the most common is nonstaining cement, which should be used for marble, limestone, terra cotta, cut stone, and glazed brick.

Types of Mortar

There are four basic types of mortar: Types M, S, N, and O. Each has a different proportion of cement, lime, and aggregate, and each has a different compressive strength. These are summarized in Table 37.1. Which mortar is specified depends on the type of masonry unit being used and the conditions of use. Generally, a job should never use a mortar that is stronger in compression than required. In addition, because lime helps retain water in the mortar for hydration, a mortar with a high lime content is appropriate for bricks with a high initial rate of absorption or for summer construction where evaporation is a factor. Table 37.2 summarizes some guidelines for mortar selection.

Grout

Grout is similar to mortar, but it is mixed to a pouring consistency and used to fill wall cavities or cores of hollow masonry units and to bond masonry to reinforcement. Grout may be fine or coarse. Coarse grout includes no. 4 aggregate (pea gravel). Fine grout is used when the dimensions of the space in which the grout is placed are less than 2 in (50).

Table 37.1
Types of Mortar

		parts by volume					aggregate ratio—measured in a damp, loose condition	min. average 28-day compressive strength	
			masonry cement						
cement	type	portland cement	M	S	N	hydrated lime or lime putty		(psi)	(kPa)
cement-lime	M	1		–		1/4		2500	17 235
	S	1		–		over 1/4 to 1/2	not less than 2 1/4 and not more than 3	1800	12 410
	N	1		–		over 1/2 to 1 1/4	times the sum of the separate volumes of	750	5170
	O	1		–		over 1 1/2 to 2 1/2	cementitious materials	350	2410
masonry cement	M	1	–	–	1	–		2500	17 235
	M	–	1	–	–				
	S	1/2	–	–	1	–		1800	12 410
	S	–	–	1	–				
	N	–	–	–	1	–		750	5170
	O	–	–	–	1	–		350	2410

Table 37.2
Selection of Mortar

		mortar type	
location	building component	1st choice	alternate
exterior, above grade	loadbearing walls	N or S	M
	nonloadbearing walls	N	S
	parapet walls	N	S
exterior, at or below grade	foundation walls, retaining walls, pavements, walks	M	S
interior	loadbearing walls	N	S or M
	nonloadbearing walls	O	N

BRICK

Types of Brick

A *brick* is a relatively small masonry unit made from burned clay, shale, or a mixture of these materials that is not less than 75% solid. The two basic types of brick are facing brick and building brick (also called *common brick*). As the name implies, *facing brick* is used for exposed locations where appearance and uniformity of size are important. *Building brick* is made without regard to color or special finish.

Building brick is graded according to resistance to exposure: SW (severe weathering), MW (moderate weathering), and NW (negligible weathering). Among other things, these grades reflect the ability of brick to resist freeze-thaw cycles. Facing brick is available in SW and MW grades and is further classified into three types: FBS, FBX, and FBA. FBS is for general use where a wide range of color and variation in size are acceptable or required. FBX is used when a high degree of mechanical perfection, narrow color range, and minimal variation in size are required. FBA is nonuniform in color, size, and texture.

Hollow brick is also available in SW and MW grades. Like facing brick, hollow brick is further classified according to its appearance. HBS is for general use where a range of size and color variation are acceptable or desired. HBX is used when a high degree of mechanical perfection, narrow color range, and minimum variation in size are required. HBA is nonuniform in color, size, and texture.

There are many sizes of brick, but not all of them are available from all manufacturers. Some typical sizes are shown in Fig. 37.1 along with the common terms used to describe the various surfaces. The most common size is manufactured to an actual dimension of 3⅝ in thick, 2¼ in high, and 7⅝ in long. With a mortar joint of ⅜ in, this gives a modular size of 4 in thick and 8 in long. Three courses equal 8 in (200), the same as a standard concrete block course. Metric bricks are 90 mm wide and 190 mm long with 10 mm mortar joints.

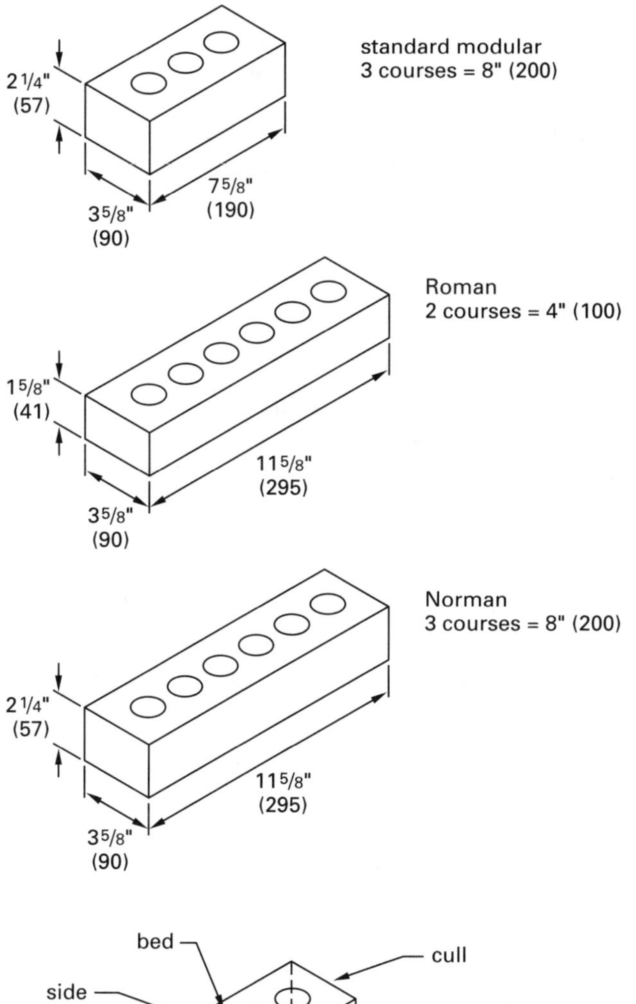

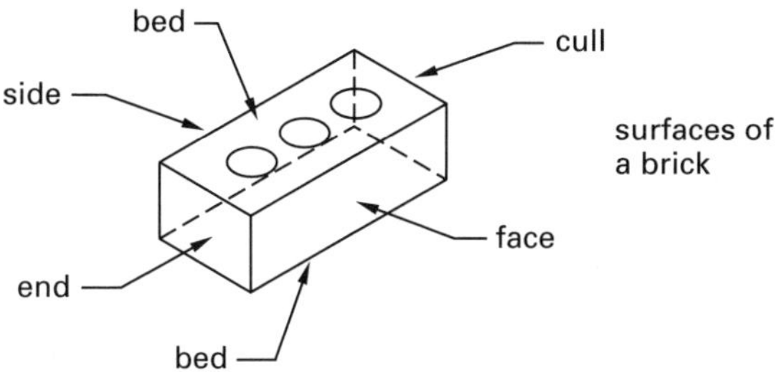

Figure 37.1 Sizes and Faces of Brick

Brick Coursing

Brick can be laid in a variety of patterns depending on which surface is oriented to the outside and what position it is in. Fig. 37.2 illustrates the methods of laying brick courses and the terms used to describe them. (A *course* is one continuous horizontal layer of masonry.)

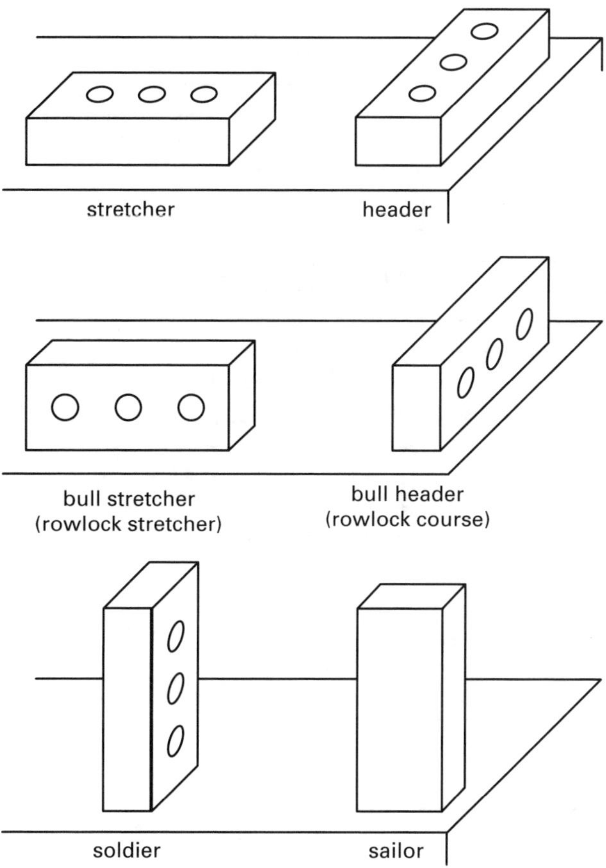

Figure 37.2 Brick Courses

The method of laying several courses in a wall is called the *bonding pattern*. Some common patterns are shown in Fig. 37.3. A brick wall is stronger if the joints do not align and the bricks overlap. Before steel joint reinforcing was used, bonding patterns were a way to accomplish this and to tie several wythes of brick together. A *wythe* is a continuous vertical section of a wall one masonry unit in thickness. For example, a header course was designed to hold a two-wythe wall together, since the length of the brick was as long as the thickness of the double wall.

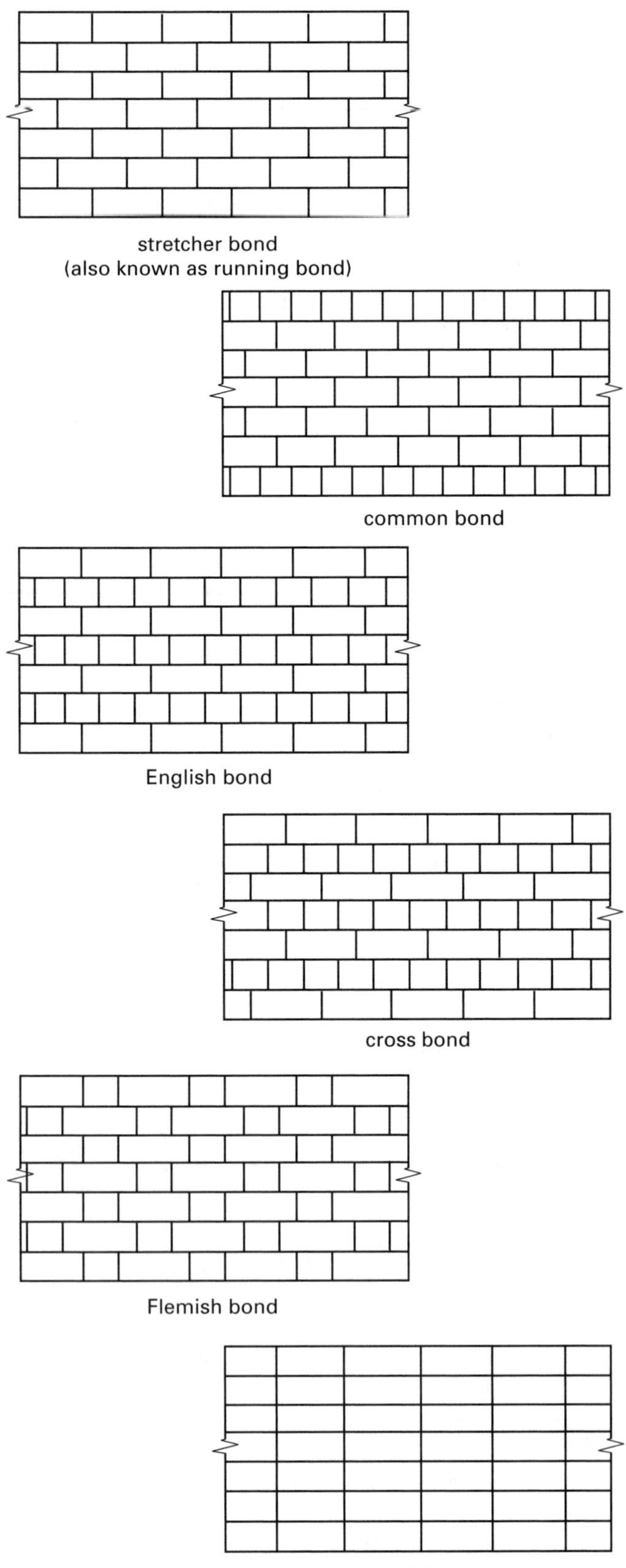

Figure 37.3 Brick Bond Patterns

With modern joint reinforcement and metal brick ties, bonding patterns are less important structurally than they once were, and brick coursing is most commonly used today for decorative purposes. Different coursing patterns can be used to differentiate among different parts of a building or to highlight wall openings and other features. Belt courses are often used to create a strong horizontal line in a masonry building. A *belt course*, sometimes called a *string course*, is a continuous band of masonry across the facade of a building or entirely around it, typically differentiated from other masonry by projecting from the face of the main surface, by being a different color or style, or by being made of a different type or thickness of masonry. If the belt course is located at the level of the window sills, it is called a *sill course*.

Brick Joints

Joints are a critical part of any masonry wall. The mortar in the joints not only holds the entire wall together, it also prevents infiltration of water and air. Bricks should be set in full beds of mortar, on both the bed joints and head joints.

After the brick is laid, the joints must be tooled. *Tooling* imparts a decorative effect to the wall, but more important, it makes the joint more watertight by compressing the mortar near the exposed surface. There are various types of mortar joints, as shown in Fig. 37.4, but only a few are recommended for exterior use because they shed water more effectively. These are the concave, flush, and vee joints. A weather-struck joint is sometimes acceptable for exterior use, but water running down the brick above the joint may not drip off and may instead run horizontally under the brick. If the joint is not tight, the water can be drawn through the joint by capillary action or by a pressure differential between the outside and inside of the wall.

In addition to the joints between individual masonry units, there must be horizontal and vertical joints to accommodate building movement caused by differential movement between materials and by temperature changes. If joints are not provided for such movement, cracking can occur in the joints or in the bricks themselves, resulting in water and air leakage and an unsightly appearance. In the worst case, stresses can be great enough without joints that the brick can crack and spall off.

There are several types of joints. Construction joints isolate the masonry from through-wall elements such as doors and windows. Control joints accommodate thermal expansion and contraction. Vertical control joints are constructed by separating two sections of masonry by about $^3/_8$ in to $^1/_2$ in (10 to 13) and filling the joint with a backing covered with a sealant. In many cases, a neoprene gasket is placed within the wall between the two sections of masonry. Expansion joints are similar to control joints and accommodate expansion from swelling of the brick. Through-building expansion

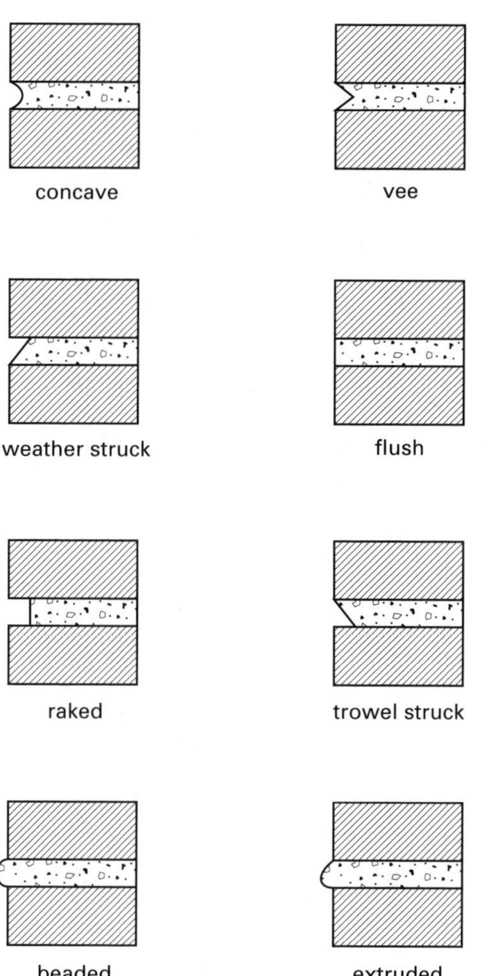

Figure 37.4 Brick Joints

joints are much larger and are used to completely separate two sections of a building.

Major expansion joints are usually spaced every 100 ft to 150 ft (30 m to 45 m) in large buildings. Expansion and control joints are spaced about every 20 ft (6 m) and at places where the wall changes direction, height, or thickness.

Horizontal expansion joints should be placed below shelf angles that support intermediate sections of brick and below beams and slabs above brick. One such detail is shown in Fig. 37.5. These types of joints prevent excessive stress from being placed on the brick from the deflection of the angle or beam above.

Brick Construction

Although brick is a basic, simple construction material, it must be designed, detailed, and installed correctly in order to function properly. There are many types of brick and masonry walls. The more common ones are shown in Fig. 37.6.

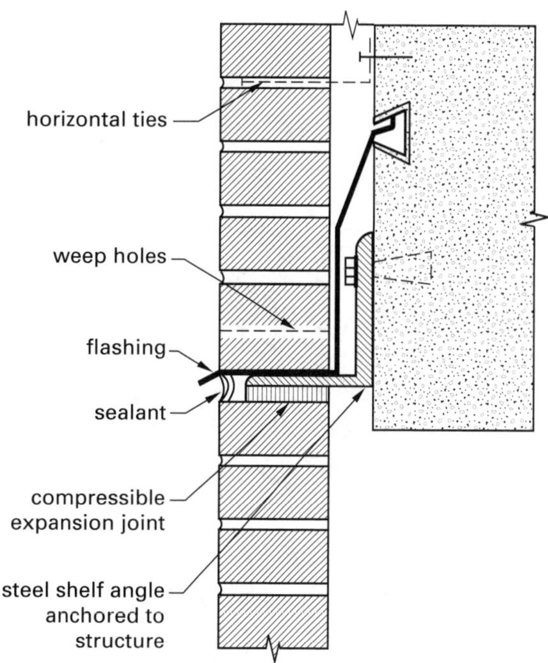

Figure 37.5 Typical Attachment of Brick Facing at Intermediate Floor

A *single-wythe wall* consists of one layer of brick that acts as either a loadbearing or nonloadbearing wall. Because it is unreinforced, the maximum ratio of unsupported height or length to thickness cannot exceed 20:1 for a solid wall or 18:1 for a hollow masonry wall.

A *cavity wall* consists of two wythes of brick separated by an air space. The two sections must be tied together. This is most often done with galvanized metal wall ties or continuous horizontal reinforcement placed 16 in (400) on center vertically.

A *reinforced grouted wall* also consists of two wythes of brick, but the cavity contains vertical and horizontal reinforcing bars and is completely filled with grout. Compared with cavity walls, grouted walls can carry heavier loads, have higher unsupported heights, and are better able to resist lateral loading.

A *veneer wall* is a single wythe of brick attached to some other type of construction, normally a wood-frame wall, as shown in Fig. 37.6(d). In a veneer wall, the masonry is for decorative and weatherproofing purposes rather than for structural support.

One of the most important considerations in designing a brick wall is watertightness. In order to accomplish this, the brick and mortar must first be properly selected for the climate conditions and loading, as previously discussed. The brick joints must be tooled correctly to shed water and

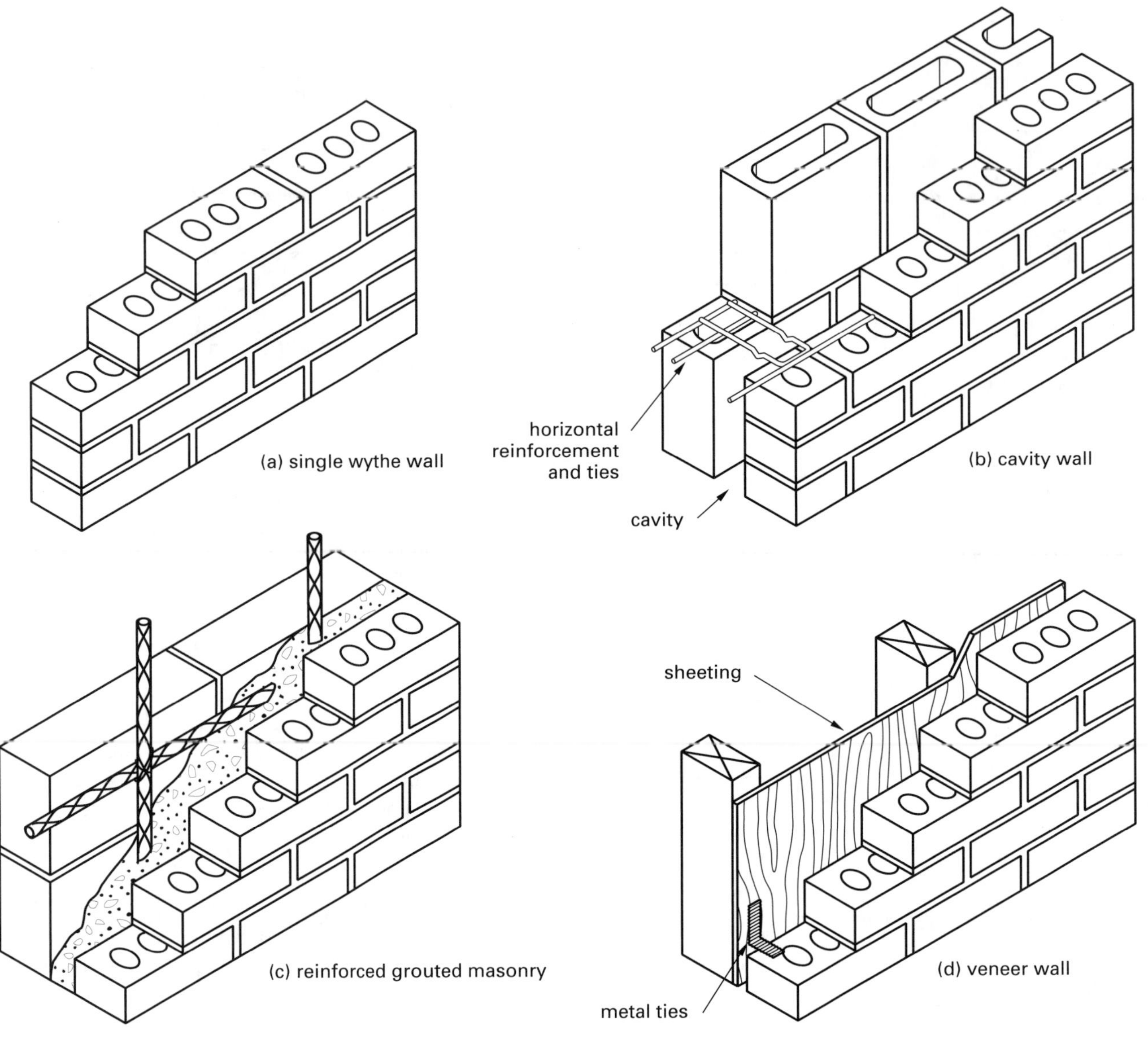

Figure 37.6 Types of Brick Walls

prevent expansion, and control joints must be located correctly to allow the wall to move without opening up cracks.

Next, the wall must be flashed and finished to prevent water from entering and to allow water that does enter to flow out. See Fig. 37.7. The tops of walls and parapets should be flashed and capped with coping, which should extend beyond the face of the wall and include drips to allow water to drain off instead of run down the wall. The slope of the coping is called the *wash*.

Base flashing should be installed at the bottom of the exterior wythe, extend up about 8 in to 10 in (200 to 250), and be set in a reglet or masonry joint in the interior wythe, as shown in Fig. 37.7. Weep holes should be located 24 in (600) on center horizontally in the lowest course of brick to allow any water that penetrates the wall to drip out. This type of detail should also be used over windows and at shelf angles, as shown in Fig. 37.5.

Brick is often used to form chimneys, both for fireplaces and for the venting of furnaces and other appliances. The top of a chimney must be at least 2 ft (610) higher than any point of the structure within a radius of 10 ft (3050). The tops of adjacent flue liners must be offset in height from 4 in to 12 in (100 to 300). If clay chimney flue liners are used in brick chimneys, they must extend a minimum of 2 in (50) above the top of the chimney cap.

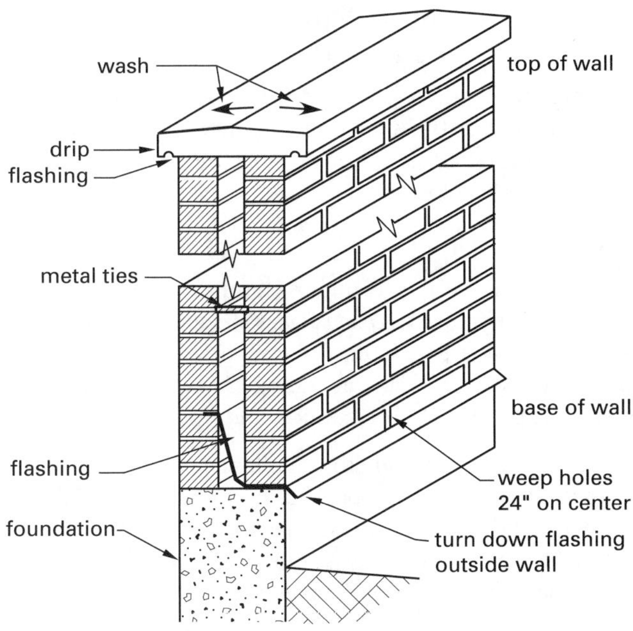

Figure 37.7 Brick Wall Construction

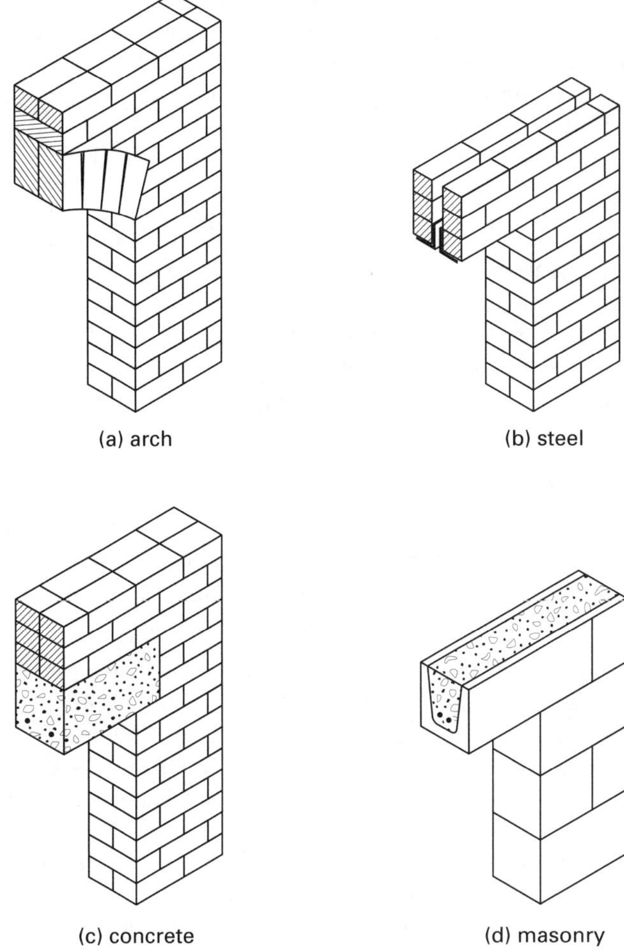

Figure 37.8 Masonry Lintels

Openings

Today, most openings in masonry construction are spanned with steel lintels. Steel lintels are often used because they are inexpensive and simple to install, and because their size and thickness can be varied to suit the span of the opening. Lintels should bear on each end of the supporting masonry such that the bearing capacity is not exceeded, but in no case should the bearing length be less than 6 in (150). However, there are several alternatives to steel lintels as shown in Fig. 37.8.

An arch is the traditional method of spanning a masonry opening because the compressive capabilities of the material are used. Alternately, a reinforced concrete beam (see Fig. 37.8(c)) or a fully grouted and reinforced concrete unit masonry bond beam (see Fig. 37.8(d)) can be used.

Regardless of the type of lintel used, there is always arch action over the opening. This is shown diagrammatically in Fig. 37.9. Unless a concentrated load or a floor load is near the top of the opening, the lintel only carries the weight of the wall above the opening in a triangular area defined by a 60° angle from each side of the opening.

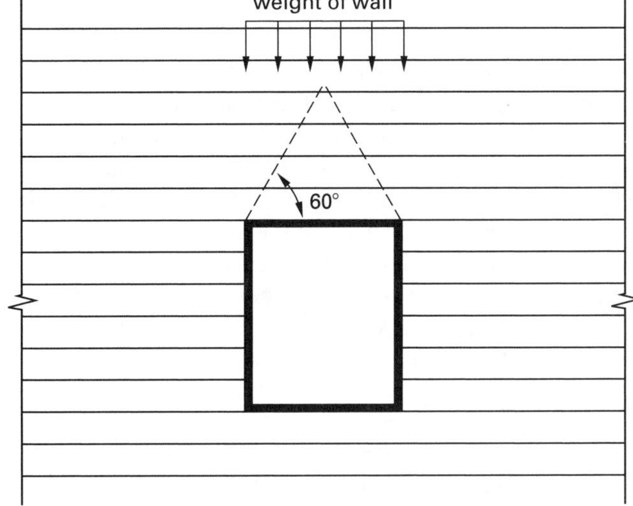

Figure 37.9 Arch Action in a Masonry Wall over an Opening

Efflorescence

Efflorescence is a white, crystalline deposit of water-soluble salts on the surface of brick masonry. It is caused when water seeps into the masonry and dissolves soluble salts present in the masonry, backup wall, mortar, or anything in contact with the wall. The dissolved salts are brought to the surface of the brick and appear when the water evaporates. Although unsightly, efflorescence is usually not harmful to the brick.

Efflorescence can be prevented or minimized by using materials with few or no soluble salts, by forming tight joints, and by detailing the wall to avoid water penetration. Both brick and mortar can be specified to contain no or limited amounts of soluble salts. If efflorescence does occur, it can be removed by dry brushing or by washing with a 5% solution of muriatic acid. A simple water wash can also be used, but this should be done in warm, dry weather so additional moisture is not added to the problem.

Cleaning and Restoration

At the completion of a job, brick should be cleaned with a mild 5% to 10% solution of muriatic acid in water and then washed off with clean water. A stiff brush can be used to remove loose mortar pieces, stains, and efflorescence.

Restoration of brick is more difficult. Over time, many problems can develop with brick. It can be physically damaged, mortar joints can deteriorate, and the entire surface can become dirty and stained. Damaged units must be carefully removed and replaced with new brick that matches the existing surface as closely as possible. If mortar has fallen out, it must be replaced with a process known as *tuck pointing* or *repointing*. In this process, the mortar in the areas to be redone is removed to about $2^1/_2$ times the depth of the joint. The joint is then cleaned and wetted with water. New mortar is pressed into the joint with a special tuck-pointing tool. High-lime mortar is best and should be applied in layers; each one applied after the previous one becomes thumbprint hard.

There are several ways to clean brick. The one used should be selected for compatibility with the nature of the soiling, the amount of cleaning desired, the surrounding environment in which the cleaning must take place, and the type of brick involved. High-pressure water washing is often effective but can wash away mortar and create swirl marks across the surface of the wall. Simply scrubbing the wall by hand with a brush and water may be required for soft brick. Acid solutions and other types of chemicals may be used to remove stubborn dirt and stains, but this, too, is not always appropriate for some brick and can damage surrounding surfaces. Abrasive cleaning using sand, glass beads, or walnut shells can be used in certain circumstances, but this can erode both brick and mortar. Refer to Ch. 2 for more information on cleaning historic structures.

OTHER UNIT MASONRY

Unit masonry is a term used to describe various types of building products assembled with mortar, of which brick is one kind. Other types of unit masonry include concrete block, clay tiles, ceramic veneer, stone, terra cotta, gypsum block, and glass block.

Concrete Block

Concrete block is the common term for concrete unit masonry, also known as *concrete masonry units* (CMUs). This building product is manufactured with cement, water, and various types of aggregate, including gravel, expanded shale or slate, expanded slag or pumice, and limestone cinders.

Concrete block is classified as hollow, loadbearing; solid, loadbearing; hollow, nonloadbearing; and solid, nonloadbearing. Solid units are those that are 75% or more solid material in any general cross section. Hollow units are those that are less than 75% solid material.

CMU dimensions are based on a nominal 4 in module with actual dimensions being $^3/_8$ in less than the nominal dimension to allow for mortar joints. Unit dimensions are referred to by width, height, and then length. One of the most common sizes is an 8 in by 8 in 16 in unit, which is actually $7^5/_8$ in wide and high and $15^5/_8$ in long. Common thicknesses are 4, 6, 8, 10, and 12 in, and common lengths are 8, 12, and 16 in. Concrete block is manufactured in a wide variety of shapes to suit particular applications. A few of the most common shapes are shown in Fig. 37.10. A metric block is 190 mm by 190 mm by 390 mm with 10 mm mortar joints.

Concrete block walls can be either single or double wythe, but they are normally single thickness, for greater economy and speed of construction. The cores allow walls to be reinforced and grouted if additional strength is required for vertical or lateral load bearing. As with brick walls, horizontal reinforcing is required every 16 in (406) on center. Walls can simply be grouted if additional fire or sound resistance is required. Figure 37.11 shows a typical reinforced, grouted concrete masonry wall. It also shows the use of a bond beam at the top of the wall that can serve as a lintel over openings, to provide bearing for the floor and roof structure, and to resist lateral loads from floor and roof diaphragms.

Because most concrete block walls consist of hollow units, it is important to understand equivalent thickness. *Equivalent thickness* is the solid thickness that would be obtained if the same amount of concrete contained in a hollow unit were recast without core holes. The value is calculated from the actual thickness of the block and the percentage of solid materials.

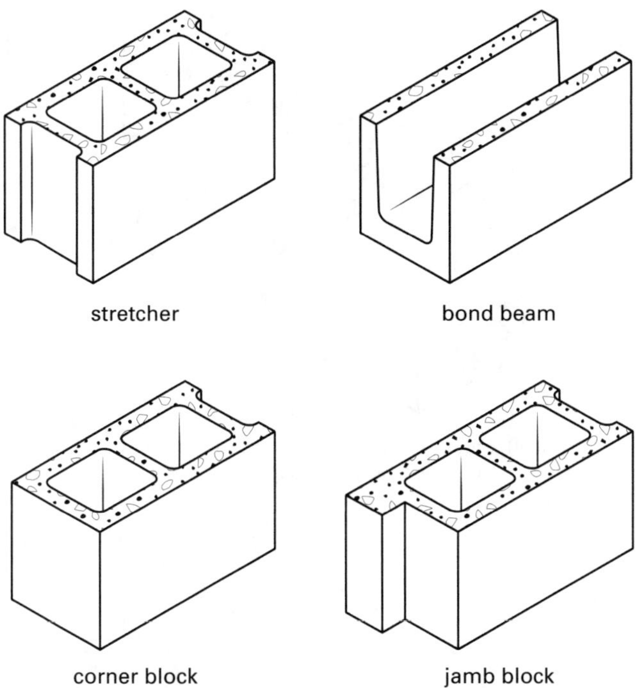

Figure 37.10 Typical Concrete Block Shapes

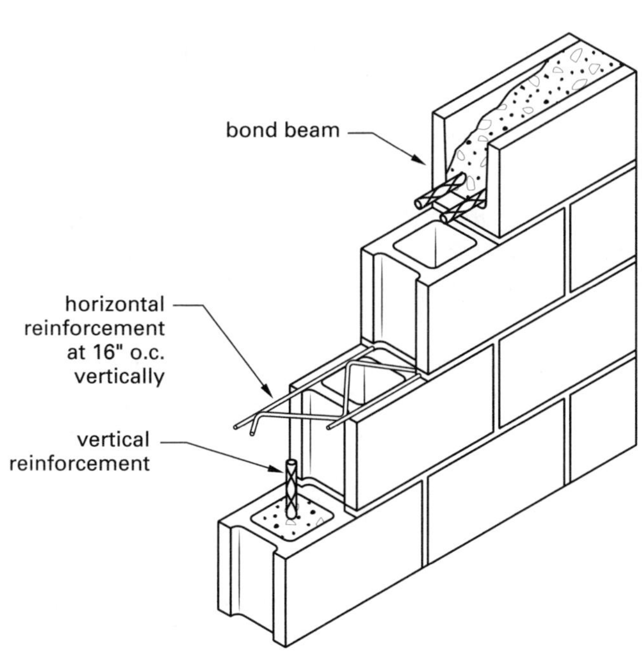

Figure 37.11 Reinforced, Grouted Concrete Masonry Wall

Example 37.1

What is the equivalent thickness of an 8 in thick concrete block that is 60% solids?

Actual thickness is $7^5/_8$ in (7.625). Equivalent thickness is then

$$(7.625 \text{ in})(0.60) = 4.58 \text{ in}$$

Fire ratings for masonry walls are based on this value and the type of material used in the manufacture of the block. Building codes give the required equivalent thicknesses for various hourly fire ratings. The designer must determine whether the thickness and type of concrete block being used meet the required fire rating.

Detailing for concrete block and brick walls is especially important to prevent cracking, leaking, and structural instability. Adequate expansion and control joints should be provided, and recommended horizontal joint reinforcing should be installed as stated previously. In addition, the connection of other materials to the masonry must be well detailed to maintain weather tightness and prevent other problems from developing.

One example of masonry detailing is shown in Fig. 37.12. This illustration shows a typical concrete block wall and parapet acting as a bearing wall for an open-web steel joist roof system. The concrete masonry is fully grouted and

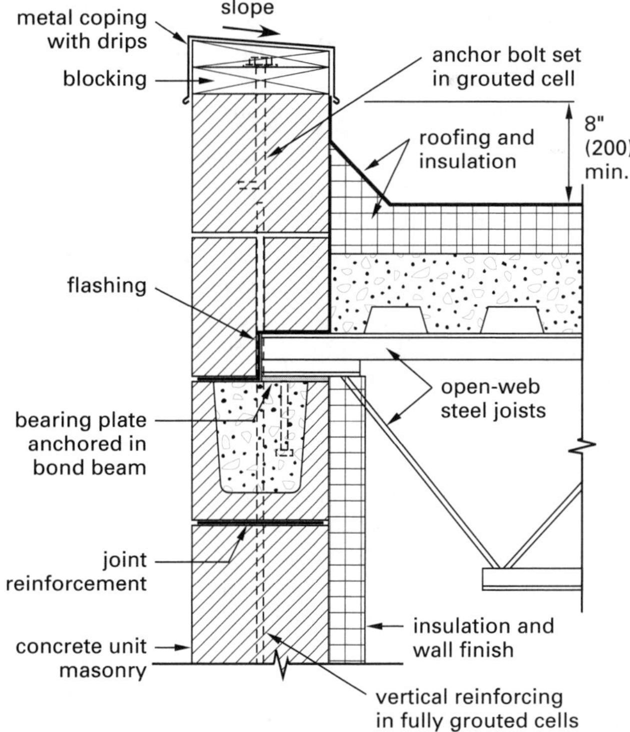

Figure 37.12 Reinforced Masonry Wall at Parapet

reinforced to provide the required bearing capacity, and a continuous bond beam with steel bearing plate is provided for attachment of the bar joist. Generally, the height of the parapet should not exceed three times its nominal thickness unless additional lateral support is provided. In this example the vertical reinforcing is continued into the parapet to anchor it to the rest of the wall and provide additional lateral support.

In this example a metal coping is used to keep water out of the wall, and it is sloped toward the roof to minimize the amount of water dripping on the side of the building. Alternately, a stone or precast concrete coping could be used if it is sloped and provided with drips to prevent water from seeping under its lower edge. To prevent leakage from moisture on the roof or from snow piled next to the parapet, the roofing is carried up under the coping. If the parapet is high, a counterflashing should be used with one edge fully embedded in a mortar joint. Additional flashing is used on the outside of the roof slab and joists.

Structural Clay Tile

Structural clay tile is made from burned clay and is formed into hollow units with parallel cells. Clay tile is available in loadbearing and nonloadbearing types and with glazed surfaces appropriate for finished exterior or interior walls.

Glazed structural clay facing tile is a loadbearing clay tile having a finish consisting of ceramic glaze fused to the body at above 1500°F (665°C). There are two grades of glazed structural tile: S grade (select) is for use with relatively narrow mortar joints, and SS grade (select sized) is for use where the variation of face dimensions must be very small.

Two types of structural clay tile are produced: side construction and end construction as shown in Fig. 37.13. Side construction tile is designed to receive its principal stress at right angles to the axis of the cells, and end construction tile is designed to receive principal stress parallel to the axis of the cells. Various sizes are produced in nominal 3, 4, 6, and 8 in widths and 6, 8, 12, and 16 in heights and lengths (76, 102, 152, and 203 mm widths and 152, 203, 305, and 406 mm heights and lengths).

Structural clay tile is used for loadbearing masonry walls that will be finished with other materials, as backup for exterior walls, and as nonloadbearing interior partitions. For interior partitions, glazed structural clay tile provides a wall with a hard, durable, decorative finish in one unit.

Terra Cotta

Terra cotta is a high-fired clay unit used for cladding and decorative purposes in building construction. Also known as *ceramic veneer*, terra cotta is made from enriched clay materials and fired at a high temperature which gives it a

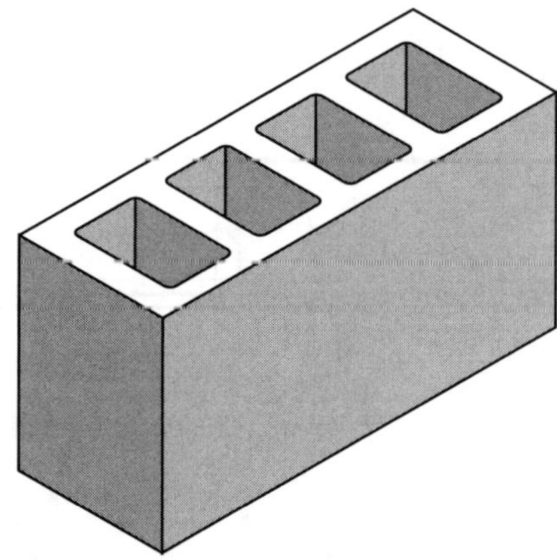

(a) end construction for loadbearing and nonloadbearing structural clay tile

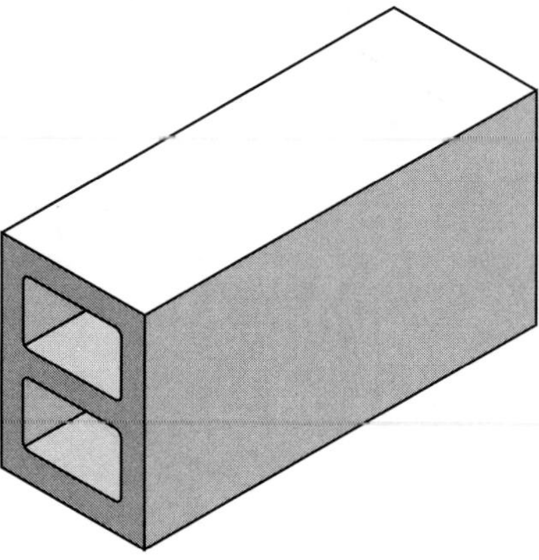

(b) side construction for structural clay facing tile

Figure 37.13 Structural Clay Tile

hardness and density that are not possible with other clay units. The base unit without the glaze is called the *bisque*. In most cases it is glazed to make it weather resistant and to provide a limitless range of colors.

Today, terra cotta is often manufactured to provide replacement pieces for building restoration. However, it has also gained popularity once again for new construction because it can be produced in a variety of custom shapes and sizes. Terra cotta can also be formed to look like stone, but with about one-tenth the weight of stone.

Terra cotta is manufactured by machine extrusion, by molding, or by hand carving for ornate work. The finished pieces are attached to a suitable substrate either by the adhesion method or the anchored method. For adhesion application, the back of the terra cotta is cast with dovetail slots and applied on a mortar bond. As with other veneer stone, building codes limit the maximum size of any one piece and the total weight to 15 lbm/ft^2 (73 kg/m^2). Adhered units cannot exceed 1$^1/_4$ in (32) in thickness.

Anchored terra cotta is attached with stainless steel or galvanized metal anchors (usually 8-gage wire) and a full grout backing. The anchors must be at least 1$^1/_4$ in (32) thick.

Because of the potential for glaze and base unit deterioration caused by moisture, terra cotta must be carefully detailed, flashed, and caulked to prevent water penetration. If moisture seeps between the bisque and the glaze, alternate freezing and thawing cycles can delaminate the glaze from the bisque. Water seeping into the clay body can also cause the clay to deteriorate.

Gypsum Block

Gypsum block or *tile* is solid or cored units cast of gypsum plaster that were previously used for nonloadbearing partitions and for fire protection of structural elements. They were available in thicknesses from 1$^1/_2$ in to 6 in with a standard face size of 12 in high and 30 in long. Gypsum block may be encountered when remodeling older buildings.

Glass Block

Glass block is manufactured as either a hollow or a solid unit with a clear, textured, or patterned face. The area inside the block is under a partial vacuum that improves the thermal insulating properties of the material. This property, along with the light-transmitting value and availability of obscuring patterns, makes glass block useful in both interior and exterior applications where a combination of light transmission, privacy, and insulation is needed. Solid block can also be used for flooring if it is correctly supported.

Generally, glass block does not provide rated fire resistance, but some assemblies are now available that qualify as 30-minute and 45-minute fire-rated enclosures in 1-hour walls. Underwriters Laboratories has classified some manufacturer's blocks for 60- or 90-minute ratings in openings up to 100 ft^2 (9.29 m^2) if no dimension is greater than 10 ft (3050).

Glass block is manufactured in a nominal thicknesses of 3 in and 4 in and in face sizes of 6 × 6, 8 × 8, 12 × 12, and 4 × 8 (152 × 152, 203 × 203, 305 × 305, and 102 × 203). The two standard thicknesses are 3$^1/_8$ in and 3$^7/_8$ in (79 and 98). The thinner block is commonly used for interior partitions. Other sizes are available from foreign manufacturers. Glass block is available in clear, textured, or patterned faces, and special blocks made by most manufacturers can be used to form 90° angles, end caps, and curves.

Glass block walls are laid in stack bond (with joints aligned rather than staggered) with Type S or N mortar and horizontal and vertical reinforcement in the joints. Because the coefficient of expansion of glass is a factor and the floor structure could experience deflection or some other building movement, it is recommended practice to provide expansion strips at the tops and sides of glass block partitions. Figure 37.14 shows typical detailing for the sill and head of an interior glass block wall.

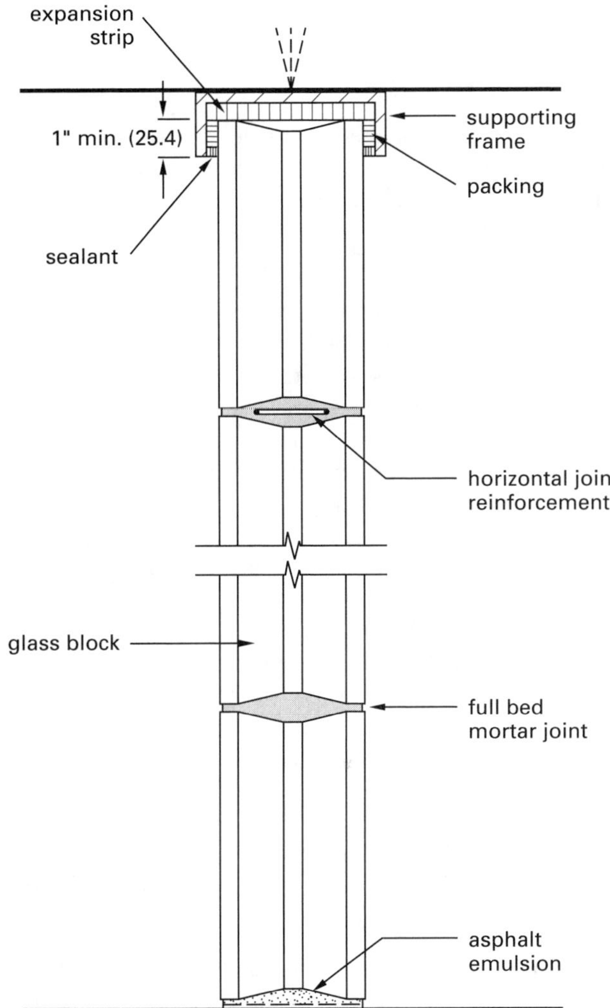

Figure 37.14 Glass Block Partition at Sill and Head

Intermediate stiffeners are required when a glass block partition exceeds the maximum sizes allowed by the building code.

Because glass block cannot be loadbearing, individual exterior panels are limited to 144 ft^2 (13.4 m^2) in total area and 15 ft (4572) in any direction. Interior panels are limited by code to 250 ft^2 (23.2 m^2) and 25 ft (7620) in any direction. Each panel must be supported with suitable structure both horizontally and vertically and with expansion joints provided at the structural support points.

Cast Stone

Cast stone is a precast concrete building product made to simulate natural stone. It is a mixture of portland cement, sand, and light aggregates. It is often used as a substitute for limestone and other smooth-faced stones for facing panels, trim, ornaments, columns, moldings, and copings, among other architectural elements.

STONE

Stone is a construction material made from various types of naturally occurring rock. *Rock* is a geologic term meaning solid and unconsolidated material in the earth's crust; whereas small, quarried pieces of rock are called *stone*.

There are three classifications of rock: igneous, sedimentary, and metamorphic. *Igneous rocks* are formed from the solidification of molten rock. Granite is a type of igneous rock. *Sedimentary rocks* consist of consolidated products of rock disintegration, sea shells, and various clays and silts. Sandstone and limestone are examples of common sedimentary rocks. *Metamorphic rocks* are formed of either igneous or sedimentary rocks that have been altered by pressure or intrusion of molten rock or other liquids over a long period of time. Marble and slate are metamorphic rocks.

Types of Construction Stone

Stone is one of civilization's oldest building materials. In the past, stone has been used as both a structural material and a finish material; however, with the increased cost of stone and the labor to place it, solid stone is seldom used any longer for structural purposes. Stone is now used in the form of thin slabs for exterior and interior finish, as flooring, countertops, stair treads, and various types of trim pieces in masonry construction. Stone chips are widely used with cement for terrazzo.

Five of the most common stones used in construction include granite, marble, limestone, slate, and sandstone. Table 37.3 lists the most common uses of the various types of stone.

Stone Finishes

A wide variety of finishes is available for the different types of stone used in construction. Each type of stone has its own nomenclature, which is summarized in Table 37.4.

Stone finishes should be selected for the conditions under which they will be used. For example, highly polished surfaces are not appropriate for flooring or stairs where a small amount of water will make them very slippery. Rough finishes may not be appropriate for exterior walls in an environment where dirt and pollution may collect and be difficult to clean off.

Table 37.3

Stones Used in Construction

types	uses
granite	exterior wall panels
	interior finish panels
	flooring
	base
	trim
	water courses
	countertops
	thresholds
	lintels
	windowsills
	stair treads
	hearths
	sculpture
	chips for terrazzo
marble	exterior wall panels
	interior finish panels
	flooring
	base
	trim
	toilet partitions
	thresholds
	tabletops
	stair treads
	hearths
	windowsills
	sculpture
	chips for terrazzo
limestone	exterior wall panels
	coping
	lintels
	sculptured trim
slate	flooring
	stair treads
	roofing
	blackboards
	countertops
sandstone	flooring
	exterior paving

Table 37.4
Types of Stone Finishes

marble finishes	
polished	a glossy surface that brings out the full color and character of the marble (not recommended for floor finishes)
honed	a satin-smooth surface with little or no gloss (recommended for commercial floors)
sandblasted	a matte-textured surface with no gloss (recommended for exterior use)
abrasive	a flat, nonreflective surface suitable for exterior use, stair treads, and other nonslip surfaces
wet-sand	a smooth surface suitable for stair treads and other nonslip surfaces
granite finishes	
polished	mirror gloss with sharp reflections
honed	dull sheen without reflections
fine-rubbed	smooth and free from scratches; no sheen
rubbed	plane surface with occasional slight "trails" or scratches
shot-ground	plane surface with pronounced circular markings or trails having no regular pattern
thermal (flame)	plane surface with flame finish applied by mechanically controlled means to ensure uniformity; surface coarseness varies, depending upon grain structure of granite
sandblasted, fine stipple	plane surface, slightly pebbled, with occasional slight trails or scratches
sandblasted, coarse stipple	coarse plane surface produced by blasting with an abrasive; coarseness varies with type of preparatory finish and grain structure of granite
8-cut	fine bush-hammered; interrupted parallel markings not over $^3/_{32}$ in (2) apart; a corrugated finish
6-cut	medium bush-hammered; markings not more than $^1/_8$ in (3) apart
4-cut	coarse bush-hammered; markings not more than $^7/_{32}$ in (5.5) apart
sawn	relatively plane surface, with texture ranging from wire sawn (a close approximation of rubbed finish) to shot sawn, with scorings $^3/_{32}$ in (2) in depth; gang saws produce parallel scorings; rotary or circular saws make circular scorings; shot-sawn surfaces are sandblasted to remove all rust stains and iron particles
limestone finishes	
smooth finish	machine finish producing a uniform honed finish; uses only select grade or standard grade
plucked	rough texture produced by rough planing the surface of the stone
machine tooled	finish made by cutting parallel, concave grooves in the stone with 4, 6, or 8 grooves to the inch; depth of the grooves range from $^1/_{32}$ in to $^1/_{16}$ in (0.8 to 1.6)
chat-sawed	coarse, pebbled surface that closely resembles the appearance of sandblasting; sometimes contains shallow saw marks or parallel scores; direction of score or saw marks will be vertical and/or horizontal in the wall unless the direction is specified
shot-sawed	coarse, uneven finish ranging from a pebbled surface to one rippled with irregular, roughly parallel grooves; steel shot used during gang-sawing rusts during process, adding permanent brown tones to the natural color variations
split face	rough, uneven, concave-convex finish produced by splitting action; limits stone sizes to 1 ft 4 in high by 4 ft 0 in long; available in ashlar or similar stone veneer only
rock face	similar to split face except that the face of the stone has been dressed by machine or by hand to produce bold convex projection along the face of the stone

Stone Coursing

Stone is classified by the way it is shaped and prepared prior to installation. Stone used with little or no shaping is called *rubble*, stone with slightly shaped edges resulting in vertical joints is called *squared stone*, and highly shaped stone is called *ashlar*. Ashlar is also referred to as *cut stone* and consists of thick pieces of stone.

Several methods are used to arrange stones in a wall. They are categorized into range, broken range, and random. *Range masonry* arranges stones in uniform courses for the entire length of the wall. In *broken range masonry*, stones are coursed for short distances. *Random masonry* is devoid of coursing or any attempt to align vertical joints. Figure 37.15 shows some common stone wall patterns.

Another commonly used classification of stone is *veneer stone*, so called because it is applied in relatively thin sheets, from $^3/_4$ in to $1^1/_4$ in (19 to 32) thick, over a structural support system. With improved cutting methods, it is also possible to cut very thin slabs, about $^3/_8$ in (10) thick, that can be mastic applied to a suitable backup wall. These tiles are commonly manufactured in small shapes, normally 12 in by 12 in (305 by 305) or similar sizes.

Stone Construction

Some types of stone work, such as steps, trim, coping, and belt courses, still employ cut stone, often called *dimension stone*. However, because the majority of stone wall finishes use veneer, it is important to know how such work is applied and anchored to structural backup walls. Many types of metal clamps and anchors are available for attaching cut stone and veneer stone to concrete, masonry, and steel construction. A few of the common methods of anchoring and forming corner joints are shown in Figs. 37.16 and 37.17. In many cases, the space around the anchoring device between the back of the stone and the structural wall is filled with plaster of paris spots to plumb the stone and hold it away from the wall. The joints of stone should be filled with nonstaining portland cement mortar. Figure 37.18 shows a typical installation of stone veneer on a concrete frame building at the roof line.

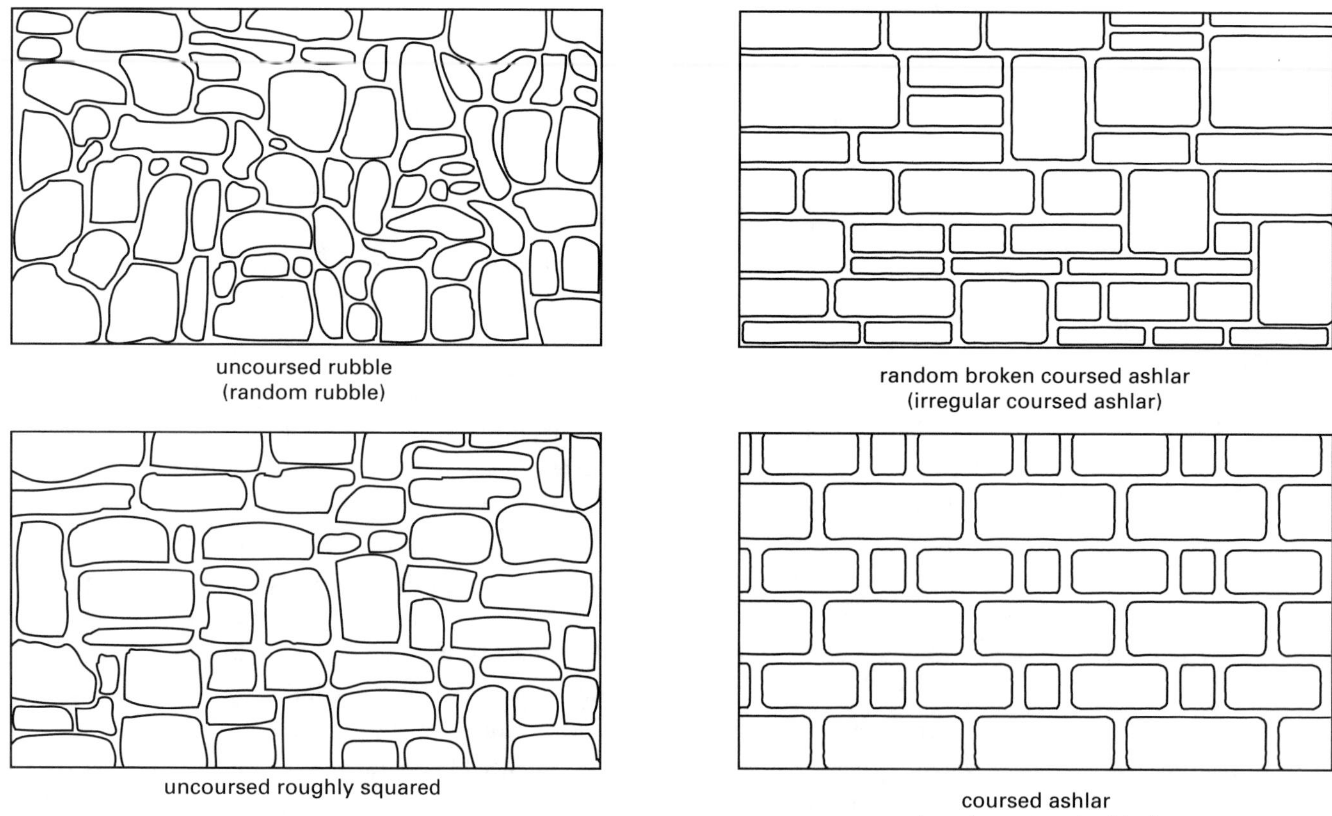

Figure 37.15 Stone Patterns

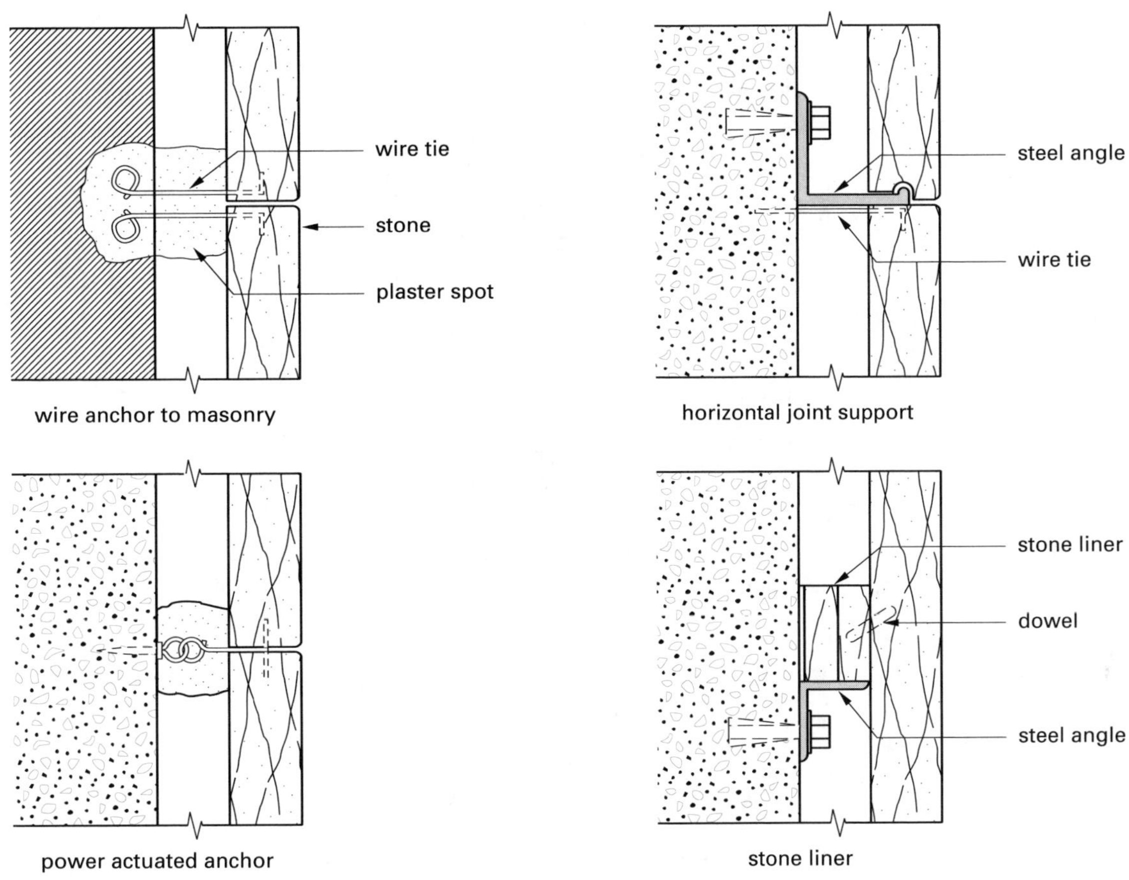

Figure 37.16 Veneer Stone Anchoring Details

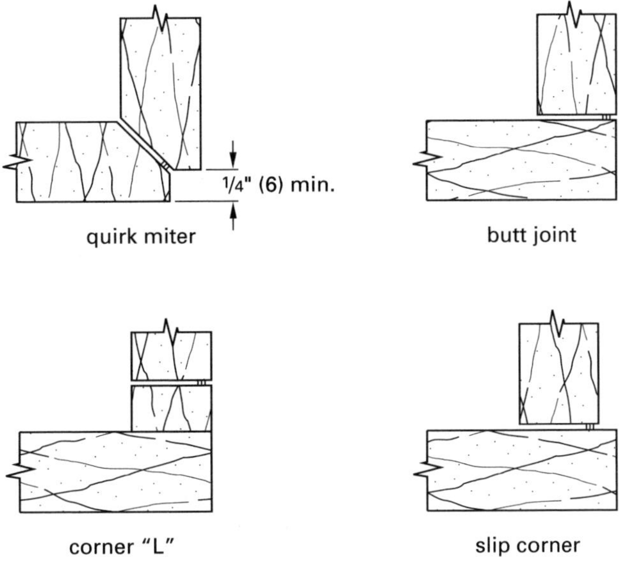

Figure 37.17 Veneer Stone Corner Joints

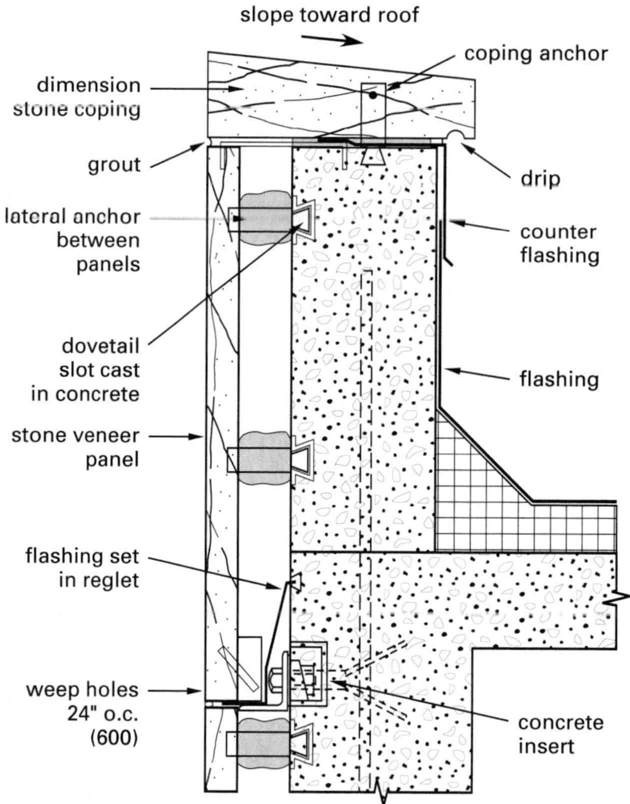

Figure 37.18 Stone Veneer at Parapet

38 METALS

Metals are the most versatile of all construction materials. Although they begin as natural elements, the process of refining, manufacturing, forming, and finishing metals allows an almost unlimited variety of forms and uses. Metals have been used in construction in a limited way for centuries, from the lead pipes of the Romans to the decorative grilles and doors of the English Medieval period. However, it has only been in the last 200 years that metals have seen widespread use in both structural and decorative applications.

HISTORY OF METALS

The first use of metals began over 3000 years before Christ when copper was produced by melting ores. Later, humans discovered that the copper could be strengthened by adding small amounts of tin to produce bronze. The Bronze Age continued until about 1200 B.C. when iron smelting was discovered and metal replaced bronze as the basic material for weapons, tools, and other utensils.

By the fourteenth century, cast iron was generally available in Europe, but its use in construction was largely restricted to door fittings, decorative grilles, and other small building parts. Structurally, iron chains were used by Brunelleschi to prevent the dome of Florence Cathedral from spreading (1463) and by Michelangelo for the same purpose on the dome of St. Peter's Cathedral (1585). Cast iron pipes were used to supply water to the gardens at Versailles around 1664.

The invention that started the widespread use of iron in construction (and that helped fuel the Industrial Revolution) occurred when Abraham Darby introduced the use of coke for smelting the metal in 1709. Substituting coke for charcoal eliminated the impurities caused by charcoal and resulted in stronger, higher quality iron. By 1876 iron was being used for roof structures in France.

In 1779, Abraham Darby III made the first major use of cast iron structural elements in a bridge over the river Severn at Coalbrookdale, England. Other cast iron bridges followed this, and at about the same time cast iron columns replaced wood columns in some English cotton mills.

As the nineteenth century began, cast iron columns were commonly used for interior columns in the English mills. In other construction, the new material was being employed for railway station roofs, exhibition halls, and greenhouses. The first use of cast iron for both columns and I-beams for the entire framework of a building was in a cotton mill at Salford, Manchester. It was built by Matthew Boulton and James Watt. Although this building still used exterior masonry bearing walls, it is considered the precursor to the steel-framed buildings in Chicago during the latter part of the century.

Notable buildings during the first half of the century included the Royal Pavilion at Brighton by John Nash (1818), the Greenhouse of the Botanical Gardens in Paris by Rouhault (1833), and the Library of Saint Geneviève in Paris by Henri Labrouste (1843). At midcentury (1851), the Crystal Palace in London became the symbol of the age when Joseph Paxton designed the huge building using prefabricated parts and plate glass, which allowed the structure to be completed in only nine months. The Crystal Palace was followed by the Eiffel Tower, built for the Paris exhibition of 1889, and by the Halle des Machines, which used a 375 ft (114 m) arch formed of cast iron.

A major technical improvement in iron construction happened in 1856 when Henry Bessemer developed the Bessemer process for making steel inexpensively. Although the process was first used to make railroad rails, it produced better-quality steel (lower carbon content) and provided the raw materials for buildings that followed. In 1868 the open-hearth process improved on this further by shortening the time required for production and allowing scrap iron to be used in larger quantities.

In the United States in 1848, James Bogardus constructed a five-story factory in New York. This building was significant because it used cast iron columns instead of masonry for the outside walls. Ten years later Bogardus designed a similar building for Harper and Brothers where he used an iron framework with large expanses of glass as infill.

The period from 1850 to the late 1880s was called the *Cast Iron Age* in the United States because of the widespread use of the material in New York, Chicago, Saint Louis, and elsewhere across the country.

In 1885 William Le Baron Jenney designed what is considered the first skyscraper. It was the ten-story Home Insurance Building in Chicago. The building utilized cast iron columns for both the interior and exterior columns and employed the new Bessemer steel girders. In addition, the building was fireproofed.

Jenney also designed the Leiter Building in Chicago. This eight-story structure was one of the first where the architecture and engineering construction were integrated into one expression. The skeleton frame determined the form even though the exterior columns were protected by masonry. Other architects were quick to adopt the new iron and steel materials. Because most of the early and innovative work occurred in Chicago, the use of the iron skeleton came to be called "Chicago Construction."

As a strictly structural device, the steel skeleton was quickly adopted. Most architects during the latter half of the nineteenth and first half of the twentieth century still cloaked the steel in masonry and other materials. It was Mies van der Rohe who was one of the first architects to make the material and its structural purpose part of the form of the building. From his early studies for glass skyscrapers in 1919 to his later work, the steel frame was always elegantly detailed and shown, even if a false grid of steel had to be applied over the fireproofed structural frame. His most notable buildings include structures for the Illinois Institute of Technology in Chicago (from 1939 on) and the 860 Lake Shore Drive apartments (1951), also in Chicago.

BASIC MATERIALS AND PROCESSES

In their natural form, metals exist in combination with other elements and substances in metallic ores. *Smelting* is the process of refining the ores to extract the pure metal. Once the basic metal is obtained, it usually undergoes further treatment to eliminate any impurities that might affect its use.

Metals for construction are seldom used in their pure form but are combined with other elements to form alloys. The addition of other substances to the base metal imparts desirable characteristics. For example, adding chromium and nickel to steel makes the steel corrosion resistant, or stainless. It is the ability to form alloys that makes metals so versatile.

Fabricating Metals

Fabrication is the process of forming and shaping refined metal into the desired condition. The most basic fabrication method is *casting*, which has been used for centuries. In this process, molten metal is poured into a form where it is allowed to cool and harden into the desired shape. The iron columns used in the nineteenth century were cast shapes. Today, the casting process is still used for decorative shapes, pipe valves, and some hardware.

Rolling is the process of passing metal through rollers to produce the needed shape. Rolling can be done while the metal is hot or cold. Hot rolling tends to eliminate flaws in the metal, whereas cold rolling increases the metal's strength and elastic limit but decreases its ductility. Most of the structural steel shapes such as wide-flange beams and channel sections are hot rolled. Many smaller, relatively thin steel shapes are cold rolled for increased strength. All metals except iron can be formed by this method.

Extruding pushes metal through a die to form a shape. Many aluminum sections are formed this way, especially decorative sections and those used for door and window frames. One advantage to the extruding process is that if a sufficiently large quantity is required, special dies can be made and custom shapes extruded for a particular job.

Drawing is similar to extruding, but the metal is pulled through a die instead of being pushed through. The drawing process usually reduces the size of the piece or changes its shape and also improves the strength and surface qualities of the metal. Drawing is applicable for all metals except iron.

There are also many ways metal can be fabricated with mechanical forming. *Bending* changes the shape of tubes and extruded shapes by passing them through various kinds of rolling machines and presses. *Brake forming* takes plates and sheets of metal and makes successive one-directional bends to fabricate the shape. *Spinning* forms round shapes on a lathe. *Embossing* makes patterns on flat sheets of metal by passing them through a machine with the embossing pattern on rollers.

Part of the fabrication process of many metals includes some type of heat treatment. Thermal treatments are used to change the strength or workability of the material. Although any metal can be heat treated, the process is most often used with steel for various structural purposes.

Annealing is a process in which the metal is reheated and slowly cooled to obtain a more ductile metal, which will have improved its machinability and cold-forming characteristics.

Quenching involves heating the metal (most often steel) to a certain temperature and then rapidly cooling it by complete submersion in water or some other liquid. This strengthens the steel.

Tempering is similar to quenching but does not involve rapid cooling. It is also used to improve the strength and workability of steel.

Case hardening produces a hard-surface steel over a relatively softer core.

Finishing Metals

There are three general types of metal finishes. Not all of these finishes are used on all metals, but the classification helps in understanding the processes involved. Each metal type has its particular finishing systems and its own terminology, which will be discussed in the individual sections concerning each metal.

Mechanical finishes alter the surface of the metal in some way. This alteration may be as simple as the way the metal comes from the final forming process or may result from more refined finishing methods, such as grinding or buffing.

Chemical finishes are produced by altering the surface of the metal with some type of chemical process. They may simply clean and prepare the surface for other types of finishes or they may protect or color the metal. Anodizing of aluminum is one type of chemical finish in which the metal is immersed in an electrolytic bath and a current is applied to the metal. In the process, the finish, which can include various colors, becomes an integral part of the aluminum structure, producing a very durable surface.

Coatings are finishes that consist of applied materials that may be for protection of the metal or purely decorative. Coatings may be clear or opaque.

In deciding on the type of finish, several considerations should be reviewed. These include appearance, the amount of protection required, initial cost, long-term or life-cycle cost, and required maintenance.

Joining Metals

There are several methods of joining metals. The selection depends on the type of metal being joined, the working space available for the operation, and the final appearance desired.

All metals can be mechanically joined using accessories such as screws, bolts, and clips. It is common to use high-strength bolts in fastening structural steel. Bolts can also be used to fasten lighter metals such as aluminum and bronze. Bolts are useful when it is necessary to join two dissimilar metals. If potentially damaging galvanic action (electrolysis) might take place between the two metals, a plastic or rubber washer is used to separate them.

Screws can be used to join light-gage metal. Self-tapping screws are typically used to fasten metal or other materials to steel studs or other light framing. Screws are also appropriate for securing light-gage metals to other substrates, such as wood. However, heavier metals must be tapped with threads before screws can be used.

Welding is the joining of two metals by heating them above their melting point. When they cool, the metals physically form one piece of metal. Welding is commonly used for joining structural steel. Welding is not appropriate for thin metals or situations where appearance is important unless the weld can be ground smooth and finished to match the adjacent metal.

Brazing is the joining of two metals at an intermediate temperature using a nonferrous filler metal with a melting point that is above 800°F (427°C) but lower than welding. Brazing is usually used for brass, bronze, and some aluminums. It results in a clean joint, although some buffing may be required if a completely smooth joint is desired.

Soldering is the joining of two metals using lead-based or tin-based alloy solder filler metal that melts below 500°F (260°C).

Metals can also be fastened with adhesives. This method is usually reserved for small trim pieces and sheet stock where the strength of the bond is not critical. Normally, adhesives are used when fastening metals to other substrates such as plywood and particle board.

Properties of Metals

In selecting, detailing, and specifying metals, the architect must have a rudimentary knowledge of several of the unique properties of the various metals. These include gage sizing, galvanic action, and coefficients of expansion.

The thickness of large steel members is usually expressed in fractions or decimals of an inch. However, sheet steel and nonferrous metals of tubing, strips, and sheets are expressed with a gage number. Gage sizing to indicate the thickness of metal started in the early days of the metal industries and was based on the weight of a square foot of a metal. Obviously, the weight would depend on the density of the metal and whether there were any coatings, such as galvanized steel. To confuse matters, different companies had their own gages and different standards have been adopted over the years. As a result, gage is only a rough approximation of a metal's thickness. Even within the same company, the actual thickness may vary even though the gage is the same. Because of the variations, it is preferable to call out the actual thickness desired in decimals of an inch or in millimeters.

Galvanic action is the corrosion resulting when dissimilar metals come in contact with each other in the presence of an electrolyte such as moisture. In the process, called *electrolysis*, a mild electric current is set up between the two metals, gradually corroding one while the other remains intact.

The following list represents the galvanic series in the presence of seawater, which is a powerful electrolyte; the metals are listed in the order of their susceptibility to corrosion. The farther apart the metals are from each other on the list, the greater the possibility for corrosion when they are in contact.

In many cases, the electromotive scale of adjacent metals in this list is so close together that few problems would be encountered. For example, the electromotive difference between brass and tin is only 0.01 V while that between zinc and aluminum is 0.24 V.

- zinc
- aluminum
- steel or iron
- 304 stainless steel (active)
- copper
- bronze
- brass
- tin
- lead
- 316 stainless steel (active)
- titanium
- 304 stainless steel (passive)
- gold

To avoid galvanic action, use identical metals when they must be in contact, or separate the metals with nonconducting materials such as neoprene, plastic, or rubber. If these precautions are not possible, use metals as close to each other on the galvanic series as possible. Electrolysis is most severe in humid, marine environments where there is an abundance of seawater; it is less severe in dry climates.

Metals expand and contract with changes in temperature more than many other materials, so it is important to allow for changes in size when designing and detailing metal building components. Table 38.1 lists some of the coefficients of thermal expansion for various metals, along with a few other materials for comparison. Most often, slip joints or expansion joints are provided to accommodate such movement when the building assembly is primarily composed of metal. When metal is used within other materials, such as an aluminum frame within a concrete opening, allowances must be made for the differential movement.

Table 38.1

Coefficients of Thermal Expansion for Metals (Temperature Range 68–212°F (20–100°C))

	coefficient of expansion	
	$\times 10^{-6}$ in/°F	$\times 10^{-6}$ mm/°C
metal		
structural steel	6.5	11.7
copper, alloy 110	9.3	16.8
stainless steel, 302	9.9	17.8
commercial bronze, alloy 220	10.2	18.1
red brass, alloy 230	10.2	18.1
aluminum	12.8	23.1
lead	15.9	28.6
other materials		
wood	2.7	4.9
glass	5.1	9.2
concrete	5.5	9.9

FERROUS METALS

There are two major classifications of metals: ferrous and nonferrous. *Ferrous metals* are those that contain a substantial amount of iron; *nonferrous metals* are those that do not. The primary types of ferrous metals used in the construction industry include iron, steel, stainless steel, and other special steel alloys.

Wrought and Cast Iron

All ferrous metals contain a majority of iron, some carbon, and other elements in the form of impurities or components mixed with the iron to form an alloy. The amount of carbon and other elements determines the strength, ductility, and other properties of the ferrous metal.

Wrought iron is iron with a very low carbon content (less than about 0.30%) and a substantial amount of slag. It is similar in chemical composition to low-carbon steel, but most of the impurities are in the slag, which is mechanically mixed with the iron. Because of its low carbon content, wrought iron is soft, ductile, and resistant to corrosion. Its use in construction is limited to ornamental iron work such as gates, grilles, and fences.

Cast iron is iron with a carbon content above 2%. With this high percentage of carbon, it is very hard, but brittle. Cast iron was used extensively in the nineteenth century for columns and beams in such structures as the Crystal Palace, mill buildings in New England, and some of the early commercial buildings in New York City.

Cast iron with a low silicon content is called white cast iron and has little use in construction unless it is processed in such a way as to produce malleable iron. Cast iron with a high silicon content is called *grey cast iron* and is used for various types of castings such as plumbing valves, pipes, and hardware.

Steel

Steel is one of the most widely used metals because of its many advantages, which include high strength, ductility, uniformity of manufacture, variety of shapes and sizes, and ease and speed of erection. *Ductility* is a property that allows steel to withstand excessive deformations due to high tensile stresses without failure. This property makes steel useful for earthquake-resistant structures. Steel is used in a variety of structural and nonstructural applications including columns, beams, concrete reinforcement, fasteners of all types, curtain wall panels, interior finish panels and trim, pipes, flashing, and electrical conduit.

Because steel is manufactured under carefully controlled conditions, its composition, size, and strength can be uniformly predicted. Therefore, steel structures do not have to be overdesigned to compensate for manufacturing or erection variables as do concrete or timber structures.

In spite of the advantages, however, steel does have properties that must be accounted for. Most notable are its reduction in strength when subjected to fire and its tendency to corrode in the presence of moisture. Steel itself does not burn, but it deforms when exposed to high temperatures. As a result, steel must be protected with fire-resistant materials, such as sprayed-on cementitious material, gypsum board, or concrete. This adds to the overall cost but is usually justified when the many advantages are considered.

As with any ferrous material, steel will rust and otherwise corrode if not protected. This can be prevented by including other elements in the steel to resist corrosion (stainless steel is an example of a material that uses this method) or by covering the steel with paint or some other type of protective coating.

Steel can also be bonderized. To *bonderize* steel (or any metal) is to coat it with an anticorrosive phosphate solution in preparation for the application of paint, enamel, or lacquer.

Steel is composed primarily of iron with small amounts of carbon and other elements that are part of the alloy, either as impurities left over from manufacturing or deliberately added to impart certain desired qualities to the alloy. In medium-carbon steel used in construction, these other elements include manganese (from 0.5% to 1.0%), silicon (from 0.25% to 0.75%), phosphorus, and sulfur. Phosphorus and sulfur in excessive amounts are harmful because they affect weldability and make steel brittle.

The percentage of carbon present affects the strength and ductility of steel. As carbon is added, the strength increases but the ductility decreases. *Low-carbon steel* contains from 0.06% to 0.30% carbon, *medium-carbon steel* has from 0.30% to 0.50% carbon, and *high-carbon steel* contains from 0.50% to 0.80% carbon. *Standard structural steel* has from 0.20% to 0.50% carbon.

The most common type of steel for structural use is ASTM A36, which means that the steel is manufactured according to the American Society for Testing and Materials (ASTM) specification number A36. The yield point for this steel is 36 ksi (248 MPa). Other high-strength steels include A242, A440, and A441 steel, which have yield points of 46 ksi or 50 ksi (317 MPa or 345 MPa).

Steel and other metals can be heat treated in a number of ways. There are many types of heat treatment used to alter the physical properties of the metal. Some of the more common for architectural metals are quenching and tempering, annealing, and case hardening. *Quenching and tempering* involves heating the steel to a certain temperature, to alter its crystalline structure, and then cooling it quickly. At this point the steel is too brittle, so it is tempered by heating it again at a lower temperature and cooling it slowly. *Annealing* is a process of heating the metal and then slowly cooling it. This relieves stresses in the metal caused by cold working, and can alter ductility, strength, and other mechanical properties. *Case hardening* is a process for heating a metal and diffusing a gas or liquid, commonly carbon or nitrogen, into its surface, creating a thin layer of a harder alloy. The metal is then given an appropriate heat treatment.

Stainless Steel

Stainless steel is a steel alloy containing a minimum of 11% chromium. In addition, nickel is often added to increase the corrosion resistance and improve cold workability. Additional trace elements such as manganese, molybdenum, and aluminum are added to impart certain characteristics.

Stainless steel is highly corrosion resistant and stronger than other architectural metals. Its resistance to corrosion results from the formation of a chromium-oxide film on the surface of the metal. If the film is scratched or otherwise damaged it will re-form as the metal is exposed to oxygen in the air. This chromium-oxide film layer gives the stainless steel *passivity*, which means that a layer of nonreactive molecules does not allow metal ions at the surface to migrate into solution. Most stainless steel remains passive, but when this layer is lost by abrasion or chemical etching that introduces free iron or chlorides, the surface can become active. The stainless steel can also become active when exposed to certain chemical agents. This affects not only resistance to corrosion but also to the position of the stainless steel in the galvanic series.

Of the nearly 40 types of stainless steel produced, only eight are used for building purposes, six for products, and two for fasteners. They are labeled by number designation of the American Iron and Steel Institute (AISI) and include the following, which are the most commonly used in construction.

- *Type 302*. This contains 18% chromium and 8% nickel and has traditionally been one of the most widely used stainless steel types. It is highly resistant to corrosion, very strong and hard, and can be easily fabricated by all standard techniques.
- *Type 304*. Type 304 has largely replaced type 302 for architectural uses because of its improved weldability. Its other properties are identical to 302.
- *Type 301*. This alloy is similar to type 302, but with slightly smaller amounts of chromium and nickel. It is still very corrosion resistant. Its advantage is its improved work-hardening properties, which can result in very high tensile strengths.
- *Type 316*. For extreme corrosive environments such as industrial plants and marine locations, this type is often used. It has a higher percentage of nickel than the other alloys and includes molybdenum.
- *Type 430*. This type does not contain any nickel, so it is less corrosion resistant than the other types. Its use is generally limited to interior applications.

Stainless steel is available in a variety of forms including sheets, wire, bars, and plates. Structural shapes of H sections, channels, tees, and angles are also available, as are custom extrusions. Stainless steel can be finished in a variety of ways, including mechanical and coatings.

The most common polished finishes for architectural work include the following.

- *No. 3 finish*: an intermediate, dull finish, coarser than no. 4.
- *No. 4 finish*: a general-purpose polished finish that is dull and prevents mirror reflection. It is one of the most frequently used architectural finishes.
- *No. 6 finish*: a dull satin finish.
- *No. 7 finish*: a highly reflective polished surface.
- *No. 8 finish*: the most reflective finish, used for mirrors and reflectors. It is seldom used for general architectural applications; a no. 7 finish is usually used instead.

There are also patterned finishes available that are produced by passing a sheet between patterned rollers. Color coatings are also available. Organic coatings consist of acrylic or other plastic-based enamels, which are fairly elastic, that can be applied to the metal prior to forming. Inorganic coatings such as porcelain enamel are less elastic but add color to the metal.

Other Alloy Steels

Various elements can be added to steel to impart certain qualities. In addition to stainless steel as described, many types of alloy structural steel are produced, which are designated by specification numbers of the American Society of Testing and Materials (ASTM).

ASTM A36 is the most common type of structural steel. It has a minimum yield point of 36,000 lbm/in^2 (248 MPa) and a carbon content from 0.25% to 0.29%. ASTM A440 is a high-strength structural steel used for bolted or riveted structures. ASTM A441 is a high-strength, low-alloy manganese vanadium steel intended for welded construction.

Weathering steel is an alloy that contains a small amount of copper. When exposed to moisture in the air or from rain, it develops a protective oxide coating with a distinctive sepia-colored finish. It is used in structures where it is difficult to maintain the steel, or it is used simply for its appearance. However, because small amounts of oxide are carried off by rain, structures using weathering steel should be detailed so the runoff does not stain other materials.

NONFERROUS METALS

Nonferrous metals are those that do not contain iron. The types most often used in construction include aluminum, copper, and copper alloys such as bronze and brass. Other nonferrous metals such as zinc, lead, and gold are of limited use in their pure state or are used in conjunction with other metals and materials.

Aluminum

Aluminum is an abundant element. The primary source of aluminum is bauxite, which is hydrated oxide of aluminum and iron with small amounts of silicon. Aluminum by itself is soft and weak; however, alloying it with manganese, zinc, magnesium, and copper improves its strength and hardness.

Aluminum is used in a wide variety of applications including structure, wall panels, curtain walls, window and door frames, and other decorative uses. In most uses, its high strength-to-weight ratio makes aluminum a desirable building material. It can be formed by casting, drawing, and rolling, although it is most often formed by extruding.

Aluminum can be finished mechanically, chemically, and with coatings. Mechanical finishes include the following.

- *Buffed finishes*: smooth specular and specular.
- *Directional textured finishes* (satin sheen with tiny, parallel scratches): fine satin, medium satin, coarse satin, hand rubbed, and brushed.
- *Nondirectional textured finishes* (formed by abrasion methods, not applicable to thicknesses under $^1/_4$ in): extra-fine matte, fine matte, medium matte, coarse matte, fine shot blast, medium shot blast, and coarse shot blast.
- *Patterned finishes*: formed by rollers and other methods.

Chemical finishing for aluminum is usually an intermediate process for some other final finishing such as cleaning, etching, or preparing for some other coating.

Coating finishes for aluminum include the most familiar *anodizing process*, which is an electrochemical process that deposits an integral coating on the metal. It is called an anodic coating and can include the familiar silvery color of aluminum or a number of colors in the black and brown ranges. The problem with this finish is that it can be scratched.

Other finishes include impregnated color coatings such as baked enamel, vitreous coatings, powder coatings, and laminated coatings.

Aluminum can be joined by screwing, bolting, welding, brazing, soldering, adhesive bonding, and with concealed fasteners. Welding, brazing, and soldering should only be used when the joint is concealed or prior to final finishing. Adhesive bonding should be limited to thin material in situations where high strength is not required.

One of the primary disadvantages of aluminum is the amount of energy required for its refining and manufacture. Although the material is recyclable, the amount of embodied energy to install a finished product into a building is considerable.

Copper and Copper Alloys

Copper is widely used in construction because of its resistance to corrosion, its workability, and its high electrical conductivity. The two primary alloys of copper are bronze and brass. Bronze, by definition, is an alloy of copper and tin, whereas brass is an alloy of copper and zinc. However, traditional nomenclature calls many true brasses by the name bronze. The confusion is clarified by referring to the alloys by their standard designation numbers developed by the Copper Development Association (CDA) or by the Unified Numbering System (UNS). Table 38.2 lists some of the alloys used in construction, including their number designations and common names as well as their nominal compositions.

Copper and copper alloys are used in a variety of applications. Of course, copper is used for electrical wiring because of its high electrical conductivity. The copper alloys are also used for hardware, curtain walls, piping, gutters, roofing, window and door frames, wall panels, railings, and many other ornamental purposes.

Copper and copper alloys can be formed by casting, rolling, bending, brake forming, extrusion, spinning, and several other methods. They are joined by mechanical fasteners, brazing, and adhesive bonding.

As with aluminum, copper alloys can be finished several ways using the three methods of mechanical finishes, chemical finishes, and coatings.

Mechanical finishes include buffed, directional textured (in a variety of grain sizes), nondirectional textured, and patterned.

Table 38.2

Composition and Description of Copper Alloys

alloy	UNS no.	name	nominal composition
110	C11000	copper	99.9% copper
220	C22000	commercial bronze	90% copper 10% zinc
230	C23000	red brass	85% copper 15% zinc
260	C26000	cartridge brass	70% copper 30% zinc
280	C28000	Muntz metal	60% copper 40% zinc
385	C38500	architectural bronze	57% copper 40% zinc 3% lead
655	C65500	silicon bronze	97% copper 3% silicon
745	C74500	nickel silver	65% copper 25% zinc 10% nickel

Chemical processing is usually used as an intermediate step in a total finishing process, but it can also be used to color the copper alloy.

Coatings can involve clear organic coatings, metallics, and oils and waxes. Although one of the advantages of copper, brass, and bronze is their ability to resist corrosion, if left unprotected many of the alloys develop a patina that is very different in color from the original finish of the metal. The distinctive green color of aged copper is the most notable example. In some cases, this is undesirable, especially in interior applications. To prevent this, various types of thin, clear organic coatings can be applied to the metal. In other situations, a coat of oil or wax can bring out the rich luster of the metal, although continued maintenance is required.

One special alloy, used primarily for roofing, is Monel metal (a trade name), which is a combination of copper and nickel with small amounts of other elements. It is also highly resistant to corrosion and is easily worked.

Miscellaneous Nonferrous Metals

Zinc is resistant to corrosion and is sometimes used for sheet roofing and flashing. Zinc fasteners are also made. The metal is more commonly used for coating steel to produce galvanized steel.

Lead is also resistant to corrosion and is occasionally used to cover complex roofing shapes because it is very easy to form around irregularities. However, its density makes it ideal for acoustical insulation, vibration control, and radiation shielding. An alloy of 75% lead and 25% tin can be used to plate steel for roofing. This is known as *terneplate*.

STRUCTURAL METALS

Steel Shapes

The two metals used in structural applications are steel and aluminum, although steel is by far the most common. The structural use of aluminum is limited to small structures or minor portions of structures. Steel is used for beams, columns, and plates; in light-gage framing such as steel studs; for floor and roof decking; as prefabricated truss joists; and for many types of fasteners.

Structural steel comes in a variety of shapes, sizes, and weights, giving the designer a great deal of flexibility in selecting an economical member that is geometrically correct for any given situation. Figure 38.1 shows the most common shapes of structural steel.

Wide-flange members are H-shaped sections used for both beams and columns. They are called wide flange because the width of the flange is greater than that of standard I-beams. Many of the wide-flange shapes are particularly suited for columns because the width of the flange is very nearly equal to the depth of the section, so they have about the same rigidity in both axes.

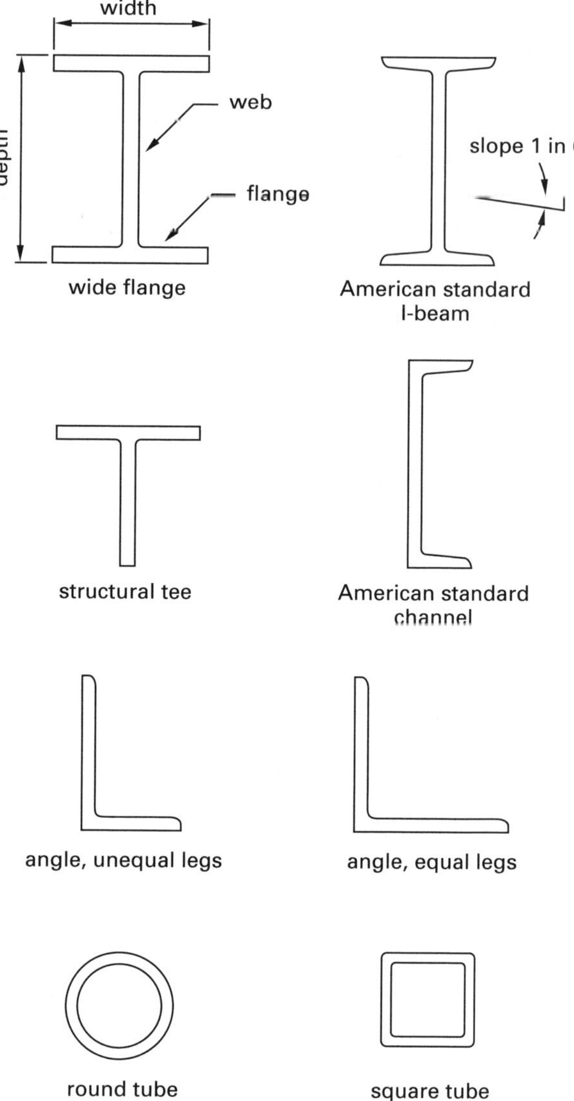

Figure 38.1 Structural Steel Shapes

Wide-flange sections are designated with the letter W followed by the nominal depth in inches (millimeters) and the weight in lbm/ft (kg/m). For example, a W18 × 85 is a wide flange nominally 18 in deep and weighing 85 lbm/ft. Because of the way these sections are rolled in the mill, the actual depth varies slightly from the nominal depth.

American standard I-beams have a relatively narrow flange width in relation to their depth, and the inside faces of the flanges have a slope of one in six. Unlike the wide flanges, the actual depth of an I-beam in any size group is also the nominal depth. The designation of depth and weight per foot for these sections is preceded with the letter S. These sections are usually used for beams only.

American standard channel sections have a flange on one side of the web only and are designated with the letter C followed by the depth and weight per foot. Like that of the American standard I-beams, the depth is constant for any size group; extra weight is added by increasing the thickness of the web and the inside face of the flanges. Channel sections are typically used to frame openings, to form stair stringers, or in other applications where a flush side is required. They are seldom used by themselves for beams or columns because they tend to buckle due to their asymmetrical shape.

Structural tees are made by cutting either a wide-flange section or I-beam in half. If cut from a wide-flange section, a tee is given the prefix designation WT and, if cut from an American standard I-beam, it is given the designation ST. A WT9 × 57, for example, is cut from a W18 × 114. Because they are symmetrical about one axis and have an open flange, tees are often used for chords of steel trusses.

Steel angles are available with either equal or unequal legs. They are designated by the letter L followed by the lengths of the angles and then followed by the thicknesses of the legs. Angles are used in pairs as members for steel trusses or singly as lintels in a variety of applications. They are also used for miscellaneous bracing of other structural members.

Square and rectangular tube sections and round pipe are also available. These are often used for light columns and as members of large trusses or space frames. *Structural tubing* of various sizes is available in several different wall thicknesses, while *structural pipe* is available in standard weight, extra strong, and double-extra strong. Each of the three weights has a standard wall thickness depending on the size. Pipe is designated by its nominal diameter, although the actual outside dimension is slightly larger, while the size designation for square or rectangular tubing refers to its actual outside dimensions. Standard designations for structural steel shapes are summarized in Table 38.3.

Finally, steel is available in bars and plates. *Bars* are considered any rectangular section 6 in (152) or less in width with a thickness of 0.203 in (5.2) and greater or sections 6 in to 8 in (152 to 203) in width with a thickness of 0.230 (5.8) and greater.

Plates are considered any section over 8 in (203) in width with a thickness of 0.230 in (5.8) and over, or sections over 48 in (1220) in width with a thickness of 0.180 in (4.6) and over.

Table 38.3

Standard Designations for Structural Shapes

structural shape	example of standard designation
wide-flange shapes	W12 × 22
American standard I-beams	S12 × 35
miscellaneous shapes	M12 × 11.8
American standard channels	C15 × 40
miscellaneous channels	MC12 × 37
angles, equal legs	L3 × 3 × 3/8
angles, unequal legs	L3 × 4 × 1/2 LLV[1]
structural tees—cut from wide flange shapes	WT7 × 15
structural tees—cut from American standard I-beams	ST9 × 35
plate	PL1/2 × 10
structural tubing	TS8 × 8 × 0.03750
pipe	pipe 4 std.

[1]LLV and LLH are used on drawings to indicate the orientation of the long leg of the angle: long leg vertical and long leg horizontal, respectively.

Open-Web Steel Joists

Open-web steel joists are standardized, shop-fabricated trusses with webs composed of linear members and chords of back-to-back steel angles. The chords are typically parallel, but some types have top chords that are pitched for roof drainage. See Fig. 38.2.

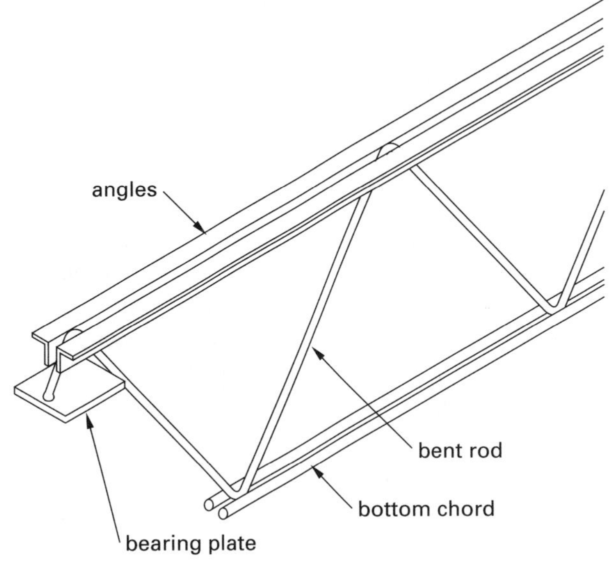

Figure 38.2 Open-Web Steel Joist

Table 38.4
Open-Web Steel Joists—Spans and Depths

series	name	span limits (ft)	span limits (m)	depths in series (in)	depths in series (mm)
K	standard	8–60	2.4–18.3	8–30	203–762
LH	long span	25–96	7.6–29.3	18–48	457–1220
DLH	deep long span	89–144	27.1–43.9	52–96	1321–2438

There are three standard series of open-web joists: the K-series, the LH-series, and the DLH-series. The typical spans and depths of each are summarized in Table 38.4. The depths in the K-series increase in 2 in (50) increments, and the depths in the LH- and DLH-series increase in 4 in (100) increments. The standard designation for an open-web joist consists of the depth, the series designation, and the particular type of chord used. For example, a 36LH13 joist is 36 in (914) deep and of the LH-series, with a number 13 chord type. Within any size group, the chord type number increases as the load-carrying capacity of that depth of joist increases.

Open-web steel joists have many advantages for spanning medium to long distances. They are lightweight and efficient structural members, they are easy and quick to erect, and the open webbing allows for ductwork and other building services to be run through the joists rather than under them. In addition, a variety of floor decking types can be used, from wood systems to steel and concrete decks. They can easily be supported by steel beams, by masonry or concrete bearing walls, or by heavier open-web joist girders.

There are also various types of composite joists that use wood top and bottom chords with steel webs. These are ideal for wood-frame buildings where wood decking is used and where spans exceed the limits of standard wood joists.

Metal Decking

Metal decking is available in steel or aluminum, although steel is the more common form. Steel decking consists of formed panels that are laid over steel beams or open-web steel joists to serve as formwork for poured concrete slabs. Before the concrete is poured, the decking also provides a convenient working deck during construction.

Steel decking is available in a wide variety of types, shapes, depths, and gages to satisfy nearly any span and loading condition. A few of the more common shapes are illustrated in Fig. 38.3. Decking is available that simply serves as a form for concrete or that is deformed to bond with the concrete and act as a composite structural material. Cellular decking provides structural support as well as raceways for power and communication cabling.

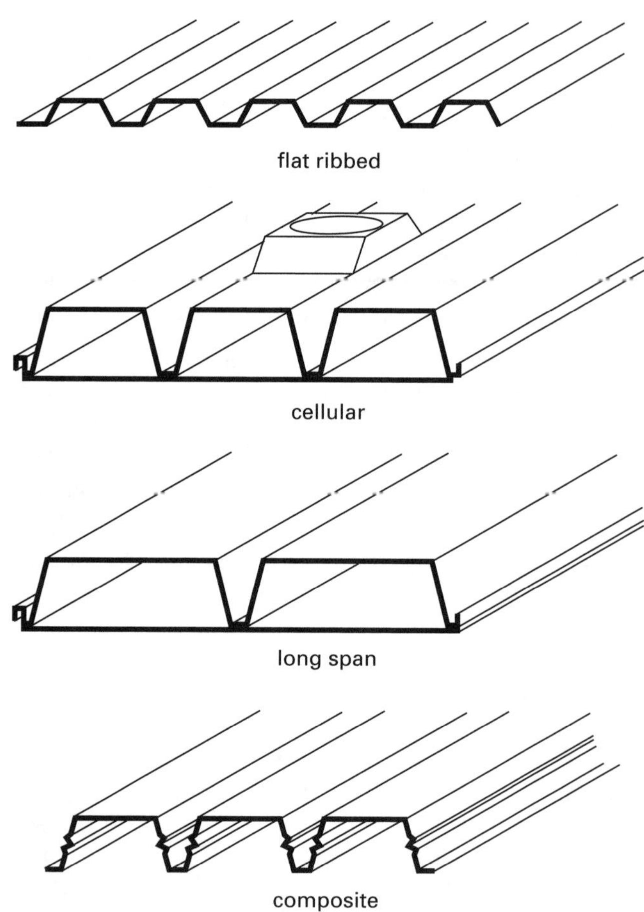

Figure 38.3 Steel Decking

Light-Gage Metal Framing

Light-gage metal framing consists of steel members with thicknesses from 10 gage to 25 gage. It is used for interior partitions, exterior bearing and nonbearing walls, joists, rafters, and similar framing. Unlike structural steel, light-gage framing comes in shapes more suitable for lighter loads and easier handling. Light-gage framing is noncombustible, is easily cut and assembled, and does not shrink or otherwise decay.

Manufacturers supply a variety of shapes, sizes, and gages for various uses. Most commonly, light-gage framing is used for interior partitions in noncombustible buildings. However, joists and deeper studs are used for floor and roof framing, as well as for some bearing wall applications. Some of the common shapes of light-gage framing are shown in Fig. 38.4.

Framing used for interior partitions ranges from 20 gage to 25 gage (0.87 to 0.48). Studs are available in depths of $1^5/_8$, $2^1/_2$, $3^5/_8$, 4, and 6 in (41.3, 63.5, 92.1, 101.6, and 152.4). For higher walls, bearing walls, and exterior walls, heavier gages and depths are available. Joists are available in depths from 6 in to 14 in (152 to 356) and in thicknesses from 10 gage to 20 gage. Light-gage joists and rafters are capable of spanning up to 40 ft (12.2 m).

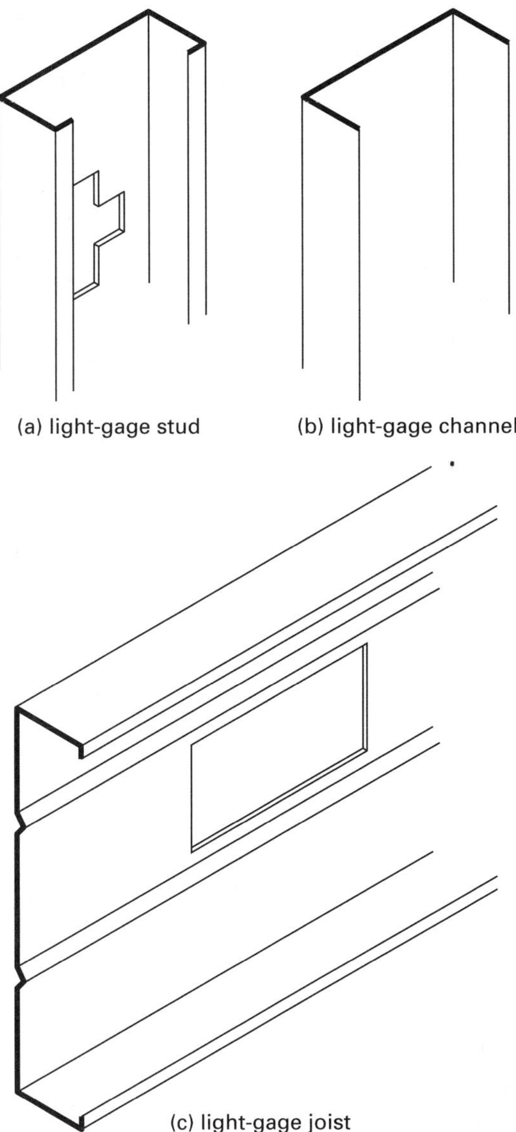

Figure 38.4 Light-Gage Metal Framing

Light-gage framing is erected with screws, bolts, or welds depending on the thickness of the member and its application.

METAL FABRICATIONS

In addition to structural metals, there are individual building components fabricated partially or entirely of steel, aluminum, or other metals that belong in the category of "metals." These include items such as spiral stairs, expansion joints, gratings, and ladders.

Spiral Stairs

Spiral stairs have a closed circular form with wedge-shaped treads supported from a central, minimum-diameter column (usually 4 in [100]). Standard prefabricated spiral stairs are commonly made from steel. Treads can be exposed steel, hardwood over a steel support, recessed steel pans for infill with concrete or stone, or particleboard over a steel support that can be finished with carpet or resilient flooring. Handrails can be specified as steel pipe, wood, or other ornamental metal. Custom spiral stairs can be fabricated of nearly any combination of steel, wood, and other ornamental metal. Spiral stairs are available in standard diameters from 3 ft 6 in to 7 ft 0 in, in 6 in increments (1067 to 2134, in 152 increments).

Spiral stairs can be fabricated with 22.5°, 27°, and 30° treads, with 30° treads being the most common. This means that there are twelve treads in a full 360° turn or three treads for each quarter circle of the stair. The riser height is set between $7^1/_2$ in and $9^1/_2$ in (190 to 240) to make up the total floor-to-floor height so each riser is the same and headroom is adequate. At the top of the stair, a square landing is used to make the transition between the stair and the rest of the floor when a square opening is used. Depending on the floor-to-floor dimension, a spiral stair must be planned so the first riser at the bottom and the last riser at the top are situated so people enter and exit the stair traveling in the right direction.

Expansion Joints

Expansion joint cover assemblies are fabrications designed to allow for major movement between independent structural units of the building. They are different from control joints or isolation joints in that the movements between adjacent portions of a building are significant—on the order of $^1/_2$ in (13) to several inches.

Expansion joints separate two sections of a building completely and continuously, from the foundation through floors, walls, and the roof. Two examples of expansion joint cover assemblies are shown in Fig. 38.5. The first, Fig. 38.5(a), illustrates an expansion joint between two floor slabs; Fig. 38.5(b) shows the separation between a floor and wall.

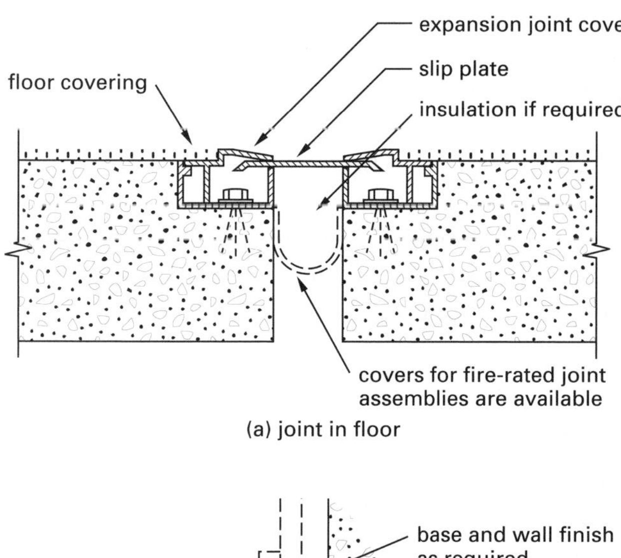

(a) joint in floor

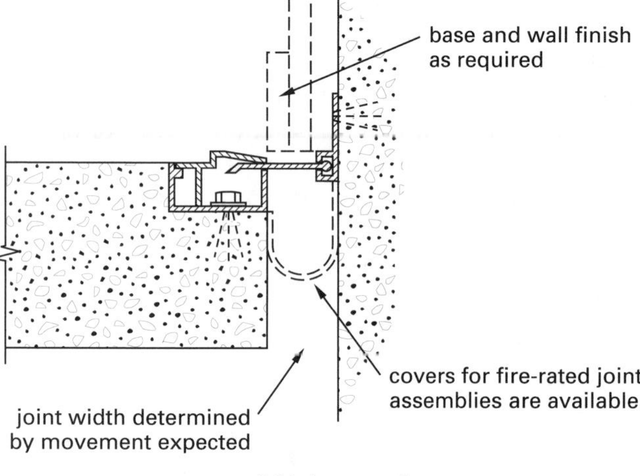

(b) joint at wall

Figure 38.5 Expansion Joint Cover Assemblies

Expansion joints that provide for lateral movement only or for both lateral and vertical movement are available. Seismic expansion joints are also available, but they require special engineering study to determine what type and amount of movement must be accommodated.

Other Miscellaneous Metal Fabrications

Other common miscellaneous metal fabrications include gratings, steel ladders for service areas, stair treads, pipe handrails and guardrails, sheet metal enclosures, prefabricated utility stairs, and protective steel bollards, bumpers, and corner guards.

ORNAMENTAL METALS

Ornamental metals include a wide variety of both functional and decorative products, such as handrails, guardrails, and elevator interiors. Metal may also be used for custom doors and door facings, partition and architectural woodwork facing, building directories and kiosks, signs, custom light fixtures, ceilings, or as part of nearly any construction assembly. The decorative options available to the architect are almost limitless. The most commonly used ornamental metals include stainless steel, the copper alloys of bronze and brass, and aluminum. Carbon steel, copper, iron, and porcelain enamel are used less frequently.

Stainless steel and copper alloys are available in several stock forms that fabricators use to construct custom assemblies. Some of the common shapes for brass and bronze are shown in Fig. 38.6. Sheet and bar stock are also available in a number of thicknesses.

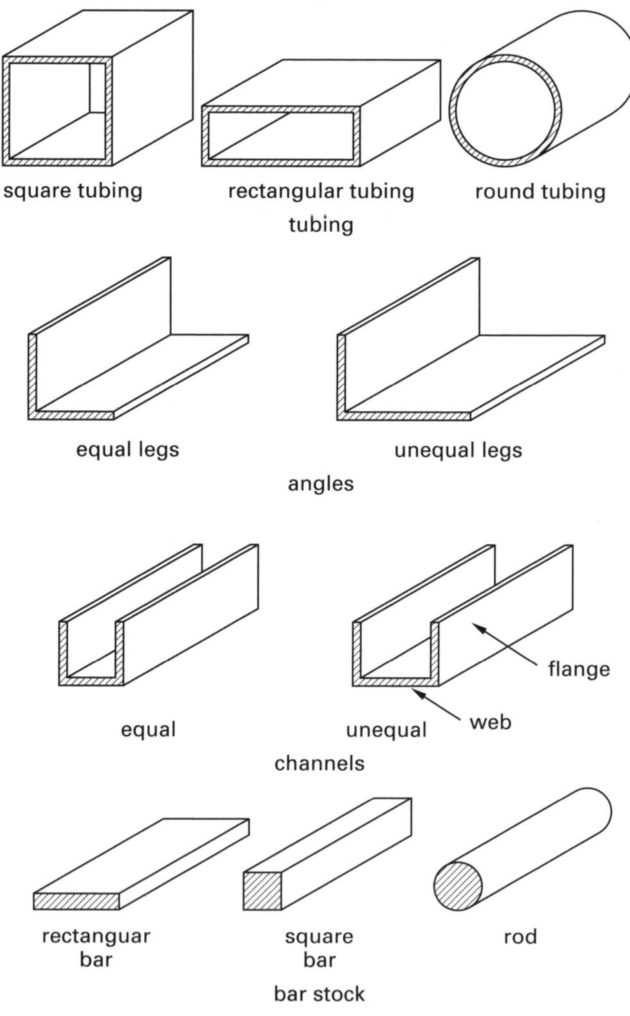

Figure 38.6 Standard Brass and Bronze Shapes

Detailing Stainless Steel

Custom details for stainless steel are developed in the same way as for plain carbon steel or any other metal. Combinations of bar, plate, tubing, sheet stock, and other shapes are detailed to nearly any configuration and in any combination. Stainless steel can be joined by welding, mechanical fasteners, and in some cases, with adhesives. For the smoothest joint, welding is preferred. However, the finish specified must make it possible to smooth and work the weld to match the adjacent finish. Some rolled and proprietary finishes cannot be matched after shop welding. When mechanical fasteners such as screws, bolts, and rivets are used, they should also be stainless steel to prevent galvanic action and rust stains caused by carbon steel fasteners. Adhesives are typically used to laminate sheet stock to other materials. In order to simplify fabrication and minimize cost, the smallest sizes and gages that satisfy the application should be used.

Detailing with Brass and Bronze

As with stainless steel, basic shapes are used to fabricate custom assemblies by various forming and fastening methods. Brass can also be extruded and cast. Extrusion is common for door and window frames, railings, and trim, whereas casting is used to manufacture hardware and plumbing fixtures.

Brass can be fabricated to any size required, but it is more economical to design and detail ornamental brass using standard shapes (see Fig. 38.6) and sizes whenever possible. Hexagonal and octagonal tubing is also available on special order as well as some T-shapes, Z-shapes, and proprietary shapes. Note that square and rectangular tubing, channels, and angles of brass have sharp corners as contrasted with the rounded corners of stainless steel and regular steel tubing, channels, and angles. Although there are some standard shapes and sizes, several manufacturers use brass to fabricate proprietary shapes and products. For example, several manufacturers produce lines of brass railings for bars, guardrails, and handrails, including brackets and other accessories for a complete installation.

Brass and bronze can be formed into an unlimited number of shapes and sizes, and different pieces can be fastened to fabricate nearly any type of detail. Brass and bronze can also be combined with other materials such as wood, plastic, and stone to construct specialty items. However, standard shapes, sizes, and metal alloys should be used to minimize cost and fabrication difficulty. Following are some general guidelines for designing and detailing with these metals.

For details with large expanses of smooth, flat sheet stock, the gage of metal must be thick enough to avoid oil canning or showing other surface imperfections. A minimum of 10-gage brass (0.1019 in [2.588]) is used when large areas are unsupported or unbacked. If the sheet has an embossed pattern, thinner material is used because the patterning imparts stiffness to the sheet. When brass is laminated to particleboard or other backing, sheets as thin as 20 gage (0.032 in [0.813]) are used. Items that are fabricated of brake-formed brass are from 14- or 12-gage (0.0640 or 0.0808 in [1.62 or 2.05]) metal.

Brass and bronze are joined with mechanical fasteners, adhesives, or by brazing or soldering. Mechanical fasteners include screws, bolts, rivets, and various types of clips in compatible alloys. In most cases the appearance of metalwork is improved if mechanical fasteners are concealed. If the installation makes it impossible to conceal fasteners, their type, size, and location should be given careful consideration based on the final installed position.

Adhesives are used for laminating sheets onto backing material or to join smaller pieces to other materials when exposed fasteners would be objectionable. Unless some additional mechanical fastening device can be incorporated into a detail, adhesive bonding should not be used alone where the metal has to support forces other than its own weight.

Brass can be joined by brazing, soldering, or welding as discussed in the earlier section on joining metals. Of the three methods, brazing is most often used for joining brass for architectural purposes. If possible, brazed joints should be concealed because the filler metal does not exactly match the brass.

Perforated Metal

Perforated metal is sheet metal that has been punched with a regular pattern of holes. Standard perforations include round and square holes as well as slots in a wide range of patterns, hole sizes, and hole spacings. For interior applications, perforated metals are used for space dividers, railing guards, shelving, furniture, supply air and return air grills, coverings for acoustical panels, custom light fixtures, or any specialty fabrication that can be constructed with sheet metal.

Architectural Mesh

Architectural mesh is a specialty metal that is most often used for elevator cab interiors, but it can be creatively applied in other architectural applications such as wall panels and door facings. Architectural mesh is formed by "weaving" thin strips of metal or heavy wire and then grinding off a portion of one face to reveal a highly textured but relatively flat surface. The final surface appearance depends on the type of weave, the type of metal used, and how much is ground off. Stainless steel and brass are the most commonly used materials.

39 STRUCTURAL AND ROUGH CARPENTRY

There are two broad categories of wood use in construction: rough carpentry and finish carpentry. *Rough carpentry* includes the structural framing, sheathing, blocking, and miscellaneous pieces necessary to prepare the building for finish work. Most rough carpentry is hidden once construction is complete, but exposed lumber such as heavy timber beams, glued-laminated members, and outdoor deck frames is considered rough carpentry.

As the name implies, *finish carpentry* includes the exposed, finished pieces of lumber necessary to complete a job, including such things as window and door trim, base, wood paneling, cabinets, and shelving. Finish carpentry work is normally done on the job site, but it also includes architectural woodwork, which is the fabrication of wood items in a manufacturing plant. Finish carpentry and architectural woodwork are reviewed in Ch. 40.

This chapter includes a general review of wood as a structural material. However, methods for calculating sizes of members and fasteners are not included.

When discussing wood as a construction material, several terms are often used interchangeably, but there is a distinction. Wood is the fibrous substance forming the trunk, stems, and branches of the tree. Lumber is the product of sawing, planing, and otherwise preparing wood to be used as construction members. Timber is lumber with a 5 in (127) minimum sectional dimension.

CHARACTERISTICS OF LUMBER

Lumber is a very versatile building material and has many advantages—it is plentiful, relatively low in cost, easy to shape and assemble, has good thermal insulating qualities, and is aesthetically pleasing. As a natural material, however, it lacks the uniform appearance and strength that manufactured materials have. Also, because of its cellular structure, it is susceptible to dimensional changes when its moisture content changes.

These disadvantages can be overcome with some of the manufactured wood products available today. A few examples of these products are plywood, glued-laminated timber, and plywood web joists.

Types and Species

There are two general classifications of wood: softwood and hardwood. These terms have nothing to do with the actual hardness of the wood, but refer to whether the wood comes from a coniferous tree or a deciduous tree. *Conifers* (softwood) are cone-bearing, needle-leaved trees that hold their foliage in the winter, such as fir, spruce, and pine. Deciduous (hardwood) trees are broad-leaved trees that lose their leaves in the winter, such as oak, walnut, and maple. Softwoods are used for structural and rough carpentry because of their greater availability and lower cost. Finish carpentry and architectural woodwork utilize both hardwoods and softwoods.

There are literally hundreds of species of softwood and hardwood available throughout the world. However, only a few are used in the United States for rough carpentry, primarily due to local availability and cost. For example, southern pine is used in the southeastern portion of the United States, whereas Douglas fir or Douglas fir-larch is used in the western region. Other commonly used species for rough carpentry include hem-fir, eastern white pine, and hemlock. Redwood and cedar are commonly used for exterior applications where resistance to moisture is required.

Strength

The strength of lumber is dependent on the direction of the load relative to the direction of the wood's grain. Lumber is strongest when the load is parallel to the direction of the grain, such as with a compressive load on a wood column. Wood can resist slightly less tensile stress parallel to the grain and even less when compressive forces are perpendicular to the grain.

Wood is weakest when horizontal shear force is induced, which occurs when bending forces are applied to a beam and the fibers tend to slip apart parallel to the grain. Allowable forces used in structural calculations are lowest for horizontal shear, and this quite often governs the design of bending members.

Defects

Because wood is a natural material, there are several types of defects that can be present in lumber. There are also many types of defects that can occur during manufacture. These affect the strength, appearance, and use of lumber and are reflected in how an individual piece of lumber is graded. Figure 39.1 shows some of the more common wood defects.

- *Knots* are the most common natural defect. A knot is a branch or limb embedded in the tree that is cut through in the process of lumber manufacture. Knots are classified according to quality, size, and occurrence. There are over 10 different types of knots.
- A *check* is a separation of the wood fibers occurring across or through the annual growth rings, a result of improper seasoning.
- A *pitch pocket* is an open area between growth rings that contains resin.
- A *shake* is a lengthwise separation of the wood that usually occurs between or through the annual growth rings.
- A *split* is similar to a check except that the separation extends completely through a piece of lumber, usually at the ends.
- A *wane* is the presence of bark or absence of wood from any cause on the edge or corner of a piece of lumber.

Warping is a common manufacturing defect. A *warp* is any variation from a true or plane surface and is usually caused by the natural shrinkage characteristics of wood and uneven drying during processing. A *bow* is a deviation parallel to the length of the lumber in line with the lumber's flat side. A *crook* is a deviation parallel to the length of the lumber perpendicular to the flat side of the piece. A *cup* is a deviation from true plane along the width of the board.

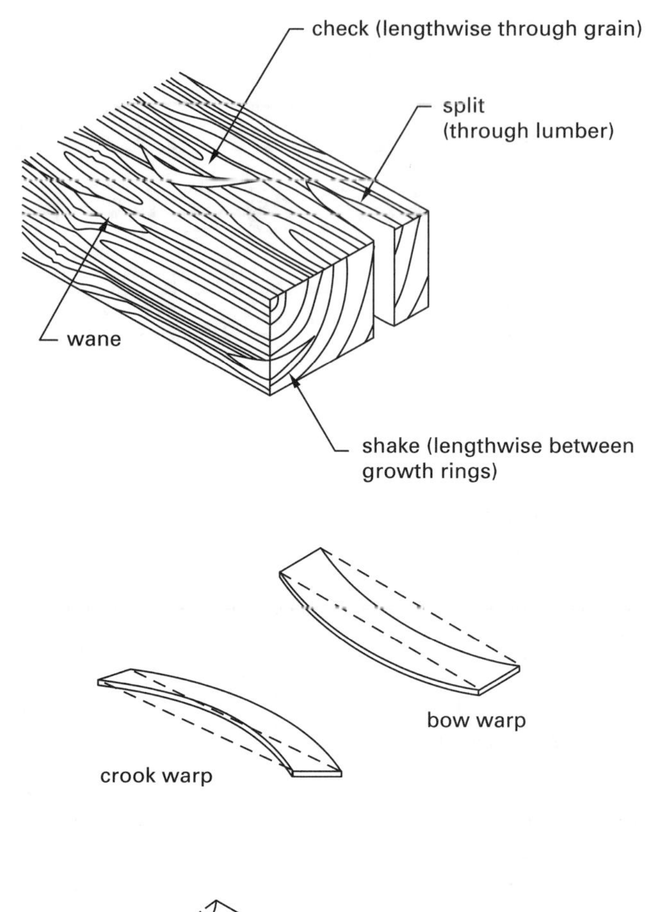

Figure 39.1 Common Wood Defects

Grading

Because a log yields lumber of varying quality, the individual sawn pieces must be categorized to allow selection of boards that are best suited for a particular purpose. For structural lumber, the primary concern is the amount of stress that a grade of lumber of a specific species can carry. For finish lumber, the primary concern is the appearance of the wood and how it accepts stain, paint, and other finishes. Load-carrying ability is affected by such things as size and number of knots, splits, and other defects.

Grading of lumber used for structural and rough carpentry purposes is done under standard rules established by several agencies certified by the American Lumber Standards Committee. The grading is done at the sawmill, either by visual inspection or machine, if the lumber is to be used for structural purposes. The resulting allowable stress values are published in tables that are used when making structural calculations.

There are two primary classifications of softwood lumber: "yard lumber," used for structural purposes and rough framing, and "factory and shop lumber," used for making door frames, windows, and finish items.

Yard lumber is further classified as boards, dimension, and timber, as shown in Fig. 39.2. Dimension lumber and timber are the two classifications used for structural purposes, and these are further classified into groups based on nominal size and use. With this system the same grade of lumber in a species may have different allowable stresses depending on which category it is in. This can be confusing, but it is critical in selecting the correct allowable stress for a particular design condition.

The five size groups (based on nominal dimensions) are as follows.

1. 2 in to 4 in (51 to 102) thick, 2 in to 4 in wide. This includes members such as 2 × 2s.
2. 2 in to 4 in (51 to 102) thick, 4 in (102) wide. This is the category for 2 × 4s, which are usually subdivided into grades of construction, standard, and utility.
3. 2 in to 4 in (51 to 102) thick, 5 in (127) wide and wider. This includes wood members such as 2 × 6s, 2 × 8s, and the like, but not 2 × 4s.
4. *Beams and stringers*. Beams and stringers are defined as members 5 in (127) wide and wider, having a depth of at least 2 in (51) greater than the width.
5. *Posts and timbers*. Posts and timbers are defined as members 5 in by 5 in (127 by 127) and larger, with a depth not more than 2 in (51) greater than the width.

These five size categories are further subdivided into smaller groups such as select structural, no. 1, no. 2, and so on. The exact nomenclature and method of subdivision vary with each grading agency and the wood species.

Machine-stress-rated lumber is based on grade designations that depend on the allowable bending stress and modulus of elasticity of the wood.

Factory and shop lumber for boards (less than 1 in [25] nominal thickness) is graded according to defects that affect the appearance and use of the wood. Exact classifications vary with the grading agency and the species of lumber, but in general factory and shop lumber is divided into select and common grades. The three select grade categories are B & Better, C Select, and D Select, with B & Better being the best and free of knots.

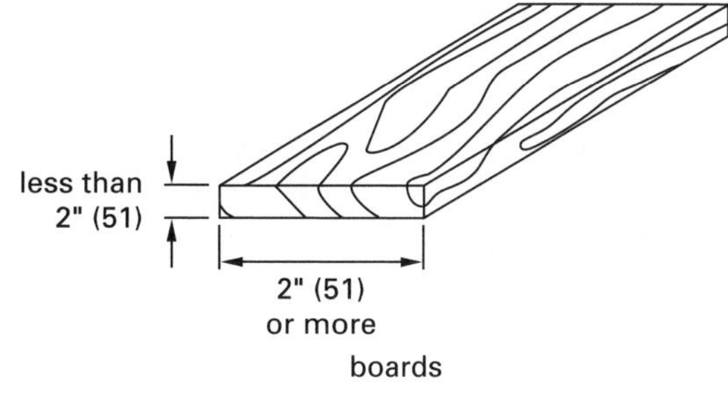

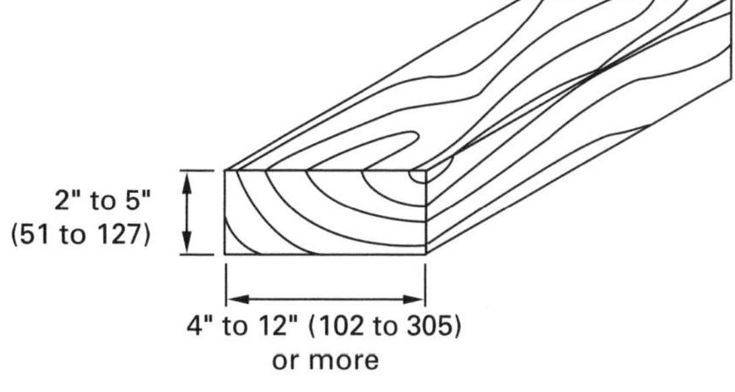

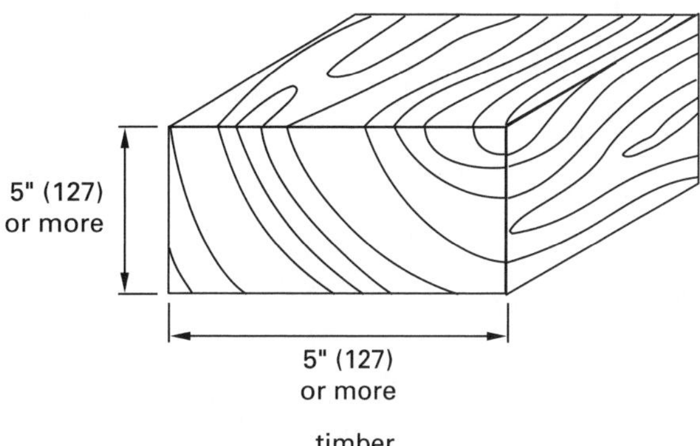

Figure 39.2 Yard Lumber Types

Common grades available include no. 1, no. 2, no. 3, no. 4, and no. 5—no. 1 common being the best. The individual grades are determined by the size and character of the knots.

Dimensioning

Lumber for rough carpentry is referred to by its nominal dimension in inches, such as 2 × 4 or 2 × 10. However, after surfacing at the mill and drying, its actual dimension is somewhat less. Table 39.1 gives the actual dimensions for various nominal sizes of sawn lumber.

Lumber is ordered and priced by the board foot. This is a measure of a quantity of lumber equal to a piece 12 in wide by 12 in long by 1 in thick. Nominal sizes are used so an actual sized piece of lumber $^3/_4$ in thick, $11^1/_4$ in wide, and 2 ft long contains 2 board feet.

Table 39.1
Nominal and Actual Sizes of Lumber

nominal size	standard dressed size (in, width × depth)
1 × 2	$^3/_4$ × 1$^1/_2$
1 × 4	$^3/_4$ × 3$^1/_2$
1 × 6	$^3/_4$ × 5$^1/_2$
1 × 8	$^3/_4$ × 7$^1/_4$
2 × 2	1$^1/_2$ × 1$^1/_2$
2 × 4	1$^1/_2$ × 3$^1/_2$
2 × 6	1$^1/_2$ × 5$^1/_2$
2 × 8	1$^1/_2$ × 7$^1/_4$
2 × 10	1$^1/_2$ × 9$^1/_4$
2 × 12	1$^1/_2$ × 11$^1/_4$
4 × 4	3$^1/_2$ × 3$^1/_2$
4 × 6	3$^1/_2$ × 5$^1/_2$
4 × 8	3$^1/_2$ × 7$^1/_4$
4 × 10	3$^1/_2$ × 9$^1/_4$
4 × 12	3$^1/_2$ × 11$^1/_4$
4 × 14	3$^1/_2$ × 13$^1/_4$
6 × 6	5$^1/_2$ × 5$^1/_2$
6 × 8	5$^1/_2$ × 7$^1/_2$
6 × 10	5$^1/_2$ × 9$^1/_2$

Moisture Content

Moisture content is defined as the weight of water in wood as a fraction of the weight of oven-dry wood. It is an important variable because it affects the amount of shrinkage, weight, and strength of the lumber, as well as the withdrawal resistance of nails.

Moisture exists in wood both in the individual cell cavities and bound chemically within cell walls. When the cell walls are completely saturated but no water exists in the cell cavities, the wood is said to have reached its *fiber saturation point*. This point averages about 30% moisture content in all woods. Above this point the wood is dimensionally stable, but as the wood dries below this point it begins to shrink.

When wood is used for structural framing and other construction purposes, it tends to absorb or lose moisture in response to the temperature and humidity of the surrounding air. As it loses moisture it shrinks, and as it gains moisture it swells. Ideally, the moisture content of wood when it is installed should be the same as the prevailing humidity to which it will be exposed. However, this is seldom possible so lumber needs to be seasoned, either by air drying or kiln drying, to reduce the moisture content to acceptable levels.

For the wood to be considered dry lumber, its moisture content cannot exceed 19%. To be grademarked "kiln dry," its moisture content cannot exceed 15%. Design values found in structural tables assume that the maximum moisture content will not exceed 19%. If it does, the allowable stresses must be decreased slightly.

Wood shrinks most in the direction perpendicular to the grain and very little parallel to the grain. When considered perpendicular to the grain, wood shrinks most in the direction of the annual growth rings (tangentially) and about half as much across the rings (radially). See Fig. 39.3. The position in the log where a piece of lumber is cut also affects the wood's shrinkage characteristics.

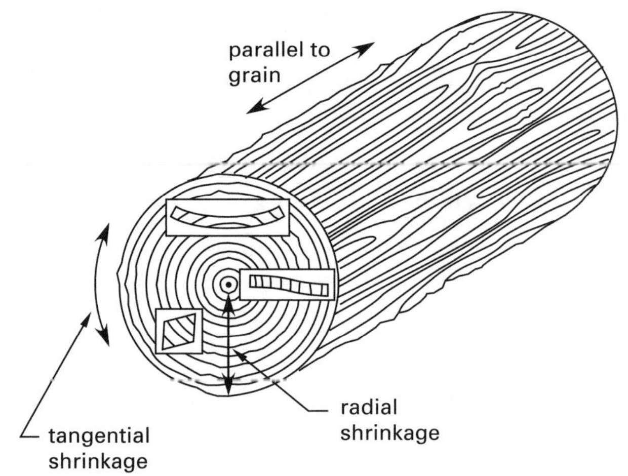

Figure 39.3 Wood Shrinkage

In detailing wood, an allowance must be made for the wood's shrinking and swelling during use, regardless of its initial moisture content. Of particular importance is the accumulated change in dimension of a series of wood members placed one on top of the next. The shrinkage of an individual member may not be significant, but the total shrinkage of several pieces may result in problems such as sagging floors, cracked plaster, distortion of door openings, and nail pops in gypsum board walls.

FRAMING

Framing is the assembly of lumber and timber components to construct a building. Because of code restrictions, structural limitations, and construction techniques, most wood construction is limited to small to moderate-sized buildings. This section discusses light frame construction; the next section reviews heavy timber construction used for larger structures.

Light Frame Construction

Light frame construction uses small, closely spaced members such as 2 × 4 or 2 × 6 studs for walls and partitions and nominal 2 in (51) thick members for floor and roof joists. Beams may be built-up sections of nominal 2 in lumber, or heavy timber or steel.

Two systems of wall framing include the platform frame (also called *western framing*) and the balloon frame. The essential difference is that the platform frame uses separate studs for each floor of the building, with the top plates, floor joists, and floor framing of the second level being constructed before the second-floor wall studs are erected. The balloon frame uses continuous wall studs from foundation to second-floor ceiling. Figure 39.4 shows the two types of framing systems.

One advantage of the platform frame is that each floor can be completed and used for constructing the next floor, and shorter studs cost less. The advantage of the balloon frame is that vertical shrinkage is minimized because most of the construction is parallel to the direction of the grain where wood shrinkage is the least.

When wood joists are framed into masonry walls instead of wood stud walls, they must rest on metal hangers attached to wood ledger strips anchored to the masonry or be fire cut, as shown in Fig. 39.5. A fire cut is required to prevent the masonry from being pushed up and out if the wood member should collapse during a fire.

Framing Openings

Openings in wood construction are required for doors, windows, stairs, and similar conditions. Because light frame construction consists of many small, closely spaced members carrying the loads, eliminating any of these studs or joists affects the structural integrity of the building. As a result, framing of openings must be capable of transferring loads from one cut member to other members. Two typical methods of framing vertical and horizontal openings are shown in Fig. 39.6. The size of header over a window opening depends on the span and usually consists of a double 2 in wide member (commonly expressed as 2 ×) bearing on studs at either side of the opening.

Plywood

Plywood consists of sheets of thin veneer glued together to form a rigid panel. Sheets are made in standard 4 ft by 8 ft sizes in thicknesses of $^1/_4$, $^3/_8$, $^1/_2$, $^5/_8$, and $^3/_4$ in. These are the most readily available, although other panel sizes and thicknesses are available. Metric plywood is 1200 mm by 2400 mm.

Plywood is graded in two ways. The first is by span rating and is used for most structural applications, including

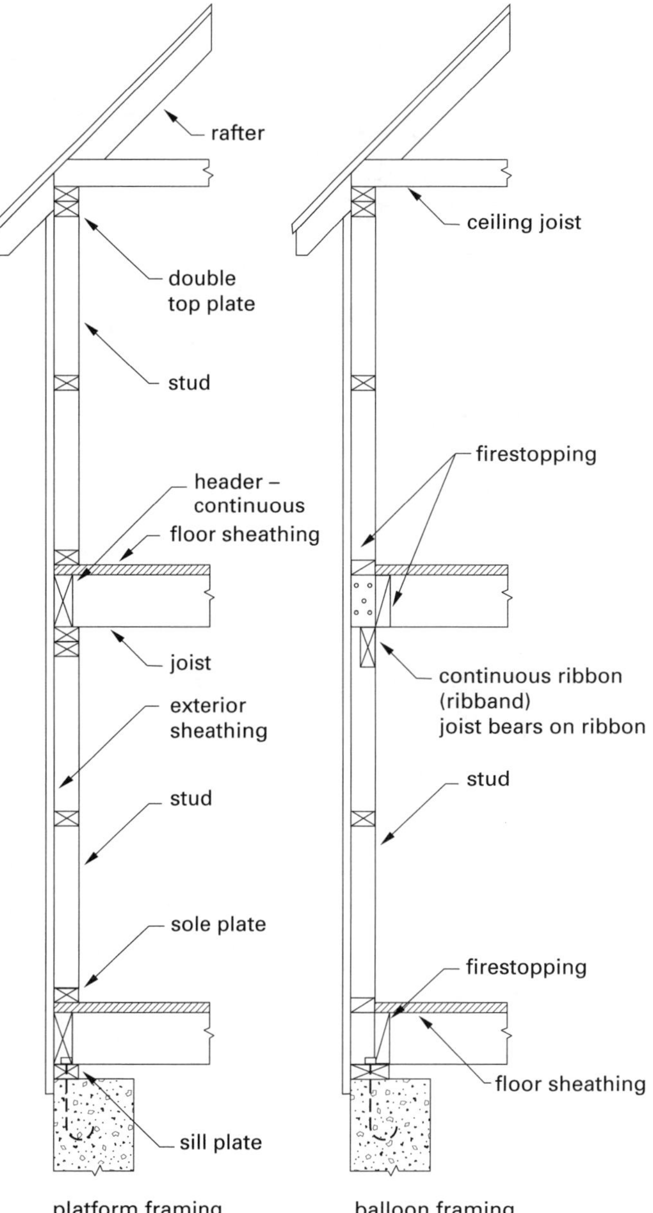

Figure 39.4 Light Frame Construction

sheathing. The span rating is a measure of the strength and stiffness of the plywood parallel to the face grain. The rating consists of two numbers, such as $^{32}/_{24}$. The first number gives the maximum spacing in inches for roof supports under average loading conditions, and the second number gives the maximum spacing in inches for floor supports under average residential loading. These spacings are allowed if the face grain is perpendicular to the direction of the supports and if the panels are continuous over three supports.

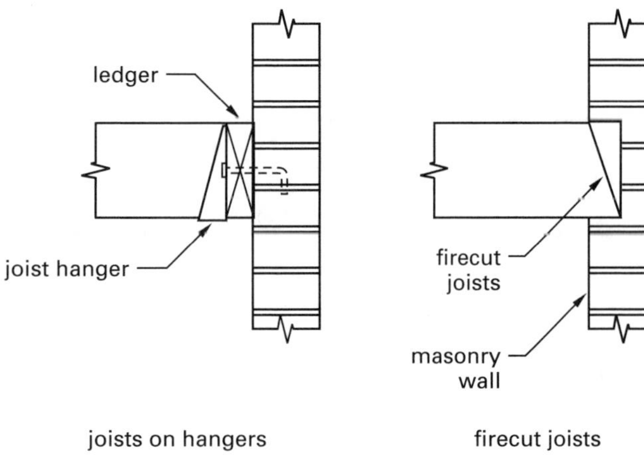

Figure 39.5 Wood Framing into Masonry

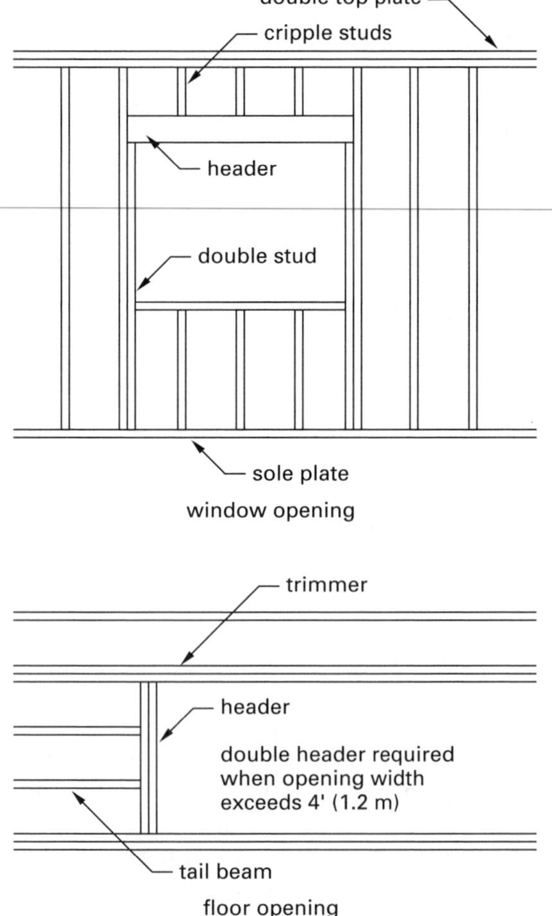

Figure 39.6 Framing for Openings

Plywood for structural uses is also classified according to the species of wood used. There are five groups. Structural I plywood is made only from woods in group 1; Structural II can be made from woods in groups 1, 2, and 3.

The other way plywood is graded is by the quality of the face veneer. Veneer grades are classified by the letters N, A, B, C, and D. *N grade* is intended for a natural finish and is made from all heartwood or all sapwood. It is free from defects but is only available on special order. *A grade* is smooth and paintable with few knots or other defects and is the best grade commonly available. *B grade* allows for plugged knotholes but has a smooth surface. *C grade* allows small knotholes and some splits, and *D grade* allows for larger knotholes. Plywood should be specified with exterior glue for outdoor locations.

Special types of plywood are also produced. These include patterned panels for exterior finish siding, marine plywood that has special glues, and overlaid plywood with a surface of resin-impregnated paper to provide a smooth surface.

Sheathing and Miscellaneous Wood Framing Members

Sheathing is thin panel material attached to framing to provide lateral support, increase rigidity, and provide a base for applying exterior finishes. For structural purposes, sheathing most often consists of plywood or particleboard nailed to the wood studs or joists. In situations where lateral stability is not critical, insulating sheathing may be used.

Particleboard is composed of small wood particles, fibers, or chips of various sizes mixed together in a binder and formed under pressure into a panel. Like plywood, it is available in several thicknesses in 4 ft by 8 ft sheets and is available in low-, medium-, and high-density forms. Metric particleboard sheets measure 1200 mm by 2400 mm. Particleboard is generally preferred for backing and framing of finish carpentry and architectural woodwork because it is less expensive and more dimensionally stable than plywood.

Oriented strand board (OSB) is an engineered panel product manufactured from precision-cut wood strands a maximum of 4 in (100) long and 0.0027 in (0.068) thick. The strands are arranged in layers at right angles to one another, much like plywood, and bonded with resin waterproof glue under heat and pressure. OSB is available in several thicknesses and sizes from standard 4 ft by 8 ft (1200 by 2400) size to much larger sizes, up to 8 ft by 28 ft (2400 by 8400). The primary strength of OSB panels is along the orientation of the chips on the face layer, which is generally parallel to the length of the panel. Although OSB is more susceptible to delamination than is plywood, it is still acceptable for use as sheathing with short-term weather exposure because of the waterproof glue used.

Medium-density fiberboard (MDF) is a panel product made from wood particles reduced to fibers in a moderate-pressure steam vessel and then combined with a resin and bonded together under heat and pressure. It is the most dimensionally stable of the mat-formed panel products. MDF has a smooth, uniform, and dense surface that makes it useful for painting, thin overlay materials, veneers, and high-pressure decorative laminate.

Hardboard is a panel product composed of inter-felted fibers consolidated under heat and pressure to a density of 31 lbm/ft^3 (497 kg/m^3) or more. It is available sanded on one or both sides and either tempered or untempered. Tempered hardboard has a greater hardness, stiffness, and weight than the untempered type.

Blocking is wood framing installed between main structural members such as studs or joists to provide extra rigidity or to provide a base for nailing other materials. For example, short pieces of lumber are often placed perpendicular to joists under the locations of interior partitions. Edge blocking is also placed at the intersection of wall and ceiling framing to provide a nailing base for the application of gypsum wallboard.

Bridging is bracing between joists that prevents the joist from buckling under load. Bridging may be solid wood blocking, 1 × 3 (actual $^3/_4$ in by $2^1/_2$ in [19 by 64]) wood cross members, or metal cross bridging. It is installed at intervals not exceeding 8 ft (2440) unless both the top and bottom edges of the joists are supported for their entire length.

Firestops are barriers installed in concealed spaces of combustible construction to prevent the spread of fire caused by drafts. Allowable materials include nominal 2 in thick wood members, gypsum board, or mineral wool. In most cases, wood blocking is used. The building code specifies where and when firestops must be installed, but in general firestopping is used in concealed spaces between floors, between a floor and ceiling or attic space, between floors under stairs, and in vertical openings around vents, chimneys, and ducts between floors.

ENGINEERED WOOD PRODUCTS

Engineered wood products include a wide range of components that are either constructed of standard wood elements (such as factory-built trusses made from 2 × 4s) or that use waste products or smaller pieces of wood to create new construction components (such as laminated veneer lumber). In some cases, wood products are used in conjunction with other materials, such as metal fasteners or insulation. Engineered wood products have the following advantages.

- better use of natural resources
- an improved product without typical wood defects
- increased strength for a given size compared with standard wood products
- consistent size and strength

Plywood Web Joists

Plywood web joists are like wood I-beams. They are fabricated with a plywood or an oriented strand board web piece fitted into grooves of chord members made of solid wood or laminated veneer lumber. They are manufactured in the same depths as standard solid wood joists and deeper. For the same depth they have a much higher load-carrying capacity than do wood joists, and they make very efficient use of wood products and only require wood from second- or third-growth timber forests. Other advantages include minimal shrinkage, ease of handling, and uniformity of size and shape. See Fig. 39.7(a).

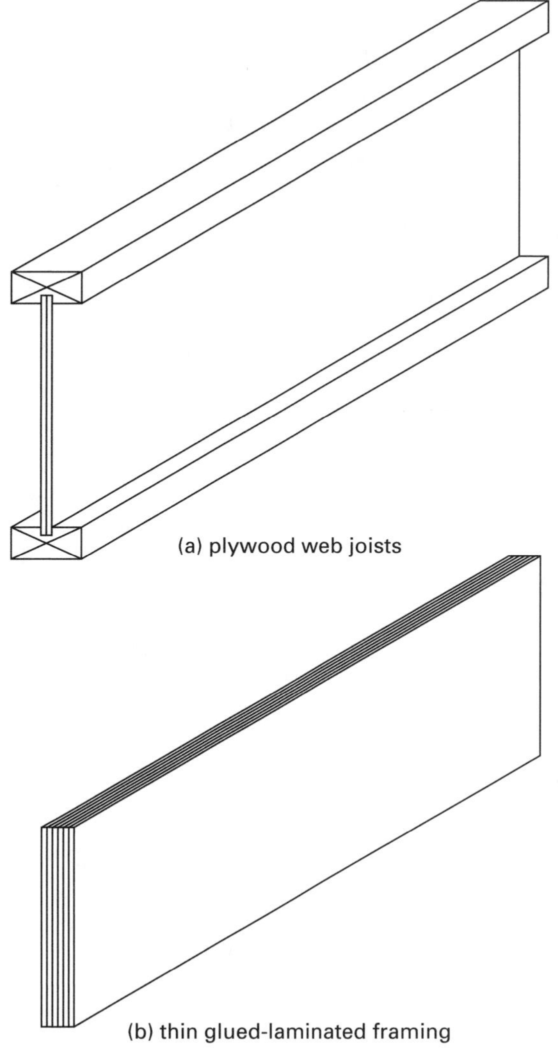

Figure 39.7 Prefabricated Structural Wood

Laminated Veneer Lumber

Laminated veneer lumber, sometimes called *thin glued-laminated framing*, is fabricated by gluing thin veneers of lumber together to build up a strong, rigid, dimensionally stable framing member than can be used like solid framing lumber. See Fig. 39.7(b). Laminated veneer lumber can be used for headers or beams and in place of studs.

Trusses

Wood trusses are factory-made assemblies consisting of relatively small wood members (normally 2 × 4s or 2 × 6s) held together with toothed plate connectors. They are available for residential and light commercial construction and can be fabricated with parallel top and bottom chords for floor framing or with sloped upper chords for roof framing. Common spacing is 24 in (600) on center. Depending on the depth of the truss and loading, floor trusses can span up to about 40 ft (12 m), and roof trusses can span up to about 70 ft (21 m). Some of the common types of trusses are shown in Fig. 39.8.

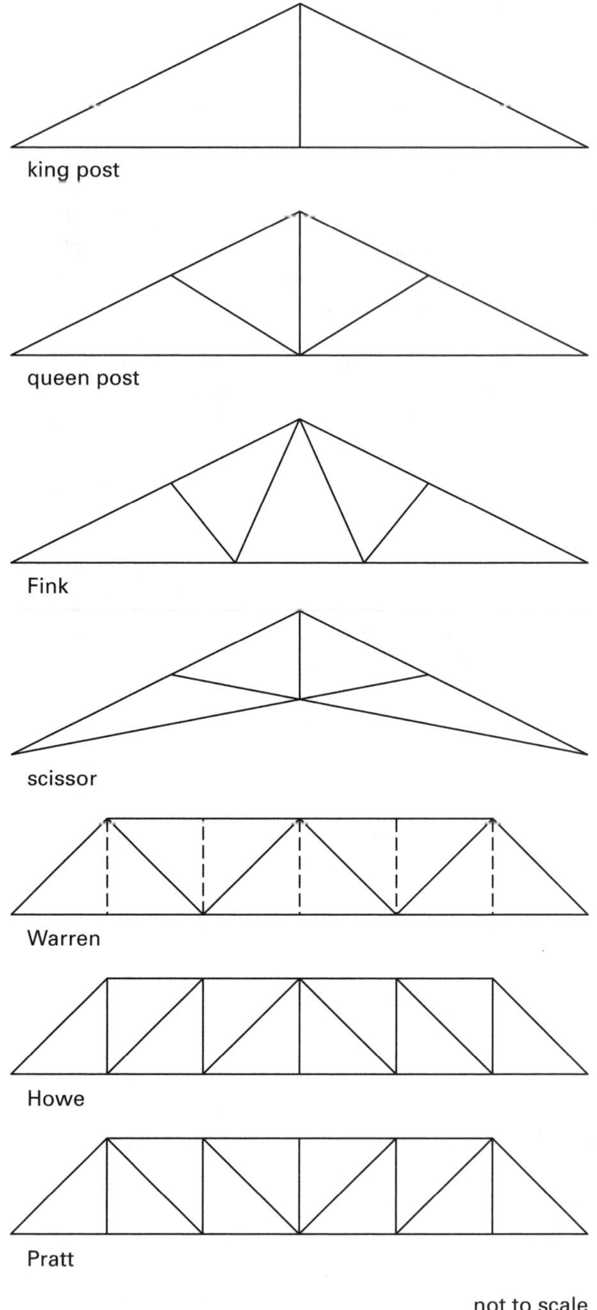

Figure 39.8 Types of Trusses

Structural Insulated Panels (SIPs)

A *structural insulated panel* (SIP) is a composite building unit consisting of two outer skins bonded to an inner core of rigid insulating material. Most SIP panels are composed of $^7/_{16}$ in (11) oriented strand board (OSB) facings with a core of molded expanded polystyrene (EPS). Other facings may include plywood, aluminum, cement board, and gypsum wallboard. However, not all units with other facings have undergone testing for building code approval. Other core materials include extruded polystyrene (XPS), urethane foam, and even compressed straw. CFC gases previously used to produce the insulation have been replaced with environmentally friendly processes.

SIPs are available in thicknesses from $4^1/_2$ in (114) to $12^1/_4$ in (311) and sizes from 4 ft by 8 ft (1200 by 2400) up to 9 ft by 28 ft (2740 by 8530). Larger sizes are also possible from some manufacturers. Custom sizes are available and are normally used to speed construction and avoid waste. They are used for residential and light commercial construction and can be used for walls, floors, and roofs.

SIPs have the following advantages.

- decreased construction time (about one-third less than for stick-built buildings)
- improved insulation value with no thermal bridges (whole-wall *R*-values of R14 for a $3^1/_2$ in (90) core vs. R9.6 for 2 × 4 studs with fiberglass insulation)
- reduced air infiltration
- stronger than conventional stud and sheathing construction
- very flat walls for subsequent finishes
- dimensional stability

Because of their composite construction, SIPs have strength in compression, bending, shear, and uplift. The erection of SIPs is accomplished by slipping the SIPs over wood plates attached to the floor. Wood splines at the vertical joints are used to fasten one panel to the next. Panels come with vertical and horizontal chases for wiring. Additional space can be made for piping or other electrical equipment by simply using a saw or hot wire to cut away the required insulation.

As a green product, SIPs require less wood than do conventional houses, use renewable resources for the facings, improve thermal performance, and reduce construction waste. Some manufactures recycle cutouts, trimmings, and EPS foam. The foam cores and water-based adhesives used have no formaldehyde content and are inert plastics. The amount of formaldehyde emitted by the OSB is less than 0.1 part per million (ppm), which is well below acceptable levels established by the U.S. Department of Housing and Urban Development.

Common coordination concerns include detailing a vapor barrier on the inside of the panel, providing seismic anchors where required, and detailing termite shields in geographical areas where they are required.

HEAVY TIMBER CONSTRUCTION

Heavy timber construction consists of exterior walls of noncombustible masonry or concrete and interior columns, girders, beams, and planking manufactured of large solid or laminated timbers. The *Uniform Building Code* requires that interior columns be at least 8 × 8 (203 × 203) in nominal size and that beams and girders supporting floors be at least 6 in (152) wide and 10 in (254) deep. Girders framed into masonry walls must be fire cut similar to the joists shown in Fig. 39.5. Floor decking must be at least 3 in (76) in nominal thickness with no concealed spaces below. Roof decking must have at least a 2 in (51) nominal thickness.

Due to the expense and limited availability of large, solid timbers today, new heavy timber construction is most typically built with glued-laminated members.

Glued-Laminated Construction

Glued-laminated wood members, or *glulams* as they are usually called, are built up from a number of individual pieces of lumber glued together and finished under factory conditions for use as beams, columns, purlins, and other structural components. Glulams are used where larger wood members are required for heavy loads or long spans and simple sawn timber pieces are not available or cannot meet the strength requirements. Glulam construction is also used where unusual structural shapes are required and appearance is a consideration. In addition to being fabricated in simple rectangular shapes, glulam members can be formed into arches, tapered forms, and pitched shapes.

Glulam members are manufactured in standard widths and depths. In most cases, 1$^1/_2$ in (38) actual depth pieces are used, so the overall depth is some multiple of 1$^1/_2$, depending on how many laminations are used. If a tight curve must be formed, $^3/_4$ in (19) thick pieces are used. Standard actual widths are 3$^1/_8$, 5$^1/_8$, 6$^3/_4$, 8$^3/_4$, 10$^3/_4$, and 12$^1/_4$ in. See Fig. 39.9.

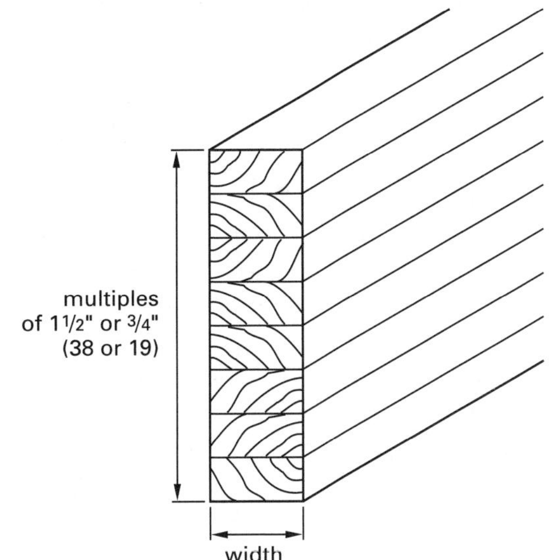

nominal width	actual width (in)	actual width (mm)
4″	3$^1/_8$″	79
6″	5$^1/_8$″	130
8″	6$^3/_4$″	171
10″	8$^3/_4$″	222
12″	10$^3/_4$″	273
14″	12$^1/_4$″	311

Figure 39.9 Glued-Laminated Beams

Because individual pieces can be selected free from certain defects and seasoned to the proper moisture content, and because the entire manufacturing process is conducted under carefully controlled conditions, the allowable stresses for glulam construction are higher than those for solid, sawn timber. Although glulam beams are usually loaded in the direction perpendicular to the laminations, they can be loaded in either direction to suit the requirements of the design.

For structural purposes, glulams are designated by size and a commonly used symbol that specifies the stress rating. Glulams are available in three appearance grades: industrial, architectural, and premium. These do not affect the structural properties but only designate the final look and finishing of the member. Industrial grade is used where appearance is not a primary concern, whereas premium is used where the finest appearance is important. Architectural grade is used where appearance is a factor but where the best grade is not required.

Planking

Wood planking, or *decking* as it is often called, is solid or laminated timber that spans beams. It is available in nominal thicknesses of 2, 3, 4, and 5 in (51, 76, 102, and 127) with actual sizes varying with the manufacturer and whether the piece is solid or laminated. All planking has some type of tongue-and-groove edging so the pieces fit solidly together and load can be distributed among adjacent pieces. Unlike sheathing, planking is intended to span greater distances between beams rather than between closely spaced joists. Common spans range from 4 ft to 20 ft (1200 to 6000), depending on the planking thickness and loads carried.

In addition to satisfying the code requirements for heavy timber construction, planking has the advantages of easy installation, attractive appearance, and efficient use of material, because the planking serves as floor structure, finish floor, and finish ceiling below. Its primary disadvantage is that there is no place to conceal insulation, electrical conduit, and mechanical services.

FASTENERS

There are many types of fasteners used for carpentry, including nails, screws, bolts, and fabricated metal fasteners.

Nails

Although they are the weakest of wood connectors, nails are the most commonly used connectors in light frame construction. The types used most frequently for structural applications include common wire nails, box nails, and common wire spikes. *Wire nails* range in size from six penny (6d) to sixty penny (60d). *Box nails* range from 6d to 40d—6d nails are 2 in (51) in length, and 60d nails are 6 in (152) long. Common wire spikes range from 10d (3 in long) to $8^1/_2$ in long and $^3/_8$ in diameter (76 to 216 mm long and 10 mm diameter). For the same pennyweight, box nails have the smallest diameter, common wire nails the next largest diameter, and wire spikes the greatest diameter.

For engineered applications, that is, where each nailed joint is specifically designed, there are tables of values giving the allowable withdrawal resistance and lateral load (shear) resistance for different sizes and penetrations of nails depending on the type of wood used. The more typical situation of most nailed wood construction is simply to use nailing schedules found in the building code. These give the minimum size, number, and penetration of nails for specific applications such as nailing studs to sole plates, joists to headers, and so forth.

There are several orientations that nails (as well as screws and lag screws) can have with wood members, which affect the holding power of the fastener. The preferable orientation is to have the fastener loaded laterally in side grain where the holding power is the greatest. The least desirable orientation is to have the nail or fastener parallel to the grain.

Screws

Wood screws are available in sizes from no. 0 (0.060 in shank diameter) to no. 24 (0.372 in shank diameter) and in lengths from $^1/_4$ in to 5 in (from 1.5 to 9.5 diameter, in lengths from 6 to 127). The most common types are flat head and round head. Because screws have a threaded design, they offer better holding power and can be removed and replaced more easily than nails. As with nails, screws are best used laterally loaded in side grain rather than in withdrawal from side grain or end grain.

Lead holes, slightly smaller than the diameter of the screw, must be drilled into the wood to permit the proper insertion of the screw and to prevent splitting of the wood.

A lag screw is threaded with a pointed end like a wood screw but has a head like a bolt. It is inserted by drilling lead holes and screwing the fastener into the wood with a wrench. A washer is used between the head and the wood.

Sizes range from $^1/_4$ in to $1^1/_4$ in (6 to 32) in diameter and from 1 in to 16 in (25 to 406) in length. Diameters are measured at the nonthreaded shank portion of the screw.

Bolts

Bolts are one of the most common forms of wood connectors for joints of moderate to heavy loading. Bolt sizes range from $^1/_4$ in to 1 in (6 to 25) in diameter and from $^1/_2$ in to 6 in (13 to 152) in length. Washers must be used under the head and nut of the bolt to prevent crushing the wood and to distribute the load.

The design requirements for bolted joints are a little more complicated than those for screwed or nailed joints. The allowable design values and the spacing of bolts are affected by such variables as the thicknesses of the main and side members, the ratio of bolt length in the main member to the bolt diameter, and the number of members joined.

Metal Fasteners

Because wood is such a common building material, there are dozens of types of special fasteners and connectors especially designed to make assembly easy, fast, and structurally sound. Hardware is available for both standard sizes of wood members and special members such as wood truss joists. Some of the common types of connection hardware are shown in Fig. 39.10.

In addition to the lightweight connectors shown in Fig. 39.10, there are special timber connectors used for heavy timber construction and for assembling wood trusses. Two of the most common types are split rings and

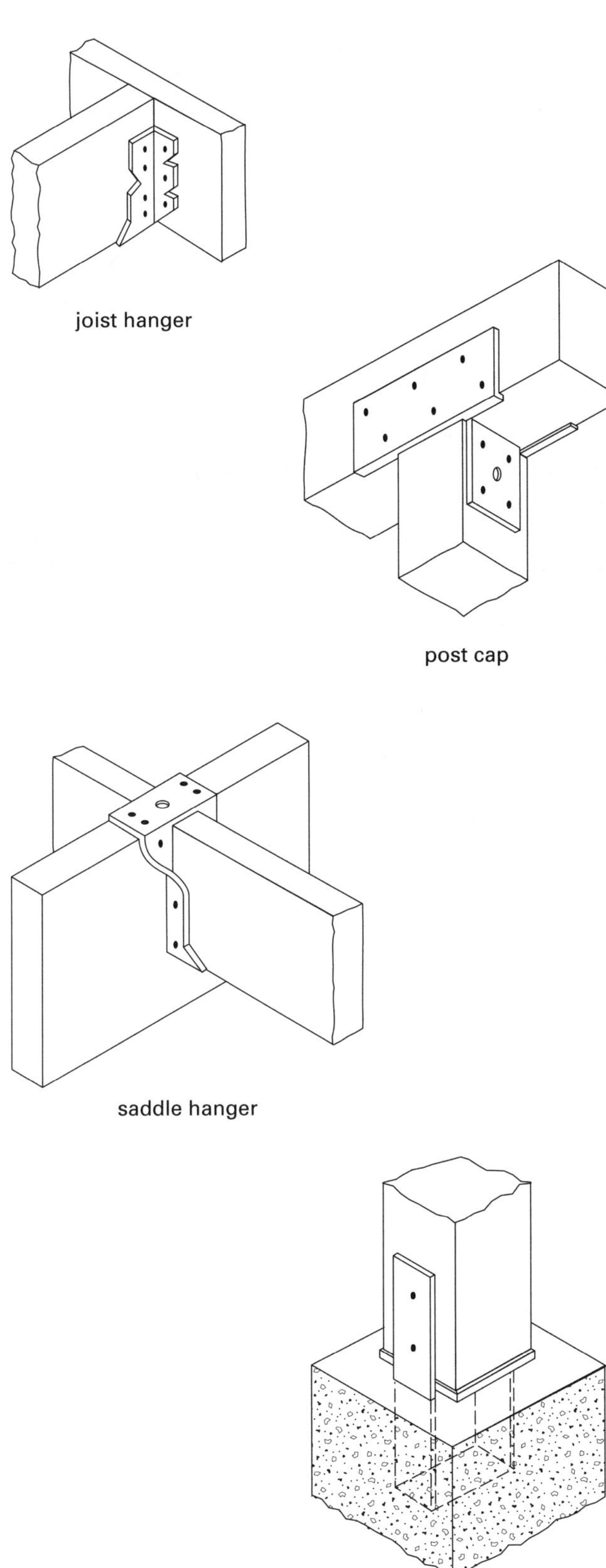

Figure 39.10 Special Connection Hardware

shear plates. Split rings are either $2^1/_2$ in or 4 in (64 or 102) in diameter and are cut through in one place in the circumference to form a tongue and slot. The ring is beveled from the central portion toward the edges. Grooves are cut in each piece of the wood members to be joined so that half the ring is in each section. The members are held together with a bolt concentric with the ring, as shown in Fig. 39.11(a).

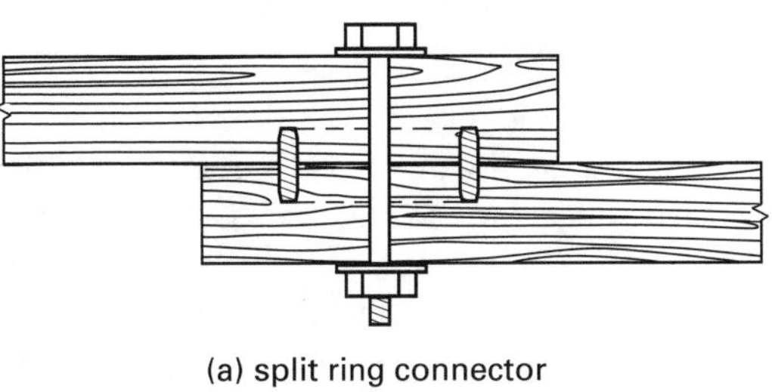

(a) split ring connector

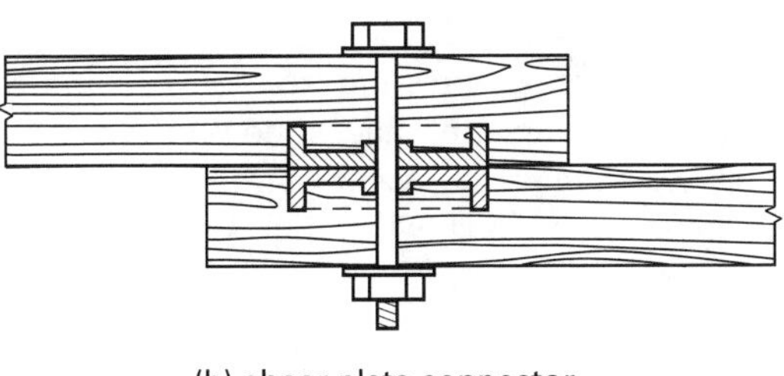

(b) shear plate connector

Figure 39.11 Timber Connectors

Shear plates are either $2^5/_8$ in or 4 in (67 or 102) in diameter and are flat plates with a flange extending from the face of the plate. There is a hole in the middle through which either a $^3/_4$ in or $^7/_8$ in (19 or 22) bolt is placed to hold the two members together. Shear plates are inserted in precut grooves in a piece of wood so that the plate is flush with one surface. (See Fig. 39.11(b).) Because of this configuration, shear plate connections can hold together either two pieces of wood or one piece of wood and a steel plate.

Split ring connectors and shear plates can transfer larger loads than can bolts or screws alone and are often used in connecting truss members. Shear plates are particularly suited for constructions that must be disassembled. Gang nail connectors are used in trusses also.

WOOD TREATMENT

As a natural material, wood is relatively durable if kept dry. Some woods, such as redwood, have naturally occurring resins that make them resistant to moisture and insect attack. However, most wood is subject to damage and decay from a number of sources and must be protected. The most common sources of attack and damage include fungi when moisture is present, insects such as termites and marine borers, and fire.

Preservatives may be applied by brushing, dipping, or pressure treatment. The most effective method is pressure treatment because the preservative is forced deep into the cells of the wood. For some applications such as marine use and protection from some insects, pressure treatment is the only satisfactory method to specify.

There are three basic types of wood preservatives: creosote, oil-borne preservatives, and waterborne preservatives. *Creosote* is a distillate of coal tar and is effective protection against insects. It is insoluble in water and is relatively easy to apply. Creosote is used mainly to protect railroad ties, marine timbers, and roadway guard posts. It is not used in building applications.

Oil-borne preservatives include *pentachlorophenol* (*penta*). This preservative is used to treat utility poles and cross arms, fresh water pilings, and bridge timbers. It is applied by brushing, dipping, or pressure treating. Penta is generally not used in building applications; however, it is sometimes used on glue-laminated beams supporting long spans in sports arenas and over swimming pools, and for similar applications.

Waterborne preservatives are the type most commonly used in residential, commercial, and industrial buildings. The types used today include *ammoniacal copper quaternary* (ACQ), also called alkaline copper quat, copper azole, and sodium borate (SBX), and variations of these three basic types. These types of treatments are clean, odorless, and nonstaining, and they leave the wood paintable. They provide protection against termites and decay. Work is continuing to develop preservatives that are totally free of metals.

Two other chemicals that have traditionally been used are chromated copper arsenate (CCA) and ammoniacal copper zinc arsenate (ACZA). However, these have been shown to be harmful to health and the environment because of their arsenic content. Chromated copper arsenate (CCA) for residential and general consumer use was phased out by the Environmental Protection Agency on December 31, 2003. Evidence had shown that arsenic could leach out of the treated wood and that disposal by burning could release toxic substances.

ACQ and copper azole are more corrosive than is CCA to fasteners and some flashing. Fasteners and connecters compatible with the chemical preservative used should be specified. Fasteners should be type 304 or 316 stainless steel or hot-dip galvanized products with a minimum G90 coating; that is, 0.90 oz/ft^2 (Z 275, 275 g/m^2). Aluminum flashing should not be used with wood treated with these preservatives. Preservatives with borates will leach out of wood when exposed to moisture, so applications with borates are limited to areas protected from moisture and not in contact with the ground. When cuts are made to treated wood, the exposed areas should be treated with a copper naphthenate solution containing at least 2% copper.

40 FINISH CARPENTRY AND ARCHITECTURAL WOODWORK

Finish carpentry is the final exposed-wood construction done on the job site. It is usually nonstructural in nature. This class of work includes exterior wood siding, interior trim, door and window framing, stair framing, shelving and cabinetry, paneling, and similar finish items.

Although finish carpentry overlaps somewhat with architectural woodwork, the latter term refers to finish lumber items fabricated in a manufacturing plant and brought to the job site for installation. Architectural woodwork items normally include fine finished cabinetry, wall paneling, custom doors, and other items that can be better made under controlled factory conditions.

FINISH CARPENTRY

Wood Species and Grading

As stated in Ch. 39, wood is classified as softwood or hardwood. *Softwoods* are those cut from coniferous trees, and *hardwoods* are those coming from deciduous trees. Finish carpentry employs both. Lower cost interior trim is usually made from the better grades of pine and fir, but when appearance is important, hardwoods such as oak, mahogany, or birch are used. Hardwoods are used almost exclusively for architectural woodwork because of their superior appearance and durability.

There are hundreds of domestic and imported wood species available for finish carpentry and architectural woodwork. However, because of cost and availability, only a few are generally used for finish carpentry and several dozen are used for architectural woodwork. Some of the common hardwood species include red and white oak, ash, walnut, cherry, mahogany, birch, poplar, and maple.

Finish carpentry lumber is graded differently than are architectural woodwork and structural lumber. The grading varies slightly from species to species, but in general the Western Wood Products Association (WWPA) classifies finish lumber into selects, finish, paneling, and commons, along with grades for siding and what the WWPA terms alternate boards. Selects are divided into B & Better (the best grade in this category), C Select, and D Select. Finish is subdivided into superior, prime, and E grades. Western red cedar, redwood, and a few other domestic species have their own grading rules. These grades are summarized in Table 40.1.

In addition to these grades, finish lumber may be specified as heartwood or sapwood. *Heartwood* comes from the center of the tree and sapwood from the perimeter. In some species, such as redwood, there is a marked color variance and resistance to decay between the two types of lumber. In some circumstances it is important to differentiate between the two.

For many types of softwood trim there is another category called *fingerjointed*. This is not really a grade but a method of manufacturing lengths of trim from shorter pieces of lumber. The ends of the short pieces are cut with finger-like projections, glued, and joined together. Fingerjointed material is less expensive than continuous molding but is only appropriate for a paint finish where the joints will be covered.

Lumber Cutting

The way lumber is cut from a log determines the final appearance of the grain pattern. There are three ways boards (also called *solid stock*) are cut from a log. Thin veneers are sliced in similar ways, but these are discussed in the next section on architectural woodwork. The three methods used are plain sawing (also called *flat sawing*), quartersawing, and rift sawing. These methods are illustrated in Fig. 40.1.

Plain sawing makes the most efficient use of the log and is the least expensive of the three methods. Because the wood is cut with various orientations to the grain of the tree, plain

Table 40.1
Selected Grades for Appearance Grades of Western Lumber

grade category	grades	description
selects	B & Better	Highest quality of select grade lumber available, with many pieces absolutely clear and free of defects.
	C Select	Appearance only slightly less than B & Better. Recommended for high-quality interior trim and cabinet work with natural stain or enamel finishes.
	D Select	Allows more defects than C Select grade but is suitable where finish requirements are less exacting.
finish	Superior; Superior VG	Highest quality of finish grade lumber available, with many pieces absolutely clear. Used for high quality trim and cabinet work where natural, stain, or enamel finishes are used and the finest appearance is required. Can be specified as VG for vertical grain.
	Prime; Prime VG	Allows slightly more defects than Superior, but can be used where finishing requirements are less exacting. Can be specified as VG for vertical grain.
	E	Boards in this grade can be cut in such a way as to produce pieces of Prime or Superior grades. E grade boards must contain two-thirds or more of such cuttings 2 in (50) or wider and 16 in (406) or longer.
paneling	any select or finish grade	C Select or any other grade can be used to produce paneling.
	selected 2 common for knotty paneling	Grade reserved for knotty paneling made from no. 2 Common grade boards (not shown in this table).

Note: Additional grades are available, but they are commonly used for other architectural purposes.

sawing results in a finished surface with the characteristic cathedral pattern shown in Fig. 40.1.

Quarter sawing is produced by cutting the log into quarters and then sawing perpendicular to a diameter line. Because the saw cut is more or less perpendicular to the grain, the resulting grain pattern is more uniformly vertical. Not only does this result in a different appearance than plain sawing, but quartersawn boards also tend to twist and cup less, shrink less in width, hold paint better, and have fewer defects.

As illustrated in Fig. 40.1, quartersawn boards cut from the edges of the log do not have the grain exactly at a 90° angle to the saw cut as do those in the middle. For an even more consistent vertical grain, *rift sawing* is used. With this method, the saw cuts from a quartered log are always made radially to the center of the tree. Because the log must be shifted after each cut and because there is a great deal of waste, rift cutting is more expensive than quartersawing.

Because of the limited availability of some species of wood and the expense of making certain cuts, not all types of lumber cutting are available in all species. In some cases, for a particular species, a veneer cut (discussed in the next section) will be available, but not the corresponding solid stock cut. The availability of cuts in the desired species should be verified before specifications are written.

Wood Siding

Wood siding consists of individual boards applied horizontally, diagonally, or vertically. When the siding is applied over wood sheathing (either plywood or particleboard), a layer of building paper is placed over the sheathing to minimize air infiltration and improve the water resistance of the wall. When the siding is applied over fiberboard or

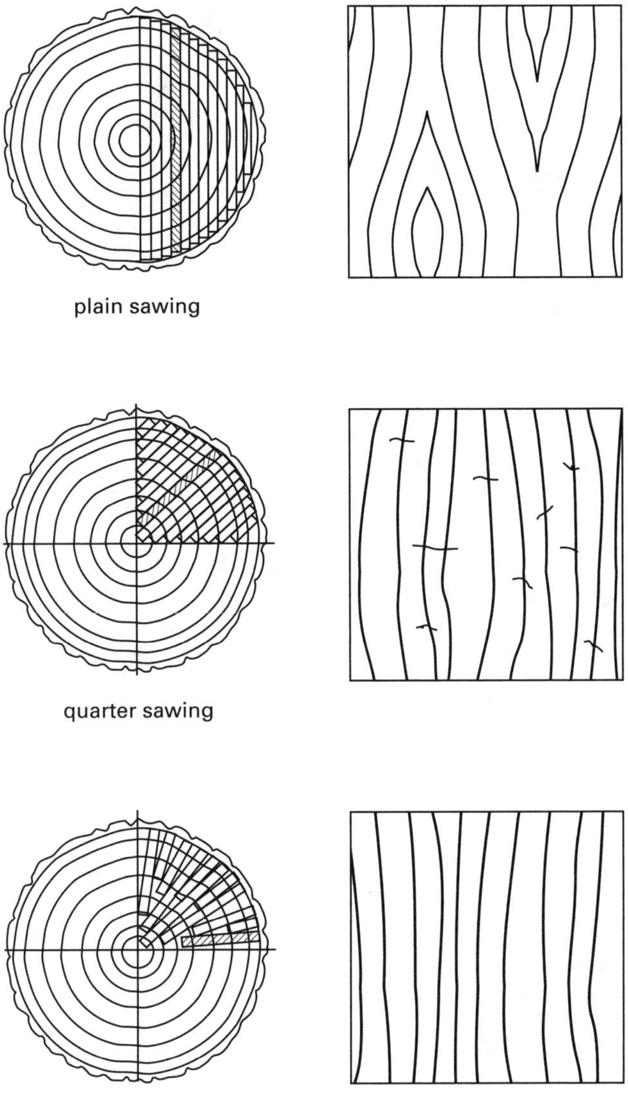

plain sawing

quarter sawing

rift sawing

Figure 40.1 Methods of Sawing Boards

insulating sheathing, an air infiltration barrier of high-density polyethylene is often used under the siding. This allows moisture vapor to pass through but minimizes air leakage.

Wood siding is milled from redwood, cedar, Douglas fir, pine, and several other species. Some, such as redwood and cypress, are naturally resistant to moisture and require less protection than varieties like pine. Siding comes in several shapes, as shown in Fig. 40.2. All are milled to allow one board to overlap.

Wood Stairs and Trim

The construction of wood stairs is considered a finish carpentry item although most utilitarian and decorative stairs are fabricated in a millshop. Stairs can range from simple

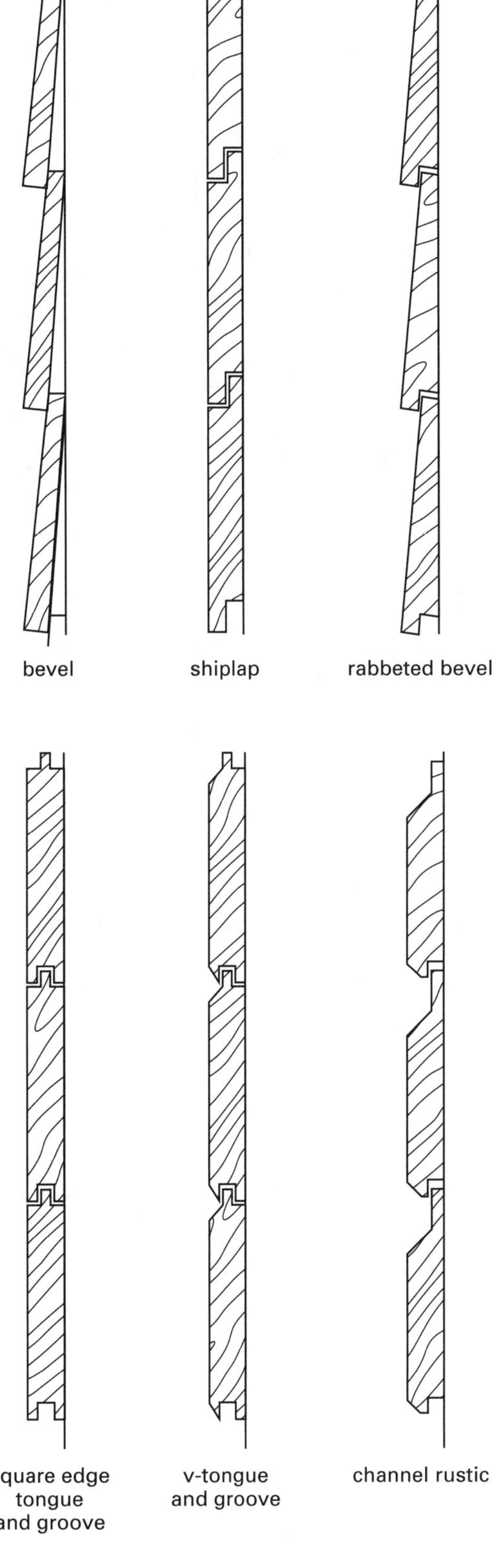

Figure 40.2 Wood Siding

utilitarian assemblies to elaborate, ornate, crafted works. A simple form of stair construction is shown in Fig. 40.3 with the primary construction elements identified.

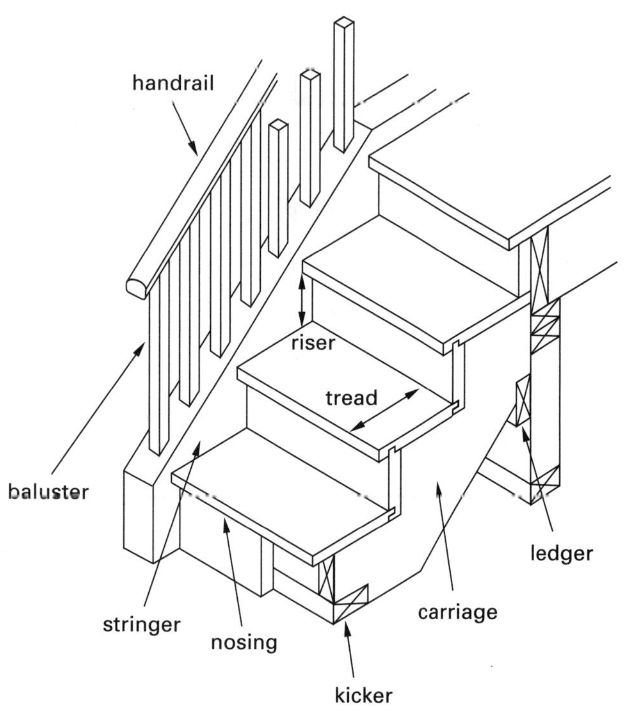

Figure 40.3 Typical Stair Construction

Interior and exterior trim is used to finish off the joints between dissimilar materials, close construction gaps between building elements, and provide decorative treatment. Simple, rectangular shapes are used for a great deal of construction trim, but there are dozens of standard, shaped molding pieces used for particular applications. Some of the more common types of interior trim are shown in Fig. 40.4.

More ornate molding sections can be built by using a combination of standard shapes or by having a millshop make a cutting blade that is used to shape special profiles.

ARCHITECTURAL WOODWORK

Architectural woodwork is custom, shop-fabricated lumber components used for interior finish construction, which includes cabinetry, paneling, custom doors and frames, shelving, custom furniture, fine stairs, and special interior trim. Architectural woodwork makes it possible to produce superior finish carpentry items because most of the work is done under carefully controlled factory conditions with machinery and finishing techniques that could never be duplicated on a job site.

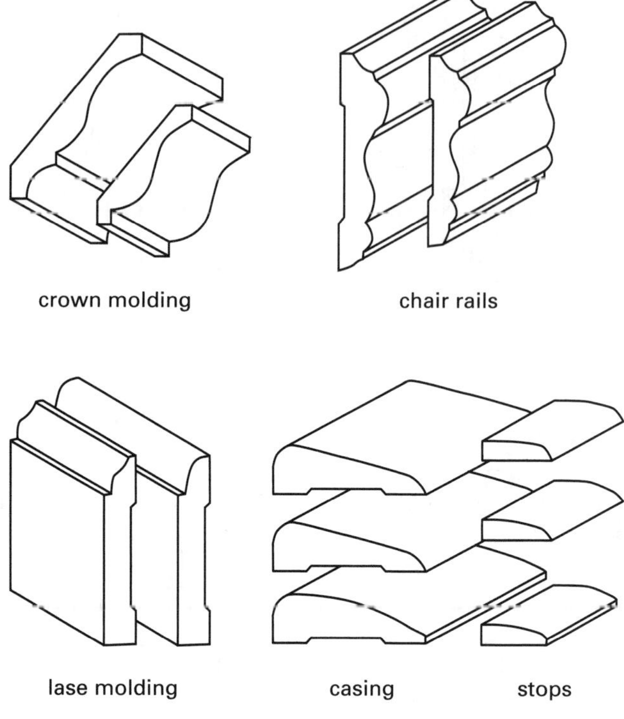

Figure 40.4 Interior Trim

Lumber for architectural woodwork and the quality of constructed woodwork items are graded differently than rough carpentry or finish carpentry. Standards for architectural woodwork are set by the Architectural Woodwork Institute (AWI) and are published in AWI's *Architectural Woodwork Standards* booklet.

Lumber is classed as Grade I, II, and III and is based on the percentage of a board that can be used by cutting out defects. There are also limitations on the types of defects that are allowed in any grade.

Construction standards, tolerances, and the finished appearance of completed components are specified as premium, custom, and economy grades. These grades apply to doors, cabinets, paneling, and other woodwork items. For example, the maximum gap between a cabinet door and frame is $^3/_{32}$ in (2.4) for premium grade, $^1/_8$ in (3) for custom grade, and $^5/_{32}$ in (4) for economy grade. A complete description for each item in each grade is given in the *Architectural Woodwork Standards* booklet.

Lumber and Veneers for Architectural Woodwork

Architects have a wider selection of solid stock and veneer for use in woodwork than for finish carpentry. Material comes from both domestic and foreign sources and varies widely in availability and cost.

Because of the limited availability of many hardwood species, most architectural woodwork is made from veneer stock. A *veneer* is a thin slice of wood cut from a log (as described in the next section) and glued to a backing of particleboard or plywood, normally $^3/_4$ in (19) thick.

Refer to Ch. 30 for more information on certified wood products and alternates to standard veneers.

Types of Veneer Cuts

Just as with solid stock, the way veneer is cut from a log affects its final appearance. There are five principal methods of cutting veneers, as shown in Fig. 40.5. Plain slicing and quarter slicing are accomplished the same way as cutting solid stock, except the resulting pieces are much thinner. Quarter slicing produces a more straight-grained pattern than does plain slicing because the cutting knife strikes the growth rings at approximately a 90° angle.

With *rotary slicing*, the log is mounted on a lathe and turned against a knife, which peels off a continuous layer of veneer. This produces a very pronounced grain pattern that is often undesirable in fine quality wood finishes, although it does produce the most veneer with the least waste.

Half-round slicing is similar to rotary slicing, but the log is cut in half and the veneer is cut slightly across the annular growth rings. This results in a pronounced grain pattern showing characteristics of both rotary-sliced and plain-sliced veneers.

Rift slicing is accomplished by quartering a log and cutting at about a 15° angle to the growth rings. Like quarter slicing, it results in a straight-grain pattern and is often used with oak to eliminate the appearance of markings perpendicular to the direction of the grain. These markings in oak are caused by *medullary rays*, which are radial cells extending from the center of the tree to its circumference.

Because the width of a piece of veneer is limited by the diameter of log or portion of log from which it is cut, several veneers must be put together on a backing panel to make up the needed size of a finished piece. The individual veneers come from the same piece of log, which is called a *flitch*. The word "flitch" is sometimes also used to describe the particular sequence in which the veneers are taken off the log as it is cut. The method of matching veneers is discussed in the following sections.

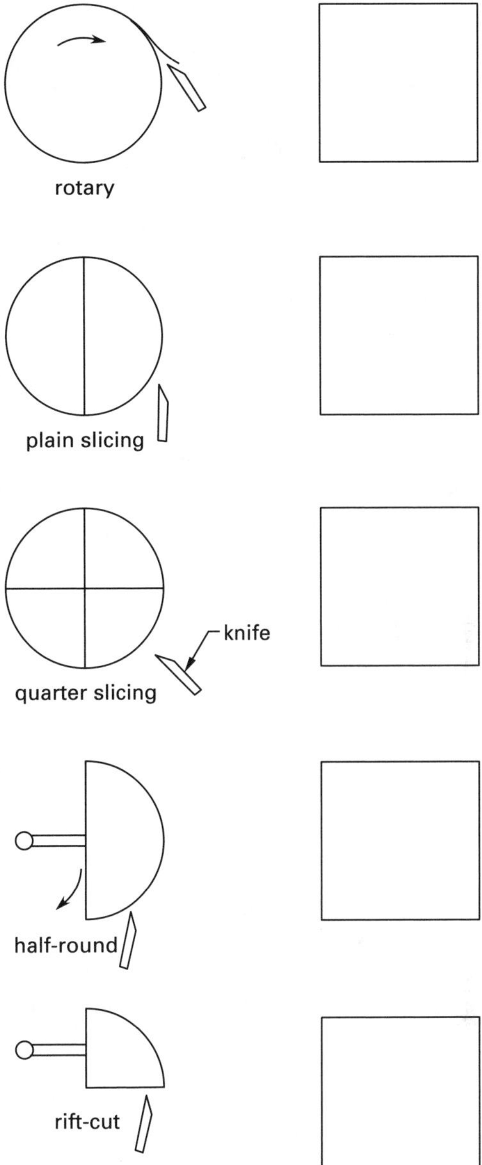

Figure 40.5 Veneer Cuts

Joinery Details

Various types of joints are used for woodwork construction to increase the strength of the joint and improve the appearance by eliminating mechanical fasteners such as screws. With the availability of high-strength adhesives, screws and other mechanical fasteners are seldom needed for the majority of the work produced in the shop. Field attachment, however, often requires the use of blind nailing or other concealed fastening to maintain the quality look of the work. Some of the common joints used in both woodwork and finish carpentry are shown in Fig. 40.6.

Cabinetwork

Architectural woodwork cabinets are built in the shop as complete assemblies and are simply set in place and

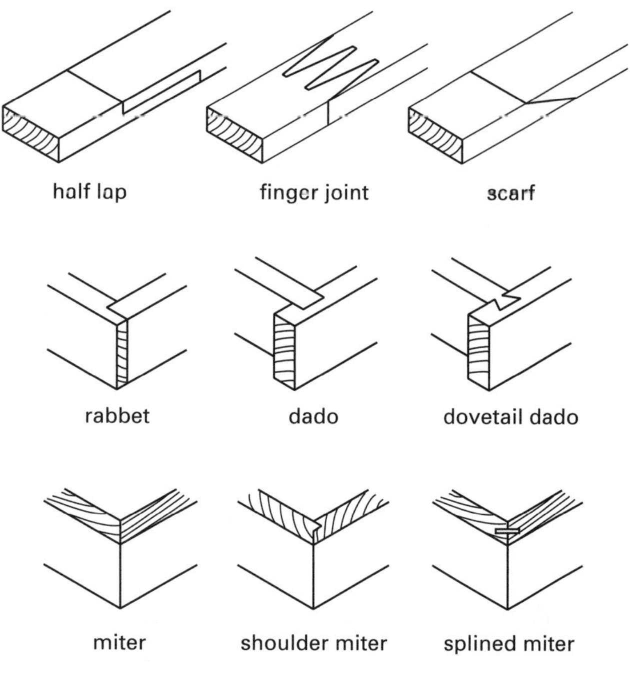

Figure 40.6 Wood Joints

attached to surrounding construction at the job site. There are several methods of detailing door and drawer fronts on cabinets, but the construction of the cabinet frames is fairly standard, as shown in Fig. 40.7.

Countertops are built separately from base cabinets and put in place in the field. This is because the countertops are built in single lengths that are much longer than any individual base cabinet. Building and installing the countertops separately also gives the installers the ability to precisely fit the countertop to the wall. This is most commonly done with a scribe piece on top of the backsplash or the back of the countertop. A *scribe piece* is an oversized piece of plastic laminate or wood that can be trimmed in the field to follow any minor irregularities of the wall. As with other woodwork components, there are hundreds of possible configurations to countertops including variations in width, materials, front edge shape and size, and backsplash shape and size. Some of the more common configurations are shown in Fig. 40.8. Figure 40.9 shows typical plastic laminate countertop edge treatments.

For both base and upper cabinets there are four basic categories of door and drawer front construction: flush, flush overlay, reveal overlay, and lipped overlay. These are shown in Fig. 40.10.

With *flush* construction, the face of a drawer or door is installed flush with the face frame. The primary disadvantage with this type of construction is its expense because of the extra care required to fit and align the doors and drawers within the frame. Another disadvantage is that, with use, the doors and drawers may sag. This results in a nonuniform spacing between fronts and may cause some doors and drawers to bind against the frame.

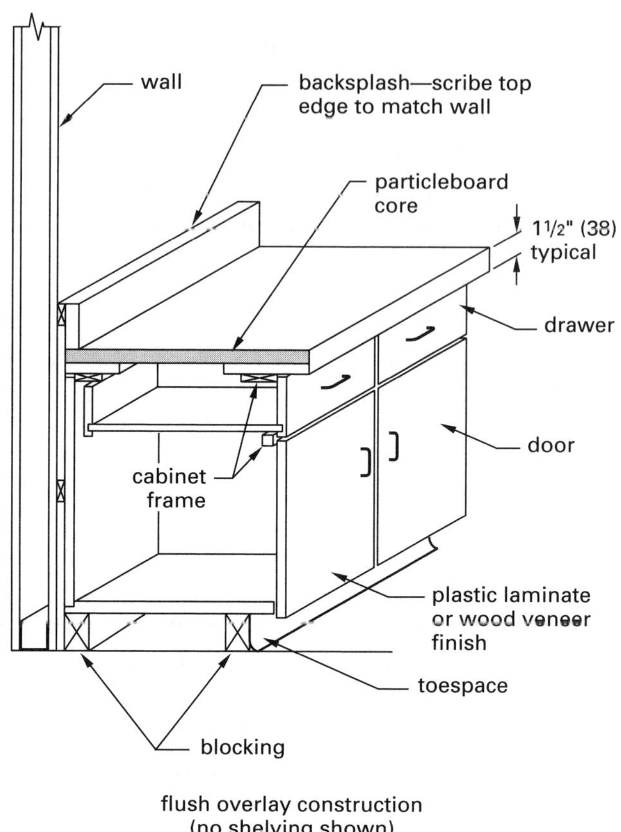

Figure 40.7 Typical Wood Cabinet

With *flush overlay* construction, the fronts of the doors and drawers overlap the face frame of the cabinet. Edges of adjacent door or drawer fronts are separated only enough to allow operation without touching, usually about 1/8 in (3) or less. Only doors and drawers are visible, and they are all flush with each other. As with flush construction, the millshop must take great care in aligning and fitting the doors and drawers so that the gap between them is uniform.

With *reveal overlay* construction, the edges of adjacent doors and door fronts are separated enough to reveal the face frame behind. This construction is less expensive than flush overlay construction because minor misalignments and sagging are not as noticeable. A variation is the *lipped overlay* construction in which part of the door or drawer overlaps the frame and covers the joint between the two pieces. See Fig. 40.10(d).

Upper cabinets are very similar in construction to base cabinets. The most notable exceptions are that they are not as

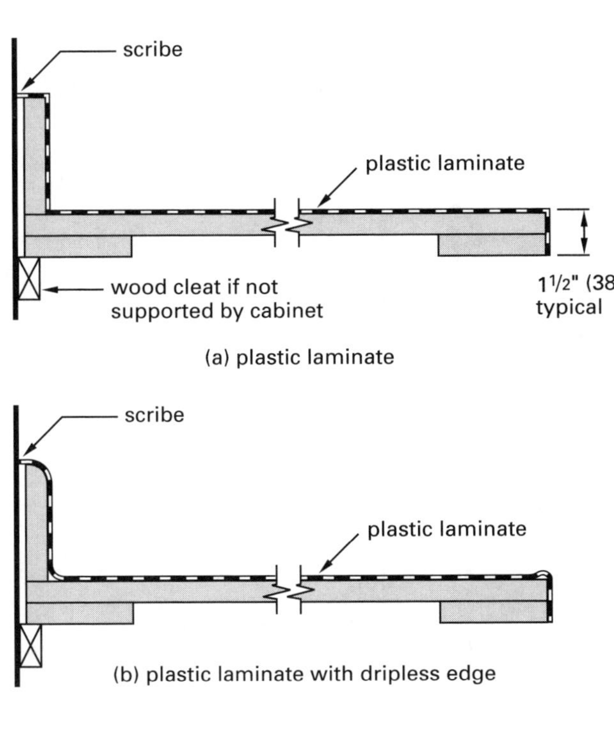

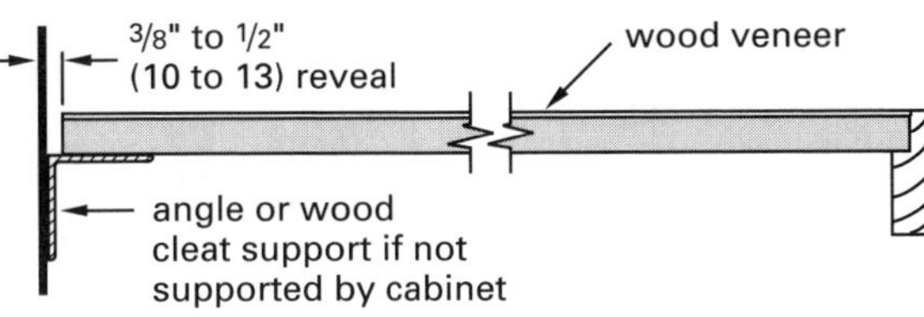

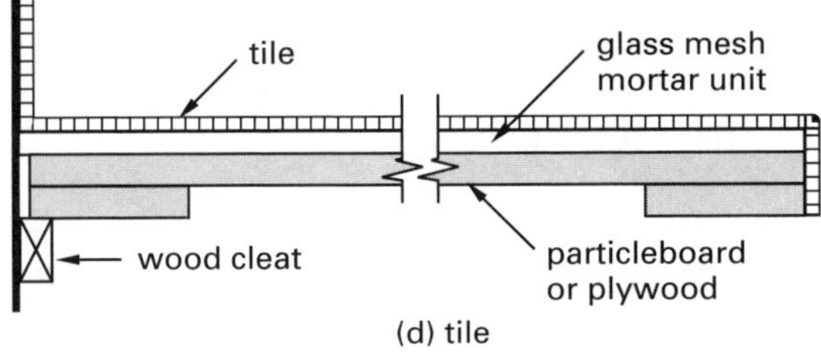

Figure 40.8 Typical Countertop Details

deep as base cabinets, and some design and detailing consideration must be given to the undersides of upper cabinets because they are visible. In addition, there must be some way to securely anchor the cabinet to the wall. In residential construction, the cabinet is attached to the wall by screwing through the cabinet back and wall finish into the wood studs. In commercial construction where metal studs are used, wood blocking is required in the stud cavity behind the wall finish. This blocking is installed as the studs are being erected and is attached to them with screws. The blocking provides a solid base for attaching the cabinets to the wall. Figure 40.11 shows a typical upper cabinet detail.

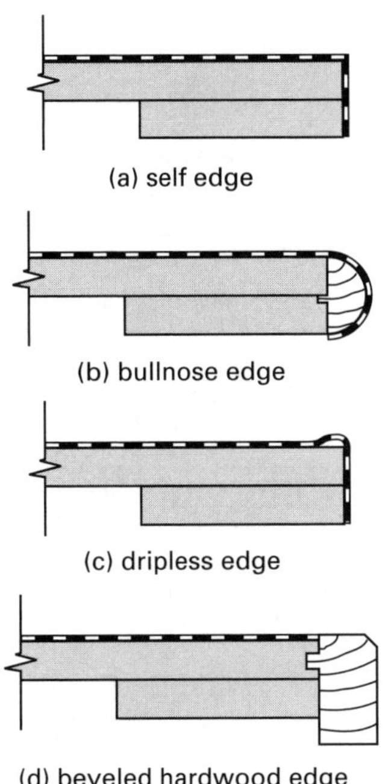

Figure 40.9 HPDL Edge Treatments

Flush Paneling

Architectural woodwork paneling includes flush or raised panel constructions used to cover vertical surfaces. As mentioned before, large, flat areas like paneling are built of thin wood veneers glued to backing panels of particleboard or plywood.

In addition to the way the veneer is cut, there are several methods of matching adjacent pieces of veneer and veneer panels in a room that affect the final appearance of the job. The three considerations, in increasing order of scale, are matching between adjacent veneer leaves, matching veneers within a panel, and matching panels within a room.

Matching adjacent veneer leaves may be done in three ways, as shown in Fig. 40.12. *Bookmatching* is the most common. As the veneers are sliced off the log, every other piece is turned over so that adjacent leaves form a symmetrical grain pattern. With *slip matching*, consecutive pieces are placed side by side with the same face sides being exposed. *Random matching* places veneers in no particular sequence, and even veneers from different flitches may be used.

Veneers must be glued to rigid panels to make installation possible. The method of doing this is the next consideration in specifying paneling. If the veneers are bookmatched, there are three ways, shown in Fig. 40.13, of matching veneers within a panel. A *running match* simply alternates bookmatched veneer pieces regardless of their width or how many must be used to complete a panel. Any portion

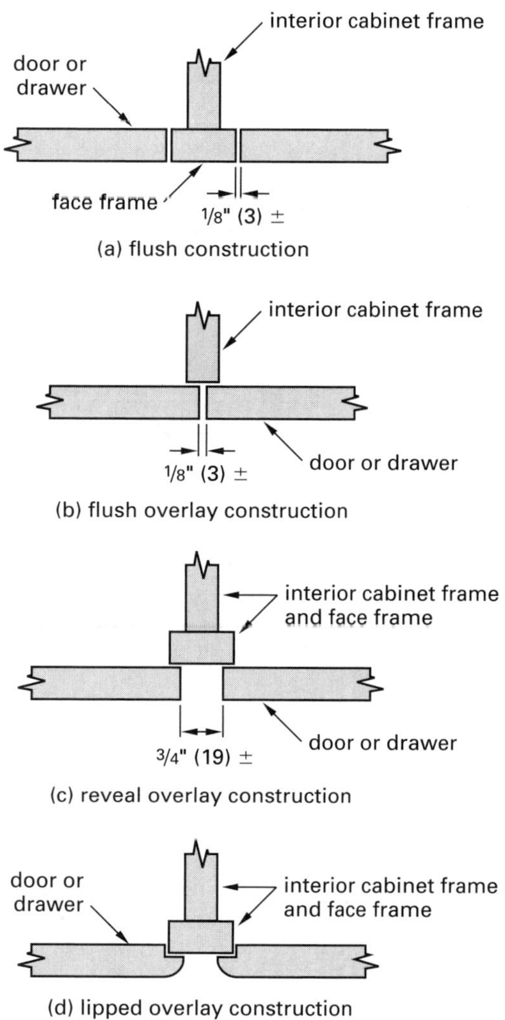

Figure 40.10 Types of Cabinet Door Framing

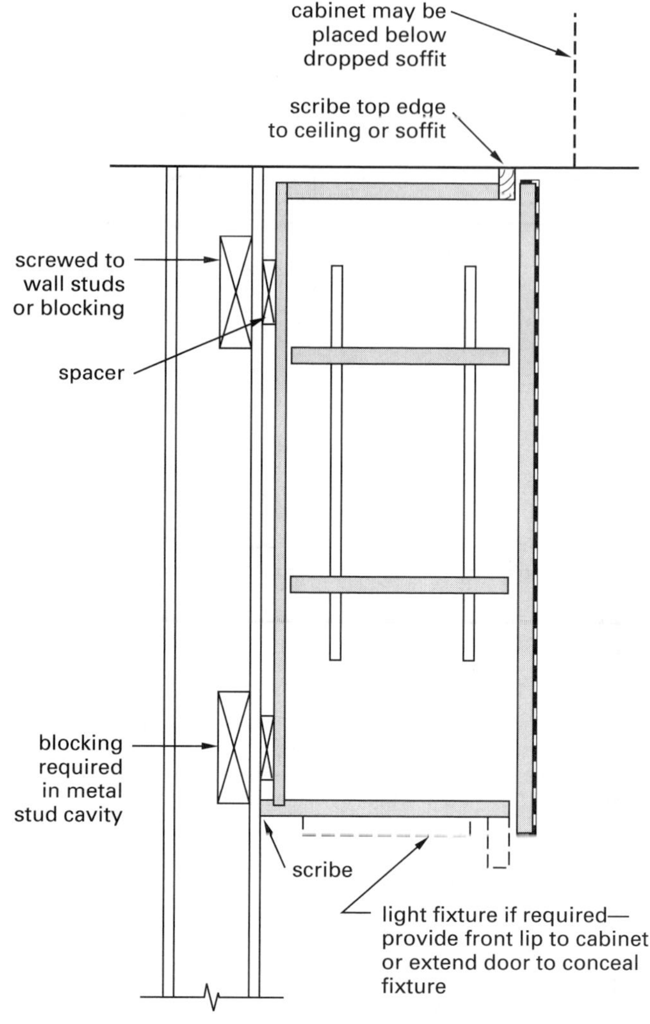

Figure 40.11 Typical Upper Cabinet

left over from the last leaf of one panel is used as the starting piece for the next. In a *balance match*, veneer pieces are trimmed to equal widths; there may be an odd or even number of veneer pieces in each panel. A *center match* has an even number of veneer leaves of uniform width so that there is symmetry about a veneer joint in the center of the panel.

There are also three ways panels can be assembled within a room to complete a project. See Fig. 40.14. The first and least expensive is called *warehouse matching*. Premanufactured panels, normally 4 ft wide by 8 ft or 10 ft long (1200 wide by 2400 or 3000 long) are assembled from a single flitch that yields from six to twelve panels. They are field cut to fit around doors, windows, and other obstructions, resulting in some loss of grain continuity.

The second method, called *sequence matching*, uses panels of uniform width manufactured for a specific job and with the veneers arranged in sequence. If some panels must be trimmed to fit around doors or other obstructions, there is a moderate loss of grain continuity.

The third and most expensive method is called *blueprint matching*. Here the panels are manufactured to precisely fit the room and line up with every obstruction so that grain continuity is not interrupted. Veneers from the same flitch are matched over doors, cabinets, and other items covered with paneling.

Joints of flush paneling may be constructed in a number of ways depending on the finish appearance desired, as shown in Fig. 40.15. Paneling is hung on a wall with either steel Z-clips or wood cleats cut at an angle to allow the individual panels to be slipped over the hanger, which is anchored to the wall structure. These methods are also illustrated in Fig. 40.15.

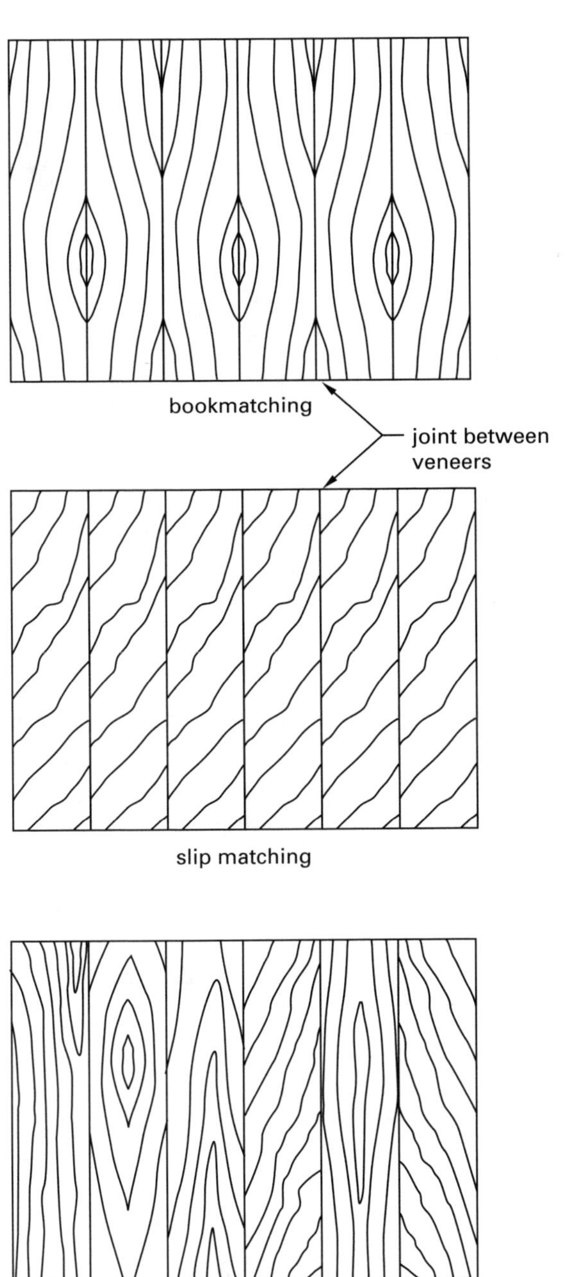

Figure 40.12 Veneer Matching

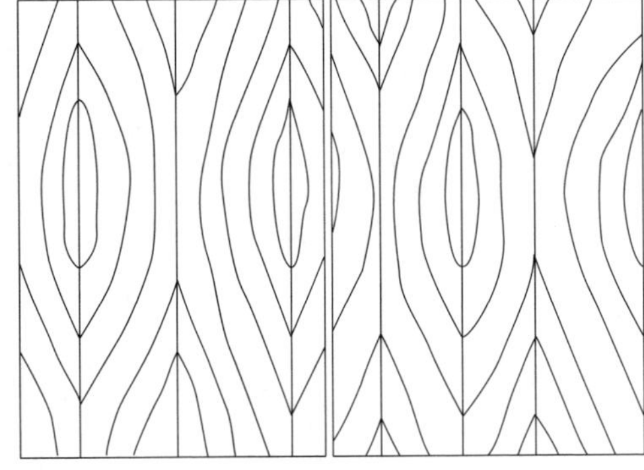

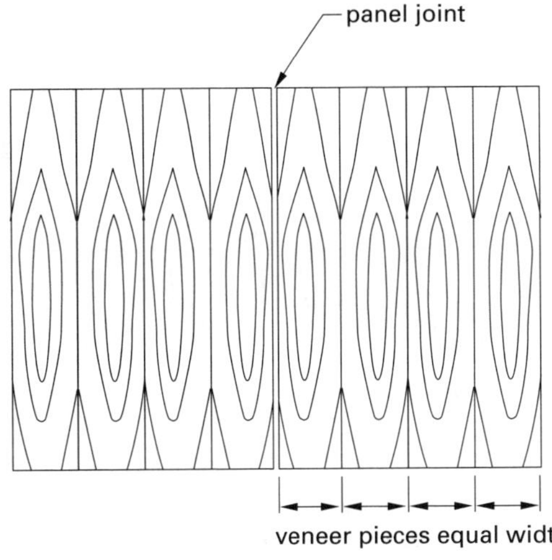

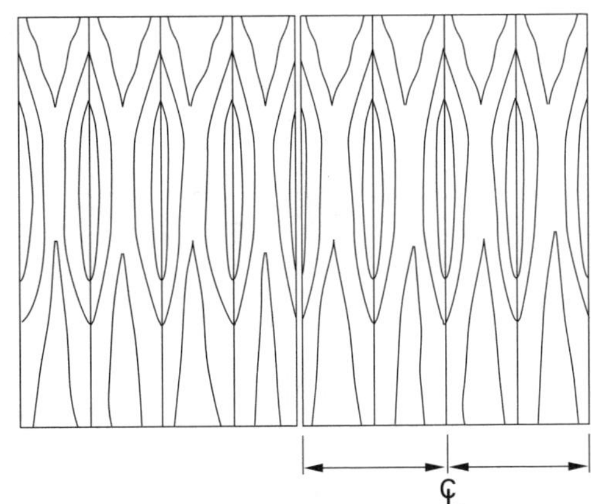

Figure 40.13 Panel Matching Veneers

Stile and Rail Paneling

Stile and rail panel construction consists of a frame of solid wood that contains individual panels. Along with various types of molding and matching doors, raised panel construction is used to detail a traditional wood-paneled room interior. See Fig. 40.16. Traditionally, the panels were also made from solid wood, but today it is more common for the panels to be veneered.

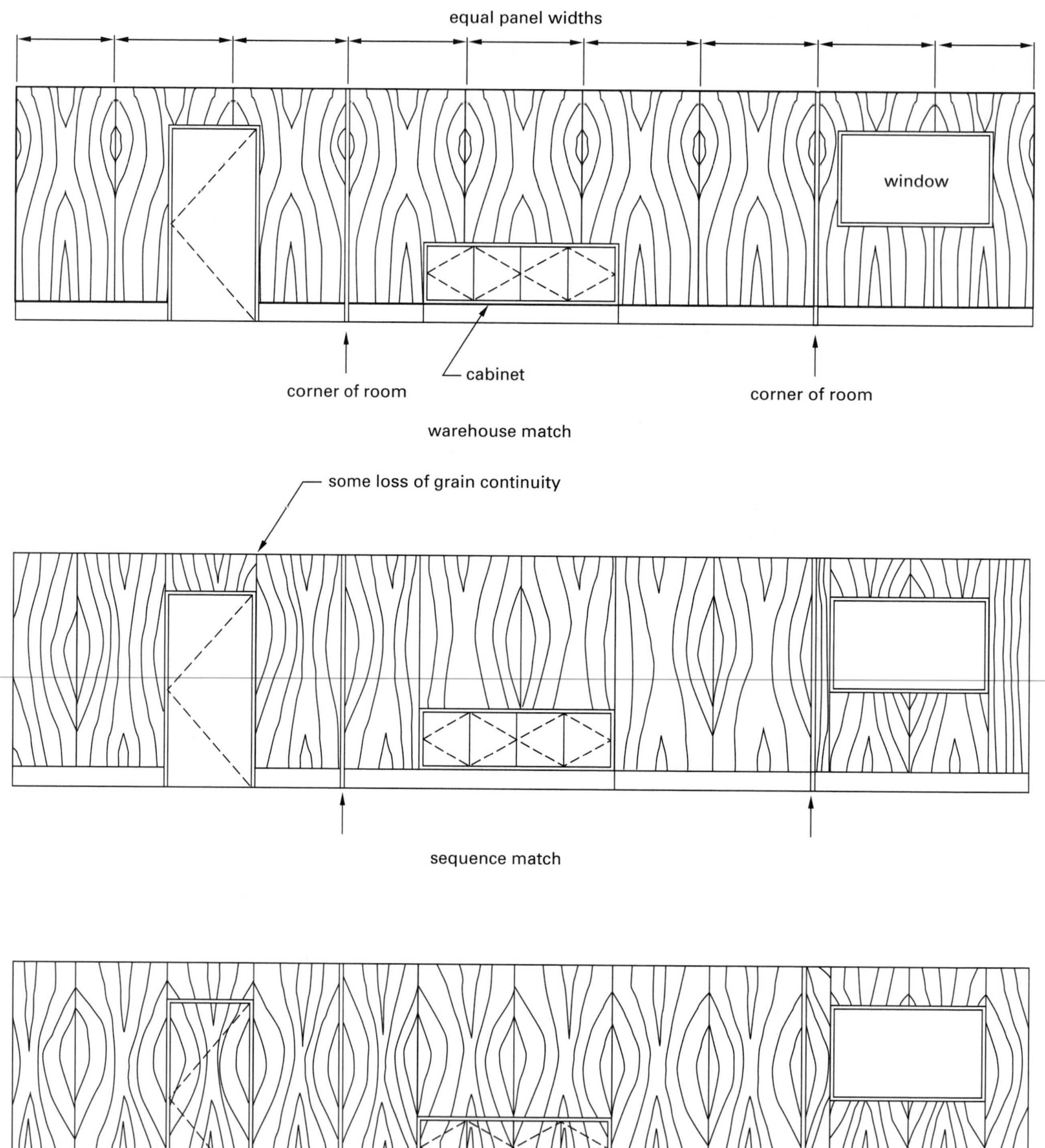

Figure 40.14 Matching Panels Within a Room

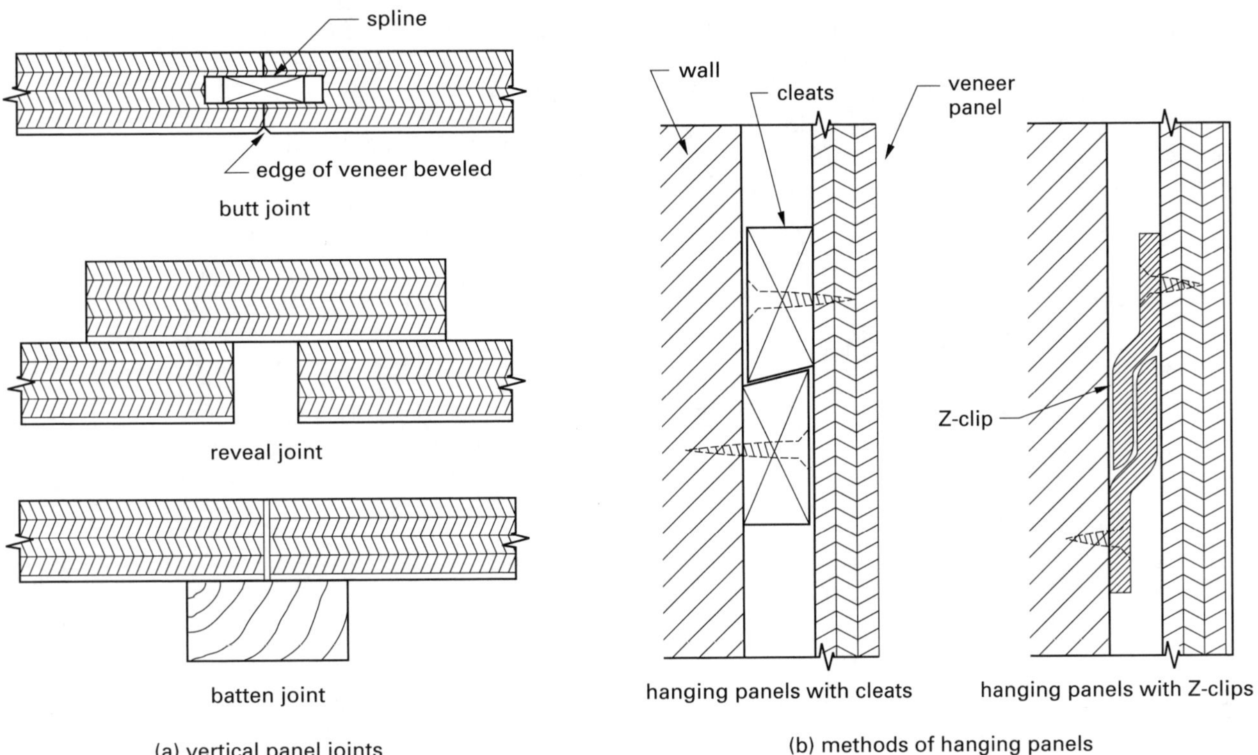

Figure 40.15 Flush Panel Joints

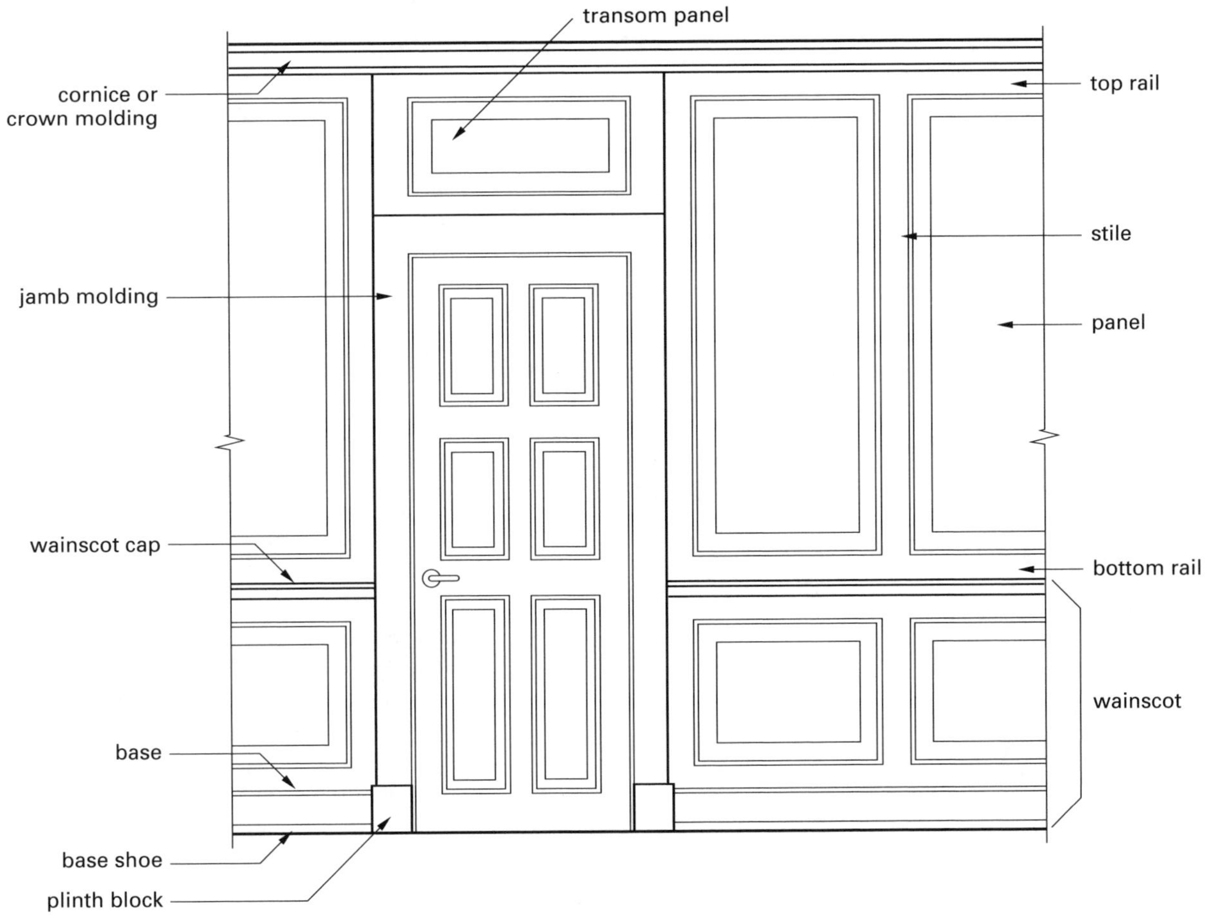

transom panel
cornice or crown molding
top rail
stile
jamb molding
panel
wainscot cap
bottom rail
wainscot
base
base shoe
plinth block

Figure 40.16 Stile and Rail Panel Construction

As shown in Fig. 40.17, the vertical frame pieces are called the *stiles*, and the horizontal members are the *rails*. The panels are held in place with grooves cut in the sides of the frames or with individual molding pieces, called sticking. The panels are set in the molding loosely to allow the panel to expand and contract with changes in the moisture content.

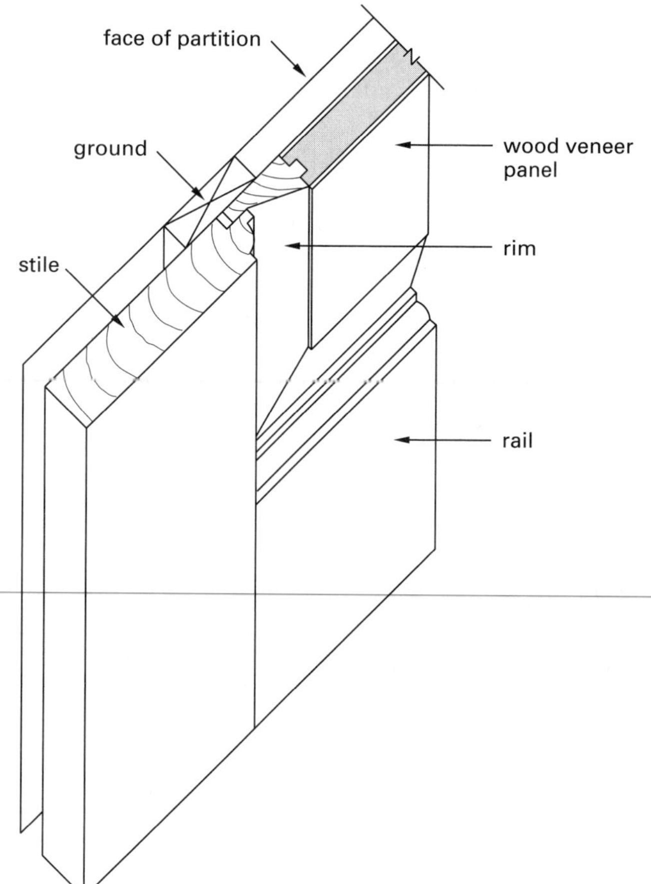

Figure 40.17 Stile and Rail Components

Stile and rail paneling may be hung on walls with wood cleats or metal Z-clips as with flush paneling, but if extensive molding is used the panels can be screwed to wood grounds behind the paneling and the fasteners concealed with the molding. Individual panels are joined with dowels or splines to keep the edges flush.

Laminates

A common finishing material used with architectural woodwork is *high-pressure decorative laminate* (HPDL). This is a thin sheet material made by impregnating several layers of kraft paper with phenolic resins and overlaying the paper with a patterned or colored sheet and a layer of melamine resin. The entire assembly is placed in a hot press under high pressure where the various layers fuse together. Plastic laminates are used for countertops, wall paneling, cabinets, shelving, and furniture.

Because laminates are very thin, they must be adhered to panel substrates such as plywood or particleboard. Smaller pieces can be glued to solid pieces of lumber. There are several types and thicknesses of plastic laminate, the most common being a general-purpose type that is 0.050 in (1.3) thick. It is used for both vertical and horizontal applications. A post-forming type, 0.040 in (1) thick, is manufactured so it can be heated and bent to a small radius.

When plastic laminate is applied to large surfaces of paneling, it must be balanced with a backing sheet to inhibit moisture absorption and to attain structural balance so that the panel does not warp.

There are several types of high-pressure decorative laminates manufactured for specific purposes. Although these generally cost more, they fill specific needs for some construction.

- *Colorthrough laminates*. These laminates are manufactured with decorative papers throughout the thickness so that the resulting sheet is a solid color. This eliminates the dark line visible at the edges of sheets when they are trimmed.
- *Fire-rated laminates*. These finishes comply with Class 1 or A ratings as long as the appropriate substrates and adhesives are selected.
- *Chemical-resistant laminates*. Special formulation of the laminate materials give these products additional resistance to strong chemicals found in laboratories, medical facilities, and photographic studios. They are available in horizontal as well as vertical thicknesses and can be post-formed for curved surfaces.
- *Static-dissipative laminates*. For areas where static control is required, such as in hospital operating rooms, electronic manufacturing plants, and computer rooms, these laminates provide a conductive layer in the sheet. When connected to suitable grounding they prevent the buildup of static charges and continuously channel them away.
- *Metal-faced laminates*. A limited number of metal finishes are available. They do not have the same wear resistance as real metal, so they should only be used on vertical surfaces subject to little abuse. They can be fabricated with standard woodworking equipment and cost much less than real metal. However, it is difficult to fabricate small, detailed items with finely crafted edges.

- *Natural wood laminates*. Thin veneers of actual wood are bonded to the standard type of laminate kraft papers and resins with this product. The laminate can be specified to provide untreated wood ready for finishing or with a protective layer of melamine resin.

Another type of laminate product is *thermoset decorative paneling*. It is made by pressing a decorative overlay from a thermoset polyester or melamine resin-impregnated saturated sheet onto a cellulosic substrate such as particleboard or medium-density fiberboard. This paneling differs from high-pressure decorative laminates in that its decorative surface is fused to the substrate of particleboard. (In contrast, the decorative surface of high-pressure laminates is a thin veneer that must be adhesive-bonded to another substrate.) Because the process is usually done with pressures lower than HPDLs, these products are sometimes called "low-pressure laminates" or melamine. The manufacturers that produce thermoset decorative panels form the American Laminators Association (ALA) and use the trade name Permalam® to identify these types of panels.

Because the decorative surface is part of the substrate, the potential problem of delamination is eliminated and the panels come ready to be fabricated. Generally, the cost of thermoset panels is less than HPDL in many cases. However, there are currently several disadvantages to thermoset decorative panels. The choices of colors, textures, and grades are limited. Thermoset panels cannot be post-formed for curves, and they should not be used for high-wear horizontal surfaces such as countertops. Only a limited number of Class I or A fire-rated panels is available from a few manufacturers. Thermoset panels are typically used for furniture, fixtures, and kitchen cabinets or where resistance to heavy use is not required.

Standing and Running Trim

Standing and running trim are similar to standard molding sections applied as finish carpentry items. Unlike moldings, however, standing and running trim are custom-fabricated to meet the requirements of a specific project.

Standing trim is woodwork of a fixed length, intended to be installed as a single piece of wood. Examples include door frame trim, door stops, window casings, and similar items. *Running trim* is woodwork of a continuing length that must be installed in several pieces fitted end to end, such as base molding, cornices, chair rails, and soffits. *Rails* are gripping or protection surfaces on corridor walls of hospitals and the like and guard rails at glass openings.

The *profile* of trim, or its *cross-sectional shape*, can be identical to the many standard shapes available in premanufactured molding, or custom profiles can be milled.

Solid Surfacing Material

Solid surfacing is a generic term for homogeneous, polymer-based surfacing materials. It can be formed into thick, flat sheets, or into shapes. It is frequently used for kitchen and bath countertops, sinks, toilet partitions, bars, and other areas where high-pressure plastic laminate might otherwise be used. It is available in a wide variety of colors and patterns. Standard thickness for countertops is $^3/_4$ in (19). Because the color is integral throughout the thickness of the material, scratches, dents, stains, and other types of minor damage can be sanded out or cleaned with a household abrasive cleanser. Because many of the available patterns resemble stone, it is often used as a lower cost, lighter weight substitute for stone tops.

Solid surfacing materials are easily fabricated and installed with normal woodworking tools. Edges can even be routed for decorative effects. When two pieces must be butted together, a two-part epoxy or liquid form of the material is used for a seamless appearance.

Moisture Content and Shrinkage

Shrinkage and swelling of lumber in architectural woodwork is not as much of a problem as for rough and finish carpentry because of the improved manufacturing methods available in the shop and the fact that solid stock and veneer can be dried or acclimated to a particular region.

However, some general guidelines should be followed. For most of the United States, the optimum moisture content of architectural woodwork for interior applications is from 5% to 10%. The relative humidity necessary to maintain this optimum level is from 25% to 55%. In the more humid southern coastal areas, the optimum moisture content is from 8% to 13%, and in the dry Southwest the corresponding values are from 4% to 9%.

Code Requirements

The various model building codes set limits on the flame-spread ratings of interior finishes based on the occupancy of the building and the use area within the building. In general, most of the model building codes regulate the use of woodwork as a wall or ceiling finish, but do not regulate the use of wood in furniture, cabinets, or trim. This includes cabinets attached to the structure.

Interior finish is defined in the IBC (and similarly in other model codes) as wall and ceiling finish including wainscoting, paneling, or other finish applied structurally or for decoration, acoustical correction, surface insulation, or similar purposes. Requirements do not apply to *trim*, which is defined as picture molds, chair rails, baseboards, and handrails; to doors and windows or their frames; or to materials that are less than $^1/_{28}$ in (0.91) thick cemented to the surface of walls or ceilings.

As discussed in Ch. 55, there are three flame-spread groupings. In the IBC these are A, B, and C, corresponding to flame-spread ratings of 0–25, 26–75, and 76–200, respectively.

Different wood species have different flame-spread ratings, but very few have ratings less than 75, so wood is generally considered a Class C material unless it is treated with a fire retardant. However, treating often darkens the wood and makes it difficult to finish.

FINISHES

Finish is used on woodwork to protect it from moisture, chemicals, and contact and to enhance its appearance. Woodwork can either be field finished or factory finished. Because more control can be achieved with a factory finish this is the preferred method, although minor cabinet and trim work is often field finished in single-family residential and small commercial construction. For high-quality woodwork, field finishing is generally limited to minor touch-up and repair.

Prior to finishing, the wood must be sanded properly and filled, if desired. On many open-grain woods such as oak, mahogany, and teak, a filler should be applied prior to finishing to give a more uniform appearance to the woodwork, but it is not required. Other types of surface preparation are also possible depending on the aesthetic effect desired. The wood may be bleached to lighten it or to provide uniformity of color. Wood may also be mechanically or physically distressed to give it an antique or aged appearance. Shading or toning can also be used to change the color of the wood and subsequent finishing operations.

Opaque Finishes

Opaque finishes include lacquer, varnish, polyurethane, and polyester. They should only be used on closed-grain woods where solid stock is used and on medium-density fiberboard where sheet materials are used.

Lacquer is a coating material with a high nitrocellulose content modified with resins and plasticizers dissolved in a volatile solvent. Catalyzed lacquers contain an extra ingredient that speeds drying time and gives the finish additional hardness.

Varnish is a material consisting of various types of resinous materials dissolved in one of several types of volatile liquids. Conversion varnish is produced with alkyd and urea formaldehyde resins. When a high solids content is specified, the finish becomes opaque.

Polyurethane is a synthetic finish that gives a very hard, durable finish. Although difficult to repair or refinish, polyurethane finishes offer superior resistance to water, to many commercial and household chemicals, and to abrasion. Opaque polyurethanes are available in sheens from dull satin to full gloss.

Polyesters are another type of synthetic finish that give the hardest, most durable finish possible. Opaque polyesters can be colored and are available only in a full-gloss sheen. Like polyurethanes, polyester finishes are very difficult to repair and refinish outside the shop, but they give very durable finishes with as much as 80% the hardness of glass.

Transparent Finishes

Transparent finishes include lacquer, varnish, vinyl, penetrating oils, polyurethane, and polyester.

Standard lacquers are easy to apply, can be repaired easily, and are relatively low in cost. However, they do not provide the chemical and wear resistance of some of the other finishes. Catalyzed lacquers for transparent finishes are more difficult to repair and refinish, but they are more durable and resistant to commercial and household chemicals. A special water-reducible acrylic lacquer is available if local regulations prohibit the use of other types of lacquers.

Conversion varnish has many of the same advantages of lacquer but can often be applied with fewer coats.

Catalyzed vinyl yields a surface that has the most chemical resistance of the standard finishes of lacquer, varnish, and vinyl. Vinyl is also very resistant to scratching, abrasion, and other mechanical damage.

Penetrating oil finishes are one of the traditional wood finishes. They are easily applied and give a rich look to wood, but they require re-oiling periodically and tend to darken with age. An oil-finish look can be achieved with a catalyzed vinyl.

As with the opaque finishes, both polyurethane and polyester provide the most durable transparent finishes possible. They are the most expensive of the finishing systems and require skilled applicators. Transparent polyurethanes are available in sheens from dull to full gloss, whereas polyesters are available only in full gloss.

Stains

Prior to applying the final finish, wood may be stained to modify its color. The two types of stains are water-based and solvent-based. Water-based stains yield a uniform color but raise the grain. Solvent-based stains dry quickly and do not raise the grain but are less uniform. Both are penetrating finishes and cannot be easily removed.

41 MOISTURE PROTECTION AND THERMAL INSULATION

Protecting buildings from water leakage and temperature transmission are two of the most troublesome technical problems an architect must solve. Water can leak into a building from underground moisture and groundwater and from precipitation on the roof and exterior walls. It can find its way into a building through a surface material such as roofing or a basement slab or through joints and penetrations between materials. Moisture can also be generated within a building from cooking, showering, or simple human habitation. This moisture must also be prevented from permeating the structure.

This chapter discusses the methods and materials used to protect a building from moisture and to control heat loss or heat gain.

DAMPPROOFING

Dampproofing is the control of moisture that is not under hydrostatic pressure. Dampproofing can apply to water-repellent coatings on concrete, masonry, and wood walls above grade, but in its most typical use the term describes the protection of slabs and foundation walls below grade that are subject to continuous exposure to moisture.

The following types of dampproofing may be used.

- *Admixtures*. Various types of admixtures can be added to concrete to make it water repellent. These include materials such as salts of fatty acids, mineral oil, and powdered iron. They may reduce the strength of the concrete, but they make it much less permeable to water.
- *Bituminous coatings*. These are asphalt or coal-tar pitch materials applied to the exterior side of the foundation wall. They may be brushed or sprayed on, can be applied either hot or cold (depending on the type), and should be applied to smooth surfaces. They do not, however, seal cracks that develop after they are applied.
- *Cementitious coatings*. One or two coats of portland cement mortar can be troweled over the surface of masonry or concrete foundation walls. Mortar coatings are often used over very rough walls to provide a smooth surface for other dampproofing materials or by themselves. Powdered iron is often added as an admixture to the mortar. As the iron oxidizes it expands and limits the amount of shrinkage of the material, making a tighter seal.
- *Membranes*. These methods include built-up layers of hot- or cold-applied asphalt felts or membranes of butyl, polyvinyl chloride, and other synthetic materials. However, membranes are usually used for waterproofing walls subject to hydrostatic pressure, and their cost and difficulty of application is usually not warranted for simple dampproofing.
- *Plastics*. Silicone and polyurethane coatings are available, but they are usually reserved for above-grade dampproofing.

WATERPROOFING

Waterproofing is the control of moisture and water that is subject to hydrostatic pressure. This may include protecting structures below the water table. Waterproofing is a more difficult technical problem than is dampproofing because of the water pressure and the need to create a continuous seal over walls, slabs, and joints in the structure.

In most cases, waterproofing membranes are used on the exteriors of the walls and slabs. These may be built-up layers of bituminous saturated felts similar to roofing, or single-ply membranes of synthetic materials such as butyl, polyvinyl chloride, or other proprietary products. When membranes are used, they are subject to puncture during backfilling operations. For this reason, a protection surface is placed over the waterproofing prior to backfilling. Figure 41.1 shows a typical installation of a waterproofed slab and foundation wall.

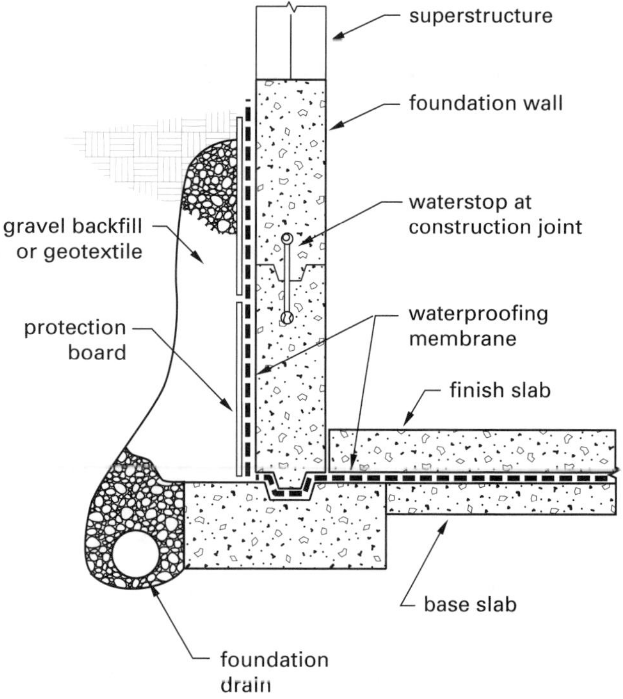

Figure 41.1 Waterproofed Wall and Slab

Joints in waterproofed walls are particularly subject to leakage. In concrete walls, *waterstops* are used to seal construction joints. Waterstops are dumbbell-shaped, continuous rubber or neoprene extrusions. Half of the waterstop is placed in the form during the first pour of concrete, and the other half is allowed to extend into the second pour.

Another method of waterproofing is the use of *bentonite panels*. These are flat packages of bentonite clay inside kraft paper packages. They are placed under slabs and against walls. After backfilling, the kraft paper deteriorates and the clay expands in the presence of moisture to form a waterproof barrier.

Of course, even when dampproofing or waterproofing a wall below grade, good construction design should include creating a positive slope away from the building to minimize water penetration around the foundation and provide some type of perimeter drainage if a heavy concentration of water is anticipated. This may include backfilling with gravel and placing perimeter foundation drains at the footing line, as discussed in Ch. 35. Hydrostatic pressure buildup can also be alleviated by using a geotextile matting over the waterproofing.

BUILDING INSULATION

Insulation is used to control unwanted heat flow, which can be from a warm building to a cold exterior or from a hot climate into a habitable space. Selecting and detailing insulation for buildings requires an understanding of the processes of heat gain and heat loss because different kinds of insulation are used to control these factors.

Methods of Heat Transfer

Heat is transferred in three ways: conduction, convection, and radiation. *Conduction* is the flow of heat within a material or between materials without displacement of the particles of the material. *Convection* is the transfer of heat within a fluid, either gas or liquid, by the movement of the fluid from an area of higher temperature to an area of lower temperature. Radiation is the transfer of heat energy through electromagnetic waves from one surface to a colder surface.

The best insulation is a vacuum. The next best insulation is air kept absolutely motionless in a space between two materials. However, this does not usually occur because convection currents carry warm air in one part of the space to the cooler parts of the space where heat is transferred by conduction. Most insulations are designed to create air pockets small enough to prevent convection but large enough to prevent the direct transfer of heat by conduction between the insulating materials.

Measuring Thermal Resistance

Thermal resistance is described with several terms, as outlined in Ch. 27. The quantity of heat used to measure transfer is the *British thermal unit* (Btu), which is the amount of heat required to raise the temperature of 1 lbm of water by 1°F. The basic unit of conductance is a material's *k*-value, or conductivity. This is the number of Btus per hour that pass through 1 ft^2 of homogeneous material 1 in thick when the temperature differential is 1°F. When the material is more than 1 in thick, the unit is *conductance*, or the *C*-value.

The more common term used is the *R*-value, or resistance of a material. Resistance is the number of hours needed for 1 Btu to pass through 1 ft^2 of a material of a given thickness when the temperature differential is 1°F. It is the reciprocal of conductance. Thus, the lower a material's *k*-value or *C*-value, the better its insulating qualities. Higher *R*-values also indicate a better insulating value.

In SI units, the joule (J) is the unit for energy, which is equal to $^1/_{4.184}$ of the amount of heat required to raise a gram of water by 1°C. 1 Btu equals 1.055 kJ. Conductivity is measured as the rate at which watts flow through 1 m^2 of homogeneous material when the temperature changes by 1K, which is the same as 1°C. Conductivity, *k*, in SI units is shown as W/m·°K or W/m·°C. Thermal resistance, *R*, in SI units is m^2·K/W.

Another rating method for foam insulation products is *long-term thermal resistance* (LTTR). It has been found that, over time, the thermal resistance of foam insulation changes due to changes in cell gas composition caused by the diffusion of air into the foam cells and the diffusion of blowing agents out of the cells. This is sometimes called *thermal drift*. LTTR is the thermal resistance value of a closed-cell foam insulation product measured after storage for five years under prescribed laboratory conditions. This has been shown to be the equivalent to the time-weighted average resistance value over a 15-year service condition. Standard test methods apply to polyisocyanurate, extruded polystyrene, and sprayed polyurethane. The LTTR value is the one that should be used for heat transfer calculations.

TYPES OF BUILDING INSULATION

The following sections describe several types of insulation used to control heat transfer by conduction, convection, and radiation. Types of insulation and their *R*-values are shown in Table 41.1. Also included are *R*-values for some common materials for comparison.

Loose-Fill Insulation

Loose-fill insulation is produced as shreds, granules, or nodules and can be poured or blown into spaces to be insulated. Loose-fill insulation is used for places where it is difficult to install other types of insulation, such as in cells of concrete block walls, plumbing chases, and attics. It is also widely used in retrofit applications because it can be blown into wall and ceiling cavities where other types of insulation cannot be installed without great difficulty.

This type of insulation is made from several materials: mineral wool, cellulose, cotton, fiberglass, perlite, and vermiculite. All loose-fill insulation will settle somewhat after installation. Cellulose settles about 20% while rock wool and fiberglass only settle about 2% to 4%. Care must also be taken when installing thick layers in ceilings because too heavy of a load will cause ceiling drywall to sag. For example, the use of cellulose or rock wool is not recommended in ceilings with $^1/_2$ in (13) wallboard on 24 in (600) centers. All loose-fill insulations require a vapor retarder or vapor barrier.

Mineral wool is a generic term for two types of product: rock wool and slag wool. *Rock wool* is manufactured by melting basalt or other rocks in a high-temperature furnace and then spinning the molten material into long fibers. Binding agents and other materials are added through various manufacturing processes to give the desired properties. *Slag wool* is manufactured from iron ore blast furnace slag using similar production methods. Slag wool accounts for about 80% of the mineral wool industry. It is formed into batts, blankets, and loose-fill material, and is used in applications similar to those of fiberglass.

The EPA recommends that rock wool insulation contain at least 50% recovered material. Most manufacturers use from 50% to 95% recycled material, with 75% postindustrial content being about average.

Cellulose insulation is made from 80% to 100% recycled paper combined with a fire-retardant additive. For loose-fill applications, a binder is added to prevent settling. Cellulose is used for loose-fill attic insulation as well as dry blown-in and wet-spray applications.

The high recycled content of cellulose insulation and its low embodied energy are its main environmental benefits. There have been concerns about the dust generated during installation and the possible toxicity of some types of fire-retardant treatments. However, with proper installation methods, detailing to isolate the insulation from interior spaces, and proper ventilation systems, dust and fibers are not a problem. A low-dust cellulose is available, and some manufacturers offer products that use only all-borate fire retardants, which are considered nontoxic.

Cotton insulation is made from pre-consumer recycled cotton denim scrap material with a small amount of polyester for binding and stability. It is made in both loose-fill and batt forms. Low-toxicity borates are added as a fire retardant. Cotton insulation has a very high recycled content and requires very little energy to manufacture.

Fiberglass insulation is produced by melting sand and recycled glass and spinning the product into thin fibers, which are held together with a binder. Fiberglass is sometimes used as loose fill but is more commonly formed into batts, either with or without a paper facing. In batt form, the insulation is placed between studs, between floor or roof joists, and in other cavities.

Fiberglass commonly contains about 30% recycled glass, and up to 90% recycled content is possible. There has been some concern that the fibers may be carcinogenic, but no long-term damage has been demonstrated. A small amount of formaldehyde is typically used in the binder, and this has also raised concern; formaldehyde-free fiberglass is available.

Perlite insulation is an expanded form of a naturally occurring siliceous volcanic rock. It is manufactured in various densities from 2 lbm/ft^3 (32 kg/m^3) to 15 lbm/ft^3 (240 kg/m^3) and in different forms including loose-fill insulation, board insulation, aggregate in lightweight concrete, and as a component in acoustical ceiling tiles. Its most common form is as loose fill used in hollow concrete unit masonry walls and

Table 41.1

R-Values for Insulation

insulation type	*R*-value/in (ft^2-hr-°F/Btu)	*R*-value/mm (m^2·K/W)	*R*-value/m (m^2·K/W)
loose fill			
cellulose	3.2–3.8	0.022–0.026	22–26
fiberglass	2.2–2.7	0.015–0.019	15–19
perlite	2.3–2.7	0.016–0.019	16–19
rock wool	3.0–3.3	0.021–0.023	21–23
vermiculite	2.1	0.015	15
batts			
fiberglass, low density	3.1–3.5	0.021–0.024	21–24
fiberglass, high density	4.3	0.030	30
mineral wool	3.5	0.024	24
boards			
polyisocyanurate	5.6–7.7 (LTTR)*	0.039 0.053	39–53
polyurethane (2.0 lbm/ft^3)	6.5 (LTTR)	0.045	45
expanded polystyrene	3.8–4.4 (LTTR)	0.026–0.030	26
extruded polystyrene	5.0 (LTTR)	0.035	30
straw	1.4–2.0	0.010–0.014	10
sprayed foam			14
polyurethane	5.0–7.0	0.035–0.049	35–49
polyicynene	3.6–4.0	0.025–0.028	25–28
soy-based polyurethane	3.7	0.026	26
sprayed fiber			
cellulose	3.5	0.024	224
fiberglass	3.0	0.021	21
rock wool	2.7	0.019	19
structural insulated panels	4.0–6.0	0.028–0.042	28–42
straw bales	2.4–3.0	0.017–0.021	17–21
autoclaved aerated concrete	1.1	0.008	8
common building materials			
air, vertical, still with two reflective surfaces	1.39	0.079	10
brick	0.12–0.10	0.0008–0.0007	0.83–0.68
concrete	0.10–0.05	0.0007–0.00035	0.69–0.35
wood, Douglas fir-larch	1.06–0.99	0.0073–0.0069	7.3–6.9

*LTTR: long-term thermal resistance

Source: U.S. Department of Energy, Office of Energy Efficiency and Renewable Energy

between walls. It is also used as insulation under floating concrete floors.

Vermiculite is a hydrated laminar magnesium-aluminum-ironsilicate. When heated during processing it forms small worm-like pieces. Although it is a fairly good insulating material, some vermiculite may contain asbestos. See Ch. 30 for information on vermiculite as a hazardous material.

Batt Insulation

Batt insulation consists of fibrous material placed on or within a kraft paper carrier. The insulation is usually mineral fiber or glass fiber. In addition to providing a means of installation and holding the insulation in place, the kraft paper also serves as a vapor retarder. Some batt insulation also comes with a reflective surface. Batts are available that have a flame-resistant facing, for use in basement walls where the insulation will be left exposed.

Batts come in standard widths designed to fit within stud and joist spacings of 16 in (406) or 24 in (610) on center. It is either friction fitted or is attached by stapling the paper flanges to the studs. Various thicknesses are available to suit the size of the cavity and the *R*-value required.

Plastic fiber insulation is made from recycled plastic (PET) milk bottles and formed into batts similar to high-density fiberglass.

Board Insulation

Board insulation is made from a variety of organic or inorganic materials formed into rigid boards. Organic board insulation is made from wood, cane fiber, or straw sandwiched between coatings of bituminous material, paper, foil, or other materials. Rigid boards can also be made with perlite or cork. However, organic board insulation has generally given way to inorganic plastics, which have much higher insulating values, about two to three times greater than for most other insulating materials of the same thickness. Inorganic board insulation is made from molded expanded polystyrene, extruded expanded polystyrene, polyisocyanurate, or polyurethane.

Originally, polystyrene foams, polyisocyanurate, and polyurethane foams were made with CFCs as the blowing agent. CFS were phased out in 1996 and replaced, in many instances, with HCFCs. However, HCFCs also cause depletion of the ozone layer. Under provisions of the Clean Air Act of 1990, the production and importation of many of the highest ozone-depletion-potential HCFCs into the United States was banned, effective January 1, 2003. This included HCFC-141b. Two blowing agents being used as a replacement are hydrocarbon (HC) and carbon dioxide (CO_2).

Expanded polystyrene (EPS) is a closed-cell material manufactured by mixing unexpanded polystyrene beads containing liquid pentane and a blowing agent. The mixture is heated to expand the beads, which are then injected into a mold to form a foam block. EPS (or *beadboard* as it is sometimes called) is manufactured in various densities for roofing and wall insulation. These densities range from 0.7 lbm/ft^3 to 3.0 lbm/ft^3 (11 kg/m^3 to 48 kg/m^3), with 1.0 lbm/ft^3 (16 kg/m^3) being the density most commonly used for insulation. The spaces between the beads can absorb water, so a vapor retarder is required if moisture migration is a concern.

Polystyrene is manufactured from petrochemicals. It has more embodied energy per insulating unit than polyisocyanurate, fiberglass, cellulose, and mineral wool. However, it is manufactured without ozone-depleting chemicals and continues to be a flexible insulation product with a high *R*-value. It can be made with recycled material, but at present few manufacturers do this.

Extruded polystyrene (XPS) is a closed-cell material manufactured by mixing polystyrene pellets with various chemicals and then introducing a blowing agent. The resulting mass is forced through an extruder, where atmospheric pressure causes the mass to expand. Densities range from 1.4 lbm/ft^3 to 3.0 lbm/ft^3 (22 kg/m^3 to 48 kg/m^3). Although more expensive than EPS, XPS foams have a higher insulative value per unit thickness and a higher compressive strength than does EPS. XPS is used for residential sheathing and wall, foundation, and roof insulation. Because of its superior resistance to water absorption, XPS is the only insulation recommended for protected membrane roof systems and below-grade insulation.

The advantages of XPS are countered by some environmental disadvantages. Petroleum products are needed in its manufacture, and the blowing agent contains ozone-depleting chemicals and can outgas styrene monomer. The blowing agent most used at present, HCFC-14b, is hydrochlorofluorocarbon based, and the United States and other countries began phasing out its production and importation in 2010. Some European manufacturers have switched to other blowing agents. Polystyrene can be recycled, but few manufacturers do this.

Polyisocyanurate insulation (commonly referred to as *polyiso*) is manufactured by combining liquid isocyanate and polyol with catalysts and additives. A blowing agent expands the material into a closed cell structure, which is then laminated between engineered facing materials. Polyisocyanurate insulation can also be blown in place.

Polyisocyanurate is used in rigid boards for above-grade applications in roof and wall assemblies. Because it can readily absorb moisture, it is not suitable for below-grade uses except on the inside of foundation walls.

Like polystyrene, polyisocyanurate requires petroleum products in its manufacture. However, the hydrocarbon-based blowing agent used to expand it has no ozone depletion potential and no global warming potential. Polyisocyanurate also makes use of recycled materials, including PET from beverage bottles. The EPA recommends that polyisocyanurate rigid foam insulation contain at least 9% recovered material.

Polyurethane is a closed-cell foam made to a density of 2 lbm/ft^3 (32 kg/m^3). Most polyurethane foams are made without the use of HCFCs and have an *R*-value of 6.5 ft^2-hr-°F/Btu to 7 ft^2-hr-°F/Btu (0.045 m^2·K/W to 0.049 m^2·K/W). These types of foam boards are more expensive than the other foam boards.

Sprayed Foam Insulation

Sprayed foam insulation uses polyurethane or polyicynene as the base material. The components of the foam are mixed at the spray head, at which time they react immediately and expand to produce low-density foam that adheres to the cavity. Sprayed foam has an excellent *R*-value with the added advantages of conforming to the shape of the cavity and sealing all cracks and openings thoroughly.

Spray polyurethane insulation is a foam plastic that is applied in the liquid state. It rapidly expands to about 30 to 50 times its original volume and cures to a solid form. The foam's density, amount of expansion, and water-resistant properties can be varied by adjusting the proportions of the component materials. As the material foams, it expands to fill all spaces and acts as an effective air barrier. Polyurethane insulation is also be made in rigid foam boards, which can be laminated with a variety of facings.

Spray polyurethane is available in either closed-cell or open-cell form. Closed-cell foams have higher densities and higher *R*-values, but some manufacturers still use an ozone-depleting blowing agent. Open-cell foams have lower *R*-values and lower densities, but the blowing agent is water and carbon dioxide, which make them environmentally more desirable.

Low-density foam is used to insulate open wall cavities, but because the foam expands so greatly, it must be cut off flush with wall studs before finish materials are applied. High-density foams used for roof insulation can effectively cover gaps and roof structure to prevent thermal bridging, while providing a base with high compressive strength for the roofing material.

While petrochemicals are required to manufacture polyurethane insulation, and some offgassing occurs, these insulation products are relatively sustainable when considering their high insulating and air-sealing properties. The EPA recommends that polyurethane foam-in-place insulation contain at least 5% recovered material.

Icynene is a brand name for a water-based, HCFC-free, low-density, open-cell polyurethane insulation. When sprayed into open wall or ceiling cavities, it expands to about 100 times its original volume and cures to a soft foam. It easily adheres to other building materials and maintains its *R*-value over time. A different formulation is available that can be used in closed cavities for retrofitting. This formulation expands less, and only in the area of least resistance, to prevent damage to walls and structure while filling the cavity.

As an alternate to petroleum-based polyurethane foams, there is a soy-based polyurethane foam that use products derived from soy beans. It is applied in the same way as other spray-on foams and has an *R*-value of about 3.7 ft^2-hr-°F/Btu per inch (0.026 m^2·K/W).

Sprayed Fiber Insulation

Sprayed fiber insulation includes cellulose, fiberglass, and rock wool mixed with an adhesive and a small amount of water to activate the adhesive. As with foam insulation, spray fiber insulation completely fills the cavities where it is installed and does a better job of filling voids than does batt insulation. Because the adhesive binds the fibers to each other and to the cavity, this type of insulation does not settle as loose-fill types do. However, because of the moisture in the spray mixture, sprayed fiber insulation must be allowed to dry thoroughly before being enclosed with gypsum wallboard or other finishes. This can take from a few days to several weeks, depending on the type of insulation, its moisture content, and the humidity when it was applied.

Cellulose is the most commonly used type of sprayed fiber insulation. It is combined with a fire retardant. Fiberglass sprayed on insulation is also known as a *blow-in-blanket system* (BIBS) and is the second most common type of sprayed fiber. It does not prevent air infiltration as well as sprayed cellulose does. Rock wool is commonly used for commercial building thermal insulation as well as fireproofing.

Radiant Barriers and Reflective Insulation

A *radiant barrier* is a single sheet of highly reflective material, usually aluminum, that faces an open airspace. It is used to reduce the passage of thermal radiation, most often by blocking summer heat gain, but sometimes to help retain winter heat. To block heat gain, a radiant barrier is placed on the outside of conventional thermal insulation, such as on top of attic insulation. Heat radiated from the hot roof deck is reflected back toward the roof, reducing the heat that would normally strike the top of the thermal insulation. To block heat loss, the reflective barrier would have to face the heated side of the insulation. When a radiant barrier is combined with a backing of insulation it is called *reflective insulation*.

Reflective surfaces have two properties that make them good for insulation. The first is *reflectivity* (also called *reflectance*), which is a measure of how much radiant heat is reflected by the material. This is a number between 0 and 1. Sometimes it is given as a percentage between 0% and 100%. Thus, when a material has a reflectivity of 0.8, it means that 80% of the radiant energy striking the material is reflected. The second property is *emissivity* (also called *emittance*), which is a measure of how much energy is emitted. All materials give off, or emit, energy by thermal radiation as a result of their temperature. Emissivity is also measured on a scale of 0 to 1. For materials that are opaque, the sum of the reflectivity and the emissivity equals one.

To be effective, radiant barriers must have a minimum reflectivity of 0.9 and a maximum emissivity of 0.1, and they must face a ventilated airspace. Some radiant barriers are manufactured with corrugations or folds that automatically provide an airspace.

Insulated Concrete Forms

Insulated concrete forms (ICF) are systems of interlocking foam insulation blocks or panels that serve as forms for pouring concrete walls and that remain in place after the concrete has cured. The foam greatly increases the insulation value of the wall and serves as a backing for gypsum wallboard finish on the inside and sheathing and exterior finish on the outside. Building codes require that a fire-resistant material be used to cover the inside layer of foam; generally $^1/_2$ in (13) drywall is acceptable. Although ICFs are typically used for foundation walls, they can be used for the entire wall structure from the footings to the roof.

The foam is typically extruded polystyrene (XPS) and comes in a variety of configurations, from preformed interlocking blocks to large panels that are held in place with plastic ties. Reinforcing steel is installed before the concrete is poured.

Structural Insulated Panels

Structural insulated panels (SIPs) are composite building units consisting of two outer skins bonded to an inner core of rigid insulating material, most commonly expanded polystyrene (EPS). Approximate *R*-values for SIPs (including OSB on each side) range from R17 for a $3^5/_8$ in (92) core to R34 for a $7^3/_8$ in (190) core. Refer to Ch. 39 for more information on SIPs.

Vapor Retarders

A *vapor retarder* is a material used to slow the transmission or diffusion of water vapor between spaces. Vapor retarders are not themselves insulation, but they play an important role in the effectiveness of other insulating materials.

Water vapor is produced in all buildings by human respiration and perspiration, by cooking, and by other activities that involve water. In addition, there is always a certain amount of humidity present in the air. Warm air is capable of holding more water than is cold air. If the temperature of the air containing a certain amount of water vapor drops, the relative humidity rises until the saturation point is reached. This is known as the *dew point*, the point at which water condenses from the vapor.

Water vapor can enter a building by diffusion through materials or by air movement, or by both. Air movement and air barriers are discussed in Ch. 29.

Vapor diffusion is the slow movement of water molecules through vapor-permeable materials. Warm, moist air generally tends to migrate into areas of cooler, drier air. Differences in temperature and relative humidity indoors and outdoors lead to differences in vapor pressure, and this causes the diffusion. In buildings, this can cause problems when the warm, moist air cools, reaches its dew point, and condenses. The condensation of moisture within a wall can degrade insulation and other building materials, promote rust, and support mold growth.

To prevent vapor migration, vapor retarders are used. These may be made of plastic sheeting (polyethylene), aluminum foil, self-adhering sheet membranes, or fluid-applied membranes. Vapor retarders may also function as air barriers if it is appropriate to place them in the same position within the wall as discussed in Ch. 29.

Different materials have different permeance ratings. As discussed in Ch. 29, *permeance* is the property of a material that prevents water vapor from diffusing through it. The basic unit of permeance is the *perm*. In customary U.S. units, a perm is one grain of moisture per hour per square foot per inch of mercury difference in vapor pressure, or 1 g/hr-ft^2-in Hg. In SI units, permeance is measured in nanograms of water per second per square meter per pascal of vapor pressure. In SI units, 1 perm equals a flow rate of 57 ng/s·m^2·Pa. Table 41.2 gives perm ratings and their corresponding terminology.

The ideal position of vapor retarders within a wall assembly is climate specific and must be considered in conjunction with the location of the air barrier. Generally, vapor retarders should be placed on the warm side of the insulation in most climatic regions.

In cold regions (generally, climate zones 6, 7, and 8), for example, vapor retarders prevent warm, moist interior air from migrating toward the cooler outdoors and condensing inside the insulation cavity or elsewhere inside the wall.

Table 41.2

Perm Rating Terminology

perm rating	term
less than 0.1	vapor impermeable
0.1 to 1	semi-impermeable
1 to 10	semipermeable
10 or over	permeable

Anything less than 1 perm is considered to be a vapor retarder (or less accurately called a vapor barrier).

(See Fig. 5.4 for the climate zone map.) They should be placed on the warmer inside of the insulation. In these regions, a *vapor-permeable* air barrier should be also placed outside the insulation to prevent air infiltration while allowing any accumulated moisture to dry out. In most cases, the air barrier is placed outside the sheathing for support, protection, and ease of construction.

In hot, humid climates (generally, climate zones 1, 2, 3A below the warm-humid line, and 3C), in air-conditioned buildings, the retarder should be placed on the warmer outside of the insulation to prevent the moist, warm air outside the building from migrating to the cooler, dehumidified interior spaces. In these climate regions, the vapor retarder should also serve as the air barrier; that is, the air barrier should be *vapor impermeable*.

In mixed climatic regions (generally, climate zones 4 and 5 and some parts of 3A, 3B, 3C, and 4B) a vapor-permeable air barrier should be placed outside the insulation with no vapor retarder. This allows any vapor or condensation to pass through the wall in either direction.

The IBC does not require the use of vapor retarders in climate zones 1, 2, and 3 for commercial buildings, or in climate zones 1, 2, 3, and 4 for residential construction as prescribed in the *International Residential Code*. When vapor retarders are required, they must have a permeance rating no greater than 1 perm (57 $ng/s \cdot m^2 \cdot Pa$).

The suggestions for mixed climates given above are general guidelines only. The local climate, interior environmental conditions, and specific building materials being used should be reviewed by the designer to determine the best use and placement of air and vapor barriers. Computer programs are available that can give a detailed analysis of heat and vapor transmission throughout the year, for a specific climatic region and for specific interior environmental conditions, through a proposed wall design. Analysis can also be done manually using the dew point method, in which a specific condition and building materials are selected and a temperature gradient line is developed from outside to inside based on the *R*-values (temperature resistance) of the individual materials.

Air Barriers

In addition to vapor retarders, air barriers are an important part of an energy-efficient building. Refer to Ch. 29 for more information on air barriers.

Sustainability Issues

As with other building materials, the sustainability of insulation involves consideration of its raw material acquisition, manufacture, use in place, and disposal or recycling potential. However, its primary purpose, that of slowing the transfer of heat, is the most important environmental consideration because the long-term energy savings from insulation generally outweigh the disadvantages that any particular insulation may have.

From the standpoint of sustainability, no insulation material is perfect; there are advantages and disadvantages to each. When other factors are considered—including required *R*-value, physical form, cost, water resistance, installation method, combustibility, vapor permeance, and others—the best insulation for the application may not be the most environmentally perfect. Insulation technology is constantly changing, however, and many of the environmentally detrimental aspects of insulation are being overcome with new materials and manufacturing techniques.

SHINGLES AND ROOFING TILE

Shingles and tiles are two of the oldest types of roofing materials. They consist of small, individual pieces of material placed in an overlapping fashion on a sloped surface in order to shed water.

Types of Roofs

Roofs are classified according to their shape. Some of the more common types are illustrated in Fig. 41.2, along with the common terms used to describe the various parts.

The amount of slope of a roof is designated by its *pitch*, which is the number of inches (mm) of rise for every 12 in (305) of horizontal projection or run. For example, a 5/12 pitch rises 5 in (127) vertically for every foot (305) of horizontal projection.

Not all roofing materials are appropriate for all pitches, although the exact pitch for any one material may affect how the roofing is detailed and installed. For example, low-slope roofs for asphalt shingles require a double layer of roofing felt rather than the normal single layer. Some general guidelines are given in Table 41.3.

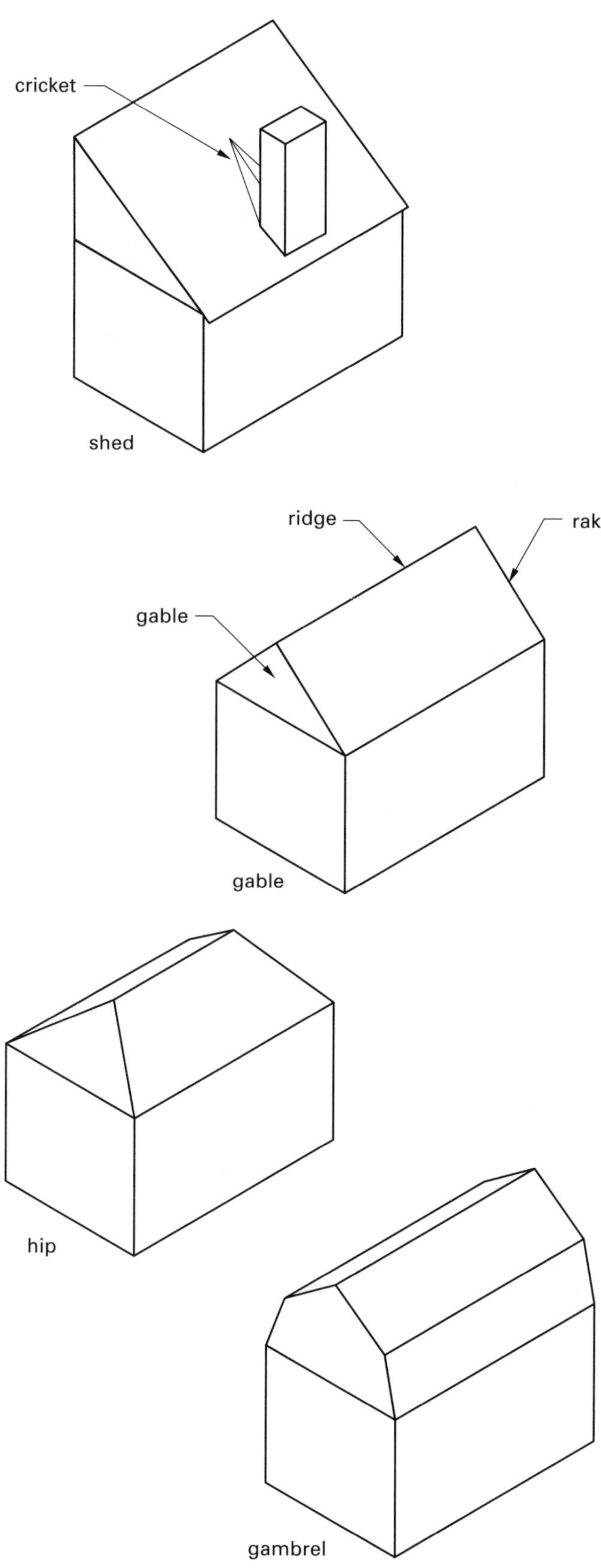

Figure 41.2 Roof Types

When describing size, estimating, and ordering materials, roofing area is referred to in squares. A square is equal to 100 ft² (9.3 m²).

Table 41.3
Recommended Slopes for Roofing

	slope—vertical rise (in/ft)		(mm/m)	
roofing type	min.	max.	min.	max.
asphalt shingles, low slope	2	4	165	330
asphalt shingles, normal	4	12	330	1000
asphalt roll roofing	1	4	82	330
wood shingles	4	–	330	–
clay tile	4	–	330	–
slate tile	4	–	330	–
metal roofing	3	–	245	–
built-up roofing	1/4	1	20	82
single-ply membranes (varies with type and method of attachment)	1/4	6	20	490

Shingles

Shingles are small, rectangular, or other-shaped units intended to shed water rather than form a watertight seal. Asphalt shingles are made from a composition of felt, asphalt, mineral stabilizers, and mineral granules. They are available in a variety of colors and shapes and are laid over an asphalt-impregnated roofing felt that is nailed to solid wood sheathing.

Wood shakes are normally manufactured from cedar and are available in a variety of grades (no. 1, blue label being the best) and finishes including smooth face and handsplit face. A typical installation is shown in Fig. 41.3. Wood shingles are typically laid over spaced sheathing so that they can breathe without a buildup of moisture.

Wood shingles are laid so that only a certain portion of each shingle is visible. This is called the *exposure*, and the dimension varies with the pitch of the roof. The edges are staggered so that joints do not coincide, and 30 lbm asphalt felt is used as an underlayment.

Roofing Tile

Roofing tile consists of slate, clay tile, and concrete tile. Because each type is heavy (10 lbm/ft², or 49 kg/m², or more), the roof structure must be sized accordingly.

Slate tile is made by splitting quarried slate into rectangular pieces from 6 in to 14 in wide and from 16 in to 24 in long (152 to 356 wide and from 406 to 610 long). Slate tile is

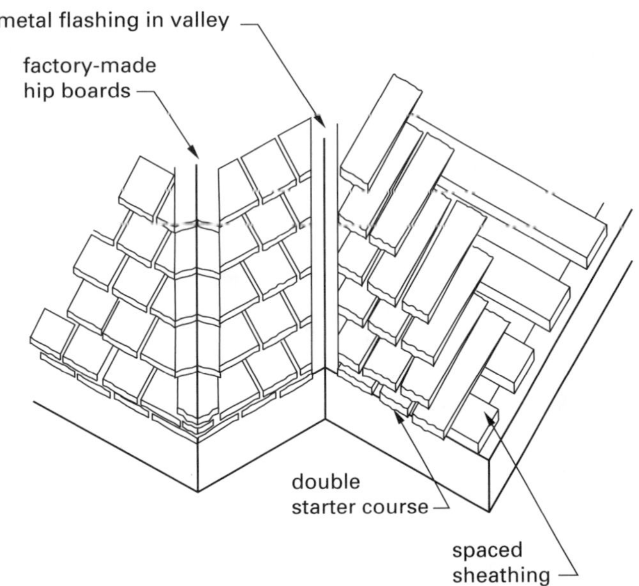

Figure 41.3 Wood Shingle Installation

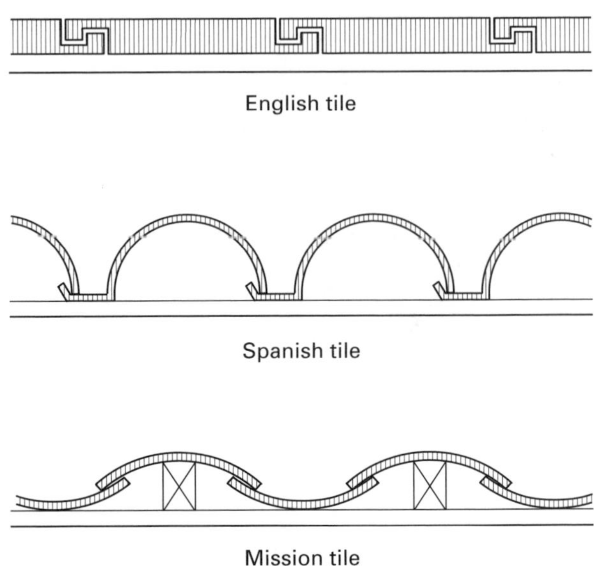

Figure 41.4 Clay Roofing Tile Profiles

about $^1/_4$ in (6) thick. It is laid over 30 lbm asphalt-saturated roofing felt on wood or nailable concrete decking. The pieces are laid like other shingles, with the sides and ends overlapping, attached with copper or galvanized nails driven through prepunched holes in the slate. Slate is very expensive as a roofing material, but it is fire resistant and very durable; most slate roofs last over 100 years.

Clay tile, available in many colors, patterns, and textures, is made from the same clay as brick and is formed into various shapes. Like slate, it is laid on roofing felt over a sloped wood or nailable deck and attached by nailing through prepunched holes. Also like slate, clay tile is expensive, but very durable, fire resistant, and attractive. Some of the available shapes are shown in Fig. 41.4.

Concrete tile, manufactured from portland cement and fine aggregates, is available in several styles, some flat and others formed to look like clay tile. It is also available in several colors. Concrete tile is less expensive than clay tile, but it is still durable and fire resistant.

PREFORMED ROOFING AND SIDING

Sheet Metal Roofing

Metal roofing is durable, attractive, and can conform to a wide variety of roof shapes. Its disadvantages include high cost and the difficulty of installing it properly. Sheet metal roofs are fabricated of individual sheets of metal joined with various types of interlocking joints. Because of the high coefficient of expansion of metals used for roofing, these joints and other parts of the roofing system must be designed to allow for expansion and contraction.

Metals used for roofing include copper, galvanized iron, aluminum, and terneplate. *Terneplate* is steel sheet coated with lead and tin. Terne-coated stainless steel is also available. Other metals that are sometimes used include stainless steel, zinc, and lead. Stainless steel is expensive but very durable and maintenance free.

Copper roofs are popular because of their long life and the attractive green patina that forms after a few years of weathering. Copper is also a good metal roofing material because a wide variety of necessary roofing accessories such as gutters, flashing, and downspouts are also made in copper.

Metal roofs are installed over asphalt roofing felt laid on top of wood or nailable concrete decking. The one exception to the underlayment is for terne or tin roofs, which require a rosin-sized paper because the asphalt can react with the tin. The minimum slope for metal roofs is 3 in 12 (75 in 305).

In most cases, standing seams are made parallel to the slope of the roof and crimped tight. Flat seams are made perpendicular to the standing seams and soldered. These connect two pieces of metal along the slope of the roof, as shown in Fig. 41.5.

The roofing is held to the sheathing or decking with metal cleats attached to the roof and spaced about 12 in (305) apart. Continuous cleats are often used at the eaves, rakes (gable ends), and flashing. In all cases, cleats, nails, and other fasteners must be of the same type of metal to avoid galvanic action.

Preformed Roof and Wall Panels

Preformed panels are shaped pieces of metal or assemblies of metal facing with insulation between that are self-supporting

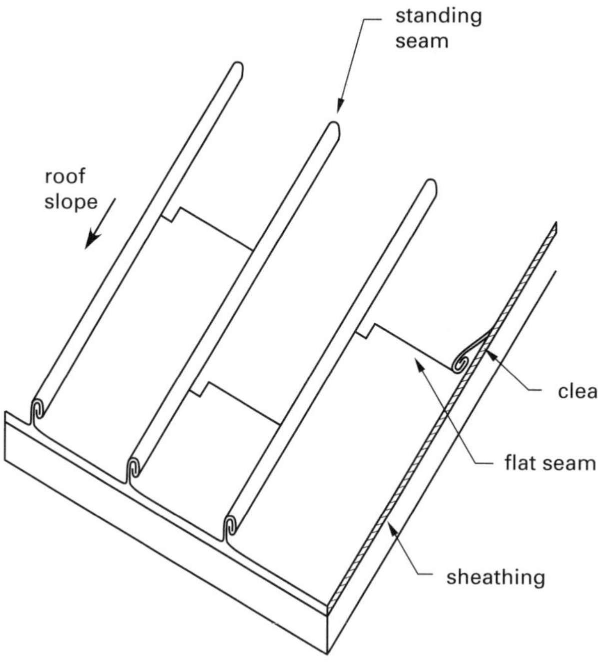

Figure 41.5 Standing Seam Metal Roof

and span intermediate supports. Roof panels span purlins, and wall panels span horizontal girts.

The simplest preformed panels are simply corrugated or fluted sheets of metal of standard widths and varying lengths. They are assembled by lapping one corrugation at the edges and overlapping the ends. Preformed panels are also made as sandwich assemblies with insulation between two finished faces, joined with interlocking edges and a weather seal. Common widths are 24, 30, and 36 in (610, 760, and 910), although others are available. These types of sandwich panels are fabricated in lengths to match the requirements of the job and usually reach from the foundation to the roof framing in one-story buildings. If two panels must be placed end to end, they are butt-jointed with flashing between.

Preformed panels are made primarily from aluminum, galvanized steel, and porcelain enamel steel. They are attached to framing with screws, clips, and proprietary fasteners. They are durable, easy and quick to install, and do not require on-site finishing. For industrial buildings and some other types of structures, a sandwich panel can serve as the interior finish as well as the exterior finish. However, preformed panels are most economical when used on large, flat, unbroken expanses of walls or roofs.

MEMBRANE ROOFING

Membrane roofing includes those materials applied in thin sheets to nearly flat roofs. It also includes liquid-applied products that can be applied to any roof slope. Although some manufacturers claim that their products are suitable for flat roofs, every roof should have at least a $^1/_4$ in/ft slope (6/305) to avoid standing water and the possibility of ponding. *Ponding* occurs when standing water causes a flat roof to deflect a little, allowing more water to collect, which causes more deflection, which in turn allows more water to collect. The process continues until the roof fails.

Built-Up Bituminous Roofing

Built-up roofing consists of several overlapping layers of bituminous saturated roofing felts cemented together with roofing cement. The bituminous material can be either asphalt or coal-tar pitch. The basic construction of such a roof is illustrated in Fig. 41.6.

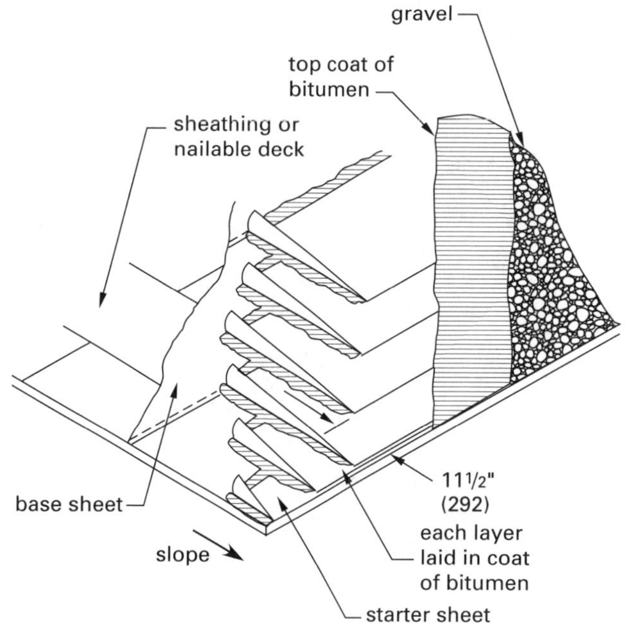

Figure 41.6 Three-Ply Built-Up Roof

Built-up roofs can be installed over nailable or non-nailable decks; the exact construction procedure changes slightly depending on which type is present. For nailable decks, a base sheet of unsaturated felt is nailed to the deck and covered with a coating of roofing cement. On non-nailable decks, the base sheet is omitted and a base coat is applied.

Three, four, or five layers of saturated roofing felts are then laid on top of each other, each layer bedded in roofing cement so that felt does not touch felt. The number of layers is determined by the type of deck used and the length of guarantee period desired. Five-ply roofs provide the most protection. A final coating of bituminous material is placed over the entire roof and covered with gravel or crushed slag. The purpose of the gravel is to protect the roofing from sunlight and other effects of weathering.

A variation of the built-up roof is the *inverted membrane roof*. Here, the built-up roof is placed on the structural decking and rigid, closed-cell insulation is placed over the roof rather than under it. The insulation is held down with gravel ballast. The purpose of this type of construction is to protect the membrane from the normal deleterious effects of expansion and contraction, drying, ultraviolet rays, and foot traffic that can cause leaks.

Built-Up Roofing Construction Details

As with any roof, built-up roofs must be designed to provide for positive drainage. As previously mentioned, the minimum roof slope should be $^1/_4$ in/ft (6/305). Nearly flat membrane roofs may be drained to interior drains, to perimeter drains, or to gutters on the low side of the roof. Crickets should be used to provide positive drainage in all directions. A *cricket* is a saddle-shaped projection on a sloping roof used to divert water around an obstacle. When a roof is surrounded on four sides with a parapet or walls, there should be *scuppers* (also called *overflow drains*) through the parapet, positioned with their low edge slightly above the top of the roof to provide a second means of drainage should the primary drains become clogged. These are usually required by building codes.

At the intersection of the roof and any vertical surface such as a wall or parapet, continuous triangular cant strips are placed in the intersection to provide positive drainage away from the joint and to give a smooth transition surface for the installation of the flashing at these points.

When objects project through a roof or roof-mounted equipment needs to be supported, the intersection of the roofing and these projections must be waterproofed. One traditional way to do this is to provide a *pitch pan*, a small metal enclosure around the projection that is filled with bituminous material. The pitch pan, however, is usually not recommended because of its tendency to leak. Projections should be treated like other joints and installed with cant strips and flashing. Roof-mounted equipment should be placed on wood curbs that are likewise flashed.

Single-Ply Roofing

Single-ply roofing is a single-membrane layer of various types of materials. Because the quality of built-up roofing is labor intensive and largely dependent on proper installation, single-ply roofing has come into widespread use. Although it too must be applied carefully, there are usually fewer installation problems. In addition, single-ply roofing is more resistant to slight building movement and the damaging effects of the weather.

There are several types of single-ply membranes. *Modified bitumens* are sheets about 50 mils (1.3) thick that are composed of bitumen, a chemical additive to enhance the elastic properties of the bitumen, and a reinforcing fabric to add tensile strength. The bitumen sheet is laid over insulation or insulating decks with a separator sheet between the deck and the membrane. These sheets allow the roof to move independently of the structure, and some sheets are designed to allow water vapor from the building to escape to the perimeter of the roof. To anchor the membrane and protect it from ultraviolet degradation, the surface is covered with gravel ballast.

Other types of membranes fall into two categories: thermoset plastics and thermoplastics. *Thermoset plastics* are those that permanently harden when they are subjected to heat and then cured. They permanently lose their shape if heated again. *Thermoplastic materials*, also called *thermoplastics*, are those that can be repeatedly softened with heat and then harden again when cooled. Thermoset roofing includes EPDM and CSPE. Thermoplastic roofing includes PVC and TPO, as well as various hybrid blends.

Ethylene propylene diene monomer (EPDM) roofing is a thermoset plastic membrane manufactured in thicknesses of 0.045 in and 0.060 in (1.1 and 1.5). It has excellent resistance to weathering, heat, and fatigue, but is only available in black. Because it is a thermoset material, seams of EPDM roofing must be sealed with adhesive or pressure-sensitive tape. EPDM can be installed loose and covered with ballast, fully adhered with adhesive, mechanically fastened, or used in a protected membrane roof system. EPDM is one of the most common types of single-ply membrane roofing materials.

Chlorosulfonated polyethylene (CSPE) roofing, also known as *Hypalon®*, is also highly resistant to weathering and is available in white. It is applied fully adhered. CSPE has generally been replaced with PVC and TPO roofing.

Polyvinyl chloride (PVC) roofing is a thermoplastic roofing manufactured in thicknesses of 0.048 in, 0.060 in, and 0.072 in (1.2, 1.5, and 1.8). PVC membranes have excellent resistance to weathering (including hail), are easy to install, and are relatively inexpensive. Seams are heat welded. PVC can be installed loose and covered with ballast, fully adhered with adhesive, mechanically fastened, or used in a protected membrane roof system. It is available in white.

Thermoplastic polyolefin (TPO) roofing is a type of single-ply roofing made with a blend of polypropylene and ethylene propylene. It can be installed loose and covered with ballast, fully adhered with adhesive, mechanically fastened, or used in a protected membrane roof system. The mechanically attached system is used where high wind uplift is a concern and for reroofing applications. It has a low installed cost relative to EPDM.

Both PVC and TPO roofing materials are white, making them good choices for cool roof systems that are used to minimize heat transfer into a building and the subsequent energy required to cool it, as well as for minimizing the heat island effect. The *heat island effect* is the unnatural buildup of heat around buildings, especially in urban areas. Some jurisdictions, such as California, even require cool roofs to minimize interior heat gain and save energy. A new, white PVC or TPO roof will reflect approximately 78% of the radiant energy striking it, compared with about 6% for a black EPDM roof.

Because PVC and TPO membranes are themoplastics they can be recycled for roofing, while thermoset membranes, such as EPDM, cannot be reused for roofing. To be recycled, EPDM roofing must be chopped up and mixed with another material to make a product, such as rubber flooring.

The commonly used single-ply membranes are available with or without reinforcing. The reinforcing is typically polyester fibers, but some products use glass fiber reinforcing. Reinforced membranes have more dimensional stability and tear strength compared with nonreinforced membranes, and they have better puncture and wind load resistance. Reinforcing also helps the roofing lie flat for easier seaming. Reinforced membranes are good choices where high wind conditions exist and where heavy foot traffic is expected. Reinforced membranes are required where the roof is fully adhered or mechanically attached. Nonreinforced membranes have a higher elongation factor, which is good for accommodating substrate movement and to bridge small gaps in the substrate. Nonreinforced membranes are less expensive and are suitable for loose-laid and ballasted roof systems and where larger sheets are wanted.

Elastic Liquid Roofing

Liquid-applied roofings include butyl, *Neoprene®*, *Hypalon®*, and other products. They are applied in liquid form in one or two coats by brushing or spraying and are air-cured to form an elastic, waterproof surface. Liquid-applied membranes are also used for below-grade waterproofing on foundation walls, tanks, and pools, and for similar applications. These products are particularly suited for roofs with complex shapes such as thin-shell concrete domes.

FLASHING

Flashing prevents water penetration and directs any water that does get into construction back to the outside. Flashing is made of galvanized steel, stainless steel, aluminum, copper, plastic, and elastomeric materials. Material selection depends on the other metals or materials it is in contact with, the configuration of the joint, the durability desired, and the cost.

Flashing protects joints wherever water penetration is anticipated or where two dissimilar surfaces meet at an angle. This may include the areas where roofs intersect parapets, areas above windows, above steel lintels supporting masonry, between butt joints of preformed siding, and elsewhere. Figure 41.7 shows some common metal flashing details, and Fig. 41.8 illustrates flashing for single-ply roofing installations. Masonry flashing details are shown in Figs. 37.5 and 37.7. In all cases, the flashing detail should allow joint movement without destroying the integrity of the flashing connection.

ROOF ACCESSORIES

Roof accessories include items in addition to the roofing itself or flashing necessary to form a complete installation. Some examples of roof accessories are expansion joints, copings, roof hatches, smoke vents, and similar fabrications.

Expansion joints are required in buildings to allow for movement caused by temperature changes in materials and differential movement between building sections. They are required at frequent intervals in long buildings—about every 100 ft to 150 ft (30.5 m to 45.7 m) in masonry buildings and about every 200 ft (61 m) in concrete buildings. They should also be located at the junctions of T-, L-, and U-shaped buildings and where a low building portion abuts a higher, heavier section. Expansion joints are particularly important in roofs because of the extremes of temperature changes and the fact that joints in the roof are exposed to the most severe weathering conditions. Figure 41.9 shows some typical roof expansion joints. Refer to Chs. 36 and 37 for a discussion of joints for concrete and masonry structures.

Smoke vents are devices that allow excess smoke to escape in the event of a fire. Exact requirements for smoke vent locations and sizes are given in the various model building codes, but in general these vents must be located in hazardous occupancies, in certain business occupancies over 50,000 ft^2 (4645 m^2), over stages, and above elevator shafts. Vents are designed to release automatically in the event of fire, usually by being spring-loaded and connected to a fusible link.

CAULKING AND SEALANTS

Sealants are flexible materials used to close joints between materials. *Sealant* is the more correct term, but the word "caulking" (sometimes spelled "calking") is often used to designate low-performance sealants employed where little movement is expected, such as between a window frame and an exterior wall. Sealants must be capable of adhering to the joints while remaining elastic and weatherproof. There are several types of sealants, each with slightly different properties and uses under various conditions. Sealants are classified as low, intermediate, and high performance, depending on the maximum amount of joint movement they can tolerate. Low-performance sealants are used in

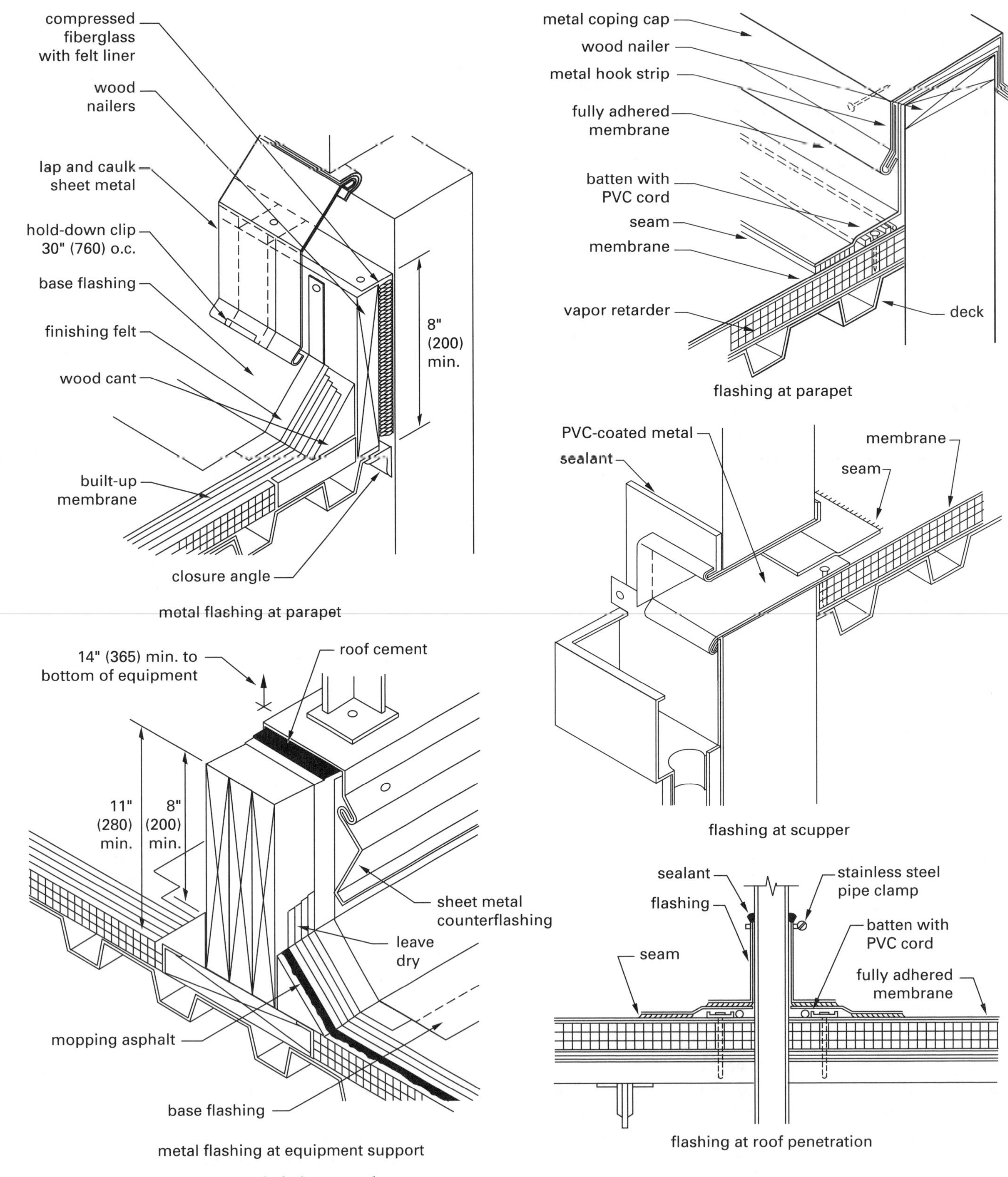

Figure 41.7 Metal Flashing Details

Figure 41.8 Elastomeric Flashing Details

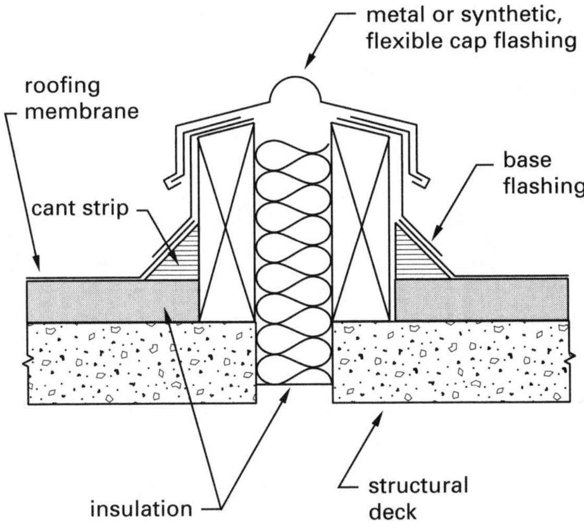

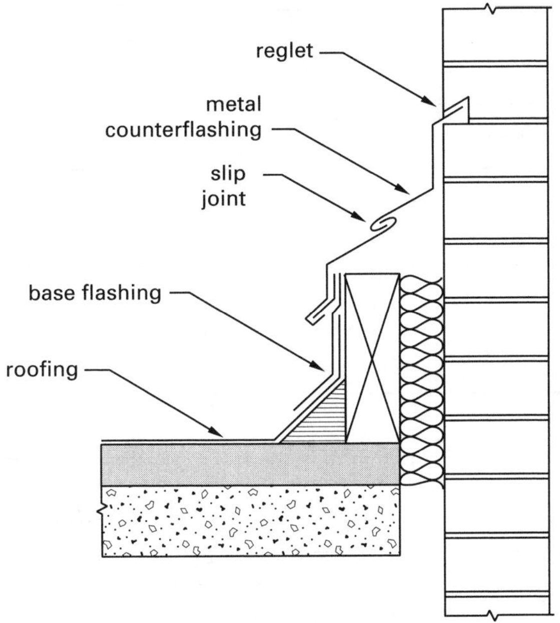

Figure 41.9 Expansion Joints

joints with ±5% movement, intermediate-performance sealants are used for joints with ±12.5% movement, and high-performance sealants are used for joints with up to about 25% movement.

The width and depth of a sealant are critical to its proper performance. See Fig. 41.10. The width is determined by the expected joint movement. The depth should be equal to the width for joints up to 1/2 in (13) wide; for joints from 1/2 in to 1 in (13 to 25), the depth should be 1/2 in (13). For wider joints, the sealant depth should not be greater than one-half the width. Joint fillers are used behind the sealant to control the depth of the sealant. Table 41.4 lists some of the common sealant types and their properties.

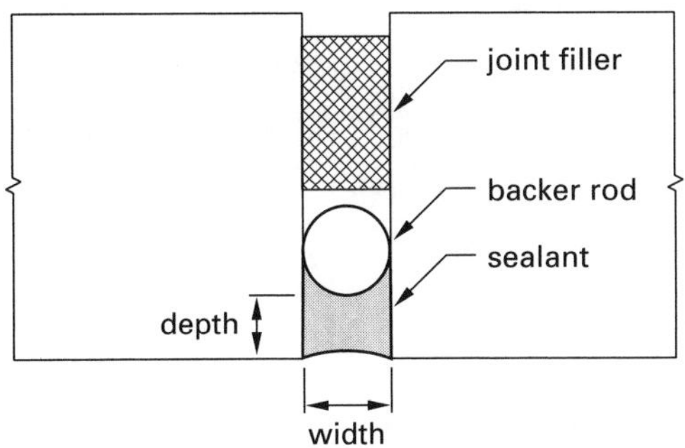

Figure 41.10 Typical Joint with Sealant

EXTERIOR INSULATION AND FINISH SYSTEMS

An *exterior insulation and finish system* (EIFS) is a cladding assembly consisting of a wet-applied cementitious finish over a rigid insulation board that is attached to building sheathing. Although portland cement stucco is included in these types of finish systems, the coating generally consists of various types of polymers (usually acrylics) or a mixture of cement and polymers. The exact formulation of an EIFS varies with each manufacturer, but there are three classifications: polymer based (Class PB), polymer modified (Class PM), and mineral based (Class MB). Class MB uses portland cement stucco in the traditional manner. A variation of the polymer-based system is the high-impact PB system, which is like the PB system but includes a heavy-duty fiberglass mesh and an additional layer of base coat.

Polymer-based systems use expanded polystyrene insulation with the base coat applied directly to the insulation with an embedded fiberglass mesh. The base coat has a high percentage of polymeric binder, which gives the system a great deal of flexibility. The finish coat, like that of the polymer-modified system, consists of acrylic polymer, sand, pigments, and other additives.

Polymer-modified systems use extruded polystyrene that is mechanically fastened to the building sheathing and structure along with the reinforcing mesh. The base coats of PM systems are thicker, from 3/16 in to 3/8 in (5 to 10), and include a higher percentage of portland cement than does the PB system. As a result, control joints are needed in PM systems to limit cracking. They should be located from 10 ft to 12 ft (3000 to 3600) apart with no section exceeding 150 ft^2 (15 m^2) in area. PM systems are more resistant to impact than are standard PB systems, and the extruded polystyrene has a slightly higher thermal resistance than does the expanded polystyrene and is more resistant to water penetration.

Table 41.4

Comparative Properties of Sealants

sealant types		oil base	butyl	acrylic, water base	acrylic, solvent base	polysulfide, one part	polysulfide, two part	polyurethane, one part	polyurethane, two part	silicone	notes
recommended maximum joint movement, %		±5	±7.5	±7.5	±12.5	±12.5 to ±25	±25	±12.5 to ±15	±25	±25	(1)
life expectancy in years		5–10	10+	10	15–20	20	20	20+	20+	20+	
maximum joint width in inches (mm)		1/4 (6)	1/2 (13)	1/2 (13)	3/4 (19)	3/4 (19)	1 (25)	3/4 (19)	1–2 (25–50)	3/4 (19)	(2)
weight shrinkage, %		10+	5–10	15	15	10	10	10	10	4	
adhesion to:	wood	•	•	•	•	•	•	•	•	•	(3)
	metal	•	•	•	•	•	•	•	•	•	
	masonry	•	•	•	•	•	•	•	•	•	(3)
	glass	•	•	•	•	•	•	•	•	•	
	plastic		•	•	•					•	
curing time in days		120	120	5	14	14+	7	7+	3–5	5	
maximum elongation, %		15	40	60	60+	300	600	300+	400+	250+	
self-leveling available		n/a	n/a		•	•	•		•	•	
nonsag available		n/a	n/a	•	•	•	•	•	•	•	
resistance to:	ultraviolet	1–2	2–3	1–3	3–4	2	2–3	3	3	5	
(see legend)	cut/tear	1	2	1–2	1	3	3	4–5	4–5	1–2	
	abrasion	1	2	1–2	1–2	1	1	3	3	1	
	weathering	1–2	2	1–3	3–4	3	3	3–4	3–4	4–5	
	oil/grease	2	1–2	2	3	3	3	3	3	2	
	compression	1	2–3	1–2	1	3	3	4	4	4–5	
	extension	1	1	1–2	1	2–3	2–3	4–5	4–5	4–5	
	water immersion	2	2–3	1	1–2	3	3	1	1	3	

(1) Some high performance urethanes and silicones have movement capabilities as high as ±50%.
(2) Figures given are conservative. Verify manufacturers' literature for specific recommendations.
(3) Primer may be required.

Legend:
1 = Poor
2 = Fair
3 = Good
4 = Very good
5 = Excellent

42 DOORS, WINDOWS, AND GLAZING

With the materials and construction systems available today, doors and windows no longer simply serve to provide passage between spaces or to admit light. Openings can be selectively designed and specified to fulfill certain functions. For example, a window can admit light but be designed to minimize sound transmission while still providing security. Or a door passage can be designed as an unobtrusive, clear opening while still providing fire protection in the event of an emergency.

DOOR OPENINGS

Both metal and wood doors can serve a variety of functions. They can control passage, provide visual and aural privacy, maintain security, supply fire resistance and weather protection, control light, and serve as radiation shielding. It is important to understand what kind of control you want in order to select the most appropriate type of door. Considerations of durability, cost, appearance, ease of use, method of construction, and availability are also important in door selection.

There are three major components of a door system: the door itself, the frame, and the hardware. Each must be coordinated with the other components and be appropriate for the circumstances and the design intent.

The common parts of a door opening are illustrated in Fig. 42.1. To differentiate the two jambs, the side where the hinge or pivot is installed is called the *hinge jamb*, and the jamb where the door closes is called the *strike side* or *strike jamb*.

There is also a standard method of referring to the way a door swings, called the *door hand* or the *handing* of a door. Handing is used by specifiers, hardware suppliers, and manufacturers to indicate exactly what kind of hardware must be supplied for a specific opening. Some hardware will only work on a door that swings a particular way because of the way the strike side of the door is beveled. Hardware that can work on any hand of door is called *reversible* or *nonhanded*.

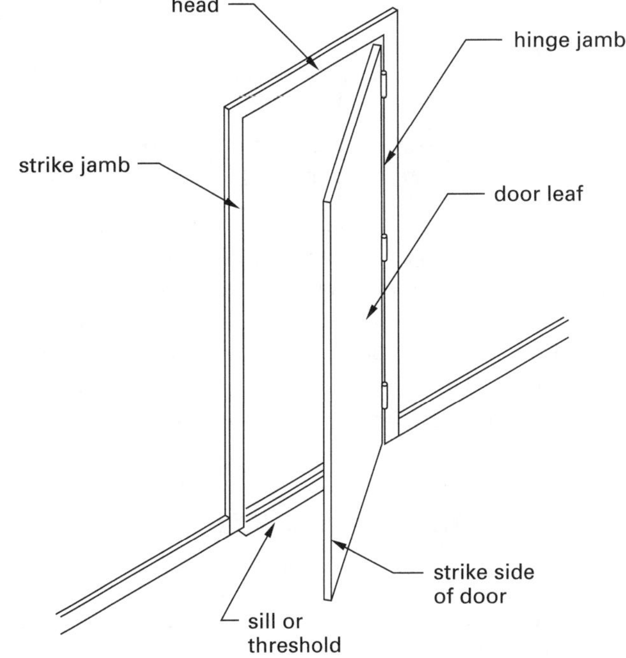

Figure 42.1 Parts of a Door

The hand of a door is determined from outside the door, as shown in Fig. 42.2. The exterior of a building is considered the outside, as is the hallway side of a room door, or the lobby side of a door opening into a room. In situations where the distinction is not clear, the outside is considered the side of the door where the hinge is not visible. When standing on the outside looking at the door, if the door hinges on the left and swings away from the viewer, it is a *left-hand door*. If it hinges on the right and swings away from the viewer, it is a *right-hand door*. If the door swings toward

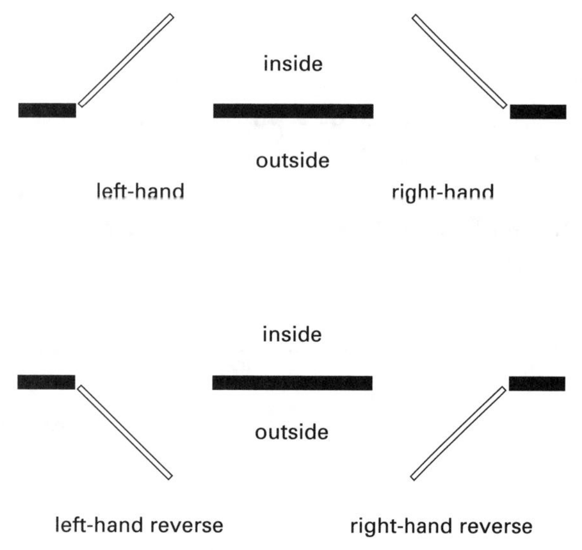

Figure 42.2 Door Handing

the viewer, it is considered a *left-hand reverse* or a *right-hand reverse*, depending on the location of the hinge or pivot.

A door can be classified by the function it serves, its operation, and the material from which it is made. Each type of classification is useful in its own way to help select the best type of door for a particular situation. Figure 42.3 illustrates some of the common types of swinging doors, and Fig. 42.4 shows doors classified by type of operation. Table 42.1 summarizes some of the advantages and disadvantages of various door types.

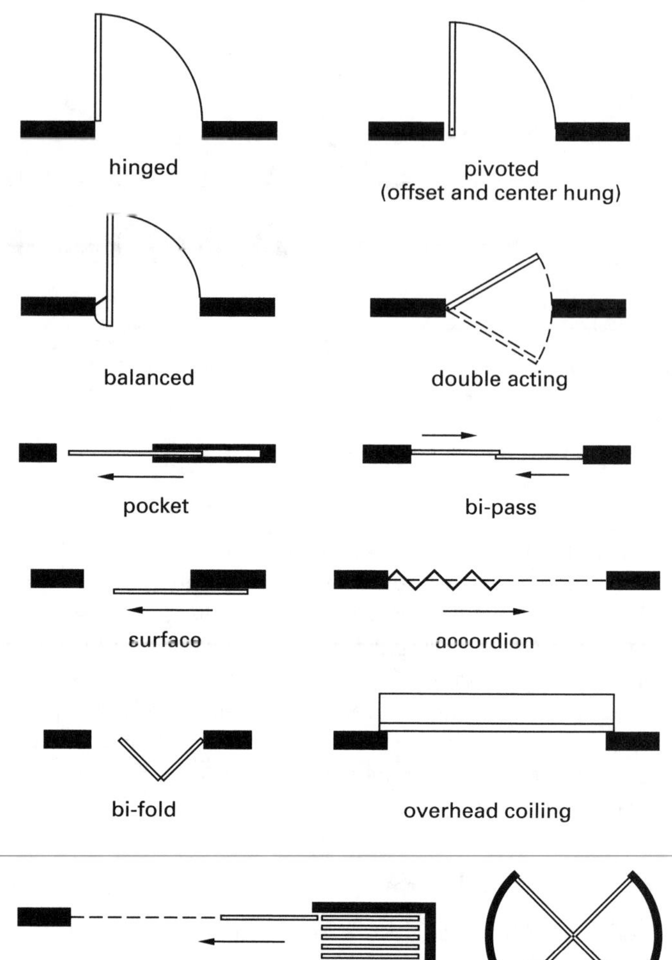

Figure 42.4 Door Classification by Operation

METAL DOORS AND FRAMES

Door Types

The three most common types of metal doors are flush, sash, and louvered. *Flush doors* have a single, smooth surface on both sides; *sash doors* contain one or more glass lites; and *louvered doors* have an opening with metal slats to provide ventilation. Paneled steel doors, which resemble wood panel doors, are also available with insulated cores for

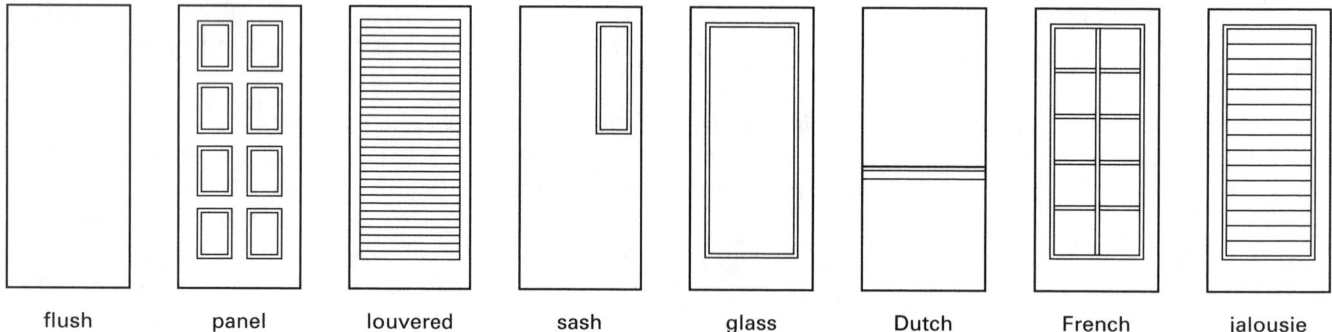

Figure 42.3 Types of Swinging Doors

Table 42.1
Door Type Advantages and Disadvantages

door operation type	advantages	disadvantages
swinging		
hinged	ease of use and installation inexpensive can be fire-rated wide variety of hinge styles	appearance of hinges sometimes undesirable
offset pivoted	ease of use closer can be part of pivot can be fire rated can accommodate very heavy doors minimal hardware appearance	more expensive than hinges floor closers require solid flooring and adequate thickness to accommodate closer
center-hung pivoted	ease of use closer can be part of pivot allows door to swing both ways support hardware fully concealed can be fire rated can accommodate very heavy doors	more expensive than hinges floor closers require solid flooring and adequate thickness to accommodate closer height limitations required to avoid bowing
balanced	little effort required to operate clear width reduced when open	expensive
double acting	easy operation both ways dangerous unless glass lite provided	cannot be used as exit door
pocket sliding	no operating space required difficult to seal against light or sound susceptible to sticking cannot be used as exit door	awkward for frequent use
bi-pass sliding	no operating space required difficult to seal cannot be used as exit door	awkward for frequent use
surface sliding	no operating space required cannot be used as exit door	appearance of hardware
bi-fold	minimum operating space cannot be used as exit door	awkward to use
accordion folding	useful for subdividing space inexpensive limited finishes and colors available	poor as a sound barrier cannot be used as exit door
operable partition	good for very large openings good sound barrier wide choice of finishes	expensive cannot be used as exit door
overhead coiling	automatic closing of large openings for security or fire separation cannot be used as exit door	visible when door closed requires large space for housing
revolving	accommodates large numbers prevents air infiltration types available for darkrooms	only appropriate for entrance doors requires large space; expensive cannot be used as exit door

residential use where energy conservation and durability are requirements in addition to a more traditional appearance.

Metal doors are available in steel, stainless steel, aluminum, and bronze, but other door materials are available on special order. The most common material is steel with a painted finish.

Construction

Steel doors, commonly referred to as *hollow metal doors*, are constructed with faces of cold-rolled sheet steel. 18-gage and 14-gage thicknesses are typically used, although 20-gage is available for light-duty doors. 16-gage is also available. The steel face is attached to cores of honeycomb kraft paper, steel ribs, hardboard, or other materials. The edges are made of steel channels, with the locations for hardware reinforced with heavier-gage steel. Mineral wool or other materials are used to provide sound-deadening qualities, if required.

Sizes

Although metal doors can be custom made in almost any practical size, standard widths are 2 ft 0 in, 2 ft 4 in, 2 ft 6 in, 2 ft 8 in, 3 ft 0 in, 3 ft 4 in, 3 ft 6 in, 3 ft 8 in, and 4 ft 0 in. Standard heights are 6 ft 8 in, 7 ft 0 in, and 8 ft 0 in. The standard thickness is 1$^3/_4$ in.

In SI units, standard widths are 610 mm, 711 mm, 762 mm, 813 mm, 914 mm, 1016 mm, 1067 mm, 1118 mm, and 1219 mm. Standard heights are 2032 mm, 2134 mm, and 2438 mm. The standard thickness is 44 mm.

Frames

Steel door frames can be used for either steel doors or wood doors and are made from sheet steel bent into the shape required for the door installation. Frames are made from 12-, 14-, or 16-gage steel, depending on location and use. The frame is mortised for the installation of hinges and door strikes and is reinforced at these points with heavier-gage steel. Two of the most common frame profiles are shown in Fig. 42.5 along with some standard dimensions and the terminology used to describe the parts. Various types of anchoring devices are used inside the frame to attach it to gypsum board, masonry, concrete, and other materials. Where a fire rating over 20 minutes is required, steel frames are used almost exclusively, although some wood frames have higher ratings.

Steel frames are manufactured in three styles: one-piece, welded frames; knock-down (KD) frames, where the two jamb sections and head section are shipped to the job site as separate pieces; or slip-on frames. One-piece frames must be set in place before the partition is constructed, whereas knock-down and slip-on frames can be set after gypsum wallboard partitions are built. Slip-on frames are

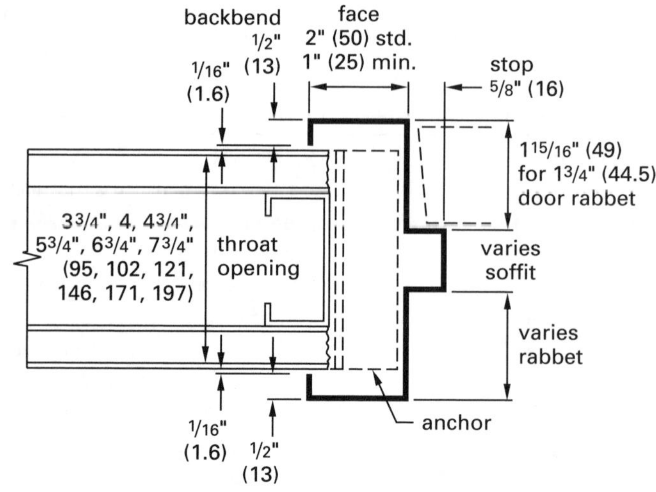

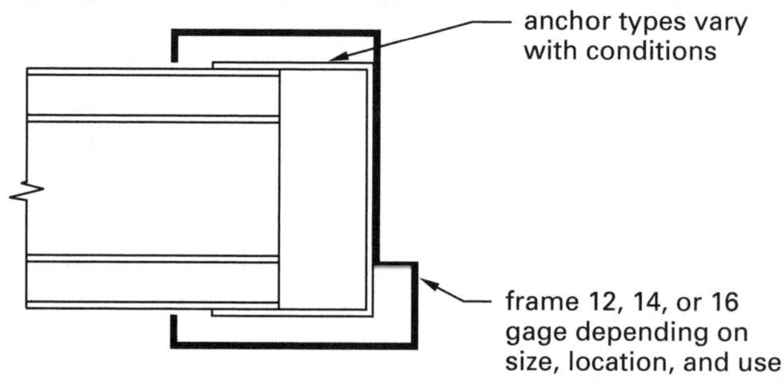

Figure 42.5 Standard Steel Door Frames

not available with welded corners and should be avoided if the appearance of a joint is objectionable.

Aluminum frames are used for both aluminum doors and wood doors. They are constructed of extruded sections and as a consequence can have thinner face dimensions and more elaborate shapes than are possible with bent steel.

Steel frames are painted, either in the shop or on site. Aluminum frames are anodized with the standard anodized colors, or they can be factory-coated with a variety of colors with baked acrylic paints and other finishes.

WOOD DOORS AND FRAMES

Wood doors are the most common types for both residential and commercial construction. They are available in a variety of styles, sizes, finishes, and methods of operation.

Door Types

Wood doors can be classed according to their operation, as shown in Fig. 42.4. *Swinging doors* are the most typical type, and they function by being hinged or pivoted on one side. They are relatively inexpensive, easy to install, and can accommodate a large volume of traffic. Double-acting doors swing in both directions when mounted on pivot hardware or special double-acting hinges.

Pocket sliding doors travel on a top track and move horizontally into a pocket built into the wall. They are good for limited space, but they are awkward to operate, and latching and sealing are difficult.

Bi-pass sliding doors also travel on a top or bottom rail and are often used for closet doors where space is limited. Bi-folding and multi-folding doors are also used for closets and other large openings where full access needs to be provided when the doors are open.

The two primary types of wood doors are the flush door and the panel door. See Fig. 42.6. *Flush doors* consist of a thin, flat veneer laminated to various types of cores as described. *Panel doors* consist of solid vertical stiles and horizontal rails that serve as a frame for flat or raised panels.

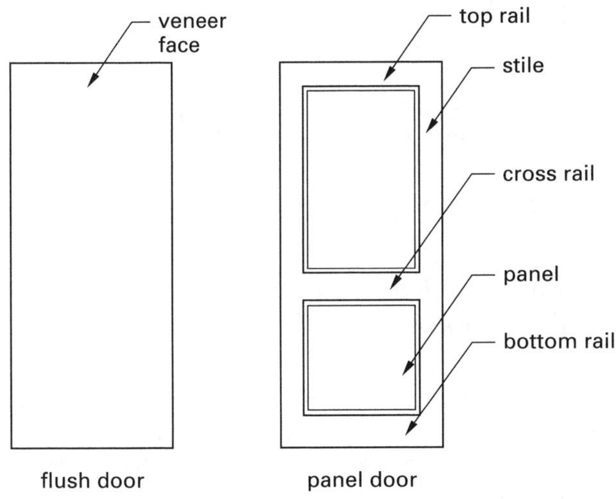

Figure 42.6 Types of Wood Doors

Construction

Wood doors are either hollow core or solid core. *Hollow-core doors* are made of one or three plies of veneer on each side of a cellular cardboard interior. The stile-and-rails frame is made of solid wood with larger blocks of solid wood where the locksets or latchsets are installed. Hollow-core doors are used in interior applications where only light use is expected and where cost is a consideration. They have no fire-resistance capabilities.

Solid-core doors are made with a variety of core types depending on the functional requirements of the door. Cores may be particleboard, stave core (solid blocks of wood), or mineral core for fire-rated doors. Solid-core doors are used for their fire-resistance properties, as acoustical barriers, for security, and for their superior durability. Solid-core doors may have a fire rating from 20 minutes to $1^1/_2$ hours. Mineral-core doors are used when fire ratings of $^3/_4$, 1, and $1^1/_2$ hours are required.

The face veneers of wood doors can be made from any available hardwood species using rotary-cut, plain-sliced, quarter-sliced, or rift-cut methods, just like wood panels. The veneers can be bookmatched, slip matched, or random matched, although bookmatching is the most common. Veneers of hardboard suitable for painting and plastic laminate are also available.

Sizes

Like metal doors, wood doors can be custom made to any size, but the standard widths are 2 ft 0 in, 2 ft 4 in, 2 ft 6 in, 2 ft 8 in, 3 ft 0 in, and 3 ft 4 in (610, 711, 762, 813, 914, and 1016). Standard heights are 6 ft 8 in and 7 ft 0 in (2032 and 2134), although higher doors, often used in commercial construction, are available. Hollow-core doors are $1^3/_8$ in (35) thick and solid-core doors are $1^3/_4$ in (44) thick; doors $2^1/_4$ in (57) thick are available for large, exterior doors and acoustical doors.

Frames

Frames for wood doors are made from wood, steel (hollow metal), and aluminum. A common wood frame jamb is illustrated in Fig. 42.7. Although the stop and casing are shown as rectangular pieces, several different profiles of trim are available and are frequently used.

The decision concerning the type of frame to use for a wood door depends on the appearance desired, the type of partition in which the opening is being installed, the fire-rating requirements, the security needed, and the durability desired. For example, wood frames may be used in 20-, 30-, and 45-minute fire door assemblies, but a 1-hour-rated door must be installed in a rated metal frame.

GLASS DOORS

Glass doors are those constructed primarily of glass with fittings to hold the pivots and other hardware. Sometimes they are called *all-glass doors*. Their strength depends on the glass rather than the framing. They are different from sash doors in that sash doors have a frame around all four sides of the door.

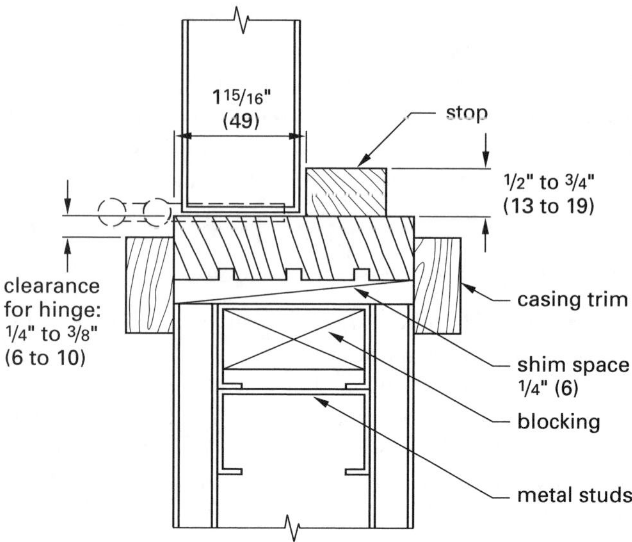

Figure 42.7 Standard Wood Door Frame

Components

Glass doors are generally constructed of 1/2 in (13) or 3/4 in (19) tempered glass with fittings and operating hardware as required by the installation. Common door sizes are 36 in (914) wide and 7 ft 0 in (2134) high, although many architects prefer to specify glass doors at the same height as that of the ceiling.

Some of the typical configurations are shown in Fig. 42.8. The minimum configuration requires some type of door pull and a corner fitting at the top and bottom to hold the pivots. In lieu of corner fittings, some manufacturers provide hinge fittings that clamp on the glass and support the door in much the same way as a standard hinged door. If a lock is required, the bottom fitting may be continuous across the door to allow for a dead bolt to be installed. Some architects prefer continuous fittings (sometimes called the shoes) on both the top and bottom.

Because a full glass door is a potential hazard and extra strength is required, the glass must be tempered. Any holes, notches, or other modification to the glass must be made before it is tempered.

Standard Assemblies

Glass doors can be used alone and set within a wall opening with or without a frame, or they can be installed between glass sidelights. If glass sidelights are used, the same type of fitting used on the door is generally used to support the sidelights. Although jamb frames of aluminum, wood, or ornamental metal can be used, they are not necessary, and the glass sidelights can be butted directly to the partition or held away a fraction of an inch.

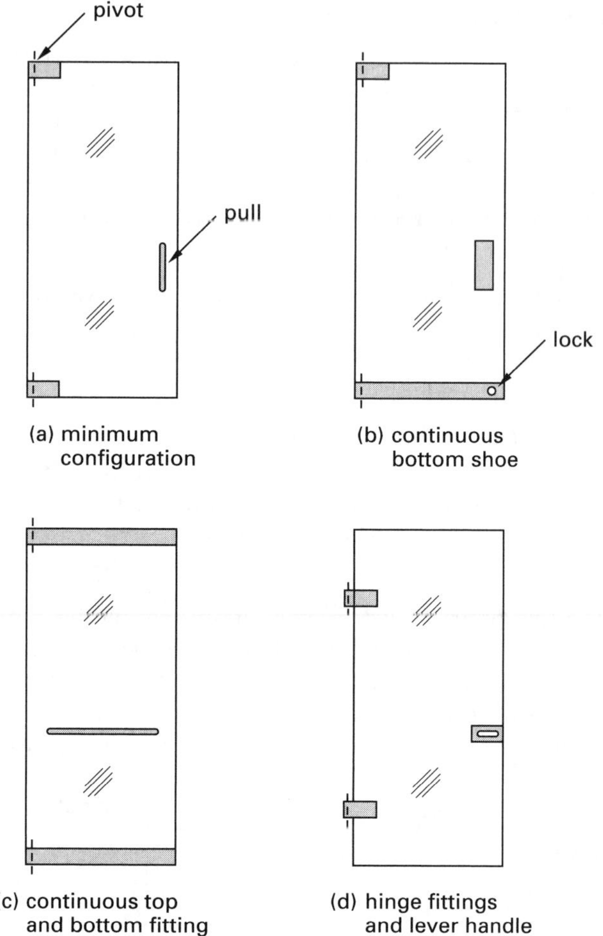

Figure 42.8 Standard Glass Door Configurations

Building Code Requirements for All-Glass Doors

Because all-glass doors cannot be fire rated, they cannot be used where a protected opening is required in a fire-rated partition. When they are allowed and serve as exit doors, the type of hardware used must conform to the requirements of the local building code. Some codes and local amendments are more restrictive than others and usually prohibit the use of a simple dead bolt in the bottom rail fitting. Instead, special panic hardware is available for glass doors that allows the door to be locked from the outside (and operated with card keys or keypads, if necessary), but still allows the door to be unlatched and opened from the inside in a single operation without any special knowledge or effort. See Fig. 42.9.

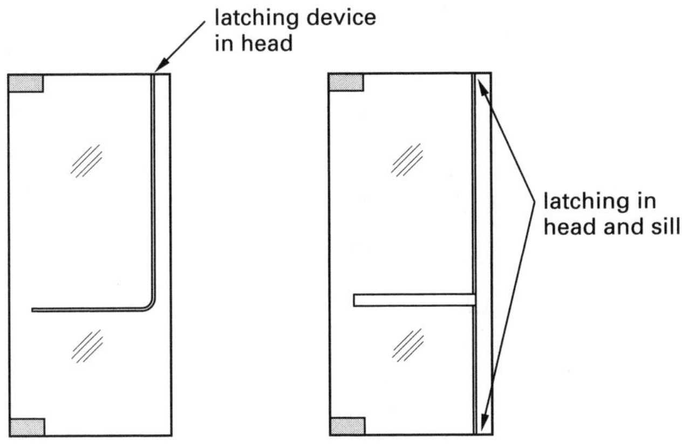

Figure 42.9 Glass Door Panic Hardware

SPECIAL DOORS

Special doors have a wide variety of applications where a special closing assembly is required. Some of the more common types of special doors include the following.

Revolving doors are assemblies of three or four leaves connected at a central point that rotate within an enclosure. They are used to control air infiltration and to allow large numbers of people to pass in and out. They are made of glass framed with aluminum, bronze, or other metals. In most cases, revolving doors do not count in determining the total exit width from a building or as a required exit. Some revolving doors are available with collapsing leaves that fold open if subjected to the force of a crowd of people pushing against them.

Overhead coiling doors are made from thin slats of metal that roll up into an enclosure above the head of the opening. They are used to close large openings such as industrial and garage doors, or as fire separations for large openings. They can be connected to fusible links so that they automatically close in the event of fire.

Sectional overhead doors also close large openings and are typically used for industrial buildings and garages. The door is made from individual sections of wood or metal that hinge as the door opens.

Other special doors include blast-resistant doors, sound-retardant doors, hangar doors, folding doors used to divide rooms, security doors, and cold-storage doors.

HARDWARE

Hardware includes the various types of finish hardware normally found on interior and exterior doors, weather stripping, electrical locking devices, and window operators. Cabinet hardware and curtain and drapery hardware are classified as a different type and included with those items.

Functions of Hardware

Hardware is a vital part of any door opening assembly. In general, hardware can be grouped according to the function it serves based on the following list.

- Hanging the door: hinges, pivots, and combination pivots and closers
- Operating the door: handles, latchsets, push plates, and pull bars
- Closing the door: door closers and combination pivots and closers
- Locking the door: locksets, dead bolts, flush bolts, electric locks, and other special devices
- Sealing the door: weather stripping, sound seals, smoke seals
- Protecting the door: kick plates, corner protection, and similar materials

Hinges

Hinging is the most common method of attaching a door to its frame. Hinges are also referred to as *butts* because they are usually attached to the butt edge of a door. Hinges consist of two leaves with an odd number of knuckles on one leaf and an even number of knuckles on the other. The knuckles are attached with a pin. The pin and knuckles form the barrel of the hinge, which is finished with a tip.

There are four basic types of hinges: full mortise, half mortise, full surface, and half surface. These are shown in Fig. 42.10.

Full mortise is the most common type and has both leaves fully mortised into the frame and edge of the door. *Half-surface hinges* have one leaf mounted on the face of the door and the other leaf mortised into the frame. *Half-mortise hinge* leaves are surface-applied to the frame and mortised into the edge of the door. *Full-surface hinges* are applied to the face of both the door and frame. The various types of hinges are used when either the door or frame cannot be mortised. For example, a half-mortise hinge may be bolted or welded to a heavy steel frame.

There are also special types of hinges. *Raised barrel hinges* are used when there is not room for the barrel to extend past the trim. The barrel is offset to allow one leaf to be mortised into the frame. *Swing clear hinges* have a special shape that allows the door to swing 90° so that the full opening of the doorway is available. See Fig. 42.11.

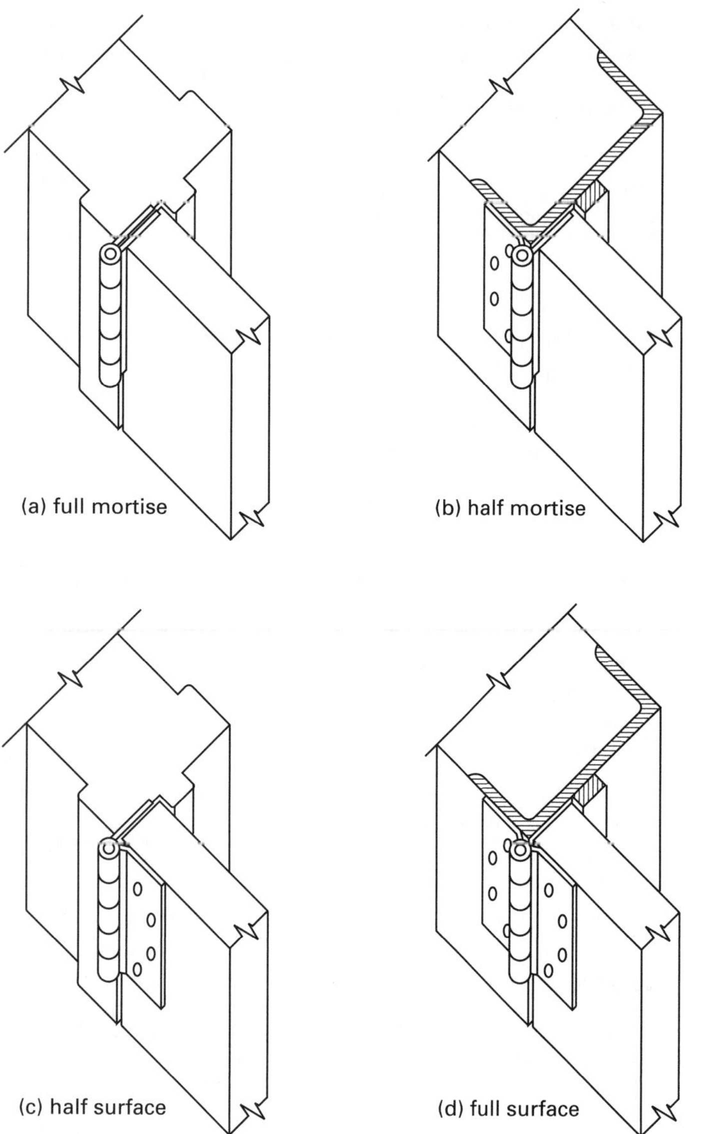

Figure 42.10 Common Hinge Types

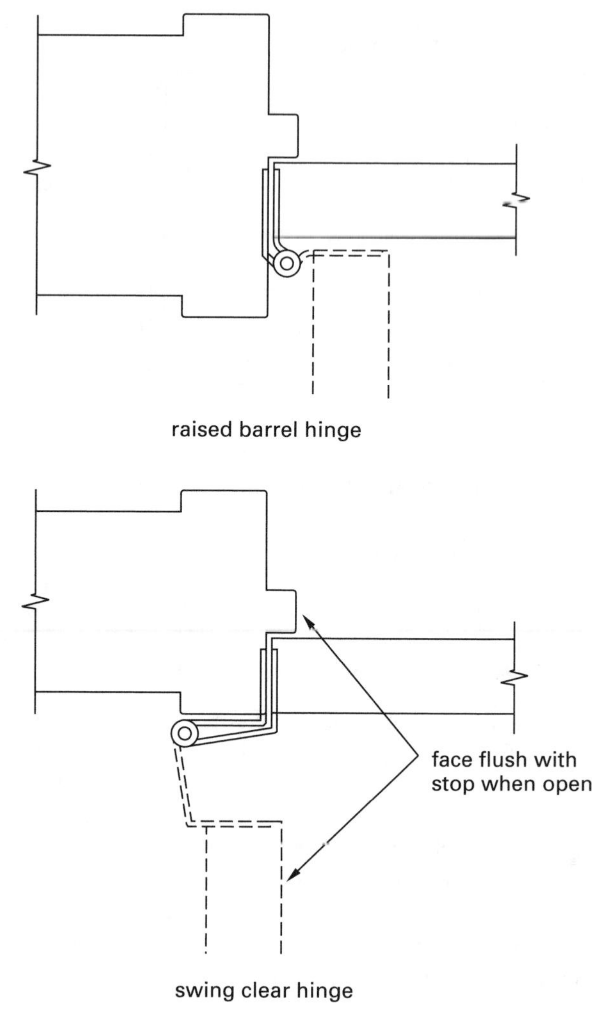

Figure 42.11 Special Hinges

Without a swing clear hinge, standard hardware decreases the opening width by the thickness of the door when it is open 90°.

Hinges are available with or without ball bearings and in three weights. Which type to use depends on the door weight and frequency of use. *Low-frequency doors*, like residential doors, can use standard-weight, plain-bearing hinges. Most commercial applications require standard-weight, ball-bearing hinges. *High-frequency applications* such as office building entrances, theaters, and so forth, require heavyweight, ball-bearing hinges. In addition, ball-bearing hinges are required for fire-rated assemblies and on all doors with closers.

The size and number of hinges for a door depend on a number of factors. The size is given by two numbers such as $4 \times 4^1/_2$. The first number is the length, which is the length of the barrel in inches, and the second number is the width, which is the dimension in inches when the hinge is open.

The width of the hinge is determined by the width of the door and the clearance required around jamb trim. One rule of thumb is that the width of the hinge equals twice the door thickness, plus trim projection, minus $^1/_2$ in (12.6). If a fraction falls between standard sizes, use the next larger size. Common hinge widths for $1^3/_4$ in (44) doors are 4 in and $4^1/_2$ in (102 and 114).

The length of the hinge is determined by the door thickness and the door width, as shown in Table 42.2.

The number of hinges is determined by the height of the door. Numbers of hinges are commonly referred to by pairs, one pair being two hinges. Doors up to 60 in (1500) high require two hinges (1 pair). Doors from 60 in to 90 in (1500

Table 42.2
How to Determine Hinge Heights

door thickness (in/mm)	door width (in/mm)	height of hinge (in/mm)
3/4 to 1 1/8	to 24	2 1/2
(19 to 29)	(610)	(63.5)
1 3/8	to 32	3 1/2
(35)	(813)	(89)
1 3/8	over 32 to 37	4
(35)	(over 813 to 940)	(102)
1 3/4	to 36	4 1/2
(44)	(to 914)	(114)
1 3/4	over 36 to 48	5
(44)	(over 914 to 1219)	(127)
1 3/4	over 48	6
(44)	(over 1219)	(152)
2, 2 1/4, 2 1/2	to 42	5 (heavy weight)
(51, 57, 64)	(to 1067)	(127)
2, 2 1/4, 2 1/2	over 42	6 (heavy weight)
(51, 57, 64)	(over 1067)	(152)

to 2290) require three hinges (11/2 pair), and doors 90 in to 120 in (2290 to 3050) require four hinges (2 pair).

Latchsets and Locksets

Latchsets and locksets are devices to hold a door in the closed position and lock it. A *latchset* only holds the door in place with no provision for locking. It has a beveled latch extending from the face of the door edge and automatically engages the strike mounted in the frame when the door is closed. A *lockset* has a special mechanism that allows the door to be locked with a key or thumbturn.

There are four types of latches and locks: mortise, preassembled, bored, and interconnected. These are shown in Fig. 42.12. Another type, the integral lock, is no longer produced in the United States, but is still found in older buildings.

A *mortise lock* or *latch* is installed in a rectangular area cut out of the door. It is generally more secure than a bored lock and offers a much wider variety of locking options. Mortise locks allow the use of a dead bolt and a latch bolt, both of which can be retracted with a single operation. A variety of knob and level handle designs can be used with the basic mechanism.

Preassembled locks and latches (also called *unit locks*) come from the factory as a complete unit. They are slid into a notch made in the edge of the door and require very little adjustment. Preassembled locks are seldom used anymore, but they are often found in older buildings.

Bored locks and latches (also called *cylindrical locks or latches*) are installed by boring holes through the face of the door and from the edge of the door to the other bored opening. They are relatively easy to install and are less expensive than mortise locks, but they offer fewer operating functions than do mortise locks. They are generally used in residential and small commercial projects.

Interconnected locks have a cylindrical lock and a dead bolt. The two locks are interconnected so that a single action of turning a knob or lever handle on the inside releases both bolts.

With all types of latches and locks, either a doorknob or lever handle may be used to operate the latching device. In most cases, a lever handle is required to meet requirements for accessibility.

The distance from the edge of the door to the center line of the doorknob or pivot of a lever handle is called the backset. Standard backsets are 2 3/4 in and 5 in (70 and 127), although others are available on special order.

Other Types of Hardware

- *Pivots*. Pivots provide an alternative way to hang doors where the visual appearance of hinges is objectionable or where a frameless door design may make it impossible to use hinges. Pivots may be center hung or offset and are mounted in the floor and head of the door. See Fig. 42.13. For large or heavy doors, an intermediate pivot is often required for offset-hung doors only. Center-hung pivots allow the door to swing in either direction and can be completely concealed, but they allow only a 90° swing. Offset pivots allow the door to swing 180°.
- *Panic hardware*. This type of operating hardware is used where required by the building code for safe egress during a panic situation. Push bars extending across the width of the door operate vertical rods that disengage latches at the top and bottom. The vertical rods can be surface mounted or concealed.
- *Push plates and pull bars*. These are used to operate a door that does not require automatic latching. They are also used on doors to toilet rooms and commercial kitchens.
- *Closers*. Closers are devices that automatically return a door to its closed position after it is opened. They also control the distance a door can be opened and thereby protect the door and surrounding construction from damage. Closers can be surface mounted on the door or head frame or concealed in the frame

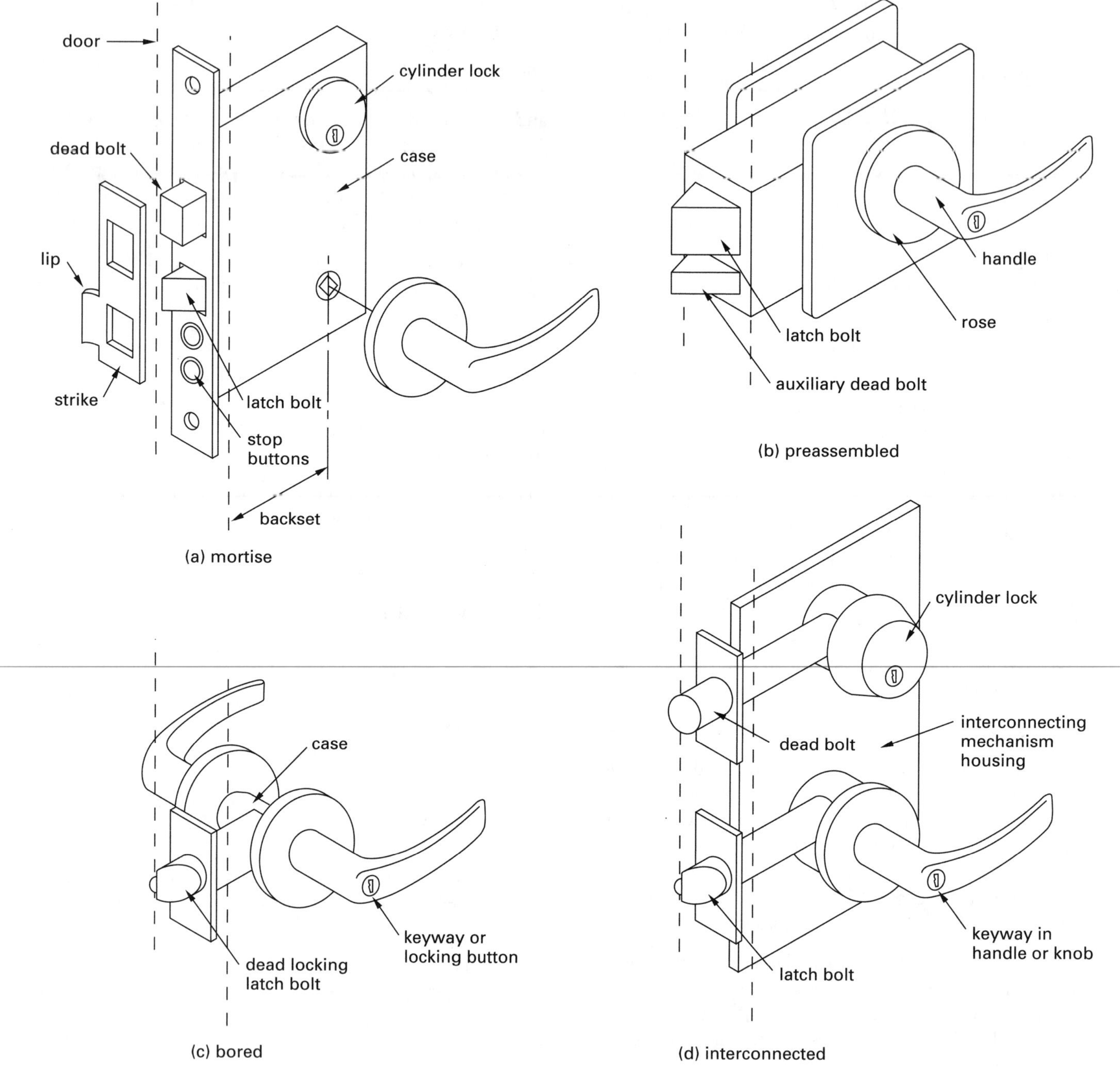

Figure 42.12 Types of Locksets

or door. Selection of a closer depends on the type, size, and weight of the door, the frequency of operation, the visual appearance desired, and the door height clearance required. Closers can also be integral with pivots mounted in the floor or ceiling, either center hung or offset.

Closers are available that have fire and smoke detectors built in so that a door may be held open during normal operation but will close when smoke is sensed.

- *Door stops and bumpers*. Some method of keeping a door from damaging adjacent construction should be provided. Closers will do this to some extent, but floor stops or wall bumpers provide more positive protection. These devices are small metal fabrications with rubber bumpers attached. See Fig. 42.14.

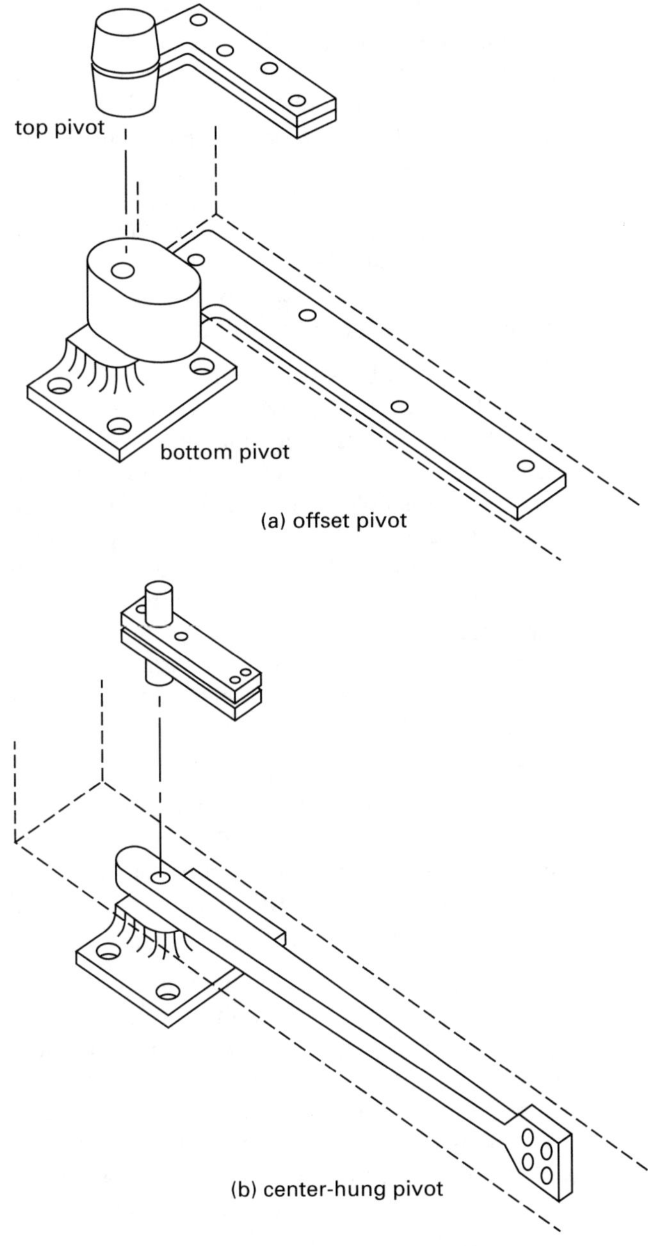

Figure 42.13 Door Pivots

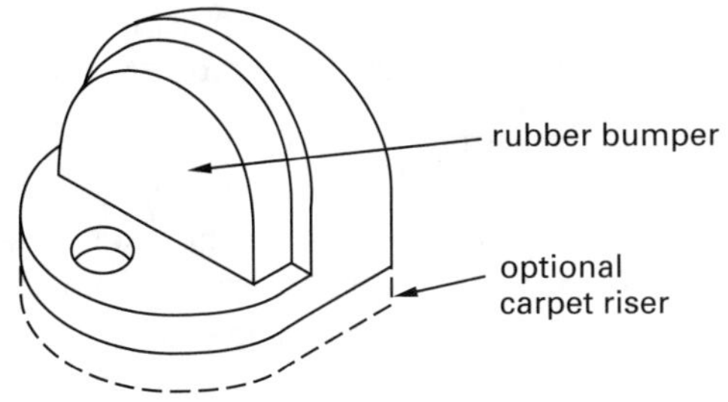

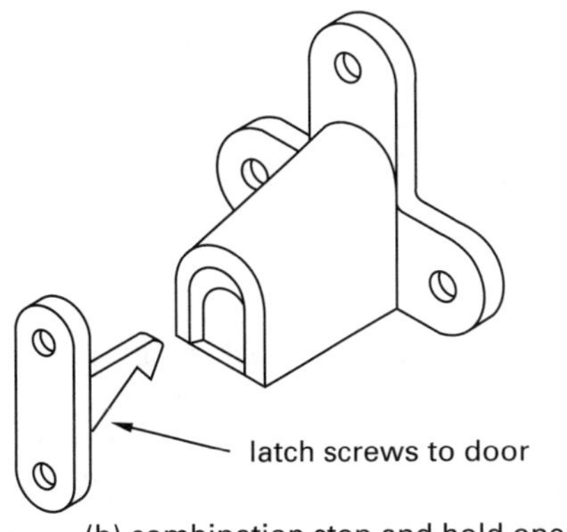

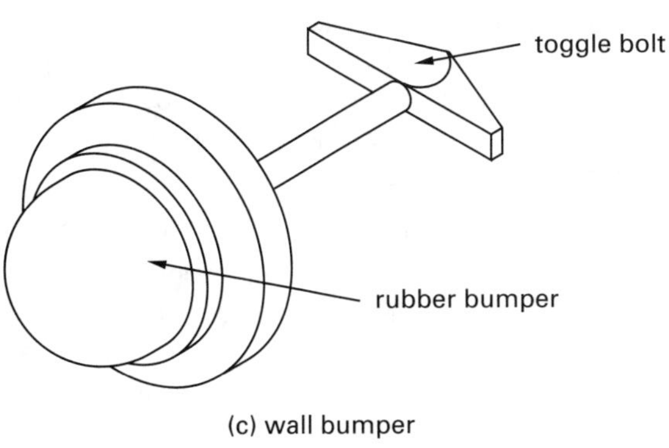

Figure 42.14 Miscellaneous Door Hardware

- *Astragals*. Astragals are vertical members used between double doors to seal the opening, act as a door stop, or provide extra security when the doors are closed. Astragals may be fixed or removable to allow for a wide opening when moving furniture.
- *Coordinators*. A door coordinator is a device used with double doors that are rabbeted or that have an astragal on the active leaf. The coordinator is mounted in or on the head of the frame, coordinating the closing sequence of the two doors so that they close completely, rather than having the leaf with the astragal close first, preventing the other leaf from closing.
- *Flush bolts*. These are used on the inactive leaf of a pair of doors to lock the doors. They may be surface mounted or mortised into the edge of the door. The active leaf then closes to the locked inactive leaf, but both can be opened when needed. Flush bolts are not allowed on exit doors.
- *Automatic door bottoms*. These are devices that are mortised or surface applied to the bottom of the door to provide a sound or light seal. When the

door is open the seal is up; as the door is closed a plunger strikes the jamb and forces the seal down.

- *Weather stripping*. Weather stripping is used along the edges and bottoms of doors to provide a tight seal against water and air infiltration. Various types of door seals are also used to provide light and sound protection on interior doors as well as sealing against the passage of smoke around fire doors. Different types of neoprene, felt, metal, vinyl, and other materials are used.

- *Thresholds*. These are used where floor materials change at a door line, where weather stripping is required, where a hard surface is required for an automatic door bottom, or where minor changes in floor level occur.

Electronic Hardware

Electronic hardware includes devices that control or monitor door openings using electric or electromechanical means. Local building codes must be consulted because some electronic hardware items do not qualify as allowable exit devices. If an exit door is electronically locked and controlled from the outside, most codes require that exiting be possible from the inside through a purely mechanical action on the locking device—that is, one that does not depend on any power supply or deactivation of the lock on the inside by the person exiting. Following are some of the most common types of electronic hardware.

- *Electric locks*. An electric lock maintains a mortise or bored lockset in the locked position until a signal is activated by some type of regulating device. Regulating devices can include wall switches, pushbuttons, card readers, key switches, computerized controls, automatic time devices, security consoles, and other sophisticated control devices. Electric locks can also be specified so that they automatically open if there is a power failure. In either case, the inside knob or handle mechanically unlatches the door for exiting at any time.

  A variation of the electric lock is the electric latch. This device is normally in a position to hold the latchbolt of the lock so that the door cannot be opened. On activation, the electric latch pivots slightly, allowing the door to be opened. From the inside, the mechanical operation of the knob or handle retracts the latch, allowing exit regardless of the position of the electric latch. Electric latches have the advantage of not requiring any power to be run to the door; all wiring is done in the door jamb. Electric locks require the use of electric hinges or other power-transfer devices to make the low-voltage wiring connections from the door frame to the mechanism in the door.

- *Electric bolts*. Electric bolts are devices separate from the operating hardware of a door. They can be mounted in the strike jamb or head of a door. In the normal, locked position, a bolt extends from the unit into a strike in the door. A pushbutton, card reader, or other regulating device activates a solenoid that retracts the bolt. Fail-safe units are available that open when there is a power failure. Electric bolts are generally not allowed on exit doors because there is no sure way to mechanically open the door if the bolt does not retract.

- *Card readers*. Card readers are one type of regulating device that reads a magnetic code on a small plastic card when the card is inserted into the reader. If the reader detects a valid code, the switch is activated and the door is unlocked. Card readers can also be used to send a signal to a central monitoring computer that keeps track of whose card was used to open which door and when the entry was made. The computer can also control the times of day when a door can be opened by particular cards. Card readers are usually mounted on the partition near the door they control, but they can also be part of the lockset, as is typically the case in hotels.

- *Keypad devices*. An alternative to the card reader is the keypad, in which a coded number must be entered to gain access. These can be separate units mounted near the door or they can be part of the door knob or lever.

- *Magnetic hold-open devices*. Although exit doors must have closers, most codes allow them to be held in an open position if they can be closed automatically upon activation of a smoke detector or other approved fire signal. One method of doing this is to use a closer with an integral smoke detector as described previously. Another way is to use a magnetic hold-open device that is an electromagnet mounted on a wall or on the floor that contacts a metal plate attached to the door. Upon activation by a central alarm signal or smoke detector or upon a power failure, the electromagnet releases and the door closes.

Finishes

Hardware is available in a variety of finishes, the choice of which is dependent primarily on the appearance desired, but also on its ability to withstand use and weathering. The finish is applied over a base metal from which the hardware is made. For most hardware items this is not critical, but for hinges and other operating hardware it can be significant.

There are five basic metals: steel, stainless steel, bronze, brass, and aluminum. Fire-rated doors must have steel or stainless steel hinges, and hardware in corrosive environments may require stainless steel or bronze base metals with compatible surface finishes.

Hardware finishes have been standardized according to numbers developed by the federal government (U.S. designations) and the Builders Hardware Manufacturers Association (BHMA). These are listed in Table 42.3.

Table 42.3

Hardware Finishes

BHMA no.	US no.	BHMA finish description
605	US3	bright brass, clear coated
606	US4	satin brass, clear coated
611	US9	bright bronze, clear coated
612	US10	satin bronze, clear coated
613	US10B	satin bronze, dark oxidized, oil rubbed
618	US14	bright nickel, clear coated
619	US15	satin nickel-plated, clear coated
622	US19	flat black
623	US20	light oxidized, statuary bronze, clear coated
624	US20A	dark statuary bronze, clear coated
625	US26	bright chromium plate
626	US26D	satin chromium plate
627	US27	satin aluminum, clear coated
628	US28	satin aluminum, clear anodized
629	US32	bright stainless steel
630	US32D	satin stainless steel

BUILDING CODE REQUIREMENTS

Doors and hardware are highly regulated by the building codes. The requirements generally fall into three major categories: exiting requirements, fire-rated assemblies, and access requirements. Many of the exit door requirements are reviewed in Ch. 55. Additional regulations specifically related to doors and hardware are included here.

The building codes regulate under what circumstances a door must provide fire protection. If a partition must have a fire rating, the openings in that partition must also be fire rated. Typical places where fire-rated doors are required include openings in stairways, in fire-rated corridors, in occupancy separation walls, and in certain hazardous locations.

The codes consider not just the door but the entire collection of door, frame, and hardware to be the fire door assembly. Every part of the assembly must be rated to make an approved opening. Doors, frames, and hardware are tested by Underwriters Laboratories (UL) and Factory Mutual (FM) according to standard ASTM and NFPA tests. If the door meets the requirements of the standard fire test, a small metal label is attached to the door, indicating its class and hourly rating. Thus, a fire-rated door is also called a *labeled door*.

Doors are rated according to the time they can withstand the standard fire test and according to the rating of assembly in which they can be installed. Time ratings, summarized in Table 42.4, range from 20 minutes to 3 hours.

Table 42.4

Fire Door Classifications

use of partition	rating of partition or wall (hours)	required door assembly rating (hours)
exit access corridors	1	0.33
fire partitions	1	$^3/_4$
fire barriers (1-hour)		
shaft and exit enclosure walls	1	1
other fire barriers	1	$^3/_4$
fire walls and fire barriers having a required fire-resistance rating greater than 1 hour	4	3
	3	3
	2	$1^1/_2$
	$1^1/_2$	$1^1/_2$
exterior walls	3	$1^1/_2$
	2	$1^1/_2$
	1	$^3/_4$

The standard test for doors is NFPA 252. This test is described in Ch. 55.

All hardware on fire doors must be tested and approved for use on fire exits. Fire doors must be operable from the inside without the use of any special knowledge or effort. This provision is intended to prohibit the use of devices such as combination locks, thumb-turn locks, and multiple locks. Some occupants in a building may not be familiar with these, or similar, devices and may find them too difficult to operate during panic conditions or when visibility is low. The code does provide for some exceptions such as in residential units, places of detention, and a few other situations.

For certain occupancies, such as educational and assembly with an occupant load over 50, panic hardware is required. This is hardware that unlatches the door when pressure is applied against a horizontal bar rather than requiring a turning motion as with a level handle or doorknob.

Fire doors must be self-closing or automatic closing. A *self-closing door* simply has a closer or other device that returns it to the closed position after someone passes through. *Automatic closing doors* are those that are normally held open, but that automatically close upon activation of a smoke detector, fire-alarm system, or other approved device.

When fire doors are closed, they must be secured with an active latch bolt. This is to secure the door during a fire, preventing fire and gas pressure from pushing the door open.

Operating devices, including door handles, pulls, latches, and locks, must be installed on the door a minimum of 34 in (864) and a maximum of 48 in (1219) above the finished floor. The only exception is that locks used only for security purposes and not used for normal operation can be at any height.

The requirements for glazing in fire door assemblies vary depending on what type of wall or partition the door is located in.

When glass is installed in fire door assemblies, it must be wire glass set in metal frames or special fire-protection-rated glass. The size of the glass is limited in area and maximum dimensions as shown in Table 42.5. Wire glass has a fire rating of 45 minutes.

Other types of fire-protection-rated glazing and fire-resistance-rated glazing may be used in lieu of wired glass if it conforms to the size limitations of NFPA 80, *Standard for Fire Doors, Fire Windows*.

Additional requirements, based on the IBC, are listed here. Verify exact requirements with the model code used in the area where the work is being done.

- A fire-rated door assembly must have a label attached to the door and frame.
- A fire door must be self-latching.
- All hardware used must be UL listed.
- A fire door must be self-closing. In some cases the code permits the door to be held open if the hold-open or closer is connected to an approved smoke or fire detector.
- A fire door must use steel hinges of the ball-bearing type.
- If a pair of doors is used, astragals or other required hardware must also be used.
- Glass (if permitted) must conform in maximum area and construction to requirements of the local code. It must be wire glass or fire-rated glass and set in a steel frame with the glass stop made of steel.
- Louvers must conform to UL requirements for maximum size and construction.

Table 42.5
Maximum Size of Wire Glass in Fire-Protection-Rated Doors

use of door	fire rating	size of glass allowed area	width	height
exit access doors in corridors	20 minute	no limit	no limit	no limit
exit access doors in other fire partitions	3/4 hour	1296 in^2 (0.84 m^2)	54 in (1372)	54 in (1372)
exit doors in 1-hour vertical shafts and exit passageways	1 hour	100 in^2 (0.065 m^2)	10 in (254)	33 in (838)
exit doors in 2-hour vertical shafts and 2-hour-rated fire barriers	1 1/2 hour	100 in^2 (0.065 m^2)	10 in (254)	33 in (838)

Accessibility requirements for doors and hardware include the following.

- Minimum width, clear of hardware, of an opened door must be 32 in (815).
- There must be adequate maneuvering clearance in front of and on the latch side of the door to operate it.
- There must be a minimum of 48 in (1220) between two doors in a series when they are open 90°.
- The maximum opening force required for various types of doors is specified by the code.
- Handles and latches must have a shape that is easy to grasp and use. This usually means lever handles or push-pull-type mechanisms.
- Thresholds with a change in level may have a vertical edge up to $^1/_4$ in (6.4) high, but must be beveled with a slope of 1:2 for heights from $^1/_4$ in to $^1/_2$ in (6.4 to 13).

WINDOWS

A *window* is an opening in a wall used to provide viewing, light transmission, solar heat (when desired), and ventilation. The standard nomenclature of a window is shown in Fig. 42.15, and the types of windows are illustrated in Fig. 42.16.

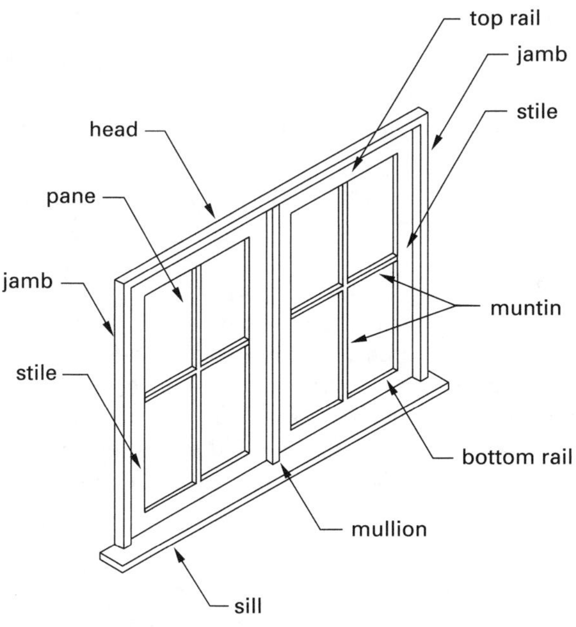

Figure 42.15 Parts of a Window

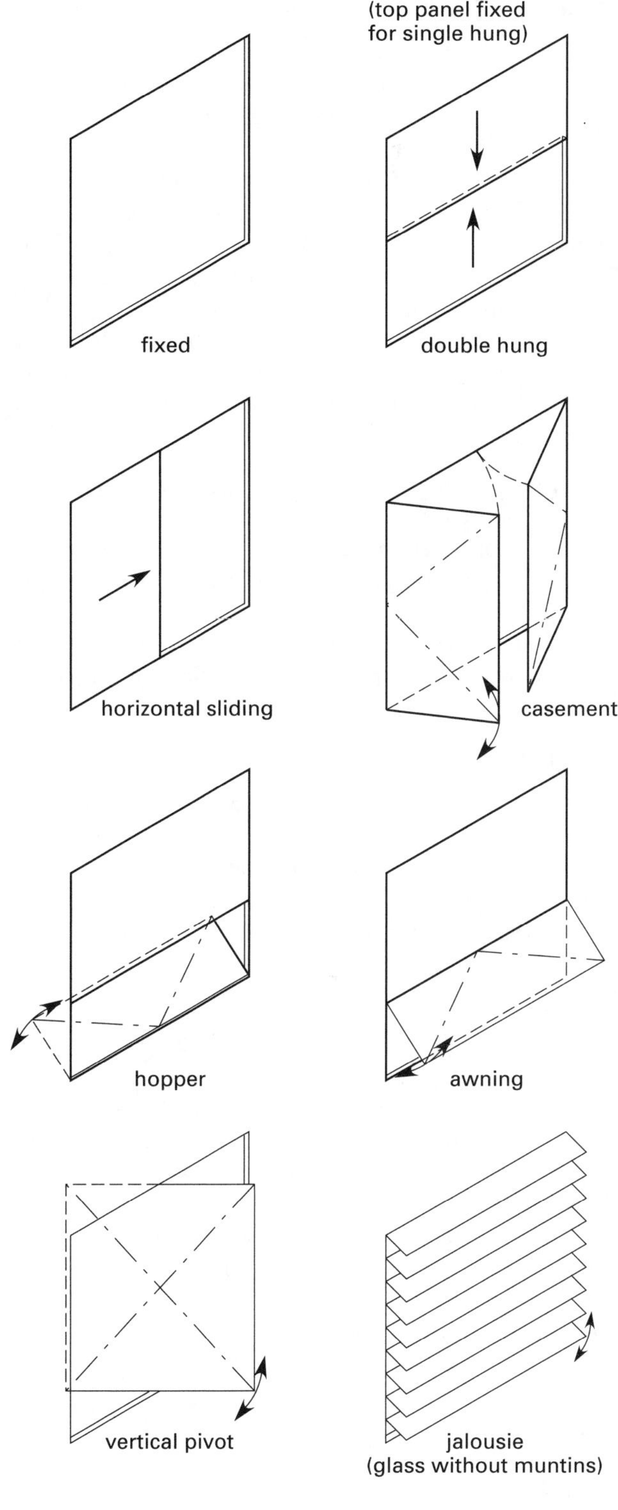

Figure 42.16 Types of Windows

Metal Windows

Metal windows are fabricated of aluminum, steel, or bronze. Aluminum is the most common metal window material because of its light weight, low cost, strength, and resistance to corrosion. A variety of finishes can be applied in the factory to make aluminum windows compatible with almost any building. Two disadvantages of aluminum are its susceptibility to galvanic action and its high heat conduction. However, both of these can be controlled. Galvanic action can be minimized or eliminated with the proper selection of fasteners and flashing; heat transmission and condensation can be prevented by specifying aluminum frames with thermal breaks. These are nonmetallic elements that connect the exterior and interior portions of a window.

Steel windows are fabricated from relatively small sections of hot- or cold-rolled steel. Because of steel's greater strength, frame sections are small compared with those aluminum. Steel windows are more expensive than aluminum ones and are used where high strength, high security, and a minimum profile size are required. They are shop painted or bonderized to improve the adhesion of site-applied paint.

Wood Windows

Wood windows are very popular because of the variety of types and sizes available, their appearance, their ease of installation, and their good insulating properties. These windows are delivered to the job site as complete manufactured units including the exterior trim. They are simply placed in a rough opening and secured to the framing. Installation of interior trim finishes the window opening.

Common types of wood windows include fixed sash, double hung, casement, and horizontal pivoted, either the awning or hopper types. Horizontal sliding units are also available. Materials used are usually pine and fir, although some other species, such as redwood and cypress, are occasionally used. Many manufacturers now provide clad wood windows. The exterior, exposed wood members are covered with a thin layer of steel or vinyl to minimize maintenance, and the interior portions are left exposed for painting or other types of wood finish.

Single-strength or double-strength glass is used for glazing windows, but most building codes now require glazing to be insulated glass in cold climates.

Skylights

Skylights are glazed openings in roofs that allow light to penetrate the interior. They are sometimes operable to allow for ventilation. Skylights may be glazed with glass or plastic, but if plastic is used it must adhere to building code restrictions on location and maximum size. If glazed with glass, the glass must be laminated or wire glass. If tempered or annealed glass is used, it must be protected from above and below with wire screening. These restrictions prevent injury to someone below if the glass breaks and falls.

A skylight should be mounted on curbs to raise the bottom edge above the roof surface, especially if the roof has a low slope. Because condensation of water vapor in a building can be a problem, skylight frames should be provided with a condensate gutter and weep holes, which allow collected water to drain to the outside.

Storefronts

Storefronts consist of extruded metal frames (usually aluminum), glass panels, doors, hardware, and miscellaneous fittings designed to be installed as one coordinated system. Storefront systems are used in one-story applications where the glass and its framing are supported within an opening rather than continuously supported across several floors as with curtain wall construction. Advantages of storefront systems include ease of construction, single-source supplying, light weight, coordinated elements, relatively low cost, and a range of styles, finishes, and sizes from which to choose.

GLASS AND GLAZING

Today's technology offers a wide variety of glass products to meet various glazing needs, ranging from simple, clear glass, to glass that can selectively transmit or reflect different wavelengths, or whose transparency can be switched on and off with electric current.

Glass is the term used to describe the actual material. Clear glass is a mixture of silica sand and small amounts of alkaline salts such as lime, potash, and soda. *Glazing* is the process of installing glass in the framing as well as installing the framing itself, or glass that has been installed through this glazing process.

Types of Glass

In selecting the type of glass to be used in a particular situation, several parameters must be considered. These include the amount of light to be transmitted, the degree of transparency, strength and security, sound isolation, insulating qualities, cost, availability, and special qualities such as radiation shielding. Following are the common types of glass available.

- *Float glass*. Float glass comprises the vast majority of glass produced in the United States. It is made by pouring molten glass on a bed of molten tin and allowing it to slowly cool, forming a smooth, flat surface. It is also called *annealed glass*.

- *Heat-strengthened glass*. This glass is produced by heating glass to about 1100°F (590°C) and slowly cooling it. Heat-strengthened glass has about twice the strength of annealed glass of the same thickness. This type of glass is used where the surface is subject to solar-induced thermal stresses and cyclic windloading.

- *Tempered glass*. Tempered glass is produced by subjecting annealed glass to a special heat treatment in which it is heated to about 1150°F (620°C) and then quickly cooled. The process sets up compressive stresses on the outer surfaces and tensile stresses inside the glass. This glass is about four times stronger than annealed glass of the same thickness. Tempered glass is available in thicknesses from $^1/_8$ in to $^7/_8$ in (3.0 to 21.0).

  In addition to its extra strength for normal glazing, tempered glass is considered safety glass, so it can be used in hazardous locations (discussed in a later section). If it breaks, it falls into thousands of very small pieces instead of dangerous shards.

- *Laminated glass*. Laminated glass consists of two or more pieces of glass bonded together by an interlayer of polyvinyl butyral resin. When laminated glass is broken, the interlayer tends to hold the pieces together even though the glass itself may be severely cracked. This type of glass is used where very strong glazing is required. It can be bullet resistant and provides high security against intentional or accidental breakage. Like tempered glass, it is considered safety glazing and can be used in hazardous locations.

  Laminated glass is also used where sound control is required. In addition to the sound control provided by the extra glass thickness, the interlayer has a damping effect on the otherwise rigid material. This glass is available in thicknesses from $^{13}/_{64}$ in to 3 in (5.2 to 76).

- *Tinted glass* or *heat-absorbing glass*. This is produced by adding various colorants to the glass material. The standard colors are bronze, gray, green, and blue. The purpose of tinted glass is to reduce the solar transmittance of the glass, which reduces the air conditioning load on the building, the brightness of the interior, and fading of fabrics and carpeting. Because tinted glass absorbs heat, it should not be used where portions of it are in direct sun and portions are shaded. The differential expansion and contraction (thermal load) will crack the glass. Because of this phenomenon, tinted glass is often heat strengthened or tempered.

  One of the important variables for tinted glass, as well as other glass materials and sun blocking devices, is the *shading coefficient*. This is the ratio of the solar heat gain through a specific fenestration to the solar heat gain through a pane of $^1/_8$ in (3.0) clear glass under identical conditions. It is used when calculating heat gain. However, the shading coefficient is a value that represents the glazing only, not the frame or spacer effects. Today, most people refer to the *solar heat-gain coefficient* (SHGC) of a window. The SHGC is the ratio of the solar heat gain through glazing or a window compared to the total solar radiation incident on the glazing or window. The SHGC is a value between 0.0 and 0.87.

- *Low-iron glass*. Low-iron glass has a reduced amount of iron oxide, which gives a light-green cast to ordinary clear float glass. Low-iron glass offers exceptional clarity, optimal light transmission, and excellent color transmission.

- *Reflective glass*. Reflective glass is clear or tinted glass coated with an extremely thin layer of metal or metallic oxide. In insulating units, this reflective layer is placed on the inside of the exterior lite of glass. Its primary purpose is to save energy by reflecting solar radiation. In addition to this, the exterior of a building with reflective glass has a mirror-like surface that may have a desired aesthetic effect. Reflective coatings come in various silver, copper, golden, and earthtone shades that can be combined with the several colors of tinted glass.

- *Insulating glass*. Insulating glass is fabricated of two or three sheets of glass separated by a hermetically sealed air space of $^1/_4$ in to $^1/_2$ in (6 to 13). Insulating glass has a much lower U-value than that of single-thickness glass and is used almost exclusively in regions where heat loss is a problem. Insulating glass can be made with heat-strengthened, tempered, reflective, tinted, and laminated glass.

- *Patterned glass*. This specialty glass is made by passing a sheet of glass through rollers on which the desired pattern is etched, which may be on one or both sides. Vision through the panel is diffused but not totally obscured; the degree of diffusion depends on the pattern and depth of etch.

- *Wire glass*. Wire glass has a mesh of wire embedded in the middle of the sheet. The surface can be either smooth or patterned. Wire glass is used primarily in fire-rated assemblies if it is not in a hazardous location. It is approximately 50% stronger than annealed glass. Wire glass cannot be tempered and does not qualify as safety glazing for hazardous locations.

- *Spandrel glass*. Spandrel glass is used as the opaque strip of glass that conceals the floor and ceiling structure in curtain wall construction. It is manufactured by permanently fusing a ceramic frit color to the back of heat-strengthened or tempered glass. It is normally manufactured and installed as a single sheet with insulation behind.

- *Low-emissivity glass*. Low-emissivity glass, or *low-ε glass* as it is sometimes called, selectively reflects and transmits certain wavelengths of the electromagnetic spectrum. It is manufactured by placing a very thin coating (just a few atoms) of metal or metal oxide on the surface of a piece of glass or a thin film. Low-ε glass works by transmitting visible light and short-wave solar radiation but reflecting long-wave heat radiation from the air and warm objects.

  Thus, in a cold climate, low-ε glass will admit solar heat gain during the day but prevent the built-up heat inside the building from escaping at night. In the summer, the same glass will reflect much of the ambient long-wave infrared heat away from the glass. In warm climates, low-ε glass can be combined with tinted or reflective glass to prevent even more heat from being transmitted to the interior of the building.

  This type of glass is used in insulated units where it is placed on the interior surface of the inside lite to reflect building heat back to the inside before it crosses the air gap. Low-ε glass can also be made by suspending a very thin layer of film in the center of the air gap, creating two air spaces. This is even more efficient than directly applying the coating to the glass, although glass made through this process is more easily damaged.

  An insulating low-ε unit with $^1/_4$ in (6) thick glass has a *U*-value of about 0.31 (1.76 W/m^2·K); an insulating unit with a low-ε film suspended in the middle has a *U*-value of about 0.23 (1.31 W/m^2·K). Standard double-pane insulating glass with a comparable air space has a *U*-value of about 0.42 (2.38 W/m^2·K).

- *Energy-efficient glazing*. Some of the types of glazing products mentioned previously are used to variously keep heat out of a building, keep heat in, or limit the amount of light coming into a building. In the past, selecting one of these objectives meant compromising on one of the others. For example, using tinted or reflective glazing to limit heat gain reduced the visible light transmittance, which was detrimental to effective daylighting. Today, however, there are many glazing products on the market that allow the designer to meet all the requirements of energy efficiency simultaneously. Some are improvements on older technologies while some are new and experimental technologies. Refer to Ch. 29 for a more detailed discussion of these products and how they are used.

- *Electrochromic glazing*. This is a general term for a type of glazing that changes from either a dark tint or a milky white opaque to a transparent state with the application of an electric current. When the current is on, the glass is transparent; when current is off, the glass darkens or turns white (depending on which type it is). There are three distinct types of this glazing currently on the market, only one of which is technically known as electrochromic glazing. The other two types are suspended particle device (SPD) and polymer-dispersed liquid crystal film. The distinction is important because each of the three types on the market at the time of this writing have slightly different characteristics, although all three depend on the application of a low electric current to keep them clear.

  Electrochromic glazing uses an inorganic ceramic thin-film coating on glass and can be manufactured to range from transparent to heavily darkened (tinted). However, it is never opaque, so it cannot be used as privacy glass. It is intended for control of light, ultraviolet energy, and solar heat gain. The amount of tinting is not just an on or off condition; it can be controlled with a simple rheostat switch.

  Suspended particle device glazing (SPD) uses a proprietary system in which light-absorbing microscopic particles are dispersed within a liquid suspension film which is then sandwiched between two pieces of transparent conductive material. The appearance of the product can range from clear to partially darkened to totally opaque, so it can be used for privacy as well as for light control and energy conservation. It can also be variably controlled with a rheostat.

  Polymer-dispersed liquid crystal film glazing is fabricated by placing the polymer film between two pieces of glass. The transparency can range from transparent to cloudy white. In its translucent state it offers total visual privacy but still allows a significant amount of light to pass through so it cannot be used for exterior light control. All of the types of electrochromic glazing are very expensive, but the first two types do offer the potential for significant energy savings, in the range of 20% to 30%.

- *Fire-rated glazing.* Aside from wire glass, there are four additional types of glazing that can be used in fire-rated openings.

  The first is a clear ceramic that has a higher impact resistance than does wire glass and a low expansion coefficient. It is available with a 1-hour rating in sizes up to 1296 in^2 (0.84 m^2) and with a 3-hour rating in sizes up to 100 in^2 (0.0645 m^2). Although some forms of ceramic glass do not meet safety glazing requirements, there are laminated assemblies that are rated up to 2 hours and are impact safety-rated.

  The second type is a special, tempered fire-protective glass. It is rated at a maximum of 30 minutes because it cannot pass the hose-stream test, but it does meet the impact safety standards of both ANSI Z97.1 and 16 CFR 1201.

  The third type consists of two or three layers of tempered glass with a clear polymer gel between them. Under normal conditions, the glass is transparent, but when subjected to fire, the gel foams and turns opaque, thus retarding the passage of heat. This product is available with 30-minute, 60-minute, and 90-minute ratings, depending on the thickness and number of glass panes used. There are restrictions on the maximum size of lites and the type of permitted framing.

  The fourth type of glazing is glass block. However, not all glass block is rated. The glass block must have been specifically tested for use in fire-rated openings and be approved by the local authority having jurisdiction.

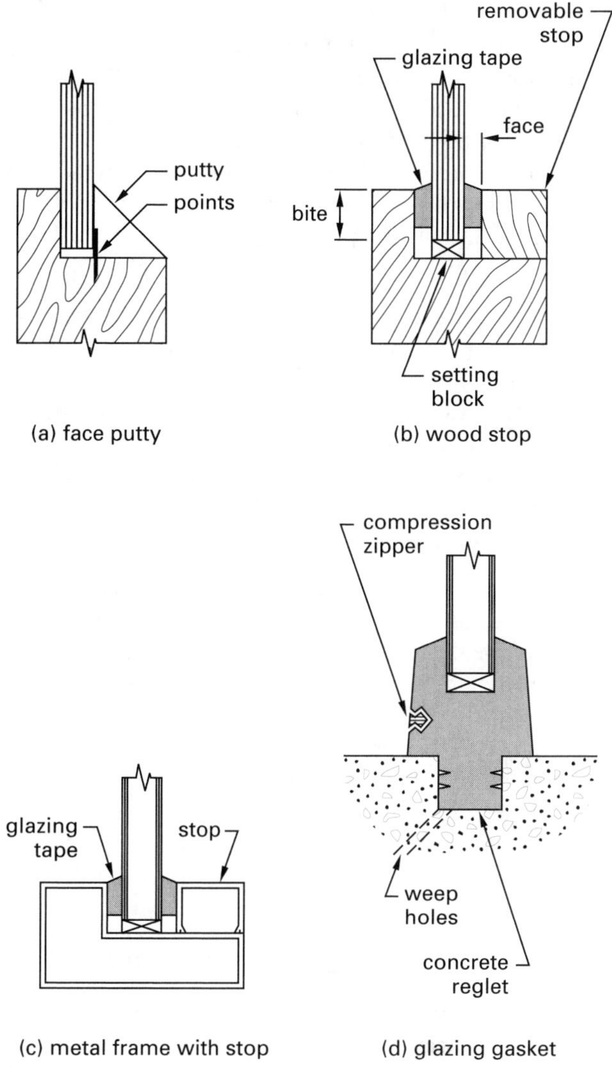

Figure 42.17 Methods of Glazing

Installation Details

There are several ways glass can be framed. Some of the more common ones are shown in Fig. 42.17. The traditional way is to place the glass in a rabbeted frame, hold it temporarily with *glaziers points* (small triangular pieces of metal), and face putty the glass in place, as shown in Fig. 42.17(a). This method is labor intensive, and the putty dries and cracks with time and must be replaced often.

Although this method is still used for single-paned glass on small residential jobs, it has been largely replaced with other methods. The glazing putty has been replaced with glazing compounds of various types that are applied like caulking and with *glazing tape*, a semi-rigid, formed material that is placed between the frame and the glass. See Fig. 42.17(b).

Glazing stops are usually required for most installations. These are removable pieces of framing that allow the glass to be installed and removed easily if it must be replaced.

Structural glazing gaskets are also used. They are fairly rigid strips of neoprene specifically designed to hold glass. Fig. 42.17(d) shows an application in a concrete reglet, but they can also be attached to metal frames. Once the glass is inserted, a compression strip is forced into a slot, which tightens the grip on the glass.

In all glazing installations, the glass should be placed on semirigid setting blocks of neoprene or other compatible elastomeric material. These prevent direct contact between the glass and frame and allow both to expand and contract and move without putting excessive stress on the glass.

Two dimensions of importance when installing exterior glazing are the face dimension and the bite, as illustrated in Fig. 42.17(b). Because glass is subject to wind loading and deflects, effectively pulling partially out of the frame, the bite must be sufficiently deep to hold the glass in place.

Some glazing installations may also be made with a *frameless glazing system*. With this method, the glass is supported at the top and bottom, and the edges are simply butt-jointed and sealed with silicon sealant. With structural glazing systems, the vertical and horizontal framing members are entirely behind the glass (on the interior of the building) and the glass is attached to it with silicon sealant. From the exterior, the installation presents a smooth, uniform appearance, broken only by the thin, butt-jointed glass units.

As an alternative, a special type of foam tape may be used to attach glass to framing. *Acrylic foam structural glazing tape* is a two-sided, pressure-sensitive, closed-cell acrylic foam used to bind a wide variety of dissimilar materials. In addition to its use in the glazing industry, it can replace liquid adhesives, screws, rivets, spot welds and other mechanical fasteners for attaching metal panels to framing and for other interior and exterior applications.

The required thickness of exterior glass depends on the size of the glazed unit and the wind loading. Tables in the building code give the minimum thicknesses for various types of glass according to these variables. The basic maximum allowable glass area, accounting for wind pressure and glass thickness, is based on float glass. Adjustment factors are provided by which the basic area is increased depending on other types of glass used. Tempered glass has the highest adjustment factor (4.00) of all the glass types. Heat-strengthened glass has an adjustment factor of 2.00; the factor for laminated glass is only 0.75.

Building Code Requirements for Glazing

Three primary glazing situations are regulated by the model codes. These are sizing of glass for wind loading, limitation on glass in fire-rated assemblies, and safety glazing subject to human impact in hazardous locations.

The codes specify the minimum thickness for glass depending on wind loading and the size of the glazed unit. The subject of maximum glass areas in fire doors was reviewed previously in this chapter.

For glass used in fire-resistance-rated partitions, the IBC differentiates between two types of glazing: fire-protection-rated glazing and fire-resistance-rated glazing.

Fire-protection-rated glazing is $^1/_4$ in thick wired glass in steel frames or other types of glazing that meet the requirements of NFPA 257, *Standard on Fire Test for Window and Glass Block Assemblies*. Such glazing must have a 45-minute rating and is limited to 1-hour-rated fire partitions or fire barriers when the fire barrier is used to separate occupancies or to separate incidental use areas. The amount of such glazing is limited to 25% of the area of the common wall within any room using the glazing. This limitation applies to partitions separating two rooms as well as a partition separating a room and a corridor. Individual lights of fire-protection-rated glazing cannot exceed 1296 in^2 in area (9 ft^2 or 0.84 m^2) and any one dimension cannot be more than 54 in (1372). The IBC accepts $^1/_4$ in wire glass as meeting the requirements for a 45-minute rating without specific testing, but other glazing must meet the NFPA 257 test requirements for a 45-minute rating.

Fire-resistance-rated glazing is glass or other glazing material that has been tested as part of a fire-resistance-rated wall assembly according to ASTM E-119. This glazing definition allows the use of special fire-rated glazing that can have fire-resistive ratings up to $1^1/_2$ hours. Refer to the previous section in this chapter for a discussion on these types of glazing products. This type of glazing may be used in partitions that must have a rating higher than 1 hour, although the glazing must have the same rating as the partition in which it is used. There are no size limitations.

In order to prevent injuries from people accidentally walking through glass doors or other openings, codes require safety glazing in hazardous locations. Hazardous locations are those subject to human impact, such as glazing in doors, glass doors, shower and bath enclosures, and certain locations in walls. A composite drawing of some situations where safety glazing is and is not required by the IBC is shown in Fig. 42.18. *Safety glazing* is considered to be tempered or laminated glass that meets the test requirements of the Code of Federal Regulations, 16 CFR 1201, *Safety Standard for Architectural Glazing Materials*.

CURTAIN WALL SYSTEMS

A *curtain wall* is an exterior wall system that is attached to the structural framework of a building and that carries no weight other than its own and wind loading that it transfers to the structure. Curtain walls can be made of preformed metal panels, precast concrete, and prefabricated marble, granite, or masonry panels, but they are usually built of aluminum framing and glass panels.

With aluminum and glass systems, the vertical mullions are attached to the floors or beams at every floor. Attachment devices allow the vertical mullions to be adjusted to provide a perfectly plumb and straight line for the entire height of the building. Horizontal mullions are attached to these vertical pieces according to the design of the system. Glass vision panels are used for window openings, whereas spandrel glass is used where floor and column lines must be concealed.

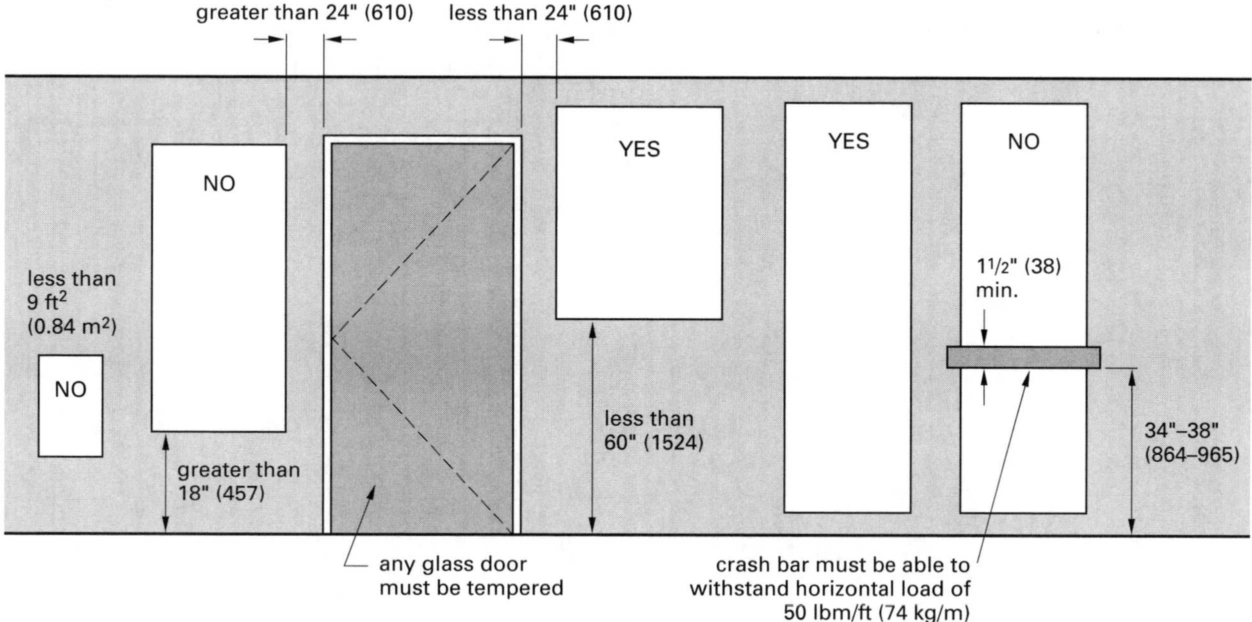

Figure 42.18 Selected Safety Glazing Locations

43 FINISH MATERIALS

LATH AND PLASTER

Plaster is a finish material made from various types of cementing compounds, fine aggregate, and water. It is applied over several kinds of base materials in two or three coats to form a smooth, level surface. Plaster is a term commonly used to describe various types of finish materials of this type used for interior applications, whereas stucco is a term reserved for exterior applications of plaster made with portland cement.

Plaster is made from gypsum and lime, aggregates of sand, vermiculite or perlite, and water. Vermiculite and perlite are used when a lightweight, fire-resistant plaster is needed. A special process is used to produce *Keene's cement*, which is a plaster that has a high resistance to abrasion and water penetration. It is used in wet areas or on walls subject to scratching or other abuse.

Stucco is made from portland cement, lime, sand, and water. It is used for exterior applications when a hard, non-water-absorbent plaster is needed. Portland cement plaster is also used as a backing for tile walls and as the scratch and brown coats under Keene's cement.

There are two common methods of applying plaster. The first is on metal lath that is attached to metal or wood studs. Metal lath is available in several types: expanded diamond mesh, paper-backed diamond mesh, flat-rib lath, and high-rib lath. See Fig. 43.1. Expanded diamond lath is a general-purpose type used for flat as well as curved surfaces. The paper-backed type has an asphalt-impregnated paper applied to it and is used as a base for portland cement plaster under ceramic tile. Rib lath is more rigid due to the one-way, V-shaped ribs about 4 in on center, and it is used for ceilings and solid partitions.

Metal lath provides a surface for the first coat of plaster to key into when the material flows around and behind the open mesh. This first coat is called the *scratch coat*. In standard plastering, the scratch coat is followed by the *brown coat* and then the final *finish coat*. The scratch and brown coats are about 1/4 in (6) thick; the finish coat is about 1/8 in (3) thick. Two-coat work combines the scratch and brown coats.

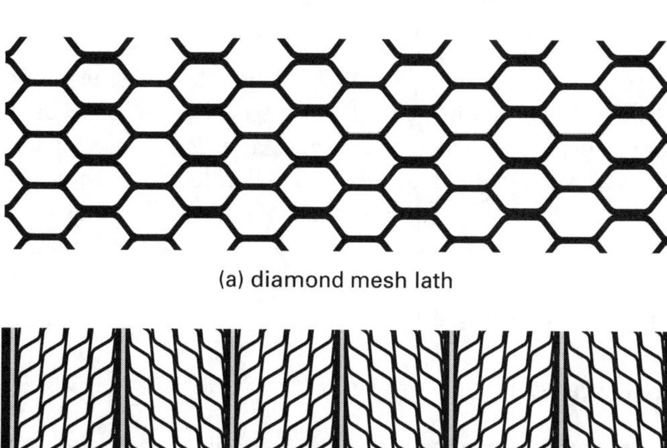
(a) diamond mesh lath

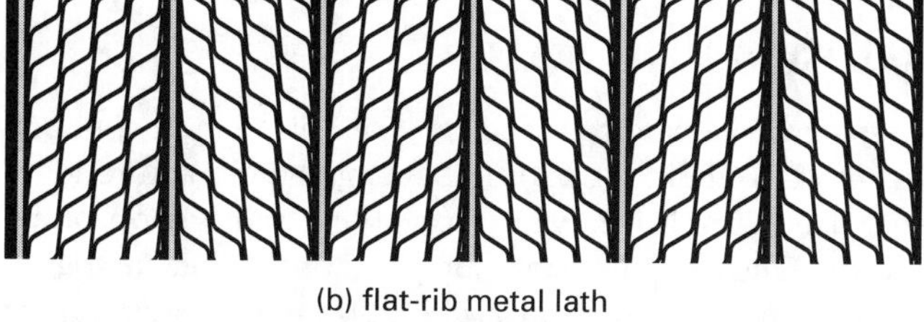
(b) flat-rib metal lath

(c) rib metal lath

Figure 43.1 Expanded Metal Lath

The other method of plastering uses *gypsum board lath* instead of metal lath. This is a special gypsum product specifically designed for plastering. Gypsum lath comes in 16 in by 48 in (906 by 1220) boards that are applied horizontally to studs, or it comes in 48 in by 96 in (1220 by 2440) sheets. One or two coats of thin veneer plaster are applied over the boards. Veneer plastering reduces labor over the traditional method because only one coat is needed.

Edges of plaster and stucco work must be finished with various types of metal trim pieces. These provide a termination point for the work and serve as screeds to give the plasterers guides for maintaining the required thickness. Common profiles include corner beads to protect outside corners; casing beads to trim doors, windows, and other openings; base screeds to finish plaster at the base of a room; and expansion joints to control cracking in the plaster or stucco surface. Stucco requires expansion joints at a minimum of every 10 ft (3000) or where it is likely to crack, such as at the corners of door and window openings.

In general, gypsum drywall systems have largely supplanted lath and plaster work because of their lower cost and faster construction sequence. However, plaster is still used where curved shapes are required and where a hard, abrasion-resistant surface is required. Stucco is still used for exterior applications regardless of the surface form of the building. Veneer plaster walls can be constructed to provide a 1- or 2-hour fire-rated partition.

GYPSUM WALLBOARD

Gypsum wallboard construction is one of the most common methods for building partitions in commercial and residential structures. It is inexpensive and can satisfy most of the performance requirements for partitions found in today's construction. *Gypsum wallboard*, also known as *drywall* or *sheetrock*, is made of a gypsum plaster core sandwiched between sheets of paper or other materials.

The advantages of gypsum wallboard include

- low installation cost
- quick and easy installation
- fire resistance
- sound control ability
- availability
- versatility: can be used for partitions, shaft enclosures, ceilings, and so on
- ease of finishing and decorating
- ease of installation of doors, windows, and other openings

Gypsum Wallboard Materials

Gypsum wallboard is manufactured in panels 4 ft (1200) wide and 8, 10, 12, and 14 ft (2400, 3000, 3600, and 4200) long. Special 1 in (25) thick coreboard used for shaft enclosures is manufactured in 2 ft (600) widths. The length used depends on the requirements of the job, but contractors generally use the longest length practical to minimize the number of joints.

Standard gypsum wallboard is available in thicknesses of $^1/_4$, $^3/_8$, $^1/_2$, and $^5/_8$ in (6.4, 9.5, 13, and 16). There is also a $^3/_4$ in (19) thick product that carries a 2-hour fire rating. This allows a 2-hour-rated partition to be constructed with a single layer without resorting to a standard two-ply application.

The thickness used depends on the particular application, the spacing of the framing, and the building code requirements. For most commercial and high-quality residential work, $^5/_8$ in (16) thick wallboard is used. A $^1/_2$ in (13) thickness is commonly used in residential projects and for some commercial applications such as furred walls.

Other applications require different wallboard thicknesses. For example, a $^3/_8$ in (9.5) thickness is used in some double-layer applications or when wallboard is applied over other finished walls in remodeling work. A thickness of $^1/_4$ in (6.4) is used for forming curved surfaces and for providing new finishes over old wall and ceiling surfaces. Double-layer applications are used when additional fire resistance is required or for extra acoustical benefits.

Gypsum wallboard is available with square edges, tapered edges, and tongue-and-groove edges. The tapered edge is the most commonly used because the slight taper allows joint compound and tape to be applied without showing a bulge in the finished surface.

Other types available include Type X for fire-rated partitions, foil-backed for vapor barriers, water-resistant for use behind tile and in other moist conditions, exterior, backing board, abuse resistant, and predecorated with vinyl wall covering already applied.

Gypsum board is applied by nailing or screwing it to wood or metal framing, or with mastic when applying it to concrete or masonry walls. The joints are finished by embedding paper or fiberglass tape in a special joint compound and allowing it to dry. Additional layers of joint compound are added and sanded smooth after each application to give a smooth-finish wall surface. Various types of textured finishes can be applied, or the surface can be left smooth for the application of other wall coverings.

Because gypsum wallboard is produced in such large quantities, its manufacture, use, and disposal have an effect on the environment. Since the 1950s, gypsum wallboard manufacturers have been using recycled paper to manufacture the surfaces of wallboard. In addition, some manufacturers are using recycled newspaper mixed with gypsum as the core material, to yield a product that is more rigid than standard wallboard yet still maintains all the other advantages of the product. About 28% of the industry's total use of gypsum is synthetic gypsum. Synthetic gypsum is chemically identical to natural, mined gypsum, but is a by-product of various manufacturing, industrial, or chemical processes. The main source of synthetic gypsum in North America is *flue-gas desulfurization*. This is the process whereby power-generating plants (and similar plants) remove polluting gases from their stacks to reduce emission of harmful materials into the atmosphere. Using this by-product allows the efficient use of refuse material that would otherwise have to be discarded.

The larger environmental concern involves the disposal of used gypsum wallboard, which cannot be reused for its original purpose when it is ripped out of an old building or a renovation project. There are some gypsum wallboard plants around the country that are recycling old drywall. The only condition is that the wallboard must be free of screws, nails, asbestos, and lead paint. Currently, the cost of collecting, separating, and transporting the old wallboard is a disincentive for recycling.

Old wallboard can also be pulverized into pieces equal to or smaller than $^1/_2$ in size and worked into the ground as a soil additive. Farmers in California and parts of Colorado use recycled gypsum as a soil conditioner for grapes, peas, and peanuts. It is also possible to work the gypsum directly into the soil around a job site, as long as the land has adequate drainage and aeration and local and state regulations allow it.

Framing

Gypsum wallboard framing for vertical construction can be either wood or metal. Wood is used in residential construction, and metal studs are commonly used in commercial construction because they are noncombustible, lightweight, nonshrinking, and easy to work with. Occasionally, wood studs are used in smaller commercial projects. Metal framing *can* be used in residential construction, but residential contractors prefer wood. Wood stud walls are also used in residential work because they can double as loadbearing walls.

Wood framing for gypsum wallboard partitions consists of 2 × 4 wood studs (actual size $1^1/_2$ in by $3^1/_2$ in [38.1 × 88.9]) spaced 16 in (406) or 24 in (610) on center, although 16 in spacing is more common, especially for residential construction. These spacings are used because they are even subdivisions of the 4 ft width and 8, 10, and 12 ft lengths of gypsum wallboard. For ceilings, the wallboard is generally attached directly to wood joists or ceiling rafters, which are also spaced 16 in on center.

Metal framing is light-gage, galvanized steel formed in a variety of sizes and shapes. Although metal stud partitions are usually not load-bearing, they can be load-bearing if heavy-gage, structural steel studs are used.

Metal studs are available in several gages (thicknesses). The most common are 25 gage (0.0188 in [0.48]), 22 gage (0.0284 in [0.72]), and 20 gage (0.0344 in [0.87]). 25 gage is most often used for studs and other metal framing. Heavier gages are used for very tall partitions, when the partition has to support unusual loads, and when framing door openings. For load-bearing partitions, exterior walls, and other heavy loading conditions, structural steel studs of 12-, 14-, 16-, or 18-gage thickness are used.

Metal studs are manufactured into a C shape with small flanges, as shown in Fig. 43.2. Openings are pre-punched along the length to allow for the passage of electrical conduit, small pipes, and other wiring. Metal studs are available in depths of $1^5/_8$, $2^1/_2$, $3^5/_8$, 4, and 6 in (41.3, 63.5, 92.1, 101.6, and 152.4).

Metal studs are placed vertically and, like wood studs, are spaced either 16 in or 24 in (406 or 610) on center, although 24 in spacing is common for most non-load-bearing commercial construction because it is more economical and minimizes construction time. Metal studs must be framed into runners at both the floor and ceiling as shown in Fig. 43.2. The runners are C-shaped metal fabrications without a flange. They have pre-punched holes and are the same widths as the studs. The runners are attached to the floor and upper support first, and then the studs are slipped into them and attached with self-tapping screws or with a crimping device. Other shapes of studs are also available for special uses such as stairway shaft framing.

The depth of the stud depends on the height of the partition, gage of the stud, number of layers of wallboard, and spacing of the studs. The most commonly used size is $2^1/_2$ in, which is sufficient for normal ceiling heights and slab-to-slab partitions and also allows enough room for electrical boxes and small pipes. Metal studs are normally spaced 16 in and 24 in on center with $^1/_2$ in or $^5/_8$ in thick gypsum board screw applied.

Wallboard Trim

Like plaster walls, gypsum wallboard must have fabricated edging. This includes cornerbead, which is used for all exterior corners not otherwise protected, and various types of edge trim. These trim pieces are shown in Fig. 43.3 and are defined as follows.

- *LC bead*: edge trim requiring finishing with joint compound

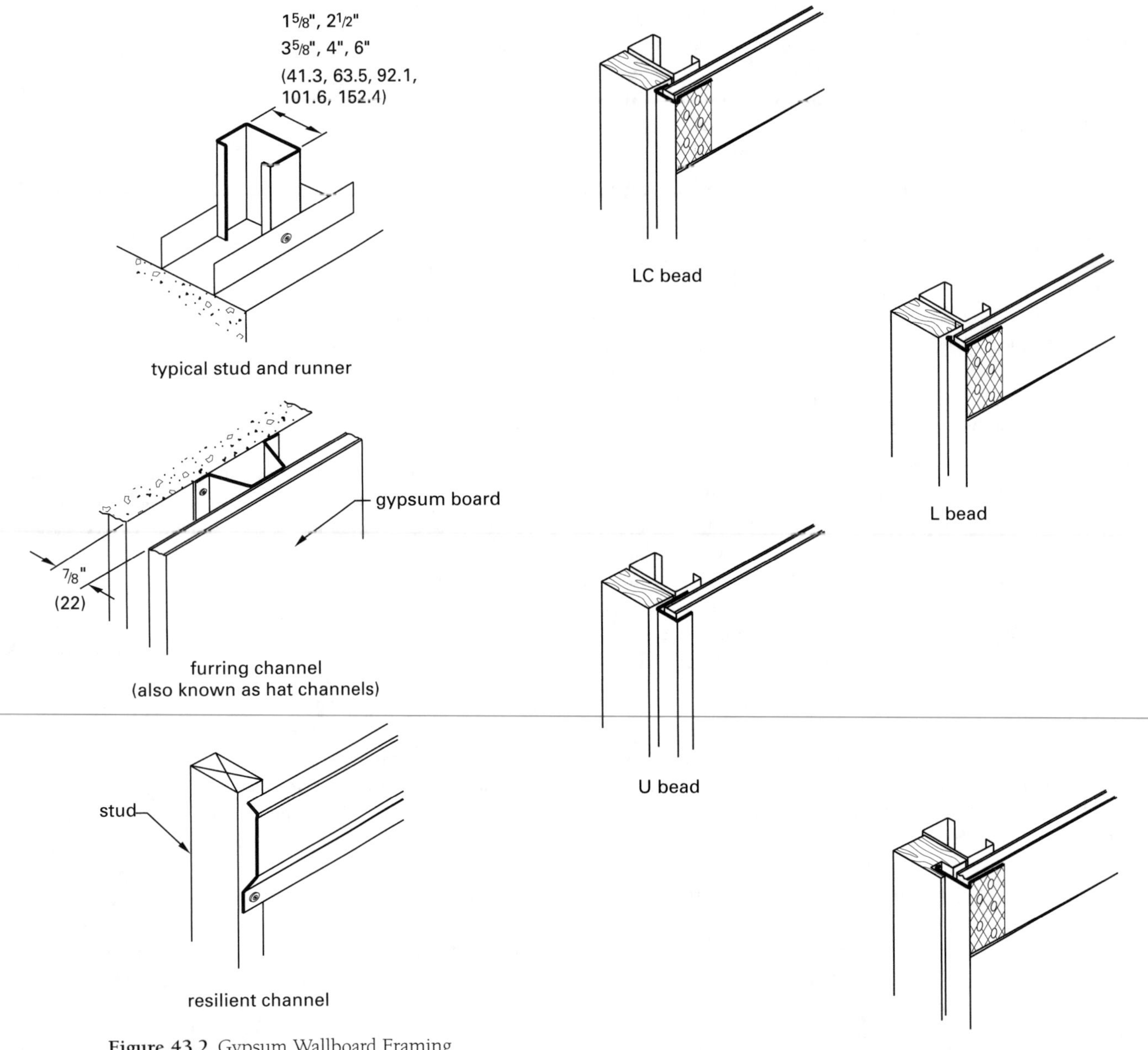

Figure 43.2 Gypsum Wallboard Framing

Figure 43.3 Gypsum Wallboard Trim

- *L bead*: edge trim without a back flange; good for installation after the wallboard has been installed. It requires finishing with joint compound.
- *LK bead*: edge trim for use with a kerfed jamb. It requires finishing with joint compound.
- *U bead*: edge trim that does not require finishing with joint compound, but does have a noticeable edge. It is sometimes called *J metal* by contractors.

Two of the most common types of gypsum wallboard construction on metal framing are shown in Fig. 43.4. The standard partition is only built up to the suspended ceiling, whereas the slab-to-slab partition is used when a complete fire-rated barrier must be constructed or when sound control is needed. By adding additional layers of Type X wallboard, fire-resistive ratings of 2, 3, and 4 hours can be obtained. Gypsum wallboard is also used for ceilings and to provide fire protection for columns, stairways, and elevator shafts. It can also be used as a base for finishing by furring over other walls.

Glass-Reinforced Gypsum

Glass-reinforced gypsum (GRG) designates a broad class of products manufactured from a high-strength, high-density gypsum reinforced with continuous-filament glass fibers or

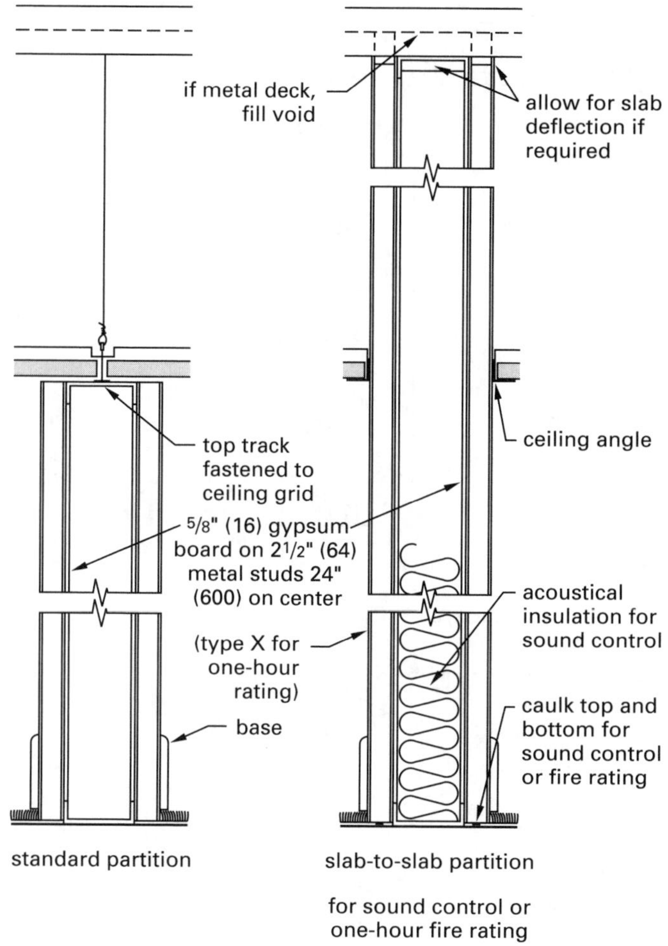

Figure 43.4 Gypsum Wallboard Partitions

chopped glass fibers. It is also known as *fiberglass-reinforced gypsum* (FRG) and *glass-fiber-reinforced gypsum* (GFRG).

GRG products are used for decorative elements such as column covers, arches, coffered ceilings, ornate moldings, light troughs, and trim. They are premanufactured products made by pouring GRG into molds. After setting, the products are shipped to the job site for installation and final finishing. They can be finished with any kind of material that can be put on plaster or gypsum wallboard. An unlimited variety of shapes can be manufactured that would otherwise be too expensive or impossible to achieve with site-fabricated lath and plaster.

TILE

Tiles are small, flat finishing units made of clay or clay mixtures. The two primary types are ceramic tile and quarry tile. The advantages of tile include durability; water resistance (if glazed); ease of installation; ease of cleaning; a wide choice of colors, sizes, and patterns; fire resistance; fade resistance; and the ability to store heat for passive solar collection.

Types of Tile

Ceramic tile is defined as a surfacing unit, usually relatively thin in relation to facial area, made from clay or a mixture of clay and other ceramic materials, having either a glazed or unglazed face, and fired above red heat in the course of manufacture to a temperature sufficiently high to produce specific physical properties and characteristics.

Quarry tile is glazed or unglazed tile, usually with 6 in^2 (3870 mm^2) or more of facial area. It is made by the extrusion process from natural clay or shale.

Some of the common types of tile are glazed wall tile, unglazed tile, ceramic mosaic tile, paver tile, quarry tile (glazed or unglazed), abrasive tile, and antistatic tile.

Ceramic mosaic tile is tile formed by either the dust-pressed or extrusion method, $^1/_4$ in to $^3/_8$ in (6 to 10) thick, and has a facial area of less than 6 in^2 (3870 mm^2).

Dust pressing uses large presses to shape the tile out of relatively dry clay. The extrusion process uses machines to cut tiles from a wetter and more malleable clay extruded through a die.

Classification of Tile

The United States tile industry classifies tile based on size: under 6 in^2 (3870 mm^2) is *mosaic tile*; over 6 in^2 is *wall tile*. Glazed and unglazed nonmosaic tile made by the extrusion method is *quarry tile*; glazed and unglazed tile over 6 in^2 made by the dust-pressed method is called *paver tile*.

Tile is often classed according to its resistance to water absorption, as follows.

- *Nonvitreous tile*: tile with water absorption of more than 7.0%
- *Semivitreous tile*: tile with water absorption of more than 3.0% but not more than 7.0%
- *Vitreous tile*: tile with water absorption of more than 0.5% but not more than 3.0%
- *Impervious tile*: tile with water absorption of 0.5% or less

Imported tile is classified differently than tile produced in the United States. European manufacturers classify tile according to its production method (either the dust-pressed or extrusion method), its degree of water absorption, its finish, and whether it is glazed or unglazed.

The classifications of abrasion resistance are: Group I, light residential; Group II, moderate residential; Group III:

maximum residential; and Group IV, highest abrasion resistance—commercial.

Tile Sizes and Shapes

Ceramic mosaic tile is available in standard nominal U.S. sizes of 1 × 1 and 2 × 2 (25 × 25 and 50 × 50) with a nominal thickness of 1/4 in (6). Some 2 × 1 tile is also available as well as tile in small hexagonal shapes. Glazed wall tile is manufactured in standard nominal sizes of 4 1/4 × 4 1/4, 6 × 4 1/2, and 6 × 6 (108 × 108, 152 × 114, and 152 × 152) with a nominal thickness of 1/4 in or 5/16 in (6 or 8). Individual manufacturers may produce other sizes as well.

Most manufacturers produce a complete line of trim pieces for ceramic tile installation. These include cove base, bullnose, inside and outside corners, and other shapes most often required. The standard trim shapes are illustrated in Fig. 43.5.

Quarry tile is available in nominal flat sizes of 3 × 3, 4 × 4, 6 × 6, 8 × 8, 8 × 4, and 6 × 3 (75 × 75, 100 × 100, 150 × 150, 200 × 200, 200 × 100, and 150 × 75) with a nominal thickness of 1/2 in (13). Trim pieces are similar in shape to that of wall tile.

Tile Installation

Tile must be installed on solid, flat substrates capable of supporting the weight of the material. There are two ways of doing this: with a full-mortar bed or with thinset mortar.

The traditional method of installing floor tile is to lay it in a thick bed of mortar. The tile and reinforced mortar bed are separated from the structural floor with a cleavage membrane (15 lbm roofing felt or 4 mil polyethylene film) to allow the two floors to move independently. This system should be used on floors where excessive deflection is expected and on precast and post-tensioned concrete floors. Because the mortar bed is reinforced with 2 in by 2 in (50 by 50), 16-gage welded wire fabric, the tile and bed are rigidly held together as a unit. In addition to providing for movement, the full-mortar bed allows for minor variations in floor level to be made up with the mortar. The tile can be set on the mortar bed while it is still plastic or on a cured mortar bed using a second coat of dry-set or latex-portland cement mortar. If a waterproof floor is required, a waterproof membrane can be used in place of the cleavage membrane. This is the preferred method for tile floors in commercial showers or where continuous wetting is present.

Thinset tile floors are laid on a suitable substrate, commonly a glass-mesh mortar unit specifically manufactured for tile installation. This is a cementitious panel nailed to the subfloor. The tile is laid on a thin coating of dry-set or latex-portland cement mortar with latex-portland cement

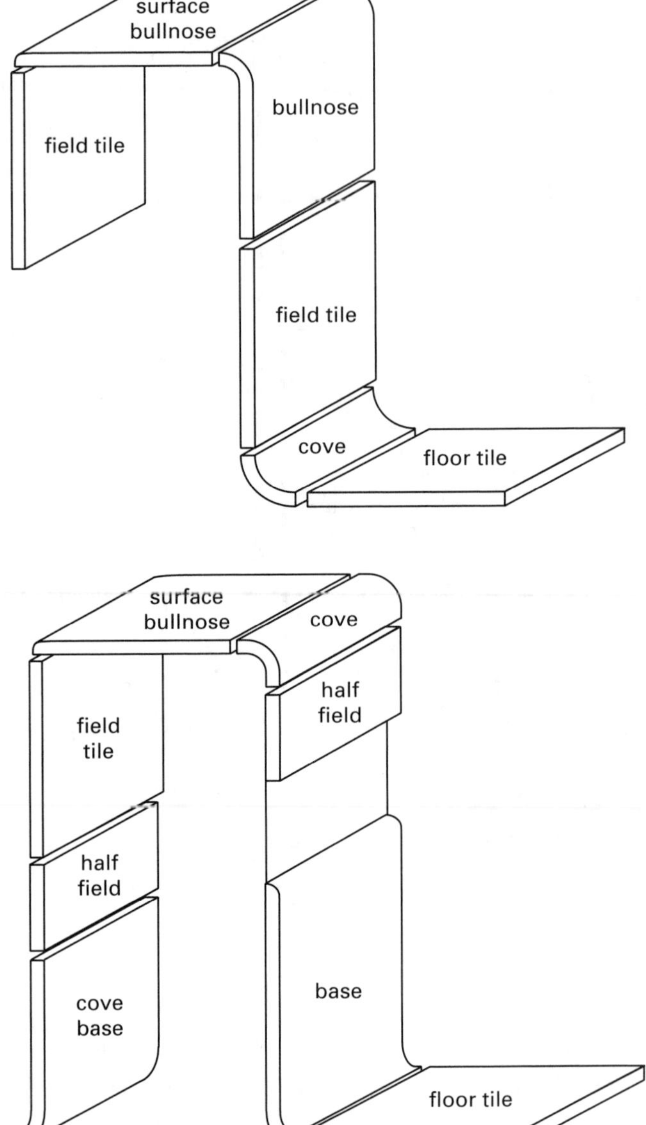

Figure 43.5 Ceramic Tile Shapes

grout. A standard sand and portland cement grout can also be used. When using thinset tile the subfloor must be level, free from dirt and other contaminants, and able to support the extra weight of the tile. If a subfloor deflects or moves in some way, a thinset tile installation will probably develop cracks.

Tile on walls can also be set with either the full-mortar bed or thinset method. The full-mortar bed method is typically used in commercial construction where extreme durability is required or in continuously wet areas, such as gang showers, laundries, pools, and tubs. For walls, instead of using welded wire fabric reinforcing, the base coat of portland cement plaster is attached to galvanized metal lath. Sometimes thinset methods are used in combination with waterproof cementitious backer boards for noncommercial construction.

TERRAZZO

Terrazzo is a composite material poured in place or precast that is used for floors, walls, stairs, and other construction elements. It consists of marble, quartz, granite, or other suitable chips, in a matrix that is cementitious, chemical, or a combination of both. Terrazzo is poured, cured, ground, and polished to produce a surface with a visible texture.

Terrazzo has many of the advantages of tile, which include durability, water resistance, ease of cleaning, a wide choice of patterns and colors, and fire resistance.

Types of Terrazzo

There are four basic types of terrazzo. *Standard terrazzo* is the most common type, using small chips no larger than $^3/_8$ in (9.5). *Venetian terrazzo* uses chips larger than $^3/_8$ in. *Palladiana terrazzo* utilizes thin random-fractured slabs of marble with standard terrazzo between. *Rustic terrazzo* has the matrix depressed to expose the chips.

An unlimited number of terrazzo finishes can be achieved by specifying various combinations of chips and matrix colors.

The most commonly used matrix is cementitious, a mixture of white portland cement, sand, and water. Modified cementitious matrices, mixing epoxy or polyacrylate with the portland cement, are used when additional chemical resistance or conductivity is required or when the installation is thinset. Resinous matrices of epoxy or polyester are used for thinset applications. Conductive floors are used where static electricity buildup must be avoided. Conductive matrices are black due to their carbon black content.

Installation of Terrazzo

Terrazzo can be installed on walls as well as on floors. The four common floor installations are shown in Fig. 43.6. The sand cushion method is the best way to avoid cracking of terrazzo, because the finish system is physically separated from the structural slab with a membrane. Because the underbed is reinforced, the terrazzo system can move independently of the structure. If floor movement or deflection is not anticipated, the bonded method can be used. Where the thickness of the installation is a problem, a monolithic or thinset method can be used.

Terrazzo is generally finished to a smooth surface with an 80-grit stone grinder, but it can be ground with a rough, 24-grit to achieve a more textured surface. Rustic terrazzo exposes some of the stone when the matrix is washed before

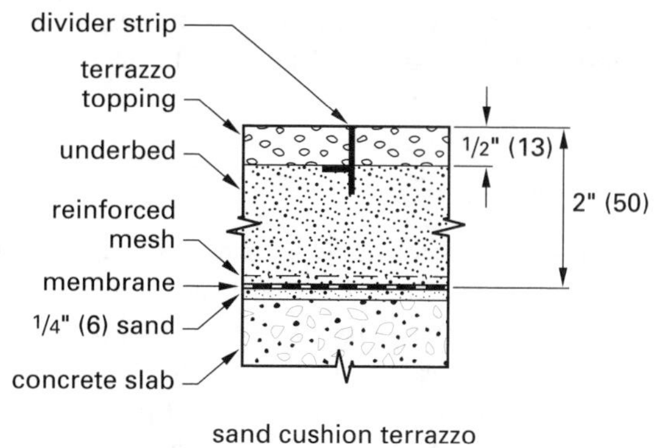

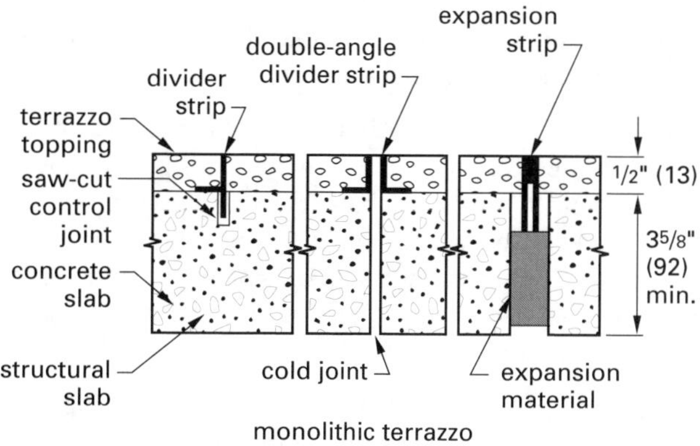

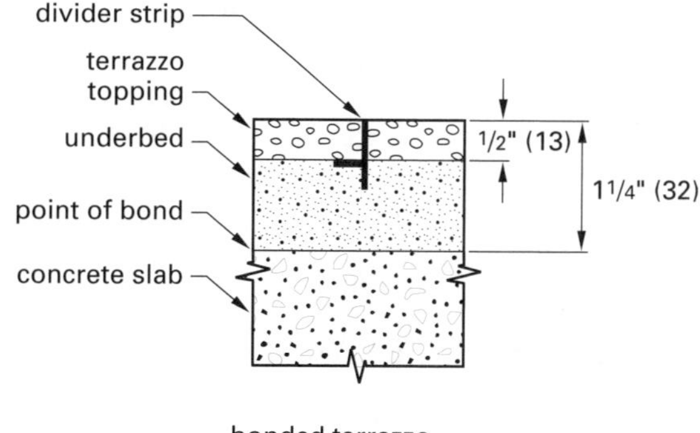

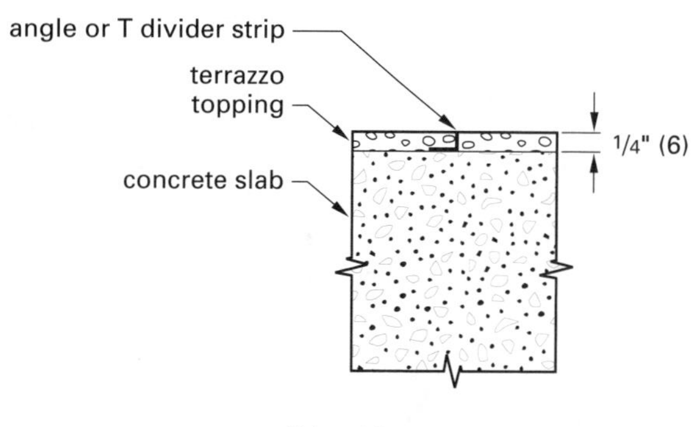

Figure 43.6 Methods of Terrazzo Installation

it has set. Terrazzo is also available as precast floor tiles in 12 in and 16 in (300 and 400) squares. It is laid in a cement mortar like stone or ceramic tile.

STONE FINISHES

Stone is often used for interior finishes of walls and floors. Commonly used types include marble, granite, and slate for flooring. Interior veneer stone is about 3/4 in to 7/8 in (19 to 22) thick and is attached to wall substrates with stainless steel wires or ties. These are anchored to the substrate and hold the stone by being set in holes or slots cut into the back or sides of the panel. Lumps of plaster of paris, called spots, are placed between the substrate and the back of the stone panel at each anchor to hold the slab in place and to allow for precise alignment before they set.

Anchoring stone inside a building is simpler than exterior stonework because there is no wind load, precipitation, or freezing and thawing to contend with, and panels are seldom stacked above each other so that the weight of the panel can be carried by the floor. For high interior spaces many of the anchoring details are similar to those of exterior work, as shown in Fig. 37.16.

Thin stone tiles are also used for interior finishing. These are about 3/8 in (10) thick and come in sizes of 1 × 1 and 1 × 2 (300 × 300 and 300 × 600). They are used for flooring and wall finish.

When stone is used for flooring it may be installed in a number of ways. These are illustrated in Fig. 43.7. Like terrazzo, stone floors are subject to cracking if bonded to a subfloor that deflects excessively. To prevent this, a membrane is used so the subfloor and stone flooring can move separately. However, on rigid structures stone may also be thinset.

ACOUSTICAL TREATMENT

The three most common acoustical treatments for ordinary construction are ceilings, special acoustical wall panels, and carpeting. Special devices used in auditoriums and similar spaces are not discussed here.

Acoustical Ceilings

In contemporary commercial construction, the ceiling is almost always a construction system separate from the structure. This allows a smooth, flat ceiling surface for partition attachment, lights, and acoustical treatment. The space above the ceiling can be used for mechanical systems, wiring, and other services.

Acoustical ceilings consist of thin panels of wood fiber, mineral fiber, or glass fiber set in a support grid of metal framing that is suspended by wires from the structure above.

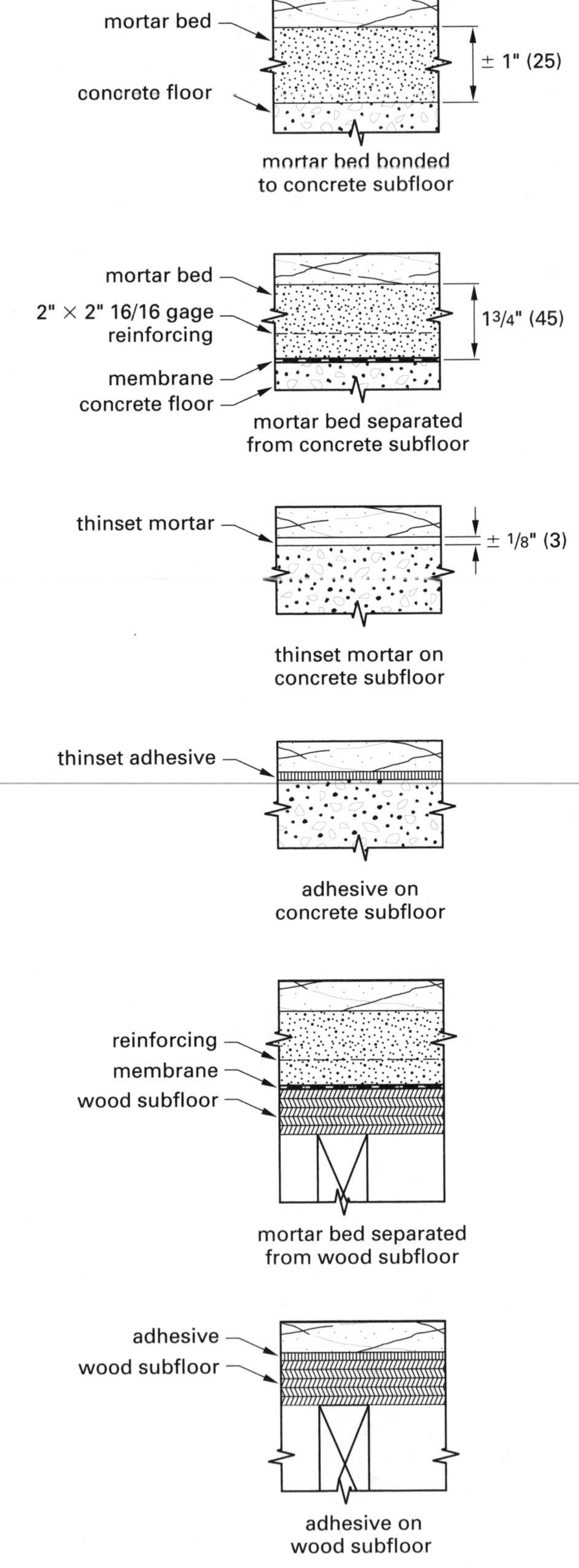

Figure 43.7 Stone Flooring Installation Methods

The tiles are perforated or fissured in various ways to absorb sound, which is the basis for the term "acoustical ceiling." It is important to remember that acoustical ceilings absorb sound, but they do not prevent sound transmission to any appreciable extent.

Acoustical ceiling tiles and the metal supporting grid are available in a variety of sizes and configurations. The most common type is the lay-in system in which tiles are simply laid on top of an exposed T-shaped grid system. See Fig. 43.8(a). A variation of this is the tegular system, which uses tiles with rabbeted edges, as shown in Fig. 43.8(b). Systems are also available in which the grid is completely concealed. These systems use 1 × 1 (300 × 300) or 1 × 2 (300 × 600) tile sizes. See Fig. 43.8(c). A typical lay-in acoustical system is shown in Fig. 43.9.

The most common tile and grid sizes for lay-in acoustical ceiling systems are 24 × 24 (600 × 600) and 24 × 48 (600 × 1200). Metric ceiling tiles are manufactured to a different size based on a 600 mm module, so they are exact multiples of 600 mm.

A 20 × 60 (500 × 1500) size is also available for use in buildings with a 5 ft working module, so three panels fit within one 60 in (1500) grid. This allows office partitions to be laid out on the 5 ft module lines without interfering with HVAC registers and with special 20 in by 48 in (500 × 1200) light fixtures located in the center of a module.

Other types of suspended systems that provide acoustical properties are also available. These include metal strip ceilings, wood grids, and fabric-covered acoustical batts. They all serve the same purpose: to absorb rather than reflect sound in order to reduce the noise level within a space.

Because suspended acoustical ceilings serve so many purposes in addition to acoustical control in today's construction, there are many elements that must be coordinated in their selection and detailing. These include determining required clearances for recessed lights; verifying clearances for ductwork; locating sprinklers, fire alarm speakers, smoke detectors, and similar items; and designing drapery pockets and other recessed fixtures.

In many cases, the space above a suspended ceiling is used as a return air plenum. Return air grilles are set in the grid, and return air is simply allowed to pass through the grilles, through the ceiling space, and back to a central return air duct or shaft that connects to the HVAC system. If this is the case the IMC requires that no combustible material be placed above the ceiling and that all plastic wiring be run in metal conduit. The IMC allows wiring used for telephone, computer, low-voltage lighting, and signal systems to be exposed if it is listed and labeled as plenum rated and installed in accordance with NFPA 70.

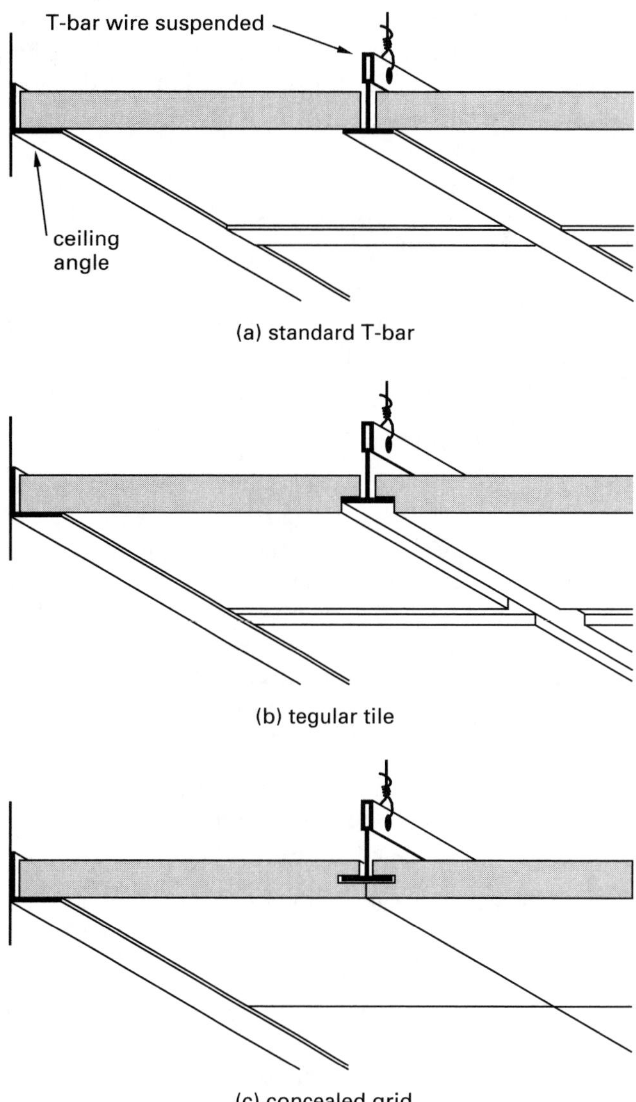

Figure 43.8 Standard Acoustical Ceiling Systems

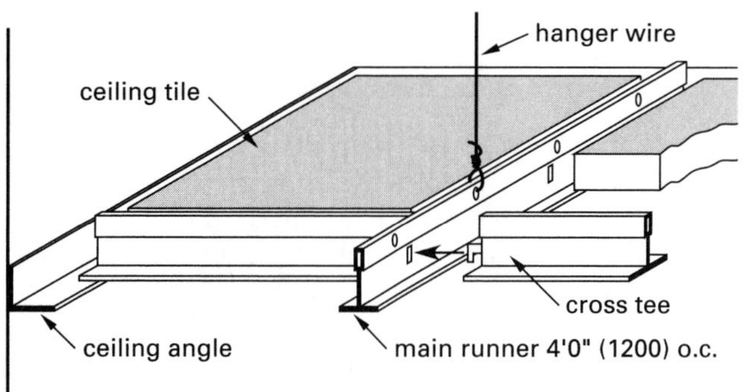

Figure 43.9 Lay-In Suspended Acoustical Ceiling

Suspended ceilings may be rated or nonrated. If they are fire rated, it means that they are part of a complete floor-ceiling or roof-ceiling assembly that is rated. Suspended ceiling systems by themselves cannot be rated. Rated acoustical ceiling systems consist of rated mineral tiles and rated grid systems, the latter of which include hold-down clips to keep the tiles in place and expansion slots to allow the grid to expand if subjected to heat.

Acoustical ceiling tiles are manufactured with varying degrees of recycled content utilizing newsprint, perlite, and ground-up pieces of old tiles. Recycled content may range for about 50% to nearly 90%.

Seismic Restraint for Suspended Ceilings

In some areas of the United States (including most of California and some portions of Idaho, Montana, Utah, Hawaii, and Alaska), special seismic-restraint detailing is required for suspended ceilings. Architects working on projects in these areas should verify the exact requirements based on the building code being used and the project's exact geographic location. When seismic restraint for suspended ceilings is required, certain criteria must be followed. Some of the more common criteria are as follows.

- Individual light fixtures and other types of equipment that are normally supported by the ceiling grid must be independently supported with wires.
- The actual weight of the ceiling system, including lights and air terminals, should be 2.5 lbm/ft^2 (12.2 kg/m^2) or less.
- The ceiling system should not be used to provide lateral support for partitions. Instead, the partitions should be braced with detailing similar to that shown in Fig. 43.10.
- Ceiling angles should provide at least a $^7/_8$ in (22) ledge, and there must be at least a $^3/_8$ in (10) clearance from the edge of the tile to the wall. This is shown in Fig. 43.11.
- The perimeter main runners and cross runners must be prevented from spreading without relying on permanent attachment to the ceiling angle.
- For ceilings in areas with very high seismic risk, the suspension system must be a heavy-duty type and must have lateral force bracing 12 ft (3600) on center in both directions, with the first point within 6 ft (1800) of each wall. As illustrated in Fig. 43.12, these points of lateral bracing must provide support in all four directions and must have rigid struts connected to the structure above to prevent uplift as well as to support gravity loads. Additional wire supports are also required for all runners at the perimeter of the room within 8 in (200) of the wall. Clearances from the end of the runners to the partition must be $^1/_2$ in (13) instead of $^3/_8$ in (9.5). The IBC requires a minimum clearance of $^3/_4$ in (19) in high-risk areas and a minimum 2 in (50) wide ceiling angle.

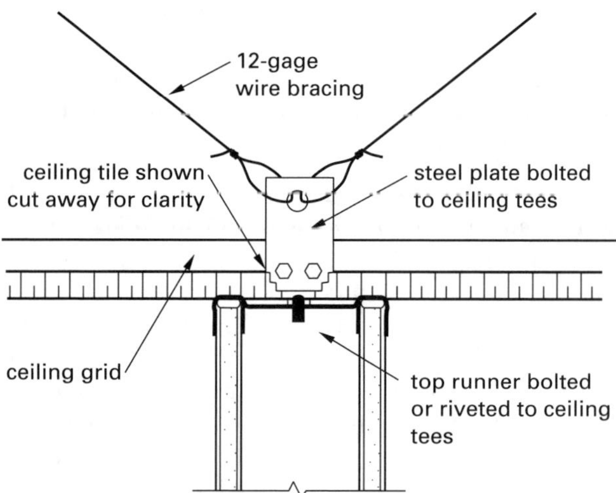

Figure 43.10 Partition Bracing for Seismic Risk Areas

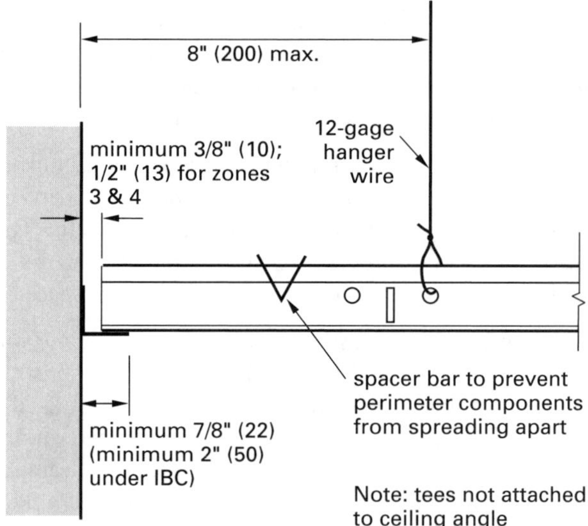

Figure 43.11 Detail of Runners at Perimeter Partition

Acoustical Wall Panels

Sound-absorbent panels can be purchased or constructed for use in spaces that require acoustical treatment in

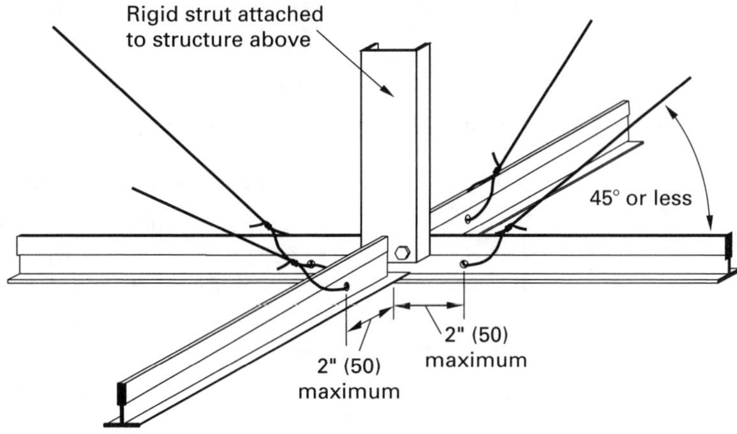

Figure 43.12 Ceiling Grid Bracing

addition to acoustical ceilings and carpeting. These are made from a sound-absorbent material such as fiberglass and are covered with a permeable material such as a loose-weave fabric. The acoustical material must be at least 1 in (25) thick in order to be effective.

WOOD FLOORING

Wood flooring offers a wide variety of appearances while providing a surface that is durable, wear resistant, and comfortable. It is available in several species and can be laid in dozens of different patterns.

Wood flooring is made from both hardwood and softwood, with the hardwoods predominating. Standard hardwoods used are red oak, white oak, maple, birch, beech, pecan, mahogany, and walnut. Softwoods used are yellow pine, fir, and western hemlock, among others.

Types of Wood Flooring

There are four basic types of wood flooring: strip flooring, plank flooring, block flooring, and solid block flooring. See Fig. 43.13.

Strip flooring is one of the most common wood flooring types and consists of thin strips from $^{3}/_{8}$ in to $^{25}/_{32}$ in (10 to 20) thick, of varying lengths, with tongue-and-groove edges. Most strip flooring is $2^{1}/_{4}$ in (57) wide, but $1^{1}/_{2}$ in (38) wide strips are also available. Strip flooring is used for residential and commercial wood floors for its appearance, warmth under foot, and resiliency, and where a durable floor is needed.

Plank flooring comes in the same thicknesses as strip flooring but is from $3^{1}/_{4}$ in to 8 in wide (83 to 203). It is laid in random lengths with the end joints staggered. Plank flooring is

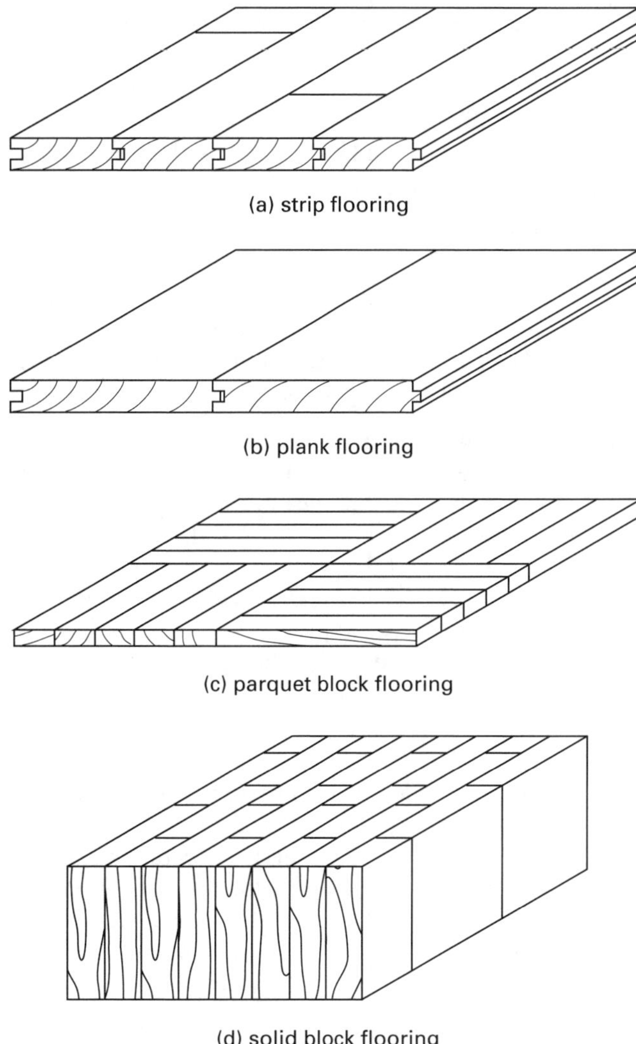

Figure 43.13 Types of Wood Flooring

used primarily in residential applications where a larger scale is desired or to emulate wider, historic planking.

Block flooring is made of preassembled wood flooring in three configurations. Unit block flooring is standard strip flooring assembled into a unit held together with steel or wood splines. Laminated block flooring is flooring made with from three to five plies of cross-laminated wood veneer. Both types of block flooring are from $^3/_8$ in to $^{25}/_{32}$ in (10 to 20) thick, in varying lengths, depending on the manufacturer. Unit and laminated block flooring can be laid in any pattern, but herringbone is one of the most common.

Parquet flooring is made of preassembled units of several small, thin slats of wood in a variety of patterns. It is available either finished or unfinished, and some manufacturers make parquet with a cellular foam resilient backing with a factory-applied adhesive for residential "peel and stick" applications. Commercial applications use nonbacked units that are field finished. Parquet flooring is usually sold in 12 in squares, $^5/_{16}$ in thick (300 mm squares, 8 mm thick), for mastic application, although some manufacturers make other sizes. Parquet flooring is easier and less expensive to install than other types of flooring and can be installed in a wide range of designs.

Solid block flooring is made from solid end-grain blocks. These are solid pieces of wood 2, $2^1/_2$, 3, and 4 in thick (50, 64, 75, and 100) laid on end with adhesive. Solid block floors are very durable and resistant to oils, mild chemicals, and indentation. They are used for industrial floors or other heavy-duty commercial applications.

There are several variations of wood floors for special uses. These include resilient and relocatable floors. *Resilient floors* are wood strip floors laid on one of three types of systems described in the next section. They provide extra buoyancy for uses like dance and theater floors. *Relocatable floors* are systems of modular units, usually 4 ft^2 (1200 mm^2), that can be quickly installed and dismantled. They are used for athletic and institutional floors where the type of flooring needs to be changed frequently.

Grades of Wood Flooring

Wood flooring is graded differently than other wood products. Grading rules are set by the various trade associations such as the National Oak Flooring Manufacturers' Association, the Maple Flooring Manufacturers' Association, the Southern Pine Inspection Bureau, the West Coast Lumber Inspection Bureau, and the Western Wood Products Association.

Unfinished oak flooring is graded as clear, select, no. 1 common, and no. 2 common. Clear is the best grade with the most uniform color. Plain sawn is standard, but quarter sawn is available on special order. Lengths of pieces are $1^1/_4$ ft (381) and up, with the average length being $3^3/_4$ ft (1143).

Beech, birch, and maple are available in first, second, and third grades along with some combination grades.

Species of Wood Flooring

In addition to the commonly used maple, oak, birch, and beech, there are many wood species, both domestic and imported, that can be used for flooring. Of the many available, two qualify as sustainable products: bamboo and palm wood.

Bamboo is not a tree, but a fast-growing grass that reaches maturity in three to four years. It can be used for flooring as well as for veneer and paneling. It can be obtained from managed forests where it is grown on steep slopes and in hill lands where other forms of agriculture are difficult to propagate.

Bamboo flooring is available in $^1/_2$ in (13) and $^3/_4$ in (19) thick strips about 3 in (76) wide or wider, depending on the manufacturer. It is milled with tongue-and-groove edges, so it can be installed like standard wood-strip flooring. It can be installed by nailing or with an adhesive.

Bamboo is almost as hard and twice as stable as red oak and maple. It is available in a natural color or a darker, amber color and is prefinished with a durable polyurethane coating.

Palm wood comes from coconut palms and is a by-product from commercial coconut plantations. Palm wood flooring is available in $^3/_4$ in by 3 in (19 by 76) wide strips with tongue-and-groove edges like those of standard strip flooring. It is harder and more stable than maple, red oak, and white oak. The flooring ranges from dark- to medium-red mahogany in color and is prefinished with polyurethane.

Finishes

Wood strip and plank flooring are usually installed unfinished for field sanding, staining, and finishing. Block flooring may come unfinished or prefinished. Parquet flooring is often impregnated with acrylic and irradiated for a very hard, durable finish. Wood may be stained and finished with wax, varnish, polyurethane, or a variety of other finishes.

Installation

Wood flooring must be installed over a suitable nailable base. Because wood swells if it gets damp, provisions must be made to prevent moisture from seeping up from below and to allow for expansion of the completed floor. Strip flooring is installed by blind nailing through the tongue. Figure 43.14 shows two methods of installing wood flooring over a concrete subfloor. In the first case, a sheet of $^3/_4$ in

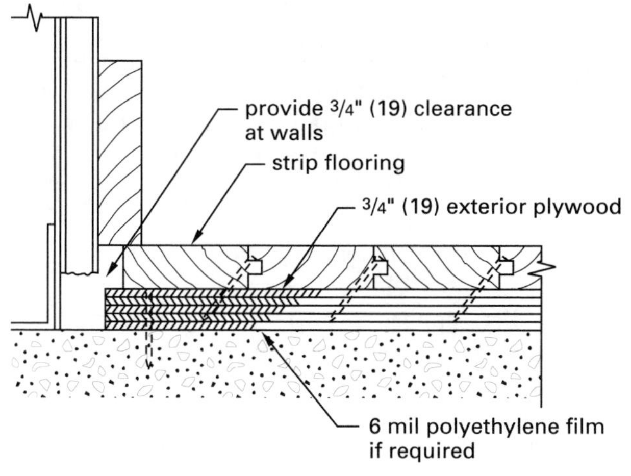

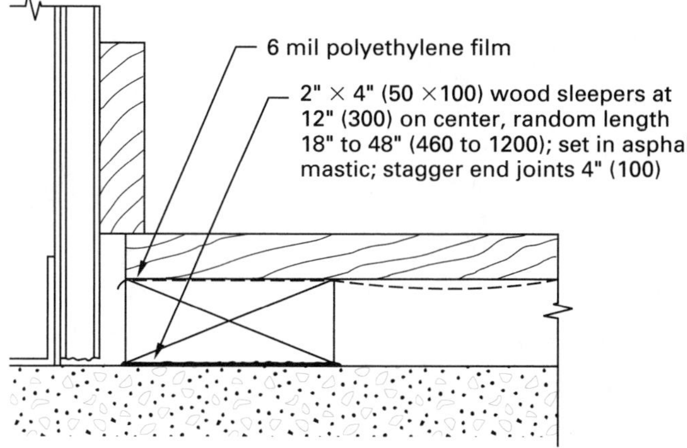

wood strip flooring over concrete

Figure 43.14 Wood Flooring Installation

(19) plywood is attached to the concrete to provide the nailable base. A layer of polyethylene film is laid down first if moisture may be a problem.

In the second case, the wood flooring is laid on wood sleepers. This method of installation not only gives a more resilient floor that is more comfortable under foot, but it also provides an airspace so that any excess moisture can escape. In both instances, a gap of at least 3/4 in (19) is left at the perimeter to allow for expansion and is concealed by the wood base.

Figure 43.15 shows the typical installation over wood framing with a plywood subfloor. A layer of 15 lbm asphalt felt may be laid to prevent squeaking and to act as a vapor barrier.

There are also resilient pads available that are used in place of sleepers for strip flooring installation. These provide an even more resilient floor and are often used for dance floors and gymnasium floors.

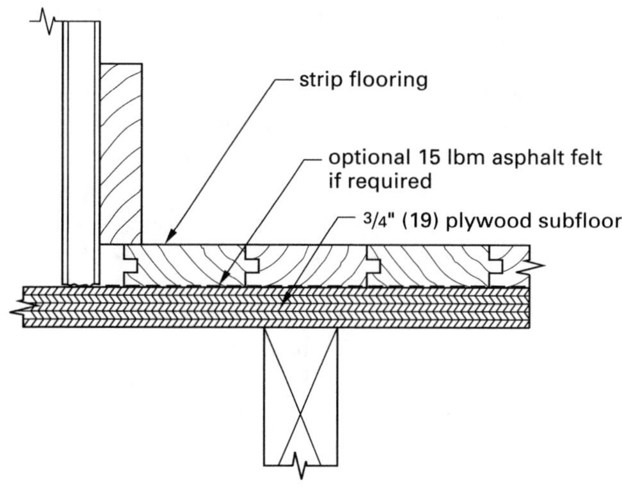

strip flooring over joists

Figure 43.15 Wood Flooring on Wood Framing

LAMINATE FLOORING

Laminate flooring is a variation of plastic laminate material. It is composed of a clear-wearing sheet over a melamine-impregnated decorative printed sheet with core layers of phenolic-impregnated kraft paper. These sheets are laminated to a high-density fiberboard core under heat and pressure and covered with a water-resistant backing sheet.

The decorative printed sheet can be made to resemble natural wood, tile, or stone, or can be printed in solid colors or even have photographic-quality images in it. Laminate flooring is available in planks (similar to wood-strip flooring but a little wider), square tiles, or rectangular blocks. It is about 5/16 in (8) thick. It is normally laid on a cushioned foam underlayment with the tongue-and-groove edges glued together. A vapor barrier is normally required when laminate flooring is laid over a concrete floor.

Laminate flooring is hard, durable, and resistant to staining. It is gaining popularity where a less-expensive alternative to wood or other types of flooring is required. It can be used in most locations but is not recommended for rest rooms or other wet areas.

RESILIENT FLOORING

Resilient flooring is a generic term describing several types of composition materials made from various resins, fibers, plasticizers, and fillers and formed under heat and pressure to produce a thin material in either sheets or tiles. Resilient flooring is applied to a subfloor of concrete, plywood, or other smooth underlayment with mastic. Some resilient floorings may only be installed above grade; others may be placed below, on, or above grade.

Resilient flooring is available in tiles or in sheet form. Sheet flooring has several advantages over tile. Although it is more difficult to install, it provides a floor with fewer seams, which makes the floor easier to clean, more hygienic, and more resistant to moisture spills. Some types of sheet flooring even allow what few seams do exist to be sealed.

Vinyl Flooring

Vinyl tile is the term commonly used to refer to flooring based on polyvinyl chloride. It is a good, durable resilient flooring resistant to indentation, abrasion, grease, water, alkalis, and some acids. Vinyl comes in a variety of colors and patterns and is easy to install. It can be used below grade, on grade, or above grade. It must be installed over a clean, dry, smooth surface. It is slightly more expensive than vinyl composition tile.

Vinyl tiles are generally 12 in (300) squares, although some are available in 9 in (225) squares and larger sizes. Either $^1/_{16}$ in or $^1/_8$ in (1.6 or 3.2) thicknesses are available, but for commercial use and better residential floors, the $^1/_8$ in thickness is preferred.

Solid sheet vinyl, like solid vinyl tile, is a homogeneous nonlayered construction of polyvinyl chloride with color and pattern extending through the entire thickness. It is very durable and resistant to indentation and rolling wheeled traffic. Because the seams can be sealed with heat welding or solvent welding, it is an excellent floor for health care facilities, clean rooms, and industrial flooring.

Vinyl Composition

Vinyl composition tile is similar to vinyl tile but includes various type of fillers that decrease the percentage of polyvinyl chloride. Although composition tile costs less than homogeneous vinyl, it has less flexibility and abrasion resistance. Because of this, through-grain types are preferred. These are tiles where the color and pattern extend uniformly through the tile thickness. Normally, this tile is applied with mastic, but peel-and-stick types are available for residential applications. Tile is also available with an attached foam backing for greater resilience.

Rubber

Rubber flooring is made from synthetic rubber and offers excellent resistance to deformation under loads while providing a very comfortable, quiet, resilient floor. Rubber, however, is not very resistant to oils or grease, is hard to clean, and can be damaged by indentation of small objects. This flooring is available with a smooth surface or with a patterned, raised surface, which allows water and dirt to lie below the wearing surface, helping to prevent slipping or excessive abrasion. Rubber flooring is available in tiles or sheet form in several sizes and thicknesses.

Rubber sheet flooring has the same properties as rubber tile, but with fewer seams. The decorative types of flooring with raised patterns are usually specified in sheet form.

Linoleum

Linoleum is one of the traditional types of sheet flooring. It is composed of oxidized linseed oil or other binders, pigments, and fillers applied over a backing of burlap or asphalt-saturated felt. Linoleum is available as plain, battleship linoleum (which is a single color), or inlaid linoleum (which consists of multicolored patterns that extend through the thickness to the backing). Linoleum has very good abrasion and grease resistance, but it has limited resistance to alkalis. A light gage is used for residential floors and a heavy gage for commercial floors.

Cork

Cork flooring is available in tile form and is used where acoustical control or resilience is desired. However, it is not resistant to staining, moisture, heavy loads, or concentrated foot traffic. It should only be used above grade and must be sealed and waxed to protect the surface.

Preparation of Substrates

Regardless of the type of resilient flooring used, preparation of the subfloor is critical to a successful installation. Because moisture is the cause of most problems, concrete floors must be dry at the time of installation. For new concrete floors, it may take 6 to 12 weeks or longer for the slab to thoroughly cure and dry. If there is any doubt, the slab should be tested for moisture. Refer to Ch. 36 for a description of some methods of testing concrete floors for moisture and alkalinity.

A slab below grade or on grade should have a vapor barrier below it to prevent moisture from migrating from the earth. The concrete must be free of any curing compounds, sealers, and hardeners that will interfere with the adhesive that will be used to bond the flooring. The slab must also be free of solvents, grease, oil, and similar compounds. The surface should be smooth and level to within $^1/_8$ in in 10 ft (3 in 3050), with no abrupt transitions or depressions. Construction and control joints should be filled and leveled with a latex patching compound.

Wood subflooring should be smooth, with all boards securely fastened. Underlayment of plywood, hardboard, or particleboard is generally recommended. The board should be underlayment grade, at least $^1/_4$ in (6) thick, and securely glued and nailed, with the joints staggered. The joints should be sanded and filled, if necessary, with all nails driven flush. Grade-level wood floors should be over a well-ventilated crawl space with a vapor barrier on the earth in the crawl space. Resilient floors may be installed over existing wood floors if they are smooth and tight and if all ridges are sanded. However, underlayment is preferred.

SEAMLESS FLOORING

Seamless flooring is a mixture of a resinous matrix, fillers, and decorative materials applied in a liquid or viscous form that cures to a hard, seamless surface. Depending on the type of matrix and specific mixture, the flooring is either poured or troweled on a subfloor. Some products are self-leveling; others must be worked to a level surface. Some products, such as epoxy terrazzo, are surface ground after they cure to produce a smooth surface.

Seamless flooring is a high-performance flooring used where special characteristics are required, such as extreme hardness, severe stain and chemical resistance, and high water resistance, and where cleanliness and ease of cleaning are required. It is used for industrial floors, commercial kitchens and food preparation plants, factories, clean rooms, laboratories, hospitals, correctional facilities, and parking garages.

Seamless flooring is applied in thicknesses from $^1/_{16}$ in to $^1/_2$ in (1.6 to 13), depending on the type of product. Mastics may be applied in thicknesses up to $1^1/_2$ in (38). Seamless flooring is applied over a suitable base of concrete or wood subflooring with the material turned up at the walls to form an integral cove base.

CARPET

Carpet is a very versatile flooring material. It is attractive, quiet, easy to install, and requires less maintenance than many other types of flooring. If its material and construction are properly specified, it is appropriate for many interior uses.

Carpet is made from several fibers and combinations of fibers including wool, nylon, acrylic, polyester, and polypropylene. Wool, of course, is a natural material and overall one of the best for carpet. It is very durable and resilient, has superior appearance characteristics, and is easy to clean and maintain. Unfortunately, it is also one of the most expensive carpet fibers.

Nylon is an economical carpet material that is very strong and wear resistant. It has a high stain resistance and is easy to clean. However, its appearance is generally less appealing than that of other fibers.

Acrylic has moderate durability, but it has a more wool-like appearance than nylon. It is easy to maintain and has a fair crush resistance. Polyester has properties similar to those of acrylic.

Polypropylene (olefin) is used for indoor-outdoor carpet and has good durability and resistance to abrasion and fading, but it is less attractive than other carpet types and has poor resiliency.

Carpet is manufactured by tufting, weaving, needle punching, and fusion bonding. *Tufting* is the most common way of producing carpet and is done by inserting pile yarns through a prewoven backing. The tops of the yarns are then cut for cut pile carpet or left as is for level loop carpet. Weaving interlaces warp and weft yarns in the traditional manner, a method that produces a very attractive, durable carpet but is the most expensive method of manufacturing carpet. *Needlepunching* pulls fibers through a backing with barbed needles. It produces carpet of limited variation in texture and accounts for a very small percentage of the total carpet market. *Fusion bonding* embeds fabric in a synthetic backing. It is used to produce carpet tiles as well as other carpet types.

The appearance and durability of carpet is affected by the amount of yarn in a given area, how tightly that yarn is packed, and the height of the yarn. The *pitch* of a carpet is the number of warp lines of yarn in a 27 in (685) width. The *stitch* is the number of lengthwise tufts in 1 in (25.4). The higher the pitch and stitch numbers, the denser the carpet. The *pile height* is the height of the fiber from the surface of the backing to the top of the pile. Generally, shorter and more tightly packed fibers result in a more durable carpet.

An important part of carpet installation is the *carpet cushion*, sometimes called *padding*. Cushion is not appropriate for all carpet installation (such as direct glue-down installation), nor is it required; however, it is recommended. Cushioning increases the life of the carpet, provides increased resiliency and comfort, helps sound absorption, lessens impact noise, and improves thermal qualities in some situations. Common cushion materials include sponge rubber, felt, urethane, and foam rubber.

Sponge rubber is made from natural or synthetic rubber and other chemicals and fillers with a facing on the top side. It is available in flat sheets or a waffled configuration.

Felt is available in four forms: hair, combination, fiber, and rubberized. Hair felt is composed of 100% animal hair. Combination felt is a mixture of animal hair and other fibers. Fiber felt is composed entirely of felt. Rubberized felt is any of the other three types with a rubberized coating on one side.

Urethane is manufactured in three different ways to produce prime, densified, or bonded sheets, each of which has a different range of densities. Thickness ranges from $^1/_4$ in to $^3/_4$ in (6 to 19).

Foam rubber is commonly applied as an integral backing to some carpet. It is natural or synthetic latex rubber with additives and with a backing on one side.

Carpet flammability is regulated in the building codes in two ways. The first limits the carpet's ability to ignite and sustain a fire if it is the first item ignited, and the second limits its flammability when subjected to the heat and flame of a fully developed fire. To prevent carpet from igniting and spreading fire when exposed to something like a dropped match, current federal law requires all carpet manufactured and sold in the United States to meet the requirements of ASTM D-2859, *Standard Test Method for Flammability of Finished Textile Floor Covering Materials*. This is more commonly known as the Methenamine Pill Test, or simply, the pill test. It is also known by its earlier designation, DOC FF-1. In this test a methenamine tablet is ignited in the center of a 9 in (229) carpet square. The distance the carpet burns beyond the center point is measured, and if the carpet burns to within 1 in (25) of the edge of an 8 in (203) distance from the center, the sample fails.

The second way of regulating carpet flammability is by limiting the degree to which a carpet sustains fire. This is done in the IBC with the flooring radiant panel test, NFPA 253 (which is discussed in the section on finishes in Ch. 55). Refer to Ch. 30 for more information on the sustainability aspects of carpet.

PAINTING

Painting is a generic term for the application of thin coatings of various materials to protect and decorate the surfaces to which they are applied. Coatings are composed of a *vehicle*, which is the liquid part of the coating, and the body and pigments if the coating is opaque. The vehicle has a nonvolatile part called the *binder* and a volatile part called the *solvent*. The binder, along with the body, forms the actual film of the coating, and the solvent dissolves the binder to allow for application of the coating. The solvent evaporates or dries, leaving the final finish. The body of most quality paints is titanium dioxide, which is white. Pigments give paint its color.

Paints are broadly classified into solvent-based and water-based types. Solvent-based coatings have binders dissolved in or containing organic solvents, and water-based coatings have binders that are soluble or dispersed in water.

Clear, solvent-based coatings include varnishes, shellac, silicone, and urethane. When a small amount of pigment is added, the coating becomes a stain, which gives color to the surface but allows the appearance of the underlying material to show through. Stains are most often used on wood. For interior applications, clear coatings can be used. It is not necessary to have a pigment to protect an interior surface as is usually required for exterior surfaces.

Oil paints use a drying oil, or curing oil, as a binder. Linseed oil was traditional, but other organic oils have also been used. Today, synthetic alkyd resin is used as the drying oil. Oil paints are durable but have a strong odor when being applied and must be cleaned up with solvents such as mineral spirits. In addition, they cannot be painted on damp surfaces or on surfaces that may become damp from behind.

In many remodeling projects old paint must be removed. If the building is old enough to have lead-based paint, local regulations may require that the lead paint be removed from some types of residential occupancies by a licensed company using approved methods for removal and disposal. Sometimes, resheathing the wall is an acceptable alternative.

Latex paints are water based, with vinyl chloride or acrylic resins as binders. Acrylic latex is better than vinyl latex. Both can be used indoors as well as outdoors and can be thinned with water.

For more durable finishes, epoxy is used as a binder for resistance to corrosion and chemicals. Epoxies also resist abrasion and strongly adhere to concrete, metal, and wood. Epoxy is considered a high-performance coating and requires skilled applicators. The fumes are noxious, so special ventilation is usually required for on-site application.

Urethane is also considered a high-performance coating. It is used for its superior resistance to abrasion, grease, alcohol, water, and fuels. Interior applications most often include clear coverings for wood floors. Exterior applications include clear or pigmented paint for anti-graffiti coatings. Polyurethane paint is sometimes used for its strictly aesthetic qualities because it can have a very high-gloss finish with an almost glass-like sheen.

Successful application of coatings depends not only on the correct selection for the intended use, but also on the surface preparation of the substrate, the primer used, and the method of application. Surfaces must be clean, dry, and free from grease, oils, and other foreign material. Application can be done by brushing, rolling, or spraying. The amount of coating material to be applied is normally specified as either wet or dry film thickness in mils (thousandths of an inch) for each coat needed. The coating should be applied under dry conditions when the temperature is between 55°F and 85°F (13°C and 29°C).

As discussed in Ch. 30, all paints and other coatings must have volatile organic compounds (VOCs) that meet the requirements of the Clean Air Act. Most paints and common architectural coatings now meet the federal requirements.

However, some specialized coatings may not, and these should be investigated before they are specified. Some jurisdictions, most notably California, have stricter standards

COLOR

Color is one of the most dominant perceptions of the physical world and one of the most powerful tools for architectural and interior design. At the same time, color is one of the most complex physical and psychological phenomena, and difficult to understand and use correctly. This section describes some fundamentals of color and its use.

Color Basics

Color is a physical property of visible light. Visible light is just one part of the larger electromagnetic spectrum, which also includes other radiation like X rays and infrared light. Each color is differentiated from the others by its wavelength. Red has the longest wavelength of the visible spectrum, while violet has the shortest wavelength. The eye and brain perceive variations in wavelengths to give the sensation of color.

When colors created with light are mixed, the wavelengths of both colors are present in the resulting light. For this reason, colors created with light are called *additive colors*. If red light is added to green light, the resulting light contains wavelengths of both colors, and this combination stimulates the eye in about the same way as yellow light stimulates it; therefore we perceive yellow light. When all the colors of light are present in equal amounts, we perceive white light.

The color of a physical object, on the other hand, is conveyed by the wavelengths of light that the object absorbs, or subtracts, from the light that strikes it. When white light strikes a blue object, the object absorbs most of the wavelengths of light except that of blue light, which is reflected to the eye. For this reason, colors created with pigments are called *subtractive colors*. When all the colors of a pigment are present in equal amounts, we perceive no color, or black. When pigments are mixed in unequal amounts, they absorb various wavelengths of the light striking them, and the wavelengths that remain in the reflected light determine the color perceived.

The three primary colors of light are red, green, and blue. In various combinations and quantities, these three colors can create the other colors. They produce white light when combined equally. The three primary colors of pigments are yellow, red, and blue. Theoretically, all other colors can be produced by mixing various proportions of the primaries. This arrangement is typically shown on a circle known as the color wheel, illustrated in Fig. 43.16.

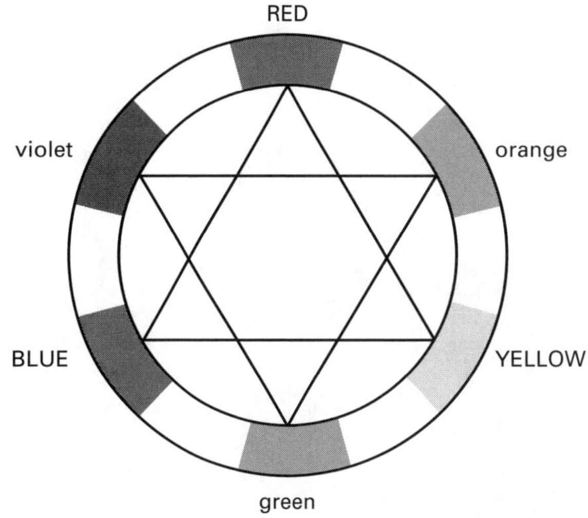

Figure 43.16 Brewster Color Wheel*

*This figure may be seen in color at **www.ppi2pass.com/ARRM/figures**

Color has three basic qualities: hue, value, and intensity (or chroma). The *hue* is the basic color; that is, the attribute by which, for example, blue is distinguished from red. The *value* describes the degree of lightness or darkness of color in relation to white and black. The *intensity* (or *chroma*) of a color is defined by the degree of purity of the hue when compared with a neutral gray of the same value. These basic qualities of color are represented diagrammatically in Fig. 43.17. When white is added to a hue, its value is raised and a tint is created. When black is added, its value is lowered and a *shade* is created. Adding gray of the same value to a hue creates a *tone*. A tone can also be created by adding the color's *complement*, the hue of the color opposite it on the color wheel.

Color Systems

Many systems have been developed to describe and quantify color. Some focus on light and some focus on pigments, while still others try to define color strictly in mathematical terms. For most interior design purposes, it is necessary to be familiar with at least two of the commonly used systems: the Brewster system and the Munsell system.

The *Brewster color system*, also known as the *Prang color system*, is the familiar color wheel that organizes color pigments by their relationship with the three *primary colors* of red, blue, and yellow. See Fig. 43.16. In this case, primary means that these colors cannot be mixed from other pigments. Mixing pairs of primary colors in equal amounts produces the *secondary colors* of violet, orange, and green. In turn, when a primary color is mixed in equal amounts with an adjacent secondary color, a *tertiary color* is created.

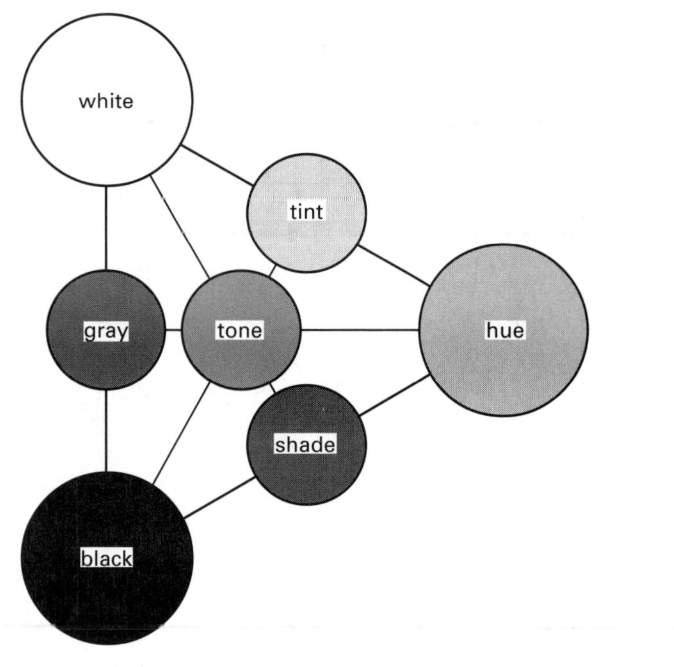

Figure 43.17 Modifying Values of a Hue*

*This figure may be seen in color at **www.ppi2pass.com/ARRM/figures**

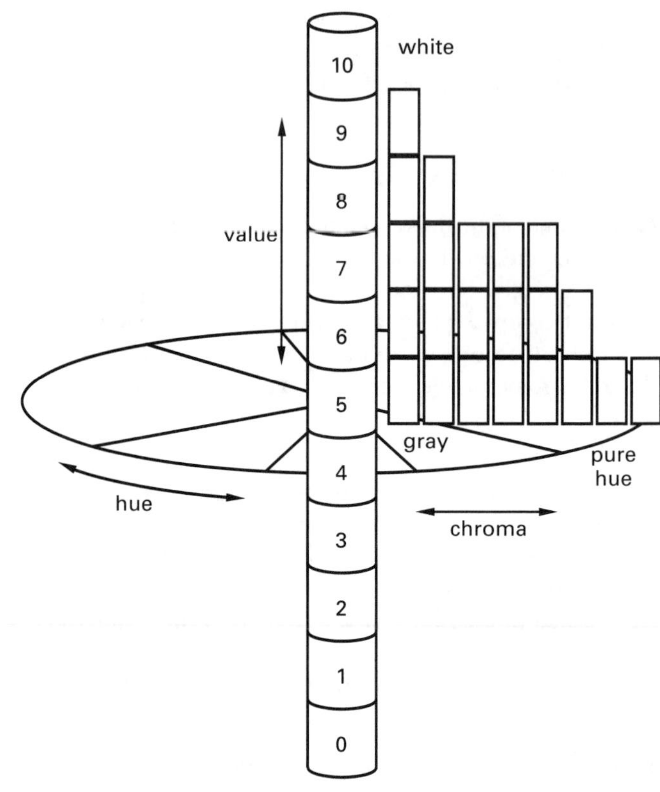

Figure 43.18 Munsell Color System

The *Munsell color system* defines color more accurately than the color wheel. It uses three scales in three dimensions to specify the values of hue, value, and chroma (intensity). Figure 43.18 shows these scales. There are five principal hues (yellow, green, blue, purple, and red), each designated by a single letter (Y, G, B, P, and R, respectively), and five intermediate hues, each halfway between two principal hues and designated by two letters (YR, GY, BG, PB, and RP). These ten hues are arranged in a circle.

To create designations for hues that lie between the principal and intermediate hues, each hue is identified with a number up to 10 (zero is not used) to indicate its position on the color wheel and the letter designation of its nearest principal or intermediate hue. The principal and intermediate hues are given the designation 5. Thus, 5GY and 5G designate green-yellow and green, respectively. Equally spaced along the color wheel from green-yellow to green are the hues 5GY, 7.5GY, 10GY, 2.5G, and 5G. This is enough detail for many uses, but when needed, the color wheel can be subdivided further, so that the ten gradations in hue from green-yellow to green are designated 5GY, 6GY, 7GY, 8GY, 9GY, 10GY, 1G, 2G, 3G, 4G, and 5G. Subdivision into even smaller gradations is possible but generally not useful.

Value (the degree of lightness or darkness) is represented by the axis through the center of the circle. The steps along this axis consist of nine neutral grays plus white and black. White is at the top of the scale and is given a value of 10, and black is at the bottom with a value of 0.

Chroma is indicated by distance from the axis. Colors that are furthest from the axis have the highest chromas; these are the hues at their purest and most saturated. Moving toward the center, colors are closer to a neutral gray.

To indicate the value and chroma of a color, the numbers are written after the hue, so that 5G 6/4 is the principal hue green with value 6 and chroma 4. A neutral gray (with no hue) is designated with the letter N, so that 1N is a very dark gray and 5N is a middle gray.

Different combinations of hue and value have different maximum chromas. For example, purples tend to reach higher chromas at full saturation than yellows do. Purples also tend to reach their maximum chromas at middle values like 5 and 6, while yellows tend to reach them at higher values like 7 and 8. For this reason, the possible distance that a color can be from the axis (which is to say, its maximum chroma) varies with both hue and value, and as a result the three-dimensional Munsell color solid is not a symmetrical form.

Effects of Adjacent Colors and Light

As with any other aspect of interior design, a single color does not exist in isolation. It affects and is affected by the colors that surround it and by the color of the light that strikes it. There are many ways in which two colors affect each other when seen together. Some of the most common examples follow.

- *Complementary colors* (those opposite each other on the color wheel) reinforce each other. This phenomenon manifests itself in several ways. For example, when someone stares at one color for some time and then looks at a white surface, an afterimage of the color's complement is seen. In addition, the color of an object will induce its complement in the surrounding background. When two complementary colors are seen adjacent to each other, each appears to heighten the other's saturation. When a small area of one color is placed against a background of its complementary color, the small area of color becomes more intense.
- When two noncomplementary colors are placed together, each appears to tint the other with its own complement. The two colors will appear to be further apart on the color wheel than they actually are.
- Two primary colors seen together will both tend to appear tinted with the third primary.
- A light color placed against a darker background will appear lighter than it is, while a dark color against a lighter background will appear darker than it actually is. Figure 43.19 shows an identical value placed against two contrasting backgrounds. This phenomenon is known as *simultaneous contrast*.
- A background color will tend to absorb the same color in a second, noncomplementary color placed over it. For example, an orange spot on a red background will appear more yellow than it is because the red background "absorbs" some of the red in the spot.
- A neutral gray will appear warm when placed on a blue background and cool when placed on a red background.

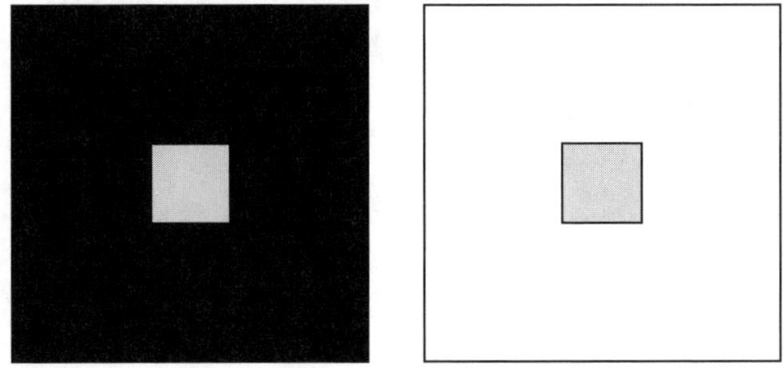

Figure 43.19 Simultaneous Contrast

One of the most important aspects of color interaction is how light affects the appearance of a color. Most light is perceived by the human eye as white, but in fact every light source produces some wavelengths more than others, so every light contains some colors more than others. For instance, incandescent light is very yellow, while midday sunlight is predominantly blue. Light from a cool white fluorescent lamp has much blue and green light in it, while light from a warm white fluorescent lamp contains much yellow and orange.

In general, when light contains a strong component of a particular hue, the light will intensify colors with similar hues and neutralize colors of complementary hues. For example, a red object seen under incandescent light will appear more intensely red and vibrant, while a blue object of the same value will appear washed out and muddy. The same blue object, however, would be rendered closer to its actual color if seen under midday light or under a cool white fluorescent light.

The amount of light also affects color. Dim lighting reduces a color's value and chroma. Strong lighting can either intensify a hue or make it appear washed out. For all these reasons, color selections should be made under the same type of lighting that will exist in the final interior installation.

44 VERTICAL TRANSPORTATION

Vertical transportation is a term that describes all the methods used to move people and materials vertically. This includes passenger and freight elevators, escalators, dumbwaiters, vertical conveyors, moving ramps, wheelchair lifts, and platform lifts, as well as stairs, ramps, and ladders.

HYDRAULIC ELEVATORS

Hydraulic elevators are one of the two major elevator types used for the movement of people and freight; the other is electric elevators. Hydraulic elevators are lifted by a plunger, or *ram*, set in the ground directly under the car and operated with oil as the pressure fluid. As a consequence, the cylinder for the ram must be extended into the ground to a depth the same as the elevator's full height.

Because the ram must be set in the ground and speed is limited, hydraulic elevators are only used for passenger and freight loads in buildings from two to six stories high, or about 50 ft (15 m). They have speeds much lower than those of electric elevators, traveling from 25 ft/min to 150 ft/min (0.13 m/s to 0.75 m/s) and are therefore not appropriate for moving large numbers of people quickly. Single-ram elevators have weight capacities from 2000 lbm to 20,000 lbm (1000 kg to 10 000 kg), and multiple-ram units can lift from 20,000 lbm to 100,000 lbm (10 000 kg to 50 000 kg).

A few variations of the standard hydraulic elevator are available. The holeless hydraulic uses a telescoping plunger set in the shaft next to the cab. Lift is provided by applying force to the upper members of the car frame. Another type uses a roller chain mounted over a wheel mounted on top of the hydraulic plunger. With this type, the plunger is mounted above the ground in the side of the shaft.

ELECTRIC ELEVATORS

Electric elevators are the most common elevator type used for passenger service. They are capable of much higher lifts and greater speeds than hydraulic types and can be precisely controlled for accelerating and decelerating. The system employs a cab suspended by cables (known as *ropes*) that are draped over a sheave and attached to a counterweight. A motor drives the sheave, which transmits lifting power to the ropes by the friction of the ropes in grooves of the sheave. For this reason, electric elevators are also referred to as *traction elevators*. The common components of a traction elevator are shown in Fig. 44.1.

Electric passenger elevators travel from 250 ft/min to 1800 ft/min (1.25 m/s to 9 m/s) and have capacities from 2000 lbm to 5000 lbm (1000 kg to 2500 kg). Higher capacities are available for electric freight elevators.

Types

The two types of electric elevators are the gearless traction and the geared traction. *Gearless traction elevators* use a direct current (dc) motor directly connected to the sheave. The brake is also mounted on the same shaft. Gearless machines that are dependable and easy to maintain are used on high-speed elevators.

The *geared traction elevator* is used for slow speeds from 25 fpm to 450 fpm (0.13 m/s to 2.25 m/s). A high-speed DC or AC motor drives a worm gear reduction assembly to provide a slow sheave speed with high torque. With the many possible variations in gear reduction ratios, sheave diameters, motor speeds, and roping arrangements, geared traction machines provide a great deal of flexibility for slow-speed, high-capacity elevators.

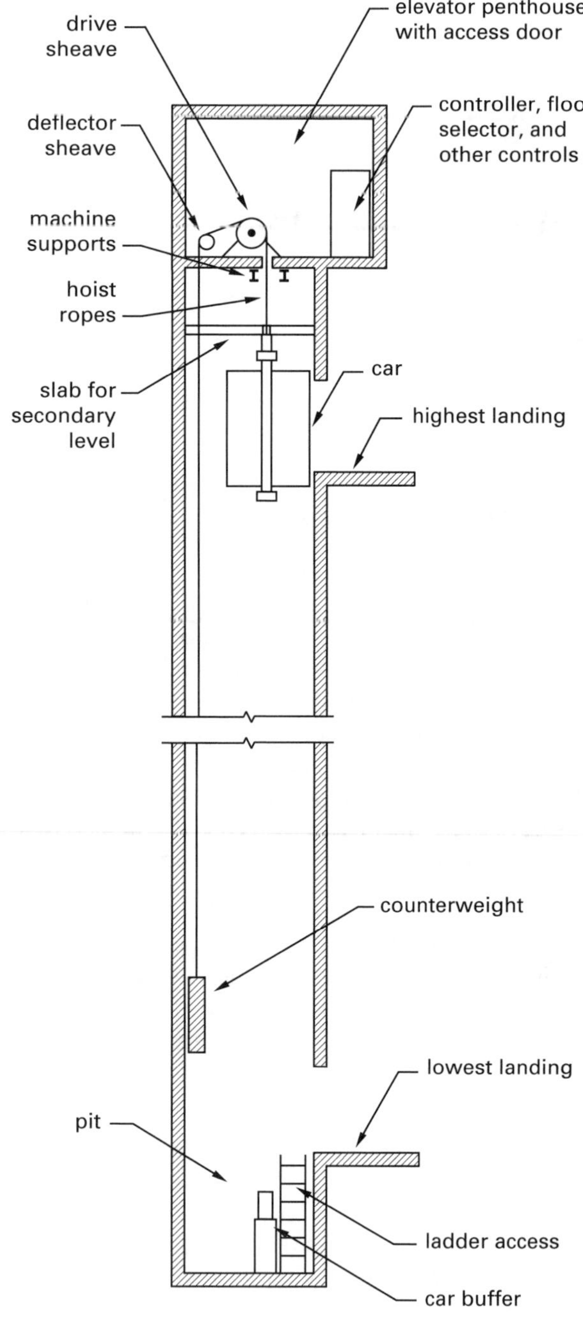

Figure 44.1 Traction Elevator

Roping

Roping refers to the arrangement of cables supporting the elevator. The simplest type is the *single wrap*, in which the rope passes over the sheave only once and is then connected to the counterweight. For high-speed elevators, additional traction is usually required so that the rope is wound over the sheave twice. This is known as a *double-wrap* arrangement. The disadvantage to double wrapping is that there are more bends in the cable and consequently a shorter rope life.

When the rope is directly connected to the counterweight, the cable travels just as far as the car, only in the opposite direction. This is known as *1:1 roping*. When the rope is wrapped around a sheave on the counterweight and connected to the top of the shaft, the rope moves twice as far as the elevator cab. This is known as *2:1 roping* and requires that less weight be lifted. Therefore, a smaller, higher-speed motor can be used, which is desirable for speeds up to 700 fpm.

Operation and Control

Operation is the term used to describe the way the electrical systems for an elevator or group of elevators answer calls for service. *Control* describes the method of coordinating and operating all the aspects of elevator service, such as travel speed, accelerating and decelerating, door opening speed and delay, leveling, and hall lantern signals.

Many types of operating methods are available. The purpose of an operating system is to coordinate elevator response to signal calls on each floor so that waiting time is minimized and the elevators operate in the most efficient manner possible.

The simplest type of system is the *single automatic*. This was the first type of automated system for elevators without attendants and consists of a single call button on each floor and a single button for each floor inside the car. The elevator can only be called if no one is using it, and once inside, the passenger has exclusive use of the car until the trip is complete. This type of system has limited use, and is therefore best for small buildings with little traffic where exclusive use is desired.

The most common type of system for many buildings is the *selective collective operation*. With this system, the elevator remembers and answers all calls in one direction and then reverses and answers all calls in the opposite direction. When the trip is complete, the elevator can be programmed to return to a home landing, usually the lobby.

The selective collective system works well for light to moderate service requirements, but for large buildings with many elevators, *group automatic operation* is employed. This is simply the control of all elevators with programmable microprocessors to respond to calls in the most efficient manner possible, taking into account all the variables involved. In addition, such things as the time of day or day of the week can be included in the programming. This provides precise response to any building's needs.

A newer method of elevator system control is the *destination floor guidance system*. This kind of system uses computer control with artificial intelligence to put riders into the same car who are going to the same floor or to floors near each other. With this system, each rider selects a destination floor in the lobby, either on a wall panel or on a kiosk, and the control system assigns a particular car based on what other riders have selected. Once in the car, the riders do not press any destination buttons; the car stops at the floors that were chosen in the lobby. The system reduces total travel time to the destination floor and results in fewer stops for each car.

Drive Control

An elevator installation contains a *drive control* that controls the speed of the motor that drives the traction machine. There are three basic types of drive controls.

The *unit multivoltage* (UMV) control system, also called the Ward-Leonard control system, uses an alternating current (AC) motor to operate a direct current (DC) generator. The DC current from the generator is then varied to run a DC traction motor. Before the advent of electronic motor control in the 1980s, this was the only way to obtain the precise motor speeds needed for smooth elevator operation. However, the system is noisy, requires three machines, and is subject to high thermal losses and low overall efficiency. Many UMV control systems are still in use, but other systems have become more common in new elevators.

The *silicon-controlled rectifier* (SCR) control system (also called a *thyristor* control system) provides variable DC voltage to a DC traction motor. This system provides good drive and leveling control, but it also has a low power factor and high thermal losses. The older AC system had many disadvantages, and the DC system is now generally used.

The *variable-voltage, variable-frequency* (VVVF) AC control system uses a rectifier and an inverter to convert AC power to DC power and then to variable-voltage, variable-frequency, three-phase AC current. This current controls a standard AC motor, which operates at the speed corresponding to the frequency of the input. The result is very accurate and efficient speed control. The VVVF control system does not have the disadvantages of the thyristor system and is energy efficient. It is useful for elevators of all speeds and travel distances, and maintenance is minimized due to its solid-state design.

Safety Devices

Modern elevators use many safety devices. The main brake on the sheave or motor shaft is normally operated by the control mechanism. If a power failure occurs, the brake is automatically applied. A governor also senses the speed of the car, and if the limit is exceeded, the brake is applied. There is also a safety rail clamp that grips the side rails if there is an emergency. In the pit of the elevator below the lowest landing, car buffers stop a car's motion if it over-travels the lowest stop; however, they are not designed to stop a free-falling elevator cab.

Hoistway door interlocks prevent the elevator from operating unless the hoistway door is closed and locked. In addition, various devices prevent the doors from closing on someone in their path. *Safety edges* are movable strips on the leading edge of the door that activate a switch to reopen the door if something contacts it. Photoelectric devices serve the same purpose. There are also proximity detectors that sense the presence of a person near the door and can stop the closing motion.

To prevent overloading of a car, sensors under the floor detect when the maximum weight is reached by deflection of the floor. This then makes a warning noise with additional loading and prevents the elevator from picking up any more people. Additional safety devices include multiple ropes, escape hatches in the top of the cab, alarm buttons on the car control panel, and telephones for direct communication in an emergency.

In the case of a power failure all cars will stop where they are, but most codes require that emergency power be available to operate at least one car at a time. This allows the unloading of occupied cars. Building codes require that if a fire alarm is activated, all cars return to the lobby without stopping and switch control to manual mode. The cars can then only be operated by fire fighting personnel using a manual key.

Elevators must also be accessible to the physically disabled. In lobbies this usually means visual signals that can be easily seen as well as audible signals indicating car approach, car landing, and directions of approach. Call buttons and raised and braille floor designations must be placed within certain height limitations. There is also a formula for calculating the minimum time between notification that a car has answered a call and the moment the doors of that car start to close, with a minimum time of 5 sec.

Elevator cars themselves must be sized to allow a person in a wheelchair to enter, maneuver within reach of the controls, and exit the car. Minimum clear door opening width is 36 in (915). All car controls must be no higher than 54 in (1370) for side approaches and 48 in (1220) for front approaches. The car controls must be designated by braille and by raised standard alphabet characters. Main entry floor, door open, door closed, emergency alarm, and emergency stop buttons must also be designated by standard raised character symbols.

ELEVATOR DESIGN

In simplest terms, elevator design involves selecting the capacity, speed, and number of elevators to adequately serve a particular building's population and then arranging the location of each elevator bank and the arrangement of the lobby. In addition, the roping method, machine room layout, control system, and cab decoration must be determined.

Capacity and Speed

Determining the number, capacity, and arrangement of elevators to serve a building is a complex process because there is an optimal interrelationship between the number of people to be served in a given time period, the maximum waiting time desired, cost, and particular requirements of the building. For example, a hospital elevator moves large numbers of people but also must have provisions for stretchers and large quantities of supplies. The elevator in a corporate headquarters building may handle a great deal of interfloor traffic, whereas one in an apartment building will primarily move people from the lobby up to their floors and back down again.

For most buildings the *handling capacity*, or number of people to be served, is usually based on a 5-minute peak period. For office buildings, this is usually the time in the morning when everyone is coming to work. The number of people a car can carry is a function of its capacity, which is measured in weight. Through experience, some general guidelines have been established for recommended capacities based on building types and rough building areas. These are shown in Table 44.1.

Table 44.1
Recommended Elevator Capacities

	building size (lbm)			service
building type	small	medium	large	elevator (lbm)
offices	2500/3000	3000/3500	3500/4000	4000–6500
garages	2500	3000	3500	–
retail	3500	3500	4000	4000–8000
hotels	3000	3500	3500	4000
apartments	2000/2500	2500	2500	4000
dormitories	3000	3000	3000	–
senior citizens	2500	2500	2500	4000

The capacities listed in Table 48.1 are in pounds. The equivalent SI units are approximate and are based on 1 kg being equal to 2.2 lbm. The corresponding SI units of elevator capacity are shown in Table 44.2.

The maximum number of passengers in a car is directly related to the capacity in weight. Table 44.3 gives the car passenger capacity based on weight capacity.

General recommended elevator speeds are also available based on the number of floors served and the general size

Table 44.2
Metric Equivalents of Elevator Capacity

capacity (lbm)	standard capacity (kg)
2000	1000
2500	1250
3000	1500
3500	1600
4000	2000
6500	3200
8000	4000

Table 44.3
Car Passenger Capacity

elevator capacity (lbm)	elevator capacity (kg)	maximum passenger capacity
2000	1000	12
2500	1250	17
3000	1500	20
3500	1600	23
4000	2000	28

of the building. The higher speed translates to shorter intervals, or waiting time, but there are some limits due to overall travel distance (number of floors). Higher-speed elevators also generally cost more. Recommended elevator speeds are shown in Table 44.4.

Number of Elevators Required

Based on the car capacity and speed, along with such particular characteristics of the elevator functioning as door opening and closing time, delays at stops, and so forth, the average round trip time can be calculated, and then the handling capacity of one car in a given 5-minute period can be determined. The exact procedure for doing this is complicated and involves probability of number of stops, highest floor reached, and other variables.

The number of elevators required is then found by taking the total number of people to be accommodated in a 5-minute peak period and dividing by the handling capacity of one car. The *interval*, or average waiting time for an elevator to arrive, can then be checked to see if it is acceptable. Recommended intervals vary with the type of building. For diversified offices the time is between 30 and 35 sec. For hotels and apartments it is from 40 to 70 sec or more.

The speeds in Table 44.4 are in feet per minute. The equivalent SI units are approximate and are based on 1 m/s being equal to about 200 ft/min. These are listed in Table 44.5.

Table 44.4
Recommended Elevator Speeds (in ft/min)

number of floors	small	medium	large	service
offices				
2–5	250	300/400	400	200
5–10	400	400	500	300
10–15	400	400/500	500/700	400
15–25	500	500/700	700	500
25–35	–	800/1000	1000	500
35–45	–	1000/1200	1200	700
45–60	–	1200/1400	1400/1600	800
over 60	–	–	1800	800
garages				
2–5	200			
5–10	200–400			
10–15	300–500			
hotels				
2–6	100–300			200
6–12	200–500			300
12–20	400–500			400
20–25	500/700			500
25–30	700/800			500
30–40	700–1000			700
40–50	1000–1200			800
apartments/dormitories, senior citizen housing				
2–6	100			200
6–12	200			200
12–20	300–500			200
20–25	400/500			300
25–30	500			300

Table 44.5
Metric Equivalents of Elevator Speed

speed (fpm)	(m/s)
100	0.5
200	1
250	1.25
300	1.5
400	2
500	2.5
700	3.5
800	4
1000	5
1200	6
1400	7
1600	8
1800	9

Location and Lobby Design

Elevators should be grouped near the center of a building whenever possible. At the lobby level, they should be easily accessible from the entrance and plainly visible from all points of access. In all but the smallest installations, there should be a minimum of two elevators so that one is available if the other is being serviced. Consideration should also be given to obvious traffic generators such as subway entrances, parking garage doors, and the like. Service elevators may be remotely located from passenger elevators as required by the building function.

Elevator lobbies should be designed so that it is easy to see all hall lanterns from one point and to minimize walking distance from any one point to the car that happens to arrive. This is especially important for barrier-free design. Adequate space must also be available so that people can wait without interfering with other circulation. There should never be more than eight cars in a group or more than four cars in a line. Figure 44.2 shows the recommended lobby layouts for various numbers of cars and the minimum space requirements based on the depth of the car.

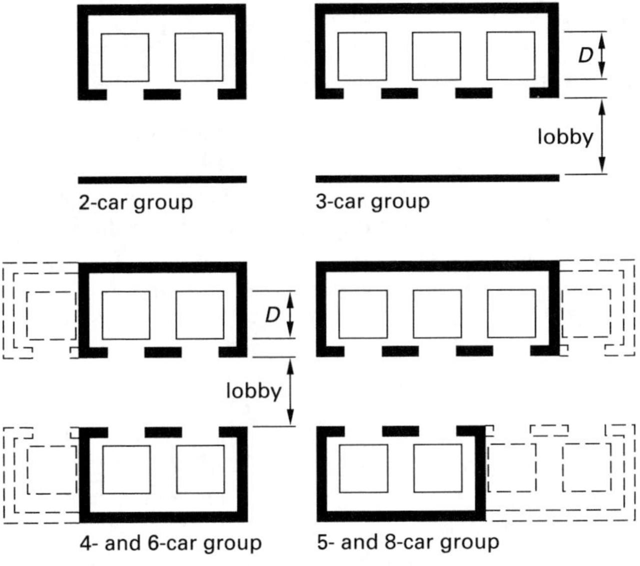

grouping	relative to D	but no less than	other
2 car	D		
3 car	$1.5 \times D$	6 ft (1800)	
4 car	1.5 to $2 \times D$	10 ft (3000)	4 cars in line $1.5 \times D$, min. 8 ft (2400)
5 car	1.5 to $2 \times D$	10 ft (3000)	
6 car	1.75 to $2 \times D$	10 ft (3000)	
8 car	$2 \times D$	max. 14 ft (4200)	lobby open both ends

Note: Maximum of 5′0″ (1500) from center line of lobby to wall for barrier-free design

Figure 44.2 Elevator Lobby Space Requirements

As buildings get taller and larger, the number of elevators required to adequately serve all floors increases, and the proportion of elevator shaft area to total floor area increases beyond economic levels. In addition, it becomes impossible for a single elevator to serve more than about 12 to 15 floors without exceeding acceptable waiting and total travel times. To solve these problems, several methods of elevatoring have been developed.

The first method simply divides the total number of elevators into banks that serve separate zones of the building. For example, the first bank may serve floors 1 through 14 while the second bank serves the lobby floor and floors 14 through 28. Additional banks can be added for taller buildings. Although this method keeps waiting and total travel times at acceptable levels, the elevator shafts still take up considerable floor space, especially on the lower floors.

The second method is the sky lobby concept. One or more intermediate lobbies are placed in very tall buildings and large capacity, high-speed elevators take people from the first floor lobby to the sky lobby where they transfer to elevators serving the upper floors. This method reduces the amount of space occupied by elevators, because the shafts do not extend the full height of the building. It also works well for multi-occupancy buildings such as those with apartments, offices, and parking.

The third method uses stacked, or double-deck, elevator cabs. At the main terminal level, traffic going to even-numbered floors is directed to one floor, and traffic going to odd-numbered floors is directed to an adjacent floor. This method effectively doubles shaft capacity, reducing the area required for elevators while decreasing the number of local stops.

Doors

Doors are an important part of elevator design because of their effect on passenger convenience and round-trip time. If a car makes 10 stops on a trip, a difference in opening and closing time of only $^1/_2$ sec can add 10 sec to the interval time and make an otherwise satisfactory design unacceptable. Doors can be either center opening or side opening and single speed or two speed. Single-speed, center-opening doors are common and allow faster passenger loading and unloading than do side-opening doors.

Two-speed, side-opening doors have two leaves, one of which telescopes past the other as they move. Two-speed, center-opening doors have four leaves. The minimum opening width is 3 ft 6 in (1070), but 4 ft 0 in (1220) is better because it allows two people to easily and quickly enter or leave at the same time.

Machine Rooms

Machine rooms are best located directly above the hoistway and must provide adequate space for the motor, sheave, brake, controller board, speed governor, floor selector mechanism, and motor generator. All of these require minimum clearances for servicing and access. The exact size varies with manufacturer and type of elevator, but in general the machine room must be about as wide as the hoistway and from 12 ft to 16 ft (3660 to 4880) deeper than the hoistway.

Minimum ceiling height ranges from 7 ft 6 in (2290) to over 10 ft 0 in (3050). In addition to this dimension, the distance from the floor of the top landing to the underside of the machine room floor can be substantial, from about 15 ft to 30 ft (4570 to 9140) depending on the type, speed, and capacity of the elevator.

FREIGHT ELEVATORS

Freight elevators are designed and intended to transport only equipment and materials and those passengers needed to handle the freight. Elevator codes classify these elevators into five groups: A, B, C1, C2, and C3. Class A is for general freight, and no item can exceed one-fourth of the rated capacity of the elevator. The rating cannot be less than 50 lbm/ft^2 (240 kg/m^2) of platform area. *Class B* elevators are those used for motor vehicle loading and are rated at no less than 30 lbm/ft^2 (150 kg/m^2). *Class C* elevators are for industrial truck loading based on 50 lbm/ft^2 (240 kg/m^2). Class C1 includes the truck; Class C2 does not include the truck; and Class C3 is for concentrated loading with the truck not carried and with increments greater than 25% rated capacity.

Freight elevators are commonly available in capacities from 2500 lbm to 8000 lbm (1250 kg to 4000 kg), with some multiple-ram hydraulic elevators capable of lifting up to 100,000 lbm (50 000 kg). Speeds range from 50 fpm to 200 fpm (0.25 m/s to 1 m/s), with speeds up to 800 fpm (4 m/s) available for very tall buildings. With freight elevators, interval time is not as important as capacity, so the speeds are much less than those of passenger elevators.

ESCALATORS

Escalators are very efficient devices for transporting large numbers of people from one level to another. They are also useful for directing the flow of traffic.

Escalators are rated by speed and size. The industry standard speed is 100 fpm (0.5 m/s). A second speed of 120 fpm (0.6 m/s) is available for transportation and sports facilities but is not used often in other applications. Three sizes are available: 32, 40, and 48 in (800, 1000, and 1200).

The actual tread widths of these sizes are 24, 32, and 40 in (600, 800, and 1000), respectively. Because the 40 in size does not increase the capacity of a 32 in escalator in actual use, the two most common sizes are 32 in and 48 in (800 and 1200).

The actual observed capacity of people using escalators is somewhat less than the theoretical maximum capacity. This is because under crowded conditions, people tend to space themselves on every other step on 32 in models and on an average of every step on 48 in models. Observed capacity ranges from 2300 people per hour for a 32 in escalator to 4500 people per hour for a 48 in model.

Escalators are housed in a trussed assembly set at a 30° angle. The motors, drives, and other mechanisms extend below the treads and floor at both the top and bottom of the assembly, so this must be taken into account when calculating head height clearance and floor-to-floor heights. See Fig. 44.3.

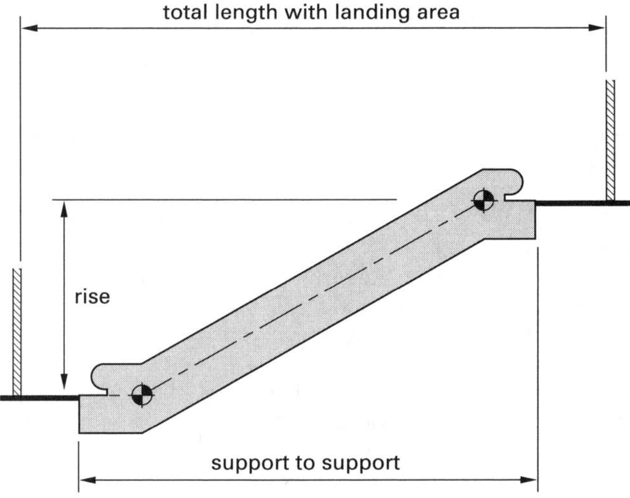

Figure 44.3 Escalator Configuration

When more than two floors are to be served by escalators, how to arrange the units can become a more complicated decision for the designer. The various possible arrangements have different advantages and disadvantages.

There are two basic arrangements. In a *crisscross arrangement*, the up and down escalators between each pair of floors form an X when viewed in elevation. This separates the entrances to the up and down escalators from a floor, which sometimes leads to confusion for riders. In a *parallel arrangement*, the up and down escalators between each pair of floors are parallel to each other, and the entrances to the up and down escalators from a floor are side by side. Each of these arrangements has two variations.

The *crisscross spiral arrangement* is the most common. After exiting at one floor, the rider makes a simple U-turn to enter the escalator that continues to the next floor. This reduces travel time for trips of two or more floors.

The *crisscross walkaround arrangement* places all the up escalators above each other and all the down escalators above each other. After exiting at one floor, the rider must walk around to the other side of the escalator area to enter the escalator that continues to the next floor. This lengthens any trip of two or more floors, but is sometimes used in retail stores so that riders will pass more displays of merchandise as they travel.

Both types of crisscross arrangement take up a total width on each floor equal to the width of two escalators.

In the *parallel spiral arrangement*, the rider can reach the escalator that continues to the next floor with a simple U-turn. This arrangement is the only one that has both advantages of reducing travel time for longer trips and placing entrances to up and down escalators near each other. But as the entrances and exits of four escalators must therefore be side by side, this arrangement requires a total width of four escalators.

The *stacked parallel arrangement* also forces the rider to walk around to the other side of the escalator area to continue to the next floor, but this arrangement takes up the width of only two escalators instead of four.

STAIRS AND RAMPS

Stairs are one of the most basic types of vertical circulation—as old as buildings themselves. Because they affect the safety of all buildings in which they are used, they must be designed correctly.

Stairways may be classified into two broad categories: those used for strictly utilitarian purposes, such as exit stairs, and monumental stairs designed to be a prominent design feature as well as provide vertical access. Whichever type is used, there are common design features that must be incorporated. This section elaborates on some of the basic building code requirements given in Ch. 55.

A stair's design and detailing begins with deciding on its basic configuration and shape, the approximate amount of space it requires, and the geometry of its layout. Some of the most common configurations are shown in Fig. 44.4. Each of these types has many variations. For example, a simple straight-run stair may be enclosed or partially open, it may be interrupted with several landings, or the landings may project from the face of the open side of the stair. L-shaped stairs can have equal or unequal legs.

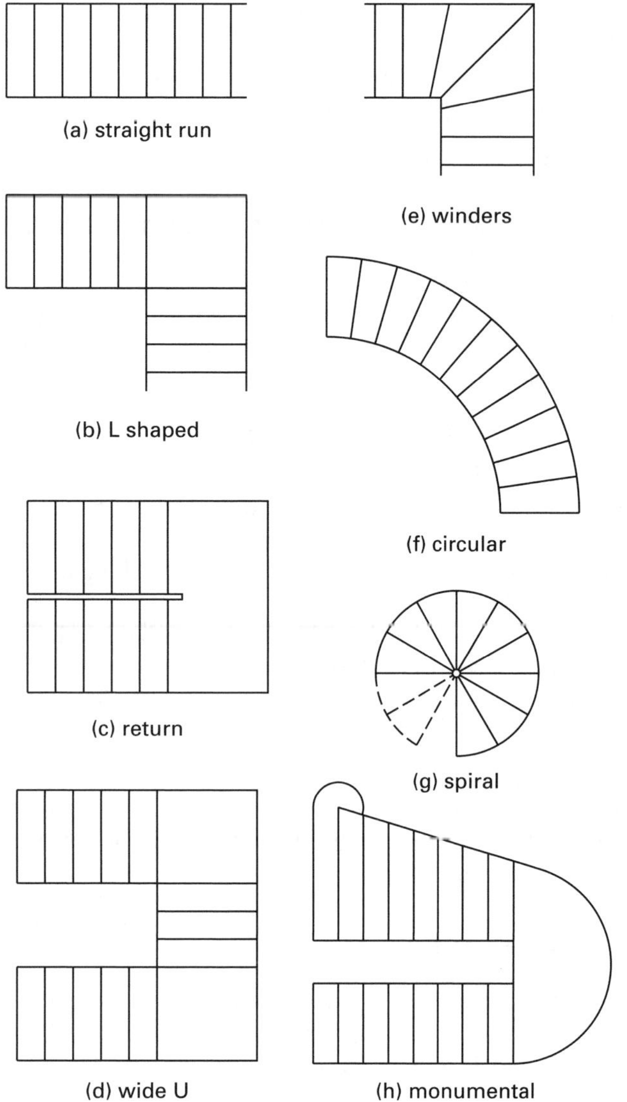

Figure 44.4 Basic Stair Configurations

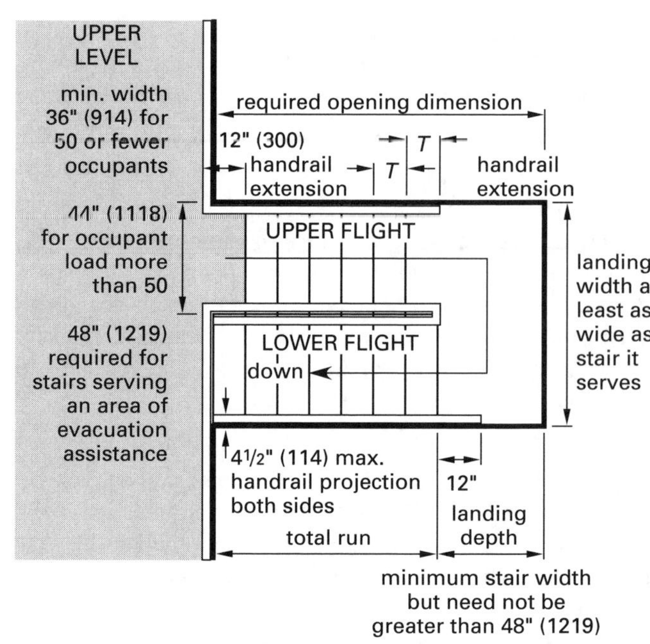

Figure 44.5 Stair Planning Guidelines

Once the basic configuration of a stairway has been determined, the width, total run, and landing depths and widths determine how much space is required. Figure 44.5 shows the minimum dimensions for laying out a stairway in plan view, including a landing. The total run depends on the depth of the treads and the number of risers and landings that will be used.

The minimum width of any stair is 36 in (914), or 44 in (1118) when the occupant load exceeds 50. Handrails may project a maximum of $4^1/_2$ in (114) on both sides of a stairway.

In addition to the requirements shown in Fig. 44.5, building codes limit the use of special types of stairs. These include winding, circular, and spiral stairways. They are only allowed as private stairways in homes, apartments, condominiums, and the like.

Winding stairways have tapered treads that are wider at one end than at the other. See Fig. 44.6(a). When circular stairways have a smaller radius than is required by code, they are classed as winding stairways. When winders are used they should all be the same shape and size.

Circular stairways have sides shaped as a circular arc. The inside, smaller arc cannot be less than twice the width of the stair. See Fig. 44.6(b). If it is, the stairway is considered a winding stairway.

Spiral stairs use wedge-shaped treads that radiate from a center support column, as shown in Fig. 44.6(c). The allowable riser height is greater than for other stairs; it must be enough to provide a minimum headroom height of 6 ft 6 in (1981) but cannot be greater than $9^1/_2$ in (241).

For enclosed exit stairways with doors adjacent to landings, the codes require that the door not intrude into the required exit path more than a certain distance, either as the door is opening or when the door is fully opened. IBC requirements are shown in Fig. 44.7. Although the dimensions in Fig. 44.7 do not include any allowance for evacuation assistance space, if it is required, these areas are normally provided in the building exit stairways.

The basic design and code requirements for vertical dimensions of stairs are shown in Fig. 55.8 along with the related discussion in that chapter.

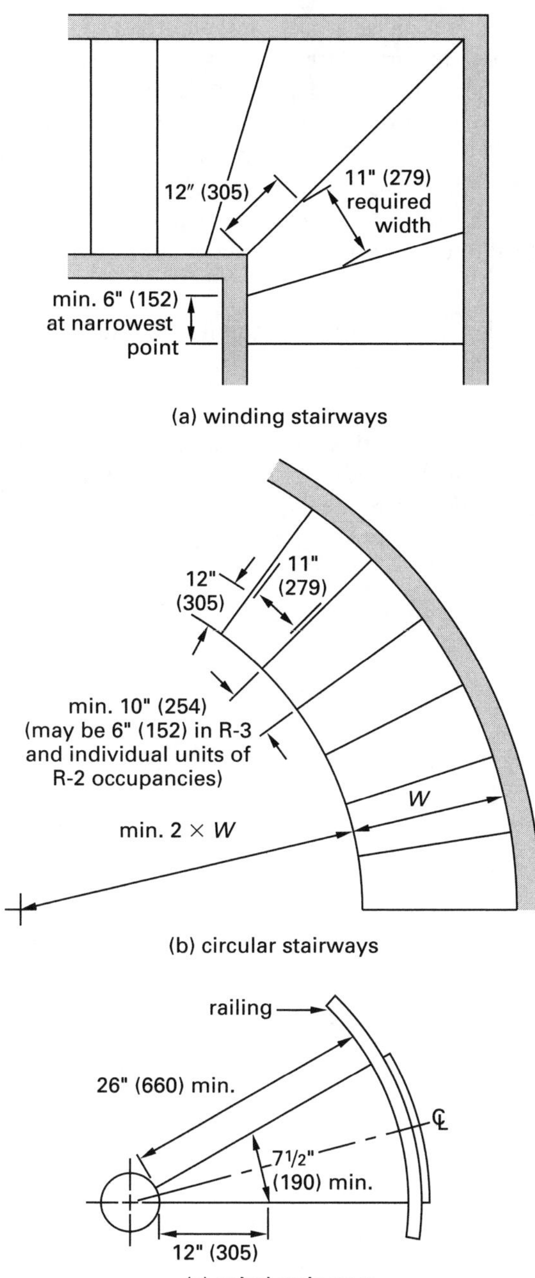

Figure 44.6 Building Code Requirements for Nonstraight Stairs

Extensive research has determined the best dimensions for the rise and treads of stairs and the safest and most comfortable proportion between the two. The maximum rise and minimum tread dimensions of 7 in and 11 in (178 and 279), respectively, represent some of the most current research, including considerations for the physically disabled. Some researchers recommend that treads be even wider, from 12 in to 14 in (305 to 356). The tread of a stair is considered the horizontal projection of the distance from the edge of one nosing to the next. It does not include any part of the tread under the nosing.

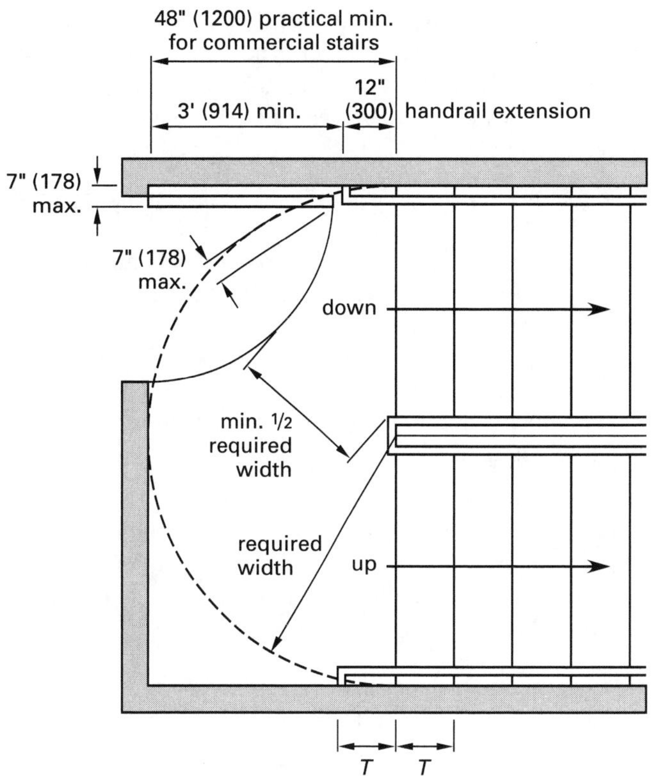

Figure 44.7 IBC Requirements for Enclosed Exit Stairs

Because stair dimensions are based on the normal stride of a person while ascending and descending a stair, various formulas have been used to determine one dimension based on the other. For example, a formula can be used to determine the total number of stairs when the total rise is known and the number of risers must be a whole number without exceeding 7 in or 8 in (178 or 203) on private stairways. Some of these formulas include the following (where R equals riser height and T equals tread depth).

$$2R + T = 25 \qquad 44.1$$

$$RT = 75 \qquad 44.2$$

$$R + T = 17 \qquad 44.3$$

$$T = 20 - \frac{4R}{3} \qquad 44.4$$

Some of these formulas are rather old and represent proportions that were comfortable for people who, on average, were slightly smaller than the average size of people today. Equation 44.1, for example, was developed in the seventeenth century and originally stipulated that twice the riser plus the tread be between 24 and 25. Now the minimum should be 25 and may be increased to 26. Of the four formulas, Eq. 44.1 gives the widest tread based on a given riser height if the value of 25 is used, and can be used in most designs. A wider tread is generally the safest, especially when descending.

The total run of a stair is calculated by taking the total rise in inches (mm) and dividing by an estimated riser height, usually 7 in (178). If the result is not a whole number, the required number of risers is the next highest whole number. This number is then divided into the total rise to obtain the actual required riser height. The number of treads for a straight-run stair is one less than the number of risers, and this number is multiplied by the tread dimension to obtain the total required run.

The maximum distance between landings is 12 ft (3660); however, some research suggests that 9 ft (2740) is a better dimension, especially for the physically disabled. The top and bottom treads should have contrasting strips at nosings for visually impaired people.

Tread design is an especially important part of stair design. The important parts of treads include their depth, material, and nosing design. The depth of treads must be enough to provide safe footing for both ascending and descending as discussed previously. The material should be a nonslip surface, but not so rough that people get their feet caught on the nosing when descending. Any nonslip material designed into the nosing should be level with the rest of the tread.

Safe and accessible design requires that nosings not be abrupt and that they have a maximum rounded edge of $^1/_2$ in (13).

Ramps are another type of vertical transportation used for minor transitions between floor levels. The requirements for ramps are covered in Ch. 56.

45 SOLVING THE ACCESSIBILITY/RAMP VIGNETTE

The Accessibility/Ramp vignette tests the candidate's understanding of accessibility requirements as they relate to the design of ramp and stair systems. A base plan, program, and code requirements are given, and the candidate must design a stair and ramp system connecting two or three floor elevations.

TIPS FOR COMPLETING THE ACCESSIBILITY/RAMP VIGNETTE

This vignette requires the candidate to design a ramp and stair system to connect two levels. It also requires the placement of an accessible exit doorway. There are usually several possible solutions to this problem. The important grading points include not exceeding the ramp slope; providing handrails (and guards) where required, with the proper extensions; maintaining minimum exit widths on both ramp and stair; including doors with the correct maneuvering clearances and swinging in the correct direction; maintaining accessible landing and turnaround dimensions (60 in [1525]); and maintaining accessibility to "leftover" spaces not used by the ramp or stair.

Use the following suggestions to generate a passing solution.

- Begin work by determining the length of ramp needed based on the given elevation change, using a slope of 1:12. By comparing this distance with the available space on the vignette (including one or more 60 in [1525] landings), it will be obvious if the ramp can be done in a single run (unlikely) or whether a switchback or L-shaped system will be required. Remember that if the code information states that the maximum total rise can only be 30 in (760) and the upper level is more than that, an intermediate landing will have to be provided, even if there is enough space for a single run of ramp.
- Before drawing the stairs, calculate how many risers will be needed. As the stairs are drawn, the tread depth will be automatically calculated and will display at the bottom of the screen.
- Avoid using angled stairs or ramps. Even if there is sufficient space for them, angled stairs or ramps would take too long to work out correctly.
- Do not overdesign by using two stairs or ramps when only one is required.
- Try to keep the access to the bottom of the stairs close to the ramp.
- Be sure to project handrails 12 in (305) beyond the tops and bottoms of ramps and stairs. Use sketch circles to help position the ends of the handrails.
- Handrails may project into the required ramp width by 4 in (101) on either side.
- Handrails may project into a 5 ft by 5 ft (1525 by 1525) space, but only if they are attached to a wall.
- Do not include more than two landings for the ramp design.
- Provide for maneuvering clearances on both the push and pull sides of doors. This element is easy to forget when time gets short. Provide 18 in (445) on the pull side of the door on the jamb strike and 12 in (305) on the push side, with a full 60 in (1525) in front of the pull side. Refer to the diagram given with the vignette's code information. Draw sketch rectangles first as a reminder of the required space adjacent to doors.
- If the problem requires the placement of an additional set of exit doors and the existing doors are double doors, place another set of double doors (not

a single door). In this case, assume that the existing double doors are required for exit width.

- When designing the ramp, work in full feet or inches so it will be easy to calculate rise and run under time pressure. For example, it is more difficult to calculate the required rise with a run of 15 ft 4 in (4675) than with a run of 15 ft (4570).
- If there is leftover space not used by the ramp or stair, make sure it is accessible by making it at least 36 in (915) wide.

SOLVING THE STAIR DESIGN VIGNETTE

46

The Stair Design vignette tests the candidate's understanding of the three-dimensional nature of stair design and of the basic functional and code issues involved. The vignette presents two background floor plans, a building section, a program, and code requirements, and the candidate must complete a floor plan with a stair system.

TIPS FOR COMPLETING THE STAIR DESIGN VIGNETTE

This vignette tests a candidate's ability to design a code-compliant stair—including landings, headroom clearances, handrails, and guards—between two or three levels while incorporating elements of accessibility. Specific code requirements are given in the program along with two background floor plans and a reference building section. Part of satisfying the code involves determining the required exit width based on occupant load and comparing this with other exit width parameters.

In some cases it is possible to see the entire stair system from the upper level. In that case no drawing of the lower level is necessary. If any portion of the stair goes under the upper landing or under any other portion of the system, then show the lower level with a cut line and the upper level with a cut line to the same run of stairs. Also, stop the railing at the cut line.

In order to solve this vignette the candidate should be familiar with the basic elements of a code-compliant stair. These include the following.

- The first step in solving the vignette is to determine if the minimum width is governed by occupant load. If the vignette states that the total occupant load is served by two exits, first divide the total by one half, and then multiply by the factor given in the code information. Compare this dimension with 44 in (118) and 48 in (1220) as described next.
- To summarize, the minimum width of stairs is determined by the largest of the following.
  - the width determined by calculation based on occupant load
  - the minimum width of 44 in (1118)
  - the minumum width of 48 in (1220) between handrails for an accessible exit when serving an area of refuge, plus an 8 in (203) allowance for handrails on both sides (4 in [102] each side), for a total of 56 in (1422)
- Before drawing the stairs, calculate how many risers will be needed. As the stairs are drawn, the tread depth is automatically calculated and displayed at the bottom of the screen.
- Stairways serving an occupant load of more than 50 must be at least 44 in (1118) wide or as wide as determined by multiplying the occupant load by 0.3 (or some other factor as defined by the code). 0.3 is the factor commonly given in the vignette sample code requirements. The greater of the two values governs unless the accessible requirement (as described next) results in a greater value.
- If the stairway is an accessible stairway that serves areas of refuge (as it typically would be on the ARE), there must be a minimum width of 48 in (1220) between handrails. Allowance for handrails must be added to this width. Although adding 3 in (915) on either side is sufficient, this vignette typically makes reference to a maximum 4 in (102) projection, so an accessible stair in this vignette should have a minimum of 56 in (1422) between walls or edges of stairs to allow for 4 in (102) of handrails on both sides.

- Maximum riser height is 7 in (178). Minimum riser height is 4 in (102).
- Minimum tread depth is 11 in (279).
- Riser height cannot vary within any flight of stairs. A flight of stairs is any run of stairs between landings.
- When landings are provided they must be at least as wide as the stairs. The depth of each landing must be at least as wide as the stairs but need not be more than 48 in (1219).
- When a door opens on a landing, it cannot reduce the required width of the landing by more than half.
- Handrails are required on *both* sides of the stair. If the stair exceeds 60 in (1524) in width, an intermediate handrail must be provided.
- Handrails must either be continuous between flights of stairs or return to a wall, a guard, or the walking surface.
- When handrails are not continuous, they must extend a minimum of 12 in (305) beyond the last riser at the top of the stairway and a distance of 12 in (305) plus the depth of one tread at the bottom of the stairway. However, the ARE vignette typically only requires a 12 in (305) extension at *both* the top and the bottom.
- Handrails must be spaced a minimum of $1^1/_2$ in (38) from the walls to which they are attached.
- The minimum headroom height of all parts of a stairway cannot be less than 80 in (2032) as measured vertically from the tread nosing or from any floor surface, including landings.
- The maximum distance between landings is 12 ft (3658) measured vertically.
- Remember that the occupant load of the lowest floor will determine the minimum width of clear path to reach the exit door on that level.
- Do not forget to provide maneuvering clearance at the strike jambs of doors: 18 in (457) on the pull side and 12 in (305) on the push side. Draw sketch rectangles as a reminder to help maintain the required clearances.
- Structure is not a consideration in this vignette, so stairs may be placed anywhere and in any configuration (straight only), with the assumption that they would be supported.
- In the problem statement, carefully read the requirements for stairway risers. If the problem states that there shall be no variation in any riser height or tread depth within the *complete stairway system*, this means that all risers and treads must have exactly the same dimensions. If the code information states that risers and treads must be the same in any flight of stairs, the riser height and tread depth between landings can be varied. In most cases, the given elevations between floors will be in even feet or half feet, or some multiple of 7 in (178). Calculate the number of risers required by dividing the total rise by either 6 in (152) or 7 in (178). The program automatically calculates the tread depth as the stairs are drawn.
- If a portion of the lower stair is under a landing or another stair, be sure to include the depth of the stair structure when calculating clearance below the stair. This depth is typically 12 in (300), to make calculations easier.
- Make sure the area of refuge is a clear space between handrails, guards, or any other obstructions.
- Remember that the top and bottom elevations of stairs must be shown along with the elevation of every landing. Even if the elevations are identical (which they should be), they must all be shown.

47 SOLVING THE ROOF PLAN VIGNETTE

The Roof Plan vignette requires that the candidate demonstrate an understanding of basic concepts related to roof design by completing the roof plan for a small building. The vignette presents a base plan of a roof, a background floor plan, and a program. The candidate must complete the roof plan by indicating slopes, directions, and elevations, along with the locations of roof accessories and equipment.

TIPS FOR COMPLETING THE ROOF PLAN VIGNETTE

This vignette requires the candidate to plan for the drainage of water on a fairly small building and add various roof features as required by the program. The roof plan can be one of the more difficult vignettes because there are so many elements, each of which must be properly placed in relation to the others. For this reason, it may make sense to do this vignette first in the section.

Following are some suggestions to help with this vignette.

- In designing the roof planes and determining elevations, start with the minimum height of the ceiling of the lower floor and work upward, adding roof structure thickness, slopes, and clerestory heights as required until the uppermost elevation is reached. Keep the total roof height to a minimum.
- Using sketch paper or sketch tools, draw a simple building elevation. This will help with the visualization of spot elevations and slope relationships (to each other and to the other requirements).
- Remember that arrows indicating slope should point in the direction of the *downward* slope.
- The roof edges above and below the clerestory must be parallel and horizontal, not sloped.
- Draw the roof planes within the building envelope, and place the gutters just outside of the building envelope. Use the *check* tool to make sure all roof planes are within the building envelope.
- Provide plumbing vents at every wall where there are fixtures.
- Be sure to place flashing around chimneys as well as around the clerestory and other intersections of roof and exterior walls.
- Unless the gutter is very short (say less than 10 ft [3 m]), show two downspouts on each end of the gutter. If the downspouts are located at the ends of gutters, they will probably be out of the way of windows as required by the program.
- Ensure that all rooms are provided with natural light. This usually means locating skylights over some interior rooms, except those that the program specifically excludes.

SECTION 8: CONSTRUCTION DOCUMENTS & SERVICES

Chapter 48: Construction Drawings and Details
Chapter 49: The Project Manual and Specifications
Chapter 50: The Primary Contractual Documents
Chapter 51: Bidding Procedures and Documents
Chapter 52: Construction Administration Services
Chapter 53: Project and Practice Management
Chapter 54: Solving the Building Section Vignette

48 CONSTRUCTION DRAWINGS AND DETAILS

Construction drawings represent the architect's final decisions concerning design, building methods, and construction technology. As such, they must show the technically correct ways of meeting the functional requirements of the design, such as keeping water out, distributing electricity, providing safe finishes, and satisfying thousands of other concerns. They must also clearly communicate the information to the contractor, material suppliers, and other people involved with the project. Finally, they must be coordinated with the specifications and the consultant's drawings. The drawings form part of the contract and are legal documents.

This chapter reviews some of the functional criteria for selecting materials and evaluating or developing details based on design development decisions and drawings. Whereas other chapters examine specific materials and construction techniques, this chapter takes a broader look at building technology. It also reviews some of the essentials in assembling a set of construction drawings and making sure they are correctly coordinated with the consultant's drawings and with the project specifications. Thorough coordination is vital in avoiding errors, cost overruns, and scheduling delays, as well as minimizing the architect's exposure to liability.

DEVELOPING AND EVALUATING CONSTRUCTION DETAILS

A building is a complex collection of component parts, all of which are connected to other parts in various ways. The manner in which an assembly of several parts is organized and connected is commonly referred to as a detail. A detail may be as simple as two bricks connected with a mortar joint or as complex as the intersection of a curtain wall, roof, ceiling, structural beam, and parapet consisting of dozens of different materials.

There are certain common functional characteristics involved with almost every category of construction detail, and the correctness of the assembly can be developed or evaluated based on these characteristics. For example, the intersection of a roof and a parapet must be designed to fulfill several functions, one of which is to drain water and avoid leakage into the structure. This holds true regardless of the roofing material or the method of wall construction. Different materials may influence certain aspects of the detail, but the intersection will always need a cant strip and positive drainage, and material expansion and contraction must be taken into account.

The following parameters cover most of the common characteristics that must be considered in a construction assembly's design or evaluation. Of course, not all of them relate to every detail, but combined with the specific information on materials given in other chapters, they should help candidates to make rational evaluations during the examination.

Compatibility with Design Intent

All building configuration begins with the desire to satisfy the program requirements and specific needs arising from these requirements. These needs and requirements must be balanced against practical considerations such as code requirements, cost, and material limitations, but even with these types of constraints there are many ways to design. Sometimes, during the long process of design and detailing, the original design intent gets lost in the practicalities of solving functional problems and making changes. A detail may work but may not look like what the client and designer originally intended.

Simple performance requirements can also be involved. This is simply the ability of the product to do its intended job. For instance, how well does an acoustical ceiling absorb sound? How slip resistant is a floor tile? In many cases, the criteria of performance can be judged against a standard test procedure.

The architect should constantly check the development of a detail against its original purpose, performance requirements, and desired appearance. For example, a client might have originally requested a simple, unobtrusive demountable partition system. Through material selection, cost analysis, and integration with other building systems, the final product may satisfy the requirements of demountability, sound transmission, cost, and finish, but may not have the clean, simple look the client wanted.

Structural Integrity

Structural integrity refers to the ability of a material or construction component to withstand the forces applied to it. These include not only the obvious natural forces of gravity, snow, wind, and seismic loading, but also other forces such as impact. The particular type of detail will determine what kinds of forces the detail must resist, and each force should be reviewed.

Some possible common forces on a detail are the following.

- live and dead loads
- wind loads
- seismic loads
- hydrostatic pressure
- forces induced by building movement
- loads induced by human use (for example, the forces produced on a door jamb through the hinge from door operation)
- loads created by one material acting as the substrate for another
- forces caused by accidental or intentional abuse
- strength properties of a material or assembly that may be necessary to resist various forces including compression, tension, shear, torsion, rupture, hardness, and impact

Safety

There are many aspects to safety, which is one of the most important elements of detailing, because the architect is responsible for protecting the health, safety, and welfare of the public. Be aware of safety concerns such as the following.

- *Structural safety*. Will the material or detail physically collapse or otherwise fail, causing harm?
- *Fire safety*. Is the material fire resistant enough for its intended use? Will it produce smoke or toxic fumes if burned? If it burns, will its failure lead to failure of adjacent construction?
- *Safety with human contact*. Is there a potential for harm when people come in contact with the material or detail? For example, will sharp edges cut people, wet floors promote slipping, or poorly designed stairs cause falls?

Security

Security is an important aspect of design today. Security can be viewed as providing protection against theft, vandalism, intentional physical harm, or a combination of all three. Common security concerns include residential and commercial burglary, employee pilferage, vandalism, sabotage or theft of company records and property, confinement of prisoners, protection of personnel, safety and confinement in psychiatric wards, abduction, and in extreme instances, terrorism.

In addition to physical barriers, security systems include methods for preventing entry, detecting intruders, controlling access to secure areas, and notification in the event of unauthorized entry or other emergencies. Refer to Ch. 32 for information on the many types of security devices.

Although the security consultant, equipment vendor, electrical engineering consultant, and contractor are responsible for designing and installing security systems and the power they need to operate, the architect is the person who must coordinate the efforts of the design team so their work fits within the overall design and construction of the project. Some of the important elements of security system coordination that may be included on the drawings and in the specifications include the following.

- Lighting required for surveillance and deterrence should be compatible with the general ambient lighting whenever possible. The electrical engineer or lighting designer should know what types of cameras are being used, in order to select the best lighting types. Lighting positions and details are shown on the architectural drawings, but detailed circuiting drawings will be produced by the electrical engineer.
- The architect must show on the architectural drawings adequate space and support for video cameras, monitors, access devices, controls, and other equipment. The actual electrical and signal circuiting will be shown on the electrical drawings.
- Conduit must be shown on the electrical consultant's drawings to accommodate signal system wiring, electric lock wiring, telecommunication wiring, and other wiring that may be provided by a separate contractor.

- Speakers that are required for public address and communication within secured areas should be shown on the architectural drawings and coordinated with other elements on the reflected ceiling plan.
- Power transfers for doors should be specified to met the necessary level of security, but should be concealed whenever possible.

Durability and Maintainability

Most building materials and details are subject to a wide range of abuses from both natural forces and human use. To the greatest extent possible, they must be able to withstand this abuse and be maintained and repaired throughout their lifetimes.

Exterior materials must have resistance to ultraviolet radiation, temperature changes, pollution, water, and atmospheric corrosion. Materials and details within human reach must be resistant to scratching and abrasion, impact, and marking.

All details must be maintainable. Can a material be cleaned easily? How will it look if it is not regularly maintained? How costly will the maintenance be? Can part of a detail be easily replaced or repaired?

Code Requirements

Of course, all details and building components must satisfy the requirements of the local building code and other statutory regulations. Checking for compliance should be an automatic reaction when developing or reviewing construction drawings. Many of these requirements have been discussed in other chapters, with reference to specific materials and areas of construction.

Construction Trade Sequence

Because all building requires the involvement of many trades and material suppliers, the best details are those that allow for construction to proceed directly from one trade to another in a timely fashion. Because labor is one of the biggest expenses of a building project, anything that can be done to minimize it saves money (within the bounds of adequate craftsmanship, of course). Organizing the detailing of a building to allow for a clear division of the labor trades can minimize interference and potential conflicts.

Each detail should be reviewed to see if its construction can proceed from one trade to another with the least amount of overlap. For example, in building a standard partition, the drywallers can install the metal framing. Then the electricians and plumbers can install conduit and piping. Then the drywallers can return, finish the wall, and leave, making way for the painters. Partition details that deviate from this standard sequence will take more time to complete and will be more costly.

Fabrication and Installation Methods

All construction details should be reviewed to ensure that they do not present building problems, such as limitations on the size and shape of assemblies due to transportation restrictions, the inability to move materials into proper position, installation difficulties, and interference with connections or construction. For example, swinging a steel beam into position and then having enough room to tighten the bolts requires certain minimum clearances. Installing a door frame in an opening requires shim space to compensate for possible deviations in plumb of the rough door opening.

Tolerances

All elements of construction are built to a different closeness to perfection. This level of perfection is typically represented by the lines and dimensions on the construction drawings. The amount of allowable variance from a given line, dimension, or size is known as *tolerance* and must be accounted for in detailing. Some construction items, such as woodwork, have a very small tolerance, sometimes as small as $^1/_{64}$ in (0.4), whereas other elements, such as poured concrete footings, may be oversized by as much as 2 in (51) and still be acceptable.

Tolerances for a great many construction components have been established by various trade organizations and are the accepted norms unless the architect specifies otherwise. However, requiring tighter tolerances than is industry standard usually requires better materials, more time, more labor, or a combination of all three. These also mean a higher cost.

Details should allow for expected tolerances. For example, a finished wood-panel wall installed over cast concrete must have enough space for shimming and blocking so that the final wall surface can be plumb, whereas the rough structural wall may be out of plumb by as much as $^1/_4$ in in a 10 ft height (6 in a 3050 height).

Clearances

A *clearance* is a gap or space designed to allow for the construction or installation of a material, construction element, or piece of equipment. Details must provide enough clearance to make construction possible. For example, the shim space around doors and windows is provided so the door or window unit can be slipped into the rough opening and leveled and plumbed before being attached to the framing. Structural steel connections made with bolts require sufficient room so an ironworker can use a pneumatic impact wrench.

Costs

There are three major elements of cost involved with building: materials, labor, and equipment. Other costs are overhead and contractor profit, which represent the initial costs of the structure and may change as the other costs fluctuate. However, there are life-cycle costs with which the architect and client must be concerned. What may be a low initial cost of an assembly may end up being a very expensive detail to maintain and ultimately replace. Refer to Ch. 30 for information on life-cycle cost analysis.

Cost control involves striking the proper balance between client needs, initial costs, and life-cycle costs. The client may want more than is affordable or may ask for the lowest initial costs without realizing that inexpensive materials will cost more in the long run. If the building is a speculative venture, low initial costs may be acceptable to the developer regardless of the consequences. It is up to the architect to make sure the client understands all the choices and ramifications of design and detailing decisions.

The cost of a portion of a building in proportion to the total cost is also an important concept to understand. If the entire building is going to cost $2 million, it does not make sense to spend a great deal of time and worry over saving $100 on one detail. On the other hand, if extensive research and study on a typical wall detail of the same building can save $30,000, then it is reasonable to make the effort. In another situation, saving a little money on quantity items is desirable. If just $100 can be trimmed from the construction of one hotel room, then saving this amount on a 2000-room hotel will add up to $200,000.

Of course, cost is directly related to the choice of materials, which is a function of the intended use, durability, strength, maintainability, and all the other considerations involved with designing a detail. Labor cost is largely determined by the effort required to build a detail so that, in general, construction costs can be minimized by developing simple details that still satisfy all other criteria. Equipment costs involve the purchase or rental of specialized machinery needed to build the project. Prefabricated concrete components may require large, expensive cranes to set them in place, but this cost may be more than offset by the savings in formwork and time delays involved with cast-in-place concrete.

Material Availability

Construction is a geographically localized industry. Not only does labor availability vary with location, but many different materials are found in different parts of the country. Of course, any material can be shipped anywhere else, but the cost may not be justified. Specifying southern pine for rough framing in Oregon does not make sense. Steel framing may be less expensive than concrete in parts of the country that are near mills, whereas the same steel building would be prohibitively expensive in other locales where concrete would be the logical choice.

Building Movement and Substrate Attachment

Because all details consist of a number of components connected with each other, it is important to understand that one material must provide an appropriate base for the attachment of another. This attachment may be done in one of three ways. The first is rigid, such as plaster fixed to lath: if one material moves, both move. The second is rigid but adjustable for installation, such as a curtain wall anchored to a floor beam. The third is flexible so that movement is allowed. An expansion joint is a typical example of this attachment.

Within each detail there must be space for the attaching device as well as clearance for workers. Problems with incompatible materials must also be considered, such as possible galvanic action or deterioration of one material from water leakage through another. If the materials are chemically bonded with sealants, mastics, paint, or other coatings, the base material must be compatible with the coating or the joining material.

In all cases, the detail must provide for expected building movement as discussed in other chapters. Movement is inevitable, whether it is from live, dead, or lateral loading; temperature changes; water absorption; or other forces. The amount of movement that will occur on a given detail varies, but it is always present.

Conformance to Industry Standards

Certain common methods of building are considered industry standards. These methods have been developed through practice and experience, from the recommendations of trade associations and testing organizations, and from building codes. A reinforced masonry wall should be built in a similar manner regardless of who designs it, who builds it, or what it is used for. The only things that may change to suit the particular needs of the building are the finish, the size of reinforcing, the type of mortar, and so on.

Conforming to these types of industry standards not only increases the likelihood that the detail will work, but also minimizes potential liability if something goes wrong. This is not to say that the architect should not try new design approaches or be creative in solving unusual technical problems, but that he or she should only do so when necessary.

Deviation from industry standards should be done only after precise definition of the performance requirements specified for the building assembly, after thorough research of the materials and construction techniques being proposed to meet the requirements, and by careful analysis of how the construction might actually perform. Then the final decision should be made by the client based on information and recommendations provided by the architect.

Resistance to Moisture and Weathering

Controlling moisture is one of the most troublesome areas of construction design and detailing and one of the most error prone. Specific methods of waterproofing are discussed in Ch. 43. Whenever water might be a problem, the detail should be carefully reviewed. These situations include all roofing details, exterior walls and wall penetrations, below-grade walls and slabs, pools, areas under and around showers and tubs, kitchens, mechanical rooms, and any other interior space where excess moisture is present.

Some of the considerations are as follows.

- *The permeability of the material itself.* Can it resist moisture, or must it be protected with a coating or by some other mechanical means?
- *The durability of the material.* Will aging, building movement, and other forms of deterioration cause the material to crack or break up, allowing water to penetrate?
- *Aggravating circumstances.* Will other conditions cause a normally water-resistant detail to leak? An exterior material may shed water but leak when wind-driven rain is forced in.
- *Joints.* Are joints constructed, flashed, and sealed so that water cannot enter? Will building movement damage the integrity of the joints?
- *Capillary action.* Are tiny joints or holes that can admit water inherent in the material? Brick mortar joints are a perfect example of this. The wrong type of joint can crack imperceptibly and let water that does not run off be sucked into the wall. A windowsill or coping without a drip can allow water to flow up the underside and into the structure.
- *Outlets.* If water does get into the structure, as is normal in some situations, is there a way for it to drain back out? Weep holes in masonry walls and curtain walls allow this to happen. A *weep hole* is a small opening or outlet in a wall or at the bottom of a window member through which accumulated condensation or water can drain to the exterior. Another example of a weep hole is the small extension of metal framing at the lower portion of skylights that collects the condensation that forms inside the glass and drips down.
- *Sealants.* Have the proper types of sealants been selected for the type of material used and for the expected movement of the joint? Is the backup material correct, and is the sealant installed with the correct dimensions?

In addition to precipitation, other forms of weathering include ultraviolet degradation, freeze-thaw cycles, and atmospheric corrosion. Materials must be selected to withstand the expected conditions.

Thermal Resistance

When necessitated by the detail's location, the detail's resistance to heat transfer, including both heat loss and heat gain, must be investigated. Of course, the resistance of the insulation must be checked, but in addition, the prudent architect will look for possible paths of air infiltration and insulation breaks where the full thickness of the insulation is not present. Exterior studs, pipes penetrating walls, and metal door frames are examples of areas where there is a weakness in the insulation value of the exterior wall.

Sustainability

With greater interest in the sustainability of buildings in general, architects must also review details, in particular, with an eye toward the environmental impact of details and how buildings are put together. Some of the same criteria for evaluating building materials that were discussed in Ch. 30 can be used as detailing guidelines for sustainability. These include the following.

- The embodied energy of the materials used in the detail should be as low as possible. This includes materials that are hidden, like blocking or bracing, as well as the obvious finish materials.
- As many of the materials and components as possible should be made from renewable materials or have recycled content.
- Details should reduce energy consumption in the building. Something as simple as adding insulation in a small gap in a detail could yield significant energy savings, especially if the detail is repeated dozens or hundreds of times in a building.
- As many of the materials and components as possible should come from local sources.
- Adhesives, cleaning compounds, and finishes should have low VOC content. For example, in some cases, mechanical fasteners can be used instead of construction mastics.
- If possible, the detail should be designed to allow for easy deconstruction so the individual components can be recycled.

Other Properties

There are many other properties of materials and construction details to review when developing or evaluating drawings. These are, when applicable, such things as acoustical properties, light reflection, abrasion resistance, resistance to termites and other insects, holding power of fasteners, resistance to fading, mildew resistance, color, and finish. Of course, no material will completely satisfy all criteria, but the architect must find the best balance.

ORGANIZATION AND LAYOUT OF CONSTRUCTION DRAWINGS

Construction drawings (also known as *working drawings*) are used more often than any other part of the contract documents. In addition to representing a correctly designed and detailed building, the drawings themselves must be accurately produced and organized to clearly communicate the architect's intent.

Organization of Construction Drawings

Construction drawings are organized in a generally standardized sequence, which has been established based on the normal sequence of construction and through practice. The drawings are usually organized in the following way.

- title and index sheet
- civil engineering drawings (if any)
- site drawings (landscape)
- architectural drawings
  - demolition plan (if any)
  - floor plans
  - reflected ceiling plans
  - roof plans
  - exterior elevations
  - interior elevations
  - building sections
  - wall sections
  - exterior details
  - interior details
  - schedules
- structural drawings
- plumbing drawings
- mechanical drawings
- electrical drawings
- other consultants' drawings, such as kitchen, acoustical, and so on

Some offices vary the exact sequence of individual sheets in the architectural portion, but the preceding method is typical. The intent is to present the information in a logical sequence so that the contractors and others can find what they need without confusion.

Sheet Organization and Layering

After the borderlines and title block are drawn, the remaining drawing area is commonly organized on a module system. The exact size of the module depends on office standards, the size of the drawing sheet, and how much of the sheet is allotted for the widths of the borderlines and the title block (usually drawn along the right side of the sheet). The typical drawing module is about 6 in square (150), but this varies slightly to provide an even division of modules within the confines of the borderline. Drawings are developed to fit within one or more modules. For example, a small detail may require only one module. A wall section may require a space one module wide and three modules high. A floor plan may require the entire sheet of modules.

Using such a system allows for the development and easy use of standard or master details that are drawn to fit within the module. This system works with either manual drafting or computer-aided drafting (CAD). A standard numbering system for the modules also makes it possible for individual drawings to be numbered early in the development of the construction drawings.

Layering of drawings is the term applied to the system of placing particular information on separate layers (or levels) in a CAD system. Layering allows information to be shown or hidden so that several drawings can be developed from one computer file of information. For example, the same partition layout layer can be used for the floor plan as well as the reflected ceiling plan of a building. Individual offices may have their own layering system or use the AIA CAD layering system.

Content and Coordination of Construction Drawings

Drawings should show the general configuration, size, shape, and location of the components of construction with general notes to explain materials, construction requirements, and dimensions, and with similar explanations of the graphic material. For comparison, Figs. 48.1 through 48.8 show various types of construction plans for the same portion of a building. Figures 48.9 through 48.13 show some of the standard symbols used on construction drawings. Detailed requirements for material quality, workmanship, and other items are contained in the technical specifications of the project manual. The following are brief descriptions of some of the more common items that should be included with the architectural drawings. This list is by no means inclusive.

- *Site plan*: vicinity map, property description, property line locations with dimensions and bearings, benchmarks, existing structures, new building location, landscaping, site improvements, fencing, roads, streets, right of way, drainage, and limit of the work of the contract

- A *benchmark* is a fixed elevation point from which all other elevations on the site and building are referenced. A benchmark may be an official surveying marker, if one exists on or near the site, or simply a nearby object that is fixed, such as the top of a manhole cover. The surveyor uses a benchmarks to lay out the vertical dimensions of the site and building and to check the accuracy of the building construction. In most architectural projects, the first floor of the building is arbitrarily set at an elevation of 100 ft (100 m) for the purposes of developing the construction drawings. This allows foundation and basement elevations to be positive numbers, while elevations above the first floor are larger than 100 ft. Used in this way, the first floor becomes a *datum*, or plane of reference from which other elevations are taken. A vertical plane may also be a datum and other horizontal dimensions referenced from it.

  The site plan will also show surveying *control points* used for horizontal measurement. These are fixed points established by the surveyor, and they usually consist of a primary system and a secondary system. The primary system is tied to the official control system of the jurisdiction (national, municipal, or other higher-order coordinate system) and normally covers the entire site. The corner points of the site are also related to the higher-order coordinate system. There are usually two or three primary control points indicated on the site plan so that dimensions can be checked and for ease of reference as the building is constructed. The secondary system is the grid reference system that is used for the building construction itself, typically based on the centerlines of the building's structural grid or the faces of major structural walls.

- *Floor plans*: building configuration with all walls shown, as well as dimensions, grade elevations at the building line, construction to remain, references to other details and elevations, room names and numbers, door swings and door numbers, window numbers, floor material indications, plumbing fixtures, built-in fixtures, stairs, special equipment, vertical transportation, and notes as required to explain items on the plan (see Fig. 48.1)

- *Roof plans*: roof outline, overall dimensions, dimensions of setbacks, slope of roof, drainage, reference to other drawing details, roof materials, penetrations through roof, and roof-mounted equipment

- *Reflected ceiling plans*: partitions extending to and through the ceiling; ceiling material and grid lines; ceiling height notes; changes in ceiling heights; locations of all lights (including exit lights), diffusers, access panels, speakers, and other equipment and ceiling penetrations; and expansion joints (see Fig. 48.2)

- *Exterior elevations*: structural grid center lines, vertical dimensions, floor-to-floor heights, opening heights, references to other details, floor lines, elevations of major elements, grade lines, foundation lines (dashed), material indications and notes, symbols for window schedule, gutters, signs and windows, doors, and all other openings

- *Building sections*: vertical dimensions, elevations of the tops of structural components and finish floor lines, general material indications, footings and foundations, references to other details, ceiling lines, and major mechanical services

- *Wall sections*: dimensions to grid center lines, face of wall dimensions to other components, vertical dimensions from foundations to parapet relating all elements to top of structural elements, material indications with notes, all connection methods, mechanical and electrical elements shown schematically, roof construction, floor construction, and foundation construction

- *Interior elevations*: vertical dimensions to critical elements, references to other details, openings in walls, wall finishes, built-in items, and locations of switches, thermostats, and other wall-mounted equipment

- *Schedules*: room finish schedule, door schedule, window schedule, and hardware schedule are common schedules found on most drawings. Others are louver, architectural woodwork, piling, and equipment schedules.

- *Structural drawings*: footing and foundation plans, rebar layout, framing plans, major structural sections, detail sections, pier reinforcing schedules, and connection details. Based on information from the structural engineer, the architect incorporates the exact sizes of structural members in the architectural details to coordinate construction details and make sure that sufficient space is provided for construction, clearances, tolerances, and finishes. Generally, only the overall outline of piers, footings, foundation walls, structural walls, and framing is shown on the architectural drawings. Elevations for tops of beams, structural walls, and floors are shown on both sets of drawings. (See Fig. 48.3.)

- *Mechanical and plumbing drawings*: location of mechanical equipment; layout of ductwork, pipes, fixtures, and other major components; plumbing isometrics; details of mechanical room layout; details, such as ductwork connections and pipe support; and equipment schedules. Generally, mechanical and plumbing items are only shown on the architectural drawings where they interface with other construction. Examples include the locations of grilles and registers on the reflected ceiling plan, the locations of sprinkler heads on the reflected ceiling plan, plumbing fixtures, ducts and piping when part of an architectural section or detail, and other situations where coordination with other construction elements is important. Because of the obvious potential for conflicts when different offices complete different drawings, coordination between the architect and the consulting engineers is critical. (See Figs. 48.4 and 48.5.)

- *Electrical drawings*: power plans; lighting plans; telecommunication plans; signal and security systems; one-line diagrams; and transformer, equipment, and fixture schedules. The number of plans will vary depending on the complexity of the project. For example, for simple projects all telecommunication and signal work may be shown on the power plan. In other cases a separate plan is developed for each system. (See Fig. 48.6.)

  The electrical drawings contain information concerning the exact circuiting of lighting and power outlets, including the number and size of conductors in each conduit, the sizes of conduits, and home runs to panel boxes. A *home run* is a graphic indication (using an arrowhead and the numbers of the circuits) that the line on the drawing connecting lights or outlets is connected to particular circuit breakers in a particular electrical panel box. This graphic device is used so that the entire line does not have to be drawn to the panel box, thereby avoiding clutter on the drawing.

  As with mechanical and plumbing work, electrical elements shown on the architectural drawings are for coordination and location only. For example, where the location of power outlets is critical, the architectural drawings may include a separate power and telephone plan with exact dimensions. The locations of luminaires are also shown on the architect's reflected ceiling plan so they can be coordinated with other ceiling-mounted equipment and architectural features. Usually, no other electrical information is given on these drawings. However, in some cases, the architect may want to show the locations of switches on the reflected ceiling plan. Compare the electrical engineer's power plan shown in Fig. 48.6 with the architect's telephone/power plan shown in Fig. 48.7, and with the architect's reflected ceiling plan shown in Fig. 48.2.

In addition to these overall views of the construction, there are corresponding details for all portions of the work.

Information Required by Building Departments

Building codes require that certain information appear on the set of construction documents submitted for plan review. Although the exact list of required information will vary from one jurisdiction to another, the following is required by the IBC and is typical of most codes.

- In general, construction documents must be of sufficient clarity to indicate the locations, nature, and extent of the proposed work and how it will conform to the code. This normally includes the standard types of drawings of floor plans, elevations, sections, and details for architectural, structural, mechanical, electrical, and other specialty construction as well as applicable schedules and written specifications.

- A site plan must be included to show the size and location of new construction and existing structures on the site, including distances from lot lines, established street grades, and the proposed finished grades. An accurate boundary survey must be shown.

- The drawings must show all portions of the means of egress. The number of occupants to be accommodated on every floor and in all rooms and spaces must be indicated.

- The exterior wall envelope must be shown in sufficient detail to determine compliance with code provisions. Manufacturing installation instructions may also have to be included to show that the weather resistance of the exterior wall envelope will be maintained.

- Fire protection shop drawings may have to be submitted to show conformance with the code.

- Structural calculations may have to be submitted.

In addition, the local authority having jurisdiction may want to see listed on the first sheet of the drawings some or all of the following information.

- names and addresses of all design professionals responsible for the work

- street address or legal description of the property
- square footage of the building
- building type and occupancy group or groups
- occupant load calculations
- the valuation of new construction represented by the plans and specifications

COORDINATION

Because the architectural construction drawings are only a part of the entire set of contract documents, they must be coordinated with other documents. Coordination is an ongoing effort during the design and production phases. Depending on how an individual office is organized, the responsibility may fall on the project architect, project manager, or job captain.

Coordination with Consultants' Work

On nearly all projects there will be several consultants working with the architect. Small- to medium-sized jobs will have structural, mechanical, and electrical consultants as a minimum. Larger projects may have additional consultants in fire protection, civil engineering, landscape architecture, food service, elevators, curtain walls, and interior design, among others.

Each discipline develops its own drawings, so coordination among everyone on the team is critical. Although all consultants must be diligent in their efforts to work with others, the primary responsibility for overall coordination is with the architect. In the office, this responsibility usually falls on the project manager, although in smaller firms or on smaller jobs the project architect may take on this task.

There are a number of ways to accomplish coordination during the design and production of contract documents. First, periodic meetings should be held to exchange information and alert everyone to the progress of the job. At these meetings, anyone may ask questions and raise issues that may affect the work of others. Second, progress prints or electronic files should be exchanged between the architect and the consultants for ongoing comparison of work being produced. Third, the project manager must be responsible for notifying all consultants, in writing, of changes made as they occur. If computer-aided drafting is being used, base sheets or electronic information can be exchanged according to the particular methods being employed. Finally, the architect must have a thorough method of checking and coordinating the entire drawing set prior to issue for bidding or negotiation.

Correlation with the Specifications

The architectural drawings must also be coordinated with the specifications. These components of the contract documents are complementary; they both give necessary information about the design of the project. Either component alone is incomplete. They should work together without duplication or overlap.

Specifications are part of the project manual and describe the types and quality of materials, quality of workmanship, methods of fabrication and installation, and general requirements related to the construction of the project. They are normally written after production of the drawings has started and materials have been selected. Because the specifications are usually written by someone not working on the drawings, there must also be close coordination within the architect's office. Again, this is usually the responsibility of the project manager. Specifications are discussed in more detail in Ch. 49.

If a computer-aided master specification system is used, there may be a sheet of drawing coordination notes produced by the system for each section of the specifications. These can be used for checking by the people producing the drawings.

BUILDING INFORMATION MODELING

In traditional drafting, either manually or with computer-aided design (CAD) software, a drawing is a two-dimensional representation of a project's three-dimensional physical aspects. *Building information modeling* (BIM) is a developing method of designing, documenting, and managing a facility. A three-dimensional computer model of the building or interior is created with BIM software. As the project develops, more detail is added to the model, which is shared with all members of the project team through computer networking. Because all the information about the building is in one model, individual drawings such as floor plans, elevations, and details can be produced easily with the appropriate commands. Three-dimensional renderings can also be produced.

A model created by BIM is considered a "smart" model because it is more than just a representation; each individual object such as a door or a partition has information attached to it. Thus, the model is useful in creating estimates of materials, door schedules, cost estimates, and the like. In addition, because the model is three-dimensional and dimensionally accurate, the software can detect interferences, such as between a structural beam and HVAC ductwork, and this can prevent problems when the job is under construction.

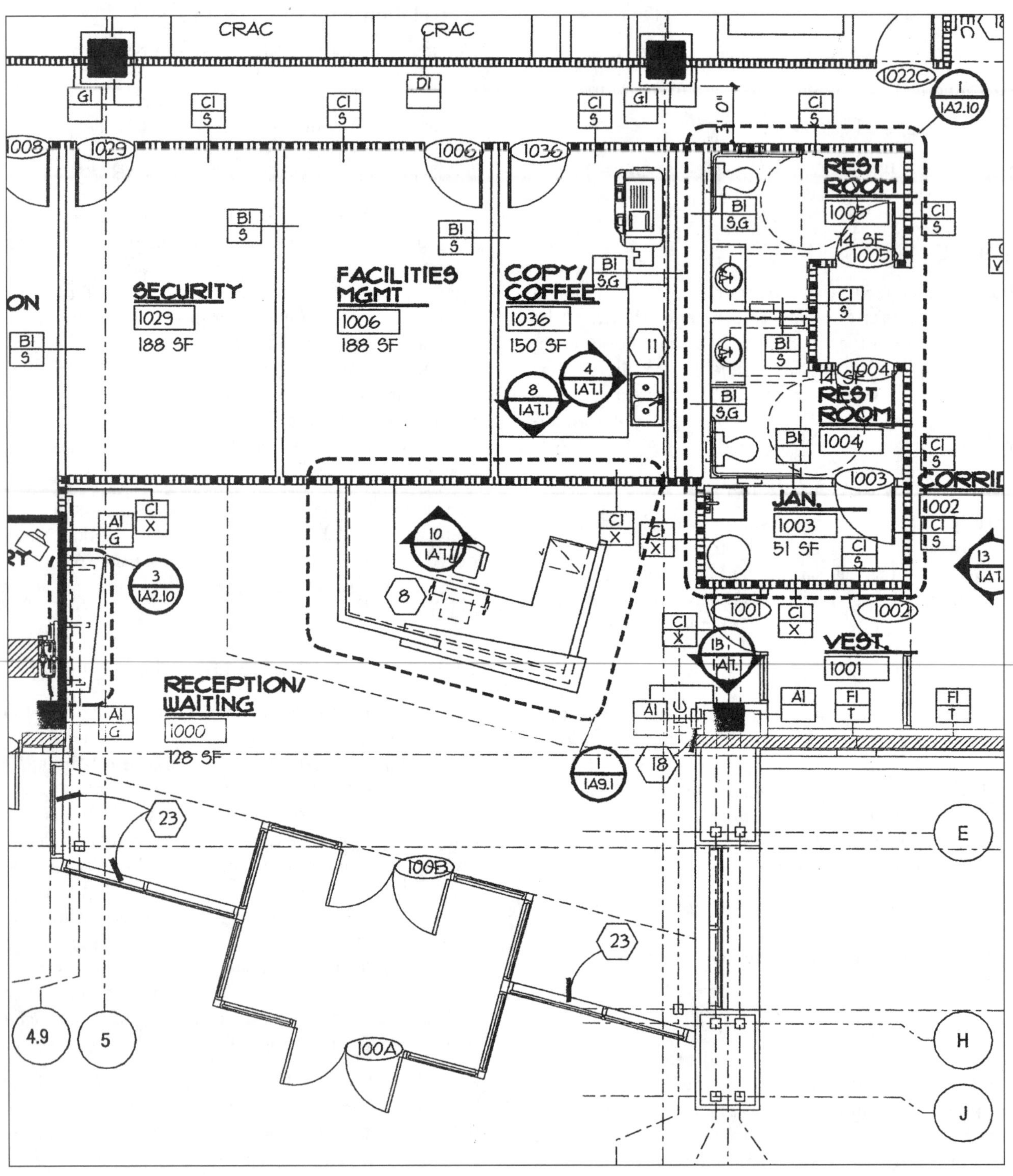

Figure 48.1 Construction Floor Plan

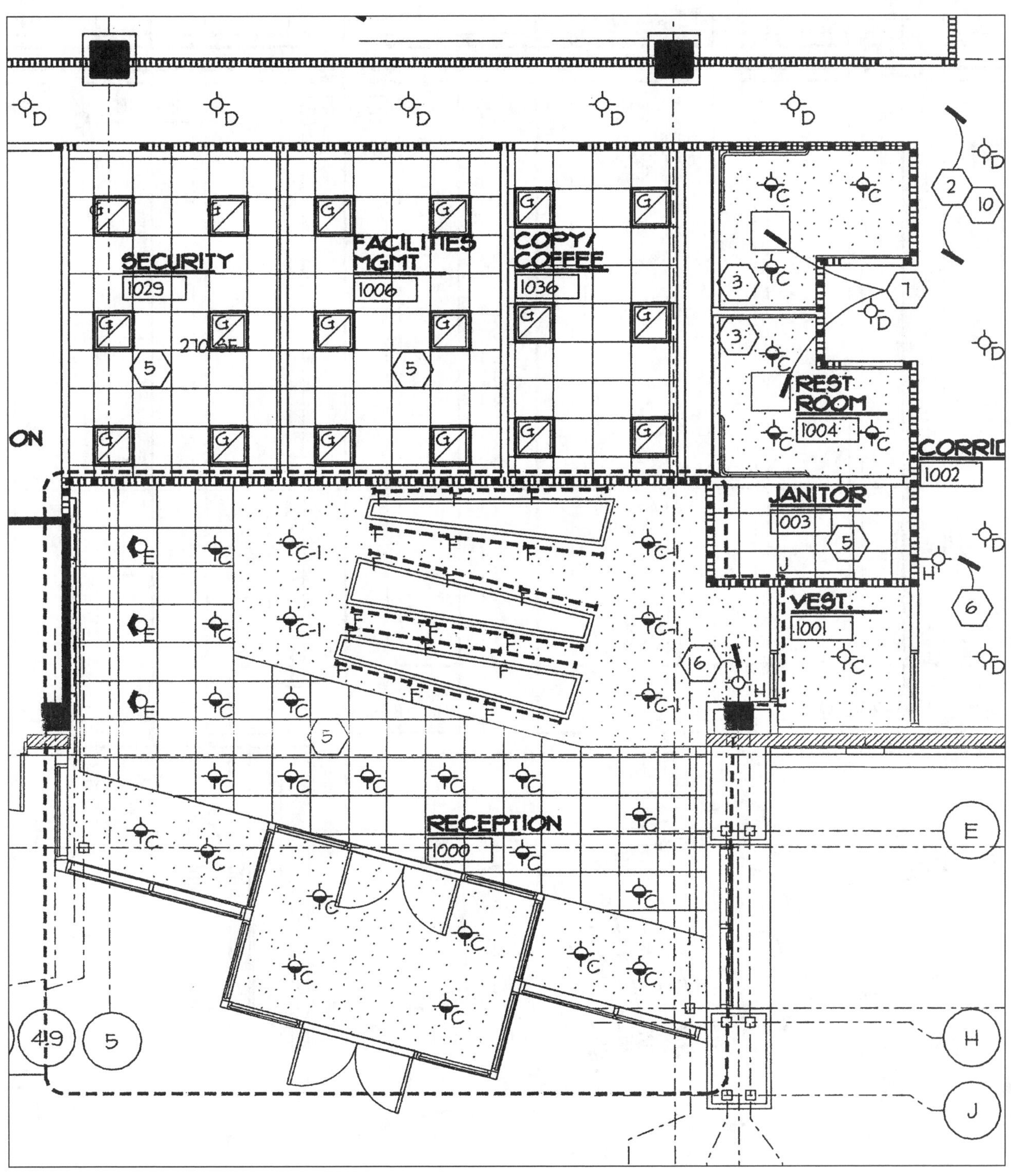

Figure 48.2 Reflected Ceiling Plan

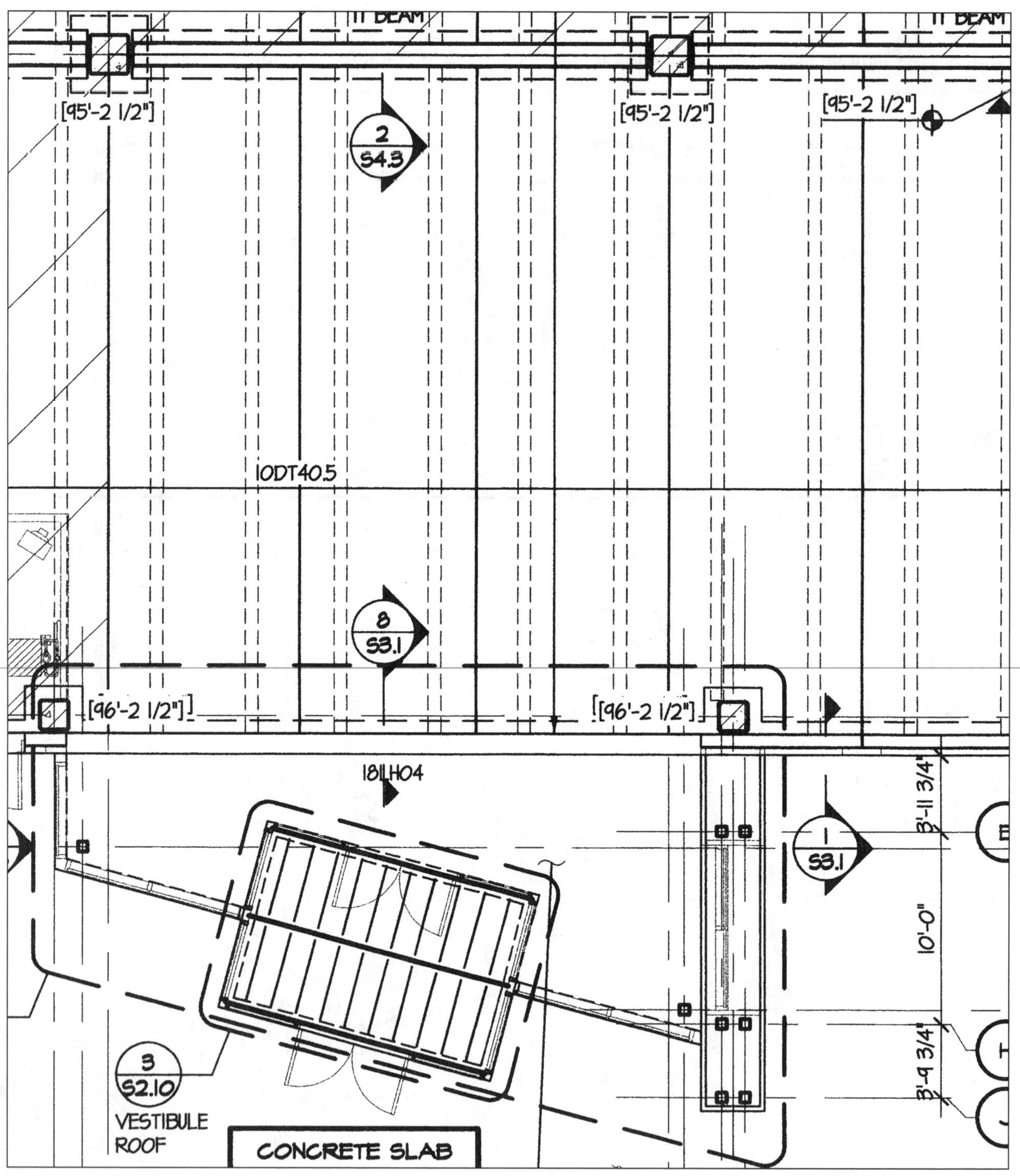

Figure 48.3 Structural Plan

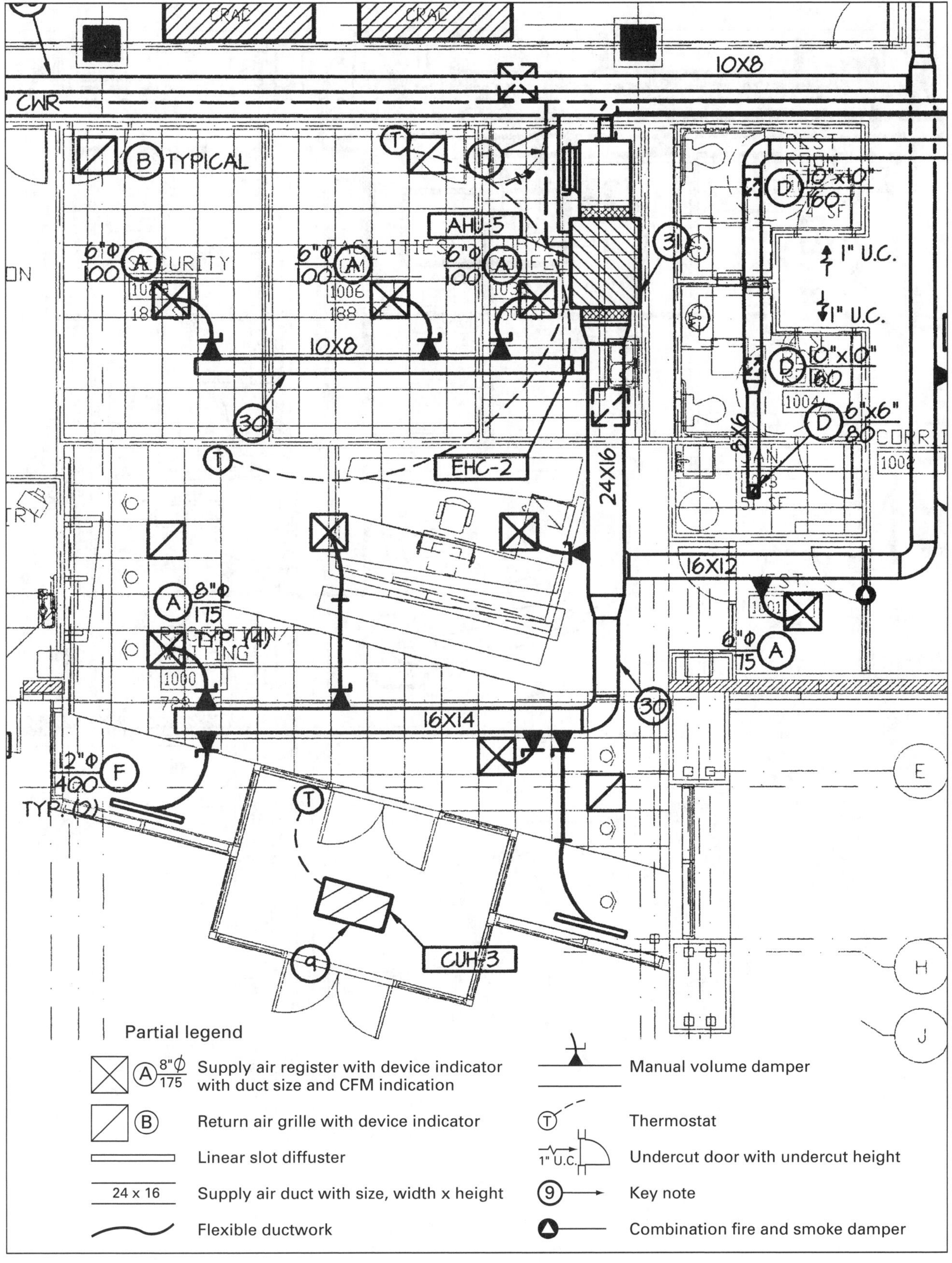

Figure 48.4 Mechanical Plan

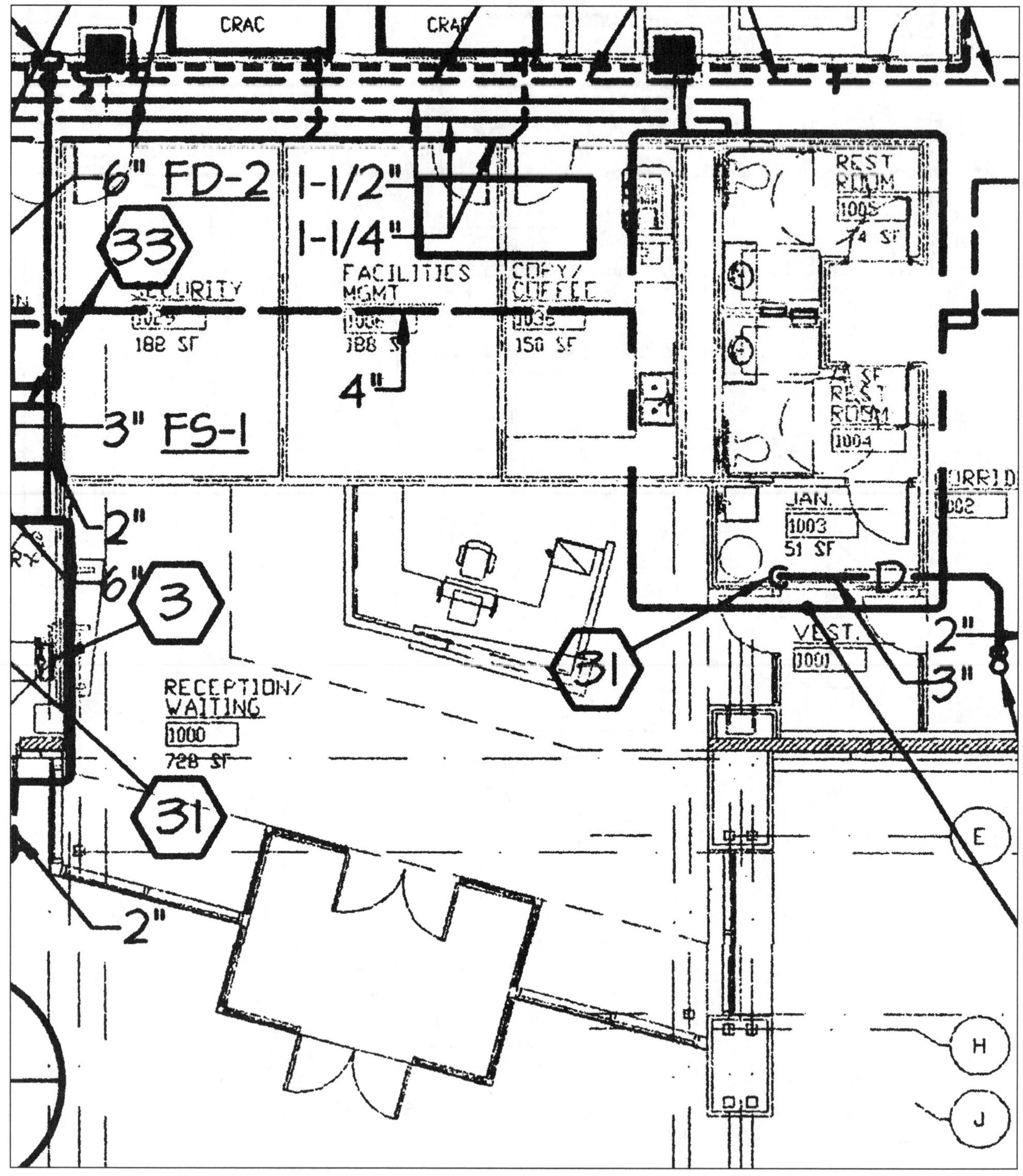

Figure 48.5 Plumbing Plan

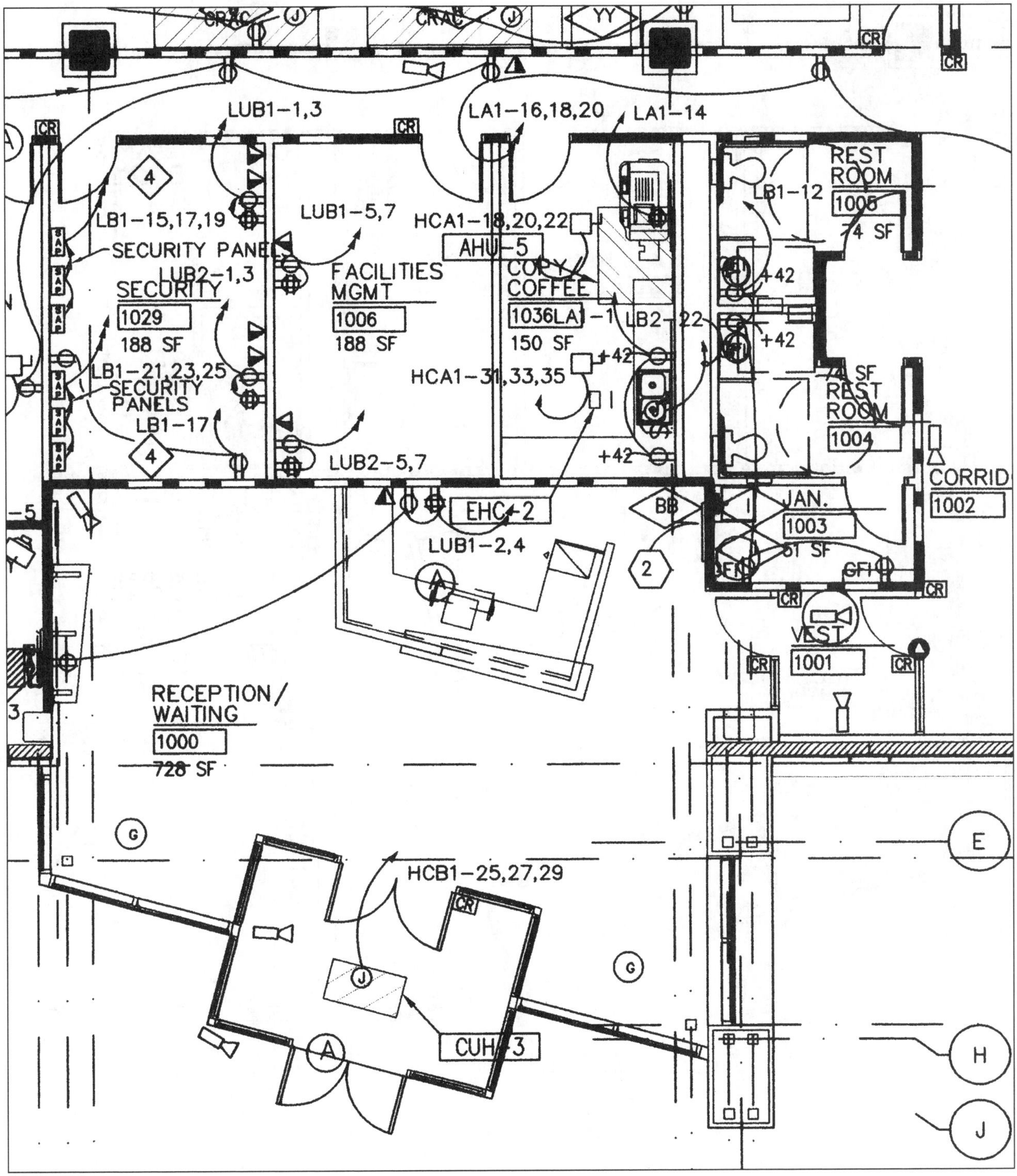

Figure 48.6 Power Plan

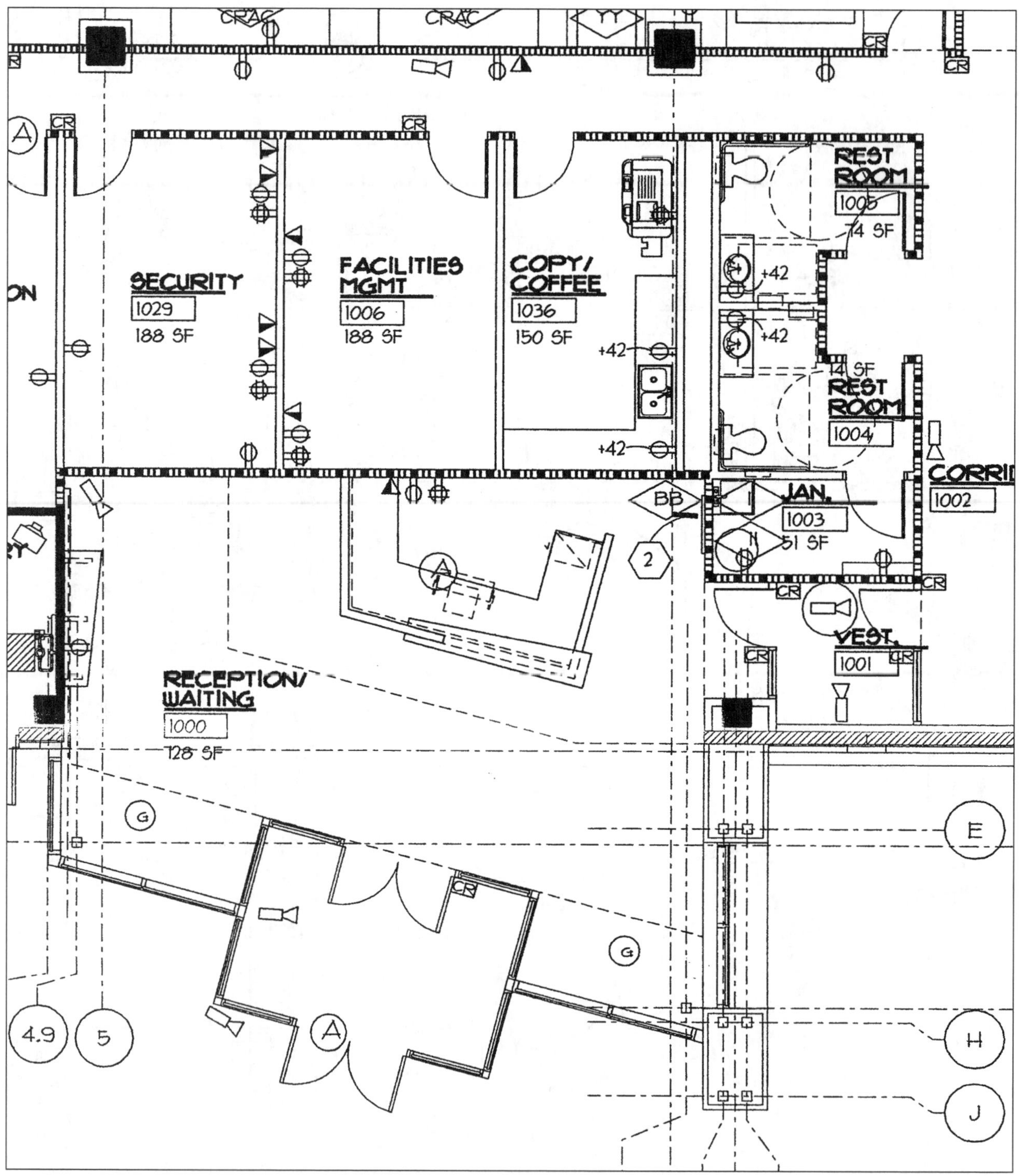

Figure 48.7 Telephone/Electrical Plan

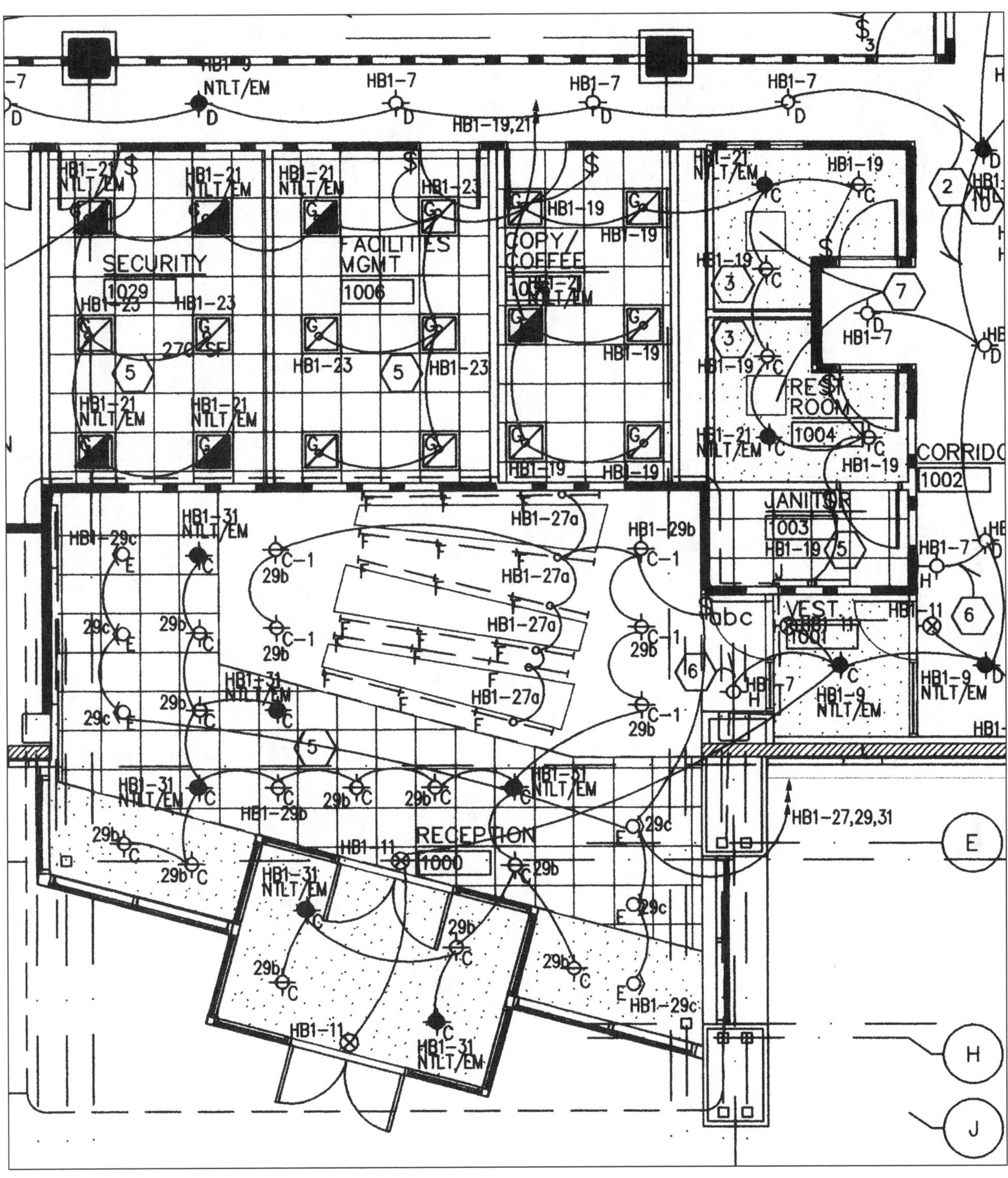

Figure 48.8 Lighting Plan

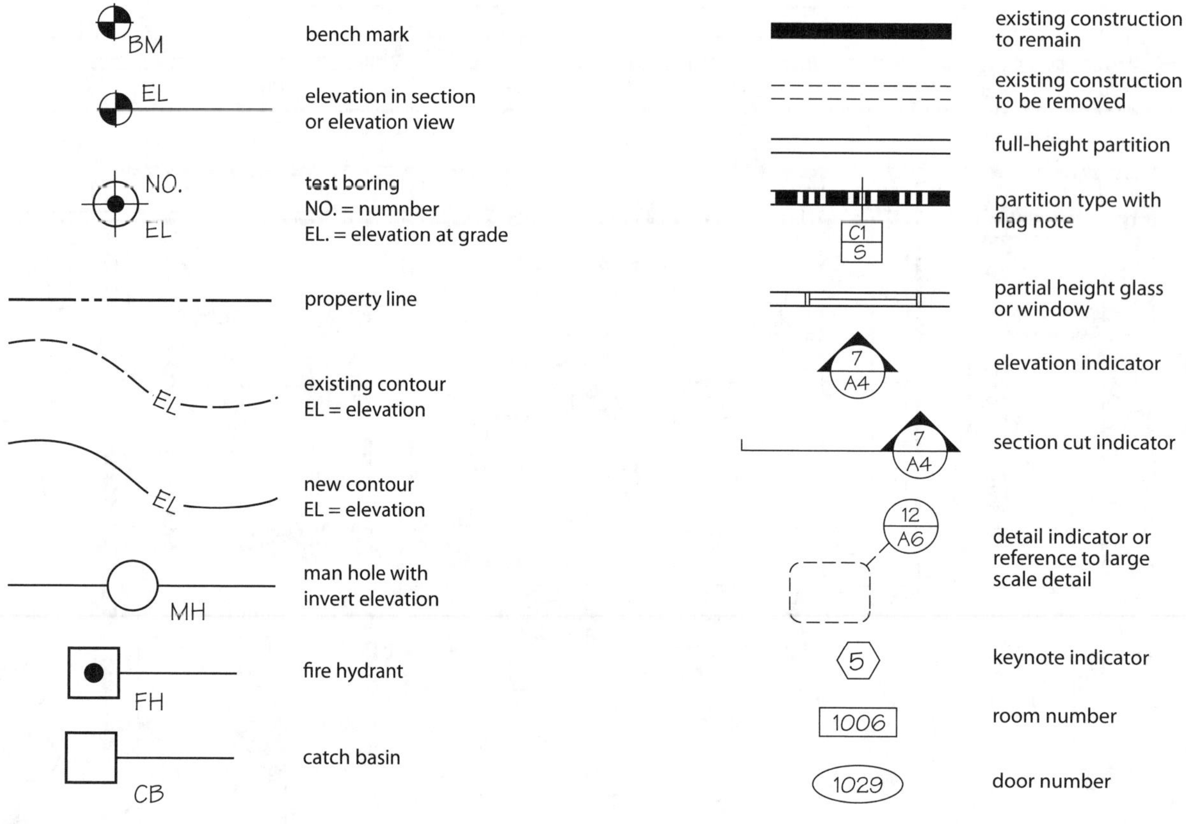

Figure 48.9 Site Plan Symbols

Figure 48.10 Architectural Symbols

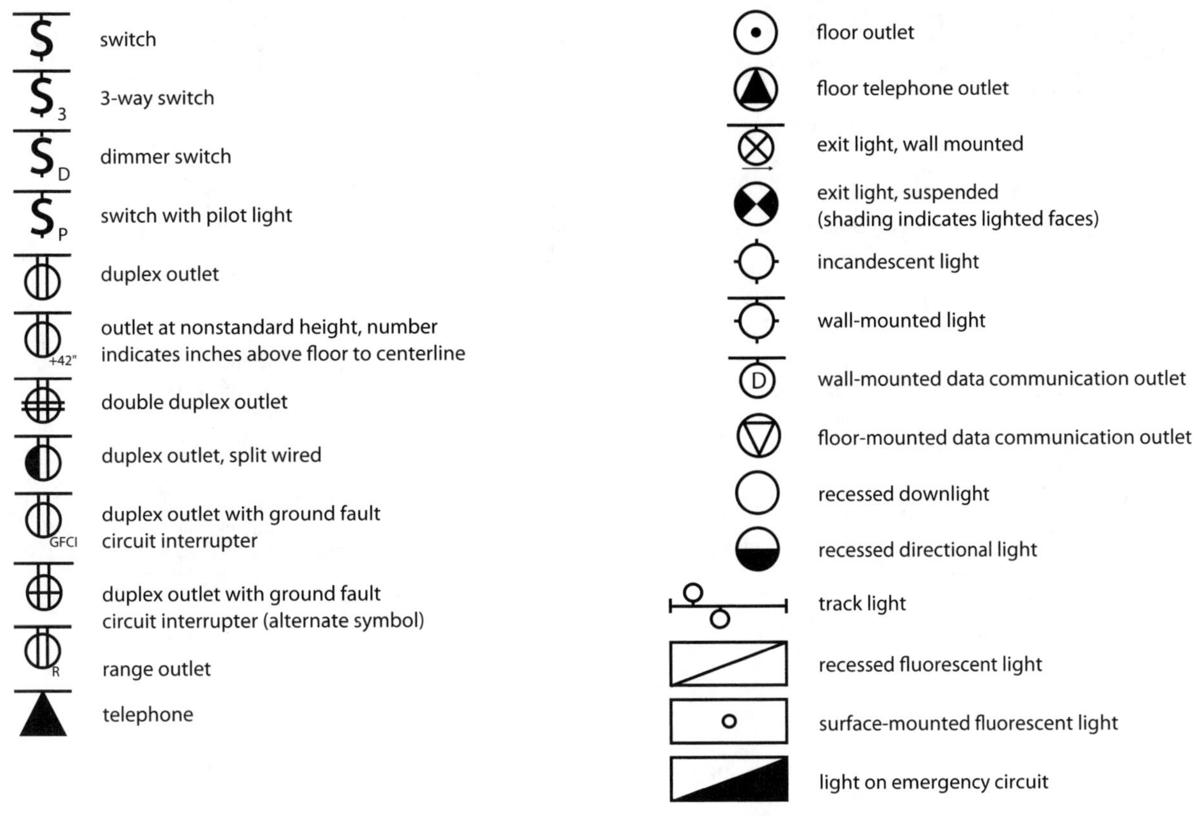

Figure 48.11 Electrical and Lighting Symbols

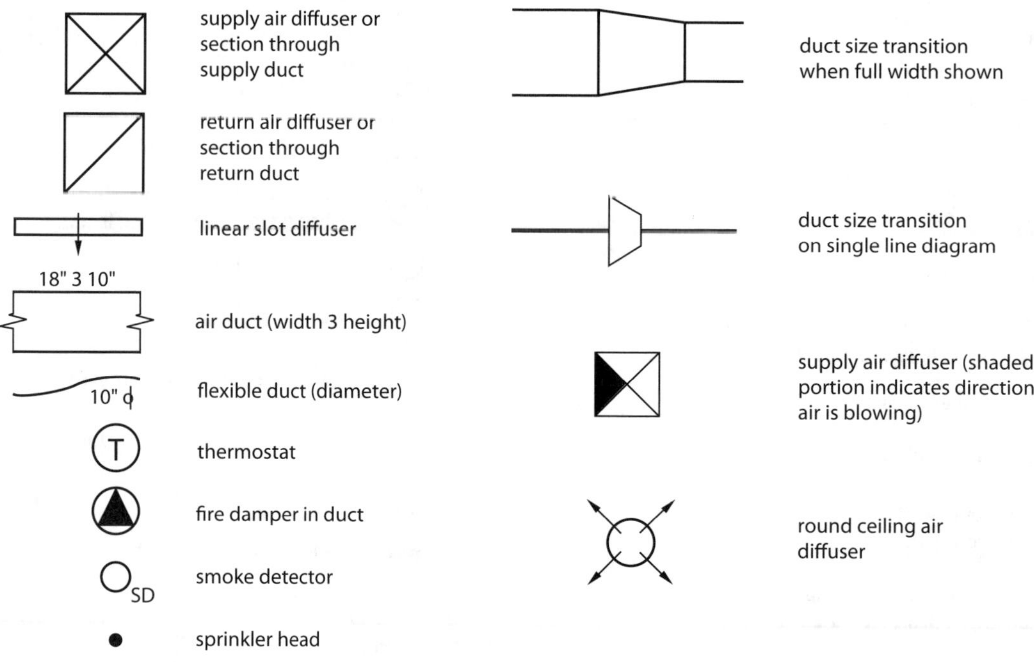

Figure 48.12 Mechanical Symbols

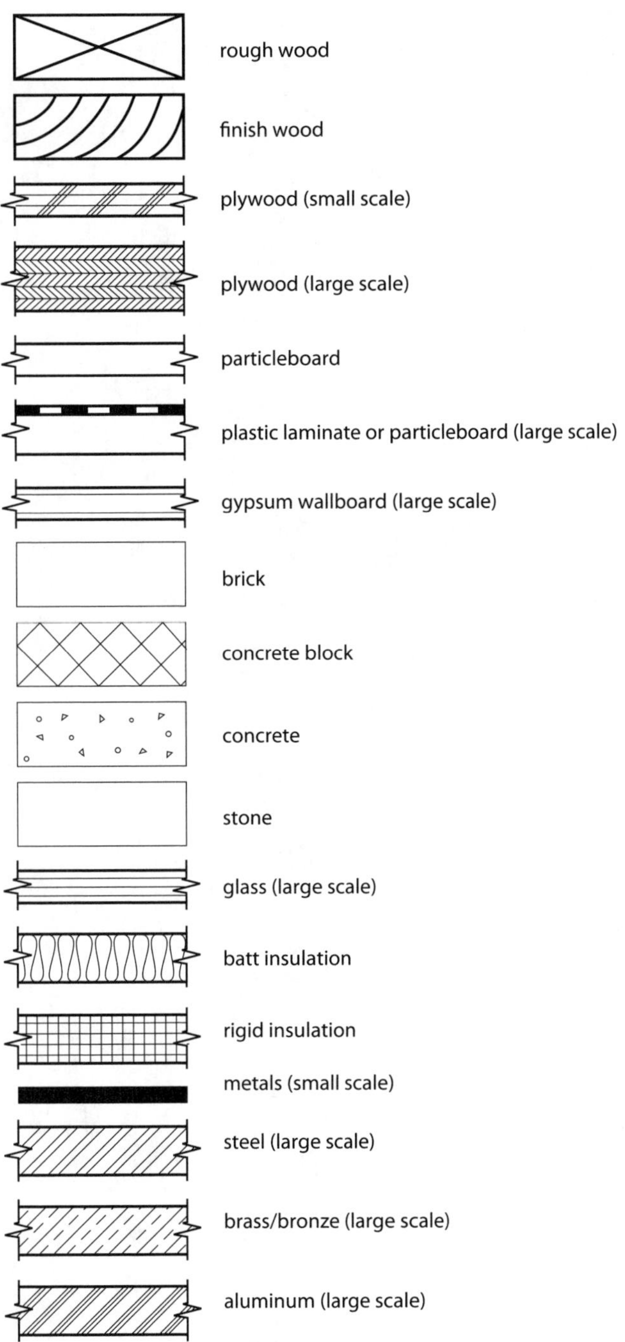

Figure 48.13 Material Indications in Section

49 THE PROJECT MANUAL AND SPECIFICATIONS

THE PROJECT MANUAL

The *project manual* is a bound book containing all contract and noncontract documents for a construction project, except the drawings. The project manual contains the technical specifications, but it also includes several other types of documents.

Organization of the Project Manual

The project manual is divided into four major parts: (1) bidding requirements; (2) parts of the contract itself, such as the agreement between owner and contractor, bond forms, and the like; (3) the general and supplementary conditions of the contract; and (4) the technical specifications.

A more detailed list of the project manual's contents might include some or all of the following.

- bidding requirements
  - invitation to bid
  - prequalification forms
  - instructions to bidders
  - information available to bidders
  - bid forms
- supplements to bid forms
  - bid security form
  - subcontractor list
  - substitution list
- contract forms
  - agreement (contract between owner and contractor)
  - performance bond
  - labor and materials payment bond
  - certificates of insurance
- general and supplementary conditions
  - general conditions of the contract (such as AIA Document 201)
  - supplementary conditions
- technical specifications

Contracts, bidding documents, and general conditions of the contract are discussed in more detail in later chapters. This chapter focuses on the technical specifications.

Coordination with the Drawings

The technical specifications and the drawings are complementary. The drawings show the general configuration and layout of the building as well as the size, shape, and dimensions of the construction. General notes to explain the graphic representation are also included. The *technical specifications* describe the quality of materials and workmanship along with general requirements for the execution of the work, standards, and other items that are more appropriately described in written, rather than graphic, form.

The drawings, technical specifications, and other parts of the project manual must be coordinated to avoid conflicting requirements, duplication, omission, and errors. There are several areas of particular concern.

First, the specifications should contain requirements for all the materials and construction indicated on the drawings. The use of one checklist by both the specifications writer and the project manager or job captain is one way to accomplish this.

Second, the terminology used in both documents should be the same. If the term *gypsum board* is used in the specifications, the term *drywall* should not be shown on the drawings.

Third, dimensions and thicknesses should only be indicated on one document. If the thickness of flashing is included in the technical specifications, there is no need to note it on the drawings.

Fourth, notes on the drawings should not describe methods of installation or material qualities; these belong in the specifications.

When there is a conflict between the drawings and the specifications, the courts have held that the specifications are more binding and take precedence over the drawings.

SPECIFICATIONS

As previously described, specifications form part of the project manual and are legal documents. As such, they must be complete, accurate, unambiguous, and exact. Because of these needs and because specifications represent complex technical information, they are difficult to write correctly. Fortunately, some standard methods of preparing specifications are in general use. These will be described in the following sections.

In addition, master specifications are available that can be used as starting documents. A master specification is a prewritten text that includes the majority of requirements for a particular specification section. Master specifications are edited by deleting unnecessary portions, adding particular requirements for a specific job, and coordinating the requirements with other specification sections and other parts of the project manual. Master specifications are available in written form and on computer disk from various commercial sources.

Computer programs based on expert system technology are also becoming available. These generate specifications through interactive sessions with the specifier and with links to some computer-aided drafting software.

Types of Specifications

There are two broad categories of specifications: prescriptive and performance.

Prescriptive specifications (also called *closed specifications*), by specifying brand names, tell the contractor exactly what product or material to use. *Performance specifications* (also called *open specifications*) tell what results the final construction assembly should achieve, but give the contractor some choice in how they will be achieved. Most specifications fall somewhere between these two extremes.

The type of specification used will depend on several factors. Public projects almost always require open specifications in order to encourage competitive bidding. In other cases, it may be preferable to use a closed specification to ensure that only one particular product is used. Whether the job is bid or a negotiated contract may also affect the choice. With bidding, it might be best to allow the contractor as much choice as possible so that he or she can find the lowest price within the context of the specification requirements.

The following types of specifications are the ones most commonly used.

Types of Prescriptive (Closed) Specifications

Proprietary specifications are the most restrictive in that they call out a specific manufacturer's product. These give the architect complete control over what is installed. They are easier than other types to write and are generally shorter. However, they do not allow for competitive bidding, and by limiting products the architect may force the contractor to get materials that may be difficult or expensive to procure in a certain geographical area or that require excessive delivery time. Further, the burden is on the specifier to call out products that meet code requirements, are within the budget, and are technically correct.

A base bid with alternates is a type of specification that calls out a proprietary product but allows the substitution of other products that the contractor thinks are equal to the one stated. This is a dangerous method of specifying because the contractor may substitute a less expensive item that he or she thinks is equal but actually is not.

There are two variations of a base bid specification. The first lists several approved manufacturers of a product. The contractor is free to bid on any one listed. This type satisfies the requirements for public work where at least three different manufacturers must be listed, but it puts the burden on the architect to make sure that every one of the approved products or manufacturers listed is equal.

The second variation is a base bid with "approved equal" language. This specification states that one product or an approved equal must be used. This means that the contractor may propose a substitution, but it is subject to review and approval by the architect before it can be incorporated into the bid. Although this gives the contractor some freedom in looking for lower-priced alternates, it also puts the burden for finding them on the contractor. However, the responsibility for fairly and accurately evaluating the proposed alternates is placed on the architect or owner. During a hectic bidding period this can be a large burden, so the specifications should clearly state how much lead time the contractor must give the architect and how alternates will be evaluated.

Types of Performance (Open) Specifications

A *descriptive specification* gives detailed written requirements for the material or product and the workmanship required for its fabrication and installation. It does not mention trade names. In its purest form, a descriptive specification is difficult to write because the architect must include all the pertinent requirements for the construction and installation of the product.

A variation of the descriptive type is a reference standard specification. This describes a material, product, or process based on requirements (reference standards) set by an accepted authority or test method. For example, a product type can be required to meet the testing standards produced by such organizations as the American Society for Testing and Materials (ASTM), the American National Standards Institute (ANSI), or Underwriters Laboratories (UL). Reference can also be made to specific trade associations, such as the Architectural Woodwork Institute, the American Iron and Steel Institute, and the Gypsum Association.

For example, in specifying gypsum wallboard the architect can state that all gypsum wallboard products must meet the requirements of ASTM C36. This particular document describes in great detail the requirements for gypsum wallboard, so they need not be repeated. The document can instead refer to a generally recognized industry standard.

Reference standard specifications are fairly easy to write and are generally short. Chances for errors are reduced and liability is minimized by using industry standards and generally recognized building methods. However, the architect must know what is in the standard and how to refer to the appropriate part of the standard if it includes more provisions than are needed for the job.

A pure performance specification is a statement setting criteria and results required of the item being specified, which can be verified by measurement, test evaluation, or other types of assurance that the final result meets the criteria. The means of achieving the required results are not specified; they are left up to the person trying to meet the specification.

A true performance specification is often used for construction components when the specifier wants to encourage new ways of achieving a particular end result. For example, a movable partition system could be specified by stating its required fire rating, acoustical properties, finish, maximum thickness, tolerances, required size, and all the other required properties. It would then be up to the contractor and manufacturer to design and develop a system to meet the criteria.

Performance specifications are difficult to write because they require that the specifier know all the criteria, state the methods for testing compliance, and be prepared for the cost consequences.

Organization of the Technical Sections

The organization of the technical sections has been standardized through general adoption of the MasterFormat™ system. This was developed by the Construction Specifications Institute and Construction Specifications Canada to standardize the numbering and format of project-related information for use in specifying, cost estimating, and data filing. The revision made in 2004 was a significant change from the previous 16-division organization that had been in use for several decades. The Construction Specifications Institute undertook the revision recognizing that the previous 16 divisions made it difficult to incorporate the increased use of building automation, signal systems, and electronic security and that the numbering system was not particularly well-suited for transportation, utility, marine, industrial, and process engineering construction.

The MasterFormat division organization is shown in Fig. 49.1. There are major subgroups, with individual divisions within each subgroup. Many of the divisions are reserved for future use to allow the system to grow as new materials and technologies emerge. Most of the divisions in the Facility Construction Subgroup are essentially the same as they were before the 2004 revision, with the same numbers as were assigned in the previous version. These include Divisions 03 through 14. Divisions 31, Earthwork, and Division 32, Exterior Improvements, are also typically used on architectural projects. The significant changes affecting architectural use include the following.

- Much of Division 01, General Requirements, covers the same material, but it has been expanded to allow for writing performance specifications for elements that overlap several specific work sections (the building envelope, for example).
- Division 02, Existing Conditions, now only covers what the name implies; namely, subsurface and other investigation, site remediation, selective demolition, and similar work. Actual site construction work groups, such as earthwork, site improvements, and planting, have been moved to the Site and Infrastructure Subgroup, Divisions 31, 32, and 33.
- Division 11, Equipment, is about the same except that equipment related to process engineering is now in the Process Equipment Subgroup, and equipment related to infrastructure is now in the Site and Infrastructure Subgroup. Most of the elements that are common to standard architectural work, such as library, audio-visual, and medical equipment, are still in Division 11.
- In Division 13, Special Construction, the work groups that deal with security access, building automation, detection and alarm, and fire suppression are now in various divisions of the Facility Services Subgroup. Special construction related to process engineering is now in the Process Equipment Subgroup.

Procurement and Contracting Requirements Group:

Division 00 – Procurement and Contracting Requirements

Specifications Group:

General Requirements Subgroup:

Division 01 – General Requirements

Facility Construction Subgroup:

Division 02 – Existing Conditions
Division 03 – Concrete
Division 04 – Masonry
Division 05 – Metals
Division 06 – Wood, Plastics, and Composites
Division 07 – Thermal and Moisture Protection
Division 08 – Openings
Division 09 – Finishes
Division 10 – Specialties
Division 11 – Equipment
Division 12 – Furnishings
Division 13 – Special Construction
Division 14 – Conveying Equipment
Division 15 Reserved for future expansion
Division 16 – Reserved for future expansion
Division 17 – Reserved for future expansion
Division 18 – Reserved for future expansion
Division 19 – Reserved for future expansion

Facility Services Subgroup:

Division 20 – Reserved for future expansion
Division 21 – Fire Suppression
Division 22 – Plumbing
Division 23 – Heating, Ventilating, and Air Conditioning
Division 24 – Reserved for future expansion
Division 25 – Integrated Automation
Division 26 – Electrical
Division 27 – Communications
Division 28 – Electronic Safety and Security
Division 29 – Reserved for future expansion

Site and Infrastructure Subgroup:

Division 30 – Reserved for future expansion
Division 31 – Earthwork
Division 32 – Exterior Improvements
Division 33 – Utilities
Division 34 – Transportation
Division 35 – Waterway and Marine
Division 36 – Reserved for future expansion
Division 37 – Reserved for future expansion
Division 38 – Reserved for future expansion
Division 39 – Reserved for future expansion

Process Equipment Subgroup:

Division 40 – Process Integration
Division 41 – Material Processing and Handling Equipment
Division 42 – Process Heating, Cooling, and Drying Equipment
Division 43 – Process Gas and Liquid Handling, Purification, and Storage Equipment
Division 44 – Pollution Control Equipment
Division 45 – Industry-Specific Manufacturing Equipment
Division 46 – Water and Wastewater Equipment
Division 47 – Reserved for future expansion
Division 48 – Electrical Power Generation
Division 49 – Reserved for future expansion

The Division Numbers and Titles used in this product are from *MasterFormat*™ 2010 Edition and the three part SectionFormat outline from *SectionFormat*™/*PageFormat*™ are published by the Construction Specifications Institute (CSI) and Construction Specifications Canada (CSC), and are used with permission from CSI, 2010.

The Construction Specifications Institute (CSI)
99 Canal Center Plaza, Suite 300
Alexandria, VA 22314
800-689-2900; 703-684-0300
CSINet URL: http://www.csinet.org

Figure 49.1 MasterFormat 2010 Divisions

- Division 15 is now reserved for future expansion and all the mechanical and plumbing work groups are now in Division 22, Plumbing, and Division 23, Heating Ventilating and Air Conditioning, of the Facility Services Subgroup. See Fig. 49.1.
- Division 16 is now reserved for future expansion, and all the electrical work groups are now in Division 26, Electrical, and Division 27, Communications of the Facility Services Subgroup. See Fig. 49.1.

Another change in the new MasterFormat system is the use of six-digit numbers for individual specification sections instead of the previous five-digit numbers. In the new system the first two numbers represent the division numbers, with a leading zero used for the single-digit divisions (02, 03, 04, etc.). The next pair of numbers (digits three and four) represents the level-two hierarchy, and the last pair of numbers represents level three in the hierarchy. This change to a six-digit format allows for flexibility and room for expansion as new materials or technologies are added.

There are often several questions on the exam asking in which CSI MasterFormat section information on a particular material will be found. Know the names of the divisions, or at least those in the facility construction subgroup and the facility services subgroup, and generally what is included in them. Following are brief summaries of what is included in each division. Study these summaries along with the more detailed level-two divisions to get familiar with the correct locations of particular construction elements in the specifications.

- *Division 00, Procurement and Contracting Requirements*: This division covers requirements for bidding and contracting including bid solicitation, instructions to bidders, information available to bidders, bid forms, the agreement (contract), bonds and certificates, and general conditions of the contract, supplementary conditions, addenda, and modifications. These parts of the contract documents are discussed in Ch. 50.

- *Division 01, General Requirements*: This division includes requirements that are applicable to the entire project or all the individual technical sections. These include a summary of the work, how pricing and payment will be handled, alternates, value analysis, contract modification procedures, unit prices, construction progress documentation, submittal procedures (for samples, shop drawings, etc.), quality control, temporary facilities at the job site, product substitution procedures, owner-furnished items, special execution requirements, and final cleaning and protection of the work.

  The term *General Requirements* should not be confused with *General Conditions* of the Contract for Construction, as discussed in Ch. 50.

- *Division 02, Existing Conditions*: This division is now used to specify site remediation, site decontamination, subsurface investigation, surveying, and selective demolition, among other items related to existing conditions on a job site.

- *Division 03, Concrete*: This division covers all aspects of concrete, including forms, reinforcement, cast-in-place concrete, precast concrete, cementitious decks and underlayment, grouts, and concrete restoration and cleaning.

- *Division 04, Masonry*: This division covers all aspects of masonry, including brick, concrete block, stone, terra cotta, simulated masonry, glass block, and masonry restoration and cleaning.

- *Division 05, Metals*: The metals division includes all types of structural steel and other structural metals, ornamental metals, metal fabrications (metal stairs, ornamental ironwork, handrails, gratings, metal castings, and stair treads and nosings), as well as expansion joint covers and metal restoration and cleaning. Light-gage metal framing for partitions is located in Division 09.

- *Division 06, Wood, Plastics, and Composites*: This division covers typical structural wood framing, rough carpentry, finish carpentry, and architectural woodwork. It also includes structural plastics, plastic fabrications, wood and plastic restoration and cleaning, and the newer plastic wood and other specialty composite materials. Note that manufactured casework is in Division 12, Furnishings.

- *Division 07, Thermal and Moisture Protection*: This is the same as the previous edition of the MasterFormat and includes dampproofing and waterproofing, insulation, vapor retarders, air barriers, shingles, roof tiles, siding, membrane roofing, flashing, joint sealers, fire and smoke protection, and roofing specialties such as roof hatches, smoke vents, roof pavers, scuppers, and gravel stops.

- *Division 08, Openings*: This was formerly called Doors and Windows but contains the same elements as before, including metal doors and frames, wood doors and frames, specialty doors, storefronts, all types of windows, skylights, hardware, curtain walls, and glazing.

- *Division 09, Finishes*: The Finishes division covers all types of finish materials, including plaster, gypsum wallboard (including metal framing), all types of floor and wall tile, terrazzo, all types of flooring materials, acoustical ceilings and other types of decorative ceilings, wall coverings, acoustical treatments, paints, and other coatings.

- *Division 10, Specialties*: The specialties division covers a long list of items including visual display boards, toilet compartments, louvers, grilles, wall and corner guards, access flooring, pre-built fireplaces, flagpoles, signage, lockers, awnings, demountable partitions, storage shelving, exterior protection (sun screens, storm panels, etc.), and toilet and bath accessories.

- *Division 11, Equipment*: This division contains information for architectural equipment including vaults and security items, teller and security equipment, church-related equipment, library equipment, theater and stage equipment, musical equipment, mercantile equipment, checkroom equipment, vending machines, audio-visual equipment, loading-dock equipment, detention equipment, athletic equipment, medical equipment, mortuary equipment, and equipment for laboratories, planetariums, observatories, and offices.

- *Division 12, Furnishings*: Division 12 includes furniture, systems furniture, art, window treatments, accessories, multiple seating, and interior plants. Note especially that this division includes manufactured casework, whereas custom casework would be in Division 06.
- *Division 13, Special Construction*: Special construction covers air-supported structures, special-purpose rooms (clean rooms, saunas, planetariums, etc.), seismic control, radiation protection, lightning protection, pre-engineered structures, hot tubs, and kennels.
- *Division 14, Conveying Equipment*: Division 14 includes elevators, escalators, dumbwaiters, moving walks, and lifts.
- *Division 21, Fire Suppression*: This division contains specifications that were previously in Division 13 and includes detection and alarms and all types of fire-suppression systems, such as wet-pipe, dry-pipe, deluge, carbon dioxide, foam, pre-action, and dry chemical systems as well as standpipes and hoses. Note that fire-related materials (doors, fire-stopping, etc.) are in their respective divisions.
- *Division 22, Plumbing*: Plumbing for buildings has been relocated from the previous Division 15. Processing piping is now in the Process Equipment Subgroup.
- *Division 23, Heating, Ventilating, and Air Conditioning*: HVAC now has its own division, relocated from the previous Division 15.
- *Division 25, Integrated Automation*: This division contains specifications for the expanding technology of integrated automation, including energy monitoring and control, environmental control, lighting control, and similar topics.
- *Division 26, Electrical*: Electrical now has its own division, with specifications for communication, sound, and video in Division 27.
- *Division 27, Communications*: This division has been established for the expanding technologies and specialized nature of computer networks and all types of communications systems (cable, telephone, internet, sound systems, etc.).
- *Division 28, Electronic Safety and Security*: This division has also been established for the expanding technologies and specialized nature of security systems, including intrusion detection, security access, video surveillance, and related topics.
- *Division 31, Earthwork*: Some of the specification items from the previous Division 2 have been moved to this division and include excavation and fill, grading, embankment, soil stabilization, erosion control, piles, caissons, and foundation walls. Most of the elements in this section are below-grade work.
- *Division 32, Exterior Improvements*: This division also contains specification items previously in Division 2 and includes mainly above-grade items like paving, utility types of fences and gates, site furnishings, play field equipment, and planting.
- *Division 33, Utilities*: Utilities contains previous Division 2 items such as water distribution, sanitary piping, septic tanks, subdrainage, storm drainage, ponds and reservoirs, and constructed wetlands.

Questions are especially difficult when they involve Divisions 10, 11, and 13. Use the following suggestions to help remember what item is in which division. Although the suggestions are sometimes superseded by exceptions, they may assist in categorizing the information. Generally, only the first two numbers (representing the division) have to be remembered if the answer choices give the full six-digit CSI number.

Division 10, Specialties, includes items that are not standard materials (like wallboard, flooring, finishes, and ceilings), are typically small scale, and are usually placed in a building in multiples. For example, visual display boards, lockers, wall and corner guards, and access flooring are typically not found in every building (they are "special"). They are small relative to the building and the spaces in the building. There is also usually more than one of them installed (more than one display board, more than one locker, and more than one corner guard).

Division 11, Equipment, includes items that are generally larger and more expensive than those in Division 10.

Division 13, Special Construction, includes much larger elements that can almost be thought of as a building within a building. Examples include air-supported structures, seismic control, and animal kennels.

Technical Section Outline and Format

The MasterFormat system also establishes a standard way of organizing any particular section. The first level of division within a section is the three-part format. This includes Part 1, General; Part 2, Products; and Part 3, Execution. All sections include these three parts; the specific articles within the parts vary with the type of material or product being specified.

Part 1 gives the general requirements for the section such as the scope of the section, submittals required, quality assurance requirements, warranties, project conditions, and specifications for the delivery, storage, and handling of materials.

Part 2 details the specifications for the materials and products themselves, including acceptable manufacturers (if applicable), standards and test methods to which the materials must conform, how items are to be fabricated, and similar concerns.

Part 3 tells how the products and materials are to be installed, applied, or otherwise put into place. This part also describes the examination and preparation required before installation, how quality control should be maintained in the field, and requirements for adjusting, cleaning, and protecting the finished work.

Figure 49.2 shows the SectionFormat™ outline, listing all the possible articles of each part.

Specifying for Sustainability

There are two main areas of a project's specifications where sustainability issues are addressed. The first is in Division 01, General Requirements, and the second is in all of the individual technical sections that cover specific materials and construction elements.

Division 01, General Requirements

In Division 01, there should be a separate specification section that applies to all the other specification sections and sets the goals and general direction of the project for sustainability and environmental quality. It is in this section that the contractor should be advised of the design requirements used by the architect and the rest of the design team in the preparation of the contract documents. These criteria can then be used if the contractor wants to propose substitutions or make enhancements.

Some of the specification articles in the general Division 01 specification section may include the following.

- A summary of the environmental goals of the project and the special requirements expected of the contractor. This summary generally includes requirements addressing three areas: resource-efficient materials and systems, energy conservation, and indoor air quality. These goals may be as simple or as complex as warranted by the project or the client's goals. If LEED certification is being sought, the individual credits required by LEED may be used to develop a list of requirements. Refer to Ch. 30 for information on LEED certification.
- Required submittals from the contractor. These may include manufacturer's certificates of recycled content, certification of wood products as coming from an accredited certifier (refer to Ch. 30 for information on wood certification), material emission testing reports, cleaning product information, and other documentation as may be required for LEED certification.

  The architect should request that the contractor submit material safety data sheets for all products that may contain hazardous materials. A *material safety data sheet* (MSDS) is a listing of product safety information prepared by manufacturers and marketers of products containing toxic chemicals. In addition to giving the basic product components, MSDSs are required to list the health effects of the material; first aid, safe storage, and disposal guidelines; protective equipment required for handling; and procedures for handling leaks and spills. They are intended for use by employers and emergency responders rather than by consumers.
- Required tests and procedures for testing materials to verify that they comply with the requirements
- A list of hazardous materials and chemicals
- A list of definitions with which the contractor may not be familiar. These may be included in this section or in individual sections if they only apply to one material, such as "certified wood product."
- A list of sources of information for product certification or sustainability that the contractor can use. This may also include trade associations and specific regulatory agencies' names and addresses.
- Requirements for the packaging of materials with recycled products
- Requirements for construction activities to minimize pollution, dust, erosion, chemical emissions, spills, and water and moisture leaks. This could include a no smoking provision for the job site.

Individual Technical Sections

The individual technical sections of the specification should contain the sustainability requirements unique to each product, such as use of local products, recycled content, requirements for VOCs, energy efficiency, cleaning and maintenance requirements, certification by a third party, and the other material criteria mentioned in Ch. 30. Generally, the sections affected will include concrete, rough carpentry, architectural woodwork, plastic products, doors, windows, gypsum wallboard, acoustical ceilings, carpeting, resilient flooring, ceramic tile, wood flooring, paints and coatings, and toilet partitions. Others should be included as needed.

PART 1 – GENERAL

SUMMARY
- Section Includes
- Products Furnished [or] Supplied But Not Installed Under This Section
- Products Installed But Not Furnished [or] Supplied Under This Section
- Related Requirements

PRICE AND PAYMENT PROCEDURES
- Allowances
- Unit Prices
- Alternates [or] Alternatives
- Measurement and Payment

REFERENCES
- Abbreviations and Acronyms
- Definitions
- Reference Standards

ADMINISTRATIVE REQUIREMENTS
- Coordination
- Preinstallation Meetings
- Sequencing
- Reference Standards

SUBMITTALS

ACTION SUBMITTALS / INFORMATIONAL SUBMITTALS
- Product Data
- Shop Drawings
- Samples
- Certificates
- Delegated Design Submittals
- Test and Evaluation Reports
- Manufacturers' Instructions
- Source Quality Control Submittals
- Field [or] Site Quality Control Submittals
- Manufacturer Reports
- Sustainable Design Submittals

SPECIAL PROCEDURES
- Submittals
- Qualification Statements

CLOSEOUT SUBMITTALS
- Maintenance Contracts
- Operation and Maintenance Data
- Bonds
- Warranty Documentation
- Record Documentation
- Sustainable Design Closeout Documentation
- Software

MAINTENANCE MATERIAL SUBMITTALS
- Spare Parts
- Extra Stock Materials
- Tools

QUALITY ASSURANCE
- Regulatory Agency Sustainability Approvals
- Qualifications
  - Manufacturers
  - Suppliers
  - Fabricators
  - Installers / Applicators / Erectors
  - Testing Agencies
  - Licensed Professionals
- Certifications
- Sustainability Standards Certifications
- Preconstruction Testing
- Field [or] Site Samples
- Mock-Ups

DELIVERY, STORAGE, AND HANDLING
- Delivery and Acceptance Requirements
- Storage and Handling Requirements
- Packaging Waste Management

FIELD [or] SITE CONDITIONS
- Ambient Conditions
- Existing Conditions

WARRANTY [or] BOND
- Manufacturer Warranty
- Special Warranty
- Extended Correction Period

PART 2 – PRODUCTS

OWNER-FURNISHED [or] OWNER-SUPPLIED PRODUCTS
- New Products
- Existing Products

[SYSTEMS] / [ASSEMBLIES] / [MANUFACTURED UNITS] / [EQUIPMENT] / [COMPONENTS] / [PRODUCT TYPES] / [MATERIALS] / [USER-DEFINED HEADING]

Manufacturers
- Manufacturer List
- Substitution Limitations
- Product Options

Description
- Regulatory Requirements
- Sustainability Characteristics

Performance / Design Criteria
- Capacities

Operation
- Operators
- Controls
- Operation Sequences

Materials

Assembly [or] Fabrication
- Factory Assembly
- Shop Fabrication
- Assembly [or] Fabrication Tolerances

Mixes

Finishes
- Primer Materials
- Finish Materials
- Shop Finishing Methods

ACCESSORIES

SOURCE QUALITY CONTROL
- Tests and Inspections
- Non-Conforming Work
- Manufacturer Services
- Coordination of Other Tests and Inspections

PART 3 – EXECUTION

INSTALLERS
- Installer List
- Substitution Limitations

EXAMINATION
- Verification of Conditions
- Preinstallation Testing
- Evaluation and Assessment

PREPARATION
- Protection of In-Place Conditions
- Surface Preparation
- Demolition / Removal

ERECTION / INSTALLATION / APPLICATION / [USER-DEFINED PROCESS]
- Special Techniques
- Interface with Other Work
- Systems Integration
- Tolerances

[REPAIR] / [RESTORATION]

RE-INSTALLATION

FIELD [or] SITE QUALITY CONTROL
- Field [or] Site Tests and Inspections
- Non-Conforming Work
- Manufacturer Services

SYSTEM STARTUP

ADJUSTING

CLEANING
- Waste Management

CLOSEOUT ACTIVITIES
- Demonstration
- Training

PROTECTION

MAINTENANCE

ATTACHMENTS

The Division Numbers and Titles used in this product are from *MasterFormat*™ 2010 Edition and the three part SectionFormat outline from *SectionFormat*™/*PageFormat*™ are published by the Construction Specifications Institute (CSI) and Construction Specifications Canada (CSC), and are used with permission from CSI, 2010.

The Construction Specifications Institute (CSI)
99 Canal Center Plaza, Suite 300
Alexandria, VA 22314
800-689-2900; 703-684-0300
CSINet URL: http://www.csinet.org

Figure 49.2 SectionFormat Outline

For actual specifying in Part 2, Products, of each specification section, the architect can use several approaches. First, the architect can write a performance specification giving the requirements for recycled content, maximum emissions of chemicals, and other criteria and the testing standard by which products must be evaluated. As stated previously in this chapter, true performance specifications are difficult to write.

Another approach is to give a list of three to five approved products that the architect knows will satisfy the requirements of the specification section. This list can contain products that have the desired recycled content or are capable of being recycled, products that have low emissions of VOCs and other hazardous chemicals, and equipment that is low polluting. Along with this, a provision can permit the contractor to submit a proposed substitution if the contractor can prove that the substitution meets all of the requirements. This puts an additional burden on the architect during the bidding or negotiation phases, when time may be short for full consideration of such substitution proposals.

Finally, if there is only one product that meets both the sustainability and aesthetic and functional requirements of the project, a proprietary specification can be written. This is typically only possible for private work, where requirements for competitive bidding are not as strict as they are for public work. Even for private work, the number of proprietary specifications should be kept to a minimum.

Specification Writing Guidelines

As previously mentioned, specifications are legal documents as well as a tool for communicating technical information to the contractor. Because of this, they must be complete, accurate, and unambiguous. The language must be precise. Some of the important things to remember are the following.

- Know what the standards and test methods referred to include and what parts of them are applicable to your project. Make sure they are the most current editions.
- Do not specify the results with the methods proposed to achieve those results, since the result may be a conflict. For instance, specifying that a brick must have certain absorption characteristics according to an ASTM test method and then specifying a particular brick that does not meet the stated requirements will result in a specification that is impossible to comply with.
- Do not include standards that cannot be measured. For example, saying that the work should be done "in a first class manner" is subject to wide interpretation.
- Avoid *exculpatory clauses*. These are phrases that try to shift responsibility to the contractor or someone else in a broad, general way. An example is something like "contractor shall be totally responsible for all ..." Unless the clause is generally accepted wording or makes sense in the context of the specification, current legal opinion disapproves of such clauses, especially when they favor the person who wrote them.
- Avoid words or phrases that are ambiguous. The combination "and/or," for example, is unclear and should be replaced with one word or the other. The abbreviation "etc." is also vague; it may include undesirable factors, and it implies that a list can go on forever. The word "any" implies that the contractor has a choice. This can be acceptable if the architect wants to allow a choice, but this is usually not the case.
- Keep the specifications as short as possible. Specification writing can be terse, even sometimes omitting words such as "all," "the," "an," and "a."
- Describe only one major idea in each paragraph. This makes reading easier and improves comprehension; it also makes changing the specification easier.

50 THE PRIMARY CONTRACTUAL DOCUMENTS

This chapter reviews the various approaches to project delivery and the primary contractual documents that formalize the delivery method selected. These include the Owner-Architect Agreement, the Owner-Contractor Agreement, and the general and supplementary conditions of the contract. Additional contractual documents, which include the drawings, specifications, change orders, and other types of forms, are discussed in other chapters. Although various types of documents used in the project delivery process may establish contractual relationships between the many parties involved, these are not part of the contract documents as formally defined.

The *contract documents* consist of the Owner-Contractor Agreement, the general conditions of the contract, the supplementary conditions of the contract (if any), the drawings, specifications, and addenda issued prior to execution of the contract, any other documents specifically listed in the agreement, and modifications issued after execution of the contract. A *modification* is a change order, a construction change directive, a written order issued by the architect for a minor change in the work, or a written amendment to the contract signed by both parties.

APPROACHES TO PROJECT DELIVERY

The term *project delivery* describes the entire sequence of events necessary to provide an owner with a completed building. It includes the selection of people who will design and construct the project, establishment of contractual relationships, and some method of organizing contractors to perform the work. This section reviews some of the elements of project delivery and discusses the three primary types.

Responsibility for Design and Construction

The traditional construction method available to owners is to hire an architect to design the project and a contractor to build the project. The architect acts as agent for the owner, looking after the owner's best interest with no financial stake in the project. The contractor, in turn, agrees to finish the project according to the plans and specifications for a fixed price within a certain time period. The owner has separate contracts with the architect and the contractor.

Another method is to have a single entity responsible for both designing and building a project. This approach allows review by construction experts during design and often includes a guaranteed cost. However, it eliminates the advantages of competitive bidding and can set up potential conflicts because the goals of designers are usually at variance with the goals of contractors. Both of these delivery approaches will be discussed later in this section.

Agency

One of the key concepts in the traditional relationships among the architect, owner, and contractor is that of agency. The legal concept of agency involves three parties: the principal, the agent, and the third party. The owner is the principal, the architect is the agent of the owner, and the contractor is the third party. The agent acts on behalf of the principal and has the authority to perform certain duties. In the performance of these duties the agent can legally bind the principal to the third party (contractor). It is therefore important that the architect understand the full extent of his or her authority and what duties are expected.

In contrast to an agent, the contractor is considered a vendor. A vendor supplies a specific product for a fixed price. Unlike the architect/agent, a vendor acts primarily in his or her own interest. Refer to Ch. 53 for more information on agency.

Contract Types

In nearly any building project, regardless of size, a number of contractual relationships are established between all the parties involved. Contract types are often classified by the primary relationship the owner has with the contractor (or contractors). This relationship is called the *prime contract*.

The most common type is the single prime contract, in which the owner has an agreement with a general contractor to build a project according to the plans and specifications. If other, specialized contractors are needed, then the general contractor subcontracts with these parties. Typical subcontractors are mechanical, electrical, plumbing, concrete, roofing, and the like. On large projects there are dozens of subcontractors and many sub-subcontractors. However, the general contractor is responsible to the owner and must coordinate the other subcontractors. The primary advantage of this method is that the owner has a single source of responsibility, which also makes the project easier for the architect to administer.

Another type is the *multiple prime contract*. With this method, major portions of the work, such as mechanical, electrical, and plumbing work, are contracted separately with the owner. Many specialty contractors favor this approach, but it makes the project more difficult for the architect to coordinate.

A third type of contract arrangement involves *many prime contracts*. This is usually applied in fast-track construction where one portion of the work needs to start before other elements are designed or ready to be priced. This arrangement is much more difficult to manage and often requires the use of a construction manager if the architect is unable to coordinate the effort.

Design-Award-Build

The design-award-build is the first and most traditional of the three common methods of project delivery. With this approach, the architect designs the project and prepares the construction drawings and specifications. These are used as the basis for costing the project and awarding a construction contract, either through competitive bidding or negotiation with one contractor. The contractor then builds the project, with the architect providing contract administration services. The owner has separate contracts with both the architect and contractor.

This method of project delivery is fairly simple because all the roles are well defined and the work proceeds in a linear fashion, from selection of the architect to final build out. Coordination problems are minimized, contract relationships are straightforward, and the owner can receive a fixed price before proceeding with construction. The disadvantage is that one phase must be completely finished before the next one proceeds. This can be a problem if the owner needs the building quickly or if extended design and construction times result in higher financing costs.

Fast-Track

When the overall time for design and construction must be compressed, a fast-track method can be used. This overlaps some of the design process with some of the construction process to reduce the total time needed for project delivery. For example, based on design development drawings, construction drawings and specifications can be completed for foundations, and this work can be begun before the architect has completed work on interior finish design. Fast-track construction requires many prime contracts and much more coordination, but it can substantially reduce the time and cost of a project.

With the fast-track delivery method, the owner may want to use the services of a construction manager (CM). A *construction manager* is a third party who advises on constructability issues, provides cost estimating during design, makes early material purchases, assists with contract negotiations, manages the construction contracts, and administers the design contracts during construction. A construction manager can also be used with standard design-award-build methods of project delivery, but this is not typical.

A construction manager can either be an independent third party who acts as the owner's agent (as does the architect) without any financial interest in the project or can be the construction contractor. If the CM is an independent advisor, the document used is often AIA A232, *General Conditions of the Contract for Construction, Construction Manager as Adviser Edition*. If the CM is a contractor, then the CM may provide the services described in addition to being financially responsible for the construction of the project, often guaranteeing the total construction cost and completion time.

The advantages of using a CM include early advice on constructability of the design as it is developed, early cost estimating and value analysis, project scheduling, professional management of multiple contracts or fast-track construction, and in some cases, a guaranteed price and completion date.

The disadvantages of using a CM include the extra costs and the more complicated management structure of having one more person on the design and build team. These disadvantages can be minimized if the contractor acts as construction manager. However, when this occurs, the advantages of competitive bidding among general contractors is lost.

Whether the CM acts as an independent agent or as a contractor (vendor), there are three common methods for establishing the total cost of a project. The first is the *fixed-price method*, also known as the *stipulated sum* or *lump sum* method, where the contractor gives the owner a set price for completing the project. With this method the owner knows the final cost before construction begins and is not responsible for cost overruns. However, the owner does not share in any savings that the contractor may realize for whatever reason. The second method is the *guaranteed maximum price* (GMP). In this case the owner has a fixed, maximum price that the contractor (or construction manager) guarantees. If the project is completed for less than this amount, the client receives the cost savings. The third method is the *cost-plus-fee method*, where the owner pays the actual cost of construction (direct plus indirect costs) plus a fee that is agreed to before construction begins.

Design-Build

With the design-build method, the owner contracts with one entity to provide both design and construction services. The design-build firm then subcontracts with others as required. There are several variations of the design-build firm. It may have its own staff of architects and construction personnel. It may primarily have a construction staff and hire architects as subcontractors. It may be a joint venture of an architect and contractor. Or it may subcontract both architecture and construction.

The design-build approach offers the owner several advantages. It is a single source of responsibility, and administering the contract is direct. The owner also has a fixed price early in the process. In addition, the total time of design and construction is usually reduced over more traditional approaches.

There are also several disadvantages. First, the owner does not have as much control over design as with other methods, once the contract is signed. Second, because this is done after the contract is signed, there can be disagreements concerning what was supposed to be included in the design. Third, the design-build firm has control over the quality of the materials and construction methods used. Fourth, in order to get what is needed, the client must develop a specific set of performance requirements.

Design-build contracts are typically used by owners who have building experience with multiple facilities and who have clearly defined needs that can be precisely stated in performance requirements.

A variation of the design-build approach is *bridging*. Bridging combines the advantages of the traditional design-bid-build process and the design-build approach.

In this approach, the owner hires an architect or engineer (referred to as the AE) to be project manager. This person (referred to as the AE/PM) acts as an advisor and works with the owner to develop the project requirements that will be used by the selected design-build firm. The AE/PM also works with public and private groups to gain necessary approvals for the project, and develops scope drawings and specifications so that design-build firms interested in bidding for the project can know the extent of the project and the owner's design intent.

Using the documents developed by the AE/PM, the owner makes the project available for bidding by design-build firms. When a design-build firm is selected, it takes over the responsibilities of the AE, and the firm produces the final, detailed construction documents. The AE/PM reviews the final documents but is not responsible for them. The design-build firm then uses the final documents in securing the necessary permits, reviewing submittals, and constructing the project.

Bridging is based on the idea that the design-build firm is in the best position to work with manufacturers, subcontractors, and other suppliers to determine the best way to construct the project at the lowest possible cost while meeting the requirements of the owner. For the owner, bridging combines an important advantage of design-build, having someone to represent the owner's interests throughout the process, with the advantages of competitive bidding, a fixed cost, and single source responsibility for construction.

Integrated Project Delivery

Integrated project delivery (IPD) is a method of completing a building project in which all participants collaborate closely from the project's earliest conceptualization to move-in. IPD assumes that the best design and the most efficient and cost-effective building can be produced when everyone works together throughout the process, without the adversarial positions that sometimes develop with the traditional design-bid-build approach.

At the beginning of the project, during what is called *conceptualization* (or *pre-design* in traditional terms), the owner, building users, architect, engineers, contractors, subcontractors, suppliers, and others begin to work together. All these people continue their collaboration as the project design is developed, finalized, and constructed. IPD depends heavily on technology, communication, and having an integrated building information model (BIM) that everyone on the team has access to.

The phases of IPD include conceptualization (pre-design), criteria design (schematic design), detailed design (design development), implementation documents (construction documents), agency review, buyout (bidding from participants not included in the integrated team), construction (construction administration), and closeout. Because more participants are involved, the early design phases may take slightly longer than with traditional approaches. The implementation documents and agency review/buyout phases, however, will take less time, and the total project delivery time will be shorter overall.

The advantages of IPD include a better design, shorter project delivery time, lower cost, quality construction, and fewer problems during construction. Although there are many details that are unique to this delivery method, such as compensation, legal responsibilities, and technology standards, IPD has the potential to improve how projects are designed and built. The AIA has developed standard documents to address these issues, including A295, *General Conditions of the Contract for Integrated Project Delivery*.

OWNER-ARCHITECT AGREEMENTS—AIA DOCUMENT B101

There are several types of owner-architect agreements published by the American Institute of Architects. The most common is AIA Document B101, *Standard Form of Agreement Between Owner and Architect*. The AIA made many changes to this document in a 2007 revision. Most notably, two earlier documents (B141 and B151) were merged into one so that the provisions of the agreement and the specific architect's scope of services are both in one document.

Two separate articles are used to describe the architect's services, one for basic services and one for additional services. Basic services include the five traditional phases of a project: schematic design, design development, construction documents, bidding or negotiation, and construction administration. Additional services include any services not described as basic services, such as programming, building information modeling, and post-occupancy evaluation. If any additional services are to be provided they must be noted in the B101 agreement and described in the agreement or in an attachment to the document.

Additional AIA standard agreements are available for large and complex projects, small projects of limited scope, jobs where construction management services are performed, interior design, and other specialized services.

Design-build contracts are typically used by owners who have building experience with multiple facilities and who have clearly defined needs that can be precisely stated in performance requirements.

Although AIA forms do not have to be used between either the owner and architect or the owner and contractor, they have been developed over many years and represent a general consensus concerning the rights and duties of the various parties involved with a construction project. A solid understanding of the provisions in the AIA documents should clarify the concept of standard contractual relationships. These are the contracts covered by the ARE.

Because the various agreements discussed in this chapter are lengthy and cover a great deal of material, it is advisable to read through the primary agreements prior to taking the exam. The remaining sections of this section will only highlight some of the more important provisions. They are based on AIA B101.

Initial Information

The first article of the first part of AIA B101 requires the architect and owner to itemize the information and assumptions about the project, if known at the time of contract execution. Information includes the project's objective; site information; the owner's program; the physical, legal, financial, and time parameters; and the key personnel for both the owner and the architect. The intent of this new article is to encourage communication at the beginning of the project. The article states that the information may materially change and if it does the owner and architect shall adjust the schedule, the architect's services, and the architect's compensation.

The Architect's Responsibilities

The architect's responsibilities are spelled out in three articles of AIA Document B101, those related to general responsibilities, basic services, and additional services. In Article 2, a *standard of care* paragraph requires the architect to perform services consistent with the professional skill and care ordinarily provided by architects practicing in the same or similar locality under the same or similar circumstances, and to perform these services as expeditiously as possible while still being consistent with such professional care and the orderly progress of the project.

The architect must not engage in any activity or accept any employment or interest that would compromise the architect's judgment. Article 2 further requires the architect and owner to list the types and amounts of insurance the architect is required to carry for the project. It specifically lists general liability, automobile liability, workers' compensation, and professional liability. If any insurance requirements placed into the agreement are in excess of the types and limits the architect normally maintains, the owner is required to reimburse the architect for any additional cost. Refer to Ch. 53 for information on types of insurance.

Article 3 states the scope of the architect's basic services. These include usual and customary structural, mechanical, and electrical engineering services. The architect must coordinate the architect's services with those provided by the owner and the owner's consultants. The architect is entitled to rely on the accuracy and completeness of information furnished by the owner and must provide prompt written notice to the owner if the architect becomes aware of any error, omission, or inconsistency in the information.

The architect must submit, for the owner's approval, a schedule for the performance of the architect's services. This schedule must include time for the owner's review, the performance of the owner's consultants, and the approval of submissions by authorities having jurisdiction. It must also include the expected dates for the start of construction and substantial completion. These time limits cannot be exceeded by the architect or owner except for reasonable cause.

One provision added to Article 3 in 2007 requires the architect to consider environmentally responsible design alternatives during the schematic design phase. These alternatives may include choices of materials, building orientation, and other considerations as long as they are consistent with the owner's program, schedule, and budget.

Other important provisions of Article 3 include the following.

- *Project administration services*. The architect must manage the architect's own services and administer the project. This includes consulting with the owner, researching design criteria, attending project meetings, coordinating both the architect's and owner's consultants, and issuing progress reports. A *progress report* may consist of copies of correspondence, memos detailing the progress of the project, architect's field reports, minutes of meetings, or any other writings that keep the owner advised.

  The architect must prepare, and keep updated, a project schedule that identifies *estimated* milestone dates for decisions required of the owner, services furnished by the architect, time required for governmental and other approvals, completion of document provided by the architect, commencement of construction, and substantial completion. The project schedule is not the construction schedule, which is prepared by the contractor and only runs from commencement of construction to the proposed date for substantial completion.

  The architect must also consider alternative materials and building systems, make presentations to the owner, submit design documents to the owner at intervals for the purposes of evaluation and approval by the owner, and assist the owner in filing documents required for approval of governmental authorities.

- *Evaluation of budget and cost of the work*. The architect must prepare a preliminary estimate of the cost of the work and update and refine it as design work progresses through the end of the preparation of construction documents. At each point, the cost estimate should be compared with the owner's budget. If the estimate exceeds the budget, the architect must make recommendations to the owner to adjust the project's size, quality, or budget, and the owner must cooperate with the architect in making the adjustments.

  All cost estimates prepared by the architect represent the best professional judgment. However, neither the architect nor the owner warrants that bids or negotiated prices will not vary from the owner's budget or from any estimate that the architect has made. Only the contractor can guarantee prices.

- *Evaluation and planning services*. The architect must provide a preliminary evaluation of the information furnished by the owner, including information about the site, program, schedule, budget, and proposed method of contracting for construction. In this evaluation the architect should review the balance between quality, cost, and time. The architect should notify the owner of any impact that the budget, schedule, site, or method of contracting may have on the project.

- *Design services*. This article covers the bulk of the architect's standard services, including schematic design, design development, and construction document production, and describes generally what is involved in each of these design phases. At the end of each phase the owner's approval is a precondition that must be received before the architect can begin work on the next phase. When schematic designs are presented to the owner, the owner is not obligated to approve the scheme if it fails to match the agreed-upon program, budget, or time frame. However, the owner must act in good faith to work with the architect as revisions are made. During the construction document production phase the architect must *assist* the owner in the development and preparation of bidding documents and the conditions of the contract for construction. By assisting, it is clear that the architect is *not* providing legal services to the owner and is *not* a party to the Owner-Contractor Agreement.

- *Construction procurement services*. During this phase the architect must *assist* the owner in obtaining competitive bids or negotiated proposals and must *assist* in awarding the contract and preparing contracts for construction. With the contract language of *assist*, the architect is acting as an agent for the owner. The architect produces the bidding documents, distributes the documents, considers requests for substitutions, holds pre-bid conferences, answers questions, prepares addenda, and participates in the opening of bids. Similar requirements are defined if the project is negotiated with a contractor. Refer to Ch. 51 for more information on bidding procedures and documents and the architect's responsibilities during this phase of the work.

- *Contract administration services*. This article of the Owner-Architect Agreement outlines the responsibilities of the architect during the construction phase of the project.

The architect must make site visits at intervals appropriate to the stage of construction to generally determine whether, when completed, the project will be in accordance with the contract documents. The architect must keep the owner informed of the progress and endeavor to protect the owner against defects. However, the architect is not required to make exhaustive or continuous on-site inspections.

The architect is not responsible for the means of construction, building techniques, or safety precautions. These are the sole responsibility of the contractor. The only time this is not true is if the architect has actually specified means and methods of construction. (This provision is in AIA Document A201, *General Conditions of the Contract for Construction*, not in AIA B101.) Refer to Ch. 52 for more information on construction administration services and the architect's responsibilities during this phase.

The owner and contractor are supposed to communicate through the architect. Communications by and with the consultants are also supposed to be through the architect.

The Owner's Responsibilities

Under AIA B101, the owner must provide the architect with information such as program, schedule, and budget. The owner must also furnish the services of consultants or authorize the architect to furnish these services as a change in services (see section on changes in services). In addition, the owner must furnish tests, inspections, and reports required by law or the contract documents, such as structural, mechanical, and chemical tests, along with tests for pollution or hazardous materials. The owner must also furnish all legal, insurance, and accounting services necessary for the project.

The owner must provide a program that gives the owner's objectives, schedule, constraints, and design criteria, including space requirements and relationships, special equipment, systems, and site requirements.

The owner must furnish land surveys to describe the legal limits of the site, grades, locations of utilities, easements, right-of-way, and other aspects of a standard survey. The architect may assist the owner in procuring these services (using AIA Document G601, *Request for Proposal—Land Survey*), but this would be an expansion of the architect's standard services.

The owner must furnish the services of a geotechnical engineer, which may include test borings, determinations of soil bearing values, percolation tests, evaluation of hazardous materials, and other investigations as may be required by the site and the project. A report with recommendations should be provided. The architect is entitled to rely on the accuracy of the geotechnical services. The architect may assist the owner in procuring these services and coordinating the necessary information. The owner also has certain responsibilities under the terms of the *General Conditions of the Contract for Construction*, AIA Document A201. Those are summarized in the next section.

Terms and Conditions of the Contract

There are many other important provisions in the Owner-Architect Agreement. These include the following.

- *Instruments of service*. The drawings, specifications, and other documents, including those in electronic form, are considered instruments of service whose authors and owners are the architect and the architect's consultants. They retain all common law, statutory, and other reserved rights, including copyrights. Under the terms of the agreement, the architect grants to the owner a license to use the instruments of service solely and exclusively for the purposes of constructing, using, maintaining, altering, and adding to the project. If the architect rightfully terminates the agreement for cause as provided for elsewhere in the agreement, this license is terminated.

  If the architect does not terminate the agreement for cause, the owner retains the license to use the instruments of service after completion of the project or the owner's termination of the agreement. If the owner later uses the instruments of service without retaining the architect, the owner agrees to release and indemnify the architect and the architect's consultants for all claims and causes of action arising from such uses.

- *Waiver of consequential damages*. Both the architect and owner waive consequential damages, which limits claims to damages resulting directly from a breach of the agreement.

- *Hazardous material*. The architect and architect's consultants have no responsibility for the discovery, presence, handling, removal, or disposal of or for the exposure of persons to hazardous materials such as asbestos, PCBs, or other toxic substances.

- *Third-party claims*. One provision states that nothing in the agreement shall create a contractual relationship with a third party against either the architect or the owner. This is to reinforce the idea of *privity*, which states that one party to a contract is protected from claims from other parties with whom there is no direct contractual relationship.

- *Causes of action.* This clause requires that any claim or cause of action taken by either the architect or the owner against the other must be initiated within a time period prescribed by applicable law (generally the law of the state in which the project is constructed), and in any case not more than 10 years after the date of substantial completion of the work. Each state defines the period of time (often referred to as the statute of limitations) within which a claim must be filed. This period generally begins at the time the problem or injury is first discovered. For example, if the client discovers a leaky roof two years after substantial completion, and state law has a five-year statute of limitations, then the claim may be filed up to seven years after substantial completion.

- *Waiver of rights.* This clause provides for a waiver of damages that are covered by property insurance during construction. It means that the owner and architect cannot sue each other for damages if they are covered by property insurance that is required by the Owner-Contractor Agreement. This is also known as a *waiver of subrogation*. A waiver of subrogation prevents the insurance company from suing any of the principal participants in the project (architect, contractor, subcontractors, engineers, and consultants) to recover what has been paid out for an insured loss.

- *Right to photograph.* The architect has the right to photograph the project and include photographs or other artistic representations of the design in the architect's promotional materials unless the owner has specifically notified the architect in writing that some or all of the portions the architect wants to photograph are confidential or proprietary information. Unless such notice has been given, the owner must give reasonable access to the completed project for photography.

- *Termination.* Either party can terminate the agreement on no less than seven days' written notice if the other party fails substantially to perform according to the terms of the agreement. The architect is also allowed to suspend performance of services on seven days' written notice to the owner if the owner fails to make fee payments when due. If the owner suspends work or terminates the agreement, the architect must be compensated for services performed prior to termination or suspension. A new clause also allows the owner to terminate the contract without cause for the owner's convenience as long as the owner gives seven days' written notice.

Cost of the Work

The *cost of the work* is defined as the cost at current market rates of labor and materials furnished by the owner and items specified or designed by the architect, including costs of management or supervision of construction provided by a separate construction manager or contractor, plus a reasonable allowance for overhead and profit. Construction cost does not include professional fees, land cost, financing costs, or other costs (such as land surveys) that are the responsibility of the owner.

The architect does not warrant that bids or negotiated costs will not vary from the owner's budget or from any estimate prepared by the architect. However, the architect must adhere to the owner's budget. If the budget is exceeded by the lowest bid or negotiated proposal, the owner has five choices: to increase the budget, to authorize rebidding or renegotiation, to terminate the project, to cooperate in revising the project scope and quality, or to implement any other mutually acceptable alternative. However, if the owner chooses to revise the project scope or quality, the architect must modify the documents for which the architect is responsible *without* any further compensation.

Additional Services Not in Agreement

Three paragraphs in the article concerned additional services cover situations in which the architect must, after the execution of the agreement, provide services not specifically listed. Except for services required due to the fault of the architect, the architect is entitled to additional compensation and an appropriate adjustment in the architect's schedule. When the architect recognizes the need to perform additional services, the architect must notify the owner with reasonable promptness and explain why the services are needed. The architect should not proceed until given written authorization by the owner. These services include the following.

- changes in initial information, previous instructions, or approvals given by the owner
- a material change in the project, which may include the owner's schedule, the budget, the delivery method, or the size, quality, or complexity of the project
- the owner's request for extensive environmentally responsible design alternatives, including LEED certification
- changes to previously prepared instruments of service made necessary by the enactment or revision of codes, laws, or regulations

- services made necessary by decisions of the owner that are not rendered in a timely manner, or by any other failure of performance by the owner or the owner's consultants
- preparation of digital data for transmission to the owner's consultants and contractors
- preparation of design and documentation for alternate bid or proposal requests proposed by the owner
- preparation for and attendance at a public presentation, meeting, or hearing
- preparation for and attendance at a dispute resolution proceeding or legal proceeding, except one to which the architect is a party
- evaluation of the qualification of bidders or persons providing proposals
- consultation concerning replacement of work resulting from fire or other cause during construction
- assistance to the initial decision maker, if this is someone other than the architect (the *initial decision maker* (IDM) is the person named in the agreement to render initial decisions on claims and to certify termination of the agreement; the architect is generally the IDM, but the owner and contractor may hire a third-party IDM for dispute resolution)

There are also situations where the architect needs to provide additional services to avoid delay in construction. In such a case, the architect may begin the service and notify the owner with reasonable promptness, explaining the facts and circumstances that have made the services necessary. If the owner determines that all or parts of these services are not required, the owner must give prompt written notice to the architect without any additional compensation to the architect. Services that fall into this category include the following.

- reviewing a contractor's submittal out of sequence from the original submittal schedule
- responding to the contractor's requests for information, when the requests are not prepared according to the contract documents or when the information requested is available to the contractor from a careful study of the contract documents, other information provided by the owner, or prior project correspondence or documentation
- preparing change orders and construction change directives that require evaluation of the contractor's proposals and supporting data
- evaluating an extensive number of claims
- evaluating substitutions proposed by the owner or contractor and making subsequent revisions to the instruments of service
- providing construction phase services 60 days or more after (1) the date of substantial completion or (2) the anticipated date of substantial completion identified in the initial information, whichever is earlier, if it affects the architect's basic services

Many services are not provided unless specifically listed in the agreement. Article 4 contains a list of additional services, and for each service the architect can indicate whether it is not provided, to be provided by the architect, or to be provided by the owner. The service can be described in the list or an exhibit can be attached to the B101 document. The AIA provides standard forms to describe many of the services listed, such as AIA Document B252, *Standard Form of Architect's Services: Architectural Interior Design*. Additional services include programming, measured drawings, building information modeling, landscape design, interior design, on-site project representation, post-occupancy evaluation, security evaluation and planning, LEED certification, and historic preservation.

Owner-Architect Dispute Resolution

The provisions for claims and disputes in the 2007 revision of AIA Document B101 are different from those in earlier AIA agreements. When one party begins a claim or cause of action, mediation must be tried first, and other forms of binding dispute resolution may not be sought unless mediation fails. *Mediation* is a process in which a neutral third party assists the disputing parties in negotiating a settlement, using preset rules established by the American Arbitration Association (AAA). Any binding dispute resolution proceedings are postponed for a period of 60 days from the date of the filing of the request for mediation. The parties to the mediation share the costs involved.

When the contract is written, the architect and owner must choose which method is to be used next if a dispute cannot be resolved by mediation. This may be arbitration, litigation, or another form to be specified in the agreement. *Arbitration* is a formal, legally binding process for resolving disputes without litigation. One or more arbiters with experience in the construction industry hear the arguments of both disputing parties and render a decision, which is binding. The arbitration proceedings are conducted according to rules and guidelines established by the AAA. A demand for arbitration must be made no earlier than the time of filing for mediation and no later than the applicable statute of limitations.

Compensation Methods

There are several methods of compensation that the owner and architect can negotiate. The following are the common types.

- *Stipulated sum (fixed fee)*. This method states a fixed sum of money that the owner will pay to the architect for a specific set of services. The money is usually paid out monthly according to the proportion of the five basic phases of services previously described. With a stipulated sum, the architect must accurately estimate the cost for the office to do the job and still make a profit. Reimbursable expenses are in addition to fees for the basic services and include such things as postage, reproduction, transportation, long-distance communication, computer-aided design and drafting equipment time, renderings, and models.
- *Cost plus fee*. With this approach the professional is compensated for the actual expenses of doing the job plus a reasonable fee for profit. The actual expenses include salaries, employee benefits, direct expenses, and office overhead. Several variations of the cost-plus-fee approach are used.

  With the *multiple of direct personnel expense*, the direct salary of employees is determined and multiplied by a factor to account for normal and required personnel expenses such as taxes, sick leave, health care, and so on. This is then increased by a multiplier that includes provisions for overhead and profit. For example, if a particular person's direct personnel expense is calculated at $30.00 per hour and the multiplier is 2.5, then the cost to the client for that person is $75.00 per hour.

  Multiple of direct salary expense is similar, except that the multiplier is larger, to provide for employee benefits.

  Hourly billing rates simply build in the multiplier to the hourly rate so that the client only sees one number for each of the types of people working on the project.
- *Percentage of construction cost*. This method is not used as much as it once was. With it, the professional fee is tied to the cost of construction as a fixed percentage. However, from the client's standpoint, the architect may be encouraged to increase the cost of construction to increase the fee or, conversely, may lose any incentive to reduce construction cost. From the architect's standpoint, the percentage method may not be good because a low-cost project may require just as much work as, or more work than, an expensive project.
- *Unit cost method*. Fees are based on a definable unit, such as square footage, for such work as tenant planning in a leased building or on a per-house basis in a large residential project.

The choice of compensation method depends on several factors. The method used should fairly compensate the architect for the actual work required and the value of that professional service. It should also allow for the rising cost of providing services, which is especially important when the project will be of long duration. Finally, the client should be comfortable with the method and understand where the money is being spent.

OWNER-CONTRACTOR AGREEMENTS—AIA DOCUMENT A101

Although the owner enters into an agreement directly with the contractor for construction of the project, the architect must be familiar with the various types of owner-contractor agreements. The variations of agreements are usually based on the method of compensation for the contractor. These will be discussed in a later section. One common document used is AIA Document A101, *Standard Form of Agreement Between Owner and Contractor, where the basis of payment is a Stipulated Sum*. Many of the provisions of this agreement are used in other agreement types and in non-AIA agreements between owner and contractor.

Identification of Contract Documents

The first article specifies that the contract documents include the agreement, the general and supplementary conditions of the contract, drawings, specifications, addenda, modifications, and other documents listed in the agreement. It makes reference to a later article in which all the documents are listed in detail. The purpose of this article is to include all the other documents by reference.

Basic Provisions

Some basic provisions are common to all contracts. These include a description of the work, the times of commencement and substantial completion, and the contract sum.

The work normally includes what is described in the contract documents, primarily the drawings and specifications. Any exclusions can be spelled out in the Owner-Contractor Agreement as well as in the contract documents when they are identified as being the responsibility of others.

The date of commencement is important because it is from this date that the construction completion time, or the *contract time*, is measured. The date can be a specific calendar day or it can be when the contractor is given a notice-to-proceed letter by the owner.

The time of substantial completion is expressed with a specific calendar date or by a number of calendar days from the date of commencement. *Substantial completion* is defined as the stage in the progress of the work when the work or designated portion thereof is sufficiently complete in accordance with the contract documents so that the owner can occupy or utilize the work for its intended use.

Completion time may be extended as provided for in the general conditions when circumstances are beyond the control of the contractor. If a particular completion date is important to the owner, provisions for liquidated damages may be included. *Liquidated damages* are monies paid by the contractor to the owner for every day the project is late. They represent actual anticipated losses the owner will incur if the project is not completed on time. For example, if an owner cannot occupy the project and must pay double rent, the liquidated damages may be the amount of extra rent.

In many cases, a liquidated damages provision is accompanied by a bonus provision so that the contractor receives a payment for early completion. This too is usually based on a realistic cost savings the owner will realize for early completion. If a penalty clause is included (which is different from liquidated damages), a bonus provision *must* also be included.

The *contract sum*, of course, states the compensation the contractor will receive for the work. The various methods of compensation are discussed in a later section.

Progress Payments

Based on applications for payment submitted by the contractor, the owner makes periodic payments, usually monthly, to the contractor on account of the contract sum. The Owner-Contractor Agreement defines how these payments are to be made.

In the AIA A101 agreement, the amount due in any time period is based on the percentage of completed work and any materials purchased and stored on site. Materials and equipment stored off site also require payment but only if approved in advance by the owner in writing. The percentage is based on a schedule of values that the contractor submits to the architect, which allocates the total contract sum to various portions of the work such as mechanical, electrical, foundations, and so forth. A certain percentage of each payment, usually 10%, called the *retainage*, is withheld until final completion of the work.

In order to receive payment, the contractor must submit an application for payment to the architect listing the completed work and stored materials according to the schedule of values. The architect then reviews the application, verifies it, and recommends payment to the owner, who then makes payment. If there is work in dispute, the architect may choose not to certify payment of all or a portion of the amount until the problem is resolved.

Owner-Contractor Dispute Resolution

As with the Owner-Architect Agreement (AIA Document B101) and the *General Conditions of the Contract for Construction* (AIA Document A201), described in the next section, the Owner-Contractor Agreement prescribes a specific procedure for dispute resolution. In an article new to the current version of the Owner-Contractor Agreement, the architect is indicated as the initial decision maker (IDM) as previously described. However, the owner and contractor can agree to appoint another person to be the IDM. This new article in the A101 agreement makes reference to Article 15 in the *General Conditions of the Contract for Construction*, where the procedures for resolving claims and disputes are described in more detail.

When disputes arise they are first referred to the IDM who reviews the claims and supporting evidence. Within 10 days of receipt of the claim the IDM must take one or more of the following actions: (1) request additional supporting information from the claimants, (2) reject the claim in whole or in part, (3) approve the claim, (4) suggest a compromise, or (5) advise the owner and contractor that the IDM is unable to resolve the claim. If the IDM renders a decision it is binding but subject to mediation. If the parties fail to resolve their dispute through mediation then it is subject to binding dispute resolution. As with the Owner-Architect Agreement, the owner and contractor must select one of three methods of binding dispute resolution when they write the contract: arbitration, litigation, or other specified means. Unlike previous editions of the AIA agreements, arbitration is not mandatory, but is now an option.

In summary, dispute resolution between the owner and the contractor is handled by the IDM and, if not resolved, by mandatory mediation which is precedent to binding resolution of arbitration, litigation, or other means.

Enumeration of Contract Documents

In this article, all of the documents are listed individually. Reference is made to the agreement itself, AIA Document A201, *General Conditions of the Contract for Construction*, any supplementary general conditions, each specification section, all the drawings, the addenda, if any, and any other documents made part of the contract.

Compensation Methods

There are several ways the contractor can be paid for the work, as mentioned in a previous section. One of the most common is the *stipulated sum*, which is a fixed price the owner agrees to pay the contractor for the work as shown in the contract documents. This is a simple way to arrange things, and owners like it because the cost is known when the bids are made or negotiation is completed. Competitive bidding always uses a stipulated-sum method.

Another method is the *guaranteed maximum price* (GMP). In this case the owner has a fixed, maximum price that the contractor (or construction manager) guarantees. If the project is completed for less than this amount, the client receives the cost savings. If the project costs exceed the GMP, the contractor must pay the excess.

Cost-plus-fee methods compensate the contractor for actual expenses of labor, materials, and subcontracts in addition to a fixed fee. Cost-plus-fee contracts have more flexibility than fixed fees and allow construction to proceed before design is complete. Their disadvantage is that the cost is not known, a problem that can be mitigated with such things as guaranteed maximums, target prices with incentives, and partial cost guarantees. Target prices establish a likely project cost, and the contractor may share in a percentage of savings below the target price or be responsible for a percentage over the price. Partial cost guarantees involve obtaining fixed prices from certain subcontractors or material suppliers.

Construction can sometimes be based on *unit prices*. Entire projects are seldom based this way, but portions of a project may be. For example, in cases where it is not possible to firmly establish quantities at the time of bid, a unit price can be set. This happens quite frequently with excavation where a cost per cubic yard of material is stated. The final quantity is then multiplied by this unit price to arrive at the total cost. In other cases where changes or additions are anticipated, the contractor can be requested to include unit prices in the bid. These can then be used to evaluate the possible cost consequences of making a change and as a check against the final cost of a change order.

GENERAL CONDITIONS OF THE CONTRACT—AIA DOCUMENT A201

The *General Conditions of the Contract for Construction*, AIA Document A201, is one of the most important parts in the entire set of contract documents. It is incorporated by specific reference into the Owner-Architect Agreement as well as the Owner-Contractor Agreement. Obtain a copy of the *General Conditions* and read the entire document prior to the exam. Many of the most important provisions will be outlined in this section. Other portions that pertain to bidding and contract administration are discussed in the following two chapters.

General Provisions

Article 1 provides basic definitions used in the *General Conditions of the Contract for Construction*. One of the most important is that of the contract documents. As stated at the beginning of this chapter, the *contract documents* consist of the agreement between owner and contractor, conditions of the contract (general, supplementary, and special conditions), the drawings, the specifications, addenda issued prior to execution of the contract, other documents listed in the agreement, and modifications issued after execution of the contract. The contract documents do *not* include other documents such as the bidding documents.

It is clearly stated that the contract documents do not create a contractual relationship between the architect and contractor, between the owner and any subcontractor, between the owner and the architect, or between any other persons other than the owner and the contractor.

One of the definitions is that of the *Work*, which means the contractor's obligations to provide improvements to the project. It is important to distinguish what is the contractor's responsibility and to define what the property insurance covers. The Work is distinguished from the *Project*, which includes the work of the contractor as well as that of separate contractors or the owner's own forces. The Work may be the whole or a part of the Project.

Article 1 defines instruments of service; this replaces the previous definition of the project manual and defines the initial decision maker, as previously discussed. *Instruments of service* are representations, in any medium, of the tangible and intangible creative work of the architect and the architect's consultants. These may include studies, surveys, models, sketches, drawings, specifications, and similar materials. Article 1 also adds a new requirement that if the parties intend to transmit information in digital form, they shall endeavor to establish protocols for the transmission of data.

The Owner

Article 2 outlines the duties, responsibilities, and rights of the owner. Among these is the responsibility of the owner to furnish reasonable evidence, at the request of the contractor, that financial arrangements have been made to fulfill the owner's obligations under the contract, in other words, to pay the contractor. However, after this initial request the contractor can only request such evidence if (1) the owner fails to make payments, (2) a change in the work materially changes the contract sum, or (3) the contractor identifies in writing a reasonable concern regarding the owner's ability to pay.

If the contractor makes a written request, the owner must give information necessary to give notice of or enforce mechanic's lien rights. This information usually means the legal description of the property and proof of legal title.

The owner must secure and pay for necessary approvals and permits required for construction of permanent structures or for changes in existing structures. Generally, these will be costs required *before* the execution of the contract, such as zoning permits, easements, assessments, environmental impact studies, and the like. However, these payments *do not* include those that the contractor must pay for after execution of the contract, such as building permits and other governmental fees and permits.

The owner must also furnish, free of charge, one copy of the contract documents for the purpose of making reproductions. The contractor is also entitled to receive any information the owner has about the site conditions. The contractor has a right to rely on the accuracy of the information furnished by the owner.

If the contractor fails to correct work not in conformance with the contract documents or persistently fails to carry out such work, the owner may order the contractor to stop the work until the cause for the order is eliminated.

The owner also has the *right to carry out the work* if the contractor fails in his or her duties to correctly do so. In order to do this the owner must give written notice to the contractor demanding correction of the problem. The contractor has ten days from receiving written notice to begin to correct the problem. If there is no response, the owner can begin work while still retaining rights to arbitration or legal action for breach of contract. The owner may execute a change order or construction change directive deducting the cost of the work from the contract sum, including compensation for the architect's services. The architect must approve the owner's actions in regard to carrying out the work as well as the amount charged to the contractor.

The Contractor

Article 3 details the responsibilities of the contractor. Before starting the work the contractor must review and study the various drawings, specifications, other contract documents, and information furnished by the owner to facilitate the contractor's work. The contractor must also observe site conditions and take any field measurements necessary.

The contractor is not liable to the owner or architect for damage resulting from errors or omissions in the contract documents unless the contractor recognized such error and knowingly failed to report it to the architect. It is also not the contractor's responsibility to ascertain that the contract documents are in accordance with building codes, ordinances, and other regulations. However, if the contractor notices some variance, he or she must notify the architect and owner in writing. If the contractor does not give this notice and performs work knowingly in variance with some regulation, the contractor assumes full responsibility for such work.

The contractor is solely responsible for the means, methods, and techniques of construction and for coordinating the work under the contract. This includes making sure that work already performed is in proper condition to receive subsequent work. It also includes controlling his or her work force, coordinating the subcontractors, and being responsible to the owner for acts and omissions of all people performing work under the contract. However, if the contract documents include specific instructions concerning the means, methods, techniques, and procedures, the contractor is only responsible for job site safety, not the results of the architect's specifications.

If the contractor wants to make a substitution, he or she can only do so with the consent of the owner, after evaluation by the architect, and in accordance with a change order.

A warranty clause states that the materials and workmanship furnished under the contract is of good quality, is free of defects, and conforms to the requirements of the contract documents. This warranty is in addition to other warranties that may be given by manufacturers or fabricators. This warranty clause is also *separate and distinct* from the one-year correction period that is outlined in a later article in the *General Conditions* on correction of work.

The contractor must secure and pay for the building permit and other permits, governmental fees, licenses, and inspections necessary for the execution of the work that are ordinarily obtained *after* the execution of the contract. The contractor must also pay sales, consumer, use, and similar taxes for work provided by the contractor.

If the contractor discovers concealed or unknown conditions that are materially different from those indicated on the contract documents, the contractor must notify the owner and architect no later than 21 days after first observance. The architect must investigate the conditions and determine if they require an increase in the contract sum, contract time, or both. If changes are justified, the architect will recommend an equitable adjustment.

During the course of the work, if the contractor encounters human remains or recognizes the existence of burial markers, archaeological sites, or wetlands not indicated in the contract documents, the contractor must immediately suspend work that would affect them and notify the owner and architect. The owner must then take any action necessary to obtain governmental authorization to resume operations. The contractor may then request adjustments in the contract time, contract sum, or both.

When developing the contract sum, the contractor must include all allowances that are listed in the contract documents. An *allowance* is a set amount of money estimated by the architect to cover a particular material or piece of equipment when the cost for that material or equipment cannot be determined precisely at the time of the bid or negotiated proposal. It is, in effect, a placeholder so some amount of money can be reserved for the item. The article on allowances further states that the allowance shall cover the cost to the contractor of the allowance item delivered at the job site and all required taxes. However, the contractor must add to the allowance the cost for unloading, handling, and installing the item as well as costs for the contractor's overhead and profit. If the costs for the allowance are more or less than the original estimate, the contract sum is adjusted accordingly by change order.

The contractor is also obligated to provide a schedule for the owner's and architect's information, to keep it up to date, and to conform to it.

The contractor must keep at the job site one set of drawings, specifications, addenda, modifications, samples, and shop drawings for the contractor's own use as well as for reference by the architect. An important part of this article requires the contractor to maintain record documents. *Record documents* are marked-up construction drawings, specifications, and other documents that record exactly how the project was built, noting any changes or deviations from the original contract documents. The architect should include the exact requirements for record documents in Division 01 of the specifications.

The article regarding shop drawings, product data, and samples states that these items are *not* contract documents and that their purpose is to demonstrate the way in which the contractor proposes to conform to the information given and the design concept expressed in the contract documents. Refer to Ch. 52 for more information on submittals.

Part of the article on shop drawings, product data, and samples states that the contractor *can* be required to provide professional design services or certifications if *specifically required* to do so by the contract documents or if the contractor needs to provide such services in order to carry out the work of the contract. The architect must specify all performance and design criteria that such services must satisfy. This requirement is sometimes called *design delegation*, but legally it is a form of design allocation by the owner because there is no contractual relationship between the architect and the contractor. Design delegation allows the use of performance specifications for products and building assemblies or allows the contractor to select the best approach to completing the work. For example, specialized temporary shoring may be required to support cutting and patching operations for a portion of the work. The contractor is responsible for doing this but may require the services of a registered professional engineer to design the shoring according to the contractor's needs.

Under a section on indemnification it is stated that, to the extent provided by law, the contractor will indemnify and hold harmless the owner, architect, architect's consultants, and agents against claims, damages, and expenses arising out of performance of the work. However, this clause does not relieve the architect of his or her liability for errors in the drawings, specifications, or administration of the contract.

To *indemnify* is to secure against loss or damage. This clause is intended to protect the owner and architect against situations where a person is injured due to the negligence of the contractor or the contractor's agents. It also is intended to protect the owner and architect against claims from property damage other than to the work itself.

The Architect

Article 4 of the *General Conditions* states the architect's roles and responsibilities in contract administration. These are discussed in more detail in Ch. 52, but in general, this article provides for the typical duties the architect performs as follows.

The architect visits the site regularly to become familiar with the progress of the work and to determine whether it is proceeding in general accordance with the contract documents. The architect is not required to make exhaustive or continuous on-site inspections.

It is reiterated in one paragraph that the architect does not have control over construction means, methods, techniques, procedures, or safety precautions.

The architect has the authority to reject work that does not conform to the contract documents. However, this authority does not give rise to any duty or responsibility to the contractor, subcontractors, or others. In addition, the architect does not have the right to stop the work if something is wrong or the architect observes some safety problem. Instead, the architect should notify both the contractor and the owner.

The architect reviews shop drawings and other submission, but only for the limited purpose of checking for conformance with the design intent expressed in the contract documents. The contractor remains responsible for the accuracy, completeness, and overall coordination of the work.

The architect prepares change orders and may authorize minor changes in the work that do not involve adjusting either the contract sum or contract time and that are not inconsistent with the intent of the contract documents.

The architect interprets and decides on matters concerning the performance of the contract if the owner or contractor requests such interpretation.

The architect's decisions concerning matters related to aesthetic effect are final if consistent with the intent shown on the contract documents.

The architect must review and respond in writing to requests for information about the contract documents. If necessary, the architect must prepare and issue supplemental drawings and specifications related to the request.

In previous versions of the *General Conditions*, the requirements for the resolution of claims and disputes were in the article defining the duties of the architect. Such requirements are now in a separate Article 15 in AIA Document A201. They specify the sequence of events discussed earlier in this chapter, referring disputes first to the IDM, then to mediation, and only then to another form of binding dispute resolution, which must be given in the agreement between the owner and contractor.

Construction by Owner or by Separate Contractors

The owner has the right to perform construction on the project with the owner's own forces and to award separate contracts for certain work. However, exercising this right does require the owner to provide for coordination of his or her own forces and to act with the same obligations and rights as would any contractor.

The contractor must work with the other separate contractors and the owner in coordinating construction schedules when requested to do so and must follow the schedules. The contractor must also allow the owner and separate contractors the opportunity to store materials and perform their work. If the contractor discovers that construction by the owner or separate contractors will adversely affect his or her work, the contractor must promptly notify the architect. The contractor must pay the owner for any costs incurred by the owner for delays or defective construction of the contractor.

Changes in the Work

Under the *General Conditions of the Contract*, changes may be made in the work after execution of the contract. These changes are made by written change order, construction change directive, or minor change in the work.

A *change order* is based on a written agreement among the owner, contractor, and architect concerning the extent of the change and how it affects construction cost and construction time. A construction change directive only requires agreement between the owner and architect and may or may not be agreed to by the contractor. A minor change in the work can be made by the architect alone.

A *construction change directive* instructs the contractor to proceed with the required changes in the work even if the contractor does not agree with the basis for adjustment in contract sum or contract time. When final determination of cost and time changes is made through submittals by the contractor and review by the architect and owner, a change order is issued. However, in the interim, the contractor may request payment for work completed in an application for payment.

The exact procedures the architect must follow for making changes are described in Ch. 52.

Time

The *contract time* is the period from the starting date established in the agreement to the time of substantial completion, including any authorized adjustments. The contractor is expected to proceed expeditiously with adequate work forces and to complete the work within the allotted time.

Payments and Completion

As mentioned previously, the contractor makes monthly applications for payment based on the percentage of work completed in accordance with a schedule of values allocated to various portions of the work. The architect reviews these applications and issues to the owner a certificate for payment or decides to withhold issuance if there are valid reasons. The exact procedures the architect must follow are described in Ch. 52.

Liens

A *mechanic's lien* is a claim by one party against the property of another party for the satisfaction of a debt and is a common method for an architect, contractor, or material supplier to gain payment. If a property carries a mechanic's lien, it cannot be sold or transferred until the lien is disposed of (or bonded), except through foreclosure. If a contractor does not pay a subcontractor or material supplier, and the subcontractor or material supplier files a mechanic's lien against the property, the owner becomes responsible for payment. If the lien is not paid, the property can be foreclosed by the lien holder, the lender, or a taxing entity.

Because the owner has no responsibility for paying subcontractors or material suppliers, ways are provided in the *General Conditions of the Contract* to protect the owner from liens. This is done by requiring the contractor to submit a release or waiver of liens to the owner before final payment is made or retainages of previous payments are released. The contractor must also furnish to the owner and architect an affidavit of payment of all debts and claims, and an affidavit of release of liens stating that all obligations have been satisfied. The release or waiver of liens is attached to this affidavit.

The exact laws governing liens and the time period during which a lien may be filed vary from state to state, so the architect and owner must be familiar with local regulations.

Protection of Persons and Property

The contractor is exclusively responsible for on-site safety and precautions against damage to persons and property. This includes the contractor's employees, other people affected by the work, the work itself, and adjacent property. Provisions concerning the discovery of asbestos, PCBs, and other hazardous materials are also included. If such substances are found or suspected by the contractor, the contractor must stop work and report the conditions to the owner and architect in writing. The owner is then required to obtain the services of a licensed laboratory to verify the presence or absence of hazardous materials reported by the contractor. The owner is responsible for removal of discovered hazardous materials, after which time work can resume upon written agreement of the owner and contractor.

When the contract documents require that hazardous materials be brought to the site, the owner is responsible for those materials, except to the extent of the contractor's fault or negligence in the use and handling of such materials. The contractor is required to indemnify the owner for any costs incurred for remediating a material or substance that the contractor brings to the site and negligently handles, or because the contractor fails to fulfill its obligations in handling hazardous materials.

If any damage to the work is sustained due to inadequate protection, the contractor must repair or correct it. However, this does not include damages caused by acts of the owner or architect.

Insurance and Bonds

For the duration of the project, both the owner and contractor must maintain insurance to protect against various types of losses. The provisions for insurance are spelled out in the *General Conditions of the Contract*. Additional provisions as required by the unique nature of each project are included in the supplementary conditions.

Although insurance is required, the architect is not responsible for giving advice to either the owner or the contractor on matters related to insurance and bonds. In fact, architects' professional liability insurance policies exclude such advice from coverage. Both the owner and contractor should receive advice from their respective legal counsels and insurance advisers as required.

The contractor must furnish liability insurance to provide coverage for the entities for whom the contractor is legally liable. This includes such coverage as workers' compensation, bodily injury or death of the contractor's employees and others, damages to the work, personal injury, motor vehicle insurance, and claims involving contractual liability. The contractor should require that all subcontractors carry similar insurance. The contractor must add the owner, architect, and architect's consultants as additional insureds for claims caused by the contractor's negligence.

The amount of coverage should not be less than the limits of liability specified in the contract or required by law, whichever is greater. It must be maintained without interruption from the beginning of the work until the date of final payment.

At the beginning of the project, the architect should write a letter to the owner reminding him or her of the owner's responsibilities under the terms of the agreement and requesting that the owner determine, with his or her legal and insurance advisers, the type and amount of coverage required. This information, including the owner's requirements on bonds, should be given to the architect for use in assisting the owner with preparing the contract and bidding documents.

The architect should also have certificates of insurance from the contractor on file and should not issue any certificate of payment until such evidence is available or until he or she has been advised by the owner that such insurance has been obtained.

The owner must also purchase and maintain the liability insurance needed to protect the owner against claims and losses arising from operations under the contract. This includes insurance for property damage and loss of use.

The owner's property insurance protects against fire, theft, vandalism, and other hazards. It must be an all-risk policy that insures against all perils that are not otherwise specifically excluded. The amount of coverage must be for the full value of the work, which is usually the contract sum plus any subsequent modifications.

This article of the *General Conditions* also gives the owner the right to require the contractor to furnish bonds covering faithful performance of the contract. A *bond*, often fully labeled a *surety bond*, is an agreement by which one party, called the *surety* (the bonding company), agrees to be responsible to another party, called the *obligee* (the owner), for the default or debts of a third party, called the *principal* (the contractor). Bonds are simply a protection for the owner against default by the contractor. Bonds are discussed in more detail in Ch. 51.

Uncovering and Correction of the Work

If the contract documents require that certain portions of the work remain uncovered for the architect's observation, and the contractor proceeds with covering them, then the contractor must uncover them at no additional charge when architect requests this in writing.

When the architect has not specifically requested to examine a portion of the work prior to its being covered, the architect may request that the work be uncovered. If the uncovered work is found *not* to be in accordance with the contract documents, the cost of uncovering, correcting, and covering the work is the responsibility of the contractor. If the uncovered work *is* found to be in conformance with the contract documents, the cost is the responsibility of the owner.

Prior to substantial completion, the contractor must correct work that has been rejected by the architect for failing to conform to the requirements of the contract documents. The contractor must bear the cost of such corrections, including testing, inspections, and compensation for the architect's services connected with the corrections. For a period of up to a year after substantial completion or within the effective dates of warranties, if any work is found not to be in accordance with the contract documents, the contractor must correct any defective work after written notice from the owner. If the contractor does not correct the work within a reasonable time, the owner may exercise his or her right to carry out the work. To do this, the owner gives the contractor another written notice and the contractor then has 10 days to correct the work. If the work is not corrected, the owner can have others correct it.

If the owner so chooses, he or she can accept nonconforming work as long as it meets code. Because this entails a change in the contract, it must be done by written change order, and if appropriate, the contract sum may be reduced.

Termination or Suspension of the Contract

Either the owner or the contractor may terminate the contract for valid reasons that are enumerated in the *General Conditions of the Contract*.

The contractor may terminate the contract if work has stopped for more than 30 days, through no fault of the contractor, for any of the following causes: a court order, an act of government, failure by the architect to issue a certificate of payment without giving a reason, repeated suspensions by the owner, or failure of the owner to provide proper evidence that financial arrangements have been made to fulfill the owner's obligations. Seven days' written notice is required.

If the architect certifies that sufficient cause exists, the owner can give seven days' written notice and terminate the contract if the contractor fails to supply enough properly skilled workers or proper materials, fails to make payment to subcontractors, disregards laws and ordinances, or is guilty of substantial breach of a provision of the contract documents. The owner may also suspend or terminate the work for convenience, without any cause.

Claims and Disputes

A new Article 15, concerning claims and disputes, is included in the most current version of AIA Document A201. This article provides the most complete description of the procedures required for dispute resolution as well as the requirements for mediation and arbitration.

A *claim* is a demand or assertion by one of the parties that seeks, as a matter of right, the payment of money or another form of relief with respect to the terms of the contract. A claim may also include other disputes between the owner and contractor arising out of or relating to the contract. Claims must be initiated by written notice, made both to the other party and to the initial decision maker, within 21 days after the occurrence of the event that gives rise to the claim or within 21 days after the claimant first discovers the condition that gives rise to the claim, whichever is later.

As described previously in the section on the Owner-Contractor Agreement, a claim is first referred to the initial decision maker. If the IDM does not render a decision or either party does not agree with the decision the claim goes to mediation. If mediation is not successful, the claim is resolved by one of the binding resolution methods agree to by the owner and contractor in their agreement: arbitration, litigation, or other method.

Claims can only be made for *direct damages*. These include the cost of repairing defective work or completing unfinished work. A clause in Article 15 specifically requires both the contractor and the owner to waive claims for indirect, or consequential, damages. *Consequential damages* are those that are not directly and immediately caused by the act of the party but from the consequences or results of such an act. For example, if a contractor does not finish a retail store by the original completion date, the owner may suffer economic loss of sales as well as the need to pay rent for an unopened store.

The consequential damages waived in Article 15 include damages incurred by the owner for rental expenses; for losses of use, income, profit, financing, business, and reputation; and for loss of management or employee productivity. They also include damages incurred by the contractor for principal office expenses; for losses of financing, business, and reputation; and for loss of profit other than anticipated profit arising directly from the work.

While the claim is being resolved, the contractor must continue diligently with performance of the contract and the owner must continue to make payments.

SUPPLEMENTARY CONDITIONS OF THE CONTRACT

Because of the unique nature of construction projects, not every condition can be covered in a standard document such as the *General Conditions of the Contract*. Each job must be customized to accommodate different clients, governmental regulation, and local laws. Information that is unique to each project can be included in one of four areas: the bidding requirements (if the information relates to bidding), the Owner-Contractor Agreement, the supplementary conditions (if the information modifies the *General Conditions*), and Division 01 (General Requirements) of the specifications. In most cases, supplementary conditions are not a separate document but are modifications made to AIA Document A201.

Some of the additional items that may be included in the supplementary conditions are

- permission for the architect to furnish the contractor with instruments of service in electronic form
- additional information and services provided by the owner
- cost for the architect to review the contractor's requests for substitutions
- provisions for the owner, instead of the contractor, to pay for utilities
- requirement that the contractor employ a superintendent to coordinate mechanical and electrical work
- provisions for fast-track scheduling
- reimbursement by the contractor for extra site visits by the architect that are made necessary by the fault of the contractor
- additional protection for the owner against claims for additional time or for consequential damages
- requirements for more detailed information on costs and overhead
- additional requirements for payment procedures
- requirements for liquidated damages and bonuses
- additional requirements for bonding and insurance

There are additional items that can be included as part of the supplementary conditions, but the above list suggests what kinds of things are often included.

In addition to the supplementary conditions, a project may require special conditions. *Special conditions* form a separate section of the conditions of the contract and are written as a separate document. They describe conditions that are unique to a particular project or project site. Special conditions differ from supplementary conditions in that they would be written only once for unique conditions. Supplementary conditions, on the other hand, accommodate different clients, governmental regulations, and local laws, and could be used several times for the same client on different projects.

51 BIDDING PROCEDURES AND DOCUMENTS

Bidding is one of the primary ways contracts are awarded. After the architect has completed the contract documents, various acceptable or invited contractors review them and submit a price for doing the work. The contractor with the lowest bid is usually awarded the contract.

Competitive bidding is popular with many owners because it usually results in the lowest construction cost. For most public agencies, open public bidding is mandatory. However, it must be done within clearly defined guidelines to protect the owner from disreputable contractors and unethical bidding practices.

Bidding is in contrast to negotiation, in which the owner, with the assistance of the architect, works out the final contract price with one contractor. The contractor with which the owner negotiates may be selected in one of two ways. In the first, the owner may know precisely which contractor he or she wants to complete the project. This knowledge may come from having worked with the contractor before, through a referral, or by reputation. In the second method, the owner may select several possible contractors to be interviewed. Each of the contractors is interviewed, and one is selected based on qualifications, and possibly a fee proposal. If requested by the owner, the architect may assist in organizing and participating in the selection interviews and the negotiation process. During the negotiation process, the contractor may point out problems, make suggestions, or propose changes in the design or specifications to reduce the cost of the project. If the agreement is negotiated with a general contractor, the subcontracts may be open to competitive bidding.

BIDDING PROCEDURES

Through many years of practice the bidding procedure has generally been standardized and codified in various industry association documents. Everyone involved with the process knows the rules and what is expected of them. This chapter reviews the common procedures and documents used during this phase of the project delivery process. The duties of the architect are given in AIA Document B101, the Owner-Contractor Agreement.

Prequalification of Bidders

Bidding may be open to any contractor or restricted to a list of contractors who have been prequalified by the owner. The purpose of prequalification of bidders is to select only those contractors who meet certain standards of reliability, experience, financial stability, and performance. An owner contemplating the construction of a multimillion-dollar laboratory building would not be comfortable reviewing the bid of a small home contractor. Once these standards have been met, the owner is better able to review contractors' bids based primarily on price, personnel, and completion time.

Prequalification is usually based on information submitted by contractors concerning their financial qualifications, personnel, experience, references, size, bonding capability, and any special qualities that make them particularly suited for the project under consideration. For public work, when prequalification is allowed, it is usually based on the financial assets and size of the firm.

Advertising for Bids

There are two ways to notify prospective bidders. The first is by advertising in newspapers and trade journals, and the second is with an invitation to bid. With an *advertisement for bids*, the following information is published in one or more newspapers.

- the fact that a call for bids is being made
- the project name and location
- the name and address of the owner and architect

- a brief description of the project, including building type, size, principal construction materials and systems, and other pertinent information
- the date, time, and location the bids are due
- how and where bidding documents can be obtained, and deposit required, if any
- the locations where bid documents may be viewed
- the type and amount of bid bonds required
- the procedures for submitting bids
- whether or not the bids will be opened publicly
- other information as required, such as the owner's right to waive irregularities of the bidding process or to accept bids other than the lowest

Advertising for bids is usually required for public work, although much private work is also advertised if it is open bidding.

For prequalified bidders, an invitation to bid is sent to the prospective bidders. The invitation contains the same information listed previously for bid advertisements. Even with a prequalified list, there should be a sufficient number of bidders to encourage price competition.

Availability of Bid Documents

Bid documents are generally made available through the architect's office. Each bidder receives the required documents including prints of the drawings, specifications, bidding documents, bid forms, and other items as required. It is general practice to require that each bidder put down a deposit on each set of documents taken up to a certain number. After bidding, the deposit may be returned when the documents are returned in usable condition. In some cases the documents are loaned with no deposit required. Extra sets of documents over a certain number can be purchased by the contractor. In most large cities, documents are also put on file in a central plan room where subcontractors and material suppliers can review them. Electronic versions of the central plan room are also available.

Substitutions

During bidding, many contractors request that substitution for some of the materials specified be considered. This most often happens when there are proprietary specifications or a very limited list of acceptable manufacturers. The conditions under which substitutions will be considered and the procedures for reviewing submissions are clearly defined in the instructions to bidders, outlined later in this chapter.

Addenda

An *addendum* is a written or graphic document issued by the architect prior to the execution of the contract that modifies or interprets the bidding documents by addition, deletion, clarification, or correction. During the bidding process, there are always questions that need answers, errors that are discovered, substitutions that are made, and changes that the owner or architect decides to make. Addenda are instruments with which to do this. They are issued prior to bidding.

When an addendum is issued, it is transmitted to all registered bidders not later than four or five days before receipt of bids to give all the bidders ample opportunity to study the document and modify their proposals accordingly.

Pre-bid Conference

On some projects it is advantageous to hold a pre-bid conference. This is a meeting with the architect, owner, and bidders during which the bidders can ask questions and the architect and owner can emphasize particularly important conditions of the project. On very large projects, there may be separate conferences for mechanical subcontract bidders, electrical bidders, and so on. During these conferences, the architect should have someone take complete notes concerning the items discussed. A copy of the notes should be sent to all bidders whether or not they were in attendance. Answers to significant questions should be formalized in an addendum.

Bid Opening

In the instructions to bidders, the date, time, and place of the bid opening is included. Unless modified by addenda, the bid opening time and method of submitting the bids should be strictly observed. Bids received after the opening time should not be accepted unless none of the bids has been opened and there are no objections from those bidders present.

Most public bid openings are conducted by the architect with the owner and bidders present. The bids are read aloud, and the presence or absence of any required supporting documentation is noted. The architect usually prepares a bid log to note the base bid amount, amounts of alternates (if any), whether receipt of addenda was acknowledged, and other pertinent information. This should be made available to the bidders in either open or private bidding.

There should be no announcement of the apparent low bid at the bid opening; the architect should thank everyone for submitting and state that the submissions will be evaluated and a decision of award made within a certain time, usually 10 days. The decision should be sent to all the bidders.

If, after the bids have been opened, a bidder discovers and can support the claim that a clerical or mathematical error has been made, the bidder is usually allowed to withdraw the bid. If it was the low bid, the next lowest bidder is accepted.

Evaluation and Awarding of Bid

The architect assists the owner in evaluating the bids. This includes not only looking for the lowest proposed contract sum, but also reviewing prices for alternates, substitutions, lists of proposed subcontractors, qualification statements, and other documentation required by the instruction to bidders.

The owner has the right to reject any or all bids, to reject bids not accompanied by the required bid bond or other documentation (if required), and to reject a bid that is in any way incomplete or irregular.

If all of the bids exceed the project budget and the Owner-Architect Agreement fixes a limit on construction, the owner has one of four courses of action.

1. to rebid (or renegotiate if a negotiated contract)
2. to authorize an increase in the construction cost and proceed with the project
3. to work with the architect in revising the scope of the project to reduce construction cost
4. to abandon the project

Rebidding seldom results in any significant reduction in cost unless the bidding marketplace is changing rapidly. If the project is revised, the architect must modify the documents without any additional compensation. As discussed in a later section, alternates are often used as a flexible method of deleting or substituting alternative materials or construction elements to help reduce costs. Because the alternates are priced along with the base bid, the owner and architect can quickly evaluate the ramifications of selecting certain alternates.

BIDDING DOCUMENTS

Bidding documents are usually prepared by the architect using standard AIA forms or forms provided by the owner. Many commercial clients who engage in a great deal of building have developed their own forms and procedures, but they are typically similar in content to the AIA forms. The bidding documents are bound into the project manual, but they are *not* part of the contract documents.

The bidding documents usually include the following.

- the advertisement or invitation to bid
- instructions to bidders
- supplementary instructions to bidders (if any)
- bid forms
- bid security information
- performance bond, if required
- labor and material payment bond, if required

Other documents that are sometimes added are qualification forms, a subcontractor list form, certificates of insurance, certificates of compliance with applicable laws and regulations, and information available to bidders, such as geotechnical data.

In addition to the bidding documents, which are not part of the contract documents, the bidding package also includes the drawings, specifications, general and supplementary conditions of the contract, special conditions (if any), addenda issued prior to the receipt of bids, and the form of agreement between owner and contractor.

Advertisement to Bid

As mentioned in the previous section, public bidding requires that bidding for the proposed building project be advertised in one or more newspapers and trade publications. If a list of prequalified bidders is being used, an invitation to bid is sent to those contractors. The advertisement or invitation to bid is also printed and bound into the project manual with the other bidding documents.

Instructions to Bidders

The instructions to bidders outline the procedures and requirements that the bidders must follow in submitting bids, how the bids will be considered, and submittals required of the successful bidder. AIA Document A701, *Instructions to Bidders*, is often used; other organizations produce similar forms. Instructions to bidders normally include the following items. (If the AIA form is being used and additional requirements must be included, it is suggested that supplementary instructions to the bidders be written.)

- *Bidder's representations*. In making a bid, the bidder represents that he or she has read and understood the documents, reviewed the plans and specifications, and visited the site to become familiar with the conditions under which the work will take place, and that the bid is based on the materials, equipment, and systems required by the bidding documents, without exception.

- *Bidding documents*. This article of the *Instructions to Bidders* states where the documents may be obtained, how many sets the bidders may have, and the amount of deposit, if any, for the documents. If the documents are returned within 10 days after receipt of bids, the deposit is returned. The cost of replacing any missing or damaged documents is deducted from the deposit. The bidder winning the contract may keep the documents, and their deposit is returned. Normally, bidding documents are not issued directly to sub-bidders unless specifically stated in the advertisement or invitation to bid.

- *Interpretation or correction of bidding documents.* This article requires the contractor to carefully study the documents and examine the site and local conditions, and to report to the architect any errors, inconsistencies, or ambiguities discovered. If the bidders or sub-bidders need clarification or interpretation of the bidding documents, they must make a written request that must reach the architect at least seven days prior to the bid date. The architect must then issue any interpretations or corrections by addendum, which is sent to all bidders. Bidders must acknowledge receipt of all addenda on the bid form.

- *Substitutions.* The materials and products described on the drawings and specifications establish a standard for the work. If the bidder wants to propose a substitution, it must meet these standards. A bidder is required to submit a request for approval at least 10 days prior to the bid opening date. The request must include the name of the material or equipment for which the substitution is submitted, along with complete backup information about the proposed substitution. The burden of proof of the merit of the substitution rests with the bidder. The architect then reviews the submission and may either reject it or approve it. If approved, the architect issues an addendum stating this fact and sends it to all the bidders. No substitutions can be considered after the contract award.

- *Addenda.* Addenda were discussed previously. According to the *Instructions to Bidders*, addenda must be transmitted to all bidders and made available for inspection wherever bidding documents are on file for that purpose. Addenda must be issued no later than four days prior to the date of bid opening.

- *Bidding procedures.* This article specifies how the bid form is to be filled in, what kind of bid security is to accompany the bid, and the procedure for submitting the bid. Bids are normally submitted in sealed envelopes, with the name of the party receiving the bid on the outside, along with the project name and the name of the entity submitting it. Bid security is described in a following section.

- *Modification or withdrawal of bid.* Bids may not be modified after the designated bid time and date. However, prior to that time a bid may be modified or withdrawn by making notice in writing over the signature of the bidder. The person receiving bids must date- and time-stamp the request. Withdrawn bids can be resubmitted if they are in full conformance with the *Instructions to Bidders*.

- *Consideration of bids.* The procedure for opening bids and reviewing them is explained in this article, including under what conditions bids may be rejected, how they will be evaluated, and conditions for award of the contract. The owner has the right to reject any or all bids. The owner also has the right to accept alternates in any order or combination and to determine the low bidder on the basis of the sum of the base bid and alternates accepted.

- *Post-bid information.* After the award of the bid, the contractor must submit to the architect AIA Document A305, *Contractor's Qualification Statement*, unless it has already been submitted as part of the bidding process. The contractor must also furnish to the owner the following.

  - a designation of the work to be performed with the contractor's own forces
  - the names of the manufacturers, the products, and the supplier of the principal items proposed for the project
  - the names of persons or companies proposed to perform major portions of the work

  If the successful bidder requests it, the owner must furnish to the bidder reasonable evidence that the financial arrangements have been made to fulfill the owner's obligations. This must be done no later than seven days prior to the expiration of the time for withdrawal of bids.

- *Performance bond and payment bond.* The required bonds and the time during which they must be delivered are outlined in this article. Normally, the cost of bonds is included in the bid number unless they are specifically required to be furnished after the receipt of bids and before execution of the contract. Performance and payment bonds are described in more detail in the following section.

Bid Forms

To ensure that all bids will be in identical form, there should be a standard form on which all the bidders enter the required information, making it easier to compare and evaluate the bids. The bid form should contain space for the amount of the base bid, written in both numbers and words, the price for the alternates (if any), unit prices (if any), and the number of calendar or work days in which the bidder proposed to complete the work. Space should be provided for the bidder to acknowledge receipt of any addenda. The bid form must be signed by someone legally empowered to bind the contractor to the owner in a contract.

Bid Security

Bid security is required to ensure that the successful bidder will enter into a contract with the owner. The form of the bid security may be a certified check, cashier's check, or bid bond. If the successful bidder does not enter into an agreement, the bid security may be retained to compensate for the difference between the low bid and the next lowest bidder. The amount of the bid security is either set as a fixed price or as a percentage of the bid; it is usually about 5% of the estimated cost of construction or the bid price.

Performance Bonds

A *performance bond* is a statement by a surety company that obligates the surety company to complete construction on the project should the contractor default on his or her obligations. If this happens, the surety company may complete construction by hiring another contractor, or it may simply supply additional money to the defaulting contractor to allow construction to proceed.

Performance bonds are usually mandatory on public work and advisable on private work. The cost of the performance bond is paid by the owner and is usually included in the amount of the construction price. The architect or owner must verify that the bond is written by a surety acceptable to issue bonds in the particular state where the construction is to take place. Some states will not accept so-called surplus-lines carriers who are not based in their state. In such cases the bond may be invalid.

Labor and Material Payment Bonds

Although a performance bond ensures the completion of the contract, it does not guarantee payment for labor and materials by the defaulting contractor. The result could be liens against the property or litigation by subcontractors and material suppliers. Because of this, a labor and material payment bond is usually required along with a performance bond to protect the owner against these possibilities.

COST CONTROL

Throughout the design process and up to completion of contract documents, the construction cost is only an estimate by the architect. It is only with bidding or final negotiation that the owner finally receives a firm price on the project. If the architect has been doing a reasonable job of tracking design changes and has a good idea of component costs, the bid price should be fairly close to the estimated amount.

Although the architect does not (and cannot) guarantee that the final construction cost will not vary from the estimate, there are several variables that can affect the final bid price.

Bidding in the Marketplace

By its very definition, bidding is a competitive activity. The price a contractor is willing to submit to an owner is, of course, dependent on the actual cost of subcontractor bids, the cost of the contractor's own labor and materials, the cost of equipment rental, the contractor's indirect costs, overhead, and profit.

Bidding is also affected by the construction marketplace, which is itself competitive. For example, if the local economy is depressed, contractors, subcontractors, and material suppliers may be willing to lower prices or reduce profit margins in order to get work and simply stay in business. In good times when work is plentiful, contractors are more selective about what jobs to bid on and what profit allowance to put in their bids. They are not as concerned about reducing prices to get jobs.

Both the architect and owner should be sensitive to these types of market conditions. If there is some flexibility in the owner's schedule, it can be advantageous to either delay or accelerate design and bidding to match favorable market conditions.

Effects of Documents on Bids

One of the variables over which the architect and owner have control is the set of contract documents. These can affect the amount of bids by what they contain and how they are put together, beyond just the amount and quality of construction they represent.

Poorly prepared drawings and specifications can raise questions in the mind of the contractor about what is specifically required, what may simply be implied, and what is omitted. To cover possible unforeseen items, the contractor may add extra money in the bid to cover these unknowns. On the other hand, a complete and clearly coordinated set of documents gives the contractor confidence in the scope and quality of the work. The contractor can then bid with more confidence only those items shown.

Alternates

An *alternate* is a request included in the bidding documents asking the contractor to supply a price for some type of variation from the base bid. This may be a change in materials or level of quality of a material, a deletion of some component, or the addition of some construction element. For example, the base bid may include carpet as a floor covering, whereas an alternate may be to substitute wood flooring for the carpet.

Alternates allow the owner some flexibility in modifying the cost of the project when the bids are in by varying the quantity or quality of the project. They also allow the owner to select certain options based on firm prices rather than on preliminary estimates.

Alternates are called *add-alternates* if they add to the base bid, or *deduct-alternates* if they reduce the base bid amount. Because alternates require more time for both the architect and bidders to prepare, they should be used carefully and should not be a substitute for conscientious cost estimating and reasonable design for the base bid amount.

For evaluating the bids, the selected alternates should be used to arrive at the lowest overall bid, but alternates should not be manipulated to favor one bidder over another.

Unit Prices

Unit prices are set costs for certain portions of work based on individual quantities. When required, they are listed on the bid form and provide a basis for determining changes to the contract. For example, a square foot cost for asphalt paving may be requested if the full extent of paving is unknown when bids are received. Even though the total cost may not be known, the unit costs of the bidders can be compared.

If unit prices are used when work is deleted from the contract, the amount of credit is usually less than the price for an additional quantity of the same item. Spaces should be provided in the bid form for both add and deduct amounts when applicable.

Allowances

As described in Ch. 50, an *allowance* is a set amount of money estimated by the architect to cover a particular material or piece of equipment when the cost for that material or equipment cannot be determined precisely at the time of the bid or negotiated proposal. For bidding, an allowance provides a way to allocate some amount of money for an item in the bid, even if the exact quantity or quality of the item is not known. The allowance (or allowances) is stated in the appropriate section (or sections) of the specifications, so all bidders are using the same amount in their bids. The contractor must add to the allowance the cost for unloading, handling, and installing the item as well as costs for the contractor's overhead and profit. If the costs for the allowance are more or less than the original estimate, the contract sum is adjusted accordingly by change order.

52 CONSTRUCTION ADMINISTRATION SERVICES

Construction of the project is one of the most important phases of project delivery. It is the culmination of a great deal of planning, design, documentation, and organization. The architect should be closely involved with this phase of the project to the extent of his or her contractual responsibilities. During this phase the architect reviews and processes shop drawings and samples, manages requests for changes in the work, observes construction to make sure it is consistent with the contract documents, evaluates and processes the contractor's requests for payment, and administers the project closeout procedures.

SUBMITTALS

After the contract is awarded, the contractor is responsible for providing submittals called for in the contract documents. These include shop drawings, samples, and product data. The submittals are sometimes prepared by the contractor, but most often they are prepared by the subcontractors, vendors, and material suppliers.

Shop drawings are drawings, diagrams, schedules, and other data prepared to show how a subcontractor or supplier proposes to supply and install work to conform to the requirements of the contract documents. As such, they are usually very detailed, showing how portions of the work will be constructed.

A *sample* is a physical example of a portion of the work intended to show exactly how a material, finish, or piece of equipment will look in the completed job. Samples become standards of appearance and workmanship by which the final work will be judged.

Product data include brochures, charts, instructions, performance data, catalog pages, and other information that illustrate some portion of the work.

Although all submittals show in detail how much of the work is going to be built and installed, they are not contract documents.

When shop drawings and other submittals are prepared by the various subcontractors and material suppliers, they are sent to the general contractor, who is responsible for reviewing and approving them. By reviewing them, the contractor represents that field measurements have been verified, materials have been checked, and other construction criteria have been coordinated. Only after this review should the contractor transmit the submittals to the architect. The contractor must give the submittals to the architect in accordance with the submittal schedule approved by the architect or, in the absence of an approved submittal schedule, with reasonable promptness and in such sequence as to cause no delay in the work.

The architect's review of submittals is only for the limited purpose of checking for conformance with information given and seeing if they conform to the design intent. The architect is not responsible for determining the accuracy of measurements and completeness of details, for verifying quantities, or for checking fabrication or installation procedures. The architect's review does not relieve the contractor of his or her responsibilities under the contract documents.

If the submittals require the review of one of the architect's consultants, the architect forwards them to the consultant, who returns the submittals to the architect after review. The architect then reviews them and returns them to the contractor, who in turn returns them to the subcontractor or material supplier who prepared them. The architect may indicate that no exceptions are taken, that marked corrections should be made, that the submittals should be revised and resubmitted, or that they are rejected.

The architect must review submittals in accordance with the submittal schedule approved by the architect or, in the absence of an approved submittal schedule, with reasonable promptness while allowing sufficient time in the architect's professional judgment to permit adequate review. The issue of time is generally dealt with in two ways. First, the contractor is required by the *General Conditions of the Contract for Construction* to prepare a construction schedule for the project, which must include a schedule of submittals that allows the architect a reasonable amount of time for review. Second, the architect may, and should, indicate in the section on submittals in Division 01 of the specifications the procedure for making submittals, including the time that the contractor must allow for the architect's review. The contractor generally takes this time to establish the construction schedule.

According to the Owner-Architect Agreement, the architect must keep a log of submittals and copies of the submittals. The log should include the submittal name or other identification and the date the submittal was received by the architect. Other dates that must also be included on the log are the date the submittal was sent from the architect to the consultant (if necessary), returned to the architect, and subsequently returned it to the contractor. The action taken should also be noted.

Shop drawings are not a way for the architect to make changes in the design or refine details. Although minor corrections and changes can be made, the contractor may request a change order if the architect's modification of the shop drawings or samples results in an increase in project cost or time.

CHANGES IN THE WORK

During construction, changes in the work are usually required. They may be necessitated by errors discovered in the drawings, unforeseen site conditions, design changes requested by the client, rulings of building officials, and many other factors. During bidding and prior to contract award, changes are made by addenda. During construction, changes in the work are accomplished in one of three ways: by minor changes in the work, by construction change directive, or by formal change order.

Minor Changes in the Work

When a change does not involve a modification of the contract sum or time and is consistent with the contract documents, the architect may issue a written order directing the contractor to make a minor change. For example, moving a door opening over 6 in before it is framed would be a minor change. The architect may issue an order for such a minor change without the approval of either the owner or contractor.

Construction Change Directive

When a change needs to be made right away but the owner and contractor cannot agree on a price or time revision, the architect may issue a construction change directive. A *construction change directive* is a written order prepared by the architect directing a change in the work before the owner and contractor agree on an adjustment in contract cost, time, or both. The construction change directive gives the owner a way to unilaterally order changes to the contract without changing the terms of the contract. It is used in the absence of total agreement on the terms of a change order. The change in the work may involve additions, deletions, or other revisions. The construction change directive must be signed by both the architect and the owner but does *not* have to be signed by the contractor.

In addition to describing the changes required, the directive should include a proposed basis for determining the adjustment of cost or time or both. If the directive involves a cost adjustment, the architect's proposed basis of adjustment must be based on one of four methods: (1) a lump sum, properly itemized, (2) unit prices previously agreed to in the specifications, (3) costs to be determined by mutual agreement on a fixed or percentage fee, or (4) as provided for in a subsequent clause and summarized in the following paragraph.

Under provisions of the *General Conditions of the Contract*, the contractor must proceed with the work and advise the architect of the contractor's agreement or disagreement with the basis for cost and time adjustment. If the contractor agrees, the change is recorded as a change order. If the contractor disagrees, the architect determines the method and adjustment based on reasonable expenditures and savings of those performing the work. In addition to the actual cost of the work, the architect must include costs related to worker's benefits, equipment rental, supplies, premiums for bonds and insurance, field supervision, permit fees, and profit.

While the parties are making a final determination of the total cost of the construction change directive, the contractor's applications for payment may include payment for work completed under the directive. The architect must make an interim determination whether the costs are justified and, if so, include them in the monthly certification for payment. The architect's interim determination adjusts the contract sum on the same basis as a change order.

Change Orders

A *change order* is a document authorizing a variation from the original contract documents that involves a change in contract price, contract time, or both. Technically, it is issued by the owner because the owner has the agreement with the contractor, but it is prepared by the architect. It must be approved by the owner, architect, and contractor.

Any of the three parties may suggest a change order, but it is normally the architect who submits a proposal request to the contractor. This request is accompanied by supporting drawings or other documents as required to fully describe the proposed change. The contractor submits his or her quotation of price and time change. If these are acceptable to the owner, the formal change order document is prepared and signed by all three parties.

FIELD ADMINISTRATION

Once the project actually gets under way, the architect has a number of responsibilities under the *Standard Form of Agreement Between Owner and Architect* and in accordance with the *General Conditions of the Contract*.

Construction Observation

If made part of the architect's services in the Owner-Architect Agreement, the architect visits the site at intervals appropriate to the stage of construction or as agreed to in writing.

The purpose of the architect's observation is (1) to become generally familiar with the progress and quality of the work and to keep the owner informed, (2) to endeavor to guard the owner against defects and deficiencies in the work, and (3) to determine, in general, if the work is progressing in such a way that, when completed, it will be in accordance with the contract documents.

During construction observation, definite lines of communication among the parties are established by the *General Conditions of the Contract for Construction*. During this time the owner and contractor must communicate through the architect, unless otherwise provided in the Owner-Architect Agreement and the *General Conditions*. Communications between the contractor and consultants should also be through the architect. Communications between the architect and the subcontractors and material suppliers should be through the contractor.

The number and timing of visits to a job site are left to the judgment of the architect based on the size and complexity of the project, the type of construction contract being used, and the exact schedule of construction operations.

During each site visit the architect should make complete notes of the observations and include these in appropriate field reports.

A field report should include the following items.

- the report name and the architect's project number
- the field report number
- the date and time of the observation, and the weather conditions at the site
- the work currently in progress
- the number of workers present at the site or an estimate of the number, if the project is large
- observations made, including any problems
- an estimate of the conformance with the schedule and the estimated percent of completion
- items to verify and action or information required
- a list of any attachments, and the name of the person making the report

Copies of the field reports are sent to the owner, to keep him or her informed of the progress of the work, and to the contractor. Unless otherwise agreed to in writing in the Owner-Architect Agreement, the architect is not responsible for exhaustive or continuous on-site inspections, nor is the architect responsible for the contractor's failure to carry out the work, or for the means, methods, or techniques of construction, or for safety precautions on the job.

Rejecting Work

Under the *General Conditions of the Contract*, the architect has the authority to reject work that does not conform to the contract documents. Because rejecting work means extra time and expense for the contractor, the reasons for rejection should be carefully documented, and the owner should be kept informed of the situation. The architect has the authority to require inspection or testing of work, whether or not such work is fabricated, installed, or completed. However, this action does not give rise to any duty or responsibility of the architect to the contractor, subcontractors, or anyone else performing portions of the work. The contractor must promptly correct work rejected by the architect or work not conforming to the contract documents, whether discovered before or after substantial completion. The contractor pays for the cost of correcting such work.

Uncovering and Correction of Work

There are two situations where work may have to be uncovered. The first occurs when a portion of the work has been covered contrary to the architect's request or to specific requirements in the contract documents. In this case, the work must be uncovered for the architect's examination, and the cost for this, and for replacing it, is paid by the contractor. The second situation occurs when the architect has not specifically made a request to view a portion of the work and the work has already been covered. If the architect then requests that the work be uncovered and it is found that the work *does* conform to the contract documents, the owner must pay for the uncovering and replacement through a change order. If the work *does not* conform, it must be corrected and replaced, and the cost must be borne by the contractor. However, if the owner or a separate contractor caused the unsatisfactory work, the owner must pay the costs.

Safety

The contractor is solely responsible for safety on the job site. If the architect volunteers suggestions or directions concerning construction means and techniques in regard to safety issues, the architect may also assume legal responsibility and be held liable for accidents or other problems.

If the architect observes an obvious safety violation, he or she should call it to the attention of both the contractor (but not suggest how it can be corrected) and owner and should follow up with a notice in writing. If the safety problem is not corrected, the architect should notify both the contractor and the owner in writing.

Field Tests

When tests and inspections are required by the contract documents, or by laws, regulations, or orders of public authorities (building departments), the contractor is responsible for making arrangements with testing agencies acceptable to the owner or with the appropriate public authorities. The contractor pays for the tests and must give the architect timely notice of when and where the test is to be made so that the architect can observe the procedure.

If the architect, owner, or public authorities require additional testing beyond what is required in the contract documents, the architect should instruct the contractor to make arrangements, but only after written authorization from the owner. In this case, the owner pays for the tests.

Regardless of whether the tests were required originally by the contract documents or later by the architect or public authorities, if a test shows that a portion of the work does not conform to the contract documents (including violating building codes or other laws), then the contractor must pay all costs required to correct the problem, including those of additional testing and compensation for the architect's services.

Documentation

During the entire construction administration phase (as well as all phases of the architect's service), the architect should keep complete documentation of the progress of the job. This includes not only the standard forms used, such as change orders, certificates of payment, and the like, but also all correspondence, meeting notes, emails, telephone logs, and similar written or electronic material that records the who, what, why, when, and how of the project. This kind of documentation is critical if disputes arise or the client objects to fee payments for extra services of the architect.

Claims

There are usually disputes and claims on any construction project, and these typically occur during the construction phase. The procedure to be followed if a claim or dispute arises is specifically outlined in the *General Conditions of the Contract*.

A *claim* is a demand or assertion by the contractor or owner seeking payment of money, an extension of time, an adjustment or interpretation of the contract terms, or other relief from terms of the contract. Claims must be made by written notice to the other party and to the architect and must be initiated within 21 days from the occurrence of what prompted the claim or 21 days after the person making the claim first recognized the problem. Whoever makes the claim must substantiate it with documentation or other evidence.

As discussed in Ch. 50, claims are first referred to the initial decision maker. The IDM is usually the architect unless the owner and contractor agreed to name a third-party IDM in the Owner-Contractor Agreement.

If the owner or contractor has a dispute or makes a claim, the IDM must take certain preliminary action within 10 days of receipt of the claim. Such action may include (a) requesting additional supporting data from the claimant, (b) suggesting a compromise, (c) accepting the claim, (d) rejecting the claim, or (e) advising the parties that the IDM unable to resolve the claim because of a lack of sufficient information, or that it would be inappropriate for the architect to resolve the claim.

In evaluating claims, the IDM may consult with or seek information from either party or from anyone with special knowledge or expertise. The IDM can ask the owner to authorize the retention of experts at the owner's expense. If the IDM asks either the owner or the contractor to respond to a claim or provide additional information, that person must respond within 10 days and must either (1) give the response or information, (2) tell the IDM when the response will be furnished, or (3) tell the IDM that no supporting data will be provided.

The approval or rejection of a claim by the IDM is final and binding on the parties but is subject to mediation and binding dispute resolution. A demand for mediation can be made by the claiming party at any time. Mediation is a condition precedent to arbitration, litigation, or the institution of other legal proceedings.

Although claims can arise from a multitude of conditions, there are two that are especially common.

- *Claims for additional time*. If the contractor feels that extra time is needed, he or she must submit the reasons for the request and include an estimate of the cost. If weather conditions are the basis for the claim, the contractor must submit evidence that weather conditions were abnormal for the time period, could not have been reasonably anticipated, and had an adverse effect on the construction schedule.

- *Claims for concealed or unknown conditions.* Sometimes there are surprises on the job site once construction begins. When this happens the contractor may make a claim for additional time or money. However, to be valid, the unknown conditions must meet two criteria: (1) they must be subsurface in nature or otherwise physically concealed, causing the site to differ from what is shown on the contract documents, or (2) they must be of an unusual nature that is different from what would ordinarily be found as part of construction activities for the project type. For example, test borings may indicate a standard type of soil, and the contractor may budget for normal excavation. If a large boulder is discovered that requires blasting or special excavation techniques, the contractor would be entitled to extra money and possibly an extension of the contract time. Claims of this type must be made within 21 days from first discovery.

Mediation and Arbitration

Mediation and *arbitration* are methods of resolving claims and disputes without the lengthy and costly procedure of litigation. Both methods make use of neutral third parties to help the parties reach a resolution. Mediation is not legally binding, while arbitration is. Under the *General Conditions of the Contract*, if a dispute cannot be resolved by the IDM, the owner and contractor must try to resolve it through mediation before they may resort to a legally binding method such as arbitration or litigation. (See also Ch. 50.)

In mediation, a mediator facilitates a discussion between the parties, helping to define and limit the issues, put the issues in perspective, and see that each side in the dispute hears and understands the opposing point of view. The mediator does not judge the case; the role of the mediator is to guide the parties toward reaching their own settlement.

Arbitration is a more formal process. Under the *General Conditions*, arbitration proceedings are conducted under the Construction Industry Arbitration Rules of the American Arbitration Association and any applicable state laws.

Under arbitration, the two parties agree to submit their claims to an arbitrator and agree to abide by the arbitrator's decision. (Sometimes a panel of three arbitrators is used.) The arbitrator is knowledgeable about the construction industry and listens to evidence, reviews documents, and hears witnesses before making a decision.

Arbitration has the advantages over litigation of speed, economy, and privacy. However, unlike a trial, there are no rules of evidence and the decision cannot be appealed.

PROGRESS PAYMENTS

During the course of a job, the contractor requests periodic payments, usually monthly, against the total contract sum. Under the *General Conditions of the Contract*, the architect is responsible for making sure that the amounts requested are consistent with the amount of work actually done and the amount of materials stored.

Intermediate Payments

In order to receive periodic payment, the contractor must submit to the architect a notarized application for payment at least 10 days before the date established for each payment in the Owner-Contractor Agreement. This application should include the value of work done up to the date of the application, in addition to the value of materials purchased and in acceptable storage but not yet incorporated into the work.

In most cases, acceptable storage means stored at the site. However, if approved in advance by the owner, payment can also be authorized for materials and equipment suitably stored off site at a location agreed to in writing. When the application for payment includes off-site storage, the amount must also include costs of applicable insurance, storage, and transportation to the site.

Certification of the application for payment constitutes a representation by the architect that the work has progressed to the point indicated and that, to the best of the architect's knowledge, information, and belief, the quality of the work is in accordance with the contract documents. Certification is not a representation that the architect has made exhaustive on-site inspections or that the architect has reviewed construction methods, techniques, or procedures. Further, certification is not a representation that the architect has reviewed copies of requisitions received from subcontractors and material suppliers or that the architect has determined how and for what purpose the contractor has used money previously paid.

The amount due to the contractor is based on the schedule of values that the contractor submits to the architect after the award of the contract. This allocates the total contract sum to various portions of work such as site work, foundations, framing, and so forth.

If the application for payment is approved, the architect signs it and sends it to the owner for payment. An amount, called the *retainage*, is withheld from each application until the end of the job or some other time during the work that is agreed on by both the contractor and the owner. The retainage gives the owner leverage in making sure the job is completed and can be used to provide money to satisfy lien claims.

The architect may withhold all or a portion of the applications for payment in order to protect the owner if the architect cannot represent that the amount of work done or materials stored is in conformance with the application. The architect may also withhold payment for any of the following reasons.

- defective work not remedied
- third-party claims or evidence of probability of third-party claims
- failure of the contractor to make payments to subcontractors
- reasonable evidence that the work cannot be completed for the unpaid balance of the contract sum
- damage to the owner or a separate contractor
- reasonable evidence that the work will not be completed on time and that the unpaid balance will not be sufficient to cover damages due to the delay
- repeated failure of the contractor to carry out the work in accordance with the contract documents

Final Payment

After the final punch list inspection, the contractor notifies the architect in writing that the work is ready for final inspection and submits a final application for payment. If, after a final inspection, the architect determines that the work is complete and acceptable under the conditions of the contract documents, a final certificate for payment is issued to the owner.

Before the certificate can be issued, however, the contractor must submit to the architect the following items.

- an affidavit that payrolls, materials, and other debts for which the owner might be responsible have been paid (AIA Document G706, *Contractor's Affidavit of Payment of Debts and Claims*, is often used)
- a certificate showing that insurance required by the contract documents to remain in force after final payment will not be canceled or allowed to expire without at least 30 days' written notice to the owner
- a written statement that the contractor knows of no reason that the insurance will not be renewable
- the consent of surety to final payment, if applicable (AIA Document G707, *Consent of Surety to Final Payment*, may be used for this purpose)
- any other data required by the owner that establish evidence of payment of obligations, such as releases and waivers of liens

If final completion is delayed through no fault of the contractor, the owner may, with certification by the architect, make partial payment for that portion completed without terminating the contract.

PROJECT CLOSEOUT

Project closeout is an important part of the construction administration phase. It is during this time that the building work is completed, the structure is made ready for occupancy, and all remaining documentation takes place.

The contractor initiates closeout procedures by notifying the architect in writing and submitting a comprehensive list of items to be completed or corrected. The contractor must proceed promptly to complete or correct these items. The architect then makes an inspection to determine if the work or a designated portion of it is substantially complete or if additional items need to be completed or corrected.

Substantial completion is the stage when the work is sufficiently complete in accordance with the contract documents so that the owner can occupy or utilize the work for its intended purpose. The date of substantial completion is important because it has legal implications. For example, in many states, the statute of limitations for errors possibly caused by the architect begins with the date of substantial completion. The date of substantial completion is also the termination of the contractor's schedule for the project. If there are bonuses or liquidated damages involved, they are based on this date.

The list of items made by the architect as a result of the inspection is called the *punch list*. It is during this inspection that the architect notes anything that needs to be completed or corrected if not in accordance with the contract documents. The contractor must correct these items, after which another inspection is called for. If the final inspection shows that the work is substantially complete, the architect issues a certificate of substantial completion. It is at this time that the final application for payment is processed.

In addition to completing the work, the contractor must also submit to the owner certain other items including the following.

- all warranties, maintenance contracts, operating instructions, certificates of inspection, and bonds
- all documentation required with the application for final payment (as described previously)
- a set of record drawings if required by the Owner-Contractor Agreement

- the certificate of occupancy as issued by the building department (part of the permit process originally paid for by the contractor)
- extra stock of materials as called for in the specifications

The contractor must also complete final cleaning, instruct the owner or owner's representatives in the operation of systems and equipment, complete the keying for locks and turn keys over to the owner, and restore all items damaged by the contractor.

If the work is not substantially complete based on the architect's inspection, the architect notifies the contractor of work that must be completed before a certificate of substantial completion can be prepared. The owner may wait for the entire project to be completed or, if appropriate, may agree with the contractor to occupy or utilize only a portion of the work.

The architect's services may terminate when the final certificate for payment is issued, if so described in the Owner-Architect Agreement. In AIA Document B201, *Standard Form of Architect's Services: Design and Construction Contract Administration*, administration services provided beyond the date of substantial completion are considered an additional service.

53 PROJECT AND PRACTICE MANAGEMENT

Project and practice management covers a wide range of services that the architect must apply throughout the entire design life cycle of a project. Most of these topics are covered in this chapter because construction documents and construction administration services are such a large part of project management, and most of the ARE test specifications related to this topic have been placed in the Construction Documents and Services division.

This chapter reviews the pertinent aspects of project and practice management that apply to all phases of the architect's work. The duties and responsibilities of the architect during construction administration are covered in Ch. 52. Also refer to Ch. 2 for more information on architectural practice and contracts during pre-design. Refer to Ch. 3 for a review of project budgeting, cost estimating, and scheduling during pre-design. Chapter 30 includes information on life-cycle cost analysis. Refer to Ch. 48 for information on the content and coordination of the architectural and consultant drawings. Project delivery methods, scope of services, and contracts are discussed in Ch. 50. Chapter 51 reviews the architect's role in construction procurement through the bidding or construction contract negotiation process.

PART 1: PRACTICE MANAGEMENT

Project and practice management are two of the most important services provided by an architect. Practice management refers to all the activities related to running a professional services business: business organization, human resources management, financial management, and marketing, as well as providing the actual services to complete projects, including project management.

BUSINESS ORGANIZATION

There are several types of organizational structures than an architect can use to conduct business. Each has its advantages and disadvantages and may be more or less appropriate depending on the number of people in the firm, the laws of the state or states where the firm is doing business, the type of practice, the size of business, and the level of risk the owner or owners want to take.

Sole Proprietorship

The simplest business type is the *sole proprietorship*. In this structure the company is owned by an individual and operates either under the individual's name or a company name. To set up a sole proprietorship, it is only necessary to establish a name and location for the business, open a company bank account, have stationery printed, and obtain whatever licenses are needed by the local jurisdiction. If employees are hired, other state and local requirements must be met.

The advantages to this form of business include the ease of setting it up, total management control by the owner, and possible tax advantages to the owner because business expenses and losses may be deducted from the gross income of the business. The primary disadvantage is that the owner is personally liable for all debts and losses of the company. For example, if a client sues the designer, his or her personal income (and possibly co-owned property of a spouse), personal property, and other assets can be seized to pay any judgments. Another disadvantage is that it is more difficult to raise capital and establish credit as a sole proprietorship unless the owner's personal credit rating and assets are adequate. Because the business depends primarily on the work and reputation of the owner, it may be difficult to sell the business, and the company usually ceases to exist when the owner quits or dies.

Partnerships

With a *general partnership*, two or more people share in the management, profits, and risks of the business. Income from the business is taxed as ordinary income on personal tax forms. If necessary, employees can be hired as with any form of business.

Partnerships are relatively easy to form (a partnership agreement is usually advisable) and provide a business with the skills and talents of several people rather than just one, as with a sole proprietorship. In most cases, partnerships are formed because each of the partners brings to the organization a particular talent such as business development, design, or technical knowledge.

The primary disadvantage is that all the partners are responsible and liable for the actions of the others. As with a sole proprietorship, the personal assets of any of the partners are vulnerable to lawsuits and other claims. Because income is taxed at individual rates, this is another disadvantage of the partnership form. On a personal level, the partners may eventually disagree on how to run the business. If one partner wants to withdraw, the partnership is usually dissolved.

A variation of the general partnership is the *limited partnership*. This type of organization has one or more general partners and other limited partners. The general partners invest in the company, manage it, and are financially responsible, as with a general partnership. The limited partners are simply investors and receive a portion of the profits. They have no say in the management of the company and are liable only to the extent of their investment. Limited partnerships have generally given way to the limited liability company, described in a following section.

Corporations

Another common form of business organization is the *corporation*, sometimes called a *C corporation*. A corporation is an association of individuals created by statutory requirements and having an existence independent from its members. The formation and conduct of corporations are governed by the laws of individual states, and formal articles of incorporation must be drawn up by an attorney and filed with the appropriate state office in order to legally form a corporation.

Because a corporation is a separate legal entity, it is financially and legally independent from the stockholders. As such, the stockholders are financially liable only for the amount of money invested in the corporation. If the corporation is sued, the personal assets of the stockholders are not at risk. This is the greatest advantage of the corporate form.

Another advantage is that a corporation is generally taxed at a lower rate than are individuals, which can result in considerable savings. However, corporations are taxed at two levels: the corporation is taxed on the profit of the corporation and then shareholders are taxed on their dividends. Additionally, corporations have a continuity independent of changes in stockholders, deaths of members of its board of directors, or changes in the principles. It is also relatively easy to raise capital for corporations by selling stock in the corporation.

The primary disadvantages of a corporation are the initial cost and the continuing paperwork and formal requirements necessary to maintain the business. These, however, are usually outweighed by the reduced liability and tax benefits.

Variations on the corporate form include the subchapter S corporation and the professional corporation. A *subchapter S corporation* (also known as an *S corporation*) has certain eligibility requirements and offers all the advantages of a standard corporation, but the profits or losses are paid or deducted from the stockholders' personal income taxes in proportion to the share of stock they hold. This can be an advantage when there are losses or the tax rates of the state shift the financial benefits when the individual is taxed rather than the corporation.

Many states allow the formation of a *professional corporation* for professionals such as architects, lawyers, doctors, accountants, and interior designers. This form of business is similar to other corporations except that liability for malpractice is generally limited to the person responsible. However, each state has its own laws regarding the burden of liability in a professional corporation.

Limited Liability Companies and Limited Liability Partnerships

A *limited liability company* (LLC) and a *limited liability partnership* (LLP) are two hybrid business organizations that combine the advantages of the corporation and the partnership. The particular requirements of LLCs and LLPs vary according to the state in which the business is established, but basically, both are formed like a partnership where the investors are called members and those who manage are called managers. Unlike partnerships, it is possible to have nonmembers as managers. The company name must include LLC or LLP in the name.

The main advantage to these types of organizations is that liability is limited to a member's investment; a member has no personal liability. In addition, they are taxed as a partnership or corporation, as the owners decide, with only one level of taxation for members, unlike a C corporation. Generally, they are easier than a corporation to set up and operate.

Joint Ventures

A *joint venture* is a temporary association of two or more persons or firms for the purpose of completing a project. It is typically used by architectural firms when a project is too large or complex to be completed by one firm alone. It can also be used when one firm may not have the experience in a particular building type that the partnering firm has.

With joint ventures, a formal, written agreement should be developed that describes the duties and responsibilities of each firm, how profits and losses should be divided, and how the work will be done. Joint ventures are treated as partnerships and cannot be sued like a corporation can. Depending on the state in which the joint venture operates, profits may be taxed as a partnership, or the individual members of the joint venture may be taxed separately.

OFFICE ORGANIZATION

In addition to the legal organization of the business, offices can be set up in various ways to complete projects. In the *departmental organization*, a project moves through the office from one department to another. There may be a marketing department, a design department, a specifications department, a contract documents department, and a construction administration department. While this type of organization is efficient and can take advantage of many types of specialists, communication among departments about any particular project can be a challenge. A departmental organization also discourages or makes it impossible for anyone to gain a breadth of experience or share their knowledge in other aspects of project planning and completion.

The *studio organization* is based on various smaller groups in the business, called studios. Each studio is responsible for completing an entire project, from initial planning to production and construction administration. Members of each studio have the necessary expertise to provide all or most of the work required of the project. Projects can be assigned to studios based on their expertise, or studios can be formed or dissolved as the need arises. For example, an office may have one studio to complete retail projects, another to do industrial work, and another to provide office planning. The advantages of the studio organization include close and immediate communication among members of the design team and the synergy that comes from sharing ideas and group problem solving. Studios also work well with a strong project manager system where the project manager has daily contact with the design and production teams as well as with the client. Sometimes the studio organization is combined with one or more departments that provide very specialized work, such as specification writing.

Smaller offices may work on a very informal basis in which the principal or the partners complete the client contact and design work and then hand off the production and administration to others in the office.

LEGAL ISSUES

There are a multitude of legal issues with which the architect should be familiar. These include not only contractual issues, but also issues such as office organizational structure, human relations, financial management, insurance, professional conduct, copyright, expert witness involvement, and obligations to the public. It is helpful to understand the fundamental principles on which contract language is based. Some of the more important ones are briefly described here.

Agency

The legal concept of *agency* is that one person, the "agent," acts on behalf of another, the "principal," in dealings with another, the "third party." In architecture, the agent is the architect, the principal is the owner or client, and the third party is the contractor. Legally speaking, when the agent consents to act on behalf of and represents the interest of the principal, the agent is empowered to create a legal relationship between the principal and third parties.

When the architect works with and conveys information to the contractor, the contractor may assume the architect has more authority than he or she has. The contractor may blame the architect for instructions the owner may not be aware of, and the owner may blame the architect for inadequately or incorrectly carrying out the wishes of the owner. The architect must be careful to act on the owner's behalf. The standard agreement forms and general conditions of the contract attempt to minimize potential problems by clearly defining duties and responsibilities of the various parties. This is one reason, for example, why change orders must be signed by the owner as well as the architect.

Duties

The law attempts to define what one person "owes" another in particular relationships, including contracts, by applying the term *duties* to a set of terms or requirements. Duties are important in the construction industry because of the multitude of formal (contractual) and informal relationships involved.

For the architect, there are three ways duty is established. The first is by the terms of a contract, whether written or oral. The standard forms of agreement established by the AIA attempt to outline the services and responsibilities of the architect as clearly as possible and state that these may not be extended without written consent of the owner. The second way duty is defined is by legislative enactment, such as building codes and architectural licensing laws. The third way duty is established is by the architect's conduct. Courts often look to the *implied duties* based on how the parties conduct themselves in the course of performing their work. Many situations may arise that are not covered by the contracts or general conditions. In these cases the architect is not free to act unilaterally without consultation with the client. The architect may be held liable for the consequences of either action or inaction.

Some examples of implied duties include the following.

- The architect has the duty to cooperate with the contractor. While some actions related to this duty are clearly stated in the contracts, others are not.
- The architect has the duty not to interfere with the contractor's work. Such interference includes actions that might cause delay or additional costs, or that cause the contractor to modify standard methods and procedures of construction.
- The architect has the duty to inform the contractor of relevant information that may affect progress of the job, including any problems or errors observed.
- The architect has the duty to assist the owner in coordinating the schedules and requirements of other contractors and vendors not under the control of the general contractor.

Liability, Negligence, and Risk Management

Liability is the legal responsibility for injury or damage to another person or property. Architects are constantly exposed to liability through their actions or inactions, or by simply being named as a responsible third party in other claims. One of the primary ways architects can be liable is through negligence. *Negligence* is the failure to use due care to avoid harming another person or property.

In order for an architect to be found negligent, three conditions must be met. First, there must be a legal duty established between the parties. Second, it must be shown that the architect breached that duty. Third, it must be shown that the breach of duty was the cause of the damage or injury suffered by the other party.

The architect is a person who represents himself or herself as having special knowledge and skill, and the law holds such professionals liable for their professional actions. However, the prevailing legal concept is that the professional is not expected to be perfect. The architect is only expected to exercise the degree of skill, knowledge, and judgment normally possessed by other professionals in similar circumstances in similar communities. The architect is expected to perform to the standards of the professional community. That is, the architect should display the generally accepted knowledge and use the generally accepted practice and procedures of that community.

Although an architect cannot totally avoid liability, he or she can limit exposure to liability through good risk management. This involves the following procedures.

- Use well-written contracts and follow them thoroughly. Standard AIA documents have been written to coordinate with each other and are based on decades of experience. If these cannot be used, employ an attorney to write your own contract or to review a client's contract.
- Maintain an active quality-control program. This should include a wide variety of elements, but the most important are establishing a well-defined program and set of objectives for the project; having standard checklists of procedures; using proven construction methods, details, and specifications; maintaining communication among everyone on the design and construction team (including the client); and making sure everyone in the office who works on the project understands the contractual obligations and their responsibilities.
- Document every decision, meeting, action, and observation throughout the entire life of the project. See the section under project management for more information on documentation. Documentation is invaluable in proving the sequence of events, who made a decision, and the standards of care the architect took to complete his or her work.
- Be very careful of last-minute changes and substitutions. About half of all claims and lawsuits are due to these types of actions, which result in modifications that the architect does not have time to fully research and consider.
- Carry sufficient liability insurance for the types of work the office does. See the following discussion on types of insurance.
- Follow the guidelines for avoiding third-party claims as discussed in the next section.

Exposure to Third-Party Claims

Through the concept of *privity*, the architect is theoretically protected from claims by parties with whom he or she has no direct contractual relationship. This is clearly stated in the *General Conditions of the Contract for Construction*, AIA A201, as an indemnification clause. An *indemnification clause* attempts to hold harmless both the owner and architect for any damages, claims, or losses resulting from the performance of any work on the project, whether by the contractor or others with whom the architect has no contractual relationship. However, in some cases courts may not support the enforcement of this clause for a variety of reasons, one of which may be that instructions the architect gave or failed to give were the primary cause of the damage or injury. In addition to making sure an indemnification clause is in the contract and general conditions, the architect can minimize third-party claims by doing the following.

- Do not include contract language that would expressly state or imply responsibility to provide management, supervision, coordination, or planning of construction, unless those services are specifically being provided.
- Be aware that actions or directions to the contractor during construction may imply that the architect's responsibility extends to portions of the work beyond what the contract requires. Do not give directions concerning methods of construction.
- Point out obvious construction safety problems to the contractor. Follow up in writing to both the contractor and owner. If the problems are not corrected, suggest to the owner that the owner stop construction until the problems are corrected.

Copyright

Copyright protection for an architectural work falls into two categories. The first is the traditional one and includes copyright for the drawings, specifications, and other pictorial or graphic representations of the architect's work. The second is for the building itself. This latter copyright protection was established under The Architectural Works Copyright Protection Act, which applies to buildings erected after December 1, 1990. With the current copyright protection, the copyright holder retains rights that include the graphic representation of a building as well as the overall form, arrangement, and composition of spaces and elements in the design. This means that an owner cannot make unauthorized copies of a building that was designed by the architect (copyright holder) or make derivative works. Derivative works are buildings designed after the original building that are either substantially similar to or modifications of the original building.

Generally, the architect owns the copyright unless the architect is an employee of the owner or the architect specifically assigns the copyright to the owner. This is something that should be clearly stated in the Owner-Architect Agreement. AIA Document B141 states that the architect is the owner of the instruments of service and shall retain all common law, statutory, and other reserved rights, including copyrights. In addition, the architect should specifically claim ownership rights of the building copyright. To do this the Owner-Architect Agreement should state that these rights belong to the architect, and the architect should register the work with the U.S. Copyright Office. Although not technically required, official registration is advisable and allows the architect to bring a lawsuit for infringement, to collect attorneys' fees, and to recover statutory damages. Registration should be made within three months of "publication," or the construction of the building.

As discussed in Ch. 50, the architect grants to the owner a license to use the instruments of service solely and exclusively for the purposes of constructing, using, maintaining, altering, and adding to the project. If the owner terminates the Owner-Architect Agreement for the owner's convenience, or if the architect terminates the agreement due to the owner's suspension of the project, the owner cannot continue to make use of the architect's instruments of service without payment of a licensing fee to the architect.

The architect can transfer copyright to the owner, if desired, or can grant a license to reproduce the building or a derivative work one or more times.

Insurance

There are many types of insurance, both required and optional, that pertain to doing business and completing a project. Each of the three primary parties to a project—the architect, owner, and contractor—must have certain kinds of insurance to protect against liability, property loss, and personal loss. Because the issue is so complex and the architect is not qualified to give insurance advice, it is best that the owner's insurance counselor give insurance recommendations for specific projects. The architect and contractor should also have their respective insurance advisers recommend needed insurance for their businesses.

Architect's Insurance

A provision added in 2007 to AIA Document B101, the Owner-Architect Agreement, requires the architect to maintain professional liability, general liability, automobile liability, and workers' compensation insurance. If the owner requires the architect to carry insurance at limits greater than the architect normally does, the owner is responsible for paying the additional cost. The following are some of the common types of insurance the architect carries.

- *Professional liability insurance*: This type of insurance protects the architect in case some action by the architect causes bodily injury, property damage, or other damage. Sometimes called *malpractice insurance* or *errors and omissions insurance*, this coverage responds to problems resulting from things such as incorrect specifications, mistakes on drawings, and negligence. However, it excludes intentional wrongful acts, claims for cost estimates being exceeded, and claims arising from express warranties.

- *General liability insurance*: This includes a range of insurance to protect against claims of property damage, liability, and personal injury caused by the architect or employees, consultants, or other people hired by the architect. Sometimes the architect will also buy insurance to cover the possibility that contractors or subcontractors do not have their own valid insurance as they should.
- *Property insurance*: Property insurance protects the architect's building and its contents against disasters such as fire, theft, and flood. Even if office space is rented, property insurance protects the contents of the office.
- *Personal injury protection*: This protects the architect against charges of slander, libel, defamation of character, misrepresentation, and other torts. A *tort* is a civil wrong (as contrasted with a criminal act) that causes injury to another person.
- *Automobile insurance*: Automobile insurance covers liability and property damage to vehicles owned and used by the business and can include protection against claims made by employees using their own cars while on company business.
- *Workers' compensation*: This insurance is mandatory in all states and protects employees in the event of injuries caused by work-related activities.

Other types of insurance that the architect may carry include health and life insurance for employees, special flood insurance, valuable papers insurance, and business life insurance.

Owner's Insurance

As stated in A201, *General Conditions of the Contract for Construction*, the owner is required to carry his or her own liability insurance as well as property insurance for the full insurable value of the work. This insures against physical loss or damage caused by fire, theft, vandalism, collapse, earthquake, flood, windstorm, or malicious mischief. It also provides for reasonable compensation for the architect's and contractor's services and expenses required as a result of insured losses. The policy must be the "all risk" type rather than the "specified peril" type. All-risk insurance is broader in coverage and includes all hazards except those that are specifically excluded by the policy. If the property insurance requires deductibles, the owner pays the costs not covered because of the deductibles. The insurance covers work stored off-site and portions of the work in transit. The owner is also required by the *General Conditions* to carry boiler and machinery insurance.

Contractor's Insurance

The *General Conditions of the Contract* require that the contractor carry insurance that will protect from the following types of claims.

- claims under workers' compensation
- claims for damages because of bodily injury, occupational sickness, or death of employees
- claims for damages of bodily injury or death to people other than employees
- claims for personal injury, which includes slander, libel, false arrest, and similar actions
- claims for damages other than to the work because of destruction of tangible property, including loss of use resulting from such damages
- claims for damages related to use of motor vehicles
- claims for bodily injury or property damage arising when an injury occurs after the job is complete and the contractor has left the site
- claims involving contractual liability insurance

PART 2: PROJECT MANAGEMENT

Project management is the coordination of the entire process of completing a job in the architect's office, from its inception to final move-in and post-occupancy follow-up. In most cases project management is the responsibility of one person. Another method of managing a project is with *partnering*. With this method, the various stakeholders of a project, such as the architect, owner, contractor, vendors, and others are brought into the decision making process. Partnering can produce much closer communication on a project and shared responsibilities. However, the day-to-day management of a project may be difficult with so many people involved. A clear line of communications and delegation of responsibility should be established and agreed to before the project begins.

PLANNING AND SCHEDULING

The project manager should be involved from the first determination of the scope of work and estimation of fees to the final follow-up. Planning involves setting requirements in three critical areas: time, fees, and quality. Time planning is scheduling the work required and making sure there are enough fees and staff to complete it. Methods of scheduling are discussed in Ch. 3.

A *fee projection* is one of the earliest and most important tasks that a project manager must complete. A fee projection takes the total fee the designer will receive for the project and allocates it to the schedule and staff members who will work on the project, after deducting amounts for profit, overhead, and other expenses that will not be used for professional time.

Ideally, fee projections should be developed from a careful projection of the scope of work, its associated costs (direct personnel expense, indirect expenses, and overhead), consultant fees, reimbursable expenses, and profit desired. These should be determined as a basis for setting the final fee agreement with the client. If this is done correctly, there should be enough money to complete the project within the allotted time.

There are many methods for estimating and allocating fees, including computer programs. Figure 53.1 shows one simple manual form that combines time scheduling with fee projections. In this example, the total working fee, that is, the fee available to pay people to do the job after subtracting for profit, consultants, and other expenses, is listed in the upper right corner of the chart. The various phases or work tasks needed to complete the job are listed in the left-hand column, and the time periods (most commonly in weeks) are listed across the top of the chart.

The project manager estimates the percentage of the total amount of work or fee that he or she thinks each phase will require. This estimate is based on experience and common rules of thumb the design office may use. The percentages are placed in the third column on the right and multiplied by the total working fee to get the allotted fee for each phase (the figure in the second column on the right). This allotted fee is then divided among the number of time periods in the schedule and placed in the individual columns under each time period.

If phases or tasks overlap (as they do in the example in Fig. 53.1), total the fees in each period and place this figure at the bottom of the chart. This dollar amount can then be divided by an average billing rate for the people working on the project to determine an approximate budgeted number of hours that the office can afford to spend on the project each week and still make a profit. Of course, if the number of hours exceeds about 40, then more than one person will be needed to do the work.

By monitoring time sheets weekly, the project manager can compare the actual hours (or fees) expended against the

Project: Mini-mall Project No.: 9274 Date: 10/14/2010
Completed by: JBL Project Manager: JBL Total Fee: $26,400

Phase or Task / Period	1	2	3	4	5	6	7	8	9	% of total fee	fee allocation by phase or task	person-hrs. est.
Date	11/16–22	11/23	11/30	12/7	12/14	12/21	12/28	1/4	1/11			
SD-design	1320	1320								10	2640	
SD presentation		1320								5	1320	
DD—arch. work			1980	1980						15	3960	
DD—consultant coord.			530	790						5	1320	
DD—approvals				1320						5	1320	
CD—plans/elevs.					1056	1056	1056	1056	1056	20	5280	
CD—details							2640	2640		20	5280	
CD—consultant coord.					440		440	440		5	1320	
CD specs.								1320	1320	10	2640	
CD—material sel.					660	660				5	1320	

budgeted fees /period	1320	2640	2510	4090	2156	1716	4136	5456	2376	100%	$26,400	
person–weeks or hours	53 / 1.3	106 / 2.6	100 / 2.5	164 / 4	108 / 2.7	86 / 2.2	207 / 5	273 / 6.8	119 / 3			
staff assigned	JLK	JLK AST JBC	JLK AST EMW-(1/2)	JLK AST JBC EMW	JLK AST EMW	JLK AST	JLK AST EMW →	JLK SBS BFD	JLK AST EMW			
actual fees expended												

Figure 53.1 Fee Projection Chart

budgeted time (or fees) and take corrective action if actual time exceeds budgeted time.

Quality planning involves determining with the client what the expectations are concerning design, cost, and other aspects of the project. Quality does not simply mean high-cost finishes, but rather the requirements of the client based on his or her needs. These needs should be clearly defined in the programming phase of a project and written down and approved by the client before design work begins.

One useful technique for developing a schedule while at the same time involving all members of the design and construction team (including the client) is to complete a *full wall schedule*. With this process vertical lines are drawn 5 in apart on an entire wall, with the space between each line representing one week. The project manager develops a preliminary list of project tasks and who may be responsible for completing the tasks. Each task is written on two 3 × 5 index cards with one labeled "start" and one labeled "finish." The names of all the people responsible for tasks are placed along the left edge of the chart. Each person is asked to place the start and finish cards where they think the activity should be placed in the total schedule to indicate the time they need allotted for the task. This large, interactive schedule, serves as a starting point for discussion among everyone on the project team. Cards can be moved around easily, and once everyone agrees to the dates the schedule can be copied in a smaller format and used by everyone on the team.

MONITORING

Monitoring is keeping track of the progress of the job to see if the planned aspects of time, fee, and quality are being accomplished. The original fee projections can be monitored by comparing weekly time sheets with the original estimate. One way of doing this manually is shown in Fig. 53.2, which shows the same example project estimated in Fig. 53.1. Some project management software performs the same monitoring function.

In this chart, the budgeted weekly fees are placed in the table under the appropriate time-period column and phase-of-work row. The actual amounts of fees expended are written next to them. At the bottom of the chart, a simple graph is plotted that shows the actual money expended against the budgeted fees.

The project manager can also plot his or her estimate of the percentage of work completed to compare with money expended. If either line begins to vary too much above the estimate, the project manager must find the problem and correct it.

Monitoring quality is sometimes more difficult. At regular times during a project, the project manager, designers, and

Project: Mini-mall		time												
Phase/People/Departments		1	2	3	4	5	6	7	8	9	10	11	12	total
schematic design	budgeted	1320	2640											
	actual	2000	2900											
design development	budgeted			2510	4090									
	actual			3200										
construction docs.	budgeted					2156	1716	4136	5456	2376				
	actual													
	budgeted													
	actual													
	budgeted													
	actual													
	budgeted													
	actual													
	budgeted													
	actual													
total (cumulative)	budgeted	1320	3960	6470	10,560	12,716	14,432	18,568	24,024	26,400				
	actual	2000	4900	8110										

(fee dollars)

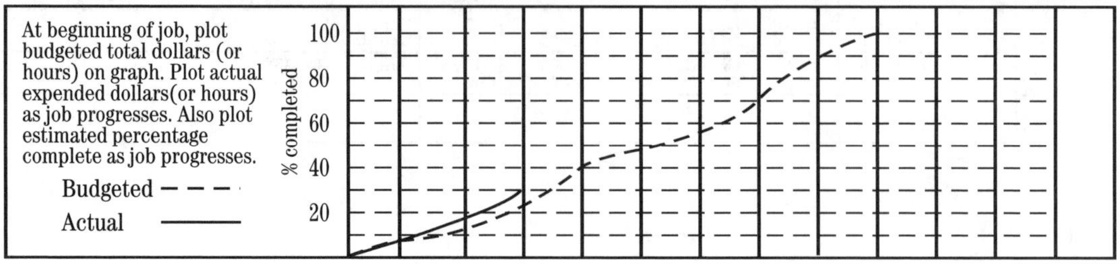

At beginning of job, plot budgeted total dollars (or hours) on graph. Plot actual expended dollars(or hours) as job progresses. Also plot estimated percentage complete as job progresses.

Budgeted – – –

Actual ———

% completed: 100, 80, 60, 40, 20

Figure 53.2 Project Monitoring Chart

office principals should review the progress of the job to determine if the original problems are being solved and if the job is being produced according to the client's and design firm's expectations. The work in progress can also be reviewed to see whether it is technically correct and if all the contractual obligations are being met.

COORDINATING

During the project, the project manager must constantly coordinate the various people involved: the architect's staff, the consultants, the client, the building code officials, and firm management. The individual efforts of the staff must also be directed on a weekly, or even daily, basis to make sure the schedule is being maintained and the necessary work is getting done.

The coordination can be done by using checklists, holding weekly project meetings to discuss issues and assign work, and exchanging drawings or project files among the consultants.

DOCUMENTATION

Everything that is done on a project must be documented in writing. This documentation provides a record in case legal problems develop and serves as a project history to use for future jobs. Documentation is also a vital part of communication. An email or written memo is more accurate, communicates more clearly, and is more difficult to forget than a simple phone call, for example.

Most design firms have standard forms or project management software for documents such as transmittals, job observation reports, time sheets, and the like. Such software makes it easy to record the necessary information. In addition, all meetings should be documented with meeting notes. Phone call logs (listing date, time, participants, and discussion topics), emails, personal daily logs, and formal communications like letters and memos should also be generated and preserved to serve as documentation.

54 SOLVING THE BUILDING SECTION VIGNETTE

The Building Section vignette requires that the candidate develop a schematic section of a two-story building given the partial floor plans where the section is cut. Additional information includes building materials, structural systems, frost depth, mechanical system information, and heights and elevations of some building elements. The section must represent the given floor plans while showing how structural elements, mechanical systems, and electrical systems are integrated into the solution. Appropriate footing and foundation depths and sizes, loadbearing walls (bearing walls) as indicated on the plan, beams, and correct thicknesses for the given floor and roof assemblies must be shown. Parapets must also be shown. Rated assemblies and fire dampers may be part of the problem.

TIPS FOR COMPLETING THE BUILDING SECTION VIGNETTE

This vignette is straightforward if the requirements are followed exactly. There is generally only one acceptable solution, with only minor variation allowed. Most mistakes are caused by not reading the problem carefully or by not accurately transferring the information from the plans to the section. For example, one common mistake is to use one size of duct to determine the required clearance under the joists when a larger duct is the one that should have been used. Also remember that the vertical dimensions developed in the section must be the *minimum* required to satisfy the problem. Using dimensions larger than necessary will downgrade the solution and may cause the solution to fail.

When working on this vignette, zoom in, use the full-screen cursor, and use the *layers* tool to draw the section with the plans visible so each plan element is placed correctly in the section. Draw the grade line completely across the section, and make sure it is in the correct position relative to the first floor elevation as shown on the first floor plan. The first floor line and the grade elevation may or may not be the same.

Consider the following suggestions to help complete this vignette successfully. They are listed in order, starting from the footings and working upward.

- Draw the footings so that their *tops* (not bottoms) are at the frost line. This gives a margin of error because the bottom of the exterior footings must be no higher than the frost line. The interior footing should be drawn under the bearing wall with its bottom at grade level. A common mistake is to draw interior footings too deep.
- For an interior footing, show the bearing wall resting directly on the footing (unless the program calls for something else), and then draw the bottoms of the slabs on top of the footing coming up to the bearing wall.
- Make sure the required ceiling heights are drawn exactly at the height required by the program.
- Make sure fire-rated walls are drawn from the slab below to the slab above, through the indicated joists. Note that the ceiling may either be drawn straight through the wall or may stop on one side of the wall and pick up again on the other side.
- Draw the floor and roof components slightly into the walls to show they are supported. However, just draw the slab on grade up to the foundation walls.
- Include space for light fixtures as called for in the program, but do not try to draw any light fixtures. (There is no tool for light fixtures.) Use sketch circles to maintain the proper clearance.
- Carefully note the largest depth of the duct in the floor under consideration. This is generally the spot where the duct exits the vertical supply riser or a

mechanical room and is the duct that must be accommodated by the section. It is typically *not* the duct dimension at the point of the section cut. However, whatever size duct is at the section cut is the one that must be drawn for that section. Remember that in plans, duct dimensions are given with the width first and then the depth; for example, a 36 in by 24 in (900 by 600) duct is 24 in (600) deep.

- Allow for the deepest combination of joist and duct indicated on the floor plans, but *draw* the sizes that occur at the section cut. In most cases, the same size joist will be used throughout a given floor, but read the plan carefully, just to make sure.
- Make sure that the joists are drawn in the direction they are shown on the plan and that they are spaced accurately if they run perpendicular to the section cut plane.
- Remember that there are five elements that determine the total distance from a floor line to the top of the floor above or the roof: the ceiling height, the allowed space for lighting, the depth of the deepest duct, the structure, and the thickness of the roof deck. In addition, if the problem requires a clerestory window in the two-story high space, that will also have to be added to develop the total height of the tall space.
- Be aware that the program automatically draws a 4 in (100) deck on top of the joists.
- Read the problem statement carefully concerning parapets. In most cases parapets are required at the edges of the roof and at any change in roof line, but sometimes they may only be required at one point or the other.
- Do not worry about space for return air ducts, flashing, roof drainage, extra structure over openings, or other such things unless a requirement is specifically stated in the program.
- Use the *layers* tool to show the base drawings so all section elements are coordinated with the base drawings.

SECTION 9: BUILDING REGULATIONS

Chapter 55: Building Codes and Regulations
Chapter 56: Barrier-Free Design

55 BUILDING CODES AND REGULATIONS

Some of the most important subject areas tested in the ARE include building codes and regulations. In all divisions of the exam the candidate is required to apply knowledge of various regulations and codes to specific areas of practice such as pre-design, building design, structures, mechanical and electrical systems, and material selection.

Because there are several model codes being used in the United States, and because each local jurisdiction may amend a model code or write their own, the ARE tests the candidate's knowledge of general principles common to all of the model codes. The *ARE Guidelines*, published by NCARB, recommends that the candidate be familiar with the latest edition of one of the model code series. This includes the model code itself and related codes, such as the *International Mechanical Code*, which is part of the series related to the *International Building Code* (IBC). Refer to the section on model building codes later in this chapter for a listing of the currently existing model codes.

On many of the vignettes, the candidate is given specific code requirements that are very similar to most model code requirements, but that may not be exactly like a particular model code. They apply only to the test division being taken.

This chapter is based on the IBC, which was first published in 2000. Most local and state jurisdictions around the United States and elsewhere have adopted the IBC or will adopt it soon, replacing their use of the *Uniform Building Code*, the *Standard Building Code*, or the *BOCA National Building Code*.

Building codes differ from zoning ordinances, easements, deed restrictions, and other regulations affecting the use and planning of land. Zoning ordinances, for example, deal with the use of a piece of property, the density of buildings within a district and on a lot, the locations of buildings on a property, parking, and loading. Refer to Ch. 2 for a more detailed discussion of zoning and other land-use regulations. Refer to Ch. 56 for a discussion of regulations dealing with barrier-free design and accessibility.

HISTORY OF BUILDING CODES

The history of building codes dates to as early as 2000 B.C. The Babylonian Law of Hammurabi required a death sentence for any builder who constructed a house that later collapsed and killed the owner. The Greeks and Romans had various types of laws governing construction and the supervision of building. The Twelve Tales of Roman law even included setback requirements to allow for repairs and to prevent the spread of fire.

In London in the year 1189, England's first building code was published as the "Henry Fitz-Elwyne Assize of Buildings." Thatched roofs were forbidden, and the construction of party walls was specified. After the Great Fire of 1666 in London, an Act of Parliament set forth requirements for the rebuilding of the city. It set up different classes of buildings, described the types of materials that should be used, and established fees to cover the cost of inspection. Nearly 200 years later, Parliament revised the law as the Metropolitan Building Act of 1844. This act further extended building laws to set building areas and heights, types of buildings, and occupancies, and even established the idea of a building official.

The development of building regulations in the United States was prompted by fires and the spread of diseases as urban areas, especially New York, grew rapidly. The first recorded code in the United States was written in 1625 for the settlement of New Amsterdam (later New York). It regulated the types of roof coverings to protect buildings from chimney sparks.

As cities were expanding during the latter half of the nineteenth century, tenements in New York and elsewhere were overcrowded, poorly ventilated, combustible, and lacked basic sanitary facilities. Insurance companies recognized that better fire protection was necessary, especially after the Chicago fire of 1871. By 1905, the National Board of Fire Underwriters wrote a model building code to decrease fire risk. This was the *National Building Code*, which was the beginning of the development of the three model building codes. In 1915, a group formed the Building Officials Conference of America and wrote what is now the *BOCA National Building Code*. The *Uniform Building Code* followed in 1927, and the *Standard Building Code* appeared in 1945. These three groups worked together in the 1990s and published a single code, the *International Building Code*, in 2000.

BUILDING REGULATIONS

Building codes are only one type of regulation affecting the design and construction of buildings. Additional requirements that may be applicable include legal and administrative regulations at the federal, state, and local levels. For example, a state may enforce environmental protection rules, while the building codes used in that state may not regulate environmental impact at all. As part of the predesign phase of a project, the architect must verify exactly which local, state, and federal regulations apply.

State and Federal Regulations

Most states have agencies that regulate building in some way. In addition to a state building code, a state government may enforce energy codes, environmental regulations, fabric flammability standards, and specific rules relating to state government buildings, institutions, and other facilities.

At the national level, several federal agencies may regulate a construction project, ranging from military construction to the building of federal prisons. Certain federal agencies may also regulate or issue rules covering a specific aspect of construction, such as the safety-glazing requirement issued by the Consumer Product Safety Commission (CPSC).

For architects, one of the most notable federal-level laws is the Americans with Disabilities Act (ADA), which regulates, among other things, removal of barriers for the physically disabled. The ADA requirements are based on the American National Standard Institute's (ANSI) ICC/ANSI A117.1, *Accessible and Usable Buildings and Facilities*. However, additional provisions are provided in the ADA regulations. Although very similar to the ICC/ANSI A117.1 standard, the ADA is not a code or standard, but is civil rights legislation. However, architects must adhere to its provisions when designing the facilities covered by the law. Chapter 56 covers requirements for barrier-free design.

Local Regulations

Local codes may include amendments to the model building code in use. These amendments usually pertain to specific concerns or needs of a geographical region or are provisions designed to alleviate local problems that are not addressed in the model codes. For example, a local amendment in a mountainous area might require a higher snowload factor for roof design based on the local climate.

Local regulations may also include requirements of agencies that govern hospitals, nursing homes, restaurants, schools, and similar institutions, as well as rules of local fire departments.

BUILDING CODES

Legal Basis of Codes

In the United States, the authority for adopting and enforcing building codes is one of the police powers given to the states by the Tenth Amendment to the United States Constitution. Each state, in turn, may retain those powers or delegate some of them to lower levels of government, such as counties or cities. Because of this division of power, the authority for adopting and enforcing building codes varies among the states.

Building codes are usually adopted and enforced by local governments, either by a municipality or, in the case of sparsely populated areas, a county or district. A few states write their own codes or adopt a model code statewide.

In Canada, the regulation of building rests with the provincial and territorial governments under the terms of the Constitution Act. The *National Building Code of Canada* (NBC) is a model code that is widely adopted by municipal bylaws or as the basis for a provincial building code. The *Canadian National Fire Code* and other complementary codes (such as the *Canadian Plumbing Code* and *Canadian Housing Code*) may also be adopted by local governments.

Codes are enacted as laws, just as any other local regulation would be. Before construction, a building code is enforced through the permit process, which requires that builders submit plans and specifications to the authority having jurisdiction (AHJ) for checking and approval before a building permit is issued. During construction, the AHJ conducts inspections to verify that building is proceeding according to the approved plans.

Even though code enforcement is the responsibility of the local building department or the AHJ, the architect is responsible for designing a building in conformance with all applicable codes and regulations. This is because an architect is required by registration laws to practice lawfully in order to protect the health, safety, and welfare of the public.

Model Building Codes

Local jurisdictions (including states) may write their own building codes, but in most cases a model code is adopted into law by reference. A model code is one that has been written by a group comprised of experts knowledgeable in the field, without reference to any particular geographical area. Adopting a model code allows a city, county, or district to have a complete, workable building code without the difficulty and expense of writing its own. If certain provisions need to be added or changed to suit the particular requirements of a municipality, the model code is enacted with modification. Even when a city or state writes its own code, that code is usually based on a model code. Exceptions include some large cities, such as New York and Chicago, and a few states that have adopted the *Life Safety Code*.

The primary model code is the IBC, published by the International Code Council (ICC). The IBC is an amalgam of the work of the three code-writing groups that previously published the three model codes in the United States. The IBC combines provisions of all three of the previous model codes and is organized in the same format that the three code-writing groups used in the most recent editions of their codes. At the time of this writing, jurisdictions in all states have adopted one or more of the family of international codes and some states have adopted the IBC on a statewide level or have used it as a basis for writing their own codes.

The *Life Safety Code*, published by the National Fire Protection Association, is also used by some jurisdictions.

The eventual use of one model code throughout the United States will bring consistency and make it easier for designers and architects to work across the country. However, to complicate matters, the National Fire Protection Association (NFPA) has written its own code. First publication of NFPA 5000™, *Building Construction and Safety Code* was in 2002. At the time of this writing, NFPA 5000 has not been well received and very few jurisdictions in the United States use it.

The material in this chapter and in this book is based on the IBC, which will most likely become the most commonly used model code in the United States. Of course, building design and construction must conform to whatever code is in force in the locale where the structure is erected. Questions on the ARE are written to test the examinee's knowledge of universal code concepts rather than to specifically address one code.

The IBC and each of the three previously published model codes are prescriptive as opposed to performance based. This means that the code describes specific materials and methods of construction, or how a building component or design must be designed as opposed to how it is supposed to function. In most cases, the codes refer to nationally recognized standards of materials and testing so that, if a building component meets the test standard, it can be used. New or untested materials and construction methods can be used if they can pass the performance-based testing or if they can otherwise be shown to meet the requirements of the code. In the future, codes may be performance based.

Building codes are written to protect the health, safety, and welfare of the public. As such, model codes are written based on the idea of the "least acceptable risk." This is the minimum level required for building and occupant safety (even though just "meeting the code" is not always the best construction for a given circumstance).

Adjuncts to Building Codes

In addition to building codes, there are companion codes that govern other aspects of construction. The same groups that publish the model building codes publish these companion codes. For example, the ICC also publishes the *International Residential Code*, the *International Fire Code*, the *International Mechanical Code*, the *International Plumbing Code*, and the *International Zoning Code*, among others.

The electrical code used by all jurisdictions is the *National Electrical Code* (NEC), published by the National Fire Protection Association (NFPA). In order to maintain greater uniformity in building regulations, the ICC does not publish an electrical code, but relies on the NEC.

Model codes also make extensive use of industry standards that are developed by trade associations, such as the Gypsum Association, government agencies, standards-writing organizations such as ASTM International and the National Fire Protection Association (NFPA), and standards-approving groups such as the American National Standards Institute (ANSI). Standards are adopted into a building code by reference name, number, and date of latest revision. For example, most codes adopt by reference the American National Standard ICC/ANSI A117.1, *Accessible and Usable Buildings and Facilities*. This standard was developed by the ICC based on previous ANSI accessibility standards and is approved by ANSI.

TESTING AND MATERIAL STANDARDS

All approved materials and construction assemblies referred to in building codes are required to be manufactured according to accepted methods or tested by approved agencies according to standardized testing procedures, or both. There are hundreds of standardized tests and product standards for building materials and constructions. Some of the more common ones are listed in this section.

As previously stated, standards are developed by trade associations, standards-writing organizations, and government agencies. By themselves, standards have no legal standing. Only when they are referred to in a building code and that code is adopted by a governmental jurisdiction do standards become enforceable.

Standards-Writing Organizations

ASTM International is one organization that publishes thousands of standards and test procedures that prescribe, in detail, such requirements as how test apparatus must be set up, how materials must be prepared, and the length of the test. If a product manufacturer has one of its materials successfully tested, it will indicate in its product literature what tests the material has passed. Standards are developed through the work of committees of experts in a particular field. Although ASTM International does not actually perform tests, its procedures and standards are used by testing agencies.

The National Fire Protection Association (NFPA) is another private, voluntary organization that develops standards related to the causes and prevention of destructive fires. NFPA publishes hundreds of codes and standards in a multivolume set that covers the entire scope of fire prevention including sprinkler systems, fire extinguishers, hazardous materials, fire fighting, and much more. As mentioned earlier in this chapter, NFPA has published its own building code, NFPA 5000.

Other standards-writing organizations are typically industry trade groups that have an interest in a particular material, product, or field of expertise. Examples of such trade groups include the American Society of Heating, Refrigerating and Air-Conditioning Engineers (ASHRAE), the Illuminating Engineering Society (IES), the Gypsum Association (GA), the American Concrete Institute (ACI), the American Iron and Steel Institute (AISI), and the American Institute of Timber Construction (AITC), among others. There are hundreds of these construction trade organizations.

The American National Standards Institute (ANSI) is a well-known organization in the field, but unlike the other standards groups ANSI does not develop or write standards. Instead, it approves standards developed by other organizations and works to avoid duplications between different standards. The ANSI approval process ensures industry consensus for a standard and avoids duplication of standards. For example, ANSI 108, *Specifications for Installation of Ceramic Tile*, was developed by the Tile Council of America and reviewed by a large committee of widely varying industry representatives. Although the ANSI approval process does not necessarily represent unanimity among committee members, it requires much more than a simple majority. It requires that all views and objections be considered and that a concerted effort be made toward their resolution.

Testing Laboratories

When a standard describes a test procedure or requires one or more tests in its description of a material or product, a testing laboratory must perform the test. A standards-writing organization may also provide testing, but in most cases a Nationally Recognized Testing Laboratory (NRTL) must perform the test. An NRTL is an independent laboratory recognized by the Occupational Safety and Health Administration (OSHA) to test products to the specifications of applicable product safety standards.

One of the best-known NTRLs is Underwriters Laboratories (UL). Among other activities, UL develops standards and tests products for safety. When a product successfully passes the prescribed test, it is given a UL label. There are several types of UL labels, and each means something different.

When a complete and total product is successfully tested, it is *listed*. This means that the product has passed the safety test and is manufactured under the UL follow-up services program. Such a product receives a *listed label*.

Another type of label is the *classified label*. This means that samples of the product were tested for certain types of uses only. In addition to the classified label, the product must also carry a statement specifying the conditions that were tested for. This allows field inspectors and others to determine if the product is being used correctly.

One of the most common uses of UL testing procedures is for doors and other opening protections. For example, fire doors are required to be tested in accordance with UL 10B, *Fire Tests of Door Assemblies*, and to carry a UL label. The results of UL tests and products that are listed are published in UL's *Building Materials Directory*.

Types of Tests and Standards

There are hundreds of types of tests and standards for building materials and assemblies that examine a wide range of properties from fire resistance to structural integrity to durability to stain resistance. Building codes indicate what tests or standards a particular type of material must satisfy in order to be considered acceptable for use. For example, gypsum wallboard must meet the standards of ASTM C1396, *Standard Specification for Gypsum Board*.

The most important types of tests for building components are those that rate the ability of a construction assembly to prevent the passage of fire and smoke from one space to another, and tests that rate the degree of flammability of a finish material. The following summaries include fire testing for building products and finishes. Flammability standards for carpet are described in Ch. 43.

Three tests are commonly used for fire-resistive assembly ratings. These include ASTM E119, NFPA 252, and NFPA 257.

ASTM E119

One of the most commonly used tests for fire resistance of construction assemblies is ASTM E119, *Standard Test Methods for Fire Tests of Building Construction and Materials*. This test involves building a sample of the wall or floor/ceiling assembly in the laboratory and applying a standard fire on one side of it using controlled gas burners. Monitoring devices measure temperature and other aspects of the test as it proceeds.

There are two parts to the E119 test, the first of which measures heat transfer through the assembly. The goal of this test is to determine the temperature at which the surface or adjacent materials on the side of the assembly not exposed to the heat source will combust. The second is the "hose stream" test, which uses a high-pressure hose stream to simulate how well the assembly stands up to impacts from falling debris and the cooling and eroding effects of water. Overall, the test evaluates an assembly's ability to prevent the passage of fire, heat, and hot gases for a given amount of time. A similar test for doors is NFPA 252, *Standard Methods of Fire Tests of Door Assemblies*.

Construction assemblies tested according to ASTM E119 are given a rating according to time. In general terms, this rating indicates the amount of time an assembly can resist a standard test fire without failing. The ratings are 1-hour, 2-hour, 3-hour, or 4-hour. Doors and other opening assemblies can also be given 20-minute, 30-minute, and 45-minute ratings.

NFPA 252

NFPA 252, *Standard Methods of Fire Tests of Door Assemblies*, evaluates the ability of a door assembly to resist the passage of flame, heat, and gases. It establishes a time-based fire-endurance rating for the door assembly, and the hose stream part of the test determines if the door will stay within its frame when subjected to a standard blast from a fire hose after the door has been subjected to the fire-endurance part of the test. Similar tests include UL10B and UL10C.

NFPA 257

NFPA 257, *Standard on Fire Test for Window and Glass Block Assemblies*, prescribes specific fire and hose stream test procedures to establish a degree of fire protection in units of time for window openings in fire-resistive walls. It determines the degree of protection to the spread of fire, including flame, heat, and hot gasses.

Flammability tests for building and finish materials determine the following.

- whether or not a material is flammable, and if so, whether it simply burns with applied heat or supports combustion (adds fuel to the fire)
- the degree of flammability (how fast fire spreads across it)
- how much smoke and toxic gas it produces when ignited

Three tests are typically used for finish materials in building construction, although not all three may be in any one building code. These include ASTM E84, NFPA 265, and NFPA 286. Refer to the section on furniture and flammability later in this chapter for tests related to fabrics and furniture.

ASTM E84

ASTM E84, *Standard Test Method for Surface Burning Characteristics of Building Materials*, is one of the most common fire testing standards. It is also known as the *Steiner tunnel test* and rates the surface burning characteristics of interior finishes and other building materials by testing a sample piece in a narrow test chamber that has a controlled flame at one end. The primary result is a material's flame-spread rating compared to glass-reinforced cement board (with a rating of 0) and red oak flooring (with an arbitrary rating of 100). ASTM E84 can also be used to generate a "smoke-developed" index.

With this test, materials are classified into one of three groups based on their flame-spread characteristics. These groups and their flame-spread indexes are given in Table 55.1.

Table 55.1

Flame-Spread Ratings

class	flame-spread index
A (I)	0–25
B (II)	26–75
C (III)	76–200

Class A is the most fire resistant. Product literature generally indicates the flame spread of the material, either by class (letter or Roman numeral) or by numerical value. Building codes then specify the minimum flame-spread requirement for various occupancies in specific areas of the building. These are discussed in the next section under Finishes.

NFPA 265

The *room corner test*, NFPA 265, is sometimes required in addition to an ASTM E84 rating for textile interior finishes or instead of it. This test determines the contribution of interior textile wall and ceiling coverings to room fire growth. It attempts to simulate real-world conditions by testing the material in the corner of a full-sized test room. It was developed as an alternate to the E84 Steiner tunnel test. For the test, the textile wall covering is applied to three sides of an 8 ft by 12 ft by 8 ft high room (2440 by 3660 by

2440). An ignition source is placed in the room and provides a heat output of 40 kW for five minutes and then 150 kW for ten minutes. The textile receives either a pass or fail rating. It passes if (1) flame does not spread to the ceiling during the 40 kW exposure and (2) other conditions are met during the 150 kW exposure, including no flashover and no spread of flame to the outer extremity of the 8 ft by 12 ft wall.

NFPA 286

NFPA 286 is the *Standard Methods of Fire Tests for Evaluating Contribution of Wall and Ceiling Interior Finish to Room Fire Growth*. This standard, which evaluates materials other than textiles, was developed to address concerns with interior finishes that do not remain in place during testing according to the E84 tunnel test. It is similar to NFPA 265 in that materials are mounted on the walls or ceilings inside a room, but with NFPA 286 more of the test room wall surfaces are covered, and ceiling materials can be tested. This test evaluates the extent to which finishes contribute to fire growth in a room by assessing factors such as heat and smoke released, combustion products released, and the potential for fire spread beyond the room.

FIRE-RESISTANCE STANDARDS

Building codes recognize that there is no such thing as a fireproof building; there are only degrees of fire resistance. Because of this, building codes specify requirements for two broad classifications of fire resistance as mentioned in the previous section: resistance of materials and assemblies, and surface burning characteristics of finish materials.

Construction Materials and Assemblies

In the first type of classification, the amount of fire resistance that a material or construction assembly must have is specified in terms of an hourly rating as determined by ASTM E119 for walls, ceiling/floor assemblies, columns, beam enclosures, and similar building elements. Codes also specify what time rating doors and glazing must have as determined by NFPA 252 or NFPA 257, respectively. For example, exit-access corridors are often required to have at least a 1-hour rating, and the door assemblies in such a corridor may be required to have a 20-minute rating.

Building codes typically include tables indicating what kinds of construction meet various hourly ratings. Other sources of information for acceptable construction assemblies include Underwriters Laboratories' *Building Materials Directory*, manufacturers' proprietary product literature, and other reference sources.

Various building elements must be protected with the types of construction specified in IBC Table 601 (see Table 55.2) and elsewhere in the code. When a fire-resistive barrier is built, any penetrations in the barrier must also be fire rated. This includes doors, windows, and ducts. Duct penetrations are protected with fire dampers placed in line with the wall. If a fire occurs, a fusible link in the damper closes a louver that maintains the rating of the wall. The fire resistance ratings of existing building components are important in determining the construction type of the building. This is discussed in more detail in a later section on classification based on construction type.

It is important to note that many materials by themselves do not create a fire-rated barrier. It is the construction assembly of which they are a part that is fire resistant. A 1-hour rated suspended ceiling, for example, must use rated ceiling tile, but it is the assembly of tile, the suspension system, and the structural floor above that carries the 1-hour rating. In a similar way, a 1-hour rated partition may consist of a layer of $^5/_8$ in (15.9) Type X gypsum board attached to both sides of a wood or metal stud according to certain conditions. A single piece of gypsum board cannot have a fire-resistance rating by itself, except under special circumstances defined by the new IBC.

Types of Fire-Resistance-Rated Walls and Partitions

One of the most common types of construction assemblies is the partition. The IBC makes important distinctions between various types of fire-resistance-rated walls and partitions. These include fire partitions, fire barriers, fire walls, and smoke barriers. Fire partitions are one of the most common fire-resistance-rated partitions used.

A *fire partition* is a wall assembly with a 1-hour fire-resistance rating used in the following designated locations.

- walls separating dwelling units such as rooms in apartments, dormitories, and assisted living facilities
- walls separating guestrooms in Group R-1 occupancies, such as hotels, as well as Group R-2 and Group I-1 occupancies
- walls separating tenant spaces in covered mall buildings
- corridor walls
- elevator lobby separation for I-2, I-3, and high-rise buildings and elsewhere where required by the code

The exceptions include (1) corridor walls permitted to be nonrated by Table 1016.1 (see Table 55.11) and (2) dwelling and guestroom separations in Types IIB, IIIB, and VB buildings equipped with automatic sprinkler systems. In these construction types, separation walls may be $^1/_2$-hour rated.

In most cases, fire partitions must provide a continuous barrier. This means that they must extend from the floor to

Table 55.2

Fire-Resistance Rating Requirements for Building Elements

BUILDING ELEMENT	TYPE I		TYPE II		TYPE III		TYPE IV	TYPE V	
	A	B	A[d]	B	A[d]	B	HT	A[d]	B
Primary structural frame[g] (see Section 202)	3[a]	2[a]	1	0	1	0	HT	1	0
Bearing walls Exterior[f, g] Interior	 3 3[a]	 2 2[a]	 1 1	 0 0	 2 1	 2 0	 2 1/HT	 1 1	 0 0
Nonbearing walls and partitions Exterior	See Table 602								
Nonbearing walls and partitions Interior[e]	0	0	0	0	0	0	See Section 602.4.6	0	0
Floor construction and secondary members (see Section 202)	2	2	1	0	1	0	HT	1	0
Roof construction and secondary members (see Section 202)	$1^1/_2$[b]	1[b, c]	1[b, c]	0[c]	1[b, c]	0	HT	1[b, c]	0

For SI: 1 foot = 304.8 mm.

a. Roof supports: Fire-resistance ratings of primary structural frame and bearing walls are permitted to be reduced by 1 hour where supporting a roof only.

b. Except in Group F-1, H, M and S-1 occupancies, fire protection of structural members shall not be required, including protection of roof framing and decking where every part of the roof construction is 20 feet or more above any floor immediately below. Fire-retardant-treated wood members shall be allowed to be used for such unprotected members.

c. In all occupancies, heavy timber shall be allowed where a 1-hour or less fire-resistance rating is required.

d. An approved automatic sprinkler system in accordance with Section 903.3.1.1 shall be allowed to be substituted for 1-hour fire-resistance-rated construction, provided such system is not otherwise required by other provisions of the code or used for an allowable area increase in accordance with Section 506.3 or an allowable height increase in accordance with Section 504.2. The 1-hour substitution for the fire resistance of exterior walls shall not be permitted.

e. Not less than the fire-resistance rating required by other sections of this code.

f. Not less than the fire-resistance rating based on fire separation distance (see Table 602).

g. Not less than the fire-resistance rating as referenced in Section 704.10

the underside of the floor or roof slab above or to the ceiling of a fire-resistance-rated floor/ceiling or roof/ceiling assembly. They must be securely attached top and bottom and extend continuously through concealed spaces, except where permitted to terminate below a fire-resistance-rated floor/ceiling or roof/ceiling assembly. There are several exceptions. Some of the more commonly used fire partitions are shown in Fig. 55.1. Refer to Sec. 709 of the IBC for complete information.

Openings in fire partitions must have a minimum rating of $^3/_4$ hour, except for corridors, which must be protected by 20-minute fire-protection assemblies.

Although two options are available to separate rooms with fire partitions (as shown in Figs. 55.1(a) and 55.1(b)) and four options are available for corridor separation, for most commercial construction, using continuous slab-to-slab partitions is usually the best option. It provides the best passive control of smoke and fire without relying on the integrity of a ceiling assembly. It is also often the easiest and least costly for contractors to construct, although there could be instances where other methods may be preferred.

A *fire barrier* is a vertical or horizontal assembly that is fire-resistance rated and is designed to restrict the spread of fire, confine it to limited areas, and/or afford safe passage for protected egress. In general terms, a fire barrier offers more protection than a fire partition. Fire barriers are used for the following purposes.

- to enclose vertical exit enclosures (stairways), exit passageways, horizontal exits, and incidental use areas
- to separate different occupancies in a mixed-occupancy situation

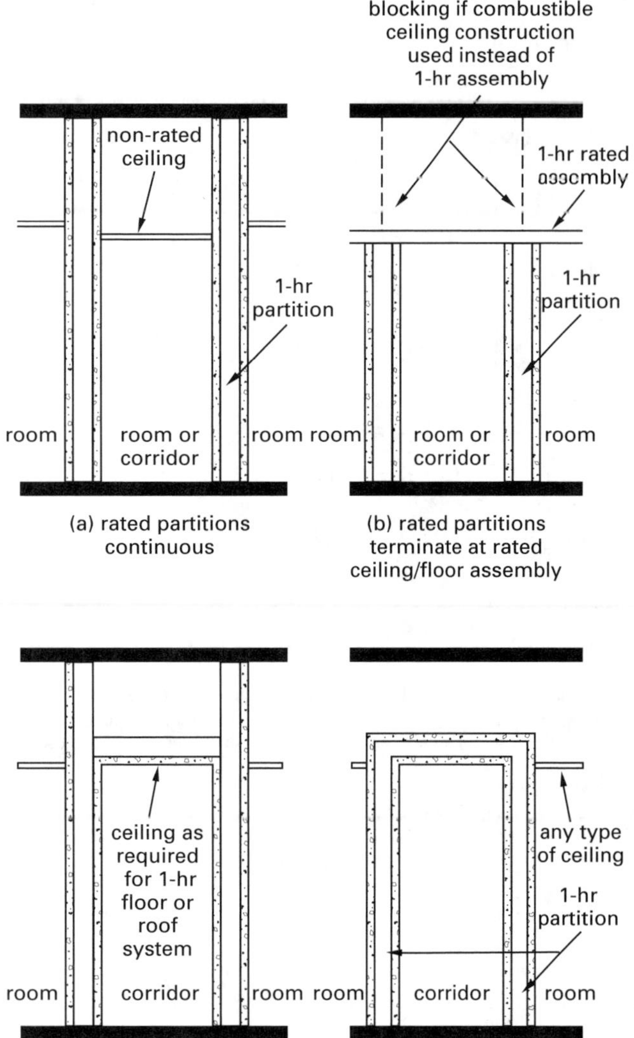

Figure 55.1 Options for Fire Partition Construction

- to separate single occupancies into different fire areas
- to otherwise provide a fire barrier where specifically required by a code provision in the IBC as well as the other international codes

Unlike fire partitions, fire barriers must always be continuous from the floor slab to the underside of the floor or roof slab above. There are only a few exceptions. Fire barriers may also be required to have a fire-resistance rating greater than 1 hour.

Openings in fire barriers are required to have a degree of protection that varies depending on the rating of the fire barrier and may range from 20 minutes to 3 hours according to IBC Table 715.4 (see Table 42.4 in Ch. 42). In any case, openings are limited to a maximum aggregate width of 25% of the length of the wall. Any single opening cannot exceed 120 ft^2 (11 m^2) in area. Exceptions to these requirements include the following.

- Openings can be greater than 120 ft^2 if adjoining fire areas are equipped throughout with an automatic sprinkler system.
- Fire doors serving an exit enclosure can exceed the previous limitation.
- Openings are not limited to 120 ft^2 or 25% of the length of the wall if the opening protective assembly has been tested according to ASTM E119 and has a fire-resistance rating equal to or greater than that of the wall. This allows the use of special fire-rated glazing.

In addition to openings, penetrations (as for pipes and conduit), joints (between the partition and other construction), ducts, and air transfer openings must also be protected as specified in the code.

A *fire wall* is a fire-resistance-rated wall that is used to separate a single structure into separate construction types or to provide for allowable area increases by creating what amounts to separate buildings even though they are attached. The unique thing about fire walls is that, in addition to providing 2- to 4-hour fire-resistance ratings, they must extend continuously from the foundation to or through the roof, and they must be designed and constructed such that, under fire conditions, the structure on one side can collapse without affecting the structural stability of the adjacent building.

A *smoke barrier* is a continuous vertical or horizontal membrane with a minimum fire-resistance rating of 1 hour that is designed and constructed to restrict the movement of smoke. It is a passive form of smoke control. Openings in smoke barriers must have at least a 20-minute rating.

Finishes

In the second type of fire-resistance classification, single layers of finish material are rated according to ASTM E84, as discussed in the previous section, and their use is restricted to certain areas of buildings based on their rating and whether or not the building is sprinklered. See Table 55.3. The purposes of this type of regulation are to control the flame-spread rate along the surface of a material and to limit the amount of combustible material in a building.

Table 55.3

Interior Wall and Ceiling Finish Requirements by Occupancy[k]

GROUP	SPRINKLERED[l]			NONSPRINKLERED		
	Exit enclosures and exit passageways[a, b]	Corridors	Rooms and enclosed spaces[c]	Exit enclosures and exit passageways[a, b]	Corridors	Rooms and enclosed spaces[c]
A-1 & A-2	B	B	C	A	A[d]	B[e]
A-3[f], A-4, A-5	B	B	C	A	A[d]	C
B, E, M, R-1	B	C	C	A	B	C
R-4	B	C	C	A	B	B
F	C	C	C	B	C	C
H	B	B	C[g]	A	A	B
I-1	B	C	C	A	B	B
I-2	B	B	B[h, i]	A	A	B
I-3	A	A[j]	C	A	A	B
I-4	B	B	B[h, i]	A	A	B
R-2	C	C	C	B	B	C
R-3	C	C	C	C	C	C
S	C	C	C	B	B	C
U	No restrictions			No restrictions		

For SI: 1 inch = 25.4 mm, 1 square foot = $0.0929 m^2$.

a. Class C interior finish materials shall be permitted for wainscotting or paneling of not more than 1,000 square feet of applied surface area in the grade lobby where applied directly to a noncombustible base or over furring strips applied to a noncombustible base and fireblocked as required by Section 803.11.1.

b. In exit enclosures of buildings less than three stories above grade plane of other than Group I-3, Class B interior finish for nonsprinklered buildings and Class C interior finish for sprinklered buildings shall be permitted.

c. Requirements for rooms and enclosed spaces shall be based upon spaces enclosed by partitions. Where a fire-resistance rating is required for structural elements, the enclosing partitions shall extend from the floor to the ceiling. Partitions that do not comply with this shall be considered enclosing spaces and the rooms or spaces on both sides shall be considered one. In determining the applicable requirements for rooms and enclosed spaces, the specific occupancy thereof shall be the governing factor regardless of the group classification of the building or structure.

d. Lobby areas in Group A-1, A-2 and A-3 occupancies shall not be less than Class B materials.

e. Class C interior finish materials shall be permitted in places of assembly with an occupant load of 300 persons or less.

f. For places of religious worship, wood used for ornamental purposes, trusses, paneling or chancel furnishing shall be permitted.

g. Class B material is required where the building exceeds two stories.

h. Class C interior finish materials shall be permitted in administrative spaces.

i. Class C interior finish materials shall be permitted in rooms with a capacity of four persons or less.

j. Class B materials shall be permitted as wainscotting extending not more than 48 inches above the finished floor in corridors.

k. Finish materials as provided for in other sections of this code.

l. Applies when the exit enclosures, exit passageways, corridors or rooms and enclosed spaces are protected by an automatic sprinkler system installed in accordance with Section 903.3.1.1 or 903.3.1.2.

The materials tested and rated according to surface burning characteristics include finishes such as wainscoting, paneling, heavy wall covering, or other finishes applied structurally or for decoration, acoustical correction, surface insulation, or similar purposes. In most cases, the restrictions do not apply to trim, such as chair rails, baseboards, and handrails, or to doors, windows, or their frames, or to materials that are less than $^1/_{28}$ in (0.9) thick cemented to the surface of noncombustible walls or ceilings.

Traditionally, the E84 test was used exclusively for interior finishes, but the IBC also allows the use of finish materials other than textiles if they meet requirements set forth in the IBC when tested in accordance with NFPA 286, *Standard Methods of Fire Tests for Evaluating Contribution of Wall and Ceiling Interior Finish to Room Fire Growth*, and when a Class A finish would otherwise be required. The NFPA 286 test was described in a previous section.

Textile wall coverings must comply with one of three conditions. They must be rated as Class A according to ASTM E84 and be protected by an automatic sprinkler system, or they must meet the requirements the Method B test protocol of NFPA 265, or they must meet the requirements of NFPA 286. Textile finishes for ceilings must meet the requirements of either ASTM E84 with sprinklers or NFPA 286.

The IBC regulates the ratings of some floor coverings, including textile coverings or those comprised of fibers—in other words, carpet. It specifically excludes traditional flooring types such as wood, vinyl, linoleum, and terrazzo.

The IBC requires textile or fiber floor coverings to be of one of two classes as defined by NFPA 253, the *flooring radiant panel test*. In this test the amount of radiant energy needed to sustain flame is measured and defined as the critical radiant flux.

Refer to Ch. 43 for a discussion of carpet flammability and tests specifically related to carpet.

Two classes are defined by the flooring radiant panel test: Class I and Class II. Class I materials have a critical radiant flux of not less than 0.45 W per square centimeter, and Class II materials have a critical radiant flux of not less than 0.22 W per square centimeter. Class I materials are more resistant to flame spread than are Class II materials. Class I finishes are typically required in vertical exits, exit passageways, and exit access corridors in Group I-1, I-2, and I-3 occupancies (hospitals, nursing homes, and detention facilities). Class II flooring is typically required in the same areas of Groups A, B, E, H, I-4, M, R-1, R-2, and S occupancies. In other areas carpet must conform to DOC FF-1 (ASTM D2859), the pill test. Refer to Ch. 43 for more information on the pill test.

The exception to this is that if the building is equipped with an automatic sprinkler system, Class II materials are permitted in any area where Class I materials would otherwise be required. In addition, materials complying with DOC FF-1 may be used in other areas.

Decorations and Trim

Curtains, draperies, hangings, and other decorative materials suspended from walls or ceilings in occupancies of Groups A, E, I, or R-1 and dormitories in Group R-2 must be flame resistant and pass the NFPA 701 vertical ignition test or must be noncombustible. In Group I-1 and I-2 occupancies, combustible decoration must be flame retardant unless quantities are so limited as to present no hazard. The amount of noncombustible decorative materials is not limited, but the amount of flame-resistant materials is limited to 10% of the aggregate area of walls and ceilings, except in A occupancies, where it is limited to 75% if the building is fully sprinklered.

Material used as interior trim must have a minimum Class C flame-spread index and smoke-developed index. Combustible trim (such as wood trim), excluding handrails and guardrails, cannot exceed 10% of the specific wall or ceiling area in which it is attached.

Refer to the definitions at the end of this chapter for an explanation of the terms used in this section.

ADMINISTRATIVE REQUIREMENTS OF BUILDING CODES

All building codes include a chapter dealing with the administration of the code itself. Provisions that are normally part of the administrative chapter include what codes apply, the duties and powers of the building official, the permit process, what information is required on construction documents, fees for services, how inspections are handled, and what kinds of inspections are required. Also included are the requirements for issuing a certificate of occupancy, instruction on how violations are handled, and the provisions for appealing the decisions of the building official concerning the application and interpretation of the code. The architect may need to coordinate with the local building official during several stages of the project from pre-design to completion of construction.

Refer to Chs. 2 and 3 for information on the architect's role in building code issues during pre-design. Refer to Ch. 48 for a discussion of the architect's responsibilities for providing required building code information on the construction documents.

REQUIREMENTS BASED ON OCCUPANCY

Occupancy refers to the type of use of a building or interior space, such as an office, a restaurant, a private residence, or a school. Uses are grouped by occupancy based on similar life-safety characteristics, fire hazards, and combustible contents.

The idea behind occupancy classification is that some uses are more hazardous than others. For example, a building where flammable liquids are used is more dangerous than a single-family residence. Also, residents of a nursing home will have more trouble exiting than will young school children who have participated in fire drills. In order to achieve equivalent safety in building design, each occupancy group varies by fire protection requirements, area and height limitations, type of construction restrictions (as described in the next section), and means of egress.

There are additional requirements for special occupancy types that include covered mall buildings, high-rise buildings, atriums, underground buildings, motor-vehicle-related occupancies, hazardous occupancies, and institutional occupancies, among others.

Occupancy Groups

Every building or portion of a building is classified according to its use and is assigned an occupancy group. This is true of the IBC and the three former U.S. model codes still used in some jurisdictions. The IBC classifies occupancies into 10 major groups.

A assembly
B business
E educational
F factory and industrial
H hazardous
I institutional
M mercantile
R residential
S storage
U utility

Six of these groups are further divided into categories to distinguish subgroups that define the relative hazard of the occupancy. For example, in the assembly group, an A-1 occupancy includes assembly places, usually with fixed seats, used to view performing arts or motion pictures, while an A-2 occupancy includes places designed for food and/or drink consumption. Table 55.4 shows a brief summary of the occupancy groups and subgroups and gives some examples of each. This table is not complete, and the IBC should be consulted for specific requirements.

If a particular project does not seem to fit any of the categories, the architect should consult with the local building official for a determination of the occupancy classification of that project.

Knowing the occupancy classification is important in determining other building requirements, such as the maximum area, the number of floors allowed, and how the building must be separated from other structures. The occupancy classification also affects the following.

- calculation of occupant load
- egress design
- interior finish requirements
- use of fire partitions and fire barriers
- fire detection and suppression systems
- ventilation and sanitation requirements
- other special restrictions particular to any given classification

Mixed Occupancy and Occupancy Separation

When a building or area of a building contains two or more occupancies, it is considered to be of mixed occupancy. This is quite common. For instance, the design of a large office space can include office occupancy (a B occupancy) adjacent to an auditorium used for training, which would be an assembly occupancy (A occupancy) if it had an occupant load over 49. Each occupancy must be separated from other occupancies with a fire barrier of the hourly rating as defined by the particular code that applies. The idea is to increase the fire protection between occupancies as the relative hazard increases.

The required hourly rating determines the specific design and detailing of the partition separating the two spaces. The IBC shows required occupancy separations in a matrix table with hourly separations ranging from 1 to 4 hours. When the building is equipped with an automated sprinkler system, the required hourly ratings are generally reduced by 1 hour.

Non-separated mixed occupancies are allowed in many cases, but when there is no separation between occupancies, the maximum allowable area and height of a building or a portion of a building is based on the most restrictive allowance for the occupancy groups under consideration.

Accessory Occupancies and Incidental Accessory Occupancies

In the IBC, there are two variations of the concept of mixed occupancies, each of which has its own particular, but related, requirements: accessory occupancies and incidental accessory occupancies.

An *accessory occupancy* is a space or room that is ancillary to a main occupancy but that does not exceed 10% of the floor area of the main occupancy. An accessory occupancy does not need to be separated from the main occupancy with a fire barrier. For example, a small gift shop in a hospital would be considered an accessory occupancy, and it would not require the 2-hour occupancy separation that would ordinarily be required between an M occupancy and an I-2 occupancy.

There are three exceptions to this. First, as long as a live/work unit complies with all other IBC requirements, portions with different uses are not considered separate occupancies. Second, most kinds of Group H (hazardous) occupancies must be separated from other occupancies.

Third, the IBC defines certain kinds of areas as incidental accessory occupancies. An *incidental accessory occupancy* is incidental to a main occupancy and has the same classification as the nearest main occupancy, but must be separated

Table 55.4
Occupancy Groups Summary

occupancy	description	examples
A-1	assembly with fixed seats for viewing of performances or movies	movie theaters, live performance theaters
A-2	assembly for food and drink consumption	bars, restaurants, clubs
A-3	assembly for worship, recreation, etc. not classified elsewhere	libraries, art museums, conference rooms > 50
A-4	assembly for viewing of indoor sports	arenas
A-5	assembly for outdoor sports	stadiums
B	business for office or service transactions	offices, banks, educational above the 12th grade, post office
E	educational by > 5 people through 12th grade	grade schools, high schools, day care if > 5 children and > 2.5 years old
F-1	factory moderate hazard	see code
F-2	factory low hazard	see code
	hazardous—see code	see code
I-1	> 16 ambulatory people on 24-hour basis	assisted living, group home, convalescent facilities
I-2	medical care on 24-hour basis	hospitals, skilled care nursing
I-3	> 5 people restrained	jails, prisons, reformatories
I-4	daycare for > 5 adults or infants (< 2.5 yrs.)	daycare for infants
M	mercantile	department stores, markets, retail stores, drug stores, sales rooms
R-1	residential for transient lodging	hotels and motels
R-2	residential with 3 or more units	apartments, dormitories, condominiums, convents
R-3	1 or 2 dwelling units with attached uses or child care < 6, less than 24-hour care	bed and breakfast, small child care
R-4	residential assisted living where number of occupants > 5 but < 16	small assisted living
dwellings	must use *International Residential Code*	
S	storage—see code	see code
U	utility—see code	see code

Note: This is just a brief summary of the groups and examples of occupancy groups. Refer to the IBC for a complete list or check with local building officials when a use is not clearly stated or described in the code.

from the main occupancy by a fire barrier, equipped with an automatic fire-extinguishing system, or both. An incidental accessory occupancy cannot exceed 10% of the area of the story where it is located. Table 55.5 lists the types of incidental accessory occupancies along with the separations or sprinkler systems required for each.

Where Table 55.5 allows a sprinkler system to substitute for a fire barrier, the incidental accessory occupancy must be separated from the main occupancy by a smoke barrier, and the sprinklers are only required in the incidental accessory occupancy area. Doors must be self-closing or automatic-closing.

CLASSIFICATION BASED ON CONSTRUCTION TYPE

Every building is classified into one of five major types of construction based on the fire-resistance rating (protection) of its major construction components. The purpose of this is to protect the structural elements of a building from fire and collapse, and to divide the building into compartments so that a fire in one area will be contained long enough to allow people to evacuate the building and firefighters to arrive.

Table 55.5

Incidental Accessory Occupancies

ROOM OR AREA	SEPARATION AND/OR PROTECTION
Furnace room where any piece of equipment is over 400,000 Btu per hour input	1 hour or provide automatic fire-extinguishing system
Rooms with boilers where the largest piece of equipment is over 15 psi and 10 horsepower	1 hour or provide automatic fire-extinguishing system
Refrigerant machinery room	1 hour or provide automatic sprinkler system
Hydrogen cutoff rooms, not classified as Group H	1 hour in Group B, F, M, S and U occupancies; 2 hours in Group A, E, I and R occupancies.
Incinerator rooms	2 hours and automatic sprinkler system
Paint shops, not classified as Group H, located in occupancies other than Group F	2 hours; or 1 hour and provide automatic fire-extinguishing system
Laboratories and vocational shops, not classified as Group H, located in a Group E or I-2 occupancy	1 hour or provide automatic fire-extinguishing system
Laundry rooms over 100 square feet	1 hour or provide automatic fire-extinguishing system
Group I-3 cells equipped with padded surfaces	1 hour
Group I-2 waste and linen collection rooms	1 hour
Waste and linen collection rooms over 100 square feet	1 hour or provide automatic fire-extinguishing system
Stationary storage battery systems having a liquid electrolyte capacity of more than 50 gallons, or a lithium-ion capacity of 1,000 pounds used for facility standby power, emergency power or uninterrupted power supplies	1 hour in Group B, F, M, S and U occupancies; 2 hours in Group A, E, I and R occupancies.
Rooms containing fire pumps in nonhigh-rise buildings	2 hours; or 1 hour and provide automatic sprinkler system throughout the building
Rooms containing fire pumps in high-rise buildings	2 hours

For SI: 1 square foot = 0.0929 m^2, 1 pound per square inch (psi) = 6.9 kPa, 1 British thermal unit (Btu) per hour = 0.293 watts, 1 horsepower = 746 watts, 1 gallon = 3.785 L.

These components, under the IBC, include the structural frame, bearing walls, nonbearing walls, exterior walls, floor construction, and roof construction. The five types of construction are Type I, II, III, IV, and V. Type I buildings are the most fire resistive, while Type V are the least fire resistive. Type I and II buildings are noncombustible, while Types III, IV, and V are considered combustible. The building type categories and fire-resistance rating requirements for each building element are shown in Table 55.2. The fire-resistance requirements for exterior, nonbearing walls are based on the distance from the building to the property line, the type of construction, and the occupancy group as shown in Table 55.6. Detailed requirements for the various construction types are contained in Ch. 6 of the IBC. It is advisable to read through this chapter and become familiar with their provisions.

In combination with occupancy groups, building type limits the area and height of buildings. For example, Type I buildings of any occupancy (except certain hazardous occupancies) can be of unlimited area and height, while Type V buildings are limited to only a few thousand square feet in area and one to three stories in height, depending on their occupancy. Limiting height and area based on construction type *and* occupancy recognizes that it becomes more difficult to fight fires, provide time for egress, and rescue people as buildings get larger and higher. It also recognizes that the type and amount of combustibles due to the building's

Table 55.6

Fire-Resistance Rating Requirements for Exterior Walls Based on Fire Separation Distance[a,e]

FIRE SEPARATION DISTANCE = X (feet)	TYPE OF CONSTRUCTION	OCCUPANCY GROUP H[f]	OCCUPANCY GROUP F-1, M, S-1[g]	OCCUPANCY GROUP A, B, E, F-2, I, R, S-2[g], U[b]
X < 5[c]	All	3	2	1
5 ≤ X <10	IA Others	3 2	2 1	1 1
10 ≤ X < 30	IA, IB IIB, VB Others	2 1 1	1 0 1	1[d] 0 1[d]
X ≥ 30	All	0	0	0

For SI: 1 foot = 304.8 mm.

a. Load-bearing exterior walls shall also comply with the fire-resistance rating requirements of Table 601.

b. For special requirements for Group U occupancies, see Section 406.1.2.

c. See Section 706.1.1 for party walls.

d. Open parking garages complying with Section 406 shall not be required to have a fire-resistance rating.

e. The fire-resistance rating of an exterior wall is determined based upon the fire separation distance of the exterior wall and the story in which the wall is located.

f. For special requirements for Group H occupancies, see Section 415.3.

g. For special requirements for Group S aircraft hangars, see Section 412.4.1.

use and construction affect its safety. Allowable height and area are discussed in the next section.

The fire zone is another consideration that is often encountered in urban areas. A municipality may, by action of the local government, divide a city into fire zones representing the degree of fire hazard. The fire hazard is usually based on factors such as density, access for fire fighting equipment, existing building heights, and so forth. The dense, central business district of a city is typically classed as fire zone 1. The local code may then restrict the types of construction that are allowed in the various fire zones.

For renovation or remodeling work, knowing the construction type is important if major changes are being made. For example, if the occupancy of a building or portion of a building is being changed from a B (business) to an A (assembly) occupancy, the architect must know the construction type to verify that the maximum area is not exceeded. If it is, a fire wall may need to be constructed or sprinklers may need to be added. In addition, construction type can affect the required fire ratings of coverings of structural elements, floor/ceiling assemblies, and openings in rated walls. For example, during a remodeling a protected beam may be damaged or changed to accommodate new construction, degrading its required fire rating. The architect would have to detail or specify repairs or new construction to return the assembly to its original rating.

Allowable Floor Area and Heights of Buildings

Chapter 5 of the IBC sets forth the requirements for determining maximum height (in stories as well as feet or meters) and area of a building based on construction type. It also gives the allowed occupancy, and then presents conditions under which the height and area may be increased. The concept is that the more hazardous a building is the smaller it should be, making it easier to fight a fire and easier for occupants to exit in an emergency.

Table 503 of the IBC gives the maximum allowable area, per floor, of a building. A portion of IBC Table 503 is reproduced in Table 55.7. This basic area can be multiplied by the number of stories up to a maximum of three stories under the IBC and up to two stories under the UBC.

If the building is equipped throughout with an approved automatic sprinkler system, the area and height can be increased. For one-story buildings, the area can be tripled, and for multistory buildings, the area can be doubled. The maximum height can be increased by 20 ft (6096), and the number of stories can be increased by one. Both area and height increases are allowed in combination.

If more than 25% of the building's perimeter is located on a public way or open space, the basic allowable area may be increased according to various formulas. Except for

Table 55.7

Allowable Building Heights and Areas[a]

Building height limitations shown in feet above grade plane. Story limitations shown as stories above grade plane. Building area limitations shown in square feet, as determined by the definition of "Area, building," per story

GROUP		TYPE OF CONSTRUCTION								
		TYPE I		TYPE II		TYPE III		TYPE IV	TYPE V	
		A	B	A	B	A	B	HT	A	B
	HEIGHT(feet)	UL	160	65	55	65	55	65	50	40
		STORIES(S) AREA (A)								
A-1	S	UL	5	3	2	3	2	3	2	1
	A	UL	UL	15,500	8,500	14,000	8,500	15,000	11,500	5,500
A-2	S	UL	11	3	2	3	2	3	2	1
	A	UL	UL	15,500	9,500	14,000	9,500	15,000	11,500	6,000
A-3	S	UL	11	3	2	3	2	3	2	1
	A	UL	UL	15,500	9,500	14,000	9,500	15,000	11,500	6,000
A-4	S	UL	11	3	2	3	2	3	2	1
	A	UL	UL	15,500	9,500	14,000	9,500	15,000	11,500	6,000
A-5	S	UL	UL	UL	UL	UL	UL	UL	UL	UL
	A	UL	UL	UL	UL	UL	UL	UL	UL	UL
B	S	UL	11	5	3	5	3	5	3	2
	A	UL	UL	37,500	23,000	28,500	19,000	36,000	18,000	9,000
E	S	UL	5	3	2	3	2	3	1	1
	A	UL	UL	26,500	14,500	23,500	14,500	25,500	18,500	9,500
F-1	S	UL	11	4	2	3	2	4	2	1
	A	UL	UL	25,000	15,500	19,000	12,000	33,500	14,000	8,500
F-2	S	UL	11	5	3	4	3	5	3	2
	A	UL	UL	37,500	23,000	28,500	18,000	50,500	21,000	13,000
H-1	S	1	1	1	1	1	1	1	1	NP
	A	21,000	16,500	11,000	7,000	9,500	7,000	10,500	7,500	NP
H-2[d]	S	UL	3	2	1	2	1	2	1	1
	A	21,000	16,500	11,000	7,000	9,500	7,000	10,500	7,500	3,000
H-3[d]	S	UL	6	4	2	4	2	4	2	1
	A	UL	60,000	26,500	14,000	17,500	13,000	25,500	10,000	5,000
H-4	S	UL	7	5	3	5	3	5	3	2
	A	UL	UL	37,500	17,500	28,500	17,500	36,000	18,000	6,500
H-5	S	4	4	3	3	3	3	3	3	2
	A	UL	UL	37,500	23,000	28,500	19,000	36,000	18,000	9,000
I-1	S	UL	9	4	3	4	3	4	3	2
	A	UL	55,000	19,000	10,000	16,500	10,000	18,000	10,500	4,500
I-2	S	UL	4	2	1	1	NP	1	1	NP
	A	UL	UL	15,000	11,000	12,000	NP	12,000	9,500	NP
I-3	S	UL	4	2	1	2	1	2	2	1
	A	UL	UL	15,000	10,000	10,500	7,500	12,000	7,500	5,000
I-4	S	UL	5	3	2	3	2	3	1	1
	A	UL	60,500	26,500	13,000	23,500	13,000	25,500	18,500	9,000
M	S	UL	11	4	2	4	2	4	3	1
	A	UL	UL	21,500	12,500	18,500	12,500	20,500	14,000	9,000
R-1	S	UL	11	4	4	4	4	4	3	2
	A	UL	UL	24,000	16,000	24,000	16,000	20,500	12,000	7,000
R-2	S	UL	11	4	4	4	4	4	3	2
	A	UL	UL	24,000	16,000	24,000	16,000	20,500	12,000	7,000
R-3	S	UL	11	4	4	4	4	4	3	3
	A	UL	UL	UL	UL	UL	UL	UL	UL	UL
R-4	S	UL	11	4	4	4	4	4	3	2
	A	UL	UL	24,000	16,000	24,000	16,000	20,500	12,000	7,000
S-1	S	UL	11	4	2	3	2	4	3	1
	A	UL	48,000	26,000	17,500	26,000	17,500	25,500	14,000	9,000
S-2[b, c]	S	UL	11	5	3	4	3	5	4	2
	A	UL	79,000	39,000	26,000	39,000	26,000	38,500	21,000	13,500
U[c]	S	UL	5	4	2	3	2	4	2	1
	A	UL	35,500	19,000	8,500	14,000	8,500	18,000	9,000	5,500

For SI: 1 foot = 304.8 mm, 1 square foot = 0.0929 m^2.

A = building area per story, S = stories above grade plane, UL = Unlimited, NP = Not permitted.

a. See the following sections for general exceptions to Table 503:

1. Section 504.2, Allowable building height and story increase due to automatic sprinkler system installation.
2. Section 506.2, Allowable building area increase due to street frontage.
3. Section 506.3, Allowable building area increase due to automatic sprinkler system installation.
4. Section 507, Unlimited area buildings.

b. For open parking structures, see Section 406.3.

c. For private garages, see Section 406.1.

d. See Section 415.5 for limitations.

Group H, Divisions 1, 2, and 5 (hazardous occupancies), a Type I building may be of unlimited floor area and unlimited height, while other construction types are limited.

The basic allowable height and building area table (Table 55.7) can be used in one of two ways. If the occupancy and construction type are known, simply find the intersection of the row designating "occupancy" and the column designating "type," read the permitted area or height, and then increase the areas according to the percentages allowed for sprinklers and perimeter open space. More often, the occupancy and required floor area are known from the building program and a determination must be made on the required construction type that will allow construction of a building that meets the client's size needs. This is typically part of the pre-design work of a project.

Occasionally, an architect may be asked to design for an occupancy different than the original occupancy of the building as part of a remodeling project. If the existing building is not large enough to accommodate the new occupancy, the project may be infeasible, or other significant steps may need to be taken to make the project work. These steps include adding a sprinkler system or adding a fire wall.

For example, consider a 12,000 ft^2 (1125 m^2), Type V-B building formerly used as a low-hazard factory (F-2 occupancy) proposed to be remodeled into a nightclub (A-2 occupancy). The IBC states the basic maximum allowable floor area for the F-2 occupancy as 13,000 ft^2 (1208 m^2) and for the A-2 occupancy as 6000 ft^2 (557 m^2) (Table 503 of the IBC, see Table 55.7). While the building would work as a factory, the entire area could not be used as a nightclub unless other steps were taken. If the client's program called for a 10,000 ft^2 nightclub, only 6000 ft^2 of the building could be used unless other changes were made, such as adding fire walls to separate the building into two areas.

Sometimes the required floor space of a project exceeds that allowed by the code and for the construction type the architect wants to use. In such cases, the architect can subdivide the building into smaller portions with fire walls. The portions thus separated are then considered separate buildings, as long as all requirements for fire walls are met. A 4-hour fire-resistive wall is required in H-1 and H-2 occupancies. A 2-hour fire wall is required in F-2, S-2, R-3, and R-4 occupancies. A 3-hour fire wall is required in other occupancies. Other codes may base the hourly ratings of fire walls (or area separation walls) on other requirements, such as the construction type, but the idea is the same—to separate one structure into two or more areas for the purpose of calculating maximum area.

Maximum Allowable Floor Area in Mixed-Occupancy Buildings

In a mixed-occupancy building, the total area of the mixed occupancies is limited, and the maximum allowable areas for the different occupancies, as given by Table 55.7, cannot simply be added together.

Each story must comply individually with the limitations on building area. Within each story, the *actual* building area divided by the *allowable* building area (from Table 55.7) is calculated for each separated occupancy, and the sum of these ratios cannot be greater than one. If the building is no more than three stories high, and each individual story complies, then the entire building complies.

However, not only must the sum of the ratios within any story be no greater than one, but the sum of the ratios within the entire building must be no greater than three. Thus, if a building is four or more stories high, it is possible for each floor to comply but not the entire building.

Location on Property

One section of Ch. 6 of the IBC contains requirements for the siting of buildings relative to adjacent property lines based on occupancy group and construction type. It does this by specifying the fire resistance of exterior, nonbearing walls based on distance from property lines. The idea behind these regulations is to prevent the spread of fire from one building to another. If the exterior wall has openings, such as windows, provisions in Ch. 7 of the IBC regulate the maximum allowable area of openings based on distance from the property lines.

As with maximum allowable area, requirements for the location of a building on a site can be approached two ways during pre-design and site planning. If the building must be placed a certain distance from the property line, then the code specifies the minimum fire-protection rating and limitations on openings. On the other hand, if for cost or other reasons the architect wants to minimize the required fire ratings or increase the allowable opening area, or both, then the minimum allowable setback can be calculated.

MEANS OF EGRESS

Means of egress, or exiting, is one of the most important provisions of any building code and one with which the architect must be intimately familiar. Several parts of the written portion of the exam will contain questions related to exiting (as well as other code issues). In addition, Interior Layout and Building Layout vignettes in the ARE require that the examinee understand how to apply exiting requirements in an actual design. Except for minor mistakes, an error in planning for exiting on these vignettes is usually enough to result in a failing score. The following sections summarize some of the more important aspects of exiting.

The Egress System

The IBC defines *means of egress* as a continuous and unobstructed path of vertical and horizontal egress travel from any point in a building or structure to a public way. The means of egress consists of three parts: the exit access, the exit, and the exit discharge. These must lead to a public way. A public way is any street, alley, or similar parcel of land essentially unobstructed from the ground to the sky that is permanently appropriated to the public for public use and has a clear width of not less than 10 ft. See Fig. 55.2.

The *exit access* is that portion of the means of egress that leads to the entrance to an exit. Exit access areas may or may not be protected depending on the specific requirements of the code, based on occupancy and construction type. They may include components such as rooms, spaces, aisles, intervening rooms, hallways, corridors, ramps, and doorways. The exit access does not provide a protected path of travel. In the IBC, even fire-protection-rated corridors are considered exit access. The exit access is the portion of the building where travel distance is measured and regulated (see the section on maximum travel distance in this chapter).

The *exit* is the portion of the egress system that provides a protected path of egress between the exit access and the exit discharge. Exits are fully enclosed and protected from all other interior spaces by fire-resistance-rated construction with protected openings (doors, glass, etc.). Exits may be as simple as an exterior exit door at ground level or may include exit enclosures for stairs, exit passageways, and horizontal exits. In the IBC, exits may also include exterior exit stairways and ramps. Depending on building height, construction type, and passageway length, exits must have either a 1- or a 2-hour rating. Travel distance is not an issue once the exit has been reached.

The *exit discharge* is the portion of the egress system between the termination of an exit and a public way. Exit discharge areas typically include portions outside the exterior walls such as exterior exit balconies, exterior exit stairways, and exit courts. Exit discharge may also include building lobbies of multistory buildings if one of the exit stairways opens onto the lobby and certain conditions are met. These conditions require that the exit door in the lobby is clearly visible, that the level of discharge is sprinklered, and that the entire area of the area of discharge is separated from areas below by the same fire-resistance rating as for the exit enclosure that opens onto it. In the IBC, exterior exit stairways and ramps are considered exits.

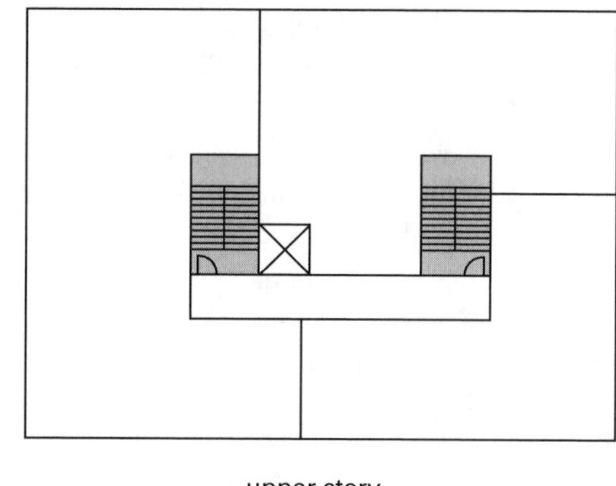

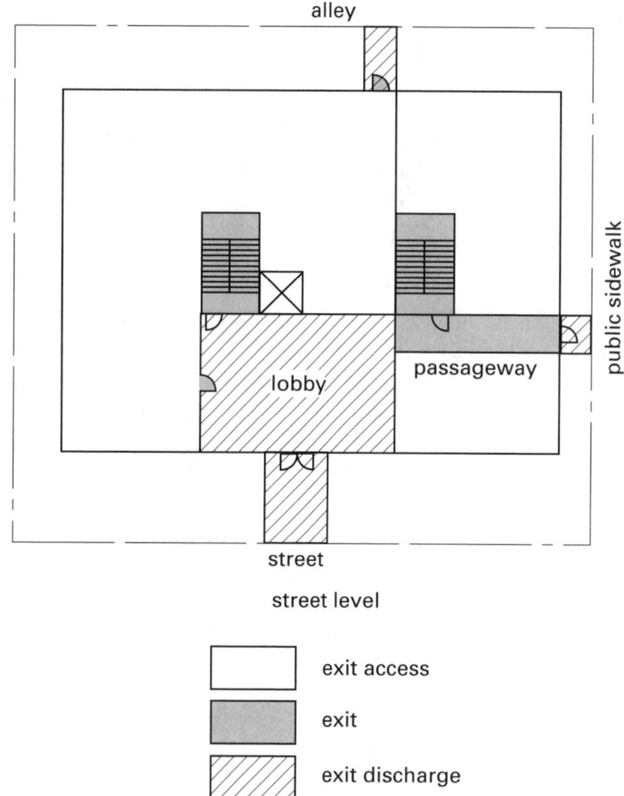

Figure 55.2 The Egress System

Occupant Load

The *occupant load* is the number of people that a building code assumes will occupy a given building or portion of a building. It is based on the occupancy classification as discussed earlier in this chapter, including assembly, business, educational, and the other categories. Occupant load assumes that certain types of use will be more densely packed with people than other types, and that exiting provisions should respond accordingly. For example, an auditorium needs more exit capacity to allow safe evacuation than does an office space with the same floor area.

The IBC requires that the occupant load be established by taking the largest number determined by one of three methods: by actual number, by table, or by combination.

In the first method, the actual number of people the building or space is designed to accommodate becomes the occupant load. For example, an auditorium with fixed seating can be calculated by counting the number of seats. However, because of the ease with which uses can change over time or how one space can be used for multiple purposes, this method is typically used only where fixed seats exist.

In the second method, the occupant load is determined by taking the area in square feet (or square meters) assigned to a particular use and dividing by an occupant load factor as given in the code. In the IBC, the occupant load factor (or floor area in square feet per occupant) is given in Table 1004.1.2, reproduced here as Table 55.8. This is the most common method of calculating occupant load. Other model codes have similar tables and use the same technique to calculate occupant load.

The *occupant load factor* is the amount of floor area presumed to be occupied by one person. It is based on the generic uses of building spaces and is *not* the same as the occupancy groups discussed earlier. The occupant load factors, over time, have been found to consistently represent the densities found in various uses. Table 55.8 also shows whether the occupant load must be calculated based on net or gross area. The gross floor area includes stairs, corridors, toilet rooms, mechanical rooms, closets, and interior partition thickness. Net floor area includes only the space actually used. Most common uses are included in the table, but the IBC gives the local building official the power to establish occupant load factors in cases where a use is not specifically listed.

In the third method, when an occupant load from an accessory space exits through a primary space, the egress facilities from the primary space occupant load must include the occupant load of the primary space plus the occupant load of the accessory space. This provision simply requires that the occupant loads should be cumulative as occupants exit through intervening spaces to an ultimate exit.

In determining the occupant load, all portions of the building are presumed to be occupied at the same time. However, the local building official may reduce the occupant load if the official determines that one area of a building would not normally be occupied while another area is occupied.

If there are mixed occupancies or uses, each area is calculated with its respective occupant load factor and then all loads are added together.

Table 55.8
Maximum Floor Area Allowances per Occupant

function of space	floor area in sq. ft. per occupant
accessory storage areas, mechanical equipment room	300 gross
agricultural building	300 gross
aircraft hangars	500 gross
airport terminal	
baggage claim	20 gross
baggage handling	300 gross
concourse	100 gross
waiting areas	15 gross
assembly	
gaming floors (keno, slots, etc.)	11 gross
assembly with fixed seats	see Sec. 1004.7
assembly without fixed seats	
concentrated (chair only—not fixed)	7 net
standing space	5 net
unconcentrated (tables and chairs)	15 net
bowling centers, allow 5 persons for each lane including 15 feet of runway, and for additional areas	7 net
business areas	100 gross
courtrooms—other than fixed seating areas	40 net
day care	35 net
dormitories	50 gross
educational	
classroom area	20 net
shops and other vocational room areas	50 net
exercise rooms	50 gross
H-5 fabrication and manufacturing areas	200 gross
industrial areas	100 gross
institutional areas	
inpatient treatment areas	240 gross
outpatient areas	100 gross
sleeping areas	120 gross
kitchens, commercial	200 gross
library	
reading rooms	50 net
stack area	100 gross
locker rooms	50 gross
mercantile	
areas on other floors	60 gross
basement and grade floor areas	30 gross
storage, stock, shipping areas	300 gross
parking garages	200 gross
residential	200 gross
skating rinks, swimming pools	
rink and pool	50 gross
decks	15 gross
stages and platforms	15 net
warehouses	500 gross

For SI: 1 square foot = 0.0929 m^2.

Example 55.1

What is the occupant load for a restaurant dining room that is 2500 ft^2 (232.5 m^2) in area?

In Table 55.8, dining rooms are included under the use "Assembly without fixed seats, unconcentrated," with an occupant load factor of 15 ft^2. Dividing 15 into 2500 gives an occupant load of 167 persons (166.67 rounded up to 167).

Example 55.2

What is the occupant load for an office with a gross area of 3700 ft^2 that also has two training classrooms of 1200 ft^2 each?

An office, as a business area, has an occupant load factor of 100 gross, so 3700 divided by 100 gives an occupant load of 37 persons. Classrooms have an occupant load factor of 20. Two classrooms of 1200 give a total of 2400 ft^2. 2400 divided by 20 gives an occupant load for the classrooms of 120. The total occupant load of all the spaces, therefore, is 37 plus 120, or 157 persons.

Required Number of Exits

The number of exits or exit access doorways from a space, a group of spaces, or an entire building is determined based on several factors. These include the occupant load and occupancy of a space, the limitations on the "common path of egress travel," which is described in the next section, and specific requirements when large occupant loads are encountered.

All buildings or portions of a building must, of course, have at least one exit. When the number of occupants exceeds the number given in the code, then at least two exits, or exit access dorways, must be provided. The idea is to have an alternate way out of a room, group of rooms, or building if one exit is blocked. The IBC requires two exits when the occupant load of a space exceeds the numbers given in Table 1015.1, reproduced as Table 55.9.

Table 55.9

Maximum Occupant Load for Spaces with One Exit

occupancy	maximum occupant load
A, B, E[a], F, M, U	49
H-1, H-2, H-3	3
H-4, H-5, I-1, I-3, I-4, R	10
S	29

a. Day care maximum occupant load is 10.

There are several exceptions where the danger to life safety is so minimal that having only one exit or exit access doorway is acceptable. One such exception is an individual dwelling unit of R-2 or R-3 occupancy with a maximum occupant load of 20 where the dwelling is equipped with a sprinkler system. Two other exceptions are the second story of an apartment with a maximum of four units and a maximum travel distance of 50 ft (15.2 m), and a business occupancy in a one-story building with a maximum occupant load of 49 and a maximum travel distance of 75 ft (23 m). Other exceptions are given in IBC Table 1021.2.

For large occupant loads, three exits are required when the occupant load is between 501 and 1000, and at least four exits are required when the occupant load exceeds 1000.

Common Path of Egress Travel

Even if the occupant load of a building space is less than that shown in Table 55.9, two exits are still required if the common path of egress travel exceeds limits given in the code. The *common path of egress travel* is that portion of an exit access that the occupants are required to traverse before two separate and distinct paths of egress travel to two exits are available. See Fig. 55.3. Even if two exits are not required based on occupant load, if the common path of travel exceeds 75 ft (32 m) for all except H-1, H-2, and H-3 occupancies, then two exits from a space are required. The distance is increased to 100 ft (30.5 m) in some occupancies if certain conditions are met. For example, in B, F, and S occupancies, if the building is fully sprinklered, the maximum length of common path of egress travel is increased to 100 ft.

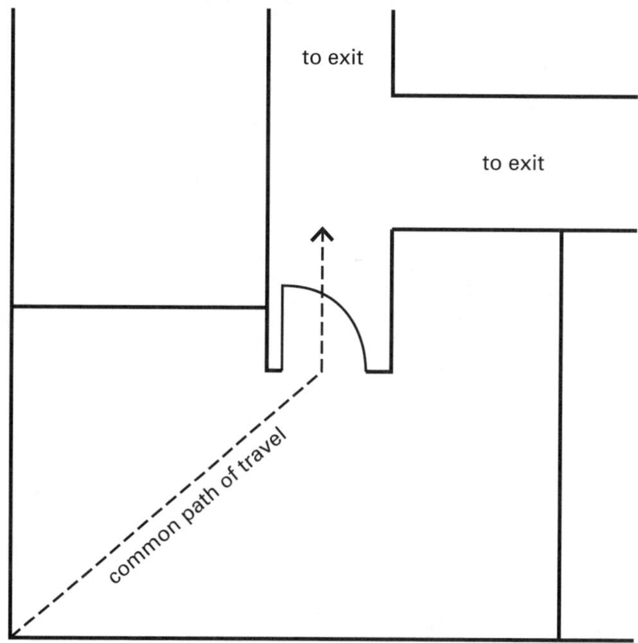

Figure 55.3 Common Path of Egress Travel

Maximum Travel Distance

Exit access travel distance is the distance that an occupant must travel from the most remote point in the occupied portions of the exit access to the entrance to the nearest exit. Because exit access areas are not protected, the code limits how far someone must travel to safety. Once a person is safely in an exit, travel distance is not an issue. Maximum travel distances are based on the occupancy of the building and whether or not the building is sprinklered. There are special requirements in the IBC as well as the older model codes that decrease the allowable travel distances in some occupancies and situations such as malls, atria, hazardous locations, educational uses, and assembly seating.

The maximum exit access travel distances are given in Table 1016.1 of the IBC. See Table 55.10. The footnotes to this table refer to other sections of the code for specific occupancy requirements.

Table 55.10

Exit Access Travel Distances[a]

occupancy	without sprinkler system (ft)	with sprinkler system (ft)
A, E, F-1, M, R, S-1	200	250[b]
I-1	not permitted	250[c]
B	200	300[c]
F-2, S-2, U	300	400[c]
H-1	not permitted	75[c]
H-2	not permitted	100[c]
H-3	not permitted	150[c]
H-4	not permitted	175[c]
H-5	not permitted	200[c]
I-2, I-3, I-4	not permitted	200[c]

For SI: 1 foot = 304.8 mm.

a. See the following sections for modifications to exit access travel distance requirements:
Section 402.4: For the distance limitation in malls.
Section 404.9: For the distance limitation through an atrium space.
Section 407.4: For the distance limitation in Group I-2.
Sections 408.6.1 and 408.8.1: For the distance limitations in Groups I-3.
Section 411.4: For the distance limitation in special amusement buildings.
Section 1014.2.2: For the distance limitation in Groups I-2 hospital suites.
Section 1015.4: For the distance limitation in refrigeration machinery rooms.
Section 1015.5: For the distance limitation in refrigerated rooms and spaces.
Section 1021.2: For buildings with one exit.
Section 1028.7: For increased limitation in assembly seating.
Section 1028.7: For increased limitation for assembly open-air seating.
Section 3103.4: For temporary structures.
Section 3104.9: For pedestrian walkways.

b. Buildings equipped throughout with an automatic sprinkler system in accordance with Section 903.3.1.1 or 903.3.1.2. See Section 903 for occupancies where automatic sprinkler systems are permitted in accordance with Section 903.3.1.2.

c. Buildings equipped throughout with an automatic sprinkler system in accordance with Section 903.3.1.1.

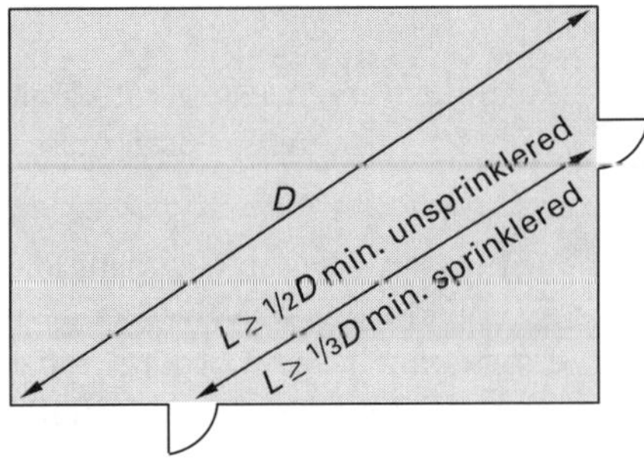

(a) exits from a room

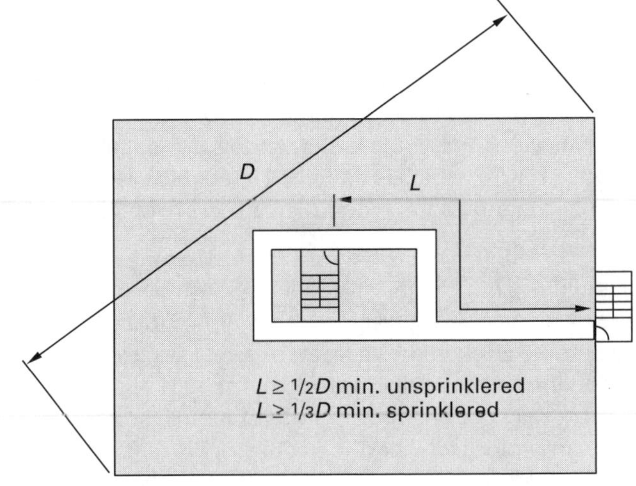

(b) exits from a building or group of rooms

Figure 55.4 Arrangement of Exits

Separation of Exits

Once the number of exits or exit access doorways required for each room, space, or group of rooms is known, the arrangement of those exits can be determined. When two exits are required in an non-sprinklered building, they must be placed a distance apart equal to not less than one-half the length of the maximum overall diagonal dimension of the building or area to be served, as measured in a straight line between the exits or exit access doorways. This rule is shown diagrammatically in Figs. 55.4(a) and 55.4(b). This requirement is intended to prevent a fire or other emergency from blocking both exits because they have been positioned too close together.

If three or more exits are required, two must conform to the one-half diagonal distance rule, and the third and additional exits must be arranged a reasonable distance apart so that if one becomes blocked, the others will be available.

In the IBC, there is a provision that reduces the minimum separation distance to one-third the maximum diagonal dimension of the room or area to be served if the building is fully sprinklered.

Exits or exit access doorways must also be located so that their availability is obvious.

Width of Exits

The required minimum width of exits is determined by multiplying the occupant load served by a factor of 0.3 in (7.62) for stairways and 0.2 in (5.08) for egress components other than stairways. The resulting number is the minimum total width in inches (millimeters). However, when the calculated width determined by these factors is less than the minimum width given elsewhere in the code (minimum corridor width, for example), the larger of the two must be used. If a greater width is specified elsewhere in the code, the larger number must be used.

For example, consider the calculated office occupant load of 157 determined in the previous example. To determine the minimum width of a corridor in this office, multiply 157 by 0.2 to get a required width of 31.4 in (798). However, elsewhere in the code the minimum width of a corridor serving an occupant load greater than 50 is given as 44 in (1118). Because 44 in is the larger of the two, it must be used as the minimum width.

If two or more exits are required, the total width must be divided such that the loss of any one means of egress does not reduce the available capacity to less than 50% of the required capacity.

The IBC also requires that if doors are part of the required egress width, their clear width must be used, not the width of the door. For example, a 36 in door actually provides about 33 in of clear width when the thickness of the door in the 90° open position and the width of the stop are subtracted from the full width.

Exiting Through Intervening Spaces

Normally, building codes intend to have means of egress from a room or space lead directly to a corridor, exit enclosure, exterior door, or some other type of exit element. However, egress can pass through an adjoining room provided that the room is accessory to the area served and the adjoining room is not an H occupancy. Additionally, there must be a discernible path of egress travel to an exit. For example, the door to a private office could lead into a larger general office area, which then leads into a corridor.

The code specifically states than egress cannot pass through kitchens, storerooms, closets, or spaces used for similar purposes. Exit access also cannot pass through a room that can be locked to prevent egress.

CORRIDORS

A *corridor* is a fully enclosed portion of an exit access that defines and provides a path of egress travel to an exit. The purpose of a corridor is to provide a space where occupants have limited choices as to paths or directions of travel. When two exits are required, corridors must be laid out so that it is possible to travel in two directions to an exit. If one path is blocked, occupants always have an alternate way out.

As part of the exit access portion of the egress system, corridors may or may not be constructed of fire-resistive construction depending on the occupancy, the occupant load, and whether or not the building is fully sprinklered. This is discussed in the next section.

As outlined in a previous section on exit width, corridors must be sized using the method of multiplying the occupant load by the appropriate factor. However, the width of an exit must not be less than 44 in (1118), with the following exceptions.

- 24 in (610): access to electrical, mechanical, and plumbing equipment
- 36 in (914): all occupancies where occupant load is less than 50
- 36 in (914): within a dwelling unit
- 72 in (1829): Group E occupancies serving occupant load of 100 or more
- 72 in (1829): Group I occupancy corridors serving health-care centers for ambulatory patients incapable of self-preservation
- 96 in (2438): Group I-2 occupancies where bed movement is required

However, the minimum width of a corridor as determined by a building code should be verified with the minimum width required by the ADA, as discussed in Ch. 56.

The width of a corridor cannot be encroached upon, with the following exceptions. See Fig. 55.5.

- Doors opening into the path of egress travel can reduce the required width up to one-half during the course of the swing, but when fully open the door cannot project more than 7 in (178) into the required width.
- Handrails cannot reduce the required means of egress width more than 7 in (178).
- Horizontal projections such as handrails, trim, fixtures, and lights can project horizontally from either side up to a maximum of $1^1/_2$ in (38).

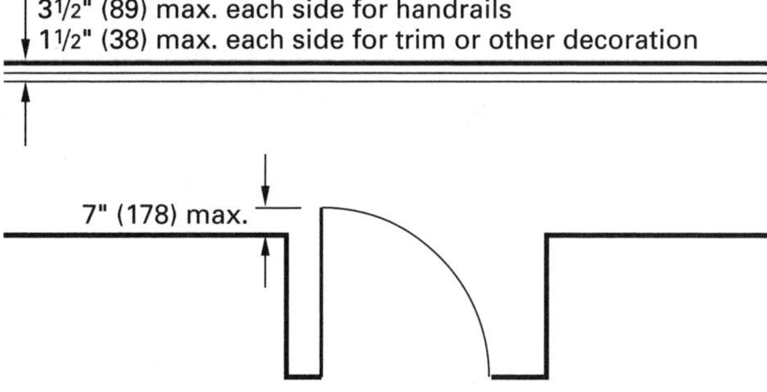

Figure 55.5 Allowable Projections into Exit Corridors

Corridor Construction

Corridors must be fire-resistance-rated according to IBC Table 1018.1, shown here as Table 55.11, and they must be constructed as fire partitions, as described in Sec. 709 of the IBC. This means that the corridor walls must extend from the floor to the underside of the structural slab above or to the underside of a fire-resistive-rated ceiling. Some of the options are shown diagrammatically in Fig. 55.1.

There are four exceptions when corridors do not have to be fire-resistance-rated. These include the following.

- Group E occupancies where classrooms and assembly rooms have half of their required egress leading directly to the exterior at ground level
- Corridors in a dwelling unit or a guestroom in a Group R occupancy
- Corridors in open parking garages
- Group B occupancies that only require one exit by other provisions in the code

Openings in Corridors

A door placed in a 1-hour corridor must have a fire rating of at least 20 minutes and must have approved smoke- and draft-control seals around it. The door also must either be maintained self-closing (with a door closer) or be automatic-closing by actuation of a smoke detector. Both the door and the frame must bear the label of an approved testing agency such as Underwriters Laboratories (UL).

Glass may be used in a 1-hour-rated corridor wall only if the glass is listed and labeled as having a $^3/_4$-hour fire-protection rating. The glass must make up no more than 25% of the area of a common wall with any room, except that if fire-resistance-rated glass is used (tested according to ASTM E119), then there is no limitation on the percentage of glass.

When a duct penetrates a rated corridor, it must be provided with a *fire damper*, which is a device that automatically closes in the event of a fire. The damper must have a fire rating of at least 20 minutes.

Glazing in fire partitions is discussed in more detail in Ch. 43. Doors are discussed in a following section.

Corridor Continuity

When a corridor is required to be fire-resistance-rated, it must be continuous to an exit and must not pass through intervening rooms. The concept is based on the idea that once an occupant reaches a certain level of safety in the egress path, that level should not be reduced as the occupant progresses through the remainder of the egress system. As with most requirements of the code, there are a few exceptions.

First, corridors may pass through foyers, lobbies, and reception rooms as long as these spaces are constructed as required for the corridors. In essence, these spaces become enlarged portions of the corridor.

The second exception allows corridors in fully sprinklered Group B buildings to pass through enclosed elevator lobbies if all areas of the building have access to at least one required exit without passing through the lobby.

Dead Ends

A dead end exists when a person in the part of the building has only one choice of direction that leads to an exit access doorway or an exit. When a corridor is required to lead to two or more exits, a person in that corridor should always have at least two choices of direction.

Table 55.11

Corridor Fire-Resistance Ratings

		required fire-resistance rating (hours)	
occupancy	occupant load served by corridor	without sprinkler system	with sprinkler system[c]
H-1, H-2, H-3	all	not permitted	1
H-4, H-5	greater than 30	not permitted	1
A, B, E, F, M, S, U	greater than 30	1	0
R	greater than 10	not permitted	0.5
I-2[a], I-4	all	not permitted	0
I-1, I-3	all	not permitted	1[b]

a. For requirements for occupancies in Group I-2, see Sections 407.2 and 407.3.
b. For a reduction in the fire-resistance rating for occupancies in Group I-3, see Section 408.8.
c. Buildings equipped throughout with an automatic sprinkler system in accordance with Section 903.3.1.1 or 903.3.1.2 where allowed.

The IBC limits the length of a dead-end corridor to 20 ft (6096). There are three exceptions based on occupancy and sprinklering.

- Group B, E, F, I-1, M, R-1, R-2, R-4, S, and U occupancies may have 50 ft (15240) dead-end corridors if the entire building is equipped with an automatic sprinkler system.
- Dead-end corridors may be 50 ft (15240) long in Group I-3 occupancies of Conditions 2, 3, or 4. These condition numbers refer to specific security arrangements in detention facilities.
- A dead-end corridor may be longer than 20 ft (6096) if its length is less than 2.5 times its width at the narrowest part.

DOORS

Because doors present a potential obstruction to egress throughout the egress system, they are highly regulated by the IBC and other model codes. Means of egress doors must meet the following design criteria.

- They must be readily distinguishable from the adjacent construction.
- They must be readily recognizable as a means-of-egress door.
- They cannot be covered with mirrors or other reflective materials.
- They cannot be concealed with curtains, drapes, decorations, or similar materials.

Doors provided in excess of the minimum required number of doors must meet the same criteria as the required doors.

Size of Doors

The minimum width of egress door openings must be sufficient for the occupant load served, but the clear width must be at least 32 in (813). The clear opening width must be measured between the face of the door and the doorstop when the door is open 90°. In practical terms, this means that 36 in doors must be used as exit doors. The maximum width of swinging egress doors is 48 in (1219). The minimum height of egress doors is 80 in (2032).

There are several exceptions to the size requirements, including doors in residential occupancies, sleeping rooms in I-3 occupancies, and others. Refer to Sec. 1008.1.1 of the IBC for details on these exceptions.

Door Swing

Egress doors must be pivoted or side-hinged. This is to ensure the egress door is familiar to the user and easy to operate. There are some exceptions to the requirement for side-swinging doors, including private garages; office areas; factory and storage areas with an occupant load of 10 or less; individual dwelling units of R-2, R-3, and R-4 occupancies; power-operated doors; and a few others. Refer to Sec. 1008.1.2 in the IBC for all of the exceptions allowed.

In most cases, special doors (such as revolving, sliding, and overhead doors) are not considered to be required exits. Power-operated doors and revolving doors are sometimes allowed if they meet certain requirements. A revolving door, for example, must have leaves that collapse under opposing pressure and must have a diameter such that at least 36 in (914) of exit width is provided when the leaves are collapsed; there must also be at least one conforming egress door in close proximity. The IBC does allow the use of a manually operated horizontal sliding door as a means-of-egress element in occupancies other then Group H, provided that the occupant load is 10 or less. For additional requirements for special doors, refer to Sec. 1008.1.4 in the IBC.

Further, egress doors must swing in the direction of travel when the area served has an occupant load of 50 or more or is a Group H occupancy. This is to prevent a door from being blocked when people are trying to get out in a panic. Candidates frequently make the mistake of not showing required doors—all building exit doors, stairway doors, and doors from spaces with a high occupant load—swinging in the direction of travel. See Fig. 55.6(a). Doors must also not swing into a required travel path such as a corridor. In many instances, exit doors must be recessed as shown in Fig. 55.6(b) to meet this requirement. Remember that recessed doors must be compensated for by providing at least 18 in (455), and preferably 24 in (610), on the pull side of the door next to the latch jamb for accessibility.

Interior swinging egress doors without closers must have a maximum opening force of 5 lbf (22 N). Other doors must have a maximum opening force of 15 lbf (67 N). The maximum allowable force to set the door in motion is 30 lbf (133 N). The door must swing to a full-open position when subjected to 15 lbf (67 N). All of these required maximum forces are measured on the latch side of the door.

Fire-Resistance Rating Requirements

Egress doors in fire-resistance-rated partitions are required to have a fire rating. The specific fire rating varies depending on the rating of the partition. These ratings are shown in Table 42.4 in Ch. 42. For most applications, four door-assembly ratings are commonly encountered. These are summarized in Table 55.12. Remember that if a building is fully sprinklered under the IBC, corridors in A, B, E, F, M, S, and U occupancies (and in some other situations) do not

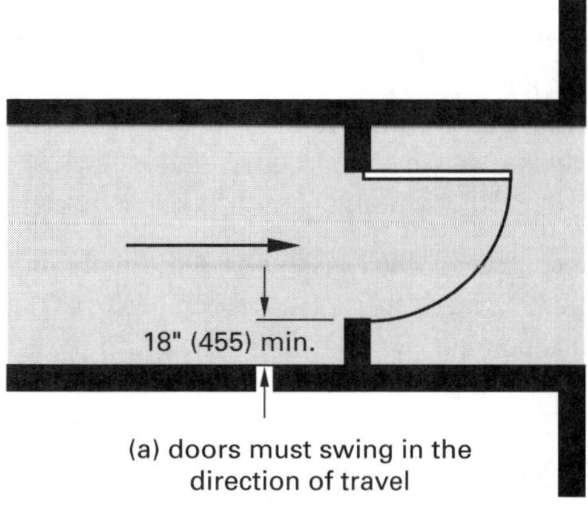

(a) doors must swing in the direction of travel

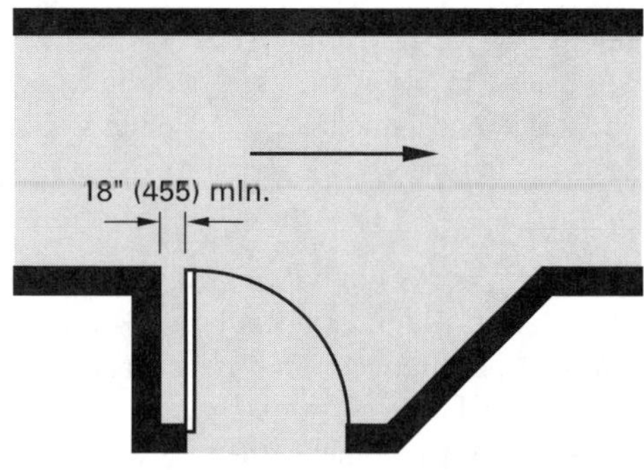

(b) doors must not swing into the required exit path more than 7 in (178)

Figure 55.6 Exit Door Swing

Table 55.12

Required Ratings of Doors Based on Partition Type

use of partition	rating of partition	required door assembly rating
corridors, smoke barriers	1 hour or less	20 minutes
fire partitions, exit passageways	1 hour	$^3/_4$ hour
exit stairs, occupancy separations, vertical shafts	1 hour	1 hour
exit stairs, fire separations	2 hours	$1^1/_2$ hour

have to have a fire rating, so fire-protection-rated doors are not required.

In addition to having a 20-minute fire rating, doors in corridors and smoke barriers must meet the requirements for positive-pressure fire testing (NFPA 252 or UL 10C, but without the hose stream test) as discussed in Ch. 42. These doors must also meet the requirements for smoke and draft control tested in accordance with UL 1784, *Standard for Safety for Air Leakage Tests for Door Assemblies*, with an artificial bottom seal installed across the full width of the bottom of the door during the test. These may need to carry an "S" label if required by the local authority having jurisdiction. Smoke barriers are commonly used to split health care and detention facilities into separate zones. They are also required in vertical shafts, vestibules to stairways, and areas of refuge.

Additional requirements for power-operated doors, horizontal sliding doors, and revolving and access-control doors, as well as for delayed-egress locks, gates, thresholds, floor elevation, and door arrangement, are given in Sec. 1008.1.4 of the IBC.

Refer to Ch. 42 for more information on building code requirements for doors, hardware, and glazing in fire-rated doors.

STAIRWAYS

A *stair* is defined by the IBC as a change in elevation accomplished by one or more risers. A *stairway* is one or more flights of stairs with the necessary landings and platforms connecting them to form a continuous passage from one level to another.

Exit Stairways

Because vertical shafts provide the most readily available path for fire and smoke spreading upward from floor to floor, interior exit stairways must be completely enclosed. In buildings four or more stories in height, they must be enclosed with 2-hour rated walls; in buildings less than four stories, 1-hour rated construction is required. The stories include basements but exclude mezzanines. Doors into 2-hour stairways must be rated as $1^1/_2$-hour doors, and doors in 1-hour stairways must have a 1-hour rating.

There are seven exceptions to the hourly rating requirements found in Sec. 1022 of the IBC. Three are commonly encountered. The first states that in other than Groups H and I occupancies, a stairway serving an occupant load less than 10 not more than one story above or below the level of exit discharge does not have to be enclosed. The second states that stairways serving and contained within a single residential dwelling unit in Group R-2 and R-3 occupancies and guestrooms in R-1 occupancies are not required to be enclosed. The third, found in Sec. 1016.1, states that in other than Group H and I occupancies, up to 50% of the number of egress stairways serving only one adjacent floor do not have to be enclosed.

Requirements for All Stairways

Stairways serving an occupant load of 50 or more must be at least 44 in (1118) wide or as wide as determined by multiplying the occupant load by 0.3, as discussed previously, whichever is greater. Stairways serving an occupant load of less than 50 must not be less than 36 in (914) wide. Handrails may project into the required width $4^1/_2$ in (114).

If the stairway is also the accessible means of egress, the minimum clear width is 48 in (1219) between handrails. Because the ARE Building Layout vignette may include an accessible stairway with an area of refuge, this stair should be made about 54 in (1372) wide. Any monumental stairs in the Building Layout vignette, however, should be wider, as suggested by the programmed space given in the problem statement.

Stair risers cannot measure less than 4 in (102) or more than 7 in (178), and the tread must not be less than 11 in (279). Risers for barrier-free stairs cannot exceed 7 in; treads must have an acceptable nosing design as shown in Fig. 55.7. For residential occupancies and private stairways in R-2 occupancies, the maximum riser may be $7^3/_4$ in (197) and the minimum tread may be 10 in (254).

There are other requirements for circular stairways, winders, spiral stairways, and stairs serving as aisles in assembly seating areas. Winding, circular, and spiral stairways may be used as exits in R-3 occupancies and in private stairways of R-1 occupancies only if they meet the requirements shown in Fig. 44.6.

Landings must be provided at the top and bottom of every stairway, and the minimum dimension in the direction of travel must not be less than the width of the stair, but need not be more than 48 in (1219) if the stair is a straight run. The maximum distance between landings is 12 ft (3658), measured vertically.

Handrails must be provided on both sides of stairs. The IBC defines a stair as containing one or more risers, so even one step generally requires handrails. Exceptions are made for decks, patios, and walkways with a single change of elevation, single risers at entrance doors of R-3 occupancies, and stairs of three risers or fewer in dwelling units of Group R-2 and R-3 occupancies. Intermediate handrails are required so that all portions of the stairway width required for egress capacity are within 30 in (762) of a handrail. Another way of stating this is that stairways wider than 5 ft (1524) must have intermediate handrails.

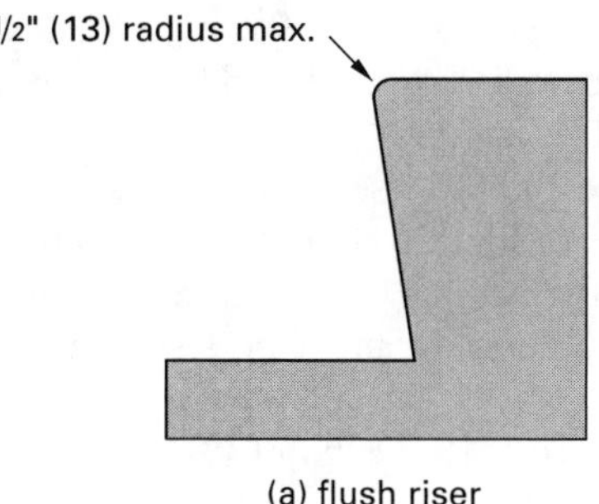

(a) flush riser

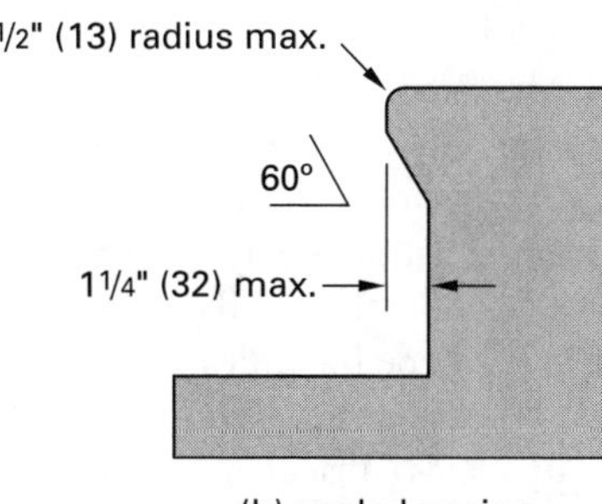

(b) angled nosing

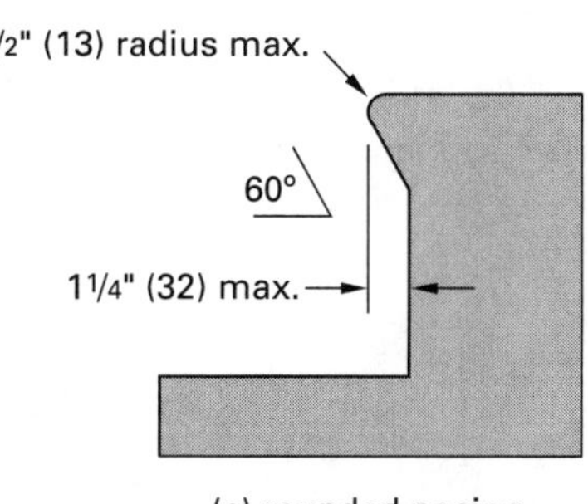

(c) rounded nosing

Figure 55.7 Acceptable Nosing Shapes for Safety and Accessibility

The exceptions to the requirement that handrails be provided on both sides include the following.

- aisle stairs with a center handrail
- stairs within dwelling units, spiral stairways, and aisle stairs serving seating only on one side
- decks, patios, and walkways that have a single change in elevation where the landing depth on each side is greater than what is required for landings
- single risers in Group R-3 occupancies at an entrance or egress door
- single risers within dwelling units of R-2 and R-3 occupancies

As shown in Fig. 55.8, the top of the handrail must be between 34 in and 38 in (864 and 965) above the nosing of the treads. The handrail must extend not less than 12 in (305) beyond the top riser and not less than the depth of one tread beyond the bottom riser. Each end must be returned to the wall or floor or terminate in a newel post. The gripping portion cannot be less than $1^1/_4$ in (32) or more than 2 in (51) in cross-sectional dimension. There must be a space at least $1^1/_2$ in (38) wide between the wall and the handrail.

When handrails are used, they must be easily graspable and mounted far enough away from the wall to allow gripping. The IBC and *ADA/ABA Guidelines* limit the size and shape of handrails, as shown in Fig. 55.9. A standard Type I handrail must have a perimeter of at least 4 in (102) and no more than $6^1/_4$ in (160). A handrail may have a perimeter greater than $6^1/_4$ in (160) if it is of Type II, with a graspable finger recess on both sides. Type II handrails are allowed in Group R-3 (residential) occupancies, within dwelling units in Group R-2 occupancies (apartments, condominiums), and in Group U occupancies that are accessory to a Group R-3 occupancy or accessory to individual dwellings in Group R-2 occupancies.

Refer to Ch. 44 for additional discussion of building code requirements for stairway layout, as well as diagrams for the code requirements described in this section. Refer to Ch. 56 for accessibility requirements.

OTHER CODE REQUIREMENTS

High-Rise Buildings

High rise buildings (those with occupied floors more than 75 ft (22 860) above the lowest level of fire department vehicle access) pose a unique problem for fire and life safety. Fire department apparatus cannot reach above this height, so special precautions need to be taken. Part of Ch. 4 of the IBC specifies the particular requirements for these buildings, which include office buildings, hotels, apartments, and other occupancies (with a few exceptions). The code requires that high-rise buildings be provided with an automatic sprinkler system, smoke detectors and alarms, communication systems, a central control station for fire department use, smoke control for exit stair enclosures, and standby power systems.

Glazing

Building codes regulate the use of glass in exterior windows (limiting the area and type based on wind loading, energy conservation, and other factors), in fire-rated assemblies, in hazardous locations subject to human impact, and in sloped glazing and skylights. Refer to Ch. 42 for more information on code requirements.

Guards (Guardrails)

A *guard* is a component whose function is to prevent falls from an elevated area. For example, an opening on the

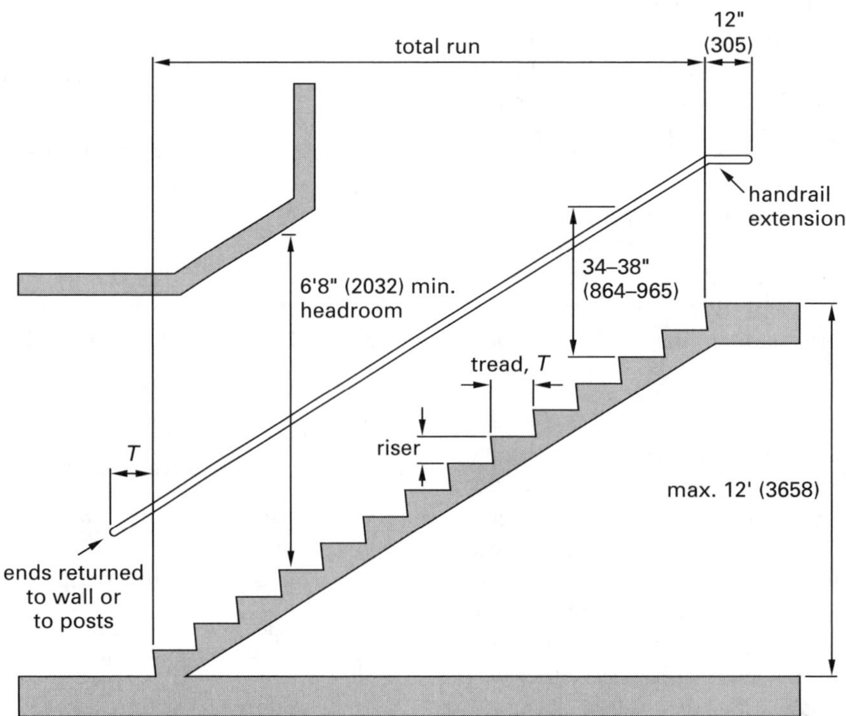

Figure 55.8 Code Requirements for Stairways

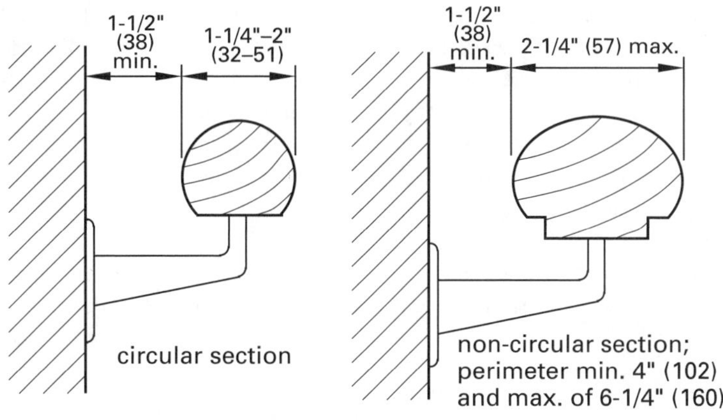

(a) type I handrails

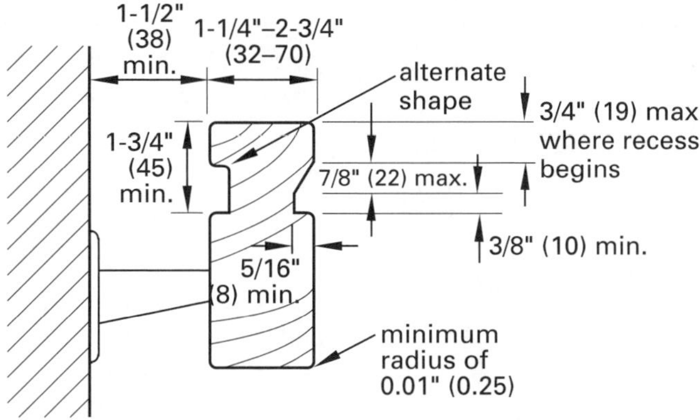

If handrails have a perimeter greater than 6-1/4" (160), they must have a graspable finger recess, as shown, or a similar profile if they meet these requirements.

(b) type II handrail

Figure 55.9 Handrail Configurations

second floor that overlooks the first floor must be protected with a guard. Guards are required along open-sided walking surfaces, mezzanines, industrial equipment platforms, stairways, ramps, and landings that are more than 30 in (762) above the floor below. There are several exceptions, including stages and raised platforms.

Guards must be a minimum of 42 in (1067) high and designed such that a 4 in diameter sphere (102) cannot pass through any opening up to a height of 34 in (864). Guards must be designed to resist a load of 50 lbf/ft (0.73 kN/m) applied in any direction at the top of the guard. There are other design requirements and exceptions, which are detailed in Sec. 1013 of the IBC.

Fire Detection and Suppression

Fire detection, alarm, and suppression systems have become important parts of a building's overall life safety and fire protection strategies. Almost all new buildings are now required to have some type of detection device, even if it is a single smoke detector in a residence. Other occupancies, such as high-rise buildings and hotels, must have elaborate detection and alarm systems, including communication devices on each floor to allow firefighters to talk with each other and occupants in the event of an emergency. Both audio and visual alarms are often required for people with hearing or visual impairments. Refer to Ch. 31 for more information on fire suppression systems and to Ch. 32 for more information on detection and alarm systems.

Mechanical Systems

The companion volumes for the IBC are the *International Mechanical Code* (IMC), the *International Fuel Gas Code* (IFGC), and the *International Energy Conservation Code* (IECC). The IMC regulates the design, installation, maintenance, alteration, and inspection of HVAC systems as well as components, equipment, and appliances included in the code, except for fuel gas-fired equipment and residential structures. An exception in the IMC requires that detached one- and two-family dwellings and multiple single-family dwellings (townhouses) not more than three stories high with separate means of egress comply with the *International Residential Code* (IRC). The IFGC regulates the installation of fuel gas distribution piping and equipment, fuel gas-fired appliances, and fuel gas-fired appliance venting systems. Together, the IMC and the IFGC cover all the currently used fuels.

Separate chapters in the IMC include requirements for ventilation; exhaust systems; duct systems; combustion air; chimneys and vents; specific appliances, fireplaces, and solid fuel-burning equipment; boilers, water heaters, and pressure vessels; refrigeration; hydronic piping; fuel oil piping and storage; and solar systems.

The IECC regulates the design and installation of HVAC systems for efficient energy use. Additionally, the IMC refers to the *International Plumbing Code* when mechanical equipment is connected to plumbing systems and to NFPA 70 for electrical wiring, controls, and connections to equipment and appliances. Refer to Chs. 27 and 28 for information on mechanical systems.

Ventilation

The IBC requires that attics, crawl spaces, and similar spaces be ventilated in order to prevent the accumulation of detrimental moisture, such as the condensation of moist air on cold surfaces. Accumulated moisture can cause dry rot on wood surfaces and rust on ferrous metals, and can lessen the effectiveness of insulation.

For an attic, the net free ventilating area must be at least 1/300 of the area of the space ventilated. At least 50% of this ventilating area must be provided by ventilators, with the rest of the required ventilation provided by eave or cornice vents. The ventilators must be located in the upper portion of the space and at least 3 ft (914) above any eave and cornice vents. At least 1 in (25) of space must be maintained between the insulation and the underside of the roof sheathing.

For a crawl space without a vapor retarder, the net free ventilation area must be at least 1/150 of the crawl space area. If the ground surface is covered with a Class I vapor retarder, the total area may be reduced to 1/1500 of the underfloor area. A Class I vapor retarder has a permeance of 0.1 perm or less. In all cases, the ventilating openings must be arranged to provide cross ventilation of the space.

Crawl spaces, attics, and other uninhabited spaces may also be mechanically ventilated. When this is done, the IMC requires a minimum exhaust rate of 0.02 cfm/ft^2 (0.00001 m^3/s·m^2) of horizontal area. The ventilation must be automatically controlled to operate whenever the relative humidity in the space exceeds 60%. In the IBC, this rate is expressed as 1.0 cfm for each 50 ft^2 (1.02 L/s for each 10 m^2) of crawl space floor area. A mechanically ventilated crawl space also requires a Class I vapor retarder.

Chimneys and Vents

The ventilation requirements for chimneys and vents are distinct from those discussed in the previous section and from the requirements for exhaust systems discussed in Ch. 28.

According to the IMC, a *chimney* is a primarily vertical structure containing one or more flues to carry gaseous products of combustion and air from a fuel-burning appliance to the outdoors. A chimney is capable of venting flue gases at higher temperatures than vents can. Chimneys may be either masonry or factory-made.

A *vent* is a pipe or factory-made component that contains a passageway for carrying combustion products and air to the atmosphere. Vents must be listed and labeled for use with specific types or classes of appliances.

One chapter of the IMC gives requirements for chimneys and vents, including size, location, construction, and installation. Requirements for factory-made fireplace chimneys are given in the IMC while requirements for masonry fireplaces are detailed in the IBC.

Plumbing Systems

The *International Plumbing Code* (IPC) is the companion volume to the IBC that regulates plumbing design and construction. Other codes have similar volumes. The IPC gives the minimum number of toilets, lavatories, drinking fountains, and other sanitary fixtures required in a building. The number required is based on occupancy and the number of people served. For convenience, these provisions are also given in Ch. 29 of the IBC. These should be considered minimum numbers, not necessarily optimum numbers. The IPC also outlines detailed requirements for plumbing system design, individual materials, and methods of installation. Refer to Ch. 31 for more information on plumbing systems.

Electrical Systems

The IBC and the other three former model codes reference the *National Electrical Code* (NEC), published by the National Fire Protection Association. As with other companion codes, the NEC details the requirements for materials and the design of the power supply and lighting systems of buildings. Refer to Ch. 32 for more information on electrical systems.

Sound Ratings

The IBC requires that wall and floor/ceiling assemblies in residential occupancies separating dwelling units or guest-rooms from each other and from public spaces be designed and constructed to provide for sound-transmission control. The code specifies a minimum sound-transmission class (STC) of 50 (45 if field tested) for walls. This provision does not apply to dwelling unit entrance doors. However, these doors must be tight fitting to the frame and sill. The minimum impact insulation class (IIC) for floors must be 50 (45 if field tested). Construction details that satisfy these requirements must be selected. For example, penetrations in sound walls must be sealed or otherwise treated to maintain the required rating. Refer to Ch. 33 for more information on acoustics.

Fireplaces

There are two basic types of fireplaces: factory-built, or prefabricated, fireplaces and traditional masonry fireplaces. A factory-built fireplace must be installed in accordance with the IMC and the manufacturer's directions, including requirements for minimum clearances between the fireplace and any combustible construction or trim nearby.

For a masonry fireplace, the IBC gives detailed requirements for its foundation, wall thickness, firebox configuration, chimney construction, and other aspects of its construction. Seismic reinforcing is required in all seismic design categories except A and B. No part of a masonry fireplace located in a building may be closer than 2 in (51) to combustible materials along the front and sides of the fireplace and no closer than 4 in (102) along its back face. The airspace created must be kept clear except for any fireblocking required at floor and ceiling penetrations.

For the interior, exposed parts of a fireplace opening, the main requirements are those for the materials and the dimensions of the hearth extensions, the trim around the opening, and the mantel. Hearth extensions must be made of concrete or masonry, supported by noncombustible materials, and reinforced to carry their own weight as well as all imposed loads. They must be a minimum of 2 in (51) thick. Figure 55.9 shows some of the required dimensions for masonry hearths and trim.

No combustible trim is allowed within 6 in (153) of the fireplace opening. Any combustible trim between 6 in (153) and 12 in (305) from the opening may only project $^1/_8$ in (3.2) from the masonry surface of the fireplace for every

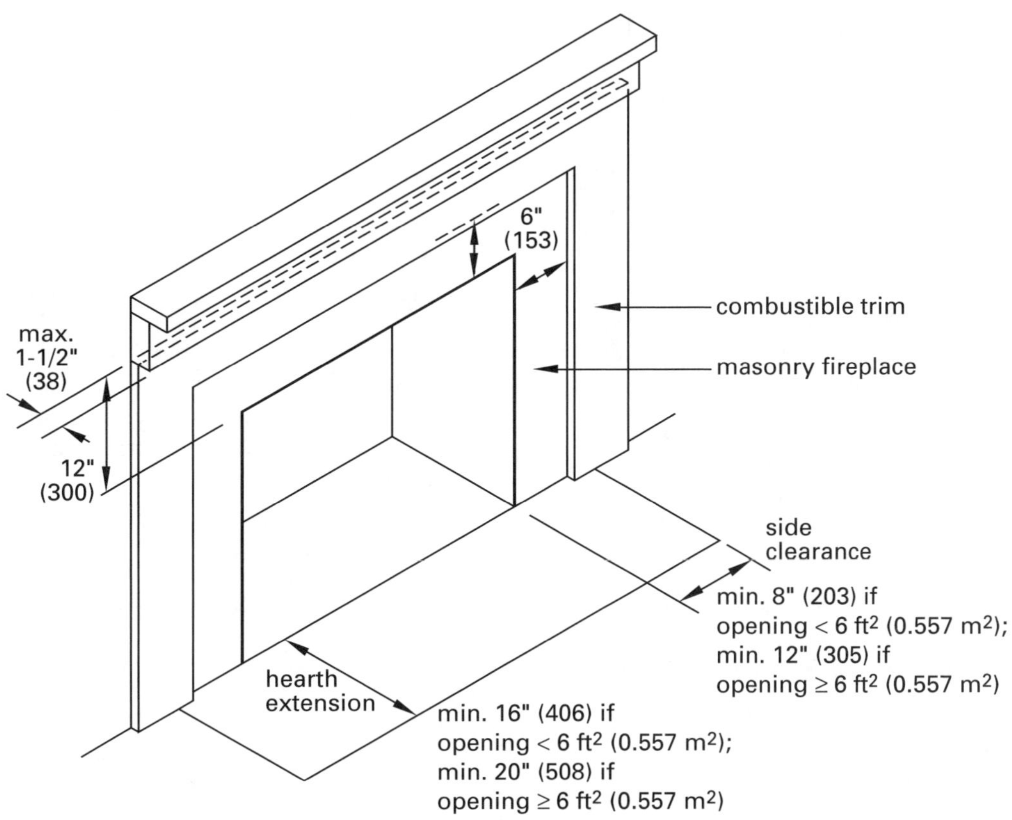

Figure 55.10 Fireplace Hearth and Trim Dimensions

1 in (25) of space between the trim and the opening. For example, at a point 6 in from the opening, any combustible trim may project only 6 times $^1/_8$ in, or $^3/_4$ in (19), out from the face of the fireplace. At 12 in from the opening, trim may project only 12 times $^1/_8$ in, or $1^1/_2$ in (38), out from the face. Beyond 12 in, combustible trim or a mantel can project any amount. Combustible materials located along the sides of the fireplace opening that project more than $1^1/_2$ in (38) from the face of the fireplace must have an additional clearance equal to the projection.

DEFINITIONS

The following terms are frequently used by building codes to precisely communicate meaning. Additional terms are defined in the main text of this chapter. Although the differences between terms are sometimes subtle, it is advisable to become familiar with them.

Area of refuge: an area where people unable to use stairways can remain temporarily while waiting for assistance

Automatic closing: as applied to a door, a door that is normally held in the open position but is released to close upon activation by a smoke detector or other type of fire alarm system. Automatic closing doors must be self-closing.

Combustible: material that will ignite and burn, either as a flame or glow, and that undergoes this process in air at pressures and temperatures that might occur during a fire in a building

Common path of egress travel: the portion of exit access that occupants must travel before two separate and distinct paths of egress travel to two exits become available

Corridor: an enclosed exit access component that defines and provides a path of egress travel to an exit. A corridor may or may not be protected depending on the particular requirements of the code.

Exit access doorway: a door or access point along the path of egress travel from an occupied room, area, or space where the path of egress enters an intervening room, corridor, unenclosed exit access stair, or unenclosed exit access ramp.

Exit court: a court or yard (considered part of an exit discharge) that provides access to a public way for one or more required exits. (In the IBC this is now called an egress court.)

Exit enclosure: a fully enclosed portion of an exit that is only used as a means of egress and that provides for a protected path of egress either in a vertical or horizontal direction. Depending on construction type, height, and building occupancy, an exit enclosure must have either a 1- or 2-hour rating, and all openings must be protected. An exit enclosure must lead to an exit discharge or the public way.

Exit passageway: a horizontal, fully enclosed portion of an exit that is only used as a means of egress. An exit passageway leads from an exit doorway to an exit discharge or a public way. A common example of an exit passageway is an exit from the door at the ground level of an interior stairway that leads through the building to an outside door.

Fire assembly: an assembly of a fire door, fire window, or fire damper, including all required anchorage, frames, sills, and hardware

Fire barrier: a fire-resistance-rated vertical or horizontal assembly of materials designed to restrict the spread of fire, in which openings are protected.

Fire door assembly: any combination of a fire door, frame, hardware, and other accessories that provides a specific degree of fire protection to an opening

Fire exit hardware: panic hardware that is listed for use on fire-door assemblies

Fire partition: a fire-resistive component used to separate dwelling units in R-2 construction, to separate guestrooms in Group R-1 construction, to separate tenant spaces in covered mall buildings, and as a corridor wall. Fire partitions are generally required to have a minimum 1-hour rated construction except in certain circumstances. They are similar to fire barriers, but the requirements for support are not as strict.

Fire-protection rating: the period of time in which an opening assembly, such as a door or window, maintains the ability to confine a fire or maintains its integrity, or both, when tested in accordance with NFPA 252, UL 10B, or UL 10C for doors, and NFPA 257 for windows. An assembly that requires a fire-protection rating must withstand fire exposure and thermal shock as with a fire-resistance rating, but not heat transmission as walls, columns, and floors do.

Fire-rated: See *Fire-protection rating*

Fire resistance: the property of a material or assembly to withstand or resist the spread of fire or give protection from it

Fire-resistance rating: the period of time a building component such as a wall, floor, roof, beam, or column is able to confine a fire or maintain its structural integrity, or both, when tested in accordance with ASTM E119, *Standard Methods for Fire Tests of Building Construction and Materials*. This is different from "fire-protection rating," which involves protected opening assemblies.

Fire-resistive construction: See *Fire resistance*

Flame resistance: the ability to withstand flame impingement or give protection from it. This applies to individual materials as well as combinations of components when tested in accordance with NFPA 701, *Standard Methods of Fire Tests for Flame-Resistant Textiles and Films*.

Flame spread: the propagation of flame over a surface

Flame-spread index: the numerical value assigned to a material tested in accordance with ASTM E84, *Standard Test Method for Surface Burning Characteristics of Building Materials*

Flammable: capable of burning with a flame and subject to easy ignition and rapid flaming combustion

Horizontal exit: an exit through a minimum 2-hour rated wall that divides a building into two or more separate exit access areas to afford safety from fire and smoke

Noncombustible: describing material that will not ignite and burn when subjected to a fire. The IBC qualifies a material as noncombustible only if it is tested in accordance with ASTM E136, *Noncombustible Material—Tests*, or if it has a structural base of noncombustible material with a surfacing not more than $^{1}/_{8}$ in (3.18) thick that has a flame-spread index no greater than 50.

Occupant load: the number of people for which the means of egress of a building or part of a building is designed

Panic hardware: a door-latching assembly that includes a device that releases the latch when a force is applied in the direction of egress travel

Self-closing: as applied to a door, a door that is equipped with a device (most commonly a door closer) that will ensure closing after the door has been opened

Stair: a change in elevation, consisting of one or more risers

Stairway: one or more flights of stairs, either exterior or interior, with the necessary landings and platforms connecting them to form a continuous and uninterrupted passage from one level to another

Travel distance: the measurement of the distance between the most remote occupied point of an area or room to the entrance of the nearest exit that serves it. It is part of the exit access and it is measured along the natural and unobstructed path of egress travel.

Trim: picture molds, chair rails, baseboards, handrails, door and window frames, and similar decorative or protective materials used in fixed applications

56 BARRIER-FREE DESIGN

Barrier-free design is an important part of the ARE, especially since the Americans with Disabilities Act (ADA) became law in 1992. Although building codes and many federal and state agencies require accessibility, the overriding regulation today is the ADA. This federal law requires, among other things, that all commercial and public accommodations be accessible to people with disabilities. Although the ADA is not a national building code and does not depend on inspection for its enforcement, building owners must comply with its requirements or be liable for civil suits. Architects are likewise responsible for designing buildings that conform to the ADA requirements as well as local building code regulations.

The ADA is a complex, four-title civil rights law. Title III, Public Accommodations and Commercial Facilities, is the part that most affects designers.

The design requirements for construction are found mainly in the *Americans with Disabilities Act and Architectural Barriers Act Accessibility Guidelines (ADA/ABA Guidelines)* published in 2004. These replaced the original *ADA Accessibility Guidelines* (ADAAG), which were Appendix A to 28 CFR 36, the *Code of Federal Regulations* rule that implemented Title III. When architects and others refer to the ADA, they are usually referring to the design criteria contained in the *ADA/ABA Guidelines*.

Other local and federal laws and regulations also govern accessibility. For example, multifamily housing is regulated mainly by the federal Fair Housing Act and by some state laws. For some federal buildings, the *Uniform Federal Accessibility Standards* govern. Although there are differences among these regulations, they all follow most of the standards set forth in ICC/ANSI A117.1, *Accessible and Usable Buildings and Facilities*, or the older version, CABO/ANSI A117.1, *American National Standard for Buildings and Facilities Providing Accessibility and Usability for Physically Handicapped People*.

The main differences among the standards are in scoping provisions, which set how many accessible elements must be provided. For example, scoping provisions tell the designer how many seats in a restaurant must allow for wheelchair access or how many housing units in a complex must be accessible.

The standards discussed in this chapter include some of the basic requirements for accessibility inside a building as defined in the ADA and with ICC/ANSI A117.1. Additional accessibility provisions for site work are discussed in Ch. 5.

ACCESSIBLE ROUTES

An *accessible route* is a continuous unobstructed path connecting all accessible elements and spaces in a building or facility. It includes corridors, doorways, floors, ramps, elevators, lifts, and clear floor space at fixtures. The standards for accessible routes are designed to accommodate a person with a severe disability who uses a wheelchair, and are also intended to provide ease of use for people with other disabilities.

Accessible routes and other clearances are based on basic dimensional requirements of wheelchairs. The minimum clear floor space required to accommodate one stationary wheelchair is 30 in by 48 in (760 by 1220). For maneuverability, a minimum 60 in (1525) diameter circle is required for a wheelchair to make a 180° turn. In place of this, a T-shaped space may be provided as shown in Fig. 56.1.

The minimum clear width for an accessible route is 36 in (915) continuously and 32 in (815) clear at a passage point such as a doorway. The passage point cannot be more than 24 in (610) long. The minimum passage width for two wheelchairs is 60 in (1525). If an accessible route is less than 60 in wide, passing spaces at least 60 in by 60 in (1525 by 1525) must be provided at intervals not to exceed 200 ft (61 m). These requirements are shown in Fig. 56.2.

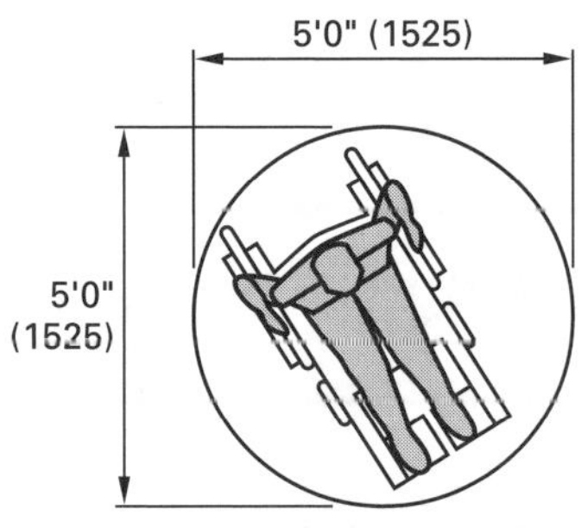

(a) turning diameter

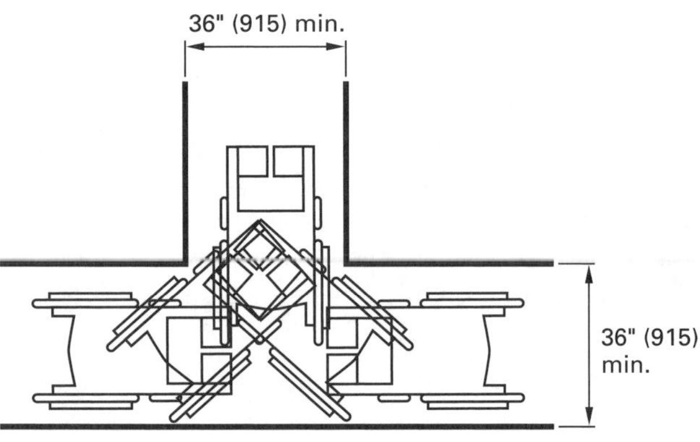

(b) T-shaped space for 180° turns

Figure 56.1 Maneuvering Clearances

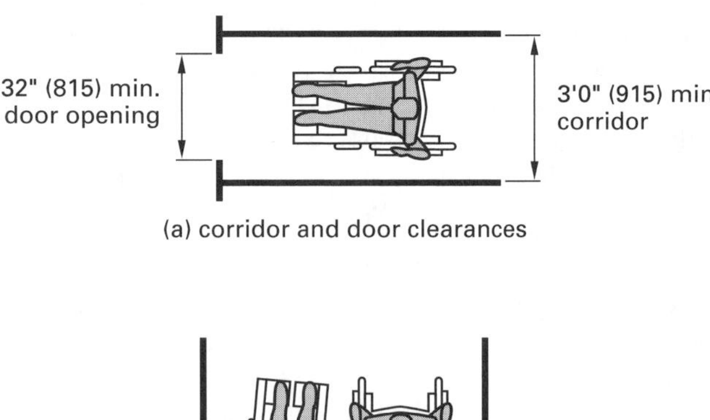

(a) corridor and door clearances

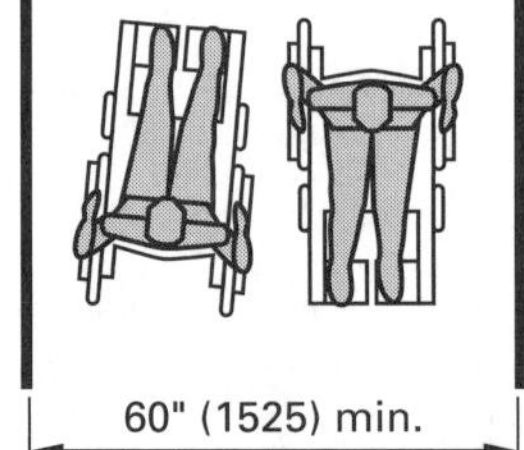

(b) minimum clear width for two wheelchairs

Figure 56.2 Wheelchair Clearances

In toilet rooms the turning space may overlap with the required clear floor space at fixtures and controls and with the accessible route. If turns in corridors or around obstructions must be made, the minimum dimensions are as shown in Fig. 56.3.

An accessible route may have a slope up to 1:20 (a 1 in rise for every 20 in of distance) or 5%. Any slope greater than this is classified as a ramp and must meet the requirements given in the section later in this chapter.

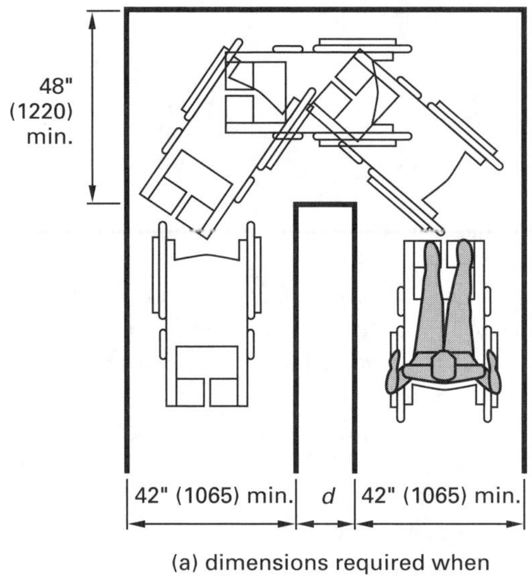

(a) dimensions required when
d is less than 48" (1220)

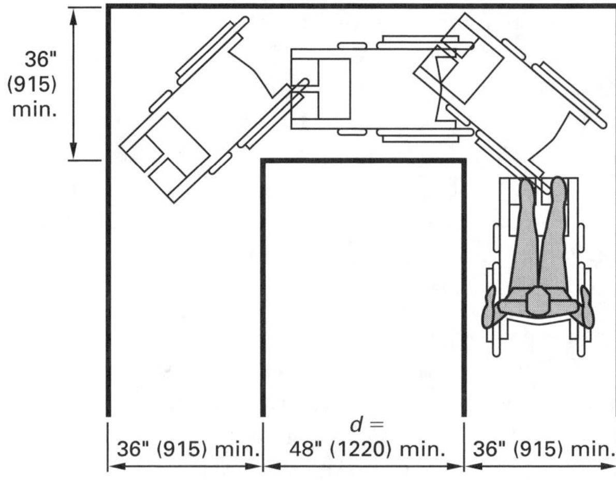

(b) dimensions required when
d is 48" (1220) or greater

Figure 56.3 Turn in Corridors or Around Obstructions

DOORWAYS

Width and Arrangement

Doors must have a minimum clear opening width of 32 in (815) when the door is opened at 90°. The maximum depth of a doorway 32 in wide is 24 in (610). If the area is deeper than this, the width must be increased to 36 in (915). See Fig. 56.4.

Maneuvering clearances are required at standard swinging doors to allow easy operation of the latch and provide for a clear swing. For single doors the clearances are shown in Fig. 56.5. For two doors in a series the minimum space is shown in Fig. 56.6. Note the 48 in (1220) space requirement. If sufficient clearance is not provided, the doors must have power-assisted mechanisms or be automatic opening.

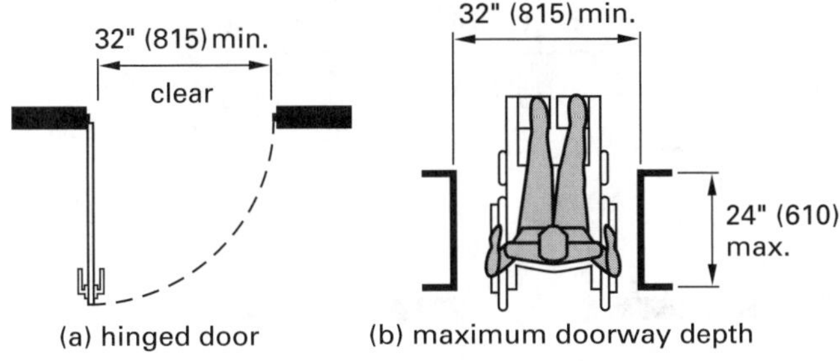

Figure 56.4 Doorway Clearances

Opening Force

The maximum opening force required to push or pull open interior hinged doors cannot be more than 5 lbf-ft (22.2 N). This force does not include the force required to retract the latch bolts or disengage other devices that may hold the door closed. Maximum opening forces may be greater if the door is a fire door and regulated by the local code jurisdiction. Automatic doors and power-assisted doors may also be used if they comply with ANSI/BHMA Standard A156.10 (automatic doors) or ANSI/BHMA 156.19 (low-powered, automatic doors).

When closers are used, the sweep period of the door must be adjusted so that from an open position of 70°, the door will take at least 3 sec to move to a point 3 in (75) from the latch as measured to the leading edge of the door.

Hardware

A threshold at a doorway cannot exceed a $^1/_4$ in (6.4) vertical change. A change in elevation between $^1/_4$ in (6.4) and $^1/_2$ in (12.7) in height must be beveled so that no part of the threshold slopes more than 1 vertical unit for each 2 horizontal units. In other words, a $^1/_4$ in (6.4) vertical change in elevation beyond the first $^1/_4$ in would have to be made over a minimum horizontal distance of $^1/_2$ in (12.7). Operating devices must have a shape that is easy to grasp. This includes lever handles, push-type mechanisms, and U-shaped handles. Round doorknobs are not allowed. If door closers are provided, they must be adjusted to slow the closing time. Hardware for accessible doors cannot be mounted more than 48 in (1220) above the finished floor.

PLUMBING FIXTURES AND TOILET ROOMS

ICC/ANSI A117.1 and the ADA govern the design of the components of toilet rooms as well as individual elements such as drinking fountains, bathtubs, and showers. As mentioned in a previous section, toilet rooms must have a minimum clear turning space of a 5 ft (1525) diameter circle in addition to the minimum access areas required at each type of fixture. The 5 ft circle can overlap with required access at controls and fixtures and with the accessible route.

Toilet Stalls

There are several acceptable layouts for toilet stalls. Minimum clearances for two standard stall layouts are shown in Fig. 56.7. The clearance depth in both cases varies depending on whether a wall-hung or floor-mounted water closet is used. In most cases, the door must provide a minimum clear opening of 32 in (815) and must swing out, away from the stall enclosure. Grab bars must also be provided as shown in the illustrations, mounted from 33 in to 36 in (840 to 915) above the floor.

In addition to the dimensional requirements shown in Fig. 56.7, the *ADA/ABA Guidelines* require that at least one ambulatory toilet stall be provided where there are six or more toilet stalls or where the combination of urinals and water closets totals six or more fixtures. An ambulatory toilet stall is shown in Fig. 56.8.

In all cases the clearance depth varies depending on whether a wall-hung or floor-mounted water closet is used.

All toilet stalls must have toe clearance below the front partition and below at least one side partition. This clearance must be a minimum of 9 in (230) above the floor and extend a minimum of 6 in (150) beyond the compartment-side face of the partition. Refer to the full text of the *ADA/ABA Guidelines* for additional requirements for children's toilets and toilet stalls.

In residential units, the edge of a lavatory may be located a minimum of 18 in (455) from the centerline of the toilet. In all other cases there must be a clear floor space as shown in Fig. 56.9.

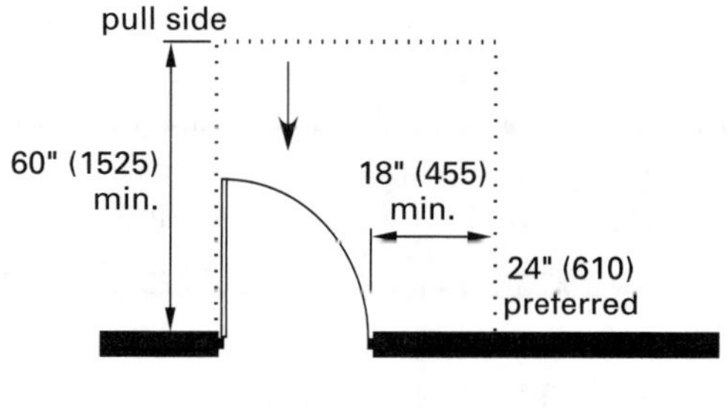

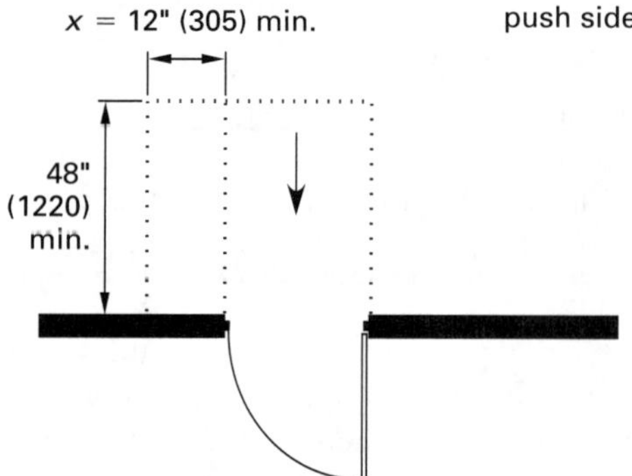

Note: x = 12" (305) if door has both closer and latch.

(a) front approaches—swinging doors

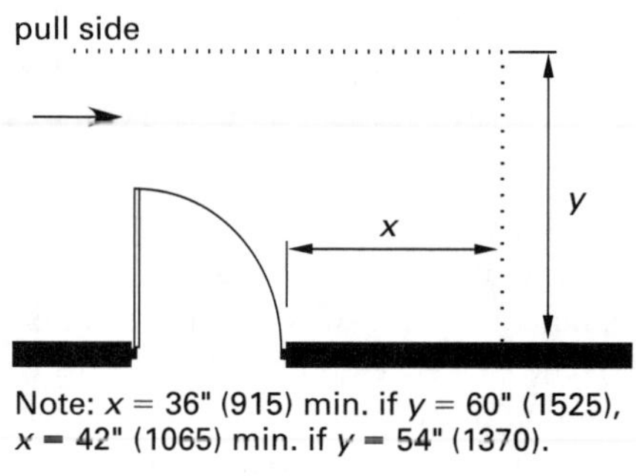

Note: x = 36" (915) min. if y = 60" (1525), x = 42" (1065) min. if y = 54" (1370).

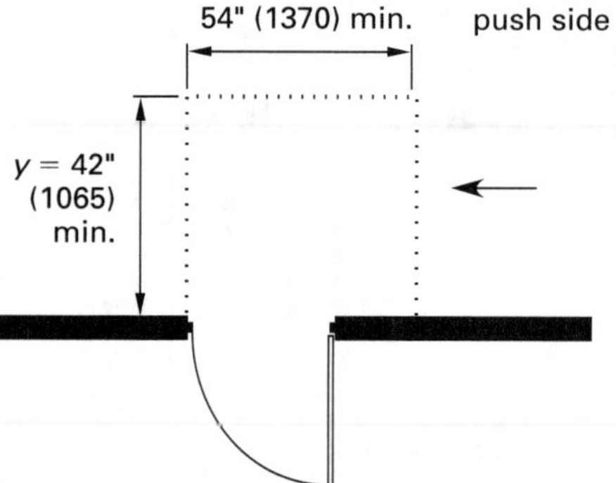

Note: y = 48" (1220) min. if door has both latch and closer.

(b) hinge side approaches—swinging doors

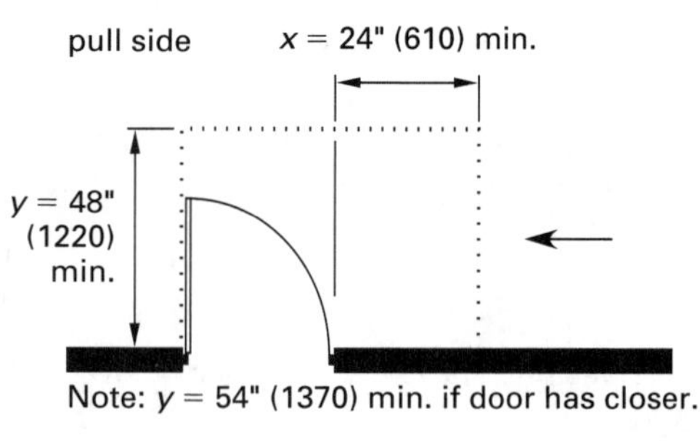

Note: y = 54" (1370) min. if door has closer.

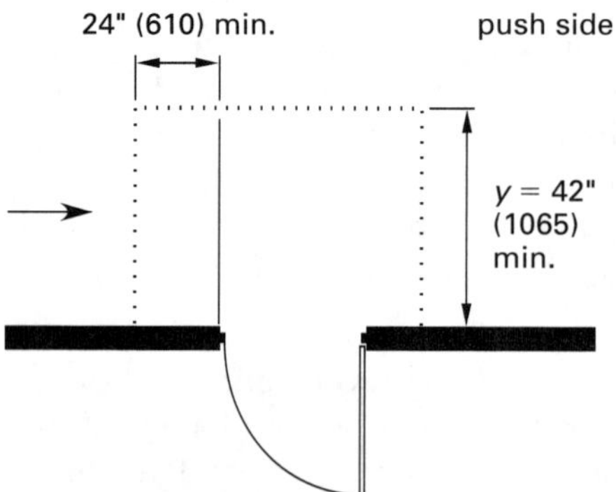

Note: y = 48" (1220) min. if door has closer.

(c) latch side approaches—swinging doors

Figure 56.5 Maneuvering Clearances at Doors

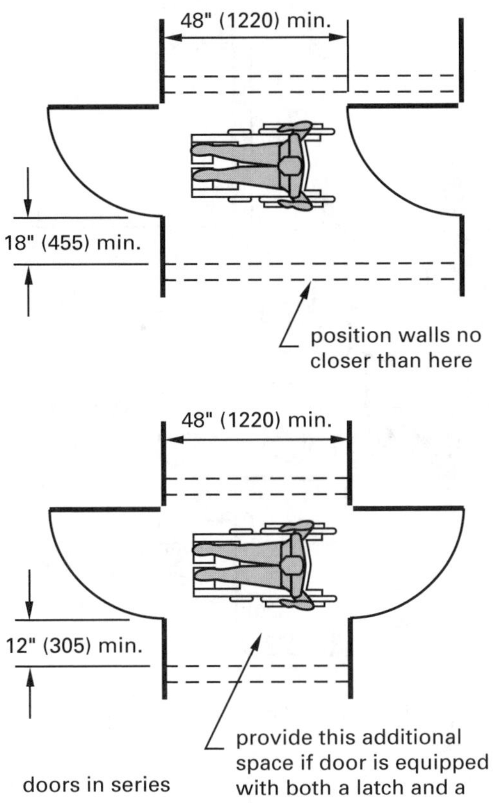

Figure 56.6 Double Door Clearances

If toilet stalls are not used, the centerline of the toilet must still be 16 in to 18 in (405 to 455) from a wall with grab bars at both the back and side of the water closet. A clear space in front of and beside open water closets should be provided as shown in Fig. 56.9. Toilet paper dispensers must be 7 in (180) minimum and 9 in (230) maximum in front of the water closet. The outlet of the dispenser must be between 15 in (380) and 48 in (1220) above the floor. It may be mounted either above or below the grab bar. If mounted above the grab bar there must be a minimum of 12 in (305) between the top of the bar and the outlet. If mounted below the grab bar, there must be a minimum clearance of $1^1/_2$ in (38) between the bottom of the bar and the top of the dispenser. Dispensers must not be of a type that controls delivery or that does not allow continuous paper flow.

Urinals

Urinals must be stall-type or wall-hung with an elongated rim at a maximum height of 17 in (430) above the floor. A clear floor space of 30 in by 48 in (760 by 1220) must be provided in front of the urinal, which may adjoin or overlap an accessible route. Urinal shields that do not extend beyond the front edge of the rim may be provided with 30 in (760) clearance between them.

Lavatories and Sinks

Lavatories must allow someone in a wheelchair to move under the sink and easily use the basin and water controls. The required dimensions are shown in Fig. 56.10. Notice

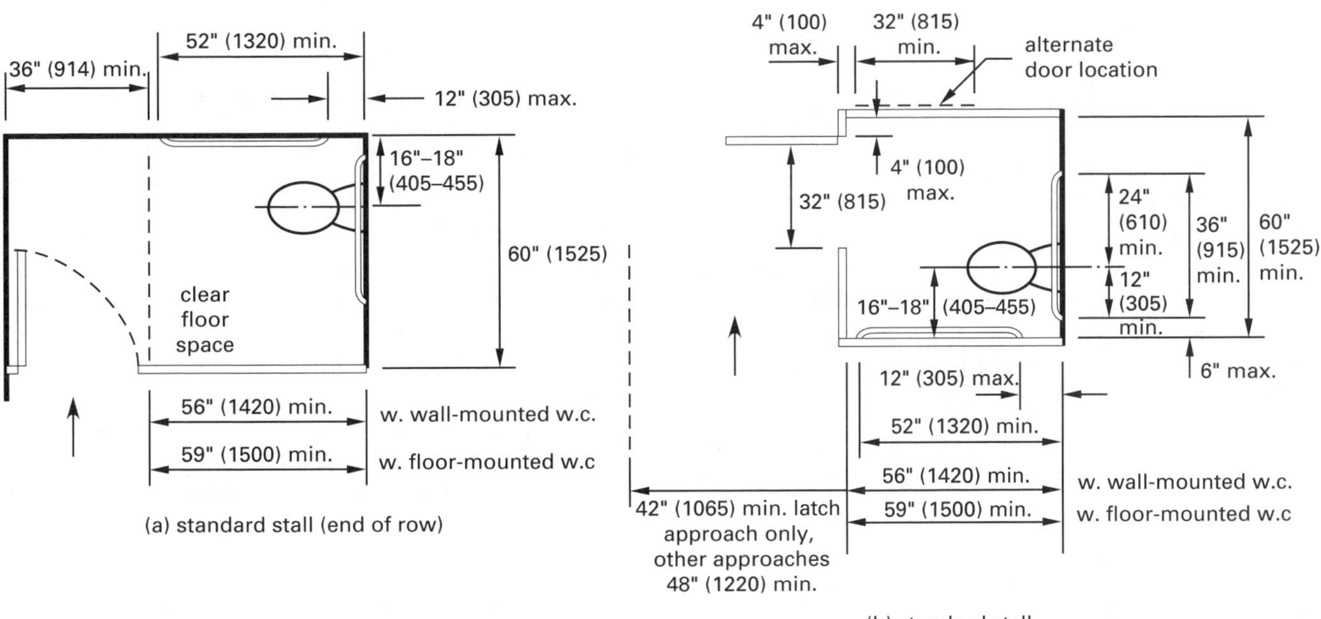

Figure 56.7 Toilet Stall Dimensions

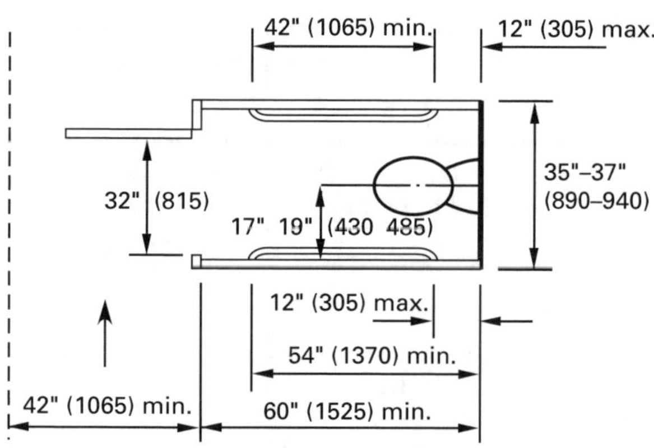

Figure 56.8 Ambulatory Toilet Stall Dimensions

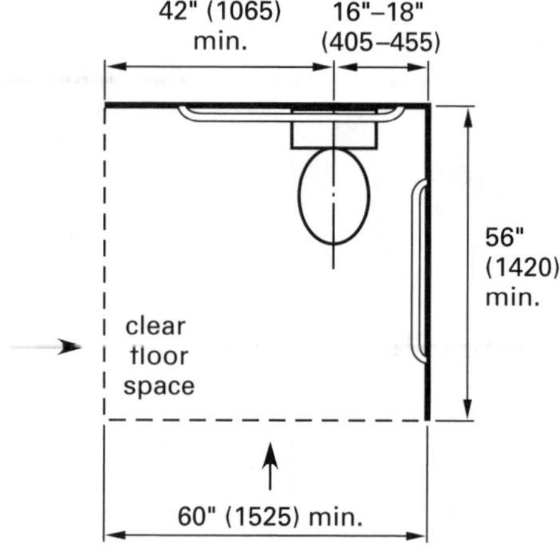

Figure 56.9 Clear Floor Space at Water Closets

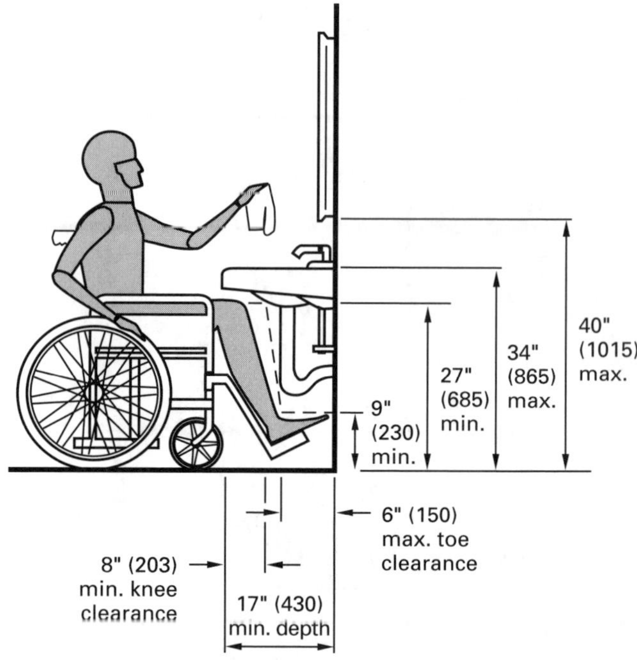

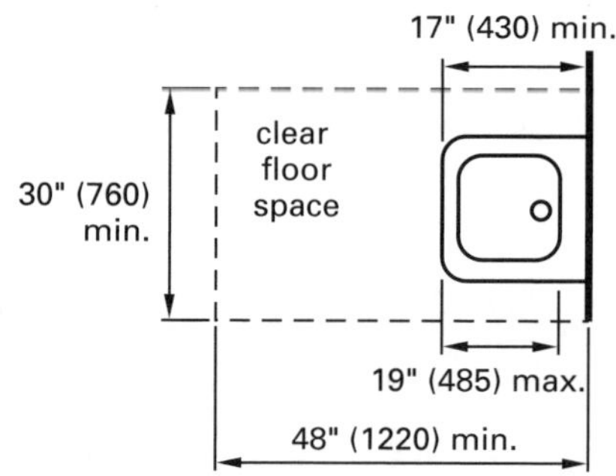

Figure 56.10 Clear Floor Space at Lavatories

that because of these clearances, wall-hung lavatories are the best type to use when accessibility is a concern. If pipes are exposed below the lavatory, they must be insulated or otherwise protected, and there must not be any sharp or abrasive surfaces under lavatories or sinks. Faucets must be operable with one hand and cannot require tight grasping, pinching, or twisting of the wrist. Lever-operated, push-type, and automatically controlled mechanisms are acceptable types.

Mirrors must be mounted with the bottom edge of the reflecting surface no higher than 40 in (1015) from the floor.

Requirements for sinks are the same as those for lavatories. The maximum depth of the sink bowl is $6^1/_2$ in (165). The clear floor space requirement is the same as it is for lavatories.

Drinking Fountains

Requirements for drinking fountains with a front approach are shown in Fig. 56.11. A drinking fountain that is freestanding or built-in without clear space below must have a clear floor space in front of it at least 30 in by 48 in wide (760 by 1220) with the long dimension parallel to the fountain, which allows a person in a wheelchair to make a parallel approach. The spout must be a maximum of 5 in (125) from the front edge of the unit, for users making a forward approach.

The IBC requires that two drinking fountains be provided, one for wheelchair users and one for persons who are standing. A combination unit that accommodates both may be provided instead.

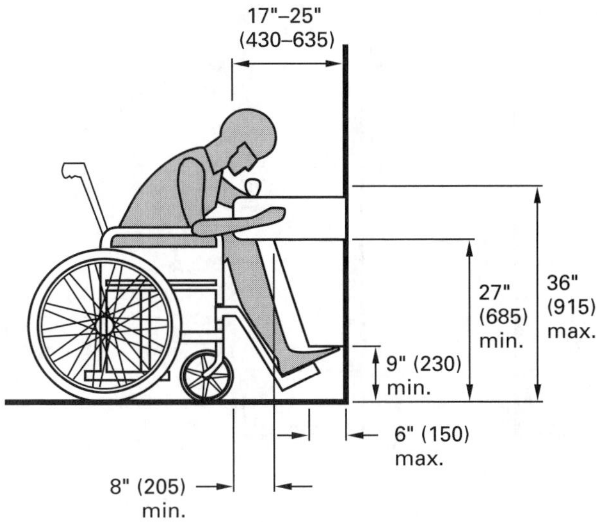

(a) spout height and knee clearance

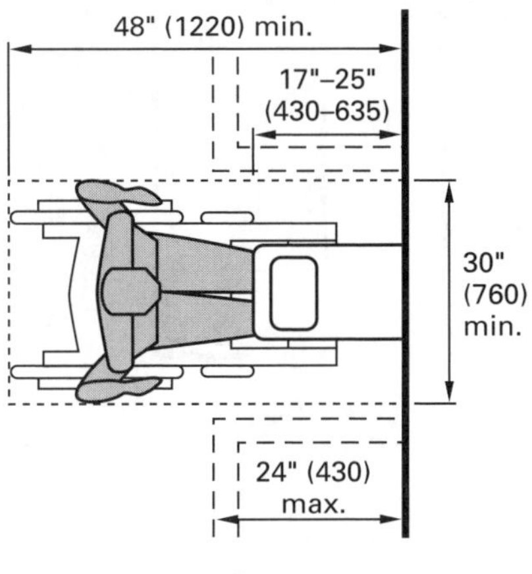

(b) clear floor space

Figure 56.11 Water Fountain Access

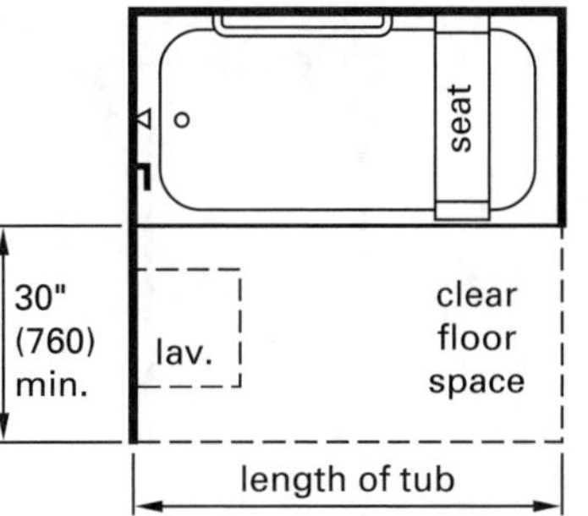

(a) with seat in tub, side approach

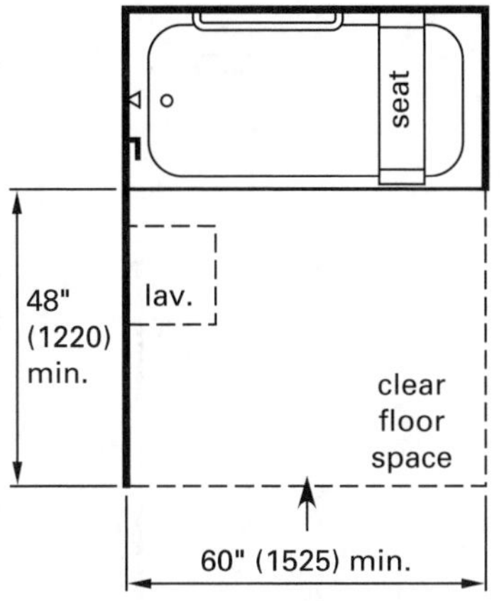

(b) with seat in tub, front approach

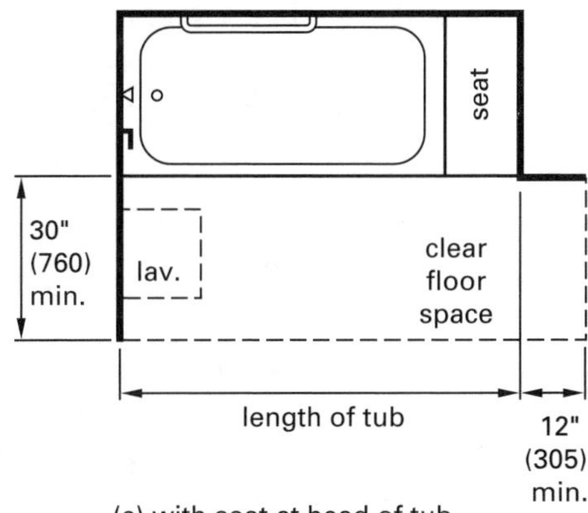

(c) with seat at head of tub

o drain
◁ shower head
┐ shower controls

Figure 56.12 Clear Floor Space at Bathtubs

Bathtubs

Bathtubs must be configured as shown in Fig. 56.12. An in-tub seat or a seat at the head of the tub must be provided as shown in the drawing. Grab bars must be provided as illustrated in Fig. 56.13. If an enclosure is provided, it cannot obstruct the controls or transfer from wheelchairs onto seats or into the tub. Enclosure tracks cannot be mounted on the rim of the tub.

Showers

Shower stalls may be one of two basic types as shown in Fig. 56.14. When facilities with accessible sleeping rooms or suites are provided, a minimum number of rooms having roll-in showers, as specified in the ADA or the Federal Fair Housing Act, is required. A seat is required in the smaller shower stall configuration, while a folding seat is required in the larger configuration if a permanent seat is provided. Grab bars must be provided and mounted from 33 in to 36 in (840 to 915) above the floor.

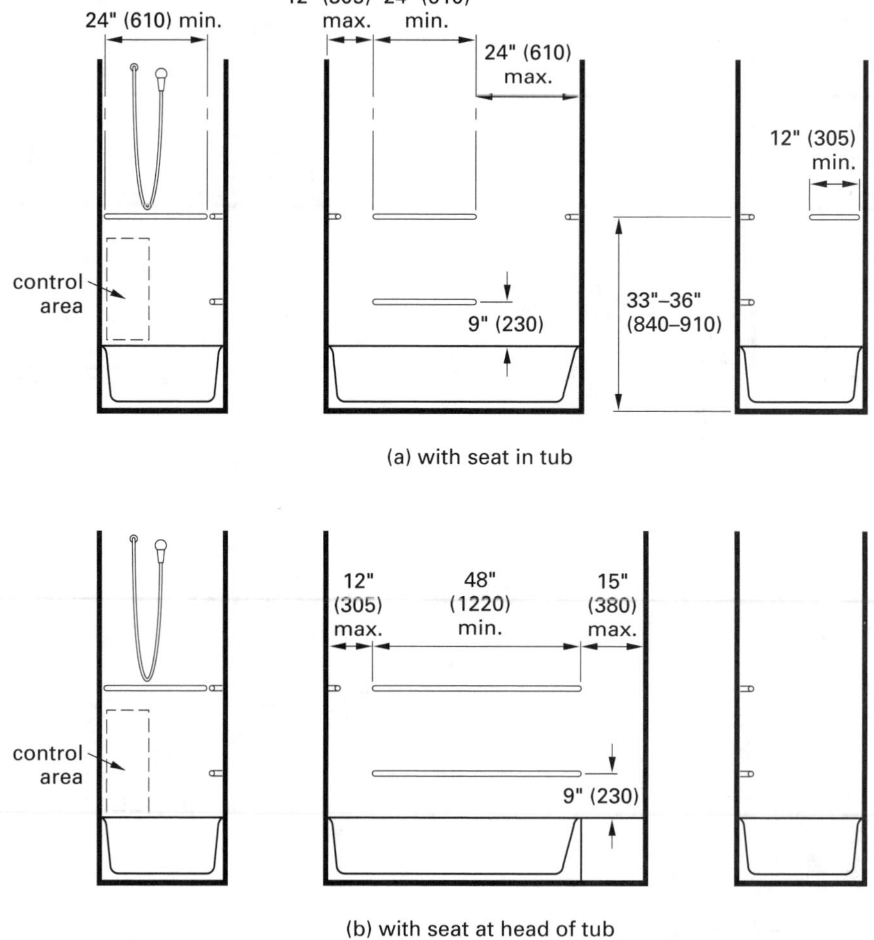

Figure 56.13 Grab Bars at Bathtubs

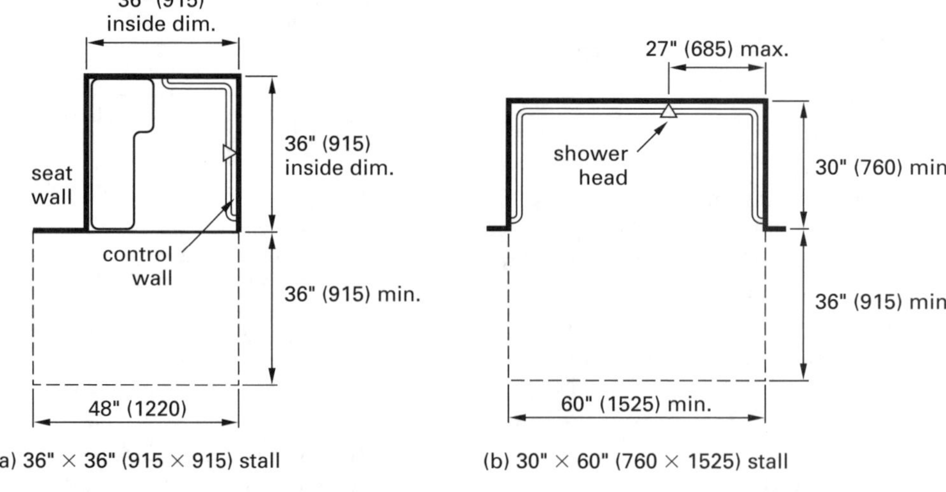

Figure 56.14 Accessible Shower Stalls

FLOOR SURFACES

Floor surfaces must be stable, firm, and slip resistant. If there is a change in level, the transition must meet the following requirements. If the change is less than $^{1}/_{4}$ in (6), it may be vertical and without edge treatment. If the change is between $^{1}/_{4}$ in and $^{1}/_{2}$ in (6 to 13), it must be beveled with a slope no greater than 1:2 ($^{1}/_{2}$ in of rise requires 1 in of length, for example). Changes greater than $^{1}/_{2}$ in (13) must be accomplished with a ramp meeting the requirements in the next section.

If carpet is used, it must have a firm cushion or backing, or it must have no cushion and a level loop, textured loop, level cut pile, or level cut/uncut pile texture with a maximum pile height of $^{1}/_{2}$ in (13). It must be securely attached to the floor and have trim along all lengths of exposed edges.

RAMPS AND STAIRS

Ramps are required to provide a smooth transition between changes in elevation for both wheelchair-bound persons as well as those whose mobility is otherwise restricted. In general, the least possible slope should be used, but in no case can a ramp have a slope greater than 1:12 (1 in rise for every 12 in of run [25 for 300]). The maximum rise for any ramp is limited to 30 in (760). Changes in elevation greater than this require a level landing before the next run of ramp is encountered. In some cases where existing conditions prevent the 1:12 slope, a 1:10 slope is permitted if the maximum rise does not exceed 6 in (150), and a 1:8 slope is permitted if the maximum rise does not exceed 3 in (75).

The minimum clear width of a ramp is 36 in (915) with landings at least as wide as the widest ramp leading to them. Landing lengths must be a minimum of 60 in (1525). If ramps change direction at a landing, the landing must be at least 60 in square.

Ramps with rises greater than 6 in (150) or lengths greater than 72 in (1830) must have handrails on both sides, with the top of the handrail from 34 in to 38 in (865 to 965) above the ramp surface. They must extend at least 12 in (305) beyond the top and bottom of the ramp segment and have a diameter or width of gripping surface from $1^{1}/_{4}$ in to $1^{1}/_{2}$ in (32 m to 38 m). Handrails are not required for ramps adjacent to seating in assembly areas.

Stairs that are required as a means of egress and stairs between floors not connected by an elevator must be designed according to certain standards specifying the configuration of treads, risers, nosings, and handrails. The maximum riser height is 7 in (180), and the treads must be a minimum of 11 in (280) as measured from riser to riser as shown in Fig. 55.8. Open risers are not permitted. The undersides of the nosings must not be abrupt and must conform to one of the styles shown in Fig. 55.7. There should be contrasting strips at the top and bottom tread nosings.

Stairway handrails must be continuous on both sides of the stairs. The inside handrail on switchback or dogleg stairs must always be continuous as it changes direction. Other handrails must extend beyond the top and bottom risers as shown in Fig. 55.8. The top of the gripping surface must be between 34 in and 38 in (865 and 965) above stair nosings. The handrail must have a diameter or width of gripping surface from $1^{1}/_{4}$ in to 2 in (32 to 51). There must be a clear space between the handrail and the wall of at least $1^{1}/_{2}$ in (38).

When an exit stairway is part of an accessible route in an unsprinklered building (not including houses), there must be a clear width of 48 in (1220) between handrails.

PROTRUDING OBJECTS

Because objects and building elements that project into corridors and other walkways present a hazard for visually impaired people, there are restrictions on their size and configuration. These are shown in Fig. 56.15 and are based on the use of a cane by people with severe vision impairments. Protruding objects with their lower edge less than 27 in (685) above the floor can be detected so they may project any amount (as long as the minimum passage width is maintained).

Regardless of the situation, protruding objects cannot reduce the clear width required for an accessible route or maneuvering space. In addition, if vertical clearance of an area adjacent to an accessible route is reduced to less than 80 in (2030), a guardrail or other barrier must be provided.

DETECTABLE WARNINGS

A *detectable warning* is a surface feature built in or applied to a walking surface or other element to warn of hazards on a circulation path. Detectable warning surfaces consist of truncated domes 0.2 in (5.1) in height spaced between 1.6 in and 2.4 in (41 to 61) on center in a square grid pattern.

Continuous detectable warning surfaces 24 in (610) wide are generally required at passenger transit platform edges where there is no guard or other protection. Other locations where detectable warning surfaces are required depend on the locally adopted regulation. Both the ADA and the IBC require detectable warning surfaces at platform boarding edges, but the IBC does not require them at bus stops. ANSI A117.1 makes reference to detectable warning surfaces in both exterior and interior locations but provides no scoping provisions stating precisely where they are required. Local codes should be verified to determine which rules might apply to a particular design project.

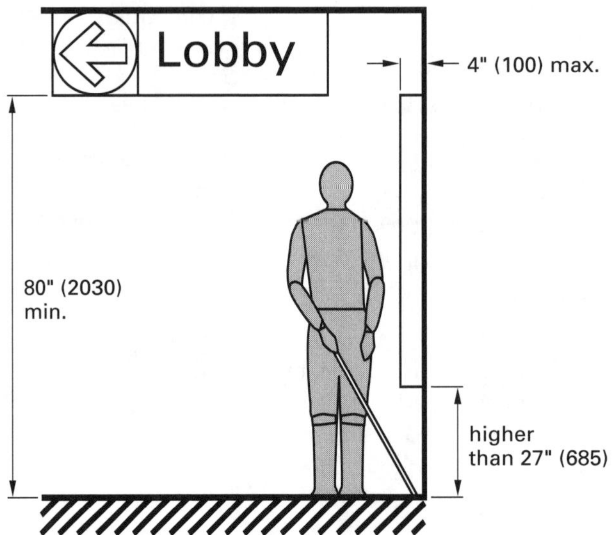

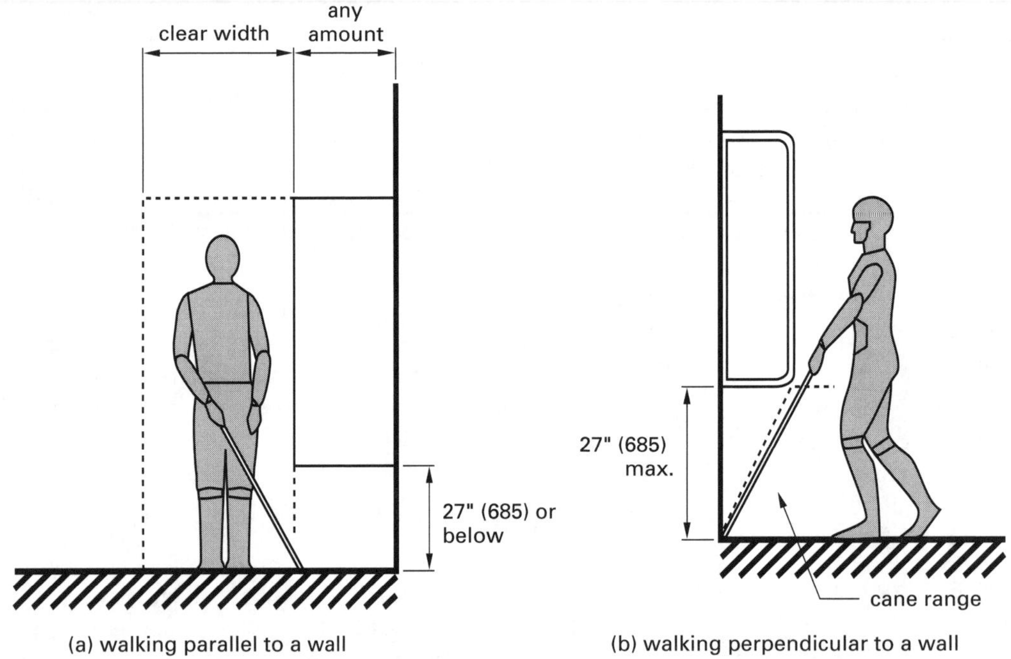

Figure 56.15 Requirements for Protruding Objects

SIGNAGE AND ALARMS

Signage that gives emergency information and general circulation directions for visually impaired people must be provided. Signage is also required for elevators.

Emergency warning systems that provide both a visual and an audible alarm are required. Audible alarms must produce a sound that exceeds the prevailing sound level in the room or space by at least 15 dB. Visual alarms must be flashing lights that have a flashing frequency of about 1 Hz (1 cycle per second).

The ADA requires that certain accessible rooms and features be clearly identified with the symbol for accessibility and that identification, directional, and information signs meet certain specifications.

Permanent rooms and spaces must be identified with signs having lettering from 5/8 in to 2 in (16 to 50) high, raised

$^1/_{32}$ in (0.8) above the surface of the sign. Lettering must be all uppercase, in sans serif or simple serif type accompanies with Grade 2 Braille. If pictograms are used, they must be at least 6 in (152) high and must be accompanies with the equivalent verbal description placed directly below the pictogram. Signs must be eggshell matte or use some other nonglare finish with characters and symbols contrasting with their background. Permanent identification signs must be mounted on the wall adjacent to the latch side of the door such that there is a minimum clear floor space of 18 in by 18 in (455 by 455) centered on the tactile characters and beyond the arc of the door swing. The mounting height to the baseline of the lowest tactile character must be 48 in (1220) minimum and 60 in (1525) maximum to the baseline of the highest tactile character. When there is no wall space to the latch side of the door, including for double-leaf doors, the sign must be placed to the right of the right-hand door.

Directional and informational signs must have lettering from $^5/_8$ in to 3 in (16 to 75) high, depending on the viewing distance, which is detailed in a table in the *ADA/ABA Guidelines*. Contrast and finish requirements are the same as those for permanent room identification. Lettering can be uppercase or lowercase.

The international symbol for accessibility is required on parking spaces, passenger loading zones, accessible entrances, and toilet and bathing facilities when not all are accessible. Building directories and temporary signs do not have to comply. Refer to the *ADA/ABA Guidelines* for the detailed requirements for signage.

TELEPHONES

If public telephones are provided, there must be at least one telephone per floor conforming to the requirements as shown in Fig. 56.16 and as specified in the ADA requirements. If there are two or more banks of telephones, there must be at least one conforming telephone per bank. When four or more public pay telephones are provided, then at least one interior public text telephone is required.

Accessible telephones may be designed for either front or side access. The dimensions required for both of these types are shown in Fig. 56.16. In either case, a clear floor space of at least 30 in by 48 in (760 by 1220) must be provided. The telephones should have pushbutton controls and telephone directories within reach of a person in a wheelchair.

The international TDD (text telephone) is required to identify the location of those phones, and volume control telephones must have a sign depicting a telephone handset with radiating sound waves. In assembly areas, permanently installed assistive listening systems must display the international symbol of access for hearing loss. See Fig. 56.17.

Refer to the ADA requirements and local codes for detailed rules on telephone types and installation requirements.

SEATING

If fixed or built-in seating or tables are provided in accessible public- or common-use areas, then at least 5%, but not less than one of the seating areas must be accessible. This includes facilities such as restaurants, nightclubs, churches, and similar spaces. In new construction and when possible in remodeling, the number of tables should be dispersed throughout the facility. If smoking and nonsmoking areas are provided, the required number of seating spaces must be proportioned among the smoking and nonsmoking areas. The area for this type of seating must comply with the dimensions shown in Fig. 56.18.

In places of assembly with fixed seating, the minimum number of wheelchair locations is given in Table 56.1. At least 1%, but not less than one of all fixed seats must be aisle seats with no armrests on the aisle side, or must have removable or folding armrests on the aisle side. Signs notifying people of the availability of these seats must be posted at the ticket office. The wheelchair areas must be an integral part of the overall seating plan and must be provided so people have a choice of admission prices and lines of sight comparable to those available for members of the general public. At least one companion seat must be provided next to each wheelchair area. Wheelchair areas must adjoin an accessible route that also serves as a means of emergency egress.

When assembly areas are part of a remodeling and it is not feasible to disperse the seating areas throughout, the accessible seating areas may be clustered. These clustered areas must have provisions for companion seating and must be located on an accessible route that also serves as a means of emergency egress.

Refer to the complete text of the ADA for requirements for audio-amplification systems, assisted listening devices, and signage required for assembly areas.

ELEVATORS

The ADA requires that elevator signals be located as shown in Fig. 56.19. The call buttons, hall lantern, and floor designators must all be located within easy reach and visual access. The call button must indicate when each call is registered and answered. The hall lantern must give a visual and audible signal. For audible signals, the lantern can sound once for up and twice for down, or it may be equipped with a verbal annunciator that sounds out "up" and "down."

Inside the car, floor buttons can be no higher than 48 in (1220) above the floor. However, when a side approach is possible and the elevator panel serves more than 16 openings, floor buttons may be a maximum of 54 in (1370) above the floor. Emergency controls must be grouped at the bottom of the panel with the centerline of the group no less than 35 in (890) above the floor. Refer to the *ADA/ABA Guidelines* for other requirements, including the minimum size of cars, door and signal timing, and safety reopening devices.

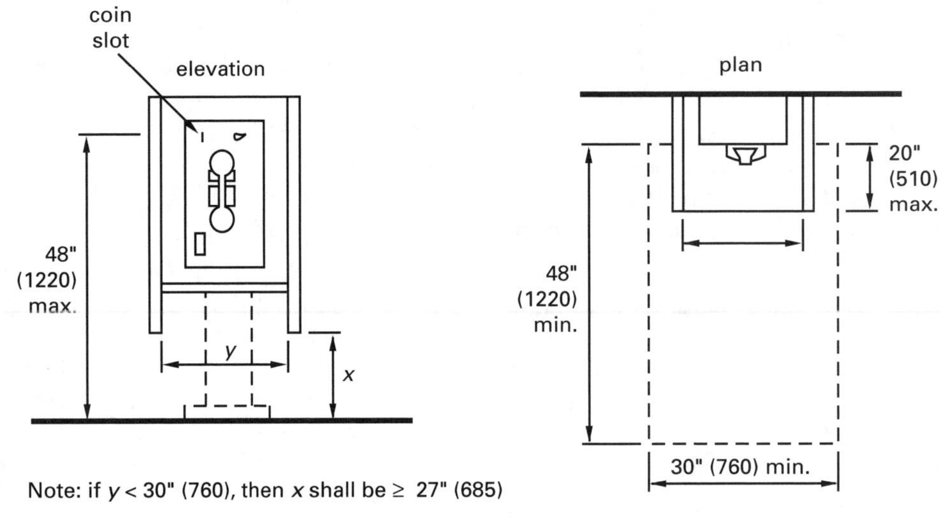

(a) forward reach possible

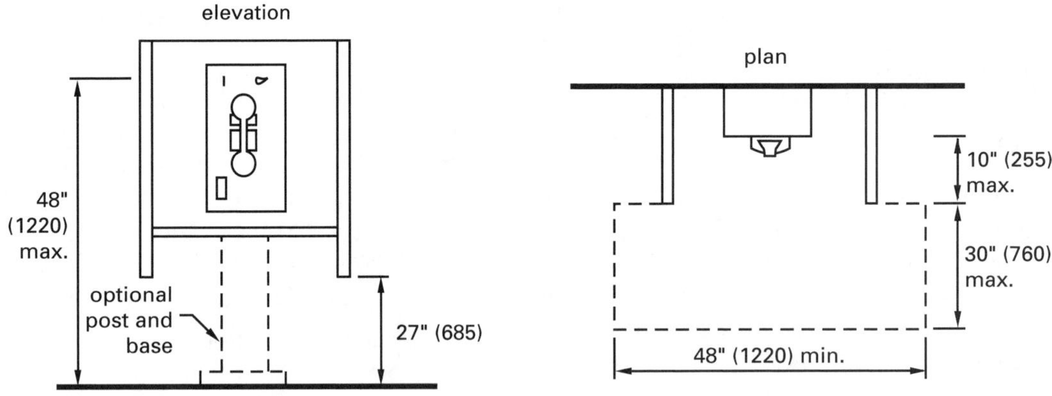

(b) side reach possible

Figure 56.16 Telephone Access

(a) TDD symbol

(b) access for hearing loss symbol

Figure 56.17 International TDD and Hearing Loss Symbols

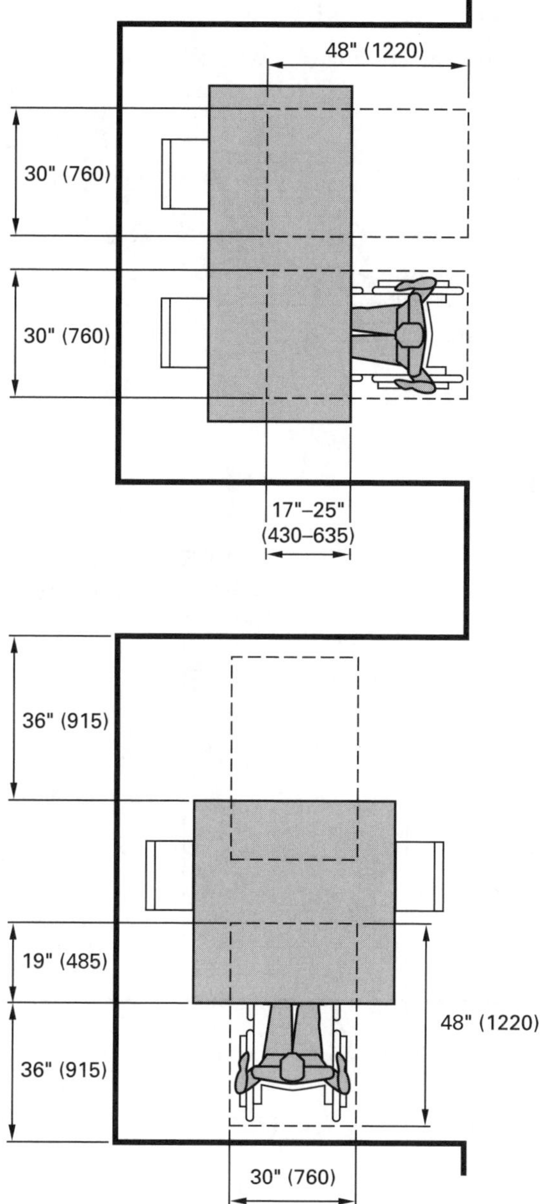

Figure 56.18 Minimum Clearances for Seating and Tables

Table 56.1

Minimum Number of Wheelchair Spaces for Assembly Areas

capacity of seating in assembly areas	number of required wheelchair locations
4 to 25	1
26 to 50	2
51 to 300	4
301 to 500	6
over 500	6, plus 1 additional space for each total capacity increase of 100

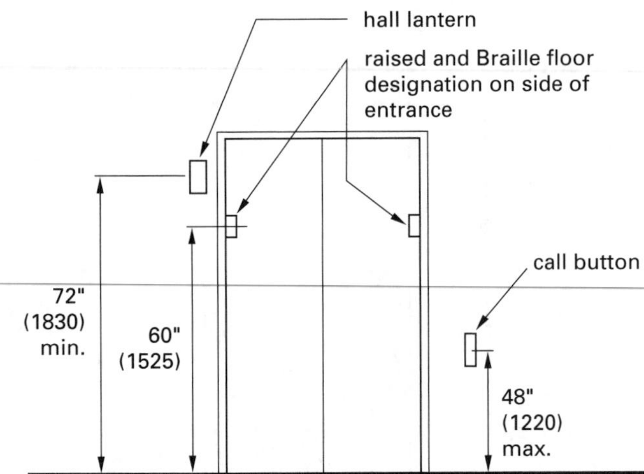

Figure 56.19 Elevator Entrances

INDEX

4-phenylcyclohexene (4-PC), 30-9

A
AAC (*see* Autoclaved aerated concrete)
AASHTO girder, 24-5
Abatement, 2-29
Aboveground drainage, 5-7
Absorption
  refrigeration, 28-3
  sound, 33-6
Acceleration, 23-3
Accelerator, 20-2, 36-6
Access
  control, 32-22
  easement, 2-19
  floor system, 17-2
  security, 5-18
Accessibility (*see also* Barrier-free design)
  in programming, 3-18
  site, 5-10
Accessibility/Ramp (vignette), 45-1
Accessible
  and Usable Buildings and Facilities, ICC/ANSI A117.1, 55-2, 55-4, 56-1
  route, 56-1, 56-9
Accessories, for concrete, 36-5, 36-11
Accessory
  building, 2-29
  lighting, 32-17
  use area, 55-11
Accidental torsion, 23-14
ACI (*see* American Concrete Institute)
  318, Building Code Requirements for Structural Concrete, 17-4, 17-5
Acid wash concrete finish, 36-10
Acoustical
  ceiling, 43-8
  ceiling tile, as a sustainable building material, 30-10
  design, rules of thumb, 33-6, 33-7
  perfume (*see* White sound)
  wall panel, 43-10
Acoustics, 24-8
  open office, 33-11
  planning concepts, 33-13
  room, 33-13
  site, 5-16
ACQ (*see* Ammoniacal copper quaternary)
Action
  arch, 21-4, 21-5, 24-2, 25-4, 25-5
  beam, 25-4, 25-5, 25-7
  dome, 25-4
  slab, 25-7
Active
  circulation, solar water heating, 31-16
  smoke control, 31-21
  solar collector, 5-7
  solar design, 29-17
Activity grouping, 3-17
Actuator, 28-15
ACZA (*see* Ammoniacal copper zinc arsenate)
ADA (*see* Americans with Disabilities Act)
Adaptive reuse, 2-20, 30-16
Add-alternate, 51-6
Addenda, 51-2, 51-4
Addition
  algebraic force, 12-7, 12-8
  graphic force, 12-7, 12-8
Additive color, 43-17
Adhesive, 30-8
  as a sustainable building material, 30-8
  for metal, 38-3
Adjacency
  diagram, 3-3, 3-4
  matrix, 3-3, 3-4
Administration, contract, 50-13
Admixture, 20-1, 20-2
  for dampproofing, 41-1
  types, 36-6
Ad valorem tax, 2-21
Advertisement for bids, 51-1, 51-3
Aerodynamic effect, 22-4
A-frame, 24-6
AFUE (*see* Annual fuel utilization efficiency)
Agency, 50-1, 53-3
Aggregate, 20-1, 20-2, 21-4
  coarse, 20-2
  concrete, 36-6
  fine, 20-2
  lightweight, 20-10
Agora, 2-1
AHJ (*see* Authority having jurisdiction)
AIA (*see also* American Institute of Architects)
  A101, Standard Form of Agreement Between Owner and Contractor, where the basis of payment is a stipulated sum, 50-9
  A201, General Conditions of the Contract, 28-4, 28-6, 50-6, 50-11, 52-1, 52-2, 52-4, 52-5
  A201Cma, General Conditions of the Contract for Construction, Construction Manager-Adviser Edition, 50-2
  A701, Instructions to Bidders, 51-3
  B101, Standard Form of Agreement Between Owner and Architect with Standard Form of Architect's Services, 28-5, 50-4, 51-1
  G706, Contractor's Affidavit of Payment of Debts and Claims, 52-6
  G707, Consent of Surety Company to Final Payment, 52-6
Air
  barrier, 29-7
  chamber, 31-9
  contaminants, 30-12
  -entraining agent, 20-2, 36-6
  infiltration, 29-7
  lock, 29-7
  movement, for human comfort, 27-3
  -supported structure, 25-6
  -to-air heat exchanger, 28-12
  quality, 2-16
  -water system, 28-6
AISC (*see* American Institute of Steel Construction)
  Steel Construction Manual, 12-6, 13-2, 13-9, 14-2, 16-8, 16-16, 16-17, 17-4, 19-4

Alarm
  barrier-free design, 56-10
  fire, 32-23
  system, 32-21
Albedo, 2-15, 2-17, 5-13
Algebraic force addition, 12-7, 12-8
Alignment, road, 2-14
Alkalinity in concrete, 36-8
Alkali-silica reaction (ASR) 36-9
All
  -air system, 28-4
  -glass doors, 42-5, 42-6
  -risk insurance, 53-6
  -water system, 28-6
Allowable
  axial compression stress, 19-11, 19-13
  bearing pressure, 15-7
  bending stress, 19-4
  bolt
    bearing, 16-8, 16-10
    shear, 16-8, 16-9
  building height, 55-14, 55-15
  deflection, 13-9, 18-8
  floor area, 55-14, 55-15
  joist span, 18-11, 18-12
  load on beams, 19-5, 19-9
  soil bearing capacity, 15-3, 15-5
  steel
    column load, 19-14
    stress, 17-3, 19-3, 19-4
  stress, 17-3
    axial compression, 19-11, 19-13
    bending, 18-5
    compression, 18-10
    design (ASD), 11-5, 17-1, 17-2, 19-1, 22-8, 23-25
    shear, 18-7, 18-8
    steel, 17-3, 19-3, 19-4
    wood, 17-3
  wood
    bending stress, 18-5
    compression stress, 18-10
    design values, 18-2, 18-3
    shear stress, 18-7
    stress, 17-3
Allowance, 50-13, 51-6
Alternate, 51-5
Alternating current, 32-2, 32-4
Alternative energy
  effects on building planning, 5-6
  source
    geothermal, 29-18
    photovoltaics, 29-18
    solar design, 29-13
    wind, 29-18
Altitude angle, 29-13, 29-14
Aluminum, 38-6
  conductor, 32-3
  door and frame, 42-4
Amenities, 2-29
American
  Association of State Highway and Transportation Official (*see also* AASHTO), 24-5
  Concrete Institute (*see also* ACI), 11-5, 15-8, 17-2, 17-4, 20-1, 20-11, 21-7
  Conference of Governmental Industrial Hygienists (ACGIH), 30-15
  Forest and Paper Association (AF&PA), 16-5, 16-6, 18-3, 18-4
  Institute of Architects (*see also* AIA), 50-4
  Institute of Steel Construction (*see also* AISC; Steel Construction Manual), 12-6, 13-2, 13-9, 14-2, 16-8, 16-9, 16-10, 16-12, 16-13, 16-16, 16-17, 17-4, 19-3, 19-6, 19-7, 19-8, 19-12, 19-13, 19-14
  Lumber Standards Committee, 18-1, 39-2
  National Standards Institute (ANSI), 55-4
  standard
    beam, 19-2, 19-3
    channel, 19-2, 19-3
    channel section, 38-8
    I-beams, 38-8
Americans with Disabilities Act (ADA), 55-2, 56-1
Ammoniacal copper
  quaternary (ACQ), 39-12
  zinc arsenate (ACZA), 39-12
Amortization, 2-29
Ampacity, 32-3
Ampere, 32-1
Amplification, 33-1
Amplitude, 32-2
Analemma, 29-19
Analysis
  dynamic, 23-2
    structural, 11-7
  earthquake, 23-16
    method, 23-1
    simplified, 23-2
  site, 2-13, 2-16
  static method, 11-7
  wind, 22-4
Anchorage, 17-1
Anchor tenant, 2-29
Angle
  bracket connection, 22-14
  double, 14-2
  of load, 16-2
  of repose, 15-6, 15-11
  steel, 19-2, 19-3
Annealing of metal, 38-3
Annual fuel utilization efficiency (AFUE), 28-15
Anodizing, 38-7
ANSI (*see* American National Standards Institute)
Anticlastic
  shape, 25-6
  shell, 25-5
Aperture, effective, 29-19
Apex, 10-8
Appearance grade, 18-2
Application for payment, 52-5
Applied concrete finish, 36-10
Appraisal, 2-29
Approved equal language, 49-2
Approximate period, 23-20, 23-21
Aquifer, 2-29, 31-1
Arbitration, 50-8, 52-5
Arch, 10-7, 21-5, 24-6
  action, 21-4, 21-5, 24-2, 25-4, 25-5, 37-7
  circular, 24-6
  concrete, 24-1, 24-6
  Gothic, 24-6
  lamella, 25-2
  parabolic, 24-6
  radial, 24-6
  steel, 24-1, 24-6
  three
    -centered, 24-6
    -hinged, 10-8
  true, 24-6
  types, 24-6
  wood, 24-1, 24-6
Architect
  as owner's agent, 50-1, 53-3
  duties, 53-4
  insurance, 53-5
  responsibilities, 50-4, 50-13, 51-1, 52-5, 53-4
  scope of services, 50-4
Architectural
  components, 23-24
  finishes for concrete, 36-10
  grade, 18-11
  mesh, 38-13
  services, during pre-design, 2-28
  woodwork, 40-1, 40-4
    cabinetwork, 40-5
    code requirements, 40-13
    finishes, 40-14
    flush paneling, 40-7
    laminates, 40-12
    stile and rail paneling, 40-9
    trim, 40-13
    veneer, 40-4
  Woodwork Institute, 40-4
Architectural Woodwork Quality Standards, 40-4
Area, 12-5, 13-10, 18-1, 18-2
  hurricane-prone, 22-4, 22-7
  metropolitan, 22-2
  net, 14-2, 16-2, 16-11
    shear, 16-11
    tension, 16-11
  of refuge, 55-30
  or room protection devices, 32-22
  projected method, 22-5, 22-7
  suburban, 22-2, 22-4
  tributary, 11-5
  urban, 22-4
Area method (budgeting), 3-11
Arterial street, 2-13
Articulation
  class (AC), 33-11

index (AI), 33-1, 33-11
Asbestos, 30-16
ban in construction, 30-17
ASCE 7, Minimum Design Loads for Buildings and Other Structures, 22-2, 22-3, 22-5, 22-6, 22-7, 23-20, 23-21
ASHRAE Standard
62-2001, Ventilation for Acceptable Indoor Air Quality, 30-15
62.2-2003, Ventilation and Acceptable Indoor Air Quality in Low-Rise Residential Buildings, 30-15
90.1, Energy Standard for Buildings Except Low-Rise Residential Buildings, 30-22
Aspdin, Joseph, 36-1
Asphaltic concrete, 35-7
ASR (*see* Alkali-silica reaction)
Assemblies, construction, fire resistance, 55-6
Assembly, 24-8, 25-9
method (budgeting), 3-11
Assessed
valuation, 2-20
value, 2-29
Assessment, special district, 2-22
ASTM International, 16-8, 19-2, 55-4
D2859, Standard Test Method for Flammability of Finished Textile Floor Covering Materials, 43-16
D5116, Standard Guide for Small-Scale Environmental Chamber Determinations of Organic Emissions from Indoor Materials/Products, 30-15
D6670, Standard Practice for Full-Scale Chamber Determination of Volatile Organic Emissions from Indoor Materials/Products, 30-15
E84, Standard Test Method for Surface Burning Characteristics of Building Materials, 55-5, 55-6, 55-8
E119, Standard Methods of Fire Tests of Building Construction and Materials, 55-5
E1333, Standard Test Method for Determining Formaldehyde Concentrations in Air and Emission Rates from Wood Products Using a Large Chamber, 30-15
E1991, Standard Guide for Environmental Life Cycle Assessment of Building Materials/Products, 30-23
E2114, Standard Terminology for Sustainability Relative to the Performance of Buildings, 30-23
E2129, Standard Practice for Data Collection for Sustainability Assessment of Building Products, 30-23
Astragal, 42-11
Atmospheric effect, 22-4
Attenuation, 33-1
Audio detector, 32-22
Auger boring, 35-3
Authority having jurisdiction (AHJ), 55-2
Autoclaved aerated concrete (AAC), 30-5, 36-7
Automatic
closing, 55-30
closing door, 42-14
door bottom, 42-11
sprinkler system, 55-14
Automobile
circulation, 5-8
insurance, 53-6
Award of bid, 51-3
Axial organization, 3-4
Azimuth, 5-3
angle, 29-13, 29-14

B

Backflow preventer, 31-18
Background noise, 33-5
Backwater valve, 31-18
Bagasse, 30-6
Balance
match, 40-8, 40-9
-point temperature, 29-19
Ballast, 32-15
roof, 41-12
Balloon framing, 21-5, 39-5
Ball penetration test, 36-8
Bamboo flooring, 30-4, 43-12
Bar
chart, 3-14
deformed, 20-3
epoxy-coated bar, 20-10
steel, 19-3
Barrel vault, 25-2, 25-4
Barrier, sound, 5-16
Barrier-free design
accessible route, 56-1, 56-9
alarm, 56-10
bathtub, 56-7
carpet, 56-9
detectable warning, 56-9
doors and hardware, 42-15
doorway, 56-3, 56-4
drinking fountain, 56-6, 56-7
floor surface, 56-9
handrail, 56-9
hardware, 56-3
lavatory and sink, 56-5
maneuvering clearance, 56-2, 56-3, 56-4
mirror, 56-6
opening force, 56-3
parking, 5-12
plumbing fixtures, 56-3
protruding object, 56-9, 56-10
ramp, 56-9, 56-9
seating, 56-11, 56-13
shower, 56-7, 56-8
signage, 56-10
stair, 56-9
telephone, 56-11
toilet room, 56-3
toilet stall, 56-3, 56-5
urinal, 56-5
wheelchair clearance, 56-2, 56-3, 56-4
Base bid specification, 49-2
Base line, 5-13
Base shear, 23-17, 23-22
distribution, 23-22
Basic
flexure formula, 18-5, 19-4
wind speed, 22-2, 22-3
Batch system, 31-17
Batt insulation, 41-5
Battery, 32-9
Beam, 13-1, 13-2, 13-3, 13-9
action, 25-4, 25-5, 25-7
allowable load on, 19-5, 19-9
American standard, 19-2, 19-3
-and-girder
concrete system, 10-4
steel system, 10-2, 10-3
and stringer, 18-2
bond, 21-3
cantilever, 13-3, 13-9
concrete, 20-5, 20-6, 20-11
grade, 15-5
moment capacity, 20-7
continuous, 13-3, 20-11, 20-12
curved, 24-5
doubly reinforced, 20-10
edge, 20-12, 20-13
effective depth, 20-6
fixed-end, 13-3, 13-9
framed connection, 16-12, 16-13, 16-14
glued-laminated, 18-11, 24-1, 24-4
grade, 15-7
inverted tee, 10-5
L-shaped, 10-5
notched, 18-9
overhanging, 13-3
plywood box, 10-2
rectangular, 10-5
simply supported, 13-3, 13-9
steel, 19-3
design, 19-4
-to-beam connection, 16-18
-to-column connection, 22-14
-to-girder connection, 16-12
under-reinforced, 20-6
wood, 18-5
Bearing
allowable
bolt, 16-8, 16-10
pressure, 15-7
soil capacity, 15-3, 15-5
-type connection, 16-7, 16-9, 16-10, 16-13
wall system, 23-6, 23-7
wood, 18-10
Bedroom community, 2-29
Behavior setting, 3-8
Belled pier, 15-7
Beltway, 2-6

Bending
  allowable
    stress, 19-4
    wood stress, 18-5
  footing, 15-7, 15-8
  of metal, 38-2
  reinforcement, 17-5
  stiffness, 12-6
  stress, 12-2, 13-2
Benefit assessment (*see* Business improvement districts)
Bent, 22-9
Bentonite, 15-5, 15-7
  panel, 41-2
Bessemer, Henry, 38-1
BIBS (*see* Blow-in-blanket system)
Bid
  award, 51-3
  forms, 51-4
  opening, 51-2
  security, 51-5
BID (*see* Business improvement district)
Bidder's representation, under AIA A701, 51-3
Bidding
  advertisement, 51-1, 51-3
  documents, 51-2, 51-3
  phase, 3-13
  procedures, under AIA A701, 51-4
  requirements, 49-1
BIM (*see* Building Information Modeling)
Biological
  contaminant, 30-12
  exposure index, 30-15
Biometric devices, 32-23
Bio-plastics, 30-7
Bioswale, 2-17
Bituminous coating, dampproofing, 41-1
Black
  -body, 32-17
  water, 30-1, 31-17
  water recycling, 30-3
Blanket loan, 2-22
Blighted area, 2-29
Blocked diaphragm, 22-12, 22-13
Block flooring, 43-12
Blocking, 39-7
Blow-in-blanket system (BIBS), 41-6
Blueprint matching, 40-8, 40-10
Board, 39-3
  insulation, 41-5
  oriented strand, 10-1
  particle, 10-1
BOCA National Building Code, 55-1, 55-3
Body temperature, 27-2
Bogardus, James, 38-2
Boiler, 28-2, 28-3
  fuel economizer, 28-11
  recuperative gas, 28-11
Boilerplate, 2-29
Bolt, 38-3, 39-10
  allowable
    bearing, 16-8, 16-10
    shear, 16-8, 16-9
  high-strength, 16-8
  lag, 16-4
  spacing, 16-12
  steel, 16-7, 16-9, 16-10
  type N, 16-8, 16-9
  type X, 16-8, 16-9
  unfinished, 16-8
  wood, 16-4
    design value, 16-4, 16-5, 16-6
Bond, 2-22
  beam, 21-3, 37-7
  labor and material payment, 51-5
  performance, 51-5
  types, 2-21
  under General Conditions of the Contract, 50-15
Bonding pattern, 37-3, 37-4
Bookmatching, 40-7, 40-9
Borehole test, 35-1
Boring, 15-1
  core, 15-1
  log, 2-12, 15-1, 15-2, 35-1, 35-2
Bottom chord, 14-1, 25-3
  grid, 25-2
Boulton, Matthew, 38-1
Boundary survey, 5-13, 5-15
Bow, 39-2
Bowstring truss, 14-1
Box
  girder, 24-5
  nail, 16-3
Brace
  chevron, 22-11
  K, 22-11
  knee, 22-11
  X, 22-11
Braced
  concentric frame, 23-7, 23-10
  eccentric frame, 23-7, 23-10
  frame, 23-6, 23-7, 23-10
Bracing of excavations, 35-5, 35-6
Brake forming, 38-2
Branch circuit, 32-6
Brasilia, 2-6
Brass, 38-7, 38-13
Brazing, 38-3
Breadbox heater, 31-17
Breast board, 35-5
Brewster color system, 43-17
BRI (*see* Building-related illness)
Brick, 37-2
  cleaning, 37-8
  construction, 37-5
  coursing, 37-3
  joint, 37-4, 37-5
  restoration, 37-8
  types, 37-2
Bridge loan, 2-22
Bridging, 14-1, 18-9, 39-7
Brightness, 32-10
  ratio, 32-11
British thermal unit, 27-1, 41-2
Brittle material, 23-6
Broadacre City, 2-4
Bronze, 38-7, 38-13
Broom finish, 36-11
Btu (*see* British thermal unit)
Bubble diagram (*see* Adjacency diagram)
Buckle, 13-9
Buckling, 25-2
Budget
  in programming, 3-9
  methods of developing, 3-11
Buffer zone, 2-29
Building
  area, programming, 3-2
  automation system, 28-14
  brick, 37-2
  Code Requirements for Structural Concrete (ACI 318), 17-4, 17-5
  commissioning, 28-14, 30-13
  configuration, 23-12
  corner, 22-8
  cost, 3-10
  deflection, 21-9
  department requirements for drawings, 48-8
  disposal, 30-16
  drain, 31-18
  drift, 11-6
  economy, 24-7, 25-9
  envelope, 10-6, 21-7, 27-6, 29-7
    security, 5-18
  frame system, 23-7, 23-10
  function, 24-6, 25-9
  height, allowable, 55-14, 55-15
  information modeling (BIM), 48-9
  insulation, 41-2
  Layout (vignette), 8-1
  location on property, 55-16
  Materials Directory, UL, 55-4, 55-6
  materials
    evaluating for sustainability, 30-4
    local, 30-4
    recycled, 30-16
    salvaged, 30-5
    sustainable, 30-3, 39-9, 43-12
  material weight, 11-2
  movement, 21-9, 23-14
    in detailing, 48-4
  orientation, 5-3, 29-1
  parts, 23-24
  portion factor, 22-4, 22-6
  product certification, for sustainability, 30-20
  rating systems, 30-18
  -related illness (BRI), 30-13
  Research Establishment (BRE) Environmental Assessment Method, 30-19
  Section (vignette), 54-1
  section, 48-7
  sewer, 5-7, 31-18
  shading, 5-3, 5-6, 29-4, 29-12
  shape, 22-10, 24-8, 29-2
  stiffness, 23-6
  style, 10-13

survey, documenting, 2-24
weight, 23-17, 23-21
Building code
adjuncts, 55-3
administrative requirements, 55-10
enforcement, 55-2
history, 55-1
in programming, 3-16
legal basis, 55-2
model, 55-3
requirements (*see also* Regulations)
accessory use area, 55-11
all-glass doors, 42-6
allowable building height, 55-14, 55-15
allowable floor area, 55-14, 55-15
as part of detailing, 48-3
common path of egress travel, 55-19
construction type, 55-12
corridor, 55-21
corridor continuity, 55-22
dead end, 55-22
definitions, 55-30
door, 42-13, 55-23
drawing information, 48-8
egress system, 55-17
electrical system, 55-28
exit, 55-16, 55-17
exiting through intervening spaces, 55-21
fire detection and suppression, 55-27
fire-resistive rating, doors, 55-23
fire-resistive rating requirements, 55-6, 55-7
glazing, 42-20, 55-26
guard, 55-26
hardware, 42-14
high-rise building, 55-26
incidental accessory occupancy, 55-11, 55-13
location on property, 55-16
maximum travel distance, 55-19
means of egress, 55-16
mechanical systems, 55-27
mixed occupancy, 55-11, 55-18
number of exits required, 55-19
occupancy, 55-10
occupancy groups, 55-11
occupancy separation, 55-11
occupant load, 55-17
plumbing systems, 55-28
separation of exits, 55-20
sound ratings, 55-29
stairways, 55-24
wood finish, 40-13
wood trim, 40-13
Built-up
roofing, 41-11
steel section, 19-12, 24-2
Bulk plane restriction, 2-18
Bull float finish, 36-10
Burnham, Daniel, 2-4
Busduct, 32-3
Bush hammering, 36-10
Business
improvement district (BID), 2-22
organization, types, 53-1
Busway, 32-3
Butt joint, 16-15, 16-16
BX cable, 32-3

C

Cabinetwork, 40-5
types, 40-6
Cable
structure, 25-7, 25-8
suspended, 10-10, 25-8
Caisson foundation, 15-6, 15-7
Calcium chloride test, 36-9
California
Safe Drinking Water and Toxic Enforcement Act of 1986 (Proposition 65), 30-15
South Coast Air Quality Management District, 30-9, 30-12
Calthorpe, Peter, 2-4
Camber, 24-4
Canada Green Building Council, 30-20
Canadian
National Building Code, 55-2
National Fire Code, 55-2
Candlepower, 32-10
distribution curve, 32-16
Cantilever, 25-3
beam, 13-3, 13-9
footing, 15-6
wall, 15-11
Capital expenditure, 2-29
Carbon fiber concrete, 36-7
Card reader, 32-22, 42-12
Carpet, 30-9, 43-15
and Rug Institute (CRI), 30-9
as a sustainable building material, 30-9
barrier-free design, 56-7
wool, 30-4
Casehardening of metal, 38-3
Cash flow, 2-29
Cast
iron, 38-4
Iron Age, 38-2
-iron pipe, 31-18
stone, 37-12
Cast-in-place
concrete, 10-3
wall, 21-7
Catalyzed lacquer, 40-14
Catch basin, 2-17, 5-7, 35-7
Catchment area, 2-8
Catenary curve, 10-10, 25-8
Caulking, 41-13
Causes of action, under AIA Document B101, 50-7
Cavity wall, 21-3, 37-5, 37-6
construction, 10-5
CC&Rs, 2-30
CCA (*see* Chromated copper arsenate)
C corporation, 53-2
Ceiling
acoustical, 43-8
acoustical tile, 30-10
seismic restraint, 43-10
Cellular metal floor, 32-4
Cellulose insulation, 30-8, 41-3, 41-6
Cement, 20-1, 20-2 (*see also* Portland cement)
high-early, 20-4
portland, 20-2, 21-4
types, 36-5
Cementitious coating, 41-1
Center match, 40-8, 40-9
Center
of gravity, 12-5
of mass, 23-14, 23-25
of rigidity, 23-14
Central
organization, 3-4
Park, New York, 2-4
Centroid, 12-5
Ceramic
tile, 30-10, 43-5
tile, as a sustainable building material, 30-10
veneer (*see* Terra cotta)
Certificate of occupancy, 2-28
Certified
rehabilitation, 2-26
wood products, 30-7
CFC (*see* Chlorofluorocarbon)
Chain of custody, 30-7
Chair (concrete formwork), 36-5
Change
in service, 50-7
in the work, 52-2
in the work, under General Conditions of the Contract, 50-14
order, 50-14, 52-2
Channel
American standard, 19-2, 19-3
slab, 24-5
Character, in programming, 3-17
Chart, sun peg, 29-14
Check
lumber defect, 39-2
property description, 5-13
valve, 31-8
Chemical
finishes of metal, 38-3
-resistant laminate, 40-12
Chevron brace, 22-11
Chicago
construction, 38-2
fire of 1871, 55-2
Chiller
dual-condenser, 28-11
gas-fired absorption-based, 28-11
Chimney, 55-28
Chlorofluorocarbon (CFC), 28-3, 29-7, 30-8, 41-5
Chlorosulfonated polyethylene (CSPE) roofing, 41-12

Chord, 22-9, 22-12
  bottom, 14-1, 25-2, 25-3
  force, 22-12
  parallel, 24-4
  pitched, 24-4
  steel joist configurations, 24-4
  top, 14-1, 25-2, 25-3
Chromated copper arsenate (CCA), 30-7
  phaseout, 39-12
Chronic inhalation reference exposure level (REL), 30-12
Circular
  arch, 24-6
  frame dome, 25-3
  stairway, 44-8, 55-24
Circulating system, hot water, 31-15
Circulation
  automobile, 5-8
  in space planning, 3-6
  patterns, in space planning, 3-6, 3-7
  pedestrian, 5-9
  service, 5-10
Cistern, 30-2
Cité industrielle, 2-3, 36-1
City
  Beautiful movement, 2-4
  development pattern, 2-4
  forms, historic, 2-1,
  planning, 2-1
    Renaissance, 2-2
    United States, 2-3
Cladding, 22-8
Claim, 50-16, 52-4
  for additional time, 52-4
  for concealed or unknown conditions, 52-5
  third-party, 28-4
Classified label, 55-4 (*see also* Listed label)
Clay, 2-12, 15-1, 15-7
  masonry compressive strength, 21-2
  roof tile, 41-10
  tile, 37-10
Clean Air Act (CAA)
  of 1970, 30-10, 30-17
  of 1990, 41-5
Cleaning
  brick, 37-8
  final, 52-6
Clearance, in detailing, 48-3
Climate
  design for, 27-9
  influences on site planning, 2-14, 5-3, 5-4
Climatic
  region, 5-4, 5-5, 27-9, 29-1, 29-3
  zone, 28-8
Clo, 27-4
Closed
  -loop system, 29-18
    active, 31-16
    solar water heating, 31-15
  specification, 49-2
Closer, 42-9
Cluster housing, 2-30
Clustered organization, 3-6
CMU (*see* Concrete masonry unit)
Coarse aggregate, 20-2
Coatings for metal, 38-3
Codes (*see also* Building code requirements, individual topics)
  in programming, 3-16
Coefficient
  of absorption, 33-6
  of earth pressure, 15-12
  of expansion, 11-7
  of heat transmission, 27-1
  of linear expansion, 12-3
  of performance (COP), 28-15
  of thermal expansion, 10-7
  of metals, 38-4
  of transmission, 32-9
  of utilization (CU), 32-18
  response modification, 23-7, 23-8, 23-17, 23-20
  seismic
    response, 23-17
    site, 23-19
  shading, 29-19
  site, 23-18
Cohesive soil, 15-12
Cold
  -drawn steel wire, 20-3
  -lain asphalt, 35-7
Collinear force, 12-1, 12-2, 12-7
Collector
  solar, 29-17
  street, 2-13
Color, 43-17
  additive, 43-17
  Brewster system, 43-17
  complementary, 43-19
  in lighting, 32-11
  Munsell system, 43-18
  Prang system, 43-17
  primary, 43-17
  rendering index (CRI), 32-18
  secondary, 43-17
  subtractive, 43-17
  system, 43-17
  temperature, 32-15, 32-17
  tertiary, 43-17
  wheel, 43-17
Colorthrough laminate, 40-12
Columbia, Maryland, new town, 2-4
Columbian Exposition, 2-4
Column, 13-9
  allowable steel load, 19-14
  capital, 10-4
  concrete, 20-13
  discontinuous, 23-16
  end condition, 13-10, 13-11, 18-10, 19-11
  independent footing, 15-6, 15-9
  intermediate, 13-10
  precast, 10-5
  short, 13-10
  slender, 13-10
  spiral, 20-14
  steel, 19-11 19-12, 19-14
  tied, 20-13
  -to-beam connection, 16-12
  -to-column connection, 16-18
  wood, 18-11
Combined
  footing, 15-6
  load, 13-9
  specular and diffuse reflection, 32-9
  stress, 12-2
Combustible, 55-30
  construction, 17-5
Comfort chart, 27-4
Commissioning, building, 28-14
Common
  area, 2-29
  brick, 37-2
  path of egress travel, 55-19, 55-30
  wire
    nail, 16-3
    spike, 16-3
Communication
  in programming, 3-17
  system, 32-21
Community planning, 2-1
Compact
  fluorescent (CF) lamps, 32-15
  section, 19-4
  stress, 17-4, 19-4
Compaction of soil, 35-5
Compartmentation, 31-20
Compensation methods
  for architect, 50-9
  for contractor, 50-10
Component factor, 22-8
Component, 23-24
Composite
  construction, 10-6
  open-web joist, 10-6, 10-7
  section, 16-19
  steel deck, 10-6, 10-7
  wood veneer, 30-6
Complementary color, 43-19
Compressed straw, 30-8
Compression, 14-1, 14-3
  allowable
    axial stress, 19-11, 19-13
    wood stress, 18-10
  flange, 19-4
  ring, 25-8
  steel, 20-10
  stress, 12-2, 13-1
  /tension diagonal, 23-10, 23-10
Compressive
  concrete
    member, 20-13
    strength, 20-2, 20-5
  masonry strength, 21-2
    clay, 21-2
    concrete, 21-2
  refrigeration, 28-3
  specified
    concrete strength, 17-4
    strength, 21-1

Compressor, 28-3
Concealed conditions, 52-5
Concentrated load, 11-3, 11-4, 13-3, 13-5, 13-6, 13-9
Concentric braced frame, 23-7, 23-10
Concept
design, 3-17
in programming, 3-16
programmatic, 3-16
Concrete, 20-1
accessories, 36-11
admixture, 36-6
aggregate, 36-6
American Institute (ACI), 11-5, 15-8, 17-2, 17-4, 20-1, 20-11, 21-7
arch, 24-1, 24-6
as a sustainable building material, 30-5
autoclaved aerated, 30-5
basic materials, 36-5
beam, 20-5, 20-6, 20-11
-and-girder system, 10-4
moment capacity, 20-7
block, 37-8
detailing, 37-9
Building Code Requirements for Structural (ACI 318), 17-4, 17-5
carbon fiber, 36-7
cast-in-place, 10-3
column, 20-13
compaction, 20-4
compressive
member, 20-13
strength, 20-2, 20-5
conduit embedded, 17-5
connection, 16-17
construction load, 17-5
crushing, 20-6
curing, 20-4, 36-8
deflection, 20-11
design, 20-5
strength of, 20-2, 20-4
finishing, 36-10
flange, 20-12
flat
plate system, 10-4
slab system, 10-4
flexural design, 20-7
form, 36-1, 36-2
insulated, 41-7
foundation wall, 15-8
grade beam, 15-5
history, 36-1
insert, 36-12
joint, 36-11
joist system, 10-4
lightweight structural, 20-2
lintel, 21-5
masonry
compressive strength, 21-2
unit (CMU), 37-8
minimum 17-5
moisture migration through, 36-3
new products, 36-7
one-way system, 10-3
paving, 35-7
placement, 20-4
placing, 36-10
post-tensioned, 10-5, 20-14, 24-5
precast, 10-3, 20-14, 36-12
connection, 16-18
wall, 21-7, 21-8
prestressed, 20-14, 24-5, 36-13
girder, 24-1
pretensioned, 20-14
reinforced construction, 10-6
reinforcement, 36-4
required shear strength, 20-9
sealer, 36-12
shear, 20-9
slab, 20-13, 36-3
and steel beam, 10-6, 10-7, 16-19
finishes, 36-10
specified compressive strength, 17-4
strength, 36-6
structural system, 10-3
support face, 20-9
testing, 17-4, 20-5, 36-8
topping, 24-5
two-way, 10-3
waffle slab system, 10-4
wall, 21-7
strength, 21-7
water-cement ratio, 36-5
web, 20-12
Concurrent force, 12-1, 12-2, 12-7, 12-8
Condenser, 28-3
Conditional use permit, 2-19, 2-30
Condominium, 2-30
Conductance, 27-1, 27-6, 41-2
Conduction, 27-2, 27-6, 41-2
Conductivity, 2-15, 27-1, 27-6, 41-2
Conductor, 32-2
electric, 32-3
in conduit, 32-3
Conduit, 48-2
electrical, 32-3
Cone (in the retina), 32-9
Connection, 22-14, 24-8
angle bracket, 22-14
beam
-to-beam, 16-18
-to-column, 22-14
-to-girder, 16-12
bearing-type, 16-7, 16-9, 16-10, 16-13
column
-to-beam, 16-12
-to-column, 16-18
concrete, 16-17
coped, 16-12
double-angle, 16-13, 16-14
footing to wall, 16-18
framed beam, 16-12, 16-13, 16-14
keyed, 16-18
main member, 16-4, 16-5, 16-6
moment, 16-12
-resisting, 22-11, 22-15, 24-2
precast concrete, 16-18
rebar, 16-18
rigid, 24-9
semirigid, 22-15
side member, 16-4, 16-5, 16-6
slip-critical, 16-8, 16-9, 16-10, 16-14
steel, 16-7
wall
panel, 21-7
-to-slab, 16-18
welded, 16-15, 22-14
wood, 16-1
Connector, 16-1
groups, 16-1
lateral load, 16-3
shear, 16-19
plate, 16-7
spacing, 16-3
split ring, 16-7
timber, 16-7
Consent of Surety Company to Final Payment, AIA G707, 52-6
Conservation easement, 2-19
Consideration of bids, under AIA A701, 51-4
Constant-volume system, 28-5
Construction
American Institute of Steel Construction (AISC), 12-6, 13-2, 13-9, 14-2, 16-8, 16-9, 16-10, 16-12, 16-13, 16-16, 16-17, 17-4, 19-3, 19-6, 19-7, 19-8, 19-12, 19-13, 19-14
by owner, under General Conditions of the Contract, 50-14
cavity wall, 10-5
change directive, 50-14, 52-2
combustible, 17-5
composite, 10-6
concrete load, 17-5
details, 48-1
double wythe, 10-5, 10-6
drawing, 48-1, 48-6
phase, 3-13
building department information, 48-8
CAD layering, 48-6
content, 48-6
coordination, 48-6
sequential organization, 48-6
sheet organization, 48-6
ease, 24-8
glued-laminated, 10-1
heavy timber, 17-5
joint, 21-10, 36-11
brick, 37-4
lift-slab, 10-3
limitations, 10-12
loan, 2-22
manager, 50-2
materials, fire resistance, 55-6
National Design Specification for Wood (NDS), 16-3, 17-3, 18-9
noncombustible, 17-5
observation, 24-10, 52-3
platform, 21-6
procurement services, under AIA Document B101, 50-5

reinforced concrete, 10-6
requirement, 17-4
schedule, 3-13, 52-2
single wythe, 10-5, 10-6
Specifications Canada, 49-3
Specifications Institute, 49-3
time, 24-7
tolerances, 48-3
trade sequence, as part of detailing, 48-3
type, 55-6, 55-12
wall, 21-1
Consultant coordination, 2-28, 48-9
Consumer Product Safety Commission (CPSC), 55-2
Contingency costs, 3-11
Continuity, 20-12
Continuous beam, 13-3, 20-11, 20-12
Contour
interval, 2-10
lines, 2-10, 5-1, 5-2, 5-3
representation on plans, 2-11, 5-9
Contract
administration services, under AIA Document B101, 50-6
administration, under General Conditions of the Contract, 50-13
documents, 50-1, 50-9, 50-11
effect on bids, 51-5
forms, 49-1
sum, definition, 50-10
time, under General Conditions of the Contract, 50-14
types, 50-1
Contractor's
Affidavit of Payment of Debts and Claims, AIA G706, 52-6
insurance, 53-6
responsibilities, 52-4, 52-6
responsibilities, under General Conditions of the Contract, 50-12
Contrast, 32-11
simultaneous, 43-19
Control joint,
brick, 37-4
concrete, 36-11
in sidewalks, 35-7
Controller, 28-15
Convection, 27-2, 27-6, 41-2
Convenience outlet (*see* Duplex receptacle)
Convergent photogrammetry, 2-24
Conversion varnish, 40-14
Convertibility, programming concept, 3-8
Conveyance, 2-30
Cool climate, design response, 27-9, 29-3
Cooling
by absorption, 28-3
by refrigeration, 28-3
displacement ventilation, 28-11
evaporative, 28-4
extract-air window, 28-14
ground-coupled heat exchanger, 28-14
ground-source heat pump, 29-18
loads, 29-2
nocturnal, 29-19
radiative, 29-19
solar-powered absorption, 28-11, 29-18
thermal energy storage, 28-12
water-loop heat pump, 28-12
Co-op, 2-30
Cooperative, 2-30
Coordination
between architect and consulting engineers, 48-7, 48-9
consultant, 2-28
drawings with specifications, 48-9
of construction drawings, 48-6
project management, 53-6
regulatory agencies during pre-design, 2-28
security system design, 48-2
with consultants' work, 48-9
Coordinator, 42-11
COP (*see* Coefficient of performance)
Coped
connection, 16-12
flange, 17-4
Coplanar force, 12-2, 12-8
Copper, 38-7
azole, 39-12
conductor, 32-3
piping, 31-5
roof, 41-10
Coproduct, 30-23
Copyright, 53-5
Core
boring, 15-1
cylinder test, 20-4, 20-5, 36-8
Cored slab, 36-12
Cork flooring, 43-14
as a sustainable building material, 30-9
Corporate space standards, 3-1
Corporation, 53-2
Correction of bidding documents, under AIA A701, 51-4
Corridor, 55-21, 55-30
construction, 55-21
continuity, 55-22
door encroachment, 55-21
openings, 55-22
width, 55-21
Cost
approach, land value, 2-20
as part of detailing, 48-4
control, 3-18, 51-5
index, 3-13
influences, 3-10
information sources, 3-12
of HVAC systems, 28-8
of project, 50-2
of the work, definition, 50-7
of the work, under AIA Document B101, 50-5
-plus-fee method, 50-3, 50-9, 50-11
types, 3-10
Costa, Lucio, 2-6
Cost factors, 24-7, 25-9
Cotton batt insulation, 30-4
Counterfort wall, 15-11
Countertop, 40-6
Covenants
conditions, and restrictions (CC&Rs), 2-30
restrictive, 2-20
Cover plate, 19-15, 24-2
CPM (*see* Critical path method)
CPSC (*see* Consumer Product Safety Commission)
CPTED (*see* Crime prevention through environmental design)
Creep, 10-7
Creosote, 39-12
CRI (*see* Carpet and Rug Institute or Color rendering index)
Cribbing, 35-5
Cricket, 41-10
Crime prevention through environmental design (CPTED), 2-8
Cripple stud, 21-6
Critical
moment section, 15-8
net section, 16-2
path method (CPM), 3-14
shear section, 15-8, 20-9
Crook, 39-2
Crowding, 2-7
Crown of road, 5-9
Crystalline cell, 29-19
CSPE (*see* Chlorosulfonated polyethylene)
CU (*see* Coefficient of utilization)
Cul-de-sac, 2-30
Cultural influence, 10-14
Cup (lumber defect), 39-2
Curing concrete, 36-8
Curtain
board, 31-21
wall, 21-1, 21-9, 42-20
system, 10-6
Curved beam, 24-5
Cylinder
mold, 20-5
test, 20-4, 20-5, 36-8

D

Dampproofing, 41-1
Darby, Abraham, 38-1
Daylight factor, 29-10, 29-19
Daylighting, 29-2, 29-10, 29-13
effective aperture, 29-11, 29-19
glazing types, 29-12
light shelf, 29-11, 29-19
visible light transmittance, 29-11, 29-20
window-to-wall ratio, 29-11, 29-20
dBA, 33-1
DCLF (*see* Design cooling load factor)
Dead
end, 55-22
load, 10-11, 11-1, 17-2, 20-5, 21-7, 21-8, 23-21
Deadband, 28-15

Decibel, 33-1, 33-2
  addition, 33-3
Decking
  metal, 38-10
  wood, 10-1, 18-13, 39-10
    laminated, 18-13
    solid, 18-13
Declination
  angle, 29-13
  magnetic, 29-15
Decoration, fire-resistive standards, 55-10
Dedication, 2-30
Deduct-alternate, 51-6
Deed restriction, 2-20
Deep long-span joist, 10-3, 19-15, 24-1, 24-3
Deep-well jet pump, 31-4
Defensible space, 2-8
Deflection, 13-3, 13-9, 18-8, 24-1, 24-9
  allowable, 13-9, 18-8
  amplification factor, 23-7, 23-26
  building, 21-9
  concrete, 20-11
  immediate, 20-11
  limitation, 20-11
  long-term, 20-9, 20-11
  maximum, 13-9
  steel design, 19-10
Deformation, 12-3
Deformed bar, 20-3
Degree day, 28-2
Deluge system, 31-22
Demand control ventilation, 30-23
Demineralization, 31-2
Demising wall, 2-30
Densification, 35-5
Density, 2-7, 3-17
Departmental organization, 53-3
Depth-to-span ratio, 24-1
Descriptive specification, 49-2
Design
  allowable
    stress (ASD), 11-5, 17-1, 17-2, 19-1, 22-8, 23-25
    wood values, 18-2, 18-3
  -award-build, 50-2
  -build contract, 50-3
  concepts, 3-16
  concrete, 20-5
  cooling load factor (DCLF), 27-8
  delegation, 50-13
  development, 3-13
  diaphragm, 22-12
  equivalent temperature difference (DETD), 27-7
  flexural concrete, 20-7
  intent, in detailing, 48-1
  load and resistance factor (LRFD), 17-1, 19-1, 22-8, 23-25
  Minimum Loads for Buildings and Other Structures (ASCE 7), 22-2, 22-3, 22-5, 22-6, 22-7, 23-20, 23-21
  National Specification for Wood Construction (NDS), 16-3, 17-3, 18-9
  one-way system, 24-6
  process, phases, 3-13
  response displacement, 23-26
  services, under AIA Document B101, 50-5
  seismic, 23-1
    category, 23-3, 23-20
  spectral response, 23-17, 23-20
  steel
    beam, 19-4
    column, 19-12, 19-14
    deflection, 19-10
    shear, 19-10
  strength, 11-5, 17-1, 22-8, 23-25
    method, 20-1
    of concrete, 20-2, 20-4, 36-6
  time scheduling, 3-13
  two-way system, 25-9
  wood bolt value, 16-4, 16-5, 16-6
  working stress, 17-1
Despoil, 2-30
Detail, construction, 48-1
Detailing
  building code requirements, 48-3
  building movement and substrate attachment, 48-4
  clearances, 48-3
  conformance to industry standards, 48-4
  construction trade sequence, 48-3
  costs, 48-4
  design intent, 48-1
  durability and maintainability, 48-3
  fabrication and installation methods, 48-3
  material availability, 48-4
  process, 48-1
  resistance to moisture and weathering, 48-5
  safety, 48-2
  security, 48-2
  structural integrity, 48-2
  sustainability, 48-5
  tolerances, 48-3
DETD (*see* Design equivalent temperature difference)
Detectable warning, barrier-free design, 56-9
Detention, 30-23
Development
  impact fee, 2-22
  length, 15-8, 16-18, 20-10
  pattern
    city, 2-4
    effects on social behavior, 2-7
  rights, 2-30
Dew point, 27-1, 27-7, 41-7
  line, 27-5
Diagonal
  bridging, 19-15
  cracking, 20-9
  tension, 15-7
    stress, 20-9
  web, 25-3
Diagram
  free-body, 12-9
  moment, 13-5, 13-6, 13-7
  shear, 13-4, 13-5, 13-6
Diaphragm, 22-9, 22-12, 22-13, 23-11
  blocked, 22-12, 22-13
  design, 22-12
  discontinuity, 23-13
  flexible, 23-11, 23-13
  horizontal, 22-12
  load distribution, 23-11
  rigid, 23-11
  unblocked, 22-13
  wood, 22-13
Differential movement, 21-9
Diffraction of sound, 5-16, 33-13
Diffuse reflection, 32-9
Diffusion, 36-3
  of sound, 33-13
Dimension
  lumber, 39-3
  stone, 37-14
Dimensioning of lumber, 39-3
Direct
  -contact water heater, 28-11
  current, 32-1, 32-4
  expansion system (DX), 28-4
  gain system, 29-15
  glare, 32-11
  lighting system, 32-16
  system
    graywater recycling, 30-3
    solar water heating, 31-15
  upfeed pumping system, 31-4
Directionality factor, 22-5
Discontinuous
  column, 23-16
  shear wall, 23-16
Discount rate, 2-30, 30-18
Disinfection, 31-3
Displacement
  design response, 23-26
  inelastic response, 23-26
  lateral, 22-2, 22-14
  ventilation, 28-11
Disposal
  of buildings, 30-16
  of gypsum wallboard, 43-3
Dispute, 50-16
District, 2-6
Diversity, 2-8
DLH-series joist, 19-15
Documentation
  of contract administration, 52-4
  project management, 53-9
Dome, 25-3
  action, 25-4
  circular frame, 25-3
  frame, 25-3, 25-4
  geodesic, 25-2, 25-3, 25-4
  Schwedler, 25-4

shear stress, 25-5
thin shell, 25-2
Door
as a sustainable building material, 30-8
building code requirements, 42-13
egress, 55-23
elevator, 44-6
encroachment, 55-21, 55-23
fire-resistive rating, 55-23
glass, 42-5
lock, electric, 32-22
major components, 42-1
opening force, 55-23
openings, 42-1
overhead coiling, 42-7
revolving, 42-7
sectional overhead, 42-7
size for egress, 55-23
steel, 42-4
swing, 55-23
types, 42-2, 42-3, 42-5
wood frame, 42-5
Doorway, barrier-free design, 56-3, 56-4
Double
angle, 14-2
-deck elevator, 44-6
envelope glazing, 28-14, 29-10
glazing, 29-9
shear, 16-2, 16-4, 16-6, 16-9
-skin
inflatable structure, 10-11
structure, 25-6
tee, 24-5
wythe construction, 10-5, 10-6
Doubly
curved, 25-4, 25-5
surface, 25-6
reinforced beam, 20-10
Doughnut circulation pattern, 3-6
Dowel, 16-18
Downfeed system, water supply, 31-4, 31-7
Downflow furnace, 28-2
Downspout, 31-20
Downzoning, 2-30
Drain, 31-20
-back system, 31-17
-down system, 31-17
field, 31-20
Drainage, 15-3
aboveground, 5-7
capacity, 5-8
easement, 30-23
of soil, 35-4
parking, 5-12
piping, 31-18
sanitary, 31-17
site, 2-12, 5-7, 35-6
slope, recommended, 2-10
storm, 31-17, 31-19
surface water, 35-7
system design, 31-18
underground, 5-7
Drain tile, 15-3
Drawing
coordination with specifications, 48-9
of metal, 38-2
Drift, 22-14, 23-26
building, 11-6
limitations, 23-26
maximum, 22-2, 22-14
story, 23-26
wind, 22-2
Drilled pier, 15-7
Drinking fountain, barrier-free design, 56-6, 56-7
Driven pile, 15-7
Drop panel, 10-4
Drive control (elevator), 44-3
Dry
-bulb temperature, 27-1, 27-3
-pipe system, 31-22
sample boring, 35-3
Drywall (*see* Gypsum wallboard)
Drywell, 31-20
Dual
-condenser chiller, 28-11
-duct system, 28-5
system, 23-18, 23-11
Duany, Andres, 2-4
Ductile, 10-2
Ductility, 19-1, 23-6, 38-5
Ductwork sizing, 28-10
Dumbbell circulation pattern, 3-6
Duplex receptacle, 32-7
location, 32-7
Durability
and maintainability, in detailing, 48-3
for sustainability, 30-5
Duties
implied, 28-4
of the architect, 28-3
DX (*see* Direct expansion system)
Dynamic
analysis, 23-2
buffer zone, 29-10
forces, 23-1
load, 11-7
structural analysis, 11-7
Dynamically sensitive, 22-4

E

Earth
crust, 23-2
sheltering, 29-4
Earthquake, 23-1
analysis, 23-16
method, 23-1
characteristics, 23-2
damage, 23-1
effects, 23-3
-induced vibration, 23-26
load, 11-6, 17-2
maximum considered, 23-3, 23-20
measurement, 23-2
-resistant structure, 23-1
simplified analysis, 23-2
Earthwork, 35-5
Easement, 2-19, 2-30
access, 2-19
conservation, 2-19
drainage, 30-23
joint use, 2-19
scenic, 2-19
support, 2-19
utility, 2-19
Eccentric braced frame, 23-7, 23-10
Ecological design, 30-1
Ecology, 2-15
Economic analysis, site, 2-20
Economizer
cycle, 28-6, 28-10
boiler fuel, 28-11
Eco-roof, 29-5
Edge, 2-6
beam, 20-12, 20-13
distance, 16-2, 16-3, 16-11
EDM (*see* Electromagnetic distance measurement)
EER (*see* Energy efficiency ratio)
Effective
aperture, 29-11, 29-19
beam depth, 20-6
depth, 15-8
flange width, 20-12, 20-13
length, 14-2, 18-10, 19-12
factor, 18-10, 21-7
temperature (ET), 27-3
Efficacy, 32-12
Efficiency, 22-10, 24-7
building, 3-2
ratio, 3-3
Efflorescence, 37-7
Egress
door, 55-23
system, 55-16
EIFS (*see* Exterior insulation and finish system)
EIS (*see* Environmental impact statement)
Elastic limit, 12-3, 23-6
Electric
arc process, 16-15
elevator, 44-1
field vector mapping (EFVM), 29-6
heating, 28-7
insulation, types, 32-3
lock, 32-22
metallic tubing (EMT), 32-3
power supply, 32-4
service, primary, 32-4
strike, 32-22
Electrical
circuit, 32-2
drawing, 48-7
impedance test, 36-9
system, building code requirements, 55-28
system materials, 32-2
Electricity, 32-1
as energy source, 28-1
primary distribution, 32-6
secondary distribution, 32-6

Electrochromic glazing, 29-10, 42-18
Electrolysis, 38-4
Electromagnetic
  distance measurement (EDM), 2-24
  lock, 32-23
Electronic
  ballast, 32-15
  hardware, 42-12
Elevation
  exterior, 48-7
  interior, 48-7
Elevator
  barrier-free design, 56-11
  design, 44-3
  door, 44-6
  electric, 44-1
  entrance, 56-14
  freight, 44-6
  hydraulic, 44-1
  lobby design, 44-5
  machine room, 44-6
  operation and control, 44-2
  safety device, 44-3
Elliptical reflector (ER) lamp, 32-13
Embodied energy, 30-4, 30-23
Embossing of metal, 38-2
Emergency
  lighting, 32-20
  power supply, 32-7
Eminent domain, 2-30
Emissivity, 27-3, 41-7
Emittance (*see* Emissivity)
EMS (*see* Energy management system)
Enclosed building, 22-4
Encroachment, 2-30
End
  distance, 16-2, 16-3
  frame, 25-5
  grain withdrawal, 16-3
  rotation, 13-10, 13-11, 18-10, 19-11, 19-12
  translation, 13-10, 13-11, 18-10, 19-11, 19-12
Energy, 32-1
  budget, 32-20
  conservation, 28-2, 3-18 (*see also* Energy efficiency, Sustainable building design)
    air barrier, 29-7
    boiler fuel economizer, 28-11
    building automation system, 28-14
    cool roof system, 41-12
    daylighting, 29-10
    direct-contact water heater, 28-11
    displacement ventilation, 28-11
    dual-condenser chiller, 28-11
    economizer cycle, 28-6, 28-10
    electric, 32-5
    energy recovery ventilator, 28-12
    energy transfer wheel, 28-13
    extract-air window, 28-14
    gas-fired absorption-based chiller, 28-11
    glazing, 29-9
    ground-coupled heat exchanger, 28-14
    heat pipe, 28-13
    heat transfer equipment, 28-12
    insulation, 29-7
    mechanical system components, 28-10
    power budget, 32-11, 32-20
    recuperative gas boiler, 28-11
    solar-powered absorption cooling, 28-11
    thermal energy storage, 28-12
    water-loop heat pump, 28-12
    water-to-water heat exchanger, 28-13
  efficiency (*see also* Energy conservation, Sustainable building design)
    air lock, 29-7
    building orientation, 29-1
    building shading, 29-3
    building shape, 29-2
    daylighting, 29-10
    double envelope, 29-10
    earth sheltering, 29-4
    glazing, 29-9, 42-18
    green roof, 29-5
    insulation, 29-7
    landscaping, 29-3
    ratio (EER), 28-15
    weather sealing, 29-7
  -efficient glazing, 42-18
  embodied, 30-5, 30-23
  management system (EMS), 28-14, 28-15
  Policy Act (EPACT) of 1992, 32-12, 32-13, 32-15
  recovery ventilator, 28-12
  sources, 28-1
  transfer wheel, 28-13
Engineered wood products, 39-7
English truss, 24-3
Enthalpy, 27-1, 27-5
  heat exchanger, 28-13
  line, 27-5
Envelope attachment, 24-9
Environmental
  controls, 3-18
  design (*see* Sustainable building design)
  impact statement (EIS), 2-15
  Protection Agency, 2-15, 30-10, 30-11, 30-17, 39-12
  psychology, 2-7, 3-8
  tobacco smoke (ETS), 30-12
EPA (*see* Environmental Protection Agency)
EPACT (*see* Energy Policy Act of 1992)
EPDM (*see* Ethylene propylene diene monomer)
Epicenter, 23-2
Epoxy-coated bar, 20-10
Equilibrium, 12-1, 13-4, 14-3
Equipment
  cost, 24-7
  heat
    gains, 27-7
    generating, 28-2
EPS (*see* Expanded polystyrene)
Equation of time, 29-19
Equidistant horizontal projection, 29-15
Equity, 2-30
Equivalent
  fluid weight, 15-12
  lateral
    force method, 23-1, 23-2, 23-17
    load, 23-3
  length of pipe, 31-14
  thickness, 37-8
Erection, 24-8, 25-9
  speed, 24-7
Erosion control, 30-2
Errors and omissions insurance (*see* Professional liability insurance)
Escalator, 44-6
Escalation rate, 2-30
ET (*see* Effective temperature)
Ethylene propylene diene monomer (EPDM) roofing, 41-12
Euler's equation, 13-10
Evaluating
  building materials, sustainability, 30-4
  existing structures, 2-23
Evaporation, 27-2
Evaporative
  cooler, 27-6
  cooling, 28-4
Evaporator, 28-3
Exaction, subdivision, 2-22
Excavation, 35-5
Exculpatory clause, 49-9
Exfiltration, 29-7
Exhaust
  mechanical system, 28-8
  outlet, location, 28-8, 28-9
Existing
  buildings, surveying, 2-23
  structures, evaluating, 2-23, 2-25
Exit, 55-16, 55-17
  access, 55-17
  access travel distance, 55-19
  court, 55-30
  discharge, 55-16, 55-17
  enclosure, 55-30
  number, 55-19
  passageway, 55-30
  separation, 55-20
  stairway, 55-24
  width, 55-20
Exiting (*see also* Means of egress), 55-16
  through intervening spaces, 55-21
Expanding grid pattern, 2-5
Expansibility, programming concept, 3-8
Expansion joint, 41-13
  brick, 37-4
  concrete, 36-11
  concrete paving, 35-7
  metal, 38-11
Expansive soil, 15-5
Exposure factor, 22-4, 22-5
Expressway, 2-13
Extensive green roof, 29-5

Exterior
elevation, 48-7
insulation and finish system (EIFS), 41-15
stairway, 5-10, 5-11
External load dominated building, 29-2
Extinguishing agents, 31-24
Extract-air window, 28-14
Extruded polystyrene (XPS), 41-3, 41-5
Extruding of metal, 38-2
Eye, in vision, 32-9

F

Fabrication
methods, in detailing, 48-3
of metal, 38-2
Facade-integrated photovoltaics, 5-7
Facing brick, 37-2
Factor
building portion, 22-4, 22-6
component, 22-8
cost, 24-7, 25-9
daylight, 29-10, 29-19
deflection amplification, 23-7, 23-26
directionality, 22-5
effective length, 18-10, 21-7
exposure, 22-4, 22-5
flat use, 18-4
glazing, 29-19
gust, 22-4, 22-5
height, 22-4, 22-5
importance, 22-5, 22-7, 23-18, 23-19
load, 20-5
and resistance design (LRFD), 17-1, 19-1, 22-8, 23-25
duration, 16-1, 17-3, 18-5
repetitive use, 17-3, 18-2, 18-4, 18-11
response modification, 23-7, 23-8, 23-17, 23-20
safety, 20-5
size, 17-3, 18-4, 18-10
strength reduction, 20-5
stress intensity, 20-6
topographic, 22-5
wet service, 18-4
wind stagnation, 22-5
Factory and shop lumber, 39-3
Facts, in programming, 3-16
Fair market value, 2-30
Fastener, for lumber, 39-10, 39-12
Fastest-mile wind, 22-2
Fast-track, 50-2
scheduling, 3-16
Federal Historic Preservation Tax Incentives program, 2-26
Federal Reserve Bank (Minneapolis), 10-10
Fee
architect's, 50-9
in lieu, 30-23
projection, 53-6
Ferrous metal 38-4
Fiber, 13-2
saturation point, 18-5, 39-4
Fiberglass
insulation, 41-3, 41-6
-reinforced gypsum, 43-5
Field
administration, 52-3
circulation pattern, 3-6
measuring, 2-24
pattern, 2-5
report, 52-3
tests, 52-4
weld, 16-16
Fill, 15-3
soil, 35-4
Fillet weld, 16-15, 16-16
Filtration, 31-2
Final
cleaning, 52-6
payment, 52-6
Financing
methods, 2-21, 2-22
public works, 2-21
Fine aggregate, 20-2
Fingerjointed trim, 40-1
Finish
architectural woodwork, 40-14
carpentry, 39-1, 40-1
grading, 40-1
fire-resistive standards, 55-8
floor, 21-6
grading, 35-5
hardware, 42-12
materials, tests for flammability, 55-5
Finishing
metal, 38-3
of concrete, 36-10
Fink truss, 24-3
Fire
area, 55-8
assembly, 55-30
barrier, 55-7, 55-30
containment, 31-20
damper, 31-21, 55-6
detection, 32-23, 55-27
door assembly, 55-30
exit hardware, 55-30
extinguisher, 31-24
extinguishing agent, 31-24
partition, 55-6, 55-30
openings, 55-8
protection, 24-8, 28-8, 31-20
rating, 55-30
-rated, 55-30
door, 42-13
glazing, 42-14, 42-19, 42-20
gypsum wallboard, 43-2
laminate, 40-12
rating, of masonry, 37-9
resistance, 10-12, 55-30
-rated glazing, 42-14, 42-20
-rated walls and partitions, 55-6
rating, 10-6, 55-30
-resistive
assemblies, tests for, 55-5
construction, 55-31
rating, door, 55-23, 55-24
rating requirements, 55-6, 55-7
standards, 55-6
decoration and trim, 55-10
finish, 55-8
-retardant
treatment, 17-3
wood treatment, 16-2
sprinkler system, 31-22
suppression, 55-27
Tests of Door Assemblies, NFPA 252, 55-5
Tests of Door Assemblies, UL 10B, 55-4
wall, 55-8, 55-14
zone, 55-14
Fireplace, 55-29
Fireproofing, 17-5
Firestop, 39-7
Fish-eye projection, 29-15
Fitting, water piping, 31-8
Fixed
-end beam, 13-3, 13-9
fee, 50-9
-price method, 50-2
Fixture, 2-30
unit, 31-11, 31-12
Flame
resistance, 55-31
spread, 55-31
index, 55-10, 55-31
rating, 55-6
Flammability
carpet, 43-16
requirements of floor coverings, 55-10
tests, 55-5
for interior finishes, 55-6
Flammable, 55-31
Flange, 24-2
Flashing, 41-13
details, 41-14
masonry, 37-5
Flat
-head screw, 16-3
-plate collectors, 29-17
-plate heat recovery unit, 28-13
sawing, 40-1
truss, 14-1
steel, 24-1
wood, 24-1
use factor, 18-4
Flex, 32-3
Flexibility, programming concept, 3-8, 3-18
Flexible
components, 23-24
diaphragm, 23-11, 23-13
metal-clad cable, 32-3
structure, 22-4
Flexural
concrete design, 20-7
shear, 15-7, 15-8
strength, 10-6
stress, 13-10
Flexure, basic formula, 18-5, 19-4

Flitch, 40-5
Float, 3-14, 36-10
  finish, 36-11
  glass, 42-16
Floating, 36-10
Flood test, 29-6
Floor
  area, allowable, 55-14, 55-15
  area ratio (FAR), 2-7, 2-18
  covering, flammability requirements, 55-10
  drain, 31-18
  plan, 48-6
  surface, barrier-free design, 56-9
Flooring
  carpet, 30-9, 43-15
  cork, 30-9, 43-14
  laminate, 43-13
  linoleum, 30-9, 43-14
  radiant panel test (NFPA 253), 55-10
  resilient, 43-13
  rubber, 43-14
  seamless, 43-15
  stone, 43-8
  types for sustainability, 30-9
  vinyl, 30-9, 43-14
  wood, 30-9, 43-11
Flow chart, water piping, 31-13
Flue-gas desulfurization, 30-10, 43-3
Fluorescent lamp, 32-12, 32-13
Flush
  bolt, 42-11
  door, 42-2, 42-5
  paneling, 40-7
Flutter, 25-6
Flutter echo, 33-13
Fly ash, 30-5, 36-6
Flying form, 36-2
Focusing collector, 29-17
Folded plate, 10-9, 25-2, 25-7
Footing
  bending, 15-7, 15-8
  cantilever, 15-6
  combined, 15-6
  friction, 15-12
  heel, 15-11
  independent column, 15-6, 15-9
  key, 15-11, 15-12
  shear, 15-7
  sliding, 15-12
  spread, 15-6, 15-8
  strap, 15-6
  toe, 15-11
  -to-wall connection, 16-18
  wall, 15-6, 15-8
Footlambert, 32-10
Force, 12-1
  algebraic addition, 12-7, 12-8
  chord, 22-12
  collinear, 12-1, 12-2, 12-7
  component, 12-8
  concurrent, 12-1, 12-2, 12-7, 12-8
  coplanar, 12-2, 12-8
  distribution, 23-22
  dynamic, 23-1
  equivalent lateral method, 23-1, 23-2, 23-17
  graphic addition, 12-7, 12-8
  horizontal component, 14-3
  lateral distribution, 22-9
  nonconcurrent, 12-2
  normal method, 22-5, 22-7
  parallel, 12-2
  perpendicular, 12-2
  polygon, 14-5, 14-6
  resultant, 12-7, 12-8
  seismic resisting system, 23-7, 23-8
  shear, 13-2
  structural, 12-2
  vertical component, 14-3
Forest
  Certification Program of SCS, 30-22
  Conservation Program, 30-7
  Stewardship Council (FSC), 30-7, 30-11
  Stewardship Council principles, 30-7
Form
  concrete, 30-5, 36-1
  insulated concrete, 41-7
  liner finish, 36-10
  ties, 36-2
Formaldehyde, 30-9, 30-11, 39-9
  -free
  -free medium-density fiberboard (MDF), 30-6, 30-11
  in furnishings, 30-11
  levels, in panel products, 30-6
Form-resistant structure, 25-6
Formwork, concrete, 36-1
Foundation, 15-1
  caisson, 15-6, 15-7
  concrete wall, 15-8
  masonry wall, 15-8
  mat, 15-6
  pile, 15-6, 15-7
  raft, 15-6
  sill, 17-4
  systems, 15-6
Four-section hyperbolic paraboloid, 25-6
Four-way switch, 32-7
Frame
  A, 24-6
  braced, 23-6, 23-7, 23-10
  building system, 23-7, 23-10
  circular dome, 25-3
  concentric braced, 23-7, 23-10
  dome, 25-3, 25-4
  eccentric braced, 23-7, 23-10
  end, 25-5
  gabled, 10-9, 24-6
  glued-laminated rigid, 24-1, 24-3
  intermediate moment-resisting, 23-8, 23-10
  moment-resisting, 22-11, 23-10
    system, 23-8, 23-10
  ordinary moment-resisting, 23-8, 23-10
  portal, 22-11
  rigid, 10-8, 24-2, 24-3
  space, 10-9, 23-6, 25-2
    support, 25-3
  special moment-resisting, 23-8, 23-10
  steel door, 42-4
  steel rigid, 24-1, 24-2
  triangulated space, 10-9
  Tudor, 24-6
  two-way truss space, 25-2
  wood door, 42-5
Framed
  beam connection, 16-12, 16-13, 16-14
  tube, 22-12
Frameless glazing system, 42-20
Framing
  balloon, 21-5
  for gypsum wallboard, 43-3
  lateral system, 22-11
  method, 22-10
  plank-and-beam, 10-1, 10-2
  platform, 21-5, 21-6
  with lumber, 39-4
Free-body diagram, 12-9
Freestanding light fixture, 32-17
Freight elevator, 44-6
French drain, 35-7
Frequency of sound, 33-1, 33-2
Friction
  footing, 15-12
  skin, 15-6
Frost, 15-5
  line, 15-5
FSC (*see* Forest Stewardship Council)
Fuel source, 28-1
  selection, 28-2
Full
  -mortar bed tile installation, 43-6
  wall schedule, 53-7
Fuller, Buckminster, 25-4
Fundamental period, 11-7, 22-2
Funicular shape, 10-7, 24-6, 25-4
Furnace, 28-2
Furnishings, as sustainable building materials, 30-10
Furniture-mounted luminaire, 32-17

G

Gabled frame, 10-9, 24-6
Gage line, 14-2
Galvanic
  action, 38-4, 48-4
  series, 38-4
Gantt chart, 3-14, 3-15
Garden
  City, 2-3
  roof, 29-5
Garnier, Tony, 2-3, 36-1
Gas
  -fired absorption-based chiller, 28-11
  for glazing fill, 29-9
  natural, 28-1
Gate valve, 31-8
Gaudi, Antonio, 10-8
Geared traction elevator, 44-1
Gearless traction elevator, 44-1

General
  and supplementary conditions, 49-1
  Conditions of the Contract for Construction, Construction Manager-Adviser Editions, AIA A201Cma, 50-2
  Conditions of the Contract, AIA A201, 49-1, 50-6, 50-11, 50-14, 52-1, 52-2, 52-4, 52-5, 28-4, 28-6
  liability insurance, 53-5
  obligation bond, 2-21
  overhead, 3-12
  partnership, 53-2
  tax, 2-21
Generator, 32-9
Geodesic dome, 25-2, 25-3, 25-4
Geotextile, 41-2
  material, 35-7
Geothermal power, 29-18
GFI (*see* Ground fault interrupter)
GFIC (*see* Ground-fault circuit interrupter)
GGBFS (*see* Ground-granulated blast-furnace slag)
Girder
  AASHTO, 24-5
  box, 24-5
  joist, 24-1, 24-4
    designation, 24-4
  plate, 19-12, 24-2
  prestressed concrete, 24-1
  steel, 24-1, 24-1
  tapered, 24-2
  transfer, 24-2
Glare, 32-11
Glass (*see also* Glazing), 42-16
  block, 37-11
  break detector, 32-22
  building code requirements, 42-20
  door, 42-5
  double, 29-9
  fiber insulation, 30-8
  -fiber-reinforced gypsum, 43-5
  fire-rated, 42-19
  in fire doors, 42-14
  installation details, 42-19
  insulating, 29-9
  low-emittance, 29-9
  -reinforced gypsum, 43-4
  sound control with, 33-9
  types, 42-16
Glaziers points, 42-19
Glazing (*see also* Glass), 42-16
  building code requirements, 42-20, 55-26
  double, 29-9
  envelope, 29-10
  electrochromic, 29-10, 42-18
  fire-rated, 42-19
  factor, 29-19
  gasket, 42-19
  photochromic, 29-10
  selection, for daylighting, 29-12
  spectrally selective, 29-9
  stops, 42-19
  switchable, 29-10
  tape, 42-19
  thermochromic, 29-10
  transition-metal hydride electrochromic, 29-10
Globe
  thermometer, 27-3
  valve, 31-8
Glued-laminated
  beam, 18-11, 24-1, 24-3, 24-4
  construction, 10-1
  wood, 39-9
    member, 18-11
Glulam (*see* Glued-laminated wood)
Gnomonic projection, 29-15
Goals, in programming, 3-16
Gothic arch, 24-6
Grade beam, 15-7
Gradient
  height, 22-2
  velocity, 22-4
Grading, 35-5
  of lumber, 39-2
Grain size and shape of soil, 35-3
Graphic
  force addition, 12-7, 12-8
  method, 14-3, 14-6
Grass slope, recommended, 2-10
Gravel, 2-12
  fill, 15-3, 15-5
Gravity
  load, 11-1
  wall, 15-11
Graywater, 30-1, 31-17
  recycling, 30-2
Great Fire of 1666 (London), 55-1
Greek cities, 2-1
Green
  building (*see* Sustainable building design)
  roof, 29-5
  Seal, 30-21
  GS-11, product standard for paint, 30-10, 30-23
  GS-13, product standard for windows, 30-8, 30-23
  label, 30-8
Greenguard Environmental Institute, 30-12, 30-15, 30-21
Greenhouse design (passive solar), 29-17
Grey
  cast iron, 38-5
  water (*see* Graywater)
Grid
  circulation pattern, 3-6
  organization, 3-4
  pattern, 2-5
Gridiron street system, 2-3
Grinding concrete finish, 36-10
Groove weld, 16-15, 16-16
Gross
  building area, 3-2
  shear stress, 17-4, 19-4
  tension stress, 17-4, 19-4
Ground
  -coupled cooling, 28-15
  -coupled heat exchanger, 28-14
  coupling, 5-6
  fault circuit interrupter (GFCI), 32-6
  fault interrupter (GFI), 32-6
  -granulated blast-furnace slag (GGBFS), 36-7
  lease, 2-30
  light, 29-19
  motion, 23-3, 23-4, 23-5
  source heat pump, 29-18
  wave, 23-2
Grounding, 32-6
Groundwater, 2-12, 15-3
Group
  automatic elevator control, 44-2
  interaction, influence on space planning, 3-9
Grout, 21-4, 37-1
  cleaned concrete finish, 36-10
Grouting
  high-lift, 21-4
  low-lift, 21-4
GSHP (*see* Ground-source heat pump)
Guaranteed maximum price, 50-3, 50-11
Guard, building code requirements, 55-26
Guardrail (*see* Guard)
Guide meridian, 5-13
Gusset plate, 14-2
Gust factor, 22-4, 22-5
Gutter, 31-20, 35-7
Gypsum
  block, 37-11
  board lath, 43-1
  deck, 36-8
  wallboard, 43-2
    as a sustainable building material, 30-10
  synthetic, 30-10
Gyration, radius of, 12-5, 12-7, 13-10, 14-2, 18-10, 19-11

H

Half-round slicing, 40-5
Hall, Edward T., 2-8, 3-8
Halogenated agents, 31-24
Halon, 31-24
Handicapped design (*see* Barrier-free design)
Handing of a door, 42-1, 42-2
Handling capacity of elevators, 44-4
Handrail
  barrier-free design, 56-9
  in corridors, 55-21
  stair, 55-24, 55-25, 55-26
Hankinson formula, 16-2, 16-4
Hard
  money loan, 2-22
  steel trowel finish, 36-11
  wired, 32-7
Hardboard, 39-7

Hardness, of water, 31-1
Hardware, 42-7
  astragal, 42-11
  automatic door bottoms, 42-11
  barrier-free design, 56-3
  building code requirements, 42-14
  closer, 42-9
  coordinator, 42-11
  electric lock, 32-22
  electronic, 42-12
  finishes, 42-12
  flush bolt, 42-11
  hinge, 42-7, 42-8
  latchset and lockset, 42-9
  panic, 42-9
  pivot, 42-9, 42-11
  threshold, 42-12
  weather stripping, 42-12
Hardwood, 39-1, 40-1
Harmonic current, 32-6
Haussmann, George-Eugène, 2-2
Hazardous material, 50-15
  mitigation, 30-16
  under AIA Document B101, 50-6
HDPE (*see* High-density polyethylene)
Headed anchor stud, 16-19
Header, 21-6
Heartwood, 40-1
Heat
  -absorbing glass, 42-17
  exchanger
    air-to-air, 28-12
    energy recovery, 28-12
    energy transfer wheel, 28-13
    enthalpy, 28-12
    flat-plate, 28-13
    for graywater, 30-3
    ground-coupled, 28-14
    heat pipe, 28-13
    runaround coil, 28-13
    water-to-water, 28-13
  gain
    calculation, 27-7
    from equipment, 27-8
    from lighting, 27-7
  -generating equipment, 28-2
  island effect, 41-13
  latent, 27-1, 27-7, 27-8
  loads, 27-6, 29-2
  loss calculation, 27-6
  of hydration, 20-4, 36-8
  pipe, 28-13
  pump, 28-1
    ground-source, 29-18
    water-loop, 28-12
  sensible, 27-1, 27-7
  specific, 27-2
  -strengthened glass, 42-16
  transfer, 41-2
  transfer equipment, 28-12
Heating (*see also* HVAC systems)
  seasonal performance factor (HSPF), 28-15
Heavy timber construction, 17-5, 39-9
Hectare, 5-16
Height
  factor, 22-4, 22-5
  -to-span ratio, 25-2
  zoning, 2-30
Helmholtz resonator, 33-8
Henry Fitz-Elwyne Assize of Buildings, 55-1
HERS (*see* Home energy rating system)
Hertz, 33-1
HFCs (*see* Hydrofluorocarbons)
Hierarchy, 3-17
High
  -carbon steel, 19-2
  -density polyethylene (HDPE), 30-7
  -early cement, 20-4
  -intensity discharge (HID) lamp, 32-15
  -lift grouting, 21-4
  -pressure decorative laminate (HPDL), 40-12
  -pressure sodium (HPS) lamp, 32-15
  -rise building, 55-26
    defined, 31-21
  -strength
    bolt, 16-8
    steel, 19-2
    steel strand, 24-5
  -velocity system, 28-5
Highest and best use, 2-20
Hinge, 42-7, 42-8
Historic
  building, masonry in, 2-27
  landmark, 2-26
  Preservation Service, 2-25
  preservation treatments, 2-26
  structure, evaluating, 2-25
  structure, survey, 2-27
History
  building codes, 55-1
  city planning, 2-1
  of concrete, 36-1
  of metal, 38-1
Holding pond, 5-8
Hole
  lead screw, 16-3
  long slotted, 16-8, 16-9
  oversized, 16-8, 16-9
  short slotted, 16-8, 16-9
  standard round, 16-8, 16-9
Hollow
  brick, 37-3
  -core door, 42-5
  core slab, 10-5
  metal door, 42-4
Home
  base, in programming, 3-17
  energy rating system (HERS), 28-15
  run, 48-7
Honeycombing, 20-4, 36-10
Hooke, Robert, 12-3
Hooke's law, 12-3
Hoop, 25-3, 25-4
Horizontal
  alignment, roads, 2-14
  bridging, 19-15
  diaphragm, 22-12
  exit, 55-31
  force component, 14-3
  furnace, 28-3
  irregularities, 23-12, 23-13
  joint
    reinforcing, 37-9
    reinforcement, 10-5, 21-3
  load distribution, 23-11
  masonry reinforcement, 10-6
  polar projection, 29-15
  projection, equidistant, 29-15
  shear, 13-2, 18-7
    stress, 18-7
  wind load, 21-7, 21-8
Hose stream test, 55-5
Hot
  -arid climate, design response, 27-9, 29-3
  -humid climate, design response, 27-9, 29-3
  water supply, 31-14
Hourly billing rates, 50-9
House
  drain, 31-18
  sewer, 31-18
Howard, Ebenezer, 2-3
Howe truss, 24-3
HPDL (*see* High-pressure decorative laminate)
HSPF (*see* Heating seasonal performance factor)
Human
  behavior, 2-7, 3-8
  comfort, 27-2
  interaction, 3-9
  metabolism, 27-2
  sensitivity to sound, 33-3
Humidity
  as component of human comfort, 27-3
  ratio, 27-6
Hurricane-prone area, 22-4, 22-7
HVAC system, 28-4
  air-water, 28-6
  all-air, 28-4
  all-water, 28-6
  constant volume, 28-5
  direct expansion, 28-4
  dual-duct, 28-5
  economizer cycle, 28-6
  for building type, 28-9
  high-velocity, 28-5
  multizone, 28-6
  reheat, 28-5
  selection, 28-7
  sizing, 28-10
  terminal reheat, 28-5
  variable air volume, 28-4
  zone reheat, 28-6
Hydrated lime, 21-4
Hydration, 20-2, 36-5
Hydraulic elevator, 44-1

Hydrochlorofluorocarbon (HCFC), 29-7
EPA phaseout, 30-8, 41-5
Hydrofluorocarbon (HFC), 28-3
Hydrologic soil group, 30-23
Hydrostatic pressure, 11-8, 15-3, 35-3, 35-6, 35-7, 41-2
Hygrometer test, 36-9
Hypalon, 41-12
Hyperbolic paraboloid, 25-2, 25-5
Hypocenter, 23-2
Hypothalamus, 27-2

I
IAQ (*see* Indoor air quality)
IBC (*see* International Building Code)
ICC (*see* Impact insulation class)
ICC/ANSI A117.1, Accessible and Usable Buildings and Facilities, 55-2, 55-4, 56-1
Ignition test, vertical, 55-10
I-joist, 30-6, 39-7
Illuminance, 32-10
Illuminating Engineering Society (IES), 32-10
Image of the City, The, 2-6
Imageability, 2-6
Immediate deflection, 20-11
Impact
assessment, 30-3
hammer test, 36-8
insulation class (IIC), 33-1, 33-12
building code requirements, 55-29
load, 11-7
noise control, 33-12
Impedance, 32-1, 32-2
Implied duties, 28-4
Importance factor, 22-5, 22-7, 23-18, 23-19
Improvement
analysis, 30-3
ratio, 2-30
Incandescent lamp, 32-12, 32-12
Incidental accessory occupancy, 55-11, 55-13
Income approach, land value, 2-20
Incremental unit, 28-4
Indemnification, 50-13
clause, 28-4
Independent column footing, 15-6, 15-9
Indirect
gain system, 29-15
heating, 31-15
lighting system, 32-16
system, solar water heating, 31-15
Indoor air
contaminants, 30-11
quality (IAQ), 28-12, 30-11
biological contaminants, 30-12
carpet, 30-9
causes of poor, 30-12
standards, 30-14
strategies for good, 30-13
symptoms of poor, 30-13
Induction system, 28-6
Industrial
grade, 18-11
Revolution, 2-2
Industry standards, 55-4
in detailing, 48-4
Inelastic response displacement, 23-26
Inertia, 23-3
moment of, 12-5, 12-6, 13-10, 18-1, 18-2
Infiltration, 27-8, 29-7
basin, 2-17
costs, 3-11
storm water, 30-23
Inflatable structure, 10-11
Inflection point, 13-7, 13-8
Infrared detector, 32-22
Inorganic board insulation, 41-5
Insert, concrete, 36-12
Insolation, 27-1
Installation methods, in detailing, 48-3
Instant start fluorescent lamp, 32-15
Instructions to Bidders, AIA A701, 51-3
Instruments of service, under AIA Document B101, 50-6
Insulated concrete form, 36-3, 41-7
Insulating glass, 29-9, 42-17
Insulation, 25-9, 29-7
as a sustainable building material, 30-8
batt, 41-5
board, 41-5
building, 41-2
cellulose, 30-8, 41-3
electric, 32-3
fiberglass, 41-3
glass fiber, 30-8
inorganic board, 41-5
loose-fill, 41-3
mineral-fiber, 30-8
movable, 29-7
organic board, 41-5
perlite, 30-8
plastic fiber, 41-5
reflective, 41-6
R-value, 41-4
sprayed fiber, 41-6
sprayed foam, 41-6
super, 29-7
transparent, 29-7
vermiculite, 30-8
Insurance
all-risk, 53-6
architect's, 53-5
automobile, 53-6
contractor's, 53-6
general liability, 53-5
owner's, 53-6
personal injury protection, 53-5
professional liability, 53-5
property, 53-5
types, 53-5
under General Conditions of the Contract, 50-15
workers' compensation, 53-6
Integrated
part load value (IPLV), 28-16
project delivery (IPD), 50-3
Intensity, 33-1
level, 33-1
Intensive green roof, 29-5
Interior
elevation, 48-7
finish, tests, 55-6
Layout (vignette), 9-1
Intermediate
column, 13-10
metal conduit (IMC), 32-3
moment-resisting frame, 23-8, 23-10
payment, 52-5
Internal
load dominated building, 29-2, 29-3
pressure, 22-4
International
Building Code (IBC), 11-2, 11-3, 11-4, 11-5, 11-7, 11-8, 15-3, 15-5, 17-1, 17-3, 17-4, 17-5, 18-8, 18-9, 19-1, 19-3, 21-2, 22-12, 22-13, 23-1, 23-4, 23-5, 23-7, 23-8, 23-9, 23-12, 23-13, 23-18, 23-19, 23-20, 55-1, 55-2, 55-3, 55-16
Energy Conservation Code, 29-7
Mechanical Code, 27-4
Plumbing Code, 31-10, 55-28
Standard Organization, 30-21
Interpretation of bidding documents, under AIA A701, 51-4
Interval (elevator design), 44-4
Intervening spaces, exiting through, 55-21
Intimate distance, 2-8
Intrusion detection, 32-21
Intumescent materials, 31-21
Inventory analysis, 30-3
Inverse
condemnation, 2-30
square law, 33-2
Inverted
membrane roof, 41-12
tee beam, 10-5
Invert elevation, 5-8
Ionization detector, 32-23
IPD (*see* Integrated project delivery)
IPLV (*see* Integrated part load value)
I-shaped joist, 10-1, 10-2
Isofootcandle chart, 32-18
Isolated T-section, 20-12, 20-13
Isolation joints, 36-12
Isolux chart, 32-18

J
Jenney, William Le Baron, 38-2
Jet pump, 31-3
John Hancock
Building (Chicago), 10-11
Tower (Chicago), 22-12
Joinery details, 40-5
Joining metal, 38-3

Joint
butt, 16-15
concrete, 36-11
construction, 21-10
horizontal reinforcement, 10-5, 21-3
lap, 16-15
metal expansion, 38-11
method, 14-3
reinforcing, horizontal, 37-9
seismic, 23-14
tee, 16-15
through
-building expansion, 21-9
-wall expansion, 21-10
use easement, 2-19
venture, 53-3
Joist, 21-6
allowable span, 18-11, 18-12
composite open-web, 10-6, 10-7
concrete system, 10-4
DLH-series, 19-15
girder, 24-1, 24-4
designation, 24-4
hanger, 16-7
Institute, Steel, 19-15, 24-3
I-shaped, 10-1, 10-2
K-series, 19-15, 19-17
LH-series, 19-15
load table, 19-17
long span, 10-3, 19-15, 24-1, 24-3
open-web, 24-3
steel, 14-1, 19-15, 24-3
steel system, 10-2, 10-3
steel chord configurations, 24-4
wood 10-1, 10-2, 18-11
Jurisdictional wetlands, 2-16

K
Katz, Peter, 2-4
K-brace, 22-11
Keene's cement, 43-1
Kelly ball test, 36-8
Keyed
connection, 16-18
slab, 16-18
Keypad device, 42-12
Kiln dry, 18-5
King post truss, 24-3
Knee brace, 22-11
Knot, 39-2
K-series joist, 19-15, 19-17
K-slump test, 36-8

L
Labeled door, 42-13
Labor and material payment bond, 51-5
Labor cost, 24-7
Labrouste, Henri, 38-1
Lacquer, 40-14
Lag
bolt, 16-4
screw, 16-4
Laitance, 36-6
Lamella
arch, 25-2
roof, 25-5
Laminate
flooring, 43-13
for woodwork, 40-12
Laminated
decking, 18-13
glass, 42-17
veneer lumber, 30-6, 39-8
Lamp
elliptical reflector, 32-13
fluorescent, 32-13, 32-15
high-intensity discharge, 32-15
high-pressure sodium, 32-15
incandescent, 32-12
low-pressure sodium, 32-15
low-voltage miniature reflector, 32-13
lumen depreciation, 32-18
metal halide, 32-15
parabolic aluminized reflector, 32-13
reflector, 32-13
tungsten halogen, 32-13
Land
sale leaseback, 2-30
value, 2-20
Landlocked, 2-30
Landmark, 2-6
Landscape slope, recommended, 2-10
Landscaping, 2-17, 5-6, 5-13, 29-3
Lap joint, 16-15
Laser scanning, 2-25
Latchset, 42-9
Latent heat, 27-1, 27-7, 27-8
Lateral
buckling, 18-9
connector load, 16-3
displacement, 22-2, 22-14
force
distribution, 22-9
-resisting element, 22-9
-resisting system, 23-11
framing system, 22-11
load, 11-6, 17-2
resisting structure, 23-6
pressure, 11-7, 15-5, 15-11
reinforcement, 20-13
support, 18-10, 19-4
ties, 20-10, 20-13, 20-14
Lath, 43-1
Lavatory and sink, barrier-free design, 56-5
Law of cosines, 1-2, 12-8
Law of sines, 1-2, 12-8
Law of Hammurabi, 55-1
LCA (*see* Life-cycle assessment analysis)
LCC (*see* Life-cycle cost analysis)
Le Corbusier, 2-4, 2-6, 36-1
Leaching field, 31-19
Lead, 30-17, 38-8
-based paint ban, 30-17
screw hole, 16-4
Leadership in Energy and Environmental Design (LEED), 29-5, 30-1
Canada, 30-20
certification, 30-19
in specifications, 49-7
credit, 29-5, 29-11, 30-1, 30-4, 30-5, 30-7, 30-9, 30-10, 30-16
LEED (*see* Leadership in Energy and Environmental Design)
Leeward wall, 22-4
pressure, 22-6
Legal
basis for building codes, 55-2
constraints, land development, 2-17
issues for architects, 28-3
L'Enfant, Pierre Charles, 2-3
Length-to-width ratio, 22-11
Letchworth, 2-3
LH-series joist, 19-15
Liability, 28-4
Lien, 2-30
under General Conditions of the Contract, 50-14
waiver, 2-30
Life
-cycle
assessment analysis (LCA), 2-21, 30-3
cost, 48-4
cost analysis (LCC), 2-21, 30-18
inventory model, 30-4
safety, 31-20
Safety Code, 32-20, 55-3
Lift-slab construction, 10-3, 36-13
Light, 32-9
-emitting diode, 32-15
frame construction, 39-5
-gage metal framing, 38-10
-gage steel stud, 21-6
ground, 29-19
level, 32-10
loss factor, 32-18
pipe, 29-12
quality, 32-17
shelf, 29-11, 29-19
source, 32-12
source, color, 32-11
transmittance, visible, 29-20
Lighting
calculations, 32-18
design, 32-10, 32-16
emergency, 32-20
fundamentals, 32-9
heat gain, 27-7
surveillance and deterrence, 48-2
system, 32-16
Lightweight
aggregate, 20-10
structural concrete, 20-2
Limited
liability company (LLC), 53-2
liability partnership (LLP), 53-2
Linear organization, 3-4
Linoleum, 30-4, 43-14
as a sustainable building material, 30-9
Lintel, 21-4, 21-5
concrete, 21-5

masonry, 21-5, 37-7
steel, 21-5
Liquid
and plastic limits of soil, 35-3
-applied roofing, 41-13
Listed label (Underwriters Laboratories), 55-4 (*see also* Classified label)
Live load, 10-11, 11-2, 17-2, 20-5
reduction, 11-3, 17-2
LLC (*see* Limited liability company)
LLP (*see* Limited liability partnership)
Load, 11-1, 12-1
allowable
on beams, 19-5, 19-9
steel column, 19-14
and resistance factor design (LRFD), 17-1, 19-1, 22-8, 23-25
angle of, 16-2
combinations, 11-5, 17-1, 22-8, 23-25
combined, 13-9
concentrated, 11-3, 11-4, 13-3, 13-5, 13-6, 13-9
concrete construction, 17-5
control, 32-5
dead, 10-11, 11-1, 17-2, 20-5, 21-7, 21-8, 23-21
diaphragm distribution, 23-11
duration factor, 16-1, 17-3, 18-5
dynamic, 11-7
earthquake, 11-6, 17-2
equivalent lateral, 23-3
factor, 20-5, 32-5
gravity, 11-1
horizontal 23-11
wind, 21-7, 21-8
impact, 11-7
joist table, 19-17
lateral, 11-6, 17-2
connector, 16-3
resisting structure, 23-6
live, 10-11, 11-2, 17-2, 20-5
reduction, 11-3, 17-2
Minimum Design Loads for Buildings and Other Structures (ASCE 7), 22-2, 22-3, 22-5, 22-6, 22-7, 23-20, 23-21
normal duration, 17-3, 18-5
oscillating, 22-2
parallel to grain, 16-2, 16-5, 16-6
partition, 11-2, 17-2
perpendicular to grain, 16-2, 16-5, 16-6
resonant, 11-7, 22-2
roof, 17-2
live, 11-5
seismic, 17-2, 21-7, 21-9
shedding, 32-5
snow, 11-3
soil, 11-7
lateral, 11-8
temperature-induced, 11-7
uniform, 11-4, 13-3, 13-5, 13-7, 13-9
vertical, 11-1
water, 11-8
wind, 11-6, 17-2
Load-bearing wall, 21-1
Loaded edge, 16-2, 16-3
Loading, 17-1
Loan, 2-22
blanket, 2-22
bridge, 2-22
construction, 2-22
hard money, 2-22
mezzanine, 2-22
mortgage, 2-22
Lobby design, for elevators, 44-5
Local
materials, for sustainability, 30-4
street, 2-13
Lockset, 42-9, 42-10
Logarithm, 1-2
London, city plan, 2-2
Long
period, 23-17, 23-19, 23-21
-period building, 23-6
slotted hole, 16-8, 16-9
span, 24-1, 24-3
joist, 10-3, 19-15, 24-1, 24-3
structures, 24-1, 25-1
-term deflection, 20-9, 20-11
-term thermal resistance (LTTR), 41-3
Loose-fill insulation, 41-3
Loudness, 33-3
Louvered door, 42-2
Low
-emissivity glass, 29-9, 42-18
-iron glass, 42-17
-lift grouting, 21-4
-pressure sodium lamps, 32-15
-voltage miniature reflector (MR) lamps, 32-13
-voltage switching, 32-7
L-shaped beam, 10-5
LTTR (*see* Long-term thermal resistance)
Lumber, 39-1
American Standards Committee, 18-1
cutting, 40-1
defects, 39-2
dimensioning, 39-3
fastener, 39-10, 39-12
for architectural woodwork, 40-4
framing, 39-4
grading, 39-2
machine stress-rated, 18-1, 18-2
moisture content, 39-4
sawn, 18-1, 18-2
shrinkage, 39-4
species, 39-1
strength, 39-1
visually graded, 18-1, 18-2
dimension, 18-3
Lumen, 32-10
Luminaire, 32-16
dirt depreciation, 32-18
types, 32-17
Luminance, 32-10
Luminous intensity, 32-10
Lump sum, 50-2
Lynch, Kevin, 2-6
M
Machine
room, elevator, 44-6
-stress-rated lumber, 18-1, 18-2, 39-3
Maekawa equation, 5-16
Magnetic
contacts, 32-21
declination, 29-15
hold-open devices, 42-12
south, 29-15
Maillart, Robert, 36-1
Main connection member, 16-4, 16-5, 16-6
Maintainability, for sustainability, 30-5
Maintenance procedures, for indoor air quality, 30-13
Malpractice insurance (*see* Professional liability insurance)
Management
Contract Form Between Owner and Construction Manager, CCA 5, 50-2
practice, 53-1
project, 53-6
Maneuvering clearance, barrier-free design, 56-2, 56-3, 56-4
Manhole, 5-8
Many prime contracts, 50-2
Mapped spectral response, 23-18
Market
approach, land value 2-20
value, 2-30
Masonry
as a sustainable building material, 30-5
bearing wall, 10-5
cement, 37-1
clay compressive strength, 21-2
compressive strength, 21-2
concrete compressive strength, 21-2
foundation wall, 15-8
horizontal reinforcement, 10-6
in historic building, 2-27
lintel, 21-5
reinforced
grouted wall, 21-2, 21-3, 21-4
hollow wall, 21-2, 21-3
structural system, 10-5
vertical reinforcement, 10-6
wall, 21-1
fire rating, 37-9
opening, 21-4
Mass distribution, 23-22
MasterFormat, 49-3
2010 divisions, 49-4
changes, 49-3
contents, 49-5
technical sections, 49-7, 49-8
Master specifications, 49-2
Material
availability, in detailing, 48-4
cost, 24-7
electrical system, 32-2
safety data sheet (MSDS), 30-13, 49-7
standards, 55-3

Mat foundation, 15-6
Matrix costing, 3-12
Mat test, 36-9
Maximum
  considered earthquake, 23-3, 23-20
  deflection, 13-9
  drift, 22-2, 22-14
  longitudinal steel percentage, 20-13
  moment, 13-6, 13-9
  resisting moment, 19-4, 19-5, 19-7, 19-8
  shear, 13-9
  steel amount, 20-6
  travel distance, 55-19
MCM nomenclature, 32-3
MCS (*see* Multiple chemical sensitivity)
MDI urea formaldehyde, 30-6
Mean radiant temperature (MRT), 27-3
Means of egress, 55-16
Measurement, existing buildings, 2-24
Mechanic's
  and materialman's lien, 2-30
  lien, 50-14
Mechanical
  and Electrical Plan (vignette), 34-1
  drawing, 48-7
  finish of metal, 38-3
  noise control, 33-12
  room space requirements, 28-10
  system, building code requirements, 55-27
Mediation, 50-8, 52-5
Medieval city, 2-1
Medium
  -carbon steel, 19-2
  -density fiberboard, 30-6, 39-7
Medullary ray, 40-5
Megalopolis, 2-6
Membrane, 25-4, 25-6
  dampproofing, 41-1
  roofing, 41-11
  structure, 25-6
MEPS (*see* Molded expanded polystyrene)
Meridian, 5-13, 25-3, 25-4
Met (*see* Metabolic unit), 27-2
Metabolic unit, 27-2
Metabolism, 27-2
Metal
  aluminum, 38-6
  architectural mesh, 38-13
  as a sustainable building material, 30-6
  basic materials, 38-2
  cast iron, 38-4
  copper and copper alloys, 38-7
  decking, 38-10
  door and frame, 42-2
  fabrications, 38-11
  -faced laminate, 40-12
  fastener for lumber, 39-10
  finishing, 38-3
  forming processes, 38-1
  framing, light-gage, 38-10
  galvanic action, 38-4
  halide lamp, 32-15
  history, 38-1
  joining, 38-3
  lath, 43-1
  lead, 38-8
  ornamental, 38-12
  perforated, 38-13
  properties of, 38-3
  roofing, 41-10
  stainless steel, 38-5
  steel, 38-5
  structural, 38-8
  stud, 21-6
  wall tie, 21-3
  window, 42-16
  wrought iron, 38-4
  zinc, 38-8
Metallocene polyolefin, 30-7
Meter, watt-hour, 32-5
Metering, 32-5
  net, 29-19
Metes and bounds, 5-16
Method
  earthquake analysis, 23-1
  equivalent lateral force, 23-1, 23-2, 23-17
  framing, 22-10
  graphic, 14-3, 14-5
  normal force, 22-5, 22-7
  of joints, 14-3
  of sections, 14-3, 14-5
  projected area, 22-5, 22-7
  static analysis, 11-7
  strength design, 20-1
Methylene-diphenyl isocyanate (MDI), 30-6
Metric units, xxxiii
Metropolitan
  area, 22-2
  Building Act of 1844, 55-1
Mezzanine loan, 2-22
Microclimate, 2-15, 5-13
Microwave detector, 32-22
Mildew, 30-12
Mild steel, 19-2
Mill levy, 2-20
Mineral-fiber insulation, 30-8
Minimum
  concrete cover, 17-5
  Design Loads for Buildings and Other Structures (ASCE 7), 22-2, 22-3, 22-5, 22-6, 22-7, 23-20, 23-21
  horizontal wall reinforcement, 21-7
  longitudinal steel percentage, 20-13
  member depth, 20-11
  property standards, 2-30
  steel amount, 20-7
  vertical wall reinforcement, 21-7
  web reinforcement, 20-9
  weld size, 16-17
Minor change in the work, 52-2
Mirror, barrier-free design, 56-6
Mixed
  flow, 3-18
  occupancy, 55-11, 55-18
Mixing of soil, 35-5
Model building code, 55-3
Modification, 50-1
  coefficient, response, 23-7, 23-8, 23-17, 23-20
  of bid, under AIA A701, 51-4
Modified
  bitumen, 41-12
Mercalli scale, 23-2, 23-3
Module size, 25-3
Modulus
  of elasticity, 12-3, 12-4, 18-8
  section, 12-5, 12-7, 13-2, 18-1, 18-2, 19-4, 19-5, 19-7, 19-8
  uniform present worth factor, 2-31
Moisture
  change, 21-9
  content, 18-4, 18-5
    in architectural woodwork, 40-13
    in concrete, 36-8
    of lumber, 39-4
  dome test, 36-8
  for sustainability, 30-5
  migration through concrete, 36-3
  protection (sustainable material), 30-8
  resistance, as part of detailing, 48-5
  test for concrete, 36-8
Mold, 30-12
Molded high-density polyurethane foam, 30-6
Moment, 12-4, 13-2
  concrete beam capacity, 20-7
  connection, 16-12
  critical section, 15-8
  diagram, 13-5, 13-6, 13-7
  maximum, 13-6, 13-9
    resisting, 19-4, 19-5, 19-7, 19-8
  negative, 20-12
  of inertia, 12-5, 12-6, 13-10, 18-1, 18-2
  overturning, 23-25
  -resisting
    connection, 22-11, 22-15, 24-2
    frame, 22-11, 23-10
    frame system, 23-8, 23-10
    intermediate frame, 23-8, 23-10
    ordinary frame, 23-8, 23-10
    special frame, 23-8, 23-10
  statical, 13-2
  torsional, 17-1
Monitoring, 53-8
Mortar, 21-2, 37-1
  joint, 37-4
  types, 37-1, 37-2
Mortgage loan, 2-22
Mosaic tile, 43-5
Movable
  equipment costs, 3-11
  insulation, 29-7
MRT (*see* Mean radiant temperature)
MSDS (*see* Material safety data sheet)
Multiple
  chemical sensitivity (MCS), 30-13
  of direct personnel expense, 50-9
  of direct salary expense, 50-9

prime contract, 50-2
shear, 16-2
wythe wall, 21-1
Multizone system, 28-6
Municipal
services, 2-14
storm sewer system, 31-20
water supply, 31-6
Munsell color system, 43-18

N
Nail, 16-3, 39-10
box, 16-3
common wire, 16-3
Nash, John, 38-1
National
Ambient Air Quality Standard, 30-15
Appliance Energy Conservation Act of 1987, 28-10
Building Code, 55-1, 55-3
Building Code of Canada (NBC), 55-2, 55-3
Design Specification for Wood Construction (NDS), 16-3, 17-3, 18-10
Electrical Code (NEC), 32-4, 32-6, 32-20, 55-3
Emission Standards for Hazardous Air Pollutants (NESHAP), 30-17
Environmental Policy Act of 1969, 2-15
Fenestration Rating Council (NFRC), 30-8
Fire Protection Association (NFPA), 31-24, 55-3, 55-4
Forest Products Association (NFPA), 16-3, 16-4, 16-7, 18-2, 18-11
Institute for Occupational Safety and Health (NIOSH), 30-17
Park Service, 2-25
VOC Emission Standards for Architectural Coatings, 30-15
Volatile Organic Compound Emission Standards for Architectural Coatings, 30-10
Nationally Recognized Testing Laboratory (NRTL), 55-4
Natural
energy sources, 28-2
features, of site, 2-12
gas, 28-1
period, 23-3
ventilation, 5-7
wood laminate, 40-13
NBC (*see* National Building Code of Canada)
NC (*see* Noise criteria)
NEC (*see* National Electrical Code)
Needs, in programming, 3-17
Negative
moment, 20-12
pressure, 22-1
rotation, 12-4, 13-4
Negligence, 53-4
Negotiation phase, 3-13
Neighborhood, 2-9
Neighbors, in programming, 3-18
Nervi, Pier Luigi, 36-1
Net
area, 14-2, 16-2, 16-11
assignable area, 3-2
leasable area, 2-31
metering, 29-19
shear area, 16-11
tension
area, 16-11
stress, 17-4, 19-4
-to-gross ratio, 3-2
Neutral axis, 13-1, 13-2
New
town concept, 2-4
urbanism, 2-4
Newman, Oscar, 2-8
Newton's law, 23-3
NFPA (*see also* National Fire Protection Association)
13, Standard for the Installation of Sprinkler Systems, 31-23
14, Standpipe and Hose System, 31-24
252, Fire Tests of Door Assemblies, 55-5
253, Standard Method of Test for Critical Radiant Flux of Floor Covering Systems Using a Radiant Heat Energy Source (Flooring radiant panel test), 55-10
257, Standard on Fire Test for Window and Glass Block Assemblies, 55-5
265, Standard Methods of Fire Tests for Evaluating Room Fire Growth Contribution of Textile Wall Covering (Room Corner Test), 55-6, 55-10
286, Standard Methods of Fire Tests for Evaluating Room Fire Growth Contribution of Wall and Ceiling Interior Finish, 55-6, 55-10
5000 Building Code, 55-3, 55-4
701, Standard Methods of Fire Tests for Flame-Resistant Textiles and Films (vertical ignition test), 55-10
NIC (*see* Noise insulation class)
Niemeyer, Oscar, 2-6
Night-cooled mass, 29-19
NIOSH (*see* National Institute for Occupational Safety and Health)
Nit, 32-10
Nocturnal cooling, 29-19
Node, 2-6
Noise, 33-1
control, mechanical, 33-12
control, room, 33-8
control, site, 5-16
criteria (NC), 33-1
criteria curve, 33-5
insulation class (NIC), 33-2
reduction, 33-4
coefficient (NRC), 33-2, 33-6
in a space, 33-7
Nominal size, 18-1
Non-bearing wall (*see* Non-load-bearing wall)
Noncombustible, 55-31
construction, 17-5
Nonconforming use, 2-19
Noncompact section, 19-4
stress, 17-4
Nonconcurrent force, 12-2
Nonferrous metal, 38-4, 38-6
Non-load-bearing wall, 10-6, 21-1
Nonmetallic sheathed cable, 32-3
Nonpotable water, 31-1
Nonrigid elements, 23-24
Nonsymmetric load-resisting elements, 23-14
Normal
force method, 22-5, 22-7
load duration, 17-3, 18-5
stress, 12-2
North American plate, 23-2
Notched beam, 18-9
Notification system, security, 32-23
NRC (*see* Noise reduction coefficient)
NRTL (*see* Nationally Recognized Testing Laboratory)
Numbered keypad, 32-22
Number of exits required, 55-19
Nylon 6, 30-9

O
Object protection, 32-22
Observation, construction, 52-3
Occupancy, 10-11, 55-10
category, 23-18
groups, 55-11, 55-12
nature, 23-18
permit, 2-31
separation, 55-11
Occupant load, 55-17, 55-31
factor, 55-18
Occupational Safety and Health Administration (OSHA), 30-11, 30-14, 55-4
Octave band, 33-2
Office organization, 53-3
Offset
grid, 25-2, 25-3
wall, 23-13, 23-16
Ohm, 32-1
Ohm's law, 32-1
Oil, 28-1
-borne preservatives, 39-12
finish for wood, 40-14
Olmsted, Frederick Law, 2-3, 2-4
One-way
cable structure, 25-8
shear, 15-9
slab, 20-11, 20-13
systems, 24-1, 25-1
concrete, 10-3
design, 24-6
long span, 24-1
selecting, 24-6
structural, 10-1

types, 24-1
On-site security, 5-18
Open
country, 22-2, 22-4
-loop system, 29-18
solar water heating, 31-15
office acoustics, 33-11
specification, 49-2
-web
joist, 24-3
matting, 15-3, 15-5
steel joist, 10-2, 10-3, 14-1, 19-15, 24-3, 38-9
Opening
force, barrier-free design, 56-3
in corridors, 55-22
in fire barrier, 55-8
in masonry, 37-7
in smoke barrier, 55-8
in wood framing, 39-5
of bids, 51-2
Operative temperature, 27-3
Ordinance of 1785, 2-3
Ordinary moment-resisting frame, 23-8, 23-10
Organic, 15-1
board insulation, 41-5
Organization
concept, space planning, 3-4, 3-5
of architect's business, 53-1
of architect's office, 53-3
Orientation
building, 5-3, 29-1
in programming, 3-18
solar, 5-3
Oriented strand board (OSB), 10-1, 30-4, 39-6
Ornamental metal, 38-12
Orthophotography, 2-24
OSB (*see* Oriented strand board)
Oscillating load, 22-2
OSHA (*see* Occupational Safety and Health Administration)
Outlet (*see also* Duplex receptacle)
location of exhaust, 28-9
Overflow drain, 41-12
Overhanging beam, 13-3
Overhead
coiling door, 42-7
costs, 3-12
Oversized hole, 16-8, 16-9
Overturning, 22-14
moment, 23-25
Owner-Architect Agreement, 2-28, 2-29, 50-4, 50-11, 52-1, 52-2, 52-7
Owner's
insurance, 53-6
responsibilities, 50-6
responsibilities, under General Conditions of the Contract, 50-11

P

Pacific plate, 23-2
Pad site, 2-31
Paint, 30-10
Palm wood flooring, 43-12
Panel door, 42-5
Paneling
flush, 40-7
stile and rail, 40-9
thermoset decorative, 40-13
Panel point, 14-1, 24-3
Panic hardware, 42-9, 55-30, 55-31
Parabolic
aluminized reflector (PAR) lamp, 32-13
arch, 24-6
curve, 10-10, 25-8
Parallel
chord, 24-4
truss, 14-1
circuit, 32-2
force, 12-2
-to-grain load, 16-2, 16-5, 16-6
Parallel, standard, 5-13
Parameter method (budgeting), 3-11
Parapet, 22-8
Paris, plan for, 2-2
Parking, 5-10
lot drainage, 5-12
security, 5-18
Parquet flooring, 43-12
Partially seasoned wood, 16-2
Particleboard, 10-1, 30-6, 39-6
Partition
controlling sound through, 33-9
fire resistance, 55-6
load, 11-2, 17-2
Partnering, 53-6
Partnership, 53-2
general, 53-2
Party wall, 2-31
Passive
circulation, solar water heating, 31-16
smoke control, 31-21
solar
cooling, 5-6
design, 29-15
heating, 5-6
Path, 2-6
Patterned glass, 42-17
Pattern of the street, 2-6
Paved slope, recommended, 2-10
Paver tile, 43-5
Paving, 35-7
pervious, 30-2
Paxton, Joseph, 38-1
Payment
final, 52-6
intermediate, 52-5
to contractor, 52-5
under General Conditions of the Contract, 50-14
PCBs (*see* Polychlorinated biphenyls)
Peak
demand control, 32-5
hourly demand, 31-15
load regulation, 32-5
Peat, 2-12
Peg chart, sun, 29-15
Pedestrian circulation, 5-9
Penetrating oil finish, 40-14
Penetrations, in fire-resistive partitions, 55-8
Pennyweight, 16-3
Pentachlorophenol (penta), 39-12
People grouping, 3-17
Percentage of construction cost, 50-9
Percolation test, 31-19
Perforated
drain tile, 35-7
metal, 38-13
Performance
bond, 51-5
under AIA A701, 51-4
specification, 49-2, 49-3
Perimeter
protection, 5-17, 32-21
stiffness, 23-15
Period, 23-3, 23-20
approximate, 23-21
fundamental, 11-7, 22-2
long, 23-17, 23-19, 23-21
natural, 23-3
short, 23-17, 23-19, 23-20
upper limit, 23-20
Perlite, 30-8, 41-3
Perm, 36-4
Permeance, 36-4
Perpendicular
force, 12-2
-to-grain load, 16-2, 16-5, 16-6
Perret, Auguste, 36-1
Perry, Clarence, 2-9
Personal
distance, 2-8
injury protection insurance, 53-5
space, 2-8
Personalization of space, 3-9
Pervious paving, 30-2
PET (*see* Polyethylene terephthalate)
pH
level,
in concrete, 36-9
of water, 31-1
test, 36-9
Phase
change material, 29-17
change system, 31-17
Phasing, 3-18
Philadelphia city plan, 2-3
Phon, 33-2
Photochromic glazing, 29-10
Photoelectric
beam, 32-22
cell, 32-22
detector, smoke, 32-23
Photogrammetry, 2-24
Photography, tool for field recording, 2-24
Photovoltaics, 5-7, 28-2, 29-18
Pier, 15-6, 15-7
belled, 15-7
drilled, 15-7

Pile
  cap, 15-7
  driven, 15-7
  foundation, 15-6, 15-7
  tapered, 15-7
Pipe
  equivalent length, 31-14
  sizing, 31-10, 31-15
  steel, 19-3
Piping
  drainage, 31-18
  plastic water, 31-8
Pitch
  pan, 41-12
  pocket, 39-2
  of roof, 41-8
Pitched
  chord, 24-4
  steel truss, 24-1
  truss, 14-1
  wood truss, 24-1
Pivot, 42-9, 42-11
PLA (*see* Polylactide)
Placement, of concrete, 36-10
Plain
  sawing, 40-1
  slicing, 40-5
Plank
  -and-beam framing, 10-1, 10-2
  flooring, 43-11
Planned unit development (PUD), 2-7
Planning
  and scheduling, 53-6
  sustainable building design, 30-1
Plan shape, 23-14
Plaster, 43-1
Plastic
  as a sustainable building material, 30-6, 30-7
  fiber insulation, 41-5
  high-density polyethylene, 30-7
  limits of soil, 35-3
  lumber, 30-7
  metallocene polyolefin, 30-7
  polyethylene terephthalate (PET), 30-7
  polylactide (PLA), 30-7
  polyolefin, 30-7
  thermoset and thermoplastics, 41-12
  water pipe, 31-8
Plasticizer, 20-2, 36-6
Plate
  concrete flat system, 10-4
  cover, 19-15, 24-2
  folded, 10-9, 25-2, 25-7
  girder, 19-15, 24-2
  gusset, 14-2
  North American, 23-2
  Pacific, 23-2
  sill, 21-6
  slippage, 23-2
  sole, 21-6
  steel, 19-3
  tectonics, 23-2
  top, 21-6
  weld, 16-18
  welding, 21-7, 21-8
Plater-Zyberk, Elizabeth, 2-4
Platform
  construction, 21-6
  framing, 21-5, 21-6, 39-5
Plumbing
  drawings, 48-7
  fixture
    barrier-free design, 56-3
    water conserving, 30-3
  system, building code requirements, 55-28
Plywood, 10-1, 39-5
  box beam, 10-2
  web joist, 39-7
PNC (*see* Preferred noise criteria)
Pneumatic structure, 25-6
Point source, lighting calculations, 32-18
Polar projection, horizontal, 29-15
Polychlorinated biphenyls (PCBs), 30-18
Polycrystalline cell, 29-19
Polyester wood finish, 40-14
Polyethylene
  sheet test, 36-9
  terephthalate (PET), 30-7, 30-9, 30-11
Polyisocyanurate (polyiso), 41-3, 41-5
Polylactide (PLA), 30-7
Polymer-dispersed liquid crystal film glazing, 42-18
Polyolefin, 30-7
Polystyrene, extruded, 41-3
Polyurethane
  for insulation, 41-3, 41-6
  sprayed insulation, 41-3
  wood finish, 40-14
Polyvinyl chloride, 30-9
  roofing, 41-12
Ponding, 24-9, 41-11
Portable fire extinguisher, 31-24
Portal frame, 22-11
Portland cement, 20-2, 21-4, 36-1, 36-5
Positive
  -and-beam system, 10-8
  and timber, 18-2
  base, 16-7
  cap, 16-7
  pressure, 22-1
  rotation, 12-4, 13-4
  -tensioned concrete, 10-5, 20-14, 24-5
  -tensioning, 20-14
    steel, 20-2
Post
  -bid information, under AIA A701, 51-4
  -consumer material, 30-4, 30-23
  -industrial, 30-23
    material, 30-4
  -tensioned concrete, 36-13
Potable water, 20-2, 30-1, 31-1
Power
  budget, 32-11
  conditioning unit, 32-6
  definition, 32-2
  factor, 32-1
  of sound, 33-2
  quality, 32-6
  supply
    electric, 32-4
    emergency, 32-9
Pozzolan, 36-7
Practice management, 53-1
Prang color system, 43-17
Pratt truss, 24-3
Preaction system, 31-22
Prebid conference, 51-2
Precast
  column, 10-5
  concrete, 10-3, 20-14, 36-12
    connection, 16-18
    wall, 21-7, 21-8
  structural members, 10-5
Pre-consumer, 30-23
Preferred noise criteria (PNC), 33-6
Preformed panel, 41-10, 41-11
Preheat fluorescent lamp, 32-15
Premium grade, 18-11
Prescriptive specification, 49-2
Preservation, 2-26
Preservative, for lumber, 39-12
Pressure
  allowable bearing, 15-7
  coefficient of earth, 15-12
  hydrostatic, 11-8, 15-3
  internal, 22-4
  lateral, 11-7, 15-5, 15-11
  leeward wall, 22-6
  loss in pipes, 31-10
  negative, 22-1
  positive, 22-1
  reducer, 31-9
  regulator, 31-9
  roof, 22-6
  sensor, 32-22
  side wall, 22-6
  tank, 31-6
  wave, 23-2
  windward wall, 22-6
Pressurized stairway, 31-21
Prestressed, 10-5
  concrete, 20-14, 24-5, 36-13
    girder, 24-1
  double tee, 24-1, 24-5
  single tee, 24-1, 24-5
Prestressing steel, 20-2, 20-14
Pretensioned concrete, 20-14, 36-13
Pretensioning, 20-14
Pretreatment, 31-2
Primary
  color, 43-17
  electrical service, 32-4
  electric distribution, 32-6
Prime contract, 50-2
Principal meridian, 5-13
Priority, 3-17
Proctor test, 15-4, 35-5
Product data, 52-1
Professional
  liability insurance, 53-5

services
costs, 3-11
during pre-design, 2-28
Profit, 3-12
Pro forma, 2-23, 2-31
Programmatic concepts, 3-3, 3-16
Programming, 3-1
building area, 3-2
codes and regulations, 3-16
process, 3-16
space relationships, 3-3
Progress
payment, 50-10, 52-5
report, 50-5
Project
administration services, under AIA Document B101, 50-5
closeout, 52-6
comparison method, 3-11
cost methods, 50-2
delivery, 50-1
financing, 2-22
management, 53-6
manual, 48-9, 49-1, 51-3
overhead, 3-12
schedule, 50-4
Projected area method, 22-5, 22-7
Projection
equidistant horizontal, 29-15
fish-eye, 29-15
gnomonic, 29-15
horizontal polar, 29-15
rectilinear, 29-14
sun path, 29-16
Propane, 28-1
Property insurance, 53-5
Proposition 65, 30-12, 30-15
Proprietary specification, 49-2
Protection
device, 32-22
persons and property, under General Conditions of the Contract, 50-15
Protruding object, barrier-free design, 56-9, 56-10
Proxemics, 3-8
Psychological influences on space planning, 3-8
Psychrometric chart, 27-5
Psychrometry, 27-5
Public
distance, 2-8
enterprise revenue bonds, 2-21
facilities, effects on city planning, 2-9
transit, 2-14
way, 55-16
works financing, 2-21
PUD (*see* Planned unit development)
Pump, heat, 28-1
Punch list, 52-6
Punching shear, 15-7
Pythagorean theorem, 12-8

Q

Quadratic equation, 13-9
Quality
of light, 32-17
planning, 28-7
Quarry tile, 43-5
Quarter slicing, 40-5
Quartersawing, 40-2
Queen post truss, 24-3
Quenching, 38-3

R

Radial
arch, 24-6
circulation pattern, 3-6
organization, 3-4
Radiant barrier, 41-6
Radiation, 27-2, 27-6
spectrum, 27-19
Radiative cooling, 5-6, 29-19
Radius of gyration, 12-5, 12-7, 13-10, 14-2, 18-10, 19-11
Radon, 30-17
Rafter, wood-trussed, 14-1, 14-2
Raft foundation, 15-6
Railroad shipping, 24-7
Rainforest Alliance, 30-7
Rainwater collection, 30-2
Raker, 35-6
Ramp, 5-10, 44-10
barrier-free design, 56-9
slope, recommended, 2-10
Random
matching, 40-7, 40-9
noise (*see* White sound)
Range, 5-13
Rapid start fluorescent lamp, 32-15
Rate-supported bond, 2-21
Ratio
depth-to-span, 24-1
height-to-span, 25-2
length-to-width, 22-11
slenderness, 10-6, 13-10, 19-11, 19-12, 21-2
span-to-depth, 20-11
water-to-cement, 20-2
window-to-wall, 29-20
Reactance, 32-1
Reaction, 13-1, 13-5
Rebar, 20-2, 20-3, 20-4, 36-4
connection, 16-18
designation, 20-3, 20-4
grades, 20-3
Recessed luminaire, 32-17
Reclaimed wood, 30-6
Reconstruction, 2-26
Record documents, 50-13
Recovered material, 30-4, 30-23
Recovery rate, 31-15
Rectangular
beam, 10-5
survey system, 2-3
tube section, 19-3
Rectified photography, 2-24
Rectilinear projection, 29-14
Recuperative gas boiler, 28-11
Recyclability, 30-16
Recycled
content, 30-4
material, 41-13, 30-16, 43-3
Recycling, 30-5, 30-16
REDM (*see* Reflectorless electromagnetic distance measurement)
Reduction rate, 11-3
Redundancy, 24-8, 25-1
Reentrant corner, 23-13, 23-14, 23-15
Reference standard specification, 49-3
Reflectance (*see* Reflectivity)
coefficient, 32-9
Reflected
ceiling plan, 48-7
glare, 32-11
Reflection, 33-13
types, 32-9
Reflective
glass, 42-17
insulation, 41-6
Reflectivity, 41-7
Reflector (R) lamp, 32-13
Reflectorless electromagnetic distance measurement (REDM), 2-23
Reform movement in city planning, 2-2
Refrigeration
absorption, 28-3
compressive, 28-3
principles, 28-3
Regulations (*see also* Building code requirements)
federal, 55-2
in programming, 3-16
local, 55-2
state, 55-2
Regulatory agency coordination, during pre-design, 2-28
Rehabilitation, 2-26
Secretary of the Interior's Standards for, 2-26
Reheat system, 28-5
Reinforced
Building Code Requirements for Concrete (ACI-318), 17-4, 17-5
concrete construction, 10-6
doubly, beam, 20-10
grouted masonry wall, 21-2, 21-3, 21-4
grouted wall, 37-5, 37-6
hollow masonry wall, 21-2, 21-3
Reinforcement
anchorage, 20-10
bending, 17-5
concrete, 36-4
horizontal
joint, 10-5, 21-3
masonry, 10-6
lateral, 20-13
minimum
horizontal wall, 21-7
vertical wall, 21-7
web, 20-9
shear, 20-9
spiral, 20-14

vertical
masonry, 10-6
wall, 21-3
web, 20-9
Reinforcing
bar, 36-4
size, 20-3
steel, 20-2
Rejecting work, 52-3
REL (*see* Chronic inhalation reference exposure level)
Relationships, in programming, 3-17
Relative
humidity test, 36-9
solar heat gain (RSHG), 28-16
Renaissance city planning, 2-2
Renewable
materials, 30-4
product, 30-23
Repetitive use factor, 17-3, 18-2, 18-4, 18-11
Repointing, 37-8
Repose, 15-6
Required concrete shear strength, 20-9
Resilient flooring, 43-13
Resistance (*see also* R-value), 27-1, 27-6
Resonant load, 11-7, 22-2
Response modification coefficient, 23-7, 23-8, 23-17, 23-20
Reston, Virginia new town, 2-4
Restoration, 2-26, 2-27
of brick, 37-8
Restriction, 2-31
Restrictive covenant, 2-20, 2-29
Resultant force, 12-7, 12-8
Retainage, 50-10, 52-5
Retaining wall, 11-7, 15-11, 15-12, 21-1
Retarder, 36-6
Reusability, 30-5
Reuse, 30-5
of materials, 30-16
Revenue bond, 2-21
Reverberation, 33-2, 33-7
time, 33-2, 33-7
Revolving door, 42-7
Ribbed slab, 20-11
Rice straw, 30-6
Richter scale, 23-2, 23-3
Rift
sawing, 40-2
slicing, 40-5
Right
-of-way, 2-19
to carry out the work, 50-12
to photograph, under AIA Document B101, 50-7
Rigid
components, 23-24
connection, 24-9
diaphragm, 23-11
elements, 23-24
frame, 10-8, 24-2, 24-3
steel conduit, 32-3
Riparian, 2-31
rights, 2-31
Rise
and tread of stairs, 44-9, 44-10
-of-temperature detector, 32-23
Riser, 55-24
Risk management, 53-4
Riveting, 16-7, 16-9
Road
alignment, 2-14
layout, 2-13, 5-8
types, 2-13
Rock
classification, 37-12
wool, 41-3
Rod (in the retina), 32-10
Rolling of metal, 38-2
Romex, 32-3
Roof
accessories, 41-13
live load, 11-5
load, 17-2
panel, preformed, 41-10
plan, 48-7
Plan (vignette), 47-1
pressure, 22-6
slope, 11-5
types, 41-8
Roofing
built-up, 41-11
liquid-applied, 41-13
membrane, 41-11
sheet metal, 41-10
single-ply, 41-12
tile, 41-9
Room
acoustics, 33-13
corner test, NFPA 265, 55-6, 55-10
noise control, 33-8
Root, John, 2-4
Roping, 44-2
Rotary slicing, 40-5
Rotation
end, 13-10, 13-11, 18-10, 19-11, 19-12
negative, 12-4, 13-4
positive, 12-4, 13-4
Rough
carpentry, 39-1
form finish, 36-10
grading, 35-5
Round head screw, 16-3
RSHG (*see* Relative solar heat gain)
Rubbed concrete finish, 36-10
Rubber flooring, 43-14
as a sustainable building material, 30-9
Runaround coil, 28-13
Running
match, 40-7, 40-9
trim, 40-13
Runoff, 5-7
coefficient, 2-12, 5-8
storm, 30-2
R-value, 27-1, 27-6, 29-7, 41-2
for insulation, 41-4

S

S corporation, 53-2
Sabin, 33-2
formula, 33-2
Saddle hanger, 16-7
Safety, 3-18, 52-4
as part of detailing, 48-2
devices, elevator, 44-3
edges for elevators, 44-3
factor, 20-5
glazing, 42-20, 42-21
Sag, 10-10, 25-7, 25-8
Sally port, 5-18
Salvaged building materials, 30-5
Sample, 52-1
Sand, 2-12
and gravel, 15-1, 20-2
Sandblasted concrete finish, 36-10
Sanitary
drainage, 31-17
sewer slope, 5-7
Sash door, 42-2
Satellite
pattern, 2-5
tenant, 2-31
Saturation line, 27-5
Savannah, Georgia, city plan, 2-3
Sawn lumber, 18-1, 18-2
SBS (*see* Sick-building syndrome)
SBX (*see* Sodium borate)
Scale
Modified Mercalli, 23-2, 23-3
Richter, 23-2, 23-3
Scenic easement, 2-19
Schedule, 48-7
construction, 3-13, 52-2
project, 50-4, 50-13
Scheduling, 3-13
critical path method, 3-14
fast-track, 3-16
Gantt chart, 3-14, 3-15
part of programming, 3-9
project management, 53-6
Schematic design, 3-13
Schwedler dome, 25-4
Scientific Certification System (SCS), 30-7, 30-22
Scissor truss, 14-1
SCM (*see* Supplementary cementitious material)
Screw, 16-3, 38-3, 39-10
flat head, 16-3
lag, 16-4
lead hole, 16-3
penetration, 16-3
round head, 16-3
wood, 16-3
Scribe, 40-6
Scrubbed concrete finish, 36-10
SCR (*see* Silicon-controlled rectifier)
SCS (*see* Scientific Certification System)
Scupper, 41-12
Sealant, 41-13
properties, 41-16

Seamless flooring, 43-15
Sears Tower (Chicago), 10-11, 22-12
Seaside, Florida, 2-4
Seasonal energy efficiency ratio (SEER), 28-16
Seasoned wood, 18-8
Seating, barrier-free design, 56-11, 56-13
Secondary
  color, 43-17
  electric distribution, 32-6
Secondhand smoke (*see* Environmental tobacco smoke)
Secretary of the Interior's Standards for Rehabilitation, 2-26
Section
  building, 48-7
  built-up steel, 19-15, 24-2
  compact, 19-4
    stress, 17-4, 19-4
  composite, 16-19
  critical
    moment, 15-8
    net, 16-2
    shear, 15-8, 20-9
  modulus, 12-5, 12-7, 13-2, 18-1, 18-2, 19-4, 19-5, 19-7, 19-8
  noncompact, 19-4
    stress, 17-4
  property, 12-5
  rectangular tube, 19-3
  square tube, 19-3
  standard rolled, 19-15
  wall, 48-7
Sections, method of, 14-3, 14-5
Sectional overhead doors, 42-7
SectionFormat outline, 49-8
Security
  as part of detailing, 48-2
  controls, 3-18
  site, 5-17
  system, 32-21
SEER (*see* Seasonal energy efficiency ratio)
Segregation, 36-10
Seismic
  design, 23-1
  category, 23-3, 23-20
  force resisting system, 23-7, 23-8
  joint, 23-14
  load, 17-2, 21-7, 21-9
  response coefficient, 23-17
  restraint for ceilings, 43-10
  site coefficient, 23-19
  use group, 23-20
Selecting
  one-way system, 24-6
  two-way system, 25-9
Selective collective elevator control, 44-2
Self
  -closing door, 42-14, 55-31
  -consolidating concrete, 36-7
Semidirect lighting system, 32-16
Semirigid connection, 22-14
Sensible heat, 27-1, 27-7
Separated flow, 3-18
Separation of exits, 55-20
Septic tank, 31-19
Sequence matching, 40-8, 40-10
Sequential flow, 3-18
Series circuit, 32-2
Service
  access, site planning, 2-14
  circulation, 5-10
  groupings, 3-17
  spaces, space planning, 3-8
Setback, 2-18, 23-15
Sewage disposal, private, 31-19
Sewer
  building, 31-18
  house, 31-18
  sanitary, 5-8
  slope, recommended, 2-10
SGS Systems and Services Certification, Inc., 30-7
Shading, 29-12
  coefficient, 29-9, 29-19, 42-17
  device, 29-4
Shadow mask, 29-15
Shake, 39-2
Shallow well, 31-3
Shear
  allowable
    bolt, 16-8, 16-9
    wood stress, 18-7
  base, 23-17, 23-22
    distribution, 23-22
  concrete, 20-9
  connector, 16-19
  critical section, 15-8, 20-9
  diagram, 13-4, 13-5, 13-6
  discontinuous wall, 23-16
  dome stress, 25-5
  double, 16-2, 16-4, 16-6, 16-9
  flexural, 15-7, 15-8
  footing, 15-7
  force, 13-2
  gross stress, 17-4, 19-4
  horizontal, 13-2, 18-7
    stress, 18-7
  maximum, 13-9
  multiple, 16-2
  net area, 16-11
  one-way, 15-9
  plane, 16-8
  plate, 39-11
  plate connector, 16-7
  punching, 15-7
  reinforcement, 20-9
  required concrete strength, 20-9
  single, 16-2, 16-4, 16-5, 16-9
  soil
    undrained strength, 23-20
    wave velocity, 23-20
  steel design, 19-10
  stress, 12-2, 13-2
  two-way, 15-7, 15-8, 15-9
  vertical, 13-2, 13-4
  wall, 21-1, 22-9, 22-10, 22-11, 22-14, 23-6, 23-7
  wave, 23-2
Sheathing, 21-5, 21-6, 39-6
Sheepsfoot roller, 35-5
Sheet
  flow, 5-7
  metal roofing, 41-10
Sheetrock (*see* Gypsum wallboard)
Shelf, light, 29-11, 29-19
Shielding effect, 22-2
Shingle, 41-9
Shipping, 24-1, 24-7, 25-9
Shock absorber, 31-9
Shop drawing, 50-13, 52-1, 52-2
  review, 24-9
Shoring, 17-5, 35-5, 35-6
Short
  column, 13-10
  period, 23-17, 23-19, 23-20
  slotted hole, 16-8, 16-9
Shower, barrier-free design, 56-7, 56-8
Shrinkage, in architectural woodwork, 40-13
SI unit, xxxiii
Sick-building syndrome (SBS), 30-13
Side
  connection member, 16-4, 16-5, 16-6
  grain withdrawal, 16-3
  wall pressure, 22-6
Sidewalk, 5-10, 35-7
Siding, wood, 40-2
Signage, barrier-free design, 56-10
Signal system, 32-21
Silica fume, 36-7
Silicon-controlled rectifier (SCR), 44-3
Sill plate, 21-6
Silt, 2-12, 15-1
Simplified earthquake analysis, 23-2
Simply supported beam, 13-3, 13-9
Simultaneous contrast, 43-19
Single
  automatic elevator control, 44-2
  membrane, 25-6
  -ply membrane for waterproofing, 41-1
  -ply roofing, 41-12
  shear, 16-2, 16-4, 16-5, 16-9
  tee, 24-5
  wythe
    construction, 10-5, 10-6
    wall, 21-1, 21-2, 21-3, 37-5, 37-6
Singly curved, 25-4
SIP (*see* Structural insulated panel)
Sisal wall covering, 30-10
Site
  acoustics, 5-16
  analysis, 2-13
    economic, 2-20
    sustainability, 2-16
    utilities, 2-14
  class definition, 23-20
  coefficient, 23-18
  Design (vignette), 6-1
  development, 2-9
  drainage, 2-12, 5-7, 35-6

evaluation, sustainable building design, 2-15
features, analysis, 2-12
Grading (vignette), 7-1
improvements, 35-7
noise, control of, 5-16
plan, 48-6
planning
climate, 2-14
landscaping, 5-6
natural cooling, 5-6
parking, 5-10
pedestrian, 5-9
roads, 2-13, 5-8
service access, 2-14, 5-10
solar orientation, 2-14, 5-3, 5-4
sustainability building design, 2-16
topography, 5-1
utilities, 5-8
utility availability, 2-14
security, 5-17
visits by architect, 50-6, 52-3
Zoning (vignette), 4-1
Sitte, Camillo, 2-2
Size
factor, 17-3, 18-4, 18-10
minimum weld, 16-17
module, 25-3
nominal, 18-1
reinforcing, 20-3
wood, 18-1
Skin friction, 15-6
-load dominant buildings, 29-2, 29-3
Skylight, 42-16
Sky-lobby, 44-6
S-label, 55-23
Slab
channel, 24-5
concrete, 20-13
flat system, 10-4
hollow core, 10-5
keyed, 16-18
one-way, 20-11, 20-13
on grade, 36-3
ribbed, 20-11
two-way, 20-13
Slate roof tile, 41-9
Slender column, 13-10
Slenderness ratio, 10-6, 13-10, 19-11, 19-12, 21-2
Sling psychrometer, 27-3
Slip
-critical connection, 16-8, 16-9, 16-10, 16-14
forming, 36-2
matching, 40-7, 40-9
Slope
analysis, 2-10
formula, 2-10
green roof, 29-5
of land, 2-10
parking lot, 5-12
pedestrian walk, 5-9
recommended for various uses, 2-10
road, 5-8
sanitary sewer, 5-8
surface drainage, 5-7, 35-6
Slump, 20-5
test, 20-4, 20-5, 36-8
SmartWood Program, 30-7
Smelting, 38-2
Smoke
barrier, 55-8
control, 28-8, 31-21
-developed index, 55-6, 55-10
tobacco, 30-12
vent, 41-13
Smokeproof enclosure, 31-21
Smooth
form finish, 36-10
rubbed concrete finish, 36-10
Snow load, 11-3
Social
behavior, 2-7
distance, 2-8
influence, 10-13
influences on space planning, 3-8
Sociofugal space, 2-7
Sociopetal space, 2-7
Sodium borate (SBX), 39-12
Soft story, 23-12, 23-16, 23-17
Softwood, 39-1, 40-1
Soil, 2-12, 15-1
allowable bearing capacity, 15-3, 15-5
classification, 2-12, 35-1
cohesive, 15-12
compaction, 15-4
densification, 15-5
density, 15-4
expansive, 15-5
group, hydrologic, 30-23
lateral load, 11-8
load, 11-7
load test, 35-3
moisture content, 15-4
profile, 23-20
shear wave velocity, 23-20
stack, 31-18
surcharging, 15-5
test, 15-3, 35-1
treatment, 15-3, 35-4
types, 35-3
uncompacted, 15-12
undrained shear strength, 23-20
Unified Classification System (USCS), 15-3, 15-4
water in, 15-3, 35-3
Solar
altitude, 5-3
angle, 5-3
cooling, passive, 5-6
constant, 29-19
day, mean, 29-20
design, 29-13
active, 29-17
collectors, 5-7
passive, 29-15
heat-gain coefficient (SHGC), 29-9, 29-19, 30-8, 42-17
orientation, 2-15, 4-1
-powered absorption cooling, 28-11
savings fraction, 29-20
south, 29-15
time, 29-20
water heating, 31-15
Soldering, 38-3
Sole
plate, 21-6
proprietorship, 53-1
Solid
block flooring, 43-12
-core doors, 42-5
decking, 18-13
stock, 40-1
surfacing, 40-13
Sound, 33-2
absorption, 33-6
coefficient, 33-2
rules of thumb, 33-7
barrier, 5-16
control, 33-8
site, 5-16
diffraction, 5-16, 33-13
intensity, 33-2
level, 33-3
masking, 33-8
power, 33-2
qualities, 33-2
ratings, building code requirements, 55-29
transmission, 33-4
class (STC), 33-2, 33-4
class (STC), building code requirements, 55-29
class ratings, 33-5
control, 33-8
South
Coast Air Quality Management District
California, 30-9, 30-11
Rule 1113, Architectural Coatings, 30-15
magnetic, 29-15
solar, 29-15
Southern Forest Products Association, 18-11
Soy-based polyurethane foam, 41-6
Space
frame, 10-9, 23-6, 25-2
support, 25-3
needs, programming, 3-1
planning
circulation patterns, 3-4
guidelines, 3-2
organization concepts, 3-4
service spaces, 3-8
relationships, in programming, 3-3
requirements
determining, 3-1, 3-2
mechanical room, 28-10
standards, corporate, 3-1

Span
  range, 24-1, 25-2
  rating, 39-5
  -to-depth ratio, 20-11
Spandrel glass, 42-18, 42-20
Special
  conditions, 50-17
  district assessments, 2-22
  moment-resisting frame, 23-8, 23-10
  tax, 2-21
  use permit, 2-31
  wind regions, 22-2, 22-3
Specific
  gravity of soil, 35-3
  heat, 27-2
  site class, 23-20
Specification
  coordination with drawings, 48-9, 49-1
  organization, 49-3
  types, 49-2
  writing guidelines, 49-9
Specified
  compressive strength, 21-1
  concrete compressive strength, 17-4
  yield point, 19-3
Specifying for sustainability, 49-7
Spectral
  energy distribution, 32-17
  response acceleration, 23-3, 23-4, 23-5, 23-19
Spectrally selective glazing, 29-9
Spectrum, radiation, 29-19
Specular reflection, 32-9
Speech privacy, 33-11
Spiral
  column, 20-14
  pitch, 20-14
  reinforcement, 20-14
  stairway, 38-11, 55-24, 44-8, 44-9
Splay corner, 23-15
Split
  lumber defect, 39-2
  ring, 39-11
  ring connector, 16-7
  -wired receptacle, 32-7
Spot zoning, 2-31
Sprayed
  fiber insulation, 41-6
  foam insulation, 41-6
  polyurethane, 41-3
  -on fireproofing, 17-5
Spread footing, 15-6, 15-8
Sprinkler system, 31-22
Square tube section, 19-3
Stability, 24-9
Stack
  effect, 29-8
  vent, 31-18
Stacked elevators, 44-6
Stain, wood, 40-14
Stainless steel, 38-5, 38-12
Stair Design (vignette), 46-1
Stairs, 55-31
  and ramps, as vertical transportation, 44-7
  barrier-free design, 56-9
  circular, 44-8
  code requirements, 44-8
  configuration, 44-7
  definition, 55-24
  design, 44-7
  exterior, 5-10, 5-11
  rise and tread, 44-9
  spiral, 38-11, 44-8, 44-9
  width, 55-24
  winding, 44-8
  wood, 40-3
Stairway, 55-24, 55-25, 55-31
  smoke control, 31-21
Standard
  Building Code, 55-1, 55-3
  Form of Agreement Between Owner and Architect with Form of Architect's Services, AIA B101, 50-4, 50-8, 51-1, 28-5
  Form of Agreement Between Owner and Contractor, where the basis of payment is a stipulated sum, AIA A101, 50-9
  for the Installation of Sprinkler Systems, NFPA 13, 31-23
  Method of Test for Critical Radiant Flux of Floor Covering Systems Using a Radiant Heat Energy Source (Flooring radiant panel test), NFPA 253, 55-10
  Methods of Fire Tests for Evaluating Room Fire Growth Contribution of Textile Wall Covering (Room Corner Test), NFPA 265, 55-6, 55-10
  Methods of Fire Tests for Evaluating Room Fire Growth Contribution of Wall and Ceiling Interior Finish, NFPA 286, 55-6, 55-9
  Methods of Fire Tests for Flame-Resistant Textiles and Films (Vertical ignition test), NFPA 701, 55-10
  Methods of Fire Tests of Building Construction and Materials, ASTM E119, 55-5
  on Fire Test for Window and Glass Block Assemblies, NFPA 257, 55-5
  parallel, 5-13
  penetration resistance, 23-20
  penetration test (SPT), 15-1, 35-1
  rolled section, 19-15
  round hole, 16-8, 16-9
  Test Method for Flammability of Finished Textile Floor Covering Materials, ASTM D2859, 43-16
  Test Method for Surface Burning Characteristics of Building Materials, ASTM E84, 55-5, 55-6, 55-8
Standards
  fire-resistance, 55-6
  for Rehabilitation, 2-26
  industry, 55-4
  material, 55-3
  testing, 55-3
  types, 55-4
  -writing organizations, 55-4
Standing and running trim, 40-13
Standpipe, 31-23
  and Hose System, NFPA 14, 31-24
Star
  pattern, 2-5
  -shaped city, 2-2
Static
  analysis method, 11-7
  -dissipative laminate, 40-12
  head, 28-10, 31-4, 31-9
Statically
  determinate, 13-3
  indeterminate, 13-3
Statical moment, 12-5, 12-6, 13-2
Statics, 12-1
Status, influence on space planning, 3-9
STC (*see* Sound transmission class)
Steam, 28-1
Steel, 19-1, 30-6, 38-5
  allowable
    column load, 19-14
    stress, 17-3, 19-3, 19-4
  American Institute of Steel Construction (AISC), 12-6, 13-2, 13-9, 14-2, 16-8, 16-9, 16-10, 16-12, 16-13, 16-16, 16-17, 17-4, 19-3, 19-6, 19-7, 19-8, 19-12, 19-13, 19-14
  angle, 19-2, 19-3
  arch, 24-1, 24-6
  bar, 19-3
  beam, 19-3
    and concrete slab, 10-6, 10-7, 16-19
    -and-girder system, 10-2, 10-3
    design, 19-4
  bolt, 16-7, 16-9, 16-10
  built-up section, 19-15, 24-2
  camber, 17-5
  cold-drawn wire, 20-3
  column, 19-11
    design, 19-12, 19-14
  composite deck, 10-6, 10-7
  composition, 19-2
  compression, 20-10
  connection, 16-7
  Construction Manual, 12-6, 13-2, 13-9, 14-2, 16-8, 16-16, 16-17, 17-4, 19-4
  deflection design, 19-10
  designation, 19-3
  door, 42-4
  frame, 42-4
  flat truss, 24-1
  girder, 24-1, 24-1
  high
    -carbon, 19-2
    -strength, 19-2, 24-5

joist chord configurations, 24-4
Joist Institute, 19-15, 19-17, 24-3
joist, open-web, 38-9
light-gage stud, 21-6
lintel, 21-5
maximum
amount, 20-6
longitudinal percentage, 20-13
medium-carbon, 19-2
mild, 19-2
minimum
amount, 20-7
longitudinal percentage, 20-13
open-web joist, 14-1, 19-15, 24-3
pipe, 19-3
pitched truss, 24-1
plate, 19-3
ponding, 17-5
post-tensioning, 20-2
prestressing, 20-2, 20-14
reinforcing, 20-2
rigid frame, 24-1, 24-2
shear design, 19-10
structural system, 10-2
temperature, 20-13
trowel finish, 36-11
truss, 24-3
type, 19-2
yielding, 20-6
Steiner tunnel test, 55-5, 55-6
Stereophotogrammetry, 2-24
Stiffener, 24-2
Stiffness
bending, 12-6
building, 23-6
perimeter, 23-15
Stile and rail
door, 42-5
paneling, 40-9
Stipulated sum, 50-2, 50-9, 50-11
Stirrup, vertical, 20-9
Stone, 37-12
cast, 37-12
construction, 37-14
coursing, 37-14, 37-14
finish, 37-12, 43-8
finish, types, 37-13
types, 37-12
veneer, 37-14
Storage
of materials, 52-5
tank system, hot water, 31-15
Storefront, 42-16
Storm
drainage, 31-17, 31-19
drainage, private, 31-20
runoff, 30-2
sewer, 5-8, 35-7
sewer, municipal, 31-20
water management, 30-2
Story drift, 23-26
Strain, 12-3
Strap footing, 15-6
Straw
board, 30-4
compressed, 30-8
particleboard, 30-6
Street, types, 2-13
Strength
clay masonry compressive, 21-2
concrete
compressive, 20-2, 20-5
masonry compressive, 21-2
wall, 21-7
design, 11-5, 17-1, 22-8, 23-25
method, 20-1
of concrete, 20-2, 20-4
flexural, 10-6
masonry compressive, 21-2
reduction factor, 20-5
required concrete shear, 20-9
soil undrained shear, 23-20
specified
compressive, 21-1
concrete compressive, 17-4
ultimate, 12-3
weld, 16-16
Stress, 12-1, 12-2, 12-3
allowable, 17-3
axial compression, 19-11, 19-13
bending, 19-4
design (ASD), 11-5, 17-1, 17-2, 19-1, 22-8, 23-25
steel, 17-3, 19-3, 19-4
wood, 17-3
wood, bending, 18-5
wood, compression, 18-10
wood, shear, 18-7
bending, 12-2, 13-2
combined, 12-2
compact section, 17-4, 19-4
compression, 12-2, 13-1
concentration, 23-14
diagonal tension, 20-9
dome shear, 25-5
flexural, 13-10
gross
shear, 17-4, 19-4
tension, 17-4, 19-4
horizontal shear, 18-7
intensity factor, 20-6
net tension, 17-4, 19-4
noncompact section, 17-4
normal, 12-2
shear, 12-2, 13-2
temperature, 24-9
tension, 12-2, 13-1
thermal, 12-3
torsion, 12-2
Whitney block, 20-6
working design, 17-1
Stressed-skin
panel, 10-2
structure, 10-10
Strip flooring, 43-11
Strong motion accelerograph, 23-3
Structural
clay tile, 37-10
components, 23-24
cost, 10-12
drawings, 48-7
dynamic analysis, 11-7
force, 12-2
glazing gasket, 42-19
grade, 18-2
insulated panel (SIP), 30-6, 39-8, 41-7
integrity, in detailing, 48-2
Layout (vignette), 26-1
lightweight concrete, 20-2
precast member, 10-5
steel, 38-8
system
concrete, 10-3
masonry, 10-5
one-way, 10-1
selection, 10-11
steel, 10-2
wood, 10-1
tee, 19-2, 19-3, 22-14
Structure
air-supported, 25-6
cable, 25-7, 25-8
-suspended, 25-8
suspension, 10-10
double skin, 25-6
inflatable, 10-11
earthquake-resistant, 23-1
flexible, 22-4
form-resistant, 25-6
inflatable, 10-11
lateral load resisting, 23-6
long span, 25-1, 24-1
membrane, 25-6
one-way cable, 25-8
pneumatic, 25-6
stressed-skin, 10-10
suspended cable, 25-2
suspension, 10-10, 25-7
thin-shell, 10-10, 25-3, 25-4
wind-resisting, 22-9
Stub bracket, 22-14
Stucco, 43-1
Stud
cripple, 21-6
headed anchor, 16-19
light-gage steel, 21-6
metal, 21-6
wall, 21-5
framing, 21-6
wood, 21-5
Studio organization, 53-3
Study period, 30-18
Styrene, 30-9
Subchapter S corporation, 53-2
Subdivision exaction, 2-22
Subfloor, 21-6
Submersible pump, 31-3
Submittal, 52-1
review, 52-1
Substantial completion, 52-6

Substitution, 50-12, 51-2
under AIA A701, 51-4
Subsurface conditions, 2-12
Suburban area, 22-2, 22-4
Suction, 11-6, 22-1
pump, 31-3
Subtractive color, 43-17
Sump, 35-7
pit, 31-18
Sun
chart, 29-14
control, 5-3
path, 5-3
projection, 29-15
peg chart, 29-15
Sunflower seed board, 30-4
Superblock, 2-6
Superflat floor finish, 36-11
Superinsulation, 29-7
Super windows, 29-9
Supplementary
cementitious material, 36-6
conditions of the contract, 49-1, 50-15, 50-17
Supplements to bid forms, 49-1
Support easement, 2-19
Surcharging of soil, 35-5
Surety bond, 50-15
Surface
burning characteristics, 55-9
-mounted luminaire, 32-17
temperature, 27-3
water drainage, 35-7
wave, 23-2
Surveying existing building, 2-23
Survey system, United States, 2-3, 5-13, 5-14
Suspended
cable structure, 25-2
luminaire, 32-17
particle device glazing, 42-18
Suspension of the contract, under General Conditions of the Contract, 50-16
Suspension structure, 10-10, 25-7
Sustainability, 30-1
building concepts, 2-16
site concepts, 2-16
specifying, 49-7
Sustainable design (*see also* Energy conservation or Energy efficiency)
building materials, 30-3, 39-9, 43-12
building rating systems, 30-18
definition, 30-1, 30-23
detailing, 48-5
evaluating building materials, 30-4
hazardous material mitigation, 30-16
indoor air quality, 30-10
life-cycle cost analysis, 30-18
product certification, 30-20
recycling and reuse, 30-16
site development, 30-1
site evaluation, 2-15
site planning, 5-6
standards, 30-22
water use, 30-1
Swamp cooler (*see* Evaporative cooling)
Switch, 32-7
Switchable glazing, 29-10
Switchgear, 32-6
Symmetric building, 23-14
Synclastic shell, 25-5
Switching, 32-7
Synthetic gypsum wallboard, 30-10
System
access floor, 17-2
bearing wall, 23-6, 23-7
building frame, 23-7, 23-10
concrete
beam-and-girder, 10-4
flat plate, 10-4
flat slab, 10-4
joist, 10-4
waffle slab, 10-4
curtain wall, 10-6
dual, 23-18, 23-11
foundation, 15-6
integration, 10-11
lateral
force-resisting, 23-11
framing, 22-11
method (budgeting), 3-11
moment-resisting frame, 23-8, 23-10
one-way, 24-1, 25-1
concrete, 10-3
design, 24-6
long span, 24-1
types, 24-1
open-web steel joist, 10-2, 10-3
post-and-beam, 10-8
seismic force resisting, 23-7, 23-8
selecting
one-way, 24-6
two-way, 25-9
steel beam-and-girder, 10-2, 10-3
one-way, 24-1, 25-1
design, 25-9
types, 25-2
Unified Soil Classification (USCS), 15-3, 15-4
Système International d'Unités (SI), xxxiii

T

TAB (*see* Testing, adjusting, and balancing)
Tangent, 2-14
Tankless
system, hot water, 31-15
Tank system, graywater recycling, 30-3
Tapered
girder, 24-2
pile, 15-7
Task-ambient lighting, 32-16, 32-17
Tax
ad valorem, 2-21
general, 2-21
incentive, 2-26
-increment financing, 2-22
special, 2-21
structure, 2-20
T-beam, 20-12
Tearing failure, 16-11
Technical
considerations, 24-8, 25-9
specifications, 49-1
Tee
double, 10-5, 24-5
inverted beam, 10-5
joint, 16-15
prestressed
double, 24-1, 24-5
single, 24-1, 24-5
single, 10-5, 24-5
structural, 19-2, 19-3, 22-14
Telephone, barrier-free design, 56-11
Temperature
as component of human comfort, 27-3
balance-point, 29-19
body, 27-2
climate, design response, 27-9, 29-3
color, 32-17
dry-bulb, 27-1, 27-3
effective, 27-3
expansion, 24-1
-induced load, 11-7
mean radiant, 27-3
movement, 21-9, 24-9
operative, 27-3
steel, 20-13
stress, 24-9
surface, 27-3
wet-bulb, 27-2, 27-3
Tempered glass, 42-17
Tempering of metal, 38-3
Tendon, 10-5, 20-14, 24-5
Tension, 14-1, 14-3
development length, 20-10
diagonal, 15-7, 23-10
stress, 20-9
gross stress, 17-4, 19-4
net
area, 16-11
stress, 17-4, 19-4
stress, 12-2, 13-1
Terminal reheat system, 28-5
Termination
of agreement, under AIA Document B101, 50-7
of the contract, under General Conditions of the Contract, 50-16
Terneplate, 38-8, 41-10
Terra cotta, 37-10
Terrazzo, 43-7
Territoriality, 2-7, 3-8
Tertiary color, 43-17
Test
core cylinder, 20-5
cylinder, 20-5
field, 52-4
flood, 29-6
for interior finish flammability, 55-6
percolation, 31-19
pit, 15-1, 35-3

Proctor, 15-4
slump, 20-5
soil, 15-3
Standard Penetration (SPT), 15-1
types, 55-4
wind tunnel, 22-2
Testing
adjusting, and balancing (TAB), 28-14, 30-13
concrete, 17-4, 20-5, 36-8
laboratories, 55-4
standards, 55-4
Textile wall covering, 55-10
Thermal
drift, 41-3
energy storage, 28-12
resistance, as part of detailing, 48-5
storage wall, 29-15
stress, 12-3
Thermochromic glazing, 29-10
Thermoplastic, 41-12
polyolefin (TPO) roofing, 41-12
Thermoset
decorative paneling, 40-13
plastics, 41-12
Thermosiphon system, 31-17
Thicknesses, metal, 38-3
Thin
-film cells, 29-19
glued-laminated framing (*see* Laminated veneer lumber)
-shell
barrel vault, 25-5
dome, 25-2
structure, 10-10, 25-3, 25-4
Thinset tile installation, 43-6
Third-party claims, 53-4
under AIA Document B101, 50-6
Three
-centered arch, 24-6
-hinged arch, 10-8
-part format of specification sections, 49-6
-second peak gust wind, 22-2
-way switch, 32-7
Threshold, 42-12, 42-15
Limit Values and Biological Exposure Indices, 30-15
Throat dimension, 16-15, 16-16
Through
-building expansion joint, 21-9
-wall expansion joint, 21-10
Thrust, 10-8, 24-6, 25-4, 25-5
Tieback, 35-6
Tied column, 20-13
Ties, 20-13, 20-14
Tile, 43-5
ceramic, 43-5
classification, 43-5
installation, 43-6
roofing, 41-9
types, 43-5
vinyl composition, 43-14
Tilt-up
construction, 36-13
panels, 10-3
Timber, 39-3
connector, 16-7
heavy construction, 17-5
Time
claim for additional, 52-4
contract, 50-14
equation of, 29-19
Tinted glass, 42-17
Titration test, 36-9
TL (*see* Transmission loss)
Tobacco smoke, 30-12
Toilet
room, barrier-free design, 56-3
stall, barrier-free design, 56-3, 56-5
Tolerance, 24-9
as part of detailing, 48-3
of concrete, 36-3
programming concept, 3-17
Tongue-and-groove edging, 18-13
Ton of refrigeration, 28-4
Tooled concrete finish, 36-10
Tooling, 37-4
Top
chord, 14-1, 25-3
grid, 25-2
plate, 21-6
Topographic factor, 22-5
Topography, 2-9, 2-10, 5-1
Torchère, 32-17
Torsion, 23-12
accidental, 23-14
stress, 12-2
Torsional
development, 23-14
irregularity, 23-13
moment, 17-1
Tort, 53-6
Township, 5-13
Tow, 36-8
Toxicity of materials, 30-5
Toxic Substances Control Act (TSCA) of 1976, 30-17, 30-23
TPO (*see* Thermoplastic polyolefin)
Transfer girder, 24-2
Transformer, 32-5
Transit
public, 2-14
Transition-metal hydride electrochromic glazing, 29-10
Translation, end, 13-10, 13-11, 18-10, 19-11, 19-12
Transmissibility, 12-1
Transmission
loss, 33-2, 33-4
of sound, 33-4
Transmittance, 32-9
visible light, 29-20
Transparent insulation, 29-7
Transportation
analysis, 2-13
effects on city planning, 2-9
public, 2-14
Transverse reinforcement, 20-10
Trap, 31-17
Travel distance, 55-31
maximum, 55-19
Tread, 55-24
Tremie, 36-10
Trenching, 35-5
Triangulated space frame, 10-9
Tributary area, 11-5
Trigonometry, 1-2
Trim, 55-31
fire-resistive standards, 55-10
wallboard, 43-3
wood, 40-13
Trombe wall, 29-15, 29-17
Truck shipping, 24-7
True arch, 24-6
Truss, 10-7, 14-1, 24-3
bowstring, 14-1
configurations, 24-3
English, 24-3
Fink, 24-3
flat, 14-1
steel, 24-1
wood, 24-1
Howe, 24-3
king post, 24-3
parallel chord, 14-1
pitched, 14-1
steel, 24-1
wood, 24-1
Pratt, 24-3
queen post, 24-3
scissor, 14-1
steel, 24-3
two-way frame, 25-2
Vierendeel, 24-4
Warren, 24-3
wood, 10-2, 24-3, 39-8
Trussed tube, 22-11, 22-12, 23-10
Tube
framed, 22-12
rectangular section, 19-3
square section, 19-3
trussed, 22-11, 22-12, 23-10
Tuck pointing, 37-8
Tudor frame, 24-6
Tuned dynamic damper, 11-7
Tungsten halogen lamp, 32-13
Turbidity, 31-1
Turbine square, 2-2
Twelve Tales of Roman law, 55-1
Two-pipe circulating system, 31-15
Two-way
concrete, 10-3
selecting system, 25-9
shear, 15-7, 15-8, 15-9
slab, 20-13
switch, 32-6
system, 24-1, 25-1
design, 25-9
types, 25-2
truss space frame, 25-2

Type
  N bolt, 16-8, 16-9
  X bolt, 16-8, 16-9
  X gypsum wallboard, 43-2

U

UBC (*see* Uniform Building Code)
UL (*see also* Underwriters Laboratories)
  10B, Fire Tests of Door Assemblies, 55-4
  Building Materials Directory, 55-4, 55-6
Ultimate strength, 12-3
Ultrasonic detector, 32-22
UMV (*see* Unit multivoltage)
Unassigned area, 3-2, 3-3
Unblocked diaphragm, 22-13
Unbraced length, 19-11
Uncompacted soil, 15-12
Unconfined compression, 35-3
Uncovering and correction of work, 52-3
  under General Conditions of the Contract, 50-15
Under-carpet wiring, 32-4
Underfloor duct, 32-4
Underground
  buildings (*see* Earth sheltering)
  drainage, 5-7
Underimproved land, 2-31
Underpinning, 35-6
Under-reinforced beam, 20-6
Underslung, 24-4
Underwriters Laboratories (UL), 55-4, 55-6
Unfinished bolt, 16-8
Unified
  Numbering System, 38-7
  Soil Classification System (USCS), 15-3, 15-4, 35-3, 35-4
Uniform
  Building Code, 55-1, 55-3
  capital recovery, 2-31
  Federal Accessible Standards Accessible and Usable Buildings and Facilities
  load, 11-4, 13-3, 13-5, 13-7, 13-9
  Mechanical Code, 55-1
  present worth factor, 2-31
  sinking fund, 2-31
Union, 31-8
Unit
  cost method, 3-13, 50-9
  loading, 15-7
  masonry, 37-7, 37-8
  mulitvoltage (UMV), 44-3
  paver, 35-7
  price, 51-6
United States
  city planning, 2-3
  Consumer Product Safety Commission (CPSC), 30-17
  Green Building Council, 30-1, 30-19
  survey system, 5-13, 5-14
Unknown conditions, 52-5
Unloaded edge, 16-2, 16-3
Upfeed system, water supply, 31-4, 31-6
Upflow furnace, 28-2
Uplift, 11-6, 22-2, 23-25
Upper limit period, 23-20
Urban
  area, 22-4
  development patterns, 2-4
Urinal, barrier-free design, 56-5
Usury, 2-31
Utilities
  analysis, 2-14
  easement, 2-19
  site design, 5-8

V

Vacuum breaker, 31-17
Valuation of land, 2-20
Value engineering, 3-10
Valves, water, 31-8
Van der Rohe, Mies, 38-2
Vapor
  barrier, 27-7, 29-7, 36-3, 36-4
  retarder, 36-4, 41-7
Variable
  air volume system (VAV), 28-4
  -voltage variable-frequency (VVVF), 44-3
Variance, 2-18, 2-31
Varnish, 40-14
Vasoconstriction, 27-2
Vasodilation, 27-2
Vaux, Calvert, 2-3
VAV (*see* Variable air volume system)
Vector quantity, 12-1
Vegetated roof cover, 29-5
Veiling reflection, 32-11
Velocity of sound, 33-2
Veneer
  architectural woodwork, 40-4, 40-5
  grades, plywood, 39-6
  stone, 37-14
  wall, 37-5, 37-6
Veneered wall, 21-2, 21-3, 21-8
Vent, 55-28
  plumbing, 31-18
  smoke, 41-13
  stack, 31-18
Ventilation, 27-4, 29-2
  and Acceptable Indoor Air Quality in Low-Rise Residential Buildings, ASHRAE Standard 62.2-2003, 30-15
  attic, 55-28
  crawl space, 55-28
  demand control, 30-23
  displacement, 28-11
  energy recovery, 28-12
  for Acceptable Indoor Air Quality, ASHRAE Standard 62-2001, 30-15
  for indoor air quality, 30-13
  mechanical, 27-4
  natural, 5-7, 27-4
Venting, plumbing systems, 31-17
Venturi pump, 31-3
Vermiculite, 41-5, 30-8, 30-17
Versatility, programming concept, 3-8
Vertical
  alignment, roads, 2-14
  force component, 14-3
  ignition test, NFPA 701, 55-10
  irregularities, 23-12, 23-13
  load, 11-1
  load-bearing wall, 21-1
  masonry reinforcement, 10-6
  shear, 13-2, 13-4
  stirrup, 20-9
  transportation, 44-1
  wall reinforcement, 21-3
Vibrator, 20-4
Vierendeel truss, 24-4
View analysis, 2-12
Viewed angle, 27-3
Vignette
  Accessibility/Ramp, 45-1
  Building Layout, 8-1
  Building Section, 54-1
  Interior Layout, 9-1
  Mechanical and Electrical Plan, 34-1
  Roof Plan, 47-1
  Site Design, 6-1
  Site Grading, 7-1
  Site Zoning, 4-1
  Structural Layout, 26-1
Vinyl
  composition tile, 43-14
  flooring, 43-14
    as a sustainable building material, 30-9
Visible light transmittance (VLT), 29-11, 29-20, 30-8
Vision, 32-9
Visual comfort probability, 32-11
Visually graded
  dimension lumber, 18-3
  lumber, 18-1, 18-2
VLT (*see* Visible light transmittance)
Volatile organic compound (VOC), 30-5, 30-10, 30-11
  in carpet, 30-9
  LEED credit, 30-8
Volt, 32-1
Voltage, to buildings, 32-4
Volume method (budgeting), 32-4
VVVF (*see* Variable-voltage variable-frequency)

W

Waiver
  of consequential damages, under AIA Document B101, 50-6
  of rights, under AIA Document B101, 50-7
  of subrogation, 50-7
Wale, 35-6
Wall
  attachment, 21-7, 21-8, 21-9, 21-10
  bearing system, 23-6, 23-7
  cantilever, 15-11
  cast-in-place, 21-7
  cavity, 21-3

concrete, 21-7
foundation, 15-8
strength, 21-7
construction, 21-1
counterfort, 15-11
covering
sisal, 30-10
textile, 55-10
curtain, 21-1, 21-9
system, 10-6
discontinuous shear, 23-15
finish
gypsum board, 30-10
paint, 30-10
sisal, 30-10
stone, 43-8
fire resistance, 55-6
footing, 15-6, 15-8
gravity, 15-11
leeward, 22-4
pressure, 22-6
load-bearing, 21-1
masonry, 21-1
bearing, 10-5
foundation, 15-8
opening, 21-4
metal, 21-3
minimum
horizontal reinforcement, 21-7
vertical reinforcement, 21-7
-mounted luminaire, 32-17
multiple wythe, 21-1
non-load-bearing, 10-6, 21-1
offset, 23-13, 23-16
openings, 21-4
overturning, 15-12
panel
acoustical, 43-10
connection, 21-7
preformed, 41-10
precast concrete, 21-7, 21-8
reinforced
grouted masonry, 21-2, 21-3, 21-4
hollow masonry, 21-2, 21-3
retaining, 11-7, 15-11, 15-12, 21-1
sections, 48-7
shear, 21-1, 22-9, 22-10, 22-11, 22-14, 23-6, 23-7
side pressure, 22-6
single wythe, 21-1, 21-2, 21-3
stud, 21-5
tile, 43-5
-to-slab connection, 16-18
veneered 21-2, 21-3, 21-8
vertical load-bearing, 21-1
vertical reinforcement, 21-3
windward, 22-4
pressure, 22-6
Wane (lumber defect), 39-2
Warehouse matching, 40-8, 40-10
Warp, 39-2
Warranty clause, 50-12
Warren truss, 24-3
Wash, 37-6
borings, 35-3
Washington, D. C., city plan, 2-3
Waste
disposal, 31-19
stack, 31-18
Water, 20-1, 20-2
-cement ratio, 36-3, 36-5
conservation, 30-5
content of soil, 35-3
for concrete, 36-5
hammer, 31-9
heater, 31-14, 31-15, 31-16
direct-contact, 28-11
in soil, 35-3
jet concrete finish, 36-10
load, 11-8
-loop heat pump, 28-12
municipal supply, 31-6
pipe sizing, 31-1, 31-10
potable, 20-2
private supply, 31-3
pump, 31-3
quality problem, 31-1
soil, 15-3
supply, 31-1
components, 31-5
design, 31-4
hot, 31-14
system design, 31-9
table, 2-12, 15-3, 35-3, 35-6
-to-cement ratio, 20-2
-to-water heat exchanger, 28-13
Tower Place (Chicago), 22-12
treatment methods, 31-2
use, sustainable building design, 30-1
well, 31-3
Waterborne preservatives, 39-12
Watercourse, 30-23
Waterproofing, 25-9, 41-1
agents for concrete, 36-6
Waterstop, 41-2
Waterway, 30-23
Watt, 32-1
-hour meter, 32-5
James, 38-1
Wave
ground, 23-2
pressure, 23-2
shear, 23-2
soil shear velocity, 23-20
surface, 23-2
Weak story, 23-12
Weather stripping, 42-12
Weathering
as part of detailing, 48-5
steel, 38-6
Web
member, 14-1, 14-2
reinforcement, 20-9
Weep hole, 37-6, 48-5
Weight
building, 23-17, 23-21
material, 11-2
equivalent fluid, 15-12
Weld, 16-15
dimension, 16-16
electrode, 16-15
field, 16-16
fillet, 16-15, 16-16
groove, 16-15, 16-16
minimum size, 16-17
penetration, 16-15
plate, 16-18, 36-12
strength, 16-16
Welded
connection, 16-15, 22-14
wire fabric, 20-2, 20-3, 20-4, 36-5
designation, 20-3, 20-4
Welding, 16-8, 16-15, 38-3
plate, 21-7, 21-8
symbol, 16-16
Well water, 31-3
Welwyn Garden City, 2-3
Western framing, 39-5
Wet
-bulb temperature, 27-2, 27-3
-pipe system, 31-22
service factor, 18-4
wood, 16-2
Wetlands, 2-16, 2-17, 2-31
Wheatgrass cabinetry, 30-4
Wheel, color, 43-17
Wheelchair
clearances, 56-2, 56-3, 56-4
spaces, minimum number, 56-14
White sound, 33-8
Whitney stress block, 20-6
Wide flange, 19-2, 19-3
properties, 19-6
section, 38-8
Width
of corridors, 55-21
of exits, 55-20
Wind, 22-1
analysis, 22-4
basic speed, 22-2, 22-3
drift, 22-2
effects, 22-1
fastest-mile, 22-2
horizontal load, 21-7, 21-8
-induced vibration, 23-26
influences on site planning, 2-14, 5-4, 5-13
load, 11-6, 17-2
measurement, 22-2
power, 29-18
pressure, 29-8
-resisting structure, 22-9
special regions, 22-2, 22-3
stagnation factor, 22-5
three-second peak gust, 22-2
tunnel test, 22-2
variables, 22-2
velocity, 11-6, 22-4
Winder stairs, 55-24
Winding stairway, 44-8

Window
  as a sustainable building material, 30-8
  metal, 42-16
  parts, 42-15
  screen, 32-22
  -to-wall ratio (WWR), 29-11, 29-20
  types, 42-15
  wood, 42-16
Windward wall, 22-4
  pressure, 22-6
Wire
  glass, 42-17
  sizes, 32-3
Wiring devices, 32-7
Withdrawal of bid, under AIA A701, 51-4
Wood
  allowable
    design values, 18-2, 18-3
    stress, 17-3
      bending, 18-5
      compression, 18-10
      shear, 18-7
  arch, 24-1, 24-6
  as a sustainable building material, 30-6
  beam, 18-5
  bearing, 18-10
  bolt, 16-4
    design value, 16-4, 16-5, 16-6
  certified, 30-7
  column, 18-11
  connection, 16-1
  crawl space, 17-4
  decay protection, 17-4
  decking, 10-1, 18-13
  density, 16-1
  diaphragm, 22-13
  door frame, 42-5
  door and frame, 42-4
  fire
    -retardant treatment, 16-2
    stop, 17-5
  flat truss, 24-1
  flooring, 43-11
    as a sustainable building material, 30-9
    finish, 43-12
    grades, 43-12
    installation, 43-12
  glued-laminated member, 18-11
  grading, 18-1
  joist, 10-1, 10-2, 18-11
  moisture content, 16-2
  National Design Specification for Construction (NDS), 16-3, 17-3, 18-10
  partially seasoned, 16-2
  pitched truss, 24-1
  planking, 18-13, 39-10
  screw, 16-3
  seasoned, 18-8
  service condition, 16-2
  shrinkage, 39-4
  siding, 40-2
  sizes, 18-1
  species, 16-1
  stairs, 40-3
  structural system, 10-1
  stud, 21-5
  treatment, 39-11
  trim, 40-13
  truss, 10-2, 24-3, 39-8
  -trussed rafter, 14-1, 14-2
  window, 42-16
  wet, 16-2
Work, 50-11
  cost of, 50-7
  rejection of, 52-3
  uncovering and correction, 52-3
Workers' compensation, 53-6
Working
  drawings (*see* Construction drawings)
  stress design, 17-1
Workplane, 29-20
Wren, Christopher, 2-2
Wright
  Frank Lloyd, 2-4, 36-1
  Henry, 2-6
Wrought iron, 38-4
WWR (*see* Window-to-wall ratio)
Wythe, 37-3

X
X-brace, 22-11
XPS (*see* Extruded polystyrene)

Y
Yard lumber, 39-3
Yield
  of water well, 31-3
  point, 12-3

Z
Zero lot line, 2-31
Zinc, 38-8
Zonal cavity method, 32-18
Zone reheat system, 28-6
Zoning, 2-17
  by law, 2-31
  ordinance, 2-7, 3-16, 55-1
  setback, 2-18